W9-CBV-145

THE RANDOM HOUSE

COMPACT WORLD ATLAS

THE RANDOM HOUSE
COMPACT
WORLD
ATLAS

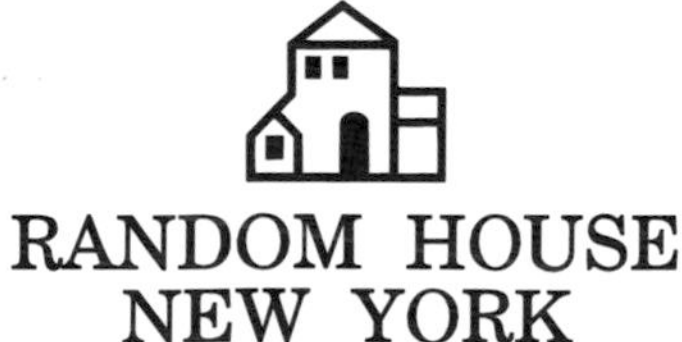

RANDOM HOUSE
NEW YORK

Copyright © 1991 by Bartholomew
Copyright © 1984 by John Bartholomew & Son Ltd

All Rights reserved under International and Pan-American Copyright Conventions.
Published in the United States by Random House, Inc., New York

This revised edition was originally published in the United Kingdom by
Bartholomew, a division of HarperCollins Publishers, Edinburgh in 1992.

This work was originally published in different form in 1984 in the United States by
Random House, Inc. as THE RANDOM HOUSE CONCISE WORLD ATLAS and in the
United Kingdom by John Bartholomew & Son Ltd. as the BARTHOLOMEW CONCISE
WORLD ATLAS. A revised edition of the 1984 edition was published in 1991 in the
United States by Random House, Inc. and in the United Kingdom by Bartholomew, a
division of HarperCollins.

Library of Congress Cataloging-in-Publication Data

The Random House compact world atlas. — Scales differ.
    p.   cm.
   Published in the U.K. under title: Bartholomew compact world
atlas.
   Includes indexes.
   1. Atlases.   I. John Bartholomew and Son.   II. Title: Compact
world atlas.
G1021.R523   1992 <G&M>
912—dc20   92-357
                                  CIP
                                  MAP

Manufactured in Hong Kong

123456789
Second Revised U.S. Edition, 1992

E/B5551

CONTENTS

viii–ix World Physical
x–xi World Political
xii–xiii World Time Zones
xiv–xv World Environment
xvi Key to Symbols

1 Arctic Ocean 1:40M
2-3 North America – Political 1:35M
4-5 Canada, West 1:15M
6-7 Canada, East 1:15M
8-9 USA, West 1:12·5M
10-11 USA, East 1:12·5M
12 USA, Alaska 1:10M
13 Canada Pacific 1:7·5M
14-15 Lower Canada, USA North-East 1:5M
16 Washington – New York – Boston 1:2·5M
17 USA, South-East 1:5M
18-19 USA, South-Central 1:5M
20 USA, Pacific NW 1:5M
21 USA, Pacific S 1:5M
22 San Francisco & Los Angeles 1:2·5M
23 Central Mexico 1:5M
24-25 Mexico & Central America 1:15M
26-27 Caribbean 1:10M

28 South America - Political 1:40M
29 South America, South 1:15M
30 South America, Central 1:15M
31 South America, NE 1:15M
32-33 South America, North 1:15M
34 Central Argentina 1:7·5M
35 South-East Brazil 1:7·5M

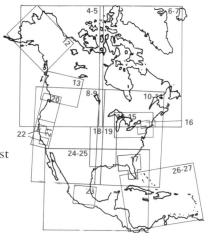

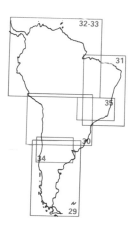

36–37	Europe – Political 1:16M
38–39	Scandinavia 1:7·5M
40–41	British Isles 1:5M
42–43	England & Wales 1:2·5M
44	Scotland, North 1:2·5M
45	Ireland 1:2·5M
46	Paris – Brussels – Ruhr 1:2·5M
47	Alps 1:2·5M
48–49	France 1:5M
50–51	Spain 1:5M
52–53	Italy 1:5M
54–55	The Balkans 1:5M
56–57	Germany & Austria 1:5M
58–59	East-Central Europe 1:5M
60–61	Central European Russia 1:10M
62	North Asia - Political 1:45M

63	Russian Federation, East 1:20M
64–65	Russian Federation, West 1:20M
66–67	South Asia – Political 1:40M
68–69	East Asia 1:20M
70–71	South-East Asia 1:20M
72–73	Central China 1:10M
74	Japan & Korea 1:10M
75	Central Japan 1:5M
76–77	Indo-China & Singapore 1:10M
78	Indonesia, Central 1:10M
79	Philippines 1:10M
80–81	Middle East 1:20M
82–83	India & West China 1:20M
84–85	India, NW & Pakistan 1:7·5M

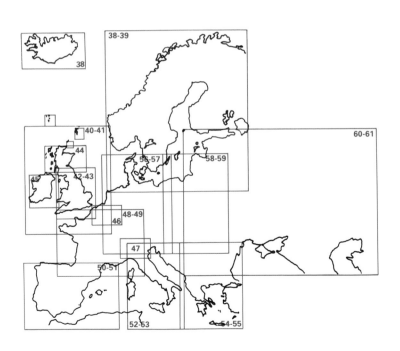

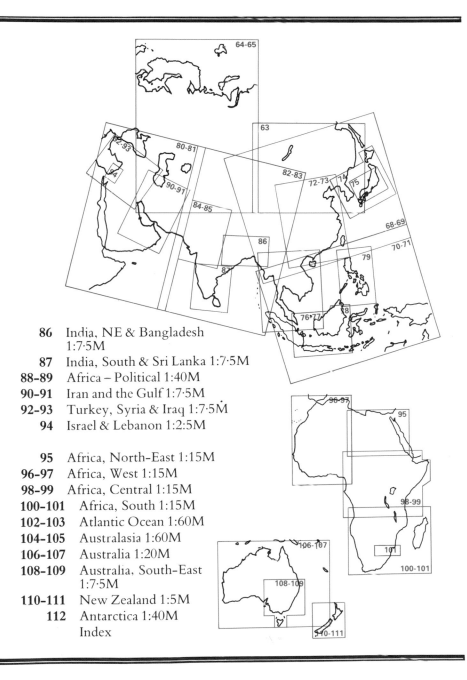

86 India, NE & Bangladesh 1:7·5M

87 India, South & Sri Lanka 1:7·5M

88–89 Africa – Political 1:40M

90–91 Iran and the Gulf 1:7·5M

92–93 Turkey, Syria & Iraq 1:7·5M

94 Israel & Lebanon 1:2·5M

95 Africa, North-East 1:15M

96–97 Africa, West 1:15M

98–99 Africa, Central 1:15M

100–101 Africa, South 1:15M

102–103 Atlantic Ocean 1:60M

104–105 Australasia 1:60M

106–107 Australia 1:20M

108–109 Australia, South-East 1:7·5M

110–111 New Zealand 1:5M

112 Antarctica 1:40M

Index

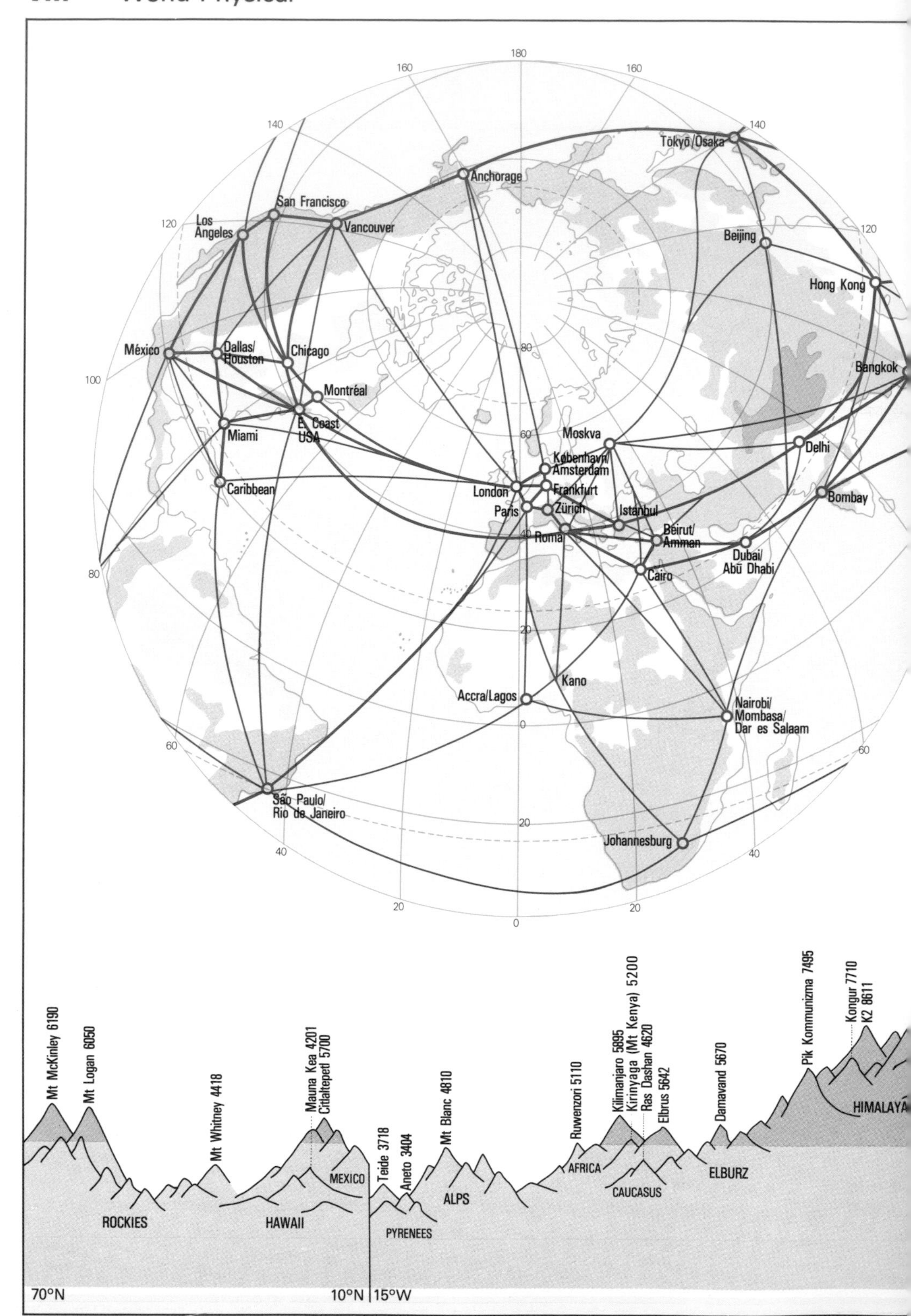

Anchorage
Tōkyō/Osaka
San Francisco
Los Angeles
Vancouver
Beijing
Hong Kong
Bangkok
México
Dallas/ Houston
Chicago
Montréal
E. Coast USA
Miami
Caribbean
Moskva
København/ Amsterdam
Frankfurt
London
Paris
Zürich
Istanbul
Roma
Beirut/ Amman
Cairo
Dubai/ Abū Dhabi
Delhi
Bombay
Kano
Accra/Lagos
Nairobi/ Mombasa/ Dar es Salaam
São Paulo/ Rio de Janeiro
Johannesburg
Mt McKinley 6190
Mt Logan 6050
Mt Whitney 4418
Mauna Kea 4201
Citlaltepetl 5700
Teide 3718
Aneto 3404
Mt Blanc 4810
Ruwenzori 5110
Kilimanjaro 5895
Kirinyaga (Mt Kenya) 5200
Ras Dashan 4620
Elbrus 5642
Damavand 5670
Pik Kommunizma 7495
Kongur 7710
K2 8611
ROCKIES
HAWAII
MEXICO
PYRENEES
ALPS
AFRICA
CAUCASUS
ELBURZ
HIMALAYA
70°N
10°N
15°W

1:150M

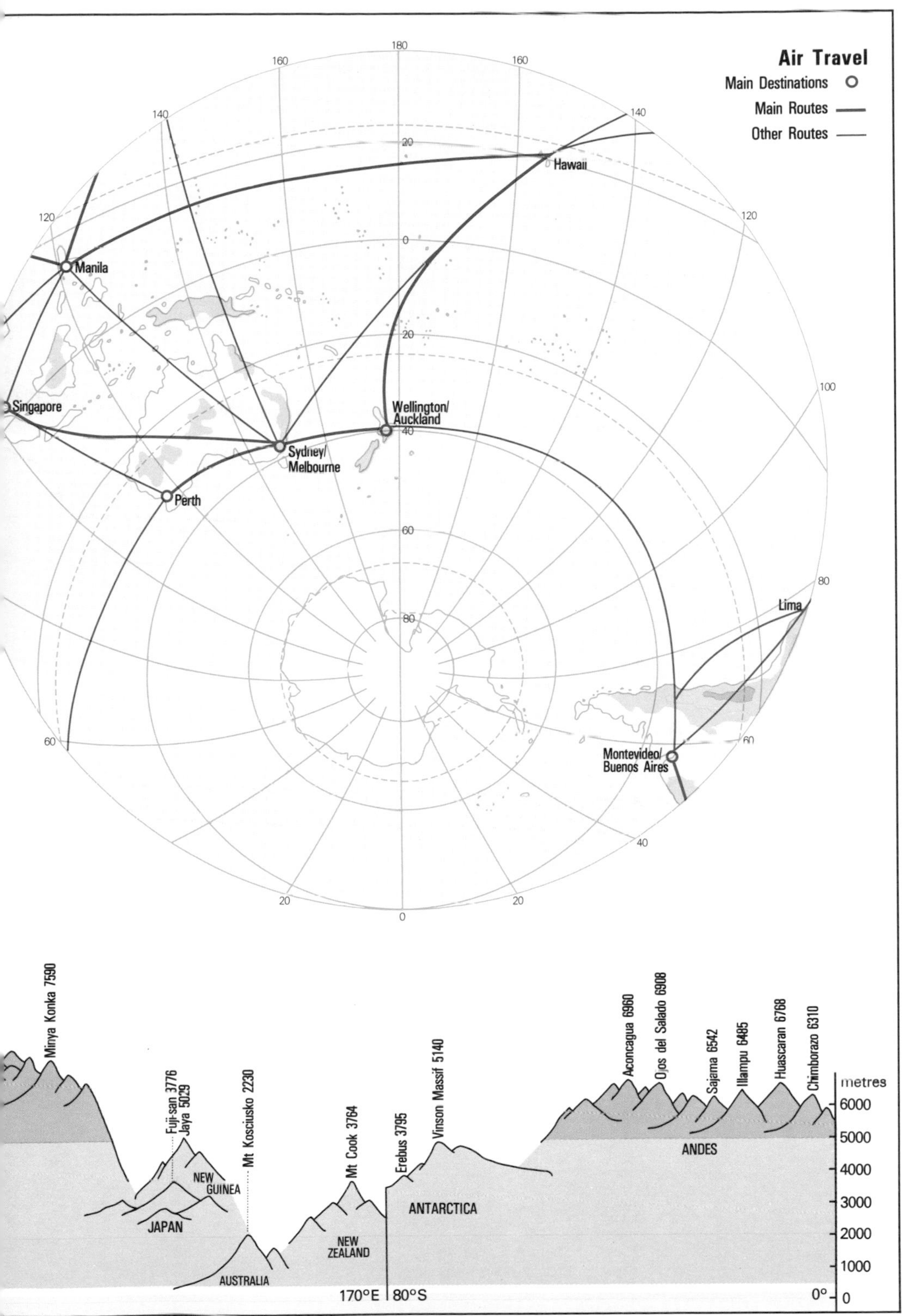

Air Travel

Main Destinations ○
Main Routes ——
Other Routes ——

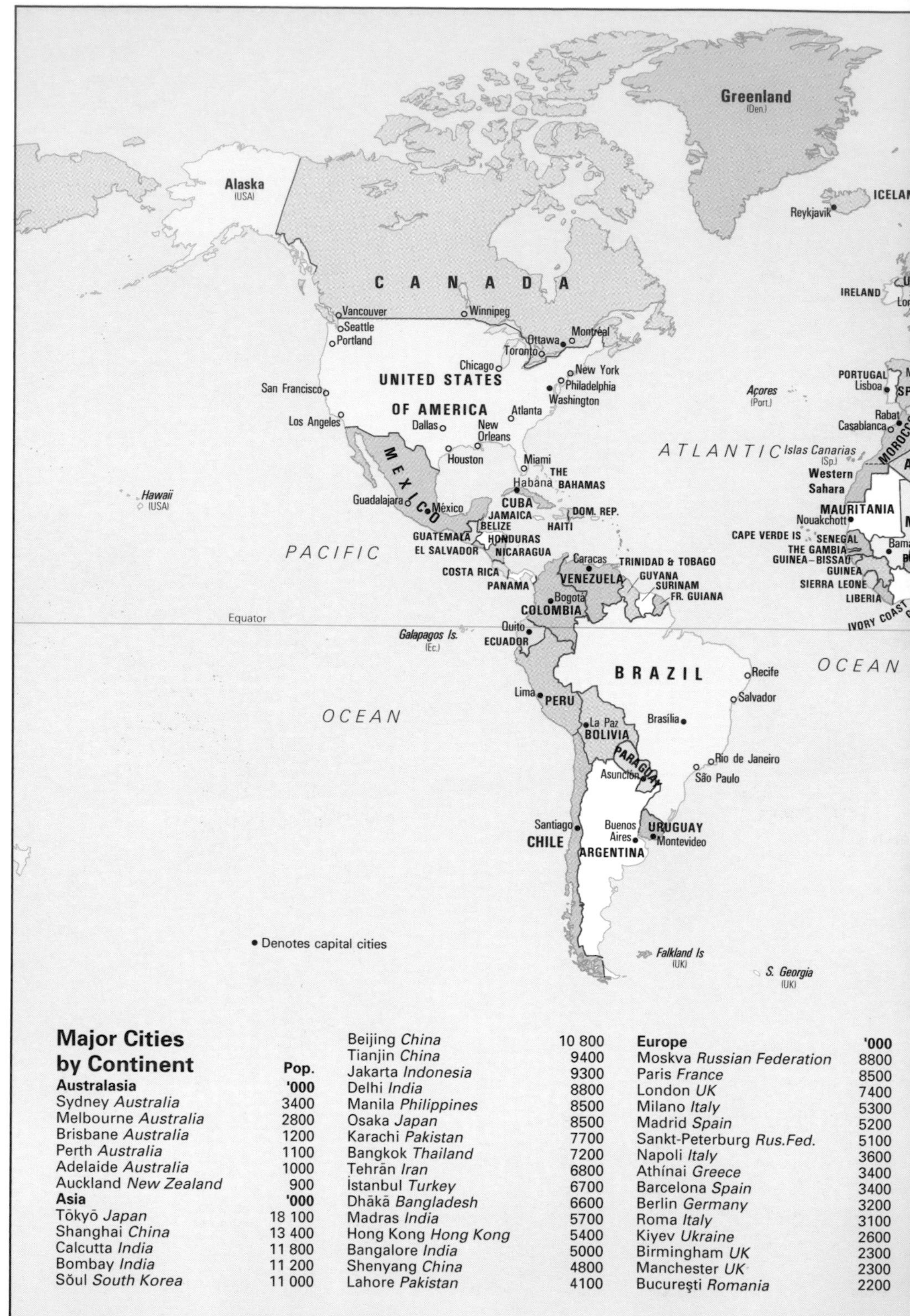

Greenland
(Den.)

ICELAND

Reykjavik

Alaska
(USA)

IRELAND   U.K
Lond

C A N A D A

Vancouver   Winnipeg
Seattle
Portland   Montréal
Ottawa   Toronto

Chicago   New York
Philadelphia
Washington

PORTUGAL   Ma
Lisboa   SPA

San Francisco   UNITED STATES
OF AMERICA   Atlanta
Los Angeles   Dallas   New
Orleans

Açores
(Port.)

Rabat
Casablanca   MOROCCO   AL

Houston   Miami
THE
Habâna   BAHAMAS

ATLANTIC   Islas Canarias
(Sp.)

Hawaii
(USA)

Guadalajara   México   CUBA
JAMAICA
BELIZE   DOM. REP.
GUATEMALA   HONDURAS   HAITI
EL SALVADOR   NICARAGUA

Western
Sahara

MAURITANIA
Nouakchott   M

CAPE VERDE IS   SENEGAL   Bamak
THE GAMBIA   BIS
GUINEA-BISSAU   GUINEA

PACIFIC

COSTA RICA   Caracas   TRINIDAD & TOBAGO
PANAMA   VENEZUELA   GUYANA
SURINAM
Bogotá   FR. GUIANA
COLOMBIA

SIERRA LEONE
LIBERIA

IVORY COAST   GH

Equator

Galapagos Is.
(Ec.)   Quito
ECUADOR

B R A Z I L   Recife   OCEAN

Lima   PERU   Salvador

OCEAN   La Paz   Brasília
BOLIVIA

PARAGUAY   Rio de Janeiro
Asunción   São Paulo

Santiago   Buenos   URUGUAY
Aires   Montevideo
CHILE   ARGENTINA

• Denotes capital cities

Falkland Is
(UK)   S. Georgia
(UK)

Major Cities by Continent

Australasia	Pop. '000
Sydney *Australia*	3400
Melbourne *Australia*	2800
Brisbane *Australia*	1200
Perth *Australia*	1100
Adelaide *Australia*	1000
Auckland *New Zealand*	900

Asia	'000
Tōkyō *Japan*	18 100
Shanghai *China*	13 400
Calcutta *India*	11 800
Bombay *India*	11 200
Sŏul *South Korea*	11 000
Beijing *China*	10 800
Tianjin *China*	9400
Jakarta *Indonesia*	9300
Delhi *India*	8800
Manila *Philippines*	8500
Osaka *Japan*	8500
Karachi *Pakistan*	7700
Bangkok *Thailand*	7200
Tehrān *Iran*	6800
İstanbul *Turkey*	6700
Dhākā *Bangladesh*	6600
Madras *India*	5700
Hong Kong *Hong Kong*	5400
Bangalore *India*	5000
Shenyang *China*	4800
Lahore *Pakistan*	4100

Europe	'000
Moskva *Russian Federation*	8800
Paris *France*	8500
London *UK*	7400
Milano *Italy*	5300
Madrid *Spain*	5200
Sankt-Peterburg *Rus.Fed.*	5100
Napoli *Italy*	3600
Athínai *Greece*	3400
Barcelona *Spain*	3400
Berlin *Germany*	3200
Roma *Italy*	3100
Kiyev *Ukraine*	2600
Birmingham *UK*	2300
Manchester *UK*	2300
Bucureşti *Romania*	2200

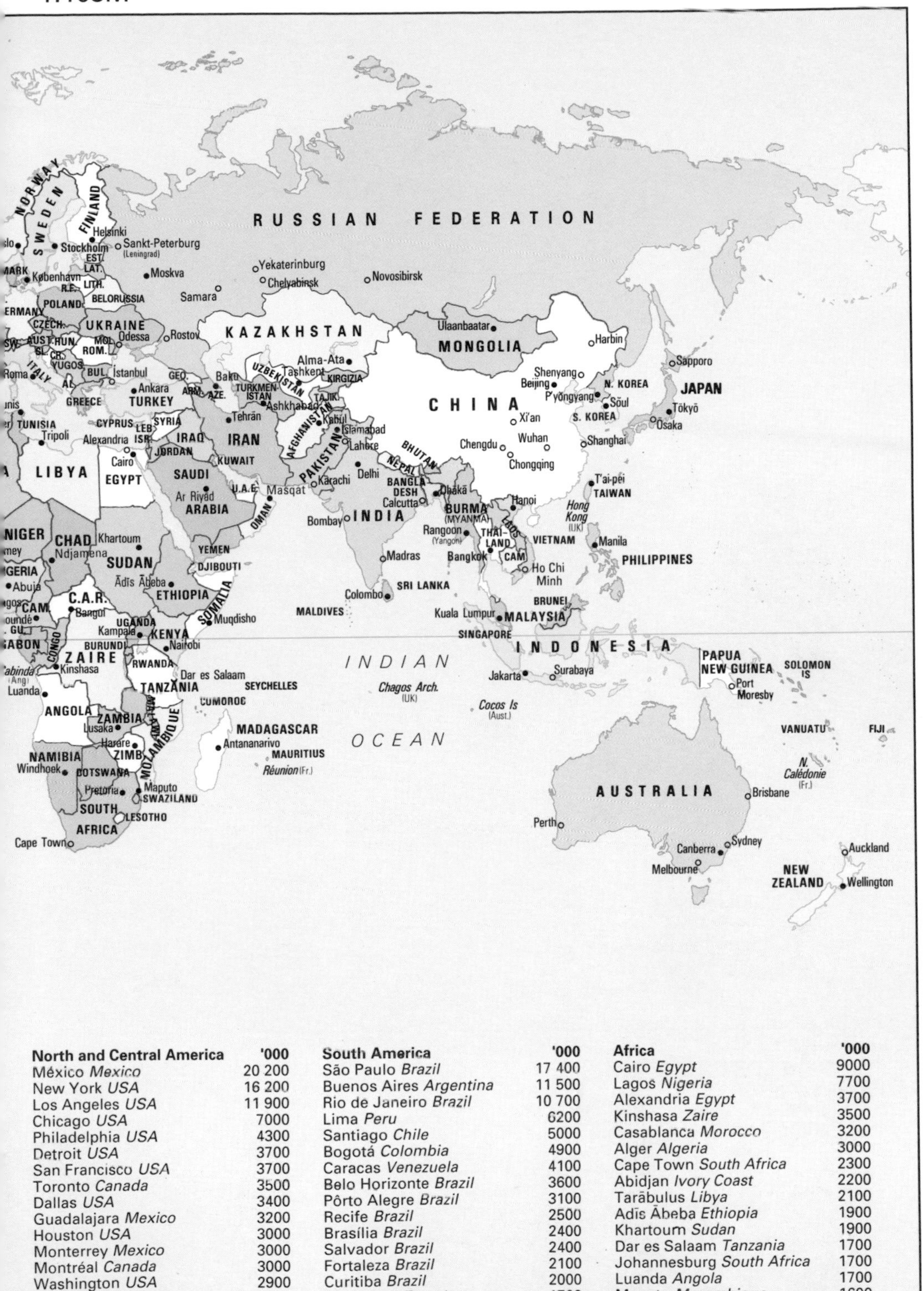

North and Central America	'000	South America	'000	Africa	'000
México *Mexico*	20 200	São Paulo *Brazil*	17 400	Cairo *Egypt*	9000
New York *USA*	16 200	Buenos Aires *Argentina*	11 500	Lagos *Nigeria*	7700
Los Angeles *USA*	11 900	Rio de Janeiro *Brazil*	10 700	Alexandria *Egypt*	3700
Chicago *USA*	7000	Lima *Peru*	6200	Kinshasa *Zaire*	3500
Philadelphia *USA*	4300	Santiago *Chile*	5000	Casablanca *Morocco*	3200
Detroit *USA*	3700	Bogotá *Colombia*	4900	Alger *Algeria*	3000
San Francisco *USA*	3700	Caracas *Venezuela*	4100	Cape Town *South Africa*	2300
Toronto *Canada*	3500	Belo Horizonte *Brazil*	3600	Abidjan *Ivory Coast*	2200
Dallas *USA*	3400	Pôrto Alegre *Brazil*	3100	Tarābulus *Libya*	2100
Guadalajara *Mexico*	3200	Recife *Brazil*	2500	Adis Ābeba *Ethiopia*	1900
Houston *USA*	3000	Brasília *Brazil*	2400	Khartoum *Sudan*	1900
Monterrey *Mexico*	3000	Salvador *Brazil*	2400	Dar es Salaam *Tanzania*	1700
Montréal *Canada*	3000	Fortaleza *Brazil*	2100	Johannesburg *South Africa*	1700
Washington *USA*	2900	Curitiba *Brazil*	2000	Luanda *Angola*	1700
Boston *USA*	2800	Guayaquil *Ecuador*	1700	Maputo *Mozambique*	1600

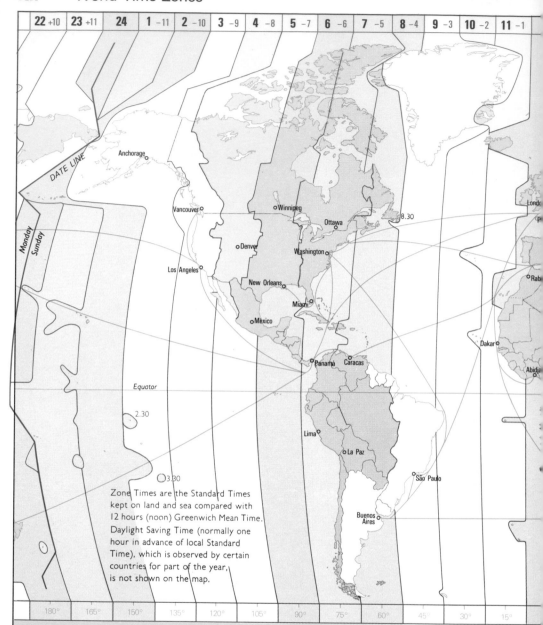

| 22 +10 | 23 +11 | 24 | 1 −11 | 2 −10 | 3 −9 | 4 −8 | 5 −7 | 6 −6 | 7 −5 | 8 −4 | 9 −3 | 10 −2 | 11 −1 |

DATE LINE

Monday / Sunday

Anchorage

Vancouver   Winnipeg   Ottawa   8.30   London

Denver   Washington   Rabat

Los Angeles

New Orleans

Miami

México

Panamá   Caracas   Dakar   Abidja

Equator

2.30

Lima

3.30   La Paz

São Paulo

Zone Times are the Standard Times
kept on land and sea compared with
12 hours (noon) Greenwich Mean Time.
Daylight Saving Time (normally one
hour in advance of local Standard
Time), which is observed by certain
countries for part of the year,
is not shown on the map.

Buenos
Aires

| 180° | 165° | 150° | 135° | 120° | 105° | 90° | 75° | 60° | 45° | 30° | 15° |

Journey Times

Sail (via Cape)
164 days

Steam (via Cape)
43 days

Steam (via Suez)
30 days

Supertanker
(via Cape)
28 days

Singapore

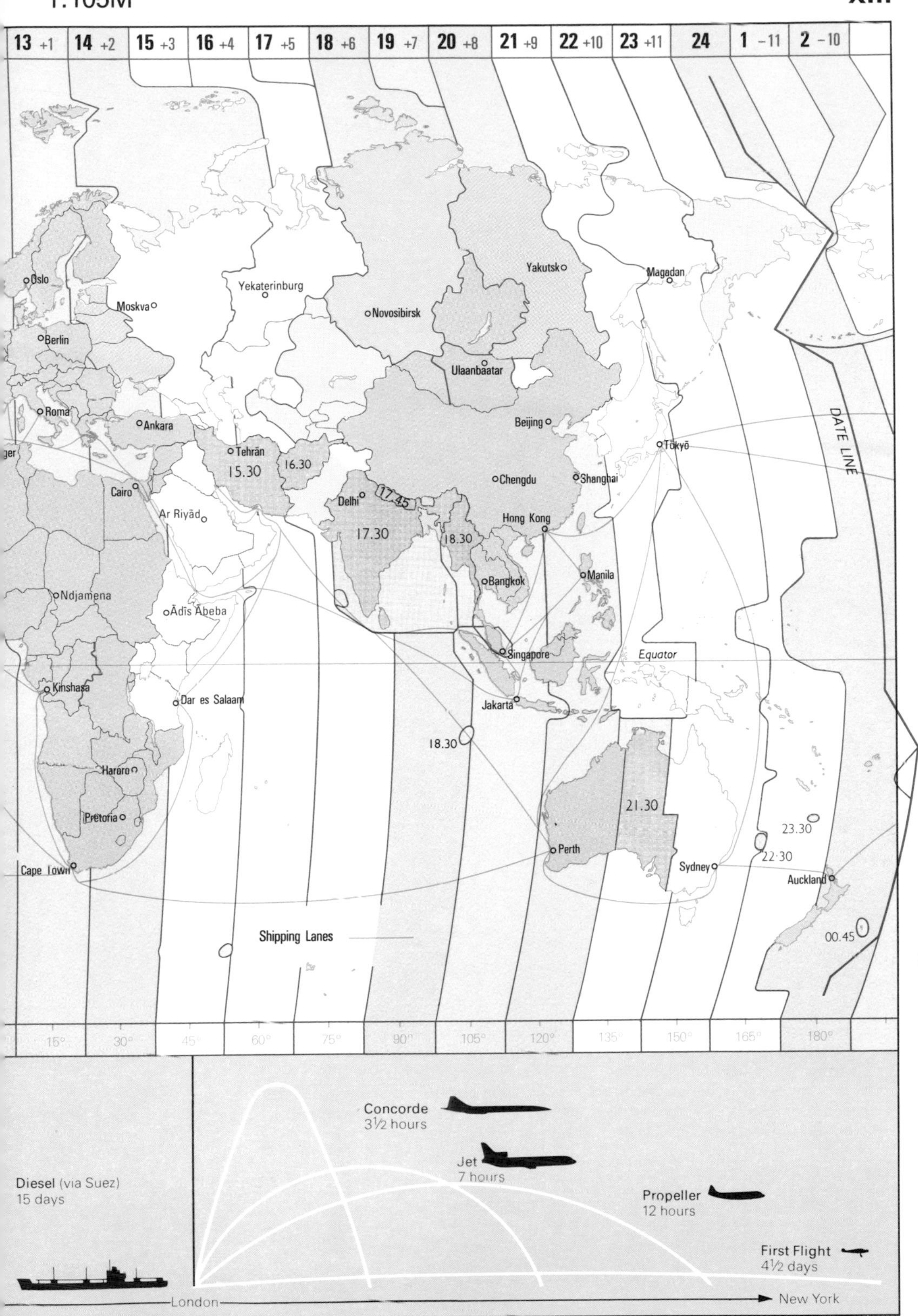

13 +1	**14** +2	**15** +3	**16** +4	**17** +5	**18** +6	**19** +7	**20** +8	**21** +9	**22** +10	**23** +11	**24**	**1** −11	**2** −10

Oslo

Moskva

Yekaterinburg

Yakutsk

Magadan

Berlin

Novosibirsk

Roma

Ulaanbaatar

Ankara

Beijing

Tōkyō

DATE LINE

Tehrān
15.30

16.30

Cairo

Chengdu

Shanghai

Ar Riyād

Delhi

17.45

Hong Kong

17.30

18.30

Ndjamena

Manila

Ādis Ābeba

Bangkok

Kinshasa

Dar es Salaam

Singapore

Equator

Jakarta

18.30

Harāre

21.30

Pretoria

23.30

Cape Town

Perth

Sydney
22.30

Auckland

Shipping Lanes

00.45

| 15° | 30° | 45° | 60° | 75° | 90° | 105° | 120° | 135° | 150° | 165° | 180° |

Diesel (via Suez)
15 days

Concorde
3½ hours

Jet
7 hours

Propeller
12 hours

First Flight
4½ days

London ────────────────────────→ New York

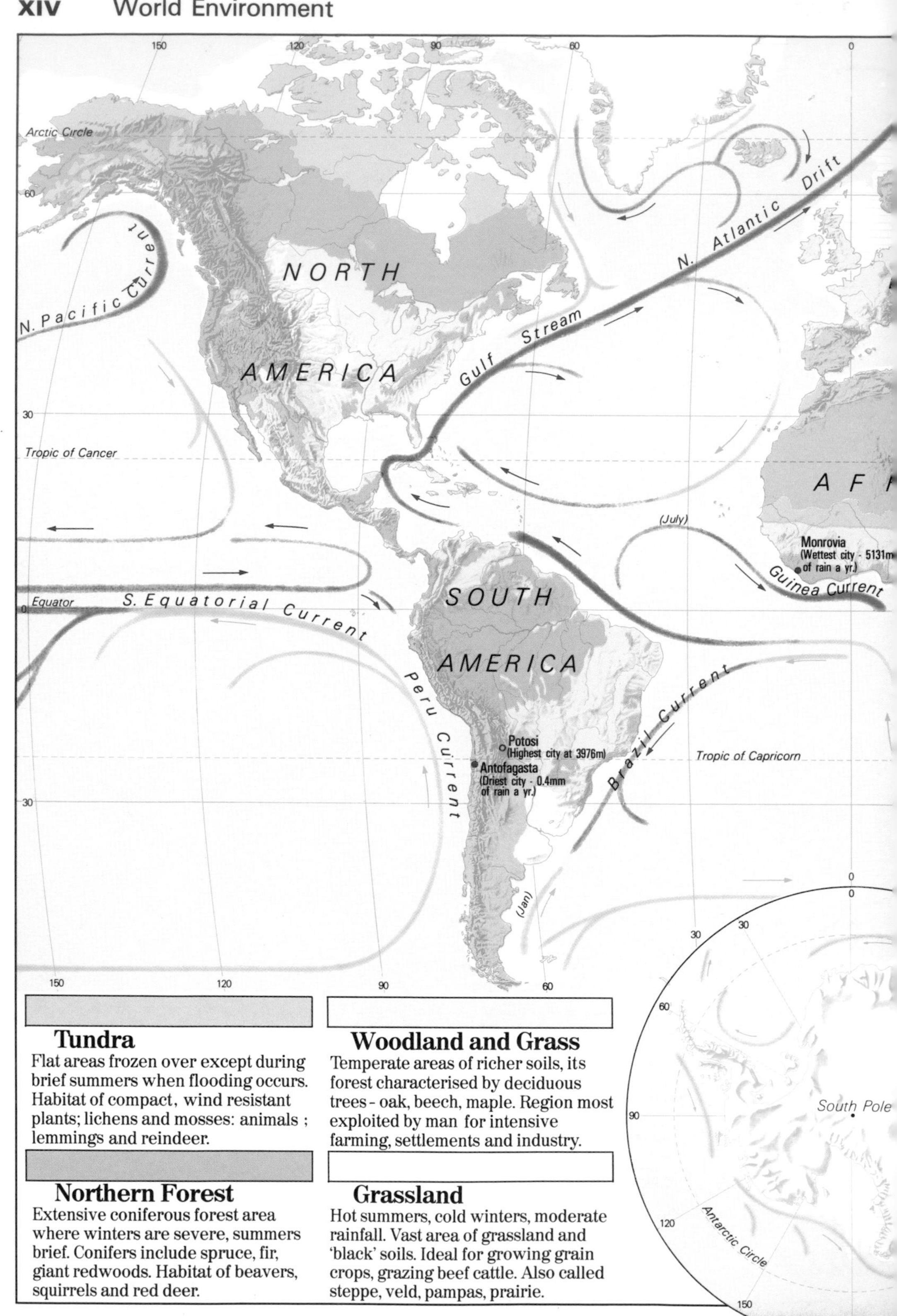

Tundra
Flat areas frozen over except during brief summers when flooding occurs. Habitat of compact, wind resistant plants; lichens and mosses: animals ; lemmings and reindeer.

Woodland and Grass
Temperate areas of richer soils, its forest characterised by deciduous trees - oak, beech, maple. Region most exploited by man for intensive farming, settlements and industry.

Northern Forest
Extensive coniferous forest area where winters are severe, summers brief. Conifers include spruce, fir, giant redwoods. Habitat of beavers, squirrels and red deer.

Grassland
Hot summers, cold winters, moderate rainfall. Vast area of grassland and 'black' soils. Ideal for growing grain crops, grazing beef cattle. Also called steppe, veld, pampas, prairie.

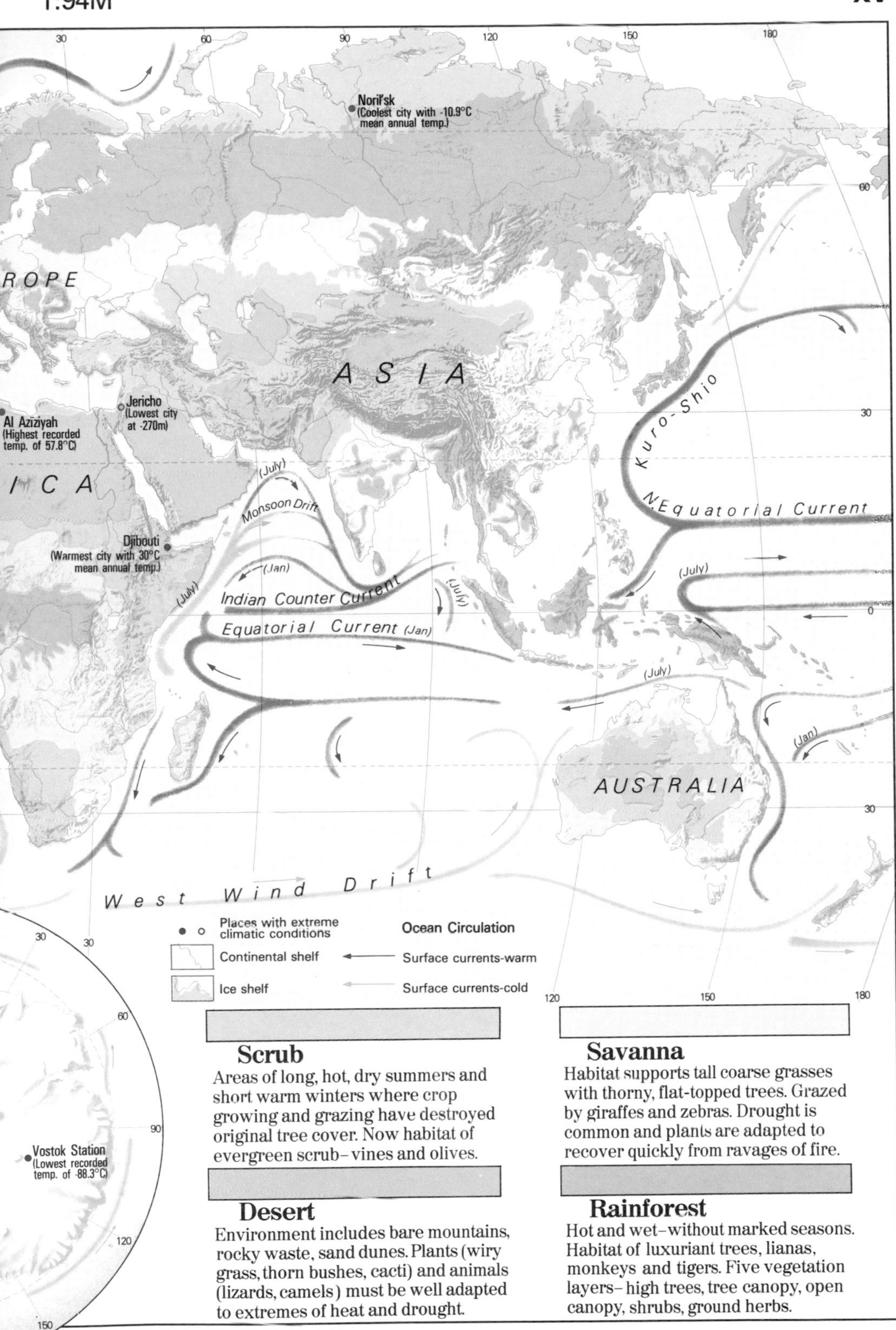

Noril'sk
(Coolest city with -10.9°C
mean annual temp.)

R O P E

A S I A

I C A

Al Aziziyah
(Highest recorded
temp. of 57.8°C)

Jericho
(Lowest city
at -270m)

Djibouti
(Warmest city with 30°C
mean annual temp.)

Kuro-Shio

(July)

Monsoon Drift

N Equatorial Current

Indian Counter Current

(Jan)

(July)

(July)

Equatorial Current (Jan)

(July)

(July)

AUSTRALIA

(Jan)

West Wind Drift

Vostok Station
(Lowest recorded
temp. of -88.3°C)

Places with extreme
climatic conditions

Ocean Circulation

Continental shelf   ⟵ Surface currents-warm

Ice shelf   ⟵ Surface currents-cold

Scrub
Areas of long, hot, dry summers and
short warm winters where crop
growing and grazing have destroyed
original tree cover. Now habitat of
evergreen scrub–vines and olives.

Savanna
Habitat supports tall coarse grasses
with thorny, flat-topped trees. Grazed
by giraffes and zebras. Drought is
common and plants are adapted to
recover quickly from ravages of fire.

Desert
Environment includes bare mountains,
rocky waste, sand dunes. Plants (wiry
grass, thorn bushes, cacti) and animals
(lizards, camels) must be well adapted
to extremes of heat and drought.

Rainforest
Hot and wet–without marked seasons.
Habitat of luxuriant trees, lianas,
monkeys and tigers. Five vegetation
layers– high trees, tree canopy, open
canopy, shrubs, ground herbs.

BOUNDARIES

▬▬▬▬	International
▬ ▬ ▬ ▬	International under Dispute
▪ ▪ ▪ ▪ ▪ ▪	Cease Fire Line
▬▬▬▬	Autonomous or State/ Administrative
▬ ▬ ▬ ▬	Maritime (National)
─ ─ ─ ─	International Date Line

COMMUNICATIONS

══════ ════	Motorway/Under Construction
───────	Major/Other Road
─ ─ ─ ─ ─	Under Construction
‧ ‧ ‧ ‧ ‧ ‧	Track
⇒──── ⇐	Road Tunnel
─ ‧ ─ ‧ ─	Car Ferry
───────	Main/Other Railway
─ ─ ─ ─ ─	Under Construction
─ ‧ ─ ‧ ─	Rail Ferry
⟶──── ⟵	Rail Tunnel
┴┴┴┴┴┴	Canal
⊕ ✈	International/Other Airport

LANDSCAPE FEATURES

	Glacier, Ice Cap
	Marsh, Swamp
	Sand Desert, Dunes
	Freshwater
	Saltwater
	Seasonal
	Salt Pan

OTHER FEATURES

	River/Seasonal
≍	Pass, Gorge
	Dam, Barrage
	Waterfall, Rapid
───────	Aqueduct
	Reef
.217 ▲4231	Spot Height, Depth/ Summit, Peak
	Well
Δ ▲	Oil/Gas Field
Gas / Oil	Oil/Natural Gas Pipeline
⌐ Gemsbok Nat. Pk ⌐	National Park
.∴UR	Historic Site

LETTERING STYLES

CANADA	Independent Nation
FLORIDA	State, Province or Autonomous Region
Gibraltar (U.K.)	Sovereignty of Dependent Territory
Lothian	Administrative Area
LANGUEDOC	Historic Region
Loire ***Vosges***	Physical Feature or Physical Region

TOWNS AND CITIES

Square symbols denote capital cities

▣	◉	**New York**	Major City
▪	●	**Montréal**	City
▢	○	Ottawa	Small City
▪	•	**Québec**	Large Town
▫	○	St John's	Town
▫	○	Yorkton	Small Town
▫	○	Jasper	Village
			Built-up-area

Depth   Sea Level   Height
0

8000m 6000m 4000m 2000m 200m   200m 500m 1000m 2000m 3000m 4000m 5000m 6000m

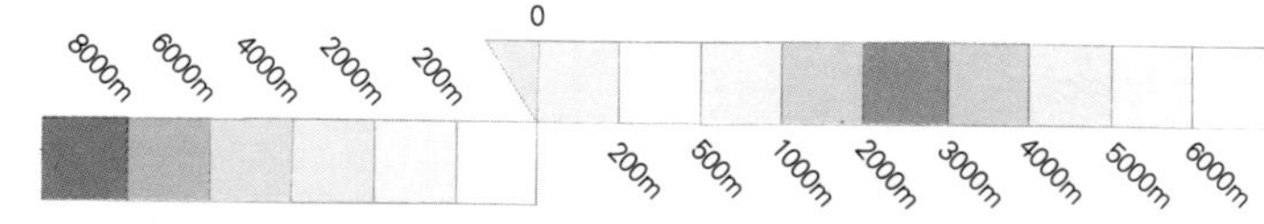

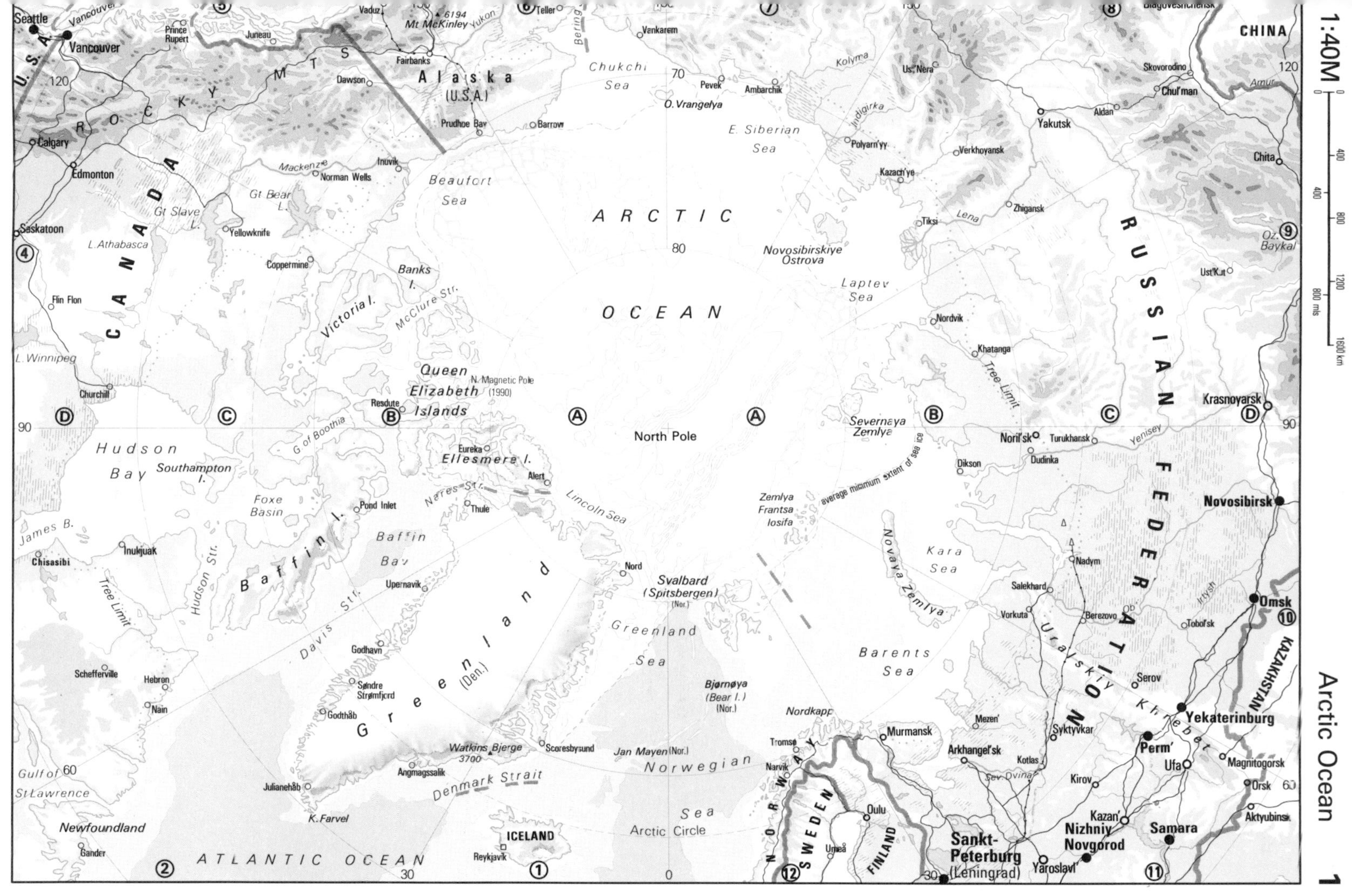

1:40M

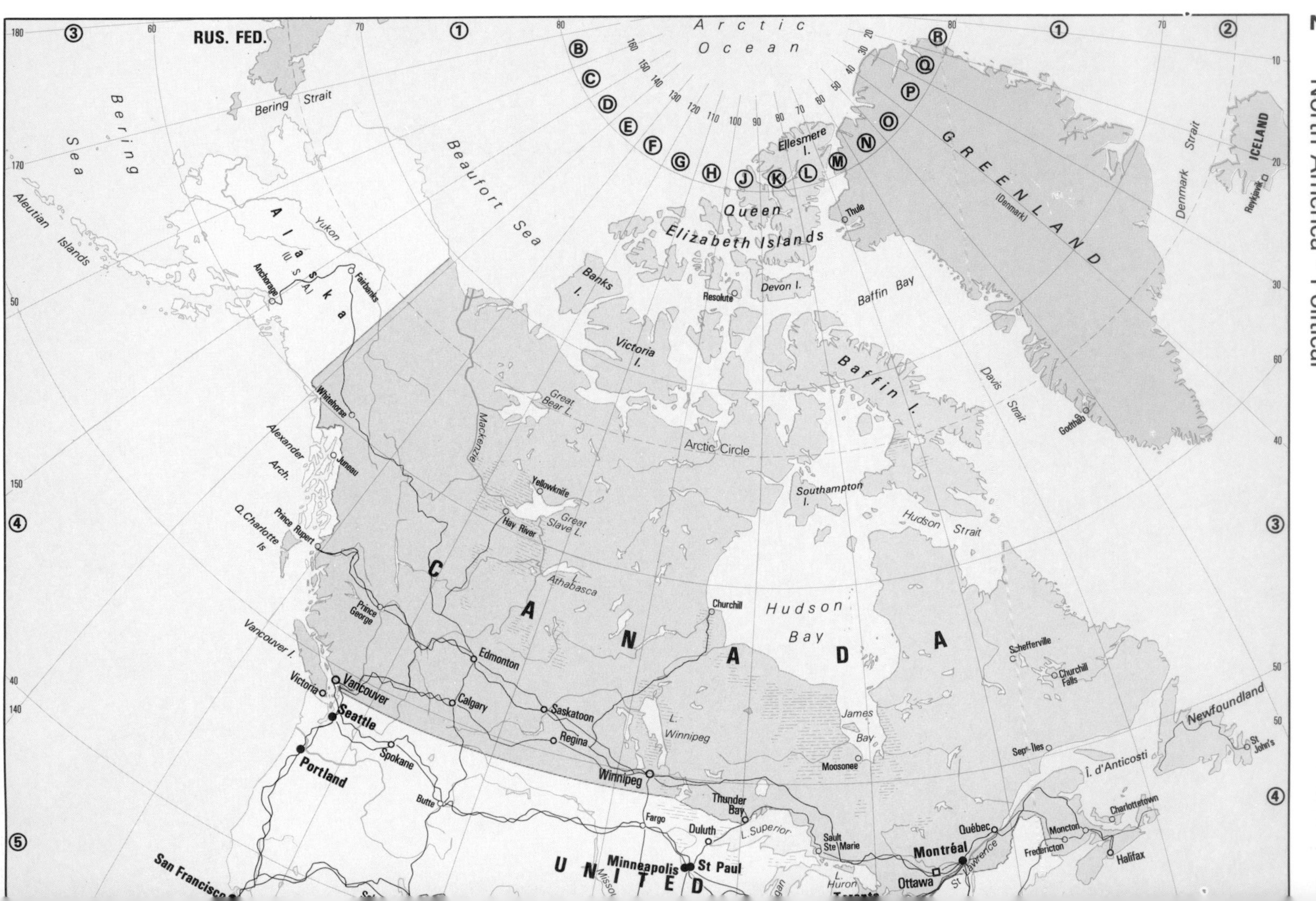
RUS. FED.
Arctic Ocean
Bering Strait
Bering Sea
Aleutian Islands
Alaska
(U S A)
Yukon
Anchorage
Fairbanks
Beaufort Sea
Queen Elizabeth Islands
Ellesmere I.
Thule
GREENLAND
(Denmark)
Denmark Strait
ICELAND
Reykjavík
Banks I.
Resolute
Devon I.
Baffin Bay
Victoria I.
Baffin I.
Davis Strait
Godthåb
Whitehorse
Great Bear L.
Mackenzie
Arctic Circle
Alexander Arch.
Juneau
Yellowknife
Southampton I.
Hay River
Great Slave L.
Hudson Strait
Q. Charlotte Is
Prince Rupert
C A N A D A
Athabasca
Churchill
Hudson Bay
Prince George
Vancouver I.
Edmonton
Schefferville
Churchill Falls
Victoria
Vancouver
Calgary
Saskatoon
L. Winnipeg
James Bay
Newfoundland
Seattle
Regina
St John's
Sept Îles
Portland
Spokane
Moosonee
Î. d'Anticosti
Winnipeg
Thunder Bay
Butte
Charlottetown
Fargo
Duluth
L. Superior
Sault Ste Marie
Québec
Moncton
Fredericton
Montréal
Halifax
San Francisco
Minneapolis
St Paul
UNITED
L. Huron
Ottawa
St Lawrence

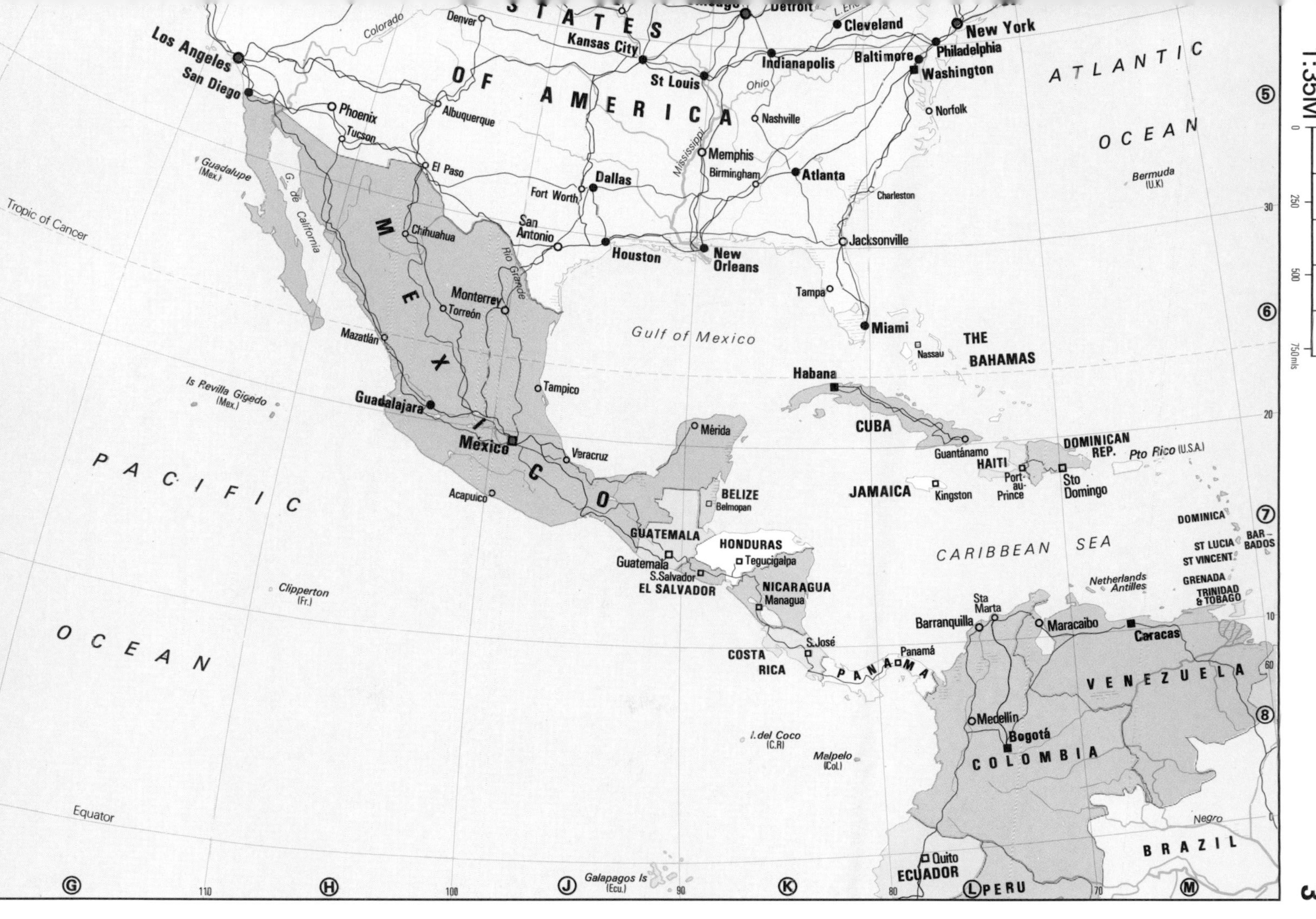

1:35M

250   500   750   1000   1250 km

250   500   750mls

ATLANTIC OCEAN

L. Erie

L. Ontario

Bermuda (U.K.)

UNITED STATES OF AMERICA

Chicago
Detroit
Cleveland
New York
Philadelphia
Baltimore
Washington
Indianapolis
Ohio
Norfolk
Nashville
Atlanta
Charleston
St Louis
Memphis
Birmingham
Jacksonville
Kansas City
Denver
Albuquerque
Dallas
Fort Worth
San Antonio
El Paso
Phoenix
Tucson
Los Angeles
San Diego
Colorado

Rio Grande
Chihuahua

MEXICO

Monterrey
Torreón
Mazatlán
Guadalajara
México
Acapulco
Tampico
Veracruz
Mérida

Tropic of Cancer

G. de California

Guadalupe (Mex.)

Is Revilla Gigedo (Mex.)

PACIFIC OCEAN

Clipperton (Fr.)

Equator

Tampa
Miami

THE BAHAMAS

Nassau

Gulf of Mexico

Habana

CUBA

Guantánamo

JAMAICA
Kingston

HAITI
Port-au-Prince

DOMINICAN REP.
Sto Domingo

Pto Rico (U.S.A)

CARIBBEAN SEA

BAR-BADOS
ST LUCIA
ST VINCENT
GRENADA
DOMINICA
TRINIDAD & TOBAGO

Netherlands Antilles

Caracas

VENEZUELA

Maracaibo
Sta Marta
Barranquilla
Medellín
Bogotá

COLOMBIA

BRAZIL

Negro

Quito

ECUADOR

PERU

Malpelo (Col.)

Galapagos Is (Ecu.)

I. del Coco (C.R)

BELIZE
Belmopan

GUATEMALA
Guatemala

EL SALVADOR
S.Salvador

HONDURAS
Tegucigalpa

NICARAGUA
Managua

COSTA RICA
S.José

PANAMA
Panamá

New Orleans
Houston

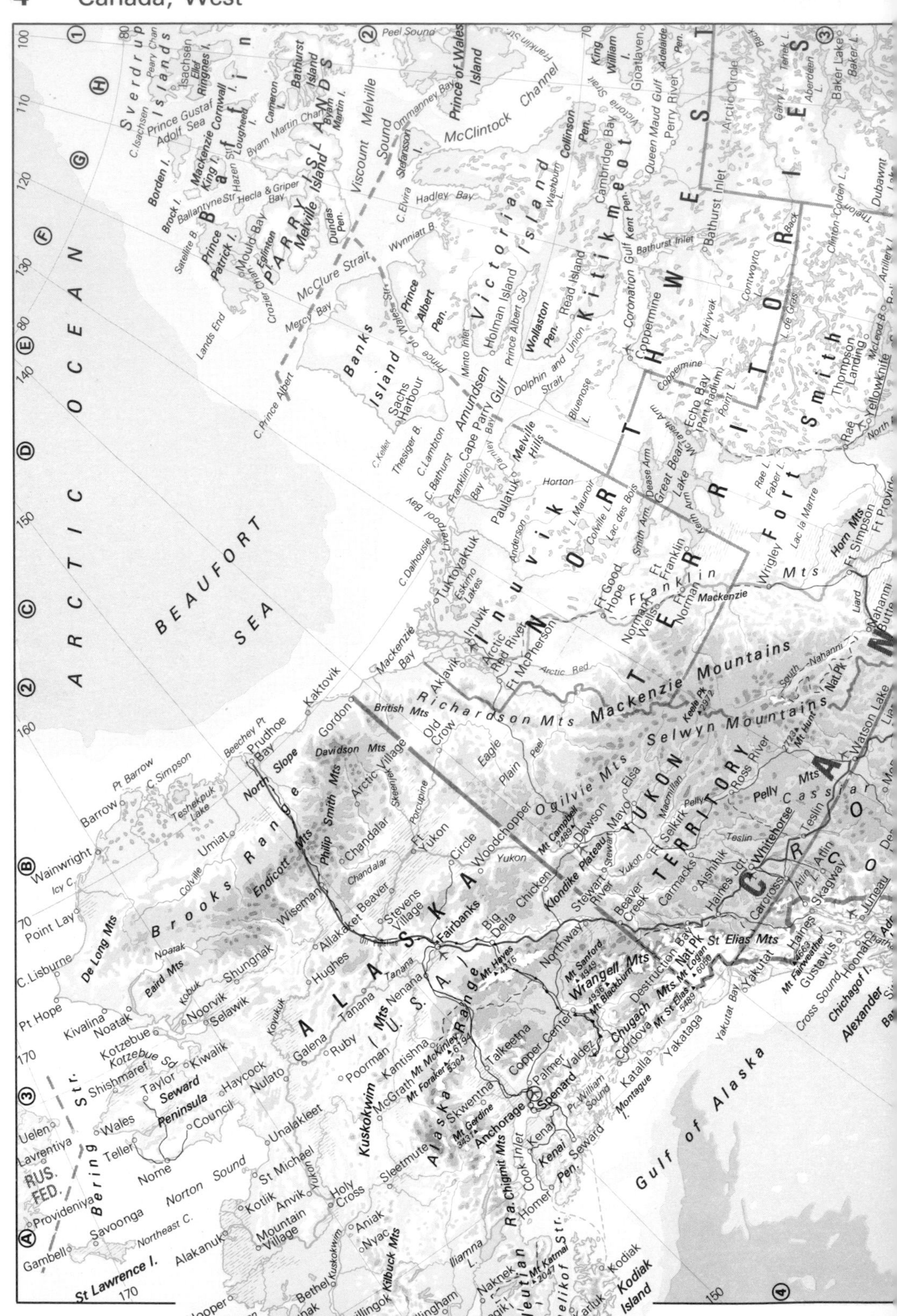
ARCTIC OCEAN
BEAUFORT SEA
Gulf of Alaska
Sverdrup Islands
PARRY ISLANDS
Banks Island
Victoria Island
Prince of Wales Island
King William I.
Melville Island
Prince Patrick I.
Borden I.
Mackenzie King I.
Brock I.
Lougheed I.
Cameron I.
Bathurst Island
Byam Martin I.
Ellef Ringnes I.
Isachsen
C.Isachsen
Peary Chan
Prince Gustaf Adolf Sea
Cornwall
Hazen Str
Byam Martin Chan
Ballantyne Str
Hecla & Griper Bay
Satellite B.
Mould Bay
Eglinton
Crozier Chan
Dundas Pen.
Viscount Melville Sound
Stefansson I.
Ommanney Bay
McClintock Channel
Peel Sound
Franklin Str
C.Elvira
Hadley Bay
Wynniatt B.
McClure Strait
Mercy Bay
Lands End
Prince of Wales Str
Prince Albert Pen.
Minto Inlet
Holman Island
Prince Albert Sd
Wollaston Pen.
Read Island
Dolphin and Union Strait
Collinson Pen.
Washburn L.
Cambridge Bay
Victoria Strait
Gjoa Haven
Queen Maud Gulf
Adelaide Pen.
Perry River
Kent Pen.
Bathurst Inlet
Coronation Gulf
Coppermine
C.Prince Albert
Sachs Harbour
Amundsen Gulf
Cape Parry
Darnley Bay
Melville Hills
Paulatuk
Horton
Bluenose L.
C.Kellet
Thesiger B.
C.Lambton
C.Bathurst
Franklin Bay
Liverpool Bay
C.Dalhousie
Anderson
L.Maunoir
Colville L.
Lac des Bois
Dease Arm
Great Bear Lake
McVicar Arm
Echo Bay (Port Radium)
Smith Arm
Keith Arm
Tuktoyaktuk
Eskimo Lakes
Mackenzie Bay
Inuvik
Aklavik
Arctic Red River
Ft McPherson
Arctic Red
Ft Good Hope
Ft Franklin
Norman Wells
Ft Norman
Franklin Mts
Mackenzie
Wrigley
Horn Mts
Ft Simpson
Ft Providence
Lac la Martre
Rae L.
Faber L.
Rae
Yellowknife
Thompson Landing
Contwoyto L.
Takiyvak L.
L.de Gras
Point L.
Coppermine
Back
Baker Lake
Aberdeen L.
Garry L.
Tehek L.
Arctic Circle
Dubawnt
Thelon
Clinton-Colden L.
Artillery L.
McLeod B.
Kitikmeot
Inuvik
Fort Smith
NORTHWEST TERRITORIES
YUKON TERRITORY
Mackenzie Mountains
Selwyn Mountains
Richardson Mts
British Mts
Keele Pk 2972
South Nahanni
Nahanni Nat.Pk
Nahanni Butte
Liard
Watson Lake
Mt Hunt 2743
Pelly Mts
Cassiar
Ross River
Macmillan
Pelly
Teslin
Whitehorse
Atlin
Atlin L.
Carcross
Skagway
Juneau
Haines
Haines Jct.
Aishihik
Carmacks
Ft Selkirk
Beaver Creek
Stewart River
Mayo
Elsa
Dawson
Mt Campbell 2489
Klondike Plateau
Ogilvie Mts
Eagle Plain
Peel
Old Crow
Porcupine
Yukon
Stewart
Kaktovik
Gordon
Beechey Pt
Prudhoe Bay
Pt Barrow
C.Simpson
Barrow
Teshekpuk Lake
Wainwright
Icy C.
Point Lay
C.Lisburne
Pt Hope
Kivalina
Noatak
Kotzebue
Kotzebue Sd
Shishmaref
Kiwalik
Taylor
Seward Peninsula
Haycock
Council
Wales
Teller
Nome
Uelen
Lavrentiya
Provideniya
RUS. FED.
Bering Str
Gambell
Savoonga
Northeast C.
St Lawrence I.
Norton Sound
Alakanuk
Kotlik
St Michael
Unalakleet
Anvik
Holy Cross
Mountain Village
Sleetmute
Aniak
Nyac
Kilbuck Mts
Kuskokwim
Kuskokwim Mts
Bethel
Hooper Bay
Hazen Bay
Tanunak
Kwigillingok
Dillingham
Iliamna L.
Naknek
Egegik
Aleutian Ra.
Mt Katmai 2047
Shelikof Str.
Karluk
Kodiak
Kodiak Island
Chigmit Mts
Cook Inlet
Kenai
Kenai Pen.
Homer
Seward
Anchorage
Spenard
Palmer
Talkeetna
Skwentna
Mt Gerdine 3431
Alaska Range
Mt McKinley 6194
Mt Foraker 5304
McGrath
Kantishna
Poorman
Ruby
Galena
Nulato
Tanana
Nenana
Hughes
Allakaket
Koyukuk
Kobuk
Shungnak
Noorvik
Selawik
Noatak
Baird Mts
De Long Mts
Brooks Range
Endicott Mts
Philip Smith Mts
Davidson Mts
North Slope
Umiat
Colville
Arctic Village
Sheenjek
Chandalar
Ft Yukon
Circle
Woodchopper
Wiseman
Beaver
Stevens Village
Fairbanks
Big Delta
Chicken
Northway
Mt Hayes 4216
Mt Sanford 4949
Wrangell Mts
Mt Blackburn 4996
Copper Center
Valdez
Chugach Mts
Cordova
Katalla
Yakataga
Pr.William Sound
Montague I.
Mt St Elias 5489
Mt Logan 6050
St Elias Mts
Destruction Bay
Yakutat
Yakutat Bay
Mt Fairweather 4663
Gustavus
Hoonah
Chichagof I.
Cross Sound
Alexander
ALASKA
U.S.A.
CANADA
COLOMBIA
N
E
H
G
F
E
D
C
B
A
1
2
3
4
100
110
120
130
140
150
160
170
80
70
60

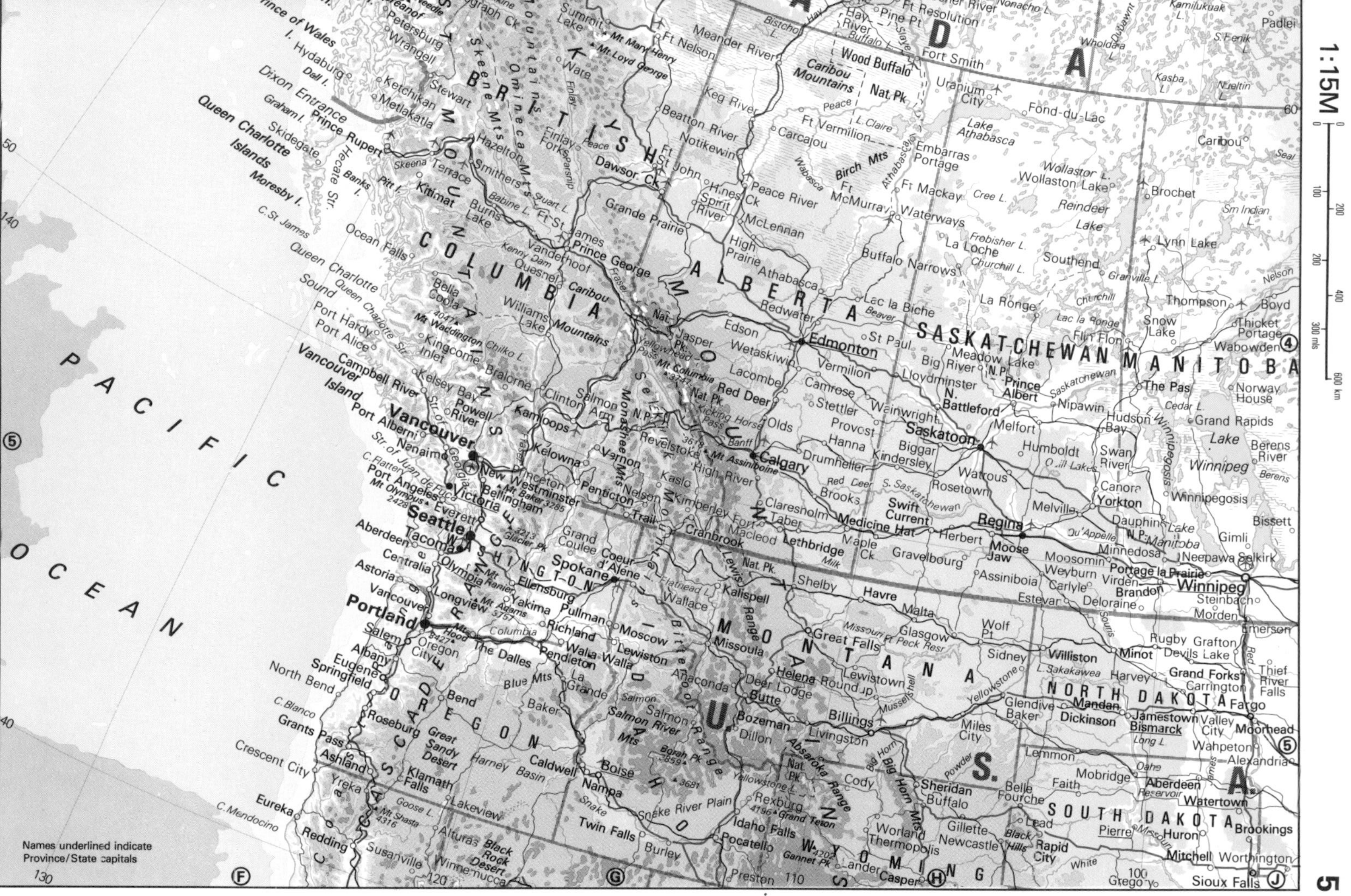
CANADA
U.S.A.
PACIFIC OCEAN
BRITISH COLUMBIA
ALBERTA
SASKATCHEWAN
MANITOBA
WASHINGTON
OREGON
IDAHO
MONTANA
WYOMING
NORTH DAKOTA
SOUTH DAKOTA
Vancouver
Victoria
Seattle
Tacoma
Portland
Spokane
Calgary
Edmonton
Regina
Saskatoon
Winnipeg
Prince George
Prince Rupert
Kamloops
Kelowna
Lethbridge
Medicine Hat
Great Falls
Helena
Billings
Boise
Bismarck
Fargo
Pierre
Olympia
Salem
Eugene
Queen Charlotte Islands
Vancouver Island
Rocky Mountains
Coast Mountains
Big Horn Mts
Absaroka Range
Bitterroot Range
Lake Athabasca
Lake Winnipeg
Lake Winnipegosis
Names underlined indicate Province/State capitals

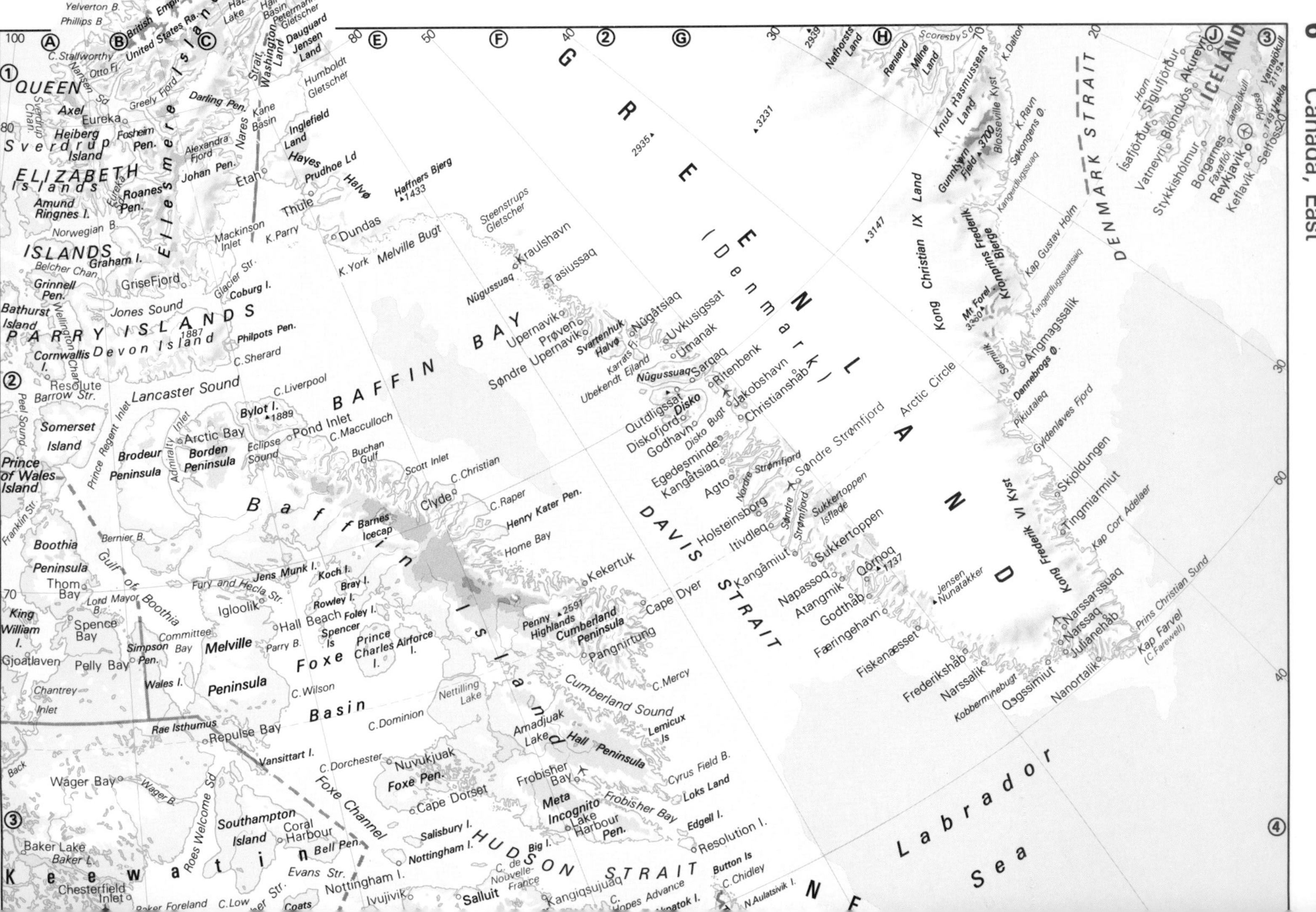
GREENLAND
(Denmark)
ICELAND
DENMARK STRAIT
DAVIS STRAIT
BAFFIN BAY
Baffin Island
Labrador Sea
HUDSON STRAIT
Foxe Basin
Foxe Channel
QUEEN ELIZABETH ISLANDS
PARRY ISLANDS
Sverdrup Islands
Ellesmere Island
Devon Island
Lancaster Sound
Jones Sound
Gulf of Boothia
Melville Peninsula
Southampton Island
Cumberland Sound
Frobisher Bay
Kong Christian IX Land
Kong Frederik VI Kyst
Arctic Circle
Reykjavík
Akureyri
Thule
Godthåb
Julianehåb
Angmagssalik
Upernavik
Umanak
Jakobshavn
Holsteinsborg
Frobisher Bay
Pangnirtung
Clyde
Pond Inlet
Arctic Bay
Resolute
Igloolik
Hall Beach
Repulse Bay
Coral Harbour
Cape Dorset
Chesterfield Inlet
Baker Lake
Spence Bay
Pelly Bay
Gjoa Haven
Nettilling Lake
Amadjuak Lake
Prince Charles I.
Bylot I.
Somerset Island
Prince of Wales Island
Boothia Peninsula
Keewatin

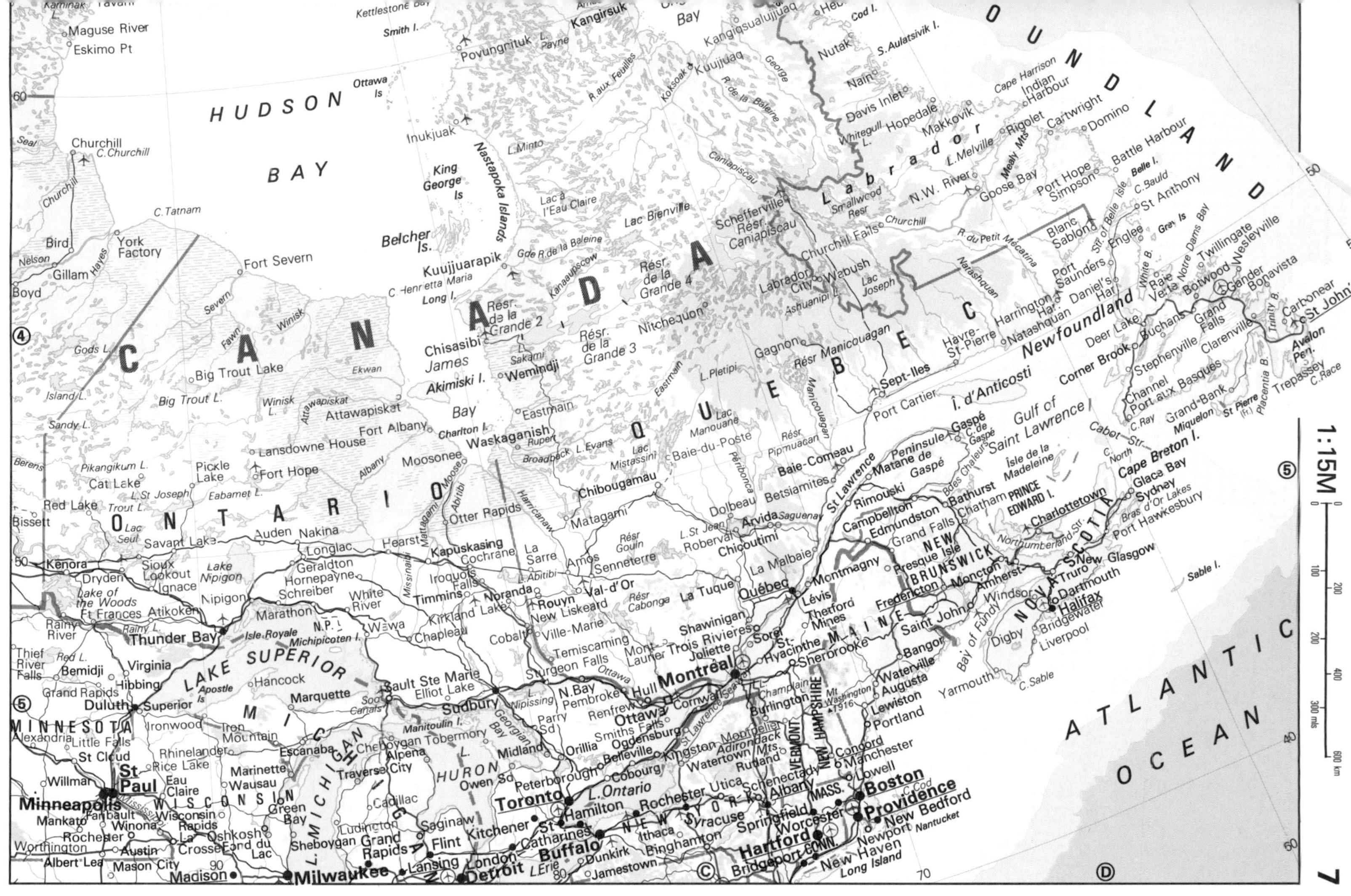
HUDSON BAY
James Bay
CANADA
ONTARIO
QUEBEC
NEWFOUNDLAND
Labrador
Newfoundland
NEW BRUNSWICK
NOVA SCOTIA
PRINCE EDWARD I.
MAINE
NEW HAMPSHIRE
VERMONT
MASS.
CONN.
NEW YORK
MINNESOTA
WISCONSIN
MICHIGAN
L. MICHIGAN
ATLANTIC OCEAN
LAKE SUPERIOR
L. HURON
L. Ontario
L. Erie
Gulf of Saint Lawrence
Î. d'Anticosti
Cape Breton I.
Sable I.
Nastapoka Islands
Belcher Is.
King George Is
Akimiski I.
Churchill
York Factory
Fort Severn
Big Trout Lake
Attawapiskat
Fort Albany
Moosonee
Kapuskasing
Timmins
Sudbury
Sault Ste Marie
Thunder Bay
Duluth
Minneapolis
St Paul
Milwaukee
Detroit
Toronto
Buffalo
Ottawa
Montréal
Québec
Chibougamau
Chicoutimi
Baie-Comeau
Sept-Iles
Schefferville
Churchill Falls
Goose Bay
Corner Brook
Gander
St John's
Halifax
Charlottetown
Saint John
Fredericton
Moncton
Bangor
Portland
Boston
Providence
Hartford
New Haven
Long Island

1:12.5M

0 100 200 300 400 500 km

0 100 200 300 mls

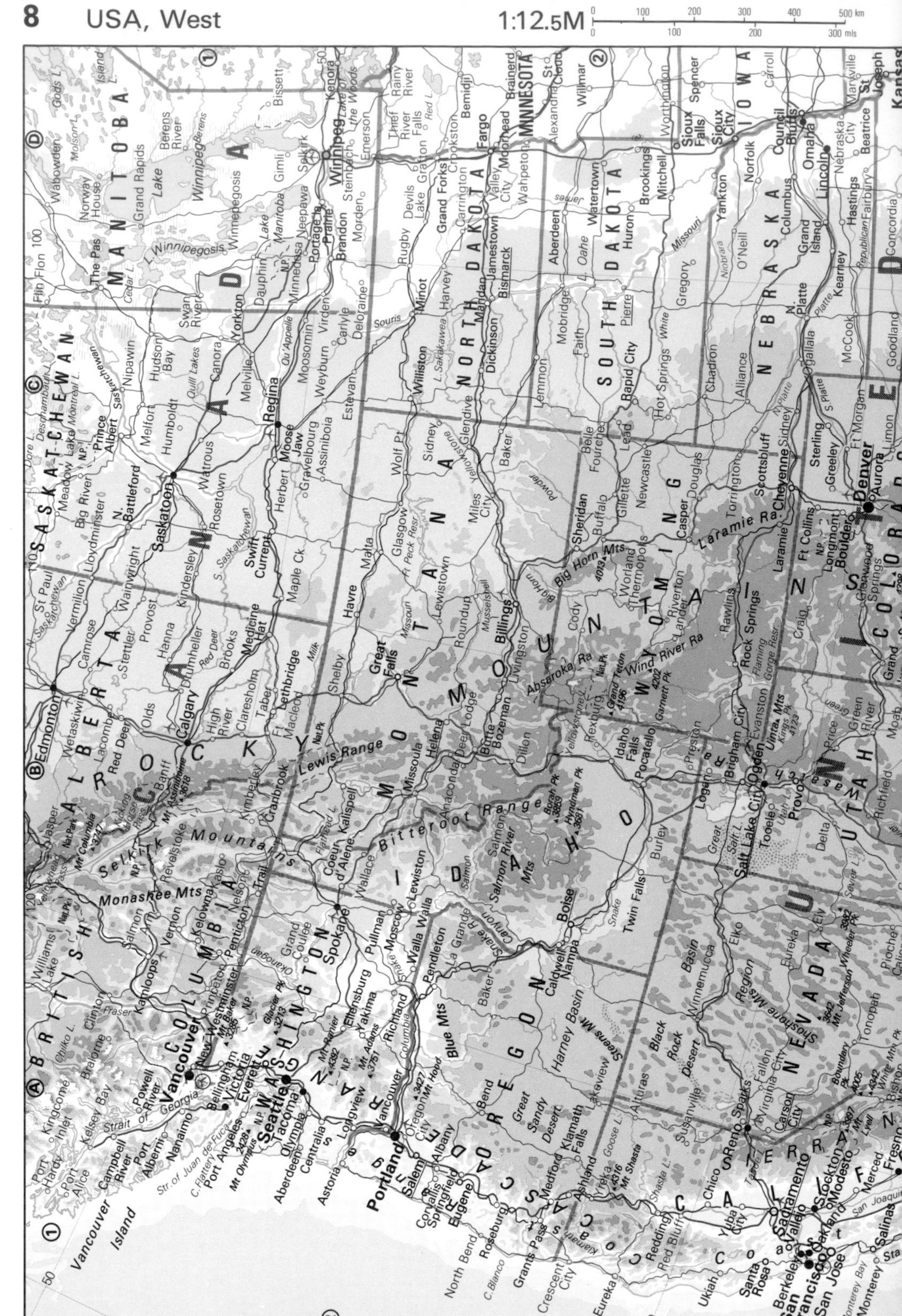

MANITOBA
SASKATCHEWAN
ALBERTA
BRITISH COLUMBIA
CANADA
NORTH DAKOTA
SOUTH DAKOTA
MINNESOTA
IOWA
NEBRASKA
MONTANA
WYOMING
IDAHO
WASHINGTON
OREGON
NEVADA
UTAH
COLORADO
CALIFORNIA
UNITED STATES
ROCKY MOUNTAINS
Lewis Range
Bitterroot Range
Selkirk Mountains
Monashee Mts
Salmon River Mts
Big Horn Mts
Wind River Ra
Absaroka Ra
Laramie Ra
Blue Mts
Great Basin
Black Rock Desert
Harney Basin
Great Sandy Desert
Vancouver Island
Strait of Georgia
Winnipeg
Regina
Saskatoon
Calgary
Edmonton
Vancouver
Victoria
Seattle
Tacoma
Olympia
Spokane
Portland
Salem
Eugene
Boise
Salt Lake City
Ogden
Provo
Helena
Great Falls
Billings
Missoula
Butte
Bismarck
Fargo
Pierre
Rapid City
Sioux Falls
Omaha
Lincoln
Cheyenne
Casper
Denver
Reno
Sacramento
San Francisco
Oakland
San Jose
Fresno

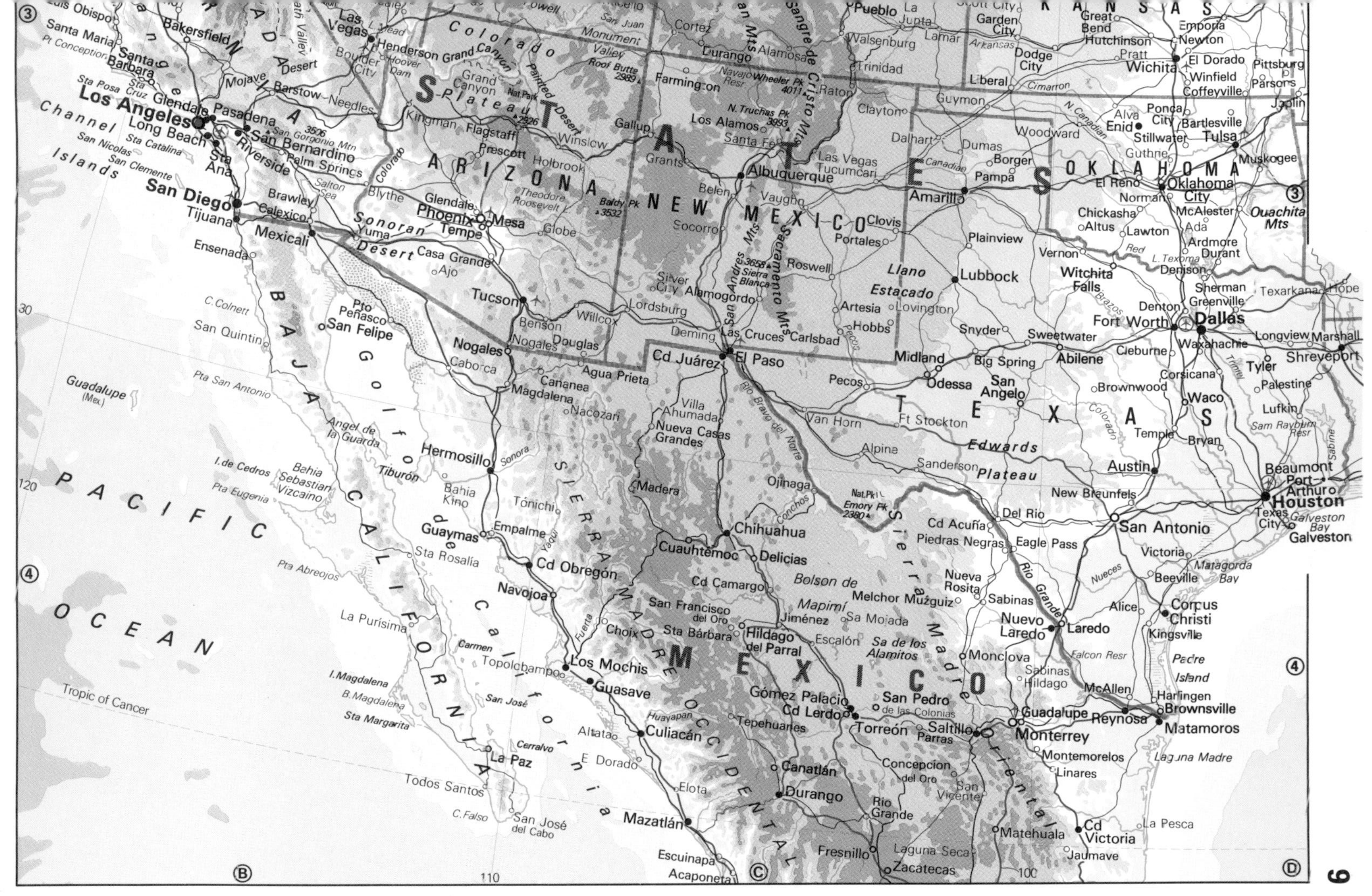
K A N S A S
O K L A H O M A
T E X A S
N E W M E X I C O
A R I Z O N A
U N I T E D S T A T E S
N E V A D A
M E X I C O
B A J A C A L I F O R N I A
Golfo de California
P A C I F I C O C E A N
Sierra Madre Oriental
S I E R R A M A D R E O C C I D E N T A L
Colorado Plateau
Painted Desert
Sonoran Desert
Llano Estacado
Edwards Plateau
Sangre de Cristo Mts
Sacramento Mts
San Andres Mts
Ouachita Mts
Bolson de Mapimí
Sa de los Alamitos
Channel Islands
Pueblo
Walsenburg
Trinidad
La Junta
Lamar
Garden City
Dodge City
Great Bend
Hutchinson
Pratt
Wichita
Emporia
Newton
El Dorado
Winfield
Coffeyville
Pittsburg
Parsons
Joplin
Liberal
Guymon
Dalhart
Dumas
Borger
Pampa
Amarillo
Clayton
Raton
Tucumcari
Las Vegas
Santa Fe
Los Alamos
Albuquerque
Belen
Socorro
Clovis
Portales
Roswell
Artesia
Hobbs
Carlsbad
Lovington
Alamogordo
Las Cruces
Deming
Silver City
Lordsburg
El Paso
Cd Juárez
Farmington
Durango
Cortez
Gallup
Grants
Flagstaff
Prescott
Winslow
Holbrook
Kingman
Phoenix
Mesa
Tempe
Glendale
Casa Grande
Tucson
Nogales
Benson
Douglas
Willcox
Yuma
Ajo
Blythe
Las Vegas
Henderson
Boulder City
Hoover Dam
Needles
Barstow
Mojave
Bakersfield
Santa Barbara
Santa Maria
Los Angeles
Long Beach
Pasadena
San Bernardino
Riverside
Sta Ana
Palm Springs
San Diego
Tijuana
Mexicali
Calexico
Brawley
Ensenada
San Quintín
San Felipe
Pto Peñasco
Caborca
Magdalena
Cananea
Agua Prieta
Nacozari
Hermosillo
Guaymas
Empalme
Cd Obregón
Navojoa
Los Mochis
Guasave
Culiacán
Mazatlán
Escuinapa
Acaponeta
La Paz
San José del Cabo
Todos Santos
Sta Rosalía
La Purísima
Chihuahua
Cuauhtémoc
Delicias
Cd Camargo
Jiménez
Hildago del Parral
Gómez Palacio
Cd Lerdo
Torreón
San Pedro de las Colonias
Durango
Fresnillo
Zacatecas
Saltillo
Monterrey
Guadalupe
Monclova
Nuevo Laredo
Laredo
Piedras Negras
Eagle Pass
Cd Acuña
Del Rio
Reynosa
McAllen
Matamoros
Brownsville
Harlingen
Cd Victoria
Linares
Montemorelos
Matehuala
Ojinaga
Villa Ahumada
Nueva Casas Grandes
Madera
Lubbock
Plainview
Snyder
Big Spring
Midland
Odessa
San Angelo
Sweetwater
Abilene
Pecos
Van Horn
Alpine
Ft Stockton
Sanderson
Wichita Falls
Vernon
Lawton
Altus
Chickasha
El Reno
Oklahoma City
Norman
Enid
Stillwater
Ponca City
Bartlesville
Tulsa
Muskogee
McAlester
Ada
Ardmore
Durant
Denison
Sherman
Denton
Fort Worth
Dallas
Greenville
Waxahachie
Corsicana
Waco
Temple
Bryan
Austin
New Braunfels
San Antonio
Victoria
Beeville
Corpus Christi
Kingsville
Alice
Tyler
Longview
Marshall
Shreveport
Texarkana
Hope
Palestine
Lufkin
Beaumont
Port Arthur
Houston
Texas City
Galveston
Rio Grande
Rio Bravo del Norte
Pecos
Colorado
Brazos
Red
Canadian
Arkansas
Cimarron
Nueces
Conchos
Laguna Madre
Tropic of Cancer
Emory Pk 2380
Wheeler Pk 4011
N. Truchas Pk 3993
Sierra Blanca 3658
Baldy Pk 3532
Roof Butte 2989
San Gorgonio Mtn 3506
Tiburón
I. de Cedros
Guadalupe (Mex.)
Sta Margarita
I. Magdalena
Cerralvo
Carmen
San José
Padre Island
Matagorda Bay
Galveston Bay
30
100
110
120
3
4
B
C
D

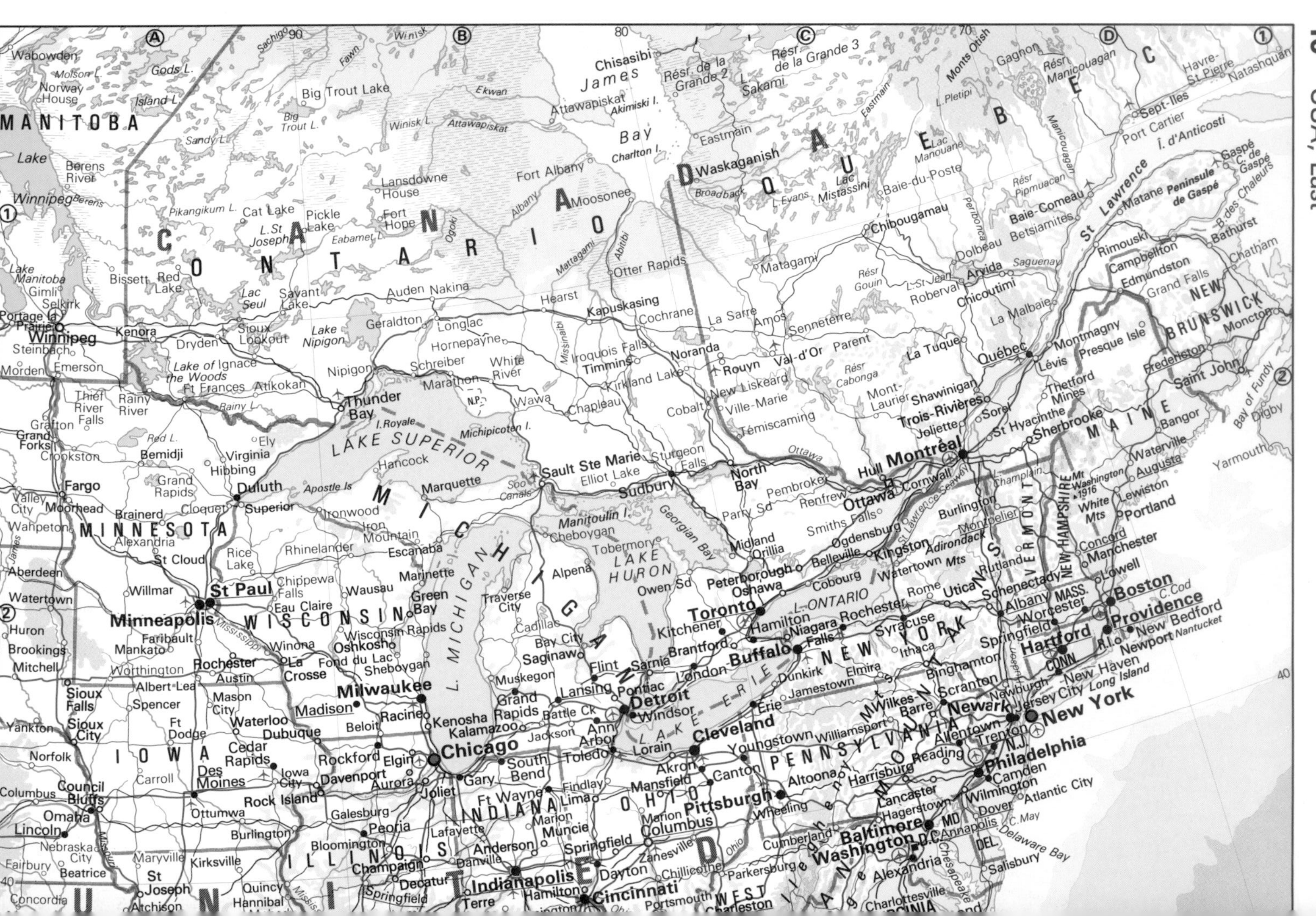

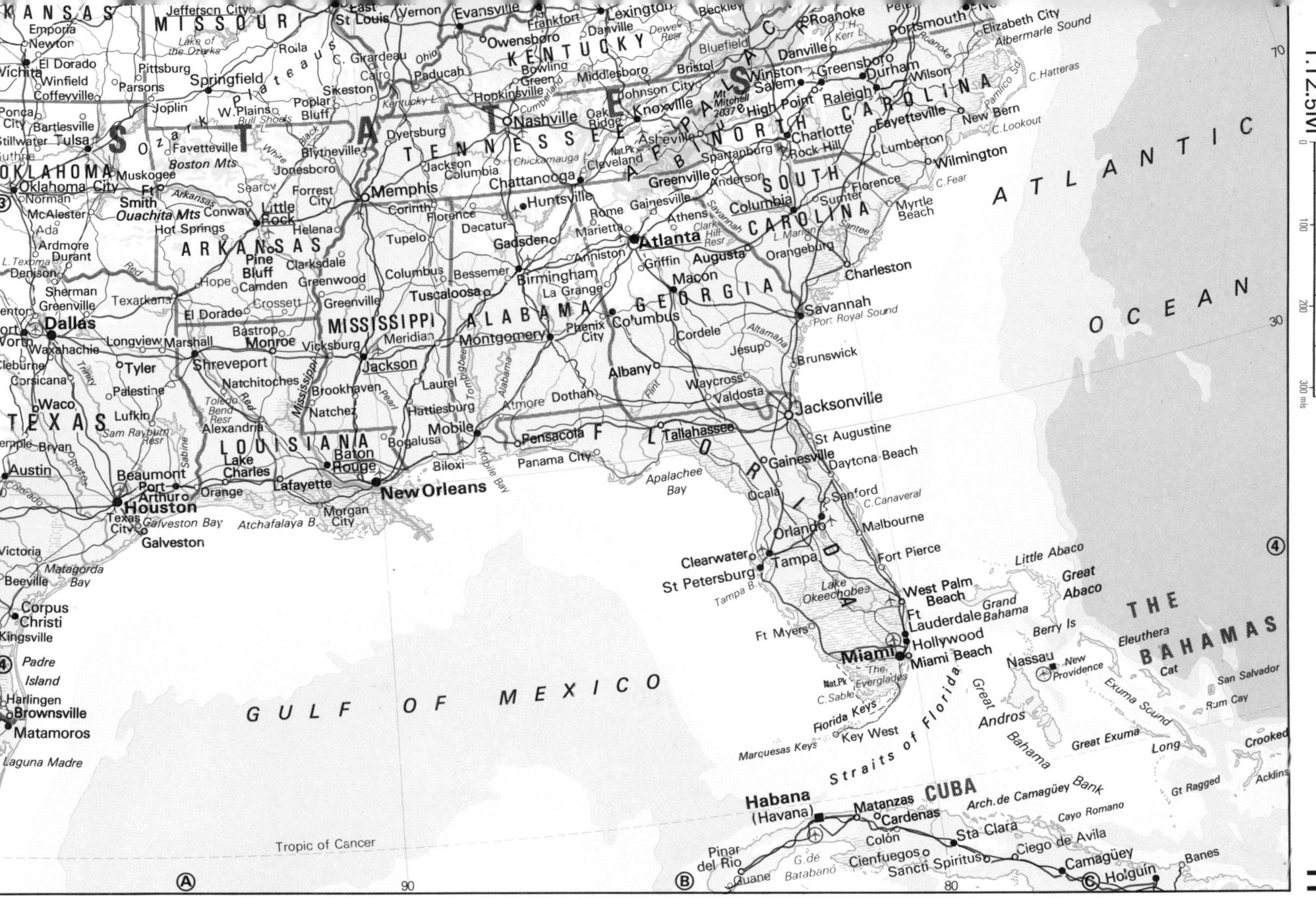
ATLANTIC OCEAN
GULF OF MEXICO
THE BAHAMAS
Straits of Florida
CUBA
KANSAS
MISSOURI
KENTUCKY
TENNESSEE
NORTH CAROLINA
SOUTH CAROLINA
GEORGIA
ALABAMA
MISSISSIPPI
LOUISIANA
ARKANSAS
OKLAHOMA
TEXAS
FLORIDA
Ozark Plateau
Dallas
Houston
New Orleans
Atlanta
Miami
Jacksonville
Memphis
Nashville
Habana (Havana)
Nassau
Tropic of Cancer

0 100 200 300 400 km
100 200 mls

Mackenzie Mountains

Canyon Range

Backbone Ranges

Richardson Mts

Ogilvie Mountains

Wernecke Mountains

YUKON

Pelly Mountains

Stikine Ranges

TERRITORY

Alexander Archipelago

St. Elias Mountains

Wrangell Mts

Chugach Mountains

Gulf of Alaska

Brooks Range

Endicott Mts

Schwatka Mts

Baird Mountains

Seward Peninsula

Norton Sound

Kuskokwim Mountains

Kuskokwim Bay

Bristol Bay

Kodiak

Talkeetna Range

Kenai Peninsula

Cook Inlet

Fairbanks

Anchorage

Nome

Whitehorse

Dawson

Juneau

Arctic Circle

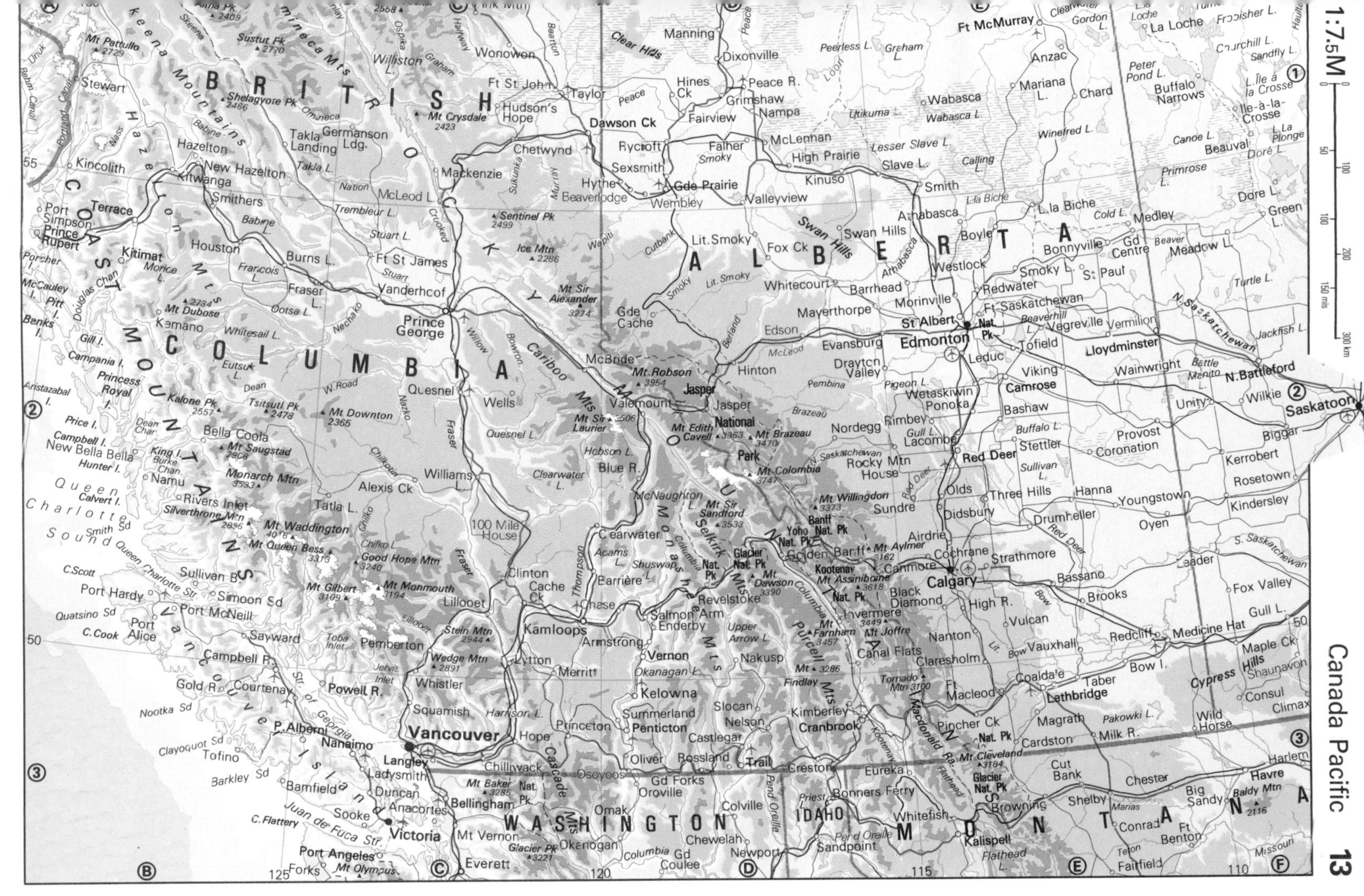

1:7.5M

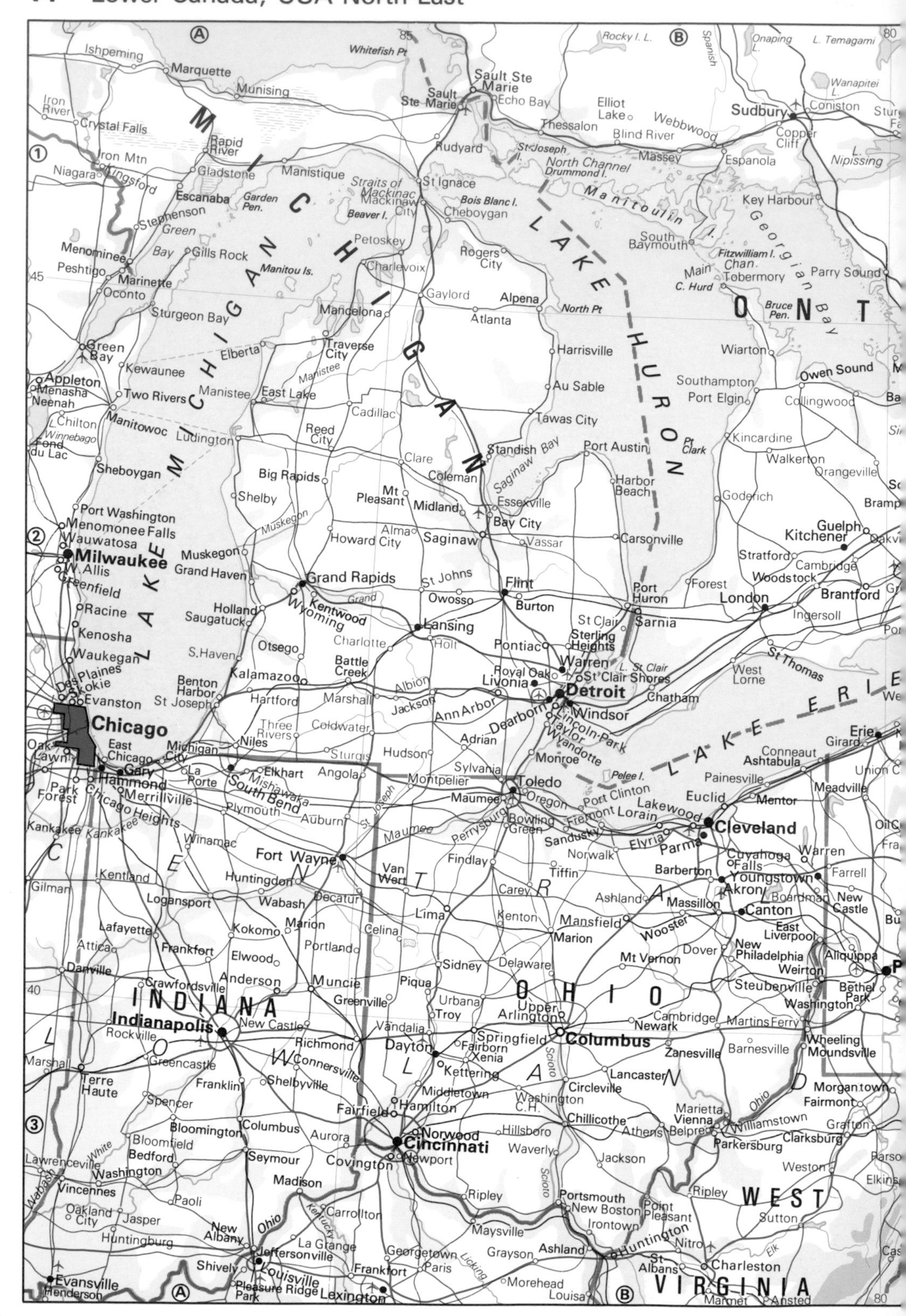
A
B
85
80
45
40
1
2
3
Ishpeming
Marquette
Munising
Whitefish Pt
Sault Ste Marie
Sault Ste Marie
Echo Bay
Rocky L. L.
Spanish
Onaping L.
L. Temagami
Wanapitei L.
Sudbury
Coniston
Iron River
Crystal Falls
Elliot Lake
Webbwood
Thessalon
Blind River
Copper Cliff
Rudyard
St Joseph I.
North Channel
Drummond I.
Massey
Espanola
L. Nipissing
Iron Mtn
Kingsford
Niagara
Rapid River
Gladstone
Manistique
Straits of Mackinac
Mackinaw City
St Ignace
Bois Blanc I.
Cheboygan
Manitoulin I.
Key Harbour
Escanaba
Garden Pen.
Beaver I.
Stephenson
Green Bay
Menominee
Peshtigo
Marinette
Oconto
Gills Rock
Manitou Is.
Petoskey
Charlevoix
Rogers City
South Baymouth
Georgian Bay
Fitzwilliam I.
Main Chan.
C. Hurd
Tobermory
Parry Sound
Gaylord
Alpena
North Pt
Bruce Pen.
Sturgeon Bay
Mancelona
Atlanta
ONT
MICHIGAN
LAKE MICHIGAN
LAKE HURON
Green Bay
Elberta
Traverse City
Harrisville
Wiarton
Kewaunee
Manistee
Owen Sound
Appleton
Menasha
Neenah
Two Rivers
Manistee
East Lake
Au Sable
Southampton
Port Elgin
Collingwood
Cadillac
Tawas City
L. Chilton
L. Winnebago
Manitowoc
Ludington
Reed City
Fond du Lac
Saginaw Bay
Standish
Port Austin
Pt Clark
Kincardine
Walkerton
Clare
Orangeville
Sheboygan
Big Rapids
Coleman
Harbor Beach
Goderich
Shelby
Mt Pleasant
Midland
Essexville
Port Washington
Muskegon
Bay City
Menomonee Falls
Wauwatosa
Alma
Howard City
Saginaw
Vassar
Carsonville
Guelph
Kitchener
Milwaukee
Muskegon
Grand Haven
W. Allis
Greenfield
Grand Rapids
St Johns
Flint
Stratford
Cambridge
Woodstock
Forest
Port Huron
London
Brantford
Owosso
Burton
Racine
Holland
Saugatuck
Grand
Kentwood
Wyoming
Lansing
St Clair
Sarnia
Ingersoll
Kenosha
Charlotte
Holt
Sterling Heights
Otsego
Pontiac
St Thomas
Waukegan
S. Haven
Battle Creek
Warren
L. St Clair
West Lorne
Des Plaines
Skokie
Kalamazoo
Royal Oak
St Clair Shores
Evanston
Benton Harbor
St Joseph
Albion
Livonia
Detroit
Chatham
Hartford
Marshall
Jackson
Ann Arbor
Windsor
Chicago
Dearborn
Lincoln Park
LAKE ERIE
Three Rivers
Coldwater
Taylor
Wyandotte
Erie
Oak Lawn
East Chicago
Michigan City
Niles
Adrian
Conneaut
Girard
Sturgis
Hudson
Monroe
Ashtabula
Gary
La Porte
Elkhart
Angola
Sylvania
Pelee I.
Painesville
Hammond
Mishawaka
South Bend
Montpelier
Toledo
Park Forest
Merrillville
Maumee
Oregon
Port Clinton
Euclid
Meadville
Chicago Heights
Plymouth
Auburn
St Joseph
Perrysburg
Bowling Green
Fremont
Lorain
Lakewood
Mentor
Kankakee
Kankakee
Winamac
Maumee
Sandusky
Cleveland
Elyria
Parma
Fort Wayne
Findlay
Norwalk
Cuyahoga Falls
Warren
Kentland
Huntingdon
Van Wert
Tiffin
Barberton
Youngstown
Farrell
Gilman
Decatur
Carey
Akron
Logansport
Wabash
Ashland
Massillon
Boardman
New Castle
Lima
Canton
Lafayette
Marion
Celina
Kenton
Mansfield
Wooster
East Liverpool
Kokomo
Marion
Attica
Frankfort
Portland
Dover
New Philadelphia
Aliquippa
Elwood
Mt Vernon
Danville
Sidney
Delaware
Weirton
Crawfordsville
Anderson
Muncie
Piqua
Steubenville
Bethel Park
INDIANA
Greenville
Urbana
OHIO
Washington
Indianapolis
New Castle
Troy
Upper Arlington
Cambridge
Newark
Martins Ferry
Rockville
Vandalia
Springfield
Columbus
Wheeling
Richmond
Dayton
Fairborn
Xenia
Zanesville
Barnesville
Moundsville
Marshall
Connersville
Scioto
Greencastle
Kettering
Terre Haute
Lancaster
Franklin
Shelbyville
Middletown
Circleville
Morgantown
Spencer
Fairfield
Hamilton
Washington C.H.
Fairmont
Marietta
Vienna
Chillicothe
Williamstown
Bloomington
Columbus
Norwood
Hillsboro
Athens
Belpre
Grafton
Bloomfield
Aurora
Cincinnati
Parkersburg
Clarksburg
Waverly
Bedford
White
Seymour
Covington
Newport
Jackson
Lawrenceville
Washington
Weston
Wabash
Vincennes
Madison
Ripley
Portsmouth
Ripley
WEST
Elkins
Carrollton
New Boston
Point Pleasant
Oakland City
Paoli
Jasper
Kentucky
Irontown
Sutton
New Albany
Ohio
Maysville
Huntington
Huntingburg
La Grange
Nitro
Jeffersonville
Georgetown
Licking
Grayson
Ashland
Elk
Shively
Louisville
Frankfort
Paris
St Albans
Charleston
Evansville
Henderson
Pleasure Ridge Park
Lexington
Morehead
Louisa
VIRGINIA
Marmet
Ansted

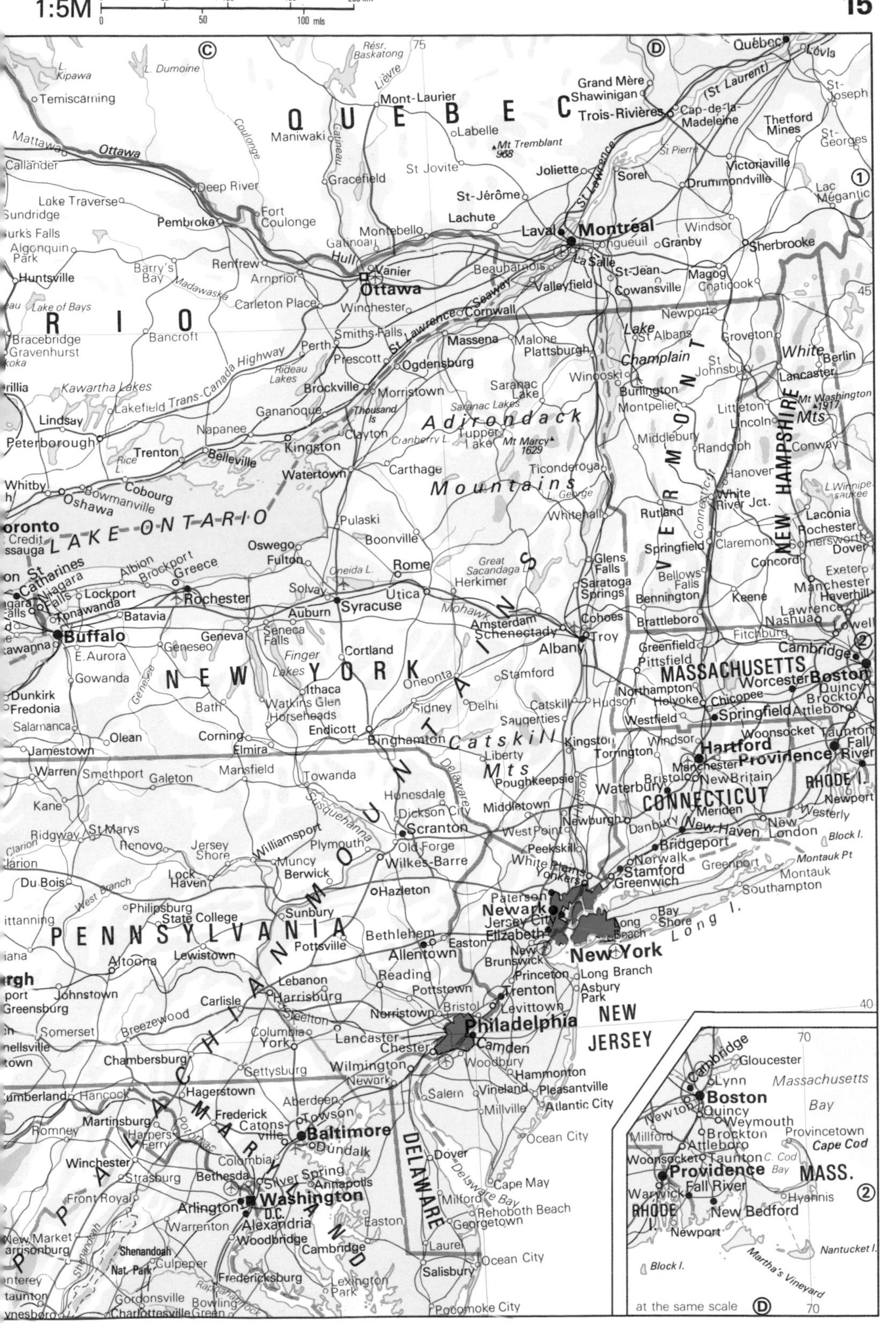
QUEBEC
Québec
Lévis
St-Joseph
Grand Mère
Shawinigan
Trois-Rivières
Cap-de-la-Madeleine
(St Laurent)
Thetford Mines
St-Georges
Victoriaville
Drummondville
Lac Mégantic
Sorel
St Pierre
Joliette
St-Jérôme
Lachute
Laval
Montréal
Longueuil
Granby
Windsor
Sherbrooke
La Salle
St-Jean
Magog
Coaticook
Cowansville
Beauharnois
Valleyfield
Cornwall
Seaway
St Lawrence
Mt Tremblant 968
Labelle
St Jovite
Mont-Laurier
Rés. Baskatong
Lièvre
Gatineau
Maniwaki
Gracefield
Montebello
Gatineau
Hull
Vanier
Ottawa
Winchester
Coulonge
L. Kipawa
L. Dumoine
Temiscaming
Mattawa
Ottawa
Callander
Deep River
Lake Traverse
Sundridge
Burk's Falls
Pembroke
Fort Coulonge
Algonquin Park
Huntsville
Renfrew
Arnprior
Barry's Bay
Madawaska
Carleton Place
Lake of Bays
RIO
Bracebridge
Gravenhurst
Muskoka
Bancroft
Smiths Falls
Perth
Rideau Lakes
Prescott
Ogdensburg
Trans-Canada Highway
Brockville
Morristown
Orillia
Kawartha Lakes
Lakefield
Gananoque
Thousand Is
Lindsay
Napanee
Kingston
Clayton
Peterborough
Trenton
Belleville
Rice L.
Watertown
Whitby
Cobourg
Bowmanville
Oshawa
LAKE ONTARIO
Toronto
Mississauga
Pulaski
Oswego
Fulton
Boonville
Rome
Oneida L.
St Catharines
Niagara Falls
Lockport
Albion
Brockport
Greece
Rochester
Tonawanda
Batavia
Solvay
Syracuse
Utica
Auburn
Buffalo
Geneva
Seneca Falls
Geneseo
E. Aurora
Gowanda
Finger Lakes
Cortland
NEW YORK
Genesee
Ithaca
Watkins Glen
Horseheads
Dunkirk
Fredonia
Bath
Salamanca
Olean
Corning
Elmira
Endicott
Binghamton
Jamestown
Warren
Smethport
Galeton
Mansfield
Towanda
Kane
Susquehanna
Ridgway
St Marys
Renovo
Clarion
Jersey Shore
Williamsport
Lock Haven
Muncy
Berwick
Du Bois
West Branch
Philipsburg
State College
Kittanning
PENNSYLVANIA
Sunbury
Pottsville
Lewistown
Altoona
Pittsburgh
Johnstown
Greensburg
Lebanon
Harrisburg
Carlisle
Steelton
Breezewood
Somerset
Columbia
York
Lancaster
Chambersburg
Gettysburg
Cumberland
Hancock
Hagerstown
Martinsburg
Romney
Harpers Ferry
Potomac
Frederick
Winchester
Strasburg
Front Royal
New Market
Harrisonburg
Shenandoah Nat. Park
Shenandoah
Culpeper
Warrenton
Staunton
Waynesboro
Gordonsville
Charlottesville
Fredericksburg
Rappahannock
Bowling Green
Massena
Malone
Plattsburgh
Saranac Lake
Saranac Lakes
Adirondack Mountains
Cranberry L.
Tupper Lake
Mt Marcy 1629
Carthage
Ticonderoga
L. George
Whitehall
Great Sacandaga L.
Herkimer
Mohawk
Amsterdam
Schenectady
Glens Falls
Saratoga Springs
Cohoes
Troy
Albany
Oneonta
Stamford
Sidney
Delhi
Catskill
Saugerties
Hudson
Catskill Mts
Liberty
Kingston
Poughkeepsie
Delaware
Honesdale
Dickson City
Scranton
Middletown
Newburgh
West Point
Old Forge
Plymouth
Wilkes-Barre
Hazleton
Peekskill
White Plains
Yonkers
Paterson
Newark
Jersey City
Elizabeth
Bethlehem
Allentown
Easton
New Brunswick
New York
Long Beach
Bay Shore
Long I.
Reading
Pottstown
Princeton
Long Branch
Asbury Park
Trenton
Levittown
Bristol
Norristown
Philadelphia
Camden
Chester
Wilmington
Newark
Woodbury
NEW JERSEY
Hammonton
Pleasantville
Atlantic City
Vineland
Salem
Millville
Aberdeen
Towson
Baltimore
Catonsville
Dundalk
Columbia
Bethesda
Silver Spring
Annapolis
Arlington
Washington D.C.
Alexandria
Woodbridge
Easton
Cambridge
MARYLAND
DELAWARE
Dover
Delaware Bay
Milford
Cape May
Ocean City
Rehoboth Beach
Georgetown
Laurel
Salisbury
Ocean City
Lexington Park
Pocomoke City
APPALACHIAN MOUNTAINS
Lake Champlain
St Albans
Newport
Winooski
Burlington
Montpelier
Middlebury
Randolph
VERMONT
Rutland
Springfield
Bellows Falls
Bennington
Brattleboro
Groveton
St Johnsbury
Littleton
Lincoln
Hanover
White River Jct.
Connecticut
Claremont
Keene
White Mts
Berlin
Lancaster
Mt Washington 1917
Conway
NEW HAMPSHIRE
L. Winnipesaukee
Laconia
Rochester
Somersworth
Dover
Concord
Exeter
Manchester
Haverhill
Lawrence
Nashua
Lowell
Fitchburg
Cambridge
Boston
Quincy
Brockton
Greenfield
Pittsfield
MASSACHUSETTS
Worcester
Northampton
Holyoke
Chicopee
Springfield
Westfield
Attleboro
Woonsocket
Taunton
Fall River
Windsor
Torrington
Hartford
Providence
Manchester
Bristol
New Britain
RHODE I.
Waterbury
CONNECTICUT
Meriden
Newport
Westerly
Danbury
New Haven
New London
Block I.
Bridgeport
Norwalk
Stamford
Greenwich
Greenport
Montauk Pt
Montauk
Southampton
45
40
75
70
1
2
C
D
Gloucester
Lynn
Massachusetts Bay
Newton
Weymouth
Milford
Provincetown
Cape Cod
C. Cod Bay
MASS.
Hyannis
Warwick
RHODE I.
New Bedford
Nantucket I.
Martha's Vineyard
at the same scale

Cobleskill Cohoes Watervliet Troy Rensselaer Hinsdale Readsboro Winchester 72 Greenville Haverhill Methuen Newburyport
Richmondville Schoharie Albany Adams Williamstown Greenfield Northfield Winchendon Nashua Dracut Lawrence Ipswich
Middleburgh Nassau Cheshire Mt Greylock 1064 Shelburne Turners Falls Fitchburg Lowell Salem Beverly
Grand Gorge Stamford Ravena N. Adams S. Deerfield Millers Falls Gardner Leominster Marlboro Cambridge Massachuse
Prattsville Coxsackie Pittsfield Dalton Northampton Amherst Barre Wachusett Resr Waltham Newton Boston
Catskill Chatham Lenox Chester Easthampton Quabbin Framingham Brookline Quincy
NEW Shandaken Catskill Hudson Stockbridge Lee Resr Worcester Norwood Weymou
Mountains Saugerties Gt Barrington Otis Westfield Monson Southboro Stoughton Brockton
Slide Mtn 1281 Canaan Springfield Milford Webster Franklin Mansfield
Ashokan Resr Kingston Millerton Mt Everett 793 Thompsonville Stafford Springs Woonsocket Attleboro Bridgewate
YORK Liberty Rhinebeck Winsted Windsor Locks Rockville Putnam Central Falls Taunton Plymouth
Ellenville New Paltz Millbrook Torrington Hartford Manchester Storrs Providence Pawtucket Middlebo
Monticello Hyde Park Amenia Bristol Willimantic Cranston Warren Fall River
CONNECTICUT New Britain Moosup Jewett Warwick RHODE Bristol New
Otisville Newburgh Poughkeepsie Wappingers Falls Waterbury Southington Colchester City Norwich ISLAND Bedford
Middletown Beacon New Milford Meriden Middletown Uncasville Jamestown Newport Falmout
Port Jervis Highland Candlewood Naugatuck Wallingford Deep River Wakefield Buzzards Vineyar
Milford Falls Carmel Brewster Hamden Seymour Norwich Rhode Island Sound Martha's Viney Have
Sussex Warwick Bethel Derby New Haven New London Westerly Nomans La
Franklin Peekskill Danbury Clinton Old Lyme Fishers I. Block Island Sd
Newton Hamburg Haverstraw Ossining New Canaan Milford Mystic Block Island
Pompton Suffern Tarrytown Bridgeport Stratford Greenport Gardiners I. Montauk Pt
Lakes Ramsey White Plains Fairfield Long Island Sound Montauk
Butler Nyack Port Chester Mattituck Sag Harbor
Dover Clifton Paterson Yonkers Huntington Riverhead East Hampton ATLANTIC
Morristown Passaic E.Orange Bronx Kings Park Southampton OCEAN
NEW Newark Queens New York Bay Shore Sayville Long Island
Bernardsville Jersey City Brooklyn Center Moriches
JERSEY Elizabeth Great South Bay
Somerville Staten I. Long Beach

Milton Bloomsburg Danville Catawissa Hazleton Lehigh Stroudsburg Newton Butler White Plains Por
Lewisburg Sunbury Mt Carmel Mahanoy Bangor Hackettstown Dover Paterson Clifton Yonkers Ches
Milroy Middleburg Shamokin Frackville City Tamaqua Belvidere Morristown Passaic New York
Burnham McClure Herndon Minersville Palmerton Washington Bernardsville Newark E.Orange Bronx
Lewistown Mifflintown Tremont Pottsville Whitehall Phillipsburg Clinton Jersey City Queens Brooklyn
Newport Lykens Pine Grove Schuylkill Haven Allentown Easton Somerville Perth Amboy Elizabeth Staten I. Long
Duncannon Millersburg Womelsdorf Hamburg Emmaus Bethlehem New Brunswick Amboy Atlantic Highlands Beac
PENN. Lebanon Boyertown Flemington South River Raritan Bay
Harrisburg Dauphin Hershey Shillington Reading Quakertown Lambertville Red Bank
Palmyra Souderton Doylestown Princeton Hightstown Long Branch
Blue Mtn Steelton Middletown Lititz Lansdale Warminster Morrisville Trenton Freehold Asbury Park
Carlisle Elizabethtown Pottstown Norristown Levittown Bordentown Lakewood Manasquan
Mt Holly Dillsburg Columbia Ephrata Phoenixville Philadelphia Lakehurst Point Pleasant
Springs Manchester Lancaster Coatesville Downingtown Willingboro Burlington Mt Holly Breton Woods
York Red Lion Parkesburg W.Chester Camden Toms River
Gettysburg Hanover Glen Rock Kennett Square Chester Woodbury NEW Chatsworth Seaside Park
Waynesboro Littlestown Stewartstown Rising Sun Penns Grove Barnegat Bay
Emmitsburg Wilmington Glassboro JERSEY Barnegat
Westminster Elkton Newark Woodstown Atco Surf City
Reisterstown Havre de Grace Salem Hammonton Mullica Tuckerton Beach Haven
Frederick Towson Bel Air Aberdeen Elmer Egg Harbor City Little Egg Harbor
MARYLAND Mt Airy Ellicott City Cockeysville Edgewood Vineland Mays Landing Great Egg Harbor
Damascus Baltimore Cecilton Bridgeton Pleasantville Atlantic City
Columbia Catonsville Dundalk Chestertown Millville Somers Point Great Egg Harbor
Leesburg Rockville Glen Burnie Dover Woodbine Ocean City
Wheaton Laurel College Centreville Smyrna Port Norris Stone Harbor
Silver Spring Park Queenstown Delaware ATLANTIC
Bethesda Bowie Annapolis Bay Cape May Wildwood OCEAN
Arlington Washington Mayo Queen Anne Greensboro Cape May
Fairfax D.C. St Michaels Denton Harrington Milford C. May Pt
Alexandria 76 Greenwood Henlopen 74

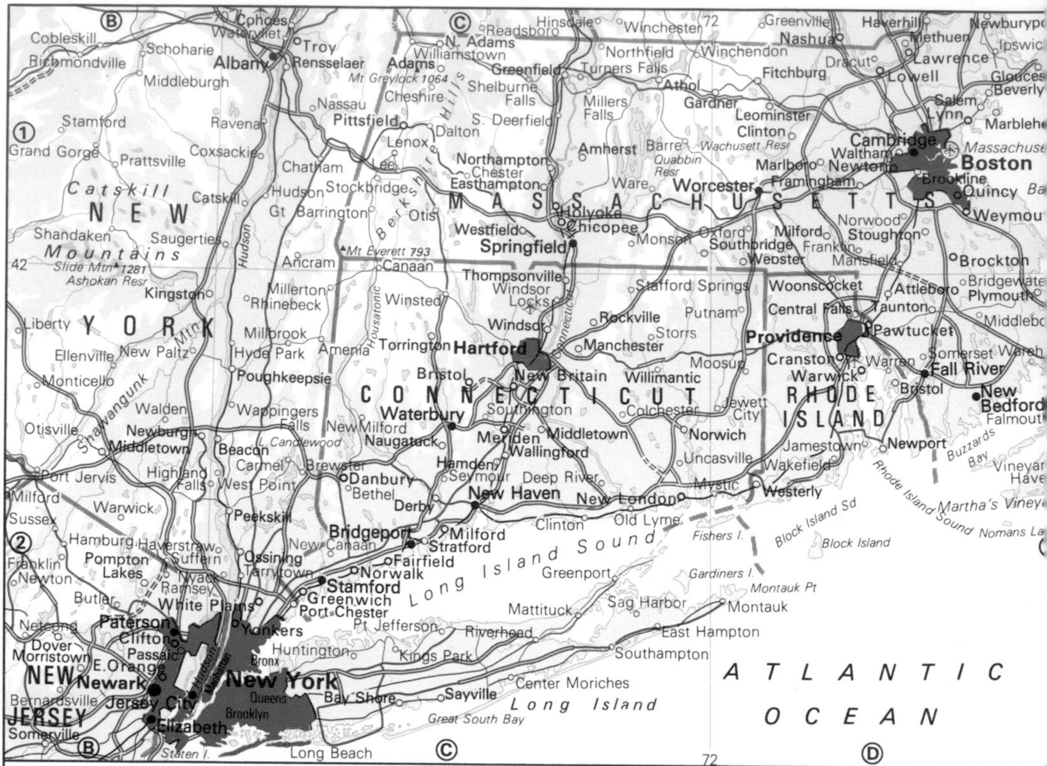

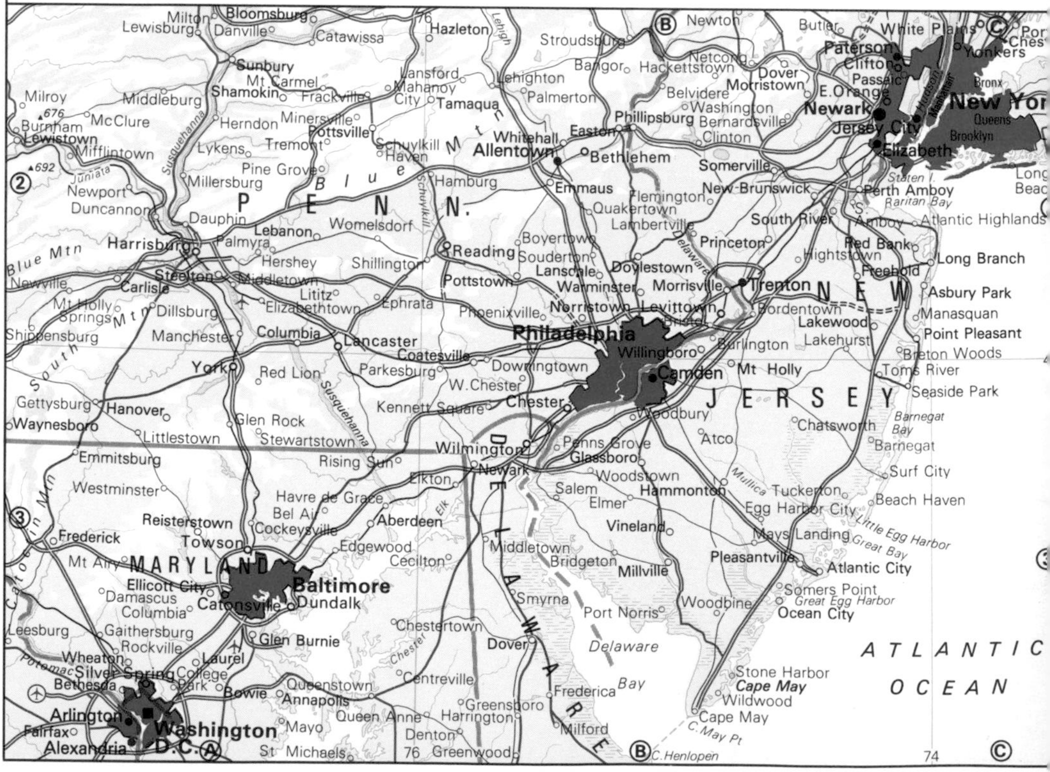

1:5M

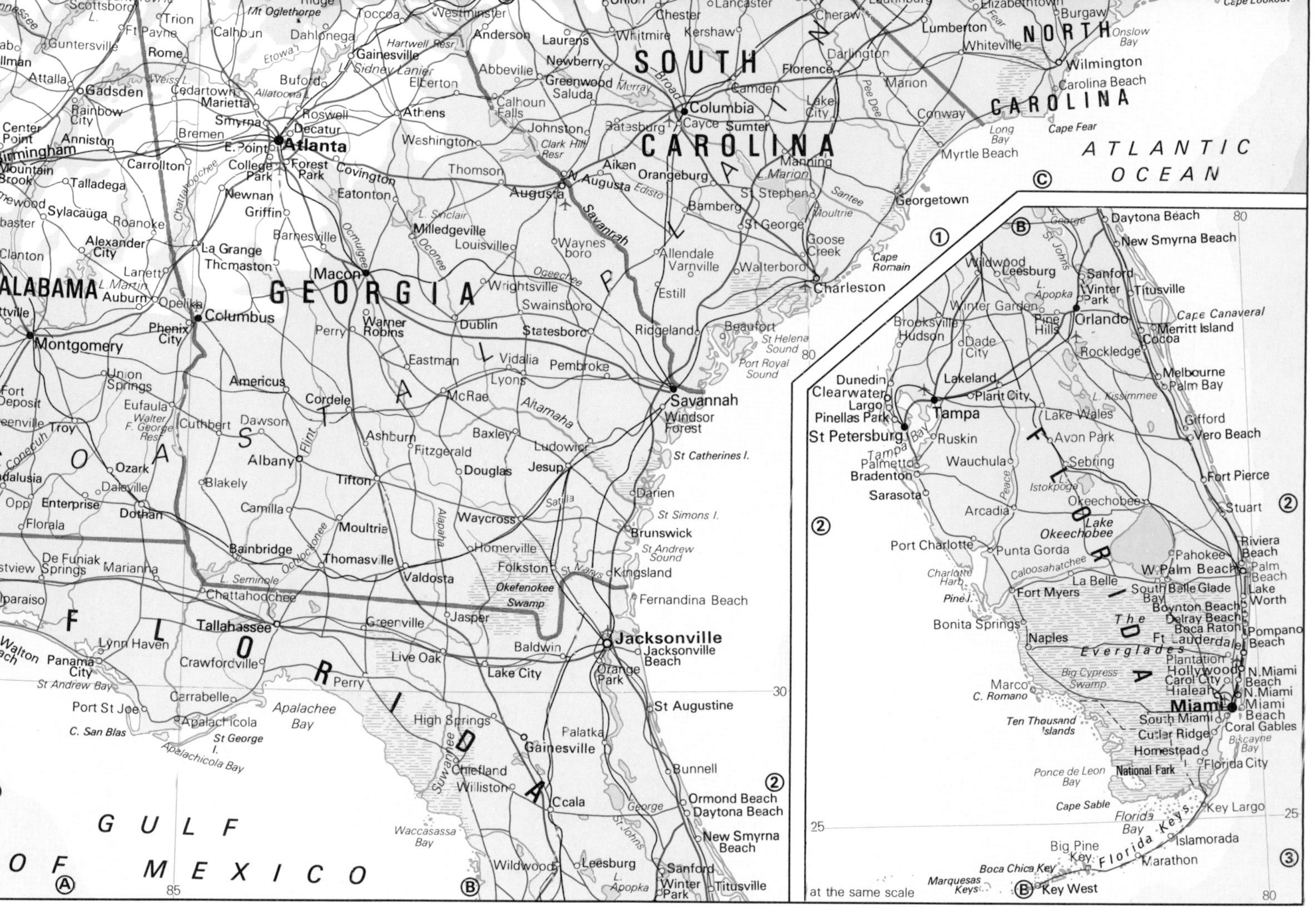

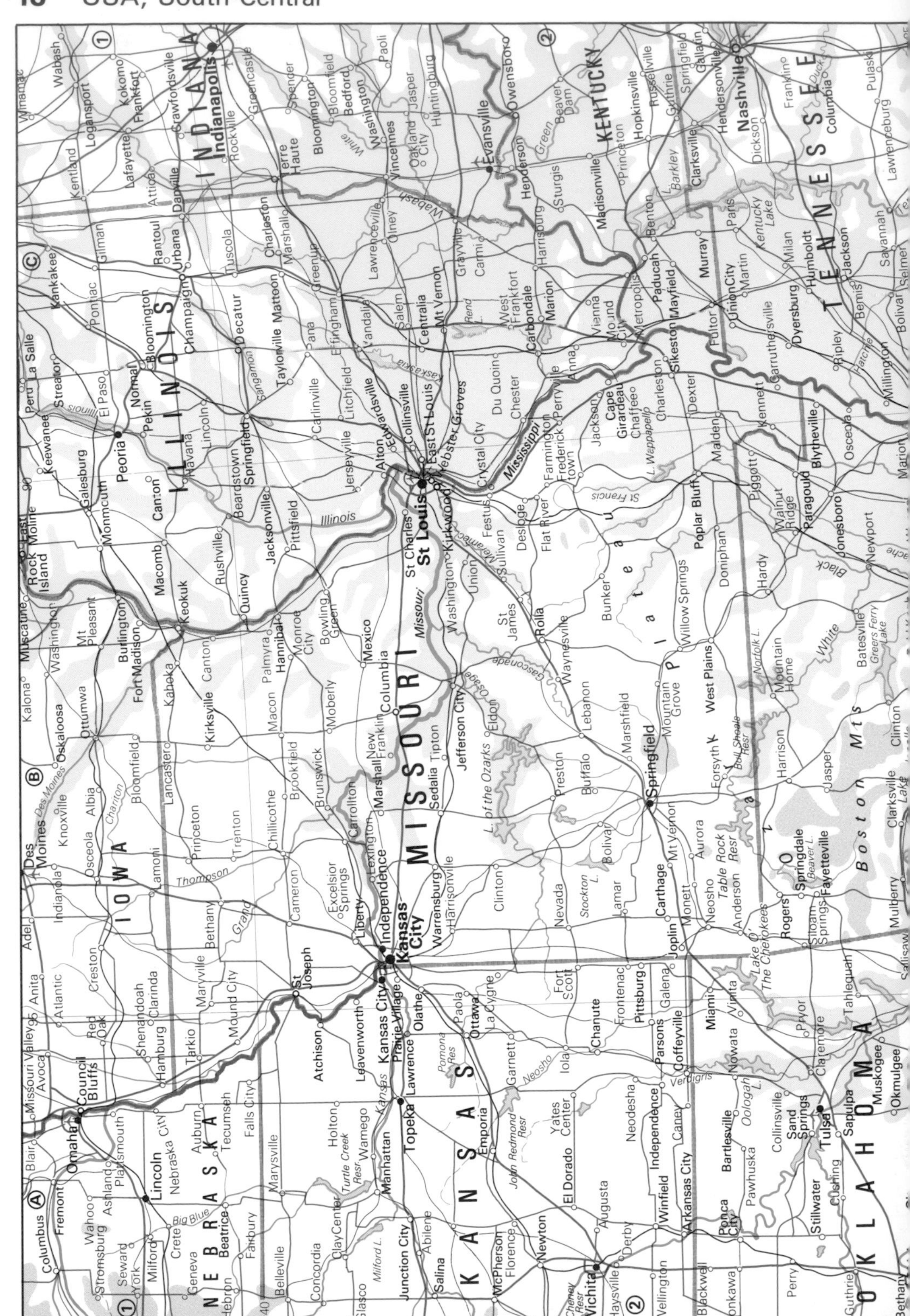
INDIANA
ILLINOIS
KENTUCKY
TENNESSEE
IOWA
MISSOURI
NEBRASKA
KANSAS
OKLAHOMA
Indianapolis
Evansville
Terre Haute
Bloomington
Lafayette
Logansport
Kokomo
Frankfort
Crawfordsville
Danville
Vincennes
Owensboro
Henderson
Madisonville
Hopkinsville
Paducah
Murray
Mayfield
Clarksville
Nashville
Columbia
Jackson
Dyersburg
Humboldt
Union City
Peoria
Springfield
Decatur
Champaign
Urbana
Bloomington
Normal
Kankakee
Galesburg
Quincy
Jacksonville
Effingham
Mattoon
Centralia
Mt Vernon
Carbondale
Marion
Alton
East St Louis
St Louis
St Charles
Kirkwood
Webster Groves
Rock Island
Moline
Burlington
Fort Madison
Keokuk
Des Moines
Ottumwa
Oskaloosa
Council Bluffs
Omaha
Lincoln
Beatrice
Hannibal
Kirksville
Columbia
Jefferson City
Rolla
Cape Girardeau
Sikeston
Poplar Bluff
Springfield
Joplin
Carthage
Sedalia
Kansas City
Independence
St Joseph
Atchison
Leavenworth
Lawrence
Topeka
Manhattan
Junction City
Salina
Emporia
Wichita
Newton
El Dorado
Winfield
Arkansas City
Ponca City
Bartlesville
Tulsa
Muskogee
Stillwater
Fayetteville
Springdale
Jonesboro
Blytheville
Mississippi
Missouri
Illinois
Wabash
Ozark Plateau
Boston Mts
L. of the Ozarks

1:5M

0 50 100 150 200 km
0 50 100 mils

ALABAMA ③

④

MISSISSIPPI

LOUISIANA

ARKANSAS

TEXAS

Ouachita Mts

New Orleans

Baton Rouge

Mobile

Birmingham

Tuscaloosa

Jackson

Shreveport

Dallas

Fort Worth

Houston

Austin

Waco

Beaumont

Lake Charles

Lafayette

Biloxi

Gulfport

Mississippi Delta

Mobile Bay

C

B

A

③

④

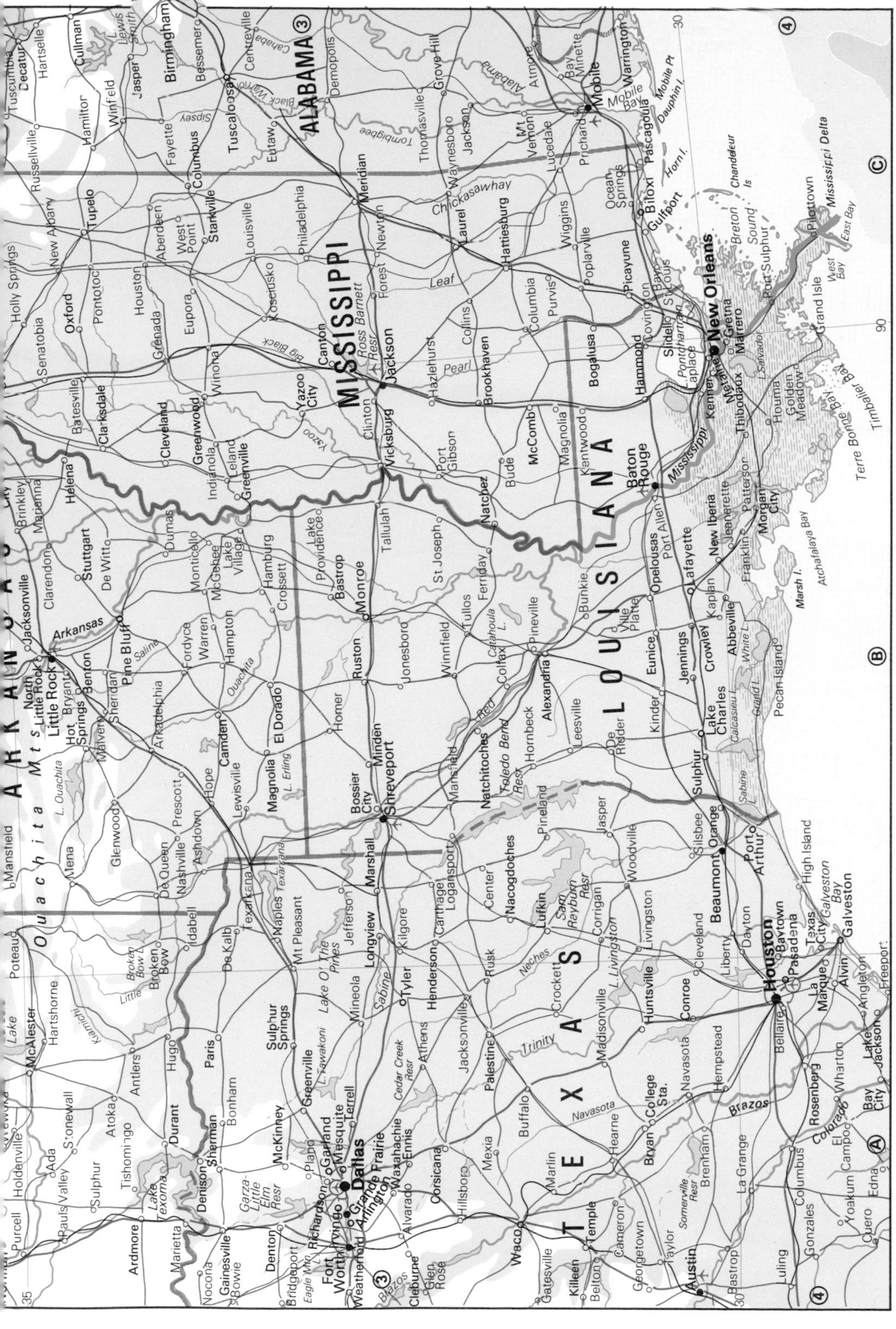

Scale bars: 0 50 100 150 200 km / 0 50 100 mils

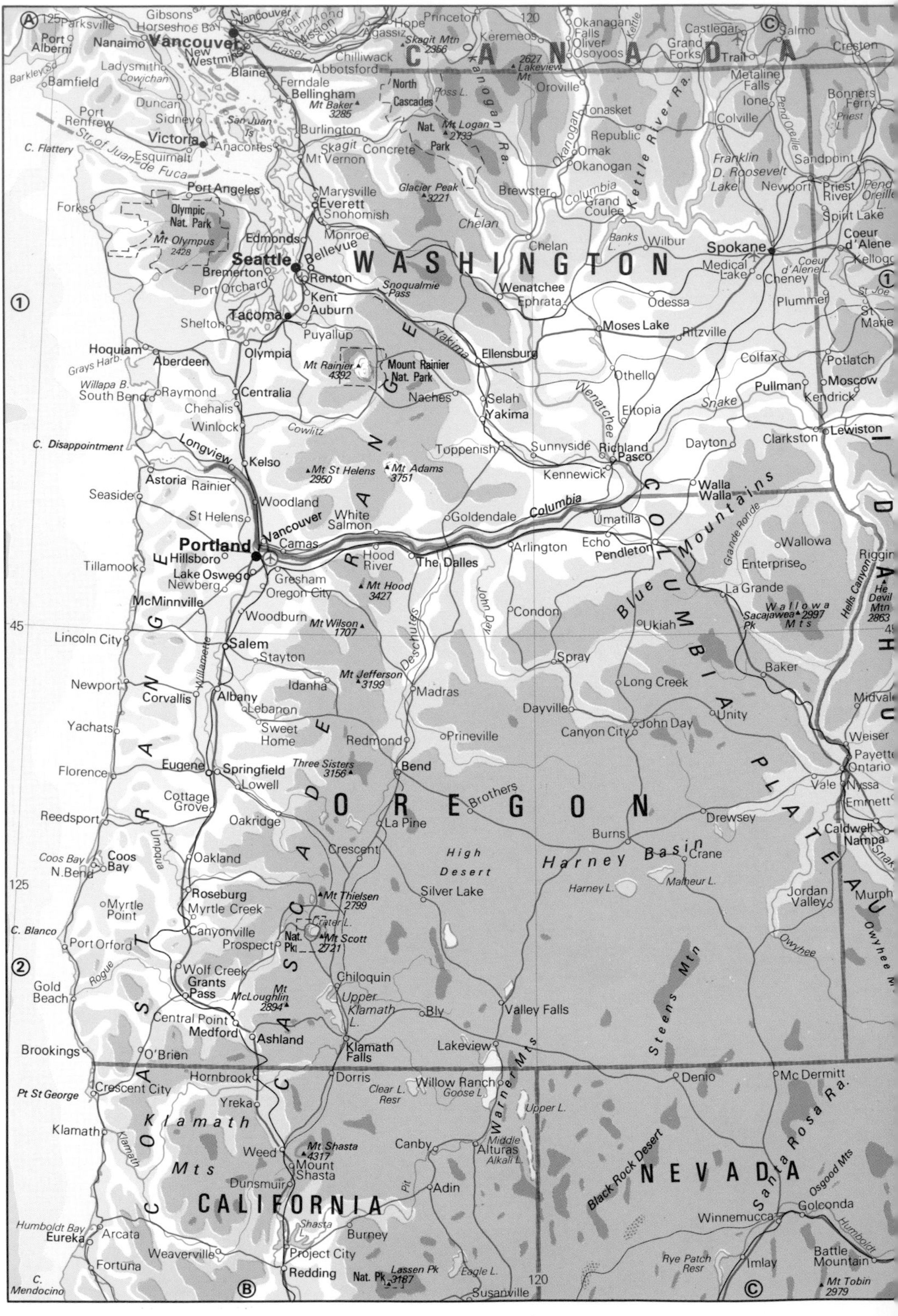

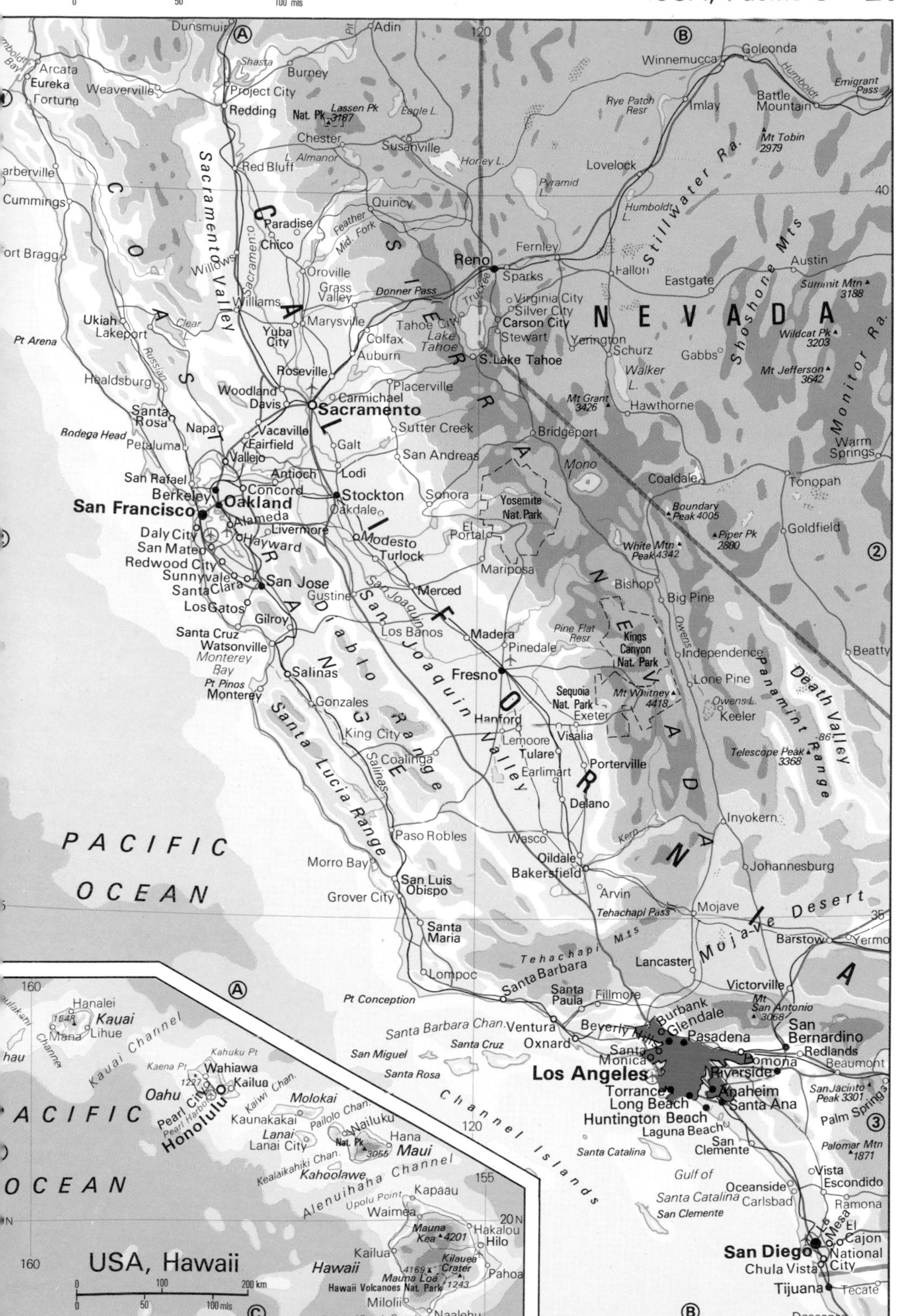
Dunsmuir
Adin
120
Winnemucca
Golconda
Arcata
Eureka
Fortuna
Weaverville
Shasta
Burney
Project City
Redding
Lassen Pk 3187
Nat. Pk
Eagle L.
Rye Patch Resr
Imlay
Battle Mountain
Emigrant Pass
Humboldt
Chester
Susanville
L. Almanor
Red Bluff
Honey L.
Mt Tobin 2979
Lovelock
Pyramid L.
Cummings
Quincy
Humboldt L.
Stillwater Ra.
Paradise
Chico
Feather
Mid. Fork
Fort Bragg
Willows
Sacramento Valley
Sacramento
Fernley
Reno
Sparks
Fallon
Austin
Oroville
Grass Valley
Donner Pass
Truckee
Eastgate
Shoshone Mts
Summit Mtn 3188
Williams
Virginia City
Silver City
Carson City
NEVADA
Ukiah
Lakeport
Clear L.
Marysville
Yuba City
Tahoe City
Lake Tahoe
Stewart
Yerington
Wildcat Pk 3203
Monitor Ra.
Pt Arena
Colfax
Auburn
S. Lake Tahoe
Schurz
Gabbs
Russian
Walker L.
Healdsburg
Roseville
Mt Jefferson 3642
Woodland
Davis
Carmichael
Placerville
Mt Grant 3426
Hawthorne
Santa Rosa
Napa
Sacramento
Vacaville
Sutter Creek
Bridgeport
Bodega Head
Petaluma
Fairfield
Galt
Warm Springs
Vallejo
San Andreas
Mono L.
Antioch
Lodi
Coaldale
Tonopah
San Rafael
Concord
Berkeley
Stockton
Sonora
Yosemite Nat. Park
Boundary Peak 4005
San Francisco
Oakland
Oakdale
Alameda
El Portal
Goldfield
Daly City
Livermore
Piper Pk 2880
San Mateo
Hayward
Modesto
Turlock
White Mtn Peak 4342
Redwood City
Mariposa
Sunnyvale
Santa Clara
San Jose
Merced
Bishop
Los Gatos
Gustine
San Joaquin
Big Pine
Gilroy
Los Banos
Madera
Pine Flat Resr
Kings Canyon Nat. Park
Santa Cruz
Watsonville
Pinedale
Owens
Monterey Bay
Independence
Beatty
Salinas
Fresno
Pt Pinos
Monterey
Lone Pine
Death Valley
Sequoia Nat. Park
Mt Whitney 4418
Gonzales
Owens L.
Diablo Range
San Joaquin Valley
Hanford
Exeter
Keeler
King City
Lemoore
Visalia
Panamint Range
Tulare
-86
Santa Lucia Range
Coalinga
Porterville
Telescope Peak 3368
Salinas
Earlimart
Delano
Inyokern
COAST RANGES
SIERRA NEVADA
CALIFORNIA
PACIFIC OCEAN
Paso Robles
Wasco
Kern
Morro Bay
Oildale
Johannesburg
Bakersfield
San Luis Obispo
Arvin
Grover City
Tehachapi Pass
Mojave
Mojave Desert
35
Santa Maria
Tehachapi Mts
Barstow
Yermo
Lancaster
Lompoc
Santa Barbara
Victorville
Pt Conception
Santa Paula
Fillmore
Mt San Antonio 3068
Burbank
Glendale
Santa Barbara Chan.
Ventura
Beverly Hills
Pasadena
San Bernardino
San Miguel
Santa Cruz
Oxnard
Santa Monica
Redlands
Pomona
Beaumont
Santa Rosa
Los Angeles
Riverside
Torrance
Anaheim
San Jacinto Peak 3301
Long Beach
Santa Ana
Palm Springs
Channel Islands
Huntington Beach
Laguna Beach
120
Santa Catalina
San Clemente
Palomar Mtn 1871
Gulf of Santa Catalina
Oceanside
Vista
Escondido
Carlsbad
San Clemente
Ramona
La Mesa
El Cajon
San Diego
National City
Chula Vista
Tijuana
Tecate
Descanso
160
Hanalei
Kauai
1548
Lihue
Kauai Channel
Kahuku Pt
Kaena Pt
Wahiawa
1227
Kailua
Oahu
Kaiwi Chan.
Pearl City
Pearl Harbor
Honolulu
Molokai
Kaunakakai
Pailolo Chan.
Nailuku
Lanai
Lanai City
Nat. Pk
3055
Hana
Maui
Kealaikahiki Chan.
Kahoolawe
Alenuihaha Channel
155
Upolu Point
Kapaau
Waimea
20 N
Mauna Kea 4201
Hakalau
Hilo
Kailua
Hawaii
4169
Mauna Loa
Kilauea Crater 1243
Pahoa
Hawaii Volcanoes Nat. Park
Milolii
Naalehu
Ka Lae (South Cape)
160
PACIFIC OCEAN
USA, Hawaii
0 100 200 km
0 50 100 mls
A
B
C
2
3

0 25 50 75 100 km
0 25 50 mls

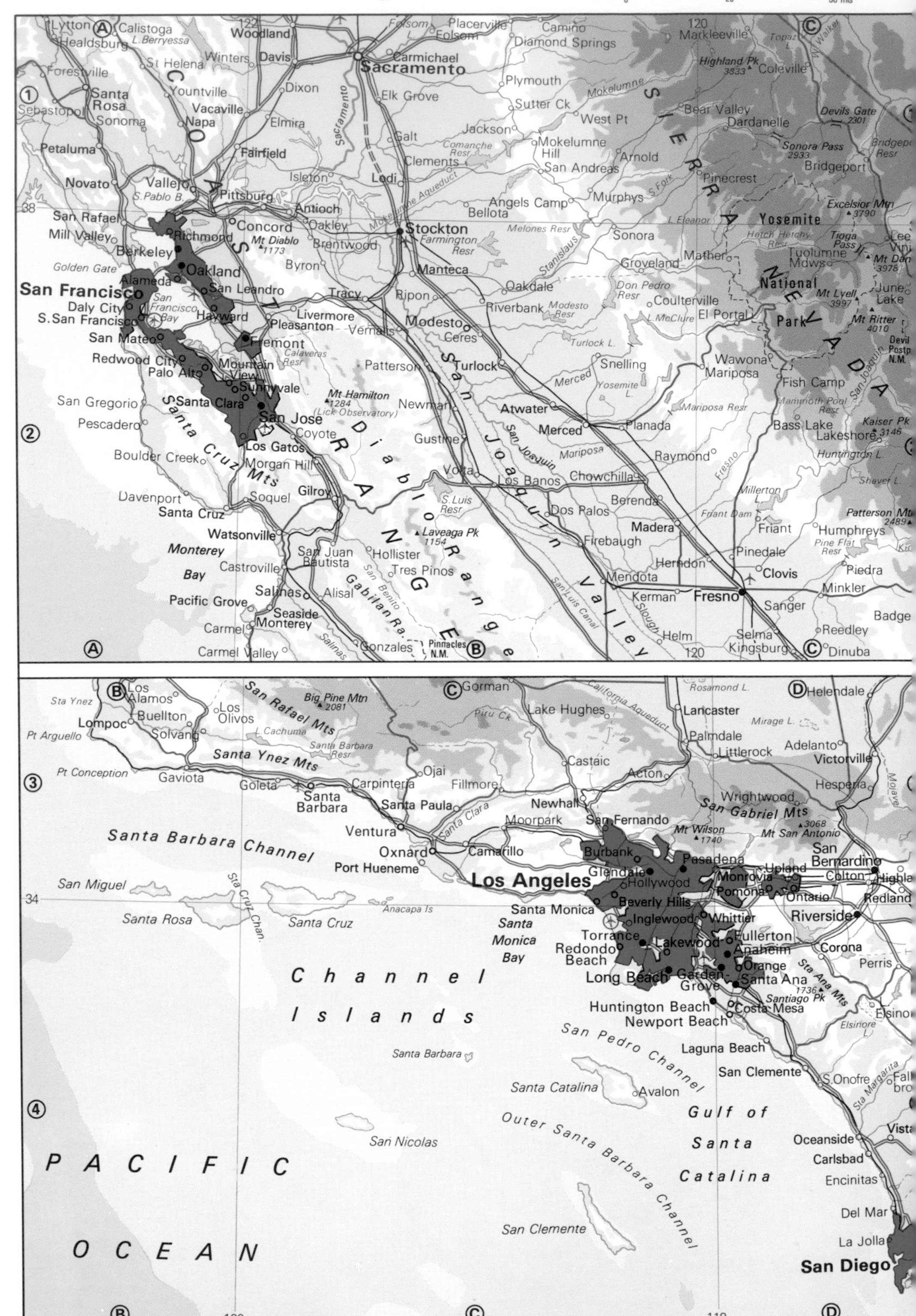

Lytton
Calistoga
Healdsburg
L. Berryessa
Woodland
Folsom
Placerville
Camino
Markleeville
Topaz L.
Forestville
St Helena
Winters
Davis
Carmichael
Sacramento
Diamond Springs
Highland Pk 3333
Coleville
Santa Rosa
Sebastopol
Sonoma
Yountville
Vacaville
Napa
Dixon
Elmira
Elk Grove
Plymouth
Sutter Ck
Mokelumne
West Pt
Bear Valley
Dardanelle
Devils Gate 2301
Petaluma
Fairfield
Galt
Jackson
Comanche Resr
Mokelumne Hill
Arnold
Sonora Pass 2933
Bridgeport Resr
Bridgeport
Novato
Vallejo
S. Pablo B.
Pittsburg
Isleton
Lodi
Clements
San Andreas
Pinecrest
Antioch
Mokelumne Aqueduct
Angels Camp
Bellota
Murphys
Excelsior Mtn 3790
San Rafael
Mill Valley
Concord
Oakley
Richmond
Mt Diablo 1173
Brentwood
Stockton
Farmington Resr
Melones Resr
L. Eleanor
Sonora
Yosemite
Hetch Hetchy Resr
Tioga Pass
Tuolumne Mdws
Mt Dana 3978
Berkeley
Golden Gate
Oakland
Byron
Manteca
Stanislaus
Groveland
Mather
National Park
Alameda
San Francisco
San Leandro
Tracy
Ripon
Oakdale
Don Pedro Resr
Coulterville
Mt Lyell 3997
June Lake
Daly City
San Francisco Bay
S.San Francisco
Hayward
Livermore
Pleasanton
Vernalis
Modesto
Riverbank
Modesto Resr
L. McClure
El Portal
Park
Mt Ritter 4010
San Mateo
Fremont
Ceres
Turlock L.
Devil Postpile N.M.
Redwood City
Palo Alto
Mountain View
Calaveras Resr
Patterson
Turlock
Merced
Snelling
Yosemite L.
Wawona
Mariposa
Fish Camp
San Gregorio
Sunnyvale
Santa Clara
Mt Hamilton 1284 (Lick Observatory)
Newman
Atwater
Mariposa Resr
Mammoth Pool Resr
Pescadero
San Jose
Coyote
Merced
Planada
Bass Lake
Kaiser Pk 3146
Lakeshore
Huntington L.
Boulder Creek
Santa Cruz Mts
Los Gatos
Gustine
San Joaquin
Mariposa
Raymond
Morgan Hill
Volta
Chowchilla
Fresno
Shaver L.
Davenport
Soquel
Gilroy
S. Luis Resr
Los Banos
Berenda
Millerton L.
Santa Cruz
Dos Palos
Friant Dam
Patterson Mtn 2489
Watsonville
Laveaga Pk 1154
Madera
Friant
Humphreys
Monterey
Firebaugh
Pine Flat Resr
Bay
Castroville
San Juan Bautista
Hollister
Tres Pinos
Herndon
Pinedale
Clovis
Piedra
Mendota
Pacific Grove
Salinas
Alisal
San Benito
Gabilan Ra.
San Luis Canal
Kerman
Fresno
Minkler
Seaside
Monterey
Slough
Sanger
Badger
Carmel
Helm
Reedley
Carmel Valley
Salinas
Gonzales
Pinnacles N.M.
Selma
Kingsburg
Dinuba
COAST RANGES
Diablo Range
San Joaquin Valley
SIERRA NEVADA
Sacramento
38
122
120
Los Alamos
Sta Ynez
Big Pine Mtn 2081
Gorman
California Aqueduct
Rosamond L.
Helendale
Buellton
Los Olivos
San Rafael Mts
Piru Ck
Lake Hughes
Lancaster
Lompoc
Solvang
L. Cachuma
Mirage L.
Pt Arguello
Santa Barbara Resr
Palmdale
Adelanto
Santa Ynez Mts
Castaic
Littlerock
Victorville
Pt Conception
Gaviota
Ojai
Acton
Hesperia
Mojave
Goleta
Carpinteria
Fillmore
Santa Barbara
Santa Paula
Newhall
Wrightwood
San Gabriel Mts
Santa Clara
Moorpark
San Fernando
3068
Mt San Antonio
Mt Wilson 1740
Santa Barbara Channel
Ventura
Oxnard
Camarillo
Burbank
San Bernardino
Port Hueneme
Pasadena
Upland
Los Angeles
Glendale
Hollywood
Monrovia
Colton
Highland
San Miguel
Sta Cruz Chan.
Pomona
Redlands
34
Beverly Hills
Ontario
Santa Rosa
Anacapa Is
Santa Monica
Santa Cruz
Inglewood
Whittier
Riverside
Santa Monica Bay
Torrance
Fullerton
Redondo Beach
Lakewood
Anaheim
Corona
Perris
Long Beach
Orange
Garden Grove
Santa Ana
Sta Ana Mts
Channel Islands
Santiago Pk 1736
Huntington Beach
Costa Mesa
Elsinore
Newport Beach
Elsinore
San Pedro Channel
Santa Barbara
Laguna Beach
San Clemente
Santa Catalina
Avalon
S. Onofre
Sta Margarita
Gulf of Santa Catalina
Outer Santa Barbara Channel
Oceanside
San Nicolas
Carlsbad
PACIFIC OCEAN
Encinitas
Del Mar
La Jolla
San Clemente
San Diego
120
118

1:5M 0 50 100 150 200 km
0 50 100 mls

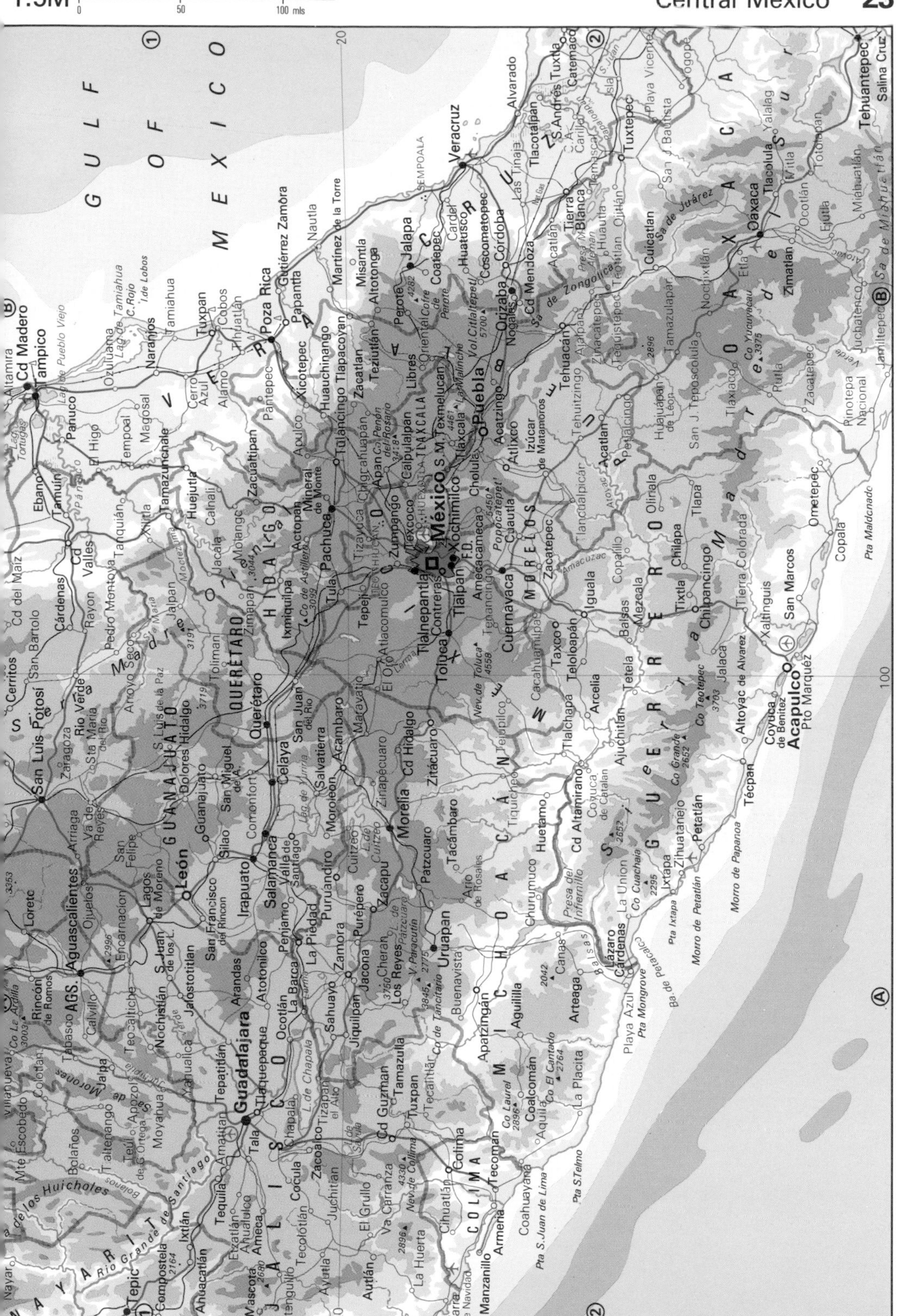
GULF OF MEXICO
Cd Madero
Tampico
Tuxpan
Poza Rica
Veracruz
Alvarado
Jalapa
Córdoba
Orizaba
Puebla
México
Pachuca
Tlaxcala
Toluca
Cuernavaca
Querétaro
Celaya
Irapuato
Salamanca
León
Guanajuato
San Luis Potosí
Aguascalientes
Guadalajara
Morelia
Uruapan
Colima
Manzanillo
Tepic
Acapulco
Chilpancingo
Oaxaca
Tehuantepec
Tuxtepec
Tehuacán
Iguala
Taxco
Zihuatanejo
Lázaro Cárdenas
HIDALGO
QUERÉTARO
GUANAJUATO
JALISCO
MICHOACÁN
MORELOS
GUERRERO
OAXACA
COLIMA
NAYARIT
Vol. Citlaltépetl 5700
Popocatépetl 5450
Nev. de Toluca 4558
Nev. de Colima 4330
L. de Chapala

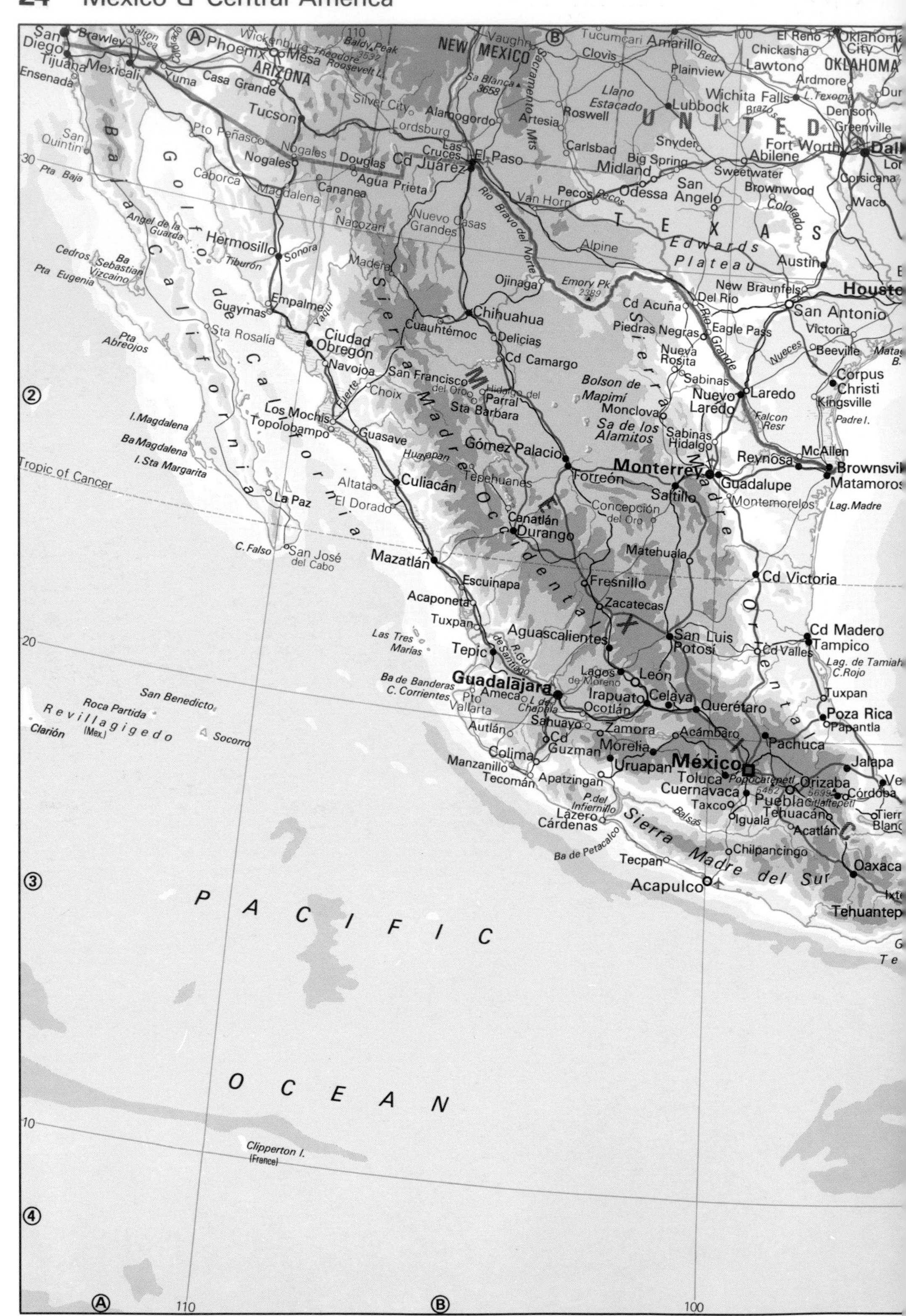

San Diego
Brawley
Salton Sea
Colorado
A
Phoenix
Wickenburg
Theodore Roosevelt L.
Baldy Peak 3537
Mesa
ARIZONA
NEW MEXICO
Vaughn
B
Tucumcari
Amarillo
Red
El Reno
Chickasha
Lawton
OKLAHOMA
Ardmore
Tijuana
Mexicali
Ensenada
Yuma
Casa Grande
Sa Blanca 3658
Sacramento Mts
Clovis
Plainview
Llano Estacado
Lubbock
Wichita Falls
L.Texoma
Denison
Greenville
Silver City
Alamogordo
Artesia
Roswell
Tucson
UNITED
Brazos
Pto Peñasco
Lordsburg
San Quintín
Baja California
Las Cruces
El Paso
Carlsbad
Snyder
Fort Worth
Abilene
Nogales
Douglas
Cd Juárez
Big Spring
Midland
Sweetwater
Corsicana
30
Pta Baja
Caborca
Agua Prieta
Cananea
Magdalena
Van Horn
Pecos
Odessa
San Angelo
Brownwood
Colorado
Waco
Golfo de California
Rio Bravo del Norte
Nacozari
Nuevo Casas Grandes
TEXAS
Ángel de la Guarda
Hermosillo
Sonora
Alpine
Edwards Plateau
Austin
Cedros
Ba Sebastián Vizcaíno
Tiburón
Pta Eugenia
Madera
Ojinaga
Emory Pk 2389
New Braunfels
Del Rio
Empalme
Guaymas
Yaqui
Chihuahua
Cd Acuña
San Antonio
Sierra Madre Occidental
Sta Rosalía
Cuauhtémoc
Rio Grande
Piedras Negras
Eagle Pass
Victoria
Pta Abreojos
Ciudad Obregón
Delicias
Nueva Rosita
Nueces
Beeville
Navojoa
Cd Camargo
Sierra Madre Oriental
Sabinas
Corpus Christi
San Francisco del Oro
Bolson de Mapimí
Fuerte
Choix
MEXICO
Hidalgo del Parral
Nuevo Laredo
Laredo
Kingsville
Monclova
Los Mochis
Sta Barbara
I.Magdalena
Topolobampo
Sa de los Alamitos
Falcon Resr
Padre I.
Ba Magdalena
Guasave
Sabinas Hidalgo
McAllen
Gómez Palacio
I.Sta Margarita
Huayapan
Reynosa
Tropic of Cancer
Tepehuanes
Torreón
Monterrey
Altata
Culiacán
Saltillo
Guadalupe
Matamoros
La Paz
El Dorado
Concepción del Oro
Montemorelos
Lag.Madre
Canatlán
Durango
C. Falso
San José del Cabo
Matehuala
Mazatlán
Escuinapa
Fresnillo
Cd Victoria
Acaponeta
Zacatecas
Tuxpan
Aguascalientes
Cd Madero
San Luis Potosí
Tampico
Las Tres Marías
Tepic
R.Gd de Santiago
Cd Valles
Lag. de Tamiahua
C.Rojo
20
Lagos de Moreno
León
Ba de Banderas
Guadalajara
Irapuato
Celaya
Tuxpan
C. Corrientes
Ameca
Pto Vallarta
L.de Chapala
Ocotlán
Querétaro
Poza Rica
San Benedicto
Sahuayo
Zamora
Papantla
Roca Partida
Revillagigedo (Mex.)
Clarión
Socorro
Autlán
Cd Guzman
Morelia
Acámbaro
Pachuca
Colima
Uruapan
México
Jalapa
Manzanillo
Tecomán
Apatzingan
Toluca
Popocatepetl 5452
Orizaba
Citlaltepetl 5699
Córdoba
Cuernavaca
Puebla
P.del Infiernillo
Taxco
Tehuacán
Lázaro Cárdenas
Balsas
Iguala
Acatlán
Ba de Petacalco
Sierra Madre del Sur
Chilpancingo
Tecpan
Oaxaca
Acapulco
Tehuantepec
PACIFIC OCEAN
10
Clipperton I. (France)
A
110
B
100

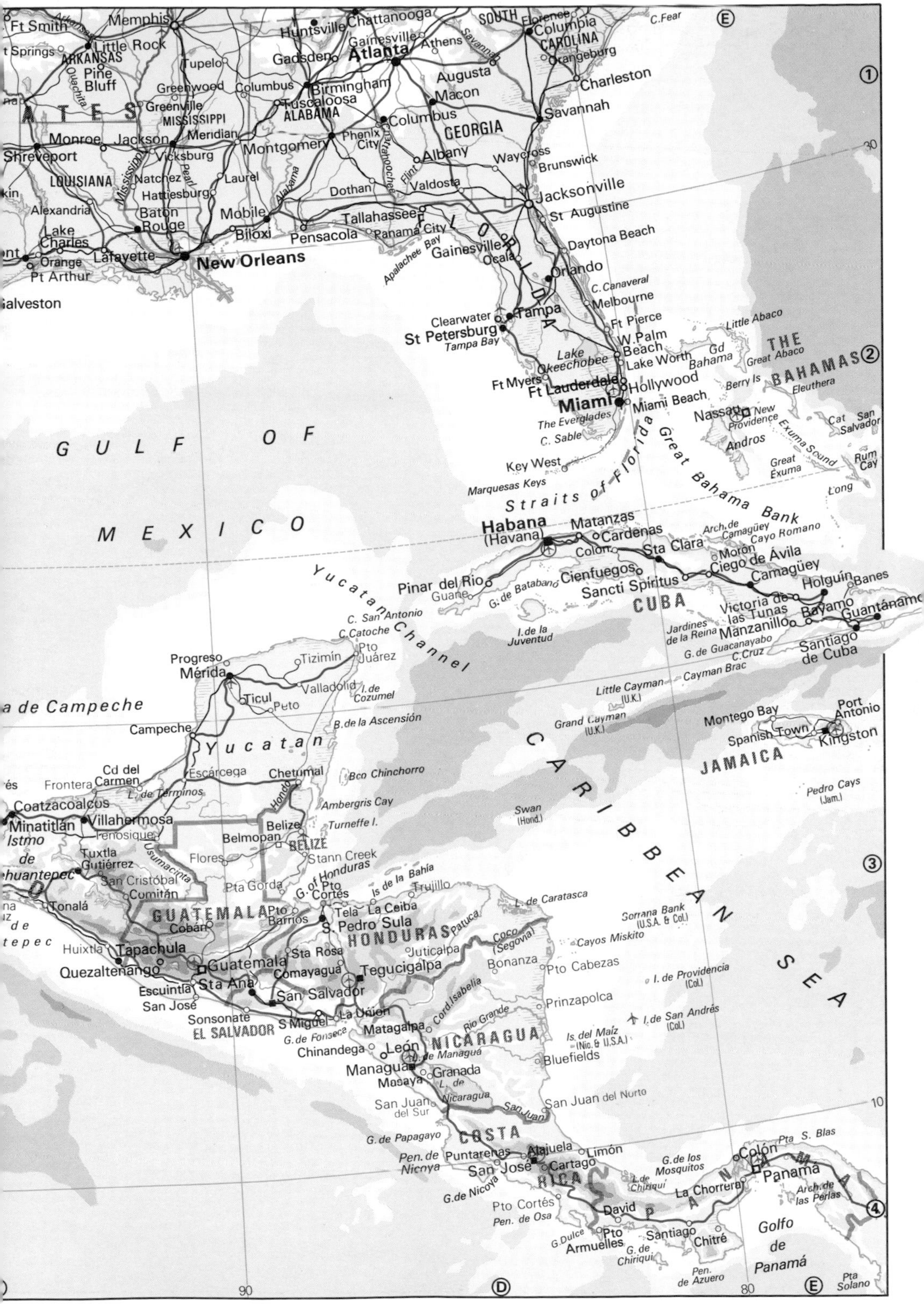

1:15M

200 400 600 km
100 200 300 mls

UNITED STATES

Ft Smith
t Springs
Memphis
Little Rock
ARKANSAS
Pine
Bluff
Huntsville
Chattanooga
Gadsden
Athens
SOUTH
Florence
Columbia
CAROLINA
C. Fear

Gainesville
Atlanta
Augusta
Orangeburg

Tupelo
Columbus
Birmingham
Macon
Charleston

Greenwood
Tuscaloosa
ALABAMA

Greenville
MISSISSIPPI
Columbus
GEORGIA
Savannah

Monroe
Jackson
Meridian
Montgomery
Phenix
City
Albany
Waycross
Brunswick

Shreveport
Vicksburg
Natchez
Laurel
Hattiesburg
Dothan
Valdosta
Jacksonville
St Augustine

LOUISIANA
Baton
Rouge
Mobile
Biloxi
Pensacola
Tallahassee
Panama City
Gainesville
Ocala
Daytona Beach

Alexandria
Lake
Charles
Lafayette
New Orleans
Apalachee Bay
FLORIDA
Orlando
C. Canaveral
Melbourne

Galveston
Pt Arthur
Orange

Clearwater
Tampa
Ft Pierce

St Petersburg
Tampa Bay
W. Palm
Beach
Little Abaco

Ft Myers
Lake
Okeechobee
Lake Worth
Gd
Bahama
Great Abaco
THE

Ft Lauderdale
Hollywood
Berry Is
BAHAMAS

Miami
Miami Beach
Nassau
New
Providence
Eleuthera

The Everglades
C. Sable
Andros
Exuma Sound
Cat
San
Salvador

GULF OF
Key West

Marquesas Keys
Straits of Florida
Great
Éxuma
Rum
Cay

MEXICO
Habana
(Havana)
Matanzas
Cárdenas
Arch. de
Camagüey
Cayo Romano
Long

Pinar del Río
Colón
Sta Clara
Morón
Ciego de Ávila
Banes

Guane
G. de Batabanó
Cienfuegos
Sancti Spíritus
CUBA
Camagüey
Holguín

Yucatan Channel
I. de la
Juventud
Jardines
de la Reina
Victoria de
las Tunas
Bayamo
Guantánamo

C. San Antonio
Pto
Juárez
G. de Guacanayabo
Manzanillo
Santiago
de Cuba

C. Catoche
Tizimín
I. de
Cozumel
C. Cruz

Progreso
Mérida
Valladolid
B. de la Ascensión
Little Cayman
(U.K.)
Cayman Brac
Montego Bay
Port
Antonio

Ticul
Peto
Bco Chinchorro
Grand Cayman
(U.K.)
Spanish Town
Kingston

Campeche
Yucatan
Escárcega
Chetumal
JAMAICA
Pedro Cays
(Jam.)

a de Campeche
Cd del
Carmen
Ambergris Cay

és
Frontera
L. de Términos
Turneffe I.
Swan
(Hond.)

Coatzacoalcos
Villahermosa
Belize
CARIBBEAN
SEA

Minatitlán
Istmo
Tenosique
Belmopan
BELIZE

de
huantepec
Tuxtla
Gutiérrez
Flores
Stann Creek

San Cristóbal
Comitán
Pta Gorda
G. of
Honduras
Is de la Bahía
Trujillo

az
tz
de
tepec
Tonalá
GUATEMALA
Pto
Barrios
Tela
La Ceiba
L. de Caratasca

Huixtla
Cobán
S. Pedro
Sula
HONDURAS
Patuca
Sorrana Bank
(U.S.A. & Col.)

Tapachula
Sta Rosa
Coco
(Segovia)
Cayos Miskito

Quezaltenango
Guatemala
Comayagua
Juticalpa
Bonanza
Pto Cabezas
I. de Providencia
(Col.)

Escuintla
Sta Ana
Tegucigalpa
Prinzapolca
I. de San Andrés
(Col.)

San José
Sonsonate
San Salvador
La Unión
Matagalpa
Rio Grande
Cord. Isabelia

EL SALVADOR
S Miguel
G. de Fonseca
Chinandega
León
NICARAGUA
Bluefields

Managua
L. de Managua
Is. del Maíz
(Nic. & U.S.A.)

Masaya
Granada
L. de
Nicaragua
San Juan del Norte

San Juan
del Sur
San Juan
G. de Papagayo

G. de Nicoya
COSTA
Pta S. Blas
Colón

Pen. de
Nicoya
Puntarenas
Alajuela
Limón
G. de los
Mosquitos
La Chorrera
Panamá
Arch. de
las Perlas

San José
Cartago
RICA
G. de
Chiriquí

Pto Cortés
Pen. de Osa
David
Santiago
Chitré
Golfo
de
Panamá

G. Dulce
Pto
Armuelles
G. de
Chiriquí
Pen.
de Azuero
Pta
Solano

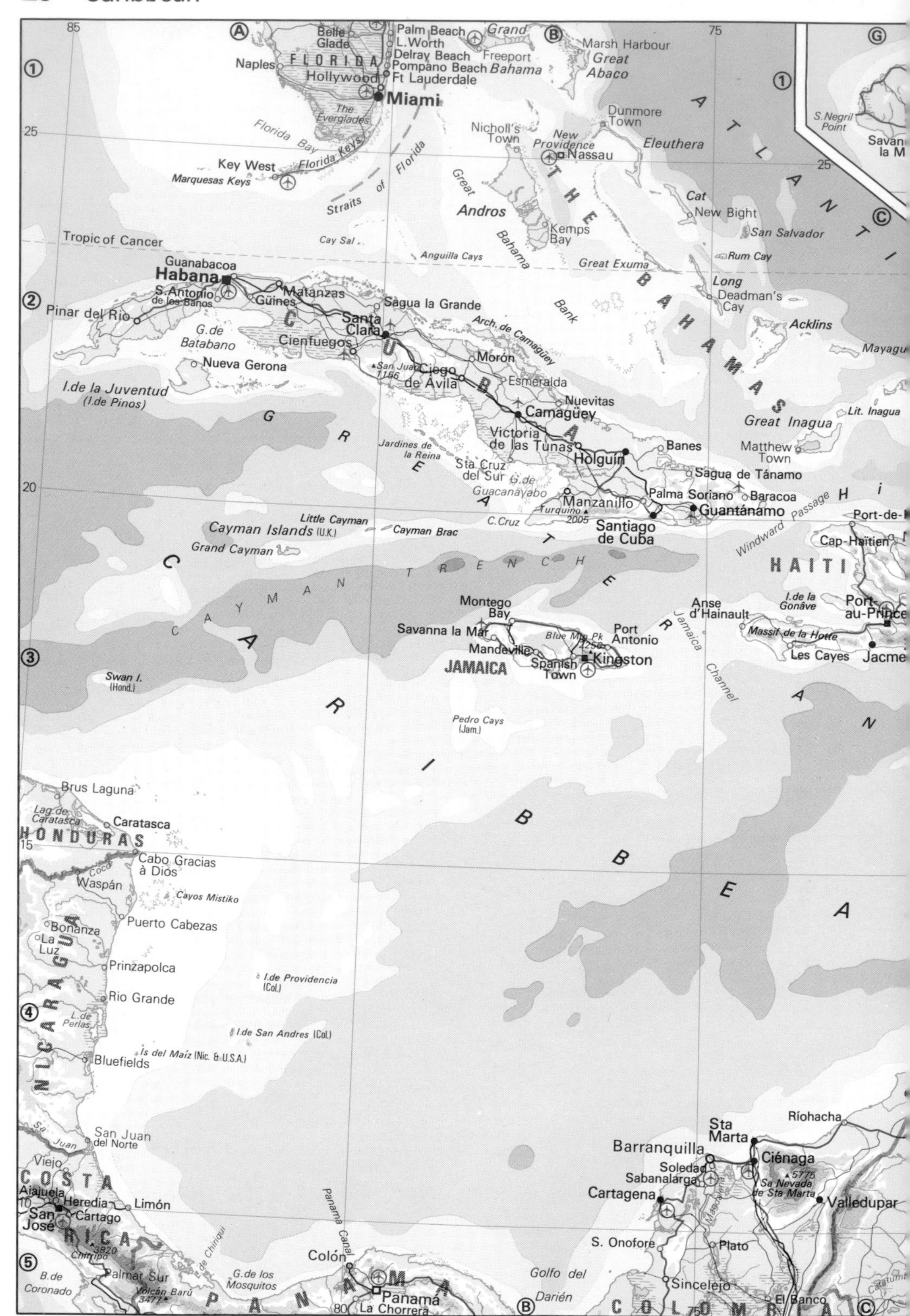

85

(A)(1)

Belle Glade
L. Worth
Palm Beach
Delray Beach
Pompano Beach
Ft Lauderdale

Naples

FLORIDA

Hollywood

Miami

The Everglades

Florida Bay

(B)
Marsh Harbour
Great Abaco

Dunmore Town

75

(G)(1)

S. Negril Point

Savan la M

25

Key West

Marquesas Keys

Florida Keys

Straits of Florida

Cay Sal

Nicholl's Town

New Providence
Nassau

Eleuthera

Cat
New Bight
San Salvador

25

(C)

Tropic of Cancer

Anguilla Cays

Great Bahama Bank

Andros

Kemps Bay

Great Exuma

Long
Deadman's Cay

Rum Cay

ATLANTI

Guanabacoa
Habana
S. Antonio de los Baños

Matanzas
Güines
Santa Clara

Sagua la Grande

Arch. de Camagüey

Bank

Acklins

Mayagu

20

Pinar del Rio

G. de Batabano

Cienfuegos

C
U
B
A

San Juan 1156
Ciego de Avila

Morón

Esmeralda

Nuevitas

Camagüey

Banes

Great Inagua

Lit. Inagua

(2)

Nueva Gerona

I. de la Juventud
(I. de Pinos)

Victoria de las Tunas

Holguin

Matthew Town

Sagua de Tánamo

20

G
R
E
A
T

Jardines de la Reina

Sta Cruz del Sur

G. de Guacanayabo

Turquino 2005

Manzanillo

C. Cruz

Palma Soriano
Santiago de Cuba

Baracoa
Guantánamo

H
I

Windward Passage

Port-de-

Cap-Haïtien

Little Cayman

Cayman Islands (U.K.)

Cayman Brac

T
H
E

T
R
E
N
C
H

Port-au-Prince

I. de la Gonâve

HAITI

Grand Cayman

(3)

Swan I. (Hond.)

C
A
Y
M
A
N

Montego Bay

Savanna la Mar

Mandeville

JAMAICA

Blue Mtn Pk 2256
Port Antonio

Spanish Town
Kingston

Jamaica

Anse d'Hainault

Massif de la Hotte

Les Cayes

Port-au-Prince

Jacme

Pedro Cays (Jam.)

Jamaica Channel

A
N

C
A
R
I
B
B
E
A

Brus Laguna

Lag. de Caratasca

Caratasca

H
O
N
D
U
R
A
S

15

Cabo Gracias à Dios

Waspán

Coco

Cayos Mistiko

Puerto Cabezas

Bonanza
La Luz

Prinzapolca

Rio Grande

I. de Providencia
(Col.)

I. de San Andres (Col.)

N
I
C
A
R
A
G
U
A

(4)

I. de Perlas

Is del Maiz (Nic. & U.S.A.)

Bluefields

Río
San Juan
del Norte

Viejo

COSTA

Alajuela
San José
Heredia
Cartago

Limón

R
I
C
A

3820
Chirripó

B. de Coronado

(5)

Palmar Sur

Volcán Barú 3477

G. de los Mosquitos

de Chiriquí

Colón

Panama Canal

PANAMA

Panamá
La Chorrera

80

(B)

Golfo del Darién

Sta Marta

Ríohacha

Barranquilla

Soledad
Sabanalarga

Ciénaga
5775
Sa Nevada de Sta Marta

Cartagena

Valledupar

S. Onofore

Plato

Sincelejo

El Banco

C O L O M B I A

(C)

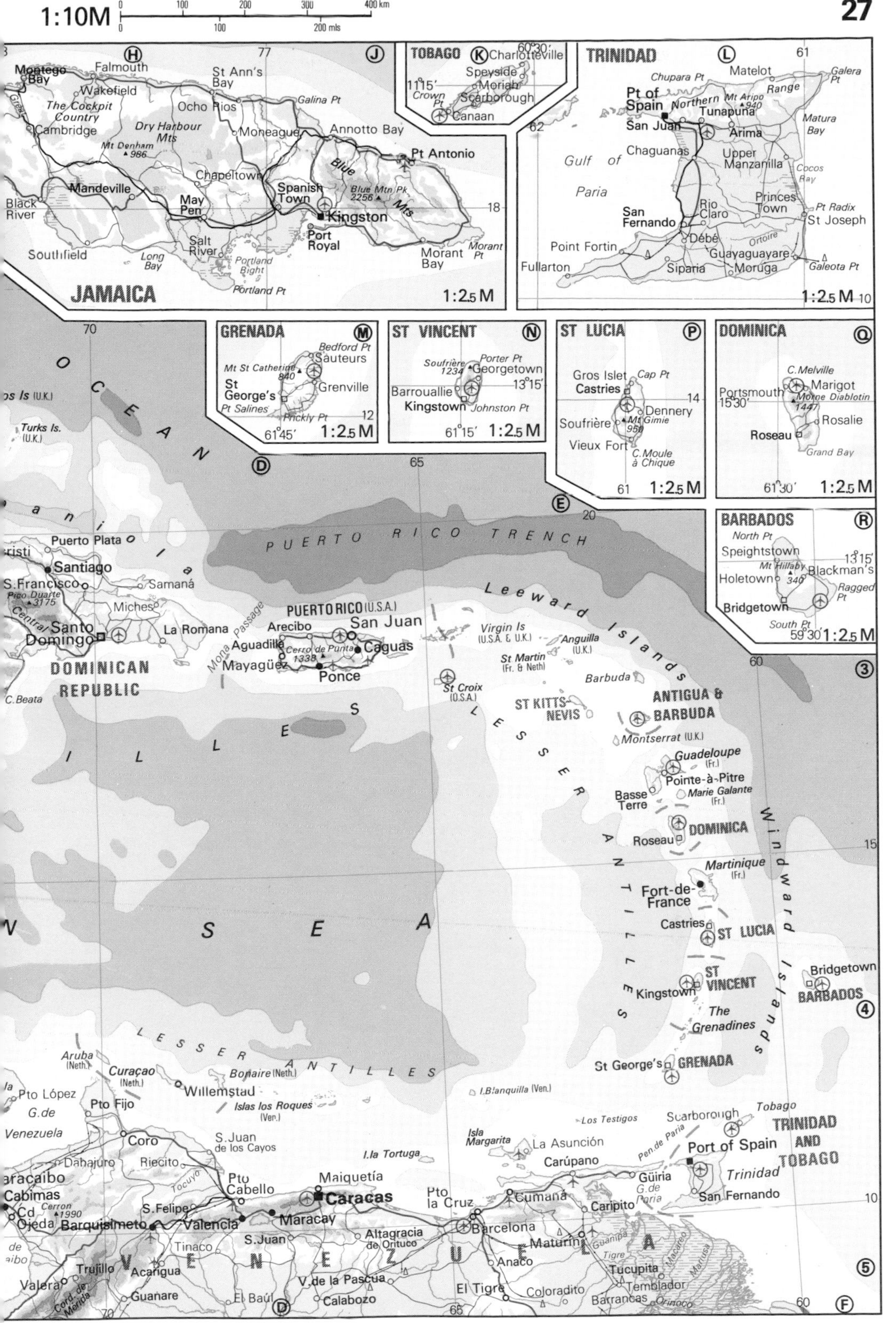

1:10M

0 100 200 300 400 km
0 100 200 mls

H Falmouth
Montego Bay
Wakefield
St Ann's Bay
The Cockpit Country
Galina Pt
J
Ocho Rios
Cambridge
Dry Harbour Mts
Moneague
Annotto Bay
Mt Denham 966
Chapelton
Pt Antonio
Blue Mtn Pk 2256
Blue Mts
Spanish Town
Mandeville
May Pen
Kingston
Black River
Salt River
Port Royal
Southfield
Long Bay
Portland Bight
Morant Pt
Morant Bay
Portland Pt

JAMAICA   1:2.5M

TOBAGO **K** Charlotteville
Speyside
11°15′ Crown Moriah
Scarborough
Canaan

TRINIDAD Matelot **L** Galera Pt 61
Chupara Pt
Pt of Spain Northern Mt Aripo 940 Tunapuna
San Juan Range Matura Bay
Chaguanas Upper Manzanilla
Gulf of Paria
Cocos Bay
62
Rio Claro Princes Town
San Fernando Pt Radix St Joseph
Point Fortin Débé Ortoire
Guayaguayare
Fullarton Siparia Moruga Galeota Pt

1:2.5M -10

GRENADA **M** Bedford Pt Sauteurs
Mt St Catherine 840
St George's Grenville
Pt Salines Prickly Pt
61°45′ 1:2.5M 12

D

ST VINCENT **N** Porter Pt
Soufrière 1234 Georgetown
13°15′
Barrouallie
Kingstown Johnston Pt
61°15′ 1:2.5M

ST LUCIA **P**
Gros Islet Cap Pt
Castries
14
Dennery
Soufrière Mt Gimie 950
C. Moule à Chique
Vieux Fort
61 1:2.5M

DOMINICA **Q**
C. Melville
Portsmouth Morne Diablotin 1447
15°30′ Marigot
Rosalie
Roseau
Grand Bay
61°30′ 1:2.5M

E 20
65

BARBADOS **R**
North Pt
Speightstown 13°15′
Mt Hillaby 340 Blackman's
Holetown Ragged Pt
Bridgetown
South Pt
59°30′ 1:2.5M
3

70

O C E A N

os Is (U.K.)
Turks Is. (U.K.)
Puerto Plata
Cristi Samaná
Santiago S.Francisco
Pico Duarte 3175
S. Miches
Santo Domingo
La Romana
C. Beata
DOMINICAN REPUBLIC

P U E R T O R I C O T R E N C H

Leeward Islands

PUERTO RICO (U.S.A.)
Arecibo San Juan
Aguadilla Caguas
Cerro de Punta 1338
Mayagüez Ponce

Mona Passage

Virgin Is (U.S.A. & U.K.)
St Martin (Fr. & Neth)
Anguilla (U.K.)
Barbuda
St Croix (U.S.A.)
ST KITTS- NEVIS
ANTIGUA & BARBUDA
Montserrat (U.K.)
Guadeloupe (Fr.)
Pointe-à-Pitre
Basse Terre Marie Galante (Fr.)
Roseau **DOMINICA**
15
Martinique (Fr.)
Fort-de-France
Castries **ST LUCIA**

L E S S E R

A N T I L L E S

C A R I B B E A N S E A

Windward Islands
Kingstown **ST VINCENT**
Bridgetown **BARBADOS**
4
The Grenadines
St George's **GRENADA**

L E S S E R A N T I L L E S

Aruba (Neth.) Curaçao (Neth.) Bonaire (Neth.)
Pto López Pto Fijo Willemstad
G.de
Venezuela
Coro Islas los Roques (Ven.)
Dabajuro Riecito S.Juan de los Cayos
I.la Tortuga
I.Blanquilla (Ven.)
Los Testigos
Isla Margarita
La Asunción
Scarborough Tobago
Pen de Paria
TRINIDAD AND TOBAGO
Port of Spain

racaibo
Cabimas Cerron 1990
Cd. S.Felipe
Ojeda Valencia
Barquisimeto Maracay
aibo Tinaco S.Juan
Trujillo Acarigua
V E N E Z U E L A
Valera Guanare El Baúl
Cord. de Mérida
70 **D** 66

Pto Cabello
Caracas
Maiquetía
Carúpano Güiria G.de Paria Trinidad
Pto la Cruz Cumaná Caripito San Fernando 10
Barcelona Caripe Maturín
Altagracia de Orituco Anaco Tigre Tucupita
S.Juan Tembladar
V.de la Pascua Calabozo Coloradito El Tigre Barrancas Orinoco
60 **F**
5

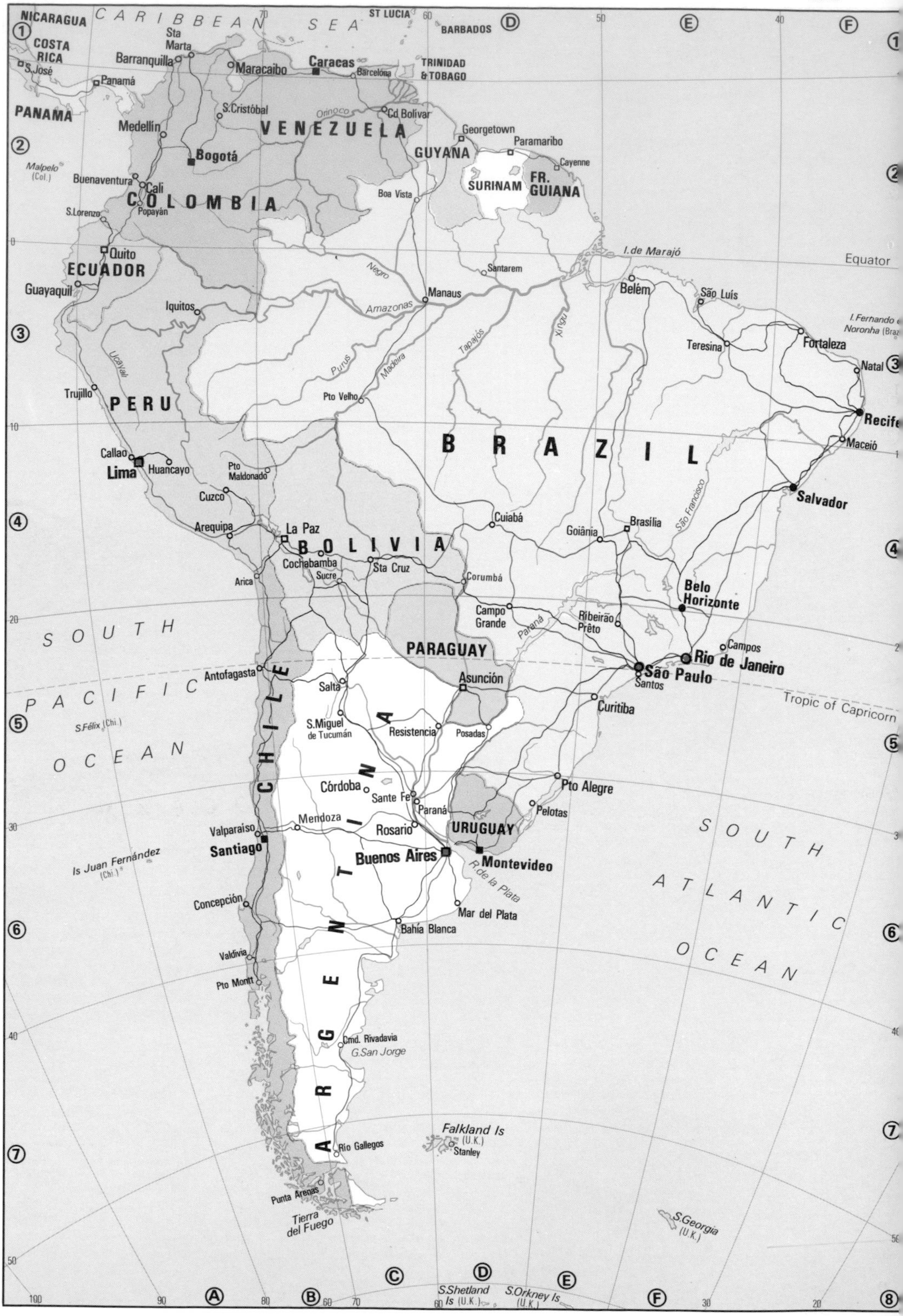

0 400 800 1200 1600 km
0 400 800 mls

NICARAGUA
CARIBBEAN SEA
ST LUCIA
BARBADOS
D
E
F
COSTA RICA
Sta Marta
TRINIDAD & TOBAGO
S.José
Barranquilla
Maracaibo
Caracas
Barcelona
PANAMA
Panamá
S.Cristóbal
Cd.Bolivar
Georgetown
Paramaribo
Medellín
VENEZUELA
GUYANA
Cayenne
Malpelo (Col.)
Bogotá
SURINAM
FR. GUIANA
Buenaventura
Cali
Boa Vista
COLOMBIA
Popayán
S.Lorenzo
Orinoco
Negro
Equator
Quito
Santarem
I. de Marajó
ECUADOR
Belém
São Luís
Guayaquil
Iquitos
Manaus
I.Fernando de Noronha (Braz)
Amazonas
Teresina
Fortaleza
Ucayali
Purus
Tapajos
Xingu
Natal
Trujillo
PERU
Pto Velho
Madeira
Recife
Maceió
Callao
Huancayo
Pto Maldonado
B R A Z I L
Lima
Cuzco
São Francisco
Salvador
Arequipa
Cuiabá
Brasília
SOUTH
La Paz
Goiânia
BOLIVIA
Cochabamba
Sta Cruz
Belo Horizonte
Arica
Sucre
Corumbá
PACIFIC
Campo Grande
Ribeirão Prêto
Campos
Antofagasta
PARAGUAY
Paraná
Rio de Janeiro
S.Félix (Chi.)
Salta
Asunción
São Paulo
Santos
OCEAN
S.Miguel de Tucumán
Resistencia
Posadas
Curitiba
Tropic of Capricorn
Córdoba
Santa Fe
Paraná
Pto Alegre
SOUTH
Is Juan Fernández (Chi.)
Mendoza
Rosario
URUGUAY
Pelotas
ATLANTIC
Valparaíso
Santiago
Buenos Aires
Montevideo
R.de la Plata
Concepción
Mar del Plata
OCEAN
Bahía Blanca
ARGENTINA
CHILE
Valdivia
Pto Montt
Cmd. Rivadavia
G.San Jorge
Falkland Is (U.K.)
Stanley
Rio Gallegos
Punta Arenas
Tierra del Fuego
S.Georgia (U.K.)
S.Shetland Is (U.K.)
S.Orkney Is (U.K.)

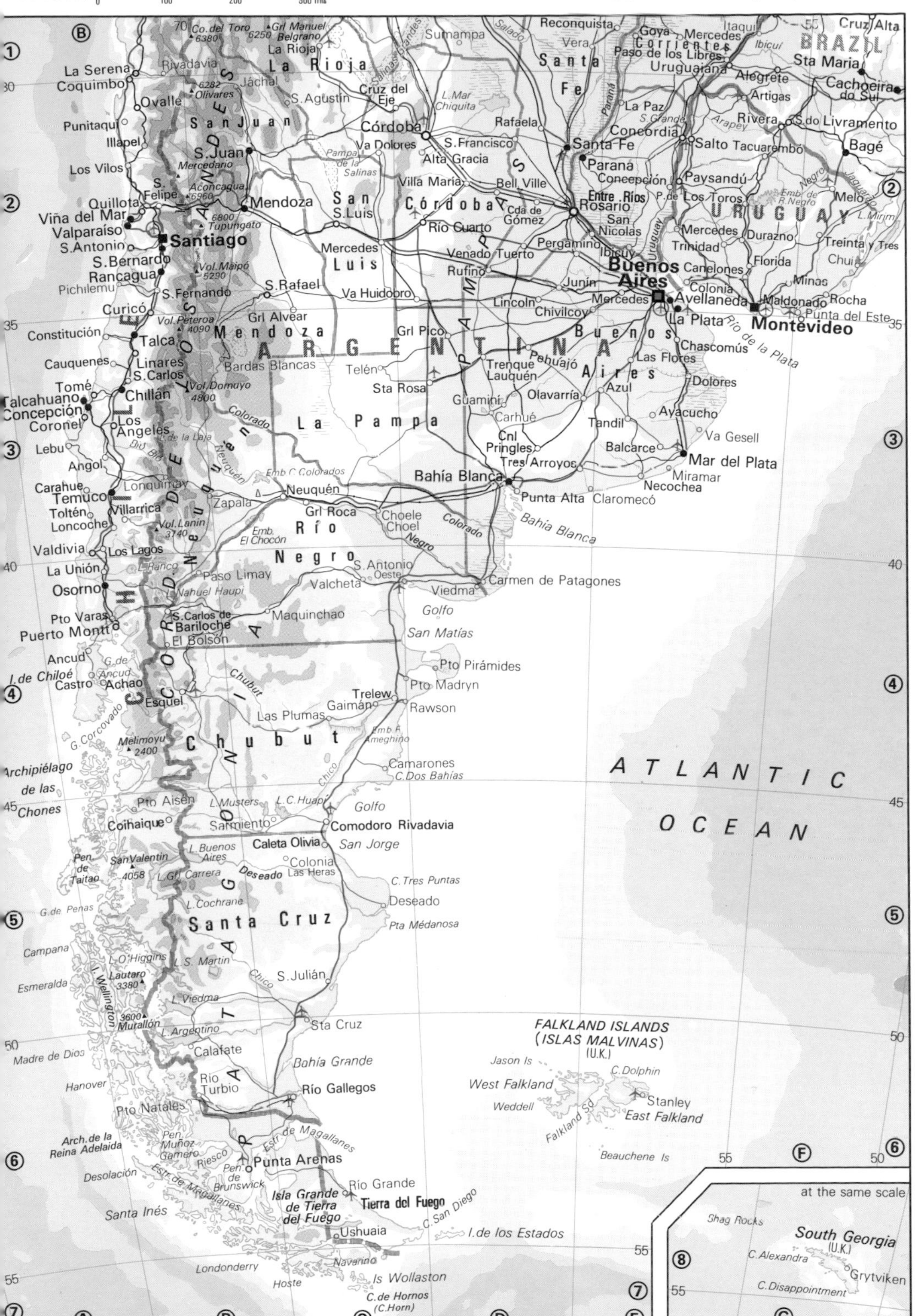

Co.del Toro 6380
Grl Manuel Belgrano 6250
La Rioja
Sumampa
Reconquista
Goya
Mercedes
Itaqui
Cruz Alta
55
BRAZIL
Rivadavia
La Serena
Coquimbo
La Rioja
Cruz del Eje
Vera
Corrientes
Paso de los Libres
Uruguaiana
Sta Maria
Cachoeira do Sul
30
Ovalle
Olivares 6282
S. Agustin
L. Mar Chiquita
Santa
Ibicuí
Artigas
Rivera
S.do Livramento
Bagé
Punitaqui
Illapel
San Juan
Córdoba
Rafaela
Fe
La Paz
S. Grande
Arapey
Salto
Tacuarembó
Los Vilos
S. Juan
Mercedario 6960
Va Dolores
S. Francisco
Pampa de las Salinas
Alta Gracia
Santa Fe
Paraná
Concepción
Entre Ríos
Concordia
Paysandú
Durazno
Negro
Emb. de R. Negro
Melo
L. Mirim
Quillota
Aconcagua 6800
Tupungato
Mendoza
San
Villa María
Bell Ville
Cda de Gómez
Rosario
San Nicolás
Trinidad
Florida
Treinta y Tres
Chuí
Viña del Mar
Valparaíso
S.Antonio
S. Felipe
S. Luis
Córdoba
Río Cuarto
Pergamino
Buenos
Canelones
Minas
Rocha
Santiago
S. Bernardo
Rancagua
Vol.Maipó 5290
Luis
Mercedes
Venado Tuerto
Rufino
Junín
Aires
Avellaneda
La Plata
Colonia
Maldonado
Punta del Este
Pichilemu
S. Fernando
S. Rafael
Va Huidobro
Lincoln
Chivilcoy
Mercedes
Montevideo
35
Curicó
Grl Alvear
Chascomús
35
Constitución
Talca
Mendoza 4090
Vol.Peteroa
Grl Pico
Buenos
Las Flores
Dolores
Cauquenes
Linares
S.Carlos
Bardas Blancas
Telén
Trenque Lauquén
Pehuajó
Aires
Azul
Tomé
Chillán
Vol.Domuyo 4800
Sta Rosa
Guaminí
Carhué
Olavarría
Tandil
Ayacucho
Va Gesell
Talcahuano
Concepción
Coronel
La Pampa
Cnl Pringles
Tres Arroyos
Balcarce
Mar del Plata
Lebu
Angol
Colorado
Neuquén
Bahía Blanca
Punta Alta
Claromecó
Miramar
Necochea
Carahue
Temuco
Toltén
Loncoche
Lonquimay
Villarrica
Vol.Lanín 3740
Zapala
Grl Roca
Choele Choel
Río
Colorado
Bahía Blanca
Valdivia
Los Lagos
La Unión
Osorno
Emb. El Chocón
Negro
S.Antonio Oeste
Carmen de Patagones
40
Pto Varas
Puerto Montt
Nahuel Haupi
Paso Limay
Valcheta
Viedma
Ancud
I. de Chiloé
Castro
Achao
G.de Ancud
Maquinchao
Golfo
San Matías
Pto Pirámides
Pto Madryn
Archipiélago de las
Chones
G. Corcovado
Chubut
Esquel
Las Plumas
Gaimán
Trelew
Rawson
Melimoyu 2400
Emb.F. Ameghino
Camarones
C.Dos Bahías
Pto Aisén
Coihaique
L.Musters
Sarmiento
L.C.Huapi
Golfo
San Jorge
Comodoro Rivadavia
45
Pen. de Taitao
San Valentín 4058
L. Buenos Aires
L.Gll Carrera
Caleta Olivia
Colonia Las Heras
C.Tres Puntas
Campana
G. de Penas
Deseado
Deseado
Esmeralda
O'Higgins
Lautaro 3380
L.S. Martín
L.Cochrane
Pta Médanosa
Santa Cruz
50
Madre de Dios
Hanover
Wellington
Mutallón 3600
L.Viedma
Chico
S. Julián
FALKLAND ISLANDS (ISLAS MALVINAS) (U.K.)
Campana
L.Argentino
Sta Cruz
Jason Is
C.Dolphin
West Falkland
Stanley
East Falkland
Arch.de la Reina Adelaida
Pen. Muñoz Gamero
Riesco
Calafate
Río Turbio
Bahía Grande
Río Gallegos
Weddell
Falkland Sd
Pto Natales
Pen. de Brunswick
Est. de Magallanes
Beauchene Is
50
55
Santa Inés
Desolación
Punta Arenas
Isla Grande de Tierra del Fuego
Tierra del Fuego
Río Grande
at the same scale
Shag Rocks
South Georgia (U.K.)
C.Alexandra
Desolación
Est. de Magallanes
C. San Diego
I. de los Estados
Londonderry
Hoste
Ushuaia
Navarino
C.Disappointment
Grytviken
55
Madre de Dios
Is Diego Ramírez
C.de Hornos (C.Horn)
Is Wollaston
75   70   65   60
55   50   45   40   35

ATLANTIC OCEAN

1:15M

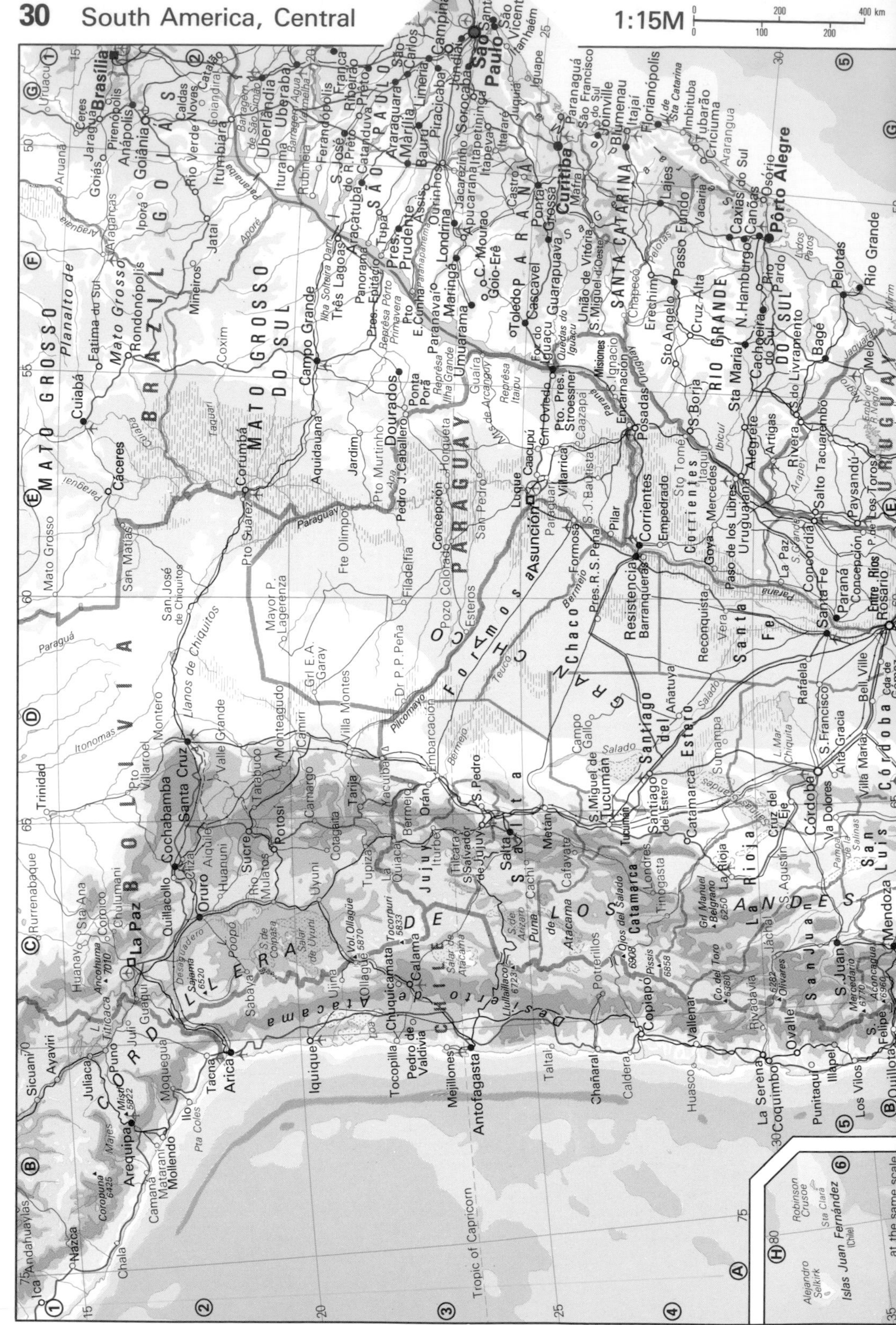

0
200
400 km
0
100
200
B R A Z I L
MATO GROSSO
MATO GROSSO DO SUL
GOIÁS
SÃO PAULO
PARANÁ
SANTA CATARINA
RIO GRANDE DO SUL
B O L I V I A
P A R A G U A Y
U R U G U A Y
CHILE
GRAN CHACO
Brasília
Goiânia
Cuiabá
Campo Grande
Corumbá
São Paulo
Santos
Curitiba
Pôrto Alegre
Florianópolis
Asunción
La Paz
Cochabamba
Santa Cruz
Sucre
Potosí
Oruro
Tarija
Arica
Iquique
Antofagasta
Copiapó
La Serena
Coquimbo
Salta
Tucumán
Córdoba
Rosario
Santa Fe
Corrientes
Resistencia
Posadas
Mendoza
Arequipa
Tropic of Capricorn
Islas Juan Fernández (Chile)
Alejandro Selkirk
Robinson Crusoe
at the same scale

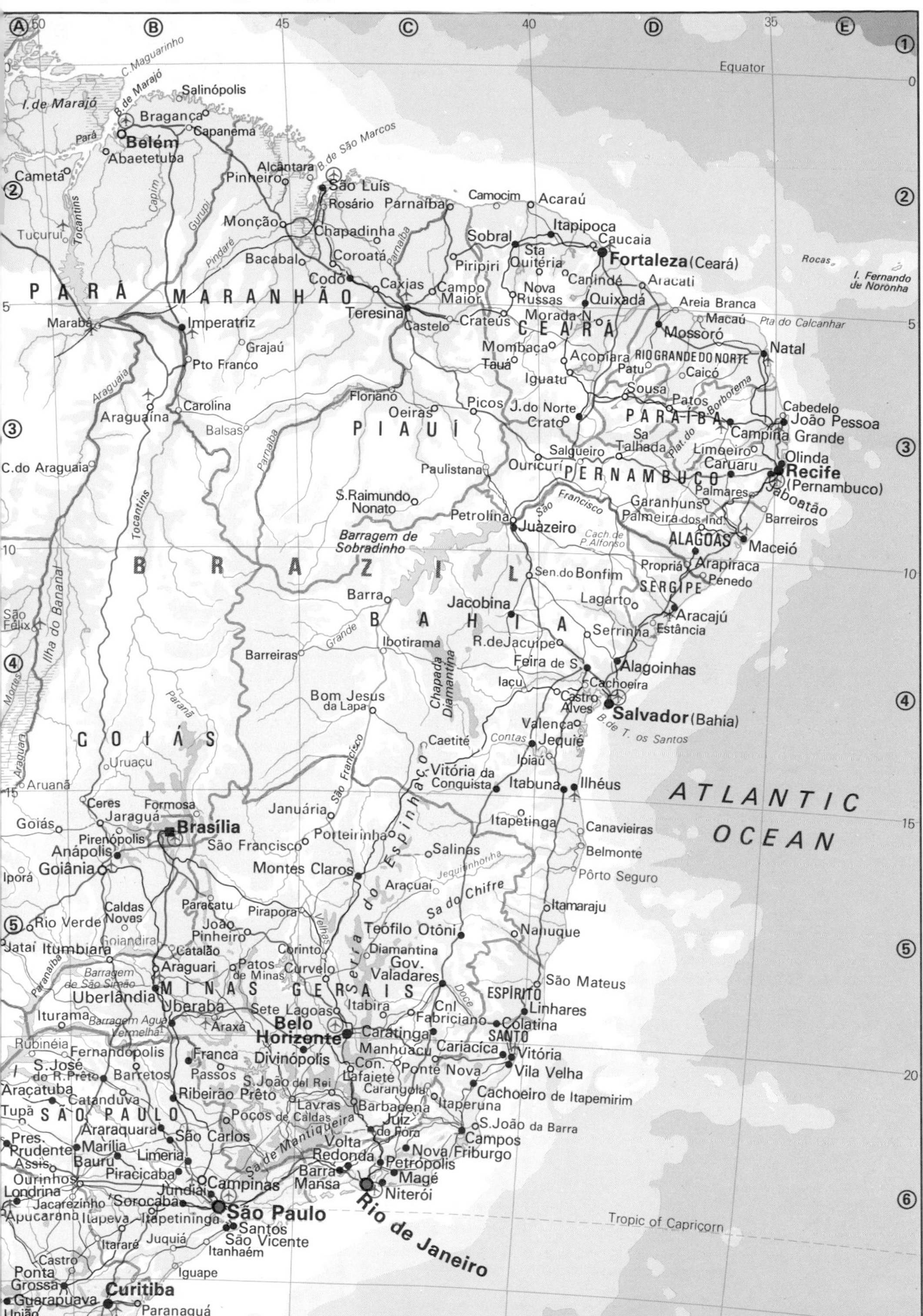

200   400   600 km
100   200   300 mls

Equator

PARÁ   **MARANHÃO**   **CEARÁ**

I. de Marajó
C. Maguarinho
B. de Marajó
Salinópolis
Bragança
Capanema
Belém
Abaetetuba
Cametá
Pará
Alcântara
Pinheiro
São Luís
Rosário
Parnaíba
Camocim
Acaraú
Tucuruí
Monção
Chapadinha
Sobral
Itapipoca
Caucaia
Rocas
I. Fernando de Noronha
Bacabal
Coroatá
Piripiri
Sta Quitéria
Fortaleza (Ceará)
Marabá
Imperatriz
Codó
Caxias
Campo Maior
Nova Russas
Canindé
Aracati
Quixadá
Areia Branca
Pto Franco
Grajaú
Teresina
Castelo
Crateús
Morada-N.
Mossoró
Macau
Pta do Calcanhar
Natal
Carolina
Balsas
Floriano
Oeiras
Picos
J. do Norte
Mombaça
Tauá
Acopiara
Iguatu
Patu
Sousa
Caicó
RIO GRANDE DO NORTE
Cabedelo
João Pessoa
Campina Grande

PIAUÍ
Crato
Salgueiro
Ouricuri
Paulistana
S.Raimundo Nonato
Petrolina
Juàzeiro
Barragem de Sobradinho

BRAZIL   **GOIÁS**   **BAHIA**   **PERNAMBUCO**   **ALAGOAS**   **SÉRGIPE**

Olinda
Recife (Pernambuco)
Palmeira dos Ind.
Maceió
Propriá
Arapiraca
Penedo
Lagarto
Aracajú
Estância
Serrinha
Alagoinhas
Salvador (Bahia)
B. de T. os Santos

ATLANTIC OCEAN

MINAS GERAIS   **ESPÍRITO**   **SÃO PAULO**

Brasília
Anápolis
Goiânia
Rio Verde
Uberlândia
Uberaba
Belo Horizonte
Divinópolis
Teófilo Otôni
Gov. Valadares
São Mateus
Linhares
Colatina
SANTO
Vitória
Vila Velha

São Paulo
Santos
Rio de Janeiro
Niterói
Petrópolis
Campos

Tropic of Capricorn

Curitiba
Paranaguá
Ponta Grossa

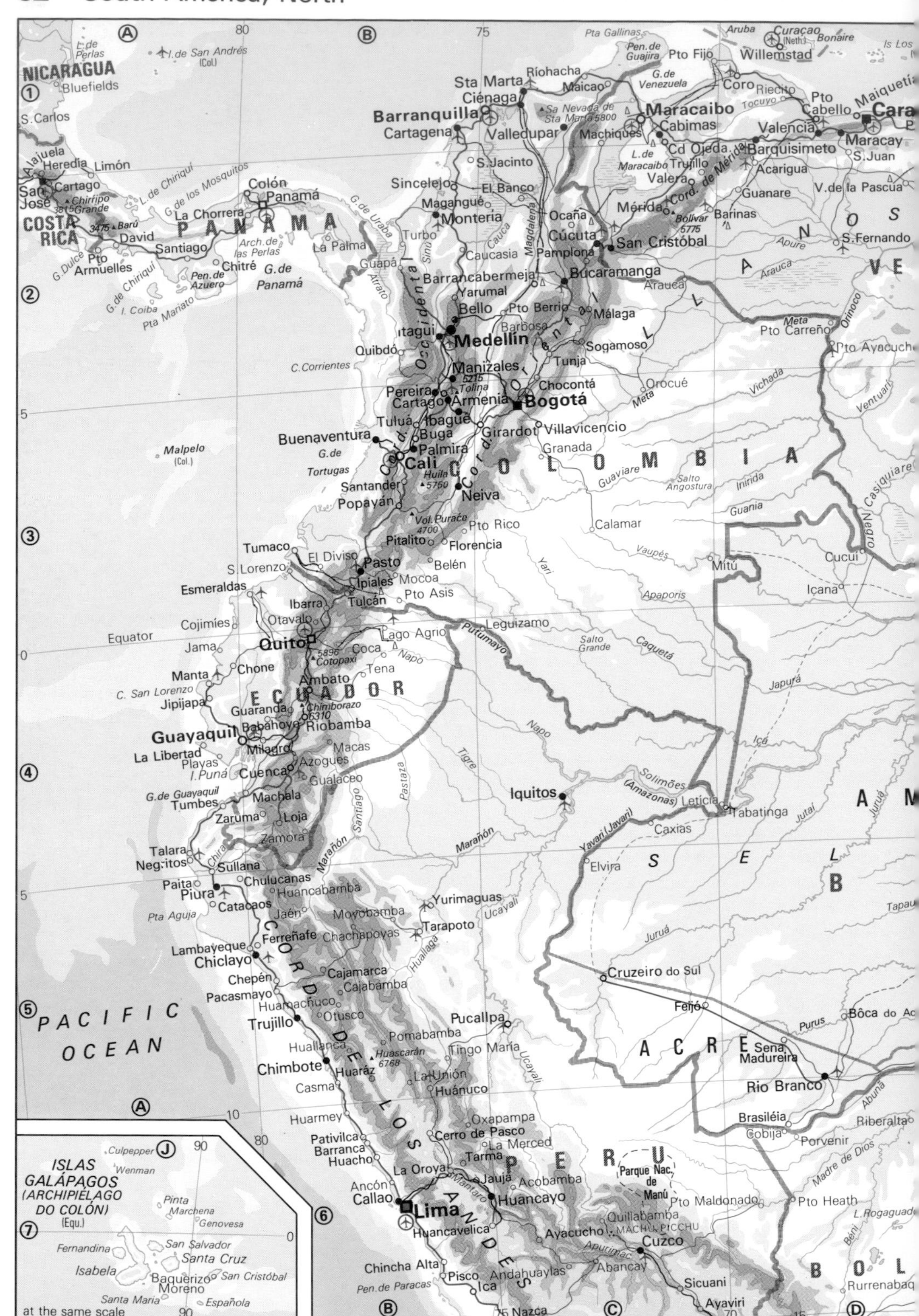

NICARAGUA
Bluefields
S. Carlos
Najuela
Heredia Limón
San Cartago
José Chirripó
COSTA 3475 Baru
RICA David Santiago
Pto
Armuelles
G. Dulce de Chiriqui
G. de Chiriqui
I. Coiba
Pta Mariato
Pto Fijo
Aruba Curaçao Bonaire
(Neth.)
Willemstad
Is Los

Colón
Panamá
P A N A M A
La Chorrera
La Palma
Arch. de
las Perlas
Pen. de Azuero
Chitré G. de Panamá

Pta Gallinas
Pen. de Guajira
Ríohacha
Sta Marta Maicao
Ciénaga
Barranquilla
Cartagena Valledupar
S. Jacinto
Sincelejo
Magangué El Banco
Monteria
Turbo
Sinú
Cauca
Caucasia
Barrancabermeja
Yarumal
Bello
Itaguí
Medellin
Manizales
Pereira
Cartago Armenia
Tuluá Ibagué
Buenaventura
Buga
Palmira
Cali
Santander
Popayán

Machiques
Maracaibo Cabimas
Cd Ojeda
L. de Maracaibo
Valera
Mérida
Ocaña
Cúcuta
Pamplona
San Cristóbal
Bucaramanga
Málaga
Barbosa
Sogamoso
Tunja
Chocontá
Bogotá
Villavicencio
Granada
Girardot
Neiva

G. de Venezuela
Coro
Riecito
Pto Cabello
Valencia
Barquisimeto
Acarigua
Guanare
Barinas
S. Fernando
Apure
Arauca
Pto Carreño
Meta
Orocué
Vichada
Meta
Inírida
Guaviare

COLOMBIA

Vol. Puracé 4700
Pitalito
Florencia
Belén
Pto Rico
Calamar
Guainía
Salto Angostura

Tumaco
S. Lorenzo
El Diviso Pasto
Esmeraldas
Ibarra
Ipiales Mocoa
Tulcán Pto Asis
Otavalo
Cojimíes
Jama
Quito
Manta
Chone
Ambato
EQUADOR
Guaranda Chimborazo 6310
Babahoyo Riobamba
Guayaquil
La Libertad Milagro
Playas Macas
I. Puná Cuenca
Tumbes Azogues
Machala Gualaceo
Zaruma
Loja
Zamora

Leguizamo
Putumayo
Lago Agrio
Coca Napo
Tena
Napo

Mitú
Vaupés
Apaporis

Iquitos

Leticia
Tabatinga
Caxias

Talara
Neg:itos
Paita
Piura
Catacaos
Sullana
Chulucanas
Huancabamba
Pta Aguja

Yurimaguas
Moyobamba
Tarapoto
Chachapoyas

Juruá
Cruzeiro do Sul
Feijó

Lambayeque
Ferreñafe
Chiclayo
Chepén
Pacasmayo
Cajamarca
Cajabamba
Jaén

Huamachuco
Otusco
Trujillo
Pomabamba
Pucallpa

Purus
Bôca do Ac
A C R E
Sena Madureira
Rio Branco
Brasiléia
Cobija
Porvenir
Riberalta

PACIFIC
OCEAN

Chimbote
Huaraz Huascarán 6768
Casma
Huarmey
Huallanca
La Unión
Huánuco
Tingo Maria
Ucayali

Pativilca
Barranca
Huacho
Ancón
Callao
Oxapampa
Cerro de Pasco
La Merced
Tarma
La Oroya
Jauja Acobamba
Huancayo
Lima
Huancavelica
Ayacucho
Parque Nac. de Manú

Quillabamba
MACHU PICCHU
Cuzco
Pto Maldonado
Pto Heath
L. Rogaguad
Rurrenabaq
B O L

P E R U

ISLAS
GALÁPAGOS
(ARCHIPIÉLAGO
DO COLÓN)
(Equ.)
Culpepper J
Wenman
Pinta
Marchena
Genovesa
Fernandina
San Salvador
Santa Cruz
Isabela
Baquerizo
Moreno San Cristóbal
Santa Maria
Española
at the same scale

Chincha Alta
Pisco
Ica
Pen. de Paracas
Andahuaylas
Abancay
Sicuani
Ayaviri
Nazca

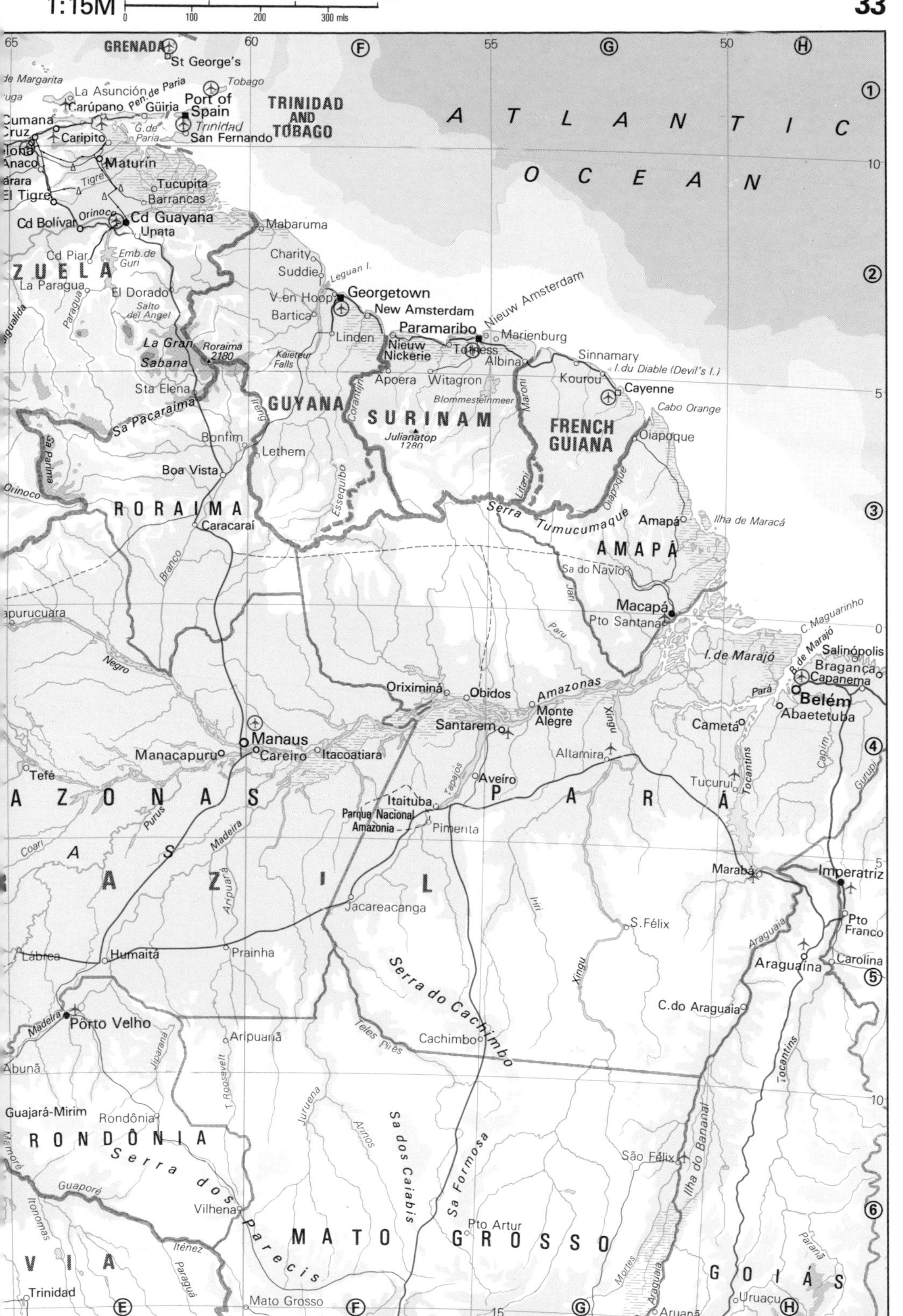

1:15M

200 400 600 km
100 200 300 mls

ATLANTIC

OCEAN

GRENADA
St George's
Tobago
TRINIDAD
AND
TOBAGO
de Margarita
La Asunción Pen.de Paria
Carúpano Güiria
Port of
Spain
G. de
Paria Trinidad
Cumana San Fernando
Cruz Caripito
ToloR Maturín
Anaco
árara Tigre Tucupita
El Tigre Barrancas
Cd Bolívar Orinoco Cd Guayana
Cd Piar Upata
Emb.de
Guri Mabaruma
La Paragua
ZUELA El Dorado Charity
Suddie
Salto V-en Hoop Georgetown
del Angel Bartica New Amsterdam
La Gran Roraima Linden Nieuw Amsterdam
Sabana 2180 Paramaribo
Nieuw Marienburg
Sta Elena Kaieteur Nickerie Totness
Falls Apoera Albina Sinnamary
Sa Pacaraima GUYANA Witagron I.du Diable (Devil's I.)
Bonfim SURINAM Kourou
Lethem Julianatop Blommesteinmeer Cayenne
Boa Vista 1280 Cabo Orange
FRENCH
RORAIMA GUIANA Oiapoque
Caracaraí Serra Tumucumaque Amapá Ilha de Maracá
AMAPÁ
Sa do Navio
puruúuara C. Maguarinho
Macapá
Pto Santana
I. de Marajó Salinópolis
Bragança
Negro de Marajó Capanema
Oriximiná Obidos Amazonas Pará Belém
Santarem Monte Abaetetuba
Tefé Manaus Alegre Cametá
Manacapuru Careiro Itacoatiara Altamira Tucuruí
AZONAS Aveiro PARÁ
A S Itaituba Marabá
Z Parque Nacional Imperatriz
I Amazônia Pimenta
L Jacareacanga Pto
Labrea Humaitá Prainha S. Félix Franco
Araguaína Carolina
Porto Velho Serra do Cachimbo C.do Araguaia
Madeira Aripuanã Cachimbo
Abunã
Guajará-Mirim Rondônia
RONDÔNIA São Félix
V Serra dos parecis
Guaporé Vilhena
I
A MATO GROSSO
Trinidad Mato Grosso GOIÁS
Aruanã Uruacu

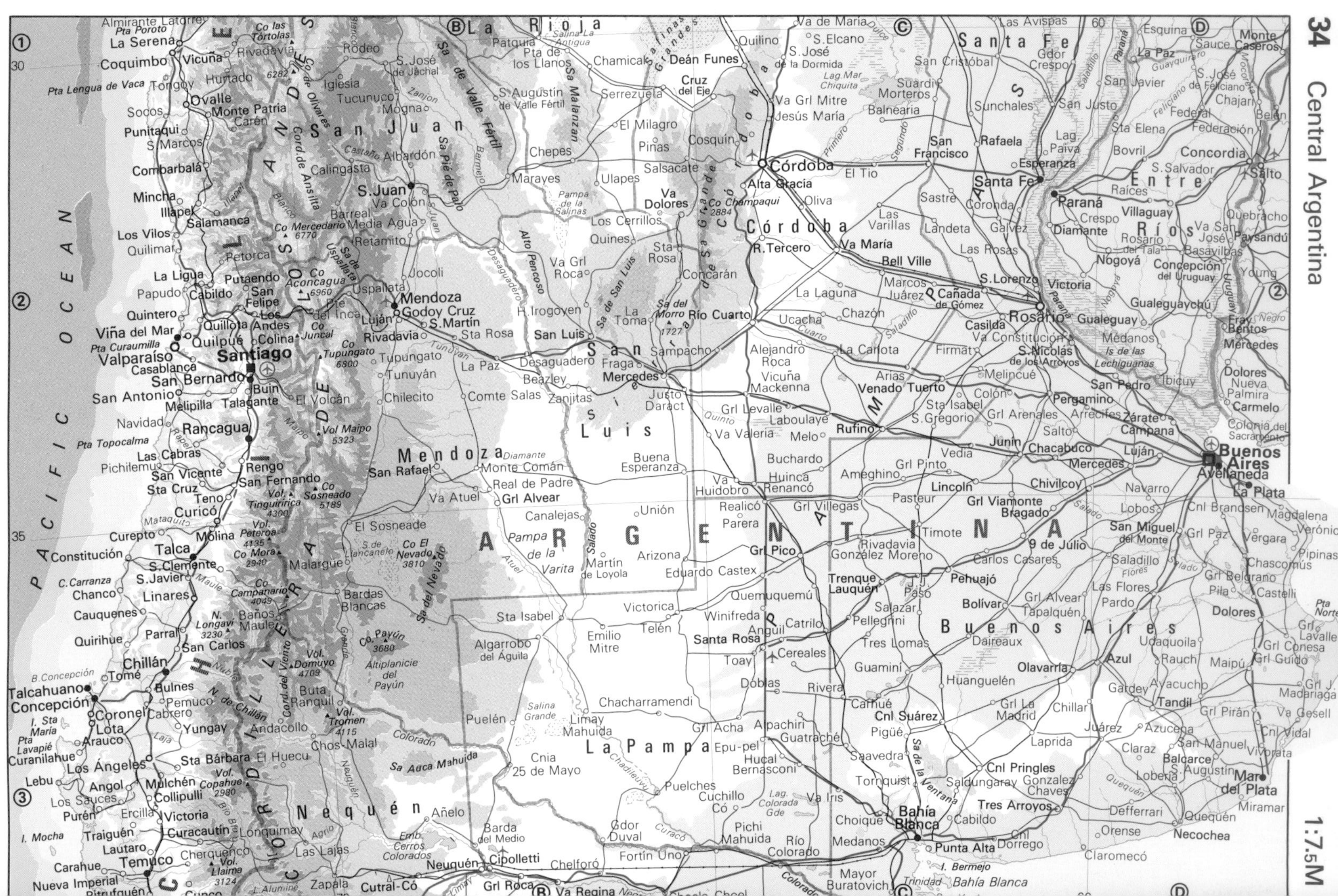
PACIFIC OCEAN
ARGENTINA
La Rioja
San Juan
Córdoba
Santa Fe
Entre Ríos
San Luis
Mendoza
La Pampa
Buenos Aires
Nequén
Buenos Aires
La Plata
Avellaneda
Mar del Plata
Bahía Blanca
Rosario
Córdoba
Santa Fe
Paraná
Mendoza
S.Juan
San Luis
Santiago
Valparaíso
Viña del Mar
Concepción
Talcahuano
Temuco
Chillán
Talca
Rancagua
Neuquén
Santa Rosa
Río Cuarto
Concordia
La Serena
Coquimbo
Ovalle
Curicó
Los Ángeles
Tandil
Azul
Olavarría
Junín
Pergamino
Venado Tuerto
Rufino
Villa María
Bell Ville
San Rafael
Necochea
Tres Arroyos
Cipolletti
Gualeguaychú
Concepción del Uruguay
Salto
Fray Bentos
Colonia del Sacramento

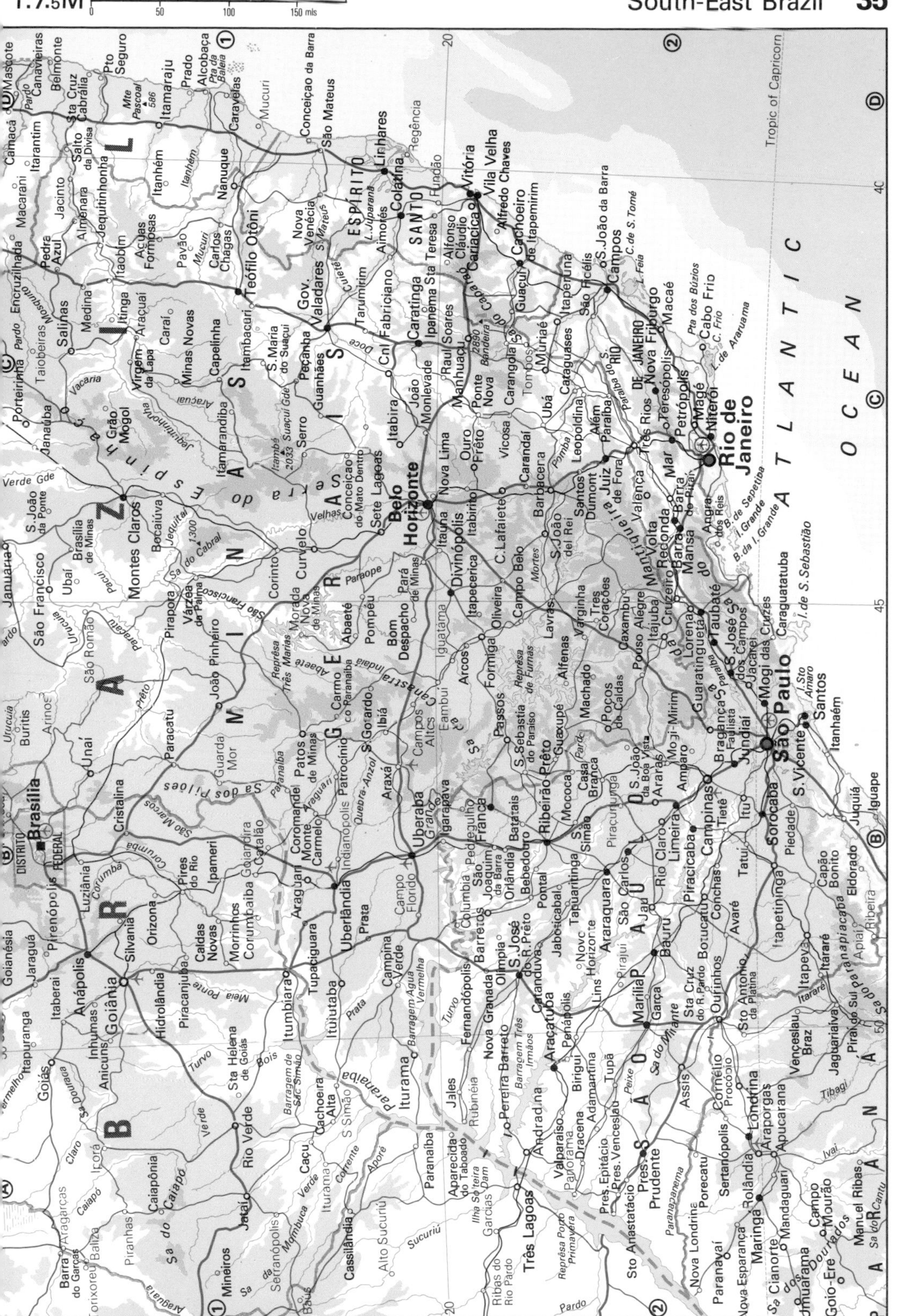
BRAZIL
MINAS GERAIS
ESPÍRITO SANTO
RIO DE JANEIRO
SÃO PAULO
PARANÁ
DISTRITO FEDERAL
ATLANTIC OCEAN
Tropic of Capricorn
Brasília
Belo Horizonte
Rio de Janeiro
São Paulo
Vitória
Vila Velha
Goiânia
Anápolis
Uberlândia
Uberaba
Montes Claros
Juiz de Fora
Campinas
Santos
Niterói
Londrina
Maringá
Ribeirão Prêto
Governador Valadares
Teófilo Otôni
Campos
Volta Redonda
Serra do Espinhaço
Serra da Canastra
Serra da Mantiqueira
São Francisco
Paranaíba
Grande
Tietê
Doce
Paraná

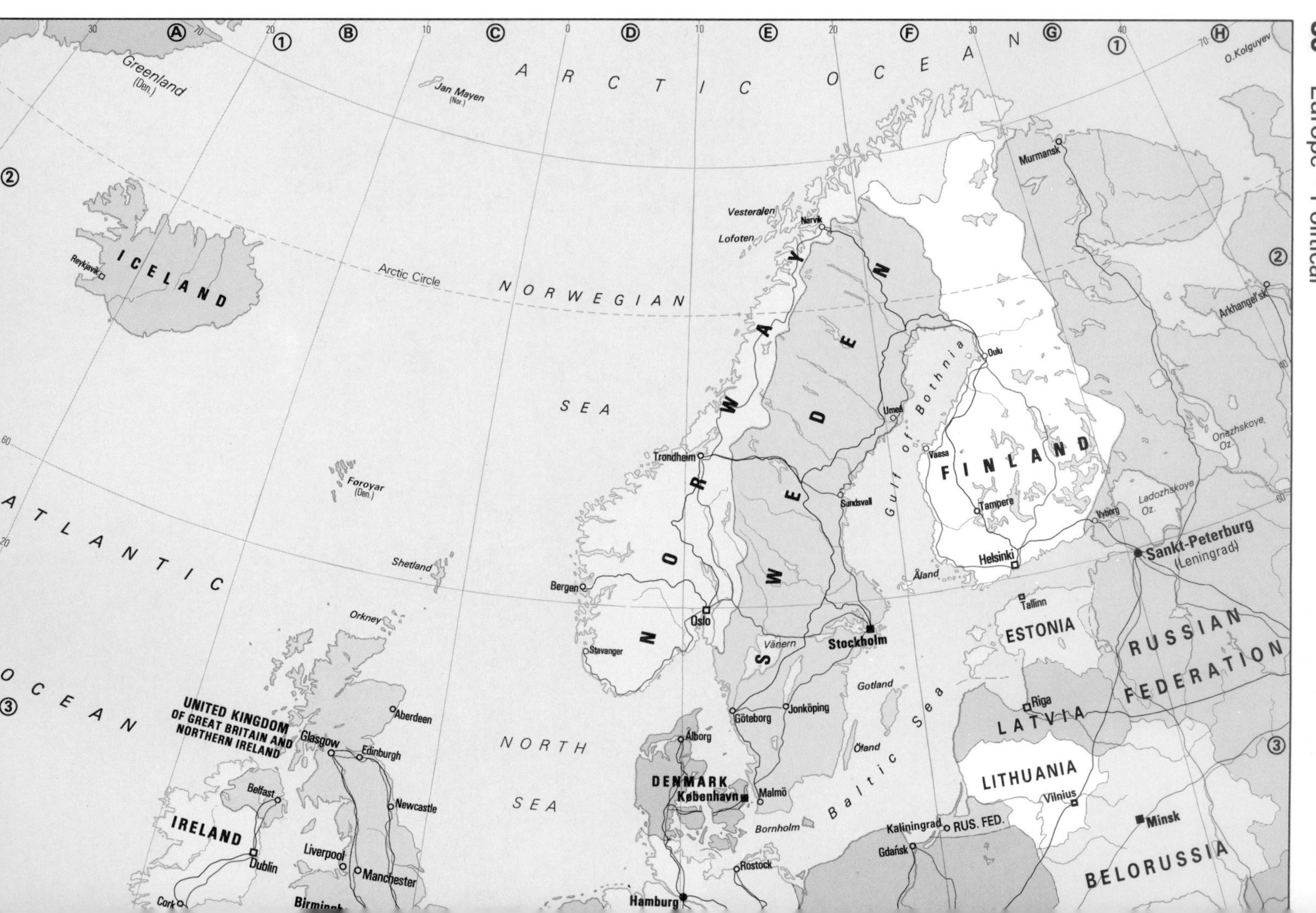
ARCTIC OCEAN
NORWEGIAN SEA
NORTH SEA
ATLANTIC OCEAN
Arctic Circle
Greenland (Den.)
Jan Mayen (Nor.)
ICELAND
Reykjavík
Føroyar (Den.)
Shetland
Orkney
UNITED KINGDOM OF GREAT BRITAIN AND NORTHERN IRELAND
Aberdeen
Edinburgh
Glasgow
Newcastle
Manchester
Liverpool
Belfast
IRELAND
Dublin
Cork
NORWAY
Bergen
Stavanger
Oslo
Trondheim
Narvik
Vesterålen
Lofoten
SWEDEN
Stockholm
Göteborg
Malmö
Jönköping
Vänern
Sundsvall
Umeå
Gotland
Öland
Bornholm
DENMARK
København
Ålborg
Hamburg
Rostock
Gulf of Bothnia
Baltic Sea
FINLAND
Helsinki
Tampere
Vaasa
Oulu
Åland
Murmansk
Arkhangel'sk
o. Kolguyev
Onezhskoye Oz.
Ladozhskoye Oz.
Vyborg
Sankt-Peterburg (Leningrad)
RUSSIAN FEDERATION
ESTONIA
Tallinn
LATVIA
Riga
LITHUANIA
Vilnius
BELORUSSIA
Minsk
RUS. FED.
Kaliningrad
Gdańsk

1:16M 0 200 400 600 km
0 100 200 300 mls

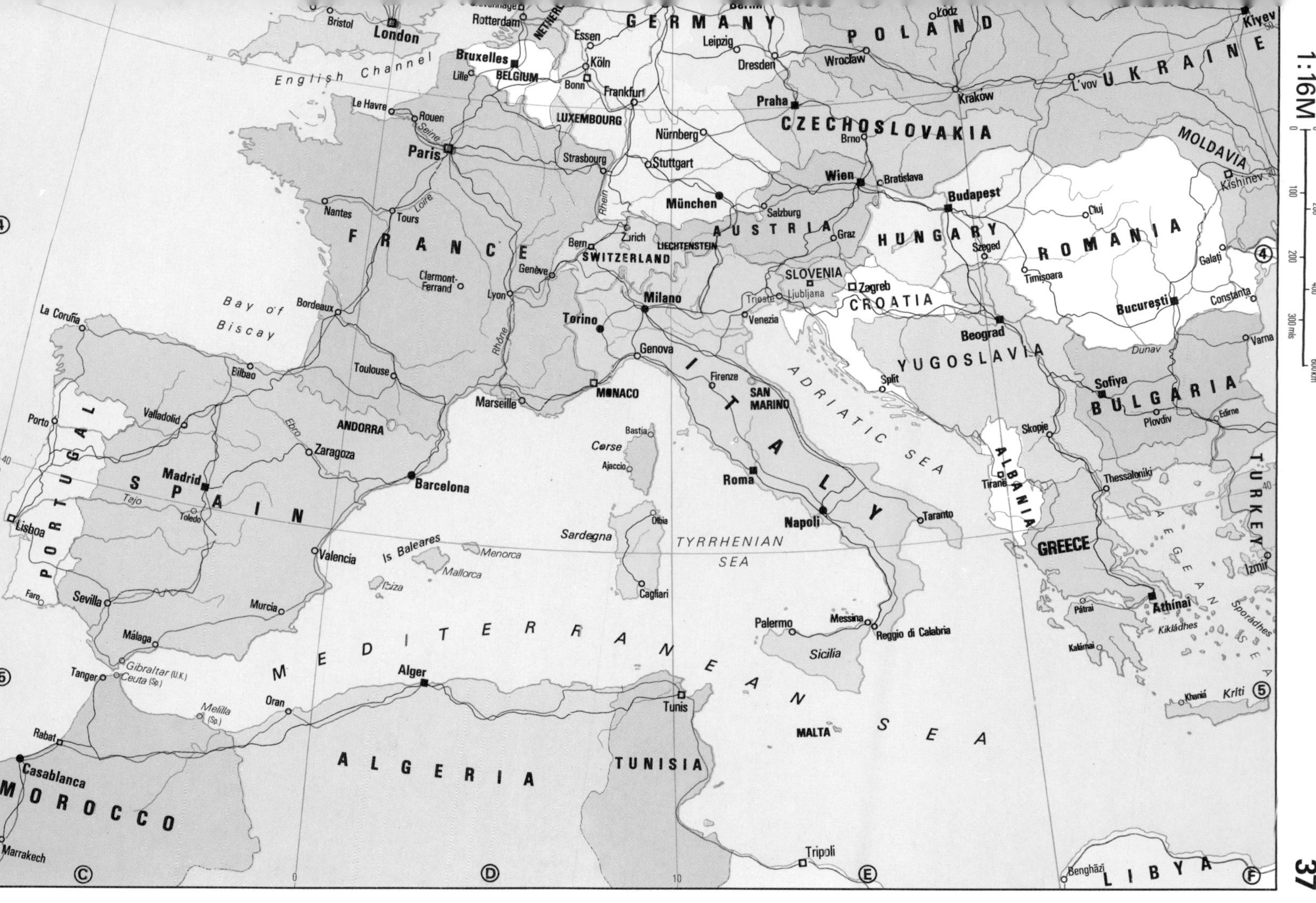

Bristol
London
English Channel
Rotterdam
Bruxelles
Lille
BELGIUM
Essen
Köln
Bonn
Frankfurt
LUXEMBOURG
GERMANY
Leipzig
Dresden
Nürnberg
Stuttgart
Strasbourg
Rhein
München
POLAND
Łódź
Wrocław
Kraków
L'vov
UKRAINE
Kiyev
Praha
CZECHOSLOVAKIA
Brno
Wien
Bratislava
MOLDAVIA
Kishinev
Le Havre
Rouen
Seine
Paris
Nantes
Tours
Loire
FRANCE
Clermont-Ferrand
Lyon
Rhône
Genève
Bern
Zürich
SWITZERLAND
LIECHTENSTEIN
AUSTRIA
Salzburg
Graz
Budapest
HUNGARY
Szeged
Cluj
ROMANIA
Timișoara
Galați
București
Constanța
Varna
Dunav
SLOVENIA
Ljubljana
Zagreb
CROATIA
Trieste
Venezia
Milano
Torino
Genova
MONACO
Marseille
Beograd
YUGOSLAVIA
Split
Sofiya
BULGARIA
Plovdiv
Edirne
Skopje
ALBANIA
Tiranë
Thessaloníki
TURKEY
İzmir
GREECE
Pátrai
Athínai
Kalámai
AEGEAN SEA
Kikládhes
Sporádhes
Khaniá
Kríti
Bay of Biscay
La Coruña
Bordeaux
Toulouse
Bilbao
Porto
PORTUGAL
Valladolid
Ebro
ANDORRA
Zaragoza
Madrid
SPAIN
Tajo
Toledo
Lisboa
Barcelona
Valencia
Is Baleares
Menorca
Mallorca
Ibiza
Faro
Sevilla
Murcia
Málaga
Gibraltar (U.K.)
Ceuta (Sp.)
Tanger
Melilla (Sp.)
Oran
Alger
Rabat
Casablanca
MOROCCO
Marrakech
ALGERIA
TUNISIA
Tunis
Firenze
SAN MARINO
ITALY
Roma
Napoli
Taranto
ADRIATIC SEA
Bastia
Corse
Ajaccio
Sardegna
Olbia
Cagliari
TYRRHENIAN SEA
Palermo
Messina
Reggio di Calabria
Sicilia
MEDITERRANEAN SEA
MALTA
Tripoli
Benghāzī
LIBYA

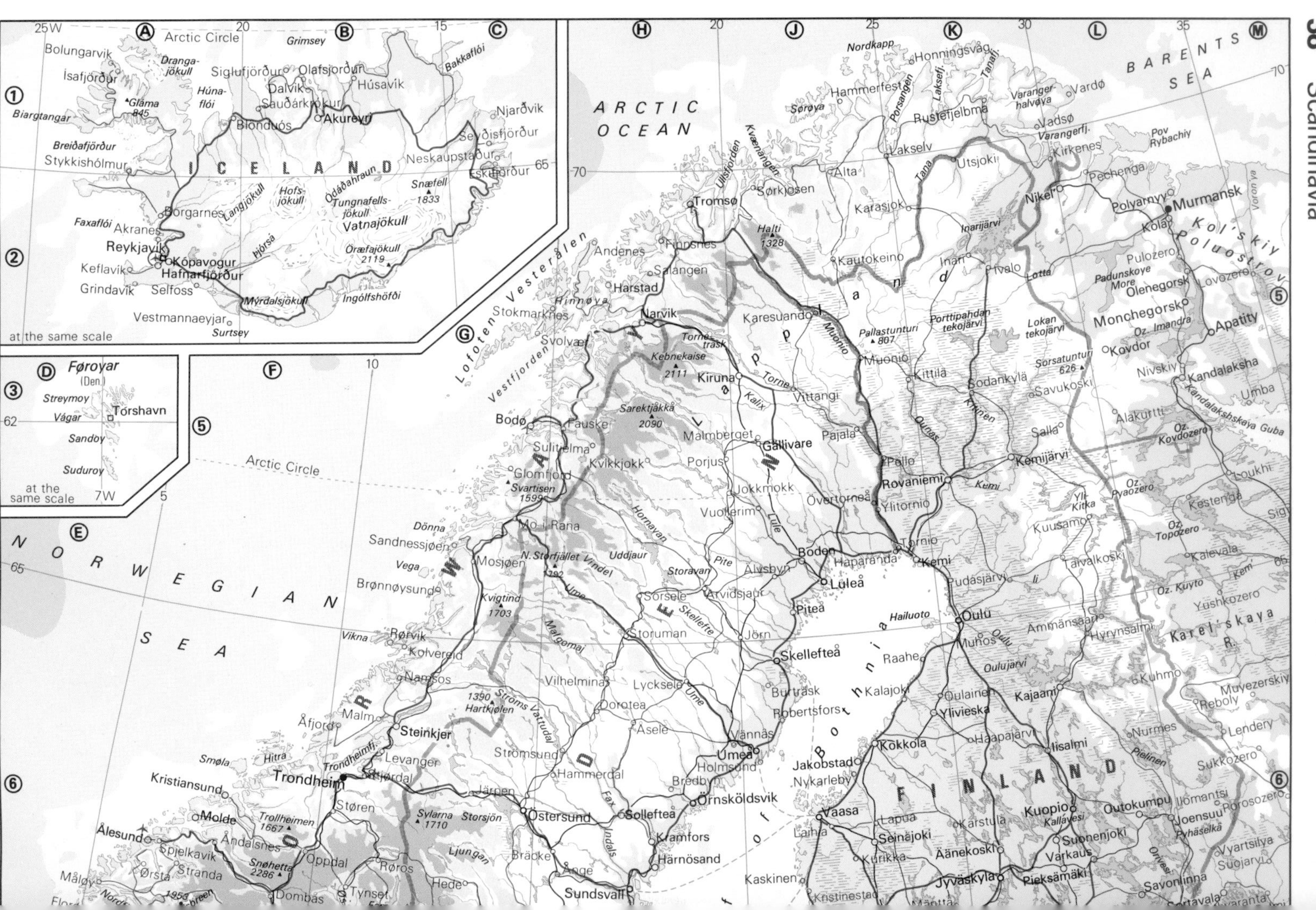
ARCTIC OCEAN
BARENTS SEA
NORWEGIAN SEA
ICELAND
FINLAND
Lapland
Gulf of Bothnia
Kol'skiy Poluostrov
Karel'skaya R.
Lofoten Vesterålen
Vestfjorden
Arctic Circle
Føroyar (Den.)
at the same scale
Reykjavik
Akureyri
Tórshavn
Tromsø
Narvik
Bodø
Trondheim
Kiruna
Gällivare
Luleå
Umeå
Östersund
Sundsvall
Oulu
Rovaniemi
Vaasa
Kuopio
Jyväskylä
Murmansk
Apatity
Kandalaksha
Monchegorsk
Hammerfest
Nordkapp
Kebnekaise 2111
Sarektjåkkå 2090
Halti 1328
Snøhetta 2286
Vatnajökull
Öræfajökull 2119

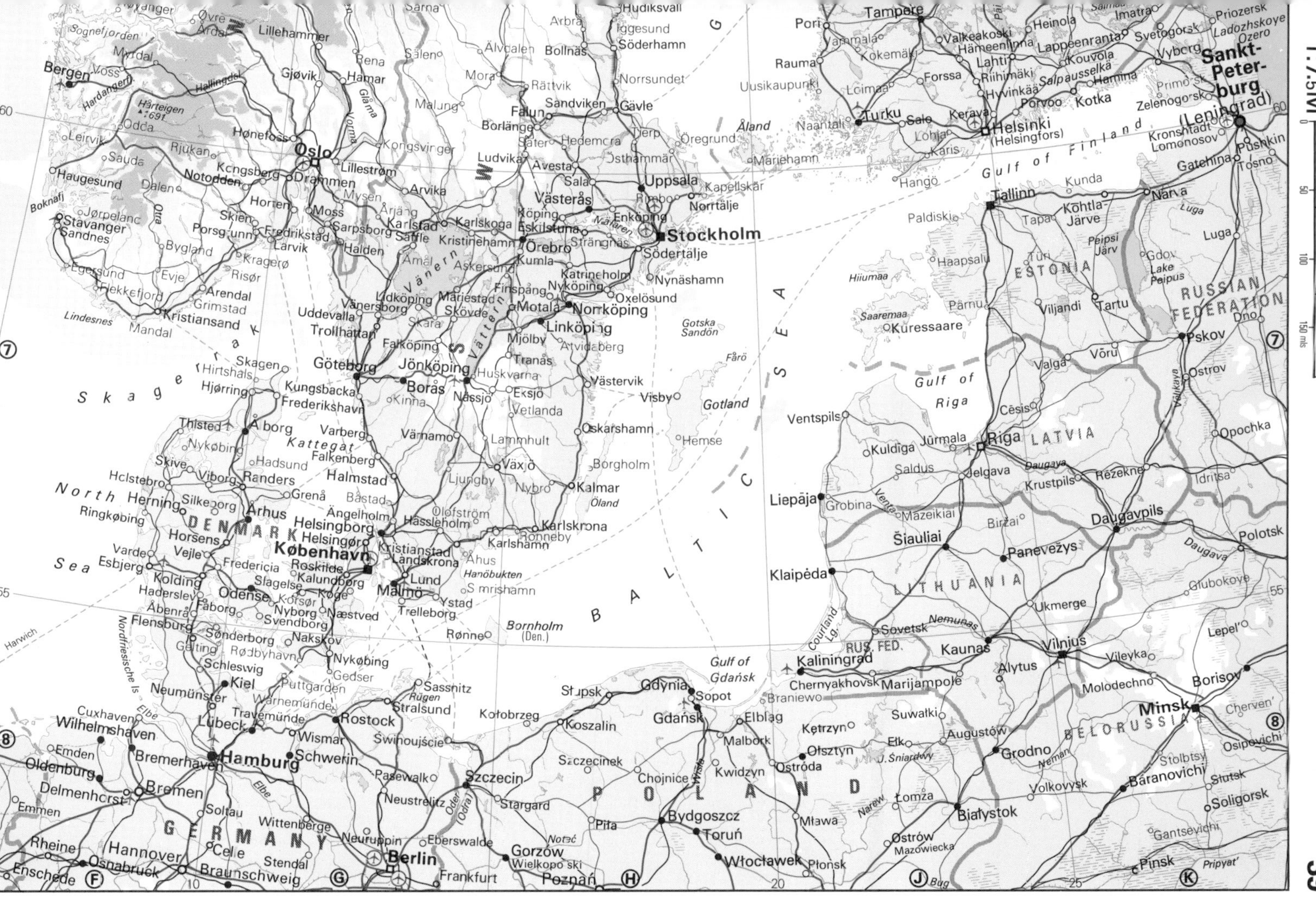

1:7.5M

1:5M

50 100 150 200 km
50 100 mils

NORTH SEA

NORWAY

Nordhordland (E)
Dale
Bergen
Sotra
Sunnhordland Stord
Leirvik
Bømlo
Skjold
Haugesund
Karmøy

Shetland
Herma Ness
Unst
Fetlar
Isbister
Yell
Whalsay
St Magnus B.
Lerwick
Foula
Sumburgh Hd

Fair Isle

Orkney
Westray
Sanday
Rousay
Stronsay
Sule Skerry
Kirkwall
Stromness
Scapa Flow
Hoy
Stack Skerry

Duncansby Hd
Wick
Thurso
Helmsdale
Dornoch Firth
Ben Hope 927
Ben More Assynt 998
Dornoch
C. Wrath
N. Rona
Sula Sgeir
Butt of Lewis
Ullapool
Dingwall
L. Ness
Inverness
Elgin
Moray Firth
Banff
Fraserburgh
Peterhead
Buchan Ness
Aberdeen
Stonehaven
Montrose
Arbroath
F. of Tay
St Andrews

Flannan Is
Stornoway
Lewis
Harris
N. Uist
The Minch
Skye
Portree
C. Kyle of Lochalsh
Mallaig
Fort William
Ben Nevis 1344
Fort Augustus
SCOTLAND
Ben Macdui 1309
Braemar
Dee
Don
Pitlochry
Grampian
Perth
F. of Forth
Kirkcaldy
Edinburgh
Berwick-upon-Tweed
Holy I.
St Abbs Hd
Galashiels
Alnwick
Morpeth
Blyth
Newcastle upon Tyne
S. Shields
Gateshead
Sunderland
Cheviots
Hawick
White Coomb 822
Moffat
Carlisle
Kirkcudbright
Nith
Dumfries
Merrick 843
Stirling
Glasgow
Motherwell
Paisley
Greenock
Kilmarnock
Ayr
Irvine
Arran
Girvan
F. of Clyde
L. Lomond
L. Awe
L. Lorn
Oban
Mull
Coll
Tiree
Rum
Iday
Colonsay
Jura
Campbeltown
Outer Hebrides
St Kilda
Barra
S. Uist

N. IRELAND
Coleraine
Ballymena
Londonderry
L. Foyle
Malin Hd
Errigal 752
Tory I.
Aran I.
Rossan Pt
Donegal
Rathlin I.
Larne
Stranraer

60
55

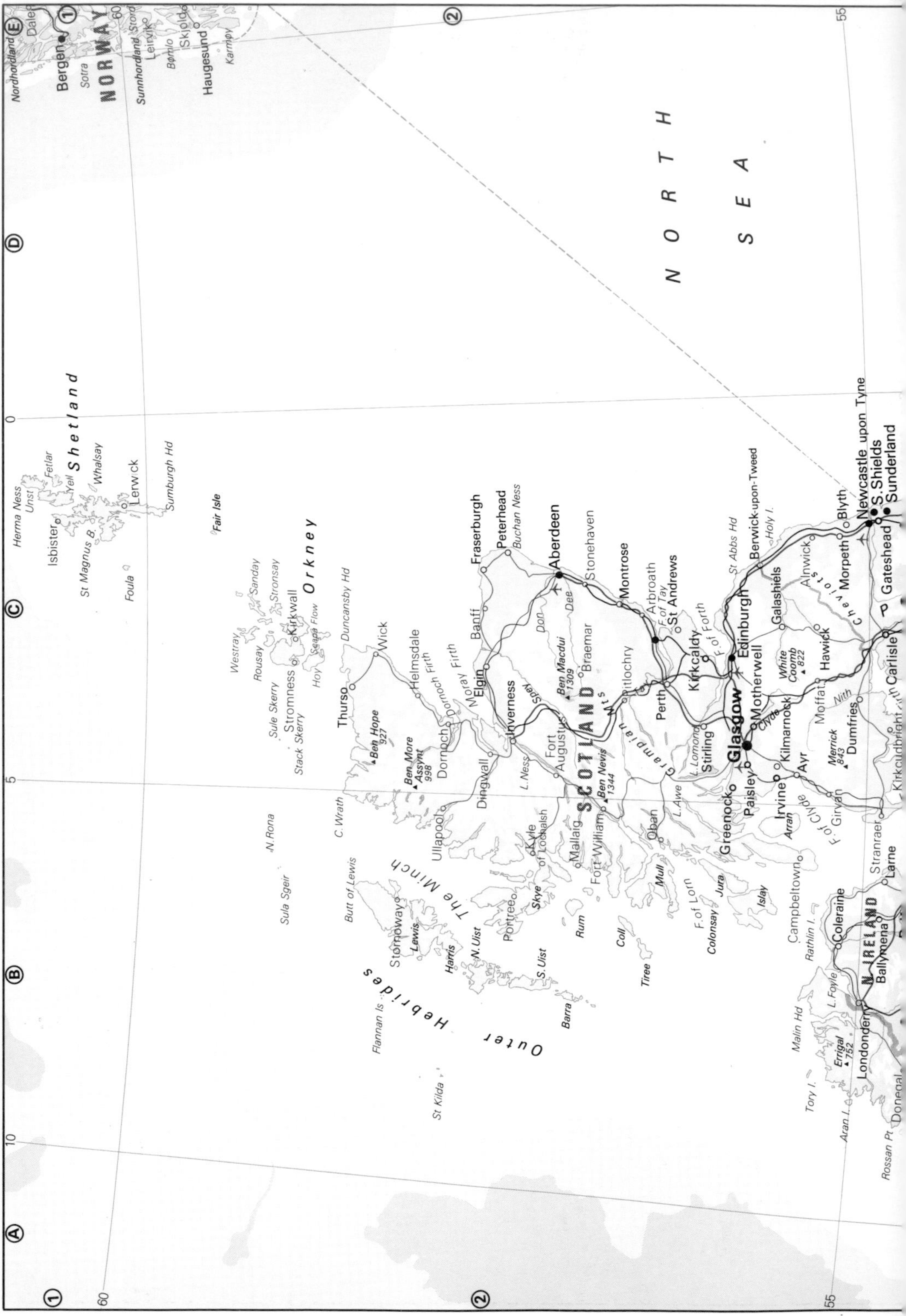

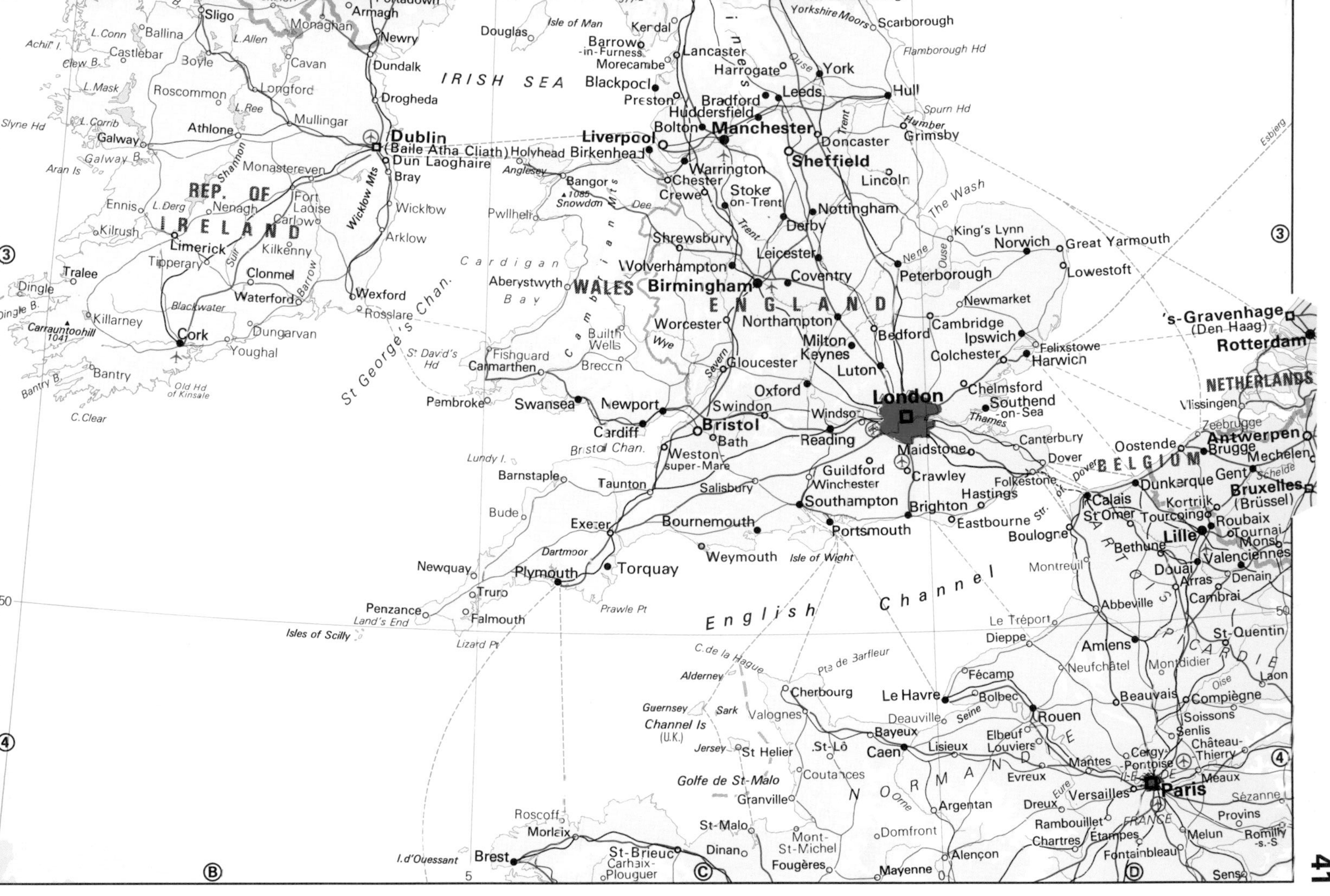

IRISH SEA
Isle of Man
Douglas
WALES
ENGLAND
REP. OF IRELAND
BELGIUM
NETHERLANDS
FRANCE
English Channel
Cardigan Bay
Cambrian Mts
St George's Chan.
Bristol Chan.
Golfe de St-Malo
Channel Is (U.K.)
NORMANDIE
PICARDIE
ARTOIS
ÎLE-DE-FRANCE
Sligo
Ballina
L.Conn
Achill I.
Castlebar
Clew B.
L.Mask
L.Corrib
Slyne Hd
Galway
Galway B.
Aran Is
Boyle
L.Allen
Roscommon
L.Ree
Longford
Cavan
Monaghan
Armagh
Portadown
Newry
Dundalk
Drogheda
Mullingar
Athlone
Shannon
Monasterevan
Dublin (Baile Atha Cliath)
Dun Laoghaire
Bray
Wicklow Mts
Wicklow
Arklow
Wexford
Rosslare
Ennis
L.Derg
Nenagh
Port Laoise
Carlow
Kilrush
Limerick
Tipperary
Suir
Kilkenny
Barrow
Clonmel
Waterford
Tralee
Dingle
Dingle B.
Killarney
Carrauntoohill 1041
Blackwater
Cork
Dungarvan
Youghal
Bantry
Bantry B.
Old Hd of Kinsale
C.Clear
Holyhead
Anglesey
Bangor
1085 Snowdon
Pwllheli
Aberystwyth
Fishguard
St David's Hd
Carmarthen
Builth Wells
Brecon
Pembroke
Swansea
Newport
Cardiff
Lundy I.
Barnstaple
Bude
Newquay
Truro
Falmouth
Penzance
Land's End
Isles of Scilly
Lizard Pt
Dartmoor
Plymouth
Torquay
Prawle Pt
Exeter
Taunton
Weston-super-Mare
Bristol
Bath
Swindon
Kendal
Barrow-in-Furness
Morecambe
Lancaster
Blackpool
Preston
Bolton
Liverpool
Birkenhead
Chester
Crewe
Warrington
Manchester
Huddersfield
Bradford
Leeds
Harrogate
Ouse
York
Yorkshire Moors
Scarborough
Flamborough Hd
Hull
Spurn Hd
Humber
Grimsby
Trent
Doncaster
Sheffield
Lincoln
Stoke-on-Trent
Dee
Nottingham
Derby
Shrewsbury
Leicester
Wolverhampton
Birmingham
Coventry
Worcester
Wye
Northampton
Severn
Gloucester
Milton Keynes
Luton
Bedford
Oxford
The Wash
King's Lynn
Nene
Ouse
Peterborough
Norwich
Great Yarmouth
Lowestoft
Newmarket
Cambridge
Ipswich
Felixstowe
Harwich
Colchester
Chelmsford
Southend-on-Sea
Thames
London
Windsor
Reading
Maidstone
Canterbury
Dover
Folkestone
Guildford
Winchester
Crawley
Hastings
Salisbury
Southampton
Brighton
Eastbourne
Bournemouth
Portsmouth
Weymouth
Isle of Wight
Esbjerg
's-Gravenhage (Den Haag)
Rotterdam
Vlissingen
Zeebrugge
Antwerpen
Oostende
Brugge
Mechelen
Gent
Schelde
Bruxelles (Brüssel)
Dover Str.
Dunkerque
Calais
St Omer
Kortrijk
Tourcoing
Roubaix
Tournai
Lille
Mons
Bethune
Valenciennes
Douai
Denain
Arras
Cambrai
Boulogne
Montreuil
Abbeville
Le Tréport
Dieppe
Amiens
St-Quentin
Neufchâtel
Montdidier
Oise
Laon
Fécamp
Le Havre
Bolbec
Seine
Beauvais
Compiègne
Soissons
Rouen
Senlis
Château-Thierry
Deauville
Elbeuf
Louviers
Cergy-Pontoise
Meaux
Mantes
Evreux
Eure
Paris
Versailles
Sézanne
Provins
Dreux
Rambouillet
Étampes
Melun
Romilly-s.-S.
Chartres
Fontainbleau
Sens
C.de la Hague
Pte de Barfleur
Alderney
Cherbourg
Guernsey
Sark
Valognes
Bayeux
Caen
Lisieux
Jersey
St Helier
St-Lô
Coutances
Orne
Argentan
Granville
Domfront
Alençon
Roscoff
Morlaix
St-Malo
Mont-St-Michel
Dinan
Fougères
Mayenne
I.d'Ouessant
Brest
St-Brieuc
Carhaix-Plouguer
50
5

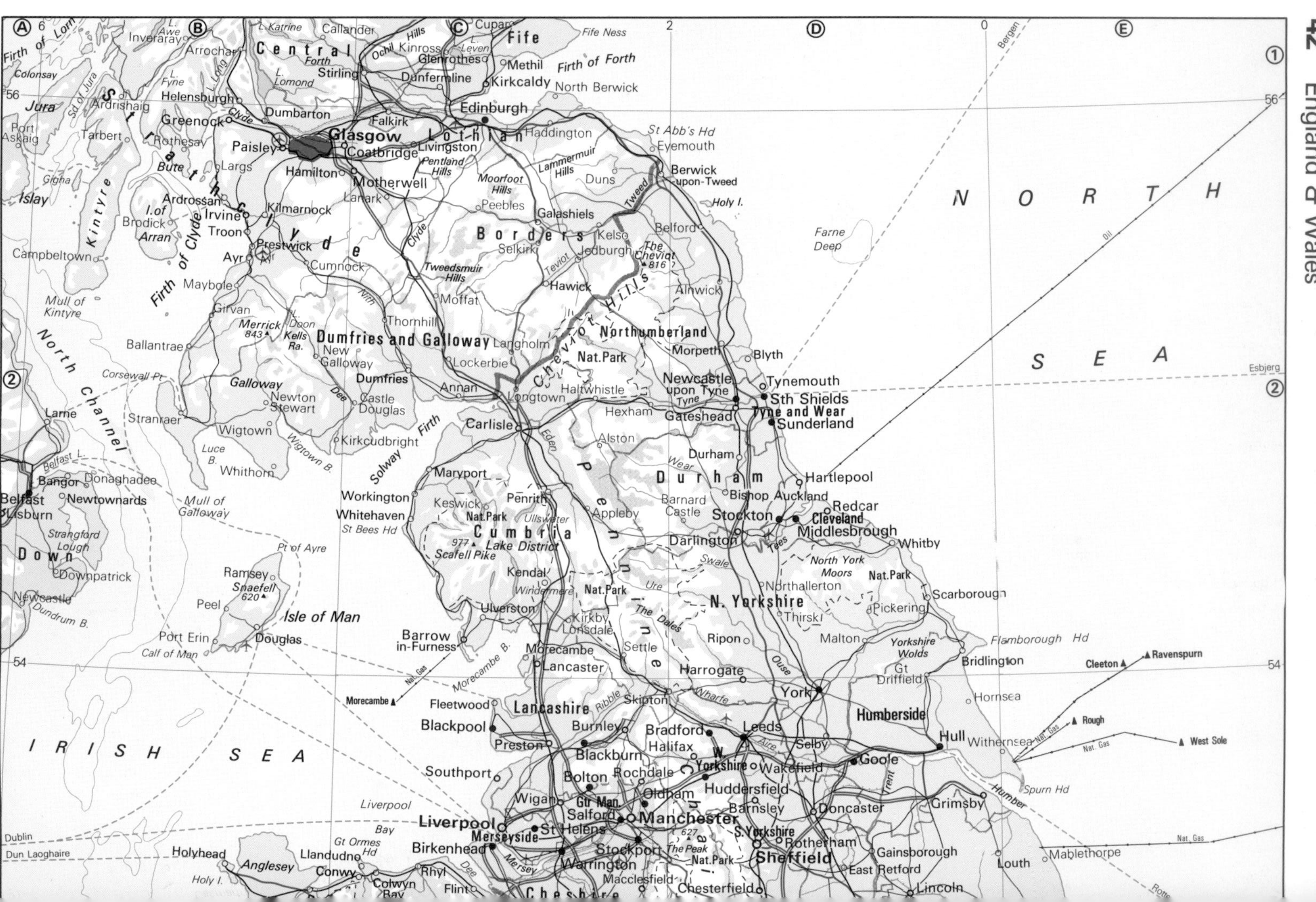
NORTH SEA
IRISH SEA
North Channel
Firth of Forth
Firth of Clyde
Solway Firth
Isle of Man
Edinburgh
Glasgow
Newcastle upon Tyne
Sunderland
Middlesbrough
Hartlepool
Durham
Carlisle
York
Leeds
Bradford
Hull
Manchester
Liverpool
Sheffield
Blackpool
Preston
Lancaster
Scarborough
Whitby
Grimsby
Lincoln
Doncaster
Belfast
Dumfries and Galloway
Borders
Lothian
Central
Strathclyde
Fife
Northumberland
Durham
Cumbria
N. Yorkshire
Humberside
Lancashire
Merseyside
Gtr Man.
Tyne and Wear
Cleveland
S. Yorkshire
W. Yorkshire
Pennine
Lake District
Cheviot Hills
Kintyre
Arran
Jura
Islay
Anglesey
Farne Deep
Flamborough Hd
Spurn Hd
Morecambe B.
Liverpool Bay
Berwick upon-Tweed
Stranraer
Ayr
Kilmarnock
Paisley
Greenock
Stirling
Falkirk
Dunfermline
Kirkcaldy
Douglas
Ramsey
Barrow in-Furness
Whitehaven
Workington
Kendal
Penrith
Darlington
Stockton
Harrogate
Ripon
Wakefield
Huddersfield
Halifax
Oldham
Rochdale
Bolton
Wigan
St Helens
Warrington
Stockport
Birkenhead
Southport
Holyhead
Llandudno
Rhyl
Larne
Bangor
Newtownards
Downpatrick
Ravenspurn
West Sole
Rough
Cleeton
Morecambe

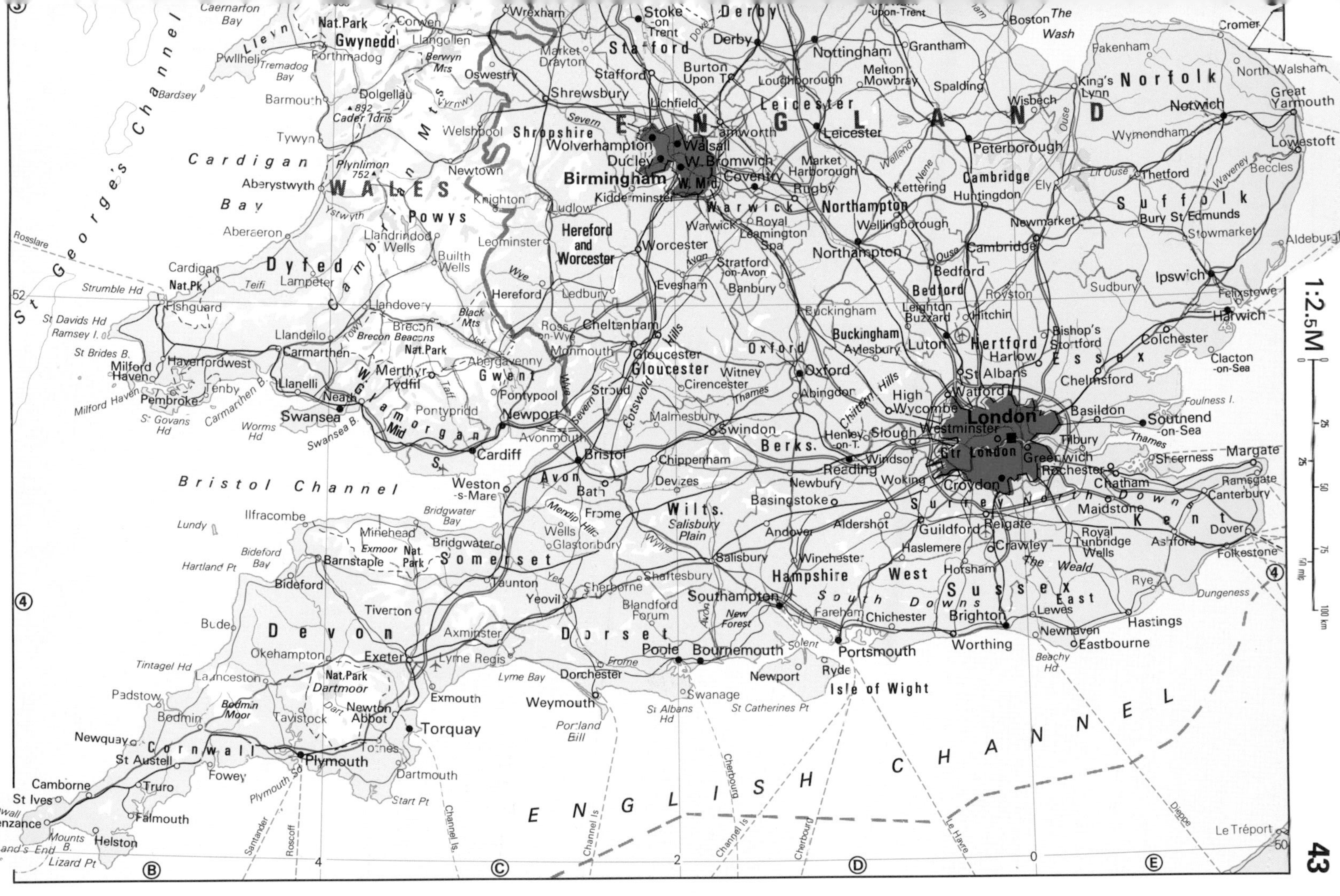
E N G L A N D
W A L E S
E N G L I S H C H A N N E L
Bristol Channel
St George's Channel
Cardigan Bay
London
Gtr London
Westminster
Croydon
Greenwich
Birmingham
W. Mid.
Wolverhampton
Walsall
W. Bromwich
Dudley
Coventry
Norfolk
Norwich
Great Yarmouth
Lowestoft
Cromer
North Walsham
King's Lynn
Fakenham
Wymondham
Thetford
Suffolk
Bury St Edmunds
Stowmarket
Ipswich
Felixstowe
Harwich
Aldeburgh
Beccles
Colchester
Clacton-on-Sea
Essex
Chelmsford
Southend-on-Sea
Basildon
Sudbury
Cambridge
Peterborough
Huntingdon
Newmarket
Ely
Wisbech
Boston
The Wash
Spalding
Grantham
Nottingham
Derby
Leicester
Loughborough
Melton Mowbray
Market Harborough
Rugby
Northampton
Kettering
Wellingborough
Bedford
Luton
Hertford
St Albans
Watford
Harlow
Hitchin
Royston
Bishop's Stortford
Buckingham
Aylesbury
High Wycombe
Oxford
Abingdon
Banbury
Witney
Swindon
Reading
Newbury
Berks.
Slough
Windsor
Woking
Guildford
Surrey
Reigate
Crawley
Horsham
Brighton
Worthing
Lewes
Newhaven
Eastbourne
Hastings
Rye
East Sussex
West Sussex
Kent
Maidstone
Rochester
Chatham
Sheerness
Margate
Ramsgate
Canterbury
Dover
Folkestone
Ashford
Royal Tunbridge Wells
Tilbury
Dungeness
Beachy Hd
Hampshire
Basingstoke
Andover
Winchester
Aldershot
Southampton
Portsmouth
Fareham
Chichester
Isle of Wight
Newport
Ryde
Bournemouth
Poole
Swanage
Dorset
Dorchester
Weymouth
Portland Bill
Salisbury
Wilts.
Salisbury Plain
Chippenham
Devizes
Bath
Bristol
Avon
Gloucester
Cheltenham
Cirencester
Stroud
Cotswold Hills
Worcester
Hereford and Worcester
Hereford
Evesham
Stratford-on-Avon
Warwick
Royal Leamington Spa
Kidderminster
Ludlow
Shrewsbury
Shropshire
Stafford
Stoke-on-Trent
Lichfield
Tamworth
Burton upon Trent
Somerset
Taunton
Yeovil
Bridgwater
Weston-s-Mare
Minehead
Exmoor Nat Park
Devon
Exeter
Torquay
Plymouth
Dartmoor
Barnstaple
Bideford
Ilfracombe
Cornwall
Truro
Falmouth
Penzance
St Ives
Newquay
Bodmin
Land's End
Lizard Pt
Cardiff
Newport
Swansea
Gwent
Mid Glamorgan
W. Glamorgan
Powys
Dyfed
Gwynedd
Aberystwyth
Carmarthen
Pembroke
Haverfordwest
Milford Haven
Fishguard
Cardigan
Brecon Beacons
Wrexham
Oswestry
Welshpool
Newtown
Dolgellau
Llandrindod Wells
Builth Wells
Cherbourg
Le Havre
Dieppe
Channel Is.
Roscoff
Santander
Rosslare

1:2.5M
0 25 50 75 100 km
0 25 50 mls

Shetland
Unst
Yell
Fetlar
Whalsay
Herma Ness
Isbister
Hillswick
The Faither
St Magnus Bay
Papa Stour
Brae
Bressay
Noss
Lerwick
Hanstolm-Bergen
Scalloway
Grutness
Fitful Hd
Sumburgh Hd
Foula
Fair Isle
Stromness
Aberdeen
at the same scale

Orkney
N. Ronaldsay
Papa Westray
Sanday
Stronsay
Westray
Eday
Shapinsay
Rousay
Kirkwall
Birsay
Mainland
Stromness
Scapa Flow
Burray
S. Ronaldsay
Hoy
Pentland Firth
Dunnet Hd
John o' Groats
Duncansby Hd
Lerwick

NORTH SEA
Long Forties
Buchan Deep
Beatrice

Burray
S. Ronaldsay
Duncansby Hd
Pentland Firth
Hoy
John o' Groats
Dunnet Hd
Thurso
Wick
Lybster
Helmsdale
Brora
Dornoch Firth
Tarbat Ness
Moray Firth
Tongue
Ben Kilbreck 961
L. Eriboll
Ben Hope 927
Durness
C. Wrath
Ben More Assynt 998
L. Shin
Lairg
Dornoch
Tain
Oykel
Lochinver
Eddrachillis Bay
Enard Bay
Ullapool
L. Broom
Ben Dearg 1081
Ben Wyvis 1045
Alness
Cromarty
Black Isle
Dingwall
Inverness
Nairn
Forres
Elgin
Lossiemouth
Keith
Banff
Deveron
Huntly
Fraserburgh
Kinnairds Hd
Peterhead
Buchan Ness
Ythan
Inverurie
Aberdeen
Girdle Ness
Stonehaven
Banchory
Dee
Ballater
Braemar
Lochnagar 1155
Don
Dufftown
Grantown-on-Spey
Spey
Grampian
Aviemore
Cairngorms
Ben Macdui 1310
Monadhliath Mts
Findhorn
Kingussie
Highland
Glen More
L. Ness
Beauly
Farrar
Fort Augustus
L. Lochy
Ben Nevis 1344
Fort William
Ben Attow 1031
Kyle of Lochalsh
L. Maree
L. Torridon
L. Ewe
Gairloch
Greenstone Pt
North Minch
Butt of Lewis
Broad B.
Stornoway
Lewis
Loch Roag
Western Isles
Harris
Tarbert
Taransay
Scarp
Sd. of Harris
Little Minch
Lochmaddy
Pabbay
North Uist
Monach Is
Benbecula
South Uist
Lochboisdale
Eriskay
Barra
Castlebay
Sd of Barra
Barra Hd
Flannan Is
Outer Hebrides
Rubha Hunish
Uig
L. Snizort
Portree
Raasay
Sd of Raasay
Isle of Skye
Cuillin Hills
Broadford
L. Bracadale
Canna
Rum
Eigg
Muck
Sd of Sleat
L. Hourn
Mallaig
L. Morar
Arisaig
L. Shiel
Ardnamurchan Pt
Coll
Tiree
Tobermory
Ulva
Staffa
Iona
Mull
Morvern
L. Sunart
Firth of Lorn
L. Linnhe
Oban
L. Etive
L. Awe
Ballachulish
Colonsay
Jura
Sd of Jura
Islay
Port Askaig
Tarbert
Ardrishaig
Inveraray
L. Fyne
Scotland
Grampian Mts
L. Ericht
L. Rannoch
Garry
Blair Atholl
Pitlochry
Tayside
Ben Lawers 1214
L. Tay
Killin
Aberfeldy
L. Earn
Crieff
Crianlarich
L. Katrine
L. Lomond
Callander
Central
Forth
Stirling
Arrochar
L. Long
Helensburgh
Dumbarton
Clyde
Greenock
Rothesay
Paisley
Glasgow
Coatbridge
Falkirk
Ochil Hills
Kinross
Dunfermline
Glenrothes
L. Leven
Perth
Sidlaw Hills
Blairgowrie
Forfar
Dundee
Tay
Cupar
Fife
St Andrews
Fife Ness
Methil
Kirkcaldy
Firth of Forth
North Berwick
Edinburgh
Livingston
Pentland Hills
Lothian
Haddington
Lammermuir Hills
St Abb's Hd
Eyemouth
Berwick
Brechin
Montrose
Arbroath
A. Esk
Oil

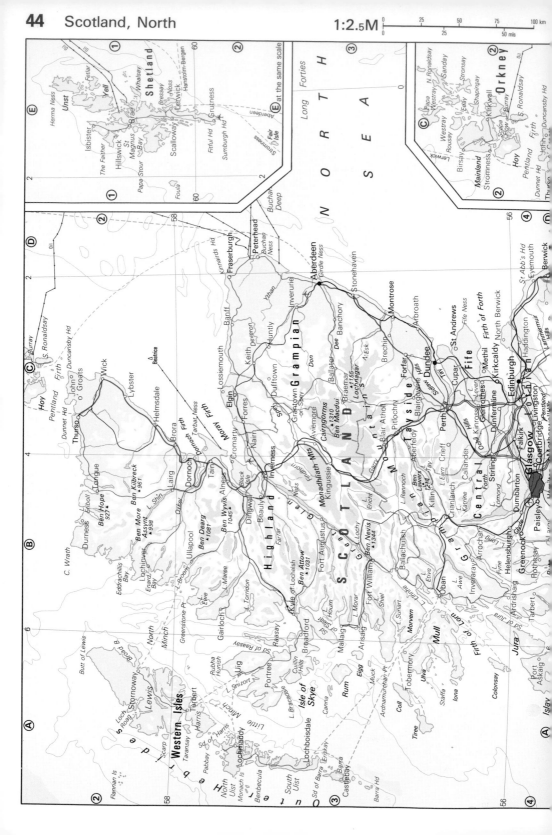

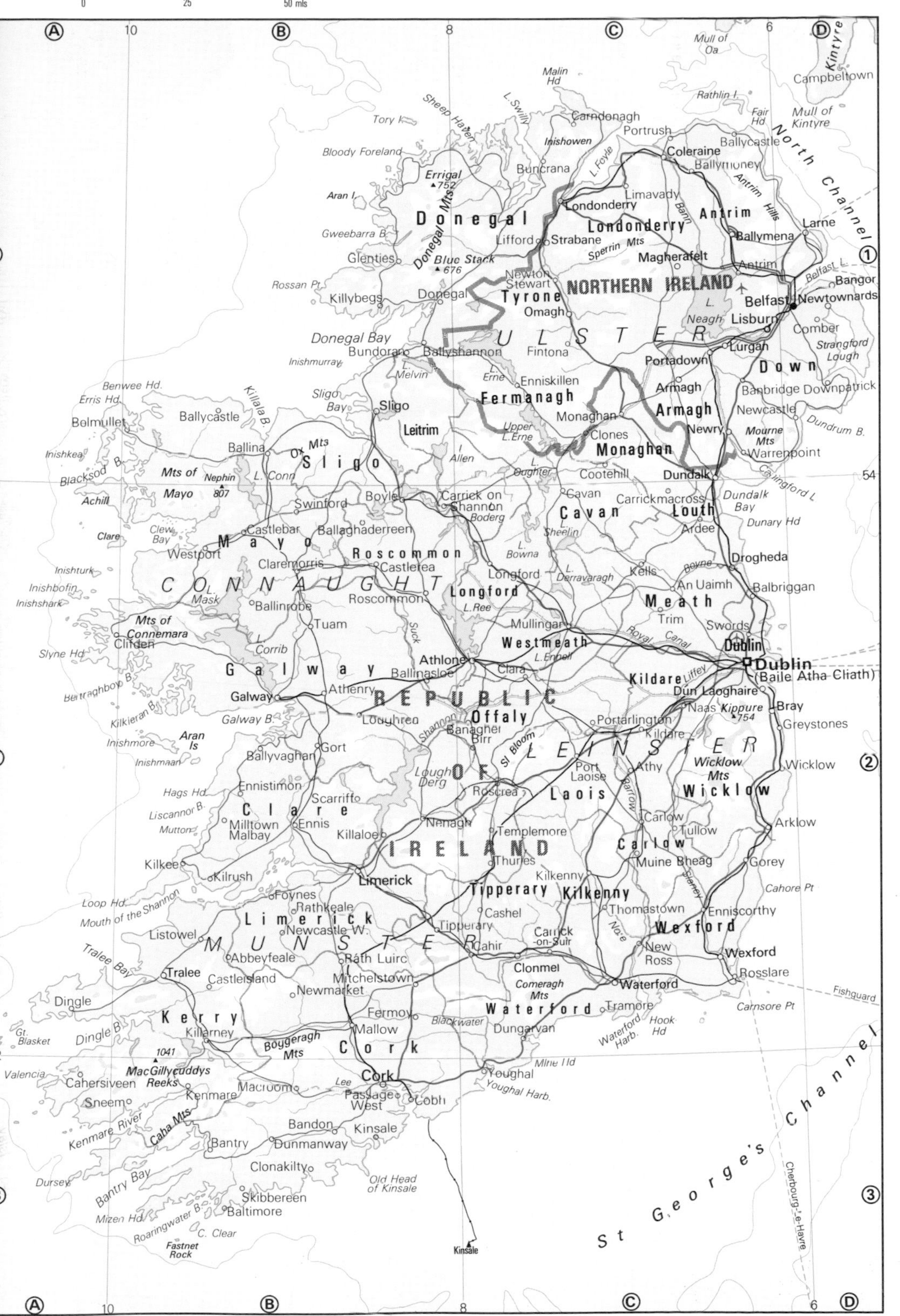

75   50   75   100 km
0   25   50 mls

A   10   B   8   C   6   D

Mull of
Oa
Campbeltown
Tory I.
Malin
Hd
Carndonagh
Portrush
Ballycastle
Rathlin I.
Fair
Hd
Mull of
Kintyre
Bloody Foreland
L. Swilly
Inishowen
Coleraine
Ballymoney
Antrim Hills
North Channel
Errigal
▲752
Buncrana
L. Foyle
Limavady
Bann
Antrim
Larne
Aran I.
Londonderry
Londonderry
Antrim
Ballymena
Belfast L.
Bangor
Gweebarra B.
Donegal
Lifford
Strabane
Sperrin Mts
Magherafelt
Antrim
Belfast
Newtownards
Glenties
Blue Stack
▲676
Newton
Stewart
NORTHERN IRELAND
L.
Neagh
Lisburn
Comber
Strangford
Lough
Rossan Pt.
Killybegs
Donegal
Tyrone
Omagh
ULSTER
Portadown
Lurgan
Down
Donegal Bay
Bundoran
Ballyshannon
Fintona
Enniskillen
Armagh
Banbridge
Downpatrick
Inishmurray
Melvin
Erne
Fermanagh
Monaghan
Armagh
Newcastle
Dundrum B.
Sligo
Bay
Sligo
Upper
L. Erne
Clones
Newry
Mourne
Mts
Warrenpoint
Benwee Hd.
Ballycastle
Leitrim
Allen
Monaghan
Cootehill
Dundalk
Carlingford L.
54
Erris Hd.
Belmullet
Ballina
Ox   Mts
L.
Oughter
Cavan
Carrickmacross
Dundalk
Bay
Dunary Hd.
Blacksod B.
Inishkea
Achill
Mts of
Mayo
Nephin
▲807
L. Conn
Swinford
Boyle
Carrick on
Shannon
Boderg
Cavan
L.
Sheelin
Kells
Ardee
Louth
Clare
Clew
Bay
Castlebar
Ballaghaderreen
L.
Bowna
Drogheda
Inishturk
Westport
Mayo
Claremorris
Castlerea
Roscommon
Longford
L.
Derravaragh
An Uaimh
Balbriggan
Inishbofin
Inishshark
CONNAUGHT
Mask
Ballinrobe
Roscommon
Mullingar
Meath
Trim
Swords
Mts of
Connemara
Tuam
Suck
L. Ree
Royal   Canal
Slyne Hd.
Clifden
Corrib
Athlone
Westmeath
L. Ennell
Dublin
Dublin
Galway
Ballinasloe
Clara
REPUBLIC
Kildare
Liffey
Dun Laoghaire
(Baile Atha Cliath)
Beltraghboy B.
Galway
Athenry
Offaly
Kildare
Naas
Kippure
▲754
Bray
Galway B.
Loughrea
Banagher
Birr
St. Bloom
Portarlington
Athy
Wicklow
Mts
Greystones
Aran
Is
Inishmore
Inishmaan
Gort
Lough
Derg
Roscrea
Port
Laoise
Wicklow
Wicklow
Hags Hd.
Ennistimon
Scarriffo
Nenagh
Carlow
Tullow
Arklow
Liscannor B.
Clare
Ennis
Killaloe
Templemore
Carlow
Mutton I.
Milltown
Malbay
Thurles
Kilkenny
Gorey
Kilkee
Kilrush
Limerick
Tipperary
Kilkenny
Thomastown
Enniscorthy
Cahore Pt.
Loop Hd.
Foynes
Rathkeale
Cashel
Wexford
Mouth of the Shannon
Listowel
Limerick
Newcastle W.
Tipperary
Carrick
-on-Suir
New
Ross
Wexford
Tralee Bay
Abbeyfeale
Rath Luirc
MUNSTER
Cahir
Clonmel
Comeragh
Mts
Waterford
Tramore
Rosslare
Fishguard
Dingle
Tralee
Castleisland
Newmarket
Mitchelstown
Waterford
Carnsore Pt.
Gt.
Blasket
Dingle B.
1041
Kerry
Killarney
Boggeragh
Mts
Fermoy
Mallow
Blackwater
Dungarvan
Waterford
Harb.
Hook
Hd.
Valencia
MacGillycuddys
Reeks
Macroom
Lee
Cork
Mine Hd
Cahersiveen
Kenmare
Cork
Youghal
Cherbourg-le-Havre
Sneem
Kenmare River
Caha Mts
Passage
West
Cobh
Youghal Harb.
Bandon
Kinsale
Dursey
Bantry
Dunmanway
Clonakilty
Old Head
of Kinsale
St   George's   Channel
Bantry Bay
Skibbereen
Baltimore
Mizen Hd.
Roaringwater B.
C. Clear
Fastnet
Rock
Kinsale

1:2.5M

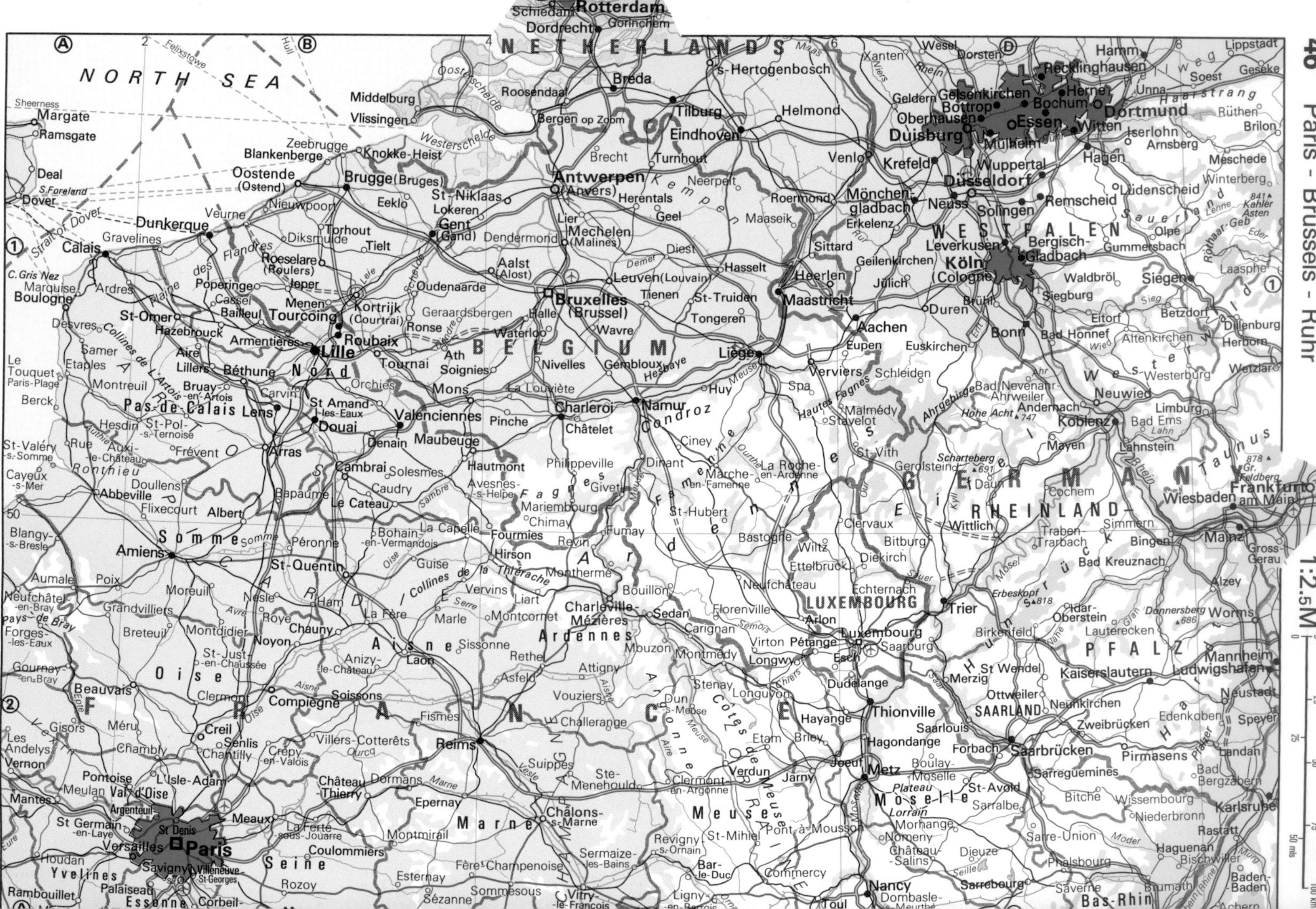

0 25 50 75 100 km
0 25 50 mls
NORTH SEA
NETHERLANDS
BELGIUM
GERMANY
FRANCE
LUXEMBOURG
SAARLAND
PFALZ
WESTFALEN
RHEINLAND
Ardennes
Aisne
Oise
Somme
Marne
Seine
Meuse
Moselle
Pas-de-Calais
Nord
Paris
Bruxelles (Brussel)
Antwerpen (Anvers)
Rotterdam
Köln (Cologne)
Düsseldorf
Duisburg
Essen
Dortmund
Frankfurt am Main
Wiesbaden
Mainz
Mannheim
Ludwigshafen
Karlsruhe
Saarbrücken
Trier
Koblenz
Bonn
Aachen
Liège
Namur
Charleroi
Lille
Gent (Gand)
Brugge (Bruges)
Oostende (Ostend)
Calais
Dunkerque
Boulogne
Amiens
Reims
Metz
Nancy
Luxembourg
Maastricht
Eindhoven
Dover
Margate

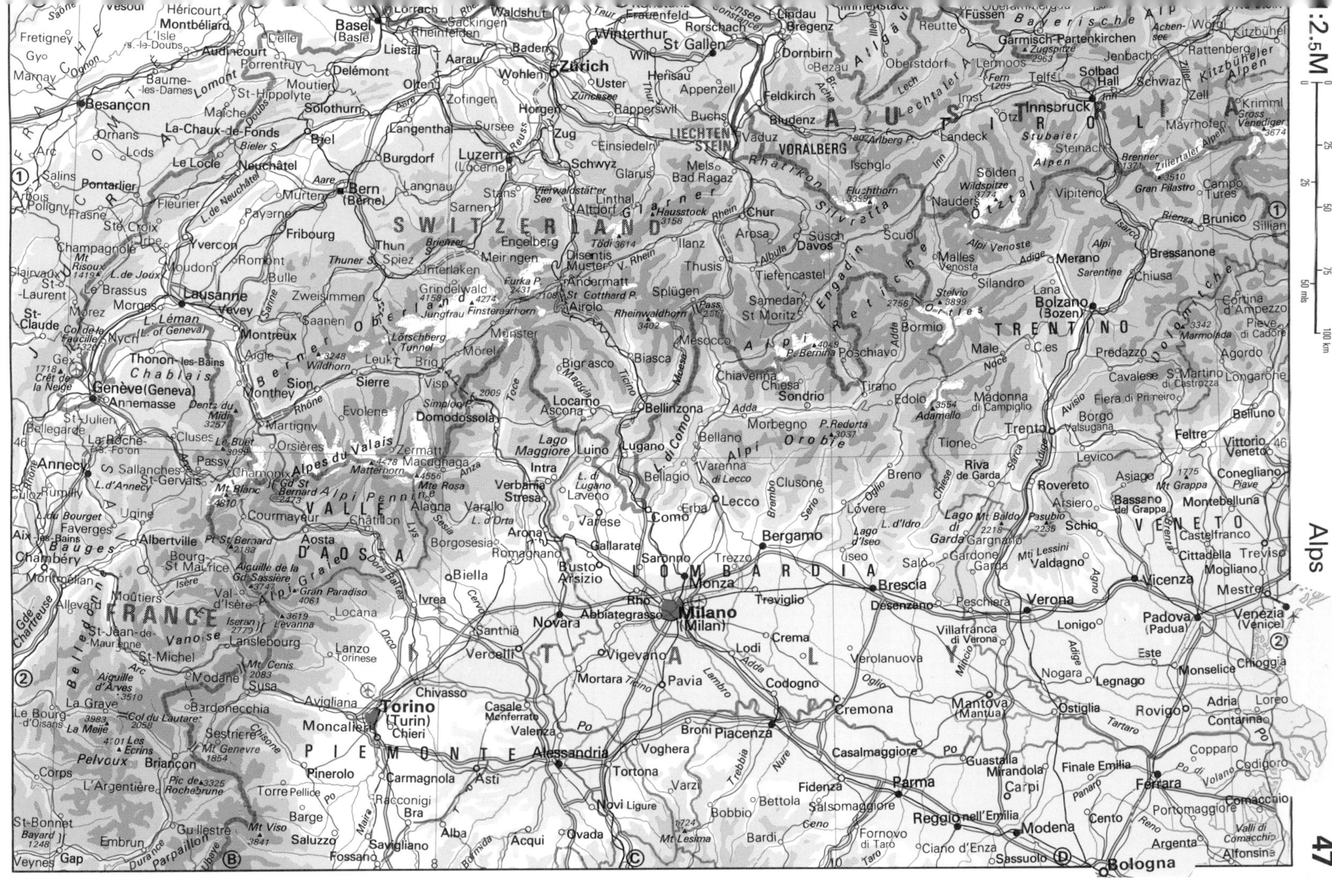
SWITZERLAND
AUSTRIA
TIROL
FRANCE
ITALY
LOMBARDIA
PIEMONTE
VENETO
TRENTINO
VALLE D'AOSTA
LIECHTENSTEIN
VORALBERG
Milano (Milan)
Torino (Turin)
Venezia (Venice)
Padova (Padua)
Bologna
Genève (Geneva)
Zürich
Bern (Berne)
Basel (Basle)
Luzern (Lucerne)
Lausanne
Innsbruck
Bolzano (Bozen)
Verona
Brescia
Bergamo
Besançon
Alessandria
Parma
Modena
Ferrara

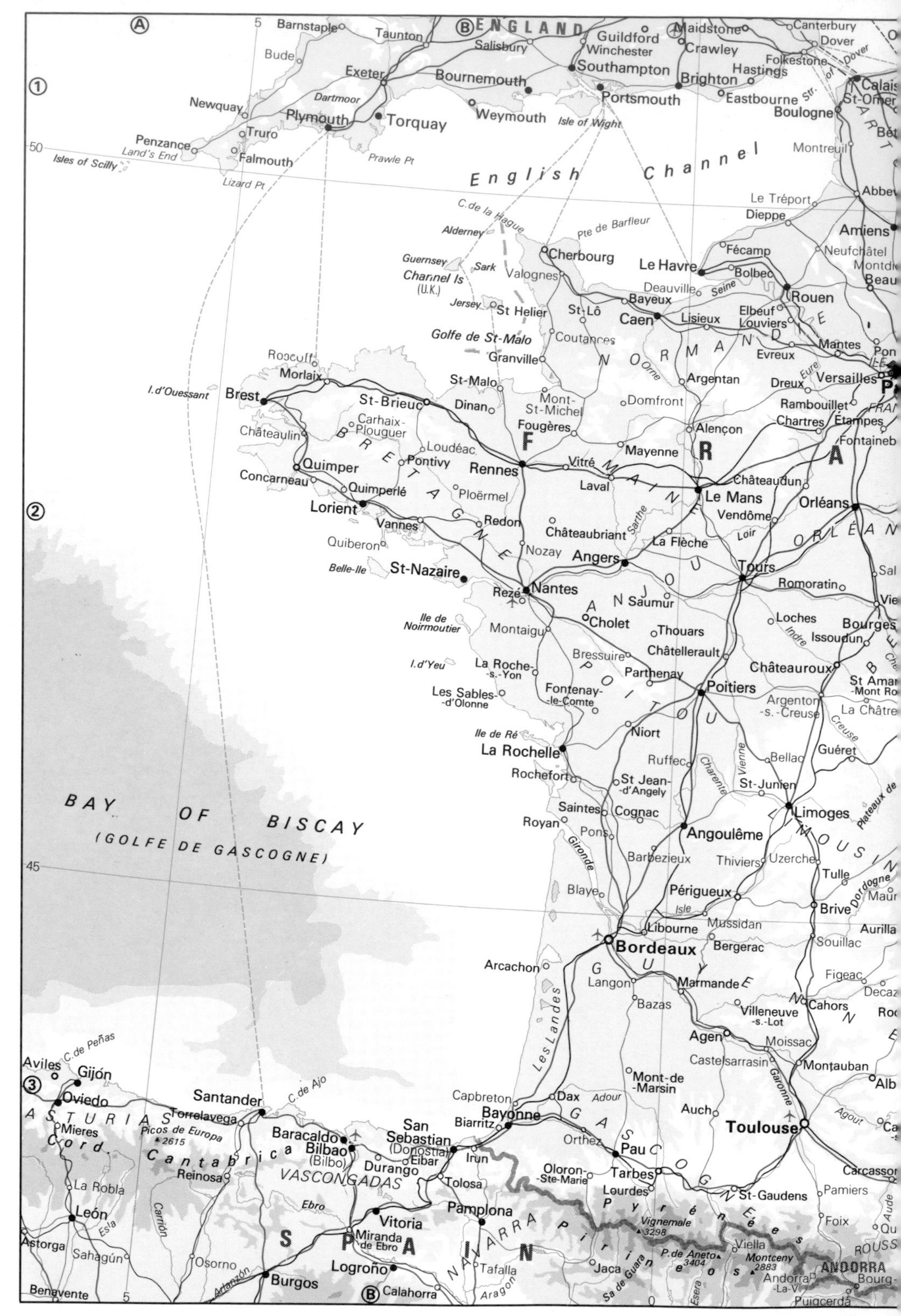

ENGLAND
Barnstaple
Taunton
Guildford
Maidstone
Canterbury
Dover
Bude
Salisbury
Winchester
Crawley
Folkestone
Exeter
Bournemouth
Southampton
Brighton
Hastings
Newquay
Dartmoor
Portsmouth
Eastbourne
Boulogne
Plymouth
Torquay
Weymouth
Isle of Wight
Calais
St-Omer
Truro
Penzance
Land's End
Falmouth
Isles of Scilly
Prawle Pt
Lizard Pt
Montreuil
English Channel
Le Tréport
Dieppe
Abbeville
Amiens
C. de la Hague
Alderney
Pte de Barfleur
Fécamp
Neufchâtel
Guernsey
Sark
Cherbourg
Le Havre
Bolbec
Channel Is (U.K.)
Valognes
Deauville
Seine
Rouen
Jersey
St Helier
St-Lô
Bayeux
Caen
Lisieux
Elbeuf
Louviers
Golfe de St-Malo
Coutances
NORMANDIE
Mantes
Evreux
Roscoff
Granville
Orne
Morlaix
St-Malo
Argentan
Dreux
Eure
Versailles
I.d'Ouessant
Brest
St-Brieuc
Dinan
Mont-St-Michel
Domfront
Rambouillet
Carhaix-Plouguer
Fougères
Alençon
Chartres
Étampes
Châteaulin
BRETAGNE
Loudéac
Fontainebleau
Pontivy
Mayenne
FRANCE
Quimper
Rennes
Vitré
MAINE
Concarneau
Laval
Châteaudun
Quimperlé
Ploërmel
Le Mans
Lorient
Orléans
Vannes
Redon
Châteaubriant
Vendôme
Sarthe
Loir
ORLÉANAIS
Quiberon
La Flèche
Nozay
Angers
Tours
Belle-Ile
St-Nazaire
ANJOU
Romorantin
Nantes
Rezé
Saumur
Ile de Noirmoutier
Cholet
Loches
Bourges
Montaigu
Thouars
Issoudun
Indre
Bressuire
Châtellerault
I.d'Yeu
La Roche-s.-Yon
POITOU
Parthenay
Châteauroux
St Amand-Mont Rond
Les Sables-d'Olonne
Fontenay-le-Comte
Poitiers
Argenton-s.-Creuse
La Châtre
Creuse
Ile de Ré
Niort
La Rochelle
Ruffec
Vienne
Charente
Bellac
Guéret
Rochefort
St Jean-d'Angely
St-Junien
Saintes
Cognac
Limoges
Royan
Pons
LIMOUSIN
Plateaux de
Angoulême
BAY OF BISCAY
(GOLFE DE GASCOGNE)
Gironde
Barbezieux
Thiviers
Uzerche
Tulle
Blaye
Périgueux
Dordogne
Isle
Brive
Libourne
Mussidan
Bordeaux
Bergerac
Souillac
Arcachon
GUYENNE
Figeac
Langon
Marmande
Bazas
Les Landes
Villeneuve-s.-Lot
Cahors
Agen
Moissac
Castelsarrasin
Montauban
Garonne
Mont-de-Marsan
C. de Peñas
Aviles
Gijón
Oviedo
Santander
C. de Ajo
Capbreton
Dax
Adour
ASTURIAS
Torrelavega
Bayonne
Auch
Toulouse
Agout
Mieres
Picos de Europa
2615
Baracaldo
Bilbao (Bilbo)
San Sebastian (Donostia)
Biarritz
GASCOGNE
Cord. Cantabrica
Eibar
Irun
Orthez
Pau
Reinosa
Durango
Oloron-Ste-Marie
Tarbes
Carcassonne
VASCONGADAS
Tolosa
Lourdes
Pamiers
La Robla
Ebro
Pamplona
Vignemale
3298
Pyrénées
St-Gaudens
Foix
León
Vitoria
Carrión
Esla
NAVARRA
Vielle
Astorga
Sahagún
Miranda de Ebro
SPAIN
P. de Aneto
3404
Montceny
2883
ROUSSILLON
Osorno
Logroño
Tafalla
Jaca
Sa de Guara
Esera
ANDORRA
Andorra-la-V
Bourg
Arlanzón
Burgos
Aragon
Benavente
Calahorra
Puigcerdá
50
45
5
0

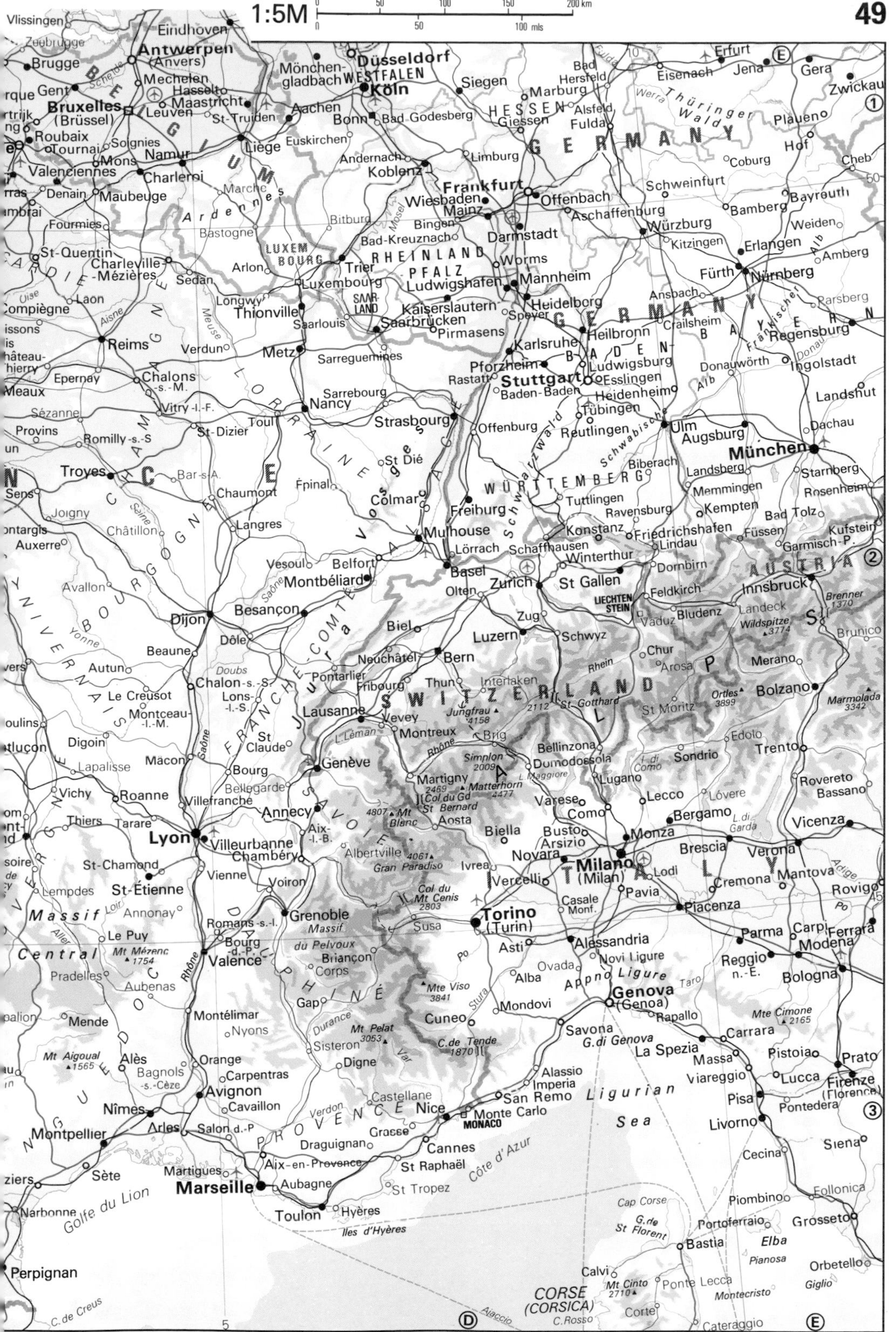
1:5M
0 50 100 150 200 km
0 50 100 mls
Vlissingen
Eindhoven
Zeebrugge
Antwerpen
(Anvers)
Brugge
Mechelen
Gent
Hasselt
Maastricht
Bruxelles
(Brüssel)
Leuven
St-Truiden
Aachen
Roubaix
Tournai
Soignies
Liège
Mons
Namur
Valenciennes
Charleroi
Denain
Maubeuge
Fourmies
St-Quentin
Charleville-
-Mézières
Sedan
Laon
Compiègne
Reims
Epernay
Chalons
-s.-M.
Meaux
Sézanne
Vitry-l.-F.
Provins
Romilly-s.-S
St-Dizier
Troyes
Bar-s-A.
Sens
Joigny
Chaumont
Châtillon
Langres
Auxerre
Avallon
Dijon
Beaune
Dôle
Autun
Le Creusot
Montceau-
-l.-M.
Digoin
Mâcon
Lapalisse
Vichy
Roanne
Thiers
Tarare
Villefranche
Lyon
Villeurbanne
St-Chamond
St-Etienne
Lempdes
Annonay
Le Puy
Mt Mézenc
1754
Pradelles
Aubenas
Mende
Mt Aigoual
1565
Alès
Bagnols
-s.-Cèze
Nîmes
Montpellier
Sète
Narbonne
Golfe du Lion
Perpignan
C. de Creus
Massif
Central
Arles
Salon d.-P
Avignon
Cavaillon
Orange
Carpentras
Nyons
Montélimar
Valence
Romans-s.-l.
Bourg
-d.-P.
Grenoble
Voiron
Vienne
Chambéry
Aix-
-l.-B.
Annecy
Bellegarde
Bourg
St
Claude
Genève
Lausanne
Vevey
Montreux
L. Léman
Fribourg
Pontarlier
Neuchâtel
Biel
Bern
Thun
Interlaken
Jungfrau
4158
Brig
Simplon
2009
Martigny
2469
Col du Gd
St Bernard
Matterhorn
4477
4807 Mt
Blanc
Aosta
Albertville
4061
Gran Paradiso
Col du
Mt Cenis
2803
Susa
Massif
du Pelvoux
Briançon
Corps
Gap
Mte Viso
3841
Sisteron
Mt Pelat
3053
Digne
C.de Tende
1870
Cuneo
Mondovi
Alba
Asti
Torino
(Turin)
Ivrea
Biella
Vercelli
Novara
Busto
Arsizio
Varese
Como
Lugano
Bellinzona
Domodossola
L. Maggiore
Lecco
Bergamo
Monza
Milano
(Milan)
Lodi
Pavia
Casale
Monf.
Alessandria
Novi Ligure
Ovada
Genova
(Genoa)
Savona
G. di Genova
Rapallo
La Spezia
Alassio
Imperia
San Remo
Monte Carlo
MONACO
Nice
Cannes
Grasse
Castellane
Draguignan
St Raphaël
St Tropez
Côte d'Azur
Aix-en-Provence
Marseille
Martigues
Aubagne
Toulon
Hyères
Iles d'Hyères
Ligurian
Sea
Cap Corse
G. de
St Florent
Bastia
Calvi
Mt Cinto
2710
Ponte Lecca
Corte
CORSE
(CORSICA)
C.Rosso
Ajaccio
Cateraggio
Portoferraio
Elba
Pianosa
Montecristo
Giglio
Orbetello
Grosseto
Piombino
Follonica
Cecina
Siena
Livorno
Pisa
Pontedera
Lucca
Viareggio
Massa
Carrara
Pistoia
Prato
Firenze
(Florence)
Mte Cimone
2165
Bologna
Modena
Reggio
n.-E.
Parma
Carpi
Ferrara
Piacenza
Cremona
Mantova
Rovigo
Brescia
Verona
Vicenza
Lóvere
L. di
Garda
Rovereto
Bassano
Trento
Sondrio
Edolo
L. di
Como
St Moritz
Ortles
3899
Bolzano
Marmolada
3342
Merano
Brunico
Brenner
1370
Wildspitze
3774
Landeck
Innsbruck
AUSTRIA
Feldkirch
Bludenz
Vaduz
LIECHTEN
STEIN
Chur
Arosa
Rhein
St Gotthard
2112
SWITZERLAND
Luzern
Schwyz
Zug
Zurich
Olten
St Gallen
Winterthur
Schaffhausen
Basel
Lörrach
Konstanz
Friedrichshafen
Lindau
Dornbirn
Ravensburg
Tuttlingen
Freiburg
Mulhouse
Belfort
Montbéliard
Vesoul
Besançon
Colmar
St Dié
Epinal
Strasbourg
Offenburg
Baden-Baden
Rastatt
Pforzheim
Stuttgart
Esslingen
Ludwigsburg
Heidenheim
Tübingen
Reutlingen
Ulm
Biberach
Memmingen
Kempten
Füssen
Garmisch-P.
Kufstein
Rosenheim
Bad Tolz
Starnberg
München
Dachau
Landsberg
Augsburg
Landshut
Ingolstadt
Donauwörth
Regensburg
Parsberg
Nürnberg
Fürth
Erlangen
Amberg
Weiden
Bamberg
Bayreuth
Ansbach
Crailsheim
Heilbronn
Heidelberg
Speyer
Karlsruhe
Mannheim
Ludwigshafen
Worms
Darmstadt
Kaiserslautern
Pirmasens
Saarbrücken
Saarlouis
SAAR-
LAND
Sarreguemines
Sarrebourg
Nancy
Toul
Metz
Thionville
Longwy
Verdun
Luxembourg
LUXEM
BOURG
Arlon
Bastogne
Trier
Bitburg
Bad-Kreuznach
Bingen
Mainz
Wiesbaden
Frankfurt
Offenbach
Aschaffenburg
Würzburg
Kitzingen
Schweinfurt
Coburg
Hof
Cheb
Plauen
Gera
Zwickau
Jena
Erfurt
Eisenach
Thüringer
Wald
Werra
Fulda
Alsfeld
Bad
Hersfeld
Marburg
Giessen
HESSEN
Limburg
Koblenz
Andernach
Siegen
Bonn
Bad Godesberg
Köln
WESTFALEN
Düsseldorf
Mönchen-
gladbach
Euskirchen
RHEINLAND
-PFALZ
BADEN-
WÜRTTEMBERG
BAYERN
GERMANY
BELGIUM
Ardennes
LORRAINE
ALSACE
Vosges
Schwarzwald
Schwäbische Alb
Fränkische Alb
Donau
FRANCHE-COMTÉ
Jura
BOURGOGNE
NIVERNAIS
CHAMPAGNE
PICARDIE
FRANCE
SAVOIE
DAUPHINÉ
PROVENCE
LANGUEDOC
AUVERGNE
ALPS
Appno Ligure
ITALY
Meuse
Marne
Aisne
Oise
Seine
Yonne
Saône
Doubs
Loire
Allier
Rhône
Durance
Verdon
Var
Stura
Po
Taro
Adige
Mosel
Schelde
Vitry
Marche
Stura
1
2
3
D
E
5
10
45
50

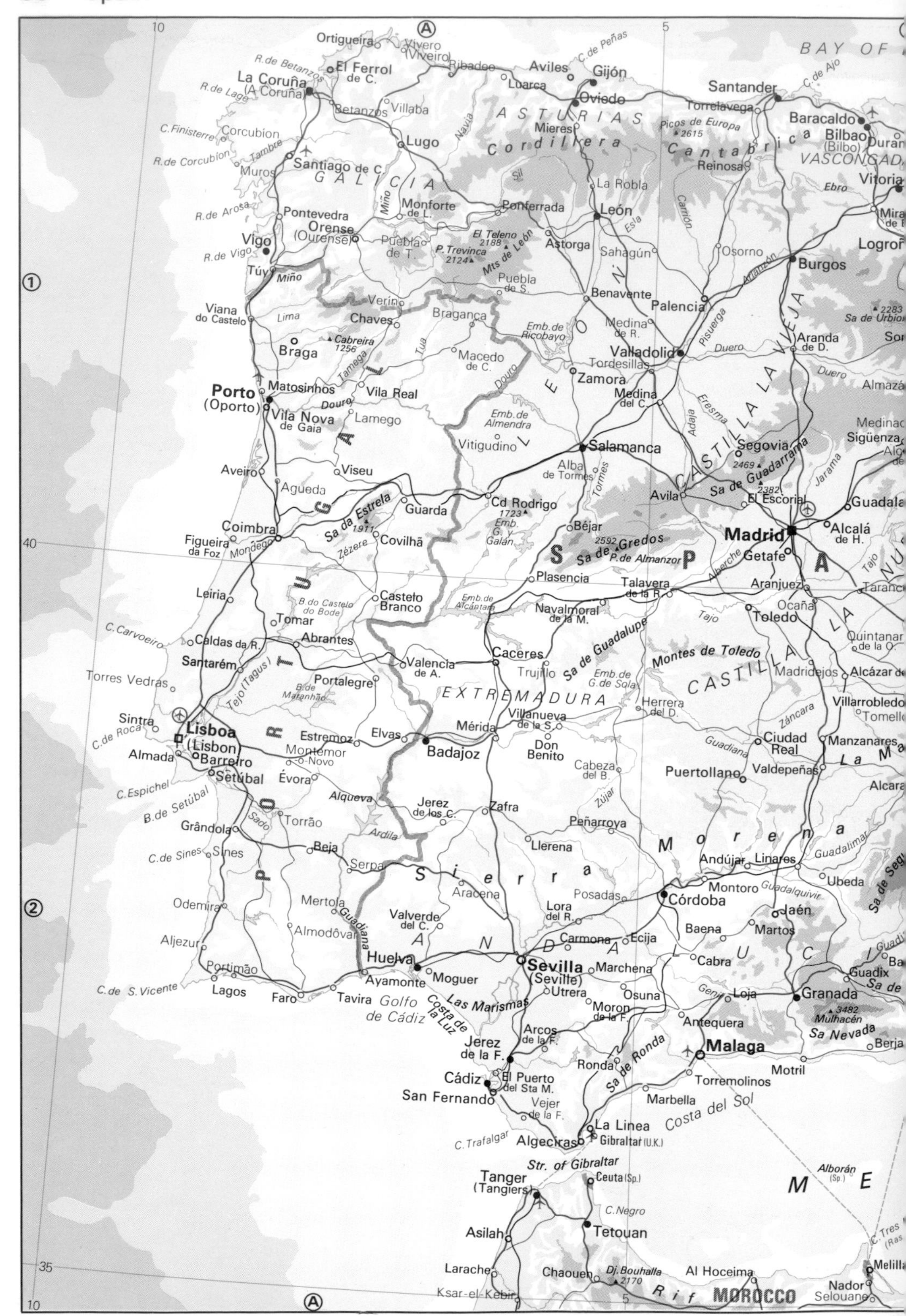

BAY OF
Ortigueira
Vivero (Viveiro)
Ribadeo
Aviles
C. de Peñas
Gijón
El Ferrol de C.
R. de Betanzos
La Coruña (A Coruña)
R. de Lage
Luarca
Oviedo
Santander
C. de Ajo
Torrelavega
Baracaldo
Bilbao (Bilbo)
Betanzos
Villaba
C. Finisterre
Corcubion
R. de Corcubion
Tambre
Santiago de C.
Muros
Lugo
Navia
ASTURIAS
Mieres
Cordillera Cantabrica
Picos de Europa
2615
Reinosa
VASCONGADAS
Vitoria
Ebro
GALICIA
Sil
La Robla
Miño
R. de Arosa
Pontevedra
Monforte de L.
Ponferrada
León
Carrión
Orense (Ourense)
Vigo
R. de Vigo
Puebla de T.
El Teleno 2188
P. Trevinca 2124
Mts de León
Astorga
Esla
Sahagún
Osorno
Logroño
Burgos
Túy
Miño
Puebla de S.
Benavente
Arlanzón
Viana do Castelo
Lima
Verín
Chaves
Bragança
Palencia
2283
Sa de Urbión
Soria
Braga
Cabreira 1256
Tamega
Tua
Emb. de Ricobayo
Medina de R.
Pisuerga
Valladolid
Aranda de D.
Duero
Macedo de C.
Tordesillas
Porto (Oporto)
Matosinhos
Vila Real
Douro
Zamora
Medina del C.
Almazán
Vila Nova de Gaia
Douro
Lamego
Emb. de Almendra
LEÓN
Eresma
Adaja
Medinaceli
Sigüenza
Vitigudino
Salamanca
Segovia
2469
Sa de Guadarrama
CASTILLA LA VIEJA
Aveiro
Viseu
Alba de Tormes
Tormes
Jarama
Agueda
Avila
2382
El Escorial
Guadalajara
Guarda
Cd Rodrigo
1723
Emb. G. y Galán
Sa da Estrela
1911
Coimbra
Béjar
Alcalá de H.
Madrid
Figueira da Foz
Mondego
Zêzere
Covilhã
2592
Sa de Gredos
P. de Almanzor
Getafe
SPAIN
Alberche
Tajo
Plasencia
Talavera de la R.
Aranjuez
Tarancón
Leiria
B. do Castelo do Bode
Castelo Branco
Emb. de Alcántara
Navalmoral de la M.
Ocaña
Tomar
Toledo
Tajo
C. Carvoeiro
Caldas da R.
Abrantes
Quintanar de la O.
Santarém
Caceres
Sa de Guadalupe
Montes de Toledo
Valencia de A.
Trujillo
Madridejos
Alcázar de
Torres Vedras
Tejo (Tagus)
Portalegre
Emb. de G. de Sola
CASTILLA LA NUEVA
B. de Maranhão
EXTREMADURA
Herrera del D.
Villarrobledo
Tomelloso
Sintra
Lisboa (Lisbon)
Villanueva de la S.
Záncara
C. de Roca
Estremoz
Elvas
Mérida
Guadiana
Ciudad Real
Manzanares
Almada
Barreiro
Montemor-o-Novo
Badajoz
Don Benito
La Mancha
Setúbal
Évora
Cabeza del B.
Puertollano
Valdepeñas
C. Espichel
Alqueva
Alcaraz
B. de Setúbal
Jerez de los C.
Zafra
Zújar
Sado
Torrão
Peñarroya
Grândola
Ardila
Llerena
Sierra Morena
Guadalimar
C. de Sines
Sines
Beja
Andújar
Linares
Serpa
Sierra
Ubeda
Aracena
Posadas
Montoro
Guadalquivir
Córdoba
Sa de Segura
Odemira
Mertola
Valverde del C.
Lora del R.
Jaén
Almodôvar
Guadiana
Baena
Martos
Aljezur
ANDALUCIA
Carmona
Ecija
Huelva
Sevilla (Seville)
Marchena
Cabra
Guadix
Portimão
Ayamonte
Moguer
Sa de Baza
C. de S. Vicente
Lagos
Faro
Tavira
Golfo de Cádiz
Costa de la Luz
Las Marismas
Utrera
Osuna
Genil
Loja
Granada
Moron de la F.
3482
Mulhacén
Sa Nevada
Arcos de la F.
Antequera
Jerez de la F.
Sa de Ronda
Malaga
Berja
Ronda
Cádiz
El Puerto del Sta M.
Torremolinos
Motril
San Fernando
Vejer de la F.
Marbella
Costa del Sol
La Linea
C. Trafalgar
Algeciras
Gibraltar (U.K.)
Str. of Gibraltar
Alborán (Sp.)
Tanger (Tangiers)
Ceuta (Sp.)
ME
C. Negro
Tetouan
Asilah
C. Tres Forcas (Ras
Larache
Chaouen
Dj. Bouhalla 2170
Al Hoceima
Melilla
Nador
Ksar-el-Kebir
Rif
MOROCCO
Selouane
10
5
40
35
①
②
Ⓐ

0 50 100 150 200 km
0 50 100 mls

FRANCE

Capbreton · Mont-de-Marsin · Dax · Auch · Albi · Castres-s.l'A · Nîmes · Salon-d.-P. · Aix-en-Provence · Aubagne

CAY · San · Biarritz · Bayonne · Orthez · Pau · St-Gaudens · Pamiers · Carcassonne · Béziers · Sète · Martigues · Marseille · Toulon · Hyères

Irun · Oloron-Ste-Marie · Lourdes · Tarbes · Foix · Quillan · Narbonne · Golfe du Lion

Tolosa · Pamplona · Pyrénées · Vignemale 3298 · Viella (Vielha) · Andorra · Bourg-Madame · Perpignan · C. de Creus

NAVARRA · Tafalla · Jaca · P. de Aneto 3404 · Monteny 2883 · Andorra-La-V. · ROUSSILLON · Costa Brava

Alfaro · Tudela · Huesca · Barbastro · Puigcerdá · Figueras (Figueres) · Gerona (Girona)

Tarazona · Alagón · Pirineos · Vich (Vic) · San Feliu de G.

Calatayud · Zaragoza · Emb. de Mequinenza · Lérida (Leida) · Sabadell · Granollers · Mataró · Badalona · Barcelona

ARAGÓN · CATALUÑA · Tarrasa · Villanueva-y-G. (Vilanova i la Geltrú)

Daroca · Caspe · Reus · Tarragona

Alcañiz · Golfo de San Jorge · C. de Tortosa

Monreal del C. · Sa de Gudar · Tortosa · Amposta

Teruel · Penarroya 2019 · Vinaroz · Benicarló · Torreblanca · C. de Caballeria · Menorca

Cuenca · Sarrion · Castellon de la P. · Is Columbretes · C. Formentor · Ciudadela · Mahón

Segorbe · Villarreal · Mallorca · Mayor 1445 · Capdepera · C. Binibeca

Emb. de Alarcon · Sagunto · Golfo de · Palma de Mallorca · Manacor

Motilla del P. · Utiel · Valencia · Santañy

La Roda · Alcira · Valencia · Ibiza · Cabrera · C. de Salinas

Albacete · Játiva · Gandia · S.Antonio Abad · Ibiza · ISLAS BALEARES (BALEARIC ISLANDS) (Sp.)

Almansa · Onteniente · Denia · C. de la Nao · Formentera

Villena · Alcoy · Benidorm

Hellin · Elda · Costa Blanca

MURCIA · Cieza · Alicante

Caravaca · Orihuela

Totana · Murcia · C. de Palos

Lorca · G. de Mazarrón · Cartagena

Aguilas · Vera

neria · C. de Gata

MEDITERRANEAN SEA

Alger (Algiers) · Harrach · Dellys · Bejaia (Bougie)

Cherchell · Boufarik · Tizi Ouzou · Kherrata

Tónès · Blida · Bouira · Djurdjura · Sétif

Bosquet · Miliana · Médéa · Bir Rabalou · Beni Mansour

Mostaganem · Khemis · Ech Cheliff · Ksar El Boukhari · Bj bou Arréridj · Mts du Hodna

Mers el Kebir · Arzew · Relizane · Massif de l'Ouarsenis · Aïn Oussera · Aïn el Hadjel · M'Sila

Oran · Sig · Mohammadia · Ouassel · Chott el Hodna

Beni-Saf · Aïn Témouchent · Mascara · Tiareto · Plat. du Sersou · Z.Chergui · Bou Saâda · Barika

Sidi-bel-Abbés · Frenda · Monts des Ouled Nail

ALGERIA

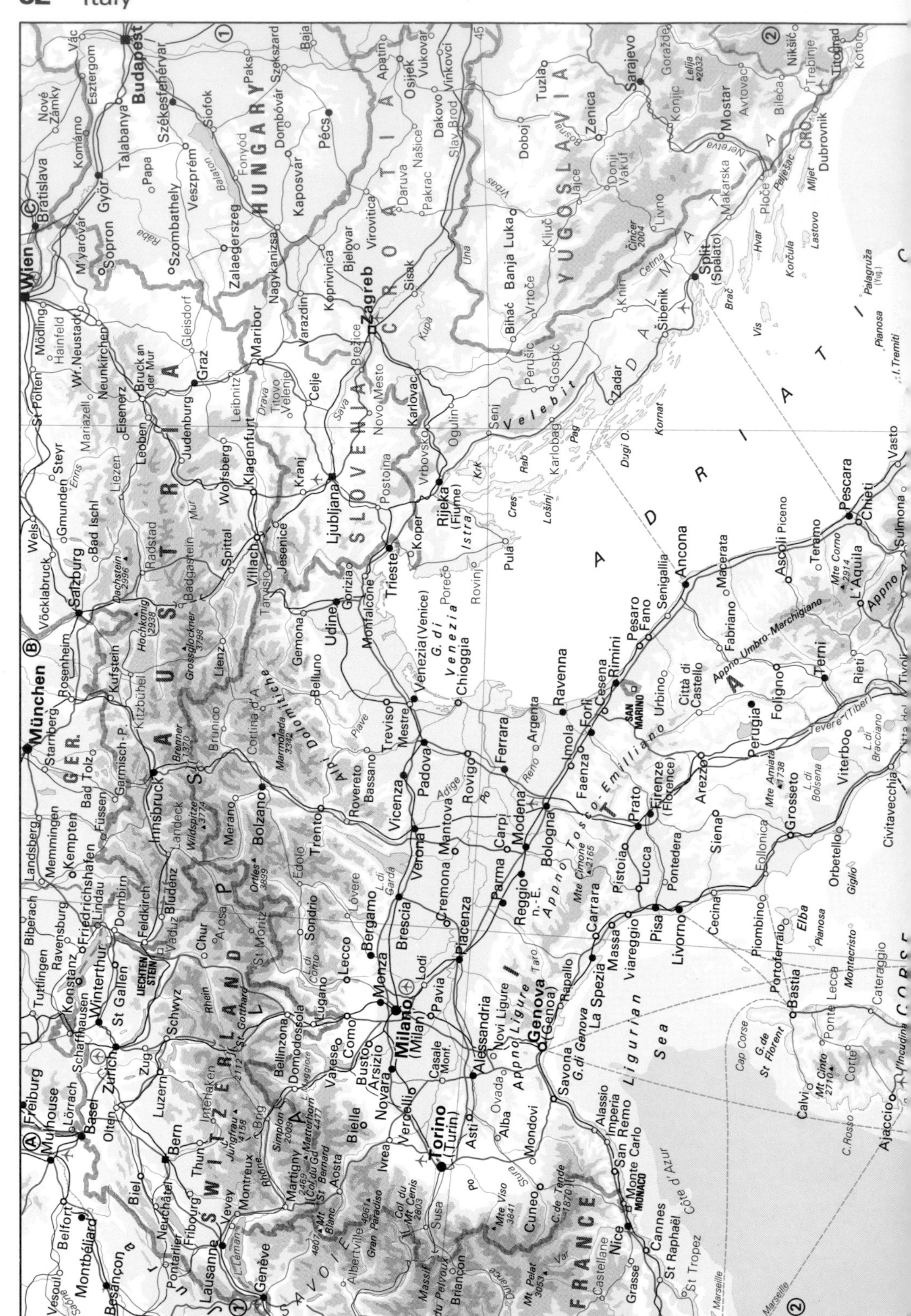

AUSTRIA
SWITZERLAND
FRANCE
GER.
HUNGARY
CROATIA
SLOVENIA
YUGOSLAVIA
LIECHTENSTEIN
SAN MARINO
MONACO
ADRIATIC
Ligurian Sea
G. di Venezia
G. di Genova
Alpi Dolomitiche
Appno Tosco-Emiliano
Appno Umbro-Marchigiano
Velebit
Istra
Elba
Corse
München
Wien
Budapest
Zagreb
Ljubljana
Sarajevo
Milano (Milan)
Torino (Turin)
Genova (Genoa)
Venezia (Venice)
Firenze (Florence)
Bologna
Verona
Trieste
Bolzano
Trento
Innsbruck
Salzburg
Graz
Zürich
Bern
Basel
Genève
Lausanne
Nice
Ancona
Pescara
Perugia
Pisa
Livorno
Rijeka (Fiume)
Split (Spalato)
Pécs
Győr
Bratislava
Ajaccio
Bastia

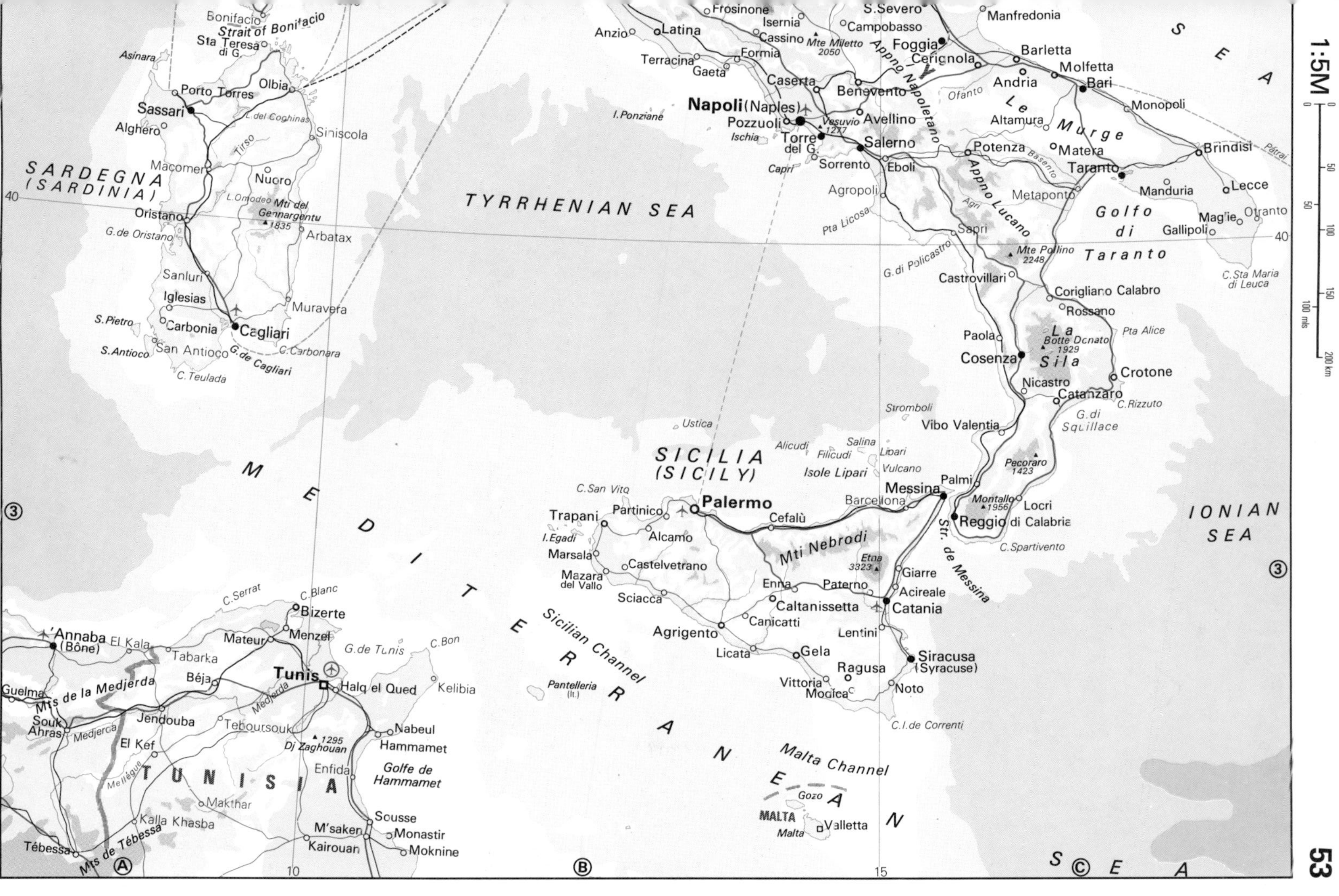
TYRRHENIAN SEA
IONIAN SEA
MEDITERRANEAN SEA
S E A
Golfo di Taranto
SICILIA (SICILY)
SARDEGNA (SARDINIA)
TUNISIA
MALTA
Sicilian Channel
Malta Channel
Str. de Messina
Strait of Bonifacio
Napoli (Naples)
Palermo
Messina
Catania
Siracusa (Syracuse)
Reggio di Calabria
Cosenza
Catanzaro
Crotone
Taranto
Brindisi
Lecce
Bari
Foggia
Salerno
Cagliari
Sassari
Tunis
Bizerte
Annaba (Bône)
Manfredonia
Barletta
Molfetta
Monopoli
Andria
Cerignola
Altamura
Matera
Potenza
Manduria
Gallipoli
Maglie
Otranto
C. Sta Maria di Leuca
Metaponto
Corigliano Calabro
Rossano
Pta Alice
C. Rizzuto
G. di Squillace
Nicastro
Locri
Pecoraro 1423
Montalto 1956
C. Spartivento
La Sila
Botte Donato 1929
Mte Pollino 2248
Appno Lucano
Appno Napoletano
Le Murge
Castrovillari
Paola
Vibo Valentia
Palmi
Sapri
G. di Policastro
Agropoli
Pta Licosa
Eboli
Sorrento
Capri
Torre del G.
Vesuvio 1277
Pozzuoli
Ischia
Avellino
Benevento
Caserta
Campobasso
S. Severo
Mte Miletto 2050
Isernia
Cassino
Frosinone
Formia
Gaeta
Terracina
Latina
Anzio
I. Ponziane
Ofanto
Basento
Agri
Pátrai
Stromboli
Lipari
Vulcano
Salina
Filicudi
Alicudi
Isole Lipari
Ustica
Barcellona
Cefalù
Mti Nebrodi
Etna 3323
Giarre
Acireale
Paterno
Lentini
Noto
C. I. de Correnti
Ragusa
Modica
Vittoria
Gela
Licata
Caltanissetta
Canicatti
Enna
Agrigento
Sciacca
Castelvetrano
Alcamo
Partinico
C. San Vito
Trapani
I. Egadi
Marsala
Mazara del Vallo
Pantelleria (It.)
Gozo
Valletta
Malta
Bonifacio
Sta Teresa di G.
Olbia
Porto Torres
Asinara
Siniscola
L. del Coghinas
Nuoro
Tirso
Mti del Gennargentu 1835
Arbatax
L. Omodeo
Macomer
Alghero
Oristano
G. de Oristano
Sanluri
Muravera
C. Carbonara
G. de Cagliari
Iglesias
Carbonia
San Antioco
S. Antioco
S. Pietro
C. Teulada
C. Blanc
C. Serrat
Menzel
Mateur
G. de Tunis
C. Bon
Kelibia
Halq el Oued
Nabeul
Hammamet
Golfe de Hammamet
Dj Zaghouan 1295
Enfida
Sousse
Monastir
Moknine
M'saken
Kairouan
Teboursouk
Medjerda
Béja
Tabarka
El Kala
Jendouba
Makthar
El Kef
Mellègue
Kalla Khasba
Mts de Tébessa
Tébessa
Mts de la Medjerda
Souk Ahras
Guelma
40
10
15
3
A
B
C

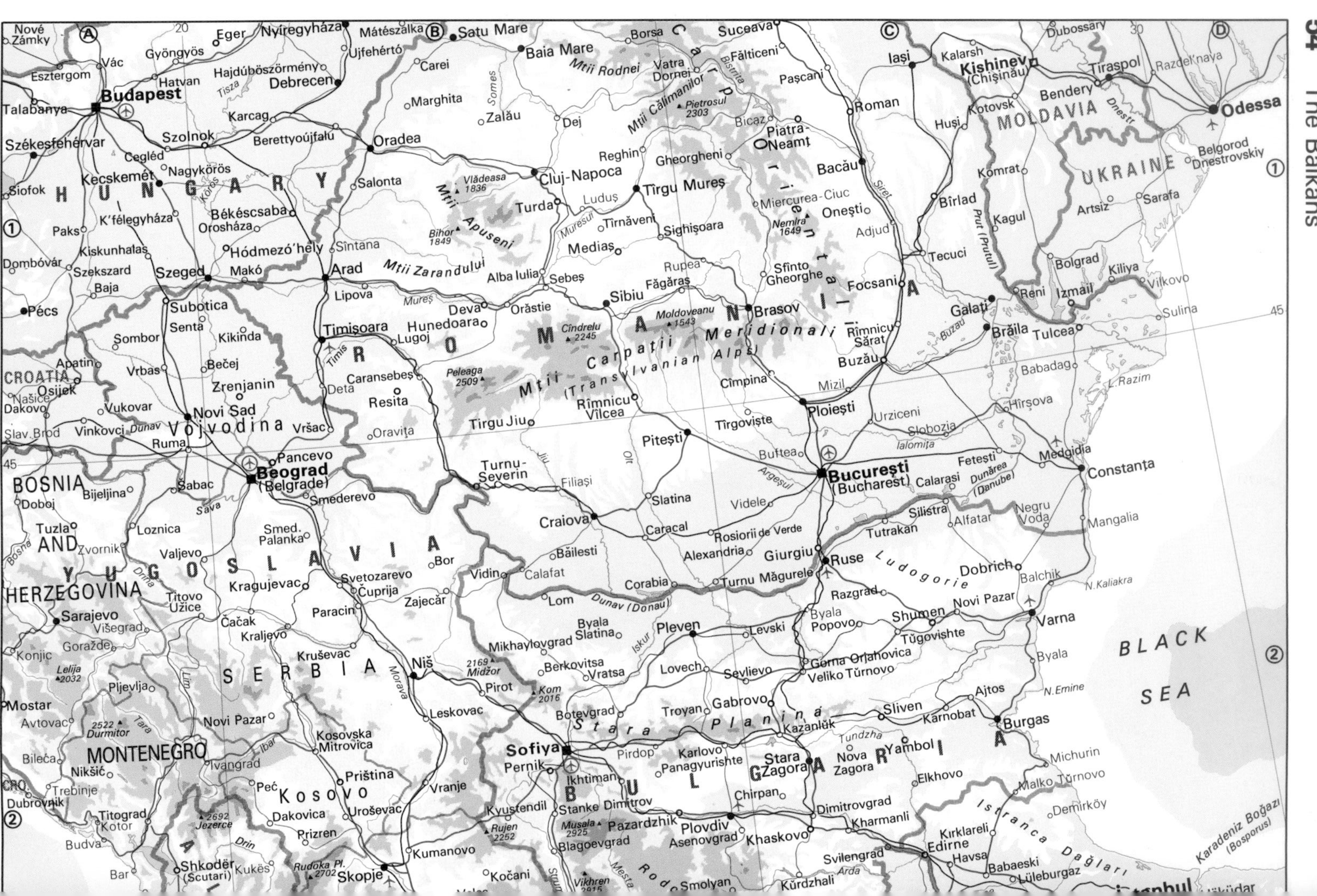
BLACK SEA
UKRAINE
MOLDAVIA
ROMANIA
HUNGARY
YUGOSLAVIA
BULGARIA
SERBIA
BOSNIA AND HERZEGOVINA
MONTENEGRO
CROATIA
Vojvodina
Kosovo
Odessa
Kishinev (Chişinău)
Tiraspol
Bendery
Iaşi
Galaţi
Brăila
Tulcea
Constanţa
Mangalia
Bucureşti (Bucharest)
Ploieşti
Braşov
Sibiu
Cluj-Napoca
Tîrgu Mureş
Oradea
Arad
Timişoara
Craiova
Piteşti
Budapest
Debrecen
Szeged
Kecskemét
Pécs
Beograd (Belgrade)
Novi Sad
Subotica
Niš
Sarajevo
Skopje
Sofiya
Plovdiv
Varna
Burgas
Ruse
Pleven
Stara Zagora
Edirne
Shkodër (Scutari)
Carpaţii Meridionali (Transylvanian Alps)
Mţii Apuseni
Stara Planina
Ludogorie
Dunav (Donau)
Prut (Prutul)
Siret
Olt
Mureş
Tisza
Sava
Drina
Morava

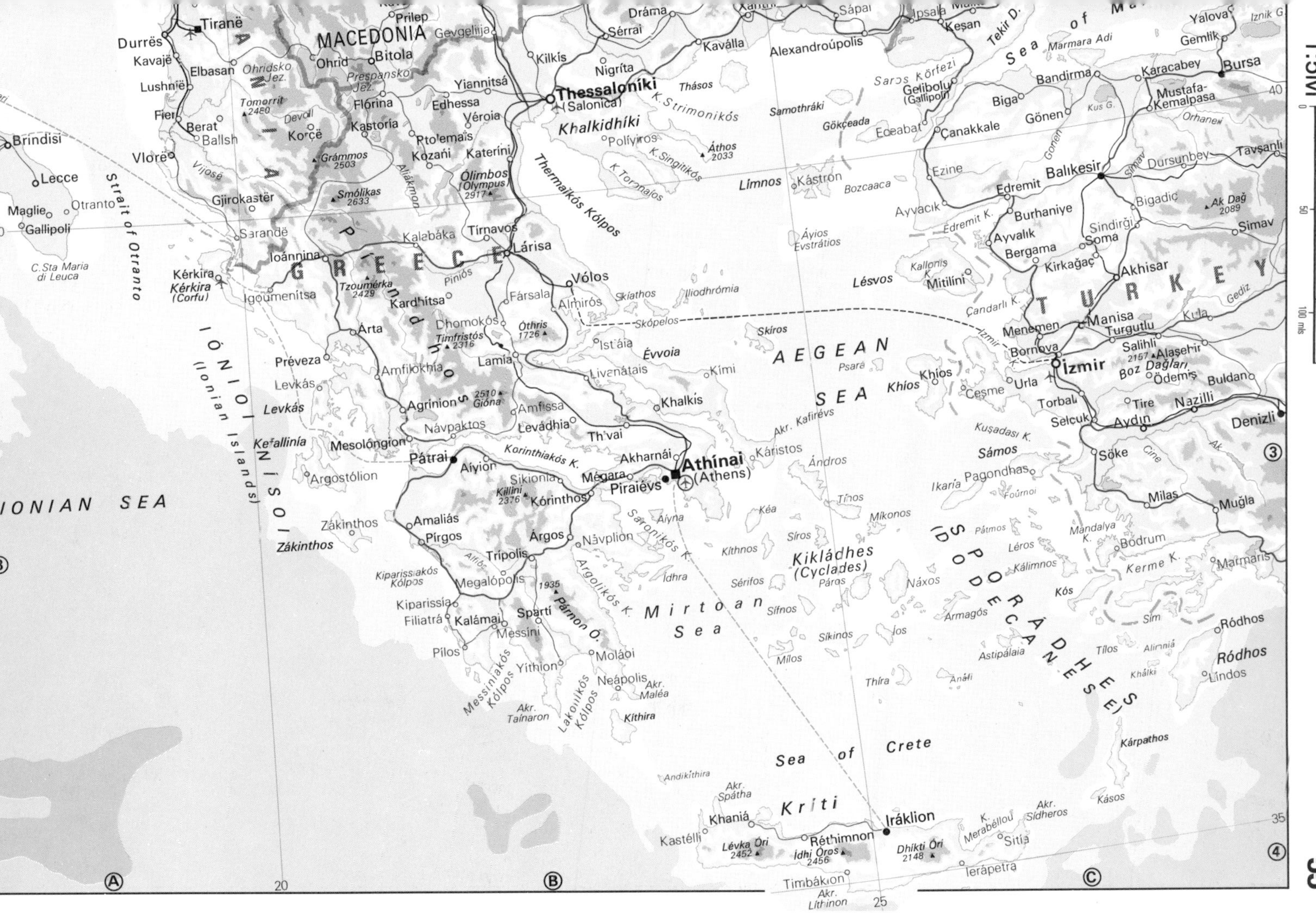

1:5M

50 · 100 · 150 · 200 km
50 · 100 mils

AEGEAN SEA
IONIAN SEA
Sea of Crete
Mirtoan Sea
Strait of Otranto
IÓNIOI NÍSOI
(Ionian Islands)
GREECE
TURKEY
MACEDONIA
DODECANESE
(DODEKÁNISOS)
Kikládhes
(Cyclades)
Athínai
(Athens)
Piraiévs
Thessaloníki
(Salonica)
Izmir
Iráklion
Kríti
Lésvos
Khíos
Sámos
Ródhos
Kárpathos
Kéa
Náxos
Thíra
Límnos
Thásos
Évvoia
Kérkira
(Corfu)
Kefallinía
Levkás
Zákinthos
Khalkidhikí
Thermaïkós Kólpos
Lárisa
Vólos
Pátrai
Kórinthos
Trípolis
Spartí
Kalámai
Ioánnina
Tiranë
Durrës
Vlorë
Brindisi
Lecce
Otranto
Bursa
Balıkesir
Manisa
Denizli
Muğla
Aydın
Kaválla
Alexandroúpolis
Khaniá
Réthimnon
Kíthira

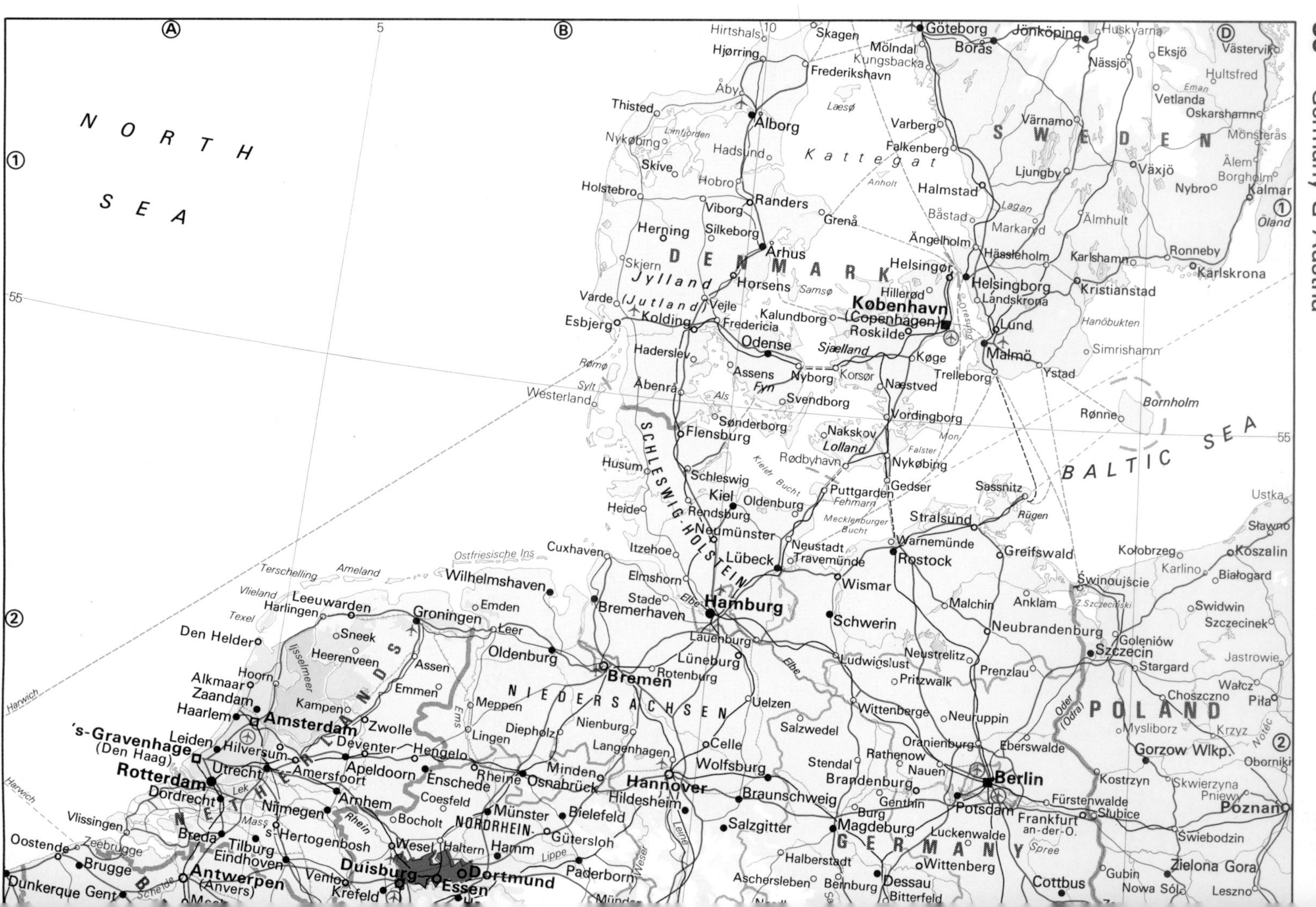
NORTH SEA
BALTIC SEA
SWEDEN
DENMARK
POLAND
GERMANY
NIEDERSACHSEN
NORDRHEIN-
SCHLESWIG-HOLSTEIN
Kattegat
Jylland (Jutland)
Sjælland
Fyn
Lolland
Falster
Bornholm
Öland
Rügen
Fehmarn
Ijsselmeer
Göteborg
Borås
Jönköping
Helsingborg
Malmö
Lund
Karlskrona
København (Copenhagen)
Roskilde
Helsingør
Ålborg
Århus
Odense
Esbjerg
Kolding
Flensburg
Kiel
Lübeck
Hamburg
Bremen
Bremerhaven
Hannover
Braunschweig
Magdeburg
Berlin
Potsdam
Rostock
Schwerin
Szczecin
Frankfurt an-der-O.
Cottbus
Oldenburg
Osnabrück
Münster
Dortmund
Essen
Duisburg
Amsterdam
Rotterdam
's-Gravenhage (Den Haag)
Utrecht
Groningen
Antwerpen (Anvers)
Brugge
Dunkerque

1:5M

0 50 100 150 200 km

0 50 100 mls

BELGIUM

LUXEMBOURG

FRANCE

GERMANY

ČESKÉ ZEMĚ

AUSTRIA

SWITZERLAND

LIECHTENSTEIN

ITALY

SLOVENIA

CROATIA

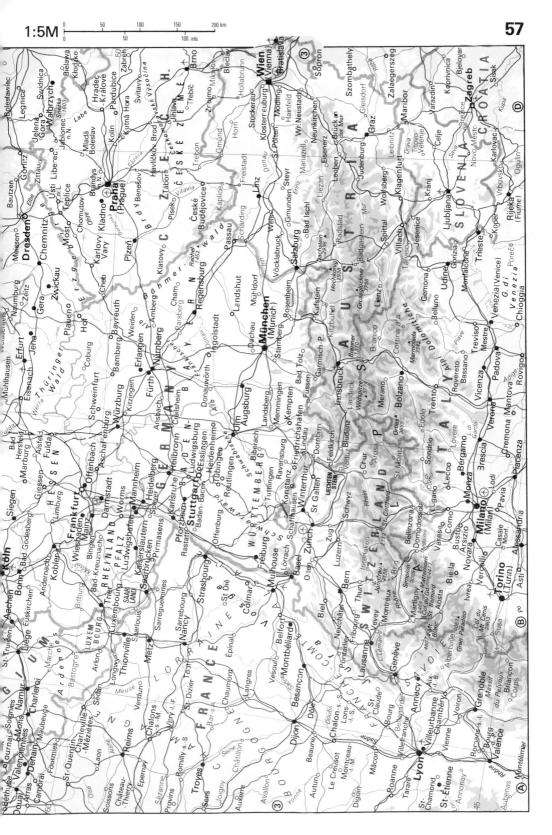

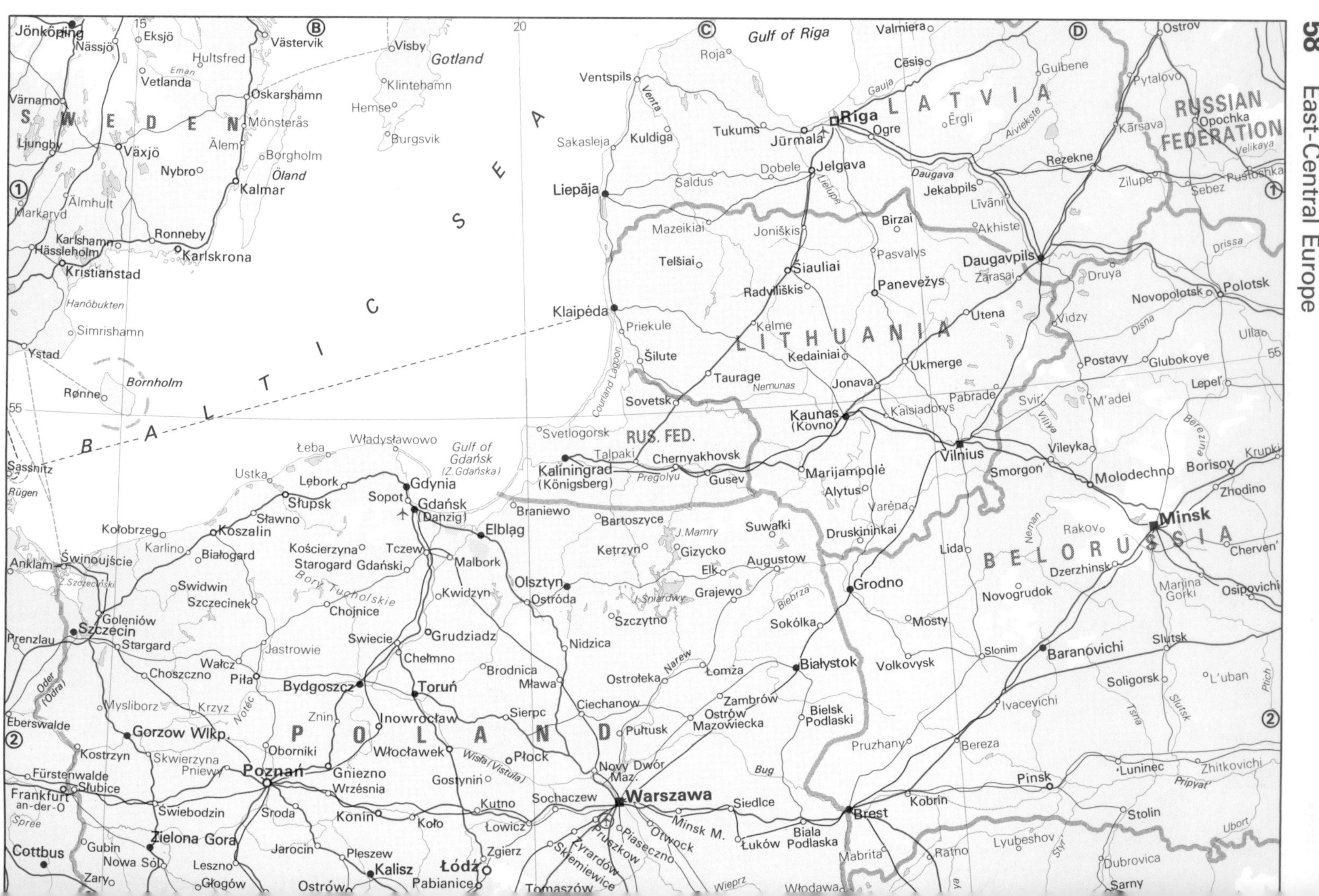

RUSSIAN FEDERATION
LATVIA
LITHUANIA
BELORUSSIA
POLAND
SWEDEN
BALTIC SEA
RUS. FED.
Gulf of Riga
Gulf of Gdańsk (Z. Gdańska)
Gotland
Öland
Bornholm
Hanöbukten
Courland Lagoon
Rügen
Jönköping
Nässjö
Eksjö
Hultsfred
Eman
Vetlanda
Västervik
Visby
Klintehamn
Hemse
Burgsvik
Värnamo
Oskarshamn
Mönsterås
Ålem
Borgholm
Ljungby
Växjö
Nybro
Kalmar
Älmhult
Markaryd
Karlshamn
Hässleholm
Ronneby
Karlskrona
Kristianstad
Simrishamn
Ystad
Rønne
Sassnitz
Ventspils
Venta
Roja
Sakasleja
Kuldiga
Tukums
Jūrmala
Riga
Ogre
Ērgli
Valmiera
Cēsis
Gauja
Gulbene
Aiviekste
Pytalovo
Ostrov
Kārsava
Opochka
Velikaya
Pustoshka
Sebez
Zilupe
Rezekne
Daugava
Jekabpils
Līvāni
Akhiste
Dobele
Jelgava
Lielupe
Saldus
Liepāja
Mazeikiai
Joniškis
Birzai
Pasvalys
Telšiai
Šiauliai
Radviliškis
Panevežys
Daugavpils
Zarasai
Druya
Drissa
Novopolotsk
Polotsk
Vidzy
Disna
Ulla
Klaipėda
Priekule
Kelme
Utena
Šilute
Kedainiai
Ukmerge
Postavy
Glubokoye
Taurage
Nemunas
Jonava
Lepel'
Sovetsk
Pabrade
Kaunas (Kovno)
Kaisiadorys
Svir'
M'adel
Viliya
Berezina
Svetlogorsk
Talpaki
Chernyakhovsk
Kaliningrad (Königsberg)
Pregolyu
Gusev
Marijampolė
Alytus
Vilnius
Smorgon'
Vileyka
Molodechno
Borisov
Krupki
Zhodino
Minsk
Rakov
Neman
Cherven'
Varėna
Druskininkai
Lida
Dzerzhinsk
Marjina Gorki
Osipovichi
Novogrudok
Grodno
Mosty
Slonim
Baranovichi
Slutsk
Soligorsk
L'uban
Ptich
Tsna
Ivacevichi
Volkovysk
Pruzhany
Bereza
Luninec
Zhitkovichi
Pripyat'
Pinsk
Kobrin
Brest
Stolin
Lyubeshov
Styr
Ubort
Ratno
Mabrita
Dubrovica
Sarny
Łeba
Władysławowo
Ustka
Lębork
Gdynia
Sopot
Gdańsk (Danzig)
Słupsk
Sławno
Kołobrzeg
Koszalin
Karlino
Białogard
Anklam
Świnoujście
Z. Szczeciński
Kościerzyna
Tczew
Starogard Gdański
Bory Tucholskie
Malbork
Elbląg
Braniewo
Bartoszyce
J. Mamry
Suwałki
Kętrzyn
Gizycko
Augustow
Ełk
Olsztyn
Ostróda
J. Śniardwy
Grajewo
Biebrza
Sokółka
Kwidzyn
Swidwin
Szczecinek
Chojnice
Goleniów
Szczecin
Prenzlau
Stargard
Jastrowie
Swiecie
Grudziadz
Szczytno
Nidzica
Chełmno
Brodnica
Mława
Ostrołeka
Narew
Łomża
Białystok
Wałcz
Choszczno
Piła
Bydgoszcz
Toruń
Zambrów
Ostrów Mazowiecka
Bielsk Podlaski
Oder (Odra)
Mysliborz
Krzyz
Noteć
Znin
Inowrocław
Sierpc
Ciechanow
Pułtusk
Eberswalde
Gorzow Wlkp.
Oborniki
Kostrzyn
Skwierzyna
Pniewy
Włocławek
Wisła (Vistula)
Płock
Nowy Dwór Maz.
Bug
Fürstenwalde
Frankfurt an-der-O
Słubice
Poznań
Gniezno
Września
Gostynin
Warszawa
Siedlce
Spree
Świebodzin
Środa
Konin
Kutno
Sochaczew
Minsk M.
Łuków
Biala Podlaska
Koło
Łowicz
Pruszków
Piaseczno
Otwock
Cottbus
Gubin
Zielona Gora
Jarocin
Pleszew
Zgierz
Żyrardów
Skiemiewice
Nowa Sól
Leszno
Kalisz
Łódź
Żary
Głogów
Ostrów
Pabianice
Tomaszów
Wieprz
Włodawa
15
20
55
B
C
D
1
2

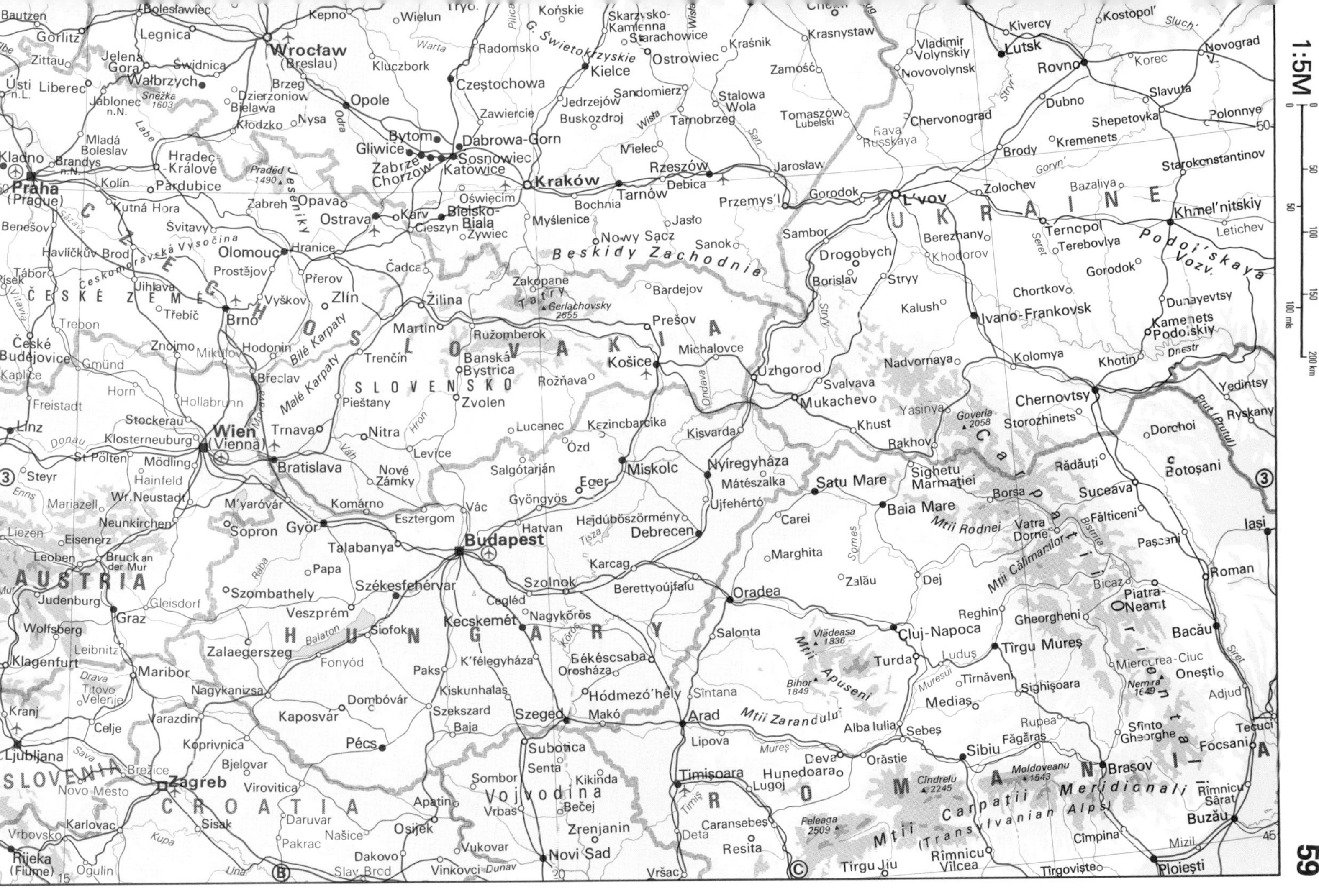

1:5M

0 50 100 150 200 km

50 100 mls

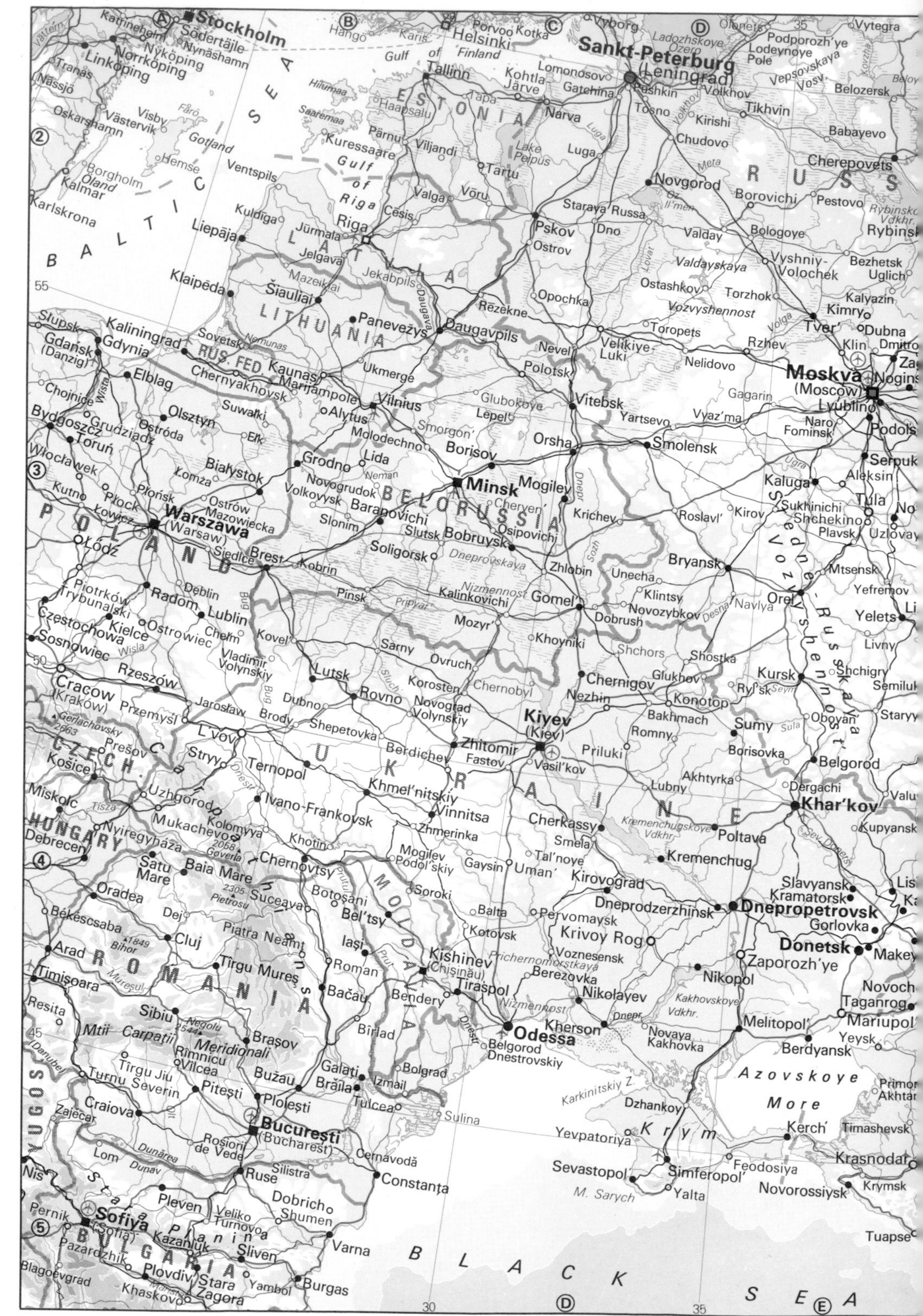

Stockholm
Helsinki
Tallinn
Sankt-Peterburg
(Leningrad)
Riga
Vilnius
Minsk
Moskva
(Moscow)
Warszawa
(Warsaw)
Kiyev
(Kiev)
Kishinev
(Chişinău)
Bucureşti
(Bucharest)
Sofiya
(Sofia)
Odessa
Kharkov
Dnepropetrovsk
Donetsk
ESTONIA
LATVIA
LITHUANIA
RUS. FED.
BELORUSSIA
POLAND
UKRAINE
MOLDAVIA
ROMANIA
BULGARIA
HUNGARY
CZECH.
RUSSIA
BALTIC SEA
BLACK SEA
Azovskoye More
Gulf of Finland
Gulf of Riga
Krym

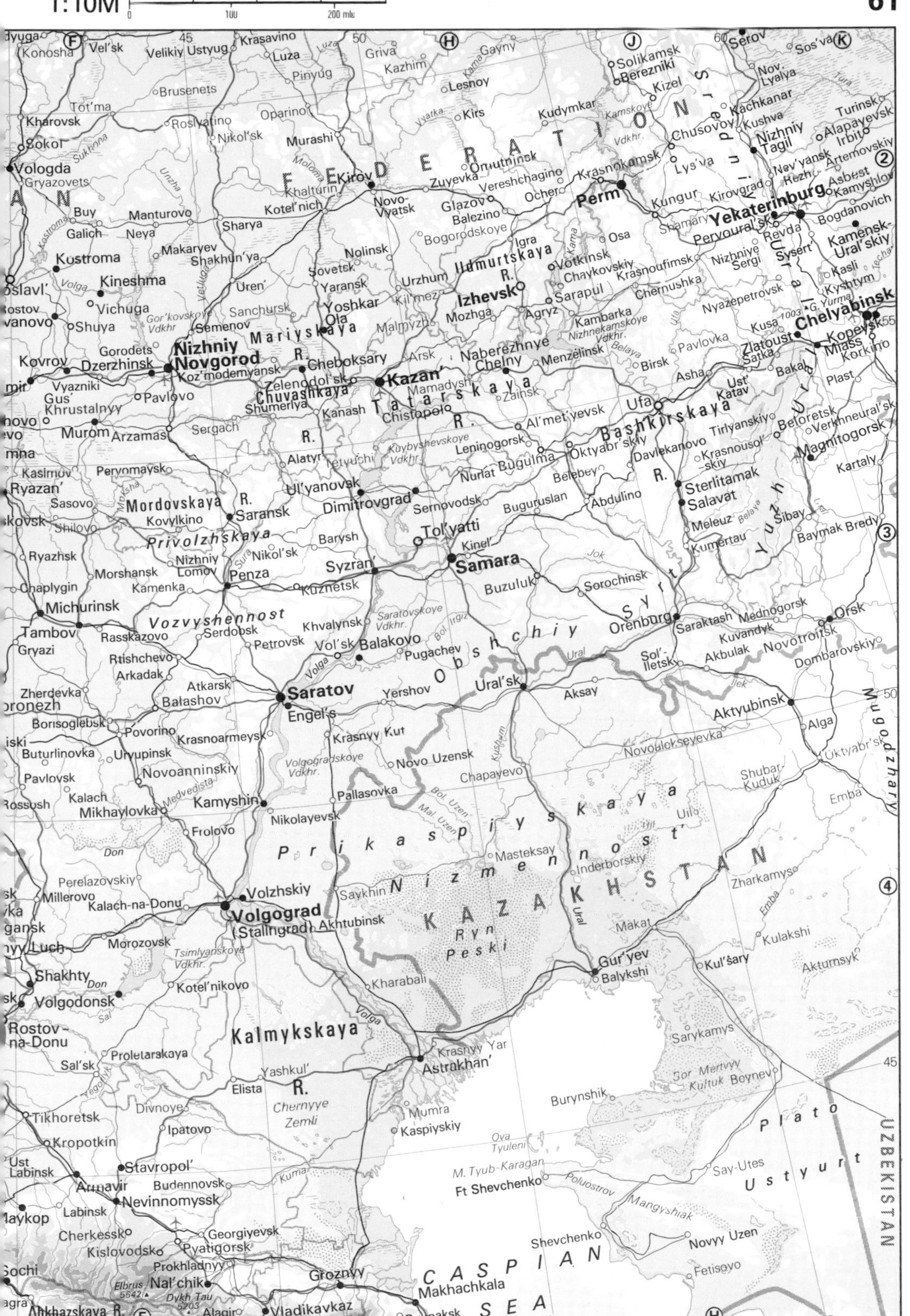

1:10M

| | 100 | 200 | 300 | 400 km |
| 100 | | 200 mls | | |

F · Vel'sk · Velikiy Ustyug · Krasavino · 50 · H · Gayny · J · Solikamsk · Serov · Sos'va · K
Konosha · Luza · Griva · Kazhim · Berezniki · Kizel · Nov. · Lyalya
Tot'ma · Brusenets · Pinyug · Oparino · Lesnoy · Kamskoye · Kudymkar · Kachkanar · Turinsk · ②
Kharovsk · Roslyatino · Nikol'sk · Murashi · Vdkhr. · Chusovoy · Nizhniy · Alapayevsk · Irbito
Sokol · FEDERATION · Vyatka · Kirs · Krasnokamsk · Lys'va · Tagil · Nev'yansk · Artemovskiy
Vologda · Kirov · Omutinsk · Zuyevka · Vereshchagino · Ocher · Perm · Kungur · Kirovgrad · Rezh · Asbest · Kamyshlov
Gryazovets · Khalturin · Novo-Vyatsk · Glazov · Balezino · Osa · Shamary · Pervoural'sk · Yekaterinburg · Bogdanovich
Buy · Manturovo · Sharya · Bogorodskoye · Igra · Votkinsk · Chaykovskiy · Krasnoufimsk · Nizhniy · Sergi · Sysert' · Kamensk-Ural'skiy
Galich · Neya · Nolinsk · Urzhum · Udmurtskaya · R. · Sarapul · Chernushka · Nyazepetrovsk · Kasli · Kyshtym
Kostroma · Makaryevo · Shakhun'ya · Sovetsk · Yaransk · Kil'mez · Mozhga · Kambarka · Pavlovka · Kusa · G. Yurma · Chelyabinsk
Kineshma · Uren' · Yoshkar · Ola · Malmyzh · Izhevsk · Agryz · Nizhnekamsk · Belaya · Zlatoust · Kopeysk
Vichuga · Semenov · Mariyskaya · R. · Arsk · Naberezhnye · Menzelinsk · Birsk · Asha · Ust'- · Miass · Korkino
Shuya · Gorodets · Koz'modemyansk · Cheboksary · Chelny · Ufa · Katav · Satka · Bakal · Plast
Nizhniy Novgorod · Dzerzhinsk · Zelenodol'sk · Kazan' · Tatarskaya · Al'met'yevsk · Davlekanovo · Tirlyanskiy · Beloretsk · Verkhneural'sk
Pavlovo · Chuvashskaya · Shumerlya · Kanash · Chistopol · R. · Zainsk · Bugul'ma · Oktyabr'skiy · Krasnousol- · Magnitogorsk
Gus'- · Khrustalnyy · Sergach · Alatyr · Tetyuchi · Kuybyshevskoye · Leninogorsk · Belebey · -skiy · Kartaly
Murom · Arzamas · Ul'yanovsk · Vdkhr. · Nurlat · Bugul'ma · Abdulino · Sterlitamak · Sibay · Baymak · Bredy
Kasimov · Pervomaysk · Mordovskaya · R. · Dimitrovgrad · Sernovodsk · Buguruslan · Salavat · Kumertau · ③
Ryazan' · Sasovo · Kovylkino · Saransk · Tol'yatti · Kinel' · Sorochinsk · Meleuz · Yuzh.
Ryazhsk · Shilovo · Nizhniy · Lomov · Barysh · Nikol'sk · Syzran · SAMARA · Buzuluk · Saraktash
Chaplygin · Morshansk · Penza · Kuznetsk · Khvalynsk · Saratovskoye · Orenburg · Mednogorsk · Orsk
Michurinsk · Kamenka · Vozvyshennost · Serdobsk · Petrovsk · Vdkhr. · Balakovo · Pugachev · Ural · Sol'- · Kuvandyk · Novotroitsk
Tambov · Rasskazovo · Vol'sk · Bol. Irgiz · Sorochinsk · Iletsk · Akbulak · Dombarovskiy
Gryazi · Rtishchevo · Atkarsk · Yershov · Ural'sk · Aksay · Ilek · Aktyubinsk · Alga
Zherdevka · Arkadak · Balashov · Saratov · Ilek
Borisoglebsk · Povorino · Krasnoarmeysk · Engel's · Krasnyy Kut · Novoalekseyevka · Uktyabr'sk · 50
Buturlinovka · Uryupinsk · Novoanninskiy · Medveditsa · Novo Uzensk · Chapayevo · Shubar- · Kuduk · Emba
Pavlovsk · Kalach · Mikhaylovka · Kamyshin · Pallasovka · Bol. Uzen · Uils
Rossosh · Frolovo · Nikolayevsk · Prikas · Mal. Uzen · Kazakhskaya
Perelazovskiy · Don · Volga · Masteksay · Inderborskiy · Zharkamys
Millerovo · Kalach-na-Donu · Volzhskiy · Saykhin · Nizmennost' · ④
gansk · Morozovsk · Volgograd · Akhtubinsk · Makat · Kulakshi
Luch · (Stalingrad) · Ryn · Gur'yev · Aktumsyk
Shakhty · Kotel'nikovo · Tsimlyanskoye · Peski · Balykshi · Kul'sary
Volgodonsk · Vdkhr. · Kharabali · Sarykamys
Rostov- · na-Donu · Kalmykskaya · Volga · Makat
Sal'sk · Proletarskaya · Yashkul' · Krasnyy Yar · Gor. Mertvyy · Plato
Tikhoretsk · Divnoye · Elista · R. · Astrakhan' · Kultuk Boyneyu · 45
Kropotkin · Ipatovo · Chernyye · Zemli · Burynshik · Ustyurt
Ust · Labinsk · Stavropol' · Mumra · Ova · Tyuleni · Say-Utes
Armavir · Budennovsk · Kaspiyskiy · Poluostrov · UZBEKISTAN
Maykop · Labinsk · Nevinnomyssk · Kuma · M. Tyub-Karagan · Mangyshlak · Novyy Uzen
Cherkessk · Georgiyevsk · Ft Shevchenko · Shevchenko · Fetisovo
Kislovodsk · Pyatigorsk · Kura · Groznyy · Makhachkala · CASPIAN
Sochi · Elbrus · Nal'chik · Vladikavkaz · Buynaksk · SEA
Abkhazskaya R. · F · Dykh Tau · Alagir · H · 55

600 1200 1800 km
300 600 900 mls

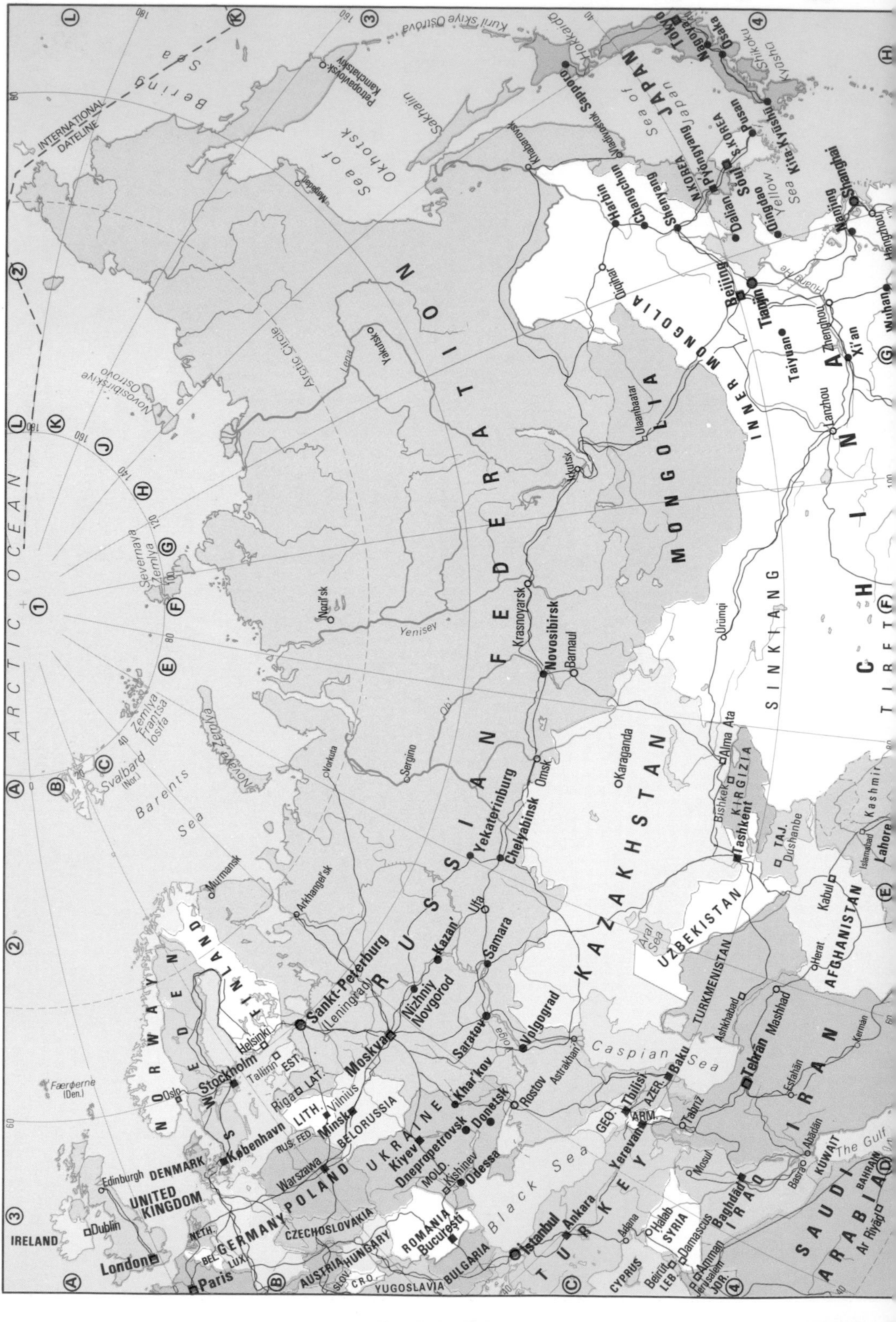

INTERNATIONAL DATELINE

Bering Sea

Kuril'skiye Ostrova

Petropavlovsk-Kamchatskiy

Sea of Okhotsk

Sakhalin

Hokkaido

JAPAN

Tokyo
Yokohama
Ōsaka
Sapporo
Shikoku
Kyūshū
Sea of Japan

N.KOREA
Pyongyang
S.KOREA
Seoul
Pusan
Kita-Kyūshū

Harbin
Changchun
Shenyang
Dalian
Qingdao
Yellow Sea
Nanjing
Shanghai
Hangzhou

Beijing
Tianjin
Wuhan
Zhengzhou
Huang He
Xi'an
Taiyuan

INNER MONGOLIA

MONGOLIA
Ulaanbaatar

Zanzhou

C H I N A

Ürümqi

SINKIANG

TIBET

R U S S I A N   F E D E R A T I O N

ARCTIC OCEAN

ARCTIC CIRCLE

Novosibirskiye Ostrova

Severnaya Zemlya

Zemlya Frantsa Iosifa

Svalbard (Nor.)

Barents Sea

Noril'sk
Yenisey
Ob'
Krasnoyarsk
Novosibirsk
Barnaul
Yakutsk

Vorkuta
Sergino
Yekaterinburg
Chelyabinsk
Omsk
Karaganda

KAZAKHSTAN

Aral Sea

Bishkek
Alma Ata
KIRGIZIA
Tashkent
UZBEKISTAN
TAJ.
Dushanbe

Kashmir
Islamabad
Lahore

Murmansk
Arkhangel'sk

N O R W A Y
S W E D E N
FINLAND

Oslo
Stockholm
Helsinki
Tallinn
EST.
Riga LAT.
LITH.
Vilnius

Sankt-Peterburg (Leningrad)

Moskva
Nizhniy Novgorod
Kazan'
Ufa
Samara
Saratov
Volgograd

Khar'kov
Rostov
Astrakhan'
Caspian Sea

Baku
AZER.
Tbilisi
GEO.
Yerevan
ARM.
Tehrān
Mashhad
Eşfahān
Kermān
Ābādān

AFGHANISTAN
Herat
Kabul
TURKMENISTAN
Ashkhabad

I R A N

Tabriz
Mosul
Baghdad
BAHRAIN
The Gulf
KUWAIT
Ar Riyāḍ

Faerøerne (Den.)

DENMARK
København
UNITED KINGDOM
Edinburgh
Dublin
IRELAND
London
Paris
NETH.
BEL.
LUX.
GERMANY
POLAND
Warszawa
CZECHOSLOVAKIA
AUSTRIA HUNGARY
Minsk
BELORUSSIA
RUS. FED.
MOLD.
Kishinev
UKRAINE
Kiyev
Dnepropetrovsk
Donetsk
Odessa
Black Sea
ROMANIA
Bucureşti
BULGARIA
YUGOSLAVIA
CRO.
SLOV.
Istanbul
Ankara
T U R K E Y
Adana
CYPRUS
SYRIA
LEB.
Beirut
Damascus
Amman
JOR.
S A U D I   A R A B I A
I R A Q
Ḥalab

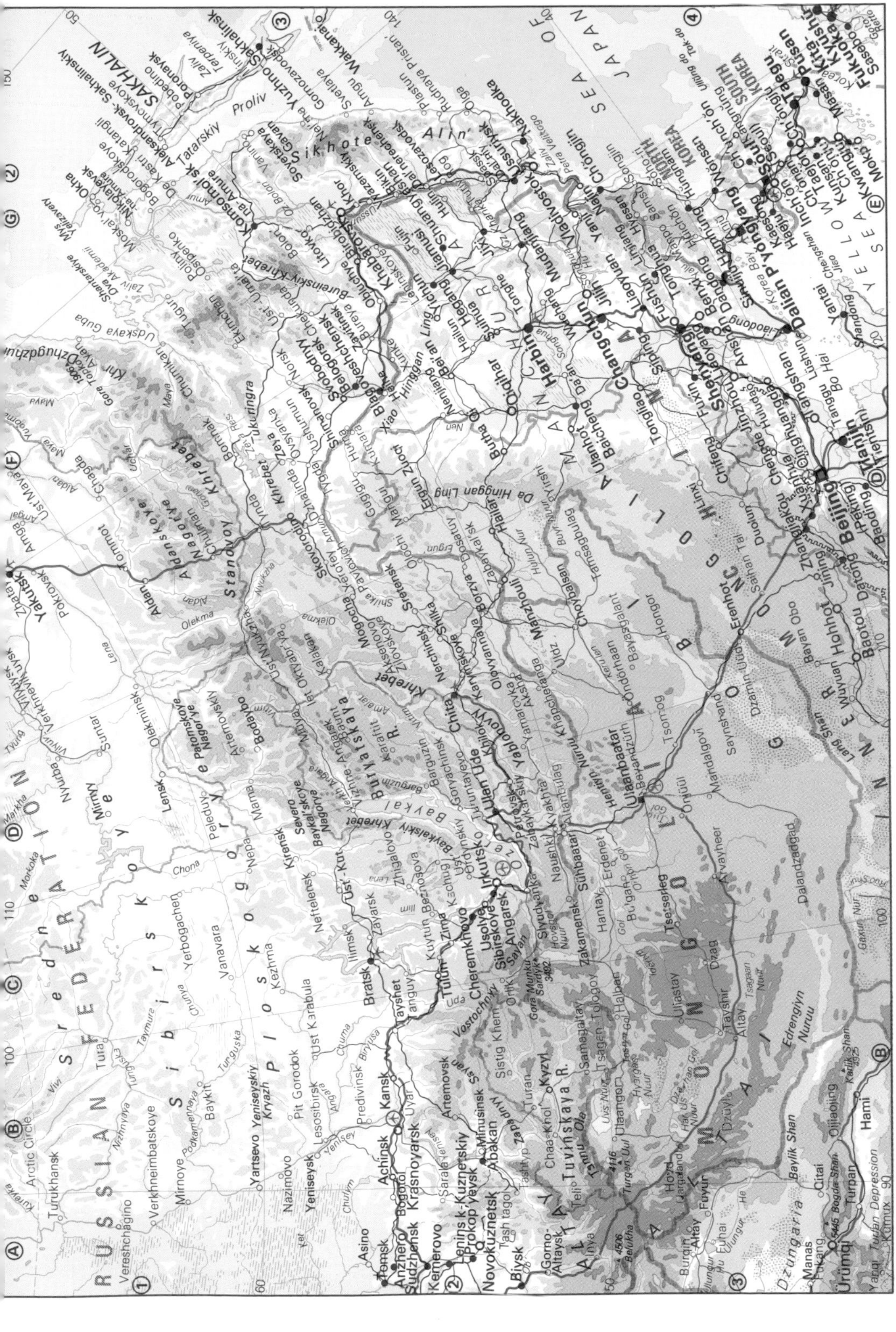

200 400 600 800 km

200 400 mils

RUSSIAN FEDERATION

Sredne Sibirskoye Ploskogorye

SAKHALIN

JAPAN SEA OF

SEA OF JAPAN

MONGOLIA

CHINA

NORTH KOREA

SOUTH KOREA

YELLOW SEA

Beijing (Peking)

Tianjin

Harbin

Changchun

Shenyang

Dalian

Vladivostok

Khabarovsk

Komsomol'sk-na-Amure

Yakutsk

Bratsk

Irkutsk

Ulan Ude

Chita

Ulaanbaatar

Krasnoyarsk

Novokuznetsk

Tomsk

Kemerovo

Baykal

Sikhote Alin'

Stanovoy Khrebet

Da Hinggan Ling

Arctic Circle

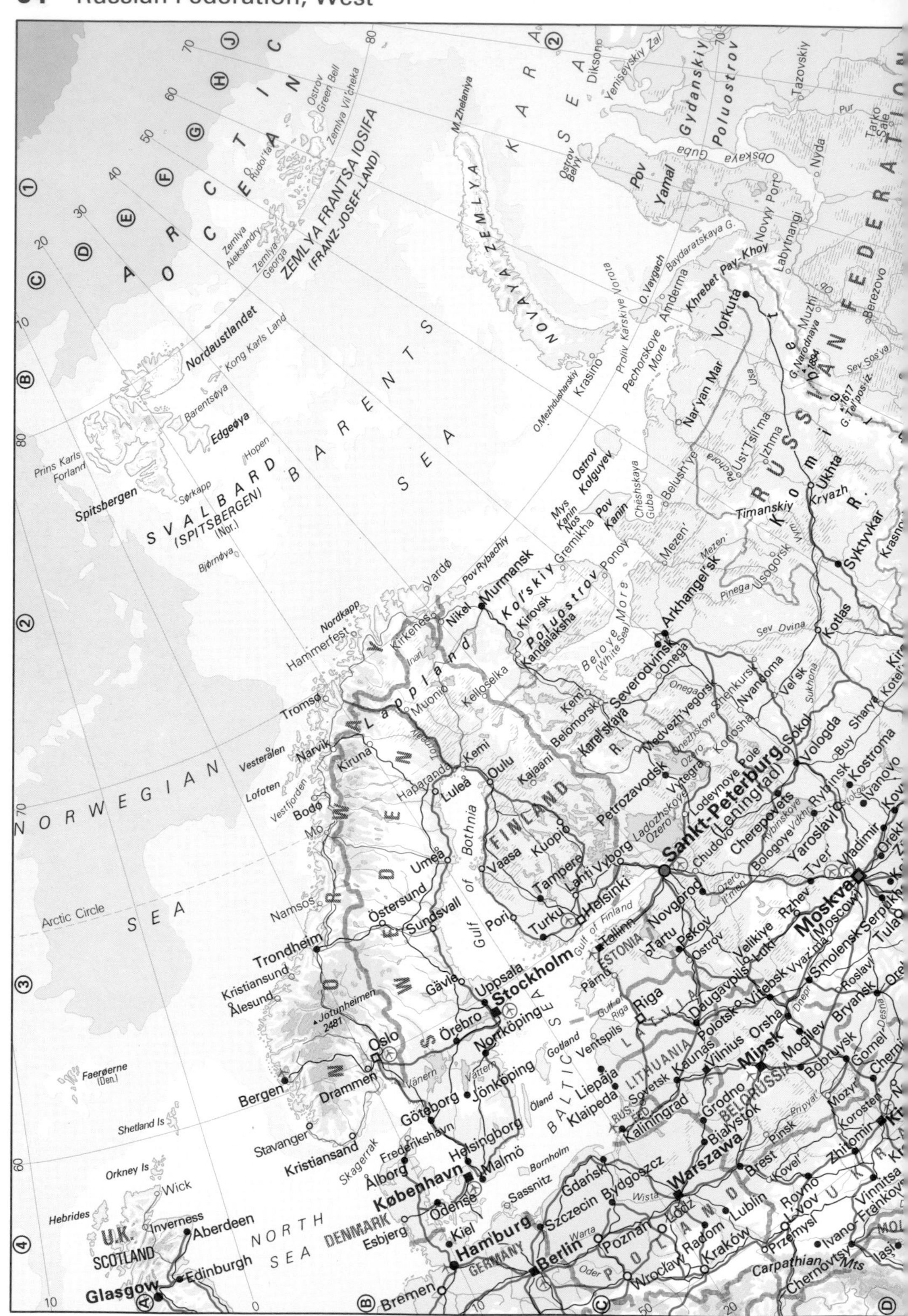
ARCTIC OCEAN
BARENTS SEA
NORWEGIAN SEA
KARA SEA
NORTH SEA
BALTIC SEA
SVALBARD (SPITSBERGEN) (Nor.)
Nordaustlandet
Spitsbergen
Edgeøya
Prins Karls Forland
ZEMLYA FRANTSA IOSIFA (FRANZ-JOSEF-LAND)
NOVAYA ZEMLYA
Pov Yamal
Gydanskiy Poluostrov
Ostrov Kolguyev
Kol'skiy Poluostrov
Beloye More (White Sea)
Gulf of Bothnia
Gulf of Finland
Lappland
FINLAND
SWEDEN
NORWAY
RUSSIAN FEDERATION
ESTONIA
LATVIA
LITHUANIA
BELORUSSIA
POLAND
GERMANY
DENMARK
U.K.
SCOTLAND
Arctic Circle
Murmansk
Arkhangel'sk
Vorkuta
Nar'yan Mar
Ukhta
Syktyvkar
Kotlas
Severodvinsk
Petrozavodsk
Sankt-Peterburg (Leningrad)
Moskva (Moscow)
Vologda
Yaroslavl'
Kostroma
Tver'
Novgorod
Pskov
Smolensk
Bryansk
Minsk
Vilnius
Kaunas
Riga
Tallinn
Helsinki
Turku
Tampere
Oulu
Stockholm
Uppsala
Göteborg
Malmö
København
Oslo
Bergen
Trondheim
Tromsø
Narvik
Bodø
Hammerfest
Nordkapp
Warszawa
Gdańsk
Kaliningrad
Berlin
Hamburg
Bremen
Kiel
Aberdeen
Edinburgh
Glasgow
Inverness
Wick
Faerøerne (Den.)
Shetland Is
Orkney Is
Hebrides

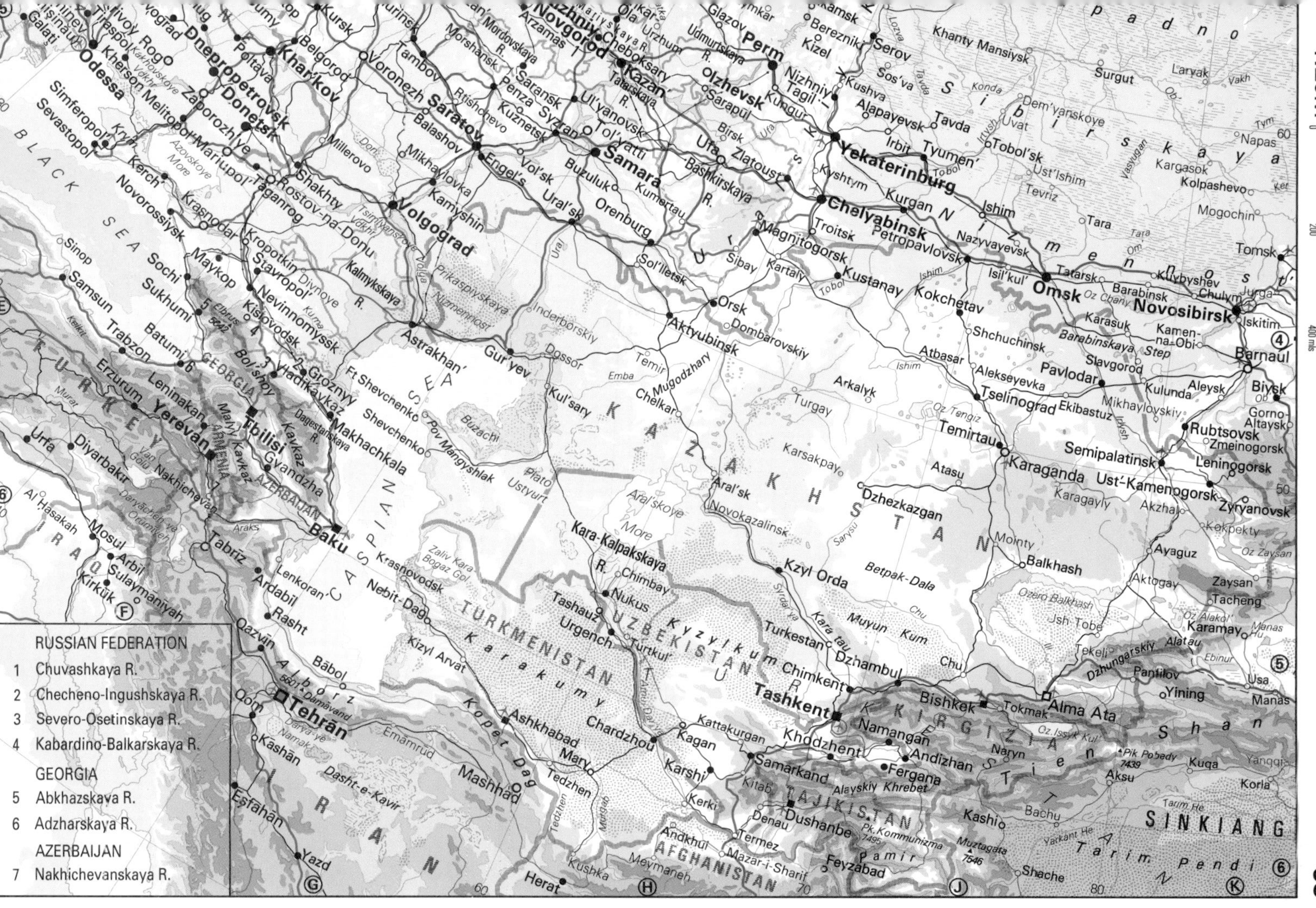

RUSSIAN FEDERATION
1 Chuvashskaya R.
2 Checheno-Ingushskaya R.
3 Severo-Osetinskaya R.
4 Kabardino-Balkarskaya R.

GEORGIA
5 Abkhazskaya R.
6 Adzharskaya R.

AZERBAIJAN
7 Nakhichevanskaya R.

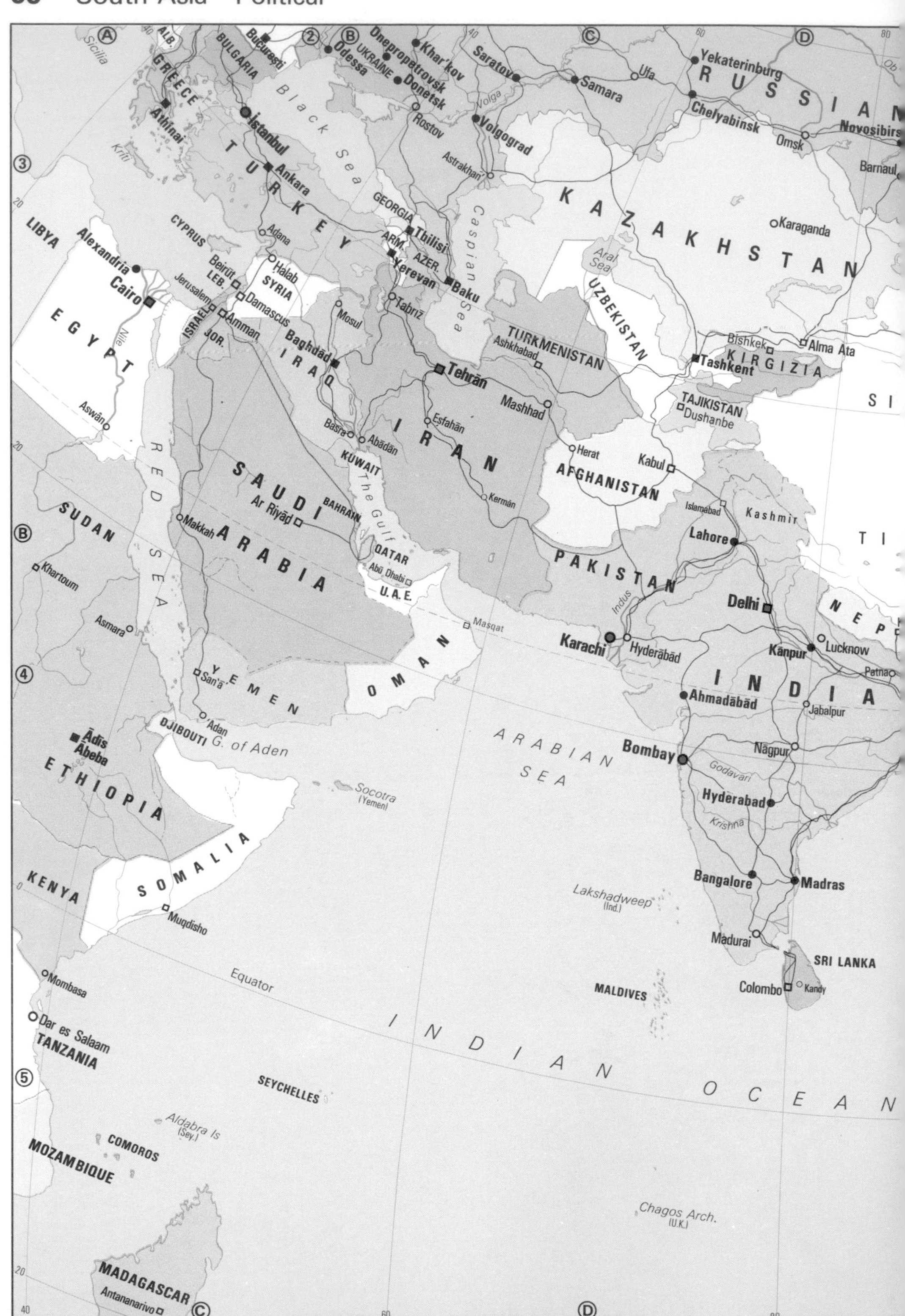
RUSSIA
KAZAKHSTAN
UZBEKISTAN
TURKMENISTAN
KIRGIZIA
TAJIKISTAN
AFGHANISTAN
PAKISTAN
INDIA
IRAN
IRAQ
SAUDI ARABIA
TURKEY
EGYPT
SUDAN
ETHIOPIA
SOMALIA
KENYA
TANZANIA
MOZAMBIQUE
MADAGASCAR
YEMEN
OMAN
SRI LANKA
MALDIVES
SEYCHELLES
COMOROS
Black Sea
Caspian Sea
Aral Sea
RED SEA
ARABIAN SEA
INDIAN OCEAN
The Gulf
G. of Aden
Equator
Tehrān
Delhi
Bombay
Karachi
Madras
Colombo
Kabul
Tashkent
Baghdād
Istanbul
Ankara
Cairo
Socotra (Yemen)
Lakshadweep (Ind.)
Chagos Arch. (U.K.)
Aldabra Is (Sey.)

400 800 1200 1600 km
400 800 mls

100 120 140 160

FEDERATION

Krasnoyarsk
Yenisey
Irkutsk
Khabarovsk
Sakhalin
Kuril'skiye Ostrova

MONGOLIA
Ulaanbaatar

INNER MONGOLIA

Qiqihar
Harbin
Changchun
Shenyang
Vladivostok
Sapporo
Hokkaidō
JAPAN

Ürümqi

N.KOREA
P'yŏngyang
Sea of
Japan
Honshū
Tōkyō
Nagoya

SINKIANG

Beijing
Tianjin
Dalian
Sŏul
S.KOREA
Pusan
Osaka

Lanzhou
Taiyuan
Zhengzhou
Huang He
Qingdao
Yellow Sea
Kita-Kyūshū
Shikoku
Kyūshū

CHINA
Xi'an
Nanjing
Shanghai

TIBET
Lhasa

Chengdu
Chongqing
Chang Jiang
Changsha
Nanchang
Wuhan
Hangzhou
Fuzhou

Guiyang
Kunming

T'ai-pei
TAIWAN
Tropic of Cancer

PACIFIC
OCEAN

Thimphu
BHUTAN
Brahmaputra
Imphal
BANGLA-DESH
Dhāka
Chittagong
Calcutta
Mandalay
BURMA (MYANMA)
Chiang Mai

Guangzhou
Macau (Port.)
Hong Kong (U.K.)
Hanoi
Haiphong
Hainan

Luzon
Manila
PHILIPPINES
Mindanao

Bay of Bengal

Rangoon (Yangon)
Moulmein
THAILAND
Vientiane
LAOS
Da Nang
VIETNAM
Mekong

SOUTH CHINA SEA

Davao

Andaman Is (Ind.)

Bangkok
CAMBODIA
Phnom Penh
Ho Chi Minh
Palawan

Sandakan
Manado
Halmahera
Irian Jaya

Surat Thani

MALAYSIA
BRUNEI
Sabah
Sarawak

Nicobar Is (Ind.)

George Town
Kuala Lumpur
SINGAPORE
BORNEO
Sulawesi
Seram

INDONESIA

SUMATERA
Padang
Palembang
JAWA
Jakarta
Surabaya
Flores
Timor
Kupang
Sumba
Darwin

AUSTRALIA

Christmas I (Aust.)
Cocos Is (Aust.)

E F G H
2 3 4 5

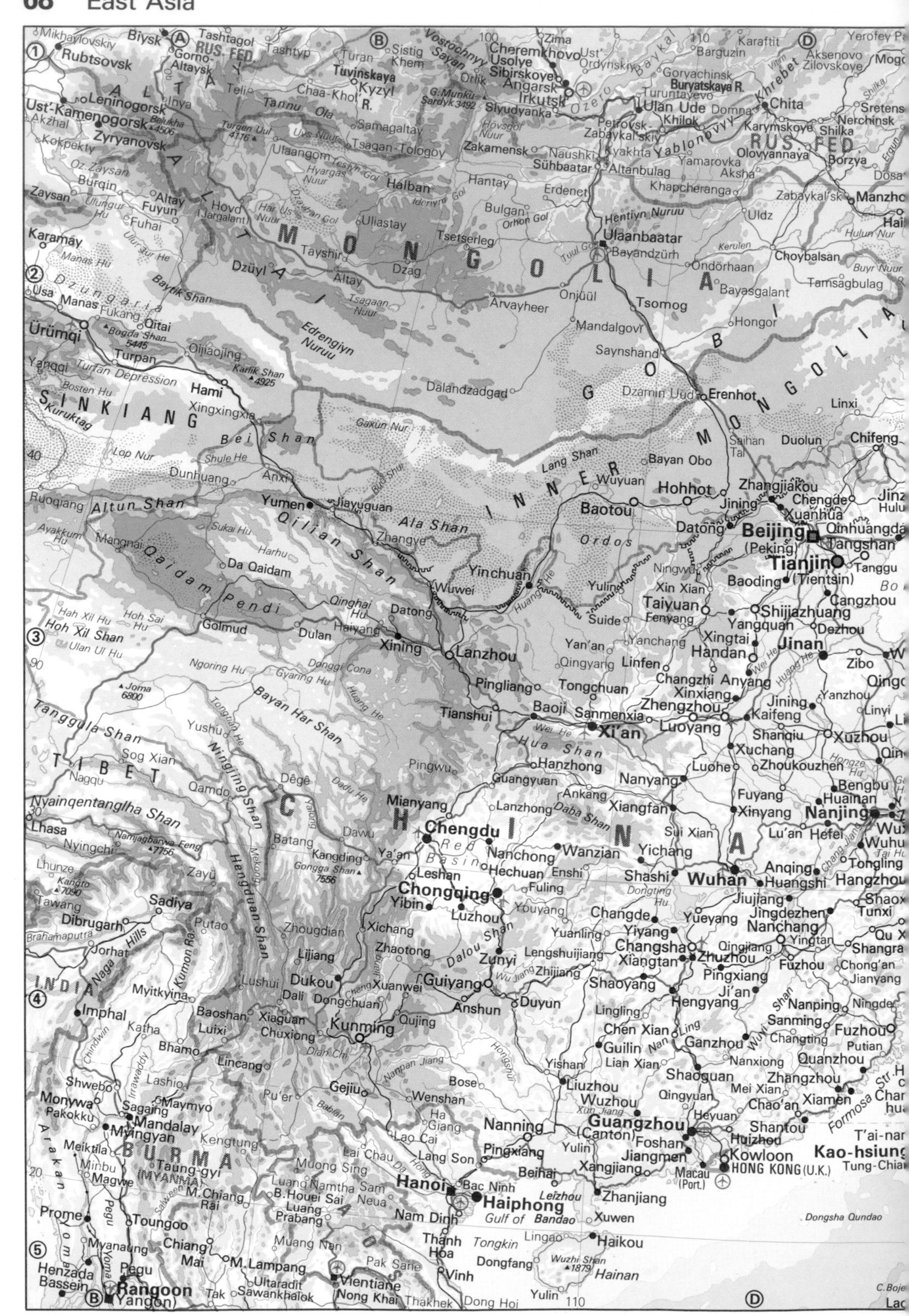

RUS. FED.
MONGOLIA
INNER MONGOLIA
SINKIANG
TIBET
CHINA
BURMA (MYANMAR)
LAOS
INDIA
ALTAI
GOBI
Mikhaylovskiy
Biysk
Rubtsovsk
Gorno-Altaysk
Tashtagol
Tashtyp
Turan
Sistig Khem
Vostochnyy Sayan
Zima
Cheremkhovo
Usolye Sibirskoye
Angarsk
Irkutsk
Ust'-Ordynskiy
Ozero Baykal
Barguzin
Karaftit
Goryachinsk
Buryatskaya R.
Yerofey Pavlovich
Aksenovo Zilovskoye
Mogocha
Tuvinskaya
Kyzyl
Chaa-Khol'
Orlik
G. Munku-Sardyk 3492
Slyudyanka
Turuntayevo
Ulan Ude
Chita
Sretensk
Nerchinsk
Shilka
Karymskoye
Khilok
Petrovsk-Zabaykal'skiy
Yablonovyy Khrebet
Leninogorsk
Ust'-Kamenogorsk
Zyryanovsk
Belukha 4506
Inya
Teli
Tannu Ola
Turgen Uul 4116
Uvs Nuur
Samagaltay
Tsagan-Tologoy
Hovsgol Nuur
Zakamensk
Naushki
Kyakhta
Sühbaatar
Altanbulag
Olovyannaya
Borzya
Yamarovka
Aksha
Khapcheranga
Dosatuy
Zabaykal'sk
Manzhouli
Hailar
Hulun Nur
Akzhal
Kokpekty
Oz. Zaysan
Burqin
Zaysan
Ulungur Hu
Altay
Fuyun
Fuhai
Hovd (Jargalant)
Har Us Nuur
Ulaangom
Hyargas Nuur
Tesiyn Gol
Halban
Hantay
Erdenet
Bulgan
Orhon Gol
Dzavhan Gol
Uliastay
Tsetserleg
Hentiyn Nuruu
Ulaanbaatar
Bayandzürh
Tuul Gol
Uldz
Kerulen
Choybalsan
Buyr Nuur
Öndörhaan
Bayasgalant
Tamsagbulag
Karamay
Manas Hu
Dzungaria
Baytik Shan
Tayshir
Dzag
Dzüyl
Altay
Tsagaan Nuur
Arvayheer
Onjüül
Tsomog
Hongor
Usa
Manas
Fukang
Qitai
Ürümqi
Bogda Shan 5445
Edrengiyn Nuruu
Mandalgovi
Saynshand
Yanqqi
Turpan
Qijiaojing
Turfan Depression
Karlik Shan 4925
Bosten Hu
Hami
Kuruktag
Xingxingxia
Dalandzadgad
Dzamin Uud
Erenhot
Linxi
Gaxun Nur
Bei Shan
Lop Nur
Shule He
Dunhuang
Anxi
Ruo Shui
Lang Shan
Saihan Tal
Duolun
Chifeng
Bayan Obo
Wuyuan
Hohhot
Zhangjiakou
Chengde
Xuanhua
Jining
Ruoqiang
Altun Shan
Yumen
Jiayuguan
Ala Shan
Baotou
Datong
Beijing (Peking)
Qinhuangdao
Tangshan
Tianjin (Tientsin)
Tanggu
Ayakkum Hu
Mangnai
Sukai Hu
Qilian Shan
Zhangye
Ordos
Harhu
Da Qaidam
Qaidam Pendi
Wuwei
Yinchuan
Huang He
Ningwu
Yulin
Xin Xian
Baoding
Cangzhou
Bo Hai
Qinghai Hu
Datong
Taiyuan
Fenyang
Shijiazhuang
Hah Xil Hu
Hoh Sai Hu
Hoh Xil Shan
Ulan Ul Hu
Golmud
Dulan
Haiyang
Xining
Lanzhou
Suide
Yan'an
Yanchang
Yangquan
Dezhou
Xingtai
Jinan
Handan
Zibo
Qingyang
Linfen
Changzhi
Anyang
Ngoring Hu
Gyaring Hu
Donggi Cona
Pingliang
Tongchuan
Xinxiang
Jining
Yanzhou
Linyi
Joma 6800
Bayan Har Shan
Tianshui
Baoji
Sanmenxia
Zhengzhou
Kaifeng
Tanggula Shan
Tongtian He
Yushu
Wei He
Xi'an
Luoyang
Shangqiu
Xuzhou
Hua Shan
Sog Xian
Ningjing Shan
Hanzhong
Xuchang
Zhoukouzhen
Nagqu
Qamdo
Dêgê
Pingwu
Guangyuan
Luohe
Hongze Hu
Bengbu
Huainan
Nyainqentanglha Shan
Dadu He
Yalong
Mianyang
Lanzhong
Ankang
Daba Shan
Nanyang
Xiangfan
Fuyang
Xinyang
Nanjing
Lhasa
Chengdu
Dawu
Red Basin
Sui Xian
Lu'an
Hefei
Wuhu
Nyingchi
Namjagbarwa Feng 7756
Batang
Kangding
Ya'an
Nanchong
Wanzian
Yichang
Tai Hu
Tongling
Lhunze
Mekong
Gongga Shan 7556
Leshan
Hechuan
Enshi
Shashi
Wuhan
Anqing
Huangshi
Hangzhou
Kangto 7090
Zayü
Hengduan Shan
Chongqing
Fuling
Dongting Hu
Jiujiang
Tawang
Sadiya
Yibin
Luzhou
Youyang
Changde
Yueyang
Jingdezhen
Tunxi
Dibrugarh
Putao
Zhougdian
Xichang
Dalou Shan
Yiyang
Nanchang
Yingtan
Brahmaputra
Jorhat
Naga Hills
Kumon Ra.
Lijiang
Zhaotong
Yuanling
Changsha
Zhuzhou
Xiangtan
Qingjiang
Shangrao
Zunyi
Lengshuijiang
Fuzhou
Chong'an
Dukou
Lushui
Dali
Xuanwei
Guiyang
Wu Jiang
Zhijiang
Shaoyang
Pingxiang
Jianyang
Myitkyina
Dongchuan
Anshun
Duyun
Hengyang
Ji'an
Imphal
Baoshan
Xiaguan
Kunming
Qujing
Lingling
Nanping
Ningde
Katha
Luixi
Chuxiong
Chen Xian
Guilin
Ganzhou
Sanming
Fuzhou
Chindwin
Bhamo
Dian Chi
Hongshui
Changting
Putian
Lincang
Nanpan Jiang
Lian Xian
Nanxiong
Quanzhou
Shwebo
Lashio
Irrawaddy
Yishan
Shaoguan
Zhangzhou
Monywa
Maymyo
Pu'er
Gejiu
Bose
Liuzhou
Qingyuan
Mei Xian
Xiamen
Formosa Str.
Pakokku
Sagaing
Mandalay
Babian
Wenshan
Wuzhou
Xun Jiang
Chao'an
Myingyan
Kengtung
Ha Giang
Nanning
Guangzhou (Canton)
Heyuan
Shantou
Meiktila
Lao Cai
Pingxiang
Yulin
Foshan
Huizhou
T'ai-nan
Minbu
Lai Chau
Lang Son
Jiangmen
Kowloon
Kao-hsiung
Magwe
Taung-gyi
Muong Sing
Beihai
Xangjiang
Macau (Port.)
HONG KONG (U.K.)
Tung-Chiang
Arakan
Salween
Luang Namtha
Sam Neua
Hanoi
Bac Ninh
Leizhou
Zhanjiang
Pegu
M. Chiang Rai
B. Houei Sai
Haiphong
Prome
Toungoo
Luang Prabang
Nam Dinh
Gulf of Tongkin
Bandao
Xuwen
Dongsha Qundao
Myanaung
Chiang Mai
Muang Nan
Thanh Hoa
Lingao
Haikou
Henzada
Bassein
M. Lampang
Pak Sane
Vinh
Dongfang
Wuzhi Shan 1879
Hainan
Rangoon (Yangon)
Tak
Uttaradit
Sawankhalok
Vientiane
Nong Khai
Thakhek
Dong Hoi
Yulin
C. Bojeador
100
110
40
90
30
20

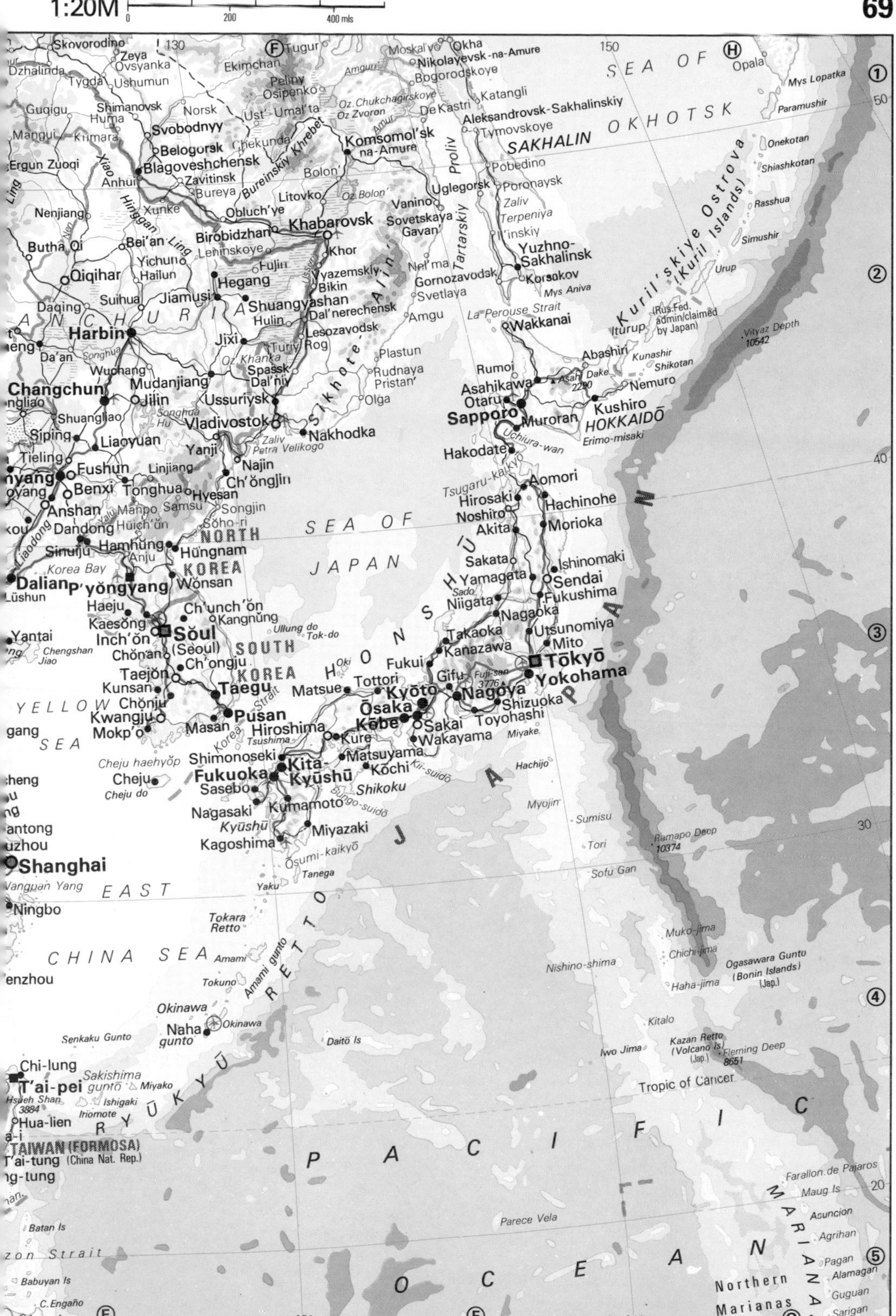

1:20M

200   400   600   800 km

200   400 mls

Skovorodino · Zeya · Tugur · SEA OF · Opala
Dzhalinda · Ovsyanka · Ekimchan · Pebiny · Moskal'vo · Okha · Mys Lopatka
Tygda · Ushumun · Osipenko · Amgun' · Nikolayevsk-na-Amure · Paramushir · 50
Guqigu · Shimanovsk · Norsk · Ust'-Umal'ta · Bogorodskoye · Katangli
Huma · Belogorsk · Oz. Chukchagirskoye · DeKastri · Onekotan
Mangui · Kumara · Svobodnyy · Oz Zvoron · Aleksandrovsk-Sakhalinskiy · Shiashkotan
Ergun Zuoqi · Blagoveshchensk · Zavitinsk · Tymovskoye · SAKHALIN · OKHOTSK · Rasshua
Anhui · Bureya · Litovko · Pobedino
Nenjiang · Bei'an · Ling · Birobidzhan · Khabarovsk · Uglegorsk · Poronaysk · Simushir
Butha Qi · Yichun · Leninskoye · Fujin · Obluch'ye · Zaliv · Urup
Qiqihar · Hailun · Hegang · Khor · Vanino · Terpeniya · Vityaz Depth
Daqing · Songhua · Suihua · Jiamusi · Yyazemskiy · Sovetskaya · Il'inskiy · 10542
Shuangyashan · Bikin · Gavan' · Gornozavodsk
Harbin · Jixi · Hulin · Dal'nerechensk · Amgu · Svetlaya · Wakkanai · Abashiri · Kunashir
Changchun · Wuchang · Mudanjiang · Oz. Khanka · Spassk · Rudnaya · La Perouse Strait · Asahikawa · Asahi Dake · Shikotan
Shuangliao · Jilin · Ussuriysk · Dal'niy · Pristan' · Mys Aniva · Nemuro
Siping · Liaoyuan · Yanji · Vladivostok · Nakhodka · Olga · Otaru · Sapporo · Muroran · HOKKAIDŌ · Erimo-misaki
Tieling · Fushun · Linjiang · Najin · Zaliv · Hakodate · Uchiura-wan
Benxi · Tonghua · Ch'ŏngjin · Petra Velikogo · Tsugaru-kaikyō · 40
Anshan · Hyesan · Songjin · Aomori
Dandong · Huich'ŏn · Samsu · Hirosaki · Hachinohe
Dalian · Hamhŭng · NORTH · Manpo · Söho-ri · Noshiro · Morioka
Lüshun · Anju · KOREA · Hŭngnam · Akita
Korea Bay · Haeju · Wŏnsan · Sakata · Ishinomaki
Yantai · Kaesŏng · Kangnŭng · Yamagata · Sendai
Chengshan · Inch'ŏn · Ullung do · Sado · Niigata · Fukushima
Jiao · Sŏul · SOUTH · Tok-do · Nagaoka
Chŏnan · (Seoul) · KOREA · Takaoka · Utsunomiya
Taejŏn · Ch'ongju · Oki · Fukui · Kanazawa · Mito · Tōkyō
Taegu · Matsue · Tottori · Gifu · Fuji-san · Yokohama
Kunsan · Chŏnju · Kyōto · Nagoya · 3776 · Shizuoka
Kwangju · Pusan · Osaka · Sakai · Toyohashi
Mokp'o · Masan · Hiroshima · Kōbe · Wakayama · Miyake
YELLOW · Kure · Matsuyama
Shimonoseki · Kita- · Kōchi · Kii-suidō · Hachijo
Cheju haehyŏp · Fukuoka · Kyūshū · Bungo-suidō
SEA · Cheju · Sasebo · Shikoku · Sumisu
Cheju do · Nagasaki · Kumamoto · Myojin
Kagoshima · Kyūshū · Miyazaki · Tori
Ōsumi-kaikyō · Sofu Gan
Shanghai · Yaku · Tanega
Ningbo · EAST · Ramapo Deep · 10374
Tokara · Muko-jima · Chichi-jima
CHINA · Retto · Amami · Nishino-shima · Haha-jima · Ogasawara Gunto · 30
Tokuno · (Bonin Islands)
SEA · Okinawa · (Jap.)
Naha · Okinawa · Kitalo
Senkaku Gunto · gunto · Iwo Jima · Kazan Retto · Fleming Deep
Chi-lung · Sakishima · Daitō Is · (Volcano Is) · 8651
T'ai-pei · gunto · Miyako · (Jap.)
Hsueh Shan · Ishigaki · Tropic of Cancer
3884 · Iriomote · Farallon de Pajaros
Hua-lien · TAIWAN (FORMOSA) · Maug Is · 20
T'ai-tung (China Nat. Rep.) · Asuncion
Agrihan
Batan Is · Pagan · Alamagan
Babuyan Is · Parece Vela · Guguan
C. Engaño · Sarigan · 5
Aparri · Northern · Anatahan
Strait · Marianas

SEA OF JAPAN

PACIFIC OCEAN

130   140

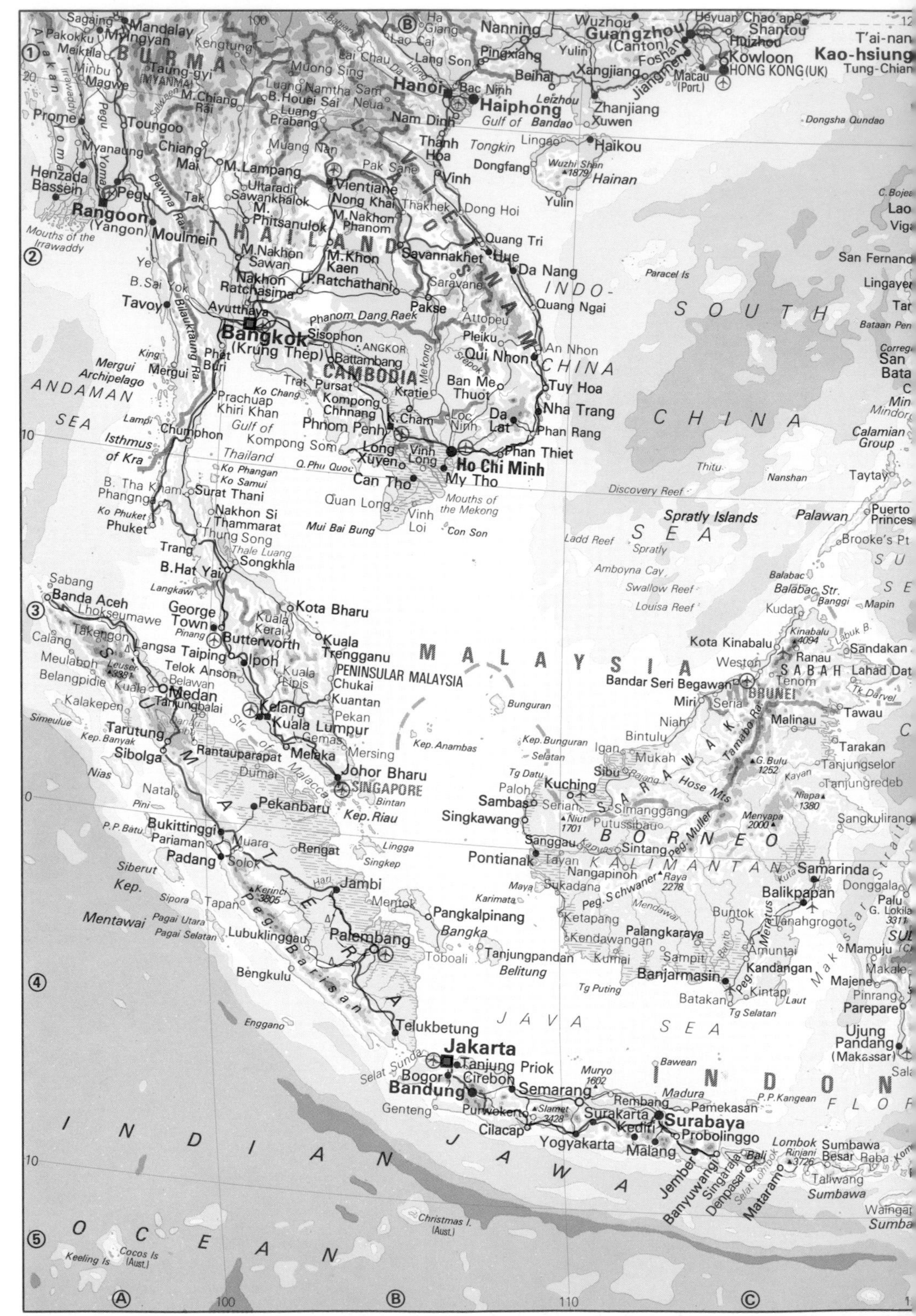

BURMA
(MYANMAR)
Mandalay
Myingyan
Meiktila
Minbu
Magwe
Taung-gyi
Kengtung
Prome
Toungoo
Myanaung
Henzada
Bassein
Pegu
Rangoon
(Yangon)
Mouths of the Irrawaddy
Moulmein
Ye
Tavoy
Mergui
Mergui Archipelago
ANDAMAN SEA
Isthmus of Kra
THAILAND
Chiang Rai
Chiang Mai
Lampang
Uttaradit
Sawankhalok
Phitsanulok
Nakhon Sawan
Nakhon Ratchasima
Ayutthaya
Bangkok
(Krung Thep)
Phet Buri
Prachuap Khiri Khan
Chumphon
Gulf of Thailand
Surat Thani
Nakhon Si Thammarat
Phuket
Phangnga
Trang
Songkhla
B.Hat Yai
Udon Thani
Nakhon Phanom
Khon Kaen
Ubon Ratchathani
LAOS
Luang Prabang
Vientiane
Nong Khai
Thakhek
Savannakhet
Saravane
Pakse
Attopeu
VIETNAM
Hanoi
Haiphong
Nam Dinh
Thanh Hoa
Vinh
Dong Hoi
Quang Tri
Hue
Da Nang
Quang Ngai
Qui Nhon
Tuy Hoa
Nha Trang
Da Lat
Phan Rang
Phan Thiet
Ho Chi Minh
My Tho
Can Tho
Mouths of the Mekong
Con Son
CAMBODIA
Sisophon
ANGKOR
Battambang
Pursat
Kompong Chhnang
Kratie
Phnom Penh
Kompong Som
Gulf of Tonkin
Nanning
Guangzhou
(Canton)
Foshan
Jiangmen
Macau
(Port.)
Kowloon
HONG KONG (UK)
Shantou
Kao-hsiung
Zhanjiang
Xuwen
Haikou
Hainan
Yulin
Paracel Is
SOUTH CHINA SEA
Spratly Islands
Palawan
Puerto Princesa
Calamian Group
San Fernando
Lingayen
MALAYSIA
PENINSULAR MALAYSIA
Kota Bharu
Kuala Trengganu
Kuantan
Ipoh
Taiping
George Town
Butterworth
Telok Anson
Kelang
Kuala Lumpur
Melaka
Mersing
Johor Bharu
SINGAPORE
Kep. Anambas
Bunguran
Kep. Riau
Lingga
Singkep
SUMATERA
Banda Aceh
Sabang
Lhokseumawe
Medan
Tanjungbalai
Sibolga
Nias
Pekanbaru
Bukittinggi
Padang
Siberut
Kep. Mentawai
Jambi
Palembang
Bengkulu
Telukbetung
Enggano
Bangka
Pangkalpinang
Belitung
Tanjungpandan
BORNEO
KALIMANTAN
SARAWAK
SABAH
BRUNEI
Bandar Seri Begawan
Kota Kinabalu
Sandakan
Tawau
Miri
Bintulu
Sibu
Kuching
Singkawang
Pontianak
Ketapang
Palangkaraya
Banjarmasin
Samarinda
Balikpapan
Tarakan
JAVA SEA
Jakarta
Tanjung Priok
Bogor
Bandung
Cirebon
Semarang
Surakarta
Yogyakarta
Surabaya
Madura
Malang
Kediri
Probolinggo
Jember
Banyuwangi
Bali
Denpasar
Lombok
Mataram
Sumbawa
JAWA
INDONESIA
Ujung Pandang
(Makassar)
Christmas I.
(Aust.)
Cocos Is
(Aust.)
Keeling Is
INDIAN OCEAN

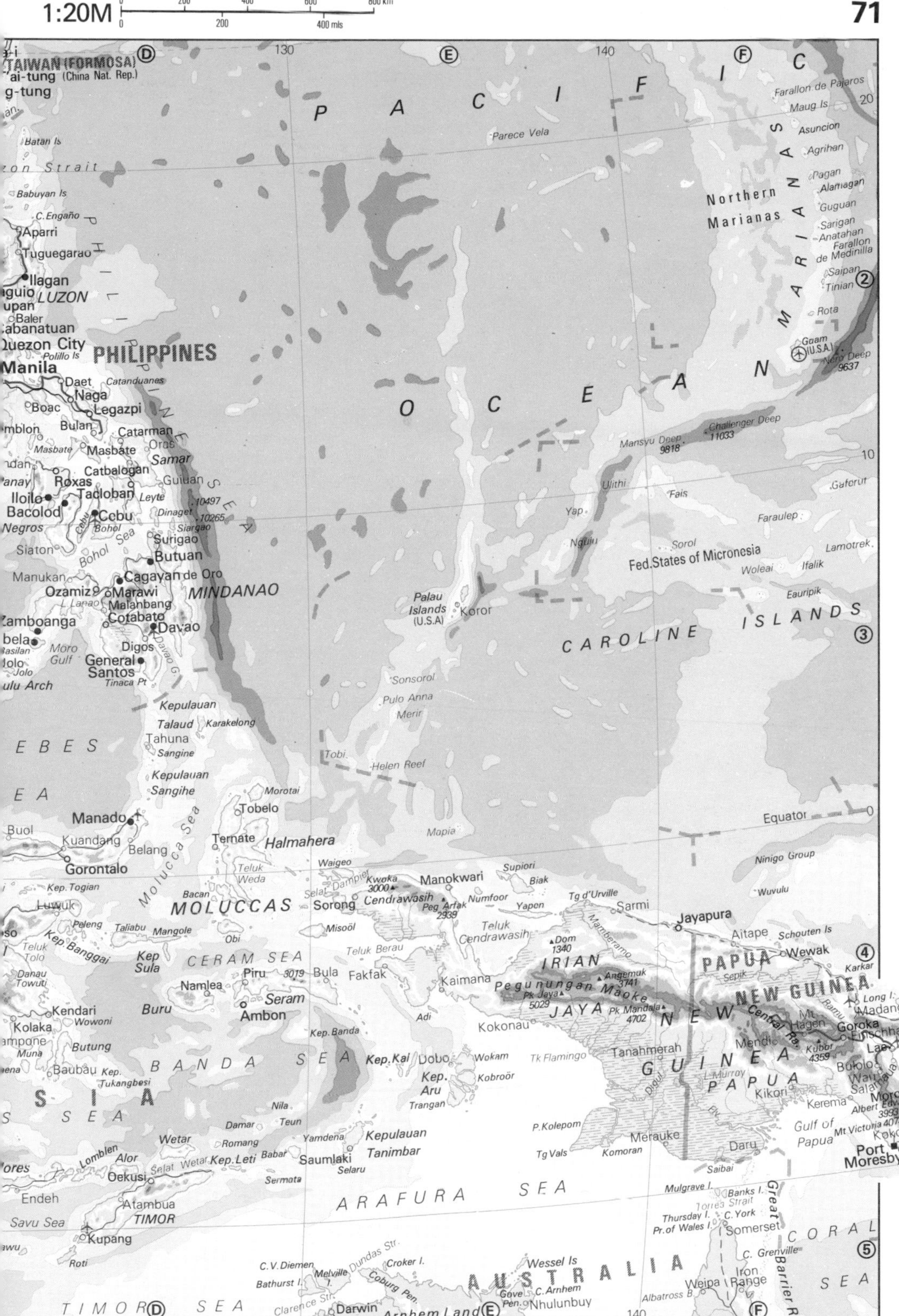
TAIWAN (FORMOSA)
(China Nat. Rep.)
P A C I F I C
O C E A N
Farallon de Pajaros
Maug Is
Asuncion
Agrihan
Pagan
Alamagan
Guguan
Sarigan
Anatahan
Farallon de Medinilla
Saipan
Tinian
Rota
Guam (U.S.A.)
Nero Deep 9637
Northern Marianas
M A R I A N A S
Parece Vela
Batan Is
Babuyan Is
C. Engaño
Aparri
Tuguegarao
Ilagan
LUZON
Baler
Cabanatuan
Quezon City
Polillo Is
Manila
PHILIPPINES
P H I L I P P I N E S E A
Daet
Catanduanes
Naga
Legazpi
Boac
Bulan
Catarman
Masbate
Oras
Samar
Catbalogan
Roxas
Guiuan
Iloilo
Tacloban
Leyte
Bacolod
Cebu
Dinagat
10497
10265
Negros
Bohol
Siargao
Surigao
Bohol Sea
Siaton
Butuan
Manukan
Cagayan de Oro
Ozamiz
Marawi
MINDANAO
L. Lanao
Malanbang
Cotabato
Zamboanga
Davao
Davao G.
Moro Gulf
Digos
General Santos
Jolo
Tinaca Pt
Challenger Deep 11033
Mansyu Deep 9818
Ulithi
Fais
Gaferut
Yap
Faraulep
Ngulu
Sorol
Lamotrek
Fed. States of Micronesia
Woleai
Ifalik
Eauripik
Palau Islands (U.S.A.)
Koror
C A R O L I N E I S L A N D S
Sonsorol
Pulo Anna
Merir
Tobi
Helen Reef
Kepulauan Talaud
Karakelong
Tahuna
Sangine
Kepulauan Sangihe
Morotai
Tobelo
Manado
Mapia
Equator
Buol
Kuandang
Ternate
Halmahera
Belang
Gorontalo
Molucca Sea
Waigeo
Teluk Weda
Kwoka 3000
Manokwari
Supiori
Biak
Ninigo Group
Kep. Togian
Selat Dampier
Cendrawasih
Peg Arfak 2939
Numfoor
Yapen
Tg d'Urville
Sarmi
Wuvulu
Luwuk
Bacan
MOLUCCAS
Sorong
Jayapura
Peleng
Taliabu
Mangole
Misoöl
Teluk Cendrawasih
Dom 1340
Mamberamo
Aitape
Schouten Is
Kep. Banggai
Obi
Teluk Tolo
Kep Sula
C E R A M S E A
Teluk Berau
IRIAN
PAPUA
Wewak
Karkar
Danau Towuti
Piru
3019
Bula
Fakfak
Kaimana
Angemuk 3741
Sepik
NEW GUINEA
Long I.
Madang
Namlea
Seram
Pegunungan Maoke
Pk Jaya 5029
Pk Mandala 4702
JAYA
Ramu
Kendari
Buru
Ambon
Adi
Kokonau
N E W
Central Ra.
Mt Hagen
Goroka
Kolaka
Wowoni
Kep. Banda
Mendi
Kubor 4359
Finschhafen
Lae
Butung
Muna
B A N D A S E A
Kep. Kai
Dobo
Wokam
Tk Flamingo
Tanahmerah
G U I N E A
Baubau
Kep. Tukangbesi
Kep. Aru
Kobroör
Digul
L. Murray
P A P U A
Kikori
Bulolo
Wau
Salamaua
Morobe
Kerema
Albert Edward 3993
Mt Victoria 4073
Kokoda
Gulf of Papua
Port Moresby
Nila
Trangan
Teun
Damar
P. Kolepom
Merauke
Daru
Wetar
Romang
Yamdena
Kepulauan Tanimbar
Tg Vals
Komoran
Saibai
Lomblen
Alor
Selat Wetar
Kep. Leti
Babar
Saumlaki
Selaru
Sermata
Oekusi
Endeh
Atambua
TIMOR
Savu Sea
Kupang
Roti
A R A F U R A S E A
Mulgrave I.
Banks I.
Torres Strait
Thursday I.
C. York
Pr. of Wales I.
Somerset
Great Barrier Rf
C O R A L S E A
C. Grenville
Iron Range
Weipa
Albatross B.
C. V. Diemen
Dundas Str.
Croker I.
Wessel Is
Melville I.
Bathurst I.
Coburg Pen.
A U S T R A L I A
Gove Pen.
C. Arnhem
Nhulunbuy
Clarence Str.
Darwin
Arnhem Land
T I M O R S E A
130
140
20
10
0

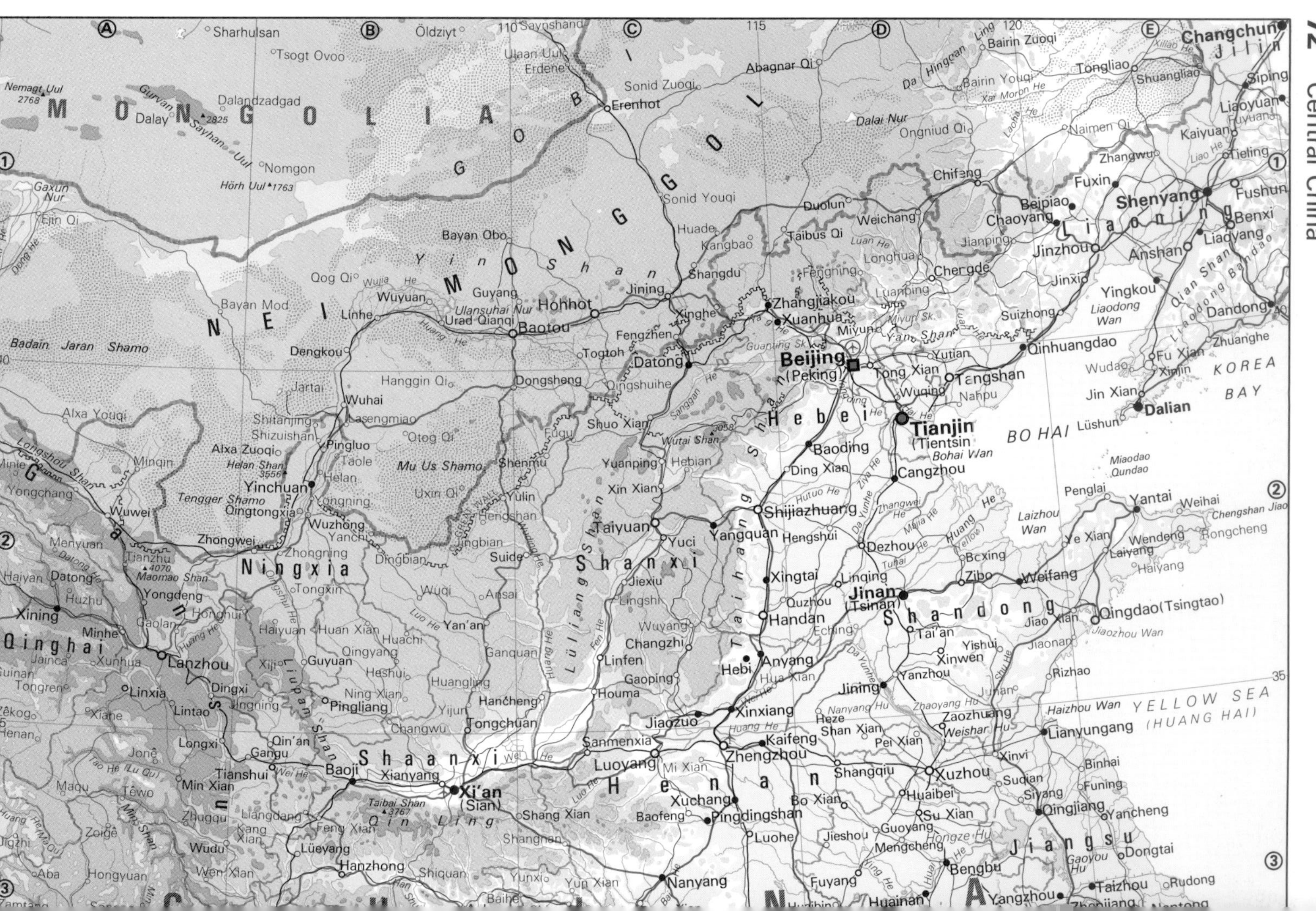
MONGOLIA
NEI MONGGOL
GOBI
Yin Shan
Ningxia
Shaanxi
Shanxi
Hebei
Henan
Shandong
Jiangsu
Liaoning
Jilin
Qinghai
KOREA BAY
BO HAI
YELLOW SEA (HUANG HAI)
Bohai Wan
Laizhou Wan
Liaodong Wan
Haizhou Wan
Jiaozhou Wan
Beijing (Peking)
Tianjin (Tientsin)
Shenyang
Dalian
Changchun
Qingdao (Tsingtao)
Jinan (Tsinan)
Xi'an (Sian)
Lanzhou
Yinchuan
Hohhot
Baotou
Taiyuan
Shijiazhuang
Zhengzhou
Luoyang
Kaifeng
Xining
Datong
Zhangjiakou
Xuanhua
Xuzhou
Tangshan
Qinhuangdao
Anshan
Fushun
Benxi
Liaoyang
Yingkou
Dandong
Jinzhou
Fuxin
Chifeng
Yantai
Weifang
Zibo
Baoding
Cangzhou
Handan
Anyang
Xinxiang
Pingdingshan
Nanyang
Baoji
Tianshui
Hanzhong
Erenhot
Jining
Lianyungang
Bengbu
Huang He
Wei He
Mu Us Shamo
Tengger Shamo
Badain Jaran Shamo
Liupan Shan
Qin Ling
Taihang Shan
Lüliang Shan
Helan Shan
Great Wall

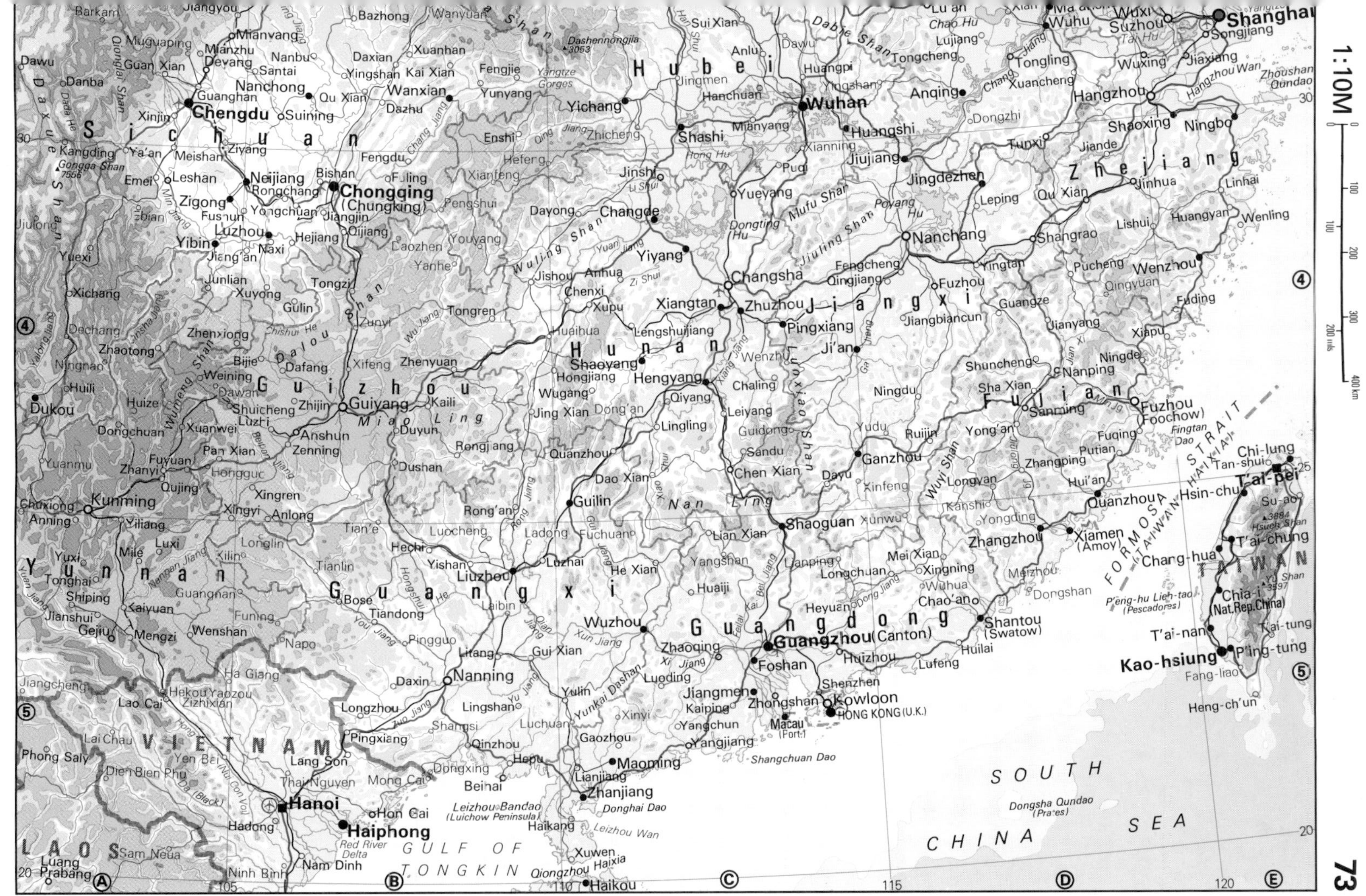
Shanghai
Suzhou
Hangzhou
Ningbo
Wenzhou
Zhejiang
Wuhan
Hubei
Yichang
Shashi
Jiujiang
Nanchang
Jiangxi
Jingdezhen
Ganzhou
Changsha
Zhuzhou
Xiangtan
Hengyang
Hunan
Fuzhou (Foochow)
Fujian
Xiamen (Amoy)
Quanzhou
Zhangzhou
Shantou (Swatow)
Guangzhou (Canton)
Guangdong
Kowloon
HONG KONG (U.K.)
Macau (Port.)
Shenzhen
Foshan
Shaoguan
Zhanjiang
Haikou
Wuzhou
Guilin
Liuzhou
Nanning
Guangxi
Guiyang
Guizhou
Chongqing (Chungking)
Chengdu
Sichuan
Kunming
Yunnan
T'ai-pei
Kao-hsiung
TAIWAN
FORMOSA STRAIT (TAIWAN HAIXIA)
SOUTH CHINA SEA
GULF OF TONGKIN
Hanoi
Haiphong
VIETNAM
LAOS

0 100 200 300 km
0 100 200 mls

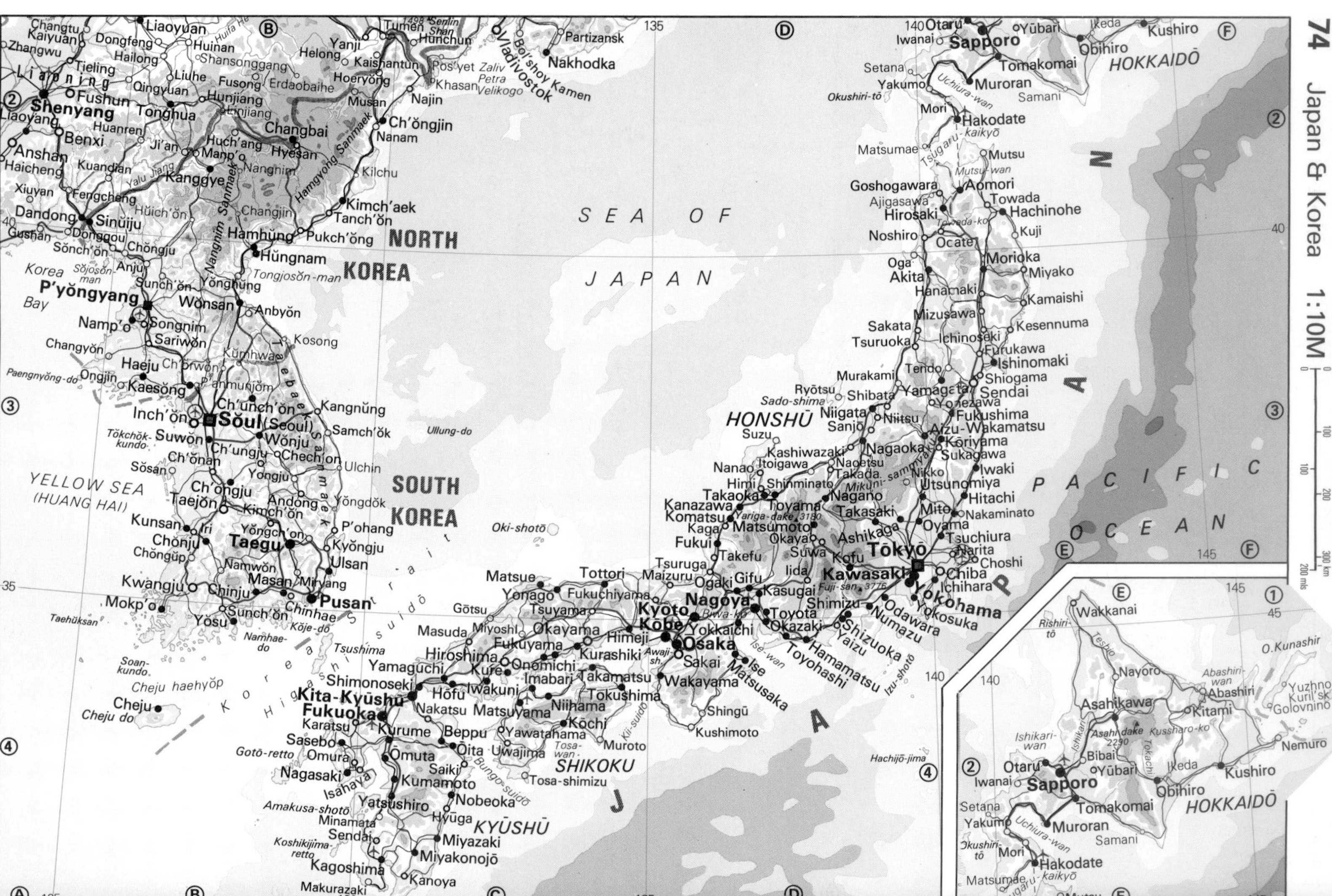

SEA OF JAPAN
PACIFIC OCEAN
JAPAN
NORTH KOREA
SOUTH KOREA
YELLOW SEA (HUANG HAI)
Korea Bay
Korea Strait
HOKKAIDŌ
HONSHŪ
SHIKOKU
KYŪSHŪ
Tōkyō
Yokohama
Kawasaki
Nagoya
Kyoto
Kobe
Ōsaka
Sapporo
Hakodate
Sendai
Niigata
Hiroshima
Kita-Kyūshū
Fukuoka
Nagasaki
Kagoshima
Sŏul (Seoul)
Pusan
Taegu
Inch'ŏn
Kwangju
P'yŏngyang
Wŏnsan
Hamhŭng
Kaesŏng
Sinŭiju
Ch'ŏngjin
Cheju
Vladivostok
Nakhodka
Shenyang
Dandong
Fushun

1:5M

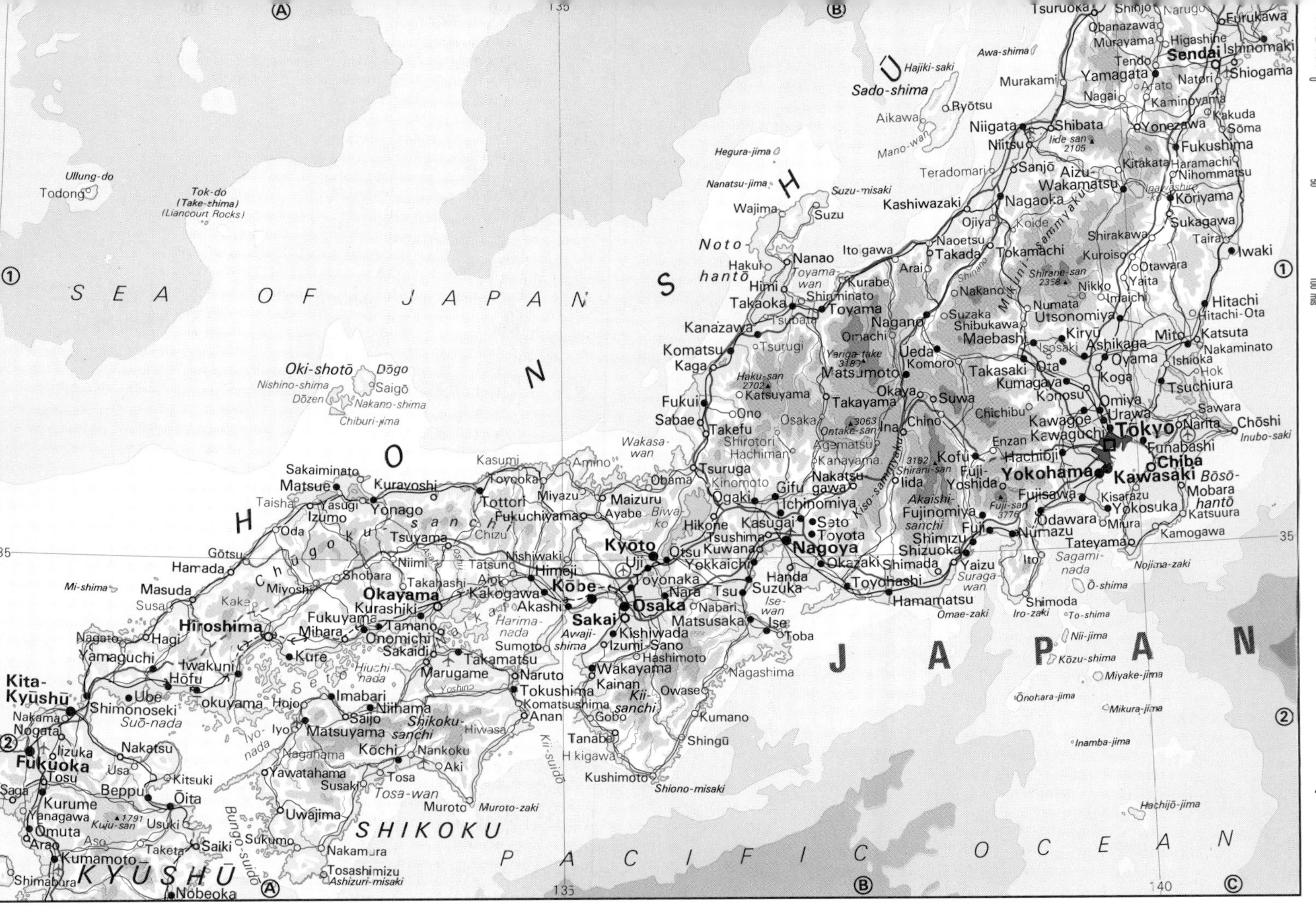

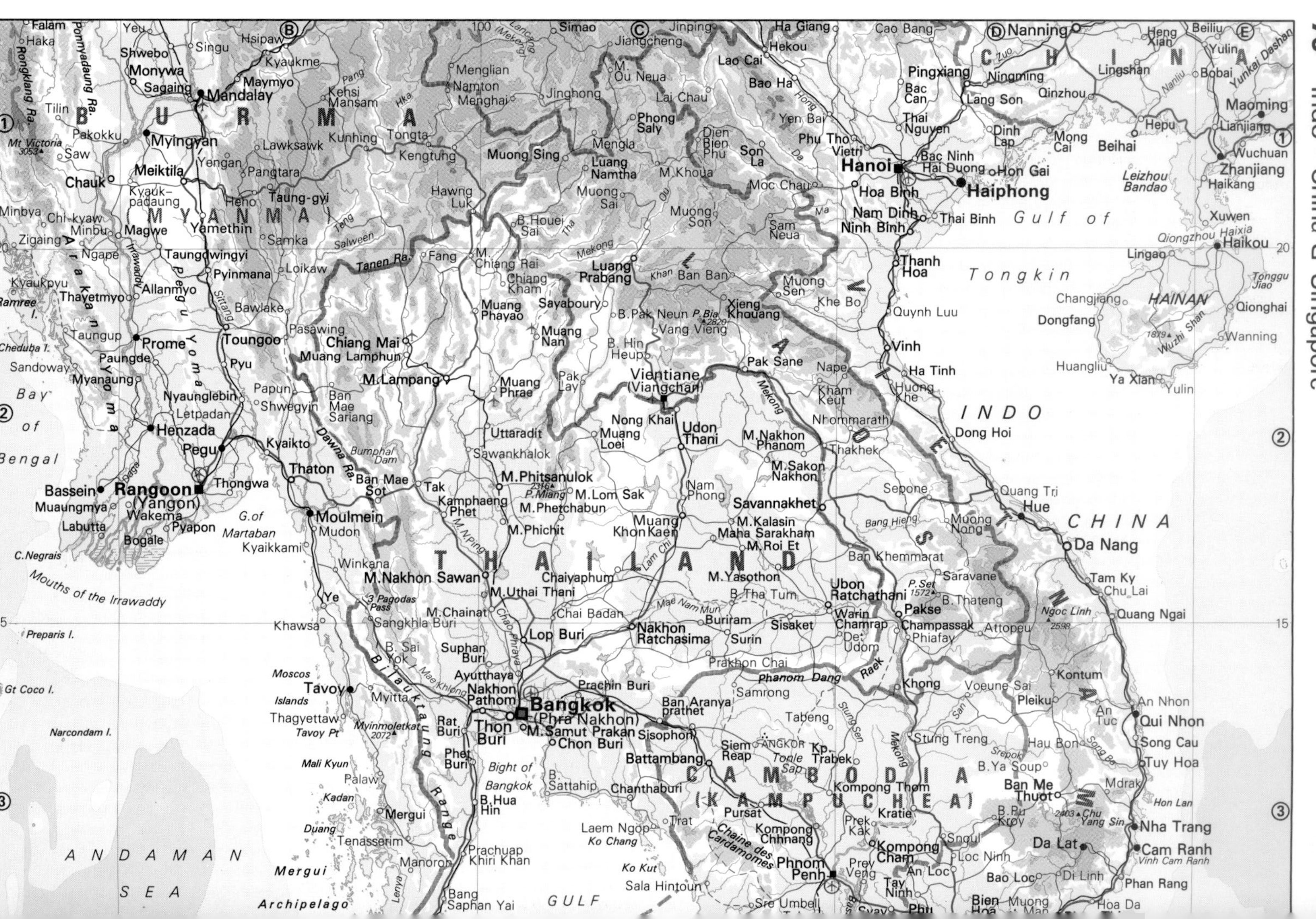
CHINA
BURMA
MYANMAR
LAOS
VIETNAM
THAILAND
CAMBODIA
(KAMPUCHEA)
INDO CHINA
HAINAN
Gulf of Tongkin
ANDAMAN SEA
Bay of Bengal
G.of Martaban
Mergui Archipelago
Mouths of the Irrawaddy
Bight of Bangkok
Leizhou Bandao
Nanning
Zhanjiang
Haikou
Hanoi
Haiphong
Vinh
Hue
Da Nang
Qui Nhon
Nha Trang
Cam Ranh
Da Lat
Vientiane (Viangchan)
Luang Prabang
Udon Thani
Savannakhet
Pakse
Nakhon Ratchasima
Bangkok (Phra Nakhon)
Chiang Mai
Phnom Penh
Battambang
Mandalay
Rangoon (Yangon)
Moulmein
Bassein
Prome
Toungoo
Pegu
Henzada
Tavoy
Mergui

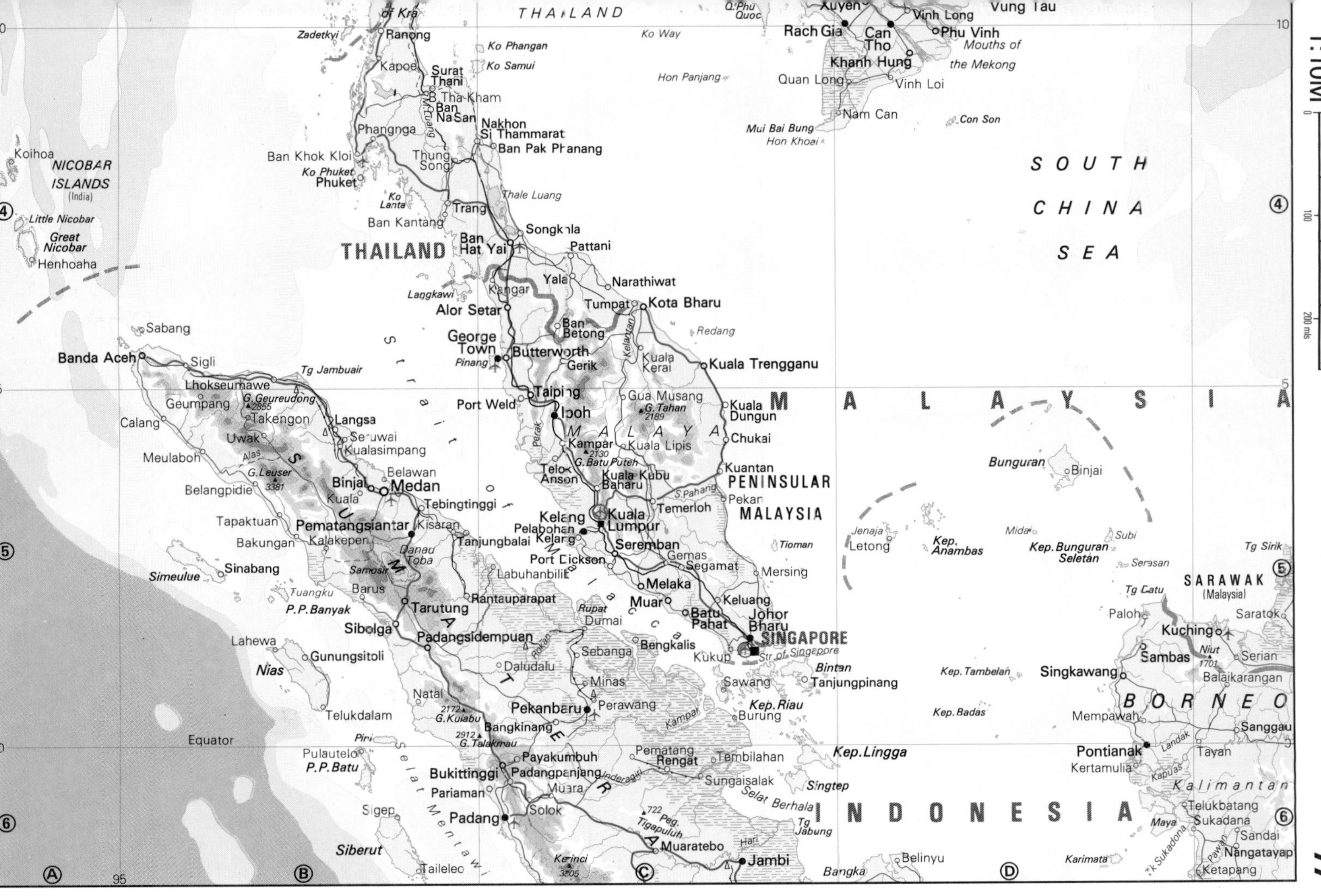

1:10M

1:10M

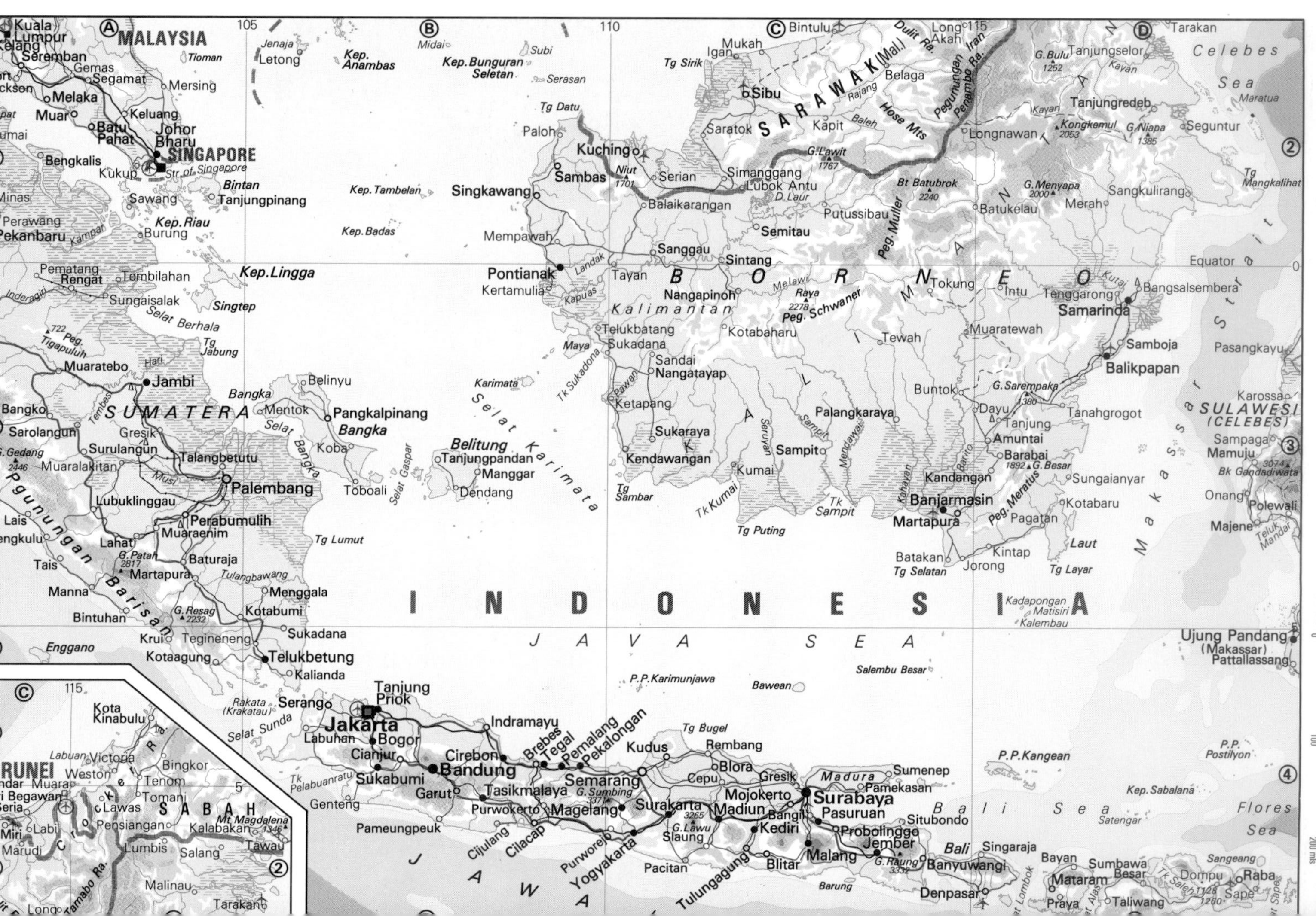

MALAYSIA
SINGAPORE
SARAWAK (Mal.)
BORNEO
Kalimantan
SUMATERA
SULAWESI (CELEBES)
INDONESIA
JAVA SEA
JAWA
Celebes Sea
Makassar Strait
Bali Sea
Flores Sea
Selat Karimata
Selat Sunda
Pegunungan Barisan
Hose Mts
Peg. Muller
Peg. Schwaner
Peg. Meratus
Equator
Kuala Lumpur
Kelang
Seremban
Melaka
Segamat
Mersing
Muar
Keluang
Batu Pahat
Johor Bharu
Str. of Singapore
Dumai
Bengkalis
Tanjungpinang
Kep. Riau
Pekanbaru
Kep. Lingga
Kep. Anambas
Kep. Bunguran Seletan
Kep. Tambelan
Kep. Badas
Singtep
Jambi
Bangka
Pangkalpinang
Palembang
Lubuklinggau
Perabumulih
Muaraenim
Lahat
Bengkulu
Kotabumi
Menggala
Telukbetung
Enggano
Belitung
Tanjungpandan
Manggar
Karimata
Kuching
Sambas
Singkawang
Pontianak
Sibu
Bintulu
Mukah
Kapit
Sanggau
Sintang
Nangapinoh
Ketapang
Sampit
Kumai
Palangkaraya
Banjarmasin
Martapura
Kotabaru
Balikpapan
Samarinda
Tanjungredeb
Tarakan
Ujung Pandang (Makassar)
Jakarta
Tanjung Priok
Bogor
Sukabumi
Bandung
Cirebon
Indramayu
Tegal
Pekalongan
Semarang
Kudus
Magelang
Yogyakarta
Surakarta
Madiun
Kediri
Surabaya
Malang
Madura
Jember
Banyuwangi
Bali
Denpasar
Mataram
Sumbawa Besar
BRUNEI
Bandar Seri Begawan
SABAH
Kota Kinabalu
Tawau
Miri

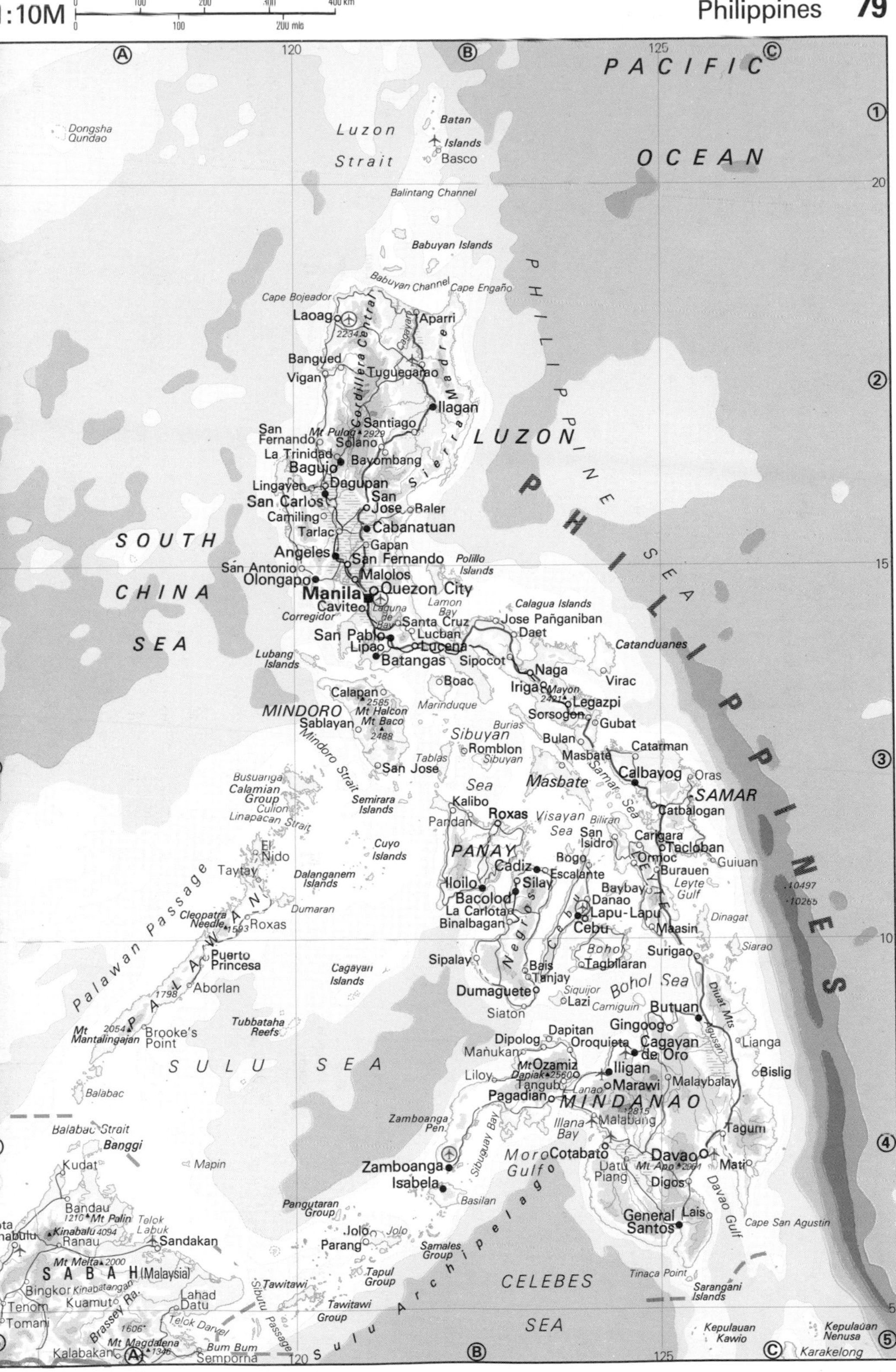

:10M

0   100   200   300   400 km
0   100   200 mia

PACIFIC

OCEAN

Luzon
Strait

Batan
Islands
Basco

Balintang Channel

Babuyan Islands

Dongsha
Qundao

Cape Bojeador
Babuyan Channel   Cape Engaño

Laoag
2234   Aparri

Bangued   Tuguegarao
Vigan

San   Mt Pulog 2929
Fernando   Santiago   Ilagan
Solano
La Trinidad   **LUZON**
Baguio   Bayombang
Lingayen   Dagupan
San Carlos   San
Camiling   Jose   Baler
Tarlac   Cabanatuan
Angeles   Gapan
San Antonio   San Fernando   Polillo
Olongapo   Malolos   Islands
Manila   Quezon City
Cavite   Lamon
Corregidor   Laguna   Bay
Santa Cruz   Jose Pañganiban
San Pablo   Lucban   Daet
Lipao   Lucena   Calagua Islands
Lubang   Batangas   Sipocot
Islands   Boac   Naga   Virac
Calapan   Marinduque   Iriga   Legazpi   *Catanduanes*
2585   Mayon
MINDORO   Mt Halcon   Sorsogon   Gubat
Sablayan   Mt Baco   Bulan   Catarman
2488   Burias
Mindoro Strait   *Sibuyan*   Masbate   Calbayog
San Jose   Romblon   Oras
Busuanga   *Tablas*   Sibuyan   **Masbate**   **SAMAR**
Calamian   Sea   Catbalogan
Group   Kalibo   *Visayan*   Biliran
Culion   Roxas   *Sea*   Cangara
Linapacan Strait   Pandan   San   Tacloban
El   **PANAY**   Isidro   Ormoc
Nido   Cadiz   Bogo   Guiuan
Taytay   Cuyo   Iloilo   Silay   Escalante   Baybay
Islands   Bacolod   Danao   *Leyte*
Dalanganem   La Carlota   Lapu-Lapu   *Gulf*
Islands   Binalbagan   Cebu   Maasin   *Dinagat*
Dumaran   Sipalay   Bais   *Bohol*   Surigao
Cleopatras   Tagbilaran   *Siargao*
Needle 1563   Roxas   Tanjay   *Siquijor*
Puerto   Cagayan   Dumaguete   Lazi   *Camiguin*   Butuan
Princesa   Islands   Siaton   *Bohol Sea*   Gingoog
Aborlan   Dapitan   Cagayan   *Dinat Mts*   Lianga
Mt   2054   Dipolog   Oroquieta   de Oro
Mantalingajan   Brooke's   Mañukan   Iligan   Malaybalay   Bislig
Point   Liloy   Mt Ozamiz   Marawi
Dapiak 2550
SULU   **SEA**   Tangub   **MINDANAO**
Tubbataha   Pagadian   *Lanao*   Malabang   Tagum
Reefs   Zamboanga   Illana   Mt Apo 2951
Balabac   Pen.   *Bay*   Davao   Mati
Zamboanga   Cotabato   Digos
Isabela   Datu   Lais
Banggi   Basilan   Piang   General   *Davao Gulf*
Kudat   Santos   Cape San Agustin
Bandau   Pangutaran
1210 Mt Palin   Group   Jolo   *Jolo*   *Samales*   *Tinaca Point*
Kinabalu 4094   Sandakan   Parang   *Group*   *Sarangani*
Ranau   *Tapul*   *Islands*
Mt Melta 2000   Tawitawi   *Group*   **CELEBES**
SABAH (Malaysia)   *Group*
Bingkor Kinabatangan   Tawitawi   *Sulu   Archipelago*
Tenom   Datu   Group   **SEA**
Tomani   1606   *Kepulauan*   *Kepulauan*
Kuamut   Brassey Ra   *Kawio*   *Nenusa*
Lahad
Kalabakan   Mt Magdalena   Telok Darvel   125   *Karakelong*
1745   Bum Bum
Semporna   120

SOUTH
CHINA
SEA

Palawan Passage

PALAWAN

Palawan Passage

Moro
Gulf

Sibuguey Bay

Negros
Panay
Cebu

120   **A**   **B**   125   **C**

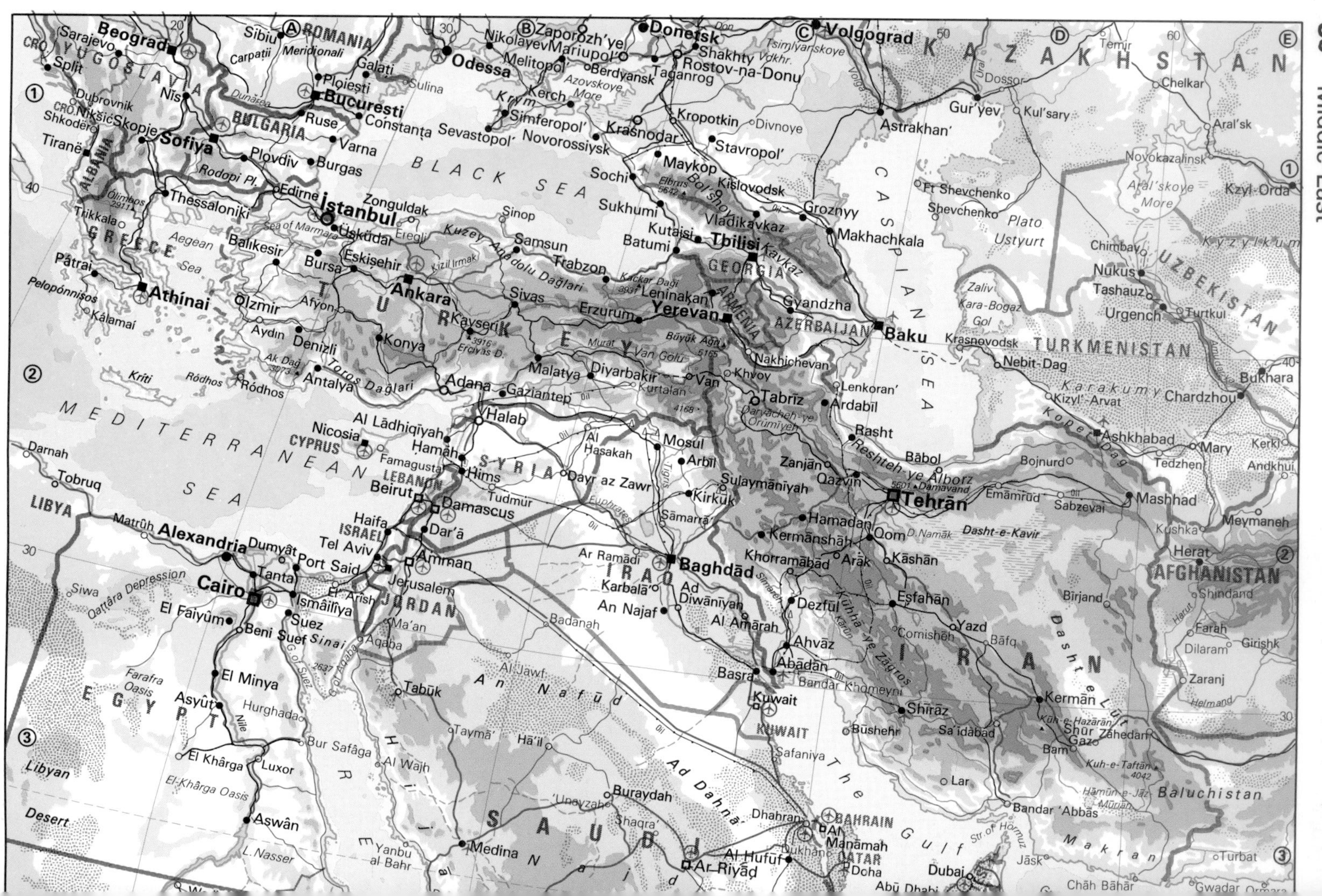
KAZAKHSTAN
UZBEKISTAN
TURKMENISTAN
AFGHANISTAN
IRAN
IRAQ
SYRIA
TURKEY
SAUDI
EGYPT
JORDAN
LEBANON
ISRAEL
KUWAIT
BAHRAIN
QATAR
CYPRUS
GEORGIA
ARMENIA
AZERBAIJAN
YUGOSLAVIA
ALBANIA
GREECE
BULGARIA
ROMANIA
LIBYA
BLACK SEA
CASPIAN SEA
MEDITERRANEAN SEA
The Gulf
Aral'skoye More
Volgograd
Astrakhan'
Gur'yev
Donetsk
Rostov-na-Donu
Odessa
Baku
Tbilisi
Yerevan
Tehrān
Mashhad
Herat
Baghdād
Basra
Kuwait
Ar Riyāḍ
Damascus
Beirut
Amman
Jerusalem
Tel Aviv
Cairo
Alexandria
Port Said
Suez
Nicosia
Ankara
Istanbul
Bucureşti
Sofiya
Beograd
Athínai
Thessaloníki
Tiranë
Skopje
Esfahān
Shīrāz
Tabrīz
Kermān
Yazd
Mosul
Halab
Adana
Konya
Izmir
Bursa
Trabzon
Erzurum
Medina
Tabūk
Dubai
Doha
Manāmah
Dhahran
Bukhara
Chardzhou
Ashkhabad
Nukus
Urgench
Tashauz
Makhachkala
Groznyy
Batumi
Sukhumi
Sochi
Krasnodar
Stavropol'
Zaporozh'ye
Mariupol'
Simferopol'
Sevastopol'
Novorossiysk
Ad Dahnā
An Nafūd
Dasht-e Lūt
Dasht-e-Kavīr
Kūhhā-ye Zāgros
Reshteh-ye Alborz
Karakumy
Baluchistan
Makran
Libyan Desert
Sinai
Aswân
Luxor
Asyût
El Minya
El Faiyûm
Tobruq
Siwa
Qattâra Depression

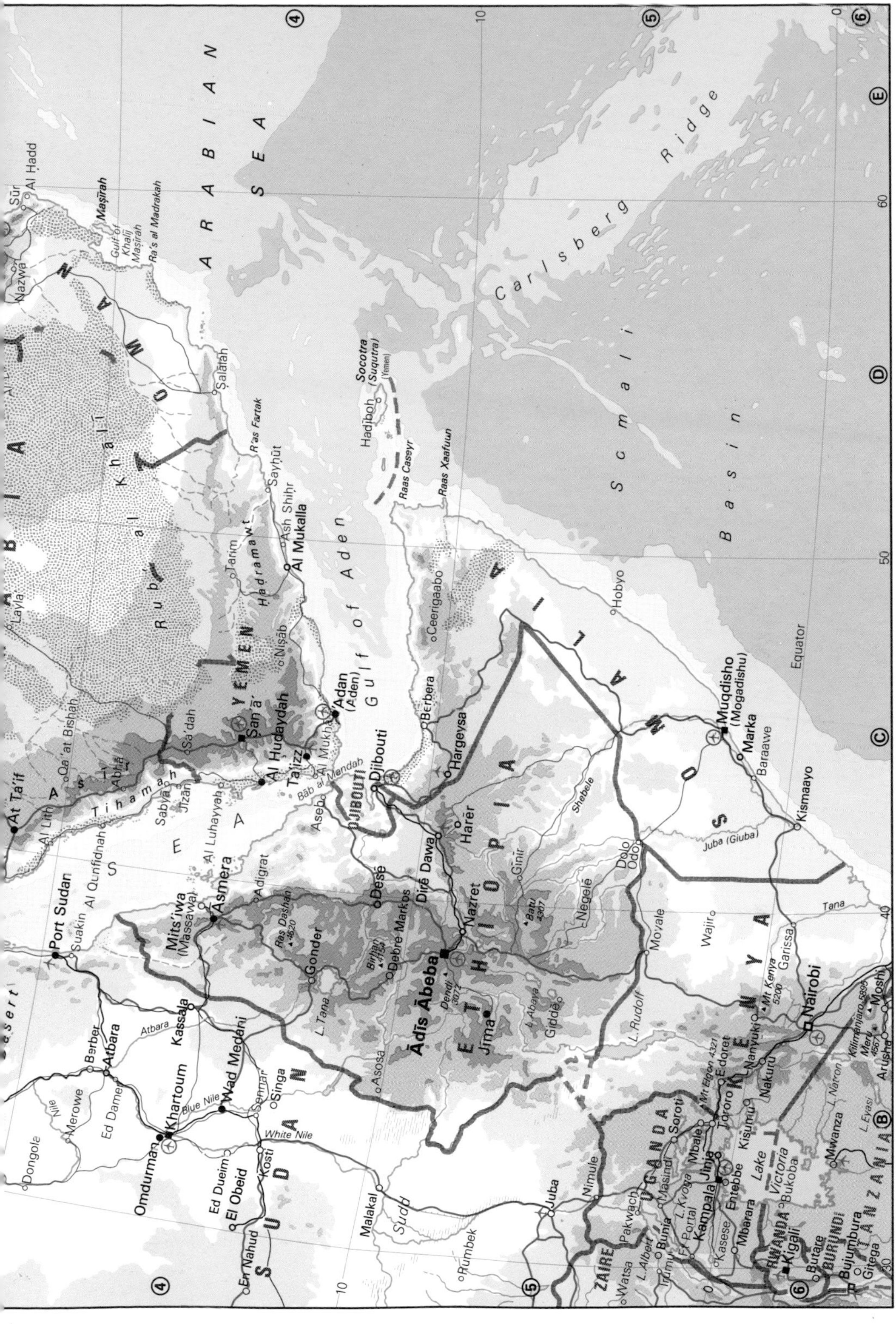

200 400 600 800 km
0
200 400 mls
0

ARABIAN SEA

Carlsberg Ridge

Socotra
(Suqutra)
(Yemen)

Somali Basin

Sūr
Al Hadd
Naziwa
Masirah
Gulf of Khalij
Masirah
Ra's al Madrakah

O M A N

Rub' al Khali

Ra's Fartak
Raas Caseyr
Hadiboh
Raas Xaafuun

Salālah
Savhūt
Ash Shihr
Al Mukalla
Tarīm
Hadramawt
An Nisāb

Layla
Al Lith
Qa' at Bīshah
YEMEN
Sa'dah
San'ā'
Al Hudaydah
Ta'izz
Al Mukhā
Adan (Aden)
Gulf of Aden

Ceerigaabo
Berbera
Hobyo

At Tā'if
A s i r
Al Luhayyah
Sabya
Jizan
Tihamah
Bāb al Mandab
Aseb
Mendab
Djibouti
Hargeysa

Muqdisho (Mogadishu)
Marka
Baraawe

Port Sudan
Suakin
Mits'iwa (Massawa)
Asmera
Adigrat
Adigrat
Ras Dashan 4620
Dese
Debre Markos
Dire Dawa
Harer
Nazret
Batu 4307
Shebele
Gīnīr
Dolo Odo
Juba (Giuba)
Kismaayo
Equator

Berber
Atbara
Kassala
Wad Medani
Gonder
Birhan
Bahir Dar
L. Tana
ADīs Ābeba
Dendi 3072
Jima
Gīdolē
A. Abaya
Negelē
Movale
Wajir
L. Rudolf
Tana

Dongola
Merowe
Ed Damer
Atbara
Nile
Khartoum
Omdurman
Blue Nile
Sennar
Singa
White Nile
Kosti
Asosa
SUDAN
ETHIOPIA
K E N Y A
Garissa
Nairobi
Mt Kenya 5200
Nanyuki
Meru 4567

Er Nahud
Ed Dueim
El Obeid
Malakal
Sudd
Juba
Rumbek
Nimule
ZAIRE
Watsa
Bunia
Pakwach
L. Albert
UGANDA
Soroti
Mbale
Tororo
Kisumu
Eldoret
Kitale
Mt Elgon 4321
Nakuru
L. Naron
L. Evasi
Mwanza
Moshi
Kilimanjaro 5895
Arusha

Butare
Kigali
RWANDA
BURUNDI
Bujumbura
Gitega
Kampala
Jinja
Entebbe
Lake Victoria
Bukoba
TANZANIA
Mbarara
L. Kivu
L. Kyoga
Kasese
Fort Portal
Masindi

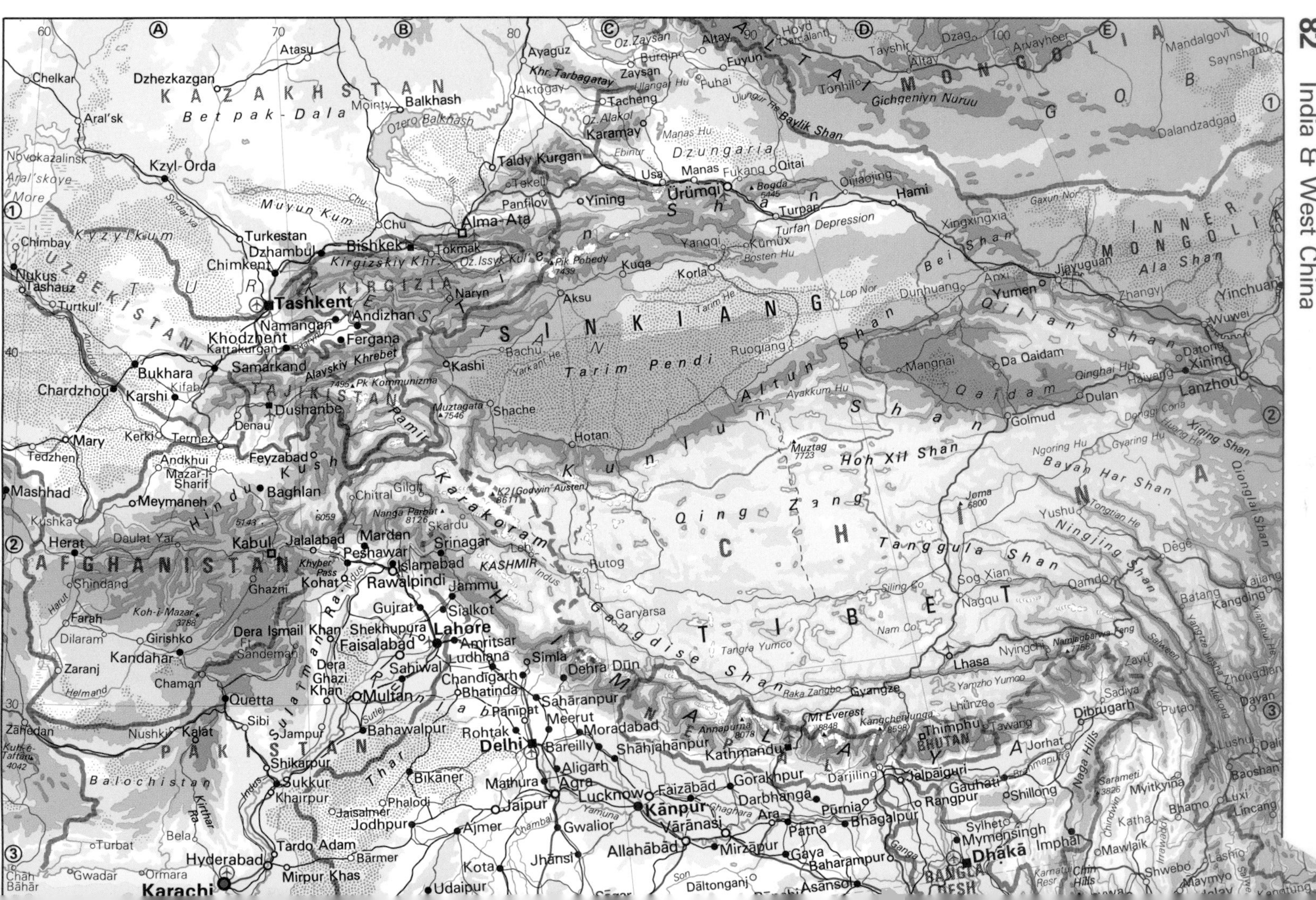

KAZAKHSTAN
UZBEKISTAN
KIRGIZIA
TAJIKISTAN
AFGHANISTAN
PAKISTAN
SINKIANG
TIBET
CHINA
MONGOLIA
INNER MONGOLIA
Tashkent
Alma-Ata
Bishkek
Dushanbe
Kabul
Islamabad
Rawalpindi
Lahore
Delhi
Karachi
Kathmandu
Thimphu
Lhasa
Ürümqi
Lanzhou
Xining
Dhākā
Kānpur
Lucknow
Tarim Pendi
Kunlun Shan
Karakoram
Hindu Kush
Qilian Shan
Altun Shan
Tanggula Shan
Gangdise Shan
Mt Everest

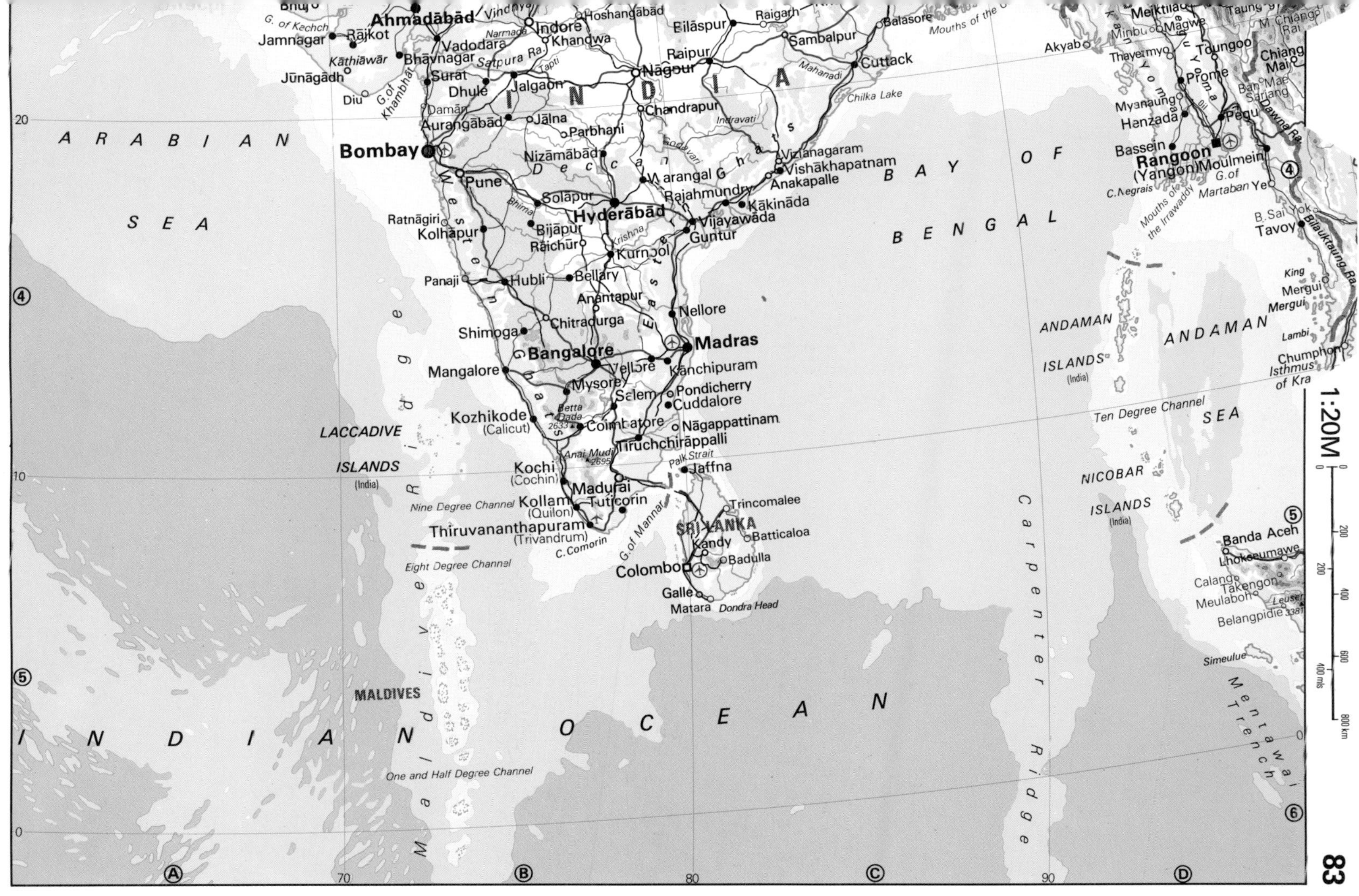

1:20M

0   200   400   600   800 km
0   200   400 mils

ARABIAN
SEA

BAY

OF

BENGAL

INDIA

DECCAN

Western   Ghats

Eastern   Ghats

ANDAMAN   SEA

Carpenter   Ridge

Mentawai
Trench

INDIAN

OCEAN

MALDIVES

LACCADIVE
ISLANDS
(India)

ANDAMAN
ISLANDS
(India)

NICOBAR
ISLANDS
(India)

SRI LANKA

Bombay
Ahmadābād
Rājkot
Jamnāgar
Junāgadh
Vadodara
Bhāvnagar
Surat
Diu
Damān
Dhule
Jalgaon
Aurangābād
Nāsik
Pune
Kolhāpur
Ratnāgiri
Panaji
Mangalore
Shimoga
Hubli
Bijāpur
Solāpur
Indore
Hoshangābād
Khandwa
Ujjain
Nāgpur
Bhir
Bilāspur
Raipur
Raigarh
Sambalpur
Balasore
Cuttack
Hyderābād
Nizāmābād
Warangal
Rāichūr
Bellary
Anantapur
Chitradurga
Bangalore
Mysore
Kozhikode
(Calicut)
Kochi
(Cochin)
Kollam
(Quilon)
Thiruvananthapuram
(Trivandrum)
Coimbatore
Salem
Tiruchchirāppalli
Madurai
Tuticorin
Nāgappattinam
Cuddalore
Pondicherry
Kānchipuram
Nellore
Madras
Guntūr
Vijayawāda
Rājahmundry
Kākināda
Anakapalle
Vishākhapatnam
Vizianagaram
Chandrapur
Farbhani
Pārbhani
Kurnool
Hyderābād

Colombo
Galle
Matara
Dondra Head
Kandy
Badulla
Batticaloa
Trincomalee
Jaffna

Banda Aceh
Lhokseumawe
Meulaboh
Calang
Takengon
Lhoksukon
Belangpidie
Simeuluë

Rangoon
(Yangon)
Moulmein
Bassein
Hanzada
Myanaung
Prome
Thayetmyo
Myaungmya
Akyabō
Toungoo
Pyu
Ban Mae
Chiang Mai
Chiang Rai
Tavoy
B. Savoy
Mergui
King
Lambi
Chumphon
Isthmus
of Kra

Mouths of the Irrawaddy

Mouths of the Ganges

Chilka Lake

Palk Strait
Gulf of Mannar
Adam's Bridge

Ten Degree Channel
Nine Degree Channel
Eight Degree Channel
One and Half Degree Channel

C. Comorin
C. Negrais

20
10
70
80
90

4
5
6

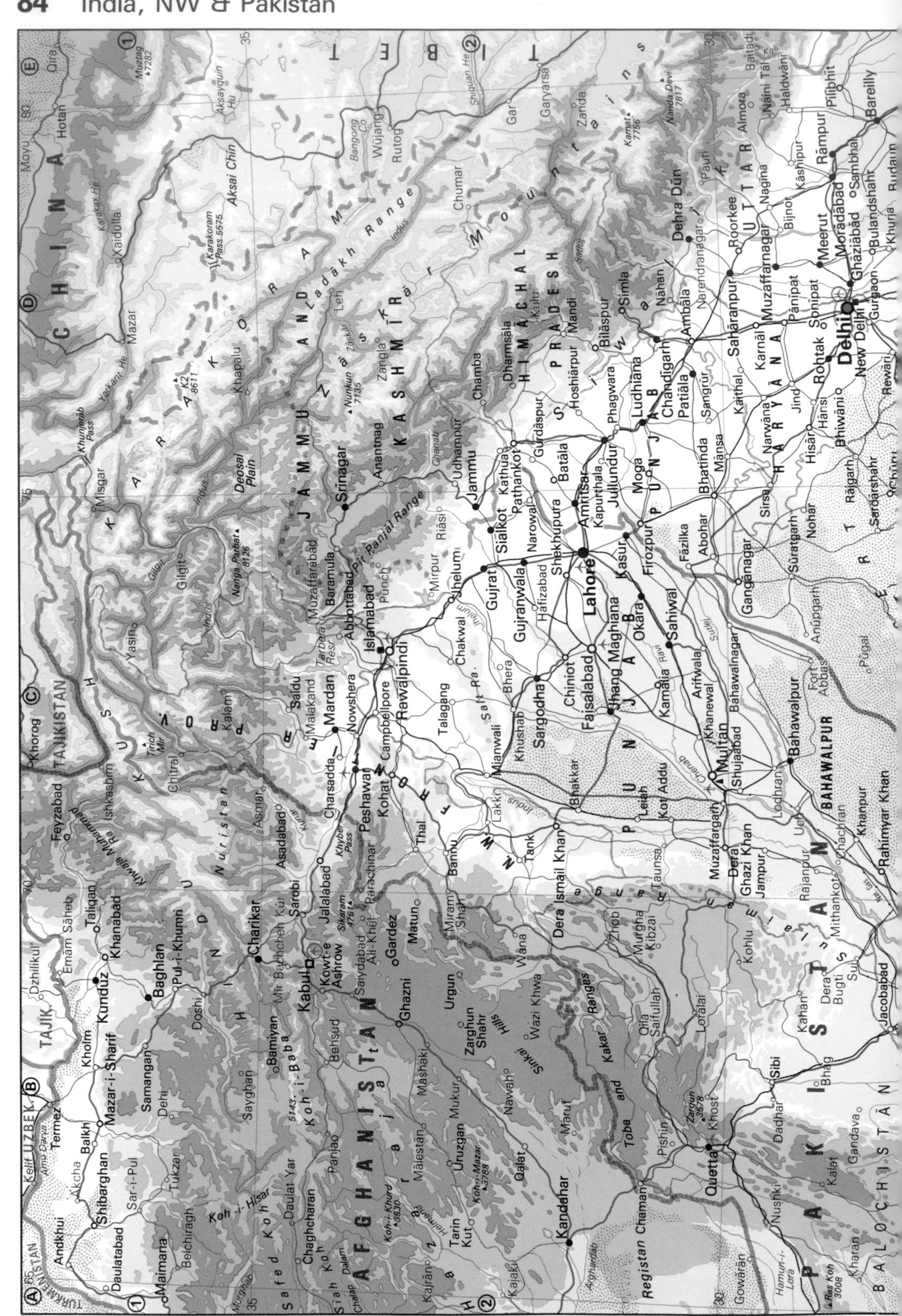
CHINA
AFGHANISTAN
PAKISTAN
TAJIKISTAN
UZBEK.
TURKMENISTAN
JAMMU AND KASHMIR
HIMACHAL PRADESH
PUNJAB
HARYANA
UTTAR PRADESH
BALOCHISTAN
N.W. FRONTIER
BAHAWALPUR
Kabul
Islamabad
Rawalpindi
Peshawar
Lahore
Delhi
New Delhi
Srinagar
Kandahar
Quetta
Multan
Faisalabad
Amritsar
Ludhiana
Chandigarh
Jammu
Simla
Meerut
Moradabad
Saharanpur
Dehra Dūn
Ghazni
Charikar
Kunduz
Baghlan
Mazar-i-Sharif
Shibarghan
Maimana
Sialkot
Gujranwala
Gujrat
Sargodha
Jhang Maghiana
Okara
Sahiwal
Bahawalpur
Dera Ghazi Khan
Dera Ismail Khan
Mardan
Sibi
Jacobabad
Hindu Kush
Karakoram
Ladakh Range
Pir Panjal Range
Toba and Kakar Ranges
Registan
Nuristan
K2 8611
Nanga Parbat 8126
Tirich Mir
Khyber Pass
Indus

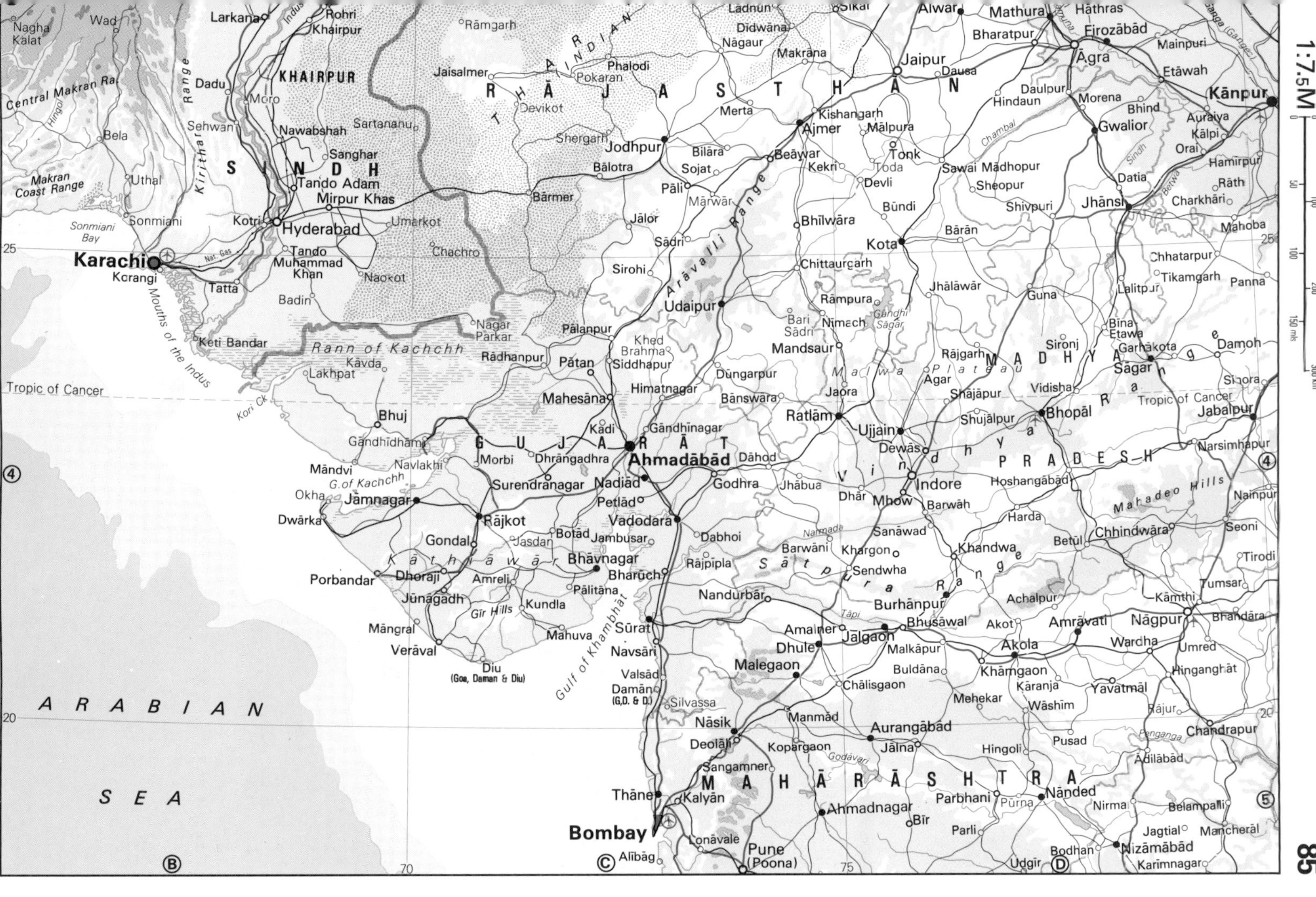

1:7.5M

100   200   300 km

50   100   150 mls

1:7.5M

0 100 200 300 km
0 50 100 150 mls

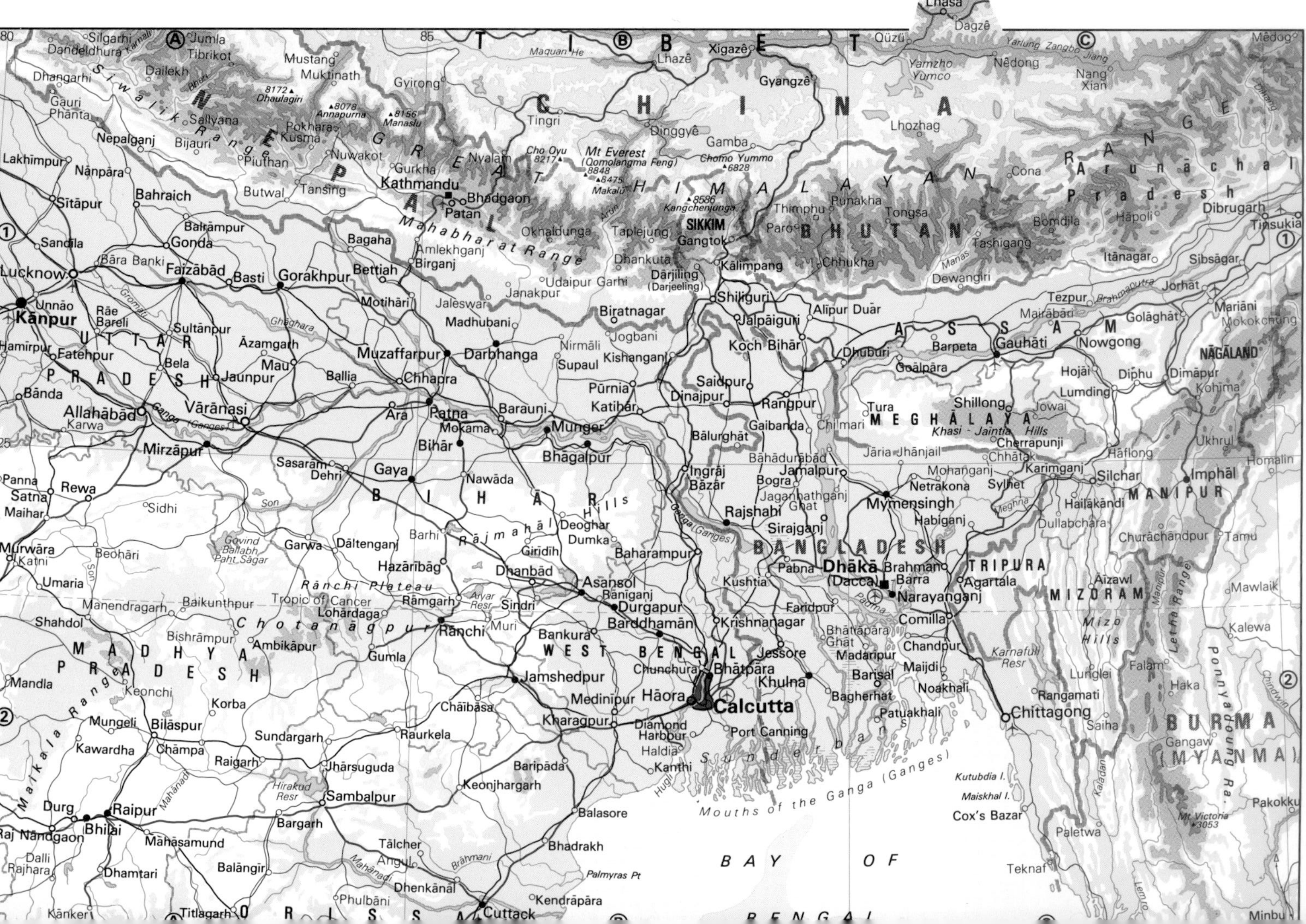

TIBET
CHINA
NEPAL
BHUTAN
SIKKIM
BANGLADESH
BURMA (MYANMA)
ASSAM
MEGHALAYA
NAGALAND
MANIPUR
MIZORAM
TRIPURA
Arunachal Pradesh
WEST BENGAL
BIHAR
ORISSA
UTTAR PRADESH
MADHYA PRADESH
GREAT HIMALAYAN RANGE
Mahabharat Range
Siwalik Range
Chotanagpur
Ranchi Plateau
Rajmahal Hills
Khasi - Jaintia Hills
Mizo Hills
Letha Range
Ponnyadoung Ra.
Maikala Range
BAY OF BENGAL
Mouths of the Ganga (Ganges)
Sundarbans
Tropic of Cancer
Mt Everest (Qomolangma Feng) 8848
Kangchenjunga 8586
Makalu 8475
Cho Oyu 8217
Dhaulagiri 8172
Manaslu 8156
Annapurna 8078
Chomo Yummo 6828
Mt Victoria 3053
Lhasa
Kathmandu
Thimphu
Dhākā (Dacca)
Calcutta
Chittagong
Patna
Vārānasi
Allahābād
Kānpur
Lucknow
Gauhāti
Shillong
Imphāl
Cuttack
Raipur
Jamshedpur
Rānchi
Gaya
Dārjiling (Darjeeling)
Gangtok
Cox's Bazar
Kutubdia I.
Maiskhal I.
Palmyras Pt

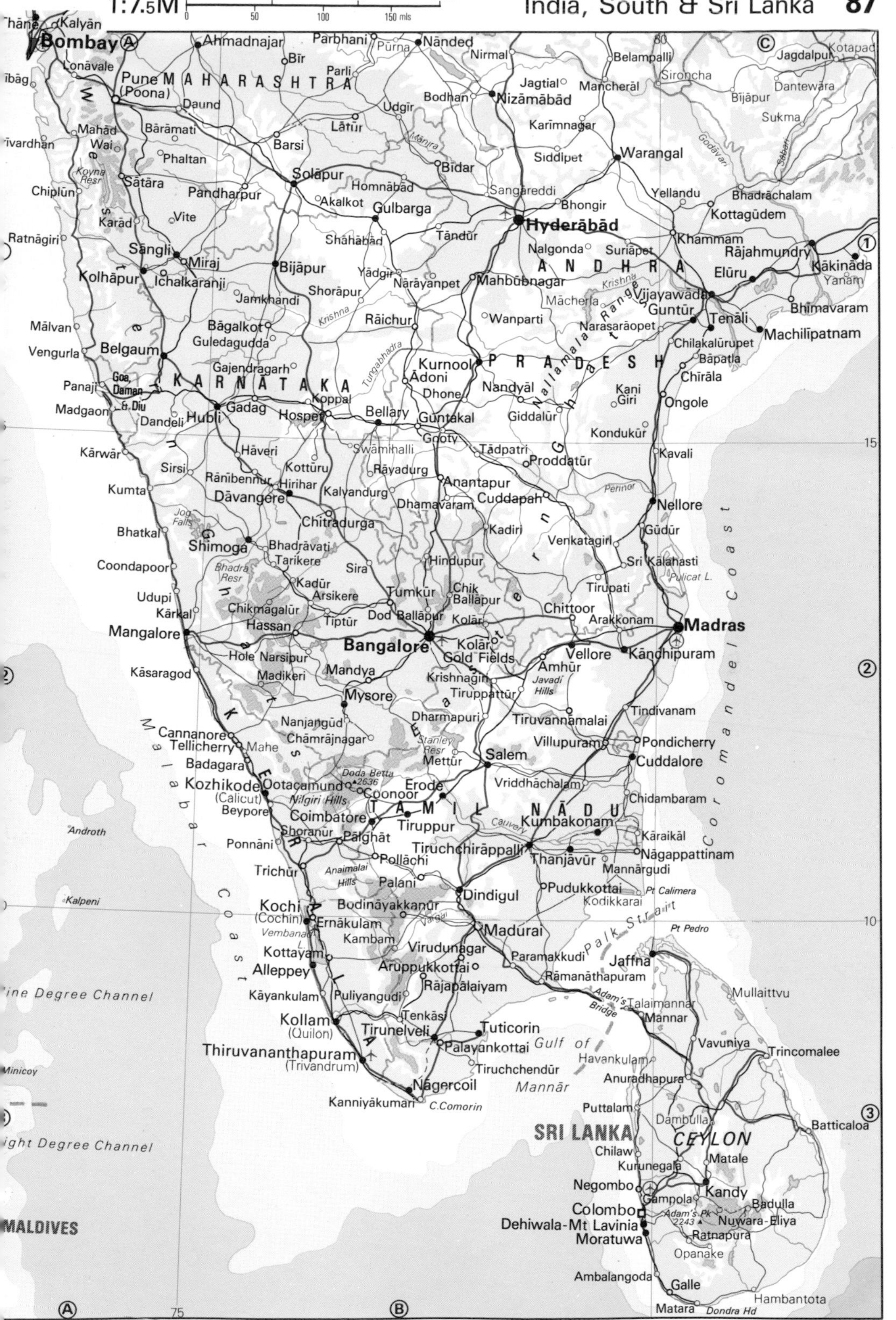
Thāne
Kalyān
Bombay
Lonāvale
Pune (Poona)
MAHARASHTRA
Ahmadnajar
Bīr
Parbhani
Pūrna
Nānded
Nirmal
Belampalli
Sironcha
Jagdalpur
Kotapad
Dantewāra
Bījāpur
Sukma
Parli
Daund
Udgīr
Bodhan
Nizāmābād
Jagtial
Mancherāl
Karīmnagar
Bārāmati
Lātūr
Barsi
Mahād
Wai
Phaltan
Mānjra
Bīdar
Siddipet
Warangal
Godāvari
Sabari
Shrivardhan
Koyna Resr
Sātāra
Solāpur
Homnābād
Sangāreddi
Yellandu
Bhadrāchalam
Chiplūn
Pandharpur
Akalkot
Gulbarga
Bhongir
Kottagūdem
Karād
Vite
Shāhābād
Tāndūr
Hyderābād
Khammam
Ratnāgiri
Sāngli
Miraj
Nalgonda
Suriāpet
Rājahmundry
Kākināda
Yanam
Kolhāpur
Ichalkaranji
Bijāpur
Yādgir
Nārāyanpet
Mahbūbnagar
ANDHRA
Elūru
Krishna
Vijayawāda
Bhīmavaram
Jamkhandi
Shorāpur
Mācherla
Guntūr
Mālvan
Bāgalkot
Rāichur
Wanparti
Narasarāopet
Tenāli
Machilīpatnam
Guledagudda
Vengurla
Belgaum
Tungabhadra
Nallamala Range
Chilakalūrupet
Gajendragarh
Kurnool
PRADESH
Bāpatla
Panaji
Goa, Daman & Diu
KARNATAKA
Ādoni
Chīrāla
Madgaon
Gadag
Koppal
Dhone
Nandyāl
Kani Giri
Ongole
Dandeli
Hubli
Hospet
Bellary
Guntakal
Giddalūr
Kondukūr
Gooty
Kārwār
Hāveri
Swāmihalli
Tādpatri
Kavali
Sirsi
Kottūru
Rāyadurg
Proddatūr
Rānibennur
Hirihar
Anantapur
Kumta
Dāvangere
Kalyandurg
Pennar
Dhamavaram
Cuddapah
Nellore
Jog Falls
Chitradurga
Bhatkal
Kadiri
Gūdūr
Shimoga
Bhadrāvati
Venkatagiri
Tarikere
Coondapoor
Bhadra Resr
Hindupur
Sri Kālahasti
Sira
Pulicat L.
Kadūr
Arsikere
Tumkūr
Chik Ballāpur
Tirupati
Udupi
Kārkal
Chikmagalūr
Tiptūr
Dod Ballāpur
Chittoor
Hassan
Kolār
Arakkonam
Mangalore
Madras
Bangalore
Kolār Gold Fields
Vellore
Kānchipuram
Hole Narsipur
Amhūr
Kāsaragod
Mandya
Madikeri
Krishnagiri
Javadi Hills
Mysore
Tiruppattūr
Tindivanam
Nanjangūd
Dharmapuri
Tiruvannāmalai
Cannanore
Chāmrājnagar
Stanley Resr
Villupuram
Pondicherry
Tellicherry
Mahe
Mettūr
Salem
Badagara
Cuddalore
Doda Betta 2636
Kozhikode (Calicut)
Ootacamund
Erode
Vriddhāchalam
Coonoor
Nilgiri Hills
Beypore
Chidambaram
Coimbatore
TAMIL NĀDU
Tiruppur
Cauvery
Kumbakonam
Androth
Shoranūr
Pālghāt
Kāraikāl
Ponnāni
Tiruchchirāppalli
Nāgappattinam
Pollāchi
Thanjāvūr
Mannārgudi
Trichūr
Anaimalai Hills
Palani
Pudukkottai
Pt Calimera
Kalpeni
Dindigul
Kodikkarai
Kochi (Cochin)
Bodināyakkanūr
Ernākulam
Vaigai
Palk Strait
Vembanad L.
Madurai
Pt Pedro
Kambam
Kottayam
Virudunagar
Paramakkudi
Jaffna
Alleppey
Aruppukkottai
Rāmanāthapuram
Rājapālaiyam
Nine Degree Channel
Kāyankulam
Puliyangudi
Mullaittivu
Adam's Bridge
Talaimannar
Tenkāsi
Mannar
Kollam (Quilon)
Tirunelveli
Tuticorin
Gulf of Mannār
Vavuniya
Palayankottai
Trincomalee
Thiruvananthapuram (Trivandrum)
Havankulam
Tiruchchendūr
Minicoy
Anuradhapura
Nāgercoil
Kanniyākumari
C.Comorin
Puttalam
Dambulla
Batticaloa
SRI LANKA
CEYLON
Eight Degree Channel
Chilaw
Matale
Kurunegala
Negombo
Kandy
Gampola
Badulla
Colombo
Adam's Pk 2243
Nuwara-Eliya
MALDIVES
Dehiwala-Mt Lavinia
Ratnapura
Moratuwa
Opanake
Ambalangoda
Galle
Hambantota
Matara
Dondra Hd
Western Ghats
Eastern Ghats
Malabar Coast
Coromandel Coast
KERALA
80
75
15
10
A
B
C
1
2
3

NORTH ATLANTIC OCEAN

UNITED KINGDOM
IRELAND Dublin
London
Edinburgh

NORWAY Oslo
SWEDEN Stockholm Göteborg
Helsinki FINLAND
Sankt-Peterburg (Leningrad)
Nizhniy Novgorod
Moskva
RUSSIAN FEDERATION
Volgograd
Samara
KAZAKHSTAN
Aral Sea
UZBEKISTAN
Amu-Darya
Syr-Darya
TURKMENISTAN
Ashkhabad
AFGHANISTAN
Mashhad
IRAN
Tehrān
OMAN
Muscat
Kuria Is.
Socotra (S.Y.)
Gulf of Aden
YEMEN
Aden
San'ā
DJIBOUTI
Asmara
Kassala
Khartoum
Omdurman
El Obeid
Atbara
Port Sudan
Blue Nile
CHAD
L. Chad
NIGER
Agadez
Niamey
BURKINA
Bobo-Dioulasso
Ouagadougou
Bamako
MALI
Tombouctou
Tamanrasset
Niger
GUINEA
GUINEA BISSAU
THE GAMBIA Banjul
Dakar SENEGAL
St-Louis
Nouakchott
MAURITANIA
Nouadhibou
Western Sahara
La'Youn
Islas Canarias (Sp.)
Madeira (Port.)
Açores (Port.)
Bay of Biscay
Bordeaux
FRANCE
Paris
Seine
Rhône
Marseille
SPAIN
Madrid
Barcelona
Lisboa
PORTUGAL
Porto
Tajo
Ebro
Islas Baleares
Corse
Sardegna
Sicilia
ITALY
Roma
Napoli
Milano
München
SWITZ.
AUSTRIA Wien
GERMANY
Berlin
Hamburg
Bruxelles
NETH.
BELG.
LUX.
Bonn
DENMARK København
Kiel
POLAND Warszawa
Kraków
CZECHOSLOVAKIA
Praha
HUNGARY Budapest
SLOV.
CROATIA Zagreb
YUGOSLAVIA
Beograd
ROMANIA Bucureşti
Danub
MOLDAVIA Kishinev
BULGARIA Sofiya
ALB.
GREECE Athínai
MACED.
Adriatic Sea
Tunis
TUNISIA
Annaba
Constantine
Oran
Alger
ALGERIA
MOROCCO
Casablanca
Rabat
Fès
Tanger
Marrakech
Agadir
SAHARA
Tropic of Cancer
In Salah
Ghudamis
Tripoli
LIBYA
Benghâzi
Sabha
Ghât
EGYPT
Cairo
Alexandria
Suez
Asyût
Aswân
L. Nasser
Nile
Port Said
Wadi Halfa
RED SEA
Mekkah
Jerusalem
Amman JORDAN
Damascus
SYRIA
Beirut LEB.
CYPRUS Nicosia
ISR.
Mediterranean Sea
TURKEY
Ankara
İstanbul
Black Sea
Odessa
UKRAINE
Kiev
Kharkov
Rostov
Don
BELORUSSIA Minsk
LITH.
LAT. Riga
EST. Tallinn
Baltic Sea
Gdańsk
Vilnius
RUS. FED.
Volga
Caspian Sea
Baku
Tbilisi GEORGIA
Yerevan
ARM.
AZE.
Tabriz
Baghdād
IRAQ
Basra
Euphrates
Tigris
KUWAIT
BAHRAIN
QATAR
UNITED ARAB EMIRATES
Abu Dhabi
SAUDI ARABIA
Ar Riyād
Shiraz
The Gulf

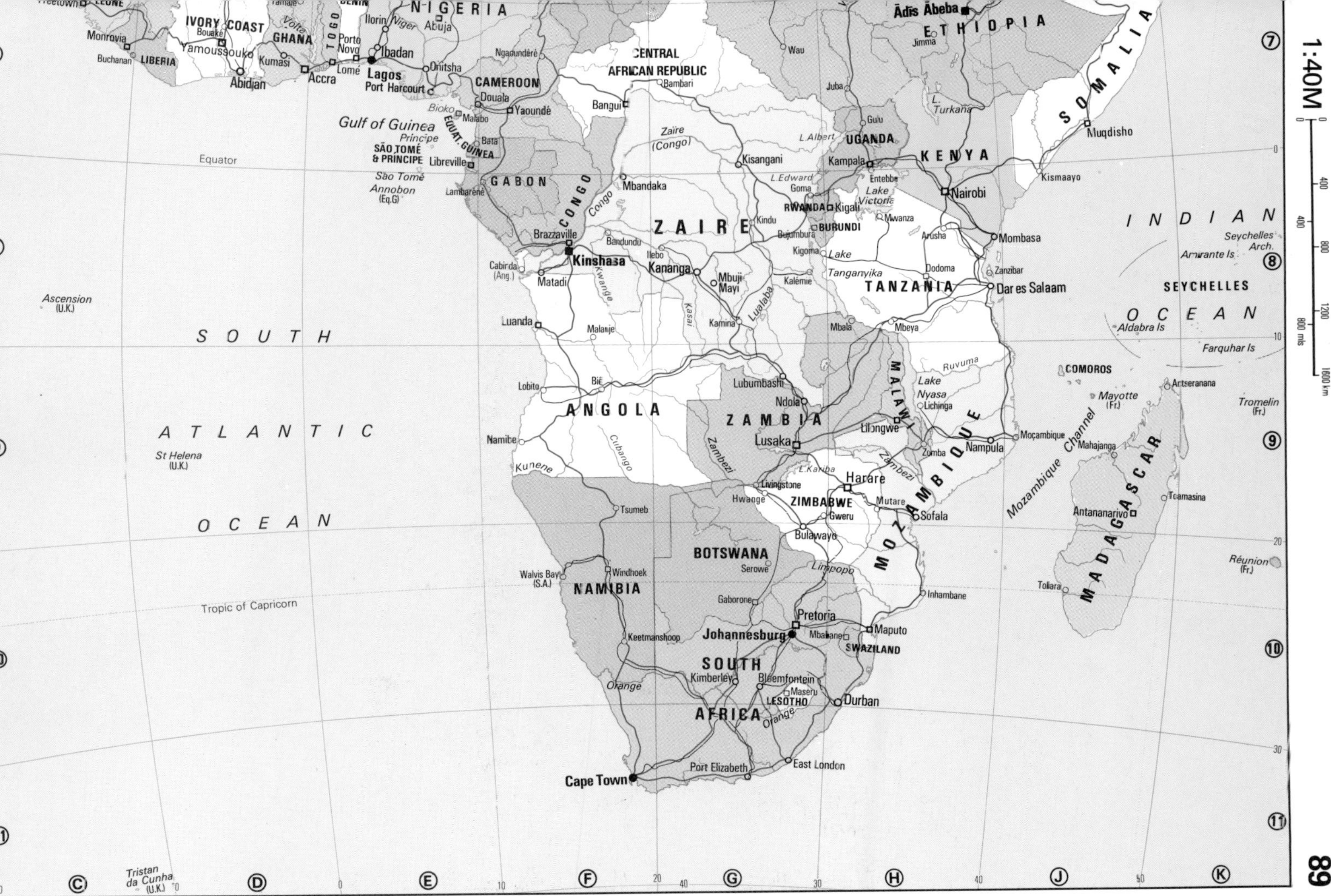

1:40M

400 800 1200 1600 km

400 800 mls

① ⑧ ⑨ ⑩ ⑪

Ⓚ

INDIAN

Seychelles
Arch.

Aruante Is.

SEYCHELLES

Tromelin
(Fr.)

Réunion
(Fr.)

OCEAN

Farquhar Is.

Aldabra Is.

Mayotte
(Fr.)

COMOROS

MADAGASCAR

Antananarivo

Toliara

Ⓙ

SOMALIA

Muqdisho

Kismaayo

Mombasa

Zanzibar

Dar es Salaam

Moçambique

Mozambique Channel

Antseranana

Toamasina

Mahajanga

Ⓗ

ETHIOPIA

Ādīs Ābeba

Jimma

Turkana

Juba

Gulu

KENYA

Nairobi

Arusha

Dodoma

TANZANIA

Mbeya

Lake
Nyasa

Lichinga

Nampula

MOZAMBIQUE

Sofala

UGANDA

Kampala

Entebbe

Lake
Victoria

Mwanza

Mbulu

Lake
Tanganyika

MALAWI

Zomba

Lilongwe

Mutare

Harare

ZIMBABWE

Gweru

Bulawayo

Inhambane

Maputo

SWAZILAND

Mbabane

Durban

East London

Ⓖ

CENTRAL
AFRICAN REPUBLIC

Wau

Bambari

Bangui

ZAIRE

Ksangani

L.Edward

Goma

RWANDA

Kigali

BURUNDI

Bujumbura

Kigoma

Kindu

Kalemie

Kananga

Kasai

Mbuji
Mayi

Kamina

ZAMBIA

Lubumbashi

Ndola

Lusaka

Kabwe

Zambezi

L.Kariba

Hwange

Kwango

BOTSWANA

Serowe

Gaborone

Johannesburg

SOUTH AFRICA

Pretoria

Bloemfontein

LESOTHO

Maseru

Kimberley

Keetmanshoop

Port Elizabeth

Ⓕ

NIGERIA

Lagos

Port Harcourt

CAMEROON

Douala

Yaoundé

Malabo

Bata

EQUAT. GUINEA

Libreville

GABON

CONGO

Brazzaville

Kinshasa

Matadi

Bandundu

Mbandaka

Ilebo

Zaire
(Congo)

Bié

ANGOLA

Luanda

Lobito

Cabinda
(Ang.)

Namibe

Kunene

Malange

Cubango

Tsumeb

NAMIBIA

Windhoek

Walvis Bay
(S.A.)

Okavango

Orange

Cape Town

Ⓔ

IVORY COAST

Abidjan

Yamoussoukro

Bouaké

LIBERIA

Monrovia

Buchanan

GHANA

Kumasi

Accra

Lomé

Porto
Novo

BENIN

Ibadan

Ilorin

Volta

São Tomé
& PRINCIPE

Príncipe

São Tomé

Annobon
(Eq.G.)

Bioko
(Eq.G.)

Gulf of Guinea

SOUTH

ATLANTIC

OCEAN

St Helena
(U.K.)

Ascension
(U.K.)

Tristan
da Cunha
(U.K.)

Equator

Tropic of Capricorn

⑦ ⑧ ⑨ ⑩ ⑪

TURKMENISTAN
Karakumy
AZERBAIJAN
ARMENIA
IRAN
Caspian Sea
Baku
Krasnovodsk
Cheleken
Nebit-Dag
Kum-Dag
Kizyl-Arvat
Ashkhabad
Bezmein
Tedzhen
Sarakhs
Mashhad
Neyshābūr
Sabzevār
Shīrvān
Quchan
Bojnūrd
Gorgān
Gonbad-e Kāvūs
Bandar-e Torkoman
Behshahr
Sārī
Bābol
Āmol
Rāmsar
Lāhījān
Bandar Anzalī
Rasht
Qazvīn
Karaj
Tehrān
Qom
Kāshān
Eşfahān
Najafābād
Shahr Kord
Yazd
Semnān
Dāmghan
Torbat-e Heydarīyeh
Torbat-e Jām
Kāshmar
Ferdows
Bīrjand
Ţabas
Ardabīl
Tabrīz
Marand
Jolfa
Nakhichevan
Marāgheh
Mīāneh
Zanjān
Hamadān
Arāk
Borūjerd
Khorramābād
Kermānshāh
Sanandaj
Dezfūl
Ahvāz
Masjed Soleymān
Reshteh-ye Alborz (Elburz Mts)
Dasht-e Kavīr
Dasht-e Lūt
Kūhhā-ye Zāgros (Zagros Mountains)
Khrebet Kopet Dag
Kūh-e Hazār Masjed
Kūh-e Karkas
Qolleh-ye Damāvand 5601

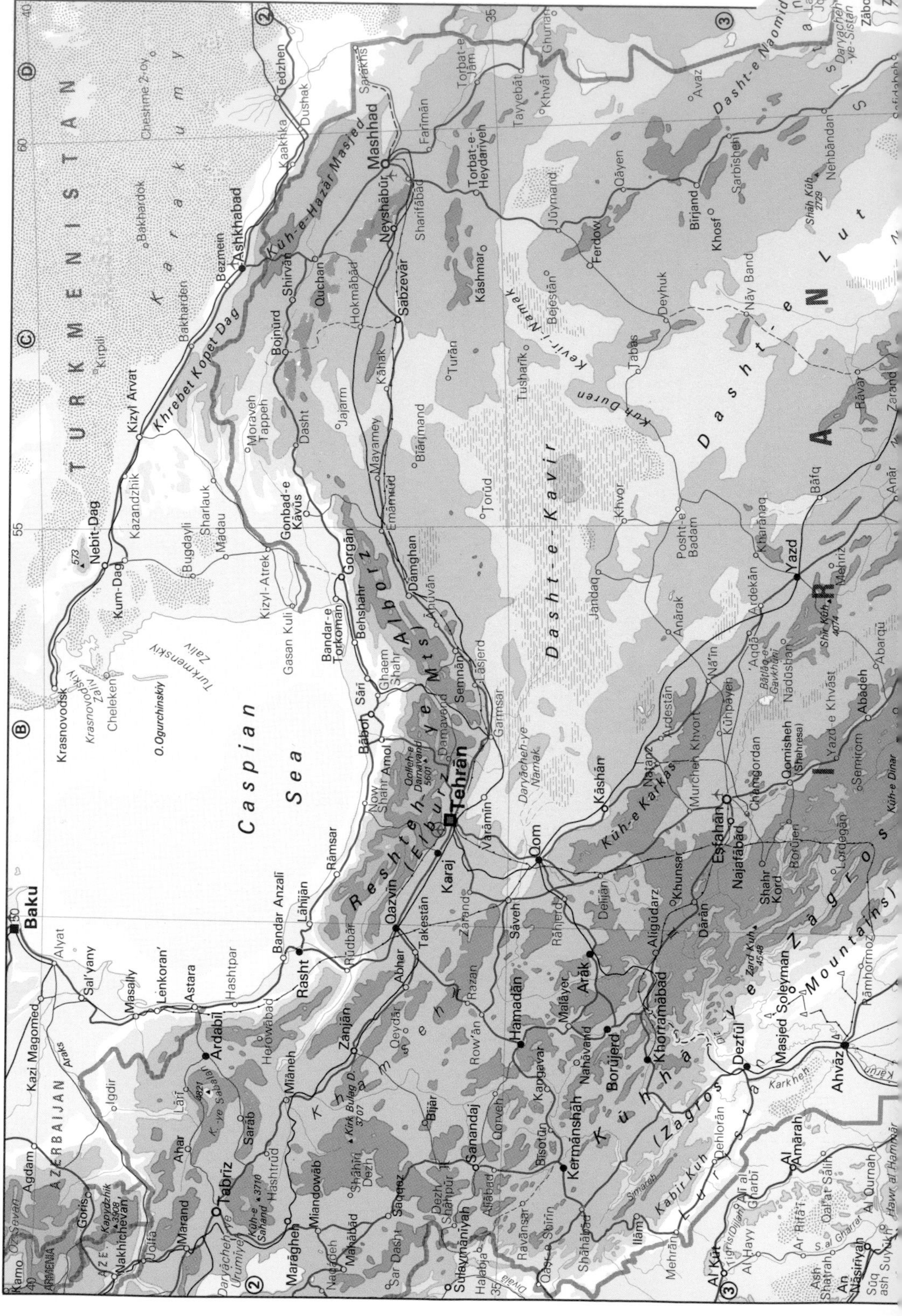

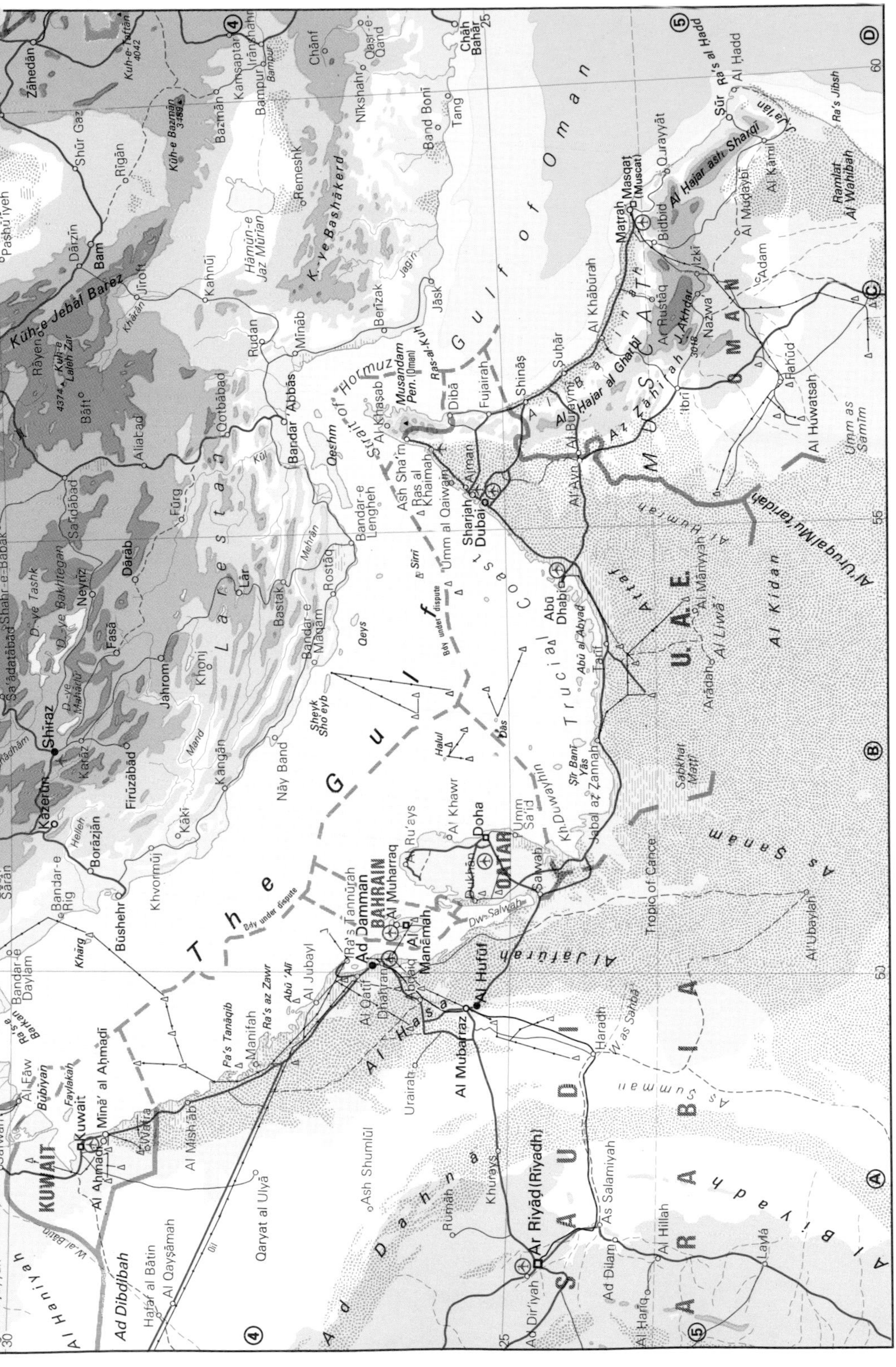

100   200   300 km
50   100   150 mls

Gulf of Oman

Strait of Hormuz

The Gulf

Coast

Trucial

Musandam Pen. (Oman)

Lārestān

Kūh-e Jebāl Barez

Kūh-e Bashākerd

Hāmūn-e Jaz Mūrīān

KUWAIT

BAHRAIN

QATAR

U.A.E.

OMAN

AL HAJAR

SAUDI ARABIA

Ar Riyāḍ (Riyadh)

Al Hufūf

Ad Dammām
Al Muharraq
Manāmah
Dhahrān
Al Qaṭīf

Doha
Umm Saʿīd
Al Khawr
Ruʿays

Abū Dhabi
Dubai
Sharjah
Ajman
Umm al Qaiwain
Ras al Khaimah
Ash Shām
Fujairah
Dibā
Al Khaṣab
Ras-al-Kuh

Masqaṭ Muscat
Maṭrāh
Bidbid
Al Khābūrah
Suhār
Shinās
Al Buraymī
Al ʿAyn
Rustāq
Nazwā
Ibrī
Ādam
Ṣūr
Raʾs al Ḥadd
Raʾs Jibsh
Ramlat Al Wahiban
Al Kāmil
Al Muḍaybī
Quraiyāt

Kermān
Shīrāz
Kāzerūn
Abādān
Kuwait
Bandar Abbās
Bushehr
Zāhedān
Bam
Bampūr

As Sanām

Ad Dahnāʾ

Al Jafūrah

Al Hasā

Tropic of Cancer

Bdy under dispute

Bdry under dispute

60   56   50

30   25

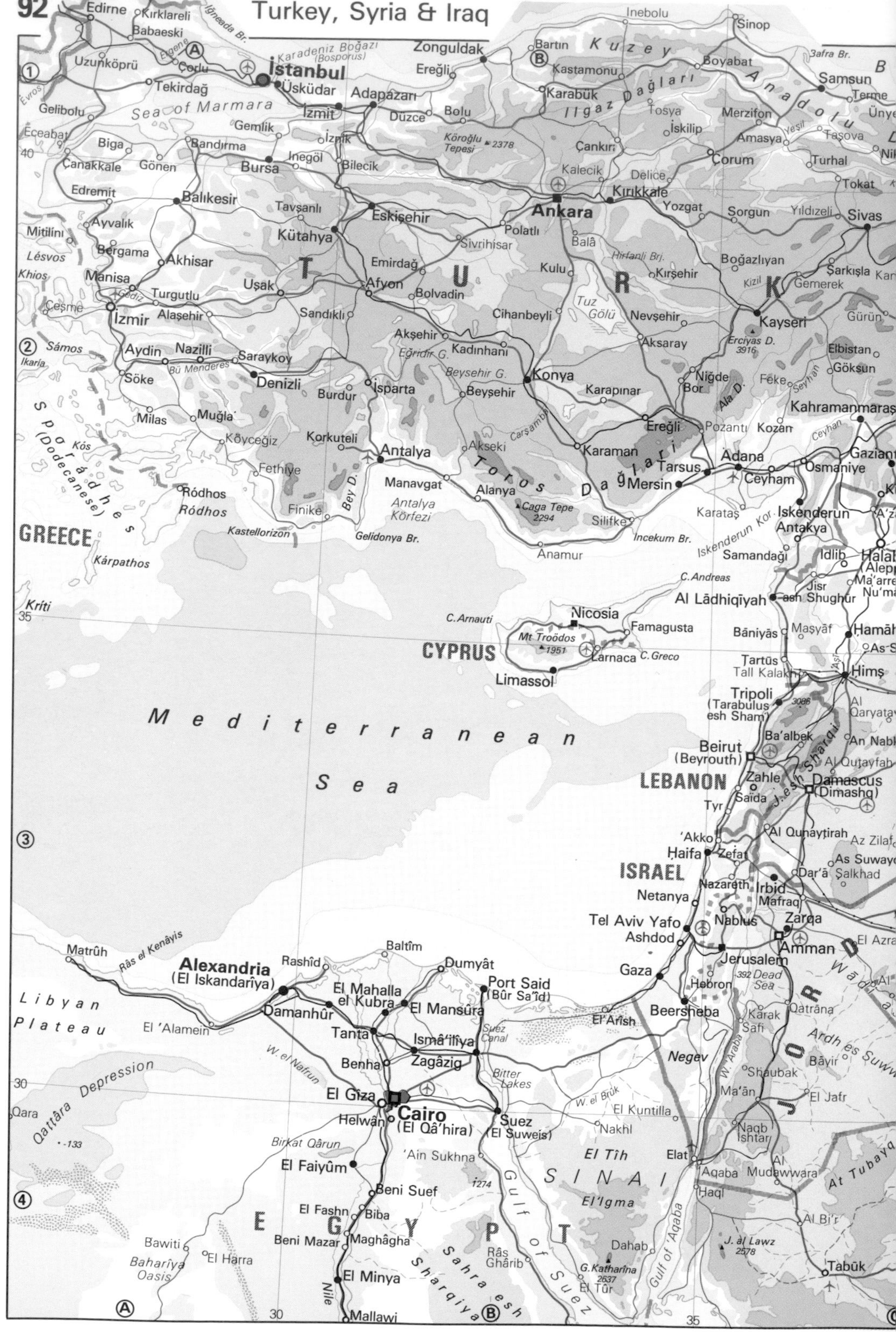
Edirne
Kırklareli
Babaeski
İğneada Br.
Uzunköprü
Çorlu
Karadeniz Boğazı (Bosporus)
İstanbul
Üsküdar
Tekirdağ
Evros
Gelibolu
Sea of Marmara
Eceabat
Gemlik
İzmit
Adapazarı
Düzce
Zonguldak
Ereğli
Bartın
Bolu
Inebolu
Sinop
Kastamonu
Karabük
Boyabat
Samsun
Terme
Ünye
Kuzey Anadolu
Ilgaz Dağları
Tosya
İskilip
Merzifon
Amasya
Yeşil
Taşova
Niksar
Çorum
Turhal
Tokat
Çankırı
Kalecik
Delice
Kırıkkale
Yozgat
Sorgun
Yıldızeli
Sivas
Köroğlu Tepesi 2378
Biga
Bandırma
Çanakkale
Gönen
Bursa
İnegöl
İznik
Bilecik
Edremit
Balıkesir
Tavşanlı
Eskişehir
Ankara
Polatlı
Sivrihisar
Balâ
Mitilíni
Ayvalık
Lésvos
Bergama
Akhisar
Kütahya
Khíos
Manisa
Gediz
Turgutlu
Uşak
Emirdağ
Afyon
Bolvadin
Kulu
Hirfanlı Brj.
Kırşehir
Boğazlıyan
Şarkışla
Kızıl
Gemerek
Çeşme
İzmir
Alaşehir
Sandıklı
Cihanbeyli
Tuz Gölü
Nevşehir
Kayseri
Gürün
TURKEY
Sámos
Ikaría
Aydın
Nazilli
Sarayköy
Büyük Menderes
Akşehir
Kadınhanı
Eğridir G.
Aksaray
Erciyas D. 3916
Elbistan
Göksun
Söke
Denizli
Beyşehir G.
Beyşehir
Konya
Niğde
Bor
Feke
Seyhan
Burdur
Isparta
Karapınar
Ala D.
Kahramanmaraş
Milas
Muğla
Kós
Köyceğiz
Korkuteli
Akseki
Çarşamba
Ereğli
Pozantı
Kozan
Ceyhan
Sporádhes (Dodecanese)
Antalya
Karaman
Tarsus
Adana
Gaziantep
Fethiye
Toros Dağları
Mersin
Ceyhan
Osmaniye
Ródhos
Bey D.
Manavgat
Alanya
Antalya Körfezi
Caga Tepe 2294
Silifke
Karataş
Iskenderun
Antakya
Finike
Kastellorizon
Gelidonya Br.
Incekum Br.
Iskenderun Kor.
GREECE
Kárpathos
Anamur
Samandağı
Idlib
Halab (Aleppo)
Ma'arrat Nu'man
C. Andreas
Jisr esh Shughur
Al Lādhiqīyah
Krítí
C. Arnauti
Nicosia
Famagusta
Bāniyās
Maşyāf
Hamāh
Mt Troödos 1951
Larnaca
C. Greco
As-Salamiyah
CYPRUS
Limassol
Ţarţūs
Tall Kalakh
Ḥimş
Tripoli (Tarabulus esh Sham)
3086
Al Qaryatayn
Mediterranean Sea
Ba'albek
An Nabk
Beirut (Beyrouth)
Al Quţayfah
LEBANON
Zahle
Damascus (Dimashq)
Saida
J. esh Sharqi
Tyr
'Akko
Al Qunayţirah
Az Zilaf
Ḥaifa
Zefat
As Suwayda
ISRAEL
Dar'ā
Şalkhad
Nazareth
Irbid
Netanya
Mafraq
Tel Aviv Yafo
Nablus
Zarqa
Ashdod
Amman
El Azraq
Matrûh
Râs el Kenâyis
Baltîm
Jerusalem
Rashîd
Dumyât
Alexandria (El Iskandarîya)
Gaza
392 Dead Sea
El Mahalla el Kubra
Port Said (Bûr Sa'îd)
Hebron
Libyan Plateau
Damanhûr
El Mansûra
El 'Arîsh
Beersheba
Karak
Qatrâna
El 'Alamein
Tanta
Ismâ'ilîya
Suez Canal
Safi
Negev
W. Araba
Ardh es Suwwan
W. el Natrun
Benha
Zagâzig
Bayir
Qattâra Depression
Bitter Lakes
Shaubak
W. el Brûk
El Giza
Ma'ān
El Jafr
Qara
Cairo (El Qâ'hira)
El Kuntilla
Helwân
Suez (El Suweis)
Nakhl
JORDAN
Naqb Ishtar
Birkat Qârun
El Tîh
'Ain Sukhna
Elat
Al Mudawwara
-133
El Faiyûm
Aqaba
At Tubayq
1274
SINAI
Beni Suef
Haql
El Fashn
Biba
El'Igma
EGYPT
Al Bi'r
Beni Mazar
Maghâgha
Bawiti
El Harra
Râs Ghârib
Dahab
J. al Lawz 2578
Baharîya Oasis
Sahra esh Sharqiya
Gulf of Suez
G. Katharîna 2637
Gulf of 'Aqaba
Tabūk
El Minya
El Tûr
Nile
Mallawi
30
35
40

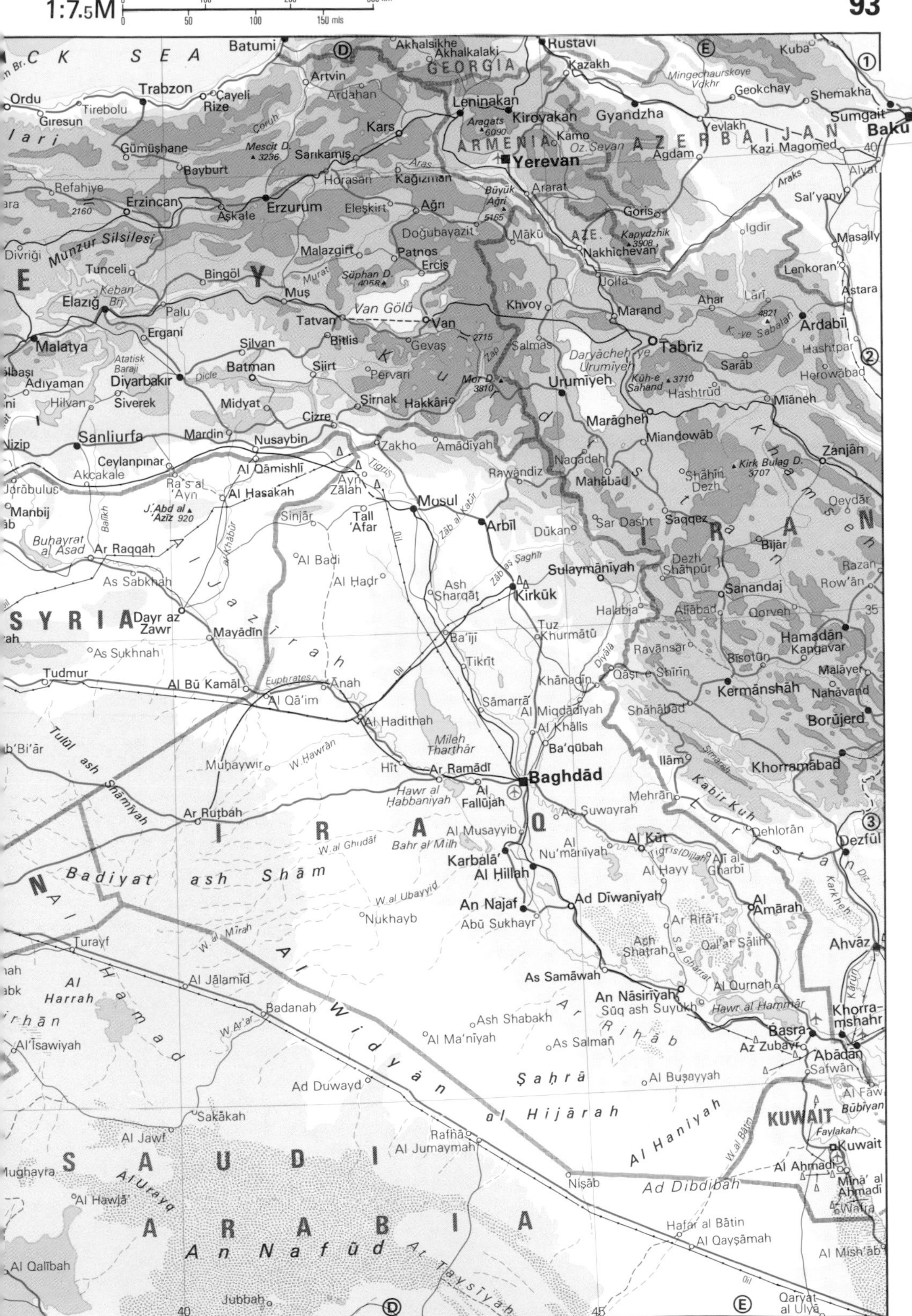

1:7.5M

100 200 300 km
50 100 150 mls

BLACK SEA
Batumi Akhalsikhe Akhalkalaki Rustavi Kuba
Ordu Tirebolu GEORGIA Kazakh Mingechaurskoye Geokchay Shemakha
Trabzon Çayeli Artvin Leninakan Kirovakan Gyandzha Vdkhr Sumgait
Giresun Rize Ardahan Aragats Kamo Yevlakh Kazi Magomed Baku
Gümüşhane Mescit D. Kars ARMENIA Oz Sevan Agdam Sal'yany
Refahiye Bayburt Sarıkamış Horasan Yerevan Goris Kapydzhik Igdir Masally
Erzincan Aşkale Erzurum Eleşkirt Ağrı Ararat Maku AZE. Nakhichevan Lenkoran
Divriği Munzur Silsilesi Doğubayazit Büyük Ağrı Astara
Tunceli Bingöl Muş Süphan D. Patnos Ercis Khvoy Marand Ahar Ardabil
Elazığ Keban Palu Murat Van Gölü Khoy Tabriz Sarab Herowabad
Malatya Ergani Silvan Tatvan Van Salmas Daryācheh ye Kuh-e Mianeh
Adiyaman Diyarbakır Batman Bitlis Gevaş Mor D. Urumiyeh Sahand Hashtrud
Hilvan Siverek Midyat Siirt Pervari Hakkâri Marāgheh Miandowāb
Şanlıurfa Mardin Cizre Zakho Amâdiyah Rawândiz Naqadeh Shahin Zanjān
Ceylanpınar Nusaybin Al Qâmishlī Ayn Mahâbâd Dezh Bijar
Akçakale Ra's al Al Hasakah Zâlah Mosul Dukan Sar Dasht Saqqez Oeydâr
Manbij J. Abd al Sinjâr Tall Arbīl Dezh Sanandaj Razan
Ar Raqqah Aziz 'Afar Ash Kirkuk Shāhpūr Aliabad Qorveh Row'ān
As Sabkhah Al Badi Sharqāt Sulaymānīyah Halabja Hamadān
SYRIA Dayr az Al Hadr Tuz Khānaqīn Qasr-e Shīrīn Bisotūn Kangavar
Zawr Mayādīn Ba'ji Khurmātū Diyala Kermānshāh Malāyer
As Sukhnah Tikrit Ravânsar Nahāvand
Tudmur Al Bū Kamāl 'Anah Sāmarrā Al Miqdādiyah Shāhābād Borūjerd
Al Qā'im Al Haditha Al Khālis Ilām Khorramābad
Tulūl ash Muhaywir Mileh Ba'qūbah Kabir Kuh
b'Bi'âr Shāmiya Hīt Tharthār Ar Ramādī Mehrān Dehlorān
Ar Rutbah Hawr al Al Baghdad Dezfūl
Habbaniyah Al Fallūjah As Suwayrah
Badiyat ash Shām Bahr al Milh Al Musayyib Al Kūt Ahvāz
Al Nu'mānīyah Al 'Ali al Dezfūl
Karbalā' Al Hillah Al Hayy Gharbi
IRAQ An Najaf Ad Diwaniyah Al Amārah
Nukhayb Abū Sukhayr Ar Rifā'ī Qal'at Sālih Ahvāz
Turayf Ash Shatrah Khorramshahr
Al Jālamīd Al As Samāwah An Nāsirīyah Hawr al Hammār Basra
Harrah Badanah Widyān Al Qurnah Az Zubayr Abādān
Al Ma'nīyah Ash Shabakh Sūq ash Suyūkh Safwān
Al 'Īsawiyah As Salmān Al Busayyah Al Faw
Ad Duwayd al Şahrā Būbiyān
Al Jawf Hijārah Al Haniyah Faylakah
Rafhā' KUWAIT
SAUDI Sakākah Al Jumaymah Kuwait
Nişāb Ad Dibdibah Al Ahmadi Mīnā' al
ARABIA An Nafūd Hafar al Bātin Ahmadi
Al Qalībah Mughayra Al Hawjā' Al Qayşāmah Al Mish'āb
Jubbah At Taysīyah Qaryat al Ulyā

1:2.5M

0 25 50 75 100 km
0 25 50 mls

Paleokhorio · Larnaca · C.Greco
Lefkara · Larnaca Bay
Zyyi · C.Kiti
CYPRUS
Limassol · Akrotiri Bay
C.Gata

Ṭarṭūs · Duraykīsh · Kafrūn Bashūr
An · Naṣirah · Tall Bīsah
Arwad · Ḥamīdīyah · Shāfita · Qal'at al Ḥiṣn · KRAK-DES CHEVALIERS · Ḥimṣ
Tall Kalakh · Homs
Kleia · Qoubayat · Al Quṣayr · Shinshār
El Mīna · Halba · El Hermel · Jūsīyah
Tripoli · Zghorta · Qornet es Saouda · Jabal Ḥalīma · Hisyāh
(Tarābulus esh Sham) · 3086 · 12464
Batroun · Amioune · Bcharre · Laboue
Jubail BYBLOS · Kartaba · Deir el Ahmar
LEBANON · Rhazir · 2659 · 'Dayr · 'Aṭiyah
Baie de St Georges · Bikfaya · 2628 · An Nabk
Jounié · Ba'albek · Yabrūd
Beirut · Ba'abda · Zahle · Rayak · Al J.Ma'lūla
(Beyrouth) · Aley · Jayrūd
Damour · Az. Zabdānī · Qutayfah
Beit ed Dine · 'Ayn el Fījah · Dúmair
Saïda · Machghárah · 1910 · Dúma 'Adhrá
(Sidon) · Barada · **Damascus** Dimáshq
Jezzine · Qatana

MEDITERRANEAN · Hásbaiya · J.ash Shaykh (Mt Hermon) · Al Kiswah
Liṭâni · Marjayoun · Dayr 'Alî
SEA · Tyr · Q.Shemona · Baniyas · **SYRIA**
(Tyre, Sour) · Jouai'ya · Mas'adah · CEASE FIRE · Ghabághib · Burâq
Enn Nâqoûra · Benn · LINES 1974 · Mismîyah
Bennt Jbail · Al Qunayṭirah · As Ṣanamayn · Khabab
Nahariyya · 1208 · Yesud · Khushnîyah · Shaqqâ
Har Meron · Hama'ala · Nawa · Al Lajâh
'Akko · Ma'alot · As Sanamayn · Izra'
(Acre) · Tarshîha · Zefat · 863 · Shahbâ
Haifa · B.of Haifa · Rama · (Safad) · Y. Tiberias · Jabal al 'Arab
(Hefa) · Q.Yam · Shefar'am · (Sea of Galilee) · Taṣil · 1735
Q. · Ata · 528 · Fíq · Shaykh Miskîn · As Suwaydâ
'Atlit · Mt Carmel · Nazareth · Ma'agan · Dar'a
Zikhron Ya'aqov · Afula · **Irbid** · W. el Zaydī · Buṣrâ ash Shâm
CAESAREA · MEGIDDO · Deir Abu · Ramtha
Pardes Hanna · ARMAGEDDON · Sa'id · Husn · Ṣalkhad
Hadera · Jenin · Beyt Shean · Ajlûn · Mafraq · Tisîyah
Netanya · Qabatiya · J. Umm ed Dara · Jarash · Sabha
Tulkarm · Tubas · 1247 · Es Samrâ
Herzliyya · Sabastiya · Far'a · Zarqa · 'Er Rummân
ISRAEL · Kefar Sava · Nablus · Qa' Khanna
Ramat Gan Yam · Petah Tiqwa · Salt · Suweilih · **Zarqa**
Tel Aviv · Ba'al Hazor · Karama · **Amman**
Yafo (Jaffa) · Lod · 1016 · Wadi es Sir · Sahâb
Rishon le Zion · Ramla · Ramallah · Naur
Rehovot · Latrun · Jericho · El Ghor · Jiza · Qasr el Kharana
Ashdod · Beit Jala · (Ariha) · 963 · Jebel
Jerusalem (El Quds) · Mâdabâ · Dab'a · Mudeisisat
Ashqelon · Bethlehem · Wad edh Dhab'i
Qiryat · (Bayt Laḥm) · Dead · Jiza
Gat · Bet Guvrin · Hebron · Sea · Khan ez Zabîb
Gaza · (El Khalil) · (Bahr Lut) · Heidan
Gaza Strip · LACHISH · Dura · En Gedi · Mazra · Rabba · Qatrâna
Khan Yunis · Sederot · Yatta · W. el Ghadaf
Rafah · P.Edh Dhahiriya · Mazra · Karak · Qâ el Hafira
Râs Burûn · Ofaqim · **Beersheba** · 1253 · Qâ'el Jinz
Sabkhet el Bardawil · Zeelim · (Be'er Sheva) · MEZADA · T.el Meise · Manzil
El 'Arîsh · Be'er · Nevatim · Arad · Mazâr
Bír Lahfân · Sheva · Safi · **JORDAN**
Haluza · Sedom · W.'el Ghadaf · Hâsâ
Revivim · Dimona · MAMSHIT · 1305
Qeziot · SHIVTA · Yeroham · Oron · W.el Hâsâ
Abu 'Aweigila · Sede · Zin · 1356 · Tafila
NIZANA · Boqer · Hazeva · J.Dasred Deir
AVEDAT · El Ghor · Rashâdîya · 1641 · Jebel Ithriyat
El Quseima · **Negev** · Dana · W.Fidan · Shaubak
EGYPT · Mizpe · Negarot · Ein · 1082
G.Maghâra · Ramon · Yahav
735 · G.Halâl · Har Ramon · Nijil
Bír Gifgâfa · 892 · 1305 · 1615 · Jum Suwwâna · Uneisa
Bír Hasana · Har Saggi · Har Hakippa · J.Atâ'ita
1006 · 467

1:15M

0	200	400	600 km
0	100	200	300 mls

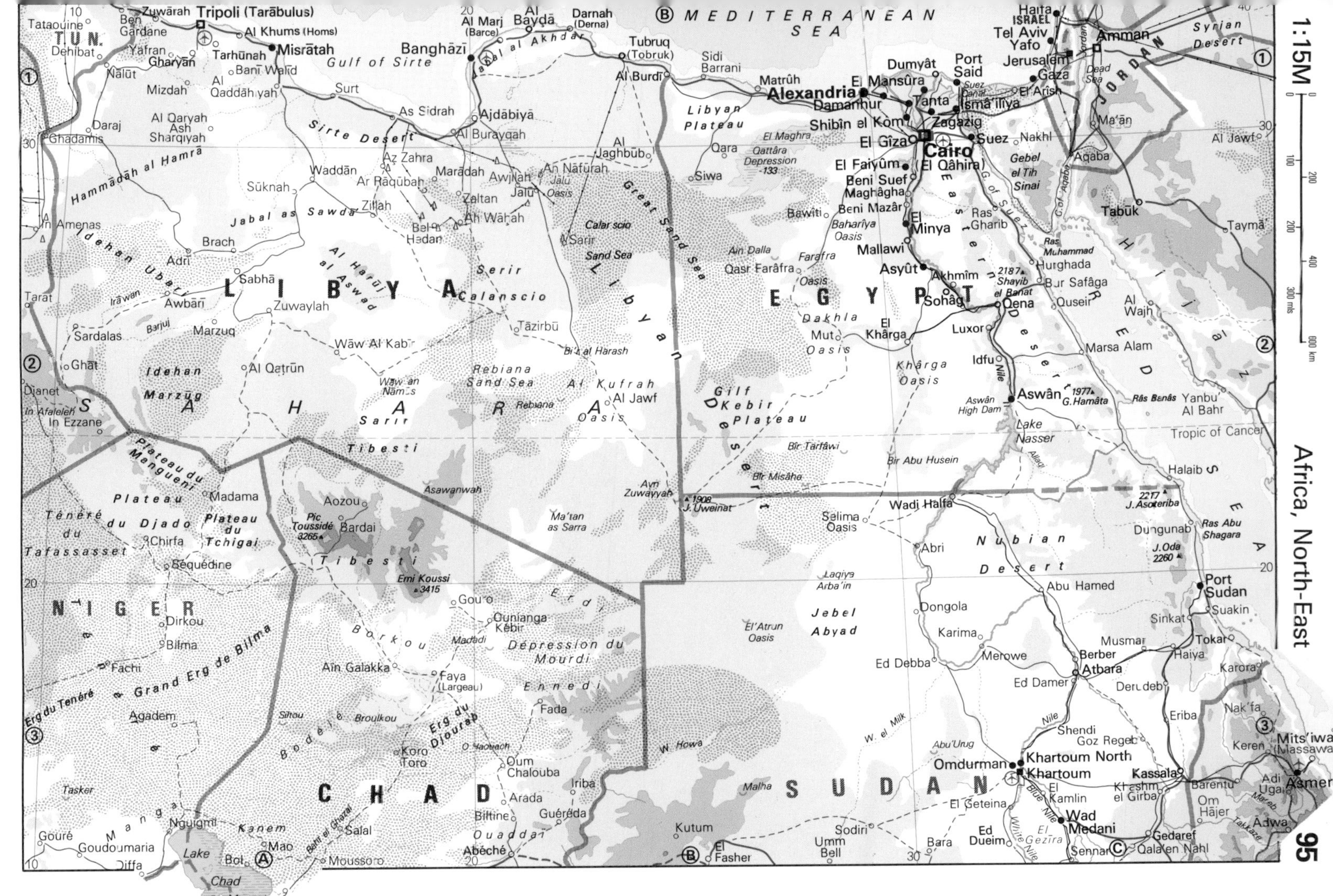

MEDITERRANEAN SEA

Syrian Desert

Hijaz

Tropic of Cancer

Amman
Haifa
ISRAEL
Tel Aviv-Yafo
Jerusalem
Gaza
El 'Arish
Nakhl
Tabūk
Al Jawf
Taymā'
Al Wajh
Yanbu'
Al Bahr
Ras Banas
J. Ascenma
2217

Port Said
Dumyāt
Alexandria
El Mansûra
Tanta
Shibîn el Kom
Zaqazig
Cairo
El Qâhira
El Gîza
Suez
Ismâ'îlîya
Bûr Safâga
Hurghada
Ghardaqa
Quseir
G. Hamâta
1977

Matrûh
Sidi Barrani
Tubruq (Tobruk)

EGYPT
El Faiyûm
Beni Suef
El Minya
Maghâgha
Beni Mazâr
Mallawi
Asyût
Sohâg
Luxor
Qena
el Shayib
Akhmîm
2187
Nile
Aswân
Aswân High Dam
Lake Nasser
Idfû
Bir Abu Husein
Halâ'ib

Libyan Plateau
Qâra
Siwa
Qattâra Depression -133
Baharîya Oasis
Farâfra
El Khârga
Khârga Oasis
Dakhla Oasis
Mut
Qasr Farâfra
'Ain Dalla
Bahariya Oasis

Nubian Desert
Abu Hamed
Wadi Halfa
Abri
Dongola
Ed Debba
Karima
Merowe

Libyan Desert

Gilf Kebir Plateau
Bir Tarfâwi
Bir Misâha
J. 'Uweinat
1902
Selîma Oasis
El'Atrun Oasis
Jaqîya Arba'în
Jebel Abyad

SUDAN
Mits'iwa
Asmera
Adi Ugri
Adwa
Keren
'Massawa
Nak'fa
J. Oda 2260
Ras Abu Shagara
Dungunâb
Suakin
Port Sudan
Sinkat
Haiya
Tokar
Eriba
Kassala
Kirshm el Girba
Gedaref
Qalâbat
Om Hâjer
Barentu
Goz Regab
Musmar
Derudeb
Atbara
Berber
Ed Damer
Shendi
Khartoum North
Omdurman
Khartoum
El Getéina
Ed Dueim
Wad Medani
El Gezira
Sennar
White Nile
Blue Nile

TUNISIA
Tataouine
Dehibat
Ben Gardane
Zuwârah
Tripoli (Tarābulus)
Al Khums (Homs)
Misrātah
Tarhūnah
Gharyān
Nālūt
Yafran
Mizdah
Al Qaryah
Ash Sharqīyah
Zliten
Al 'Azīzīyah
Bani Walīd

LIBYA
Surt
As Sidrah
Ras Lanuf
Banghāzī
Ajdābīyah
Al Marj (Barce)
Al Baydā
Darnah (Derna)
Al Burdi
Tubruq
Jaghbūb
Jālū
Awjilah
Jalu Oasis
Calanscio Sand Sea
Siwa
Al Jaghbūb
Great Sand Sea
Sand Sea

Marādah
Zaltan
Waddān
Ar Raqūbah
Hadan
Al Harāsh
Tāzirbū
Rebiana Sand Sea
Rebiana
Al Kufrah
Al Jawf
Ayn Zuwayyah
Ma'tan as Sarra
Asawqnwah
Ma'tan Bishārah

Sarīr
Serir

Al Harūj al Aswad
Waddān
Wāw Al Kabir
Wāw an Nāmūs

Tibesti
Aozou
Bardaï
Pic Toussidé 3265
Emi Koussi 3415
Zouar

Jabal as Sawdā'
Sūknah
Sabhā
Zuwaylah
Al Qaṭrūn

Ubari
Idehan Ubari
Brāk
Murzūq
Idehan Marzūq
Mizdah
Awbāri
Barjūj
Ghāt
Sardalas

NIGER
In Ezzane
Djanet
In Amenas
Tarat
In Afaleleh
Séguédine
Chirfa
Madama
Plateau du Manguéni
Plateau du Djado
Dirkou
Bilma
Fachi
Agadem
Ténéré du Tafassasset
Grand Erg de Bilma
Tasker
Goure
Goudoumaria

CHAD
Mao
Lake Chad
Bol
Nguigmi
Kanem
Bahr el Ghazal
Moussoro
Salal
Massakori
Abéché
Ouaddaï
Biltine
Arada
Iriba
Guéréda
Oum Chalouba
Kalait
Ain Galakka
Koro Toro
Faya (Largeau)
Ounianga Kébir
Gouro
Madadi
Fada
Ennedi
Borkou
Erdi
Ma
Broukou
Depression du Mourdi
Djourab
Erg du Ténéré
Sirte Desert
Gulf of Sirte

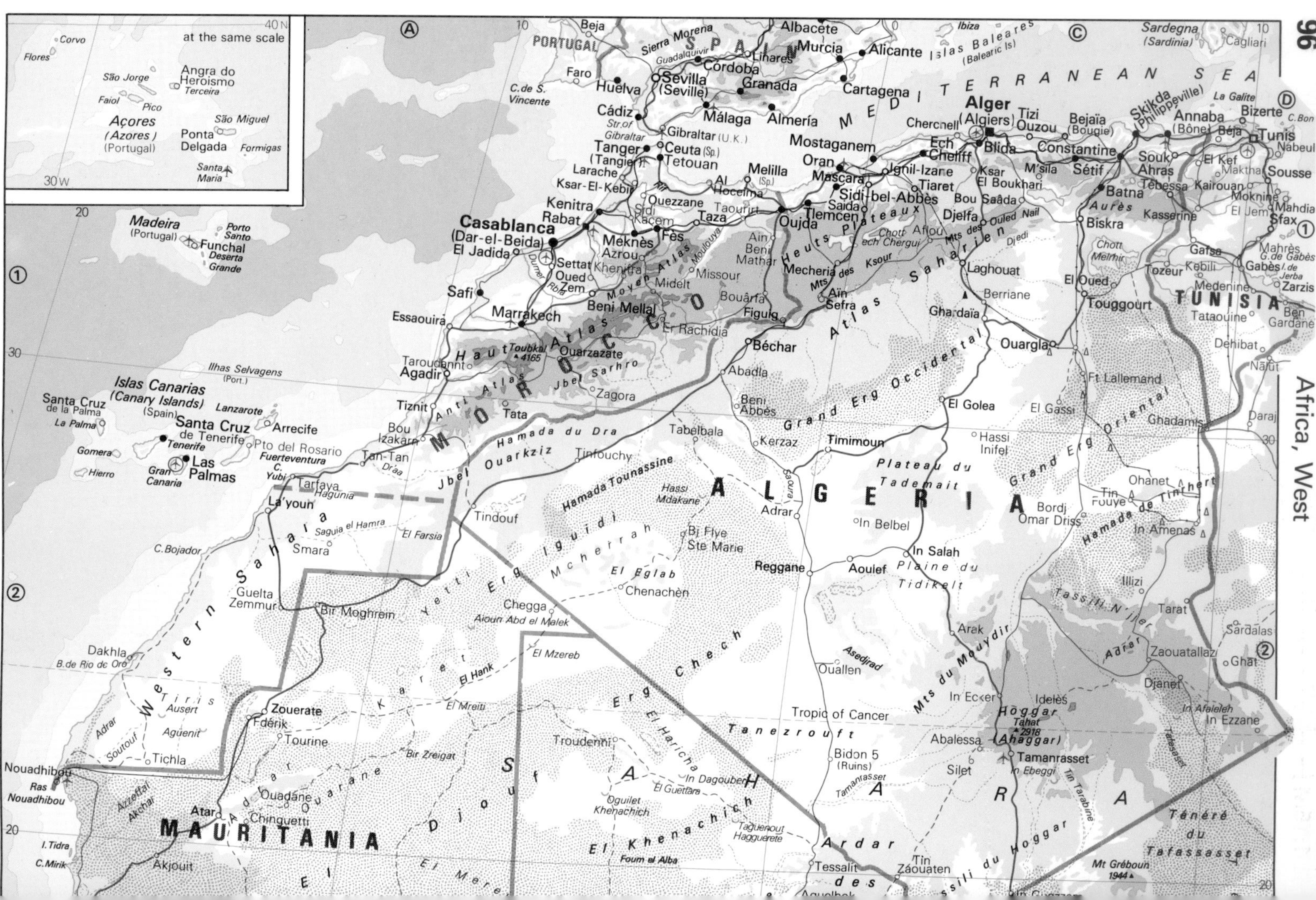
MEDITERRANEAN SEA
SPAIN
PORTUGAL
MOROCCO
ALGERIA
TUNISIA
MAURITANIA
Western Sahara
SAHARA
Alger (Algiers)
Tunis
Casablanca (Dar-el-Beida)
Rabat
Oran
Constantine
Marrakech
Tanger (Tangier)
Gibraltar (U.K.)
Sevilla (Seville)
Granada
Málaga
Alicante
Cartagena
Murcia
Almería
Córdoba
Fès
Meknès
Tlemcen
Oujda
Ghardaia
Ouargla
El Golea
In Salah
Tamanrasset
Béchar
Tindouf
Reggane
Adrar
Timimoun
Agadir
Safi
Essaouira
La'youn
Smara
Zouerate
Atar
Nouadhibou
Dakhla
Islas Canarias (Canary Islands) (Spain)
Las Palmas
Santa Cruz de Tenerife
Madeira (Portugal)
Funchal
Açores (Azores) (Portugal)
at the same scale
Ponta Delgada
Angra do Heroísmo
Grand Erg Occidental
Grand Erg Oriental
Plateau du Tademait
Hoggar (Ahaggar)
Erg Chech
Tropic of Cancer
Haut Atlas
Hamada du Dra

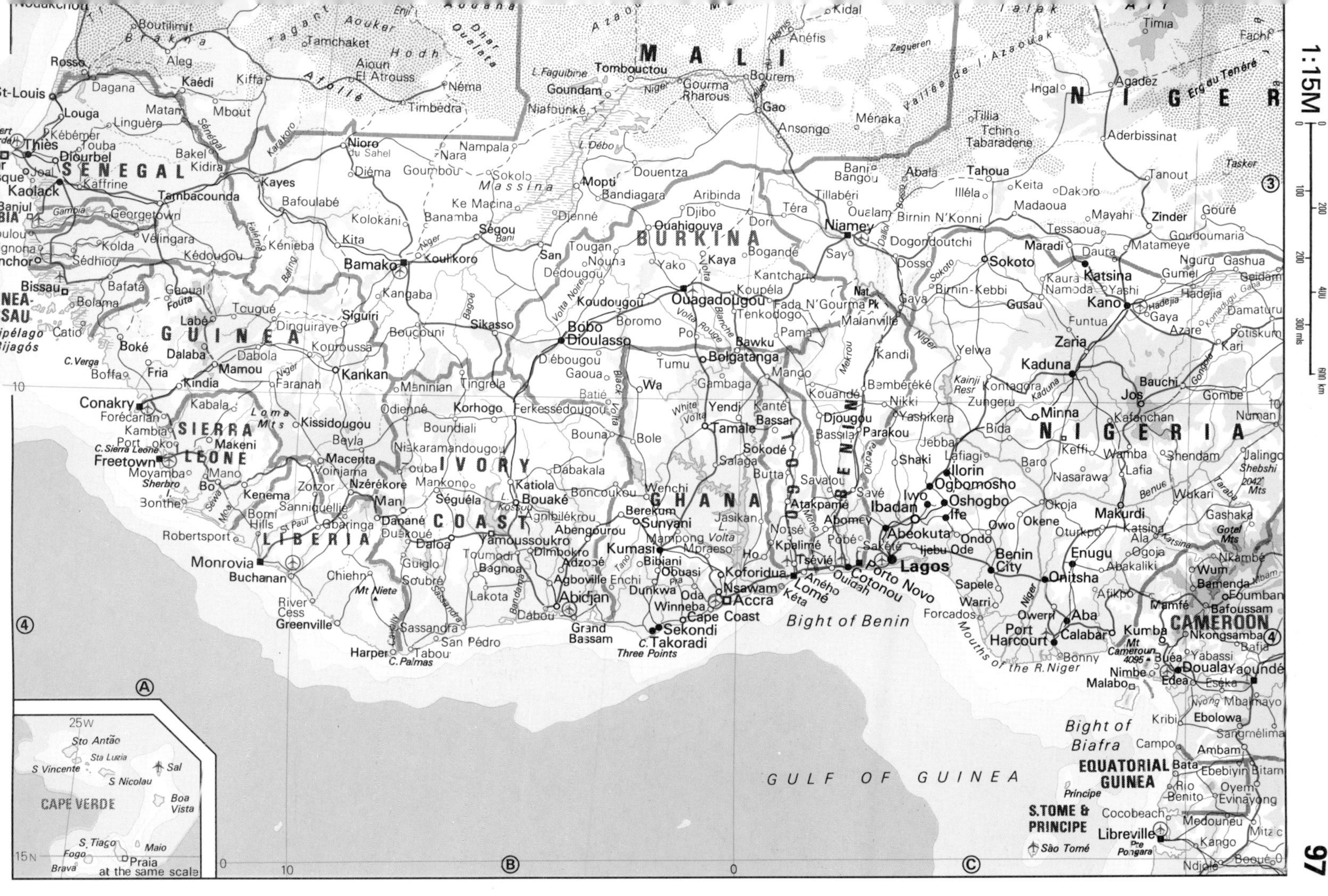
MALI
NIGER
BURKINA
NIGERIA
GHANA
TOGO
BENIN
IVORY COAST
LIBERIA
SIERRA LEONE
GUINEA
GUINEA-BISSAU
SENEGAL
CAMEROON
EQUATORIAL GUINEA
S.TOME & PRINCIPE
GULF OF GUINEA
Bight of Benin
Bight of Biafra
Mouths of the R. Niger
CAPE VERDE
at the same scale
Lagos
Ibadan
Kano
Kaduna
Accra
Kumasi
Abidjan
Bamako
Niamey
Ouagadougou
Conakry
Freetown
Monrovia
Lomé
Cotonou
Porto Novo
Bissau
Douala
Libreville
Malabo
São Tomé
Praia

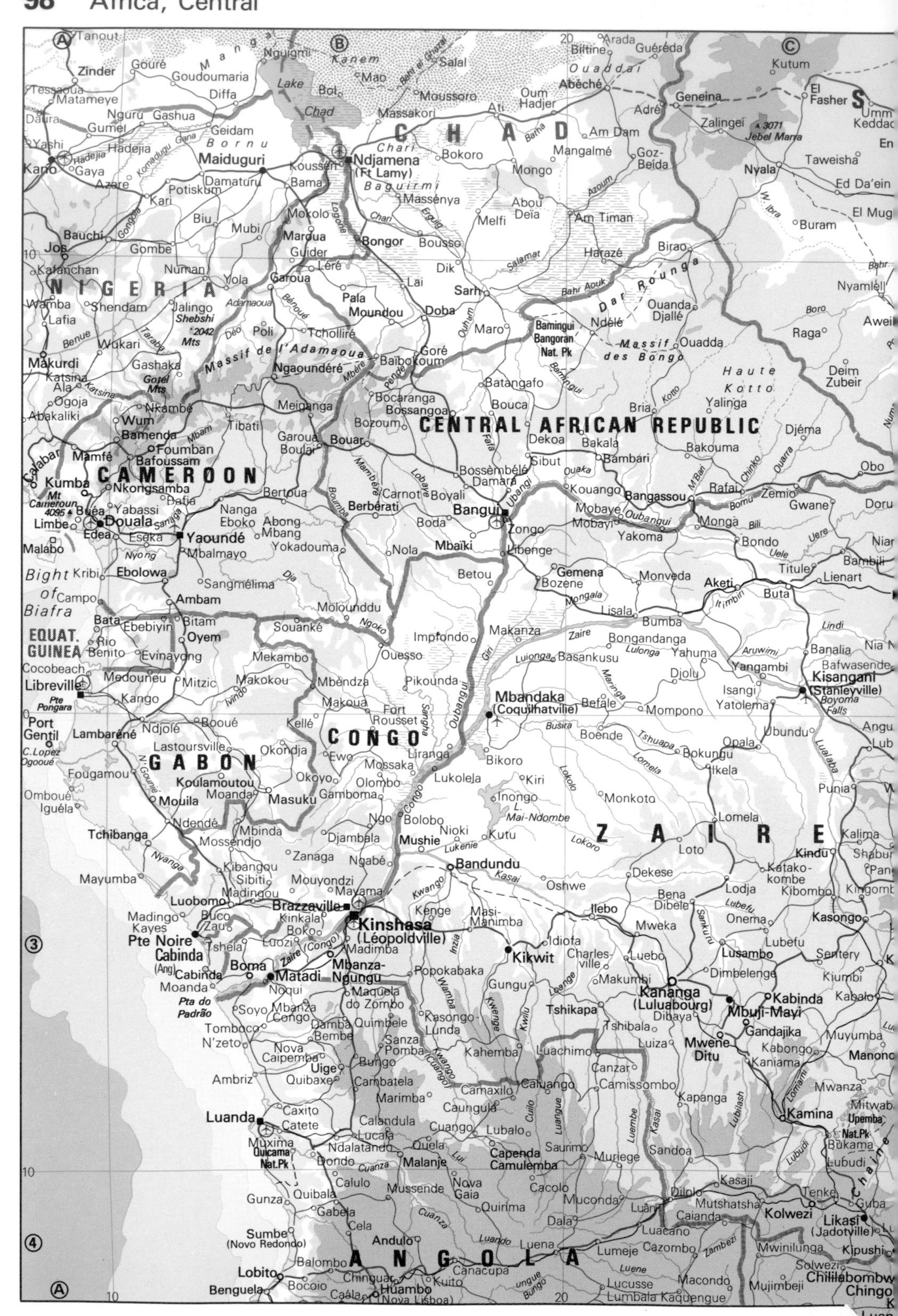
A
B
C
Tanout
Zinder
Gouré
Manga
Nguigmi
Kanem
Mao
Salal
Bahr el Ghazal
Goudoumaria
Diffa
Tessaoua
Matameye
Daura
Nguru
Gashua
Gumel
Geidam
Bornu
Lake Chad
Bol
Moussoro
Massakori
Ati
Oum Hadjer
Biltine
Arada
Guéréda
Ouaddai
Abéché
Adré
Geneina
Kutum
El Fasher
Umm Keddad
Zalingei
3071
Jebel Marra
Am Dam
Mangalmé
Goz-Beïda
Nyala
Taweisha
Ed Da'ein
El Mug
Buram
Yashi
Hadejia
Kano
Gaya
Azare
Komadugu Gana
Maiduguri
Kousseri
Ndjamena
(Ft Lamy)
Chari
Bokoro
Mongo
C H A D
Baguirmi
Massenya
Bama
Damaturu
Potiskum
Kari
Biu
Mubi
Mokolo
Logone
Erguig
Abou Deïa
Melfi
Am Timan
Azoum
Batha
Bauchi
Gongola
Jos
Gombe
Kafanchan
Maroua
Guider
Bongor
Bousso
Harazé
Birao
Numan
Léré
Lai
Dik
Salamat
Bahr Aouk
Dar Rounga
Yola
Garoua
Sarh
NIGERIA
Wamba
Lafia
Shendam
Jalingo
Shebshi Mts
2042
Adamaoua
Bénoué
Pala
Moundou
Doba
Ouham
Maro
Bamingui Bangoran Nat. Pk
Ndélé
Ouanda Djallé
Nyamlell
Boro
Raga
Awei
Benue
Wukari
Taraba
Déo
Poli
Tcholliré
Massif de l'Adamaoua
Massif des Bongo
Ouadda
Haute Kotto
Deim Zubeir
Makurdi
Gashaka
Gotel Mts
Katsina Ala
Katsina
Ngaoundéré
Mbéré
Pende
Baïbokoum
Goré
Batangafo
Bamingui
Kotto
Ogoja
Abakaliki
Nkambé
Wum
Bamenda
Mbam
Tibati
Meiganga
Bocaranga
Bossangoa
Bouca
Bria
Yalinga
Foumban
Bafoussam
Mamfé
Calabar
Garoua Boulai
Bouar
Bozoum
CENTRAL AFRICAN REPUBLIC
Djéma
Dekoa
Bakala
Fafa
Sibut
Bambari
Bakouma
Kumba
CAMEROON
Mt Cameroun 4095
Nkongsamba
Bafia
Buéa
Limbe
Yabassi
Douala
Edea
Sanaga
Bertoua
Mambéré
Lobaye
Carnot
Boyali
Bossèmbélé
Damara
Ouaka
Kouango
Bangassou
Rafai
Chinko
Ouarra
M'Bari
Obo
Zemio
Bomu
Gwane
Doru
Malabo
Eséka
Yaoundé
Mbalmayo
Nyong
Nanga Eboko
Abong Mbang
Yokadouma
Boumba
Berbérati
Boda
Bangui
Ubangi
Zongo
Mobaye
Mobayi
Oubangui
Yakoma
Monga
Bili
Bondo
Uere
Uele
Niar
Bambili
Bight of Biafra
Kribi
Campo
Ebolowa
Sangmélima
Dja
Ambam
Nola
Mbaïki
Libenge
Betou
Gemena
Bozene
Monveda
Aketi
Titule
Lienart
Buta
Itimbiri
Mongala
Lisala
Bumba
Moloundou
Ngoko
EQUAT. GUINEA
Bata
Ebebiyin
Bitam
Oyem
Rio Benito
Evinayong
Cocobeach
Souanké
Mekambo
Impfondo
Makanza
Zaire
Bongandanga
Lulonga
Yahuma
Aruwimi
Lindi
Banalia
Bafwasende
Libreville
Pte Pongara
Medouneu
Mitzic
Makokou
Ivindo
Kango
Ouesso
Mbendza
Pikounda
Giri
Luilonga
Basankusu
Maringa
Djolu
Yangambi
Isangi
Kisangani
(Stanleyville)
Yatolema
Boyoma Falls
Makoua
Fort Rousset
Sangha
Oubangui
Mbandaka
(Coquilhatville)
Befale
Mompono
Port Gentil
C. Lopez
Ogooué
Lambaréné
Ndjolé
Booué
Kellé
Lastoursville
Okondja
CONGO
GABON
Ewo
Liranga
Busira
Boende
Tshuapa
Bokungu
Lomela
Opala
Ubundu
Lualaba
Angu
Lub
Fougamou
Ngounié
Koulamoutou
Moanda
Masuku
Okoyo
Mossaka
Olombo
Gamboma
Lukolela
Bikoro
Kiri
Lokolo
Ikela
Omboué
Iguéla
Mouila
Inongo
L. Mai-Ndombe
Monkota
Punia
Tchibanga
Ndendé
Mbinda
Mossendjo
Nyanga
Djambala
Ngo
Bolobo
Mushie
Nioki
Lukenie
Kutu
ZAIRE
Lomela
Lokoro
Kalima
Kindu
Shabunda
Mayumba
Kibangou
Sibiti
Madingou
Zanaga
Ngabé
Mouyondzi
Mayama
Bandundu
Kasai
Oshwe
Dekese
Loto
Katako-kombe
Kibombo
Kingombe
Pangi
Luobomo
Madingo Kayes
Pte Noire
Buco Zau
Brazzaville
Kinkala
Boko
Kinshasa
(Léopoldville)
Kwango
Kenge
Masi-Manimba
Inzia
Ilebo
Bena Dibele
Sankuru
Lubefu
Lodja
Onema
Kasongo
Cabinda
(Ang)
Tshela
Luozi
Zaire (Congo)
Madimba
Mbanza-Ngungu
Boma
Matadi
Noqui
Kikwit
Idiofa
Charlesville
Mweka
Luebo
Makumbi
Lusambo
Sentery
Kiumbi
Moanda
Pta do Padrão
Soyo
Mbanza Congo
Maquela do Zombo
Popokabaka
Wamba
Gungu
Kwenge
Loange
Tshikapa
Kananga
(Luluabourg)
Dibaya
Dimbelenge
Mbuji-Mayi
Kabinda
Kabalo
Tomboco
N'zeto
Damba
Quimbele
Bembe
Kasongo-Lunda
Kwilu
Tshibala
Luiza
Mwene Ditu
Gandajika
Muyumba
Kabongo
Kaniama
Manono
Ambriz
Nova Caipemba
Uige
Quibaxe
Sanza Pomba
Bungo
Kwango (Cuango)
Kahemba
Luachimo
Canzar
Camissombo
Cambatela
Camaxilo
Caluango
Kapanga
Mwanza
Lomami
Lubilash
Caxito
Luanda
Catete
Marimba
Calandula
Caungula
Cuango
Lubalo
Cuilo
Luengue
Luembe
Kasai
Kamina
Mitwaba
Upemba Nat. Pk
Muxima
Quiçama Nat. Pk
Lucala
Ndalatando
Quela
Lui
Capenda Camulemba
Saurimo
Muriege
Sandoa
Bukama
Lubudi
Chaîne
Dondo
Cuanza
Malanje
Calulo
Mussende
Nova Gaia
Cacolo
Kasaji
Dilolo
Tenke
Gunza
Quibala
Gabela
Quirima
Muconda
Mutshatsha
Kolwezi
Guba
Likasi
(Jadotville)
Cela
Dala
Luau
Caianda
Sumbe
(Novo Redondo)
Andulo
Luando
Luena
Luacano
Zambezi
Mwinilunga
Kipushi
Lobito
Balombo
ANGOLA
Canacupa
Lumeje
Cazombo
Solwezi
Chililabombwe
Benguela
Bocoio
Chinguar
Huambo
(Nova Lisboa)
Kuito
Caála
Bungo
Lucusse
Lumbala Kaquengue
Macondo
Mujimbeji
Chingola
Luanshya
10
20
0
3
4

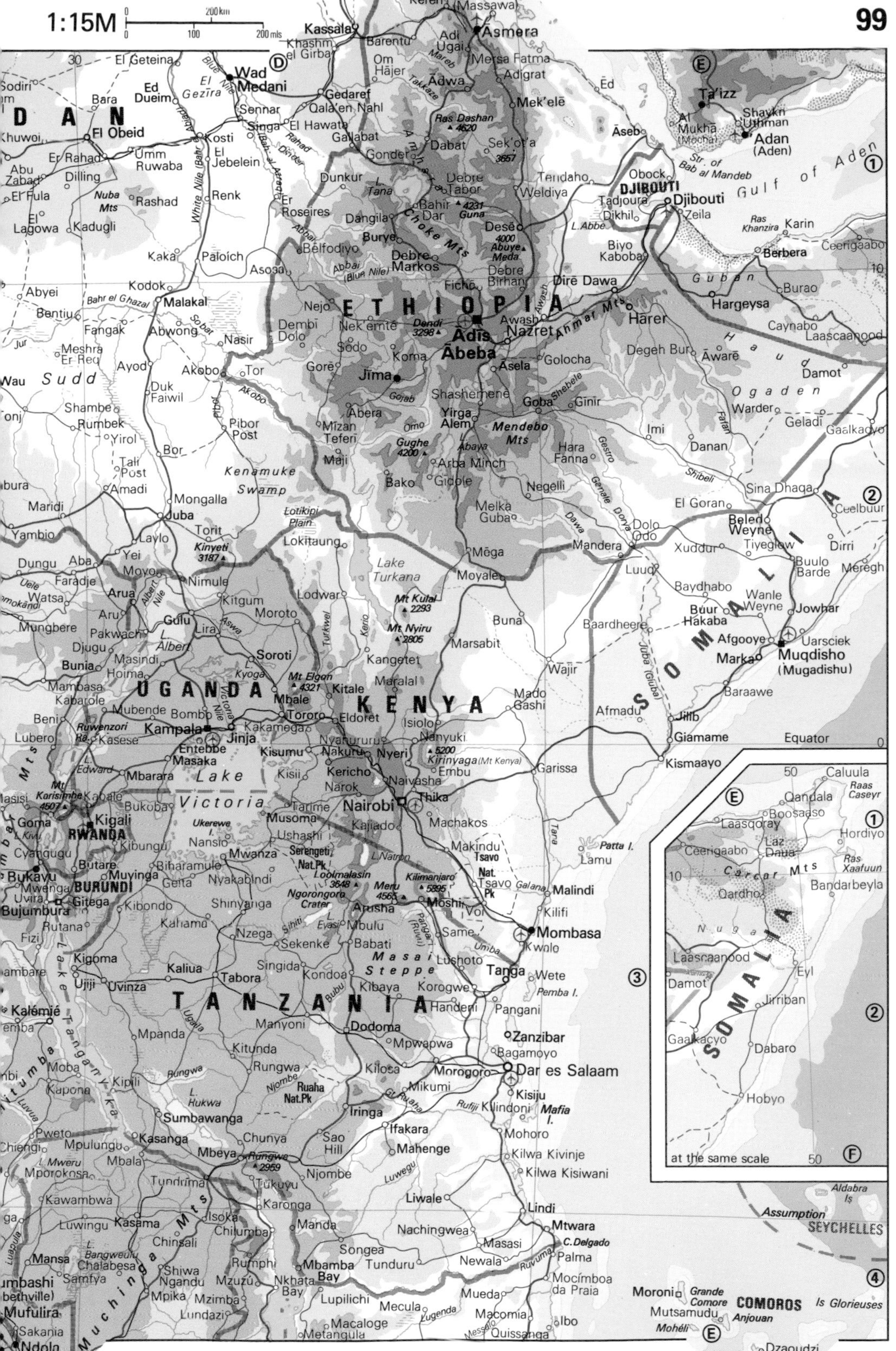

1:15M

200 km
100   200 mls

ETHIOPIA

SOMALIA

KENYA

UGANDA

TANZANIA

RWANDA

BURUNDI

DJIBOUTI

Gulf of Aden

COMOROS

SEYCHELLES

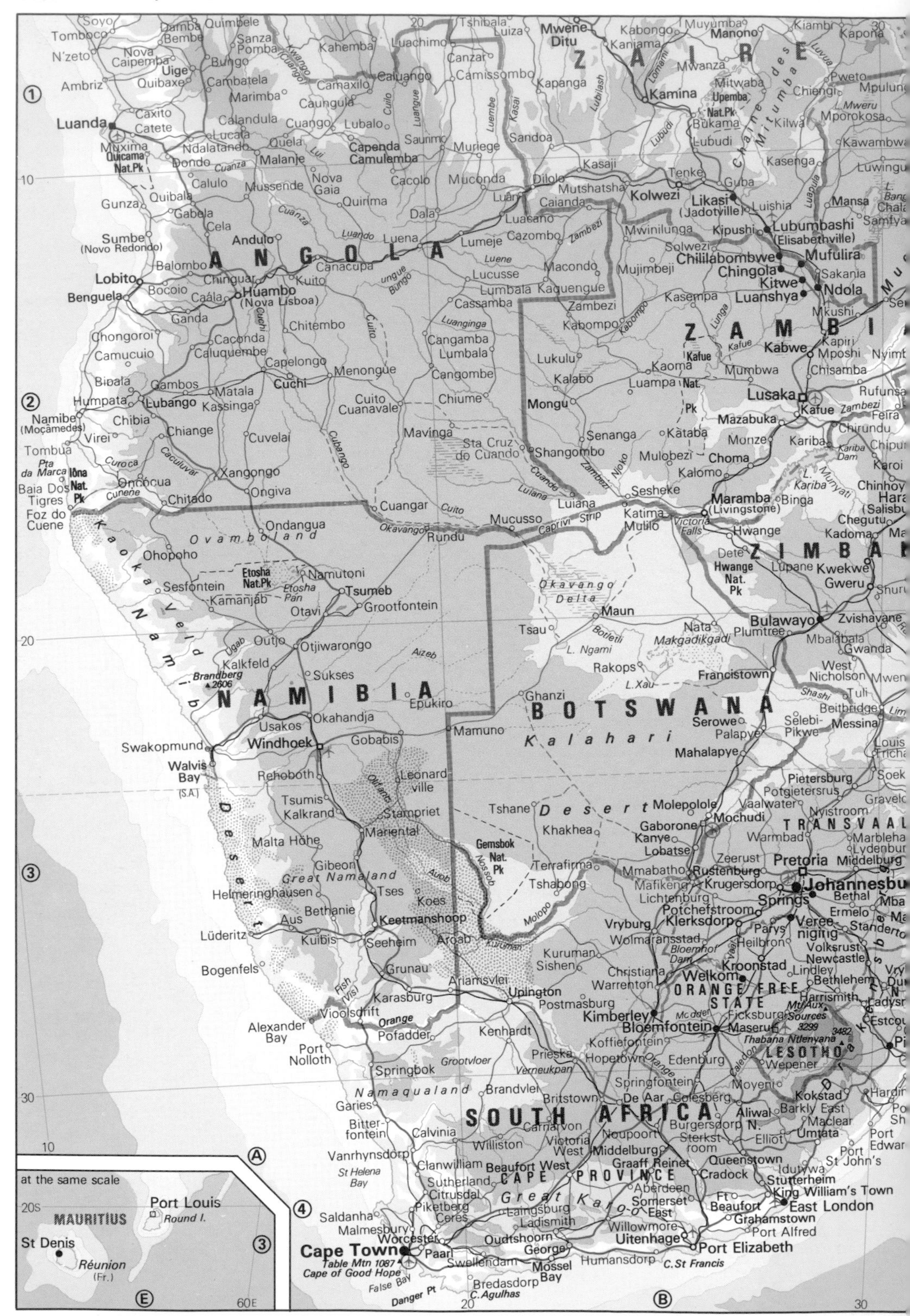
ANGOLA
ZAIRE
ZAMBIA
NAMIBIA
BOTSWANA
ZIMBABWE
SOUTH AFRICA
TRANSVAAL
ORANGE FREE STATE
CAPE PROVINCE
LESOTHO
Soyo
Tomboco
N'zeto
Ambriz
Damba
Bembe
Quimbele
Nova Caipemba
Uige
Quibaxe
Sanza Pomba
Bungo
Cambatela
Marimba
Luanda
Caxito
Catete
Muxima
Quicama Nat.Pk
Calandula
Lucala
Ndalatando
Dondo
Cuanza
Malanje
Calulo
Mussende
Nova Gaia
Quibala
Gunza
Gabela
Cela
Sumbe (Novo Redondo)
Andulo
Balombo
Lobito
Benguela
Bocoio
Chinguar
Huambo (Nova Lisboa)
Caála
Ganda
Kuito
Canacupa
Chitembo
Caconda
Caluquembe
Chongoroi
Camucuio
Capelongo
Cuchi
Menongue
Bibala
Gambos
Matala
Humpata
Lubango
Kassinga
Namibe (Moçamedes)
Chibia
Virei
Chiange
Cuvelai
Tombua
Pta da Marca
Iôna Nat. Pk
Baia Dos Tigres
Foz do Cuene
Curoca
Caculuvar
Oncócua
Xangongo
Cunene
Chitado
Ongiva
Cuito Cuanavale
Cubango
Cuangar
Cuito
Kahemba
Luachimo
Camaxilo
Caluango
Caungula
Cuango
Lubalo
Quela
Capenda Camulemba
Saurimo
Muriege
Cacolo
Muconda
Quirima
Dala
Luena
Luando
Lumeje
Cazombo
Lucusse
Lumbala Kaquengue
Cassamba
Luanginga
Cangamba
Lumbala
Cangombe
Chiume
Mavinga
Sta Cruz do Cuando
Tshibala
Luiza
Mwene Ditu
Canzar
Camissombo
Kapanga
Sandoa
Dilolo
Kasaji
Mutshatsha
Caiandi
Luacano
Luau
Kabongo
Kaniama
Kamina
Manono
Muyumba
Mwanza
Mitwaba
Upemba Nat.Pk
Bukama
Lubudi
Tenke
Kolwezi
Likasi (Jadotville)
Guba
Lubumbashi (Elisabethville)
Kipushi
Mwinilunga
Solwezi
Mujimbeji
Chililabombwe
Chingola
Kitwe
Luanshya
Mufulira
Sakania
Ndola
Kasempa
Zambezi
Macondo
Kabompo
Mkushi
Kapiri Mposhi
Kabwe
Kafue
Mumbwa
Chisamba
Lusaka
Kaoma
Lukulu
Kalabo
Luampa
Mongu
Senanga
Kataba
Mazabuka
Monze
Kariba
Choma
Mulobezi
Kalomo
Shangombo
Sesheke
Luiana
Katima Mulilo
Maramba (Livingstone)
Victoria Falls
Binga
Hwange
Hwange Nat. Pk
Dete
Lupane
Kwekwe
Gweru
Kadoma
Chegutu
Chinhoyi
Karoi
Chirundu
L. Kariba
Kiambi
Kapona
Pweto
Chiengi
Mpulungu
L. Mweru
Kilwa
Mporokosa
Kawambwa
Kasenga
Luwingu
Mansa
Luishia
Samfya
Chaîne des Mitumba
Mucusso
Caprivi Strip
Rundu
Okavango
Ovamboland
Ondangua
Ohopoho
Etosha Nat.Pk
Etosha Pan
Namutoni
Tsumeb
Sesfontein
Kamanjab
Otavi
Grootfontein
Outjo
Otjiwarongo
Kalkfeld
Brandberg 2606
Sukses
Kaokoveld
Namib Desert
Epukiro
Okahandja
Usakos
Swakopmund
Windhoek
Gobabis
Walvis Bay (S.A.)
Rehoboth
Leonardville
Olifants
Tsumis
Kalkrand
Stampriet
Mariental
Malta Höhe
Gibeon
Great Namaland
Helmeringhausen
Tses
Koes
Bethanie
Aus
Lüderitz
Keetmanshoop
Kuibis
Seeheim
Aroab
Bogenfels
Grunau
Karasburg
Fish
Vioolsdrift
Orange
Alexander Bay
Pofadder
Port Nolloth
Springbok
Okavango Delta
Maun
Tsau
Nata
Makgadikgadi
Botletli
L. Ngami
Rakops
Francistown
L. Xau
Ghanzi
Mamuno
Kalahari Desert
Serowe
Palapye
Mahalapye
Tshane
Molepolole
Mochudi
Gaborone
Kanye
Lobatse
Khakhea
Gemsbok Nat. Pk
Nossob
Terrafirma
Tshabong
Molopo
Auob
Bulawayo
Plumtree
Zvishavane
Mbalabala
Gwanda
West Nicholson
Shashi
Tuli
Beitbridge
Messina
Selebi-Pikwe
Pietersburg
Potgietersrus
Vaalwater
Nylstroom
Warmbad
Marble Hall
Lydenburg
Zeerust
Pretoria
Middelburg
Mmabatho
Rustenburg
Mafikeng
Krugersdorp
Johannesburg
Lichtenburg
Springs
Bethal
Potchefstroom
Ermelo
Klerksdorp
Vereeniging
Parys
Standerton
Vryburg
Wolmaransstad
Heilbron
Volksrust
Newcastle
Bloemhof Dam
Kroonstad
Lindley
Kuruman
Sishen
Christiana
Welkom
Bethlehem
Warrenton
Harrismith
Upington
Ariamsvlei
Postmasburg
Kimberley
Bloemfontein
Ficksburg
Mt Aux Sources 3299
Maseru
Thabana Ntlenyana 3482
Kenhardt
Koffiefontein
Prieska
Hopetown
Edenburg
Wepener
Grootvloer
Verneukpan
Springfontein
Moyeni
Namaqualand
Brandvlei
Britstown
De Aar
Colesberg
Aliwal N.
Kokstad
Barkly East
Maclear
Garies
Bitterfontein
Calvinia
Williston
Carnarvon
Victoria West
Noupoort
Burgersdorp
Sterkstroom
Elliot
Umtata
Vanrhynsdorp
Clanwilliam
Beaufort West
Middelburg
Graaff Reinet
Queenstown
Port St John's
St Helena Bay
Sutherland
Cradock
Idutywa
Stutterheim
Citrusdal
Great Karoo
Aberdeen
King William's Town
Saldanha
Piketberg
Laingsburg
Somerset East
Ft Beaufort
East London
Malmesbury
Ceres
Ladismith
Grahamstown
Worcester
Willowmore
Port Alfred
Cape Town
Oudtshoorn
Uitenhage
Port Elizabeth
Table Mtn 1087
Cape of Good Hope
Paarl
George
Swellendam
Mossel Bay
Humansdorp
C. St Francis
False Bay
Bredasdorp
Danger Pt
C. Agulhas
at the same scale
MAURITIUS
Port Louis
Round I.
St Denis
Réunion (Fr.)
20S
60E
10
20
30
1
2
3
4
A
B
E

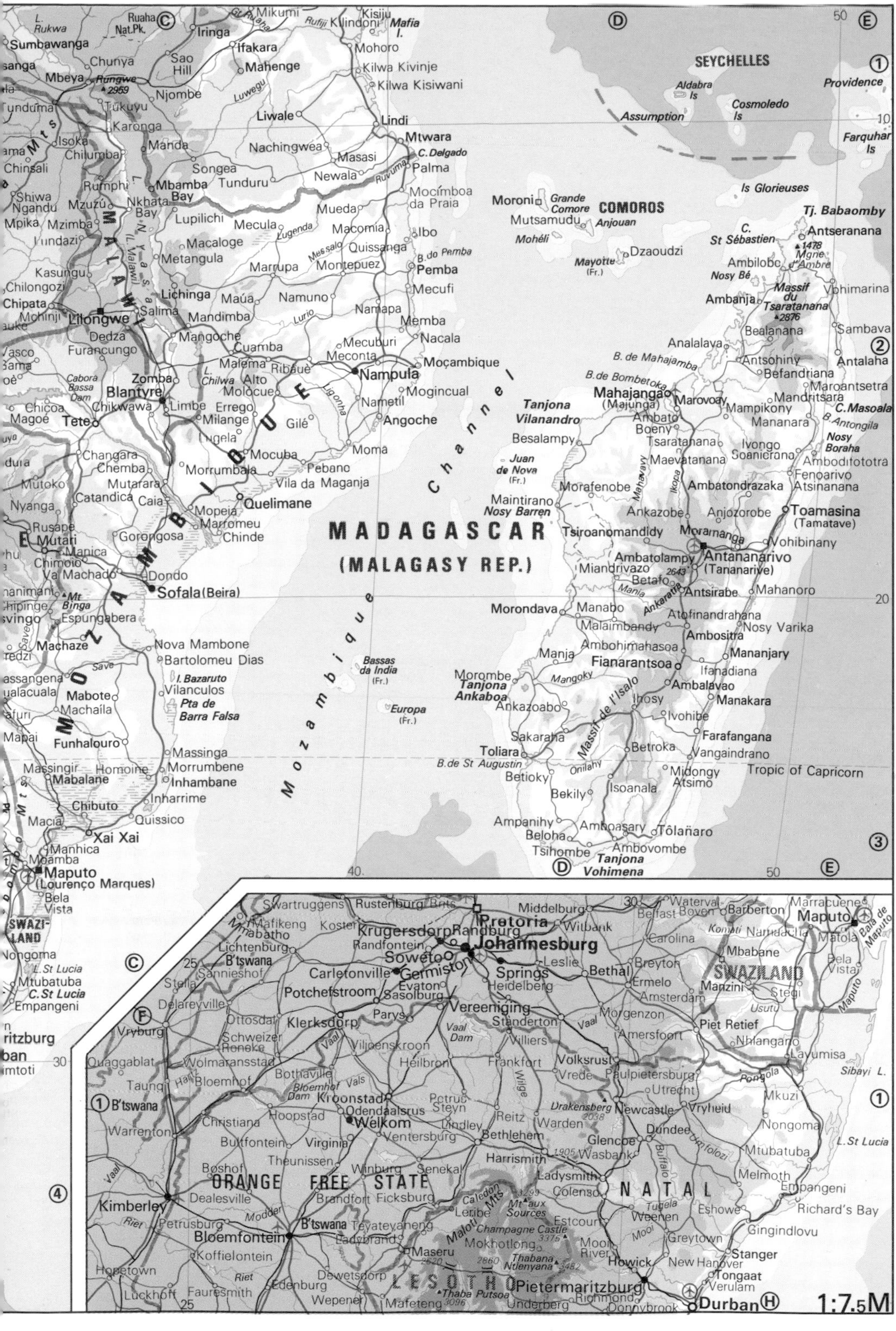

L. Rukwa Sumbawanga sanga Chunya Mbeya ·Rungwe *2959 tunduma Tukuyu Karonga Isoka Chilumba Chinsali Shiwa Ngandu Mzuzu Nkhata Bay Mpika Mzimba Yundazi Metangula Kasungu Chilongozi Chipata Mchinji Lilongwe Dedza Salima Mandimba Vasco Furancungo Gama Cabora Bassa Dam Zomba Chilwa Blantyre Chikwawa Limbe Errego Chicoa Magoé Teté Milange Fingela Mocuba Changara Chemba Morrumbala Mutoko Mutarara Nyanga Catandica Caia Rusape Mutati Gorongosa Chimoio Va' Machado Dondo Sofala (Beira)

Ruaha Nat.Pk. Iringa Mikumi Rufiji Kilindoni Mafia I. Kisiju Ifakara Mahenge Mohoro Kilwa Kivinje Sao Hill Njombe Liwale Kilwa Kisiwani Lindi Manda Nachingwea Mtwara C. Delgado Songea Tunduru Newala Palma Mocimboa da Praia Mbamba Bay Mueda Macomia Lupilichi Mecula Ilbo Quissanga Macaloge Montepuez Pemba Marrupa Mecufi Namuno Namapa Memba Meconta Nacala Mecuburi Moçambique Malema Ribauè Nampula Alto Molócuè Mogincual Nametil Angoche Gilé Moma Pebane Vila da Maganja

SEYCHELLES Aldabra Is Providence Assumption Is Cosmoledo Is Farquhar Is Is Glorieuses Moroni Grande Comore COMOROS Tj. Babaomby Mutsamudu Anjouan Antseranana Mohéli C. St Sébastien *1478 Mgne d'Ambre Mayotte (Fr.) Dzaoudzi Ambilobe Nosy Bé Massif du Tsaratanana *2876 Vohimarina Ambanja Sambava Analalava Antsohihy Befandriana B. de Mahajamba Antalaha B. de Bombetoka Mahajanga (Majunga) Marovoay Mampikony Mandritsara C. Masoala Tanjona Vilanandro Ambato Boeny Tsaratanana Mananara B. Antongila Besalampy Maevatanana Ivongo Soanierana Nosy Boraha Juan de Nova (Fr.) Morafenobe Ankazobe Anjozorobe Ambodifototra Fenoarivo Atsinanana Maintirano Nosy Barren Tsiroanomandidy Moramanga Toamasina (Tamatave)

MADAGASCAR (MALAGASY REP.) Ambatolampy Antananarivo (Tananarive) Vohibinany Miandrivazo Betafo Antsirabe Mahanoro Morondava Manabo Atofinandrahana Malaimbandy Ambohimahasoa Ambositra Nosy Varika Manja Fianarantsoa Ambalavao Mananjary Morombe Tanjona Ankaboa Mangoky Ifanadiana Manakara Ankazoabo Massif de l'Isalo Ihosy Ivohibe Sakaraha Farafangana Betroka Vangaindrano Toliara Onilahy Midongy Atsimo Tropic of Capricorn B. de St Augustin Betioky Isoanala Ampanihy Ambosary Tôlanaro Beloha Ambovombe Tsihombe Tanjona Vohimena

Mozambique Channel

MOZAMBIQUE Manica Mt Binga * Espungabera Machaze Nova Mambone Bartolomeu Dias I. Bazaruto Mabote Vilanculos Machaila Pta de Barra Falsa Funhalouro Massinga Morrumbene Massingir Homoíne Mabalane Inhambane Mapai Inharrime Chibuto Quissico Macia Xai Xai Manhica Moamba Maputo (Lourenço Marques) Bela Vista SWAZILAND Nongoma L. St Lucia Mtubatuba C. St Lucia Empangeni maritzburg ban imtoti

Bassas da India (Fr.) Europa (Fr.)

1:7.5M inset

Swartruggens Rustenburg Brits Middelburg Waterval Barberton Marracuene Mafikeng Koster Krugersdorp Randburg **Pretoria** Witbank Belfast Bovon Komati Namaacha **Maputo** Matola Baia de Maputo Lichtenburg Randfontein **Johannesburg** Carolina Mbabane Bela Vista Carletonville Germiston Springs Leslie Bethal Breyten SWAZILAND Sannieshof Potchefstroom Sasolburg Heidelberg Ermelo Manzini Usutu Delareyville Parys Vereeniging Standerton Amsterdam Klerksdorp Standerton Morgenzon Piet Retief Nhlangano Vryburg Schweizer Reneke Viljoenskroon Vaal Dam Villiers Amersfoort Layumisa Quaggablat Wolmaransstad Bothaville Heilbron Frankfort Vrede Paulpietersburg Sibayi L. Taung Bloemhof Vals Reitz Warden Utrecht Mkuzi B'tswana Christiana Hoopstad Odendaalsrus Petrus Steyn Lindley Bethlehem Drakensberg Newcastle Vryheid Ngonoma Warrenton Welkom Ventersburg Harrismith Glencoe Dundee L.St Lucia Mtubatuba **ORANGE FREE STATE** Dealesville Brandfort Ficksburg Ladysmith Colenso Wasbank Melmoth Kimberley B'tswana Teyateyaneng Calédon Mooi **NATAL** Weenen Eshowe Richard's Bay Petrusburg Maseru Champagne Castle Estcourt River Greytown Gingindlovu Bloemfontein Mokhotlong Thabana Ntlenyana *3482 Mooi New Hanover Stanger Koffiefontein LESOTHO Howick Tongaat Verulam Hopetown Edenburg Thaba Putsoa Pietermaritzburg Richmond **Durban**

1:7.5M

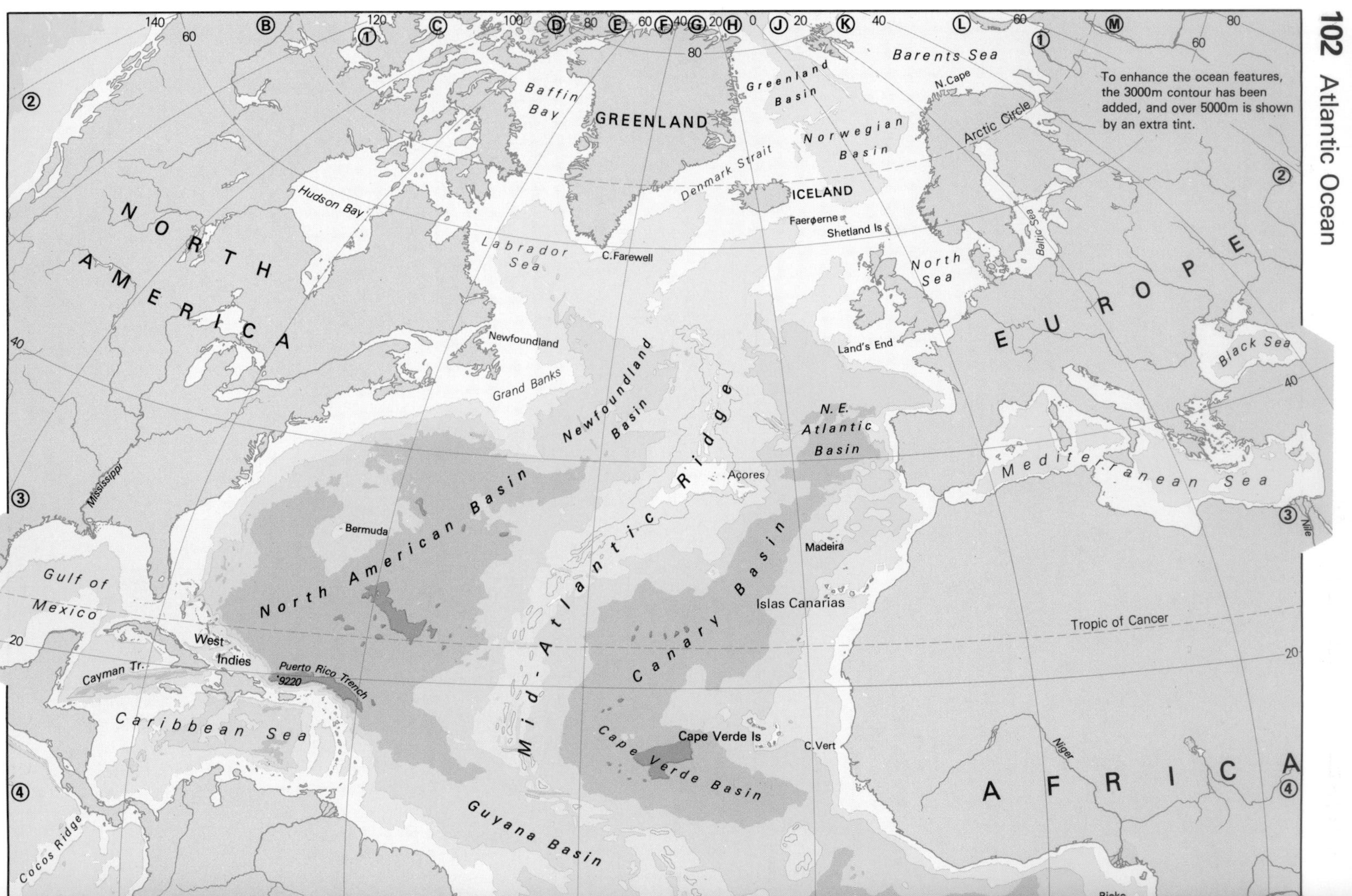
To enhance the ocean features, the 3000m contour has been added, and over 5000m is shown by an extra tint.
NORTH AMERICA
EUROPE
AFRICA
GREENLAND
ICELAND
Barents Sea
N.Cape
Arctic Circle
Baltic Sea
Black Sea
Nile
Mediterranean Sea
Tropic of Cancer
Niger
North Sea
Norwegian Basin
Greenland Basin
Denmark Strait
Faerøerne
Shetland Is
Land's End
N.E. Atlantic Basin
Madeira
Islas Canarias
C.Vert
Cape Verde Is
Cape Verde Basin
Canary Basin
Açores
Mid-Atlantic Ridge
Newfoundland Basin
C.Farewell
Baffin Bay
Labrador Sea
Newfoundland
Grand Banks
Hudson Bay
North American Basin
Bermuda
Puerto Rico Trench
9220
West Indies
Caribbean Sea
Cayman Tr.
Gulf of Mexico
Mississippi
Guyana Basin
Cocos Ridge

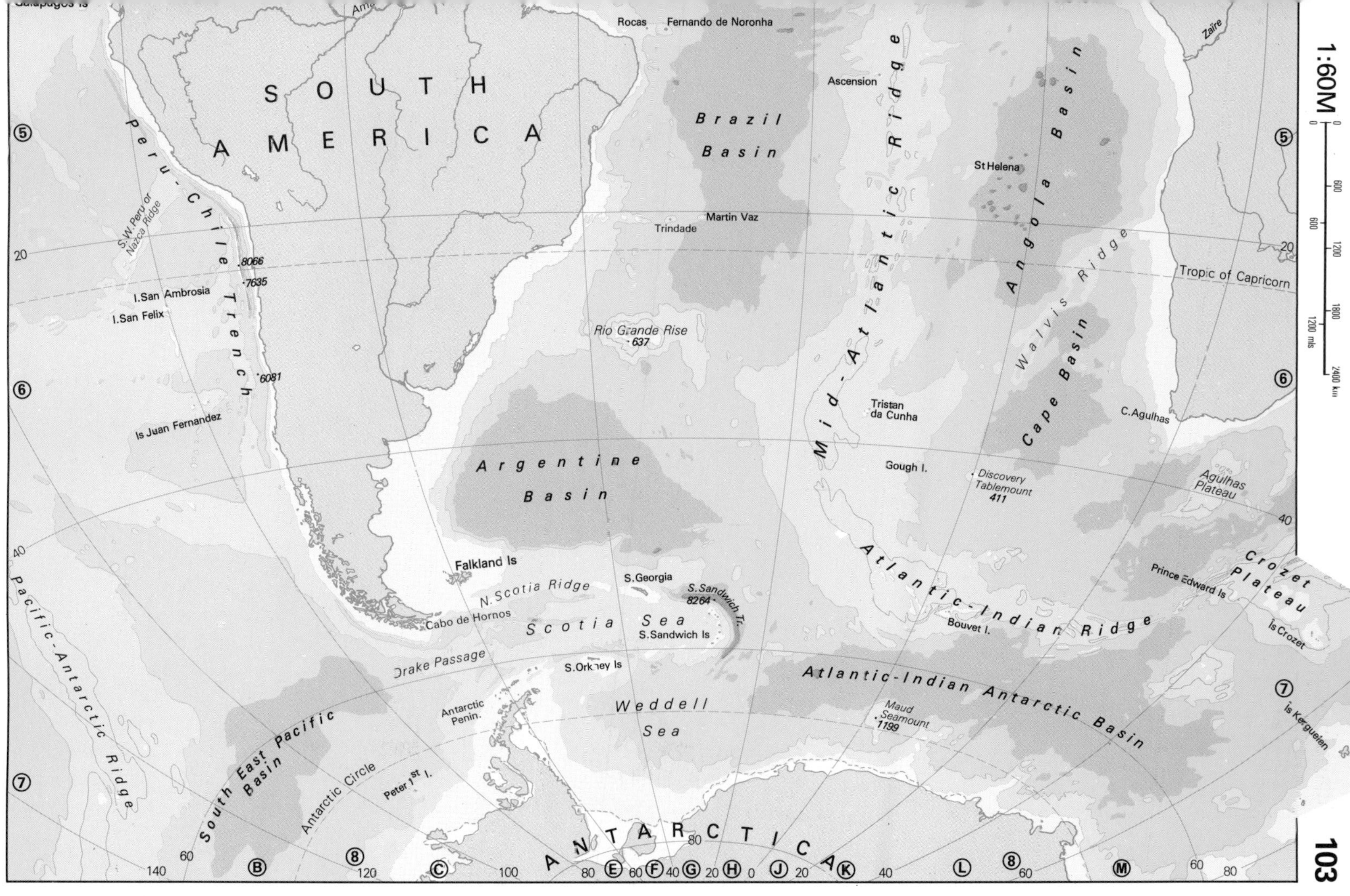

600 1200 1800 2400 km
600   1200 mls

Zaïre

Tropic of Capricorn

Agulhas Plateau

Crozet Plateau

Is Crozet

Prince Edward Is

Is Kerguelen

C. Agulhas

Cape Basin

Walvis Ridge

Angola Basin

St Helena

Discovery Tablemount 411

Atlantic-Indian Ridge

Atlantic-Indian Antarctic Basin

Bouvet I.

Maud Seamount 1199

Mid-Atlantic Ridge

Tristan da Cunha

Gough I.

Ascension

Brazil Basin

Fernando de Noronha

Rocas

Martin Vaz

Trindade

Rio Grande Rise 637

Argentine Basin

S. Georgia

S. Sandwich Tr. 8264

S. Sandwich Is

Scotia Sea

Weddell Sea

A N T A R C T I C A

N. Scotia Ridge

Falkland Is

S. Ork'ey Is

Cabo de Hornos

Drake Passage

Antarctic Penin.

S O U T H   A M E R I C A

Andes

Peru-Chile Trench

8066
7635
6081

I. San Ambrosia

I. San Felix

Is Juan Fernandez

S. W. Peru or Nazca Ridge

Antarctic Circle

Peter I. Is

Pacific

South East Pacific Basin

Pacific-Antarctic Ridge

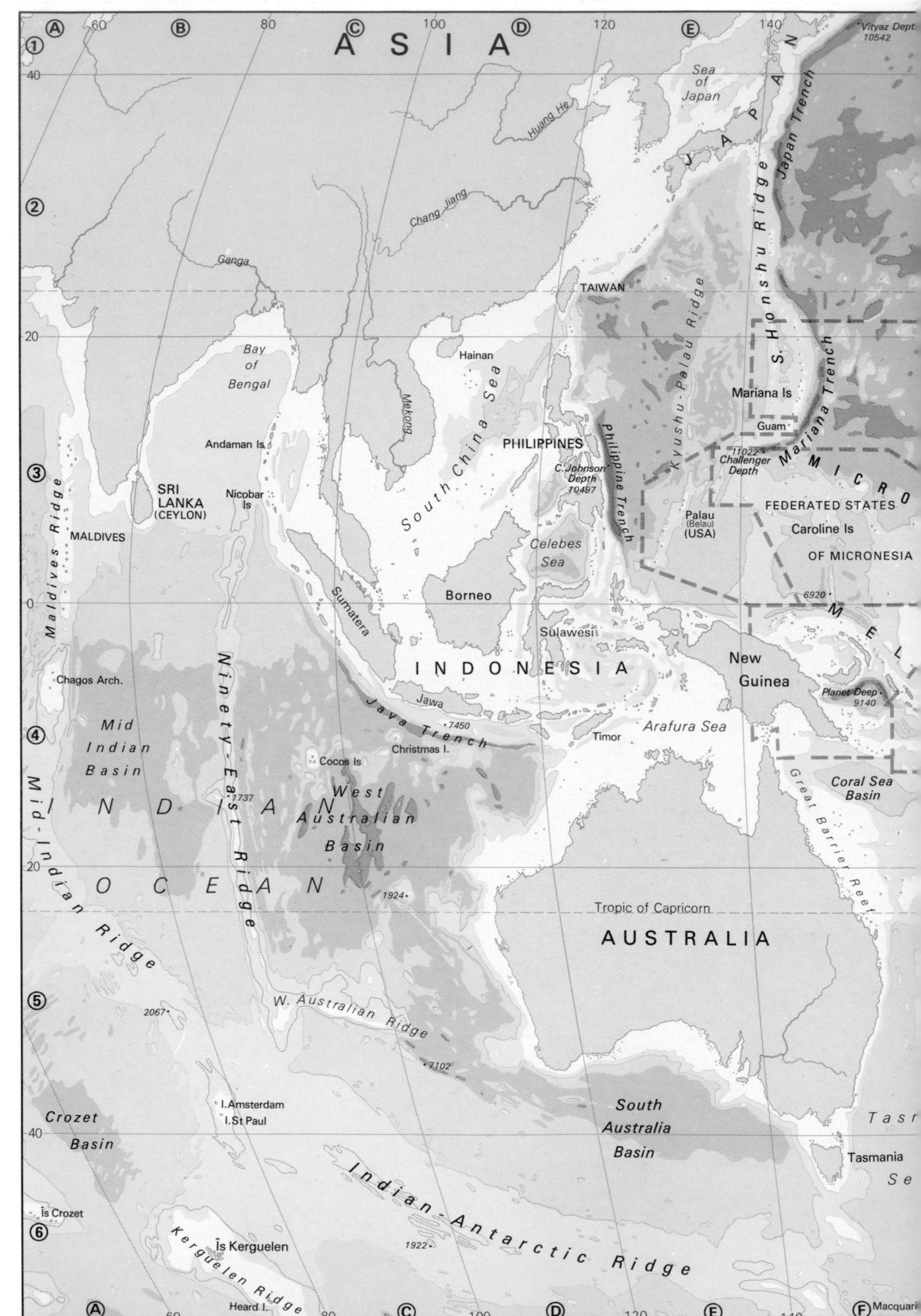

Ⓐ 60 Ⓑ 80 Ⓒ 100 Ⓓ 120 Ⓔ 140

① 40

A S I A

Sea of Japan

② *Chang Jiang*

Huang He

Ganga

J A P A N

Vityaz Dept. 10542

Japan Trench

20

Bay of Bengal

Hainan

TAIWAN

Mekong

S. Honshu Ridge

Andaman Is.

③ PHILIPPINES

C. Johnson Depth 10497

Mariana Is

Guam

MICRO

SRI LANKA (CEYLON)

Nicobar Is

Maldives Ridge

South China Sea

Kyushu-Palau Ridge

Philippine Trench

11022 Challenger Depth

Mariana Trench

MALDIVES

Celebes Sea

Palau (Belau) (USA)

FEDERATED STATES

Caroline Is

OF MICRONESIA

Chagos Arch.

Sumatera

Borneo

Sulawesi

I N D O N E S I A

6920

M E L I

New Guinea

④ *Mid Indian Basin*

Ninety-East Ridge

Java Trench

Jawa

7450

1737

Cocos Is

West Australian Basin

Christmas I.

Timor

Arafura Sea

Planet Deep 9140

Coral Sea Basin

Great Barrier Reef

I N D I A N

M I D - I N D I A N

O C E A N

1924

Tropic of Capricorn

A U S T R A L I A

W. Australian Ridge

⑤ *2067*

7102

Tas

Mid-Indian Ridge

I. Amsterdam

I. St Paul

Crozet Basin

South Australia Basin

Tasmania

Se

40

Îs Crozet

⑥ Îs Kerguelen

Kerguelen Ridge

1922

Indian-Antarctic Ridge

Heard I.

Macquari

Ⓐ 60 Ⓒ 80 Ⓒ 100 Ⓓ 120 Ⓔ 140 Ⓕ

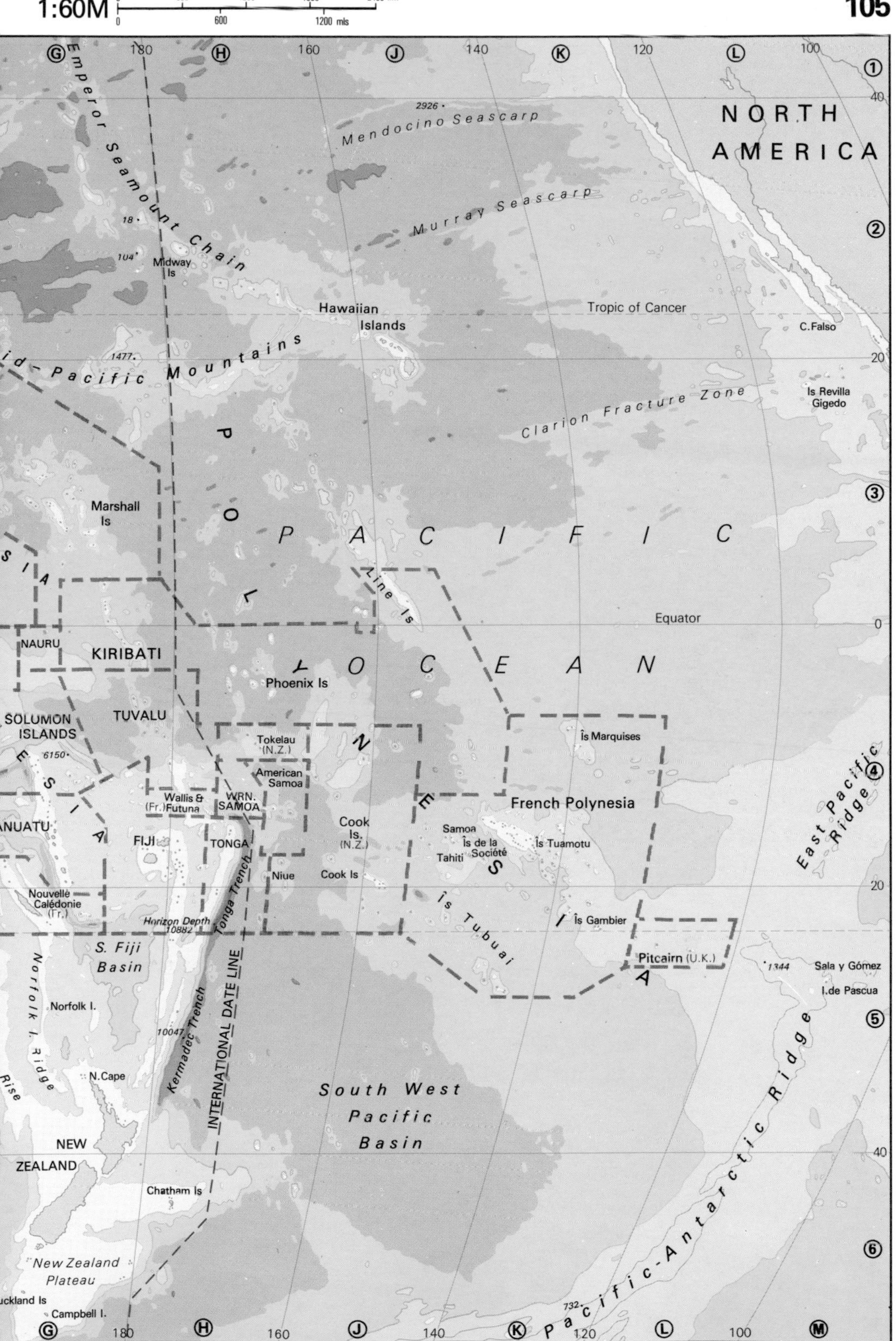

1:60M

600 1200 1800 2400 km
600 1200 mls

NORTH AMERICA

Mendocino Seascarp
2926·

Murray Seascarp

Emperor Seamount Chain

18·
104· Midway Is

Hawaiian Islands

Tropic of Cancer

C.Falso

Mid-Pacific Mountains
1477·

Clarion Fracture Zone

Is Revilla Gigedo

Marshall Is

P O L Y N E S I A

P A C I F I C

Line Is

Equator

NAURU

KIRIBATI

Phoenix Is

O C E A N

TUVALU

SOLOMON ISLANDS
6150·

Tokelau (N.Z.)

American Samoa

Îs Marquises

French Polynesia

East Pacific Ridge

VANUATU

Wallis & (Fr.)Futuna

WRN. SAMOA

Cook Is. (N.Z.)

Samoa
Îs de la Société
Tahiti

Îs Tuamotu

FIJI

TONGA

Niue

Cook Is

Îs Tubuai

Nouvelle Calédonie (Fr.)

Horizon Depth 10882

Îs Gambier

Pitcairn (U.K.)

1344·

Sala y Gómez

I.de Pascua

S. Fiji Basin

Norfolk I. Ridge

Norfolk I.

Rise

N.Cape

South West Pacific Basin

Pacific-Antarctic Ridge

NEW ZEALAND

Chatham Is

New Zealand Plateau

Auckland Is

Campbell I.

732·

INTERNATIONAL DATE LINE

Kermadec Trench
10047·

Tonga Trench

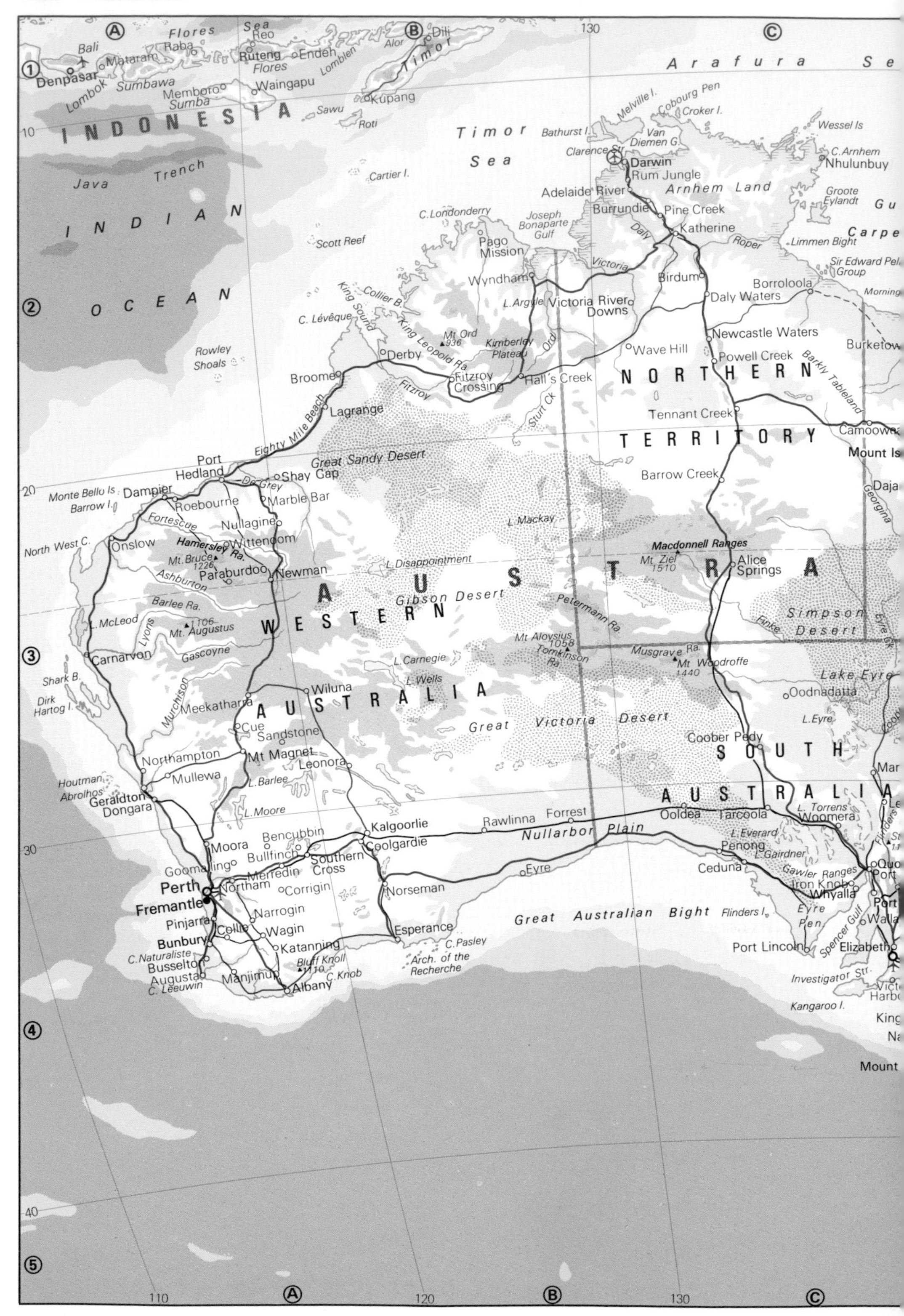
INDONESIA
Bali
Denpasar
Mataram
Lombok
Sumbawa
Flores Sea
Raba
Reo
Ruteng
Endeh
Flores
Lomblen
Alor
Dili
Timor
Memboro
Sumba
Waingapu
Sawu
Kupang
Roti
Arafura Sea
Timor Sea
Java Trench
INDIAN OCEAN
Cartier I.
Scott Reef
Rowley Shoals
Melville I.
Bathurst I.
Cobourg Pen
Croker I.
Van Diemen G.
Clarence Str.
Darwin
Rum Jungle
Adelaide River
Arnhem Land
Wessel Is
C. Arnhem
Nhulunbuy
Groote Eylandt
Burrundie
Pine Creek
Katherine
Daly
Roper
Limmen Bight
Sir Edward Pellew Group
C. Londonderry
Joseph Bonaparte Gulf
Pago Mission
Victoria
Wyndham
Birdum
Borroloola
Daly Waters
Collier B.
King Sound
C. Lévêque
King Leopold Ra.
Mt Ord 936
L. Argyle
Victoria River Downs
Kimberley Plateau
Ord
Newcastle Waters
Wave Hill
Powell Creek
Barkly Tableland
Derby
Broome
Fitzroy Crossing
Fitzroy
Hall's Creek
NORTHERN TERRITORY
Lagrange
Eighty Mile Beach
Sturt Ck
Tennant Creek
Camooweal
Mount Isa
Great Sandy Desert
Port Hedland
De Grey
Shay Gap
Barrow Creek
Monte Bello Is
Barrow I.
Dampier
Roebourne
Marble Bar
Fortescue
Nullagine
Wittenoom
Hamersley Ra.
Mt. Bruce 1226
Onslow
North West C.
L. Mackay
Macdonnell Ranges
Mt. Ziel 1510
Alice Springs
Georgina
L. Disappointment
Paraburdoo
Newman
Ashburton
AUSTRALIA
Gibson Desert
Petermann Ra.
Simpson Desert
Finke
Barlee Ra.
L. McLeod
Lyons
1106 Mt. Augustus
WESTERN AUSTRALIA
Gascoyne
Carnarvon
Mt Aloysius 1058
Tomkinson Ra.
Musgrave Ra.
Mt Woodroffe 1440
Lake Eyre
Shark B.
Dirk Hartog I.
L. Carnegie
L. Wells
Wiluna
Oodnadatta
Murchison
Meekatharra
L. Eyre
Cue
Sandstone
Great Victoria Desert
Coober Pedy
SOUTH AUSTRALIA
Northampton
Mt Magnet
Mullewa
Leonora
L. Barlee
Houtman Abrolhos
Geraldton
Dongara
L. Moore
Ooldea
Tarcoola
L. Torrens
Woomera
Kalgoorlie
Rawlinna
Forrest
Nullarbor Plain
L. Everard
Moora
Bencubbin
Bullfinch
Coolgardie
Southern Cross
Merredin
Goomalling
Penong
L. Gairdner
Ceduna
Gawler Ranges
Iron Knob
Whyalla
Eyre
Perth
Fremantle
Northam
Corrigin
Norseman
Narrogin
Pinjarra
Collie
Wagin
Bunbury
Esperance
Great Australian Bight
Flinders I.
Eyre Pen
Spencer Gulf
Katanning
C. Pasley
Port Lincoln
Elizabeth
C. Naturaliste
Busselton
Bluff Knoll 1110
Arch. of the Recherche
Augusta
C. Leeuwin
Manjimup
Albany
C. Knob
Investigator Str.
Kangaroo I.
Mount
A
B
C
1
2
3
4
5
10
20
30
40
110
120
130

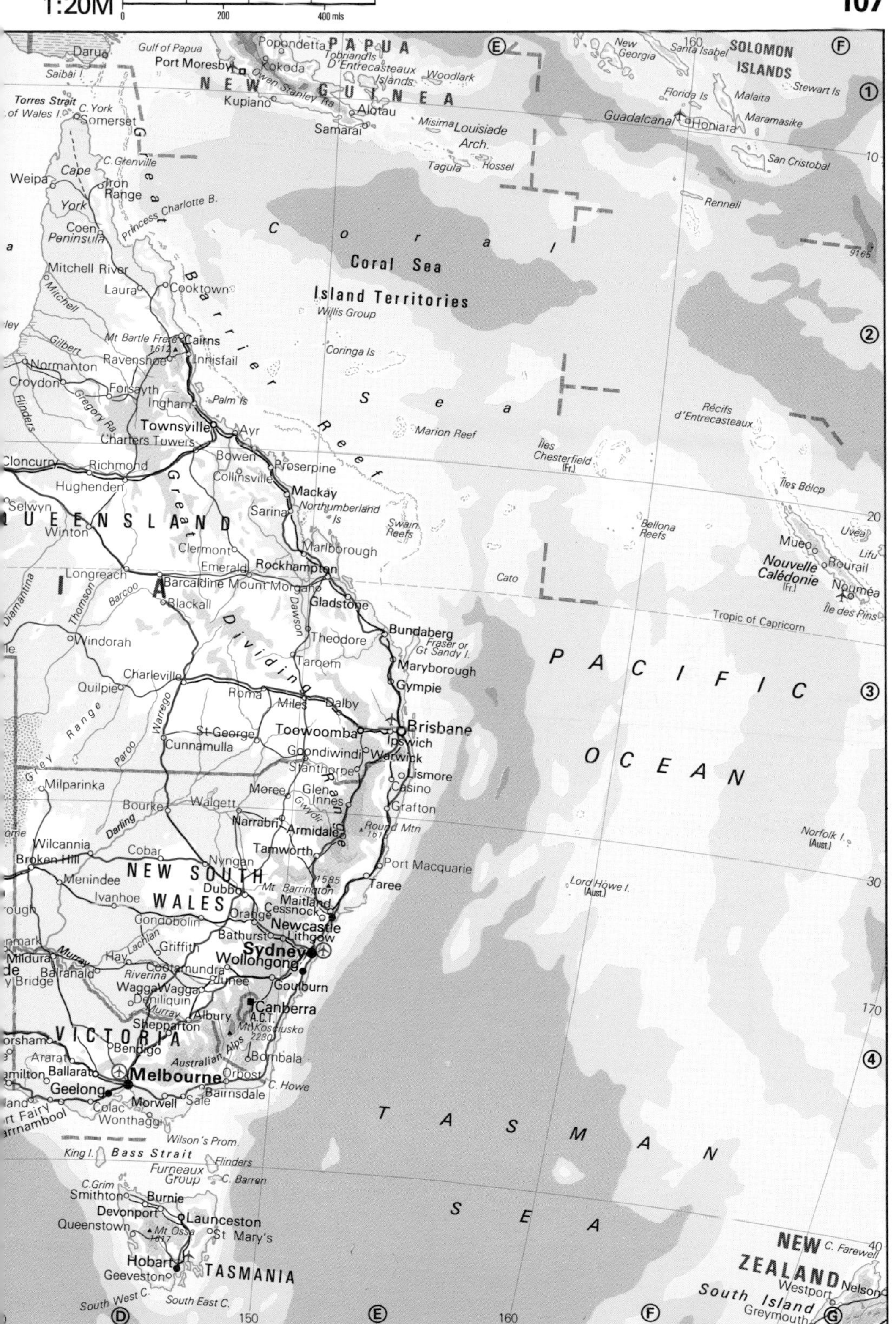

Darua
Gulf of Papua
Popondetta
Rokoda
PAPUA
New Georgia
Santa Isabel
SOLOMON ISLANDS
Port Moresby
Tobriand Is
D'Entrecasteaux
Islands
Woodlark
NEW GUINEA
Torres Strait
of Wales I.
Saibai I.
C. York
Somerset
Kupiano
Owen Stanley Ra.
Alotau
Floride Is
Malaita
Maramasike
Guadalcanal
Honiara
Stewart Is

Weipa
Cape
York
C. Grenville
Iron
Range
Samarai
Misima
Louisiade
Arch.
Tagula
Rossel
San Cristobal
Rennell

Coen
Peninsula
Princess Charlotte B.

Mitchell River
Laura
Cooktown
Coral Sea
Island Territories
Willis Group

Normanton
Croydon
Mt Bartle Frere
1612
Cairns
Ravenshoe
Innisfail
Coringa Is
Récifs
d'Entrecasteaux
Îles Bélcp

Forsayth
Palm Is
Ingham
Townsville
Charters Towers
Ayr
Marion Reef
Îles
Chesterfield
(Fr.)

QUEENSLAND
Bowen
Collinsville
Proserpine
Mackay
Sarina
Northumberland
Is
Swain
Reefs
Bellona
Reefs
Muéo
Uvéa
Lifu
Nouvelle
Calédonie
(Fr.)
Bourail
Nouméa
Île des Pins

PACIFIC

OCEAN

Brisbane

NEW SOUTH

WALES

Sydney

Canberra

VICTORIA

Melbourne

TASMAN

SEA

TASMANIA

Hobart

NEW

ZEALAND
South Island

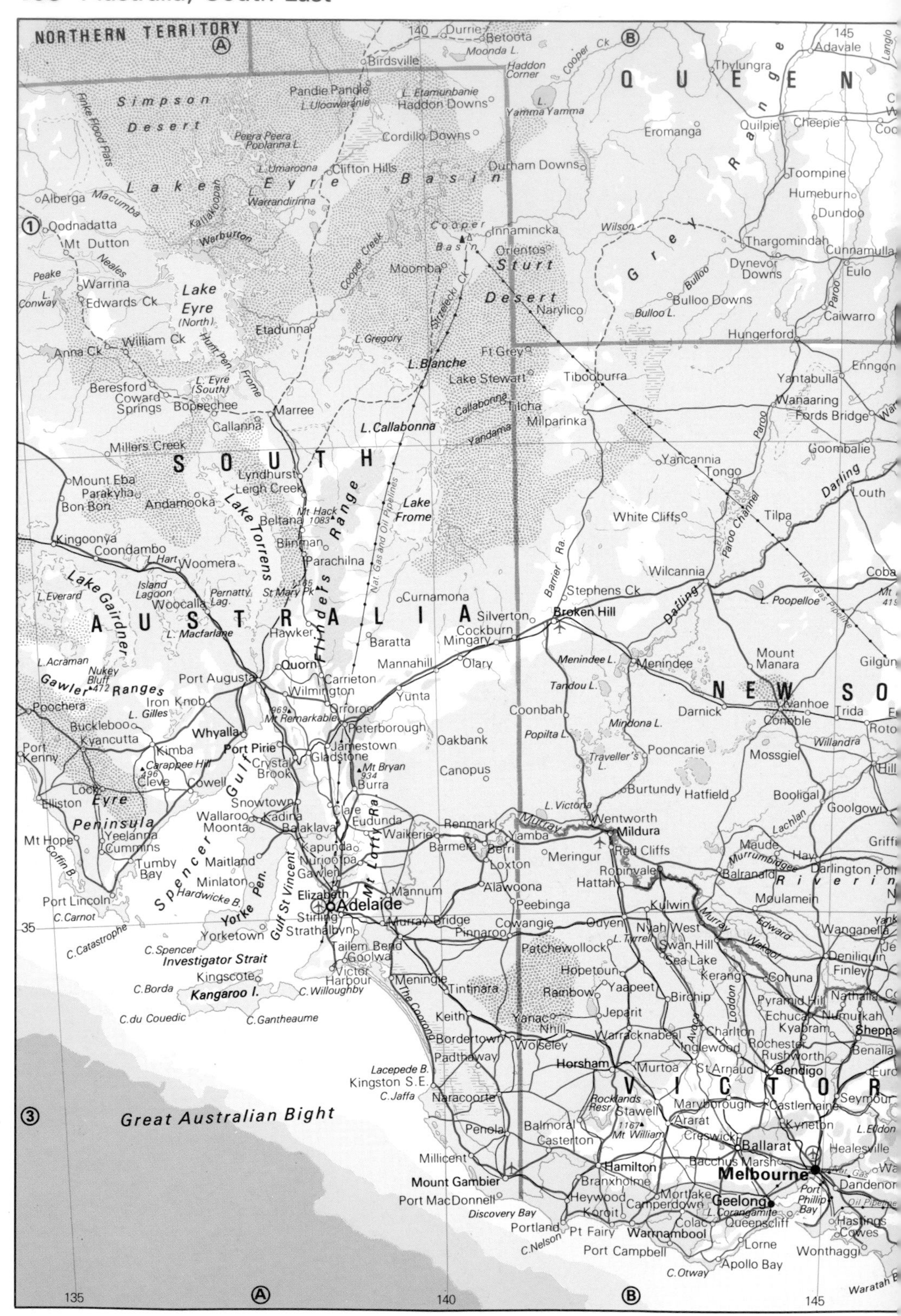
NORTHERN TERRITORY
A
B
140
145
135
35
1
3
Durrie
Betoota
Moonda L.
Birdsville
Haddon Corner
Cooper Ck
Q U E E N
Adavale
Thylungra
Grey Range
Langlo
Simpson Desert
Finke Flood Flats
Pandie Pandie
L. Uloowaranie
L. Etamunbanie
Haddon Downs
L. Yamma Yamma
Eromanga
Quilpie
Cheepie
Peera Peera Poolanna L.
Cordillo Downs
Lake Eyre Basin
L. Umaroona
Clifton Hills
Durham Downs
Toompine
Humeburn
Dundoo
Alberga
Macumba
Kallakoopah
Warrandirinna
Warburton
Oodnadatta
Mt Dutton
Neales
Cooper Creek
Cooper Basin
Innamincka
Wilson
Thargomindah
Cunnamulla
Orientos
Sturt Desert
Peake
Warrina
L. Conway
Edwards Ck
Lake Eyre (North)
Moomba
Strzelecki Ck
Dynevor Downs
Eulo
Bulloo
Bulloo Downs
Bulloo L.
Paroo
Caiwarro
Narylico
Etadunna
Hungerford
Anna Ck
William Ck
Hunt Pen
Frome
L. Gregory
L. Blanche
Ft Grey
Enngonia
Beresford
L. Eyre (South)
Lake Stewart
Tibooburra
Yantabulla
Coward Springs
Bopeechee
Marree
Callabonna
Tilcha
Milparinka
Wanaaring
Fords Bridge
Callanna
L. Callabonna
Yandama
Goombalie
Millers Creek
SOUTH
Yancannia
Tongo
Mount Eba
Parakylia
Lyndhurst
Leigh Creek
Darling
Louth
Bon Bon
Andamooka
Lake Torrens
Mt Hack 1083
Lake Frome
Nat. Gas and Oil Pipelines
White Cliffs
Tilpa
Paroo Channel
Beltana
Kingoonya
Coondambo
Blinman
Flinders Range
L. Hart
Woomera
Parachilna
Barrier Ra.
Wilcannia
Cobar
Lake Gairdner
Island Lagoon
L. Everard
Pernatty Lag.
St Mary Pk 1165
Curnamona
Stephens Ck
L. Poopelloe
Woocalla
Broken Hill
AUSTRALIA
Silverton
Nat. Gas Pipeline
L. Macfarlane
Hawker
Cockburn
Mingary
Baratta
L. Acraman
Quorn
Mannahill
Olary
Menindee L.
Menindee
Mount Manara
Gilgunnia
Nukey Bluff 472
Port Augusta
Carrieton
Tandou L.
Gawler Ranges
Wilmington
Yunta
NEW SO
Iron Knob
Poochera
L. Gilles
969 Mt Remarkable
Orroroo
Coonbah
Darnick
Ivanhoe
Trida
Buckleboo
Whyalla
Peterborough
Mindona L.
Conoble
Roto
Kyancutta
Port Kenny
Kimba
Port Pirie
Jamestown
Oakbank
Popilta L.
Willandra
Carappee Hill 496
Crystal Brook
Gladstone
Mt Bryan 934
Traveller's L.
Pooncarie
Mossgiel
Cleve
Cowell
Canopus
Hillston
Lock
Eyre Peninsula
Elliston
Burra
Burtundy
Hatfield
Booligal
Snowtown
Spencer Gulf
Clare
L. Victoria
Goolgowi
Wallaroo
Kadina
Eudunda
Mt Lofty Ra.
Renmark
Wentworth
Mildura
Moonta
Balaklava
Waikerie
Murray
Yamba
Lachlan
Griffith
Mt Hope
Yeelanna
Cummins
Kapunda
Barmera
Berri
Red Cliffs
Maude
Coffin B.
Tumby Bay
Maitland
Nuriootpa
Loxton
Meringur
Murrumbidgee
Hay
Darlington Point
Minlaton
Yorke Pen.
Gawler
Robinvale
Balranald
Riverina
Port Lincoln
Hardwicke B.
Gulf St Vincent
Elizabeth
Mannum
Alawoona
Hattah
C. Carnot
Adelaide
Peebinga
Kulwin
Moulamein
Stirling
Murray Bridge
Cowangie
Ouyen
Nyah West
Edward
Yanko
Jerilderie
C. Catastrophe
Yorketown
Strathalbyn
Pinnaroo
L. Tyrrell
Swan Hill
Wakool
Wanganella
C. Spencer
Tailem Bend
Goolwa
Patchewollock
Sea Lake
Deniliquin
Investigator Strait
Victor Harbour
Hopetoun
Kerang
Cohuna
Finley
Kingscote
Meningie
Tintinara
Yaapeet
Loddon
Pyramid Hill
Nathalia
C. Borda
Kangaroo I.
C. Willoughby
The Coorong
Rainbow
Birchip
Echuca
Numurkah
C. du Couedic
C. Gantheaume
Keith
Yanac
Jeparit
Charlton
Kyabram
Shepparton
Nhill
Avoca
Bordertown
Wolseley
Warracknabeal
Inglewood
Rochester
Benalla
Padthaway
Rushworth
Horsham
Murtoa
St Arnaud
Bendigo
Lacepede B.
Kingston S.E.
VICTORIA
Euroa
C. Jaffa
Naracoorte
Rocklands Resr
Stawell
Maryborough
Castlemaine
Seymour
Great Australian Bight
1167 Mt William
Ararat
Kyneton
L. Eildon
Penola
Balmoral
Creswick
Ballarat
Casterton
Healesville
Millicent
Bacchus Marsh
Hamilton
Melbourne
Nat. Gas
Mount Gambier
Branxholme
Dandenong
Port MacDonnell
Heywood
Mortlake
Geelong
Port Phillip Bay
Oil Pipeline
Discovery Bay
Koroit
Camperdown
L. Corangamite
Portland
Pt Fairy
Colac
Queenscliff
Hastings
Cowes
C. Nelson
Warrnambool
Lorne
Port Campbell
Wonthaggi
Apollo Bay
C. Otway
Waratah B.

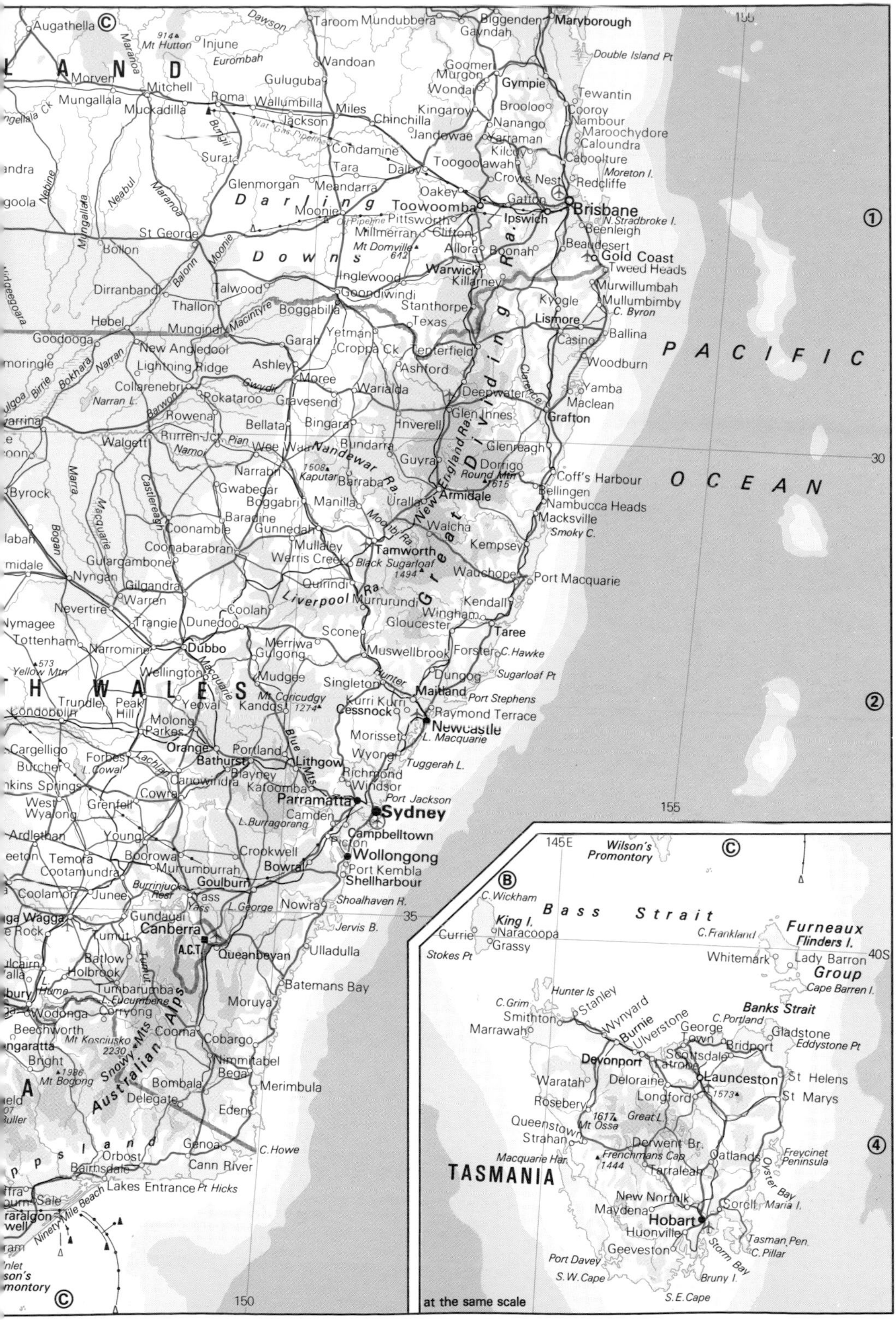

100　200　300 km
50　100　150 mls

Augathella C
Morven
Mungallala
Mitchell
Muckadilla
Roma
Wallumbilla
Miles
Chinchilla
Jackson
Condamine
Surat
Tara
Dalby
Glenmorgan
Meandarra
Oakey
Toowoomba
Pittsworth
Millmerran
Clifton
Allora
Boonah
Mt Domville
Warwick
Killarney
Inglewood
Goondiwindi
Stanthorpe
Texas
Dirranbandi
Talwood
Boggabilla
Yetman
Tenterfield
Goodooga
Hebel
Mungindi
Macintyre
Garah
Ashford
New Angledool
Lightning Ridge
Croppa Ck
Collarenebri
Rokataroo
Gravesend
Moree
Warialda
Ashley
Narran L.
Bellata
Bingara
Inverell
Walgett
Burren-Jc
Narrabri
Kaputar
Barraba
Guyra
Round Mtn
Coff's Harbour
Gwabegar
Boggabri
Manilla
Uralla
Armidale
Bellingen
Nambucca Heads
Baradine
Gunnedah
Walcha
Macksville
Smoky C.
Coonabarabran
Mullaley
Werris Creek
Tamworth
Kempsey
Wauchope
Black Sugarloaf
Quirindi
Port Macquarie
Coolah
Murrurundi
Wingham
Kendall
Dunedoo
Gloucester
Taree
Merriwa
Scone
Muswellbrook
Forster
C. Hawke
Gulgong
Mudgee
Singleton
Dunoog
Sugarloaf Pt
Dubbo
Wellington
Hunter
Maitland
Port Stephens
Mt Coricudgy
Kurri Kurri
Cessnock
Raymond Terrace
Newcastle
Yeoval
Kandos
Morisset
L. Macquarie
Parkes
Orange
Portland
Wyong
Tuggerah L.
Forbes
Molong
Blayney
Richmond
Windsor
Carcowidra
Kaloomba
Port Jackson
Cowra
Grenfell
Camden
Parramatta
L. Burragorang
Sydney
Young
Boorowa
Cropwell
Campbelltown
Cootamundra
Wollongong
Junee
Goulburn
Port Kembla
Shellharbour
Wagga Wagga
Gundagai
L. George
Nowra
Shoalhaven R.
Tumut
Jervis B.
Canberra
Queanbeyan
Ulladulla
A.C.T.
Batemans Bay
Holbrook
Tumbarumba
Moruya
Corryong
Cobargo
Cooma
Nimmitabel
Bega
Bombala
Merimbula
Delegate
Eden
Genoa
Orbost
C. Howe
Cann River
Lakes Entrance
Pt Hicks

Taroom
Mundubbera
Biggenden
Maryborough
Gayndah
Goomeri
Murgon
Gympie
Wondai
Tewantin
Cooroy
Nambour
Kingaroy
Nanango
Yarraman
Maroochydore
Caloundra
Kilcoy
Toogoolawah
Caboolture
Crows Nest
Moreton I.
Gatton
Redcliffe
Ipswich
Brisbane
Beenleigh
N. Stradbroke I.
Beaudesert
Gold Coast
Tweed Heads
Murwillumbah
Mullumbimby
Kyogle
C. Byron
Lismore
Ballina
Casino
Woodburn
Deepwater
Yamba
Glen Innes
Maclean
Glencoe
Grafton
Glen Elgh
Dorrigo

Darling Downs
Nandewar Ra.
Liverpool Ra.
Great Dividing Ra.
New England Ra.
New South WALES
Snowy Mts
Australian Alps

PACIFIC OCEAN

Gippsland
Bairnsdale
Sale
Traralgon
Wilson's Promontory

145E
Wilson's Promontory
C. Wickham
C. Frankland
B A S S　S t r a i t
King I.
Naracoopa
C. Portland
Furneaux
Flinders I.
Currie
Grassy
Whitemark
Lady Barron
Group
Stokes Pt
40S
Cape Barren I.
Hunter Is
Stanley
Banks Strait
Eddystone Pt
C. Grim
Smithton
Wynyard
Burnie
Ulverstone
George Town
Gladstone
Marrawah
Waratah
Penguin
Scottsdale
Bridport
Devonport
Latrobe
St Helens
Deloraine
Launceston
Rosebery
Longford
St Marys
Queenstown
Great L.
Mt Ossa
Strahan
Derwent Br.
Oatlands
Freycinet Peninsula
Macquarie Har.
Frenchmans Cap
Tarraleah
Oyster Bay
TASMANIA
Maria I.
New Norfolk
Sorell
Tasman Pen.
Maydena
Hobart
C. Pillar
Port Davey
Huonville
Geeveston
Storm Bay
S.W. Cape
Bruny I.
S.E. Cape

at the same scale

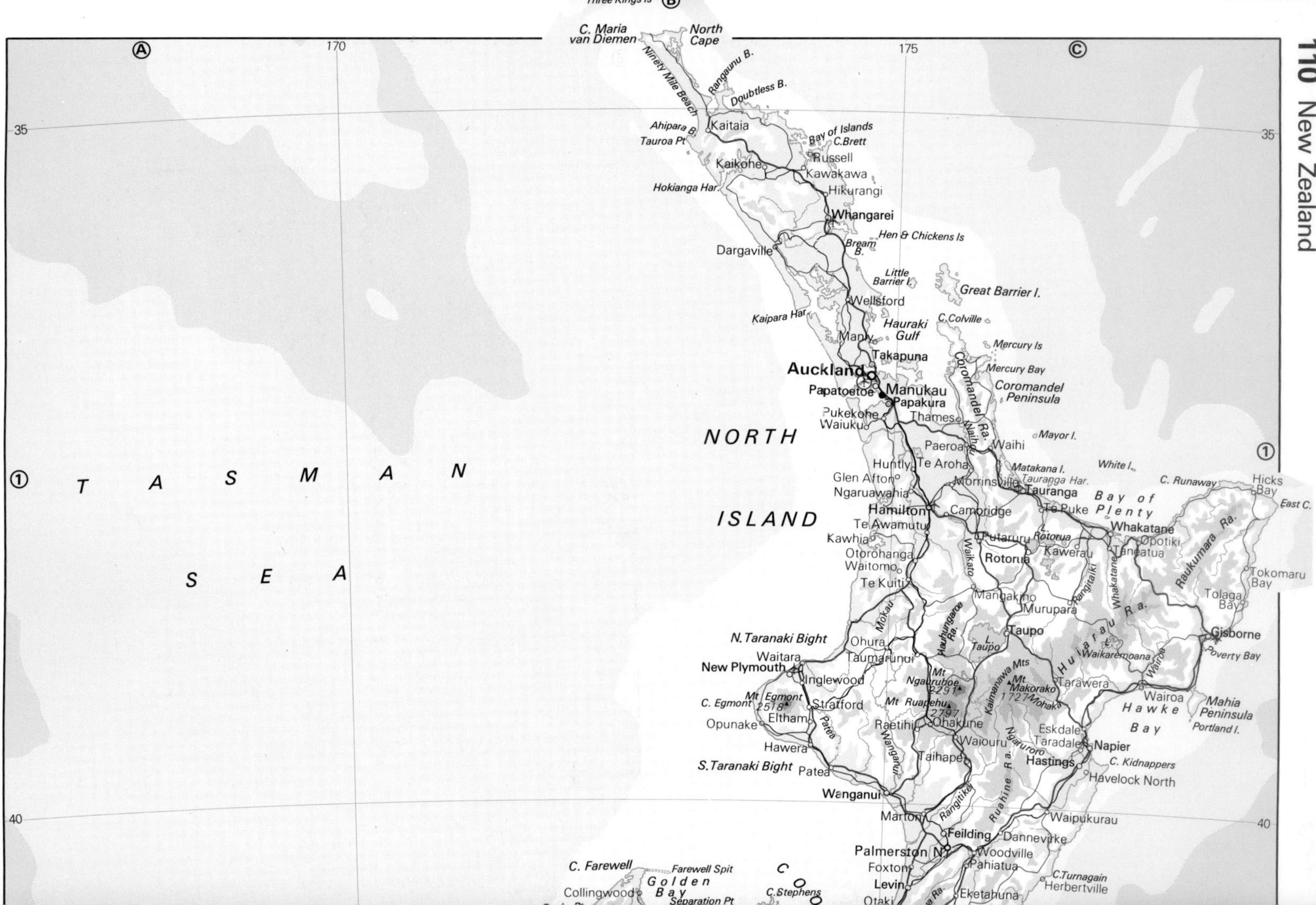

Three Kings Is
C. Maria van Diemen
North Cape
Ninety Mile Beach
Rangaunu B.
Doubtless B.
Ahipara B.
Tauroa Pt
Kaitaia
Bay of Islands
C.Brett
Russell
Kaikohe
Kawakawa
Hokianga Har.
Hikurangi
Whangarei
Hen & Chickens Is
Bream B.
Dargaville
Little Barrier I.
Great Barrier I.
Wellsford
Kaipara Har
C.Colville
Hauraki Gulf
Manly
Mercury Is
Takapuna
Mercury Bay
Auckland
Coromandel Ra.
Coromandel Peninsula
Papatoetoe
Manukau
Papakura
Pukekohe
Thames
Waiuku
Waihou
NORTH
Mayor I.
Paeroa
Waihi
Huntly
Te Aroha
Matakana I.
White I.
Tauranga Har.
Glen Afton
Morrinsville
C. Runaway
Hicks Bay
Ngaruawahia
Tauranga
Bay of Plenty
East C.
Hamilton
Cambridge
Te Puke
ISLAND
Te Awamutu
Whakatane
L. Rotorua
Raukumara Ra.
Kawhia
Putaruru
Opotiki
Taneatua
Otorohanga
Rotorua
Kawerau
Waitomo
Waikato
Rangitaiki
Whakatane
Tokomaru Bay
Te Kuiti
Mangakino
Mokau
Murupara
Tolaga Bay
Hauhungaroa Ra.
Huiarau Ra.
Taupo
L. Taupo
Gisborne
N.Taranaki Bight
Ohura
Waikaremoana
Waitara
Taumarunui
Wairoa
Poverty Bay
New Plymouth
Kaimanawa Mts
Inglewood
Mt Ngauruhoe 2291
Mt Makorako 1727
Mohaka
Tarawera
Mt Egmont 2518
C. Egmont
Stratford
Mt Ruapehu 2797
Wairoa
Mahia Peninsula
Hawke Bay
Opunake
Eltham
Patea
Raetihi
Ohakune
Portland I.
Waiouru
Eskdale
Taradale
Napier
Ngaruroro
Hawera
Wanganui
Taihape
Hastings
C. Kidnappers
S.Taranaki Bight
Patea
Ruahine Ra.
Havelock North
Wanganui
Marton
Rangitikei
Waipukurau
Feilding
Dannevirke
Palmerston N.
Woodville
C. Farewell
Farewell Spit
Foxton
Pahiatua
C.Turnagain
Golden Bay
Herbertville
Collingwood
C.Stephens
Levin
Separation Pt
Otaki
Eketahuna
TASMAN SEA
A
B
C
1
170
175
35
40

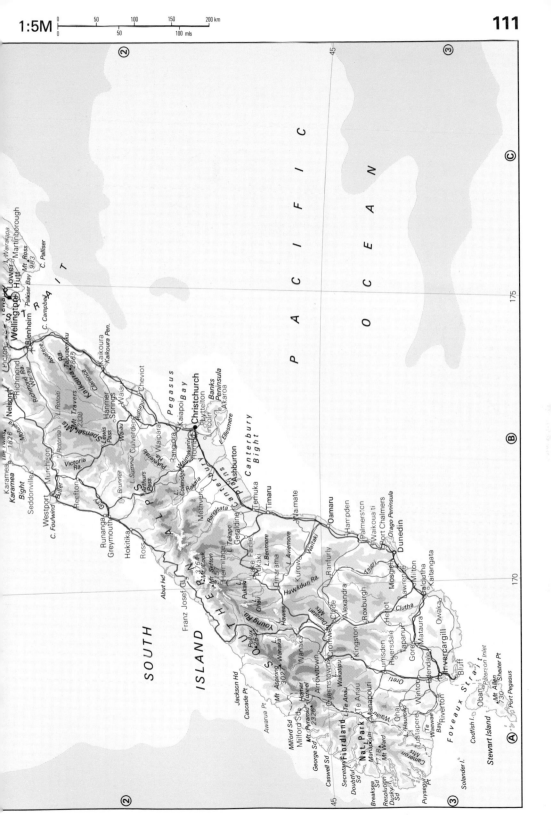

SOUTH

ISLAND

S O U T H E R N

A L P S

Franz Josef Gln.

R. Mt Cook
3764

Mt Sefton

Pollux
2536

Mt Aspiring
3027

Haast Pass

Pyramid Tunnel
2328

Fiordland Nat. Park

Jackson Hd

Cascade Pt

Awarua Pt

Milford Sd
Milford Sd

George Sd

Caswell Sd

Secretary I.

Doubtful
Sd

Breaksea
Sd

Resolution
I.

Dusky
Sd

Puysegur Pt

Solander I.

Mt Ward
1863

Te Anau

L. Te Anau

Manapouri

L. Manapouri

Cameron Mts

Takitimu
Mts

Wakatipu

Queenstown

Arrowtown

Cromwell

Kingston

Te Waewae
Bay

Ohai

Nightcaps

Winton

Riverton

Otautau

Invercargill

Bluff

Oban

Mt Anglem
730

Sheter Pt

Paterson Inlet

Codfish I.

Stewart Island

Port Pegasus

F o v e a u x   S t r a i t

Lumsden

Mataura

Gore

Balclutha

Milton

Clutha

Kaitangata

Taieri

Dunedin

Port Chalmers

Otago Peninsula

Waikouaiti

Palmerston

Hampden

Oamaru

Waitaki

L. Aviemore

L. Benmore

Kurow

Oamaru

Ranfurly

Naseby

Clyde

Alexandra

Roxburgh

Clutha

Heriot

Tapanui

Clinton

Balfour

Edendale

Waipahi

Mossburn

Riversdale

Manuherikia

Wanaka

L. Wanaka

Hawea

L. Hawea

Pukaki

L. Pukaki

Tekapo

L. Tekapo

Young Ra.

Ohau

L. Ohau

Twizel

Fairlie

Geraldine

Temuka

Timaru

Waimate

Hawkdun Ra.

Pareora

Rangitata

Ashburton

Methven

Mt Somers

Rakaia

Coleridge

Culverden

Waiau

Waiau

Waipara

Hanmer
Springs

Lewis
Pass

Reefton

Maruia

Springs

Murchison

Victoria
Ra.

Brunner

Greymouth

Runanga

Grey

Hokitika

Ross

Abut Hd

Westport
C. Foulwind

Seddonville

Buller

Karamea, the Twins
1826

Karamea
Bight

Richmond
Mount

Richmond Ra.

Nelson

Mt Arthur
1826

Motueka

Spenser Mts
Mt Travers
2338

Arthurs
Pass

Otira

Kaikoura

Kaikoura Pen.

Cheviot

Clarence

Kaikoura
Ra. 2665

Clarence

Hundalee

Waiau

Rotoiti

Rotoroa

Tophouse

Blenheim

Picton

Tory Cowal

Wairau

Awatere

C. Campbell

Cloudy Bay

Wellington

Lower
Hutt

Martinborough

Waitapu

C. Palliser

Palliser Bay

Mt Ross
983

Waikawa

Richmond

Waimea

Pegasus
Bay

Christchurch

Lyttelton

Banks
Peninsula

Akaroa

Kaiapoi

Lincoln

Ellesmere

Darfield

Rangiora

Amberley

Waimakariri

Selwyn

Waipara

C a n t e r b u r y

B i g h t

P A C I F I C

O C E A N

45

175

170

45

② ③

④

① ②

③

1:40M

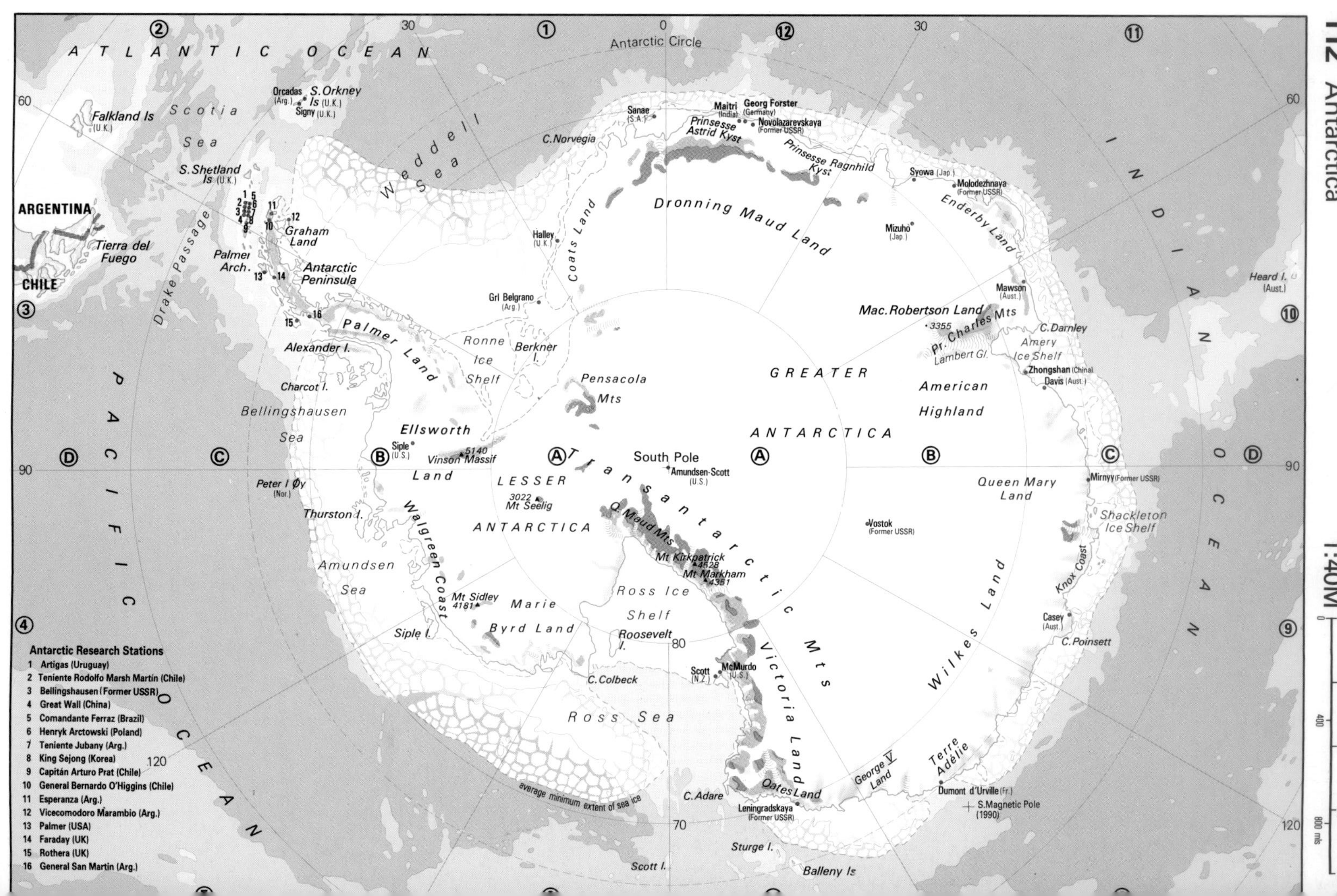

0   400   800   1200   1600 km
0   400   800   mls

Antarctic Research Stations
1 Artigas (Uruguay)
2 Teniente Rodolfo Marsh Martin (Chile)
3 Bellingshausen (Former USSR)
4 Great Wall (China)
5 Comandante Ferraz (Brazil)
6 Henryk Arctowski (Poland)
7 Teniente Jubany (Arg.)
8 King Sejong (Korea)
9 General Bernardo O'Higgins (Chile)
10 General Arturo Prat (Chile)
11 Esperanza (Arg.)
12 Vicecomodoro Marambio (Arg.)
13 Palmer (USA)
14 Faraday (UK)
15 Rothera (UK)
16 General San Martín (Arg.)

Index

In the index, the first number refers to the page, and the following letter and number to the section of the map in which the index entry can be found. For example, 48C2 **Paris** means that Paris can be found on page 48 where column C and row 2 meet.

Abbreviations used in the index

Afghan	Afghanistan	Germ	Germany	Phil	Philippines	Arch	Archipelago
Alb	Albania	Hung	Hungary	Pol	Poland	B	Bay
Alg	Algeria	Ind	Indonesia	Port	Portugal	C	Cape
Ant	Antarctica	Irish Rep	Ireland	Rom	Romania	Chan	Channel
Arg	Argentina	Leb	Lebanon		Russian	Gl	Glacier
Aust	Australia	Lib	Liberia	Russian Fed	Federation	I(s)	Island(s)
Bang	Bangladesh	Liech	Liechtenstein	S Arabia	Saudi Arabia	Lg	Lagoon
Belg	Belgium	Lux	Luxembourg	Scot	Scotland	L	Lake
Bol	Bolivia	Madag	Madagascar	Sen	Senegal	Mt(s)	Mountain(s)
Bulg	Bulgaria	Malay	Malaysia	S Africa	South Africa	O	Ocean
Burk	Burkina	Maur	Mauritania	S Yemen	South Yemen	P	Pass
Camb	Cambodia	Mor	Morocco	Switz	Switzerland	Pen	Peninsula
Can	Canada	Mozam	Mozambique	Tanz	Tanzania	Plat	Plateau
CAR	Central African Republic	Neth	Netherlands	Thai	Thailand	Pt	Point
Czech	Czechoslovakia	NZ	New Zealand	Turk	Turkey	Res	Reservoir
Den	Denmark	Nic	Nicaragaua		United States	R	River
Dom Rep	Dominican Republic	N Ire	Northern Ireland	USA	of America	S	Sea
El Sal	El Salvador	Nig	Nigeria	Urug	Uruguay	Sd	Sound
Eng	England	Nor	Norway	Ven	Venezuela	Str	Strait
Eq Guinea	Equatorial Guinea	Pak	Pakistan	Viet	Vietnam	V	Valley
Eth	Ethiopia	PNG	Papua New Guinea	Yugos	Yugoslavia		
Fin	Finland	Paar	Paraguay	Zim	Zimbabwe		

A

57B2 **Aachen** Germany
46C1 **Aalst** Belg
38K6 **Äänekoski** Fin
47C1 **Aarau** Switz
47B1 **Aare** *R* Switz
72A3 **Aba** China
97C4 **Aba** Nig
99D2 **Aba** Zaire
91A3 **Ābādān** Iran
90B3 **Ābādeh** Iran
96B1 **Abadla** Alg
35B1 **Abaeté** Brazil
35B1 **Abaeté** *R* Brazil
31B2 **Abaetetuba** Brazil
72D1 **Abagnar Qi** China
97C4 **Abakaliki** Nig
63B2 **Abakan** Russian Fed
97C3 **Abala** Niger
96C2 **Abalessa** Alg
32C6 **Abancay** Peru
90B3 **Abarqū** Iran
74E2 **Abashiri** Japan
74E2 **Abashiri-wan** *B* Japan
71F4 **Abau** PNG
99D2 **Abaya** *L* Eth
99D1 **Abbai** *R* Eth
99E1 **Abbe** *L* Eth
48C1 **Abbeville** France
19B4 **Abbeville** Louisiana, USA
17B1 **Abbeville** S Carolina, USA
45B2 **Abbeyfeale** Irish Rep
47C2 **Abbiategrasso** Italy
20B1 **Abbotsford** Can
84C2 **Abbottabad** Pak
61H3 **Abdulino** Russian Fed
98C1 **Abéché** Chad
39F7 **Abenrå** Den
97C4 **Abeokuta** Nig
99D2 **Abera** Eth
43B3 **Aberaeron** Wales
15C3 **Aberdeen** Maryland, USA
100B4 **Aberdeen** S Africa
44C3 **Aberdeen** Scot
8D2 **Aberdeen** S Dakota, USA
8A2 **Aberdeen** Washington, USA
4J3 **Aberdeen L** Can
44C3 **Aberfeldy** Scot
43C4 **Abergavenny** Wales
43B3 **Aberystwyth** Wales
81C4 **Abha** S Arabia
90A2 **Abhar** Iran
97B4 **Abidjan** Ivory Coast
18A2 **Abilene** Kansas, USA
9D3 **Abilene** Texas, USA
43D4 **Abingdon** Eng
7B4 **Abitibi** *R* Can
7C5 **Abitibi,L** Can
61F5 **Abkhazskaya Respublika,** Georgia
84C2 **Abohar** India
97C4 **Abomey** Benin
98B2 **Abong Mbang** Cam
79A4 **Aborlan** Phil
98B1 **Abou Deïa** Chad
91A4 **Abqaiq** S Arabia
50A2 **Abrantes** Port
95C2 **Abri** Sudan
106A3 **Abrolhos** *Is* Aust
8B2 **Absaroka Range** *Mts* USA
91B5 **Abū al Abyad** *I* UAE
91A4 **Abū 'Ali** *I* S Arabia
91B5 **Abū Dhabi** UAE
95C3 **Abu Hamed** Sudan
97C4 **Abuja** Nig
33D5 **Abunã** Brazil
32D6 **Abunã** *R* Bol
93D3 **Abū Sukhayr** Iraq
111B2 **Abut Head** *C* NZ
95C3 **Abu 'Urug** *Well* Sudan
99D1 **Abuye Meda** *Mt* Eth
99C1 **Abu Zabad** Sudan
99D2 **Abwong** Sudan
56B1 **Aby** Den
94B3 **Aby 'Aweigîla** *Well* Egypt
99C2 **Abyei** Sudan
24B2 **Acambaro** Mexico
24B2 **Acaponeta** Mexico
24B3 **Acapulco** Mexico
31D2 **Acaraú** Brazil
32D2 **Acarigua** Ven
24C3 **Acatlán** Mexico
23B2 **Acatzingo** Mexico
97B4 **Accra** Ghana
85D4 **Achalpur** India
29B4 **Achao** Chile
47D1 **Achensee** *L* Austria
46E2 **Achern** Germany
41A3 **Achill** *I* Irish Rep
63B2 **Achinsk** Russian Fed
53C3 **Acireale** Italy
26C2 **Acklins** *I* Caribbean S
32C6 **Acobamba** Peru
29B2 **Aconcagua** *Mt* Chile
31D3 **Acopiara** Brazil
88B4 **Açores** *Is* Atlantic O
A Coruña = La Coruña
47C2 **Acqui** Italy
108A2 **Acraman,L** Aust
Acre = 'Akko
32C5 **Acre** State, Brazil
22C3 **Acton** USA
23B1 **Actopan** Mexico
19A3 **Ada** USA
50B1 **Adaja** *R* Spain
91C5 **Adam** Oman
35A2 **Adamantina** Brazil
98B2 **Adamaoua Region,** Nig/Cam
47D1 **Adamello** *Mt* Italy
16C1 **Adams** USA
87B3 **Adam's Bridge** India/ Sri Lanka
13D2 **Adams L** Can
8A2 **Adams,Mt** USA
87C3 **Adam's Peak** *Mt* Sri Lanka
81C4 **'Adan** Yemen
92C2 **Adana** Turk
60D5 **Adapazari** Turk
112B7 **Adare,C** Ant
108B1 **Adavale** Aust
47C2 **Adda** *R* Italy
91A4 **Ad Dahna'** Region, S Arabia
96A2 **Ad Dakhla** Mor
81C4 **Ad Dāli'** Yemen
91B4 **Ad Damman** S Arabia
91A4 **Ad Dibdibah** Region, S Arabia
91A5 **Ad Dilam** S Arabia
91A5 **Ad Dir'iyah** S Arabia
93D3 **Ad Diwanīyah** Iraq
93D3 **Ad Duwayd** S Arabia
106C4 **Adelaide** Aust
4J3 **Adelaide Pen** Can
22D3 **Adelanto** USA
Aden = 'Adan
81C4 **Aden,G of** Yemen/ Somalia
97C3 **Aderbissinat** Niger
94C2 **Adhra** Syria
71E4 **Adi** *I* Indon
52B1 **Adige** *R* Italy
99D1 **Adigrat** Eth
85D5 **Adilābād** India
20B2 **Adin** USA
15D2 **Adirondack Mts** USA
99D2 **Adis Abeba** Eth
95C3 **Adi Ugai** Eth
93C2 **Adıyaman** Turk
54C1 **Adjud** Rom
4E4 **Admiralty I** USA
6B2 **Admiralty Inlet** *B* Can
87B1 **Adoni** India
48B3 **Adour** *R* France
96A2 **Adrar** Region, Maur
96C2 **Adrar** *Mts* Alg
96A2 **Adrar Soutouf** Region, Mor
98C1 **Adré** Chad
95A2 **Adri** Libya
47E2 **Adria** Italy

14B2 **Adrian** Michigan, USA
52B2 **Adriatic S** S Europe
99D1 **Ādwa** Eth
97B4 **Adzopé** Ivory Coast
55B3 **Aegean** *S* Greece
80E2 **Afghanistan** Republic, Asia
99E2 **Afgooye** Somalia
97C4 **Afikpo** Nig
38G6 **Åfjord** Nor
96C1 **Aflou** Alg
99E2 **Afmadu** Somalia
97A3 **Afollé** Region, Maur
94B2 **Afula** Israel
92B2 **Afyon** Turk
95A3 **Agadem** Niger
97C3 **Agadez** Niger
96B1 **Agadir** Mor
85D4 **Agar** India
86C2 **Agartala** India
20B1 **Agassiz** Can
97B4 **Agboville** Ivory Coast
93E1 **Agdam** Azerbaijan
75B1 **Agematsu** Japan
48C3 **Agen** France
90A3 **Agha Jārī** Iran
96A2 **Aghwinit** *Well* Mor
47D2 **Agno** *R* Italy
47E1 **Agordo** Italy
48C3 **Agout** *R* France
85D3 **Āgra** India
93D2 **Ağri** Turk
53C2 **Agri** *R* Italy
53B3 **Agrigento** Italy
55B3 **Agrínion** Greece
34A3 **Agrio** *R* Chile
53B2 **Agropoli** Italy
61H2 **Agryz** Russian Fed
6E3 **Agto** Greenland
27D3 **Aguadilla** Puerto Rico
24B1 **Agua Prieta** Mexico
24B2 **Aguascalientes** Mexico
23A1 **Aguascalientes** State, Mexico
35C1 **Aguas Formosas** Brazil
50A1 **Agueda** Port
96C3 **Aguelhok** Mali
50B2 **Aguilas** Spain
23A2 **Aguililla** Mexico
100B4 **Agulhas,C** S Africa
79C4 **Agusan** *R* Phil
Ahaggar = **Hoggar**
93E2 **Ahar** Iran
110B1 **Ahipara B** NZ
85C4 **Ahmadābād** India
87A1 **Ahmadnagar** India
99E2 **Ahmar** *Mts* Eth
46D1 **Ahr** *R* Germany
46D1 **Ahrgebirge** Region, Germany
23A1 **Ahuacatlán** Mexico
23A1 **Ahualulco** Mexico
39G7 **Åhus** Sweden
90B2 **Ahuvān** Iran
90A3 **Ahvāz** Iran
26A4 **Aiajuela** Costa Rica
47B1 **Aigle** Switz
47B2 **Aiguille d'Arves** *Mt* France
47B2 **Aiguille de la Grand Sassière** *Mt* France
75B1 **Aikawa** Japan
17B1 **Aiken** USA
73A5 **Ailao Shan** *Upland* China
35C1 **Aimorés** Brazil
96B1 **Ain Beni Mathar** Mor
95B2 **Ain Dalla** *Well* Egypt
51C2 **Aïn el Hadjel** Alg
95A3 **Aïn Galakka** Chad
96B1 **Aïn Sefra** Alg
92B4 **'Ain Sukhna** Egypt
75A2 **Aioi** Japan
96B2 **Aioun Abd el Malek** *Well* Maur
97B3 **Aïoun El Atrouss** Maur
30C2 **Aiquile** Bol
97C3 **Aïr** *Desert Region* Niger
13E2 **Airdrie** Can
46B1 **Aire** France
42D3 **Aire** *R* Eng
46C2 **Aire** *R* France
6C3 **Airforce I** Can
47C1 **Airolo** Switz
4E3 **Aishihik** Can
12G2 **Aishihik L** Can
46B2 **Aisne** Department, France
49C2 **Aisne** *R* France
71F4 **Aitape** PNG
58D1 **Aiviekste** *R* Latvia
72B2 **Aixa Zuogi** China
49D3 **Aix-en-Provence** France
47A2 **Aix-les-Bains** France
86B2 **Aiyar Res** India
55B3 **Aíyion** Greece
55B3 **Aíyna** *I* Greece
86C2 **Āīzawl** India
100A3 **Aizeb** *R* Namibia
74E3 **Aizu-Wakamatsu** Japan
52A2 **Ajaccio** Corse
23B2 **Ajalpan** Mexico
95B1 **Ajdābiyā** Libya
74E2 **Ajigasawa** Japan
94B2 **Ajlūn** Jordan
91C4 **Ajman** UAE
85C3 **Ajmer** India
9B3 **Ajo** USA
23A2 **Ajuchitan** Mexico
55C3 **Ak** *R* Turk
75B1 **Akaishi-sanchi** *Mts* Japan
87B1 **Akalkot** India
111B2 **Akaroa** NZ
75A2 **Akashi** Japan
61J3 **Akbulak** Russian Fed
93C2 **Akçakale** Turk
96A2 **Akchar** *Watercourse* Maur
55C3 **Akdağ** *Mt* Turk
98C2 **Aketi** Zaïre
93D1 **Akhalkalaki** Georgia
93D1 **Akhalsikhe** Georgia
55B3 **Akharnái** Greece
12D3 **Akhiok** USA
92A2 **Akhisar** Turk
58D1 **Akhiste** Latvia
95C2 **Akhmîm** Egypt
61G4 **Akhtubinsk** Russian Fed
60D4 **Akhtyrka** Ukraine
75A2 **Aki** Japan
7B4 **Akimiski I** Can
74E3 **Akita** Japan
96A3 **Akjoujt** Maur
94B2 **'Akko** Israel
4E3 **Aklavik** USA
97B3 **Aklé Aouana** *Desert Region* Maur
99D2 **Akobo** Sudan
99D2 **Akobo** *R* Sudan
84B1 **Akoha** Afghan
85D4 **Akola** India
85D4 **Akot** India
6D3 **Akpatok I** Can
55B3 **Ákra Kafirévs** *C* Greece
55B3 **Ákra Maléa** *C* Greece
38A2 **Akranes** Iceland
55C3 **Ákra Sídheros** *C* Greece
55B3 **Ákra Spátha** *C* Greece
55B3 **Ákra Taínaron** *C* Greece
10B2 **Akron** USA
94A1 **Akrotiri B** Cyprus
84D1 **Aksai Chin** *Mts* China
92B2 **Aksaray** Turk
61H3 **Aksay** Kazakhstan
84D1 **Aksayquin Hu** *L* China
92B2 **Akşehir** Turk
92B2 **Akseki** Turk
63D2 **Aksenovo Zilovskoye** Russian Fed
68D1 **Aksha** Russian Fed
82C1 **Aksu** China
65J5 **Aktogay** Kazakhstan
61J4 **Aktumsyk** Kazakhstan
65G4 **Aktyubinsk** Kazakhstan
38B1 **Akureyri** Iceland
65K5 **Akzhal** Kazakhstan
11B3 **Alabama** State, USA
11B3 **Alabama** *R* USA
17A1 **Alabaster** USA
92C2 **Ala Dağlari** *Mts* Turk
61F5 **Alagir** Russian Fed
47B2 **Alagna** Italy
31D3 **Alagoas** State, Brazil
31D4 **Alagoinhas** Brazil
51B1 **Alagón** Spain
93E4 **Al Ahmadi** Kuwait
25D3 **Alajuela** Costa Rica
12B2 **Alakanuk** USA
38L5 **Alakurtti** Russian Fed
93E3 **Al Amārah** Iraq
21A2 **Alameda** USA
23B1 **Alamo** Mexico
9C3 **Alamogordo** USA
9C3 **Alamosa** USA
39H6 **Åland** *I* Fin
92B2 **Alanya** Turk
17B1 **Alapaha** *R* USA
65H4 **Alapayevsk** Russian Fed
92A2 **Alaşehir** Turk
68C3 **Ala Shan** *Mts* China
4C3 **Alaska** State, USA
4D4 **Alaska,G of** USA
12C3 **Alaska Pen** USA
4C3 **Alaska Range** *Mts* USA
52A2 **Alassio** Italy
12D1 **Alatna** *R* USA
61G3 **Alatyr** Russian Fed
108B2 **Alawoona** Aust
91C5 **Al'Ayn** UAE
82B2 **Alayskiy Khrebet** *Mts* Tajikistan
49D3 **Alba** Italy
92C2 **Al Bāb** Syria
51B2 **Albacete** Spain
50A1 **Alba de Tormes** Spain
93D2 **Al Badi** Iraq
54B1 **Alba Iulia** Rom
54A2 **Albania** Republic, Europe
106A4 **Albany** Aust
17B1 **Albany** Georgia, USA
15D2 **Albany** New York, USA
8A2 **Albany** Oregon, USA
7B4 **Albany** *R* Can
34B2 **Albardón** Arg
91C5 **Al Batinah** Region, Oman
71F5 **Albatross B** Aust
95B1 **Al Bayḍā** Libya
11C3 **Albemarle Sd** USA
50B1 **Alberche** *R* Spain
108A1 **Alberga** Aust
46B1 **Albert** France
5G4 **Alberta** Province, Can
99D2 **Albert,L** Uganda/Zaïre
10A2 **Albert Lea** USA
99D2 **Albert Nile** *R* Uganda
49D2 **Albertville** France
48C3 **Albi** France
18B1 **Albia** USA
33G2 **Albina** Suriname
14B2 **Albion** Michigan, USA
15C2 **Albion** New York, USA
92C4 **Al Bi'r** S Arabia
91A5 **Al Biyadh** Region, S Arabia
50B2 **Alborán** *I* Spain
39G7 **Ålborg** Den
93D3 **Al Bū Kamāl** Syria
47C1 **Albula** *R* Switz
9C3 **Albuquerque** USA
91C5 **Al Buraymi** Oman
95A1 **Al Burayqah** Libya
95B1 **Al Burdī** Libya
107D4 **Albury** Aust
93E3 **Al Buṣayyah** Iraq
50B1 **Alcalá de Henares** Spain
53B3 **Alcamo** Italy
51B1 **Alcaniz** Spain
31C2 **Alcântara** Brazil
50B2 **Alcaraz** Spain
50B2 **Alcázar de San Juan** Spain
51B2 **Alcira** Spain
35D1 **Alcobaça** Brazil
50B1 **Alcolea de Pinar** Spain
51B2 **Alcoy** Spain
51C2 **Alcudia** Spain
89J8 **Aldabra** *Is* Indian O
63E2 **Aldan** Russian Fed
63E2 **Aldanskoye Nagor'ye** *Upland* Russian Fed
43E3 **Aldeburgh** Eng
48B2 **Alderney** *I* UK
43D4 **Aldershot** Eng
97A3 **Aleg** Maur
30E4 **Alegrete** Brazil
34C2 **Alejandro Roca** Arg
30H6 **Alejandro Selkirk** *I* Chile
63G2 **Aleksandrovsk Sakhalinskiy** Russian Fed
65J4 **Alekseyevka** Kazakhstan
60E3 **Aleksin** Russian Fed
58B1 **Ālem** Sweden
35C2 **Além Paraíba** Brazil
49C2 **Alençon** France
21C4 **Alenuihaha Chan** Hawaiian Is
Aleppo = **Ḥalab**
6D1 **Alert** Can
49C3 **Alès** France
52A2 **Alessandria** Italy
64B3 **Ålesund** Nor
12C3 **Aleutian Range** *Mts* USA
4E4 **Alexander Arch** USA
100A3 **Alexander Bay** S Africa
17A1 **Alexander City** USA
112C3 **Alexander I** Ant
111A3 **Alexandra** NZ
29G8 **Alexandra,C** South Georgia
6C2 **Alexandra Fjord** Can
95B1 **Alexandria** Egypt
11A3 **Alexandria** Louisiana, USA
10A2 **Alexandria** Minnesota, USA
10C3 **Alexandria** Virginia, USA
55C2 **Alexandroúpolis** Greece
13C2 **Alexis Creek** Can
94B2 **Aley** Leb
65K4 **Aleysk** Russian Fed
93D3 **Al Fallūjah** Iraq
51B1 **Alfaro** Spain
54C2 **Alfatar** Bulg
93E3 **Al Fāw** Iraq
35B2 **Alfensas** Brazil
55B3 **Alfiós** *R* Greece
47D2 **Alfonsine** Italy
35C2 **Alfonzo Cláudio** Brazil
35C2 **Alfredo Chaves** Brazil
61J4 **Alga** Kazakhstan
34B3 **Algarrobo del Águila** Arg
50A2 **Algeciras** Spain
96C1 **Alger** Alg

96B2 **Algeria** Republic, Africa
53A2 **Alghero** Sardegna
Algiers = Alger
15C1 **Algonquin Park** Can
91C5 **Al Hadd** Oman
93D3 **Al Hadithah** Iraq
92C3 **Al Hadithah** S Arabia
93D2 **Al Haḍr** Iraq
91C5 **Al Hajar al Gharbī** *Mts* Oman
91C5 **Al Hajar ash Sharqī** *Mts* Oman
93C3 **Al Hamad** *Desert Region* Jordan/ S Arabia
93E4 **Al Haniyah** *Desert Region* Iraq
91A5 **Al Harīq** S Arabia
93C3 **Al Harrah** *Desert Region* S Arabia
95A2 **Al Harūj al Aswad** *Upland* Libya
91A4 **Al Hasa** Region, S Arabia
93D2 **Al Hasakah** Syria
93C4 **Al Hawjā'** S Arabia
93E3 **Al Hayy** Iraq
94C2 **Al Hījānah** Syria
93D3 **Al Hillah** Iraq
91A5 **Al Hillah** S Arabia
96B1 **Al Hoceima** Mor
91A4 **Al Hufūf** S Arabia
91B5 **Al Humrah** Region, UAE
91C5 **Al Huwatsah** Oman
90A2 **Alīābad** Iran
91C4 **Aliabad** Iran
55B2 **Aliákmon** *R* Greece
93E3 **Alī al Gharbī** Iraq
87A1 **Alībāg** India
51B2 **Alicante** Spain
9D4 **Alice** USA
106C3 **Alice Springs** Aust
53B3 **Alicudi** *I* Italy
84D3 **Aligarh** India
90A3 **Aligūdarz** Iran
84B2 **Ali-Khel** Afghan
55C3 **Alimniá** *I* Greece
86B1 **Alīpur Duār** India
14B2 **Aliquippa** USA
22B2 **Alisal** USA
93C3 **Al' Isawiyah** S Arabia
100B4 **Aliwal North** S Africa
95B2 **Al Jaghbūb** Libya
93D3 **Al Jālamīd** S Arabia
95B2 **Al Jawf** Libya
93C4 **Al Jawf** S Arabia
93D2 **Al Jazīrah** *Desert Region* Syria/Iraq
50A2 **Aljezur** Port
91A4 **Al Jubayl** S Arabia
91C5 **Al Kāmil** Oman
93D2 **Al Khābūr** *R* Syria
91C5 **Al Khābūrah** Oman
93D3 **Al Khālis** Iraq
91C4 **Al Khasab** Oman
91B4 **Al Khawr** Qatar
95A1 **Al Khums** Libya
91B5 **Al Kidan** Region, S Arabia
94C2 **Al Kiswah** Syria
56A2 **Alkmaar** Neth
95B2 **Al Kufrah Oasis** Libya
93E3 **Al Kūt** Iraq
92C2 **Al Lādhiqīyah** Syria
86A1 **Allahābād** India
94C2 **Al Lajāh** *Mt* Syria
12D1 **Allakaket** USA
76B2 **Allanmyo** Burma
95C2 **'Allaqi** *Watercourse* Egypt
17B1 **Allatoona L** USA
15C2 **Allegheny** *R* USA
10C3 **Allegheny Mts** USA
17B1 **Allendale** USA
111A3 **Allen,Mt** NZ
15C2 **Allentown** USA
87B3 **Alleppey** India
49C2 **Aller** *R* France
47D1 **Allgäu** *Mts* Germany
8C2 **Alliance** USA
81C3 **Al Līth** S Arabia
91B5 **Al Liwā** Region, UAE
109D1 **Allora** Aust
14B2 **Alma** Michigan, USA
82B1 **Alma Ata** Kazakhstan
50A2 **Almada** Port
Al Madinah = Medina
71F2 **Almagan** *I* Pacific O
91B4 **Al Manāmah** Bahrain
93D3 **Al Ma'nīyah** Iraq
21A1 **Almanor,L** USA
51B2 **Almansa** Spain
13B1 **Alma Peak** *Mt* Can
91B5 **Al Māriyyah** UAE
95B1 **Al Marj** Libya
50B1 **Almazán** Spain
35C1 **Almenara** Brazil
50B2 **Almeria** Spain
61H3 **Al'met'yevsk** Russian Fed
56C1 **Älmhult** Sweden
93E3 **Al Miqdādīyah** Iraq
112C3 **Almirante Brown** *Base* Ant
34A1 **Almirante Latorre** Chile
55B3 **Almirós** Greece
91A4 **Al Mish'āb** S Arabia
50A2 **Almodôvar** Port
84D3 **Almora** India
91A4 **Al Mubarraz** S Arabia
92C4 **Al Mudawwara** Jordan
91C5 **Al Mudaybi** Oman
91B4 **Al Muharraq** Bahrain
81C4 **Al Mukallā** Yemen
81C4 **Al Mukhā** Yemen
93D3 **Al Musayyib** Iraq
44B3 **Alness** Scot
93E3 **Al Nu'mānīyah** Iraq
42D2 **Alnwick** Eng
71D4 **Alor** *I* Indon
77C4 **Alor Setar** Malay
Alost = Aalst
107E2 **Alotau** PNG
106B3 **Aloysius,Mt** Aust
34C3 **Alpachiri** Arg
14B1 **Alpena** USA
47B2 **Alpes du Valais** *Mts* Switz
52B1 **Alpi Dolomitiche** *Mts* Italy
47B2 **Alpi Graie** *Mts* Italy
9C3 **Alpine** Texas, USA
47C1 **Alpi Orobie** *Mts* Italy
47B2 **Alpi Pennine** *Mts* Italy
47C1 **Alpi Retiche** *Mts* Switz
47D1 **Alpi Venoste** *Mts* Italy
52A1 **Alps** *Mts* Europe
95A1 **Al Qaddāhiyah** Libya
94C1 **Al Qadmūs** Syria
93D3 **Al Qā'im** Iraq
93C4 **Al Qalībah** S Arabia
93D2 **Al Qāmishlī** Syria
95A1 **Al Qaryah Ash Sharqiyah** Libya
92C3 **Al Qaryatayn** Syria
91A4 **Al Qātif** S Arabia
95A2 **Al Qatrūn** Libya
91A4 **Al Qayşāmah** S Arabia
94C2 **Al Quatayfah** Syria
50A2 **Alqueva** *R* Port
92C3 **Al Qunayţirah** Syria
81C4 **Al Qunfidhah** S Arabia
93E3 **Al Qurnah** Iraq
94C1 **Al Quşayr** Syria
92C3 **Al Qutayfah** Syria
56B1 **Als** *I* Den
49D2 **Alsace** Region, France
57B2 **Alsfeld** Germany
42C2 **Alston** Eng
38J5 **Alta** Nor
29D2 **Alta Gracia** Arg
27D5 **Altagracia de Orituco** Ven
68A2 **Altai** *Mts* Mongolia
17B1 **Altamaha** *R* USA
33G4 **Altamira** Brazil
23B1 **Altamira** Mexico
53C2 **Altamura** Italy
68C1 **Altanbulag** Mongolia
71F4 **Altape** PNG
24B2 **Altata** Mexico
63A3 **Altay** China
63B3 **Altay** Mongolia
63A2 **Altay** *Mts* Russian Fed
47C1 **Altdorf** Switz
46D1 **Altenkirchen** Germany
34B3 **Altiplanicie del Payún** *Plat* Arg
47B1 **Altkirch** France
101C2 **Alto Molócue** Mozam
10A3 **Alton** USA
15C2 **Altoona** USA
34B2 **Alto Pencoso** *Mts* Arg
35A1 **Alto Sucuriú** Brazil
23B2 **Altotonga** Mexico
23A2 **Altoyac de Alvarez** Mexico
82C2 **Altun Shan** *Mts* China
20B2 **Alturas** USA
9D3 **Altus** USA
91B5 **Al'Ubaylah** S Arabia
93C4 **Al Urayq** *Desert Region* S Arabia
91B5 **Al'Uruq al Mu'taridah** Region, S Arabia
9D2 **Alva** USA
23B2 **Alvarado** Mexico
19A3 **Alvarado** USA
39G6 **Älvdalen** Sweden
19A4 **Alvin** USA
38J5 **Alvsbyn** Sweden
80B3 **Al Wajh** S Arabia
85D3 **Alwar** India
93D3 **Al Widyān** *Desert Region* Iraq/S Arabia
72A2 **Alxa Yougi** China
93E2 **Alyat** Azerbaijan
39J8 **Alytus** Lithuania
46E2 **Alzey** Germany
23B2 **Amacuzac** *R* Mexico
99D2 **Amadi** Sudan
93D2 **Amādīyah** Iraq
6C3 **Amadjuak L** Can
74B4 **Amakusa-shotō** *I* Japan
39G7 **Åmål** Sweden
63D2 **Amalat** *R* Russian Fed
55B3 **Amaliás** Greece
85D4 **Amalner** India
69E4 **Amami** *I* Japan
69E4 **Amami gunto** *Arch* Japan
100C4 **Amanzimtoti** S Africa
33G3 **Amapá** Brazil
33G3 **Amapá** State, Brazil
9C3 **Amarillo** USA
60E5 **Amasya** Turk
23A1 **Amatitan** Mexico
Amazonas = Solimões
32D4 **Amazonas** State, Brazil
28C3 **Amazonas** *R* Brazil
84D2 **Ambāla** India
87C3 **Ambalangoda** Sri Lanka
101D3 **Ambalavao** Madag
98B2 **Ambam** Cam
101D2 **Ambanja** Madag
1C7 **Ambarchik** Russian Fed
32B4 **Ambato** Ecuador
101D2 **Ambato-Boeny** Madag
101D2 **Ambatolampy** Madag
101D2 **Ambatondrazaka** Madag
57C3 **Amberg** Germany
25D3 **Ambergris Cay** *I* Belize
86A2 **Ambikāpur** India
101D2 **Ambilobe** Madag
101D3 **Amboasary** Madag
101D2 **Ambodifototra** Madag
101D3 **Ambohimahasoa** Madag
71D4 **Ambon** Indon
101D3 **Ambositra** Madag
101D3 **Ambovombe** Madag
98B3 **Ambriz** Angola
98C1 **Am Dam** Chad
64H3 **Amderma** Russian Fed
24B2 **Ameca** Mexico
23B2 **Amecameca** Mexico
34C2 **Ameghino** Arg
56B2 **Ameland** *I* Neth
16C2 **Amenia** USA
112B10 **American Highland** *Upland* Ant
105H4 **American Samoa** *Is* Pacific O
17B1 **Americus** USA
101G1 **Amersfoort** S Africa
112C10 **Amery Ice Shelf** Ant
55B3 **Amfilokhía** Greece
55B3 **Amfissa** Greece
63F1 **Amga** Russian Fed
63F1 **Amgal** *R* Russian Fed
69F2 **Amgu** Russian Fed
69F1 **Amgun'** *R* Russian Fed
99D1 **Amhara** *Region* Eth
7D5 **Amherst** Can
16C1 **Amherst** Massachusetts, USA
87B2 **Amhūr** India
48C2 **Amiens** France
75B1 **Amino** Japan
94B1 **Amioune** Leb
89K8 **Amirante Is** Indian O
86B1 **Amlekhgan** Nepal
92C3 **Amman** Jordan
38K6 **Ämmänsaario** Fin
56B2 **Ammersfoort** Neth
90B2 **Amol** Iran
55C3 **Amorgós** *I* Greece
7C5 **Amos** Can
Amoy = Xiamen
101D3 **Ampanihy** Madag
35B2 **Amparo** Brazil
51C1 **Amposta** Spain
85D4 **Amrāvati** India
85C4 **Amreli** India
84C2 **Amritsar** India
56A2 **Amsterdam** Neth
101H1 **Amsterdam** S Africa
15D2 **Amsterdam** USA
98C1 **Am Timan** Chad
88L3 **Amu Darya** *R* Uzbekistan
6A2 **Amund Ringes I** Can
4F2 **Amundsen G** Can
112B4 **Amundsen S** Ant
80E **Amundsen-Scott** *Base* Ant
78D3 **Amuntai** Indon
63E2 **Amur** *R* Russian Fed
33E2 **Anaco** Ven
8B2 **Anaconda** USA
20B1 **Anacortes** USA
55C3 **Anáfi** *I* Greece
93D3 **'ānah** Iraq
21B3 **Anaheim** USA
87B2 **Anaimalai Hills** India
83C4 **Anakapalle** India
12E1 **Anaktuvuk P** USA

Analalaya

101D2 **Analalaya** Madag
92B2 **Anamur** Turk
75A2 **Anan** Japan
87B2 **Anantapur** India
84D2 **Anantnag** India
31B5 **Anápolis** Brazil
90C3 **Anär** Iran
90B3 **Anärak** Iran
71F2 **Anatahan** I
Pacific O
30D4 **Añatuya** Arg
74B3 **Anbyön** N Korea
22C4 **Ancapa Is** USA
4D3 **Anchorage** USA
30C2 **Ancohuma** Mt Bol
32B6 **Ancón** Peru
52B2 **Ancona** Italy
16C1 **Ancram** USA
29B4 **Ancud** Chile
34A3 **Andacollo** Arg
108A1 **Andado** Aust
32C6 **Andahuaylas** Peru
38F6 **Andalsnes** Nor
50A2 **Andalucia** Region,
Spain
17A1 **Andalusia** USA
83D4 **Andaman Is** Burma
83D4 **Andaman S** Burma
108A2 **Andamooka** Aust
38H5 **Andenes** Nor
47C1 **Andermatt** Switz
57B2 **Andernach**
Germany
14A2 **Anderson** Indiana,
USA
18B2 **Anderson** Missouri,
USA
17B1 **Anderson** S Carolina,
USA
4F3 **Anderson** R Can
87B1 **Andhra Pradesh**
State, India
55B3 **Andikíthira** I Greece
65J5 **Andizhan**
Uzbekistan
65H6 **Andkhui** Afghan
74B3 **Andong** S Korea
51C1 **Andorra** Principality,
SW Europe
51C1 **Andorra-La-Vella**
Andorra
43D4 **Andover** Eng
35A2 **Andradina** Brazil
12B2 **Andreafsky** USA
92B2 **Andreas,C** Cyprus
53C2 **Andria** Italy
11C4 **Andros** I The
Bahamas
55B3 **Ándros** I Greece
87A2 **Androth** I India
50B2 **Andújar** Spain
100A2 **Andulo** Angola
97C4 **Anécho** Togo
97C3 **Anéfis** Mali
34B3 **Añelo** Arg
63C2 **Angarsk** Russian
Fed
38H6 **Ånge** Sweden
24A2 **Angel de la Guarda** I
Mexico
79B2 **Angeles** Phil
39G7 **Angelholm** Sweden
109C1 **Angellala Creek** R
Aust
22B1 **Angels Camp** USA
71E4 **Angemuk** Mt Indon
48B2 **Angers** France
76C3 **Angkor** Hist Site
Camb
41C3 **Anglesey** I Wales
19A4 **Angleton** USA
6G3 **Angmagssalik**
Greenland
101D2 **Angoche** Mozam
29B3 **Angol** Chile
14B2 **Angola** Indiana, USA
100A2 **Angola** Republic,
Africa
103H6 **Angola Basin**
Atlantic O
12H3 **Angoon** USA
48C2 **Angoulême** France
96A1 **Angra do Heroismo**
Açores

35C2 **Angra dos Reis**
Brazil
34C3 **Anguil** Arg
27E3 **Anguilla** I
Caribbean S
26B2 **Anguilla Cays** Is
Caribbean S
86B2 **Angul** India
99C3 **Angumu** Zaire
56C1 **Anholt** I Den
73C4 **Anhua** China
72D3 **Anhui** Province,
China
12C2 **Aniak** USA
35B1 **Anicuns** Brazil
46B2 **Anizy-le-Château**
France
4C3 **Anjak** USA
48B2 **Anjou** Republic,
France
101D2 **Anjouan** I Comoros
101D2 **Anjozorobe** Madag
74B3 **Anju** N Korea
72B3 **Ankang** China
92B2 **Ankara** Turk
101D2 **Ankaratra** Mt
Madag
101D3 **Ankazoabo** Madag
101D2 **Ankazobe** Madag
56C2 **Anklam** Germany
76D3 **An Loc** Viet
73B4 **Anlong** China
73C3 **Anlu** China
18C2 **Anna** USA
96C1 **'Annaba** Alg
92C3 **An Nabk** S Arabia
92C3 **An Nabk** Syria
108A1 **Anna Creek** Aust
80C3 **An Nafūd** Desert
S Arabia
93D3 **An Najaf** Iraq
42C2 **Annan** Scot
15C3 **Annapolis** USA
86A1 **Annapurna** Mt
Nepal
14B2 **Ann Arbor** USA
94C1 **An Nāsirah** Syria
93E3 **An Nāsiriyah** Iraq
47B2 **Annecy** France
47B1 **Annemasse** France
76D3 **An Nhon** Viet
73A5 **Anning** China
17A1 **Anniston** USA
89E8 **Annobon** I Eq
Guinea
49C2 **Annonay** France
27J1 **Annotto Bay**
Jamaica
73D3 **Anqing** China
72B2 **Ansai** China
57C3 **Ansbach** Germany
26C3 **Anse d'Hainault**
Haiti
72E1 **Anshan** China
73B4 **Anshun** China
97C3 **Ansongo** Mali
14B3 **Ansted** USA
92C2 **Antakya** Turk
101E2 **Antalaha** Madag
92B2 **Antalya** Turk
92B2 **Antalya Körfezi** B
Turk
101D2 **Antananarivo**
Madag
112C1 **Antarctic Circle** Ant
112C3 **Antarctic Pen** Ant
50B2 **Antequera** Spain
96B2 **Anti-Atlas** Mts Mor
7D5 **Anticosti, Î. d'** Can
27E3 **Antigua** I
Caribbean S
**Anti Lebanon = Jebel
esh Sharqi**
21A2 **Antioch** USA
19A3 **Antlers** USA
30B3 **Antofagasta** Chile
45C1 **Antrim** County, N Ire
45C1 **Antrim** N Ire
45C1 **Antrim Hills** N Ire
101D2 **Antseranana** Madag
101D2 **Antsirabe** Madag
101D2 **Antsohihy** Madag
76D3 **An Tuc** Viet
46C1 **Antwerpen** Belg

45C2 **An Uaimh** Irish Rep
84C3 **Anupgarh** India
87C3 **Anuradhapura**
Sri Lanka
Anvers = Antwerpen
4B3 **Anvik** USA
63B3 **Anxi** China
72C2 **Anyang** China
72A3 **A'nyêmaqên Shan**
Upland China
47C2 **Anza** R Italy
13E1 **Anzac** Can
65K4 **Anzhero-Sudzhensk**
Russian Fed
53B2 **Anzio** Italy
74E2 **Aomori** Japan
52A1 **Aosta** Italy
97B3 **Aoukar** Desert
Region Maur
96C2 **Aoulef** Alg
95A2 **Aozou** Chad
30E3 **Apa** R Brazil/Par
11B4 **Apalachee B** USA
17B2 **Apalachicola** USA
17A2 **Apalachicola B** USA
23B2 **Apan** Mexico
64E3 **Apatity** Russian
Fed
32C3 **Apaporis** R
Colombia
35A2 **Aparecida do
Taboado** Brazil
79B2 **Aparri** Phil
54A1 **Apatin** Croatia
64E3 **Apatity** Russian Fed
24B3 **Apatzingan** Mexico
56B2 **Apeldoorn** Neth
35B2 **Apiai** Brazil
33F2 **Apoera** Surinam
108B3 **Apollo Bay** Aust
79C4 **Apo,Mt** Mt Phil
17B2 **Apopka,L** USA
30F2 **Aporé** R Brazil
10A2 **Apostle Is** USA
10A2 **Apostle L** USA
23A1 **Apozol** Mexico
11B3 **Appalachian Mts**
USA
52B2 **Appennino Abruzzese**
Mts Italy
52A2 **Appennino Ligure**
Mts Italy
53C2 **Appennino Lucano**
Mts Italy
53B2 **Appennino
Napoletano** Mts
Italy
52B2 **Appennino Tosco-
Emilliano** Mts Italy
52B2 **Appennino Umbro-
Marchigiano** Mts
Italy
47C1 **Appenzell** Switz
42C2 **Appleby** Eng
14A2 **Appleton** Wisconsin,
USA
30F3 **Apucarana** Brazil
23B1 **Apulco** Mexico
32D2 **Apure** R Ven
32C6 **Apurimac** R Peru
92C4 **'Aqaba** Jordan
92B4 **'Aqaba,G of** Egypt/
S Arabia
90B3 **'Aqdā** Iran
30E3 **Aquidauana** Brazil
23A2 **Aquila** Mexico
86A1 **Ara** India
17A1 **Arab** USA
81D4 **Arabian S** Asia/
Arabian Pen
31D4 **Aracajú** Brazil
30E3 **Aracanguy, Mts de**
Par
31D2 **Aracati** Brazil
30F3 **Araçatuba** Brazil
50A2 **Aracena** Spain
31C5 **Araçuai** Brazil
94B3 **Arad** Israel
60B4 **Arad** Rom
98C1 **Arada** Chad
91B5 **'Arādah** UAE
106C1 **Arafura S** Indon/Aust
30F2 **Aragarças** Brazil
51B1 **Aragón** Region,

Spain
50B1 **Aragon** R Spain
33G6 **Araguaia** R Brazil
31B3 **Araguaina** Brazil
31B5 **Araguari** Brazil
35B1 **Araguari** R Brazil
75B1 **Arai** Japan
96C2 **Arak** Alg
90A3 **Arāk** Iran
76A2 **Arakan Yoma** Mts
Burma
87B2 **Arakkonam** India
93E2 **Araks** R Azerbaijan
**Aral S = Aral'skoye
More**
80E1 **Aral'sk** Kazakhstan
65G5 **Aral'skoye More** S
Kazakhstan/
Uzbekistan
40B2 **Aran** I Irish Rep
50B1 **Aranda de Duero**
Spain
23A1 **Arandas** Mexico
50B1 **Aranjuez** Spain
75A2 **Arao** Japan
97B3 **Araouane** Mali
29E2 **Arapey** R Urug
31D4 **Arapiraca** Brazil
35A2 **Araporgas** Brazil
30G4 **Ararangua** Brazil
31B6 **Araraquara** Brazil
35B2 **Araras** Brazil
93D2 **Ararat** Armenia
107D4 **Ararat** Aust
93D1 **Aras** R Turk
75C1 **Arato** Japan
32D2 **Arauca** R Ven
34A3 **Arauco** Chile
32C2 **Arauea** Colombia
85C4 **Arāvalli Range** Mts
India
31B5 **Araxá** Brazil
99D2 **Arba Minch** Eth
53A3 **Arbatax** Sardegna
93D2 **Arbil** Iraq
47A1 **Arbois** France
39H6 **Arbrå** Sweden
44C3 **Arbroath** Scot
47A1 **Arc** France
47B2 **Arc** R France
48B3 **Arcachon** France
17B2 **Arcadia** USA
20B2 **Arcata** USA
23A2 **Arcelia** Mexico
26B2 **Archipiélago de
Camaguey** Arch
Cuba
29B6 **Archipiélago de la
Reina Adelaida** Arch
Chile
29B4 **Archipiélago de las
Chones** Arch Chile
32B2 **Archipiélago de las
Perlas** Arch Panama
35B2 **Arcos** Brazil
50A2 **Arcos de la Frontera**
Spain
6B2 **Arctic Bay** Can
1C1 **Arctic Circle**
4E3 **Arctic Red** Can
4E3 **Arctic Red R** Can
4D3 **Arctic Village** USA
54C2 **Arda** R Bulg
65F6 **Ardabil** Iran
93D1 **Ardahan** Turk
39F6 **Ardal** Nor
96C2 **Ardar des Iforas**
Upland Alg/Mali
45C2 **Ardee** Irish Rep
90B3 **Ardekän** Iran
46C2 **Ardennes**
Department, France
57A2 **Ardennes** Region,
Belg
90B3 **Ardestan** Iran
92C3 **Ardh es Suwwan**
Desert Region
Jordan
50A2 **Ardila** R Port
109C2 **Ardlethan** Aust
9D3 **Ardmore** USA
44A3 **Ardnamurchan** Pt
Scot
46A1 **Ardres** France

44B3 **Ardrishaig** Scot
42B2 **Ardrossan** Scot
27D3 **Arecibo** Puerto Rico
31D2 **Areia Branca** Brazil
21A2 **Arena,Pt** USA
39F7 **Arendal** Nor
30B2 **Arequipa** Peru
52B2 **Arezzo** Italy
52B2 **Argenta** Italy
49C2 **Argentan** France
46B2 **Argenteuil** France
28C7 **Argentina** Republic, S America
103F7 **Argentine Basin** Atlantic O
48C2 **Argenton-sur-Creuse** France
54C2 **Argeş** *R* Rom
84B2 **Arghardab** *R* Afghan
55B3 **Argolikós Kólpos** *G* Greece
46C2 **Argonne** Region, France
55B3 **Árgos** Greece
55B3 **Argostólion** Greece
22B3 **Arguello,Pt** USA
106B2 **Argyle,L** Aust
56C1 **Århus** Den
100A3 **Ariamsvlei** Namibia
50B1 **Arlanzón** *R* Spain
34C2 **Arias** Arg
97B3 **Aribinda** Burkina
30B2 **Arica** Chile
84C2 **Arifwala** Pak
Arihā = Jericho
27L1 **Arima** Trinidad
35B1 **Arinos** Brazil
33F6 **Arinos** *R* Brazil
23A2 **Ario de Rosales** Mexico
27L1 **Aripo,Mt** Trinidad
33E5 **Aripuana** Brazil
33E5 **Aripuanã** *R* Brazil
44B3 **Arisaig** Scot
87B2 **Ariskere** India
13B2 **Aristazabal I** Can
34B3 **Arizona** Arg
9B3 **Arizona** State, USA
39G7 **Arjäng** Sweden
61F3 **Arkadak** Russian Fed
19B3 **Arkadelphia** USA
65H4 **Arkaly** Kazakhstan
11A3 **Arkansas** State, USA
11A3 **Arkansas** *R* USA
18A2 **Arkansas City** USA
64F3 **Arkhangel'sk** Russian Fed
41B3 **Arklow** Irish Rep
47D1 **Arlberg P** Austria
49C3 **Arles** France
19A3 **Arlington** Texas, USA
15C3 **Arlington** Virginia, USA
20B1 **Arlington** Washington, USA
97C3 **Arlit** Niger
57B3 **Arlon** Belg
Armageddon = Megiddo
45C1 **Armagh** County, N Ire
45C1 **Armagh** N Ire
61F5 **Armavir** Russian Fed
23A2 **Armena** Mexico
32B3 **Armenia** Colombia
65F5 **Armenia** Republic, Europe
107E4 **Armidale** Aust
13D2 **Armstrong** Can
7C3 **Arnaud** *R* Can
92B2 **Arnauti** *C* Cyprus
56B2 **Arnhem** Neth
106C2 **Arnhem,C** Aust
106C2 **Arnhem Land** Aust
22B1 **Arnold** USA
15C1 **Arnprior** Can
46E1 **Arnsberg** Germany
100A3 **Aroab** Namibia
47C2 **Arona** Italy
12B2 **Aropuk L** USA
52A1 **Arosa** Switz
97A3 **Arquipélago dos Bijagós** *Arch* Guinea-Bissau
93D3 **Ar Ramādī** Iraq
42B2 **Arran** *I* Scot
93C2 **Ar Raqqah** Syria
95A2 **Ar Rāqūbah** Libya
49C1 **Arras** France
96A2 **Arrecife** Canary Is
34C2 **Arrecifes** Arg
23A1 **Arriaga** Mexico
93E3 **Ar Rifā't** Iraq
93E3 **Ar Rihāb** *Desert Region* Iraq
91A5 **Ar Riyāḍ** S Arabia
44B3 **Arrochar** Scot
111A2 **Arrowtown** NZ
23B1 **Arroyo Seco** Mexico
91B4 **Ar Ru'ays** Qatar
91C5 **Ar Rustaq** Oman
93D3 **Ar Rutbah** Iraq
47D2 **Arsiero** Italy
49D2 **Arsizio** Italy
61G2 **Arsk** Russian Fed
55B3 **Árta** Greece
23A2 **Arteaga** Mexico
63B2 **Artemovsk** Russian Fed
63D2 **Artemovskiy** Russian Fed
9C3 **Artesia** USA
111B2 **Arthurs P** NZ
112C2 **Artigas** *Base* Ant
29E2 **Artigas** Urug
4H3 **Artillery L** Can
48C1 **Artois** Region, France
112C2 **Arturo Prat** *Base* Ant
93D1 **Artvin** Turk
99D2 **Aru** Zaïre
33G6 **Aruanã** Brazil
27C4 **Aruba** *I* Caribbean S
86B1 **Arun** *R* Nepal
86C1 **Arunāchal Pradesh** Union Territory, India
87B3 **Aruppukkottai** India
99D3 **Arusha** Tanz
98C2 **Aruwimi** *R* Zaïre
68C2 **Arvayheer** Mongolia
47B2 **Arve** *R* France
7C5 **Arvida** Can
38H5 **Arvidsjaur** Sweden
39G7 **Arvika** Sweden
21B2 **Arvin** USA
94B1 **Arwad** *I* Syria
61F2 **Arzamas** Russian Fed
84C2 **Asadabad** Afghan
75A2 **Asahi** *R* Japan
74E2 **Asahi dake** *Mt* Japan
74E2 **Asahikawa** Japan
86B2 **Asansol** India
95A2 **Asawanwah** *Well* Libya
61K2 **Asbest** Russian Fed
15D2 **Asbury Park** USA
103H5 **Ascension** *I* Atlantic O
57B3 **Aschaffenburg** Germany
56C2 **Aschersleben** Germany
52B2 **Ascoli Piceno** Italy
47C1 **Ascona** Switz
99E1 **Aseb** Eth
96C2 **Asedjirad** *Upland* Alg
99D2 **Asela** Eth
38H6 **Åsele** Sweden
54B2 **Asenovgrad** Bulg
46C2 **Asfeld** France
61J2 **Asha** Russian Fed
17B1 **Ashburn** USA
111B2 **Ashburton** NZ
106A3 **Ashburton** *R* Aust
92B3 **Ashdod** Israel
19B3 **Ashdown** USA
11B3 **Asheville** USA
109D1 **Ashford** Aust
43E4 **Ashford** Eng
74D3 **Ashikaga** Japan
75A2 **Ashizuri-misaki** *Pt* Japan
65G6 **Ashkhabad** Turkmenistan
10B3 **Ashland** Kentucky, USA
18A1 **Ashland** Nebraska, USA
14B2 **Ashland** Ohio, USA
8A2 **Ashland** Oregon, USA
109C1 **Ashley** Aust
16B2 **Ashokan Res** USA
94B3 **Ashqelon** Israel
93D3 **Ash Shabakh** Iraq
91C4 **Ash Sha'm** UAE
93D2 **Ash Sharqāt** Iraq
93E3 **Ash Shatrah** Iraq
81C4 **Ash Shihr** Yemen
91A4 **Ash Shumlul** S Arabia
14B2 **Ashtabula** USA
7D4 **Ashuanipi L** Can
92C3 **'Aṣī** *R* Syria
47D2 **Asiago** Italy
53A2 **Asinara** *I* Medit S
65K4 **Asino** Russian Fed
93D2 **Aşkale** Turk
39G7 **Askersund** Sweden
84C1 **Asmar** Afghan
95C3 **Asmera** Eth
75A2 **Aso** Japan
99D1 **Asosa** Eth
111A2 **Aspiring,Mt** NZ
93C2 **As Sabkhah** Syria
91A5 **As Salamiyah** S Arabia
92C2 **As Salamīyah** Syria
93D3 **As Salmān** Iraq
86C1 **Assam** State, India
93E3 **As Samāwah** Iraq
91B5 **As Ṣanām** Region, S Arabia
94C2 **As Sanamayn** Syria
56B2 **Assen** Neth
56B1 **Assens** Den
95A1 **As Sidrah** Libya
5H5 **Assiniboia** Can
5G4 **Assiniboine,Mt** Can
30F3 **Assis** Brazil
93C3 **As Sukhnah** Syria
91A5 **As Summan** Region, S Arabia
99E3 **Assumption** *I* Seychelles
92C3 **As Suwaydā'** Syria
93D3 **As Suwayrah** Iraq
93E2 **Astara** Azerbaijan
52A2 **Asti** Italy
55C3 **Astipálaia** *I* Greece
50A1 **Astorga** Spain
8A2 **Astoria** USA
61G4 **Astrakhan'** Russian Fed
50A1 **Asturias** Region, Spain
30E4 **Asunción** Par
99D2 **Aswa** *R* Uganda
80B3 **Aswân** Egypt
95C2 **Aswân High Dam** Egypt
95C2 **Asyût** Egypt
92C3 **As Zilaf** Syria
97C4 **Atakpamé** Togo
71D4 **Atambua** Indon
6E3 **Atangmik** Greenland
96A2 **Atar** Maur
65J5 **Atasu** Kazakhstan
95C3 **Atatisk Baraji** *Res* Turkmenistan
95C3 **Atbara** Sudan
65H4 **Atbasar** Kazakhstan
11A4 **Atchafalaya B** USA
10A3 **Atchison** USA
16B3 **Atco** USA
23A1 **Atenguillo** Mexico
52B2 **Atessa** Italy
46B1 **Ath** Belg
13E2 **Athabasca** Can
5G4 **Athabasca** *R* Can
5H4 **Athabasca L** Can
45B2 **Athenry** Irish Rep
Athens = Athínai
11B3 **Athens** Georgia, USA
14B3 **Athens** Ohio, USA
19A3 **Athens** Texas, USA
55B3 **Athínai** Greece
41B3 **Athlone** Irish Rep
16C1 **Athol** USA
55B2 **Áthos** *Mt* Greece
45C2 **Athy** Irish Rep
98B1 **Ati** Chad
7A5 **Atikoken** Can
61F3 **Atkarsk** Russian Fed
18B2 **Atkins** USA
23B2 **Atlacomulco** Mexico
11B3 **Atlanta** Georgia, USA
14B2 **Atlanta** Michigan, USA
18A1 **Atlantic** USA
10C3 **Atlantic City** USA
16B2 **Atlantic Highlands** USA
103H8 **Atlantic Indian Basin** Atlantic O
103H7 **Atlantic Indian Ridge** Atlantic O
96C1 **Atlas Saharien** *Mts* Alg
4E4 **Atlin** Can
4E4 **Atlin L** Can
94B2 **'Atlit** Israel
23B2 **Atlixco** Mexico
11B3 **Atmore** USA
101D3 **Atofinandrahana** Madag
12D3 **Atognak I** USA
19A3 **Atoka** USA
23A1 **Atotonilco** Mexico
23B2 **Atoyac** *R* Mexico
32B2 **Atrato** *R* Colombia
91B5 **Attaf** Region, UAE
81C3 **At Tā'if** S Arabia
94C2 **At Tall** Syria
17A1 **Attalla** USA
7B4 **Attauapiskat** Can
7B4 **Attauapiskat** *R* Can
93D3 **At Taysīyah** *Desert Region* S Arabia
14A2 **Attica** Indiana, USA
46C2 **Attigny** France
15D2 **Attleboro** Massachusetts, USA
76D3 **Attopeu** Laos
92C4 **At Tubayq** *Upland* S Arabia
34B3 **Atuel** *R* Arg
39H7 **Atvidaberg** Sweden
22B2 **Atwater** USA
49D3 **Aubagne** France
46C2 **Aube** Department, France
49C3 **Aubenas** France
17A1 **Auburn** Alabama, USA
21A2 **Auburn** California, USA
14A2 **Auburn** Indiana, USA
18A1 **Auburn** Nebraska, USA
15C2 **Auburn** New York, USA
20B1 **Auburn** Washington, USA
48C3 **Auch** France
110B1 **Auckland** NZ
105G6 **Auckland Is** NZ
48C3 **Aude** *R* France
7B4 **Auden** Can
47B1 **Audincourt** France
109C1 **Augathella** Aust
57C3 **Augsburg** Germany
106A4 **Augusta** Aust
11B3 **Augusta** Georgia, USA
18A2 **Augusta** Kansas, USA
10D2 **Augusta** Maine, USA
12D3 **Augustine I** USA
58C2 **Augustow** Pol
106A3 **Augustus,Mt** Aust

Aumale

46A2 **Aumale** France
85D3 **Auraiya** India
85D5 **Aurangābād** India
96C1 **Aurès** Mts Alg
48C3 **Aurillac** France
8C3 **Aurora** Colorado, USA
10B2 **Aurora** Illinois, USA
14B3 **Aurora** Indiana, USA
18B2 **Aurora** Mississippi, USA
100A3 **Aus** Namibia
14B2 **Au Sable** USA
10A2 **Austin** Minnesota, USA
21B2 **Austin** Nevada, USA
9D3 **Austin** Texas, USA
107D4 **Australian Alps** Mts Aust
37E4 **Austria** Federal Republic, Europe
46A1 **Authie** R France
24B3 **Autlán** Mexico
49C2 **Autun** France
49C2 **Auvergne** Region, France
49C2 **Auxerre** France
46B1 **Auxi-le-Châteaux** France
49C2 **Avallon** France
22C4 **Avalon** USA
7E5 **Avalon Pen** Can
35B2 **Avaré** Brazil
90D3 **Avaz** Iran
94B3 **Avedat** Hist Site Israel
33F4 **Aveiro** Brazil
50A1 **Aveiro** Port
29E2 **Avellaneda** Arg
53B2 **Avellino** Italy
46B1 **Avesnes-sur-Helpe** France
39H6 **Avesta** Sweden
52B2 **Avezzano** Italy
44C3 **Aviemore** Scot
111B2 **Aviemore,L** NZ
47B2 **Avigliana** Italy
49C3 **Avignon** France
50B1 **Avila** Spain
50A1 **Aviles** Spain
47D1 **Avisio** R Italy
108B3 **Avoca** R Aust
43C4 **Avon** County, Eng
43D4 **Avon** R Dorset, Eng
43D3 **Avon** R Warwick, Eng
43C4 **Avonmouth** Wales
17B2 **Avon Park** USA
46B2 **Avre** R France
54A2 **Avtovac** Bosnia & Herzegovina, Yugos
94C2 **A'waj** R Syria
74D4 **Awaji-shima** B Japan
99E2 **Awarē** Eth
111A2 **Awarua Pt** NZ
99E2 **Awash** Eth
99E2 **Awash** R Eth
75B1 **Awa-shima** I Japan
111B2 **Awatere** R NZ
95A2 **Awbāri** Libya
98C2 **Aweil** Sudan
95B2 **Awjilah** Libya
96A2 **Awserd** Well Mor
6A2 **Axel Heiburg I** Can
43C4 **Axminster** Eng
75B1 **Ayabe** Japan
29E3 **Ayacucho** Arg
32C6 **Ayacucho** Peru
65K5 **Ayaguz** Kazakhstan
82C2 **Ayakkum Hu** L China
50A2 **Ayamonte** Spain
63F2 **Ayan** Russian Fed
32C6 **Ayauiri** Peru
92A2 **Aydin** Turk
55C3 **Áyios Evstrátios** I Greece
43D4 **Aylesbury** Eng
13D2 **Aylmer,Mt** Can
94C2 **'Ayn al Fijah** Syria
93D2 **Ayn Zālah** Iraq

95B2 **Ayn Zuwayyah** Well Libya
99D2 **Ayod** Sudan
107D2 **Ayr** Aust
42B2 **Ayr** Scot
42B2 **Ayr** R Scot
42B2 **Ayre,Pt of** Eng
54C2 **Aytos** Bulg
76C3 **Aytthaya** Thai
23A1 **Ayutla** Mexico
55C3 **Ayvacik** Turk
55C3 **Ayvalik** Turk
86A1 **Azamgarh** India
97B3 **Azaouad** Desert Region Mali
97D3 **Azare** Nig
92C2 **A'Zāz** Syria
Azbine = Aïr
65F5 **Azerbaijan** Republic, Russian Fed
32B4 **Azogues** Ecuador
Azores = Açores
98C1 **Azoum** R Chad
60E4 **Azovskoye More** S Russian Fed/Ukraine
96B1 **Azrou** Mor
34D3 **Azucena** Arg
32A2 **Azuero,Pen de** Panama
29E3 **Azúl** Arg
94C2 **Az-Zabdānī** Syria
91C5 **Az Zāhirah** Mts Oman
95A2 **Az Zahra** Libya
96A2 **Azzeffal** R Maur
93E3 **Az Zubayr** Iraq

B

94B2 **Ba'abda** Leb
92C3 **Ba'albek** Leb
94B3 **Ba'al Hazor** Mt Israel
99E2 **Baardheere** Somalia
54C2 **Babadag** Rom
92A1 **Babaeski** Turk
32B4 **Babahoyo** Ecuador
81C4 **Bāb al Mandab** Str Djibouti/Yemen
71D4 **Babar** I Indon
99D3 **Babati** Tanz
60E2 **Babayevo** Russian Fed
14B2 **Baberton** USA
13B1 **Babine** R Can
5F4 **Babine L** Can
90B2 **Bābol** Iran
79B2 **Babuyan Chan** Phil
79B2 **Babuyan Is** Phil
31C2 **Bacabal** Brazil
71D4 **Bacan** I Indon
60C4 **Bacău** Rom
76D1 **Bac Can** Viet
108B3 **Bacchus Marsh** Aust
82B2 **Bachu** China
4J3 **Back** R Can
12J2 **Backbone Ranges** Mts Can
76D1 **Bac Ninh** Viet
79B3 **Bacolod** Phil
79B3 **Baco,Mt** Phil
87B2 **Badagara** India
72A1 **Badain Jaran Shamo** Desert China
50A2 **Badajoz** Spain
51C1 **Badalona** Spain
93D3 **Badanah** S Arabia
46D2 **Bad Bergzabern** Germany
46D1 **Bad Ems** Germany
47C1 **Baden** Switz
57B3 **Baden-Baden** Germany
57B3 **Baden-Württemberg** State, Germany
57C3 **Badgastein** Austria
22C2 **Badger** USA
57B2 **Bad-Godesberg** Germany
57B2 **Bad Hersfeld** Germany
46D1 **Bad Honnef** Germany
85B4 **Badin** Pak
52B1 **Bad Ischl** Austria

93C3 **Badiyat ash Sham** Desert Region Jordan/Iraq
57B3 **Bad-Kreuznach** Germany
46D1 **Bad Nevenahr-Ahrweiler** Germany
47C1 **Bad Ragaz** Switz
57C3 **Bad Tolz** Germany
87C3 **Badulla** Sri Lanka
50B2 **Baena** Spain
97A3 **Bafatá** Guinea-Bissau
4H2 **Baffin** Region Can
6C2 **Baffin B** Greenland/Can
6C2 **Baffin I** Can
98B2 **Bafia** Cam
97A3 **Bafing** R Mali
97A3 **Bafoulabé** Mali
98B2 **Bafoussam** Cam
90C3 **Bāfq** Iran
60E5 **Bafra Burun** Pt Turk
91C4 **Bāft** Iran
98C2 **Bafwasende** Zaïre
86A1 **Bagaha** India
87B1 **Bāgalkot** India
99D3 **Bagamoyo** Tanz
29F2 **Bagé** Brazil
93D3 **Baghdād** Iraq
86B2 **Bagherhat** Bang
91C3 **Bāghin** Iran
84B1 **Baghlan** Afghan
49C3 **Bagnols-sur-Cèze** France
97B3 **Bagoé** R Mali
79B2 **Baguio** Phil
86B1 **Bāhādurābād** India
11C4 **Bahamas,The** Is Caribbean S
86B2 **Baharampur** India
92A4 **Baharîya Oasis** Egypt
84C3 **Bahawalpur** Pak
84C3 **Bahawalpur** Province, Pak
85C3 **Bahawathagar** Pak
Bahia = Salvador
31C4 **Bahia** State, Brazil
29D3 **Bahía Blanca** Arg
29D3 **Bahía Blanca** B Arg
34A3 **Bahía Concepción** B Chile
35C2 **Bahia da Ilha Grande** B Brazil
24B2 **Bahia de Banderas** B Mexico
24C2 **Bahia de Campeche** B Mexico
25D3 **Bahia de la Ascension** B Mexico
24B3 **Bahia de Petacalco** B Mexico
96A2 **Bahia de Rio de Oro** B Mor
35C2 **Bahia de Sepetiba** B Brazil
29C6 **Bahia Grande** B Arg
9B4 **Bahia Kino** Mexico
24A2 **Bahia Magdalena** B Mexico
24A2 **Bahia Sebastia Vizcaino** B Mexico
99D1 **Bahar Dar** Eth
86A1 **Bahraich** India
80D3 **Bahrain** Sheikdom, Arabian Pen
93D3 **Bahr al Milh** L Iraq
98C2 **Bahr Aouk** R Chad/CAR
Bahrat Lut = Dead S
98C2 **Bahr el Arab** Watercourse Sudan
99D2 **Bahr el Ghazal** R Sudan
98B1 **Bahr el Ghazal** Watercourse Chad
101H1 **Baia de Maputo** B Mozam
31B2 **Baia de Marajó** B Brazil
101D2 **Baiá de Pemba** B Mozam

31C2 **Baia de São Marcos** B Brazil
50A2 **Baia de Setúbal** B Port
31D4 **Baia de Todos os Santos** B Brazil
100A2 **Baia dos Tigres** Angola
60B4 **Baia Mare** Rom
98B2 **Baïbokoum** Chad
69E2 **Baicheng** China
101E2 **Baie Antongila** B Madag
7D5 **Baie-Comeau** Can
101D2 **Baie de Bombetoka** B Madag
101D2 **Baie de Mahajamba** B Madag
101D3 **Baie de St Augustin** B Madag
94B2 **Baie de St Georges** B Leb
10D2 **Baie des Chaleurs** B Can
7C4 **Baie-du-Poste** Can
72B3 **Baihe** China
72C3 **Bai He** R China
93D3 **Ba'iji** Iraq
86A2 **Baikunthpur** India
Baile Atha Cliath = Dublin
54B2 **Bäilesti** Rom
46B1 **Bailleul** France
72A3 **Baima** China
17B1 **Bainbridge** USA
12B2 **Baird Inlet** USA
4B3 **Baird Mts** USA
72D1 **Bairin Youqi** China
72D1 **Bairin Zuoqi** China
107D4 **Bairnsdale** Aust
79B4 **Bais** Phil
54A1 **Baja** Hung
9B3 **Baja California** State, Mexico
24A1 **Baja California** Pen Mexico
61J2 **Bakal** Russian Fed
98C2 **Bakala** CAR
97A3 **Bakel** Sen
8C2 **Baker** Montana, USA
8B2 **Baker** Oregon, USA
6A3 **Baker Foreland** Pt Can
4J3 **Baker L** Can
4J3 **Baker Lake** Can
8A2 **Baker,Mt** USA
9B3 **Bakersfield** USA
90C2 **Bakharden** Turkmenistan
90C2 **Bakhardok** Turkmenistan
60D3 **Bakhmach** Ukraine
38C1 **Bakkaflói** B Iceland
99D2 **Bako** Eth
98C2 **Bakouma** CAR
65F5 **Baku** Azerbaijan
92B2 **Balã** Turk
79A4 **Balabac** I Phil
70C3 **Balabac** Str Malay
78C2 **Balaikarangan** Indon
108A2 **Balaklava** Aust
61G3 **Balakovo** Russian Fed
86A2 **Balāngir** India
61F3 **Balashov** Russian Fed
86B2 **Balasore** India
80A3 **Balât** Egypt
52C1 **Balaton** L Hung
45C2 **Balbriggan** Irish Rep
29E3 **Balcarce** Arg
54C2 **Balchik** Bulg
111B3 **Balclutha** NZ
18B2 **Bald Knob** USA
17B1 **Baldwin** USA
9C3 **Baldy Peak** Mt USA
Balearic Is = Islas Baleares
78C2 **Baleh** R Malay
79B2 **Baler** Phil
61H2 **Balezino** Russian Fed
106A1 **Bali** I Indon
92A2 **Balıkesir** Turk

93C2 **Balīkh** *R* Syria	91A3 **Bandar Khomeynī** Iran	72B3 **Baoji** China	16B3 **Barnegat** USA
78D3 **Balikpapan** Indon	78C2 **Bandar Seri Begawan** Brunei	76D3 **Bao Loc** Viet	16B3 **Barnegat B** USA
79B2 **Balintang Chan** Phil	71D4 **Banda S** Indon	68B4 **Baoshan** China	6C2 **Barnes Icecap** Can
78C4 **Bali S** Indon	91C4 **Band Boni** Iran	72C1 **Baotou** China	17B1 **Barnesville** Georgia, USA
35A1 **Baliza** Brazil	35C2 **Bandeira** *Mt* Brazil	87C1 **Bāpatla** India	14B3 **Barnesville** Ohio, USA
84B1 **Balkh** Afghan	97B3 **Bandiagara** Mali	46B1 **Bapaume** France	42D3 **Barnsley** Eng
65J6 **Balkhash** Kazakhstan	60C5 **Bandirma** Turk	93D3 **Ba'Qūbah** Iraq	43B4 **Barnstaple** Eng
44B5 **Ballachulish** Scot	45B3 **Bandon** Irish Rep	32J7 **Baquerizo Morena** Ecuador	97C4 **Baro** Nig
45B2 **Ballaghaderreen** Irish Rep	98B3 **Bandundu** Zaïre	54A2 **Bar** Montenegro, Yugos	86C1 **Barpeta** India
42B2 **Ballantrae** Scot	78B4 **Bandung** Indon	99D1 **Bara** Sudan	32D1 **Barquisimeto** Ven
4G2 **Ballantyne Str** Can	25E2 **Banes** Cuba	99E2 **Baraawe** Somalia	31C4 **Barra** Brazil
87B2 **Ballapur** India	13D2 **Banff** Can	78D3 **Barabai** Indon	44A3 **Barra** *I* Scot
107D4 **Ballarat** Aust	44C3 **Banff** Scot	86A1 **Bāra Banki** India	109D2 **Barraba** Aust
44C3 **Ballater** Scot	5G4 **Banff** *R* Can	65J4 **Barabinsk** Russian Fed	23A2 **Barra de Navidad** Mexico
112C7 **Balleny Is** Ant	13D2 **Banff Nat Pk** Can	65J4 **Barabinskaya Step** *Steppe* Kazakhstan/ Russian Fed	35C2 **Barra de Pirai** Brazil
86A1 **Ballia** India	87B2 **Bangalore** India		35A1 **Barragem de São Simão** *Res* Brazil
109D1 **Ballina** Aust	98C2 **Bangassou** CAR	50B1 **Baracaldo** Spain	35A1 **Barra do Garças** Brazil
41B3 **Ballina** Irish Rep	70C3 **Banggi** *I* Malay	26C2 **Baracoa** Cuba	35B1 **Barragem Agua Vermelha** *Res* Brazil
45B2 **Ballinasloe** Irish Rep	95B1 **Banghāzī** Libya	94C2 **Baradá** *R* Syria	50A2 **Barragem do Castelo do Bode** *Res* Port
45B2 **Ballinrobe** Irish Rep	76D2 **Bang Hieng** *R* Laos	109C2 **Baradine** Aust	50A2 **Barragem do Maranhão** *Res* Port
55A2 **Ballsh** Alb	78B3 **Bangka** *I* Indon	87A1 **Bārāmati** India	
45B1 **Ballycastle** Irish Rep	78A3 **Bangko** Indon	84C2 **Baramula** Pak	35A2 **Barragem Três Irmãos** *Res* Brazil
45C1 **Ballycastle** N Ire	76C3 **Bangkok** Thai	85D3 **Bārān** India	44A3 **Barra Head** *Pt* Scot
45C1 **Ballymena** N Ire	82C3 **Bangladesh** Republic, Asia	79B3 **Barangas** Phil	31C6 **Barra Mansa** Brazil
45C1 **Ballymoney** N Ire	84D2 **Bangong Co** *L* China	4E4 **Baranof I** USA	32B6 **Barranca** Peru
45B1 **Ballyshannon** Irish Rep	10D2 **Bangor** Maine, USA	60C3 **Baranovichi** Belorussia	32C2 **Barrancabermeja** Colombia
45B2 **Ballyvaghan** Irish Rep	45D1 **Bangor** N Ire	108A2 **Baratta** Aust	33E2 **Barrancas** Ven
108B3 **Balmoral** Aust	16B2 **Bangor** Pennsylvania, USA	86B1 **Barauni** India	30E4 **Barranqueras** Arg
34C2 **Balnearia** Arg	42B3 **Bangor** Wales	31C6 **Barbacena** Brazil	32C1 **Barranquilla** Colombia
84B3 **Balochistān** Region, Pak	78D3 **Bangsalsembera** Indon	27F4 **Barbados** *I* Caribbean S	44A3 **Barra,Sound of** *Chan* Scot
100A2 **Balombo** Angola	76B3 **Bang Saphan Yai** Thai	51C1 **Barbastro** Spain	16C1 **Barre** USA
109C1 **Balonn** *R* Aust	79B2 **Bangued** Phil	101H1 **Barberton** S Africa	34B2 **Barreal** Arg
85C3 **Balotra** India	98B2 **Bangui** CAR	48B2 **Barbezieux** France	31C4 **Barreiras** Brazil
86A1 **Balrāmpur** India	100C2 **Bangweulu** *L* Zambia	32C2 **Barbosa** Colombia	50A2 **Barreiro** Port
107D4 **Balranald** Aust	77C4 **Ban Hat Yai** Thai	27E3 **Barbuda** *I* Caribbean S	31D3 **Barreiros** Brazil
31B3 **Balsas** Brazil	76C2 **Ban Hin Heup** Laos	107D3 **Barcaldine** Aust	107D5 **Barren,C** Aust
23B2 **Balsas** Mexico	76C1 **Ban Houei Sai** Laos	**Barce = Al Marj**	12D3 **Barren Is** USA
24B3 **Balsas** *R* Mexico	76B3 **Ban Hua Hin** Thai	53C3 **Barcellona** Italy	31B6 **Barretos** Brazil
60C4 **Balta** Ukraine	97B3 **Bani** *R* Mali	51C1 **Barcelona** Spain	13E2 **Barrhead** Can
39H7 **Baltic S** N Europe	97C3 **Bani Bangou** Niger	33E1 **Barcelona** Ven	14C2 **Barrie** Can
92B3 **Baltim** Egypt	95A1 **Bani Walid** Libya	107D3 **Barcoo** *R* Aust	13C2 **Barrière** Can
45B3 **Baltimore** Irish Rep	92C2 **Bāniyās** Syria	34B3 **Barda del Medio** Arg	108B2 **Barrier Range** *Mts* Aust
10C3 **Baltimore** USA	94B2 **Baniyas** Syria	95A2 **Bardai** Chad	107E4 **Barrington,Mt** Aust
86B1 **Bālurghāt** India	52C2 **Banja Luka** Bosnia & Herzegovina, Yugos	29C3 **Bardas Blancas** Arg	27N2 **Barrouaillie** St Vincent
61H4 **Balykshi** Kazakhstan	78C3 **Banjarmasin** Indon	86B2 **Barddhamān** India	4C2 **Barrow** USA
91C4 **Bam** Iran	97A3 **Banjul** The Gambia	59C3 **Bardejov** Czech	45C2 **Barrow** *R* Irish Rep
98B1 **Bama** Nig	77B4 **Ban Kantang** Thai	47C2 **Bardi** Italy	106C3 **Barrow Creek** Aust
97B3 **Bamako** Mali	76D2 **Ban Khemmarat** Laos	47B2 **Bardonecchia** Italy	106A3 **Barrow I** Aust
98C2 **Bambari** CAR	77B4 **Ban Khok Kloi** Thai	43B3 **Bardsey** *I* Wales	42C2 **Barrow-in-Furness** Eng
17B1 **Bamberg** USA	71F5 **Banks I** Aust	84D3 **Bareilly** India	4C2 **Barrow,Pt** USA
57C3 **Bamberg** Germany	5E4 **Banks I** British Columbia, Can	64D2 **Barentsøya** *I* Barents S	6A2 **Barrow Str** Can
98C2 **Bambili** Zaïre	4F2 **Banks I** Northwest Territories, Can	64E2 **Barents S** Russian Fed	15C1 **Barry's Bay** Can
35B2 **Bambui** Brazil	20C1 **Banks L** USA	95C3 **Barentu** Eth	87B1 **Barsi** India
98B2 **Bamenda** Cam	111B2 **Banks Pen** NZ	86A2 **Bargarh** India	9B3 **Barstow** USA
13C3 **Bamfield** Can	109C4 **Banks Str** Aust	47B2 **Barge** Italy	49C2 **Bar-sur-Aube** France
98B2 **Bamingui** *R* CAR	86B2 **Bankura** India	63D2 **Barguzin** Russian Fed	33F2 **Bartica** Guyana
98B2 **Bamingui Bangoran** *National Park* CAR	76B2 **Ban Mae Sariang** Thai	63D2 **Barguzin** *R* Russian Fed	92B1 **Bartın** Turk
84B2 **Bamiyan** Afghan	76B2 **Ban Mae Sot** Thai	86B2 **Barhi** India	107D2 **Bartle Frere,Mt** Aust
91D4 **Bampur** Iran	76D3 **Ban Me Thuot** Viet	53C2 **Bari** Italy	9D3 **Bartlesville** USA
91D4 **Bampur** *R* Iran	45C1 **Bann** *R* N Ire	51D2 **Barika** Alg	101C3 **Bartolomeu Dias** Mozam
98C2 **Banalia** Zaïre	77R4 **Ban Na San** Thai	32C2 **Barinas** Ven	58C2 **Bartoszyce** Pol
97B3 **Banamba** Mali	84C2 **Bannu** Pak	86B2 **Baripāda** India	78C4 **Barung** *I* Indon
76C3 **Ban Aranyaprathet** Thai	34A3 **Baños Maule** Chile	85C4 **Bari Sādri** India	85D4 **Barwāh** India
76C2 **Ban Ban** Laos	76C2 **Ban Pak Neun** Laos	86C2 **Barisal** Bang	85C4 **Barwāni** India
77C4 **Ban Betong** Thai	77C4 **Ban Pak Phanang** Thai	78C3 **Barito** *R* Indon	109C1 **Barwon** *R* Aust
45C1 **Banbridge** N Ire	76D3 **Ban Ru Kroy** Camb	95A2 **Barjuj** *Watercourse* Libya	61G3 **Barysh** Russian Fed
43D3 **Banbury** Eng	76B3 **Ban Sai Yok** Thai	73A3 **Barkam** China	98B2 **Basankusu** Zaïre
44C3 **Banchory** Scot	76C3 **Ban Sattahip** Thai	18C2 **Barkley,L** USA	34D2 **Basavilbas** Arg
25D3 **Banco Chinchorro** *Is* Mexico	59B3 **Banská Bystrica** Czech	13B3 **Barkley Sd** Can	79B1 **Basco** Phil
15C1 **Bancroft** Can	85C4 **Bānswāra** India	100B4 **Barkly East** S Africa	52A1 **Basel** Switz
86A1 **Bānda** India	77B4 **Ban Tha Kham** Thai	106C2 **Barkly Tableland** *Mts* Aust	53C2 **Basento** *R* Italy
70A3 **Banda Aceh** Indon	76D2 **Ban Thateng** Laos	46C2 **Bar-le-Duc** France	13E2 **Bashaw** Can
97B4 **Bandama** *R* Ivory Coast	76C2 **Ban Tha Tum** Thai	106A3 **Barlee,L** Aust	79B1 **Bashi Chan** Phil
91C4 **Bandar Abbās** Iran	41B3 **Bantry** Irish Rep	106A3 **Barlee Range** *Mts* Aust	61H3 **Bashkirskaya Respublika** Russian Fed
90A2 **Bandar Anzalī** Iran	41A3 **Bantry B** Irish Rep	53C2 **Barletta** Italy	79B4 **Basilan** *I* Phil
99F2 **Bandarbeyla** Somalia	76D3 **Ban Ya Soup** Viet	85C3 **Barmer** India	43E4 **Basildon** Eng
91B4 **Bandar-e Daylam** Iran	78C4 **Banyuwangi** Indon	108B2 **Barmera** Aust	43D4 **Basingstoke** Eng
91B4 **Bandar-e Lengheh** Iran	72C3 **Baofeng** China	43B3 **Barmouth** Wales	
91B4 **Bandar-e Māqām** Iran	76C1 **Bao Ha** Viet	42D2 **Barnard Castle** Eng	
91B4 **Bandar-e Rig** Iran		65K4 **Barnaul** Russian Fed	
90B2 **Bandar-e Torkoman** Iran			

Basin Region

Basin Region USA
93E3 Basra Iraq
46D2 Bas-Rhin
Department, France
76D3 Bassac R Camb
13E2 Bassano Can
52B1 Bassano Italy
47D2 Bassano del Grappa
Italy
97C4 Bassari Togo
101C3 Bassas da India I
Mozam Chan
76A2 Bassein Burma
27E3 Basse Terre
Guadeloupe
97C4 Bassila Benin
22C2 Bass Lake USA
107D4 Bass Str Aust
39G7 Båstad Sweden
91B4 Bastak Iran
86A1 Basti India
52A2 Bastia Corse
57B3 Bastogne Belg
19B3 Bastrop Louisiana,
USA
19A3 Bastrop Texas, USA
98A2 Bata Eq Guinea
78C3 Batakan Indon
84D2 Batala India
68B3 Batang China
98B2 Batangafo CAR
79B1 Batan Is Phil
35B2 Batatais Brazil
15C2 Batavia USA
109D3 Batemans Bay Aust
17B1 Batesburg USA
18B2 Batesville Arkansas,
USA
19C3 Batesville
Mississippi, USA
43C4 Bath Eng
15C2 Bath New York,
USA
98B1 Batha R Chad
107D4 Bathurst Aust
7D5 Bathurst Can
4F2 Bathurst,C Can
106C2 Bathurst I Aust
4H2 Bathurst I Can
4H3 Bathurst Inlet B
Can
97B3 Batié Burkina
90B3 Bātlāq-e-Gavkhūnī
Salt Flat Iran
109C3 Batlow Aust
93D2 Batman Turk
96C1 Batna Alg
11A3 Baton Rouge USA
94B1 Batroun Leb
76C3 Battambang Camb
87C3 Batticaloa Sri Lanka
13F2 Battle R Can
10B2 Battle Creek USA
7E4 Battle Harbour Can
20C2 Battle Mountain
USA
78D2 Batukelau Indon
65F5 Batumi Georgia
77C5 Batu Pahat Malay
78A3 Baturaja Indon
94B2 Bat Yam Israel
71D4 Baubau Indon
97C3 Bauchi Nig
47B2 Bauges Mts France
7E4 Bauld,C Can
47B1 Baumes-les-Dames
France
63D2 Baunt Russian Fed
31B6 Bauru Brazil
35A1 Baus Brazil
57C2 Bautzen Germany
78C4 Baween I Indon
95B2 Bawiti Egypt
97B3 Bawku Ghana
76B2 Bawlake Burma
108A2 Bawlen Aust
17B1 Baxley USA
25E2 Bayamo Cuba
78D4 Bayan Indon
68C2 Bayandzürh
Mongolia
68B3 Bayan Har Shan Mts
China
72A1 Bayan Mod China

72B1 Bayan Obo China
47A2 Bayard P France
12J3 Bayard,Mt Can
63D3 Bayasgalant
Mongolia
79B3 Baybay Phil
93D1 Bayburt Turk
10B2 Bay City Michigan,
USA
19A4 Bay City Texas, USA
92B2 Bay Daǧlari Turk
64H3 Baydaratskaya Guba
B Russian Fed
99E2 Baydhabo Somalia
48B2 Bayeux France
47D1 Bayerische Alpen
Mts Germany
57C3 Bayern State,
Germany
92C3 Bāyir Jordan
63C2 Baykalskiy Khrebet
Mts Russian Fed
63B1 Baykit Russian Fed
63B3 Baylik Shan Mts
China/Mongolia
61J3 Baymak Russian
Fed
79B2 Bayombang Phil
48B3 Bayonne France
57C3 Bayreuth Germany
19C3 Bay St Louis USA
15D2 Bay Shore USA
15C1 Bays,L of Can
68A2 Baytik Shan Mts
China
Bayt Lahm =
Bethlehem
19B4 Baytown USA
50B2 Baza Spain
59D3 Bazaliya Ukraine
48B3 Bazas France
73B3 Bazhong China
91D4 Bazmān Iran
94C1 Bcharre Leb
16B3 Beach Haven USA
43E4 Beachy Head Eng
16C2 Beacon USA
101D2 Bealanana Madag
18B1 Beardstown USA
Bear I = Bjørnøya
22B1 Bear Valley USA
8D2 Beatrice USA
44C2 Beatrice Oilfield N
Sea
13C1 Beatton R Can
5F4 Beatton River Can
29E6 Beauchene Is
Falkland Is
109D1 Beaudesert Aust
1B5 Beaufort S Can
100B4 Beaufort West
S Africa
15D1 Beauharnois Can
44B3 Beauly Scot
21B3 Beaumont California,
USA
11A3 Beaumont Texas,
USA
49C2 Beaune France
48C2 Beauvais France
13F1 Beauval Can
12E1 Beaver Alaska, USA
13F2 Beaver R
Saskatchewan, Can
4D3 Beaver Creek Can
12E1 Beaver Creek USA
18C2 Beaver Dam
Kentucky, USA
13E2 Beaverhill L Can
14A1 Beaver I USA
18B2 Beaver L USA
13D1 Beaverlodge Can
85C3 Beawar India
34B2 Beazley Arg
35B2 Bebedouro Brazil
43E3 Beccles Eng
54B1 Bečej Serbia, Yugos
96B1 Béchar Alg
12C3 Becharof L USA
11B3 Beckley USA
43D3 Bedford County, Eng
43D3 Bedford Eng
14A3 Bedford Indiana,
USA

27M2 Bedford Pt Grenada
4D2 Beechey Pt USA
109C3 Beechworth Aust
109D1 Beenleigh Aust
92B3 Beersheba Israel
Beër Sheva =
Beersheba
94B3 Beér Sheva R Israel
9D4 Beeville USA
98C2 Befale Zaïre
101D2 Befandriana Madag
109C3 Bega Aust
91B3 Behbehān Iran
12H3 Behm Canal Sd
USA
90B2 Behshahr Iran
84B2 Behsud Afghan
69E2 Bei'an China
73B5 Beihai China
72D2 Beijing China
76E1 Beiliu China
73B4 Beipan Jiang R
China
72E1 Beipiao China
Beira = Sofala
92C3 Beirut Leb
68B2 Bei Shan Mts China
94B2 Beit ed Dine Leb
94B3 Beit Jala Israel
50A2 Beja Port
96C1 Beja Tunisia
96C1 Bejaïa Alg
50A1 Béjar Spain
90C3 Bejestān Iran
59C3 Békéscsaba Hung
101D3 Bekily Madag
86A1 Bela India
85B3 Bela Pak
78C2 Belaga Malay
16A3 Bel Air USA
87B1 Belamoalli India
71D3 Belang Indon
70A3 Belangpidie Indon
Belau = Palau Is.
101C3 Bela Vista Mozam
70A3 Belawan Indon
61J2 Belaya R Ukraine
6A2 Belcher Chan Can
7C4 Belcher Is Can
84B1 Belchiragh Afghan
61H3 Belebey Russian
Fed
99E2 Beled Weyne
Somalia
31B2 Belém Brazil
32B3 Belén Colombia
34D2 Belén Urug
9C3 Belen USA
45D1 Belfast N Ire
101H1 Belfast S Africa
45D1 Belfast Lough
Estuary N Ire
99D1 Belfodiyo Eth
42D2 Belford Eng
49D2 Belfort France
87A1 Belgaum India
56A2 Belgium Kingdom,
N W Europe
60E3 Belgorod Russian
Fed
60D4 Belgorod
Dnestrovskiy Ukraine
Belgrade = Beograd
95A2 Bel Hedan Libya
78B3 Belinyu Indon
78B3 Belitung I Indon
25D3 Belize Belize
25D3 Belize Republic,
Cent America
48C2 Bellac France
5F4 Bella Coola Can
47C2 Bellagio Italy
19A4 Bellaire USA
47C1 Bellano Italy
87B1 Bellary India
109C1 Bellata Aust
47B2 Belledonne Mts
France
8C2 Belle Fourche USA
49D2 Bellegarde France
17B2 Belle Glade USA
7E4 Belle I Can
48B2 Belle-Ile I France
7E4 Belle Isle,Str of Can

7C5 Belleville Can
18A2 Belleville Kansas,
USA
20B1 Bellevue
Washington, USA
109D2 Bellingen Aust
8A2 Bellingham USA
112C2 Bellingshausen Base
Ant
112C3 Bellingshausen S
Ant
52A1 Bellinzona Switz
32B2 Bello Colombia
107E3 Bellona Reefs
Nouvelle Calédonie
22B1 Bellota USA
15D2 Bellows Falls USA
6B3 Bell Pen Can
52B1 Belluno Italy
29D2 Bell Ville Arg
31D5 Belmonte Brazil
25D3 Belmopan Belize
45B1 Belmullet Irish Rep
69E1 Belogorsk Russian
Fed
101D3 Beloha Madag
31C5 Belo Horizonte
Brazil
10B2 Beloit Wisconsin,
USA
64E3 Belomorsk Russian
Fed
61J3 Beloretsk Russian
Fed
60C3 Belorussia Republic,
Europe
101D2 Belo-Tsiribihina
Madag
64E3 Beloye More S
Russian Fed
60E1 Beloye Ozero L
Russian Fed
60E1 Belozersk Russian
Fed
14B3 Belpre USA
108A2 Beltana Aust
19A3 Belton USA
59D3 Bel'tsy Moldavia
16B2 Belvidere New
Jersey, USA
98B3 Bembe Angola
97C3 Bembéréke Benin
10A2 Bemidji USA
39G6 Bena Nor
98C3 Bena Dibele Zaïre
108C3 Benalla Aust
44B3 Ben Attow Mt Scot
50A1 Benavente Spain
44A3 Benbecula I Scot
106A4 Bencubbin Aust
8A2 Bend USA
44B3 Ben Dearg Mt Scot
60C4 Bendery Moldavia
107D4 Bendigo Aust
57C3 Benešov Czech
53B2 Benevento Italy
83C4 Bengal,B of Asia
96D1 Ben Gardane
Tunisia
72D3 Bengbu China
78A2 Bengkalis Indon
78A3 Bengkulu Indon
100A2 Benguela Angola
92B3 Benha Egypt
44B2 Ben Hope Mt Scot
99C2 Beni Zaïre
32D6 Béni R Bol
96B1 Beni Abbes Alg
51C1 Benicarló Spain
7A5 Benidji USA
51B2 Benidorm Spain
51C2 Beni Mansour Alg
95C2 Beni Mazar Egypt
96B1 Beni Mellal Mor
97C4 Benin Republic,
Africa
97C4 Benin City Nig
95C2 Beni Suef Egypt
44B2 Ben Kilbreck Mt
Scot
44B3 Ben Lawers Mt UK
109C4 Ben Lomond Mt
Aust
44C3 Ben Macdui Mt Scot

44B2 Ben More Assynt *Mt* Scot
111B2 Benmore,L NZ
44B3 Ben Nevis *Mt* Scot
15D2 Bennington USA
94B2 Bennt Jbail Leb
98B2 Bénoué *R* Cam
9B3 Benson Arizona, USA
99C2 Bentiu Sudan
19B3 Benton Arkansas, USA
18C2 Benton Kentucky, USA
14A2 Benton Harbor USA
97C4 Benue *R* Nig
45B1 Benwee Hd *C* Irish Rep
44B3 Ben Wyvis *Mt* Scot
72E1 Benxi China
54B2 Beograd Serbia, Yugos
86A2 Beohari India
74C4 Beppu Japan
55A2 Berat Alb
95C3 Berber Sudan
99E1 Berbera Somalia
98B2 Berbérati CAR
46A1 Berck France
60C4 Berdichev Ukraine
60E4 Berdyansk Ukraine
97B4 Berekum Ghana
22B2 Berenda USA
5J4 Berens *R* Can
5J4 Berens River Can
108A1 Beresford Aust
59C3 Berettyoújfalu Hung
58D2 Bereza Belorussia
59C3 Berezhany Ukraine
65G4 Berezniki Russian Fed
60D4 Berezovka Ukraine
64H3 Berezovo Russian Fed
92A2 Bergama Turk
52A1 Bergamo Italy
39F6 Bergen Nor
46C1 Bergen op Zoom Neth
48C3 Bergerac France
46D1 Bergisch-Gladbach Germany
12F2 Bering Gl USA
1C6 Bering Str USA/ Russian Fed
91C4 Berizak Iran
50B2 Berja Spain
8A3 Berkeley USA
112B2 Berkner I Ant
54B2 Berkovitsa Bulg
43D4 Berkshire County, Eng
16C1 Berkshire Hills USA
13D2 Berland *R* Can
56C2 Berlin Germany
56C2 Berlin State, Germany
15D2 Berlin New Hampshire, USA
30D3 Bermejo Bol
30D4 Bermejo *R* Arg
3M5 Bermuda *I* Atlantic O
52A1 Bern Switz
16B2 Bernardsville USA
34C3 Bernasconi Arg
56C2 Bernburg Germany
47B1 Berner Oberland *Mts* Switz
6B2 Bernier B Can
57C3 Berounka *R* Czech
108B2 Berri Aust
96C1 Berriane Alg
48C2 Berry Region, France
22A1 Berryessa,L USA
11C4 Berry Is The Bahamas
98B2 Bertoua Cam
45B2 Bertraghboy B Irish Rep
15C2 Berwick USA
42C2 Berwick-upon-Tweed Eng
43C3 Berwyn *Mts* Wales

101D2 Besalampy Madag
49D2 Besançon France
59C3 Beskidy Zachodnie *Mts* Pol
93C2 Besni Turk
94B3 Besor *R* Israel
11B3 Bessemer USA
101D2 Betafo Madag
50A1 Betanzos Spain
94B3 Bet Guvrin Israel
101G1 Bethal S Africa
100A3 Bethanie Namibia
18B1 Bethany Missouri, USA
18A2 Bethany Oklahoma, USA
4B3 Bethel Alaska, USA
16C2 Bethel Connecticut, USA
14B2 Bethel Park USA
15C3 Bethesda USA
94B3 Bethlehem Israel
101G1 Bethlehem S Africa
15C2 Bethlehem USA
48C1 Bethune France
101D3 Betioky Madag
108B1 Betoota Aust
98B2 Betou Congo
82A1 Betpak Dala *Steppe* Kazakhstan
101D3 Betroka Madag
7D5 Betsiamites Can
86A1 Bettiah India
12D1 Bettles USA
47C2 Béttola Italy
85D4 Betul India
85D3 Betwa *R* India
46D1 Betzdorf Germany
12C3 Beverley,L USA
16D1 Beverly USA
21B3 Beverly Hills USA
97B4 Beyla Guinea
87B2 Beypore India
Beyrouth = Beirut
92B2 Beyşehir Turk
92B2 Beysehir Gölü *L* Turk
94B2 Beyt Shean Israel
47C1 Bezau Austria
60E2 Bezhetsk Russian Fed
49C3 Béziers France
90C2 Bezmein Turkmenistan
63C2 Beznosova Russian Fed
86B1 Bhadgaon Nepal
87C1 Bhadrachalam India
86B2 Bhadrakh India
87B2 Bhadra Res India
87B2 Bhadravati India
84B3 Bhag Pak
86B1 Bhagalpur India
84C2 Bhakkar Pak
82D3 Bhamo Burma
85D4 Bhandara India
85D3 Bharatpur India
85C4 Bharuch India
86B2 Bhatiapara Ghat Bang
84C2 Bhatinda India
87A2 Bhatkal India
86B2 Bhatpara India
85C4 Bhavnagar India
84C2 Bhera Pak
86A1 Bheri *R* Nepal
86A2 Bhilai India
85C3 Bhilwara India
87C1 Bhimavaram India
85D3 Bhind India
84D3 Bhiwani India
87B1 Bhongir India
85D4 Bhopal India
86B2 Bhubaneshwar India
85B4 Bhuj India
85D4 Bhusawal India
82C3 Bhutan Kingdom, Asia
71E4 Biak *I* Indon
58C2 Biala Podlaska Pol
58B2 Bialograd Pol
58C2 Bialystok Pol
38A1 Biargtangar *C* Iceland

90C2 Biarjmand Iran
48B3 Biarritz France
47C1 Biasca Switz
92B4 Biba Egypt
74E2 Bibai Japan
100A2 Bibala Angola
57B3 Biberach Germany
97B4 Bibiani Ghana
54C1 Bicaz Rom
97C4 Bida Nig
87B1 Bidar India
91C5 Bidbid Oman
43B4 Bideford Eng
43B4 Bideford B Eng
96C2 Bidon 5 Alg
58C2 Biebrza Pol
52A1 Biel Switz
59B2 Bielawa Pol
56B2 Bielefeld Germany
47B1 Bieler See *L* Switz
52A1 Biella Italy
58C2 Bielsk Podlaski Pol
76D3 Bien Hoa Viet
53B2 Biferno *R* Italy
92A1 Biga Turk
55C3 Bigadiç Turk
19C3 Big Black *R* USA
18A1 Big Blue *R* USA
17B2 Big Cypress Swamp USA
4D3 Big Delta USA
49D2 Bigent Germany
13F2 Biggar Can
5H4 Biggar Kindersley Can
109D1 Biggenden Aust
12G3 Bigger,Mt Can
8C2 Bighorn *R* USA
76C3 Bight of Bangkok *B* Thai
97C4 Bight of Benin *B* W Africa
97C4 Bight of Biafra *B* Cam
6C3 Big I Can
47C1 Bignasco Switz
97A3 Bignona Sen
21B2 Big Pine USA
17B2 Big Pine Key USA
22C3 Big Pine Mt USA
14A2 Big Rapids USA
5H4 Big River Can
9C3 Big Spring USA
7A4 Big Trout L Can
7B4 Big Trout Lake Can
52C2 Bihać Bosnia & Herzegovina, Yugos
86B1 Bihar India
86B2 Bihar State, India
99D3 Biharamulo Tanz
60B4 Bihor *Mt* Rom
87B1 Bijapur India
87C1 Bijapur India
90A2 Bijar Iran
86A1 Bijauri Nepal
54A2 Bijeljina Bosnia & Herzegovina, Yugos
73B4 Bijie China
84D3 Bijnor India
84C3 Bijnot Pak
84C3 Bikaner India
94B2 Bikfaya Leb
69F2 Bikin Russian Fed
98B3 Bikoro Zaïre
85C3 Bilara India
84D2 Bilaspur India
86A2 Bilaspur India
76B3 Bilauktaung Range *Mts* Thai
50D1 Bilbao Spain
Bilbo = Bilbao
59B3 Bilé *R* Czech
54A2 Bileča Bosnia & Herzegovina, Yugos
92B1 Bilecik Turk
98C2 Bili *R* Zaïre
79B3 Biliran *I* Phil
8C2 Billings USA
95A3 Bilma Niger
11B3 Biloxi USA
98C1 Biltine Chad
85D4 Bina-Etawa India
79B3 Binalbagan Phil
101C2 Bindura Zim

100B2 Binga Zim
101C2 Binga *Mt* Zim
109D1 Bingara Aust
57B3 Bingen Germany
10C2 Binghamton USA
78D1 Bingkor Malay
93D2 Bingöl Turk
72D3 Binhai China
78A2 Bintan *I* Indon
78A3 Bintuhan Indon
78C2 Bintulu Malay
29B3 Bío Bío *R* Chile
102J4 Bioko *I* Atlantic O
87B1 Bir India
95B2 Bir Abu Husein *Well* Egypt
95B2 Bi'r al Harash *Well* Libya
98C1 Birao CAR
86B1 Biratnagar Nepal
12E1 Birch Creek USA
108B3 Birchip Aust
5G4 Birch Mts Can
7A4 Bird Can
106C3 Birdsville Aust
106C2 Birdum Aust
86A1 Birganj Nepal
94A3 Bir Gifgafa *Well* Egypt
94A3 Bir Hasana *Well* Egypt
35A2 Birigui Brazil
90C3 Birjand Iran
92B4 Birkat Qarun *L* Egypt
46B2 Birkenfeld Germany
42C3 Birkenhead Eng
60C4 Birlad Rom
94A3 Bir Lahfân *Well* Egypt
43C3 Birmingham Eng
11B3 Birmingham USA
95B2 Bir Misâha *Well* Egypt
96A2 Bir Moghrein Maur
97C3 Birnin Kebbi Nig
97C3 Birni N'Konni Nig
69F2 Birobidzhan Russian Fed
45C2 Birr Irish Rep
51C2 Bir Rabalou Alg
109C1 Birrie *R* Aust
44C2 Birsay Scot
61J2 Birsk Russian Fed
95B2 Bir Tarfâwi *Well* Egypt
63B2 Biryusa Russian Fed
39J7 Biržai Lithuania
96B2 Bir Zreigat *Well* Maur
48A2 Biscay,B of France/ Spain
17B2 Biscayne B USA
46D2 Bischwiller France
73B4 Bishan China
82B1 Bishkek Kirgizia
8B3 Bishop USA
42D2 Bishop Auckland Eng
43E4 Bishop's Stortford Eng
86A2 Bishrampur India
96C1 Biskra Alg
79C4 Bislig Phil
8C2 Bismarck USA
90A3 Bisotün Iran
97A3 Bissau Guinea-Bissau
10A1 Bissett Can
5G4 Bistcho L Can
54C1 Distrita *R* Rom
98B2 Bitam Gabon
57B3 Bitburg Germany
46D2 Bitche France
93D2 Bitlis Turk
55B2 Bitola Macedonia, Yugos
56C2 Bitterfeld Germany
100A4 Bitterfontein S Africa
92B3 Bitter Lakes Egypt
8B2 Bitteroot Range *Mts* USA
74D3 Biwa-ko *L* Japan

99E1 **Biyo Kaboba** Eth
65K4 **Biysk** Russian Fed
96C1 **Bizerte** Tunisia
51C2 **Bj bou Arréridj** Alg
52C1 **Bjelovar** Croatia
96B2 **Bj Flye Ste Marie** Alg
64C2 **Bjørnøya** *I* Barents S
12F1 **Black** *R* USA
18B2 **Black** *R* USA
107D3 **Blackall** Aust
42C3 **Blackburn** Eng
4D3 **Blackburn,Mt** USA
13E2 **Black Diamond** Can
5H5 **Black Hills** USA
44B3 **Black Isle** *Pen* Scot
27R3 **Blackman's** Barbados
43C4 **Black Mts** Wales
43C3 **Blackpool** Eng
27H1 **Black River** Jamaica
8B2 **Black Rock Desert** USA
65E5 **Black S** Asia/Europe
45A1 **Blacksod B** Irish Rep
109D2 **Black Sugarloaf** *Mt* Aust
97B3 **Black Volta** *R* Ghana
41B3 **Blackwater** *R* Irish Rep
18A2 **Blackwell** USA
54B2 **Blagoevgrad** Bulg
63E2 **Blagoveshchensk** Russian Fed
20B1 **Blaine** USA
44C3 **Blair Atholl** Scot
44C3 **Blairgowrie** Scot
17B1 **Blakely** USA
108A1 **Blanche,L** Aust
34A2 **Blanco** *R* Arg
34B1 **Blanco** *R* Arg
8A2 **Blanco,C** USA
7E4 **Blanc Sablon** Can
43C4 **Blandford Forum** Eng
46A2 **Blangy-sur-Bresle** France
46B1 **Blankenberge** Belg
101C2 **Blantyre** Malawi
48B2 **Blaye** France
109C2 **Blayney** Aust
111B2 **Blenheim** NZ
96C1 **Blida** Alg
14B1 **Blind River** Can
108A2 **Blinman** Aust
78C4 **Blitar** Indon
15D2 **Block I** USA
16D2 **Block Island Sd** USA
101G1 **Bloemfontein** S Africa
101G1 **Bloemhof** S Africa
101G1 **Bloemhof Dam** *Res* S Africa
33F3 **Blommesteinmeer** *L* Surinam
38A1 **Blonduós** Iceland
45B1 **Bloody Foreland** *C* Irish Rep
14A3 **Bloomfield** Indiana, USA
18B1 **Bloomfield** Iowa, USA
10B2 **Bloomington** Illinois, USA
14A3 **Bloomington** Indiana, USA
16A2 **Bloomsburg** USA
78C4 **Blora** Indon
6H3 **Blosseville Kyst** *Mts* Greenland
57B3 **Bludenz** Austria
11B3 **Bluefield** USA
32A1 **Bluefields** Nic
26B3 **Blue Mountain Peak** *Mt* Jamaica
16A2 **Blue Mt** USA
109D2 **Blue Mts** Aust
27J1 **Blue Mts** Jamaica
8A2 **Blue Mts** USA
Blue Nile = Bahr el Azraq
99D1 **Blue Nile** *R* Sudan
4G3 **Bluenose L** Can
11B3 **Blue Ridge Mts** USA
13D2 **Blue River** Can
45B1 **Blue Stack** *Mt* Irish Rep
111A3 **Bluff** NZ
106A4 **Bluff Knoll** *Mt* Aust
30G4 **Blumenau** Brazil
49D2 **Blundez** Austria
20B2 **Bly** USA
12E3 **Blying Sd** USA
42D2 **Blyth** Eng
9B3 **Blythe** USA
11B3 **Blytheville** USA
97A4 **Bo** Sierra Leone
79B3 **Boac** Phil
72D2 **Boading** China
14B2 **Boardman** USA
63C3 **Boatou** China
33E3 **Boa Vista** Brazil
97A4 **Boa Vista** *I* Cape Verde
76E1 **Bobai** China
47C2 **Bóbbio** Italy
97B3 **Bobo Dioulasso** Burkina
60C3 **Bobruysk** Belorussia
17B2 **Boca Chica Key** *I* USA
32D5 **Bōca do Acre** Brazil
35C1 **Bocaiúva** Brazil
98B2 **Bocaranga** CAR
17B2 **Boca Raton** USA
59C3 **Bochnia** Pol
56B2 **Bocholt** Germany
46D1 **Bochum** Germany
100A2 **Bocoio** Angola
98B2 **Boda** CAR
63D2 **Bodaybo** Russian Fed
21A2 **Bodega Head** *Pt* USA
95A3 **Bodélé** *Region* Chad
38J5 **Boden** Sweden
47C1 **Bodensee** *L* Switz/Germany
87B1 **Bodhan** India
87B2 **Bodināyakkanūr** India
43B4 **Bodmin** Eng
43B4 **Bodmin Moor** *Upland* Eng
38G5 **Bodø** Nor
55C3 **Bodrum** Turk
98C3 **Boende** Zaïre
97A3 **Boffa** Guinea
76B2 **Bogale** Burma
19C3 **Bogalusa** USA
109C2 **Bogan** *R* Aust
97B3 **Bogandé** Burkina
6H3 **Bogarnes** Iceland
92C2 **Boğazlıyan** Turk
61K2 **Bogdanovich** Russian Fed
68A2 **Bogda Shan** *Mt* China
100A3 **Bogenfels** Namibia
109D1 **Boggabilla** Aust
109C2 **Boggabri** Aust
45B2 **Boggeragh Mts** Irish Rep
79B3 **Bogo** Phil
109C3 **Bogong,Mt** Aust
78B4 **Bogor** Indon
61H2 **Bogorodskoye** Russian Fed
32C3 **Bogotá** Colombia
63A2 **Bogotol** Russian Fed
86B2 **Bogra** Bang
72D2 **Bo Hai** *B* China
46B2 **Bohain-en-Vermandois** France
72D2 **Bohai Wan** *B* China
57C3 **Böhmer-Wald** *Upland* Germany
79B4 **Bohol** *I* Phil
79B4 **Bohol S** Phil
35A1 **Bois** *R* Brazil
14B1 **Bois Blanc I** USA
8B2 **Boise** USA
96A2 **Bojador,C** Mor
79B2 **Bojeador,C** Phil
90C2 **Bojnūrd** Iran
97A3 **Boké** Guinea
109C1 **Bokhara** *R* Aust
39F7 **Boknafjord** *Inlet* Nor
98B3 **Boko** Congo
76C3 **Bokor** Camb
98C3 **Bokungu** Zaïre
98B1 **Bol** Chad
23A1 **Bolaãnos** Mexico
97A3 **Bolama** Guinea-Bissau
23A1 **Bolanos** *R* Mexico
48C2 **Bolbec** France
97B4 **Bole** Ghana
59B2 **Boleslawiec** Pol
97B3 **Bolgatanga** Ghana
60C4 **Bolgrad** Ukraine
34C3 **Bolivar** Arg
18B2 **Bolivar** Missouri, USA
18C2 **Bolivar** Tennessee, USA
30C2 **Bolivia** Republic, S America
38H6 **Bollnas** Sweden
109C1 **Bollon** Aust
32C2 **Bollvar** *Mt* Ven
52B2 **Bologna** Italy
60D2 **Bologoye** Russian Fed
69F2 **Bolon'** Russian Fed
61G3 **Bol'shoy Irgiz** *R* Russian Fed
74C2 **Bol'shoy Kamen** Russian Fed
65F5 **Bol'shoy Kavkaz** *Mts* Georgia
61G4 **Bol'shoy Uzen** *R* Kazakhstan
9C4 **Bolson de Mapimi** *Desert* Mexico
43C3 **Bolton** Eng
92B1 **Bolu** Turk
38A1 **Bolungarvik** Iceland
92B2 **Bolvadin** Turk
52B1 **Bolzano** Italy
98B3 **Boma** Zaïre
107D4 **Bombala** Aust
87A1 **Bombay** India
99D2 **Bombo** Uganda
35B1 **Bom Despacho** Brazil
86C1 **Bomdila** India
97A4 **Bomi Hills** Lib
31C4 **Bom Jesus da Lapa** Brazil
63E2 **Bomnak** Russian Fed
99C2 **Bomokandi** *R* Zaïre
98C2 **Bomu** *R* CAR/Zaïre
27D4 **Bonaire** *I* Caribbean S
12F2 **Bona,Mt** USA
25D3 **Bonanza** Nic
7E5 **Bonavista** Can
108A2 **Bon Bon** Aust
98C2 **Bondo** Zaïre
97B4 **Bondoukou** Ivory Coast
Bône = 'Annaba
33E3 **Bonfim** Guyana
98C2 **Bongandanga** Zaïre
98B1 **Bongor** Chad
19A3 **Bonham** USA
53A2 **Bonifacio** Corse
52A2 **Bonifacio,Str of** *Chan* Medit S
Bonin Is = Ogasawara Gunto
17B2 **Bonita Springs** USA
57B2 **Bonn** Germany
20C1 **Bonners Ferry** USA
12H1 **Bonnet Plume** *R* Can
13E2 **Bonnyville** Can
97A4 **Bonthe** Sierra Leone
99E1 **Booaaso** Somalia
108B2 **Booligal** Aust
109D1 **Boonah** Aust
15C2 **Boonville** USA
109C2 **Boorowa** Aust
6A2 **Boothia,G of** Can
6A2 **Boothia Pen** Can
98B3 **Booué** Gabon
108A1 **Bopeechee** Aust
99D2 **Bor** Sudan
92B2 **Bor** Turk
54B2 **Bor** Serbia, Yugos
8B2 **Borah Peak** *Mt* USA
39G7 **Borås** Sweden
91B4 **Borāzjān** Iran
108A3 **Borda,C** Aust
48B3 **Bordeaux** France
4G2 **Borden I** Can
6B2 **Borden Pen** Can
16B2 **Bordentown** USA
42C2 **Borders** Region, Scot
108B3 **Bordertown** Aust
96C2 **Bordi Omar Dris** Alg
8D1 **Borens River** Can
38A2 **Borgarnes** Iceland
9C3 **Borger** USA
39H7 **Borgholm** Sweden
47C2 **Borgosia** Italy
47D1 **Borgo Valsugana** Italy
59C3 **Borislav** Ukraine
61F3 **Borisoglebsk** Russian Fed
60C3 **Borisov** Belorussia
60E3 **Borisovka** Russian Fed
95A3 **Borkou** *Region* Chad
39H6 **Borlänge** Sweden
47C2 **Bormida** Italy
47D1 **Bormio** Italy
67F5 **Borneo** *I* Malay/Indon
39H7 **Bornholm** *I* Den
55C3 **Bornova** Turk
98C2 **Boro** *R* Sudan
97B3 **Boromo** Burkina
60D2 **Borovichi** Russian Fed
106C2 **Borroloola** Aust
54B1 **Borsa** Rom
90A3 **Borūjed** Iran
90B3 **Borūjen** Iran
58B2 **Bory Tucholskie** Region, Pol
63D2 **Borzya** Russian Fed
73B5 **Bose** China
101G1 **Boshof** S Africa
54A2 **Bosna** *R* Bosnia & Herzegovina, Yugos
37E4 **Bosnia & Herzegovina** Republic, Yugos
75C1 **Bōsō-hantō** *B* Japan
Bosporus = Karadeniz Boğazi
51C2 **Bosquet** Alg
98B2 **Bossangoa** CAR
98B2 **Bossèmbélé** CAR
19B3 **Bossier City** USA
65K5 **Bosten Hu** *L* China
43D3 **Boston** Eng
10C2 **Boston** USA
11A3 **Boston Mts** USA
85C4 **Botād** Iran
54B2 **Botevgrad** Bulg
101G1 **Bothaville** S Africa
64C3 **Bothnia,G of** Sweden/Fin
100B3 **Botletli** *R* Botswana
60C4 **Botosani** Rom
100B3 **Botswana** Republic, Africa
53C3 **Botte Donato** *Mt* Italy
46D1 **Bottrop** Germany
35B2 **Botucatu** Brazil
7E5 **Botwood** Can
89D7 **Bouaké** Ivory Coast
98B2 **Bouar** CAR
96B1 **Bouârfa** Mor
98B2 **Bouca** CAR
51C2 **Boufarik** Alg
Bougie = Bejaïa
97B3 **Bougouni** Mali
46C2 **Bouillon** France
96B2 **Bou Izakarn** Mor
46D2 **Boulay-Moselle** France

8C2 **Boulder** Colorado, USA
9B3 **Boulder City** USA
22A2 **Boulder Creek** USA
48C1 **Boulogne** France
98B2 **Boumba** R CAR
97B4 **Bouna** Ivory Coast
8B3 **Boundary Peak** Mt USA
97B4 **Boundiali** Ivory Coast
107F3 **Bourail** Nouvelle Calédonie
97B3 **Bourem** Mali
49D2 **Bourg** France
49D2 **Bourg de Péage** France
48C2 **Bourges** France
48C3 **Bourg-Madame** France
49C2 **Bourgogne** Region, France
47B2 **Bourg-St-Maurice** France
108C2 **Bourke** Aust
43D4 **Bournemouth** Eng
96C1 **Bou Saâda** Alg
98B1 **Bousso** Chad
97A3 **Boutilmit** Maur
103J7 **Bouvet** I Atlantic O
34D2 **Bovril** Arg
13E2 **Bow** R Can
107D2 **Bowen** Aust
19A3 **Bowie** Texas, USA
13E2 **Bow Island** Can
11B3 **Bowling Green** Kentucky, USA
18B2 **Bowling Green** Missouri, USA
14B2 **Bowling Green** Ohio, USA
15C3 **Bowling Green** Virginia, USA
15C2 **Bowmanville** Can
109D2 **Bowral** Aust
13C2 **Bowron** R Can
72D3 **Bo Xian** China
72D2 **Boxing** China
92B1 **Boyabat** Turk
98B2 **Boyali** CAR
5J4 **Boyd** Can
16B2 **Boyertown** USA
13E2 **Boyle** Can
41B3 **Boyle** Irish Rep
45C2 **Boyne** R Irish Rep
17B2 **Boynoton Beach** USA
98C2 **Boyoma Falls** Zaïre
55C3 **Bozca Ada** I Turk
55C3 **Boz Dağlari** Mts Turk
8B2 **Bozeman** USA
Bozen = Bolzano
98B2 **Bozene** Zaïre
98B2 **Bozoum** CAR
47B2 **Bra** Italy
52C2 **Brač** I Croatia
15C1 **Bracebridge** Can
95A2 **Brach** Libya
38H6 **Bräcke** Sweden
17B2 **Bradenton** USA
42D3 **Bradford** Eng
44E1 **Brae** Scot
44C3 **Braemar** Scot
50A1 **Braga** Port
34C3 **Bragado** Arg
50A1 **Bragana** Port
31B2 **Bragança** Brazil
35B2 **Bragança Paulista** Brazil
86C2 **Brahman-Baria** Bang
86B2 **Brahmani** R India
86C1 **Brahmaputra** R India
7E5 **Braie Verte** Can
60C4 **Brăila** Rom
10A2 **Brainerd** USA
97A3 **Brakna** Region, Maur
5F4 **Bralorne** Can
14C2 **Brampton** Can
33E3 **Branco** R Brazil
100A3 **Brandberg** Mt Namibia

56C2 **Brandenburg** Germany
56C2 **Brandenburg** State, Germany
101G1 **Brandfort** S Africa
8D2 **Brandon** Can
100B4 **Brandvlei** S Africa
57C2 **Brandys nad Lebem** Czech
58B2 **Braniewo** Pol
10B2 **Brantford** Can
108B3 **Branxholme** Aust
7D5 **Bras D'Or** L Can
35C1 **Brasila de Minas** Brazil
32D6 **Brasiléia** Brazil
31B5 **Brasilia** Brazil
54C1 **Brasov** Rom
78D1 **Brassay Range** Mts Malay
59B3 **Bratislava** Czech
63C2 **Bratsk** Russian Fed
15D2 **Brattleboro** USA
56C2 **Braunschweig** Germany
97A4 **Brava** I Cape Verde
9B3 **Brawley** USA
45C2 **Bray** Irish Rep
6C3 **Bray** I Can
13D2 **Brazeau** R Can
13D2 **Brazeau,Mt** Can
28D4 **Brazil** Republic, S America
103G5 **Brazil Basin** Atlantic O
9D3 **Brazos** R USA
98B3 **Brazzaville** Congo
57C3 **Brdy** Upland Czech
111A3 **Breaksea Sd** NZ
110B1 **Bream B** NZ
78B4 **Brebes** Indon
44C3 **Brechin** Scot
46C1 **Brecht** Belg
59B3 **Břeclav** Czech
43C4 **Brecon** Wales
43C4 **Brecon Beacons** Mts Wales
43B3 **Brecon Beacons Nat Pk** Wales
56A2 **Breda** Neth
100B4 **Bredasdorp** S Africa
38H6 **Bredbyn** Sweden
61J3 **Bredy** Russian Fed
15C2 **Breezewood** USA
47C1 **Bregenz** Austria
47C1 **Bregenzer Ache** R Austria
38A1 **Breiðafjörður** B Iceland
47C2 **Brembo** R Italy
17A1 **Bremen** USA
56B2 **Bremen** Germany
56B2 **Bremerhaven** Germany
20B1 **Bremerton** USA
19A3 **Brenham** USA
57C3 **Brenner** P Austria/ Italy
47D2 **Breno** Italy
47D2 **Brenta** R Italy
22B2 **Brentwood** USA
52B1 **Brescia** Italy
Breslau = Wrocław
47D1 **Bressanone** Italy
44E1 **Bressay** I Scot
48B2 **Bressuire** France
58C2 **Brest** Belorussia
48B2 **Brest** France
48B2 **Bretagne** Region, France
46B2 **Breteuil** France
16B2 **Breton Woods** USA
110B1 **Brett,C** NZ
109C1 **Brewarrina** Aust
16C2 **Brewster** New York, USA
20C1 **Brewster** Washington, USA
101G1 **Breyten** S Africa
52C1 **Brežice** Slovenia
98C2 **Bria** CAR
49D3 **Briancon** France
49C2 **Briare** France

21B2 **Bridgeport** California, USA
15D2 **Bridgeport** Connecticut, USA
19A3 **Bridgeport** Texas, USA
22C1 **Bridgeport Res** USA
16B3 **Bridgeton** USA
27F4 **Bridgetown** Barbados
7D5 **Bridgewater** Can
16D2 **Bridgewater** USA
43C4 **Bridgwater** Eng
43C4 **Bridgwater B** Eng
42D2 **Bridlington** Eng
109C4 **Bridport** Aust
47B1 **Brienzer See** L Switz
46C2 **Briey** France
52A1 **Brig** Switz
8B2 **Brigham City** USA
109C3 **Bright** Aust
43D4 **Brighton** Eng
46E1 **Brilon** Germany
55A2 **Brindisi** Italy
19B3 **Brinkley** USA
107E3 **Brisbane** Aust
15D2 **Bristol** Connecticut, USA
43C4 **Bristol** Eng
15D2 **Bristol** Pennsylvania, USA
16D2 **Bristol** Rhode Island, USA
11B3 **Bristol** Tennessee, USA
12B3 **Bristol B** USA
43B4 **Bristol Chan** Eng/ Wales
4D3 **British** Mts USA
5F4 **British Columbia** Province, Can
6B1 **British Empire Range** Mts Can
101G1 **Brits** S Africa
100B4 **Britstown** S Africa
48C2 **Brive** France
59B3 **Brno** Czech
17B1 **Broad** R USA
7C4 **Broadback** R Can
44A2 **Broad Bay** Inlet Scot
44B3 **Broadford** Scot
5H4 **Brochet** Can
4G2 **Brock** I Can
15C2 **Brockport** USA
16D1 **Brockton** USA
15C2 **Brockville** Can
6B2 **Brodeur Pen** Can
42B2 **Brodick** Scot
58B2 **Brodnica** Pol
60C3 **Brody** Ukraine
19B3 **Broken Bow** Oklahoma, USA
19B3 **Broken Bow L** USA
107D4 **Broken Hill** Aust
47C2 **Broni** Italy
38G5 **Brønnøysund** Nor
16C2 **Bronx** Borough, New York, USA
79A4 **Brooke's Point** Phil
18B2 **Brookfield** Missouri, USA
11A3 **Brookhaven** USA
20B2 **Brookings** Oregon, USA
8D2 **Brookings** South Dakota, USA
16D1 **Brookline** USA
16C2 **Brooklyn** Borough, New York, USA
5G4 **Brooks** Can
12C3 **Brooks,L** USA
12A1 **Brooks Mt** USA
4C3 **Brooks Range** Mts USA
17B2 **Brooksville** USA
109D1 **Brooloo** Aust
106B2 **Broome** Aust
44C2 **Brora** Scot
20B2 **Brothers** USA
95A3 **Broulkou** Chad
13E3 **Browning** USA
9D4 **Brownsville** USA

9D3 **Brownwood** USA
46B1 **Bruay-en-Artois** France
106A3 **Bruce,Mt** Aust
14B1 **Bruce Pen** Can
59B3 **Brück an der Mur** Austria
Bruges = Brugge
46B1 **Brugge** Belg
46D1 **Brühl** Germany
78C2 **Brunei** Sultanate, S E Asia
52B1 **Brunico** Italy
111B2 **Brunner,L** NZ
11B3 **Brunswick** Georgia, USA
18B2 **Brunswick** Mississippi, USA
29B6 **Brunswick,Pen de** Chile
109C4 **Bruny I** Aust
61F1 **Brusenets** Russian Fed
26A3 **Brus Laguna** Honduras
Brüssel = Bruxelles
56A2 **Bruxelles** Belg
9D3 **Bryan** USA
108A2 **Bryan,Mt** Aust
60D3 **Bryansk** Russian Fed
19B3 **Bryant** USA
59B2 **Brzeg** Pol
93E4 **Būbiyan** I Kuwait/ Iraq
99D3 **Bubu** R Tanz
32C2 **Bucaramanga** Colombia
44D3 **Buchan** Oilfield N Sea
97A4 **Buchanan** Lib
44D3 **Buchan Deep** N Sea
6C2 **Buchan G** Can
40C2 **Buchan Ness** Pen Scot
7E5 **Buchans** Can
34C2 **Buchardo** Arg
Bucharest = București
47C1 **Buchs** Switz
43D3 **Buckingham** Eng
12B1 **Buckland** USA
12B1 **Buckland** R USA
108A2 **Buckleboo** Aust
98B3 **Buco Zau** Congo
54C2 **București** Rom
59B3 **Budapest** Hung
84D3 **Budaun** India
43B4 **Bude** Eng
19B3 **Bude** USA
61F5 **Budennovsk** Russian Fed
54A2 **Budva** Montenegro, Yugos
98A2 **Buea** Cam
22B3 **Buellton** USA
34B2 **Buena Esperanza** Arg
32B3 **Buenaventura** Colombia
23A2 **Buenavista** Mexico
29E2 **Buenos Aires** Arg
29D3 **Buenos Aires** State, Arg
18B2 **Buffalo** Mississipi, USA
10C2 **Buffalo** New York, USA
8C2 **Buffalo** South Dakota, USA
19A3 **Buffalo** Texas, USA
8C2 **Buffalo** Wyoming, USA
101H1 **Buffalo** R S Africa
13E2 **Buffalo L** Alberta, Can
5G3 **Buffalo L** Northwest Territories, Can
5H4 **Buffalo Narrows** Can
17B1 **Buford** USA
54C2 **Buftea** Rom
59C2 **Bug** R Pol/Ukraine
32B3 **Buga** Colombia

90B2 **Bugdayli**
Turkmenistan
61H3 **Bugulma** Russian
Fed
61H3 **Buguruslan** Russian
Fed
93C2 **Buhayrat al Asad** *Res*
Syria
41C3 **Builth Wells** Wales
34A2 **Buin** Chile
99C3 **Bujumbura** Burundi
98C3 **Bukama** Zaïre
99C3 **Bukavu** Zaïre
80E2 **Bukhara** Uzbekistan
78C2 **Bukit Batubrok** *Mt*
Indon
70B4 **Bukittinggi** Indon
99D3 **Bukoba** Tanz
78D3 **Buku Gandadiwata**
Mt Indon
71E4 **Bula** Indon
79B3 **Bulan** Phil
84D3 **Bulandshahr** India
100B3 **Bulawayo** Zim
55C3 **Buldan** Turk
85D4 **Buldāna** India
68C2 **Bulgan** Mongolia
54B2 **Bulgaria**
Republic, Europe
47B1 **Bulle** Switz
111B2 **Buller** *R* NZ
109C3 **Buller,Mt** Aust
106A4 **Bullfinch** Aust
108B1 **Bulloo** *R* Aust
108B1 **Bulloo Downs** Aust
108B1 **Bulloo L** Aust
18B2 **Bull Shoals Res** USA
34A3 **Bulnes** Chile
71F4 **Bulolo** PNG
101G1 **Bultfontein** S Africa
98C2 **Bumba** Zaïre
76B2 **Bumphal Dam** Thai
99D2 **Buna** Kenya
106A4 **Bunbury** Aust
45C1 **Buncrana** Irish Rep
107E3 **Bundaberg** Aust
109D2 **Bundarra** Aust
85D3 **Bündi** India
45B1 **Bundoran** Irish Rep
109C1 **Bungil** *R* Aust
98B3 **Bungo** Angola
75A2 **Bungo-suidō** *Str*
Japan
70B3 **Bunguran** *I* Ind
99D2 **Bunia** Zaïre
18B2 **Bunker** USA
19B3 **Bunkie** USA
17B2 **Bunnell** USA
78C3 **Buntok** Indon
71D3 **Buol** Indon
94C2 **Burāg** Syria
98C1 **Buram** Sudan
99E2 **Burao** Somalia
79B3 **Burauen** Phil
80C3 **Buraydah** S Arabia
21B3 **Burbank** USA
109C2 **Burcher** Aust
92B2 **Burdur** Turk
63F3 **Bureinskiy Khrebet**
Mts Russian Fed
56C2 **Burg** Germany
54C2 **Burgas** Bulg
17C1 **Burgaw** USA
47B1 **Burgdorf** Switz
100B4 **Burgersdorp** S Africa
50B1 **Burgos** Spain
58B1 **Burgsvik** Sweden
55C3 **Burhaniye** Turk
85D4 **Burhānpur** India
79B3 **Burias** *I* Phil
76C2 **Buriram** Thai
35B1 **Buritis** Brazil
13B2 **Burke Chan** Can
106C2 **Burketown** Aust
97B3 **Burkina** Republic,
Africa
15C1 **Burks Falls** Can
8B2 **Burley** USA
10A2 **Burlington** Iowa,
USA
16B2 **Burlington** New
Jersey, USA
10C2 **Burlington** Vermont,
USA

20B1 **Burlington**
Washington, USA
83D3 **Burma** Republic, Asia
20B2 **Burney** USA
16A2 **Burnham** USA
107D5 **Burnie** Aust
42C3 **Burnley** Eng
20C2 **Burns** USA
5F4 **Burns Lake** Can
82C1 **Burqin** China
108A2 **Burra** Aust
109D2 **Burragorang,L** Aust
44C2 **Burray** *I* Scot
109C2 **Burren Junction** Aust
109C2 **Burrinjuck Res** Aust
60C5 **Bursa** Turk
80B3 **Bur Safâga** Egypt
Bûr Sa'îd = Port Said
14B2 **Burton** USA
43D3 **Burton upon Trent**
Eng
38J6 **Burträsk** Sweden
108B2 **Burtundy** Aust
71D4 **Buru** Indon
99C3 **Burundi** Republic,
Africa
78A2 **Burung** Indon
63D2 **Buryatskaya**
Respublika, Russian
Fed
99D1 **Burye** Eth
61H4 **Burynshik**
Kazakhstan
43E3 **Bury St Edmunds**
Eng
91B4 **Būshehr** Iran
98B3 **Busira** *R* Zaïre
58C2 **Buskozdroj** Pol
94C2 **Busrā ash Shām**
Syria
106A4 **Busselton** Aust
49D2 **Busto** Italy
52A1 **Busto Arsizio** Italy
79A3 **Busuanga** *I* Phil
98C2 **Buta** Zaïre
34B3 **Buta Ranquil** Arg
99C3 **Butare** Rwanda
42B2 **Bute** *I* Scot
69E2 **Butha Qi** China
14C2 **Butler** USA
8B2 **Butte** USA
77C4 **Butterworth** Malay
40B2 **Butt of Lewis** *C* Scot
6D3 **Button Is** Can
79C4 **Butuan** Phil
71D4 **Butung** *I* Indon
61F3 **Buturlinovka** Russian
Fed
86A1 **Butwal** Nepal
99E2 **Buulo Barde** Somalia
99E2 **Buur Hakaba**
Somalia
61F2 **Buy** Russian Fed
72B1 **Buyant Ovvo**
Mongolia
61G5 **Buynaksk** Russian
Fed
63D3 **Buyr Nuur** *L*
Mongolia
93D2 **Büyük Ağri** *Mt* Turk
92A2 **Büyük Menderes** *R*
Turk
54C1 **Buzău** Rom
54C1 **Buzau** *R* Rom
61H3 **Buzuluk** Russian Fed
16D2 **Buzzards B** USA
54C2 **Byala** Bulg
54B2 **Byala Slatina** Bulg
4H2 **Byam Martin** *Chan*
Can
4H2 **Byam Martin I** Can
Byblos = Jubail
94B1 **Byblos** Hist Site, Leb
58B2 **Bydgoszcz** Pol
39F7 **Bygland** Nor
6C2 **Bylot I** Can
109C2 **Byrock** Aust
22B2 **Byron** USA
109D1 **Byron,C** Aust
59B2 **Bytom** Pol

C

30E4 **Caacupé** Par
100A2 **Caála** Angola

13B2 **Caamano Sd** Can
30E4 **Caazapá** Par
79B2 **Cabanatuan** Phil
31E3 **Cabedelo** Brazil
50A2 **Cabeza del Buey**
Spain
34C3 **Cabildo** Arg
34A2 **Cabildo** Chile
32C1 **Cabimas** Ven
98B3 **Cabinda** Angola
98B3 **Cabinda** Province,
Angola
27C3 **Cabo Beata** Dom Rep
51C2 **Cabo Binibeca** *C*
Spain
53A3 **Cabo Carbonara** *C*
Sardegna
34A3 **Cabo Carranza** *C*
Chile
50A2 **Cabo Carvoeiro** *C*
Port
9B3 **Cabo Colnett** *C*
Mexico
32B2 **Cabo Corrientes** *C*
Colombia
24B2 **Cabo Corrientes** *C*
Mexico
26B3 **Cabo Cruz** *C* Cuba
50B1 **Cabo de Ajo** *C* Spain
51C1 **Cabo de Caballeria** *C*
Spain
51C1 **Cabo de Creus** *C*
Spain
50B2 **Cabo de Gata** *C*
Spain
29C7 **Cabo de Hornos** *C*
Chile
51C2 **Cabo de la Nao** *C*
Spain
50A1 **Cabo de Peñas** *C*
Spain
50A2 **Cabo de Roca** *C* Port
51C2 **Cabo de Salinas** *C*
Spain
35C2 **Cabo de São Tomé** *C*
Brazil
50A2 **Cabo de São Vicente**
C Port
50A2 **Cabo de Sines** *C*
Port
51C1 **Cabo de Tortosa** *C*
Spain
29C4 **Cabo Dos Bahias** *C*
Arg
50A2 **Cabo Espichel** *C* Port
9B4 **Cabo Falso** *C* Mexico
51B2 **Cabo Ferrat** *C* Alg
50A1 **Cabo Finisterre** *C*
Spain
51C1 **Cabo Formentor** *C*
Spain
35C2 **Cabo Frio** Brazil
35C2 **Cabo Frio** *C* Brazil
26A4 **Cabo Gracias à Dios**
Honduras
31B2 **Cabo Maguarinho** *C*
Brazil
50A2 **Cabo Negro** *C* Mor
109D1 **Caboolture** Aust
33G3 **Cabo Orange** *C*
Brazil
21B3 **Cabo Punta Banda** *C*
Mexico
101C2 **Cabora Bassa Dam**
Mozam
24A1 **Caborca** Mexico
24C2 **Cabo Rojo** *C* Mexico
23B1 **Cabos** Mexico
29C6 **Cabo San Diego** *C*
Arg
32A4 **Cabo San Lorenzo** *C*
Ecuador
53A3 **Cabo Teulada** *C*
Sardegna
50A2 **Cabo Trafalgar** *C*
Spain
50B2 **Cabo Tres Forcas** *C*
Mor
29C5 **Cabo Tres Puntas** *C*
Arg
7D5 **Cabot Str** Can
50B2 **Cabra** Spain
50A1 **Cabreira** *Mt* Port
51C2 **Cabrera** *I* Spain

34A3 **Cabrero** Chile
51B2 **Cabriel** *R* Spain
23B2 **Cacahuamilpa**
Mexico
54B2 **Čačak** Serbia, Yugos
23B2 **C A Carillo** Mexico
30E2 **Cáceres** Brazil
50A2 **Caceres** Spain
18B2 **Cache** *R* USA
13C2 **Cache Creek** Can
30C4 **Cachi** Arg
33G5 **Cachimbo** Brazil
31D4 **Cachoeira** Brazil
35A1 **Cachoeira Alta** Brazil
31D3 **Cachoeira de Paulo**
Alfonso *Waterfall*
Brazil
29F2 **Cachoeira do Sul**
Brazil
31C6 **Cachoeiro de**
Itapemirim Brazil
22C3 **Cachuma,L** USA
100A2 **Cacolo** Angola
100A2 **Caconda** Angola
35A1 **Caçu** Brazil
100A2 **Caculuvar** *R* Angola
59B3 **Čadca** Czech
43C3 **Cader Idris** *Mts*
Wales
10B2 **Cadillac** USA
79B3 **Cadiz** Phil
50A2 **Cadiz** Spain
48B2 **Caen** France
42B3 **Caernarfon** Wales
43B3 **Caernarfon B** Wales
94B2 **Caesarea** *Hist Site*
Israel
31C4 **Caetité** Brazil
30C4 **Cafayate** Arg
92B2 **Caga Tepe** Turk
79B2 **Cagayan** *R* Phil
79B4 **Cagayan de Oro** Phil
79B4 **Cagayan Is** Phil
53A3 **Cagliari** Sardegna
27D3 **Caguas** Puerto Rico
45B3 **Caha Mts** Irish Rep
45A3 **Cahersiveen**
Irish Rep
45C2 **Cahir** Irish Rep
45C2 **Cahone Pt** Irish Rep
48C3 **Cahors** France
101C2 **Caia** Mozam
100B2 **Caianda** Angola
35A1 **Caiapó** *R* Brazil
35A1 **Caiapônia** Brazil
31D3 **Caicó** Brazil
26C2 **Caicos Is**
Caribbean S
11C4 **Caicos Pass** The
Bahamas
12C2 **Cairn Mt** USA
44C3 **Cairngorms** *Mts*
Scot
107D2 **Cairns** Aust
92B3 **Cairo** Egypt
11B3 **Cairo** USA
108B1 **Caiwarro** Aust
32B5 **Cajabamba** Peru
32B5 **Cajamarca** Peru
27D5 **Calabozo** Ven
54B2 **Calafat** Rom
29B6 **Calafate** Arg
79B3 **Calagua Is** Phil
51B1 **Calahorra** Spain
48C1 **Calais** France
30C3 **Calama** Chile
32C3 **Calamar** Colombia
79A3 **Calamian Group** *Is*
Phil
98B3 **Calandula** Angola
70A3 **Calang** Indon
95B2 **Calanscio Sand Sea**
Libya
79B3 **Calapan** Phil
54C2 **Calarasi** Rom
51B1 **Calatayud** Spain
22B2 **Calaveras Res** USA
79B3 **Calbayog** Phil
19B4 **Calcasieu L** USA
86B2 **Calcutta** India
50A2 **Caldas da Rainha**
Port
31B5 **Caldas Novas** Brazil
30B4 **Caldera** Chile

8B2 **Caldwell** USA
29C5 **Caleta Olivia** Arg
9B3 **Calexico** USA
5G4 **Calgary** Can
17B1 **Calhoun** USA
17B1 **Calhoun Falls** USA
32B3 **Cali** Colombia
8B3 **Caliente** Nevada, USA
8A3 **California** State, USA
22C3 **California Aqueduct** USA
87B2 **Calimera,Pt** India
34B2 **Calingasta** Arg
22A1 **Calistoga** USA
108B1 **Callabonna** *R* Aust
108A1 **Callabonna,L** Aust
15C1 **Callander** Can
44B3 **Callander** Scot
108A1 **Callanna** Aust
32B6 **Callao** Peru
13E1 **Calling L** Can
23B1 **Calnali** Mexico
17B2 **Caloosahatchee** *R* USA
109D1 **Caloundra** Aust
23B2 **Calpulalpan** Mexico
53B3 **Caltanissetta** Italy
98B3 **Caluango** Angola
100A2 **Calulo** Angola
100A2 **Caluquembe** Angola
99F1 **Caluula** Somalia
13B2 **Calvert I** Can
52A2 **Calvi** Corse
23A1 **Calvillo** Mexico
100A4 **Calvinia** S Africa
25E2 **Camagüey** Cuba
25E2 **Camagüey,Arch de** *Is* Cuba
30B2 **Camaná** Peru
30C3 **Camargo** Bol
22C3 **Camarillo** USA
29C4 **Camarones** Arg
20B1 **Camas** USA
98B3 **Camaxilo** Angola
98B3 **Cambatela** Angola
76C3 **Cambodia** Republic, S E Asia
43B4 **Camborne** Eng
49C1 **Cambrai** France
43C3 **Cambrian Mts** Wales
14B2 **Cambridge** Can
43D3 **Cambridge** County, Eng
43E3 **Cambridge** Eng
27H1 **Cambridge** Jamaica
15C3 **Cambridge** Maryland, USA
15D2 **Cambridge** Massachussets, USA
110C1 **Cambridge** NZ
14B2 **Cambridge** Ohio, USA
4H3 **Cambridge Bay** Can
60E5 **Cam Burun** *Pt* Turk
11A3 **Camden** Arkansas, USA
109D2 **Camden** Aust
15D3 **Camden** New Jersey, USA
17B1 **Camden** South Carolina, USA
18B2 **Cameron** Missouri, USA
19A3 **Cameron** Texas, USA
4H2 **Cameron I** Can
111A3 **Cameron Mts** NZ
98A2 **Cameroon** Federal Republic, Africa
98A2 **Cameroun** *Mt* Cam
31B2 **Cametá** Brazil
79B4 **Camiguin** *I* Phil
79B2 **Camiling** Phil
17B1 **Camilla** USA
22B1 **Camino** USA
30D3 **Camiri** Bol
31C2 **Camocim** Brazil
98C3 **Camissombo** Angola
106C2 **Camooweal** Aust
34D2 **Campana** Arg
29A5 **Campana** *I* Chile
13B2 **Campania I** Can
111B2 **Campbell,C** NZ
13D2 **Campbell I** Can
105G6 **Campbell I** NZ
4E3 **Campbell,Mt** Can
84C2 **Campbellpore** Pak
5F5 **Campbell River** Can
7D5 **Campbellton** Can
109D2 **Campbelltown** Aust
42B2 **Campbeltown** Scot
25C3 **Campeche** Mexico
108B3 **Camperdown** Aust
31D3 **Campina Grande** Brazil
31B6 **Campinas** Brazil
35B1 **Campina Verde** Brazil
98A2 **Campo** Cam
53B2 **Campobasso** Italy
35B2 **Campo Belo** Brazil
35B1 **Campo Florido** Brazil
30D4 **Campo Gallo** Arg
30F3 **Campo Grande** Brazil
31C2 **Campo Maior** Brazil
30F3 **Campo Mourão** Brazil
35C2 **Campos** Brazil
35B1 **Campos Altos** Brazil
47D1 **Campo Tures** Italy
76D3 **Cam Ranh** Viet
5G4 **Camrose** Can
100A2 **Camucuio** Angola
27K1 **Canaan** Tobago
16C1 **Canaan** USA
100A2 **Canacupa** Angola
2F3 **Canada** Dominion, N America
29D2 **Cañada de Gomez** Arg
9C3 **Canadian** *R* USA
60C5 **Canakkale** Turk
34B3 **Canalejas** Arg
13D2 **Canal Flats** Can
24A1 **Cananea** Mexico
102G3 **Canary Basin** Atlantic O
Canary Is = Islas Canarias
23A2 **Canas** Mexico
24B2 **Canatlán** Mexico
11B4 **Canaveral,C** USA
31D5 **Canavieiras** Brazil
107D4 **Canberra** Aust
20B2 **Canby** California, USA
55C3 **Çandarli Körfezi** *B* Turk
16C2 **Candlewood,L** USA
29E2 **Canelones** Urug
18A2 **Caney** USA
100A2 **Cangamba** Angola
100B2 **Cangombe** Angola
72D2 **Cangzhou** China
7D4 **Caniapiscau** *R* Can
7D4 **Caniapiscau,L** Can
53B3 **Canicatti** Italy
31D2 **Canindé** Brazil
92B1 **Çankırı** Turk
13D2 **Canmore** Can
44A3 **Canna** *I* Scot
87B2 **Cannanore** India
49D3 **Cannes** France
109C3 **Cann River** Aust
30F4 **Canôas** Brazil
13F1 **Canoe L** Can
9C3 **Canon City** USA
108B2 **Canopus** Aust
5H4 **Canora** Can
109C2 **Canowindra** Aust
45C2 **Cansore Pt** Irish Rep
43E4 **Canterbury** Eng
111B2 **Canterbury Bight** *B* NZ
111B2 **Canterbury Plains** NZ
77D4 **Can Tho** Viet
Canton = Guangzhou
19C3 **Canton** Mississippi, USA
18B1 **Canton** Missouri, USA
10B2 **Canton** Ohio, USA
12E2 **Cantwell** USA
20C2 **Canyon City** USA
12J2 **Canyon Range** *Mts* Can
20B2 **Canyonville** USA
98C3 **Canzar** Angola
76D1 **Cao Bang** Viet
31B2 **Capanema** Brazil
35B2 **Capão Bonito** Brazil
48B3 **Capbreton** France
24B2 **Cap Corrientes** *C* Mexico
52A2 **Cap Corse** *C* Corse
48B2 **Cap de la Hague** *C* France
15D1 **Cap-de-la-Madeleine** Can
6C3 **Cap de Nouvelle-France** *C* Can
51C2 **Capdepera** Spain
23A2 **Cap de Tancitiario** *C* Mexico
109C4 **Cape Barren I** Aust
103J6 **Cape Basin** Atlantic O
7E5 **Cape Breton I** Can
97B4 **Cape Coast** Ghana
15D2 **Cape Cod B** USA
6C3 **Cape Dorset** Can
17C1 **Cape Fear** *R* USA
18C2 **Cape Girardeau** USA
6B3 **Cape Henrietta Maria** Can
Cape Horn = Cabo de Hornos
104E3 **Cape Johnston Depth** Pacific O
35C1 **Capelinha** Brazil
4B3 **Cape Lisburne** USA
100A2 **Capelongo** Angola
15D3 **Cape May** USA
5F5 **Cape Mendocino** USA
98B3 **Capenda Camulemba** Angola
4F2 **Cape Perry** Can
100B4 **Cape Province** S Africa
7A4 **Cape Tatnam** Can
100A4 **Cape Town** S Africa
102G4 **Cape Verde** *Is* Atlantic O
102G4 **Cape Verde Basin** Atlantic O
12F3 **Cape Yakataga** USA
107D2 **Cape York Pen** Aust
46A1 **Cap Gris Nez** *C* France
26C3 **Cap-Haitien** Haiti
31B2 **Capim** *R* Brazil
112C2 **Capitán Arturo Prat** *Base* Ant
27P2 **Cap Moule à Chique** *C* St Lucia
53C3 **Capo Isola de Correnti** *C* Italy
53C3 **Capo Rizzuto** *C* Italy
55A3 **Capo Santa Maria di Leuca** *C* Italy
53B3 **Capo San Vito** Italy
53C3 **Capo Spartivento** *C* Italy
27P2 **Cap Pt** St Lucia
53B2 **Capri** *I* Italy
100B2 **Caprivi Strip** Region, Namibia
52A2 **Cap Rosso** *C* Corse
102H4 **Cap Vert** *C* Sen
32C4 **Caquetá** *R* Colombia
54B2 **Caracal** Rom
33E3 **Caracaraí** Brazil
32D1 **Caracas** Ven
35B2 **Caraguatatuba** Brazil
29B3 **Carahue** Chile
35C1 **Caraí** Brazil
35C2 **Carandaí** Brazil
31C6 **Carangola** Brazil
54B1 **Caransebeş** Rom
108A2 **Carappee Hill** *Mt* Aust
26A3 **Caratasca** Honduras
35C1 **Caratinga** Brazil
51B2 **Caravaca** Spain
35D1 **Caravelas** Brazil
18C2 **Carbondale** Illinois, USA
53A3 **Carbonia** Sardegna
7E5 **Carborear** Can
5G4 **Carcaion** Can
99E1 **Carcar Mts** Somalia
48C3 **Carcassonne** France
4E3 **Carcross** Can
23B2 **Cardel** Mexico
25D2 **Cardenas** Cuba
23B1 **Cárdenas** Mexico
43C4 **Cardiff** Wales
43B3 **Cardigan** Wales
43B3 **Cardigan B** Wales
13E2 **Cardston** Can
54B1 **Carei** Rom
33F4 **Careiro** Brazil
34A2 **Carén** Chile
14B2 **Carey** USA
48B2 **Carhaix-Plouguer** France
29D3 **Carhué** Arg
31C6 **Cariacica** Brazil
5J4 **Caribou** Can
5G4 **Caribou Mts** Alberta, Can
5F4 **Caribou Mts** British Columbia, Can
79B3 **Carigara** Phil
46C2 **Carignan** France
33E1 **Caripito** Ven
15C1 **Carleton Place** Can
101G1 **Carletonville** S Africa
18C2 **Carlinville** USA
42C2 **Carlisle** Eng
15C2 **Carlisle** USA
34C3 **Carlos** Arg
35C1 **Carlos Chagas** Brazil
45C2 **Carlow** County, Irish Rep
45C2 **Carlow** Irish Rep
21B3 **Carlsbad** California, USA
9C3 **Carlsbad** New Mexico, USA
5H5 **Carlyle** Can
12G2 **Carmacks** Can
47B2 **Carmagnola** Italy
43B4 **Carmarthen** Wales
43B4 **Carmarthen B** Wales
22B2 **Carmel** California, USA
16C2 **Carmel** New York, USA
94B2 **Carmel,Mt** Israel
34D2 **Carmelo** Urug
22B2 **Carmel Valley** USA
9B4 **Carmen** *I* Mexico
29D4 **Carmen de Patagones** Arg
18C2 **Carmi** USA
21A2 **Carmichael** USA
35B1 **Carmo do Paranaiba** Brazil
50A2 **Carmona** Spain
106A3 **Carnarvon** Aust
100B4 **Carnarvon** S Africa
35D1 **Carncacá** Brazil
45C1 **Carndonagh** Irish Rep
106B3 **Carnegi,L** Aust
98B2 **Carnot** CAR
108A2 **Carnot,C** Aust
17B2 **Carol City** USA
31B3 **Carolina** Brazil
101H1 **Carolina** S Africa
17C1 **Carolina Beach** USA
104F3 **Caroline Is** Pacific O
60B4 **Carpathians** *Mts* E Europe
59D3 **Carpatii Orientali** *Mts* Rom
106C2 **Carpentaria,G of** Aust
83C5 **Carpenter Ridge** Indian O
49D3 **Carpentras** France
52B2 **Carpi** Italy
22C3 **Carpinteria** USA
17B2 **Carrabelle** USA
52B2 **Carrara** Italy
41B3 **Carrauntoohill** *Mt* Irish Rep
45C2 **Carrickmacross** Irish Rep
45B2 **Carrick on Shannon** Irish Rep
45C2 **Carrick-on-Suir** Irish Rep
108A2 **Carrieton** Aust

Carrington

8D2 **Carrington** USA
50B1 **Carrión** R Spain
10A2 **Carroll** USA
17A1 **Carrollton** Georgia, USA
14A3 **Carrollton** Kentucky, USA
18B2 **Carrollton** Missouri, USA
18C2 **Carruthersville** USA
60E5 **Carsamba** Turk
92B2 **Carsamba** R Turk
8B3 **Carson City** USA
14B2 **Carsonville** USA
26B4 **Cartagena** Colombia
51B2 **Cartagena** Spain
32B3 **Cartago** Colombia
25D4 **Cartago** Costa Rica
111C2 **Carterton** NZ
18B2 **Carthage** Missouri, USA
15C2 **Carthage** New York, USA
19B3 **Carthage** Texas, USA
106B2 **Cartier** I Timor S
7E4 **Cartwright** Can
31D3 **Caruaru** Brazil
33E1 **Carúpano** Ven
46B1 **Carvin** France
34A2 **Casablanca** Chile
96B1 **Casablanca** Mor
35B2 **Casa Branca** Brazil
9B3 **Casa Grande** USA
52A1 **Casale Monferrato** Italy
47D2 **Casalmaggiore** Italy
34C3 **Casares** Arg
13C3 **Cascade Mts** Can/USA
111A2 **Cascade Pt** NZ
8A2 **Cascade Range** Mts USA
30F3 **Cascavel** Brazil
53B2 **Caserta** Italy
112C9 **Casey** Base Ant
45C2 **Cashel** Irish Rep
34C2 **Casilda** Arg
107E3 **Casino** Aust
32B5 **Casma** Peru
51B1 **Caspe** Spain
8C2 **Casper** USA
65G6 **Caspian S** Asia/Europe
14C3 **Cass** USA
100B2 **Cassamba** Angola
46B1 **Cassel** France
12J3 **Cassiar** Can
4E3 **Cassiar Mts** Can
35A1 **Cassilândia** Brazil
53B2 **Cassino** Italy
22C3 **Castaic** USA
34B2 **Castaño** R Arg
47D2 **Castelfranco** Italy
49D3 **Castellane** France
34D3 **Castelli** Arg
51B2 **Castellón de la Plana** Spain
31C3 **Castelo** Brazil
50A2 **Castelo Branco** Port
48C3 **Castelsarrasin** France
53B3 **Castelvetrano** Italy
108B3 **Casterton** Aust
50B2 **Castilla La Nueva** Region, Spain
50B1 **Castilla La Vieja** Region, Spain
41B3 **Castlebar** Irish Rep
44A3 **Castlebay** Scot
42C2 **Castle Douglas** Scot
20C1 **Castlegar** Can
45B2 **Castleisland** Irish Rep
108B3 **Castlemain** Aust
45B2 **Castlerea** Irish Rep
109C2 **Castlereagh** Aust
48C3 **Castres-sur-l'Agout** France
27E4 **Castries** St Lucia
29B4 **Castro** Arg
30F3 **Castro** Brazil
31D4 **Castro Alves** Brazil
53C3 **Castrovillari** Italy
22B2 **Castroville** USA
111A2 **Caswell Sd** NZ

25E2 **Cat** I The Bahamas
79B3 **Catabalogan** Phil
32A5 **Catacaos** Peru
35C2 **Cataguases** Brazil
19B3 **Catahoula L** USA
35B1 **Catalão** Brazil
51C1 **Cataluña** Region, Spain
30C4 **Catamarca** Arg
30C4 **Catamarca** State, Arg
101C2 **Catandica** Mozam
79B3 **Catanduanes** I Phil
31B6 **Catanduva** Brazil
53C3 **Catania** Italy
53C3 **Catanzaro** Italy
79B3 **Catarman** Phil
108A2 **Catastrophe,C** Aust
26C5 **Catatumbo** R Ven
16A2 **Catawissa** USA
23B2 **Catemaco** Mexico
49D3 **Cater** Corse
52A2 **Cateraggio** Corse
98B3 **Catete** Angola
97A3 **Catio** Guinea-Bissau
7A4 **Cat Lake** Can
13D3 **Catlegar** Can
107E3 **Cato** I Aust
25D2 **Catoche,C** Mexico
16A3 **Catoctin Mt** USA
15C3 **Catonsville** USA
34C3 **Catrilo** Arg
15D2 **Catskill** USA
15D2 **Catskill Mts** USA
32C2 **Cauca** R Colombia
31D2 **Caucaia** Brazil
32B2 **Caucasia** Colombia
Caucasus = Bol'shoy Kavkaz
46B1 **Caudry** France
98B3 **Caungula** Angola
29B3 **Cauquenes** Chile
87B2 **Cauvery** R India
49D3 **Cavaillon** France
47D1 **Cavalese** italy
97B4 **Cavally** R Lib
45C2 **Cavan** County, Irish Rep
45C2 **Cavan** Irish Rep
79B3 **Cavite** Phil
31C2 **Caxias** Brazil
32C4 **Caxias** Brazil
30F4 **Caxias do Sul** Brazil
98B3 **Caxito** Angola
17B1 **Cayce** USA
93D1 **Cayeli** Turk
33G3 **Cayenne** French Guiana
46A1 **Cayeux-sur-Mer** France
25E3 **Cayman Brac** I Caribbean S
26A3 **Cayman Is** Caribbean S
26A3 **Cayman Trench** Caribbean S
99E2 **Caynabo** Somalia
25E2 **Cayo Romana** I Cuba
25D3 **Cayos Miskitos** Is Nic
26A2 **Cay Sal** I Caribbean S
100B2 **Cazombo** Angola
Ceará = Fortaleza
31C3 **Ceara** State, Brazil
79B3 **Cebu** Phil
79B3 **Cebu** I Phil
16B3 **Cecilton** USA
52B2 **Cecina** Italy
8B3 **Cedar City** USA
19A3 **Cedar Creek Res** USA
5J4 **Cedar L** Can
10A2 **Cedar Rapids** USA
17A1 **Cedartown** USA
24A2 **Cedros** I Mexico
106C4 **Ceduna** Aust
99E2 **Ceelbuur** Somalia
99E1 **Ceerigaabo** Somalia
53B3 **Cefalù** Italy
59B3 **Cegléd** Hung
100A2 **Cela** Angola
24B2 **Celaya** Mexico
Celebes = Sulawesi
70C3 **Celebes S** S E Asia

14B2 **Celina** USA
52C1 **Celje** Slovenia
56C2 **Celle** Germany
71E4 **Cendrawasih** Pen Indon
47C2 **Ceno** R Italy
19B3 **Center** USA
16C2 **Center Moriches** USA
17A1 **Center Point** USA
47D2 **Cento** Italy
44B3 **Central** Region, Scot
98B2 **Central African Republic** Africa
16D2 **Central Falls** USA
18C2 **Centralia** Illinois, USA
8A2 **Centralia** Washington, USA
20B2 **Central Point** USA
71F4 **Central Range** Mts PNG
16A3 **Centreville** Maryland, USA
78C4 **Cepu** Indon
Ceram = Seram
71D4 **Ceram Sea** Indon
34C3 **Cereales** Arg
31B5 **Ceres** Brazil
100A4 **Ceres** S Africa
22B2 **Ceres** USA
48C2 **Cergy-Pontoise** France
53C2 **Cerignola** Italy
60C5 **Cernavodä** Rom
9C4 **Cerralvo** I Mexico
23A1 **Cerritos** Mexico
34B2 **Cerro Aconcagua** Mt Arg
23B1 **Cerro Azul** Mexico
34A3 **Cerro Campanario** Mt Chile
34C2 **Cerro Champaqui** Mt Arg
23A2 **Cerro Cuachaia** Mt Mexico
23B1 **Cerro de Astillero** Mexico
34B2 **Cerro de Olivares** Mt Arg
32B6 **Cerro de Pasco** Peru
27D3 **Cerro de Punta** Mt Puerto Rico
23A2 **Cerro El Cantado** Mt Mexico
34B3 **Cerro El Nevado** Mt Arg
23A2 **Cerro Grande** Mts Mexico
34A2 **Cerro Juncal** Mt Arg/Chile
23A1 **Cerro la Ardilla** Mts Mexico
34B1 **Cerro las Tortolas** Mt Chile
23A2 **Cerro Laurel** Mt Mexico
34A2 **Cerro Mercedario** Mt Arg
34A3 **Cerro Mora** Mt Chile
27C4 **Cerron** Mt Ven
34B3 **Cerro Payún** Mt Arg
23B2 **Cerro Penón del Rosario** Mt Mexico
34B2 **Cerro Sosneado** Mt Arg
23A2 **Cerro Teotepec** Mt Mexico
34B2 **Cerro Tupungato** Mt Arg
23B2 **Cerro Yucuyacau** Mt Mexico
47C2 **Cervo** R Italy
52B2 **Cesena** Italy
60B2 **Cēsis** Latvia
57C3 **České Budějovice** Czech
57C3 **České Zemé** Region, Czech
59B3 **Českomoravská Vysočina** U Czech
55C3 **Çeşme** Turk
107E4 **Cessnock** Aust
52C2 **Cetina** R Croatia

96B1 **Ceuta** N W Africa
92C2 **Ceyham** Turk
92C2 **Ceyhan** R Turk
93C2 **Ceylanpınar** Turk
Ceylon = Sri Lanka
63B2 **Chaa-Khol** Russian Fed
48C2 **Chaâteaudun** France
47B1 **Chablais** Region, France
34C2 **Chacabuco** Arg
32B5 **Chachapoyas** Peru
34B3 **Chacharramendi** Arg
84C3 **Chachran** Pak
30D4 **Chaco** State, Arg
98B1 **Chad** Republic, Africa
98B1 **Chad** L C Africa
34B3 **Chadileuvu** R Arg
8C2 **Chadron** USA
18C2 **Chaffee** USA
85A3 **Chagai** Pak
63F2 **Chagda** Russian Fed
84B2 **Chaghcharan** Afghan
104B4 **Chagos Arch** Indian O
27L1 **Chaguanas** Trinidad
91D4 **Chāh Bahār** Iran
76C2 **Chai Badan** Thai
76C3 **Chaine des Cardamomes** Mts Camb
98C4 **Chaine des Mitumba** Mts Zaïre
76C2 **Chaiyaphum** Thai
34D2 **Chajari** Arg
84C2 **Chakwal** Pak
30B2 **Chala** Peru
100C2 **Chalabesa** Zambia
84A2 **Chalap Dalam** Mts Afghan
73C4 **Chaling** China
85C4 **Chalisgaon** India
12F1 **Chalkyitsik** USA
46C2 **Challerange** France
46C2 **Châlons sur Marne** France
49C2 **Chalon sur Saône** France
57C3 **Cham** Germany
84B2 **Chaman** Pak
84D2 **Chamba** India
85D3 **Chambal** R India
15C3 **Chambersburg** USA
49D2 **Chambéry** France
46B2 **Chambly** France
85A3 **Chambor Kalat** Pak
90B3 **Chamgordan** Iran
34B2 **Chamical** Arg
47B2 **Chamonix** France
86A2 **Champa** India
49C2 **Champagne** Region, France
101G1 **Champagne Castle** Mt Lesotho
47A1 **Champagnole** France
10B2 **Champaign** USA
76D3 **Champassak** Laos
10C2 **Champlain,L** USA
87B2 **Chāmrājnagar** India
30B4 **Chañaral** Chile
34A3 **Chanco** Chile
4D3 **Chandalar** USA
4D3 **Chandalar** R USA
84D2 **Chandigarh** India
86C2 **Chandpur** Bang
85D5 **Chandrapur** India
91D4 **Chānf** Iran
101C2 **Changara** Mozam
74B2 **Changbai** China
69E2 **Changchun** China
73C4 **Changde** China
68E4 **Chang-hua** Taiwan
76D2 **Changjiang** China
73D3 **Chang Jiang** R China
74B2 **Changjin** N Korea
73C4 **Changsha** China
72E3 **Changshu** China
74A2 **Changtu** China
72B2 **Changwu** China
74B3 **Changyön** N Korea
72C2 **Changzhi** China
73E3 **Changzhou** China
48B2 **Channel Is** Europe
9B3 **Channel Is** USA

7E5	**Channel Port-aux-Basques** Can
76C3	**Chanthaburi** Thai
46B2	**Chantilly** France
18A2	**Chanute** USA
73D5	**Chaoàn** China
73D5	**Chao'an** China
73D3	**Chao Hu** L China
76C3	**Chao Phraya** R Thai
72E1	**Chaoyang** China
31C4	**Chapada Diamantina** Mts Brazil
31C2	**Chapadinha** Brazil
23A1	**Chapala** Mexico
23A1	**Chapala,Lac de** L Mexico
61H3	**Chapayevo** Kazakhstan
30F4	**Chapecó** Brazil
27H1	**Chapeltown** Jamaica
7B5	**Chapleau** Can
61E3	**Chaplygin** Russian Fed
112C3	**Charcot I** Ant
80E2	**Chardzhou** Turkmenistan
48C2	**Charente** R France
98B1	**Chari** R Chad
98B1	**Chari Baguirmi** Region, Chad
84B1	**Charikar** Afghan
18B1	**Chariton** R USA
33F2	**Charity** Guyana
85D3	**Charkhāri** India
46C1	**Charleroi** Belg
18C2	**Charleston** Illinois, USA
18C2	**Charleston** Missouri, USA
11C3	**Charleston** S Carolina, USA
10B3	**Charleston** W Virginia, USA
98C3	**Charlesville** Zaïre
107D3	**Charleville** Aust
49C2	**Charleville-Mézières** France
14A1	**Charlevoix** USA
14B2	**Charlotte** Michigan, USA
11B3	**Charlotte** N Carolina, USA
17B2	**Charlotte Harbor** B USA
10C3	**Charlottesville** USA
7D5	**Charlottetown** Can
27K1	**Charlotteville** Tobago
108B3	**Charlton** Aust
10C1	**Charlton I** Can
84C2	**Charsadda** Pak
107D3	**Charters Towers** Aust
48C2	**Chartres** France
29E3	**Chascomús** Arg
13D2	**Chase** Can
48B2	**Châteaubriant** France
48C2	**Châteaudun** France
48B2	**Châteaulin** France
48C2	**Châteauroux** France
46D2	**Château-Salins** France
49C2	**Château-Thierry** France
46C1	**Châtelet** Belg
48C2	**Châtellerault** France
43E4	**Chatham** Eng
7D5	**Chatham** New Brunswick, Can
16C1	**Chatham** New York, USA
14B2	**Chatham** Ontario, Can
13A2	**Chatham Sd** Can
12H3	**Chatham Str** USA
49C2	**Châtillon** France
47B2	**Châtillon** Italy
16B3	**Chatsworth** USA
17B1	**Chattahoochee** USA
17A1	**Chattahoochee** R USA
11B3	**Chattanooga** USA
76A1	**Chauk** Burma
49D2	**Chaumont** France
46B2	**Chauny** France
77D3	**Chau Phu** Viet
50A1	**Chaves** Port
61H2	**Chaykovskiy** Russian Fed
50B2	**Chazaouet** Alg
34C2	**Chazón** Arg
32C2	**Chcontá** Colombia
57C2	**Cheb** Czech
65F4	**Cheboksary** Russian Fed
10B2	**Cheboygan** USA
74B3	**Chech'on** S Korea
85C3	**Chechro** Pak
18A2	**Checotah** USA
76A2	**Cheduba I** Burma
108B1	**Cheepie** Aust
96B2	**Chegga** Maur
100C2	**Chegutu** Zim
20B1	**Chehalis** USA
74B4	**Cheju** S Korea
74B4	**Cheju do** I S Korea
74B4	**Cheju-haehyöp** Str S Korea
63F2	**Chekunda** Russian Fed
20B1	**Chelan,L** USA
90B2	**Cheleken** Turkmenistan
34B3	**Chelforo** Arg
80D1	**Chelkar** Kazakhstan
59C2	**Chelm** Pol
58B2	**Chelmno** Pol
43E4	**Chelmsford** Eng
43C4	**Cheltenham** Eng
65H4	**Chelyabinsk** Russian Fed
101C2	**Chemba** Mozam
57C2	**Chemnitz** Germany
84D2	**Chenab** R India/Pak
96B2	**Chenachane** Alg
20C1	**Cheney** USA
18A2	**Cheney Res** USA
72D1	**Chengda** China
73A3	**Chengdu** China
72E2	**Chengshan Jiao** Pt China
73C4	**Chenxi** China
73C4	**Chen Xian** China
73D3	**Cheo Xian** China
32B5	**Chepén** Peru
34B2	**Chepes** Arg
48C2	**Cher** R France
23A2	**Cheran** Mexico
17C1	**Cheraw** USA
48B2	**Cherbourg** France
96C1	**Cherchell** Alg
63C2	**Cheremkhovo** Russian Fed
60E2	**Cherepovets** Russian Fed
60D4	**Cherkassy** Ukraine
61F5	**Cherkessk** Russian Fed
60D3	**Chernigov** Ukraine
60D2	**Chernobyl** Ukraine
60C4	**Chernovtsy** Ukraine
61J2	**Chernushka** Russian Fed
60B3	**Chernyakhovsk** Russian Fed
61G4	**Chernyye Zemli** Region, Russian Fed
18A2	**Cherokees,L o'the** USA
34A3	**Cherquenco** Chile
86C1	**Cherrapunji** India
60C3	**Cherven'** Belorussia
59C2	**Chervonograd** Ukraine
10C3	**Chesapeake** B USA
42C3	**Cheshire** County, Eng
16C1	**Cheshire** USA
64F3	**Chëshskaya Guba** B Russian Fed
21A1	**Chester** California, USA
42C3	**Chester** Eng
18C2	**Chester** Illinois, USA
16C1	**Chester** Massachusets, USA
15C3	**Chester** Pennsylvania, USA
17B1	**Chester** S Carolina, USA
16A3	**Chester** R USA
42D3	**Chesterfield** Eng
6A3	**Chesterfield Inlet** Can
16A3	**Chestertown** USA
25D3	**Chetumal** Mexico
13C1	**Chetwynd** Can
12A2	**Chevak** USA
111D2	**Cheviot** NZ
40C2	**Cheviots** Hills Eng/Scot
13D3	**Chewelah** USA
8C2	**Cheyenne** USA
86A1	**Chhapra** India
86C1	**Chhātak** Bang
85D4	**Chhatarpur** India
86D4	**Chhindwāra** India
86B1	**Chhuka** Bhutan
73E5	**Chia'i** Taiwan
100A2	**Chiange** Angola
76C2	**Chiang Kham** Thai
76B2	**Chiang Mai** Thai
47C1	**Chiavenna** Italy
74E3	**Chiba** Japan
86B2	**Chibāsa** India
100A2	**Chibia** Angola
7C4	**Chibougamou** Can
75A1	**Chiburi-jima** I Japan
101C3	**Chibuto** Mozam
10B2	**Chicago** USA
14A2	**Chicago Heights** USA
12G3	**Chichagof I** USA
43D4	**Chichester** Eng
75B1	**Chichibu** Japan
69G4	**Chichi-jima** I Japan
11B3	**Chickamauga L** USA
19C3	**Chickasawhay** R USA
9D3	**Chickasha** USA
12F2	**Chicken** USA
32A5	**Chiclayo** Peru
8A3	**Chico** USA
29C4	**Chico** R Arg
101C2	**Chicoa** Mozam
15D2	**Chicopee** USA
7C5	**Chicoutimi** Can
101C3	**Chicualacuala** Mozam
87B2	**Chidambaram** India
6D3	**Chidley,C** Can
17B2	**Chiefland** USA
99C3	**Chiengi** Zambia
47B2	**Chieri** Italy
46C2	**Chiers** R France
47C1	**Chiesa** Italy
47D2	**Chiese** R Italy
52B2	**Chieti** Italy
72D1	**Chifeng** China
12C3	**Chiginigak,Mt** USA
4C3	**Chigmit Mts** USA
23B2	**Chignahuapán** Mexico
12C3	**Chignik** USA
24D2	**Chihuahua** Mexico
87B2	**Chik Ballāpur** India
87B2	**Chikmagalūr** India
12C2	**Chikuminuk L** USA
101C2	**Chikwawa** Malawi
76A1	**Chi-kyaw** Burma
87C1	**Chilakalūrupet** India
23B2	**Chilapa** Mexico
87B3	**Chilaw** Sri Lanka
28B6	**Chile** Republic
34B2	**Chilecito** Mendoza, Arg
100B2	**Chililabombwe** Zambia
86B2	**Chilka** L India
13C2	**Chilko** R Can
5F4	**Chilko L** Can
13C2	**Chilkotin** R Can
34A3	**Chillán** Chile
34D3	**Chillar** Arg
18B2	**Chillicothe** Missouri, USA
14B3	**Chillicothe** Ohio, USA
13C3	**Chilliwack** Can
86B1	**Chilmari** India
101C2	**Chilongozi** Zambia
20B2	**Chiloquin** USA
24C3	**Chilpancingo** Mexico
43D4	**Chiltern Hills** Upland Eng
14A2	**Chilton** USA
101C2	**Chilumba** Malawi
69E4	**Chi-lung** Taiwan
101C2	**Chilwa** L Malawi
100C2	**Chimanimani** Zim
46C1	**Chimay** Belg
65G5	**Chimbay** Uzbekistan
32B4	**Chimborazo** Mt Ecuador
32B5	**Chimbote** Peru
65H5	**Chimkent** Kazakhstan
101C2	**Chimoio** Mozam
67E3	**China** Republic, Asia
	China National Republic = Taiwan
25D3	**Chinandega** Nic
32B6	**Chincha Alta** Peru
109D1	**Chinchilla** Aust
101C2	**Chinde** Mozam
86C2	**Chindwin** R Burma
100B2	**Chingola** Zambia
100A2	**Chinguar** Angola
96A2	**Chinguetti** Maur
74B3	**Chinhae** S Korea
100C2	**Chinhoyi** Zim
12D3	**Chiniak,C** USA
84C2	**Chiniot** Pak
74B3	**Chinju** S Korea
98C2	**Chinko** R CAR
75B1	**Chino** Japan
101C2	**Chinsali** Zambia
52B1	**Chioggia** Italy
101C2	**Chipata** Zambia
101C3	**Chipinge** Zim
87A1	**Chiplūn** India
43C4	**Chippenham** Eng
10A2	**Chippewa Falls** USA
32A4	**Chira** R Peru
87C1	**Chirāla** India
101C3	**Chiredzi** Zim
95A2	**Chirfa** Niger
32A2	**Chiriqui** Mt Panama
54C2	**Chirpan** Bulg
32A2	**Chirripo Grande** Mt Costa Rica
100B2	**Chirundu** Zim
100B2	**Chisamba** Zambia
7C4	**Chisasibi** Can
73B4	**Chishui He** R China
	Chişinău = Kishinev
47B2	**Chisone** R Italy
61H2	**Chistopol** Russian Fed
68D1	**Chita** Russian Fed
100A2	**Chitado** Angola
100A2	**Chitembo** Angola
12F2	**Chitina** USA
12F2	**Chitina** R USA
87B2	**Chitradurga** India
84C1	**Chitral** Pak
32A2	**Chitré** Panama
86C2	**Chittagong** Bang
85C4	**Chittaurgarh** India
87B2	**Chittoor** India
100B2	**Chiume** Angola
47D1	**Chiusa** Italy
47B2	**Chivasso** Italy
100C2	**Chivhu** Zim
29D2	**Chivilcoy** Arg
100C2	**Chivu** Zim
75A1	**Chizu** Japan
29C3	**Choele Choel** Arg
34C3	**Choique** Arg
24B2	**Choix** Mexico
58B2	**Chojnice** Pol
99D1	**Choke Mts** Eth
48B2	**Cholet** France
23B2	**Cholula** Mexico
100B2	**Choma** Zambia
86B1	**Chomo Yummo** Mt China/India
57C2	**Chomutov** Czech
63C1	**Chona** R Russian Fed
74B4	**Ch'ŏnan** S Korea
76C3	**Chon Buri** Thai
32A4	**Chone** Ecuador
74B2	**Ch'ŏngjin** N Korea
74B3	**Chongju** N Korea

Ch'ŏngju

74B3 Ch'ŏngju S Korea
100A2 Chongoroi Angola
73B4 Chongqing China
74B3 Chŏngŭp S Korea
74B3 Chŏnju S Korea
86B1 Chooyu Mt China/Nepal
59D3 Chortkov Ukraine
74B3 Ch'ŏrwŏn N Korea
59B2 Chorzow Pol
74E3 Choshi Japan
34A3 Chos-Malal Arg
58B2 Choszczno Pol
86A2 Chotanāgpur Region, India
96C1 Chott Melrhir Alg
22B2 Chowchilla USA
63D3 Choybalsan Mongolia
6A3 Chrantrey Inlet B Can
111B2 Christchurch NZ
101G1 Christiana S Africa
6D2 Christian,C Can
12H3 Christian Sd USA
6E3 Christianshab Greenland
104D4 Christmas I Indian O
65J5 Chu Kazakhstan
65J5 Chu R Kazakhstan
29C4 Chubut State, Arg
29C4 Chubut R Arg
60D2 Chudovo Russian Fed
Chudskoye Ozero = Peipus, Lake
4D3 Chugach Mts USA
12E2 Chugiak USA
75A1 Chūgoku-sanchi Mts Japan
29F2 Chui Brazil
29B3 Chuillán Chile
77C5 Chukai Malay
76D2 Chu Lai Viet
21B3 Chula Vista USA
12E2 Chulitna USA
63E2 Chulman Russian Fed
32A5 Chulucanas Peru
30C2 Chulumani Bol
65K4 Chulym Russian Fed
63A2 Chulym R Russian Fed
63B2 Chuma R Russian Fed
84D2 Chumar India
63F2 Chumikan Russian Fed
77B3 Chumphon Thai
74B3 Ch'unch'ŏn S Korea
86B2 Chunchura India
74B3 Ch'ungju S Korea
Chungking = Chongqing
99D3 Chunya Tanz
63C1 Chunya R Russian Fed
27L1 Chupara Pt Trinidad
30C3 Chuquicamata Chile
52A1 Chur Switz
86C2 Churāchāndpur India
7A4 Churchill Can
7D4 Churchill R Labrador, Can
7A4 Churchill R Manitoba, Can
7A4 Churchill,C Can
7D4 Churchill Falls Can
5H4 Churchill L Can
84C3 Chūru India
23A2 Churumuco Mexico
61J2 Chusovoy Russian Fed
61G2 Chuvashkaya Respublika, Russian Fed
68B4 Chuxiong China
76D3 Chu Yang Sin Mt Viet
78B4 Cianjur Indon
47D2 Ciano d'Enza Italy
35A2 Cianorte Brazil
58C2 Ciechanow Pol
25E2 Ciego de Avila Cuba

32C1 Ciénaga Colombia
25D2 Cienfuegos Cuba
59B3 Cieszyn Pol
51B2 Cieza Spain
92B2 Cihanbeyli Turk
23A2 Cihuatlán Mexico
78B4 Cijulang Indon
78B4 Cilacap Indon
54C1 Cîmpina Rom
51C1 Cinca R Spain
52C2 Činčer Mt Bosnia & Herzegovina, Yugos
10B3 Cincinnati USA
54B1 Cindrelu Mt Rom
55C3 Cine R Turk
46C1 Ciney Belg
34B3 Cipolletti Arg
4D3 Circle Alaska, USA
14B3 Circleville USA
78B4 Cirebon Indon
43D4 Cirencester Eng
47D2 Citadella Italy
24C3 Citlaltepetl Mt Mexico
100A4 Citrusdal S Africa
52B2 Citta del Vaticano Italy
52B2 Città di Castello Italy
24B2 Ciudad Acuña Mexico
23A2 Ciudad Altamirano Mexico
33E2 Ciudad Bolivar Ven
24B2 Ciudad Camargo Mexico
25C3 Ciudad del Carmen Mexico
23B1 Ciudad del Maiz Mexico
51C1 Ciudadela Spain
33E2 Ciudad Guayana Ven
24B3 Ciudad Guzman Mexico
23A2 Ciudad Hidalgo Mexico
24B1 Ciudad Juárez Mexico
9C4 Ciudad Lerdo Mexico
24C2 Ciudad Madero Mexico
23B2 Ciudad Mendoza Mexico
24B2 Ciudad Obregon Mexico
27C4 Ciudad Ojeda Ven
33E2 Ciudad Piar Ven
50B2 Ciudad Real Spain
50A1 Ciudad Rodrigo Spain
24C2 Ciudad Valles Mexico
24C2 Ciudad Victoria Mexico
52B2 Civitavecchia Italy
93D2 Cizre Turk
43E4 Clacton-on-Sea Eng
5G4 Claire,L Can
14C2 Clairton USA
47A1 Clairvaux France
17A1 Clanton USA
100A4 Clanwilliam S Africa
45C2 Clara Irish Rep
34D3 Claraz Arg
45B2 Clare County, Irish Rep
14B2 Clare USA
45A2 Clare I Irish Rep
15D2 Claremont USA
18A2 Claremore USA
45B2 Claremorris Irish Rep
109D1 Clarence R Aust
111B2 Clarence R NZ
106C2 Clarence Str Aust
12H3 Clarence Str USA
19B3 Clarendon USA
7E5 Clarenville Can
5G4 Claresholm Can
18A1 Clarinda USA
15C2 Clarion Pennsylvania, USA
24A3 Clarión I Mexico
15C2 Clarion R USA
105J3 Clarion Fracture Zone Pacific O

11B3 Clark Hill Res USA
14B2 Clark,Pt Can
14B3 Clarksburg USA
11A3 Clarksdale USA
12C3 Clarks Point USA
20C1 Clarkston USA
18B2 Clarksville Arkansas, USA
35A1 Claro R Brazil
29D3 Claromecó Arg
18A2 Clay Center USA
44D2 Claymore Oilfield N Sea
13B3 Clayoquot Sd Can
9C3 Clayton New Mexico, USA
15C2 Clayton New York, USA
41B3 Clear C Irish Rep
12E3 Cleare,C USA
13D1 Clear Hills Mts Can
21A2 Clear L USA
20B2 Clear Lake Res USA
13D2 Clearwater Can
11B4 Clearwater USA
13E1 Clearwater R Can
13C2 Clearwater L Can
9D3 Cleburne USA
42E2 Cleeton Oilfield North Sea
22B1 Clements USA
79A3 Cleopatra Needle Mt Phil
107D3 Clermont Aust
46B2 Clermont France
46C2 Clermont-en-Argonne France
49C2 Clermont-Ferrand France
46D1 Clervaux Germany
47D1 Cles Italy
108A2 Cleve Aust
42D2 Cleveland County, Eng
19B3 Cleveland Mississippi, USA
10B2 Cleveland Ohio, USA
11B3 Cleveland Tennessee, USA
19A3 Cleveland Texas, USA
41B3 Clew B Irish Rep
45A2 Clifden Irish Rep
109D1 Clifton Aust
16B2 Clifton New Jersey, USA
108A1 Clifton Hills Aust
13F3 Climax Can
18B2 Clinton Arkansas, USA
5F4 Clinton Can
16C2 Clinton Connecticut, USA
16D1 Clinton Massachusetts, USA
19B3 Clinton Mississippi, USA
18B2 Clinton Missouri, USA
16B2 Clinton New Jersey, USA
4H3 Clinton-Colden L Can
24B3 Clipperton I Pacific O
30C2 Cliza Bol
45B3 Clonakilty Irish Rep
107D3 Cloncurry Aust
45C1 Clones Irish Rep
45C2 Clonmel Irish Rep
10A2 Cloquet USA
12C2 Cloudy Mt USA
22C2 Clovis California, USA
9C3 Clovis New Mexico, USA
60B4 Cluj Rom
54B1 Cluj-Napoca Rom
47B1 Cluses France
47C2 Clusone Italy
111A3 Clutha R NZ
43C3 Clwyd County, Wales
6D2 Clyde Can
111A3 Clyde NZ
42B2 Clyde R Scot
23A2 Coahuayana Mexico

23A2 Coalcomán Mexico
13E2 Coaldale Can
21B2 Coaldale USA
21A2 Coalinga USA
33E5 Coari R Brazil
17A1 Coastal Plain USA
4E4 Coast Mts Can
8A2 Coast Ranges Mts USA
42B2 Coatbridge Scot
23B2 Coatepec Mexico
16B3 Coatesville USA
15D1 Coaticook Can
6B3 Coats I Can
112B1 Coats Land Region, Ant
25C3 Coatzacoalcos Mexico
7C5 Cobalt Can
25C3 Cobán Guatemala
107D4 Cobar Aust
109C3 Cobargo Aust
45B3 Cobh Irish Rep
32D6 Cobija Bol
16B1 Cobleskill USA
51B2 Cobo de Palos C Spain
7C5 Cobourg Can
106C2 Cobourg Pen Aust
57C2 Coburg Germany
32B4 Coca Ecuador
17B2 Coca USA
30C2 Cochabamba Bol
46D1 Cochem Germany
Cochin = Kochi
13E2 Cochrane Alberta, Can
7B5 Cochrane Ontario, Can
108B2 Cockburn Aust
16A3 Cockeysville USA
27H1 Cockpit Country,The Jamaica
25D3 Coco R Honduras/Nic
98A2 Cocobeach Gabon
27L1 Cocos B Trinidad
104C4 Cocos Is Indian O
23A1 Cocula Mexico
10C2 Cod,C USA
111A3 Codfish I NZ
7D4 Cod I Can
47E2 Codigoro Italy
31C2 Codó Brazil
47C2 Codogno Italy
8C2 Cody USA
56B2 Coesfeld Germany
8B2 Coeur d'Alene USA
9D3 Coffeyville USA
108A2 Coffin B Aust
109D2 Coff's Harbour Aust
23B2 Cofre de Perote Mt Mexico
48B2 Cognac France
15D2 Cohoes USA
108B3 Cohuna Aust
29B5 Coihaique Chile
87B2 Coimbatore India
50A1 Coimbra Port
32A3 Cojimies Ecuador
107D4 Colac Aust
31C5 Colatina Brazil
112B6 Colbeck,C Ant
43E4 Colchester Eng
16C2 Colchester USA
47B1 Col de la Faucille France
13E2 Cold L Can
52A1 Col du Grand St Bernard P Italy/Switz
47B2 Col du Lautaret P France
52A1 Col du Mont Cenis P France/Italy
14B2 Coldwater USA
12F1 Coleen R USA
14B2 Coleman Michigan, USA
101G1 Colenso S Africa
45C1 Coleraine N Ire
111B2 Coleridge,L NZ
100B4 Colesberg S Africa
22C1 Coleville USA

21A2 **Colfax** California, USA
19B3 **Colfax** Louisiana, USA
20C1 **Colfax** Washington, USA
24B3 **Colima** Mexico
23A2 **Colima** State, Mexico
34A2 **Colina** Chile
44A3 **Coll** *I* Scot
109C1 **Collarenebri** Aust
52A2 **Colle de Tende** *P* France/Italy
12E2 **College** USA
17B1 **College Park** Georgia, USA
16A3 **College Park** Washington, USA
19A3 **College Station** USA
106A4 **Collie** Aust
106B2 **Collier B** Aust
46A1 **Collines de L'Artois** *Mts* France
46B2 **Collines De Thiérache** France
14B2 **Collingwood** Can
110B2 **Collingwood** NZ
19C3 **Collins** Mississippi, USA
4H2 **Collinson Pen** Can
107D3 **Collinsville** Aust
18C2 **Collinsville** Illinois, USA
18A2 **Collinsville** Oklahoma, USA
34A3 **Collipulli** Chile
49D2 **Colmar** France
Cologne = Köln
35B2 **Colômbia** Brazil
32B3 **Colombia** Republic, S America
15C3 **Colombia** USA
87B3 **Colombo** Sri Lanka
25D2 **Colon** Cuba
32B2 **Colón** Panama
29E2 **Colonia** Urug
34D2 **Colonia del Sacramento** Urug
34B3 **Colonia 25 de Mayo** Arg
29C5 **Colonia Las Heras** Arg
44A3 **Colonsay** *I* Scot
23A1 **Colontlán** Mexico
27E5 **Coloradito** Ven
8C3 **Colorado** State, USA
9B3 **Colorado** *R* Arizona, USA
29D3 **Colorado** *R* Buenos Aires, Arg
9D3 **Colorado** *R* Texas, USA
9B3 **Colorado Plat** USA
8C3 **Colorado Springs** USA
22D3 **Colton** USA
16A3 **Columbia** Maryland, USA
19C3 **Columbia** Mississippi, USA
10A3 **Columbia** Missouri, USA
15C2 **Columbia** Pennsylvania, USA
11B3 **Columbia** S Carolina, USA
11B3 **Columbia** Tennessee, USA
13D2 **Columbia** *R* Can
8A2 **Columbia** *R* USA
5G4 **Columbia,Mt** Can
20C1 **Columbia Plat** USA
11B3 **Columbus** Georgia, USA
14A3 **Columbus** Indiana, USA
11B3 **Columbus** Mississippi, USA
8D2 **Columbus** Nebraska, USA
10B2 **Columbus** Ohio, USA
19A4 **Columbus** Texas, USA
20C1 **Colville** USA
4C3 **Colville** *R* USA
110C1 **Colville,C** NZ
4F3 **Colville L** Can
42C3 **Colwyn Bay** Wales
47E2 **Comacchio** Italy
22B1 **Comanche Res** USA
112C2 **Comandante Ferraz** *Base* Ant
25D3 **Comayagua** Honduras
34A2 **Combarbalá** Chile
45C2 **Comeragh** *Mts* Irish Rep
86C2 **Comilla** Bang
25C3 **Comitán** Mexico
46C2 **Commercy** France
6B3 **Committees B** Can
52A1 **Como** Italy
29C5 **Comodoro Rivadavia** Arg
23A1 **Comonfort** Mexico
87B3 **Comorin,C** India
101D2 **Comoros** *Is* Indian O
49C2 **Compiègne** France
23A1 **Compostela** Mexico
34B2 **Comte Salas** Arg
86C1 **Cona** China
97A4 **Conakry** Guinea
34B2 **Concarán** Arg
48B2 **Concarneau** France
35D1 **Conceiçao da Barra** Brazil
31B3 **Conceição do Araguaia** Brazil
35C1 **Conceiçao do Mato Dentro** Brazil
29B3 **Concepción** Chile
30E3 **Concepción** Par
29E2 **Concepción** *R* Arg
24B2 **Concepcion del Oro** Mexico
34D2 **Concepcion del Uruguay** Arg
9A3 **Conception,Pt** USA
35B2 **Conchas** Brazil
9C4 **Conchos** *R* Mexico
21A2 **Concord** California, USA
10C2 **Concord** New Hampshire, USA
29E2 **Concordia** Arg
8D3 **Concordia** USA
20B1 **Concrete** USA
109D1 **Condamine** Aust
107D4 **Condobolin** Aust
20B1 **Condon** USA
46C1 **Condroz** *Mts* Belg
17A1 **Conecuh** *R* USA
47E2 **Conegliano** Italy
89F8 **Congo** Republic, Africa
89F8 **Congo** *R* Congo
Congo,R = Zaïre
14B1 **Coniston** Can
45B2 **Connaught** Region, Irish Rep
14B2 **Conneaut** USA
10C2 **Connecticut** State, USA
15D2 **Connecticut** *R* USA
15C2 **Connellsville** USA
45B2 **Connemara,Mts of** Irish Rep
14A3 **Connersville** USA
108B2 **Conoble** Aust
19A3 **Conroe** USA
35C2 **Conselheiro Lafaiete** Brazil
77D4 **Con Son** *Is* Viet
Constance,L = Bodensee
60C5 **Constanta** Rom
96C1 **Constantine** Alg
12C3 **Constantine,C** USA
29B3 **Constitución** Chile
13F3 **Consul** Can
47E2 **Contarina** Italy
31C4 **Contas** *R* Brazil
23B2 **Contreras** Mexico
4H3 **Contuoyto L** Can
11A3 **Conway** Arkansas, USA
15D2 **Conway** New Hampshire, USA
17C1 **Conway** South Carolina, USA
108A1 **Conway,L** Aust
42C3 **Conwy** Wales
106C3 **Coober Pedy** Aust
110B2 **Cook** *Str* NZ
13B2 **Cook,C** Can
4C3 **Cook Inlet** *B* USA
105H4 **Cook Is** Pacific O
111B2 **Cook,Mt** NZ
107D2 **Cooktown** Aust
109C2 **Coolabah** Aust
108C1 **Cooladdi** Aust
109C2 **Coolah** Aust
109C2 **Coolamon** Aust
106B4 **Coolgardie** Aust
109C3 **Cooma** Aust
109C2 **Coonabarabran** Aust
109C2 **Coonambie** Aust
108B2 **Coonbah** Aust
108A2 **Coondambo** Aust
87A2 **Coondapoor** India
108C1 **Coongoola** Aust
87B2 **Coonoor** India
108B1 **Cooper Basin** Aust
106C3 **Cooper Creek** Aust
108B1 **Cooper Creek** *R* Aust
108A3 **Coorong,The** Aust
109D1 **Cooroy** Aust
20B2 **Coos B** USA
20B2 **Coos Bay** USA
107D4 **Cootamundra** Aust
45C1 **Cootehill** Irish Rep
23B2 **Copala** Mexico
23B2 **Copalillo** Mexico
Copenhagen = København
30B4 **Copiapó** Chile
47D2 **Copparo** Italy
12F2 **Copper** *R* USA
4D3 **Copper Centre** USA
14B1 **Copper Cliff** Can
4G3 **Coppermine** Can
4G3 **Coppermine** *R* Can
Coquilhatville = Mbandaka
30B4 **Coquimbo** Chile
54B2 **Corabia** Rom
17B2 **Coral Gables** USA
6B3 **Coral Harbour** Can
107D2 **Coral S** Aust/PNG
104F4 **Coral Sea Basin** Pacific O
107E2 **Coral Sea Island Territories** Aust
108B3 **Corangamite,L** Aust
33F3 **Corantijn** *R* Surinam/Guyana
46B2 **Corbeil-Essonnes** France
50A1 **Corcubion** Spain
11B3 **Cordele** USA
50A1 **Cordillera Cantabrica** *Mts* Spain
26C3 **Cordillera Central** *Mts* Dom Rep
79B2 **Cordillera Central** *Mts* Phil
34B2 **Cordillera de Ansita** *Mts* Arg
32B5 **Cordillera de los Andes** *Mts* Peru
30C4 **Cordillera del Toro** *Mt* Arg
32C2 **Cordillera de Mérida** Ven
34A3 **Cordillera de Viento** *Mts* Arg
25D3 **Cordillera Isabelia** *Mts* Nic
32B3 **Cordillera Occidental** *Mts* Colombia
32B3 **Cordillera Oriental** *Mts* Colombia
108B1 **Cordillo Downs** Aust
29D2 **Córdoba** Arg
24C3 **Córdoba** Mexico
50B2 **Córdoba** Spain
29D2 **Córdoba** State, Arg
4D3 **Cordova** USA
Corfu = Kérkira
109D2 **Coricudgy,Mt** Aust
53C3 **Corigliano Calabro** Italy
11B3 **Corinth** Mississippi, USA
31C5 **Corinto** Brazil
45B2 **Cork** County, Irish Rep
41B3 **Cork** Irish Rep
92A1 **Çorlu** Turk
31C5 **Cornel Fabriciano** Brazil
35A2 **Cornelio Procópio** Brazil
7E5 **Corner Brook** Can
109C3 **Corner Inlet** *B* Aust
15C2 **Corning** USA
7C5 **Cornwall** Can
43B4 **Cornwall** County, Eng
43B4 **Cornwall,C** Eng
4H2 **Cornwall I** Can
6A2 **Cornwallis I** Can
32D1 **Coro** Ven
31C2 **Coroatá** Brazil
30C2 **Coroico** Bol
35B1 **Coromandel** Brazil
87C2 **Coromandel Coast** India
110C1 **Coromandel Pen** NZ
110C1 **Coromandel Range** *Mts* NZ
22D4 **Corona** California, USA
13E2 **Coronation** Can
4G3 **Coronation G** Can
34C2 **Coronda** Arg
29B3 **Coronel** Chile
34D3 **Coronel Brandsen** Arg
34C3 **Coronel Dorrego** Arg
35C1 **Coronel Fabriciano** Brazil
30E4 **Coronel Oviedo** Par
29D3 **Coronel Pringles** Arg
34C3 **Coronel Suárez** Arg
34D3 **Coronel Vidal** Arg
30B2 **Coropuna** *Mt* Peru
109C3 **Corowa** Aust
49D3 **Corps** France
9D4 **Corpus Christi** USA
9D4 **Corpus Christi,L** USA
79B3 **Corregidor** *I* Phil
35A1 **Corrente** *R* Mato Grosso, Brazil
30E4 **Corrientes** Arg
30E4 **Corrientes** State, Arg
19B3 **Corrigan** USA
106A4 **Corrigin** Aust
107E2 **Corringe Is** Aust
109C3 **Corryong** Aust
52A2 **Corse** *I* Medit S
42B2 **Corsewall** *Pt* Scot
Corsica = Corse
9D3 **Corsicana** USA
52A2 **Corte** Corse
9C3 **Cortez** USA
52B1 **Cortina d'Ampezzo** Italy
15C2 **Cortland** USA
23A2 **Coruca de Catalan** Mexico
93D1 **Çoruh** *R* Turk
60E5 **Çorum** Turk
30E2 **Corumbá** Brazil
35B1 **Corumba** *R* Brazil
35B1 **Corumbaiba** Brazil
20B2 **Corvallis** USA
96A1 **Corvo** *I* Açores
43C3 **Corwen** Wales
23B2 **Coscomatopec** Mexico
53C3 **Cosenza** Italy
101D1 **Cosmoledo** *Is* Seychelles
34C2 **Cosquín** Arg
51B2 **Costa Blanca** Region, Spain
51C1 **Costa Brava** Region, Spain
50B2 **Costa de la Luz** Region, Spain
50B2 **Costa del Sol** Region, Spain
22D4 **Costa Mesa** USA
25D3 **Costa Rica** Republic, Cent America

79B4 **Cotabato** Phil
30C3 **Cotagaita** Bol
49D3 **Côte d'Azur** Region, France
46C2 **Côtes de Meuse** *Mts* France
97C4 **Cotonou** Benin
32B4 **Cotopaxi** *Mt* Ecuador
43C4 **Cotswold Hills** *Upland* Eng
20B2 **Cottage Grove** USA
56C2 **Cottbus** Germany
108A3 **Couedic,C du** Aust
20C1 **Couer d'Alene L** USA
46B2 **Coulommiers** France
15C1 **Coulonge** *R* Can
22B2 **Coulterville** USA
4B3 **Council** USA
8D2 **Council Bluffs** USA
58C1 **Council Lagoon** *Lg* Lithuania/Russian Fed
47B2 **Courmayeur** Italy
13B3 **Courtenay** Can
Courtrai = Kortrijk
48B2 **Coutances** France
43D3 **Coventry** Eng
50A1 **Covilhã** Spain
17B1 **Covington** Georgia, USA
19B3 **Covington** Louisiana, USA
109C2 **Cowal,L** Aust
108B3 **Cowangie** Aust
15D1 **Cowansville** Can
108A1 **Coward Springs** Aust
108A2 **Cowell** Aust
108C3 **Cowes** Aust
20B1 **Cowichan L** Can
20B1 **Cowiltz** *R* USA
109C2 **Cowra** Aust
30F2 **Coxim** Brazil
16C1 **Coxsackie** USA
86C2 **Cox's Bazar** Bang
22B2 **Coyote** USA
23A2 **Coyuca de Benitez** Mexico
59B2 **Cracow** Pol
100B4 **Cradock** S Africa
8C2 **Craig** USA
57C3 **Crailsheim** Germany
54B2 **Craiova** Rom
15D2 **Cranberry L** USA
5G5 **Cranbrook** Can
20C2 **Crane** Oregon, USA
16D2 **Cranston** USA
20B2 **Crater L** USA
20B2 **Crater Lake Nat Pk** USA
31C3 **Crateus** Brazil
31D3 **Crato** Brazil
14A2 **Crawfordsville** USA
17B1 **Crawfordville** USA
43D4 **Crawley** Eng
5H4 **Cree L** Can
46B2 **Creil** France
47C2 **Crema** Italy
52B1 **Cremona** Italy
46B2 **Crépy-en-Valois** France
52B2 **Cres** *I* Yugos
20B2 **Crescent City** USA
34C2 **Crespo** Arg
13D3 **Creston** Can
18B1 **Creston** USA
17A1 **Crestview** USA
108B3 **Creswick** Aust
47A1 **Crêt de la Neige** *Mt* France
Crete = Kriti
18A1 **Crete** USA
55B3 **Crete,S of** Greece
48C2 **Creuse** *R* France
43C3 **Crewe** Eng
44B3 **Crianlarich** Scot
30G4 **Criciuma** Brazil
44C3 **Crieff** Scot
12G3 **Crillon,Mt** USA
35B1 **Cristalina** Brazil
52C1 **Croatia** Republic, Europe
78D1 **Crocker Range** *Mts* Malay
19A3 **Crockett** USA

106C2 **Croker I** Aust
44C3 **Cromarty** Scot
43E3 **Cromer** Eng
111A3 **Cromwell** NZ
11C4 **Crooked** *I* The Bahamas
13C2 **Crooked** *R* Can
8D2 **Crookston** USA
109C2 **Crookwell** Aust
109D1 **Croppa Creek** Aust
11A3 **Crossett** USA
12G3 **Cross Sd** USA
53C3 **Crotone** Italy
19B3 **Crowley** USA
27K1 **Crown Pt** Tobago
109D1 **Crows Nest** Aust
107D2 **Croydon** Aust
43D4 **Croydon** Eng
104B5 **Crozet Basin** Indian O
4F2 **Crozier Chan** Can
30F4 **Cruz Alta** Brazil
25E3 **Cruz,C** Cuba
29D2 **Cruz del Eje** Arg
35C2 **Cruzeiro** Brazil
32C5 **Cruzeiro do Sul** Brazil
13C1 **Crysdale,Mt** Can
108A2 **Crystal Brook** Aust
18B2 **Crystal City** Missouri, USA
14A1 **Crystal Falls** USA
101C2 **Cuamba** Mozam
100B2 **Cuando** *R* Angola
100A2 **Cuangar** Angola
Cuango,R = Kwango,R
34C2 **Cuarto** *R* Arg
24B2 **Cuauhtémoc** Mexico
23B2 **Cuautla** Mexico
25D2 **Cuba** Republic, Caribbean S
100A2 **Cubango** *R* Angola
100A2 **Cuchi** Angola
100A2 **Cuchi** *R* Angola
34C3 **Cuchillo Có** Arg
32D3 **Cucui** Brazil
32C2 **Cúcuta** Colombia
87B2 **Cuddalore** India
87B2 **Cuddapah** India
106A3 **Cue** Aust
32B4 **Cuenca** Ecuador
51B1 **Cuenca** Spain
24C3 **Cuernavaca** Mexico
19A4 **Cuero** USA
30E2 **Cuiabá** Brazil
30E2 **Cuiabá** *R* Brazil
23B2 **Cuicatlan** Mexico
35C1 **Cuieté** *R* Brazil
44A3 **Cuillin Hills** *Mts* Scot
98B3 **Cuilo** *R* Angola
100A2 **Cuito** *R* Angola
100A2 **Cuito Cunavale** Angola
23A2 **Cuitzeo** Mexico
77D3 **Cu Lao Hon** *I* Viet
109C3 **Culcairn** Aust
109C1 **Culgoa** *R* Aust
24B2 **Culiacán** Mexico
79A3 **Culion** *I* Phil
17A1 **Cullman** USA
47A2 **Culoz** France
15C3 **Culpeper** USA
32J7 **Culpepper** *I* Ecuador
17B2 **Culter Ridge** USA
111B2 **Culverden** NZ
33E1 **Cumaná** Ven
10C3 **Cumberland** Maryland, USA
11B3 **Cumberland** *R* USA
6D3 **Cumberland Pen** Can
6D3 **Cumbernauld Sd** Can
42C2 **Cumbria** Eng
21A2 **Cummings** USA
108A2 **Cummins** Aust
42B2 **Cumnock** Scot
34A3 **Cunco** Chile
100A2 **Cunene** *R* Angola/ Namibia
52A2 **Cuneo** Italy
107D3 **Cunnamulla** Aust
44C3 **Cupar** Scot
54B2 **Čuprija** Serbia, Yugos

27D4 **Curaçao** *I* Caribbean S
34A3 **Curacautin** Chile
34B3 **Curaco** *R* Arg
34A3 **Curanilahue** Chile
34A3 **Curepto** Chile
29B2 **Curicó** Chile
30G4 **Curitiba** Brazil
108A2 **Curnamona** Aust
100A2 **Curoca** *R* Angola
31C5 **Curvelo** Brazil
18A2 **Cushing** USA
13D2 **Cutbank** *R* Can
17B1 **Cuthbert** USA
34B3 **Cutral-Có** Arg
86B2 **Cuttack** India
100A2 **Cuvelai** Angola
56B2 **Cuxhaven** Germany
14B2 **Cuyahoga Falls** USA
79B3 **Cuyo Is** Phil
32C6 **Cuzco** Peru
99C3 **Cyangugu** Zaïre
Cyclades = Kikládhes
13F3 **Cypress Hills** *Mts* Can
92B3 **Cyprus** Republic, Medit S
6D3 **Cyrus Field B** Can
59B3 **Czechoslovakia** Republic, Europe
59B2 **Częstochowa** Pol

D

76C1 **Da** *R* Viet
69E2 **Da'an** China
94C3 **Dab'a** Jordan
27C4 **Dabajuro** Ven
99E2 **Dabaro** Somalia
73B3 **Daba Shan** *Mts* China
99D1 **Dabat** Eth
85C4 **Dabhoi** India
73C3 **Dabie Shan** *Mts* China
97A3 **Dabola** Guinea
97B4 **Dabou** Ivory Coast
59B2 **Dabrowa Gorn** Pol
57C3 **Dachau** Germany
52B1 **Dachstein** *Mt* Austria
73A3 **Dada He** *R* China
17B2 **Dade City** USA
84B3 **Dadhar** Pak
85B3 **Dadu** Pak
68C3 **Dadu He** *R* China
79B3 **Daet** Phil
73B4 **Dafang** China
76B2 **Daga** *R* Burma
99E2 **Dagabur** Eth
97A3 **Dagana** Sen
65F5 **Dagestanskay Respublika,** Russian Fed
79B2 **Dagupan** Phil
92B4 **Dahab** Egypt
63E3 **Da Hinggan Ling** *Mts* China
17B1 **Dahlonega** USA
85C4 **Dāhod** India
51C2 **Dahra** Region, Alg
86A1 **Dailekh** Nepal
34C3 **Daireaux** Arg
69F4 **Daitō** *Is* Pacific O
106C3 **Dajarra** Aust
97A3 **Dakar** Sen
95B2 **Dakhla Oasis** Egypt
97C3 **Dakoro** Niger
54B2 **Dakovica** Serbia, Yugos
54A1 **Dakovo** Croatia
100B2 **Dala** Angola
97A3 **Dalaba** Guinea
72D1 **Dalai Nur** *L* China
68C2 **Dalandzadgad** Mongolia
79B3 **Dalanganem Is** Phil
76D3 **Da Lat** Viet
72A1 **Dalay** Mongolia
107E3 **Dalby** Aust
39F7 **Dalen** Nor
42C2 **Dales,The** *Upland* Eng
17A1 **Daleville** USA
9C3 **Dalhart** USA
4E2 **Dalhousie,C** Can

72E2 **Dalian** China
9D3 **Dallas** USA
20B1 **Dalles,The** USA
5E4 **Dall I** USA
86A2 **Dalli Rajhara** India
97C3 **Dallol** *R* Niger
97C3 **Dallol Bosso** *R* Niger
52C2 **Dalmatia** *Region* Bosnia & Herzegovina, Yugos
69F2 **Dal'nerechensk** Russian Fed
97B4 **Daloa** Ivory Coast
73B4 **Dalou Shan** *Mts* China
86A2 **Dāltenganj** India
17B1 **Dalton** Georgia, USA
16C1 **Dalton** Massachusetts, USA
106C2 **Daly** *R* Aust
21A2 **Daly City** USA
106C2 **Daly Waters** Aust
79B4 **Damaguete** Phil
85C4 **Damān** India
92B3 **Damanhūr** Egypt
71D4 **Damar** *I* Indon
98B2 **Damara** CAR
92C3 **Damascus** Syria
16A3 **Damascus** USA
97D3 **Damaturu** Nig
90B2 **Damavand** Iran
98B3 **Damba** Angola
87C3 **Dambulla** Sri Lanka
90B2 **Damghan** Iran
85D4 **Damoh** India
99E2 **Damot** Eth
94B2 **Damour** Leb
106A3 **Dampier** Aust
94B3 **Daná** Jordan
22C2 **Dana,Mt** USA
97B4 **Danané** Lib
76D2 **Da Nang** Viet
79B3 **Danao** Phil
70A3 **Danau Tobu** *L* Indon
71D4 **Danau Tuwuti** *L* Indon
73A3 **Danbu** China
15D2 **Danbury** USA
86A1 **Dandeldhura** Nepal
87A1 **Dandeli** India
108C3 **Dandenong** Aust
74A2 **Dandong** China
100A4 **Danger Pt** S Africa
99D1 **Dangila** Eth
6D1 **Danguard Jenson Land** *Region* Can
7E4 **Daniels Harbour** Can
6G3 **Dannebrogs Øy** *I* Greenland
110C2 **Dannevirke** NZ
87C1 **Dantewära** India
Danube = Donau
10B2 **Danville** Illinois, USA
11B3 **Danville** Kentucky, USA
16A2 **Danville** Pennsylvania, USA
11C3 **Danville** Virginia, USA
Danzig = Gdańsk
73C4 **Dao Xian** China
73B4 **Daozhen** China
79B4 **Dapiak,Mt** Phil
79B4 **Dapitan** Phil
68B3 **Da Qaidam** China
69E2 **Daqing** China
94C2 **Dar'a** Syria
91B4 **Dārāb** Iran
95A1 **Daraj** Libya
90B3 **Dārān** Iran
92C3 **Dar'a Salkhad** Syria
86B1 **Darbhanga** India
22C1 **Dardanelle** USA
18B2 **Dardanelle,L** USA
Dar-el-Beida = Casablanca
99D3 **Dar es Salaam** Tanz
110B1 **Dargaville** NZ
17B1 **Darien** USA
Darjeeling = Dārjiling
86B1 **Dārjiling** India
107D4 **Darling** *R* Aust
109C1 **Darling Downs** Aust
6C1 **Darling Pen** Can

108B2 **Darlington** Aust
42D2 **Darlington** Eng
17C1 **Darlington** USA
5/R3 **Darmstadt** Germany
95B1 **Darnah** Libya
108B2 **Darnick** Aust
4F3 **Darnley B** Can
112C10 **Darnley,C** Ant
51B1 **Daroca** Spain
98C2 **Dar Rounga** Region, CAR
43C4 **Dart** R Eng
41C3 **Dartmoor** Moorland Eng
43C4 **Dartmoor Nat Pk** Eng
7D5 **Dartmouth** Can
43C4 **Dartmouth** Eng
107D1 **Daru** PNG
52C1 **Daruvar** Croatia
106C2 **Darwin** Aust
91B4 **Daryacheh-ye Bakhtegan** L Iran
91B4 **Daryacheh-ye Maharlu** L Iran
90B3 **Daryacheh-ye Namak** Salt Flat Iran
90D3 **Daryacheh-ye-Sistan** Salt L Iran/Afghan
91B4 **Daryacheh-ye Tashk** L Iran
80C2 **Daryacheh-ye Orumiyeh** L Iran
91C4 **Darzin** Iran
91B4 **Das** I UAE
73C3 **Dashennonglia** Mt China
90C2 **Dasht** Iran
90B3 **Dasht-e-Kavir** Salt Desert Iran
90C3 **Dasht-e Lut** Salt Desert Iran
90D3 **Dasht-e Naomid** Desert Region Iran
85D3 **Datia** India
72A2 **Datong** China
72C1 **Datong** China
72A2 **Datong He** R China
79B4 **Datu Piang** Phil
39K7 **Daugava** R Latvia
60C2 **Daugavpils** Latvia
6D1 **Dauguard Jensen Land** Greenland
84A1 **Daulatabad** Afghan
85D3 **Daulpur** India
46D1 **Daun** Germany
87A1 **Daund** India
5H4 **Dauphin** Can
16A2 **Dauphin** USA
49D2 **Dauphiné** Region, France
97C3 **Daura** Nig
85D3 **Dausa** India
87B2 **Davangere** India
79C4 **Davao** Phil
79C4 **Davao G** Phil
22A2 **Davenport** California, USA
10A2 **Davenport** Iowa, USA
32A2 **David** Panama
4D3 **Davidson Mts** USA
21A2 **Davis** USA
112C10 **Davis Base** Ant
7D4 **Davis Inlet** Can
6E3 **Davis Str** Greenland/Can
61J3 **Davlekanovo** Russian Fed
47C1 **Davos** Switz
99E2 **Dawa** R Eth
73A4 **Dawan** China
84B2 **Dawat Yar** Afghan
91B4 **Dawhat Salwah** B Qatar/S Arabia
76B2 **Dawna Range** Mts Burma
4E3 **Dawson** Can
17B1 **Dawson** Georgia, USA
107D3 **Dawson** R Aust
5F4 **Dawson Creek** Can
13D2 **Dawson,Mt** Can
12G2 **Dawson Range** Mts Can

73A3 **Dawu** China
73C3 **Dawu** China
48B3 **Dax** France
73B3 **Daxian** China
73B5 **Daxin** China
73A3 **Daxue Shan** Mts China
73C4 **Dayong** China
94C2 **Dayr'Ali** Syria
94C1 **Dayr'Atiyah** Syria
93D2 **Dayr az Zawr** Syria
10B3 **Dayton** Ohio, USA
19B4 **Dayton** Texas, USA
20C1 **Dayton** Washington, USA
11B4 **Daytona Beach** USA
73C4 **Dayu** China
78D3 **Dayu** Indon
72D2 **Da Yunhe** R China
20C2 **Dayville** USA
73B3 **Dazhu** China
100B4 **De Aar** S Africa
26C2 **Deadman's Cay** The Bahamas
92C3 **Dead S** Israel/Jordan
46A1 **Deal** Eng
101G1 **Dealesville** S Africa
13B2 **Dean** R Can
13B2 **Dean Chan** Can
34C2 **Deán Funes** Arg
14B2 **Dearborn** USA
4F3 **Dease Arm** B Can
4E4 **Dease Lake** Can
9B3 **Death V** USA
48C2 **Deauville** France
97B4 **Debakala** Ivory Coast
12B2 **Debauch Mt** USA
27L1 **Débé** Trinidad
59C2 **Debica** Pol
58C2 **Deblin** Pol
97B3 **Débo,L** Mali
59C3 **Debrecen** Hung
99D2 **Debre Birhan** Eth
99D1 **Debre Markos** Eth
99D1 **Debre Tabor** Eth
11B3 **Decatur** Alabama, USA
17B1 **Decatur** Georgia, USA
10B3 **Decatur** Illinois, USA
14B2 **Decatur** Indiana, USA
48C3 **Decazeville** France
73A4 **Dechang** China
97B3 **Dédougou** Burkina
101C2 **Dedza** Malawi
42B2 **Dee** R Dumfries and Galloway, Scot
42C3 **Dee** R Eng/Wales
44C3 **Dee** R Grampian, Scot
15C1 **Deep River** Can
16C2 **Deep River** USA
109D1 **Deepwater** Aust
7E5 **Deer Lake** Can
8B2 **Deer Lodge** USA
34D3 **Defferrari** Arg
17A1 **De Funiak Springs** USA
68B3 **Dêgê** China
99E1 **Degeh Bur** Eth
106A3 **De Grey** R Aust
91B3 **Deh Bid** Iran
84B1 **Dehi** Afghan
96D1 **Dehibat** Tunisia
87B3 **Dehiwala-Mt Lavinia** Sri Lanka
90A3 **Dehloran** Iran
84D2 **Dehra Dun** India
86A2 **Dehri** India
98C2 **Deim Zubeir** Sudan
94B2 **Deir Abu Sa'id** Jordan
94C1 **Deir el Ahmar** Leb
60B4 **Dej** Rom
19B3 **De Kalb** Texas, USA
63G2 **De Kastri** Russian Fed
98C3 **Dekese** Zaïre
98B2 **Dekoa** CAR
106B1 **Dekusi** Indon
9B3 **Delano** USA
10C3 **Delaware** State, USA
14B2 **Delaware** USA

15C2 **Delaware** R USA
10C3 **Delaware B** USA
109C3 **Delegate** Aust
47B1 **Delemont** Switz
101D2 **Delgado** C Mozam
84D3 **Delhi** India
15D2 **Delhi** New York, USA
97B1 **Delice** Turk
24B2 **Delicias** Mexico
90B3 **Delijan** Iran
47B1 **Delle** France
22D4 **Del Mar** USA
39F8 **Delmenhorst** Germany
4B3 **De Long** Mts USA
109C4 **Deloraine** Aust
5H5 **Deloraine** Can
17B2 **Delray Beach** USA
9C4 **Del Rio** USA
8B3 **Delta** USA
12E2 **Delta** R USA
12E2 **Delta Junction** USA
99D2 **Dembi Dolo** Eth
46C1 **Demer** R Belg
9C3 **Deming** USA
54C2 **Demirköy** Turk
49C1 **Denain** France
82A2 **Denau** Uzbekistan
42C3 **Denbigh** Wales
12B2 **Denbigh,C** USA
78B3 **Dendang** Indon
46C1 **Dendermond** Belg
99D2 **Dendi** Mt Eth
46B1 **Dèndre** R Belg
72B1 **Dengkou** China
72C3 **Deng Xian** China
Den Haag = 's-Gravenhage
27H1 **Denham,Mt** Jamaica
56A2 **Den Helder** Neth
51C2 **Denia** Spain
107D4 **Deniliquin** Aust
20C2 **Denio** USA
9D3 **Denison** Texas, USA
12D3 **Denison,Mt** USA
92A2 **Denizli** Turk
39F7 **Denmark Kingdom, Europe**
1C1 **Denmark Str** Greenland/Iceland
27P2 **Dennery** St Lucia
78D4 **Denpasar** Indon
16B3 **Denton** Maryland, USA
9D3 **Denton** Texas, USA
107E1 **D'Entrecasteaux Is** PNG
47B1 **Dents du Midi** Mt Switz
8C3 **Denver** USA
98B2 **Déo** R Cam
86B2 **Deoghar** India
85C5 **Deolāli** India
84D1 **Deosai Plain** India
95B3 **Dépression du Mourdi** Chad
19B3 **De Queen** USA
84C3 **Dera** Pak
84B3 **Dera Bugti** Pak
84C2 **Dera Ismail Khan** Pak
106B2 **Derby** Aust
16C2 **Derby** Connecticut, USA
43D3 **Derby** County, Eng
43D3 **Derby** Eng
18A2 **Derby** Kansas, USA
60E3 **Dergachi** Ukraine
19B3 **De Ridder** USA
Derna = Darnah
95C3 **Derudeb** Sudan
109C4 **Derwent Bridge** Aust
34B2 **Desaguadero** Arg
34B2 **Desaguadero** R Arg
30C2 **Desaguadero** R Bol
21B3 **Descanso** Mexico
20B2 **Deschutes** R USA
99D1 **Desë** Eth
29C5 **Deseado** Arg
29C5 **Deseado** R Arg
47D2 **Desenzano** Italy
96A1 **Deserta Grande** I Medeira
30C4 **Desierto de Atacama** Desert Chile

18B2 **Desloge** USA
10A2 **Des Moines** Iowa, USA
60D3 **Desna** R Russian Fed
29B6 **Desolación** I Chile
14A2 **Des Plaines** USA
56C2 **Dessau** Germany
12G2 **Destruction Bay** Can
46A1 **Desvres** France
54B1 **Deta** Rom
100B2 **Dete** Zim
10B2 **Detroit** USA
76D3 **Det Udom** Thai
54B1 **Deva** Rom
56B2 **Deventer** Neth
44C3 **Deveron** R Scot
85C3 **Devikot** India
22C2 **Devil Postpile Nat Mon** USA
22C1 **Devils Gate** P USA
Devil's Island = Isla du Diable
8D2 **Devils Lake** USA
12H3 **Devils Paw** Mt Can
43D4 **Devizes** Eng
85D3 **Devli** India
55B2 **Devoll** R Alb
43B4 **Devon** County, Eng
6A2 **Devon I** Can
107D5 **Devonport** Aust
86C1 **Dewangiri** Bhutan
85D4 **Dewās** India
101G1 **Dewetsdorp** S Africa
11B3 **Dewey Res** USA
19B3 **De Witt** USA
18C2 **Dexter** Missouri, USA
73A3 **Deyang** China
90C3 **Deyhuk** Iran
90A3 **Dezful** Iran
72D2 **Dezhou** China
90A2 **Dezh Shahpur** Iran
91B4 **Dhahran** S Arabia
86C2 **Dhākā** Bang
87B2 **Dhamavaram** India
86A2 **Dhamtari** India
86B2 **Dhanbād** India
86A1 **Dhangarhi** Nepal
86B1 **Dhankuta** Nepal
85D4 **Dhār** India
87B2 **Dharmapuri** India
84D2 **Dharmsāla** India
97B3 **Dhar Oualata** Desert Region Maur
86A1 **Dhaulagiri** Mt Nepal
86B2 **Dhenkānai** India
94B3 **Dhibah** Jordan
55C3 **Dhikti Óri** Mt Greece
55C3 **Dhodhekánisos** Is Greece
55B3 **Dhomokós** Greece
87B1 **Dhone** India
85C4 **Dhoraji** India
85C4 **Dhrāngadhra** India
86B1 **Dhuburi** India
85C4 **Dhule** India
22B2 **Diablo,Mt** USA
21A2 **Diablo Range** Mts USA
34C2 **Diamante** Arg
34B2 **Diamante** R Arg
31C5 **Diamantina** Brazil
107D3 **Diamantina** R Aust
86B2 **Diamond Harbours** India
22B1 **Diamond Springs** USA
91C4 **Dibā** UAE
98C3 **Dibaya** Zaïre
86C1 **Dibrugarh** India
8C2 **Dickinson** USA
15C2 **Dickson City** USA
92D2 **Dicle** R Turk
13E2 **Didsbury** Can
85C3 **Didwāna** India
97B3 **Diebougou** Burkina
46D2 **Diekirch** Lux
97B3 **Diéma** Mali
76C1 **Dien Bien Phu** Viet
56B2 **Diepholz** Germany
48C2 **Dieppe** France
46C1 **Diest** Belg
46D2 **Dieuze** France
7D5 **Digby** Can

49D3 **Digne** France
49C2 **Digoin** France
79C4 **Digos** Phil
71E4 **Digul** R Indon
86C1 **Dihang** R India
Dijlah = Tigris
49C2 **Dijon** France
98B2 **Dik** Chad
99E1 **Dikhil** Djibouti
46B1 **Diksmuide** Belg
18I0 **Dikson** Russian Fed
82A2 **Dilaram** Afghan
106B1 **Dili** Indon
76D3 **Di Linh** Viet
46E1 **Dillenburg** Germany
99C1 **Dilling** Sudan
12C3 **Dillingham** USA
8B2 **Dillon** USA
16A2 **Dillsburg** USA
100B2 **Dilolo** Zaïre
Dimashq = Damascus
98C3 **Dimbelenge** Zaïre
97B4 **Dimbokro** Ivory Coast
54C2 **Dimitrovgrad** Bulg
61G3 **Dimitrovgrad** Russian Fed
94B3 **Dimona** Israel
86C1 **Dimpāpur** India
79C3 **Dinagat** I Phil
86B1 **Dinajpur** India
48B2 **Dinan** France
46C1 **Dinant** Belg
92B2 **Dinar** Turk
99D1 **Dinder** R Sudan
87B2 **Dindigul** India
72B2 **Dingbian** China
86B1 **Dinggyē** China
41A3 **Dingle** Irish Rep
41A3 **Dingle** B Irish Rep
97A3 **Dinguiraye** Guinea
44B3 **Dingwall** Scot
72A2 **Dingxi** China
72D2 **Ding Xian** China
76D1 **Dinh Lap** Viet
22C2 **Dinuba** USA
97A3 **Diouloulou** Sen
86C1 **Diphu** India
99E2 **Dirē Dawa** Eth
106A3 **Dirk Hartog** I Aust
95A3 **Dirkou** Niger
109C1 **Dirranbandi** Aust
99E2 **Dirri** Somalia
29G8 **Disappointment,C** South Georgia
20B1 **Disappointment,C** USA
106B3 **Disappointment,L** Aust
108B3 **Discovery B** Aust
103J7 **Discovery Tablemount** Atlantic O
47C1 **Disentis Muster** Switz
6E3 **Disko** Greenland
6E3 **Disko Bugt** B Greenland
6E3 **Diskorjord** Greenland
58D1 **Disna** R Belorussia
35B1 **Distrito Federal** Federal District, Brazil
85C4 **Diu** India
79C4 **Diuat Mts** Phil
31C6 **Divinópolis** Brazil
61F4 **Divnoye** Russian Fed
93C2 **Divriği** Turk
22B1 **Dixon** California, USA
5E4 **Dixon Entrance** Sd Can/USA
13D1 **Dixonville** Can
93E3 **Diyālā** R Iraq
65F6 **Diyarbakir** Turk
90A3 **Diz** R Iran
98B2 **Dja** R Cam
96C1 **Djadi** R Alg
95A2 **Djado,Plat du** Niger
98B3 **Djambala** Congo
96C2 **Djanet** Alg
50A2 **Djebel Bouhalla** Mt Mor
96C1 **Djelfa** Alg
98C2 **Djéma** CAR

97B3 **Djenné** Mali
97B3 **Djibo** Burkina
99E1 **Djibouti** Djibouti
99E1 **Djibouti** Republic, E Africa
98C2 **Djolu** Zaïre
97C4 **Djougou** Benin
99D2 **Djugu** Zaïre
38C2 **Djúpivogur** Iceland
51C2 **Djurdjura** Mts Alg
60E2 **Dmitrov** Russian Fed
60D4 **Dnepr** R Ukraine
60D4 **Dneprodzerzhinsk** Ukraine
60E4 **Dnepropetrovsk** Ukraine
60C3 **Dneprovskaya Nizmennost'** Region, Belorussia
60B4 **Dnestr** R Ukraine
60D2 **Dno** Russian Fed
98B2 **Doba** Chad
58C1 **Dobele** Latvia
34C3 **Doblas** Arg
71E4 **Dobo** Indon
54A2 **Doboj** Bosnia & Herzegovina, Yugos
54B2 **Dobreta-Turnu-Severin** Rom
54C2 **Dobrich** Bulg
60D3 **Dobrush** Belorussia
31C5 **Doce** R Brazil
30D3 **Doctor R P Peña** Arg
87B2 **Dod** India
87B2 **Doda Betta** Mt India
Dodecanese = Sporádhes
9C3 **Dodge City** USA
99D3 **Dodoma** Tanz
75A1 **Dōgo** I Japan
97C3 **Dogondoutchi** Niger
93D2 **Doğubayazit** Turk
91B4 **Doha** Qatar
7C5 **Dolbeau** Can
49D2 **Dôle** France
43C3 **Dolgellau** Wales
47D1 **Dolomitiche** Mts Italy
99E2 **Dolo Odo** Eth
29E3 **Dolores** Arg
34D2 **Dolores** Urug
23A1 **Dolores Hidalgo** Mexico
4G3 **Dolphin and Union Str** Can
29E6 **Dolphin,C** Falkland Is
71E4 **Dom** Mt Indon
65G4 **Dombarovskiy** Russian Fed
38F6 **Dombas** Nor
46D2 **Dombasle-sur-Meurthe** France
54A1 **Dombóvár** Hung
48B2 **Domfront** France
27E3 **Dominica** I Caribbean S
27C3 **Dominican Republic** Caribbean S
6C3 **Dominion,C** Can
7E4 **Domino** Can
68D1 **Domna** Russian Fed
52A1 **Domodossola** Italy
78D4 **Dompu** Indon
29B3 **Domuyo** Mt Arg
109D1 **Domville,Mt** Aust
44C3 **Don** R Scot
61F4 **Don** R Russian Fed
45C1 **Donaghadee** N Ire
57C3 **Donau** R Germany
57C3 **Donauwörth** Germany
50A2 **Don Benito** Spain
42D3 **Doncaster** Eng
98B3 **Dondo** Angola
101C2 **Dondo** Mozam
87C3 **Dondra Head** C Sri Lanka
45B1 **Donegal** County, Irish Rep
40B3 **Donegal** Irish Rep
40B3 **Donegal** B Irish Rep
45B1 **Donegal Mts** Irish Rep
60E4 **Donetsk** Ukraine
73C4 **Dong'an** China

106A3 **Dongara** Aust
73A4 **Dongchuan** China
76D2 **Dongfang** China
74B2 **Dongfeng** China
70C4 **Donggala** Indon
68B3 **Donggi Cona** L China
74A3 **Donggou** China
73C5 **Donghai Dao** I China
72A1 **Dong He** R China
76D2 **Dong Hoi** Viet
73C5 **Dong Jiang** R China
95C3 **Dongola** Sudan
73D5 **Dongshan** China
68D4 **Dongsha Qundao** I China
72C2 **Dongsheng** China
72E3 **Dongtai** China
73C4 **Dongting Hu** L China
73B5 **Dongxing** China
73D3 **Dongzhi** China
18B2 **Doniphan** USA
52C2 **Donji Vakuf** Bosnia & Herzegovina, Yugos
38G5 **Dönna** I Nor
21A2 **Donner** P USA
46D2 **Donnersberg** Mt Germany
101G1 **Donnybrook** S Africa
Donostia = San Sebastian
22B2 **Don Pedro Res** USA
12D1 **Doonerak,Mt** USA
79B4 **Dopolong** Phil
73A3 **Do Qu** R China
47B2 **Dora Baltea** R Italy
49D2 **Dorbirn** Austria
43C4 **Dorchester** Eng
6C3 **Dorchester,C** Can
48C2 **Dordogne** R France
56A2 **Dordrecht** Neth
13F2 **Dore** R Can
13F2 **Dore Lake** Can
97B3 **Dori** Burkina
46B2 **Dormans** France
57B3 **Dornbirn** Austria
44B3 **Dornoch** Scot
44B3 **Dornoch Firth** Estuary Scot
38H6 **Dorotea** Sweden
109D2 **Dorrigo** Aust
20B2 **Dorris** USA
43C4 **Dorset** County, Eng
46D1 **Dorsten** Germany
56B2 **Dortmund** Germany
98C2 **Doruma** Zaïre
63D2 **Dosatuy** Russian Fed
84B1 **Doshi** Afghan
22B2 **Dos Palos** USA
97C3 **Dosso** Niger
65G5 **Dossor** Kazakhstan
11B3 **Dothan** USA
49C1 **Douai** France
98A2 **Douala** France
109D1 **Double Island Pt** Aust
49D2 **Doubs** R France
111A3 **Doubtful Sd** NZ
97B3 **Douentza** Mali
9C3 **Douglas** Arizona, USA
42B2 **Douglas** Eng
17B1 **Douglas** Georgia, USA
8C2 **Douglas** Wyoming, USA
12A1 **Douglas,C** USA
13B2 **Douglas Chan** Can
12D3 **Douglas,Mt** USA
46B1 **Doullens** France
45C1 **Doun** County, N Ire
30F3 **Dourados** Brazil
50A1 **Douro** R Port
15C3 **Dover** Delaware, USA
43E4 **Dover** Eng
15D2 **Dover** New Hampshire, USA
16B2 **Dover** New Jersey, USA
14B2 **Dover** Ohio, USA
43D3 **Dover** R Eng
41D3 **Dover,Str of** UK/ France

16B3 **Downington** USA
42B2 **Downpatrick** N Ire
13C2 **Downton,Mt** Can
16B2 **Doylestown** USA
75A1 **Dōzen** I Japan
96A2 **Dr'aa** R Mor
35A2 **Dracena** Brazil
16D1 **Dracut** USA
49D3 **Draguignan** France
101C3 **Drakensberg** Mts S Africa
101G1 **Drakensberg** Mt S Africa
103E7 **Drake Pass** Pacific/ Atlantic O
55B2 **Dráma** Greece
39G7 **Drammen** Nor
38A1 **Drangajökull** Iceland
52C1 **Drava** R Slovenia
13D2 **Drayton Valley** Can
49C2 **Dreaux** France
57C2 **Dresden** Germany
48C2 **Dreux** France
20C2 **Drewsey** USA
54B2 **Drin** R Alb
54A2 **Drina** R Bosnia & Herzegovina/Serbia
58D1 **Drissa** R Belorussia
45C2 **Drogheda** Irish Rep
59C3 **Drogobych** Ukraine
112B12 **Dronning Maud Land** Region, Ant
30D3 **Dr P.P. Pená** Par
5G4 **Drumheller** Can
14B1 **Drummond I** USA
15D1 **Drummondville** Can
58C2 **Druskininksi** Lithuania
12G3 **Dry B** USA
7A5 **Dryden** Can
27H1 **Dry Harbour Mts** Jamaica
76B3 **Duang** I Burma
91C4 **Dubai** UAE
5H3 **Dubawnt** R Can
4H3 **Dubawnt L** Can
107D4 **Dubbo** Aust
45C2 **Dublin** County, Irish Rep
45C2 **Dublin** Irish Rep
17B1 **Dublin** USA
60E2 **Dubna** Russian Fed
60C3 **Dubno** Ukraine
15C2 **Du Bois** USA
13B2 **Dubose,Mt** Can
58D2 **Dubrovica** Ukraine
54A2 **Dubrovnik** Croatia
10A2 **Dubuque** USA
46D2 **Dudelange** Lux
1C10 **Dudinka** Russian Fed
43C3 **Dudley** Eng
97B4 **Duekoué** Ivory Coast
50B1 **Duero** R Spain
44C3 **Dufftown** Scot
52B2 **Dugi Otok** I Croatia
56B2 **Duisburg** Germany
93E3 **Dūkan** Iraq
99D2 **Duk Faiwil** Sudan
91B4 **Dukhān** Qatar
73A4 **Dukou** China
68B3 **Dulan** China
34C2 **Dulce** R Arg
78C2 **Dulit Range** Mts Malay
86C2 **Dullabchara** India
10A2 **Duluth** USA
94C2 **Dūmā** Syria
78A2 **Dumai** Indon
79A3 **Dumaran** I Phil
9C3 **Dumas** USA
94C2 **Dumayr** Syria
42B2 **Dumbarton** Scot
42C2 **Dumfries** Scot
42B2 **Dumfries and Galloway** Region, Scot
86B2 **Dumka** India
15C1 **Dumoine,L** Can
112C8 **Dumont d'Urville** Base Ant
95C1 **Dumyat** Egypt
54C2 **Dunărea** R Rom
45C2 **Dunary Head** Pt Irish Rep

54B2 **Dunav** *R* Bulg
59D3 **Dunayevtsy** Ukraine
13C3 **Duncan** Can
16A2 **Duncannon** USA
44C2 **Duncansby Head** *Pt* Scot
45C1 **Dundalk** Irish Rep
16A3 **Dundalk** USA
45C2 **Dundalk B** Irish Rep
6D2 **Dundas** Greenland
4G2 **Dundas Pen** Can
71E5 **Dundas Str** Aust
101H1 **Dundee** S Africa
44C3 **Dundee** Scot
108B1 **Dundoo** Aust
42B2 **Dundrum** *B* N Ire
111B3 **Dunedin** NZ
17B2 **Dunedin** USA
109C2 **Dunedoo** Aust
44C3 **Dunfermline** Scot
85C4 **Dungarpur** India
45C2 **Dungarvan** Irish Rep
43E4 **Dungeness** Eng
109D2 **Dungog** Aust
99C2 **Dungu** Zaïre
95C2 **Dungunab** Sudan
68B2 **Dunhuang** China
46B1 **Dunkerque** France
10C2 **Dunkirk** USA
99D1 **Dunkur** Eth
97B4 **Dunkwa** Ghana
41B3 **Dun Laoghaire** Irish Rep
45B3 **Dunmanway** Irish Rep
26B1 **Dunmore Town** The Bahamas
44C2 **Dunnet Head** *Pt* Scot
42C2 **Duns** Scot
20B2 **Dunsmuir** USA
111A2 **Dunstan Mts** NZ
46C2 **Dun-sur-Meuse** France
72D1 **Duolun** China
18C2 **Du Quoin** USA
94B3 **Dura** Israel
49D3 **Durance** *R* France
24B2 **Durango** Mexico
50B1 **Durango** Spain
9C3 **Durango** USA
29E2 **Durano** Urug
9D3 **Durant** USA
94C1 **Duraykīsh** Syria
101H1 **Durban** S Africa
46D1 **Duren** Germany
86A2 **Durg** India
86B2 **Durgapur** India
42D2 **Durham** County, Eng
42D2 **Durham** Eng
11C3 **Durham** N Carolina, USA
16D1 **Durham** New Hampshire, USA
108B1 **Durham Downs** Aust
54A2 **Durmitor** *Mt* Montenegro, Yugos
44B2 **Durness** Scot
55A2 **Durrës** Alb
108B1 **Durrie** Aust
45A3 **Dursey** *I* Irish Rep
55C3 **Dursunbey** Turk
110B2 **D'Urville I** NZ
90D2 **Dushak** Turkmenistan
73B4 **Dushan** China
82A2 **Dushanbe** Tajikistan
111A3 **Dusky Sd** NZ
56B2 **Düsseldorf** Germany
73B4 **Duyun** China
92B1 **Düzce** Turk
60C2 **Dvina** *R* Latvia
85B4 **Dwārka** India
6D3 **Dyer,C** Can
11B3 **Dyersburg** USA
43B3 **Dyfed** County, Wales
61F5 **Dykh Tau** *Mt* Russian Fed
108B1 **Dynevor Downs** Aust
68B2 **Dzag** Mongolia
63C3 **Dzamin Uüd** Mongolia
101D2 **Dzaoudzi** Mayotte
68C2 **Dzarnïn Uüd** Mongolia
68B2 **Dzavhan Gol** *R* Mongolia
80E1 **Dzehezkazgan** Kazakhstan
61F2 **Dzerzhinsk** Russian Fed
63E2 **Dzhalinda** Russian Fed
65J5 **Dzhambul** Kazakhstan
60D4 **Dzhankoy** Ukraine
65H4 **Dzhezkazgan** Kazakhstan
84B1 **Dzhilikul'** Tajikistan
65J5 **Dzhungarskiy Alatau** *Mts* Kazakhstan
59B2 **Dzierzoniow** Pol
63B3 **Dzüyl** Mongolia
82C1 **Dzungaria** Basin, China

E

7B4 **Eabamet L** Can
12F2 **Eagle** Alaska, USA
20B2 **Eagle L** California, USA
19A3 **Eagle Mountain L** USA
9C4 **Eagle Pass** USA
4E3 **Eagle Plain** Can
12E2 **Eagle River** USA
21B2 **Earlimart** USA
17B1 **Easley** USA
15C2 **East Aurora** USA
43E4 **Eastbourne** Eng
14A2 **East Chicago** USA
69E3 **East China Sea** China/Japan
83B4 **Eastern Ghats** *Mts* India
29E6 **East Falkland** *I* Falkland Is
12E1 **East Fork** *R* USA
21B2 **Eastgate** USA
16C1 **Easthampton** USA
16C2 **East Hampton** USA
14A2 **East Lake** USA
14B2 **East Liverpool** USA
100B4 **East London** S Africa
7C4 **Eastmain** Can
7C4 **Eastmain** *R* Can
17B1 **Eastman** USA
15C3 **Easton** Maryland, USA
15C2 **Easton** Pennsylvania, USA
16B2 **East Orange** USA
105L4 **East Pacific Ridge** Pacific O
17B1 **East Point** USA
42D3 **East Retford** Eng
11A3 **East St Louis** USA
1B7 **East Siberian S** Russian Fed
43E4 **East Sussex** County, Eng
17B1 **Eatonton** USA
10A2 **Eau Claire** USA
71F3 **Eauripik** *I* Pacific O
23B1 **Ebano** Mexico
98B2 **Ebebiyin** Eq Guinea
56C2 **Eberswalde** Germany
73A4 **Ebian** China
65K5 **Ebinur** *L* China
53C2 **Eboli** Italy
98B2 **Ebolowa** Cam
51B1 **Ebro** *R* Spain
92A1 **Eceabat** Turk
96C1 **Ech Cheliff** Alg
72D2 **Eching** China
20C1 **Echo** USA
4G3 **Echo Bay** Can
46D2 **Echternach** Lux
108B3 **Echuca** Aust
50A2 **Ecija** Spain
6B2 **Eclipse Sd** Can
32B4 **Ecuador** Republic, S America
99E1 **Ed** Eth
44C2 **Eday** *I* Scot
98C1 **Ed Da'ein** Sudan
95C3 **Ed Damer** Sudan
95C3 **Ed Debba** Sudan
44B2 **Eddrachillis** *B* Scot
99D1 **Ed Dueim** Sudan
109C4 **Eddystone Pt** Aust
98A2 **Edea** Cam
109C3 **Eden** Aust
42C2 **Eden** *R* Eng
101G1 **Edenburg** S Africa
111A3 **Edendale** NZ
46E2 **Edenkoben** Germany
46E1 **Eder** *R* Germany
6D3 **Edgell I** Can
64D2 **Edgeøya** *I* Barents S
16A3 **Edgewood** USA
94B3 **Edh Dhahiriya** Israel
55B2 **Edhessa** Greece
44C3 **Edinburgh** Scot
60C5 **Edirne** Turk
17B1 **Edisto** *R* USA
13D2 **Edith Cavell,Mt** Can
20B1 **Edmonds** USA
5G4 **Edmonton** Can
7D5 **Edmundston** Can
19A4 **Edna** USA
12H3 **Edna Bay** USA
52B1 **Edolo** Italy
94B3 **Edom** Region, Jordan
92A2 **Edremit** Turk
55C3 **Edremit Körfezi** *B* Turk
68B2 **Edrengiyn Nuruu** *Mts* Mongolia
5G4 **Edson** Can
34C3 **Eduardo Castex** Arg
12J2 **Eduni,Mt** Can
108B3 **Edward** *R* Aust
99C3 **Edward,L** Uganda/Zaïre
108A1 **Edwards Creek** Aust
9C3 **Edwards Plat** USA
18C2 **Edwardsville** USA
12H3 **Edziza,Mt** Can
12B2 **Eek** USA
46B1 **Eeklo** Belg
10B3 **Effingham** USA
6E3 **Egedesminde** Greenland
12C3 **Egegik** USA
59C3 **Eger** Hung
39F7 **Egersund** Nor
16B3 **Egg Harbor City** USA
4G2 **Eglinton I** Can
110B1 **Egmont,C** NZ
110B1 **Egmont,Mt** NZ
92B2 **Eğridir Gölü** *L* Turk
95B2 **Egypt** Republic, Africa
50B1 **Eibar** Spain
49C2 **Eibeuf** France
46D1 **Eifel** Region, Germany
44A3 **Eigg** *I* Scot
83B5 **Eight Degree Chan** Indian O
106B2 **Eighty Mile Beach** Aust
108C3 **Eildon,L** Aust
56B2 **Eindhoven** Neth
47C1 **Einsiedeln** Switz
94B3 **Ein Yahav** Israel
57C2 **Eisenach** Germany
57C3 **Eisenerz** Austria
46D1 **Eitorf** Germany
72A1 **Ejin qi** China
23B2 **Ejutla** Mexico
110C2 **Eketahuna** NZ
65J4 **Ekibastuz** Kazakhstan
63F2 **Ekimchan** Russian Fed
92B3 **Ek Mahalla el Kubra** Egypt
39H7 **Eksjo** Sweden
10B1 **Ekwen** *R* Can
92A3 **El'Alamein** Egypt
92B3 **El'Arîsh** Egypt
92B4 **Elat** Israel
95B3 **El'Atrun Oasis** Sudan
93C2 **Elazig** Turk
92C3 **El Azraq** Jordan
52B2 **Elba** *I* Italy
95C2 **El Balyana** Egypt
32C2 **El Banco** Colombia
55B2 **Elbasan** Alb
27D5 **El Baúl** Ven
57C2 **Elbe** *R* Germany
94C1 **El Bega'a** *R* Leb
14A2 **Elberta** USA
8C3 **Elbert,Mt** USA
17B1 **Elberton** USA
92C2 **Elbistan** Turk
58B2 **Elblag** Pol
29B4 **El Bolson** Arg
61F5 **Elbrus** *Mt* Russian Fed
Elburz Mts = Reshteh-ye Alborz
21B3 **El Cajon** USA
19A4 **El Campo** USA
51B2 **Elche** Spain
51B2 **Elda** Spain
32B3 **El Diviso** Colombia
96B2 **El Djouf** *Desert Region* Maur
18B2 **Eldon** USA
11A3 **El Dorado** Arkansas, USA
35B2 **Eldorado** Brazil
9D3 **El Dorado** Kansas, USA
24B2 **El Dorado** Mexico
33E2 **El Dorado** Ven
99D2 **Eldoret** Kenya
22C1 **Eleanor,L** USA
96B2 **El Eglab** Region, Alg
50B1 **El Escorial** Spain
93D2 **Eleşkirt** Turk
11C4 **Eleuthera** *I* The Bahamas
92B4 **El Faiyûm** Egypt
96B2 **El Farsia** *Well* Mor
98C1 **El Fasher** Sudan
92B4 **El Fashn** Egypt
50A1 **El Ferrol del Caudillo** Spain
99C1 **El Fula** Sudan
96C1 **El Gassi** Alg
99D1 **El Geteina** Sudan
99D1 **El Gezīra** Region, Sudan
94B3 **El Ghor** *V* Israel/Jordan
10B2 **Elgin** Illinois, USA
44C3 **Elgin** Scot
92B3 **El Gîza** Egypt
96C1 **El Golea** Alg
99D2 **Elgon,Mt** Uganda/Kenya
99E2 **El Goran** Eth
23A2 **El Grullo** Mexico
96B2 **El Guettara** *Well* Mali
96B2 **El Haricha** *Desert Region* Mali
92A4 **El Harra** Egypt
51C2 **El Harrach** Alg
99D1 **El Hawata** Sudan
23B1 **El Higo** Mexico
34A3 **El Huecu** Arg
92B4 **El'Igma** *Desert Region* Egypt
12B2 **Elim** USA
4H2 **Elira,C** Can
Elisabethville = Lubumbashi
39K6 **Elisenvaara** Fin
El Iskandarîya = Alexandria
61F4 **Elista** Russian Fed
106C4 **Elizabeth** Aust
15D2 **Elizabeth** USA
11C3 **Elizabeth City** USA
17C1 **Elizabethtown** N Carolina, USA
16A2 **Elizabethtown** Pennsylvania, USA
96B1 **El Jadida** Mor
92C3 **El Jafr** Jordan
99D1 **El Jebelein** Sudan
96D1 **El Jem** Tunisia
58C2 **Elk** Pol
16B3 **Elk** *R* Maryland, USA
14B3 **Elk** *R* W Virginia, USA
95C3 **El Kamlin** Sudan
22B1 **Elk Grove** USA
El Khalil = Hebron
80B3 **El Khârga** Egypt

El-Khârga Oasis

80B3 **El-Khârga Oasis** Egypt
14A2 **Elkhart** USA
96B2 **El Khenachich** *Desert Region* Mali
54C2 **Elkhovo** Bulg
14C3 **Elkins** USA
8B2 **Elko** USA
16B3 **Elkton** USA
92B3 **El Kuntilla** Egypt
99C1 **El Lagowa** Sudan
4H2 **Ellef Ringnes I** Can
8A2 **Ellensburg** USA
16B2 **Ellenville** USA
6B2 **Ellesmere I** Can
111B2 **Ellesmere,L** NZ
16A3 **Ellicott City** USA
100B4 **Elliot** S Africa
7B5 **Elliot Lake** Can
94B3 **El Lisan** *Pen* Jordan
112B3 **Ellsworth Land** *Region* Ant
95B1 **El Maghra** *L* Egypt
92B3 **El Mansûra** Egypt
16B3 **Elmer** USA
96B3 **El Merelé** *Desert Region* Maur
34B2 **El Milagro** Arg
94B1 **El Mina** Leb
92B4 **El Minya** Egypt
22B1 **Elmira** California, USA
10C2 **Elmira** New York, USA
96B2 **El Mreitl** *Well* Maur
56B2 **Elmshorn** Germany
98C1 **El Muglad** Sudan
96B2 **El Mzereb** *Well* Mali
79A3 **El Nido** Phil
99D1 **El Obeid** Sudan
23A2 **El Oro** Mexico
96C1 **El Oued** Alg
9C3 **El Paso** USA
21A2 **El Porta** USA
22C2 **El Portal** USA
50A2 **El Puerto del Sta Maria** Spain
     El Qâhira = Cairo
     El Quds = Jerusalem
94B3 **El Quseima** Egypt
9D3 **El Reno** USA
4E3 **Elsa** Can
25D3 **El Salvador** Republic, Cent America
22D4 **Elsinore L** USA
34B3 **El Sosneade** Arg
57C2 **Elsterwerde** Germany
     El Suweis = Suez
50A1 **El Teleno** *Mt* Spain
110B1 **Eltham** NZ
33E2 **El Tigre** Ven
92B4 **El Tih** *Desert Region* Egypt
34C2 **El Tío** Arg
20C1 **Eltopia** USA
92B4 **El Tûr** Egypt
87C1 **Elûru** India
50A2 **Elvas** Port
32C5 **Elvira** Brazil
34A2 **El Volcán** Chile
14A2 **Elwood** USA
43E3 **Ely** Eng
10A2 **Ely** Minnesota, USA
8B3 **Ely** Nevada, USA
14B2 **Elyria** USA
90B2 **Emāmrúd** Iran
84B1 **Emām Sāheb** Afghan
58B1 **Eman** *R* Sweden
61J4 **Emba** Kazakhstan
61J4 **Emba** *R* Kazakhstan
29C3 **Embalse Cerros Colorados** *L* Arg
51B2 **Embalse de Alarcón** *Res* Spain
50A2 **Embalse de Alcántarà** *Res* Spain
50A1 **Embalse de Almendra** *Res* Spain
50A2 **Embalse de Garcia de Sola** *Res* Spain
33E2 **Embalse de Guri** *L* Ven

51B1 **Embalse de Mequinenza** *Res* Spain
50A1 **Embalse de Ricobayo** *Res* Spain
29E2 **Embalse de Rio Negro** *Res* Urug
29C3 **Embalse El Chocón** *L* Arg
29C4 **Embalse Florentine Ameghino** *L* Arg
50A1 **Embalse Gabriel y Galan** *Res* Spain
30D3 **Embarcación** Arg
5G4 **Embarras Portage** Can
47B2 **Embrun** France
99D3 **Embu** Kenya
56B2 **Emden** Germany
73A4 **Emei** China
107D3 **Emerald** Aust
7D4 **Emeri** Can
5J5 **Emerson** Can
21B1 **Emigrant P** USA
95A3 **Emi Koussi** *Mt* Chad
34B3 **Emilo Mitre** Arg
92B2 **Emirdağ** Turk
16B2 **Emmaus** USA
56B2 **Emmen** Neth
20C2 **Emmett** USA
16A3 **Emmitsburg** USA
12B2 **Emmonak** USA
9C4 **Emory Peak** *Mt* USA
24A2 **Empalme** Mexico
101H1 **Empangeni** S Africa
30E4 **Empedrado** Arg
105G1 **Emperor Seamount Chain** Pacific O
18A2 **Emporia** Kansas, USA
56B2 **Ems** *R* Germany
44B2 **Enard B** Scot
23A1 **Encarnacion** Mexico
30E4 **Encarnación** Par
97B4 **Enchi** Ghana
22D4 **Encinitas** USA
35C1 **Encruzilhada** Brazil
106B1 **Endeh** Indon
13D2 **Enderby** Can
112C11 **Enderby Land** Region, Ant
15C2 **Endicott** USA
12D1 **Endicott Mts** USA
47D1 **Engadin** *Mts* Switz
79B2 **Engaño,C** Phil
94B3 **En Gedi** Israel
47C1 **Engelberg** Switz
61G3 **Engel's** Russian Fed
78A4 **Enggano** *I* Indon
41C3 **England** Country, UK
7E4 **Englee** Can
41C3 **English Channel** Eng/France
97B3 **Enji** *Well* Maur
39H7 **Enkoping** Sweden
53B3 **Enna** Italy
99C1 **En Nahud** Sudan
95B3 **Ennedi** *Region* Chad
109C1 **Enngonia** Aust
41B3 **Ennis** Irish Rep
19A3 **Ennis** Texas, USA
45C2 **Enniscorthy** Irish Rep
45C1 **Enniskillen** N Ire
45B2 **Ennistimon** Irish Rep
94B2 **Enn Nâqoúra** Leb
57C3 **Enns** *R* Austria
39F8 **Enschede** Neth
24A1 **Ensenada** Mexico
73B3 **Enshi** China
99D2 **Entebbe** Uganda
17A1 **Enterprise** Alabama, USA
20C1 **Enterprise** Oregon, USA
97C4 **Enugu** Nig
75B1 **Enzan** Japan
49C2 **Epernay** France
16A2 **Ephrata** Pennsylvania, USA
20C1 **Ephrata** Washington, USA
49D2 **Épinal** France
46A2 **Epte** *R* France
100A3 **Epukiro** Namibia

34C3 **Epu pel** Arg
90B3 **Eqlid** Iran
89D7 **Equator**
98A2 **Equatorial Guinea** Republic, Africa
47C2 **Erba** Italy
46D2 **Erbeskopf** *Mt* Germany
34A3 **Ercilla** Chile
93D2 **Erciş** Turk
92C2 **Erciyas Daglari** *Mt* Turk
74B2 **Erdaobaihe** China
72C1 **Erdene** Mongolia
68C2 **Erdenet** Mongolia
95B3 **Erdi** *Region* Chad
30F4 **Erechim** Brazil
92B1 **Ereğli** Turk
92B2 **Ereğli** Turk
68D2 **Erenhot** China
50B1 **Eresma** *R* Spain
46D1 **Erft** *R* Germany
57C2 **Erfurt** Germany
93C2 **Ergani** Turk
96B2 **Erg Chech** *Desert Region* Alg
95A3 **Erg du Djourab** *Desert* Chad
97D3 **Erg Du Ténéré** *Desert Region* Niger
92A1 **Ergene** *R* Turk
96B2 **Erg Iguidi** *Region* Alg
58D1 **Ergli** Latvia
98B1 **Erguig** *R* Chad
68D1 **Ergun'** *R* China/Russian Fed
63E2 **Ergun Zuoqi** China
95C3 **Eriba** Sudan
10C2 **Erie** USA
10B2 **Erie,L** Can/USA
42B2 **Erin Port** Eng
44A3 **Eriskay** *I* Scot
46D1 **Erkelenz** Germany
57C3 **Erlangen** Germany
19B3 **Erling,L** USA
101G1 **Ermelo** S Africa
87B3 **Ernäkulam** India
87B2 **Erode** India
108B1 **Eromanga** Aust
96B1 **Er Rachidia** Mor
99D1 **Er Rahad** Sudan
101C2 **Errego** Mozam
40B2 **Errigal** *Mt* Irish Rep
41A3 **Erris Head** *Pt* Irish Rep
99D1 **Er Roseires** Sudan
94B2 **Er Rummān** Jordan
57C2 **Erzgebirge** *Upland* Germany
93C2 **Erzincan** Turk
65F6 **Erzurum** Turk
48C3 **Esara** *R* Spain
56B1 **Esbjerg** Den
9C4 **Escalón** Mexico
10B2 **Escanaba** USA
25C3 **Escárcega** Mexico
46C2 **Esch** Lux
21B3 **Escondido** USA
24B2 **Escuinapa** Mexico
25C3 **Escuintla** Guatemala
98B2 **Eséka** Cam
51C1 **Esera** *R* Spain
90B3 **Esfahān** Iran
101H1 **Eshowe** S Africa
110C1 **Eskdale** NZ
38C1 **Eskifjörður** Iceland
39H7 **Eskilstuna** Sweden
4E3 **Eskimo L** Can
7A3 **Eskimo Point** Can
92B2 **Eskisehir** Turk
50A1 **Esla** *R* Spain
29A5 **Esmeralda** *I* Chile
32B3 **Esmeraldas** Ecuador
26B2 **Esmerelda** Cuba
49C3 **Espalion** France
14B1 **Espanola** Can
32J7 **Española** *I* Ecuador
106B4 **Esperance** Aust
34C2 **Esperanza** Arg
112C2 **Esperanza** *Base* Ant
35C1 **Espírito Santo** State, Brazil
101C3 **Espungabera** Mozam

29B4 **Esquel** Arg
20B1 **Esquimalt** Can
34D2 **Esquina** Arg
94C2 **Es Samra** Jordan
96B1 **Essaouira** Mor
96A2 **Es Semara** Mor
56B2 **Essen** Germany
33F3 **Essequibo** *R* Guyana
43E4 **Essex** County, Eng
14B2 **Essexville** USA
57B3 **Esslingen** Germany
46B2 **Essonne** France
31D4 **Estância** Brazil
101G1 **Estcourt** S Africa
47D2 **Este** Italy
46B2 **Esternay** France
30D3 **Esteros** Par
5H5 **Estevan** Can
17B1 **Estill** USA
60B2 **Estonia** Republic, Europe
29B6 **Estrecho de Magallanes** *Str* Chile
50A2 **Estremoz** Port
59B3 **Esztergom** Hung
108A1 **Etadunna** Aust
46C2 **Etam** France
48C2 **Etampes** France
108A1 **Etamunbanie,L** Aust
46A1 **Etaples** France
85D3 **Etāwah** India
99D2 **Ethiopia** Republic, Africa
23B2 **Etla** Mexico
53B3 **Etna** *Mt* Italy
12H3 **Etolin I** USA
12A2 **Etolin Str** USA
6C2 **Eton** Can
100A2 **Etosha Nat Pk** Namibia
100A2 **Etosha Pan** *Salt L* Namibia
17B1 **Etowah** *R* USA
46D2 **Ettelbruck** Lux
109C2 **Euabalong** Aust
14B2 **Euclid** USA
109C3 **Eucumbene,L** Aust
108A2 **Eudunda** Aust
19A2 **Eufala L** USA
17A1 **Eufaula** USA
8A2 **Eugene** USA
108C1 **Eulo** Aust
19B3 **Eunice** Louisiana, USA
46D1 **Eupen** Germany
93D3 **Euphrates** *R* Iraq
19C3 **Eupora** USA
48C2 **Eure** *R* France
20B2 **Eureka** California, USA
6B1 **Eureka** Can
8B3 **Eureka** Nevada, USA
6B2 **Eureka** *Sd* Can
108C3 **Euroa** Aust
109C1 **Eurombah** *R* Aust
101D3 **Europa** *I* Mozam Chan
57B2 **Euskirchen** Germany
13B2 **Eutsuk L** Can
13D2 **Evansburg** Can
6B1 **Evans,C** Can
7C4 **Evans,L** Can
6B3 **Evans Str** Can
14A2 **Evanston** Illinois, USA
8B2 **Evanston** Wyoming, USA
11B3 **Evansville** Indiana, USA
101G1 **Evaton** S Africa
106C4 **Everard,L** Aust
82C3 **Everest,Mt** China/Nepal
8A2 **Everett** Washington, USA
16C1 **Everett,Mt** USA
11B4 **Everglades,The** *Swamp* USA
43D3 **Evesham** Eng
98B2 **Evinayong** Eq Guinea
39F7 **Evje** Nor
47B1 **Evolène** Switz
50A2 **Évora** Port
48C2 **Evreux** France

55B3 Évvoia / Greece
98B3 Ewo Congo
22C1 Excelisor Mt USA
18B2 Excelsior Springs USA
21R2 Exeter California, USA
43C4 Exeter Eng
15D2 Exeter New Hampshire, USA
43C4 Exmoor Nat Pk Eng
43C4 Exmouth Eng
50A2 Extremadura Region, Spain
25E2 Exuma Sd The Bahamas
99D3 Eyasi L Tanz
42C2 Eyemouth Scot
99E2 Eyl Somalia
106B4 Eyre Aust
106C3 Eyre Creek R Aust
106C3 Eyre,L Aust
106C4 Eyre Pen Aust
79B3 Eyte / Phil
23A1 Ezatlan Mexico
55C3 Ezine Turk

F
4G3 Faber L Can
39G7 Fåborg Den
52B2 Fabriano Italy
95A3 Fachi Niger
95B3 Fada Chad
97C3 Fada N'Gourma Burkina
52B2 Faenza Italy
6E3 Faeringehavn Greenland
98B2 Fafa R CAR
99E2 Fafan R Eth
54B1 Fágáras Rom
46C1 Fagnes Region, Belg
97B3 Faguibine,L L Mali
91C5 Fahud Oman
96A1 Faiol / Açores
4D3 Fairbanks USA
14B3 Fairborn USA
8D2 Fairbury USA
16A3 Fairfax USA
21A2 Fairfield California, USA
16C2 Fairfield Connecticut, USA
14B3 Fairfield Ohio, USA
45C1 Fair Head Pt N Ire
40C2 Fair Isle / Scot
111B2 Fairlie NZ
14B3 Fairmont W Virginia, USA
13D1 Fairview Can
4E4 Fairweather,Mt USA
71F3 Fais / Pacific O
84C2 Faisalabad Pak
8C2 Faith USA
44E1 Faither,The Pen Scot
86A1 Faizābād India
43E3 Fakenham Eng
39G7 Faköping Sweden
86C2 Falam Burma
24C2 Falcon Res Mexico/ USA
97A3 Falémé R Mali/Sen
39G7 Falkenberg Sweden
42C2 Falkirk Scot
29D6 Falkland Is Dependency, S Atlantic
29E6 Falkland Sd Falkland Is
22D4 Fallbrook USA
8R3 Fallon USA
15D2 Fall River USA
18A1 Falls City USA
43B4 Falmouth Eng
27H1 Falmouth Jamaica
16D2 Falmouth Massachusetts, USA
100A4 False B S Africa
24A2 Falso,C Mexico
56C2 Falster / Den
54C1 Fălticeni Rom
39H6 Falun Sweden
92B2 Famagusta Cyprus

46C1 Famenne Region, Belg
76B2 Fang Thai
99D2 Fangak Sudan
73E5 Fang liao Taiwan
52B2 Fano Italy
112C3 Faraday Base Ant
99C2 Faradje Zaïre
101D3 Farafangana Madag
95B2 Farafra Oasis Egypt
80E2 Farah Afghan
71F2 Farallon de Medinilla / Pacific O
97A3 Faranah Guinea
71F3 Faraulep / Pacific O
43D4 Fareham Eng
        Farewell,C = Kap Farvel
107G5 Farewell,C NZ
110B2 Farewell Spit Pt NZ
8D2 Fargo USA
94B2 Fari'a R Israel
10A2 Faribault USA
86B2 Faridpur Bang
90C2 Farimān Iran
18B2 Farmington Missouri, USA
9C3 Farmington New Mexico, USA
22B2 Farmington Res USA
42D2 Farne Deep N Sea
13D2 Farnham,Mt Can
12H2 Faro Can
50A2 Faro Port
39H7 Fåro / Sweden
89K9 Farquhar Is Indian O
44B3 Farrar R Scot
14B2 Farrell USA
55B3 Fársala Greece
91B4 Fasā Iran
45B3 Fastnet Rock Irish Rep
60C3 Fastov Ukraine
86A1 Fatehpur India
13D1 Father Can
30F2 Fatima du Sul Brazil
101G1 Fauresmith S Africa
47B2 Faverges France
7B4 Fawn R Can
38H6 Fax R Sweden
38A2 Faxaflói B Iceland
95A3 Faya Chad
11A3 Fayetteville Arkansas, USA
11C3 Fayetteville N Carolina, USA
93E4 Faylakah / Kuwait
84C2 Fāzilka India
96A2 Fdérik Maur
11C3 Fear,C USA
21A2 Feather Middle Fork R USA
48C2 Fécamp France
34U2 Federación Arg
34D2 Federal Arg
71F3 Federated States of Micronesia Is Pacific O
56C2 Fehmarn / Germany
32C5 Feijó Brazil
73C5 Feilai Xai Bei Jiang R China
110C2 Feilding NZ
100C2 Feira Zambia
31D4 Feira de Santan Brazil
92C2 Feke Turk
57B3 Feldkirch Austria
34D2 Feliciano R Arg
41D3 Felixstowe Eng
47D1 Feltre Italy
38G6 Femund L Nor
74A2 Fengcheng China
73B4 Fengdu China
72D1 Fenging China
73B3 Fengjie China
72B3 Feng Xian China
72C1 Fengzhen China
72C2 Fen He R China
101D2 Fenoarivo Atsinanana Madag
60E5 Feodosiya Ukraine
90C3 Ferdow Iran

46B2 Fère-Champenoise France
82B2 Fergana Uzbekistan
45C1 Fermanagh County, N Ire
45B2 Fermoy Irish Rep
47D1 Fern Mt Austria
32J7 Fernandina / Ecuador
17B1 Fernandina Beach USA
103G5 Fernando de Noronha / Atlantic O
35A2 Fernandópolis Brazil
20B1 Ferndale USA
21B2 Fernley USA
52B2 Ferrara Italy
32B5 Ferreñafe Peru
19B3 Ferriday USA
96B1 Fès Mor
18B2 Festus USA
54C2 Feteşti Rom
92A2 Fethiye Turk
61H5 Fetisovo Kazakhstan
44E1 Fetlar / Scot
84C1 Feyzabad Afghan
101D3 Fianarantsoa Madag
99D2 Fichè Eth
101G1 Ficksburg S Africa
47D2 Fidenza Italy
55A2 Fier Alb
47D1 Fiera Di Primeiro Italy
44C3 Fife Region, Scot
44C3 Fife Ness Pen Scot
48C3 Figeac France
50A1 Figueira da Foz Port
51C1 Figueras Spain
        Figueres = Figueras
96B1 Figuig Mor
105G4 Fiji Is Pacific O
30D3 Filadelfia Par
54B2 Filiaşi Rom
55B3 Filiatrá Greece
53B3 Filicudi / Italy
21B3 Fillmore California, USA
44B3 Findhorn R Scot
10B2 Findlay USA
13D2 Findlay,Mt Can
15C2 Finger Lakes USA
101C2 Fingoè Mozam
92B2 Finike Turk
106C3 Finke R Aust
108A1 Finke Flood Flats Aust
64D3 Finland Republic, N Europe
39J7 Finland,G of N Europe
5F4 Finlay R Can
5F4 Finlay Forks Can
108C3 Finley Aust
38H5 Finnsnes Nor
71F4 Finschhafen PNG
47C1 Finsteraarhorn Mt Switz
56C2 Finsterwalde Germany
45C1 Fintona N Ire
111A3 Fiordland Nat Pk NZ
94B2 Fiq Syria
93C2 Firat R Turk
22B2 Firebaugh USA
52B2 Firenze Italy
34C2 Firmat Arg
85D3 Firozābād India
84C2 Firozpur India
39H7 Firspång Sweden
42B2 Firth of Clyde Estuary Scot
44C3 Firth of Forth Estuary Scot
44A3 Firth of Lorn Estuary Scot
40C2 Firth of Tay Estuary Scot
91B4 Firūzābād Iran
100A3 Fish R Namibia
22C2 Fish Camp USA
16C2 Fishers I USA
6B3 Fisher Str Can
43B4 Fishguard Wales
6E3 Fiskenaesset Greenland

46B2 Fismes France
15D2 Fitchburg USA
44E2 Fitful Head Pt Scot
17B1 Fitzgerald USA
10bB2 Fitzroy R Aust
106B2 Fitzroy Crossing Aust
14B1 Fitzwilliam I Can
        Fiume = Rijeka
99C3 Fizi Zaïre
9B3 Flagstaff USA
42D2 Flamborough Head C Eng
8C2 Flaming Gorge Res USA
44A2 Flannan Isles Is Scot
12J2 Flat R Can
13E3 Flathead R USA
8B2 Flathead L USA
18B2 Flat River USA
8A2 Flattery,C USA
42C3 Fleetwood Eng
39F7 Flekkefjord Nor
69G4 Fleming Deep Pacific O
16B2 Flemington USA
56B2 Flensburg Germany
47B1 Fleurier Switz
106C4 Flinders / Aust
107D4 Flinders / Aust
107D2 Flinders R Aust
106C4 Flinders Range Mts Aust
5H4 Flin Flon Can
10B2 Flint USA
42C3 Flint Wales
11B3 Flint R USA
46B1 Flixecourt France
17A1 Florala USA
        Florence = Firenze
11B3 Florence Alabama, USA
18A2 Florence Kansas, USA
20B2 Florence Oregon, USA
11C3 Florence S Carolina, USA
32B3 Florencia Colombia
46C2 Florenville Belg
25D3 Flores Guatemala
96A1 Flores / Açores
106B1 Flores / Indon
34D3 Flores R Arg
70C4 Flores S Indon
31C3 Floriano Brazil
30G4 Florianópolis Brazil
25D2 Florida State, USA
29E2 Florida Urug
17B2 Florida B USA
17B2 Florida City USA
107E1 Florida Is Solomon Is
11B4 Florida Keys Is USA
11B4 Florida,Strs of USA
55B2 Flórina Greece
38F6 Floro Nor
47D1 Fluchthorn Mt Austria
54C1 Focsani Rom
53C2 Foggia Italy
97A4 Fogo / Cape Verde
48C3 Foix France
6C3 Foley L Can
52B2 Foligno Italy
43E4 Folkestone Eng
17B1 Folkston USA
52B2 Follonica Italy
22B1 Folsom USA
22B1 Folsom L L USA
5H4 Fond-du-Lac Can
10B2 Fond du Lac USA
48C2 Fontainebleau France
18B2 Fontenac USA
48B2 Fontenay-le-Comte France
52C1 Fonyód Hung
        Foochow = Fuzhou
12D2 Foraker,Mt USA
46D2 Forbach France
109C2 Forbes Aust
97C4 Forcados Nig
38F6 Forde Nor
108C1 Fords Bridge Aust
19B3 Fordyce USA

97A4 **Forécariah** Guinea
6G3 **Forel,Mt** Greenland
14B2 **Forest** Can
17B1 **Forest Park** USA
22A1 **Forestville** USA
44C3 **Forfar** Scot
46A2 **Forges-les-Eaux** France
20B1 **Forks** USA
52B2 **Forli** Italy
51C2 **Formentera** *I* Spain
53B2 **Formia** Italy
96A1 **Formigas** *I* Açores
Formosa = Taiwan
30E4 **Formosa** Arg
31B5 **Formosa** Brazil
30D3 **Formosa** State, Arg
73D5 **Formosa Str** Taiwan/China
47D2 **Fornovo di Taro** Italy
38D3 **Føroyar** *Is* N Atlantic O
44C3 **Forres** Scot
106B4 **Forrest** Aust
11A3 **Forrest City** USA
107D2 **Forsayth** Aust
39J6 **Forssa** Fin
109D2 **Forster** Aust
18B2 **Forsyth** Missouri, USA
84C3 **Fort Abbas** Pak
7B4 **Fort Albany** Can
31D2 **Fortaleza** Brazil
44B3 **Fort Augustus** Scot
100B4 **Fort Beaufort** S Africa
21A2 **Fort Bragg** USA
8C2 **Fort Collins** USA
15C1 **Fort Coulogne** Can
27E4 **Fort de France** Martinique
17A1 **Fort Deposit** USA
10A2 **Fort Dodge** USA
106A3 **Fortescue** *R* Aust
7A5 **Fort Frances** Can
4F3 **Fort Franklin** Can
4F3 **Fort Good Hope** Can
108B1 **Fort Grey** Aust
44B3 **Forth** *R* Scot
7B4 **Fort Hope** Can
34B3 **Fortin Uno** Arg
4F3 **Fort Laird** Can
96C1 **Fort Lallemand** Alg
Fort Lamy = Ndjamena
11B4 **Fort Lauderdale** USA
4F3 **Fort Liard** Can
5G4 **Fort Mackay** Can
5G5 **Fort Macleod** Can
5G4 **Fort McMurray** Can
4E3 **Fort McPherson** Can
18B2 **Fort Madison** USA
8C2 **Fort Morgan** USA
11B4 **Fort Myers** USA
5F4 **Fort Nelson** Can
4F3 **Fort Norman** Can
17A1 **Fort Payne** USA
8C2 **Fort Peck Res** USA
11B4 **Fort Pierce** USA
4G3 **Fort Providence** Can
5G3 **Fort Resolution** Can
98B3 **Fort Rousset** Congo
5F4 **Fort St James** Can
13C1 **Fort St John** Can
13E2 **Fort Saskatchewan** Can
18B2 **Fort Scott** USA
4E3 **Fort Selkirk** Can
7B4 **Fort Severn** Can
61H5 **Fort Shevchenko** Kazakhstan
4F3 **Fort Simpson** Can
5G3 **Fort Smith** Can
4G3 **Fort Smith** Region, Can
11A3 **Fort Smith** USA
9C3 **Fort Stockton** USA
20B2 **Fortuna** California, USA
5G4 **Fort Vermillion** Can
17A1 **Fort Walton Beach** USA
10B2 **Fort Wayne** USA
44B3 **Fort William** Scot
9D3 **Fort Worth** USA
12F2 **Fortymile** *R* USA
12E1 **Fort Yukon** USA
73C5 **Foshan** China
47B2 **Fossano** Italy
12G3 **Foster,Mt** USA
98B3 **Fougamou** Gabon
48B2 **Fougères** France
44D1 **Foula** *I* Scot
43E4 **Foulness I** Eng
111B2 **Foulwind,C** NZ
98B2 **Foumban** Cam
49C1 **Fourmies** France
55C3 **Foúrnoi** *I* Greece
97A3 **Fouta Djallon** *Mts* Guinea
111B3 **Foveaux** *Str* NZ
43B4 **Fowey** Eng
13D2 **Fox Creek** Can
6B3 **Foxe Basin** *G* Can
6B3 **Foxe Chan** Can
6C3 **Foxe Pen** Can
110C2 **Foxton** NZ
13F2 **Fox Valley** Can
45B2 **Foynes** Irish Rep
100A2 **Foz do Cuene** Angola
30F4 **Foz do Iquaçu** Brazil
16A2 **Frackville** USA
34B2 **Fraga** Arg
16D1 **Framingham** USA
31B6 **Franca** Brazil
49C2 **France** Republic, Europe
10A2 **Frances** Can
12J2 **Frances** *R* Can
49D2 **Franche Comté** Region, France
100B3 **Francistown** Botswana
13B2 **Francois L** Can
14A2 **Frankfort** Indiana, USA
11B3 **Frankfort** Kentucky, USA
101G1 **Frankfort** S Africa
57B2 **Frankfurt** Germany
46E1 **Frankfurt am Main** Germany
56C2 **Frankfurt-an-der-Oder** Germany
57C3 **Fränkischer Alb** *Upland* Germany
14A3 **Franklin** Indiana, USA
19B4 **Franklin** Louisiana, USA
16D1 **Franklin** Massachusetts, USA
16B2 **Franklin** New Jersey, USA
14C2 **Franklin** Pennsylvania, USA
4F2 **Franklin B** Can
20C1 **Franklin D Roosevelt** *L* USA
4F3 **Franklin Mts** Can
4J2 **Franklin Str** Can
111B2 **Franz Josef Glacier** NZ
Franz-Joseph-Land = Zemlya Frantsa Iosifa
5F5 **Fraser** *R* Can
44C3 **Fraserburgh** Scot
107E3 **Fraser I** Aust
13B2 **Fraser L** Can
47B1 **Frasne** France
47C1 **Frauenfield** Switz
34D2 **Fray Bentos** Urug
40C2 **Frazerburgh** Scot
16B3 **Frederica** USA
56B1 **Fredericia** Den
15C3 **Frederick** Maryland, USA
15C3 **Fredericksburg** Virginia, USA
12H3 **Frederick Sd** USA
18B2 **Fredericktown** USA
7D5 **Fredericton** Can
6E3 **Frederikshab** Greenland
39G7 **Frederikshavn** Den
15C2 **Fredonia** USA
39G7 **Fredrikstad** Nor
16B2 **Freehold** USA
26B1 **Freeport** The Bahamas
19A4 **Freeport** Texas, USA
97A4 **Freetown** Sierra Leone
57B3 **Freiburg** Germany
57C3 **Freistadt** Austria
106A4 **Fremantle** Aust
22B2 **Fremont** California, USA
18A1 **Fremont** Nebraska, USA
14B2 **Fremont** Ohio, USA
33G3 **French Guiana** Dependency, S America
109C4 **Frenchmans Cap** *Mt* Aust
105J4 **French Polynesia** *Is* Pacific O
24B2 **Fresnillo** Mexico
8B3 **Fresno** USA
22C2 **Fresno** *R* USA
47A1 **Fretigney** France
46B1 **Frévent** France
109C4 **Freycinet Pen** Aust
97A3 **Fria** Guinea
22C2 **Friant** USA
22C2 **Friant Dam** USA
52A1 **Fribourg** Switz
57B3 **Friedrichshafen** Germany
6D3 **Frobisher B** Can
6D3 **Frobisher Bay** Can
5H4 **Frobisher L** Can
61F4 **Frolovo** Russian Fed
43C4 **Frome** Eng
108A1 **Frome** *R* Aust
43C4 **Frome** *R* Eng
106C4 **Frome,L** Aust
25C3 **Frontera** Mexico
15C3 **Front Royal** USA
53B2 **Frosinone** Italy
73C5 **Fuchuan** China
73E4 **Fuding** China
24B2 **Fuerte** *R* Mexico
30E3 **Fuerte Olimpo** Par
96A2 **Fuerteventura** *I* Canary Is
72C2 **Fugu** China
68A2 **Fuhai** China
91C4 **Fujairah** UAE
75B1 **Fuji** Japan
73D4 **Fujian** Province, China
69F2 **Fujin** China
75B1 **Fujinomiya** Japan
74D3 **Fuji-san** *Mt* Japan
75B1 **Fujisawa** Japan
75B1 **Fuji-Yoshida** Japan
63A3 **Fukang** China
74C3 **Fukuchiyima** Japan
74D3 **Fukui** Japan
74C4 **Fukuoka** Japan
74E3 **Fukushima** Japan
74C4 **Fukuyama** Japan
57B2 **Fulda** Germany
57B2 **Fulda** *R* Germany
73B4 **Fuling** China
27L1 **Fullarton** Trinidad
22D4 **Fullerton** USA
18C2 **Fulton** Kentucky, USA
15C2 **Fulton** New York, USA
46C1 **Fumay** France
75C1 **Funabashi** Japan
96A1 **Funchal** Medeira
35C1 **Fundão** Brazil
7D5 **Fundy,B of** Can
101C3 **Funhalouro** Mozam
72D3 **Funing** China
73B5 **Funing** China
97C3 **Funtua** Nig
73D4 **Fuqing** China
101C2 **Furancungo** Mozam
91C4 **Fūrg** Iran
47C1 **Furka** *P* Switz
107D5 **Furneaux Group** *Is* Aust
56C2 **Fürstenwalde** Germany
57C3 **Fürth** Germany
74D3 **Furukawa** Japan
6B3 **Fury and Hecla St** Can
74A2 **Fushun** Liaoning, China
73A4 **Fushun** Sichuan, China
74B2 **Fusong** China
57C3 **Füssen** Germany
72E2 **Fu Xian** China
72E1 **Fuxin** China
72D3 **Fuyang** China
72E1 **Fuyuan** Liaoning, China
73A4 **Fuyuan** Yunnan, China
68A2 **Fuyun** China
73D4 **Fuzhou** China
56C1 **Fyn** *I* Den

G

99E2 **Gaalkacyo** Somalia
21B2 **Gabbs** USA
100A2 **Gabela** Angola
96D1 **Gabe's** Tunisia
22B2 **Gabilan Range** *Mts* USA
98B3 **Gabon** Republic, Africa
100B3 **Gaborone** Botswana
54C2 **Gabrovo** Bulg
91B3 **Gach Sārān** Iran
17A1 **Gadsden** Alabama, USA
10A1 **Gads L** Can
53B2 **Gaeta** Italy
71F3 **Gaferut** *I* Pacific O
96C1 **Gafsa** Tunisia
60D2 **Gagarin** Russian Fed
97B4 **Gagnoa** Ivory Coast
7D4 **Gagnon** Can
61F5 **Gagra** Georgia
86B1 **Gaibanda** India
29C4 **Gaimán** Arg
17B2 **Gainesville** Florida, USA
17B1 **Gainesville** Georgia, USA
19A3 **Gainesville** Texas, USA
42D3 **Gainsborough** Eng
108A2 **Gairdner,L** Aust
44B3 **Gairloch** Scot
16A3 **Gaithersburg** USA
87B1 **Gajendragarh** India
73D4 **Ga Jiang** *R* China
99D3 **Galana** *R* Kenya
103D5 **Galapagos Is** Pacific O
42C2 **Galashiels** Scot
54C1 **Galaţi** Rom
4C3 **Galena** Alaska, USA
18B2 **Galena** Kansas, USA
27L1 **Galeota Pt** Trinidad
27L1 **Galera Pt** Trinidad
10A2 **Galesburg** USA
15C2 **Galeton** USA
61F2 **Galich** Russian Fed
50A1 **Galicia** Region, Spain
Galilee,S of = Tiberias,L
27J1 **Galina Pt** Jamaica
99D1 **Gallabat** Sudan
47C2 **Gallarate** Italy
87C3 **Galle** Sri Lanka
51B1 **Gállego** *R* Spain
Gallipoli = Gelibolu
55A2 **Gallipoli** Italy
38J5 **Gällivare** Sweden
42B2 **Galloway** District
42B2 **Galloway,Mull of** *C* Scot
8C3 **Gallup** USA
22B1 **Galt** USA
96A2 **Galtat Zemmour** Mor
25C2 **Galveston** USA
11A4 **Galveston B** USA
34C2 **Galvez** Arg
49D3 **Galvi** Corse
45B2 **Galway** County, Irish Rep
41B3 **Galway** Irish Rep
41B3 **Galway** *B* Irish Rep
86B1 **Gamba** China
97B3 **Gambaga** Ghana

4A3 **Gambell** USA
97A3 **Gambia** *R* The Gambia/Sen
97A3 **Gambia,The** Republic, Africa
98B3 **Gamboma** Congo
100A2 **Gambos** Angola
87C3 **Gampola** Sri Lanka
99E2 **Ganale Dorya** *R* Eth
15C2 **Gananoque** Can
Gand = Gent
100A2 **Ganda** Angola
98C3 **Gandajika** Zaïre
84B3 **Gandava** Pak
7E5 **Gander** Can
85C4 **Gāndhīdhām** India
85C4 **Gāndhīnagar** India
85D4 **Gāndhi Sāgar** *L* India
51B2 **Gandia** Spain
86B2 **Ganga** *R* India
85C3 **Ganganar** India
86C2 **Gangaw** Burma
72A2 **Gangca** China
82C2 **Gangdise Shan** *Mts* China
Ganges = Ganga
86B1 **Gangtok** India
72B3 **Gangu** China
8C2 **Gannett Peak** *Mt* USA
72B2 **Ganquan** China
108A3 **Gantheaume** *C* Aust
39K8 **Gantsevichi** Belorussia
73D4 **Ganzhou** China
97C3 **Gao** Mali
72A2 **Gaolan** China
72C2 **Gaoping** China
97B3 **Gaoua** Burkina
97A3 **Gaoual** Guinea
72D3 **Gaoyou Hu** *L* China
73C5 **Gaozhou** China
49D3 **Gap** France
79B2 **Gapan** Phil
84D2 **Gar** China
109C1 **Garah** Aust
31D3 **Garanhuns** Brazil
21A1 **Garberville** USA
35B2 **Garça** Brazil
35A2 **Garcias** Brazil
47D2 **Garda** Italy
9C3 **Garden City** USA
14A1 **Garden Pen** USA
34D3 **Gardey** Arg
84B2 **Gardez** Afghan
16C2 **Gardiners I** USA
16D1 **Gardner** USA
47D2 **Gardone** Italy
47D2 **Gargano** Italy
85D4 **Garhākota** India
61K2 **Gari** Russian Fed
100A4 **Garies** S Africa
99D3 **Garissa** Kenya
19A3 **Garland** USA
57C3 **Garmisch-Partenkirchen** Germany
90B2 **Garmsar** Iran
18A2 **Garnett** USA
8B2 **Garnett Peak** *Mt* USA
48C3 **Garonne** *R* France
44B3 **Garry** *R* Scot
78B4 **Garut** Indon
86A2 **Garwa** India
14A2 **Gary** USA
82C2 **Garyarsa** China
4H3 **Gary L** Can
19A3 **Garza-Little Elm** *Res* USA
90B2 **Gasan Kuli** Turkmenistan
48B3 **Gascogne** Region, France
18B2 **Gasconade** *R* USA
106A3 **Gascoyne** *R* Aust
98B2 **Gashaka** Nig
97D3 **Gashua** Nig
10D2 **Gaspé** Can
10D2 **Gaspé,C. de** Can
94A1 **Gata,C** Cyprus
60C2 **Gatchina** Russian Fed
42D2 **Gateshead** Eng
19A3 **Gatesville** USA
15C1 **Gatineau** Can
15C1 **Gatineau** *R* Can
109D1 **Gatton** Aust
86C1 **Gauhāti** India
58C1 **Gauja** *R* Latvia
86A1 **Gauri Phanta** India
22B3 **Gaviota** USA
39H6 **Gävle** Sweden
108A2 **Gawler Ranges** *Mts* Aust
72A1 **Gaxun Nur** *L* China
86A2 **Gaya** India
97C3 **Gaya** Niger
14B1 **Gaylord** USA
109D1 **Gayndah** Aust
61H1 **Gayny** Russian Fed
60C4 **Gaysin** Ukraine
92B3 **Gaza** Israel
92C2 **Gaziantep** Turk
97B4 **Gbaringa** Lib
58B2 **Gdańsk** Pol
58B2 **Gdańsk,G of** Pol
39K7 **Gdov** Russian Fed
58B2 **Gdynia** Pol
94A3 **Gebel Halâl** *Mt* Egypt
95C2 **Gebel Hamata** *Mt* Egypt
92B4 **Gebel Katherina** *Mt* Egypt
94A3 **Gebel Libni** *Mt* Egypt
94A3 **Gebel Maghâra** *Mt* Egypt
99D1 **Gedaref** Sudan
55C3 **Gediz** *R* Turk
56C2 **Gedser** Den
46C1 **Geel** Belg
108B3 **Geelong** Aust
109C4 **Geeveston** Aust
97D3 **Geidam** Nig
46D1 **Geilenkirchen** Germany
99D3 **Geita** Tanz
73A5 **Gejiu** China
53B3 **Gela** Italy
99E2 **Geladī** Eth
46D1 **Geldern** Germany
55C2 **Gelibolu** Turk
92B2 **Gelidonya Burun** Turk
46D1 **Gelsenkirchen** Germany
39F8 **Gelting** Germany
77C5 **Gemas** Malay
46C1 **Gembloux** Belg
98B2 **Gemena** Zaïre
92C2 **Gemerek** Turk
92A1 **Gemlik** Turk
52B1 **Gemona** Italy
100B3 **Gemsbok** *Nat Pk* Botswana
98C1 **Geneina** Sudan
34C3 **General Acha** Arg
34C3 **General Alvear** Buenos Aires, Arg
34B2 **General Alvear** Mendoza, Arg
34C2 **General Arenales** Arg
34D3 **General Belgrano** Arg
112B2 **General Belgrano** *Base* Ant
112C2 **General Bernardo O'Higgins** *Base* Ant
34D3 **General Conesa** Buenos Aires, Arg
30D3 **General Eugenio A Garay** Par
34D3 **General Guido** Arg
34C3 **General La Madrid** Arg
34C2 **General Levalle** Arg
30C4 **General Manuel Belgrano** *Mt* Arg
34D3 **General Paz** Buenos Aires, Arg
34C3 **General Pico** Arg
34C2 **General Pinto** Arg
34D3 **General Pirán** Arg
29C3 **General Roca** Arg
112C3 **General San Martin** *Base* Ant
79C4 **General Santos** Phil
34C3 **General Viamonte** Arg
34C3 **General Villegas** Arg
15C2 **Genesee** *R* USA
15C2 **Geneseo** USA
Geneva = Genève
18A1 **Geneva** Nebraska, USA
15C2 **Geneva** New York, USA
Geneva,L of = LacLéman
52A1 **Genève** Switz
50B2 **Genil** *R* Spain
Genoa = Genova
109C3 **Genoa** Aust
52A2 **Genova** Italy
32J7 **Genovesa** *I* Ecuador
46B1 **Gent** Belg
78B4 **Genteng** Indon
56C2 **Genthin** Germany
93E1 **Geokchay** Azerbaijan
100B4 **George** S Africa
7D4 **George** *R* Can
109C2 **George,L** Aust
17B2 **George,L** Florida, USA
15D2 **George,L** New York, USA
111A2 **George Sd** NZ
109C4 **George Town** Aust
15C3 **Georgetown** Delaware, USA
33F2 **Georgetown** Guyana
14B3 **Georgetown** Kentucky, USA
77C4 **George Town** Malay
27N2 **Georgetown** St Vincent
17C1 **Georgetown** S Carolina, USA
19A3 **Georgetown** Texas, USA
97A3 **Georgetown** The Gambia
112C8 **George V Land** Region, Ant
65F5 **Georgia** Republic, Europe
112C12 **Georg Forster** *Base* Ant
17B1 **Georgia** State, USA
14B1 **Georgian B** Can
13C3 **Georgia,Str of** Can
106C3 **Georgina** *R* Aust
61F5 **Georgiyevsk** Russian Fed
57C2 **Gera** Germany
46B1 **Geraardsbergen** Belg
111B2 **Geraldine** NZ
106A3 **Geraldton** Aust
10B2 **Geraldton** Can
94B3 **Gerar** *R* Israel
4C3 **Gerdine,Mt** USA
12E2 **Gerdova Peak** *Mt* USA
77C4 **Gerik** Malay
60B4 **Gerlachovsky** *Mt* Pol
13C1 **Germanson Lodge** Can
56C2 **Germany** Republic, Europe
101G1 **Germiston** S Africa
46D1 **Gerolstein** Germany
51C1 **Gerona** Spain
46E1 **Geseke** Germany
99E2 **Gestro** *R* Eth
50B1 **Getafe** Spain
16A3 **Gettysburg** Pennsylvania, USA
93D2 **Gevaş** Turk
55B2 **Gevgeliija** Macedonia, Yugos
47B1 **Gex** France
94C2 **Ghabāghib** Syria
96C1 **Ghadamis** Libya
90B2 **Ghaem Shahr** Iran
86A1 **Ghāghara** *R* India
97B4 **Ghana** Republic, Africa
100B3 **Ghanzi** Botswana
96C1 **Ghardaïa** Alg
95A1 **Gharyan** Libya
95A2 **Ghāt** Libya
84D3 **Ghaziābād** India
84C3 **Ghazi Khan** Pak
84B2 **Ghazni** Afghan
54C1 **Gheorgheni** Rom
88E4 **Ghudamis** Alg
90D3 **Ghurian** Afghan
95B2 **Gialo** Libya
99E2 **Giamame** Somalia
53C3 **Giarre** Italy
100A3 **Gibeon** Namibia
50A2 **Gibraltar** Colony, SW Europe
50A2 **Gibraltar,Str of** Spain/Africa
106B3 **Gibson Desert** Aust
20B1 **Gibsons** Can
87B1 **Giddalūr** India
99D2 **Gīdolē** Eth
57B2 **Giessen** Germany
17B2 **Gifford** USA
74D3 **Gifu** Japan
42B2 **Gigha** *I* Scot
52B2 **Giglio** *I* Italy
50A1 **Gijón** Spain
107D2 **Gilbert** *R* Aust
13C2 **Gilbert,Mt** Can
101C2 **Gilé** Mozam
94B2 **Gilead** Region, Jordan
95B2 **Gilf Kebir Plat** Egypt
109C2 **Gilgandra** Aust
84C1 **Gilgit** Pak
84C1 **Gilgit** *R* Pak
108C2 **Gilgunnia** Aust
7A4 **Gillam** Can
108A2 **Gilles** *L* Aust
13B2 **Gill I** Can
14A1 **Gills Rock** USA
14A2 **Gilman** USA
22B2 **Gilroy** USA
8D1 **Gimli** Can
101H1 **Gingindlovu** S Africa
79C4 **Gingoog** Phil
99E2 **Gīnīr** Eth
55B3 **Gióna** *Mt* Greece
109C3 **Gippsland** *Mts* Aust
14B2 **Girard** USA
32C3 **Girardot** Colombia
44C3 **Girdle Ness** *Pen* Scot
93C1 **Giresun** Turk
85C4 **Gir Hills** India
98B2 **Giri** *R* Zaïre
86B2 **Girīdīh** India
Girona = Gerona
48B2 **Gironde** *R* France
42B2 **Girvan** Scot
111C2 **Gisborne** NZ
46A2 **Gisors** France
99C3 **Gitega** Burundi
Giuba,R = Juba,R
54C2 **Giurgiu** Rom
46C1 **Givet** Belg
58C2 **Gizycko** Pol
55B2 **Gjirokastër** Alb
4J3 **Gjoatlaven** Can
39G6 **Gjøvik** Nor
7D5 **Glace Bay** Can
12G3 **Glacier Bay Nat Mon** USA
13E3 **Glacier Nat Pk** USA/Can
20B1 **Glacier Peak** *Mt* USA
6B2 **Glacier Str** Can
107E3 **Gladstone** Queensland, Aust
108A2 **Gladstone** S Aust, Aust
109C4 **Gladstone** Tasmania, Aust
14A1 **Gladstone** USA
38A1 **Glama** *Mt* Iceland
39G6 **Glåma** *R* Nor
46D2 **Glan** *R* Germany
47C1 **Glarner** *Mts* Switz
47C1 **Glarus** Switz
18A2 **Glasco** USA
8C2 **Glasgow** Montana, USA
42B2 **Glasgow** Scot
16B3 **Glassboro** USA
43C4 **Glastonbury** Eng
61H2 **Glazov** Russian Fed
59B3 **Gleisdorf** Austria
110C1 **Glen Afton** NZ

16A3 **Glen Burnie** USA
101H1 **Glencoe** S Africa
9B3 **Glendale** Arizona, USA
22C3 **Glendale** California, USA
12E2 **Glenhallen** USA
109D1 **Glen Innes** Aust
109C1 **Glenmorgan** Aust
109D2 **Glenreagh** Aust
16A3 **Glen Rock** USA
19A3 **Glen Rose** USA
44C3 **Glenrothes** UK
15D2 **Glens Falls** USA
45B1 **Glenties** Irish Rep
19B3 **Glenwood** Arkansas, USA
8C3 **Glenwood Springs** USA
39F6 **Glittertind** Mt Nor
59B2 **Gliwice** Pol
9B3 **Globe** USA
58B2 **Głogów** Pol
38G5 **Glomfjord** Nor
109D2 **Gloucester** Aust
43C4 **Gloucester** Eng
16D1 **Gloucester** USA
58D1 **Glubokoye** Belorussia
60D3 **Glukhov** Russian Fed
59B3 **Gmünd** Austria
57C3 **Gmunden** Austria
58B2 **Gniezno** Pol
100A3 **Goabeg** Namibia
87A1 **Goa, Daman and Diu** Union Territory, India
86C1 **Goālpāra** India
99D2 **Goba** Eth
100A3 **Gobabis** Namibia
34C2 **Gobernador Crespo** Arg
34B3 **Gobernador Duval** Arg
72B1 **Gobi** Desert China/ Mongolia
75B2 **Gobo** Japan
87B1 **Godag** India
87C1 **Godāvari** R India
14B2 **Goderich** Can
6E3 **Godhavn** Greenland
85C4 **Godhra** India
34B2 **Godoy Cruz** Arg
7A4 **Gods L** Can
6E3 **Godthab** Greenland
Godwin Austen = K2
35B1 **Goiandira** Brazil
35B1 **Goianésia** Brazil
35B1 **Goiânia** Brazil
35A1 **Goiás** Brazil
31B4 **Goiás** State, Brazil
35A2 **Goio-Erê** Brazil
99D2 **Gojab** R Eth
55C2 **Gökçeada** I Turk
55C3 **Gökova Körfezi** B Turk
92C2 **Göksun** Turk
63C3 **Gol** R Mongolia
86C1 **Golāghāt** India
93C2 **Gölbaşi** Turk
20C2 **Golconda** USA
20B2 **Gold Beach** USA
109D1 **Gold Coast** Aust
13D2 **Golden** Can
110B2 **Golden B** NZ
20B1 **Goldendale** USA
22A2 **Golden Gate** Chan USA
19B4 **Golden Meadow** USA
21B2 **Goldfield** USA
13B3 **Gold River** Can
56C2 **Goleniów** Pol
22C3 **Goleta** USA
52A2 **Golfe d'Ajaccio** G Corse
96D1 **Golfe de Gabes** G Tunisia
Golfe de Gascogne = Biscay,Bay of
52A2 **Golfe de St Florent** G Corse
48B2 **Golfe de St-Malo** B France

49C3 **Golfe du Lion** G France
29B4 **Golfo Corcovado** G Chile
50B2 **Golfo de Almeira** G Spain
29B4 **Golfo de Ancud** G Chile
25D2 **Golfo de Batabano** G Cuba
50A2 **Golfo de Cadiz** G Spain
53A3 **Golfo de Cagliari** G Sardegna
24A1 **Golfo de California** G Mexico
25D4 **Golfo de Chiriqui** G Panama
25D3 **Golfo de Fonseca** G Honduras
26B2 **Golfo de Guacanayabo** G Cuba
32A4 **Golfo de Guayaquil** G Ecuador
26B5 **Golfo del Darien** G Colombia/Panama
32A2 **Golfo de los Mosquitos** G Panama
25D3 **Golfo del Papagaya** G Nic
51B2 **Golfo de Mazarrón** G Spain
25D4 **Golfo de Nicoya** G Costa Rica
53A3 **Golfo de Oristano** G Sardegna
25E4 **Golfo de Panamá** G Panama
25D3 **Golfo de Papagayo** G Costa Rica
27E4 **Golfo de Paria** G Ven
29B5 **Golfo de Penas** G Chile
49D3 **Golfo de St Florent** G Corse
51C1 **Golfo de San Jorge** G Spain
24C3 **Golfo de Tehuantepec** G Mexico
32B3 **Golfo de Torugas** G Colombia
32B2 **Golfo de Uraba** G Colombia
51C2 **Golfo de Valencia** G Spain
27C4 **Golfo de Venezuela** G Ven
52A2 **Golfo di Genova** G Italy
53C3 **Golfo di Policastro** G Italy
53C3 **Golfo di Squillace** G Italy
53C2 **Golfo di Taranto** G Italy
52B1 **Golfo di Venezia** G Italy
25D4 **Golfo Dulce** G Costa Rica
29C5 **Golfo San Jorge** G Arg
29D4 **Golfo San Matías** G Arg
68B3 **Golmud** China
99E2 **Golocha** Eth
12B2 **Golovin B** USA
74F2 **Golovnino** Russian Fed
99C3 **Goma** Zaïre
97D3 **Gombe** Nig
60D3 **Gomel** Belorussia
96A2 **Gomera** I Canary Is
24B2 **Gómez Palacio** Mexico
63E2 **Gonam** R Russian Fed
90C2 **Gonbad-e Kāvūs** Iran
86A1 **Gonda** India
85C4 **Gondal** India
99D1 **Gonder** Eth
92A1 **Gönen** Turk

55C3 **Gonen** R Turk
73A4 **Gongga Shan** Mt China
72A2 **Gonghe** China
97D3 **Gongola** R Nig
22B2 **Gonzales** California, USA
19A4 **Gonzales** Texas, USA
34C3 **Gonzalez Chaves** Arg
13C2 **Good Hope Mt** Can
8C2 **Goodland** USA
12B3 **Goodnews Bay** USA
109C1 **Goodooga** R Aust
42D3 **Goole** Eng
108C2 **Goolgowi** Aust
108A3 **Goolwa** Aust
106A4 **Goomalling** Aust
108C2 **Goombalie** Aust
109D1 **Goomeri** Aust
109D1 **Goomeri** Aust
109D1 **Goondiwindi** Aust
7E4 **Goose Bay** Can
17C1 **Goose Creek** USA
20B2 **Goose L** USA
87B1 **Gooty** India
63C2 **Gora Munku Sardyk** Mt Mongolia/Russian Fed
64H3 **Gora Narodnaya** Mt Russian Fed
64G3 **Gora Tel'pos-iz** Russian Fed
54A2 **Goražde** Bosnia & Herzegovina, Yugos
4D3 **Gordon** USA
13E1 **Gordon L** Can
15C3 **Gordonsville** USA
98B2 **Goré** Chad
99D2 **Gorē** Eth
111A3 **Gore** NZ
63F2 **Gore Topko** Mt Russian Fed
45C2 **Gorey** Irish Rep
90B2 **Gorgān** Iran
93E2 **Goris** Armenia
52B1 **Gorizia** Italy
61F2 **Gor'kovskoye Vodokhranilishche** Res Russian Fed
57C2 **Gorlitz** Germany
60E4 **Gorlovka** Ukraine
22C3 **Gorman** USA
54C2 **Gorna Orjahovica** Bulg
68A1 **Gorno-Altaysk** Russian Fed
69G2 **Gornozavodsk** Russian Fed
61F2 **Gorodets** Russian Fed
59C3 **Gorodok** Ukraine
59D3 **Gorodok** Ukraine
71F4 **Goroka** PNG
86A1 **Gorokhpur** India
101C2 **Gorongosa** Mozam
71D3 **Gorontalo** Indon
61K2 **Goro Yurma** Mt Russian Fed
45B2 **Gort** Irish Rep
63C2 **Goryachinsk** Russian Fed
59D3 **Goryn'** R Ukraine
59C2 **Góry Świetokrzyskie** Upland Pol
64G3 **Gory Tel'pos-iz'** Mt Russian Fed
39H8 **Gorzow Wielkopolski** Pol
74E2 **Goshogawara** Japan
52C2 **Gospić** Croatia
54B2 **Gostivar** Macedonia, Yugos
58B2 **Gostynin** Pol
39G7 **Göteborg** Sweden
98B2 **Gotel** Mts Nig
39H7 **Gotland** I Sweden
74B4 **Gotō-retto** I Japan
39H7 **Gotska Sandön** I Sweden
74C3 **Gōtsu** Japan
98B1 **Goudoumaria** Niger
103H7 **Gough** I Atlantic O
109C2 **Goulburn** Aust
97B3 **Goumbou** Mali

97B3 **Goundam** Mali
98B1 **Gouré** Niger
97B3 **Gourma Rharous** Mali
46A2 **Gournay-en-Bray** France
95A3 **Gouro** Chad
71E5 **Gove Pen** Aust
60B4 **Goverla** Mt Ukraine
35C1 **Governador Valadares** Brazil
86A2 **Govind Ballabh Paht Sägar** L India
15C2 **Gowanda** USA
84B3 **Gowärän** Afghan
30E4 **Goya** Arg
98C1 **Goz-Beida** Chad
53B3 **Gozo** I Medit S
95C3 **Goz Regeb** Sudan
100B4 **Graaff-Reinet** S Africa
15C1 **Gracefield** Can
109D1 **Grafton** Aust
8D2 **Grafton** N Dakota, USA
14B3 **Grafton** W Virginia, USA
5E4 **Graham** I Can
13C1 **Graham** R Can
13E1 **Graham L** Can
100B4 **Grahamstown** S Africa
31B3 **Grajaú** Brazil
58C2 **Grajewo** Pol
55B2 **Grámmos** Mt Greece/Alb
44C3 **Grampian** Region, Scot
44B3 **Grampian** Mts Scot
32C3 **Granada** Colombia
25D3 **Granada** Nic
50B2 **Granada** Spain
15D1 **Granby** Can
96A2 **Gran Canaria** I Canary Is
30D4 **Gran Chaco** Region Arg
14A2 **Grand** R Michigan, USA
18B1 **Grand** R Missouri, USA
27Q2 **Grand B** Dominica
11C4 **Grand Bahama** I The Bahamas
7E5 **Grand Bank** Can
102F2 **Grand Banks** Atlantic O
97B4 **Grand Bassam** Ivory Coast
9B3 **Grand Canyon** USA
26A3 **Grand Cayman** I Caribbean S
13E2 **Grand Centre** Can
20C1 **Grand Coulee** USA
34B3 **Grande** R Arg
31C4 **Grande** R Bahia, Brazil
35B1 **Grande** R Minas Gerais/São Paulo, Brazil
13D2 **Grande Cache** Can
47A2 **Grande Chartreuse** Region, France
101D2 **Grande Comore** I Comoros
13D1 **Grande Prairie** Can
19A3 **Grande Prairie** USA
95A3 **Grand Erg de Bilma** Desert Niger
96B2 **Grand erg Occidental** Mts Alg
96C2 **Grand erg Oriental** Mts Alg
7C4 **Grande Rivière de la Baleine** R Can
20C1 **Grande Ronde** R USA
7D5 **Grand Falls** New Brunswick, Can
7E5 **Grand Falls** Newfoundland, Can
20C1 **Grand Forks** Can
8D2 **Grand Forks** USA
16B1 **Grand Gorge** USA

14A2 **Grand Haven** USA
19C3 **Grand Isle** USA
19B4 **Grand L** USA
15D1 **Grand Mère** Can
50A2 **Grândola** Port
5J4 **Grand Rapids** Can
14A2 **Grand Rapids**
Michigan, USA
10A2 **Grand Rapids**
Minnesota, USA
47B2 **Grand St Bernard** *P*
Italy/Switz
8B2 **Grand Teton** *Mt*
USA
8B2 **Grand Teton Nat Pk**
USA
46A2 **Grandvilliers** France
25D1 **Grangeburg** USA
51C1 **Granollers** Spain
52A1 **Gran Paradiso** *Mt*
Italy
47D1 **Gran Pilastro** *Mt*
Austria/Italy
43D3 **Grantham** Eng
21B2 **Grant,Mt** USA
44C3 **Grantown-on-Spey**
Scot
9C3 **Grants** USA
20B2 **Grants Pass** USA
48B2 **Granville** France
6H4 **Granville L** Can
35C1 **Grão Mogol** Brazil
49D3 **Grasse** France
21A2 **Grass Valley** USA
5H5 **Gravelbourg** Can
46B1 **Gravelines** France
100C3 **Gravelotte** S Africa
15C2 **Gravenhurst** Can
109D1 **Gravesend** Aust
12H3 **Gravina I** USA
12B2 **Grayling** USA
20B1 **Grays Harbor** *B*
USA
14B3 **Grayson** USA
18C2 **Grayville** USA
59B3 **Graz** Austria
27H1 **Great** *R* Jamaica
11C4 **Great Abaco** *I*
The Bahamas
106B4 **Great Australian**
Bight *G* Aust
16B3 **Great B** New Jersey,
USA
25E2 **Great Bahama Bank**
The Bahamas
110C1 **Great Barrier I** NZ
107D2 **Great Barrier Reef** *Is*
Aust
16C1 **Great Barrington**
USA
4F3 **Great Bear L** Can
9D2 **Great Bend** USA
107D3 **Great Dividing Range**
Mts Aust
42D2 **Great Driffield** Eng
16B3 **Great Egg Harbor** *B*
USA
112B10 **Greater Antarctic**
Region, Ant
26B2 **Greater Antilles** *Is*
Caribbean S
43D4 **Greater London**
Metropolitan County,
Eng
43C3 **Greater Manchester**
County, Eng
25E2 **Great Exuma** *I*
The Bahamas
8B2 **Great Falls** USA
44B3 **Great Glen** *V* Scot
86B1 **Great Himalayan**
Range *Mts* Asia
11C4 **Great Inagua** *I*
The Bahamas
100B4 **Great Karroo** *Mts*
S Africa
109C4 **Great L** Aust
100A3 **Great Namaland**
Region, Namibia
42C3 **Great Ormes Head** *C*
Wales
11C4 **Great Ragged** *I*
The Bahamas
99D3 **Great Ruaha** *R* Tanz

15D2 **Great Sacandaga L**
Can
8B2 **Great Salt L** USA
95B2 **Great Sand Sea**
Libya/Egypt
106B3 **Great Sandy Desert**
Aust
8A2 **Great Sandy Desert**
USA
Great Sandy I =
Fraser I
4G3 **Great Slave L** Can
16C2 **Great South B** USA
106B3 **Great Victoria Desert**
Aust
112C2 **Great Wall** *Base* Ant
72B2 **Great Wall** China
43E3 **Great Yarmouth**
Eng
94B1 **Greco,C** Cyprus
55B3 **Greece**
Republic, Europe
15C2 **Greece** USA
8C2 **Greeley** USA
6B1 **Greely Fjord** Can
14A1 **Green B** USA
14A2 **Green Bay** USA
14A3 **Greencastle** Indiana,
USA
16C1 **Greenfield**
Massachusetts, USA
14A2 **Greenfield**
Wisconsin, USA
13F2 **Green Lake** Can
6F2 **Greenland**
Dependency,
N Atlantic O
102H1 **Greenland Basin**
Greenland S
1B1 **Greenland S**
Greenland
42B2 **Greenock** Scot
16C2 **Greenport** USA
16B3 **Greensboro**
Maryland, USA
11C3 **Greensboro** N
Carolina, USA
15C2 **Greensburg**
Pennsylvania, USA
44B3 **Greenstone** *Pt* Scot
18C2 **Greenup** USA
17A1 **Greenville** Alabama,
USA
97B4 **Greenville** Lib
19B3 **Greenville**
Mississippi, USA
16D1 **Greenville**
N Hampshire, USA
14B2 **Greenville** Ohio, USA
17B1 **Greenville** S
Carolina, USA
19A3 **Greenville** Texas,
USA
43E4 **Greenwich** Eng
16C2 **Greenwich** USA
16B3 **Greenwood**
Delaware, USA
19B3 **Greenwood**
Mississippi, USA
17B1 **Greenwood** S
Carolina, USA
18B2 **Greers Ferry L** USA
108A1 **Gregory,L** Aust
107D2 **Gregory Range** *Mts*
Aust
56C2 **Greifswald** Germany
64F3 **Gremikha** Russian
Fed
56C1 **Grenå** Den
19C3 **Grenada** USA
27E4 **Grenada** *I*
Caribbean S
27E4 **Grenadines,The** *Is*
Caribbean S
109C2 **Grenfell** Aust
49D2 **Grenoble** France
27M2 **Grenville** Grenada
107D2 **Grenville,C** Aust
20B1 **Gresham** USA
78C4 **Gresik** Jawa, Indon
78A3 **Gresik** Sumatera,
Indon
19B4 **Gretna** USA
111B2 **Grey** *R* NZ

12G2 **Grey Hunter Pk** *Mt*
Can
7E4 **Grey Is** Can
16C1 **Greylock,Mt** USA
111B2 **Greymouth** NZ
107D3 **Grey Range** *Mts*
Aust
45C2 **Greystones** Irish Rep
101H1 **Greytown** S Africa
101F1 **Griekwastad** S Africa
17B1 **Griffin** USA
108C2 **Griffith** Aust
107D5 **Grim,C** Aust
15C2 **Grimsby** Can
42D3 **Grimsby** Eng
38B1 **Grimsey** *I* Iceland
13D1 **Grimshaw** Can
39F7 **Grimstad** Nor
47C1 **Grindelwald** Switz
6A2 **Grinnell Pen** Can
6B2 **Grise Fjord** Can
61H1 **Griva** Russian Fed
39J7 **Grobina** Latvia
58C2 **Grodno** Belorussia
86A1 **Gromati** *R* India
56B2 **Groningen** Neth
106C2 **Groote Eylandt** *I*
Aust
100A2 **Grootfontein**
Namibia
100B3 **Grootvloer** *Salt L*
S Africa
27P2 **Gros Islet** St Lucia
46E1 **Grosser Feldberg** *Mt*
Germany
52B2 **Grosseto** Italy
46E2 **Gross-Gerau**
Germany
57C3 **Grossglockner** *Mt*
Austria
47E1 **Gross Venediger** *Mt*
Austria
12C3 **Grosvenor,L** USA
22B2 **Groveland** USA
21A2 **Grover City** USA
15D2 **Groveton** USA
61G5 **Groznyy** Russian Fed
58B2 **Grudziadz** Pol
100A3 **Grünau** Namibia
44E2 **Grutness** Scot
61F3 **Gryazi** Russian Fed
61E2 **Gryazovets** Russian
Fed
29G8 **Grytviken** South
Georgia
45A2 **Gt Blasket** *I*
Irish Rep
35C2 **Guaçui** Brazil
23A1 **Guadalajara** Mexico
50B1 **Guadalajara** Spain
107E1 **Guadalcanal** *I*
Solomon Is
50B2 **Guadalimar** *R* Spain
51B1 **Guadalope** *R* Spain
50B2 **Guadalqivir** *R* Spain
24B2 **Guadalupe** Mexico
3G6 **Guadalupe** *I* Mexico
27E3 **Guadeloupe** *I*
Caribbean S
50B2 **Guadian** *R* Spain
50A2 **Guadiana** *R* Port
50B2 **Guadix** Spain
32D6 **Guajará Mirim** Brazil
32C1 **Guajira,Pen de**
Colombia
32B4 **Gualaceo** Ecuador
34D2 **Gualeguay** Arg
34D2 **Gualeguaychú** Arg
71F2 **Guam** *I* Pacific O
34C3 **Guamini** Arg
77C5 **Gua Musang** Malay
23A1 **Guanajuato** Mexico
23A1 **Guanajuato** State,
Mexico
32D2 **Guanare** Ven
25D2 **Guane** Cuba
73C5 **Guangdong**
Province, China
73A3 **Guanghan** China
72C3 **Guanghua** China
73A4 **Guangmao Shan** *Mt*
China
73B5 **Guangnan** China
72B3 **Guangyuan** China

73D4 **Guangze** China
6/F3 **Guangzhou** China
35C1 **Guanhães** Brazil
32D3 **Guania** *R* Colombia
27E5 **Guanipa** *R* Ven
26B2 **Guantánamo** Cuba
72D1 **Guanting Shuiku** *Res*
China
73B5 **Guanxi** Province,
China
73A3 **Guan Xian** China
32B2 **Guapa** Colombia
33E6 **Guaporé** *R* Brazil/Bol
30C2 **Guaqui** Bol
32B4 **Guaranda** Ecuador
30F4 **Guarapuava** Brazil
35B2 **Guaratinguetá** Brazil
50A1 **Guarda** Port
35B1 **Guarda Mor** Brazil
9C4 **Guasave** Mexico
47D2 **Guastalla** Italy
25C3 **Guatemala**
Guatemala
25C3 **Guatemala** Republic,
Cent America
34C3 **Guatraché** Arg
32C3 **Guavrare** *R*
Colombia
35B2 **Guaxupé** Brazil
27L1 **Guayaguayare**
Trinidad
32A4 **Guayaquil** Ecuador
24A2 **Guaymas** Mexico
34D2 **Guayquiraro** *R* Arg
100B2 **Guba** Zaïre
99E2 **Guban** *Region*
Somalia
79B3 **Gubat** Phil
56C2 **Gubin** Pol
87B2 **Güdür** India
14B2 **Guelpho** Can
26A2 **Guenabacoa** Cuba
98C1 **Guéréda** Chad
48C2 **Guéret** France
48B2 **Guernsey** *I* UK
23A2 **Guerrero** State,
Mexico
99D2 **Gughe** *Mt* Eth
63E2 **Gugigu** China
71F2 **Guguan** *I* Pacific O
109C2 **Guiargambone** Aust
73C4 **Guidong** China
97B4 **Guiglo** Ivory Coast
73C5 **Gui Jiang** *R* China
43D4 **Guildford** Eng
73C4 **Guilin** China
47B2 **Guillestre** France
72A2 **Guinan** China
97A3 **Guinea** Republic,
Africa
102H4 **Guinea Basin** Atlantic
O
97A3 **Guinea-Bissau**
Republic, Africa
97C4 **Guinea,G of** W Africa
26A2 **Güines** Cuba
97B3 **Guir** *Well* Mali
84C2 **Guiranwala** Pak
33E1 **Güiria** Ven
46B2 **Guise** France
79C3 **Guiuan** Phil
73B5 **Gui Xian** China
73B4 **Guiyang** China
73B4 **Guizhou** Province,
China
85C4 **Gujarat** State, India
84C2 **Gujrat** Pak
87B1 **Gulbarga** India
58D1 **Gulbene** Latvia
87B1 **Guledagudda** India
80D3 **Gulf,The** S W Asia
109C2 **Gulgong** Aust
73B4 **Gulin** China
12E2 **Gulkana** USA
12E2 **Gulkana** *R* USA
13E2 **Gull L** Can
13F2 **Gull Lake** Can
55C3 **Gülluk Körfezi** *B*
Turk
99D2 **Gulu** Uganda
109C1 **Guluguba** Aust
97C3 **Gumel** Nig
46D1 **Gummersbach**
Germany

86A2 **Gumpla** India
93C1 **Gümüşhane** Turk
85D4 **Guna** India
99D1 **Guna** *Mt* Eth
109C3 **Gundagai** Aust
98B3 **Gungu** Zaïre
6H3 **Gunnbjørn Fjeld** *Mt* Greenland
109D2 **Gunnedah** Aust
87B1 **Guntakal** India
17A1 **Guntersville** USA
17A1 **Guntersville L** USA
87C1 **Guntür** India
77C5 **Gunung Batu Putch** *Mt* Malay
78D3 **Gunung Besar** *Mt* Indon
78D2 **Gunung Bulu** *Mt* Indon
78A3 **Gunung Gedang** *Mt* Indon
78C2 **Gunung Lawit** *Mt* Malay
78C4 **Gunung Lawu** *Mt* Indon
78D2 **Gunung Menyapa** *Mt* Indon
78D2 **Gunung Niapa** *Mt* Indon
78A3 **Gunung Patah** *Mt* Indon
78C4 **Gunung Raung** *Mt* Indon
78A3 **Gunung Resag** *Mt* Indon
78D3 **Gunung Sarempaka** *Mt* Indon
78C4 **Gunung Sumbing** *Mt* Indon
77C5 **Gunung Tahan** *Mt* Malay
78A2 **Gunung Talakmau** *Mt* Indon
100A2 **Gunza** Angola
72D3 **Guoyang** China
84D2 **Gurdāspur** India
84D3 **Gurgaon** India
86A1 **Gurkha** Nepal
92C2 **Gürün** Turk
31B2 **Gurupi** *R* Brazil
100C2 **Guruve** Zim
72A1 **Gurvan Sayhan Uul** *Upland* Mongolia
61H4 **Gur'yev** Kazakhstan
97C3 **Gusau** Nig
58C2 **Gusev** Russian Fed
74A3 **Gushan** China
61F2 **Gus'khrustalnyy** Russian Fed
12G3 **Gustavus** USA
22B2 **Gustine** USA
11B3 **Guston** USA
56B2 **Gütersloh** Germany
18C2 **Guthrie** Kentucky, USA
18A2 **Guthrie** Oklahoma, USA
23B1 **Gutiérrez Zamora** Mexico
33F3 **Guyana** Republic, S America
102F4 **Guyana Basin** Atlantic O
72C1 **Guyang** China
48B3 **Guyenne** Region, France
9C3 **Guymon** USA
109D2 **Guyra** Aust
72B2 **Guyuan** China
109C2 **Gwabegar** Aust
85D3 **Gwalior** India
100B3 **Gwanda** Zim
98C2 **Gwane** Zaïre
82A3 **Gwardar** Pak
45B1 **Gweebarra B** Irish Rep
89G9 **Gwelo** Zim
43C4 **Gwent** County, Wales
100B2 **Gweru** Zim
109C1 **Gwydir** *R* Aust
43C3 **Gwynedd** Wales
65F5 **Gyandzha** Azerbaijan
86B1 **Gyangzê** China

68B3 **Gyaring Hu** *L* China
64J2 **Gydanskiy Poluostrov** *Pen* Russian Fed
86B1 **Gyirong** China
6F3 **Gyldenløues** Greenland
109D1 **Gympie** Aust
59B3 **Gyöngyös** Hung
59B3 **Györ** Hung

H

38K6 **Haapajärvi** Fin
60B2 **Haapsalu** Estonia
56A2 **Haarlem** Neth
46D1 **Haarstrang** Region, Germany
25D2 **Habana** Cuba
86C2 **Habiganj** Bang
74D4 **Hachijō-jima** *I* Japan
75B1 **Hachiman** Japan
74E2 **Hachinohe** Japan
75B1 **Hachioji** Japan
16B2 **Hackettstown** USA
108A2 **Hack,Mt** *Mt* Aust
42C2 **Haddington** Scot
108B1 **Haddon Corner** Aust
108B1 **Haddon Downs** Aust
97D3 **Hadejia** Nig
97C3 **Hadejia** *R* Nig
94B2 **Hadera** Israel
56B1 **Haderslev** Den
81D4 **Hadiboh** Socotra
4H2 **Hadley B** Can
73B5 **Hadong** Vietnam
81C4 **Haḍramawt** Region, Yemen
56C1 **Hadsund** Den
74B3 **Haeju** N Korea
91A4 **Hafar al Bāṭin** S Arabia
6D2 **Haffners Bjerg** *Mt* Greenland
84C2 **Hafizabad** Pak
86C1 **Hāflong** India
38A2 **Hafnafjörður** Iceland
12B3 **Hagemeister** *I* USA
56B2 **Hagen** Germany
15C3 **Hagerstown** USA
75A2 **Hagi** Japan
73A5 **Ha Giang** Vietnam
46D2 **Hagondange** France
45B2 **Hags Hd** *C* Irish Rep
46D2 **Haguenan** France
96A2 **Hagunia** *Well* Mor
69G4 **Haha-jima** *I* Japan
68B3 **Hah Xil Hu** *L* China
74A2 **Haicheng** China
76D1 **Hai Duong** Viet
94B2 **Haifa** Israel
94B2 **Haifa,B** of Israel
72D2 **Hai He** *R* China
73C5 **Haikang** China
76E1 **Haikou** China
80C3 **Ha'īl** S Arabia
86C2 **Hailakāndi** India
63D3 **Hailar** China
74B2 **Hailong** China
69E2 **Hailun** China
38J5 **Hailuoto** *I* Fin
76D2 **Hainan** *I* China
12G3 **Haines** USA
12G2 **Haines Junction** Can
59B3 **Hainfeld** Austria
73B5 **Haiphong** Vietnam
26C3 **Haiti** Republic, Caribbean S
95C3 **Haiya** Sudan
72A2 **Haiyan** China
72B2 **Haiyuan** China
72D3 **Haizhou Wan** *B* China
59C3 **Hajdúböszörmény** Hung
75B1 **Hajiki-saki** *Pt* Japan
86C2 **Haka** Burma
21C4 **Hakalau** Hawaiian Is
93D2 **Hakkâri** Turk
74E2 **Hakodate** Japan
75B1 **Hakui** Japan
75B1 **Haku-san** *Mt* Japan
92C2 **Halab** Syria
93E3 **Halabja** Iraq
95C2 **Halaib** Sudan
94C1 **Halba** Leb

68B2 **Halban** Mongolia
56C2 **Halberstadt** Germany
79B3 **Halcon,Mt** Phil
39G7 **Halden** Nor
86B2 **Haldia** India
84D3 **Haldwāni** India
13C1 **Halfway** *R* Can
7D5 **Halifax** Can
42D3 **Halifax** Eng
6D1 **Hall Basin** *Sd* Can
6B3 **Hall Beach** Can
46C1 **Halle** Belg
56C2 **Halle** Germany
112B1 **Halley** *Base* Ant
39F6 **Hallingdal** *R* Nor
6D3 **Hall Pen** Can
106B2 **Hall's Creek** Aust
71D3 **Halmahera** *I* Indon
39G7 **Halmstad** Sweden
56B2 **Haltern** Germany
38J5 **Halti** *Mt* Nor
42C2 **Haltwhistle** Eng
91B4 **Halul** *I* Qatar
94B3 **Haluza** *Hist Site* Israel
75A2 **Hamada** Japan
96C2 **Hamada de Tinrhert** *Desert Region* Alg
96B2 **Hamada du Dra** *Upland* Alg
90A3 **Hamadān** Iran
96B2 **Hamada Tounassine** Region, Alg
92C2 **Hamāh** Syria
75B2 **Hamamatsu** Japan
39G6 **Hamar** Nor
87C3 **Hambantota** Sri Lanka
19B3 **Hamburg** Arkansas, USA
18A1 **Hamburg** Iowa, USA
16B2 **Hamburg** Pennsylvania, USA
56B2 **Hamburg** Germany
16C2 **Hamden** USA
39J6 **Hämeeninna** Fin
106A3 **Hamersley Range** *Mts* Aust
74B2 **Hamgyong Sanmaek** *Mts* N Korea
74B2 **Hamhüng** N Korea
68B2 **Hami** China
94B1 **Hamidīyah** Syria
108B3 **Hamilton** Aust
14C2 **Hamilton** Can
110C1 **Hamilton** NZ
14B3 **Hamilton** Ohio, USA
42B2 **Hamilton** Scot
22B2 **Hamilton,Mt** USA
38K6 **Hamina** Fin
86A1 **Hamirpur** India
56B2 **Hamm** Germany
95A2 **Hammādāh al Hamra** *Upland* Libya
38H6 **Hammerdal** Sweden
38J4 **Hammerfest** Nor
14A2 **Hammond** Illinois, USA
19B3 **Hammond** Louisiana, USA
16B3 **Hammonton** USA
111B3 **Hampden** NZ
43D4 **Hampshire** County, Eng
19B3 **Hampton** Arkansas, USA
91C4 **Hāmūn-e Jaz Mūrīan** *L* Iran
84B3 **Hamun-i-Lora** *Salt L* Pak
21C4 **Hana** Hawaiian Is
21C4 **Hanalei** Hawaiian Is
74E3 **Hanamaki** Japan
72C2 **Hancheng** China
73C3 **Hanchuan** China
15C3 **Hancock** Maryland, USA
10B2 **Hancock** Michigan, USA
75B2 **Handa** Japan
72C2 **Handan** China
99D3 **Handeni** Tanz
72B2 **Hanggin Qi** China

39J7 **Hangö** Fin
73E3 **Hangzhou** China
73E3 **Hangzhou Wan** *B* China
111B2 **Hanmer Springs** NZ
13E2 **Hanna** Can
18B2 **Hannibal** USA
56B2 **Hannover** Germany
39G7 **Hanöbukten** *B* Sweden
76D1 **Hanoi** Viet
16A3 **Hanover** USA
29B6 **Hanover** *I* Chile
72B3 **Han Shui** China
73C3 **Han Shui** *R* China
85D3 **Hänsi** India
68C2 **Hantay** Mongolia
72B3 **Hanzhong** China
86B2 **Hãora** India
38J5 **Haparanda** Sweden
86C1 **Häpoli** India
92C4 **Haql** S Arabia
91A5 **Haradh** S Arabia
99E2 **Hara Fanna** Eth
75C1 **Haramachi** Japan
101C2 **Harare** Zim
'98C1 **Harazé** Chad
14B2 **Harbor Beach** USA
85D4 **Harda** India
39F6 **Hardangerfjord** *Inlet* Nor
46D2 **Hardt** Region, Germany
108A2 **Hardwicke B** Aust
18B2 **Hardy** USA
99E2 **Harēr** Eth
99E2 **Hargeysa** Somalia
94B3 **Har Hakippa** *Mt* Israel
68B3 **Harhu** *L* China
78A3 **Hari** *R* Indon
75A2 **Harima-nada** *B* Japan
56B2 **Harlingen** Neth
9D4 **Harlingen** USA
43E4 **Harlow** Eng
94B2 **Har Meron** *Mt* Israel
20C2 **Harney Basin** USA
20C2 **Harney L** USA
38H6 **Härnösand** Sweden
63B3 **Har Nuur** *L* Mongolia
97B4 **Harper** Lib
12F2 **Harper,Mt** USA
15C3 **Harpers Ferry** USA
94B3 **Har Ramon** *Mt* Israel
7C4 **Harricanaw** *R* Can
16B3 **Harrington** USA
7E4 **Harrington Harbour** Can
44A3 **Harris** *District* Scot
18C2 **Harrisburg** Illinois, USA
16A2 **Harrisburg** Pennsylvania, USA
101G1 **Harrismith** S Africa
18B2 **Harrison** USA
15C3 **Harrisonburg** USA
7E4 **Harrison,C** Can
13C3 **Harrison L** Can
18B2 **Harrisonville** USA
44A3 **Harris,Sound of** Chan Scot
14B2 **Harrisville** USA
42D3 **Harrogate** Eng
94B3 **Har Saggi** *Mt* Israel
38H5 **Harstad** Nor
12G2 **Hart** *R* Can
39F6 **Härteigen** *Mt* Nor
16C2 **Hartford** Connecticut, USA
14A2 **Hartford** Michigan, USA
38G6 **Hartkjølen** *Mt* Nor
108A2 **Hart,L** Aust
43B4 **Hartland Pt** Eng
42D2 **Hartlepool** Eng
19A3 **Hartshorne** USA
17B1 **Hartwell Res** USA
101F1 **Hartz** *R* S Africa
68B2 **Har Us Nuur** *L* Mongolia
43E4 **Harwich** Eng
84D3 **Haryāna** State, India
94B3 **Hāsā** Jordan

Hoh Xil Shan

94B2 Häsbaiya Leb
43D4 Haselmere Eng
75B2 Hashimoto Japan
90A2 Hashtpar Iran
90A2 Hashtrüd Iran
87B2 Hassan India
56B2 Hasselt Belg
96C2 Hassi Inifel Alg
96B2 Hassi Mdakane Well Alg
96C1 Hassi Messaoud Alg
108C3 Hastings Aust
43E4 Hastings Eng
8D2 Hastings Nebraska, USA
110C1 Hastings NZ
108B2 Hatfield Aust
12B1 Hatham Inlet USA
85D3 Häthras India
76D2 Ha Tinh Viet
108B2 Hattah Aust
11C3 Hatteras,C USA
19C3 Hattiesburg USA
59B3 Hatvan Hung
76D3 Hau Bon Viet
99E2 Haud Region, Eth
39F7 Haugesund Nor
110C1 Hauhungaroa Range Mts NZ
13F1 Haultain R Can
110B1 Hauraki G NZ
111A3 Hauroko,L NZ
47C1 Hausstock Mt Switz
96B1 Haut Atlas Mts Mor
98C2 Haute Kotto Region, CAR
46C1 Hautes Fagnes Mts Belg
46B1 Hautmont Belg
96B1 Hauts Plateaux Mts Alg
90D3 Hauzdar Iran
18B1 Havana USA
Havana = Habana
87B3 Havankulam Sri Lanka
110C1 Havelock North NZ
43B4 Haverfordwest Wales
16D1 Haverhill USA
87B2 Häveri India
16C2 Haverstraw USA
59B3 Havlíčkův Brod Czech
8C2 Havre USA
16A3 Havre de Grace USA
7D4 Havre-St-Pierre Can
54C2 Havsa Turk
21C4 Hawaii I Hawaiian Is
21C4 Hawaii Volcanoes Nat Pk Hawaiian Is
111A2 Hawea,L NZ
110B1 Hawera NZ
42C2 Hawick Scot
111A2 Hawkdun Range Mts NZ
110C1 Hawke B NZ
109D2 Hawke,C Aust
108A2 Hawker Aust
76B1 Hawng Luk Burma
93D3 Hawr al Habbaniyah L Iraq
93E3 Hawr al Hammár L Iraq
21B2 Hawthorne USA
108B2 Hay Aust
5G3 Hay R Can
46D2 Hayange France
4B3 Haycock USA
7A4 Hayes R Can
6D2 Hayes Halvø Region Greenland
12E2 Hayes,Mt USA
5G3 Hay River Can
18A2 Haysville USA
22A2 Hayward California, USA
86B2 Hazärïbäg India
46B1 Hazebrouck France
19B3 Hazelhurst USA
4G2 Hazel Str Can
5F4 Hazelton Can
13B1 Hazelton Mts Can
6C1 Hazen L Can

94B3 Hazeva Israel
16B2 Hazleton USA
22A1 Healdsburg USA
108C3 Healesville Aust
12E2 Healy USA
104B6 Heard I Indian O
19A3 Hearne USA
10B2 Hearst Can
72D2 Hebei Province, China
109C1 Hebel Aust
72C2 Hebi China
72C2 Hebian China
7D4 Hebron Can
94B3 Hebron Israel
18A1 Hebron Nebraska, USA
5E4 Hecate Str Can
12I3 Heceta I USA
73B5 Hechi China
4G2 Hecla and Griper B Can
111C2 Hector,Mt NZ
38G6 Hede Sweden
39H6 Hedemora Sweden
20C1 He Devil Mt USA
56B2 Heerenveen Neth
46C1 Heerlen Neth
Hefa = Haifa
73D3 Hefei China
73B4 Hefeng China
69F2 Hegang China
75B1 Hegura jima I Japan
94B3 Heidan R Jordan
56B2 Heide Germany
101G1 Heidelberg Transvaal, S Africa
57B3 Heidelberg Germany
63E2 Heihe China
101G1 Heilbron S Africa
57B3 Heilbronn Germany
56C2 Heiligenstadt Germany
38K6 Heinola Fin
73B4 Hejiang China
6J3 Hekla Mt Iceland
76C1 Hekou Viet
73A5 Hekou Yaozou Zizhixian China
72B2 Helan China
72B2 Helan Shan Mt China
19B3 Helena Arkansas, USA
8B2 Helena Montana, USA
22D3 Helendale USA
71E3 Helen Reef I Pacific O
44B3 Helensburgh Scot
91B4 Helleh R Iran
51B2 Hellin Spain
20C1 Hells Canyon R USA
46D1 Hellweg Region, Germany
22B2 Helm USA
80E2 Helmand R Afghan
100A3 Helmeringhausen Namibia
46C1 Helmond Neth
44C2 Helmsdale Scot
74B2 Helong China
39G7 Helsingborg Sweden
Helsingfors = Helsinki
56C1 Helsingør Den
38J6 Helsinki Fin
43B4 Helston Eng
92B4 Helwân Egypt
19A3 Hempstead USA
39H7 Hemse Sweden
72A3 Henan China
72C3 Henan Province, China
110B1 Hen and Chicken Is NZ
14A3 Henderson Kentucky, USA
9B3 Henderson Nevada, USA
19B3 Henderson Texas, USA
73E5 Heng-ch'un Taiwan
68B4 Hengduan Shan Mts China

56R2 Hengelo Neth
72B2 Hengshan China
72D2 Hengshui China
76D1 Heng Xian China
73C4 Hengyang China
77A4 Henhoaha Nicobar Is
43D4 Henley-on-Thames Eng
16B3 Henlopen,C USA
7B4 Henrietta Maria,C Can
18A2 Henryetta USA
112C2 Henryk Arctowski Base Ant
6D3 Henry Kater Pen Can
68C2 Hentiyn Nuruu Mts Mongolia
76B2 Henzada Burma
73B5 Hepu China
80E2 Herat Afghan
5H4 Herbert Can
110C2 Herbertville NZ
46E1 Herborn Germany
26A4 Heredia Costa Rica
43C3 Hereford Eng
43C3 Hereford & Worcester County, Eng
46C1 Herentals Belg
47B1 Héricourt France
18A2 Herington USA
111A3 Heriot NZ
47C1 Herisau Switz
15D2 Herkimer USA
44E1 Herma Ness Pen Scot
109C2 Hermidale Aust
111B2 Hermitage NZ
Hermon,Mt = Jebel ash Shaykh
24A2 Hermosillo Mexico
16A2 Herndon Pennsylvania, USA
22C2 Herndon California, USA
46D1 Herne Germany
56B1 Herning Den
90A2 Herowäbad Iran
50A2 Herrera del Duque Spain
16A2 Hershey USA
43D4 Hertford County, Eng
94B2 Herzliyya Israel
46C1 Hesbaye Region, Belg
46B1 Hesdin France
72B2 Heshui China
22D3 Hesperia USA
12H2 Hess R Can
57B2 Hessen State, Germany
22C2 Hetch Hetchy Res USA
42C2 Hexham Eng
73C5 He Xian China
73C5 Heyuan China
108B3 Heywood Aust
72D2 Heze China
17D2 Hialeah USA
10A2 Hibbing USA
110C1 Hicks Bay NZ
109C3 Hicks,Pt Aust
23B1 Hidalgo State, Mexico
24B2 Hidalgo del Parral Mexico
35B1 Hidrolândia Brazil
96A2 Hierro I Canary Is
75C1 Higashine Japan
74B4 Higashi-suidō Str Japan
20B2 High Desert USA
19B4 High Island USA
44B3 Highland Region, Scot
22D3 Highland USA
22C1 Highland Peak Mt USA
16B2 Highlands Falls USA
11B3 High Point USA
13D1 High Prairie Can
5G4 High River Can
17B2 High Springs USA
16B2 Hightstown USA
43D4 High Wycombe Eng

39J7 Hiiumaa I Estonia
80B3 Hijäz Region, S Arabia
75B2 Hikigawa Japan
75B1 Hikone Japan
110B1 Hikurangi NZ
9C4 Hildago Mexico
9C4 Hildago del Parral Mexico
56B2 Hildesheim Germany
27R3 Hillaby,Mt Barbados
66C1 Hillerød Den
14B3 Hillsboro Ohio, USA
20B1 Hillsboro Oregon, USA
19A3 Hillsboro Texas, USA
108C2 Hillston Aust
44E1 Hillswick Scot
21C4 Hilo Hawaiian Is
93C2 Hilvan Turk
56B2 Hilversum Neth
84D2 Himachal Pradesh State, India
82B3 Himalaya Mts Asia
85C4 Himatnagar India
74C4 Himeji Japan
74D3 Himi Japan
92C3 Hims Syria
12E2 Hinchinbrook Entrance USA
12E2 Hinchinbrook I USA
85D3 Hindaun India
84B1 Hindu Kush Mts Afghan
87B2 Hindupur India
13D1 Hines Creek Can
85D4 Hinganghät India
69E2 Hinggan Ling Upland China
85B3 Hingol R Pak
85D5 Hingoli India
38H5 Hinnøya I Nor
16C1 Hinsdale USA
13D2 Hinton Can
34B2 Hipolito Itrogoyen Arg
86A2 Hirakud Res India
92B2 Hirfanli Baraji Res Turk
87B2 Hirihar India
74E2 Hirosaki Japan
74C4 Hiroshima Japan
46C2 Hirson France
54C2 Hirşova Rom
56B1 Hirtshals Den
84D3 Hisär India
26C3 Hispaniola I Caribbean S
94C1 Hisyah Syria
93D3 Hit Iraq
74E3 Hitachi Japan
75C1 Hitachi-Ota Japan
43D4 Hitchin Eng
38F6 Hitra I Nor
75A2 Hiuchi-nada B Japan
75A2 Hiwasa Japan
56B1 Hjørring Den
76B1 Hka R Burma
97C4 Ho Ghana
76D1 Hoa Binh Viet
76D3 Hoa Da Viet
109C4 Hobart Aust
9C3 Hobbs USA
56B1 Hobro Den
13C2 Hobson L Can
99E2 Hobyo Somalia
76D3 Ho Chi Minh Viet
57C3 Hochkonig Mt Austria
54B1 Hódmező'hely Hung
59B3 Hodonin Czech
74B2 Hoeryong N Korea
57C2 Hof Germany
38B2 Hofsjökull Mts Iceland
74C4 Höfu Japan
96C2 Hoggar Upland Alg
46D1 Hohe Acht Mt Germany
72C1 Hohhot China
6J3 Höhn Iceland
68B3 Hoh Sai Hu L China
82C2 Hoh Xil Shan Mts China

99D2 **Hoima** Uganda
86C1 **Hojāi** India
75A2 **Hojo** Japan
110B1 **Hokianga Harbour** *B* NZ
111B2 **Hokitika** NZ
74E2 **Hokkaidō** Japan
90C2 **Hokmābād** Iran
109C3 **Holbrook** Aust
9B3 **Holbrook** USA
19A2 **Holdenville** USA
87B2 **Hole Narsipur** India
27R3 **Holetown** Barbados
26B2 **Holguín** Cuba
111B2 **Holitika** NZ
12C2 **Holitna** *R* USA
59B3 **Hollabrunn** Austria
14A2 **Holland** USA
22B2 **Hollister** USA
19C3 **Holly Springs** USA
22C3 **Hollywood** California, USA
17B2 **Hollywood** Florida, USA
4G2 **Holman Island** Can
38J6 **Holmsund** Sweden
94B2 **Holon** Israel
56B1 **Holstebro** Den
6E3 **Holsteinborg** Greenland
14B2 **Holt** USA
18A2 **Holton** USA
12C2 **Holy Cross** USA
42B3 **Holyhead** Wales
42D2 **Holy I** Eng
43B3 **Holy I** Wales
16C1 **Holyoke** Massachusetts, USA
86C2 **Homalin** Burma
6D3 **Home B** Can
12D3 **Homer** Alaska, USA
19B3 **Homer** Louisiana, USA
111A2 **Homer Tunnel** NZ
17B1 **Homerville** USA
17B2 **Homestead** USA
17A1 **Homewood** USA
87B1 **Homnābād** India
101C3 **Homoine** Mozam
25D3 **Hondo** *R* Mexico
25D3 **Honduras** Republic, Cent America
25D3 **Honduras,G of** Honduras
39G6 **Hønefoss** Nor
15C2 **Honesdale** USA
21A1 **Honey L** USA
76C1 **Hong** *R* Viet
76D1 **Hon Gai** Viet
73A4 **Hongguo** China
73C4 **Hong Hu** *L* China
72B2 **Honghui** China
73C4 **Hongjiang** China
73C5 **Hong Kong** Colony, S E Asia
68D2 **Hongor** Mongolia
73B5 **Hongshui He** *R* China
72A3 **Hongyuan** China
72D3 **Hongze Hu** *L* China
107E1 **Honiara** Solomon Is
77C4 **Hon Khoai** *I* Camb
76D3 **Hon Lan** *I* Viet
38K4 **Honnigsvåg** Nor
21C4 **Honolulu** Hawaiian Is
77C4 **Hon Panjang** *I* Viet
74D3 **Honshu** *I* Japan
20B1 **Hood,Mt** USA
20B1 **Hood River** USA
45C2 **Hook Head** *C* Irish Rep
12G3 **Hoonah** USA
12A2 **Hooper Bay** USA
101G1 **Hoopstad** S Africa
56A2 **Hoorn** Neth
9B3 **Hoover Dam** USA
12E2 **Hope** Alaska, USA
19B3 **Hope** Arkansas, USA
13C3 **Hope** Can
7D4 **Hopedale** Can
64D2 **Hopen** *I* Barents S
6D3 **Hopes Advance,C** Can
108B3 **Hopetoun** Aust
100B3 **Hopetown** S Africa
18C2 **Hopkinsville** USA
20B1 **Hoquiam** USA
93D1 **Horasan** Turk
99F1 **Hordiyo** Somalia
47C1 **Horgen** Switz
105H5 **Horizon Depth** Pacific O
91C4 **Hormuz,Str of** Oman/Iran
59B3 **Horn** Austria
6H3 **Horn** *C* Iceland
38H5 **Hornavan** *L* Sweden
19B3 **Hornbeck** USA
20B2 **Hornbrook** USA
111B2 **Hornby** NZ
7B5 **Hornepayne** Can
4F3 **Horn Mts** Can
42D3 **Hornsea** Eng
72B1 **Horn Uul** *Mt* Mongolia
30E3 **Horqueta** Par
15C2 **Horseheads** USA
56C1 **Horsens** Den
20B1 **Horseshoe Bay** Can
108B3 **Horsham** Aust
43D4 **Horsham** Eng
39G7 **Horten** Nor
4F3 **Horton** *R* Can
78C2 **Hose Mts** Malay
85D4 **Hoshangābād** India
84D2 **Hoshiārpur** India
87B1 **Hospet** India
29C7 **Hoste** *I* Chile
82B2 **Hotan** China
19B3 **Hot Springs** Arkansas, USA
8C2 **Hot Springs** S. Dakota, USA
4G3 **Hottah** Can
46A2 **Houdan** France
72C2 **Houma** China
19B4 **Houma** USA
16C2 **Housatonic** *R* USA
13B2 **Houston** Can
19C3 **Houston** Mississippi, USA
19A4 **Houston** Texas, USA
106A3 **Houtman** *Is* Aust
68B2 **Hovd** Mongolia
68C1 **Hövsgol Nuur** *L* Mongolia
14A2 **Howard City** USA
12C1 **Howard P** USA
109C3 **Howe,C** Aust
101H1 **Howick** S Africa
44C2 **Hoy** *I* Scot
39F6 **Høyanger** Nor
59B2 **Hradeç-Králové** Czech
59B3 **Hranice** Czech
59B3 **Hron** *R* Czech
73E5 **Hsin-chu** Taiwan
73E5 **Hsüeh Shan** *Mt* Taiwan
72B2 **Huachi** China
32B6 **Huacho** Peru
72C1 **Huade** China
72D3 **Huaibei** China
72D3 **Huaibin** China
72D3 **Huai He** *R* China
73C4 **Huaihua** China
73C5 **Huaiji** China
72D3 **Huainan** China
69E4 **Hua-lien** Taiwan
32B5 **Huallaga** *R* Peru
32B5 **Huallanca** Peru
32B5 **Huamachuco** Peru
100A2 **Huambo** Angola
30C2 **Huanay** Bol
32B5 **Huancabamba** Peru
32B6 **Huancavelica** Peru
32B6 **Huancayo** Peru
73D3 **Huangchuan** China
Huang Hai = Yellow S
72D2 **Huang He** *R* China
72B2 **Huangling** China
76D2 **Huangliu** China
73C3 **Huangpi** China
73D3 **Huangshi** China
34C3 **Huanguelén** Arg
73E4 **Huangyan** China
74B2 **Huanren** China
32B5 **Huānuco** Peru
30C2 **Huanuni** Bol
72B2 **Huan Xian** China
32B5 **Huaráz** Peru
32B6 **Huarmey** Peru
32B5 **Huascarán** *Mt* Peru
30B4 **Huasco** Chile
23B2 **Huatusco** Mexico
23B1 **Huauchinango** Mexico
23B2 **Huautla** Mexico
72C2 **Hua Xian** China
24B2 **Huayapan** *R* Mexico
73C3 **Hubei** Province, China
87B1 **Hubli** India
34C3 **Hucal** Arg
74B2 **Huch'ang** N Korea
42D3 **Huddersfield** Eng
39H6 **Hudiksvall** Sweden
17B2 **Hudson** Florida, USA
14B2 **Hudson** Michigan, USA
16C1 **Hudson** New York, USA
16C1 **Hudson** *R* USA
7B4 **Hudson B** Can
5H4 **Hudson Bay** Can
13C1 **Hudson's Hope** Can
6C3 **Hudson Str** Can
76D2 **Hue** Viet
23B1 **Huejutla** Mexico
50A2 **Huelva** Spain
23A2 **Hueramo** Mexico
51B2 **Húercal Overa** Spain
51B1 **Huesca** Spain
23B2 **Huexotla** *Hist Site* Mexico
107D3 **Hughenden** Aust
12D1 **Hughes** USA
86B2 **Hugli** *R* India
19A3 **Hugo** USA
73D4 **Hui'an** China
110C1 **Huiarau Range** *Mts* NZ
74B2 **Huich'ŏn** N Korea
74B2 **Huifa He** *R* China
32B3 **Huila** *Mt* Colombia
73D5 **Huilai** China
73A4 **Huili** China
74B2 **Huinan** China
34C2 **Huinca Renancó** Arg
25C3 **Huixtla** Mexico
73A4 **Huize** China
73C5 **Huizhou** China
23B2 **Hujuápan de Léon** Mexico
69F2 **Hulin** China
15C1 **Hull** Can
42D3 **Hull** Eng
58B1 **Hultsfred** Sweden
63D3 **Hulun Nur** *L* China
69E1 **Huma** China
33E5 **Humaita** Brazil
100B4 **Humansdorp** S Africa
42D3 **Humber** *R* Eng
42D3 **Humberside** County, Eng
5H4 **Humboldt** Can
20C2 **Humboldt** *R* USA
20B2 **Humboldt B** USA
6D2 **Humboldt Gletscher** *Gl* Greenland
21B2 **Humboldt L** USA
108C1 **Humeburn** Aust
109C3 **Hume,L** Aust
100A2 **Humpata** Angola
22C2 **Humphreys** USA
38A1 **Húnaflóri** *B* Iceland
73C4 **Hunan** Province, China
74C2 **Hunchun** China
13C2 **Hundred Mile House** Can
54B1 **Hunedoara** Rom
59B3 **Hungary** Republic, Europe
108B1 **Hungerford** Aust
74B3 **Hŭngnam** N Korea
74B2 **Hunjiang** China
46D2 **Hunsrück** Mts, Germany
109D2 **Hunter** *R* Aust
13B2 **Hunter I** Can
109C4 **Hunter Is** Aust
12D2 **Hunter,Mt** USA
14A3 **Huntingburg** USA
43D3 **Huntingdon** Eng
14A2 **Huntingdon** Indiana, USA
14B3 **Huntington** W Virginia, USA
22C4 **Huntington Beach** USA
22C2 **Huntington L** USA
110C1 **Huntly** NZ
44C3 **Huntly** Scot
12J2 **Hunt,Mt** Can
108A1 **Hunt Pen** Aust
17A1 **Huntsville** Alabama, USA
15C1 **Huntsville** Can
19A3 **Huntsville** Texas, USA
76D2 **Huong Khe** Viet
71F4 **Huon Peninsula** *Pen* PNG
109C4 **Huonville** Aust
14B1 **Hurd,C** Can
80B3 **Hurghada** Egypt
8D2 **Huron** S. Dakota, USA
14B1 **Huron,L** Can/USA
34A2 **Hurtado** Chile
111B2 **Hurunui** *R* NZ
38B1 **Husavik** Iceland
54C1 **Huşi** Rom
39G7 **Huskvarna** Sweden
12C1 **Huslia** USA
94B2 **Husn** Jordan
56B2 **Husum** Germany
109C1 **Hutton,Mt** Aust
72D2 **Hutuo He** *R* China
46C1 **Huy** Belg
72A2 **Huzhu** China
52C2 **Hvar** *I* Croatia
100B2 **Hwange** Zim
100B2 **Hwange Nat Pk** Zim
15D2 **Hyannis** USA
68B2 **Hyaryas Nuur** *L* Mongolia
5E4 **Hydaburg** Can
16C2 **Hyde Park** USA
87B1 **Hyderābād** India
85B3 **Hyderabad** Pak
49D3 **Hyères** France
12J2 **Hyland** *R* Can
8B2 **Hyndman Peak** *Mt* USA
38K6 **Hyrynsalmi** Fin
13D1 **Hythe** Can
74C4 **Hyūga** Japan
39J6 **Hyvikää** Fin

I

31C4 **Iaçu** Brazil
54C2 **Ialomiţa** *R* Rom
54C1 **Iaşi** Rom
97C4 **Ibadan** Nig
32B3 **Ibagué** Colombia
54B2 **Ibar** *R* Montenegro/Serbia, Yugos
32B3 **Ibarra** Ecuador
35B1 **Ibiá** Brazil
30E4 **Ibicui** *R* Brazil
34D2 **Ibicuy** Arg
51C2 **Ibiza** Spain
51C2 **Ibiza** *I* Spain
101D2 **Ibo** Mozam
31C4 **Ibotirama** Brazil
91C5 **'Ibrī** Oman
32B6 **Ica** Peru
32D4 **Icá** *R* Brazil
32D3 **Icana** Brazil
38A1 **Iceland** Republic, N Atlantic O
13C2 **Ice Mt** Can
87A1 **Ichalkaranji** India
74E3 **Ichihara** Japan
75B1 **Ichinomiya** Japan
74E3 **Ichinoseki** Japan
12F3 **Icy B** USA
4B2 **Icy C** USA
19B3 **Idabell** USA
8B2 **Idaho Falls** USA
20B2 **Idanha** USA
46D2 **Idar Oberstein** Germany

Isla de Lobos

95A2 Idehan Marzūg *Desert* Libya
95A2 Idehan Ubari *Desert* Libya
96C2 Idelés Alg
68B2 Iderlym Gol *R* Mongolia
95C2 Idfu Egypt
55B3 Idhi Oros *Mt* Greece
55B3 Idhra *I* Greece
98B3 Idiofa Zaïre
12C2 Iditarod *R* USA
92C2 Idlib Syria
39K7 Idritsa Russian Fed
100B4 Idutywa S Africa
55C3 Ierápetra Greece
46B1 Ieper Belg
63D2 Iet Oktyobr'ya Russian Fed
99D3 Ifakara Tanz
71F3 Ifalik *I* Pacific O
101D3 Ifanadiana Madag
97C4 Ife Nig
97C3 Iférouane Niger
78C2 Igan Malay
35B2 Igaranava Brazil
93E2 Igdir Iran
39H6 Iggesund Sweden
34B2 Iglesia Arg
53A3 Iglesias Sardegna
6B3 Igloolik Can
10A2 Ignace Can
55B3 Igoumenítsa Greece
61H2 Igra Russian Fed
23B2 Iguala Mexico
35B2 Iguape Brazil
35B2 Iguatama Brazil
31D3 Iguatu Brazil
98A3 Iguéla Gabon
101D3 Ihosy Madag
74D3 Iida Japan
75B1 Iide-san *Mt* Japan
38K6 Iisalmi Fin
75A2 Iizuka Japan
97C4 Ijebu Ode Nig
56B2 Ijsselmeer *S* Neth
55C3 Ikaría *I* Greece
74E2 Ikeda Japan
98C3 Ikela Zaïre
54R2 Ikhtiman Bulg
12D3 Ikolik,C USA
101D2 Ikopa *R* Madag
79B2 Ilagan Phil
90A3 Ilām Iran
47C1 Ilanz Switz
13F1 Ile à la Crosse Can
13F1 Ile à la Crosse,L Can
89G8 Ilebo Zaïre
96D1 Ile de Jerba *I* Tunisia
48B2 Ile de Noirmoutier *I* France
48B2 Ile de Ré *I* France
107F3 Ile des Pins *I* Nouvelle Calédonie
48A2 Ile d'Ouessant *I* France
48B2 Ile d'Yeu *I* France
61J3 Ilek *R* Russian Fed
107F2 Iles Bélep Nouvelle Calédonie
107E2 Iles Chesterfield Nouvelle Calédonie
49D3 Iles d'Hyères *Is* France
43B4 Ilfracombe Eng
92B1 Ilgaz Dağları *Mts* Turk
101C3 Ilha Bazaruto *I* Mozam
33G3 Ilha De Maracá *I* Brazil
33G4 Ilha de Marajó *I* Brazil
35B2 Ilha de São Sebastião *I* Brazil
33G6 Ilha do Bananal *Region* Brazil
35C2 Ilha Grande *I* Brazil
35B2 Ilha Santo Amaro *I* Brazil
96A1 Ilhas Selvegens *I* Atlantic O

35A2 Ilha Solteira Dam Brazil
31D4 Ilhéus Brazil
12C3 Iliamna L USA
12D2 Iliamna V USA
79B4 Iligan Phil
63C2 Ilim *R* Russian Fed
63C2 Ilimsk Russian Fed
63G3 Il'inskiy Russian Fed
55R3 Iliodhrómia *I* Greece
79B4 Illana B Phil
34A2 Illapel Chile
34A2 Illapel *R* Chile
97C3 Illéla Niger
47D1 Iller *R* Germany
4C4 Illiamna L USA
10A2 Illinois State, USA
18B2 Illinois *R* USA
96C2 Illizi Alg
30B2 Ilo Peru
79B3 Iloilo Phil
38L6 Ilomantsi Fin
97C4 Ilorin Nig
75A2 Imabari Japan
75B1 Imalchi Japan
60C1 Imatra Fin
30G4 Imbituba Brazil
99E2 Imi Eth
20C2 Imlay USA
47D1 Immenstadt Germany
52B2 Imola Italy
31B3 Imperatriz Brazil
52A2 Imperia Italy
98B2 Impfondo Congo
86C2 Imphāl India
47D1 Imst Austria
12B1 Imuruk L USA
75B1 Ina Japan
96C2 In Afahleleh *Well* Alg
75B2 Inamba-jima *I* Japan
96C2 In Amenas Alg
38K5 Inari Fin
38K5 Inarijärvi *L* Fin
75C1 Inawashiro-ko *L* Japan
96C2 In Belbel Alg
60E5 Ince Burun *Pt* Turk
92B2 Incekum Burun *Pt* Turk
74B3 Inch'ŏn S Korea
96B2 In Dagouber *Well* Mali
35B1 Indaia *R* Brazil
38H6 Indals *R* Sweden
21B2 Independence California, USA
18A2 Independence Kansas, USA
18B2 Independence Missouri, USA
78A3 Inderagiri *R* Indon
61H4 Inderborskly Kazakhstan
83B3 India Federal Republic, Asia
14A2 Indiana State, USA
15C2 Indiana USA
104C6 Indian-Antarctic Ridge Indian O
14A3 Indianapolis USA
— Indian Desert = Thar Desert
7E4 Indian Harbour Can
104B4 Indian O
18B1 Indianola Iowa, USA
19B3 Indianola Mississippi, USA
35B1 Indianópolis Brazil
76D2 Indo China *Region*, S E Asia
70C4 Indonesia Republic, S E Asia
85D4 Indore India
78B4 Indramayu Indon
48C2 Indre *R* France
85B3 Indus *R* Pak
60D5 Inebdu Turk
96C2 In Ebeggi *Well* Alg
96C2 In Ecker Alg
92A1 Inegöl Turk
96D2 In Ezzane Alg
97C3 Ingal Niger
14B2 Ingersoll Can

107D2 Ingham Aust
6D2 Inglefield Land *Region* Can
110B1 Inglewood NZ
109D1 Inglewood Queensland, Aust
22C4 Inglewood USA
108B3 Inglewood Victoria, Aust
38B2 Ingólfshöfði *I* Iceland
57C3 Ingolstadt Germany
86B2 Ingrāj Bāzār India
96C3 In-Guezzam *Well* Alg
101C3 Inhambane Mozam
101C3 Inharrime Mozam
35B1 Inhumas Brazil
32D3 Inírida *R* Colombia
45A2 Inishbofin *I* Irish Rep
45A1 Inishkea *I* Irish Rep
45B2 Inishmaan *I* Irish Rep
45B2 Inishmore *I* Irish Rep
45B1 Inishmurray *I* Irish Rep
45C1 Inishowen District, Irish Rep
45A2 Inishshark *I* Irish Rep
45A2 Inishturk *I* Irish Rep
109C1 Injune Aust
12H3 Inklin Can
12H3 Inklin *R* Can
12C1 Inland L USA
47D1 Inn *R* Austria
108B1 Innamincka Aust
68C2 Inner Mongolia Autonomous Region, China
107D2 Innisfail Aust
12C2 Innoko *R* USA
57C3 Innsbruck Austria
98B3 Inongo Zaïre
58B2 Inowrocław Pol
96C2 In Salah Alg
47B1 Interlaken Switz
24C3 Intexpec Mexico
47C2 Intra Italy
78D3 Intu Indon
75C1 Inubo-saki *C* Japan
7C4 Inukjuak Can
4E3 Inuvik Can
4F3 Inuvik *Region* Can
44B3 Inveraray Scot
111A3 Invercargill NZ
109D1 Inverell Aust
13D2 Invermere Can
44B3 Inverness Scot
44C3 Inverurie Scot
108A3 Investigator Str Aust
68A1 Inya Russian Fed
21B2 Inyokern USA
98B3 Inzia *R* Zaïre
55B3 Ioánnina Greece
18A2 Iola USA
44A3 Iona *I* Scot
100A2 Iôna Nat Pk Angola
20C1 Ione USA
— Ionian Is = Ionioi Nísoi
55A3 Ionian S Italy/Greece
55B3 Ionioi Nísoi *Is* Greece
55C3 Ios *I* Greece
10A2 Iowa *R* USA
10A2 Iowa City USA
35B1 Ipameri Brazil
35C1 Ipanema Brazil
61F4 Ipatovo Russian Fed
32B3 Ipiales Colombia
77C5 Ipoh Malay
30F2 Iporá Brazil
55C2 Ipsala Turk
109D1 Ipswich Aust
43E3 Ipswich Eng
16D1 Ipswich USA
30B3 Iquique Chile
32C4 Iquitos Peru
55C3 Iráklion Greece
80D2 Iran Republic, S W Asia
91D4 Irānshahr Iran
23A1 Irapuato Mexico

93D3 Iraq Republic, S W Asia
95A2 Irā Wan *Watercourse* Libya
94B2 Irbid Jordan
61K2 Irbit Russian Fed
36C3 Ireland Republic, NW Europe
33F3 Ireng *R* Guyana
74B3 Iri S Korea
71E4 Irian Jaya Province, Indon
95B3 Iriba Chad
79B3 Iriga Phil
99D3 Iringa Tanz
69E4 Iriomote *I* Japan
33G5 Iriri *R* Brazil
42B3 Irish S Eng/Irish Rep
12D1 Irkillik *R* USA
63C2 Irkutsk Russian Fed
65J4 Irlysh *R* Kazakhstan
108A2 Iron Knob Aust
14A1 Iron Mountain USA
107D2 Iron Range Aust
14A1 Iron River USA
14B3 Irontown USA
10A2 Ironwood USA
10B2 Iroquois Falls Can
75B2 Iro-zaki *C* Japan
76A2 Irrawaddy,Mouths of the Burma
65H4 Irtysh *R* Russian Fed
51B1 Irun Spain
42B2 Irvine Scot
19A3 Irving USA
79B4 Isabela Phil
32J7 Isabela *I* Ecuador
4H2 Isachsen Can
4H2 Isachsen,C Can
6H3 Isafjörður Iceland
74C4 Isahaya Japan
98C2 Isangi Zaïre
47D1 Isar *R* Germany
47D1 Isarco *R* Italy
44E1 Isbister Scot
47D1 Ischgl Austria
53B2 Ischia *I* Italy
75B2 Ise Japan
47D2 Iseo Italy
46D1 Iserlohn Germany
53B2 Isernia Italy
75R2 Ise-wan *B* Japan
69E4 Ishigaki *I* Japan
74E2 Ishikari *R* Japan
74E2 Ishikari-wan *B* Japan
65H4 Ishim Russian Fed
65H4 Ishim *R* Kazakhstan
74E3 Ishinomaki Japan
75C1 Ishioka Japan
84C1 Ishkashim Afghan
14A1 Ishpeming USA
65J4 Isil'kul Russian Fed
99D2 Isiolo Kenya
98C2 Isiro Zaïre
92C2 Iskenderun Turk
92C2 Iskenferun Körfezi *B* Turk
92B1 Iskilip Turk
65K4 Iskitim Russian Fed
54B2 Iskur *R* Bulg
12H3 Iskut *R* Can/USA
23B2 Isla Mexico
34C3 Isla Bermejo *I* Arg
27E4 Isla Blanquilla Ven
32A2 Isla Coiba *I* Panama
9B4 Isla de Cedros *I* Mexico
29B4 Isla de Chiloé *I* Chile
25D2 Isla de Cozumel *I* Mexico
26C3 Isla de la Gonâve *I* Cuba
26A2 Isla de la Juventud *I* Cuba
34D2 Isla de las Lechiguanas *I* Arg
3K8 Isla del Coco *I* Costa Rica
25D3 Isla del Maiz *I* Caribbean S
23B1 Isla de Lobos *I* Mexico

Isla de los Estados

29D6 Isla de los Estados / Arg
28E2 Isla de Marajó / Brazil
105L5 Isla de Pascua / Pacific O
26A4 Isla de Providencia / Caribbean S
26A4 Isla de San Andres / Caribbean S
30G4 Isla de Santa Catarina / Brazil
33G2 Isla du Diable / French Guiana
31E2 Isla Fernando de Noronha / Brazil
29C6 Isla Grande de Tierra del Fuego / Arg/Chile
27D4 Isla la Tortuga / Ven
84C2 Islamabad Pak
24A2 Isla Magdalena / Mexico
27E4 Isla Margarita Ven
34A3 Isla Mocha Chile
17B2 Islamorada USA
10A1 Island L Can
108A2 Island Lg Aust
110B1 Islands,B of NZ
32A4 Isla Puná / Ecuador
103D6 Isla San Ambrosia / Pacific O
103D6 Isla San Felix / Pacific O
24A2 Isla Santa Margarita / Mexico
34A3 Isla Santa Maria / Chile
51C2 Islas Baleares Is Spain
96A2 Islas Canarias Is Atlantic O
51C2 Islas Columbretes Is Spain
25D3 Islas de la Bahia Is Honduras
26A4 Islas del Maíz Is Caribbean S
33E1 Islas de Margarita Is Ven
29C7 Islas Diego Ramirez Is Chile
32J7 Islas Galapagos Is Pacific O
30H6 Islas Juan Fernández Chile
32D1 Islas los Roques Is Ven
Islas Malvinas = Falkland Is
105L3 Islas Revilla Gigedo Is Pacific O
29C7 Islas Wollaston Is Chile
97A3 Isla Tidra / Maur
29B5 Isla Wellington / Chile
48C2 Isle R France
104B5 Isle Amsterdam / Indian O
43D4 Isle of Wight / Eng
10B2 Isle Royale / USA
104B5 Isle St Paul / Indian O
104A6 Isles Crozet / Indian O
105J4 Isles de la Société Pacific O
105K5 Îsles Gambier Is Pacific O
101D2 Isles Glorieuses Is Madag
104B6 Isles Kerguelen Is Indian O
105K4 Îsles Marquises Is Pacific O
105J4 Îsles Tuamotu Is Pacific O
105J5 Isles Tubai Is Pacific O
22B1 Isleton USA
92B3 Ismâ'iliya Egypt
101D3 Isoanala Madag
101C2 Isoka Zambia
53B3 Isola Egadi / Italy

52B2 Isola Ponziane / Italy
53B3 Isole Lipari Is Italy
52C2 Isoles Tremiti Is Italy
75B1 Isosaki Japan
92B2 Isparta Turk
94B2 Israel Republic, S W Asia
51C2 Isser R Alg
48C2 Issoire France
49C2 Issoudun France
92A1 Istanbul Turk
55B3 Istiáia Greece
25C3 Istmo de Tehuantepec Isthmus Mexico
17B2 Istokpoga,L USA
52B1 Istra Pen Croatia
35B1 Itaberai Brazil
35C1 Itabira Brazil
35C2 Itabirito Brazil
31D4 Itabuna Brazil
33F4 Itacoatiara Brazil
32B2 Itagui Colombia
33F4 Itaituba Brazil
30G4 Itajai Brazil
35B2 Itajuba Brazil
52B2 Italy Repubic, Europe
35D1 Itamaraju Brazil
35C1 Itamarandiba Brazil
35C1 Itambacuri Brazil
35C1 Itambé Mt Brazil
86C1 Itânagar India
35B2 Itanhaém Brazil
35C1 Itanhém Brazil
35C1 Itanhém R Brazil
35C1 Itaobím Brazil
35B2 Itapecerica Brazil
35C2 Itaperuna Brazil
31C5 Itapetinga Brazil
35B2 Itapetininga Brazil
35B2 Itapeva Brazil
31D2 Itapipoca Brazil
35B1 Itapuranga Brazil
30E4 Itaqui Brazil
35C1 Itarantim Brazil
35B2 Itararé Brazil
35B2 Itararé R Brazil
35C2 Itaúna Brazil
33E6 Iténez R Brazil/Bol
15C2 Ithaca USA
98C2 Itimbiri R Zaïre
35C1 Itinga Brazil
6E3 Itivdleg Greenland
75B2 Ito Japan
74D3 Itoigawa Japan
33E6 Itonomas R Bol
35B2 Itu Brazil
35B1 Itumbiara Brazil
35A1 Iturama Brazil
30C3 Iturbe Arg
35B1 Iturutaba Brazil
56B2 Itzehoe Germany
58D2 Ivacevichi Belorussia
35A2 Ivai R Brazil
38K5 Ivalo Fin
54A2 Ivangrad Montenegro, Yugos
108B2 Ivanhoe Aust
59C3 Ivano-Frankovsk Ukraine
61F2 Ivanovo Russian Fed
65H3 Ivdel' Russian Fed
98B2 Ivindo R Gabon
101D3 Ivohibe Madag
101D2 Ivongo Soanierana Madag
97B4 Ivory Coast Republic, Africa
52A1 Ivrea Italy
6C3 Ivujivik Can
74E3 Iwaki Japan
74C4 Iwakuni Japan
74E2 Iwanai Japan
97C4 Iwo Nig
69G4 Iwo Jima / Japan
23B1 Ixmiquilpa Mexico
23A2 Ixtapa Mexico
23A1 Ixtlán Mexico
75A2 Iyo Japan
75A2 Iyo-nada B Japan
65G4 Izhevsk Russian Fed
64G3 Izhma Russian Fed
91C5 Izki Oman
60C4 Izmail Ukraine

92A2 İzmir Turk
55C3 İzmir Körfezi B Turk
92A1 İzmit Turk
92A1 İznik Turk
55C2 İznik Golü L Turk
94C2 İzra' Syria
23B2 Izúcar de Matamoros Mexico
75B2 Izumi-sano Japan
75A1 Izumo Japan
74D4 Izu-shotō Is Japan

J

95B1 Jabal al Akhdar Mts Libya
94C2 Jabal al 'Arab Syria
95A2 Jabal as Sawdā Mts Libya
91B5 Jabal az Zannah UAE
94C1 Jabal Halimah Mt Leb/Syria
83B3 Jabalpur India
59B2 Jablonec nad Nisou Czech
31D3 Jaboatão Brazil
35B2 Jaboticabal Brazil
51B1 Jaca Spain
23B1 Jacala Mexico
33F5 Jacareacanga Brazil
35B2 Jacarei Brazil
30F3 Jacarezinho Brazil
29C2 Jáchal Arg
35C1 Jacinto Brazil
13F2 Jackfish L Can
109C1 Jackson Aust
22B1 Jackson California, USA
14B2 Jackson Michigan, USA
19B3 Jackson Mississippi, USA
18C2 Jackson Missouri, USA
14B3 Jackson Ohio, USA
11B3 Jackson Tennessee, USA
111B2 Jackson,C NZ
111A2 Jackson Head Pt NZ
19B3 Jacksonville Arkansas, USA
17B1 Jacksonville Florida, USA
18B2 Jacksonville Illinois, USA
17C1 Jacksonville N Carolina, USA
19A3 Jacksonville Texas, USA
17B1 Jacksonville Beach USA
26C3 Jacmel Haiti
84B3 Jacobabad Pak
31C4 Jacobina Brazil
23A2 Jacona Mexico
Jadotville = Likasi
32B5 Jaén Peru
50B2 Jaén Spain
Jaffa = Tel Aviv Yafo
108A3 Jaffa,C Aust
87B3 Jaffna Sri Lanka
86B2 Jagannathganj Ghat Bang
87C1 Jagdalpur India
91C4 Jagin R Iran
87B1 Jagtial India
29F2 Jaguarão R Brazil
35B2 Jaguarialva Brazil
91B4 Jahrom Iran
85D5 Jäina India
72A2 Jainca China
85D3 Jaipur India
85C3 Jaisalmer India
90C2 Jajarm Iran
52C2 Jajce Bosnia & Herzegovina, Yugos
78B4 Jakarta Indon
6E3 Jakobshavn Greenland
38J6 Jakobstad Fin
23B2 Jalaca Mexico
84B2 Jalai-Kut Afghan
23B2 Jalapa Mexico
35A2 Jales Brazil
86B1 Jaleswar Nepal

85D4 Jalgaon India
97D4 Jalingo Nig
51B1 Jalón R Spain
85C3 Jālor India
23A1 Jalostotitlan Mexico
86B1 Jalpáiguri India
23B1 Jalpan Mexico
95B2 Jālū Oasis Libya
32A4 Jama Ecuador
26B3 Jamaica / Caribbean S
26B3 Jamaica Chan Caribbean S
86B2 Jamalpur Bang
78A3 Jambi Indon
85C4 Jambussar India
7B4 James B Can
5J5 Jamestown USA
108A2 Jamestown Aust
8D2 Jamestown N. Dakota, USA
15C2 Jamestown New York, USA
16D2 Jamestown Rhode Island, USA
23B2 Jamiltepec Mexico
87B1 Jamkhandi India
84C2 Jammu India
84D2 Jammu and Kashmir State, India
85B4 Jamnagar India
84C3 Jampur Pak
38K6 Jämsä Fin
86B2 Jamshedpur India
86B1 Janakpur Nepal
35C1 Janaúba Brazil
90B3 Jandaq Iran
109D1 Jandowae Aust
1B1 Jan Mayen / Norwegian S
35C1 Januária Brazil
85D4 Jaora India
51 Japan Empire, E Asia
74C3 Japan,S of S E Asia
104F2 Japan Trench Pacific O
32D4 Japurá R Brazil
93C2 Jarābulus Syria
35B1 Jaraguá Brazil
50B1 Jarama R Spain
94B2 Jarash Jordan
30E3 Jardim Brazil
51B2 Jardin R Spain
26B2 Jardines de la Reina Is Cuba
Jargalant = Hovd
33G3 Jari R Brazil
86C1 Jaria Jhānjail Bang
46C2 Jarny France
58B2 Jarocin Pol
59C2 Jaroslaw Pol
38G6 Järpen Sweden
72B2 Jartai China
85C4 Jasdan India
97C4 Jasikan Ghana
91C4 Jāsk Iran
59C3 Jaslo Pol
29D6 Jason Is Falkland Is
18B2 Jasper Arkansas, USA
13D2 Jasper Can
17B1 Jasper Florida, USA
14A3 Jasper Indiana, USA
19B3 Jasper Texas, USA
13D2 Jasper Nat Pk Can
58B2 Jastrowie Pol
35A1 Jatai Brazil
51B2 Játiva Spain
35B2 Jau Brazil
32B6 Jauja Peru
86A1 Jaunpur India
Java = Jawa
87B2 Javadi Hills India
Javari = Yavari
70B4 Java S Indon
106A2 Java Trench Indon
78B4 Jawa / Indon
71F4 Jayapura Indon
94C2 Jayrūd Syria
96B2 Jbel Ouarkziz Mts Mor
96B1 Jbel Sarhro Mt Mor
19B4 Jeanerette USA
97C4 Jebba Nig

93D2 **Jebel 'Abd al 'Azīz** *Mt* Syria
95B3 **Jebel Abyad** Sudan
91C5 **Jebel Akhdar** *Mt* Oman
92C4 **Jebel al Lawz** *Mt* S Arabia
94B2 **Jebel ash Shaykh** *Mt* Syria
95C2 **Jebel Asoteriba** *Mt* Sudan
94B3 **Jebel Ed Dabab** *Mt* Jordan
94B3 **Jebel el Ata'ita** *Mt* Jordan
92C3 **Jebel esh Sharqi** *Mts* Leb/Syria
94C3 **Jebel Ithrīyat** *Mt* Jordan
91C5 **Jebel Ja'lan** *Mt* Oman
94B2 **Jebel Liban** *Mts* Leb
94C2 **Jebel Ma'lūlā** *Mt* Syria
98C1 **Jebel Marra** *Mt* Sudan
94C3 **Jebel Mudeisisat** *Mt* Jordan
95C2 **Jebel Oda** *Mt* Sudan
94B3 **Jebel Qasr ed Deir** *Mt* Jordan
94B2 **Jebel Um ed Daraj** *Mt* Jordan
95B2 **Jebel Uweinat** *Mt* Sudan
42C2 **Jedburgh** Scot
Jedda = Jiddah
59C2 **Jedrzejów** Pol
19B3 **Jefferson** Texas, USA
11A3 **Jefferson City** USA
8B3 **Jefferson,Mt** USA
14A3 **Jeffersonville** USA
60C2 **Jekabpils** Latvia
59B2 **Jelena Gora** Pol
60B2 **Jelgava** Latvia
78C4 **Jember** Indon
57C2 **Jena** Germany
78B2 **Jenaja** *I* Indon
47D1 **Jenbach** Austria
94B2 **Jenin** Israel
19B3 **Jennings** USA
59B2 **Jeseniky** *Upland* Czech
6F3 **Jensen Nunatakker** *Mt* Greenland
6B3 **Jens Munk** *I* Can
108B3 **Jeparit** Aust
31D4 **Jequié** Brazil
35C1 **Jequital** *R* Brazil
35C1 **Jequitinhonha** Brazil
31C5 **Jequitinhonha** *R* Brazil
50A2 **Jerez de la Frontera** Spain
50A2 **Jerez de los Caballeros** Spain
94B3 **Jericho** Israel
108C3 **Jerilderie** Aust
48B2 **Jersey** *I* UK
10C2 **Jersey City** USA
15C2 **Jersey Shore** USA
18B2 **Jerseyville** USA
92C3 **Jerusalem** Israel
109D3 **Jervis B** Aust
13C2 **Jervis Inlet** *Sd* Can
52B1 **Jesenice** Slovenia
86B2 **Jessore** Bang
11B3 **Jesup** USA
34C2 **Jesus Maria** Arg
16D2 **Jewett City** USA
54A2 **Jezerce** *Mt* Alb
58C2 **Jezioro Mamry** *L* Pol
58C2 **Jezioro Śniardwy** *L* Pol
94B2 **Jezzine** Leb
85C4 **Jhābua** India
85D4 **Jhālāwār** India
84C2 **Jhang Maghiana** Pak
85D3 **Jhānsi** India
86A2 **Jhārsuguda** India
84C2 **Jhelum** Pak
84C2 **Jhelum** *R* Pak
11C3 **J H Kerr L** USA
84D3 **Jhunjhunūn** India
69F2 **Jiamusi** China
73C4 **Ji'an** Jiangxi, China
74B2 **Ji'an** Jilin, China
73D4 **Jiande** China
73B4 **Jiang'an** China
73D4 **Jiangbiancun** China
73A5 **Jiangcheng** China
73B3 **Jiang Jiang** *R* China
73C5 **Jiangmen** China
72D3 **Jiangsu** Province, China
73C4 **Jiangxi** Province, China
73A3 **Jiangyou** China
72D1 **Jianping** China
73A5 **Jianshui** China
73D4 **Jian Xi** *R* China
73D4 **Jianyang** China
72E2 **Jiaonan** China
72E2 **Jiao Xian** China
72E2 **Jiaozhou Wan** *B* China
72C2 **Jiaozuo** China
73E3 **Jiaxiang** China
68B3 **Jiayuguan** China
81B3 **Jiddah** S Arabia
72D3 **Jieshou** China
72C2 **Jiexiu** China
72A3 **Jigzhi** China
59B3 **Jihlava** Czech
99E2 **Jilib** Somalia
69E2 **Jilin** China
51B1 **Jiloca** *R* Spain
99D2 **Jima** Eth
9C4 **Jiménez** Coahuila, Mexico
72D2 **Jinan** China
84D3 **Jind** India
72B2 **Jingbian** China
73D4 **Jingdezhen** China
76C1 **Jinghong** China
73C3 **Jingmen** China
72B2 **Jingning** China
73B4 **Jing Xiang** China
73D4 **Jinhua** China
72C1 **Jining** Nei Monggol, China
72D2 **Jining** Shandong, China
99D2 **Jinja** Uganda
76C1 **Jinping** China
73A4 **Jinsha Jiang** *R* China
73C4 **Jinshi** China
72E1 **Jinxi** China
72E2 **Jin Xian** China
72E1 **Jinzhou** China
33E5 **Jiparaná** *R* Brazil
32A4 **Jipijapa** Ecuador
23A2 **Jiquilpan** Mexico
91C4 **Jiroft** Iran
99E2 **Jirriban** Somalia
73B4 **Jishou** China
92C2 **Jisr ash Shughūr** Syria
54B2 **Jiu** *R* Rom
73D4 **Jiujiang** China
73A4 **Jiulong** China
73D4 **Jiulong Jiang** *R* China
69F2 **Jixi** China
94B3 **Jiza** Jordan
81C4 **Jīzan** S Arabia
97A3 **Joal** Sen
35C1 **João Monlevade** Brazil
31E3 **João Pessoa** Brazil
35B1 **João Pirheiro** Brazil
34B2 **Jocoli** Arg
85C3 **Jodhpur** India
38K6 **Joensuu** Fin
46C2 **Joeuf** France
13D2 **Joffre,Mt** Can
86B1 **Jogbani** India
87A2 **Jog Falls** India
101G1 **Johannesburg** S Africa
21B2 **Johannesburg** USA
6C2 **Johan Pen** Can
12D1 **John** *R* USA
20C2 **John Day** USA
20B1 **John Day** *R* USA
44C2 **John O'Groats** Scot
18A2 **John Redmond Res** USA
11B3 **Johnson City** Tennessee, USA
17B1 **Johnston** USA
27N2 **Johnston Pt** St Vincent
15C2 **Johnstown** Pennsylvania, USA
77C5 **Johor Bharu** Malay
49C2 **Joigny** France
30G4 **Joinville** Brazil
61H3 **Jok** *R* Russian Fed
38H5 **Jokkmokk** Sweden
93E2 **Jolfa** Iran
10B2 **Joliet** USA
7C5 **Joliette** Can
79B4 **Jolo** Phil
79B4 **Jolo** *I* Phil
82D2 **Joma** *Mt* China
58C1 **Jonava** Lithuania
72A3 **Jonê** China
11A3 **Jonesboro** Arkansas, USA
19B3 **Jonesboro** Louisiana, USA
6B2 **Jones Sd** Can
58C1 **Joniškis** Lithuania
39G7 **Jönköping** Sweden
11A3 **Joplin** USA
92C3 **Jordan** Kingdom, S W Asia
94B2 **Jordan** *R* Israel
20C2 **Jordan Valley** USA
86C1 **Jorhāt** India
38J5 **Jörn** Sweden
78C3 **Jorong** Indon
39F7 **Jørpeland** Nor
79B3 **Jose Pañganiban** Phil
106B2 **Joseph Bonaparte G** Aust
64B3 **Jotunheimen** *Mt* Nor
94B2 **Jouai'ya** Leb
94B2 **Jounié** Leb
86C1 **Jowai** India
99E2 **Jowhar** Somalia
12H2 **Joy,Mt** Can
5F5 **Juan de Fuca,Str of** Can/USA
101D2 **Juan de Nova** *I* Mozam Chan
34D3 **Juárez** Arg
31C3 **Juàzeiro** Brazil
31D3 **Juazeiro do Norte** Brazil
99D2 **Juba** Sudan
99E2 **Juba** *R* Somalia
94B1 **Jubail** Leb
93D3 **Jubbah** S Arabia
96A2 **Juby,C** Mor
51B2 **Jucar** *R* Spain
23B2 **Juchatengo** Mexico
23A1 **Juchipila** *R* Mexico
23A1 **Juchitlan** Mexico
57C3 **Judenburg** Austria
30B2 **Juilaca** Peru
73C4 **Juiling Shan** *Hills* China
31C6 **Juiz de Fora** Brazil
30C3 **Jujuy** State, Arg
30C2 **Juli** Peru
33F3 **Julianatop** *Mt* Surinam
6F3 **Julianehab** Greenland
46D1 **Jülich** Germany
84D2 **Jullundur** India
86A1 **Jumla** Nepal
94B3 **Jum Suwwāna** *Mt* Jordan
85C4 **Jūnāgadh** India
72D2 **Junan** China
9D3 **Junction City** USA
31B6 **Jundiaí** Brazil
4E4 **Juneau** USA
107D4 **Junee** Aust
22C2 **June Lake** USA
52A1 **Jungfrau** *Mt* Switz
16A2 **Juniata** *R* USA
29D2 **Junín** Arg
73A4 **Junlian** China
31B6 **Juquiá** Brazil
99C2 **Jur** *R* Sudan
42B2 **Jura** *I* Scot
49D2 **Jura** *Mts* France
44B3 **Jura,Sound of** *Chan* Scot
94B3 **Jurf ed Darāwīsh** Jordan
65K4 **Jurga** Russian Fed
60B2 **Jūrmala** Latvia
32D4 **Juruá** *R* Brazil
33F6 **Juruena** *R* Brazil
94C1 **Jūsīyah** Syria
34B2 **Justo Daract** Arg
32D4 **Jutai** *R* Brazil
25D3 **Juticalpa** Honduras
Jutland = Jylland
90C3 **Jūymand** Iran
56B1 **Jylland** *Pen* Den
38K6 **Jyväskyla** Fin

K

82B2 **K2** *Mt* China/India
90C2 **Kaakhka** Turkmenistan
101H1 **Kaapmuiden** S Africa
71D4 **Kabaena** *I* Indon
97A4 **Kabala** Sierra Leone
99D3 **Kabale** Rwanda
98C3 **Kabalo** Zaïre
98C3 **Kabambare** Zaïre
99D2 **Kabarole** Uganda
98C3 **Kabinda** Zaïre
90A3 **Kabir Kuh** *Mts* Iran
100B2 **Kabompo** Zambia
100B2 **Kabompo** *R* Zambia
98C3 **Kabongo** Zaïre
84B2 **Kabul** Afghan
85B4 **Kachchh,G of** India
61J2 **Kachkanar** Russian Fed
63C2 **Kachug** Russian Fed
76B3 **Kadan** Burma
78D3 **Kadapongan** *I* Indon
85C4 **Kadi** India
108A2 **Kadina** Aust
92B2 **Kadinhanı** Turk
87B2 **Kadiri** India
60E4 **Kadiyevka** Ukraine
100B2 **Kadoma** Zim
99C1 **Kadugli** Sudan
97C3 **Kaduna** Nig
97C3 **Kaduna** *R* Nig
87B2 **Kadūr** India
97A3 **Kaédi** Maur
21C4 **Kaena Pt** Hawaiian Is
74B3 **Kaesŏng** N Korea
97C4 **Kafanchan** Nig
97A3 **Kaffrine** Sen
94C1 **Kafrūn Bashūr** Syria
100B2 **Kafue** Zambia
100B2 **Kafue** *R* Zambia
100B2 **Kafue Nat Pk** Zambia
74D3 **Kaga** Japan
65H6 **Kagan** Kazakhstan
93D1 **Kağizman** Turk
74C4 **Kagoshima** Japan
90C2 **Kāhak** Iran
99D3 **Kahama** Tanz
84B3 **Kahan** Pak
78C3 **Kahayan** *R* Indon
98B3 **Kahemba** Zaïre
46E1 **Kahler Asten** *Mt* Germany
91C4 **Kahnūj** Iran
18B1 **Kahoka** USA
21C4 **Kahoolawe** *I* Hawaiian Is
92C2 **Kahramanmaraş** Turk
21C4 **Kahuku Pt** Hawaiian Is
111B2 **Kaiapoi** NZ
33F2 **Kaieteur Fall** Guyana
72C3 **Kaifeng** China
110B1 **Kaikohe** NZ
111B2 **Kaikoura** NZ
111B2 **Kaikoura Pen** NZ
111B2 **Kaikoura Range** *Mts* NZ
73B4 **Kaili** China
21C4 **Kailua** Hawaiian Is
71E4 **Kaimana** Indon
75B2 **Kainan** Japan
97C3 **Kainji Res** Nig

110B1 **Kaipara Harbour** *B* NZ
73C5 **Kaiping** China
96D1 **Kairouan** Tunisia
22C2 **Kaiser Peak** *Mt* USA
57B3 **Kaiserslautern** Germany
74B2 **Kaishantun** China
58D2 **Kaisiadorys** Lithuania
110B1 **Kaitaia** NZ
111A3 **Kaitangata** NZ
84D3 **Kaithal** India
21C4 **Kaiwi Chan** Hawaiian Is
73B3 **Kai Xian** China
73A5 **Kaiyuan** Liaoning, China
74A2 **Kaiyuan** Yunnan, China
12C2 **Kaiyuh Mts** USA
38K6 **Kajaani** Fin
84B2 **Kajaki** Afghan
99D3 **Kajiado** Kenya
84B2 **Kajrān** Afghan
99D1 **Kaka** Sudan
99D2 **Kakamega** Kenya
75A2 **Kake** Japan
12H3 **Kake** USA
12D3 **Kakhonak** USA
65E5 **Kakhovskoye Vodokhranilishche** *Res* Ukraine
91B4 **Kākī** Iran
87C1 **Kākināda** India
75A2 **Kakogawa** Japan
4D2 **Kaktovik** USA
75C1 **Kakuda** Japan
55B3 **Kalabáka** Greece
78D1 **Kalabakan** Malay
100B2 **Kalabo** Zambia
61F3 **Kalach** Russian Fed
61F4 **Kalach-na-Donu** Russian Fed
86C2 **Kaladan** *R* Burma
21C4 **Ka Lae** *C* Hawaiian Is
100B3 **Kalahari Desert** Botswana
38J6 **Kalajoki** Fin
63D2 **Kalakan** Russian Fed
70A3 **Kalakepen** Indon
84C1 **Kalam** Pak
55B3 **Kalámai** Greece
10B2 **Kalamazoo** USA
84B3 **Kalat** Pak
92B1 **Kalecik** Turk
78D3 **Kalembau** *I* Indon
99C3 **Kalémié** Zaïre
38L5 **Kalevala** Russian Fed
86C2 **Kalewa** Burma
12D2 **Kalgin I** USA
106B4 **Kalgoorlie** Aust
78B4 **Kalianda** Indon
79B3 **Kalibo** Phil
98C3 **Kalima** Zaïre
78C3 **Kalimantan** Province, Indon
55C3 **Kálimnos** *I* Greece
86B1 **Kālimpang** India
60B3 **Kaliningrad** Russian Fed
60C3 **Kalinkovichi** Belorussia
8B2 **Kalispell** USA
58B2 **Kalisz** Pol
99D3 **Kaliua** Tanz
38J5 **Kalix** *R* Sweden
100A3 **Kalkfeld** Namibia
100A3 **Kalkrand** Namibia
108A1 **Kallakoopah** *R* Aust
38K6 **Kallávesi** *L* Fin
55C3 **Kallonis Kólpos** *B* Greece
39H7 **Kalmar** Sweden
61G4 **Kalmykskaya Respublika,** Russian Fed
100B2 **Kalomo** Zambia
18B1 **Kalona** USA
13B2 **Kalone Peak** *Mt* Can
87A2 **Kalpeni** *I* India
85D3 **Kalpi** India
53A3 **Kalsat Khasba** Tunisia
12B2 **Kalskag** USA

12C2 **Kaltag** USA
60E3 **Kaluga** Russian Fed
39G7 **Kalundborg** Den
59C3 **Kalush** Ukraine
87B2 **Kalyandurg** India
60E2 **Kalyazin** Russian Fed
61H1 **Kama** *R* Russian Fed
74E3 **Kamaishi** Japan
84C2 **Kamalia** Pak
110C1 **Kamanawa Mts** NZ
100A2 **Kamanjab** Namibia
84D2 **Kamat** *Mt* India
87B3 **Kamban** India
61H2 **Kambarka** Russian Fed
97A4 **Kambia** Sierra Leone
59D3 **Kamenets Podolskiy** Ukraine
61F3 **Kamenka** Russian Fed
65K4 **Kamen-na-Obi** Russian Fed
61K2 **Kamensk-Ural'skiy** Russian Fed
5H3 **Kamilukuak L** Can
98C3 **Kamina** Zaïre
7A3 **Kaminak L** Can
75C1 **Kaminoyama** Japan
5F4 **Kamloops** Can
93E1 **Kamo** Armenia
75C1 **Kamogawa** Japan
99D2 **Kampala** Uganda
77C5 **Kampar** Malay
78A2 **Kampar** *R* Indon
56B2 **Kampen** Neth
76B2 **Kamphaeng Phet** Thai
77C3 **Kampot** Camb
 **Kampuchea =
 Cambodia**
91D4 **Kamsaptar** Iran
61J2 **Kamskoye Vodokhranilishche** *Res* Russian Fed
85D4 **Kāmthi** India
61G3 **Kamyshin** Russian Fed
61K2 **Kamyshlov** Russian Fed
7C4 **Kanaaupscow** *R* Can
98C3 **Kananga** Zaïre
61G2 **Kanash** Russian Fed
75B1 **Kanayama** Japan
74D3 **Kanazawa** Japan
4C3 **Kanbisha** USA
87B2 **Kānchipuram** India
84B2 **Kandahar** Afghan
64E3 **Kandalaksha** Russian Fed
38L5 **Kandalakshskaya Guba** *B* Russian Fed
97C3 **Kandi** Benin
109C2 **Kandos** Aust
87C3 **Kandy** Sri Lanka
15C2 **Kane** USA
6C1 **Kane Basin** *B* Can
98B1 **Kanem** *Desert Region* Chad
97B3 **Kangaba** Mali
92C2 **Kangal** Turk
6E3 **Kangâmiut** Greenland
91B4 **Kangān** Iran
77C4 **Kangar** Malay
106C4 **Kangaroo I** Aust
6E3 **Kangâtsiaq** Greenland
90A3 **Kangavar** Iran
72C1 **Kangbao** China
82C3 **Kangchenjunga** *Mt* Nepal
73A4 **Kangding** China
6G3 **Kangerdlugssuaq** *B* Greenland
6G3 **Kangerdlugssvatsaiq** *B* Greenland
99D2 **Kangetet** Kenya
74B2 **Kanggye** N Korea
7D4 **Kangiqsualujjuaq** Can
6C3 **Kangiqsujuaq** Can
7C3 **Kangirsuk** Can
74B3 **Kangnŭng** S Korea
98B2 **Kango** Gabon

68B4 **Kanĝto** *Mt* China
72B3 **Kang Xian** China
77D4 **Kanh Hung** Viet
98C3 **Kaniama** Zaïre
87B1 **Kani Giri** India
39J6 **Kankaanpää** Fin
14A2 **Kankakee** USA
14A2 **Kankakee** *R* USA
97B3 **Kankan** Guinea
86A2 **Känker** India
87B3 **Kanniyākuman** India
97C3 **Kano** Nig
74C4 **Kanoya** Japan
86A1 **Kānpur** India
9D3 **Kansas** State, USA
18A2 **Kansas** *R* USA
10A3 **Kansas City** USA
73D5 **Kanshi** China
63B2 **Kansk** Russian Fed
97C3 **Kantchari** Burkina
86B2 **Kanthi** India
12D2 **Kantishna** USA
12D2 **Kantishna** *R* USA
100B3 **Kanye** Botswana
68D4 **Kao-hsiung** Taiwan
100A2 **Kaoka Veld** *Plain* Namibia
97A3 **Kaolack** Sen
100B2 **Kaoma** Zambia
21C4 **Kapaau** Hawaiian Is
98C3 **Kapanga** Zaïre
6F3 **Kap Cort Adelaer** *C* Greenland
6H3 **Kap Dalton** *C* Greenland
39H7 **Kapellskär** Sweden
6F3 **Kap Farvel** *C* Greenland
6G3 **Kap Gustav Holm** *C* Greenland
100B2 **Kapiri** Zambia
78C2 **Kapit** Malay
19B3 **Kaplan** USA
57C3 **Kaplice** Czech
77B4 **Kapoe** Thai
99C3 **Kapona** Zaïre
52C1 **Kaposvár** Hung
6C2 **Kap Parry** *C* Can
6H3 **Kap Ravn** *C* Greenland
78B3 **Kapuas** *R* Indon
108A2 **Kapunda** Aust
84D2 **Kapurthala** India
7B5 **Kapuskasing** Can
109D2 **Kaputar** *Mt* Aust
93E2 **Kapydzhik** *Mt* Armenia
6D2 **Kap York** *C* Greenland
92B1 **Karabük** Turk
55C2 **Karacabey** Turk
85B4 **Karachi** Pak
87A1 **Karād** India
60E5 **Kara Daglari** *Mt* Turk
54C5 **Karadeniz Boğazi** *Sd* Turk
68D1 **Karaftit** Russian Fed
65J5 **Karaganda** Kazakhstan
65J5 **Karagayly** Kazakhstan
87B2 **Kāraikāl** India
90B2 **Karaj** Iran
92C3 **Karak** Jordan
65G5 **Kara Kalpakskaya Respublika,** Uzbekistan
84D1 **Karakax He** *R* China
71D3 **Karakelong** *I* Indon
84D1 **Karakoram** *Mts* India
84D1 **Karakoram** *P* India/China
97A3 **Karakoro** *R* Maur/Sen
65G6 **Karakumy** *Desert* Russian Fed
94B3 **Karama** Jordan
92B2 **Karaman** Turk
65K5 **Karamay** China
111B2 **Karamea** NZ
111B2 **Karamea Bight** *B* NZ
85D4 **Kāranja** India
92B2 **Karapınar** Turk
64H2 **Kara S** Russian Fed

100A3 **Karasburg** Namibia
38K5 **Karasjok** Nor
65J4 **Karasuk** Russian Fed
92C2 **Karataş** Turk
65H5 **Kara Tau** *Mts* Kazakhstan
76B3 **Karathuri** Burma
74B4 **Karatsu** Japan
91B4 **Karāz** Iran
93D3 **Karbalā'** Iraq
59C3 **Karcag** Hung
55B3 **Kardhitsa** Greece
64E3 **Karel'skaya Respublika,** Russian Fed
38J5 **Karesvando** Sweden
96B2 **Karet** *Desert Region* Maur
65K4 **Kargasok** Russian Fed
97D3 **Kari** Nig
100B3 **Kariba** Zim
100B2 **Kariba** *L* Zim/Zambia
100B2 **Kariba Dam** Zim/Zambia
95C3 **Karima** Sudan
78B3 **Karimata** *I* Indon
86C2 **Karimganj** Bang
87B1 **Karimnagar** India
99E1 **Karin** Somalia
39J6 **Karis** Fin
99C3 **Karishimbe** *Mt* Zaïre
55B3 **Káristos** Greece
87A2 **Kārkal** India
71F4 **Karkar** *I* PNG
90A3 **Karkheh** *R* Iran
60D4 **Karkinitskiy Zaliv** *B* Ukraine
63B3 **Karlik Shan** *Mt* China
58B2 **Karlino** Pol
52C2 **Karlobag** Croatia
52C1 **Karlovac** Croatia
54B2 **Karlovo** Bulg
57C2 **Karlovy Vary** Czech
39G7 **Karlshamn** Sweden
39G7 **Karlskoga** Sweden
39H7 **Karlskrona** Sweden
57B3 **Karlsruhe** Germany
39G7 **Karlstad** Sweden
12D3 **Karluk** USA
86C2 **Karnafuli Res** Bang
84D3 **Karnal** India
87A1 **Karnataka** State, India
54C2 **Karnobat** Bulg
100B2 **Karoi** Zim
99D3 **Karonga** Malawi
95C3 **Karora** Sudan
78D3 **Karossa** Indon
55C3 **Kárpathos** *I* Greece
6E2 **Karrats Fjord** Greenland
93D1 **Kars** Turk
65H4 **Karsakpay** Kazakhstan
58D1 **Kārsava** Latvia
80E2 **Karshi** Uzbekistan
38J6 **Karstula** Fin
94B1 **Kartaba** Leb
54C2 **Kartal** Turk
61K3 **Kartaly** Russian Fed
90A3 **Kārūn** *R* Iran
86A1 **Karwa** India
87A2 **Kārwār** India
68D1 **Karymskoye** Russian Fed
98B3 **Kasai** *R* Zaïre
100B2 **Kasaji** Zaïre
101C2 **Kasama** Zambia
99D3 **Kasanga** Tanz
87A2 **Kāsaragod** India
5H3 **Kasba L** Can
100B2 **Kasempa** Zambia
100B2 **Kasenga** Zaïre
99D2 **Kasese** Uganda
90B3 **Kāshān** Iran
12C2 **Kashegelok** USA
82B2 **Kashi** China
84D3 **Kāshipur** India
74D3 **Kashiwazaki** Japan
90C2 **Kashmar** Iran
66D3 **Kashmir** State, India
61F3 **Kasimov** Russian Fed

18C2 **Kaskaskia** *R* USA
38J6 **Kaskinen** Fin
61K2 **Kasli** Russian Fed
5G5 **Kaslo** Can
98C3 **Kasonga** Zaïre
98B3 **Kasongo-Lunda** Zaïre
55C3 **Kásos** *I* Greece
61G4 **Kaspiyskiy** Russian Fed
95C3 **Kassala** Sudan
56B2 **Kassel** Germany
96C1 **Kasserine** Tunisia
100A2 **Kassinga** Angola
92B1 **Kastamonou** Turk
55B3 **Kastélli** Greece
92A2 **Kastellorizon** *I* Greece
55B2 **Kastoría** Greece
55C3 **Kástron** Greece
74D3 **Kasugai** Japan
75A1 **Kasumi** Japan
101C2 **Kasungu** Malawi
84C2 **Kasur** Pak
100B2 **Kataba** Zambia
98C3 **Katako-kombe** Zaïre
4D3 **Katalla** USA
63G2 **Katangli** Russian Fed
106A4 **Katanning** Aust
55B2 **Kateríni** Greece
5E4 **Kates Needle** *Mt* Can/USA
82D3 **Katha** Burma
106C2 **Katherine** Aust
85C4 **Kāthiāwār** *Pen* India
86B1 **Kathmandu** Nepal
84D2 **Kathua** India
86B1 **Katihār** India
100B2 **Katima Mulilo** Namibia
4C4 **Katmai,Mt** USA
12D3 **Katmai Nat Mon** USA
86A2 **Katni** India
109D2 **Katoomba** Aust
59B2 **Katowice** Pol
39H7 **Katrineholm** Sweden
97C3 **Katsina** Nig
97C4 **Katsina Ala** Nig
75C1 **Katsuta** Japan
75C1 **Katsuura** Japan
75B1 **Katsuy** Japan
65H6 **Kattakurgan** Uzbekistan
39G7 **Kattegat** *Str* Den/Sweden
21C4 **Kauai** *I* Hawaiian Is
21C4 **Kauai Chan** Hawaiian Is
21C4 **Kaulakahi Chan** Hawaiian Is
21C4 **Kaunakaki** Hawaiian Is
60B3 **Kaunas** Lithuania
97C3 **Kaura Namoda** Nig
38J5 **Kautokeino** Nor
55B2 **Kavadarci** Macedonia, Yugos
55A2 **Kavajë** Alb
87B2 **Kavali** India
55B2 **Kavála** Greece
85B4 **Kāvda** India
75B1 **Kawagoe** Japan
75B1 **Kawaguchi** Japan
110B1 **Kawakawa** NZ
99C3 **Kawambwa** Zambia
86A2 **Kawardha** India
15C2 **Kawartha Lakes** Can
74D3 **Kawasaki** Japan
110C1 **Kawerau** NZ
110B1 **Kawhia** NZ
97B3 **Kaya** Burkina
12F3 **Kayak I** USA
78D2 **Kayan** *R* Indon
87B3 **Kāyankulam** India
97A3 **Kayes** Mali
92C2 **Kayseri** Turk
1B8 **Kazach'ye** Russian Fed
93E1 **Kazakh** Azerbaijan
65G5 **Kazakhstan** Republic, Asia
61G2 **Kazan'** Russian Fed
54C2 **Kazanlŭk** Bulg
69G4 **Kazan Retto** *Is* Japan
91B4 **Kāzerūn** Iran
61H1 **Kazhim** Russian Fed
93E1 **Kazi Magomed** Azerbaijan
59C3 **Kazincbarcika** Hung
55B3 **Kéa** *I* Greece
21C4 **Kealaikahiki Chan** Hawaiian Is
8D2 **Kearney** USA
93C2 **Keban Baraji** *Res* Turk
97A3 **Kébémer** Sen
96C1 **Kebili** Tunisia
94C1 **Kebīr** *R* Leb/Syria
38H5 **Kebrekaise** *Mt* Sweden
59B3 **Kecskemét** Hung
58C1 **Kedainiai** Lithuania
97A3 **Kédougou** Sen
12J2 **Keele** *R* Can
12H2 **Keele Pk** *Mt* Can
21B2 **Keeler** USA
15D2 **Keene** New Hampshire, USA
100A3 **Keetmanshoop** Namibia
18C1 **Keewanee** USA
6A3 **Keewatin** *Region* Can
55B3 **Kefallinía** *I* Greece
94B2 **Kefar Sava** Israel
97C4 **Keffi** Nig
38A2 **Keflavik** Iceland
5G4 **Keg River** Can
76B1 **Kehsi Mansam** Burma
108B3 **Keith** Aust
44C3 **Keith** Scot
4F3 **Keith Arm** *B* Can
6D3 **Kekertuk** Can
85D3 **Kekri** India
77C5 **Kelang** Malay
77C4 **Kelantan** *R* Malay
84B1 **Kelif** Turkmenistan
92C1 **Kelkit** *R* Turk
98B3 **Kellé** Congo
4F2 **Kellet,C** Can
20C1 **Kellogg** USA
64D3 **Kelloselka** Fin
45C2 **Kells** Irish Rep
42B2 **Kells Range** *Hills* Scot
58C1 **Kelme** Lithuania
5G5 **Kelowna** Can
5F4 **Kelsey Bay** Can
42C2 **Kelso** Scot
20B1 **Kelso** USA
64E3 **Kem'** Russian Fed
38L6 **Kem'** *R* Russian Fed
97B3 **Ke Macina** Mali
13B2 **Kemano** Can
65K4 **Kemerovo** Russian Fed
38J5 **Kemi** Fin
38K5 **Kemi** *R* Fin
38K5 **Kemijärvi** Fin
46C1 **Kempen** Region, Belg
26B2 **Kemps Bay** The Bahamas
109D2 **Kempsey** Aust
57C3 **Kempten** Germany
12D2 **Kenai** USA
12D3 **Kenai Mts** USA
12D2 **Kenai Pen** USA
99D2 **Kenamuke Swamp** Sudan
42C2 **Kendal** Eng
109D2 **Kendall** Aust
71D4 **Kendari** Indon
78C3 **Kendawangan** Indon
86B2 **Kendrāpāra** India
20C1 **Kendrick** USA
97A4 **Kenema** Sierra Leone
98B3 **Kenge** Zaïre
76B1 **Kengtung** Burma
100B3 **Kenhardt** S Africa
97A3 **Keniéba** Mali
96B1 **Kenitra** Mor
45B3 **Kenmare** Irish Rep
45B3 **Kenmare** *R* Irish Rep
19B4 **Kenner** USA
18C2 **Kennett** USA
16B3 **Kennett Square** USA
20C1 **Kennewick** USA
5F4 **Kenny Dam** Can
7A5 **Kenora** Can
10B2 **Kenosha** USA
43E4 **Kent** County, Eng
20B1 **Kent** Washington, USA
14A2 **Kentland** USA
14B2 **Kenton** USA
4H3 **Kent Pen** Can
11B3 **Kentucky** State, USA
11B3 **Kentucky L** USA
19B3 **Kentwood** Louisiana, USA
14A2 **Kentwood** Michigan, USA
99D2 **Kenya** Republic, Africa
Kenya,Mt = Kirinyaga
18B1 **Keokuk** USA
86A2 **Keonchi** India
86B2 **Keonjhargarh** India
71E4 **Kepaluan Tanimbar** *Arch* Indon
6H3 **Keplavik** Iceland
59B2 **Kepno** Pol
78B2 **Kepulauan Anambas** *Arch* Indon
71E4 **Kepulauan Aru** *Arch* Indon
78B2 **Kepulauan Badas** *Is* Indon
71E4 **Kepulauan Banda** *Arch* Indon
71D4 **Kepulauan Banggai** *I* Indon
78B2 **Kepulauan Bunguran Seletan** *Arch* Indon
71E4 **Kepulauan Kai** *Arch* Indon
71D4 **Kepulauan Leti** *I* Indon
78A3 **Kepulauan Lingga** *Is* Indon
70A4 **Kepulauan Mentawi** *Arch* Indon
78A2 **Kepulauan Riau** *Arch* Indon
78D4 **Kepulauan Sabalana** *Arch* Indon
71D3 **Kepulauan Sangihe** *Arch* Indon
71D4 **Kepulauan Sula** *I* Indon
71D3 **Kepulauan Talaud** *Arch* Indon
78B2 **Kepulauan Tambelan** *Is* Indon
71E4 **Kepulauan Tanimbar** *I* Indon
71D4 **Kepulauan Togian** *I* Indon
71D4 **Kepulauan Tukambesi** *Is* Indon
87B2 **Kerala** State, India
108B3 **Kerang** Aust
39K6 **Kerava** Fin
60E4 **Kerch'** Ukraine
71F4 **Kerema** PNG
20C1 **Keremeps** Can
95C3 **Keren** Eth
104B6 **Kerguelen Ridge** Indian O
99D3 **Kericho** Kenya
70B4 **Kerinci** *Mt* Indon
99D2 **Kerio** *R* Kenya
80E2 **Kerki** Turkmenistan
55A3 **Kérkira** Greece
55A3 **Kérkira** *I* Greece
91C3 **Kerman** Iran
22B2 **Kerman** USA
90A3 **Kermānshāh** Iran
21B2 **Kern** *R* USA
13F2 **Kerrobert** Can
45B2 **Kerry** County, Irish Rep
17B1 **Kershaw** USA
78B3 **Kertamulia** Indon
63D3 **Kerulen** *R* Mongolia
96B2 **Kerzaz** Alg
55C2 **Keşan** Turk
74E3 **Kesennuma** Japan
38L5 **Kesten'ga** Russian Fed
42C2 **Keswick** Eng
65K4 **Ket** *R* Russian Fed
97C4 **Kéta** Ghana
78C3 **Ketapang** Indon
5E4 **Ketchikan** USA
97C3 **Ketia** Niger
85B4 **Keti Bandar** Pak
58C2 **Ketrzyn** Pol
43D3 **Kettering** Eng
14B3 **Kettering** USA
20C1 **Kettle** *R* Can
20C1 **Kettle River Range** *Mts* USA
7C3 **Kettlestone B** Can
90C3 **Kevir-i Namak** *Salt Flat* Iran
14A2 **Kewaunee** USA
14B1 **Key Harbour** Can
17B2 **Key Largo** USA
11B4 **Key West** USA
63C2 **Kezhma** Russian Fed
54A1 **K'félegháza** Hung
12B2 **Kgun L** USA
94C2 **Khabab** Syria
62H3 **Khabarovsk** Russian Fed
85B3 **Khairpur** Pak
85B3 **Khairpur** Region, Pak
100B3 **Khakhea** Botswana
55C3 **Khálki** *I* Greece
55B2 **Khalkidhíki** *Pen* Greece
55B3 **Khalkís** Greece
61G2 **Khalturin** Russian Fed
85C4 **Khambhāt,G of** India
85D4 **Khāmgaon** India
76C2 **Kham Keut** Laos
87C1 **Khammam** India
90A2 **Khamseh** *Mts* Iran
76C2 **Khan** *R* Laos
84B1 **Khanabad** Afghan
93E3 **Khānaqīn** Iraq
85D4 **Khandwa** India
84C2 **Khanewal** Pak
94C3 **Khan ez Zabib** Jordan
77D4 **Khanh Hung** Viet
55B3 **Khaniá** Greece
84C3 **Khanpur** Pak
65H3 **Khanty-Mansiysk** Russian Fed
94B3 **Khan Yunis** Egypt
84D1 **Khapalu** India
68C2 **Khapcheranga** Russian Fed
61G4 **Kharabali** Russian Fed
86B2 **Kharagpur** India
91C4 **Khārān** Iran
84B3 **Kharan** Pak
90B3 **Kharānaq** Iran
91B4 **Khārg** *Is* Iran
95C2 **Khârga Oasis** Egypt
85D4 **Khargon** India
60E4 **Khar'kov** Ukraine
54C2 **Kharmanli** Bulg
61F2 **Kharovsk** Russian Fed
95C3 **Khartoum** Sudan
95C3 **Khartoum North** Sudan
74C2 **Khasan** Russian Fed
95C3 **Khashm el Girba** Sudan
86C1 **Khasi-Jaintīa Hills** India
54C2 **Khaskovo** Bulg
1B9 **Khatanga** Russian Fed
76B3 **Khawsa** Burma
76C2 **Khe Bo** Viet
85C4 **Khed Brahma** India
51C2 **Khemis** Alg
96B1 **Khenifra** Mor
51D2 **Kherrata** Alg
60D4 **Kherson** Ukraine
63D2 **Khilok** Russian Fed
55C3 **Khíos** Greece
55C3 **Khíos** *I* Greece
60C4 **Khmel'nitskiy** Ukraine

59C3 **Khodorov** Ukraine
82A1 **Khodzhent**
Tajikistan
84B1 **Kholm** Afghan
76D3 **Khong** Laos
91B4 **Khonj** Iran
69F2 **Khor** Russian Fed
91A3 **Khoramshahr** Iran
91B5 **Khōr Duwayhin** B
UAE
84C1 **Khorog** Tajikistan
90A3 **Khorramābad** Iran
90C3 **Khosf** Iran
84B2 **Khost** Pak
60C4 **Khotin** Ukraine
12C2 **Khotol** Mt USA
60C3 **Khoyniku** Belorussia
63F2 **Khrebet Dzhugdzhur**
Mts Russian Fed
90C2 **Khrebet Kopet Dag**
Mts Turkmenistan
64H3 **Khrebet Pay-khoy**
Mts Russian Fed
82C1 **Khrebet Tarbagatay**
Mts Kazakhstan
63E2 **Khrebet Tukuringra**
Mts Russian Fed
86B2 **Khulna** Bang
84D1 **Khunjerab** P China/
India
90B3 **Khunsar** Iran
91A4 **Khurays** S Arabia
86B2 **Khurda** India
84D3 **Khurja** India
84C2 **Khushab** Pak
94B2 **Khushnīyah** Syria
59C3 **Khust** Ukraine
99C1 **Khuwei** Sudan
85B3 **Khuzdar** Pak
90D3 **Khvāf** Iran
61G3 **Khvalynsk** Russian
Fed
90C3 **Khvor** Iran
91B4 **Khvormūj** Iran
93D2 **Khvoy** Iran
84C1 **Khwaja Muhammad**
Mts Afghan
84C2 **Khyber P** Afghan/Pak
99C3 **Kiambi** Zaïre
19A3 **Kiamichi** R USA
12B1 **Kiana** USA
98B3 **Kibangou** Congo
99D3 **Kibaya** Tanz
98C3 **Kibombo** Zaïre
99D3 **Kibondo** Tanz
99D3 **Kibungu** Rwanda
55B2 **Kičevo** Macedonia,
Yugos
5G4 **Kicking Horse P** Can
97C3 **Kidal** Mali
43C3 **Kidderminster** Eng
97A3 **Kidira** Sen
110C1 **Kidnappers,C** NZ
56C2 **Kiel** Germany
59C2 **Kielce** Pol
56C2 **Kieler Bucht** B
Germany
Kiev = Kiyev
80E2 **Kifab** Uzbekistan
97A3 **Kiffa** Maur
89H8 **Kigali** Rwanda
12A2 **Kigluaik Mts** USA
99C3 **Kigoma** Tanz
75B2 **Kii-sanchi** Mts Japan
74C4 **Kii-suido** B Japan
54B1 **Kikinda** Serbia,
Yugos
55B3 **Kikládhes** Is Greece
71F4 **Kikori** PNG
98B3 **Kikwit** Zaïre
21C4 **Kilauea Crater** Mt
Hawaiian Is
4C3 **Kilbuck Mts** USA
74B2 **Kilchu** N Korea
109D1 **Kilcoy** Aust
45C2 **Kildare** County,
Irish Rep
45C2 **Kildare** Irish Rep
19B3 **Kilgore** USA
99D3 **Kilifi** Kenya
99D3 **Kilimanjaro** Mt Tanz
99D3 **Kilindoni** Tanz
92C2 **Kilis** Turk
45B2 **Kilkee** Irish Rep

45C2 **Kilkenny** County,
Irish Rep
45C2 **Kilkenny** Irish Rep
45B2 **Kilkieran B** Irish Rep
55B2 **Kilkis** Greece
45B1 **Killala B** Irish Rep
45B2 **Killaloe** Irish Rep
109D1 **Killarney** Aust
41B3 **Killarney** Irish Rep
19A3 **Killeen** USA
12D1 **Killik** R USA
44B3 **Killin** Scot
55B3 **Killini** Mt Greece
45B1 **Killybegs** Irish Rep
42B2 **Kilmarnock** Scot
61H2 **Kil'mez** Russian Fed
99D3 **Kilosa** Tanz
41B3 **Kilrush** Irish Rep
99C3 **Kilwa** Zaïre
99D3 **Kilwa Kisiwani** Tanz
99D3 **Kilwa Kivinje** Tanz
108A2 **Kimba** Aust
12F2 **Kimball,Mt** USA
13D3 **Kimberley** Can
101F1 **Kimberley** S Africa
106B2 **Kimberley Plat** Aust
74B2 **Kimch'aek** N Korea
74B3 **Kimch'ŏn** S Korea
55B3 **Kimi** Greece
60E2 **Kimry** Russian Fed
70C3 **Kinabalu** Mt Malay
78D1 **Kinabatangan** R
Malay
14B2 **Kincardine** Can
13B1 **Kincolith** Can
19B3 **Kinder** USA
13F2 **Kindersley** Can
97A3 **Kindia** Guinea
98C3 **Kindu** Zaïre
61H3 **Kinel'** Russian Fed
61F2 **Kineshma** Russian
Fed
109D1 **Kingaroy** Aust
21A2 **King City** USA
5F4 **Kingcome Inlet** Can
7C4 **King George Is** Can
107D4 **King I** Aust
13B2 **King I** Can
106B2 **King Leopold Range**
Mts Aust
9B3 **Kingman** USA
98C3 **Kingombe** Zaïre
108A2 **Kingoonya** Aust
22C2 **Kingsburg** USA
21B2 **Kings Canyon Nat Pk**
USA
108A3 **Kingscote** Aust
106B2 **King Sd** Aust
112C2 **King Sejong** Base
Ant
14A1 **Kingsford** USA
17B1 **Kingsland** USA
43E3 **King's Lynn** Eng
16C2 **Kings Park** USA
8B2 **Kings Peak** Mt USA
107C4 **Kingston** Aust
7C5 **Kingston** Can
25E3 **Kingston** Jamaica
15D2 **Kingston** New York,
USA
111A3 **Kingston** NZ
27E4 **Kingstown** St
Vincent
9D4 **Kingsville** USA
44B3 **Kingussie** Scot
4J3 **King William I** Can
100B4 **King William's Town**
S Africa
98B3 **Kinkala** Congo
39G7 **Kinna** Sweden
44D3 **Kinnairds Head** Pt
Scot
75B1 **Kinomoto** Japan
44C3 **Kinross** Scot
45B3 **Kinsale** Irish Rep
98B3 **Kinshasa** Zaïre
78D3 **Kintap** Indon
42B2 **Kintyre** Pen Scot
13D1 **Kinuso** Can
99D2 **Kinyeti** Mt Sudan
55B3 **Kiparissia** Greece
55B3 **Kiparissiakós Kólpos**
G Greece
15C1 **Kipawa,L** Can

99D3 **Kipili** Tanz
12B3 **Kipnuk** USA
45C2 **Kippure** Mt
Irish Rep
100B2 **Kipushi** Zaïre
63C2 **Kirensk** Russian Fed
65J5 **Kirgizia** Republic,
Asia
82B1 **Kirgizskiy Khrebet**
Mts Kirgizia
98B3 **Kiri** Zaïre
105G4 **Kiribati** Is Pacific O
92B2 **Kırıkkale** Turk
99D3 **Kirinyaga** Mt Kenya
60D2 **Kirishi** Russian Fed
85B3 **Kirithar Range** Mts
Pak
55C3 **Kirkağaç** Turk
90A2 **Kirk Bulāg Dāgh** Mt
Iran
42C2 **Kirkby** Eng
44C3 **Kirkcaldy** Scot
42B2 **Kirkcudbright** Scot
38K5 **Kirkenes** Nor
7B5 **Kirkland Lake** Can
112A **Kirkpatrick,Mt** Ant
10A2 **Kirksville** USA
93D2 **Kirkūk** Iraq
44C2 **Kirkwall** Scot
18B2 **Kirkwood** USA
60D3 **Kirov** Russian Fed
61G2 **Kirov** Russian Fed
93D1 **Kirovakan** Armenia
61J2 **Kirovgrad** Russian
Fed
60D4 **Kirovograd** Ukraine
61H2 **Kirs** Russian Fed
92B2 **Kirşehir** Turk
56C2 **Kiruna** Sweden
75B1 **Kiryū** Japan
98C2 **Kisangani** Zaïre
75B1 **Kisarazu** Japan
86B1 **Kishanganj** India
85C3 **Kishangarh** India
60C4 **Kishinev** Moldavia
75B2 **Kishiwada** Japan
99D3 **Kisii** Kenya
99D3 **Kisiju** Tanz
59B3 **Kiskunhalas** Hung
65F5 **Kislovodsk** Russian
Fed
99E3 **Kismaayo** Somalia
75B1 **Kiso-sammyaku** Mts
Japan
97A4 **Kissidougou** Guinea
17B2 **Kissimmee,L** USA
99D3 **Kisumu** Kenya
59C3 **Kisvárda** Hung
97B3 **Kita** Mali
65H6 **Kitab** Uzbekistan
75C1 **Kitakata** Japan
74C4 **Kita-Kyūshū** Japan
99D2 **Kitale** Kenya
69G4 **Kitalo** I Japan
74E2 **Kitami** Japan
7B5 **Kitchener** Can
99D2 **Kitgum** Uganda
55B3 **Kithira** I Greece
55B3 **Kithnos** I Greece
94A1 **Kiti,C** Cyprus
4H3 **Kitikmeot** Region
Can
5F4 **Kitimat** Can
38K5 **Kitnen** R Fin
75A2 **Kitsuki** Japan
15C2 **Kittanning** USA
38J5 **Kittilä** Fin
99D3 **Kitunda** Tanz
13B1 **Kitwanga** Can
100B2 **Kitwe** Zambia
57C3 **Kitzbühel** Austria
47E1 **Kitzbühler Alpen** Mts
Austria
57C3 **Kitzingen** Germany
98C3 **Kiumbi** Zaïre
12B1 **Kivalina** USA
59D2 **Kivercy** Ukraine
99C3 **Kivu,L** Zaïre/Rwanda
4B3 **Kiwalik** USA
60D3 **Kiyev** Ukraine
61J2 **Kizel** Russian Fed
92C2 **Kizil** R Turk
80D2 **Kizyl-Arvat**
Turkmenistan

90B2 **Kizyl-Atrek**
Turkmenistan
57C2 **Kladno** Czech
57C3 **Klagenfurt** Austria
60B2 **Klaipēda** Lithuania
8A2 **Klamath** USA
20B2 **Klamath** R USA
8A2 **Klamath Falls** USA
20B2 **Klamath Mts** USA
57C3 **Klatovy** Czech
12H3 **Klawak** USA
94B1 **Kleiat** Leb
101G1 **Klerksdorp** S Africa
60E2 **Klin** Russian Fed
58B1 **Klintehamn** Sweden
60D3 **Klintsy** Russian Fed
52C2 **Ključ** Bosnia &
Herzegovina, Yugos
59B2 **Kłodzko** Pol
12G2 **Klondike** R Can/USA
4D3 **Klondike Plat** Can/
USA
59B3 **Klosterneuburg**
Austria
12G2 **Kluane** R Can
12G2 **Kluane L** Can
12G2 **Kluane Nat Pk** Can
59B2 **Kluczbork** Pol
12G3 **Klukwan** USA
12E2 **Klutina L** USA
12E2 **Knight I** USA
43C3 **Knighton** Wales
52C2 **Knin** Croatia
106A4 **Knob,C** Aust
46B1 **Knokke-Heist** Belg
112C9 **Knox Coast** Ant
11B3 **Knoxville** Tennessee,
USA
6H3 **Knud Ramsussens**
Land Region
Greenland
78B3 **Koba** Indon
6F3 **Kobbermirebugt**
Greenland
74D4 **Kobe** Japan
56C1 **København** Den
57B2 **Koblenz** Germany
60B3 **Kobrin** Russian Fed
71E4 **Kobroör** I Indon
12C1 **Kobuk** R USA
54B2 **Kočani** Macedonia,
Yugos
76C3 **Ko Chang** I Thai
86B1 **Koch Bihār** India
47D1 **Kochel** Germany
6C3 **Koch I** Can
87B3 **Kochi** India
74C4 **Kōchi** Japan
12D3 **Kodiak** USA
12D3 **Kodiak I** USA
87B2 **Kodikkarai** India
99D2 **Kodok** Sudan
100A3 **Koes** Namibia
101G1 **Koffiefontein**
S Africa
97B4 **Koforidua** Ghana
74D3 **Kōfu** Japan
75B1 **Koga** Japan
39G7 **Køge** Den
84C2 **Kohat** Pak
84B2 **Koh-i-Baba** Mts
Afghan
84B1 **Koh-i-Hisar** Mts
Afghan
84B2 **Koh-i-Khurd** Mt
Afghan
86C1 **Kohima** India
84B1 **Koh-i-Mazar** Mt
Afghan
84B3 **Kohlu** Pak
60C2 **Kohtla Järve** Estonia
75B1 **Koide** Japan
12F2 **Koidern** Can
77A4 **Koihoa** Is Nicobar Is
74B4 **Kōje-do** I S Korea
65H4 **Kokchetav**
Kazakhstan
39J6 **Kokemaki** L Fin
38J6 **Kokkola** Fin
107D1 **Kokoda** PNG
14A2 **Kokomo** USA
71E4 **Kokonau** Indon
65K5 **Kokpekty** Kazakhstan
7D4 **Koksoak** R Can

Kulal,Mt

100B4 **Kokstad** S Africa
76C3 **Ko Kut** I Thai
38L5 **Kola** Russian Fed
71D4 **Kolaka** Indon
77B4 **Ko Lanta** I Thai
87B3 **Kollam** India
87B2 **Kolär** India
87B2 **Kolär Gold Fields** India
97A3 **Kolda** Sen
39F7 **Kolding** Den
87A1 **Kolhāpur** India
12C3 **Koliganek** USA
59B2 **Kolin** Czech
57B2 **Köln** Germany
58R2 **Kolo** Pol
58B2 **Kolobrzeg** Pol
97B3 **Kolokani** Mali
60E2 **Kolomna** Russian Fed
60C4 **Kolomyya** Ukraine
65K4 **Kolpashevo** Russian Fed
55C3 **Kólpos Merabéllou** B Greece
55B2 **Kólpos Singitikós** G Greece
55B2 **Kólpos Strimonikós** G Greece
55B2 **Kólpos Toronaíos** G Greece
38L5 **Kol'skiy Poluostrov** Pen Russian Fed
38G6 **Kolvereid** Nor
100B2 **Kolwezi** Zaïre
1C7 **Kolyma** R Russian Fed
54B2 **Kom** Mt Bulg/Serbia, Yugos
99D2 **Koma** Eth
97D3 **Komaduga Gana** R Nig
59B3 **Komárno** Czech
101H1 **Komati** R S Africa
74D3 **Komatsu** Japan
75A2 **Komatsushima** Japan
64G3 **Komi Respublika,** Russian Fed
70C4 **Komodo** I Indon
71E4 **Komoran** I Indon
75B1 **Komoro** Japan
55C2 **Komotini** Greece
76D3 **Kompong Cham** Camb
76C3 **Kompong Chhnang** Mts Camb
77C3 **Kompong Som** Camb
76C3 **Kompong Thom** Camb
76D3 **Kompong Trabek** Camb
63F? **Komsomol'sk na Amure** Russian Fed
65H4 **Konda** R Russian Fed
99D3 **Kondoa** Tanz
87B1 **Kondukür** India
6G3 **Kong Christian IX Land** Region Greenland
6F3 **Kong Frederik VI Kyst** Mts Greenland
64C2 **Kong Karls Land** Is Barents S
78D2 **Kongkemul** Mt Indon
98C3 **Kongolo** Zaïre
39F7 **Kongsberg** Den
39G6 **Kongsvinger** Nor
Königsberg = Kaliningrad
58B2 **Konin** Pol
54A2 **Konjic** Bosnia & Herzegovina, Yugos
61F1 **Konosha** Russian Fed
75B1 **Konosu** Japan
60D3 **Konotop** Ukraine
59C2 **Końskie** Pol
49D2 **Konstanz** Germany
97C3 **Kontagora** Nig
76D3 **Kontum** Viet
92B2 **Konya** Turk

13D3 **Kootenay** R Can
85C5 **Kopargaon** India
6J3 **Kópasker** Iceland
38A2 **Kópavogur** Iceland
52B1 **Koper** Slovenia
80D2 **Kopet Dag** Mts Iran/ Turkmenistan
61K2 **Kopeysk** Russian Fed
77C4 **Ko Phangan** I Thai
77B4 **Ko Phuket** I Thai
39H7 **Köping** Sweden
87B1 **Koppal** India
52C1 **Koprivnica** Croatia
85B4 **Korangi** Pak
87C1 **Koraput** India
86A2 **Korba** India
57B2 **Korbach** Germany
4B3 **Korbuk** R USA
55B2 **Korçë** Alb
52C2 **Korčula** I Croatia
72E2 **Korea B** China/Korea
74B4 **Korea Str** S Korea/ Japan
59D2 **Korec** Ukraine
92B1 **Körğlu Tepesi** Mt Turk
97B4 **Korhogo** Ivory Coast
85B4 **Kori Creek** India
55B3 **Korinthiakós Kólpos** G Greece
55B3 **Kórinthos** Greece
74E3 **Kōriyama** Japan
61K3 **Korkino** Russian Fed
92B2 **Korkuteli** Turk
82C1 **Korla** China
52C2 **Kornat** I Croatia
60D5 **Köroğlu Tepesi** Mt Turk
99D3 **Korogwe** Tanz
108B3 **Koroit** Aust
71E3 **Koror** Palau Is, Pacific O
59C3 **Körös** R Hung
60C3 **Korosten** Ukraine
95A3 **Koro Toro** Chad
12B3 **Korovin** I USA
69G2 **Korsakov** Russian Fed
39G7 **Korsør** Den
46B1 **Kortrijk** Belg
55C3 **Kós** I Greece
77C4 **Ko Samui** I Thai
58B2 **Koscierzyna** Pol
107D4 **Kosciusko** Mt Aust
12H3 **Kosciusko I** USA
74B4 **Koshikijima-retto** I Japan
59C3 **Košice** Czech
74B3 **Kosong** N Korea
54B2 **Kosovo** Aut Republic, Serbia, Yugos
97B4 **Kossou** L Ivory Coast
101G1 **Koster** S Africa
99D1 **Kosti** Sudan
59D2 **Kostopol'** Ukraine
61F2 **Kostroma** Russian Fed
56C2 **Kostrzyn** Pol
39H8 **Koszalin** Pol
85D3 **Kota** India
78A4 **Kotaagung** Indon
78C3 **Kotabaharu** Indon
78D3 **Kotabaru** Indon
77C4 **Kota Bharu** Malay
78A3 **Kotabum** Indon
84C2 **Kot Addu** Pak
78D1 **Kota Kinabulu** Malay
87C1 **Kotapad** India
61G2 **Kotel'nich** Russian Fed
61F4 **Kotel'nikovo** Russian Fed
39K6 **Kotka** Fin
64F3 **Kotlas** Russian Fed
12B2 **Kotlik** USA
54A2 **Kotor** Montenegro, Yugos
60C4 **Kotovsk** Ukraine
85B3 **Kotri** Pak
87C1 **Kottagüdem** India
87B3 **Kottayam** India
98C2 **Kotto** R CAR
87B2 **Kottüru** India

12B1 **Kotzebue** USA
4B3 **Kotzebue Sd** USA
97C3 **Kouande** Benin
98C2 **Kouango** CAR
97B3 **Koudougou** Burkina
98B3 **Koulamoutou** Gabon
97B3 **Koulikoro** Mali
97B3 **Koupéla** Burkina
33G2 **Kourou** French Guiana
97B3 **Kouroussa** Guinea
98B1 **Kousséri** Cam
39K6 **Kouvola** Fin
38L5 **Kovdor** Russian Fed
60B3 **Kovel'** Ukraine
Kovno = Kaunas
61F2 **Kovrov** Russian Fed
61F3 **Kovylkino** Russian Fed
60E1 **Kovzha** R Russian Fed
77C4 **Ko Way** I Thai
73C5 **Kowloon** Hong Kong
84B2 **Kowt-e-Ashrow** Afghan
92A2 **Köyceğğiz** Turk
38L5 **Koydor** Russian Fed
87A1 **Koyna Res** India
12B2 **Koyuk** USA
12B1 **Koyuk** R USA
12C2 **Koyukuk** USA
12C1 **Koyukuk** R USA
92C2 **Kozan** Turk
55B2 **Kozani** Greece
87B2 **Kozhikode** India
61G2 **Koz'modemyansk** Russian Fed
75B2 **Kōzu-shima** I Japan
39F7 **Kragerø** Nor
54B2 **Kragujevac** Serbia, Yugos
77B3 **Kra,Isthmus of** Burma/Malay
Krakatau = Rakata
94C1 **Krak des Chevaliers** Hist Site Syria
Kraków = Cracow
54B2 **Kraljevo** Serbia, Yugos
60E4 **Kramatorsk** Ukraine
38H6 **Kramfors** Sweden
52B1 **Kranj** Slovenia
61G1 **Krasavino** Russian Fed
64G2 **Krasino** Russian Fed
59C2 **Kraśnik** Pol
61G3 **Krasnoarmeysk** Russian Fed
60E5 **Krasnodar** Russian Fed
61J2 **Krasnokamsk** Russian Fed
61K2 **Krasnotur'insk** Russian Fed
61J2 **Krasnoufimsk** Russian Fed
61J3 **Krasnousol'-skiy** Russian Fed
65G3 **Krasnovishersk** Russian Fed
65G5 **Krasnovodsk** Turkmenistan
63B2 **Krasnoyarsk** Russian Fed
59C2 **Krasnystaw** Pol
61G3 **Krasnyy Kut** Russian Fed
60E4 **Krasnyy Luch** Ukraine
61G4 **Krasnyy Yar** Russian Fed
76D3 **Kratie** Camb
6E2 **Kraulshavn** Greenland
56B2 **Krefeld** Germany
60D4 **Kremenchug** Ukraine
60D4 **Kremenchugskoye Vodokhranilische** Res Ukraine
59D2 **Kremenets** Ukraine
98A2 **Kribi** Cam
60D3 **Krichev** Belorussia
47E1 **Krimml** Austria
87B1 **Krishna** R India

87D2 **Krishnagiri** India
86B2 **Krishnangar** India
39F7 **Kristiansand** Nor
39G7 **Kristianstad** Sweden
64B3 **Kristiansund** Nor
39G7 **Kristinehamn** Sweden
38J6 **Kristiinankaupunki** Fin
55B3 **Kriti** I Greece
60D4 **Krivoy Rog** Ukraine
52B1 **Krk** I Croatia
6G3 **Kronpris Frederik Bjerge** Mts Greenland
39K7 **Kronshtadt** Russian Fed
101G1 **Kroonstad** S Africa
65F5 **Kropotkin** Russian Fed
101G1 **Krugersdorp** S Africa
78A4 **Krui** Indon
55A2 **Kruje** Alb
58D2 **Krupki** Belorussia
12B1 **Krusenstern,C** USA
54B2 **Kruševac** Serbia, Yugos
39K7 **Krustpils** Latvia
12G3 **Kruzof I** USA
65E5 **Krym** Pen Ukraine
60E5 **Krymsk** Russian Fed
58B2 **Krzyz** Pol
96C1 **Ksar El Boukhari** Alg
96B1 **Ksar el Kebir** Mor
70A3 **Kuala** Indon
77C5 **Kuala Dungun** Malay
77C4 **Kuala Kerai** Malay
77C5 **Kuala Kubu Baharu** Malay
77C5 **Kuala Lipis** Malay
77C5 **Kuala Lumpur** Malay
77C4 **Kuala Trengganu** Malay
78D1 **Kuamut** Malay
74A2 **Kuandian** China
77C5 **Kuantan** Malay
93E1 **Kuba** Azerbaijan
71F4 **Kubar** PNG
78C2 **Kuching** Malay
70C3 **Kudat** Malay
78C4 **Kudus** Indon
61H2 **Kudymkar** Russian Fed
57C3 **Kufstein** Austria
90C3 **Kuh Duren** Upland Iran
91C4 **Kūh e Bazmān** Mt Iran
90B3 **Küh-e Dinar** Mt Iran
90C2 **Küh-e-Hazār Masjed** Mts Iran
91C4 **Küh-e Jebāl Barez** Mts Iran
90B3 **Küh-e Karkas** Mts Iran
91C4 **Kuh-e Laleh Zar** Mt Iran
90A2 **Kuh-e Sahand** Mt Iran
91C4 **Kuh e Taftān** Mt Iran
90A2 **Kühhaye Sabalan** Mts Iran
90A3 **Kühhā-ye Zāgros** Mts Iran
38K6 **Kuhmo** Fin
90B3 **Kühpäyeh** Iran
90C3 **Kühpäyeh** Mt Iran
91C4 **Küh ye Bashäkerd** Mts Iran
90A2 **Küh ye Sabalan** Mt Iran
100A3 **Kuibis** Namibia
4B4 **Kuigillingok** USA
100A2 **Kuito** Angola
12H3 **Kuiu I** USA
74E2 **Kuji** Japan
75A2 **Kuju-san** Mt Japan
12C3 **Kukaklek L** USA
54B2 **Kukës** Alb
77C5 **Kukup** Malay
91C4 **Kül** R Iran
55C3 **Kula** Turk
61J4 **Kulakshi** Kazakhstan
99D2 **Kulal,Mt** Kenya

55B2 **Kulata** Bulg
60B2 **Kuldīga** Latvia
61H4 **Kul'sary** Kazakhstan
84D2 **Kulu** India
92B2 **Kulu** Turk
65J4 **Kulunda** Russian Fed
108B2 **Kulwin** Aust
61G5 **Kuma** *R* Russian Fed
75B1 **Kumagaya** Japan
78C3 **Kumai** Indon
74C4 **Kumamoto** Japan
75B2 **Kumano** Japan
54B2 **Kumanovo** Macedonia, Yugos
63E2 **Kumara** China
97B4 **Kumasi** Ghana
98A2 **Kumba** Cam
87B2 **Kumbakonam** India
61J3 **Kumertau** Russian Fed
74B3 **Kŭmhwa** S Korea
39H7 **Kumla** Sweden
87A2 **Kumta** India
82C1 **Kümüx** China
84C2 **Kunar** *R* Afghan
39K7 **Kunda** Estonia
85C4 **Kundla** India
84B1 **Kunduz** Afghan
89F9 **Kunene** *R* Angola
39G7 **Kungsbacka** Sweden
61J2 **Kungur** Russian Fed
76B1 **Kunhing** Burma
82B2 **Kunlun Shan** *Mts* China
73A4 **Kunming** China
74B3 **Kunsan** S Korea
38K6 **Kuopio** Fin
52C1 **Kupa** *R* Croatia/ Bosnia & Herzegovina, Yugos
106B2 **Kupang** Indon
107D2 **Kupiano** PNG
12H3 **Kupreanof I** USA
60E4 **Kupyansk** Ukraine
82C1 **Kuqa** China
75B1 **Kurabe** Japan
74C4 **Kurashiki** Japan
75A1 **Kurayoshi** Japan
54C2 **Kŭrdzhali** Bulg
74C4 **Kure** Japan
60B2 **Kuressaare** Estonia
63A1 **Kureyka** *R* Russian Fed
65H4 **Kurgan** Russian Fed
88K6 **Kuria Muria Is** Oman
38J6 **Kurikka** Fin
Kuril Is = Kuril'skoye Osrova
69H2 **Kuril'skiye Ostrova** Russian Fed
87B1 **Kurnool** India
75C1 **Kuroiso** Japan
111B2 **Kurow** NZ
109D2 **Kurri Kurri** Aust
60E3 **Kursk** Russian Fed
Kurskiy Zaliv = Courland Lagoon
68A2 **Kuruktag** *R* China
100B3 **Kuruman** S Africa
74C4 **Kurume** Japan
87C3 **Kurunegala** Sri Lanka
65K5 **Kurunktag** *R* China
61J2 **Kusa** Russian Fed
55C3 **Kuşadasi Körfezi** *B* Turk
55C2 **Kus Golü** *L* Turk
74D4 **Kushimoto** Japan
74E2 **Kushiro** Japan
86B2 **Kushtia** Bang
61H3 **Kushum** *R* Kazakhstan
80E2 **Kushra** Afgan
65G4 **Kushva** Russian Fed
12B2 **Kuskokwim** *R* USA
12B3 **Kuskokwim B** USA
12C2 **Kuskokwim Mts** USA
86A1 **Kusma** Nepal
74E2 **Kussharo-ko** *L* Japan
65H4 **Kustanay** Kazakhstan
92A2 **Kütahya** Turk
78D3 **Kutai** *R* Indon
59B3 **Kutná Hora** Czech
58B2 **Kutno** Pol
98B3 **Kutu** Zaïre
86C2 **Kutubdia I** Bang
98C1 **Kutum** Sudan
7D4 **Kuujjuaq** Can
7C4 **Kuujjuarapik** Can
38K5 **Kuusamo** Fin
61J3 **Kuvandyk** Russian Fed
93E4 **Kuwait** Kuwait
80C3 **Kuwait** Sheikdom, S W Asia
75B1 **Kuwana** Japan
65J4 **Kuybyshev** Russian Fed
61G3 **Kuybyshevskoye Vodokhranilishche** *Res* Russian Fed
63C2 **Kuytun** Russian Fed
60E5 **Kuzey Anadolu Daglari** *Mts* Turk
61G3 **Kuznetsk** Russian Fed
38J4 **Kvaenangen** *Sd* Nor
12C3 **Kvichak** USA
12C3 **Kvichak** *R* USA
12C3 **Kvichak B** USA
38G5 **Kvigtind** *Mt* Nor
38H5 **Kvikkjokk** Sweden
99D3 **Kwale** Kenya
74B3 **Kwangju** S Korea
98B3 **Kwango** *R* Zaïre
100B2 **Kwekwe** Zim
12B2 **Kwethluk** USA
12B2 **Kwethluk** *R* USA
58B2 **Kwidzyn** Pol
71E4 **Kwoka** *Mt* Indon
108C3 **Kyabram** Aust
76B2 **Kyaikkami** Burma
76B2 **Kyaikto** Burma
68C1 **Kyakhta** Russian Fed
108A2 **Kyancutta** Aust
76B1 **Kyaukme** Burma
76B1 **Kyauk-padaung** Burma
76A2 **Kyaukpyu** Burma
40B2 **Kyle of Lochalsh** Scot
46D1 **Kyll** *R* Germany
108B3 **Kyneton** Aust
99D2 **Kyoga** *L* Uganda
109D1 **Kyogle** Aust
74B3 **Kyŏngju** S Korea
74D3 **Kyoto** Japan
65H4 **Kyshtym** Russian Fed
74C4 **Kyūshū** *I* Japan
104E3 **Kyushu-Palau Ridge** Pacific O
54B2 **Kyustendil** Bulg
68B1 **Kyzyl** Russian Fed
65H5 **Kyzylkum** *Desert* Uzbekistan
65H5 **Kzyl Orda** Kazakhstan

L

99E2 **Laascaanood** Somalia
46E1 **Laasphe** Germany
99E1 **Laasqoray** Somalia
33E1 **La Asunción** Ven
96A2 **Laâyoune** Mor
23A1 **La Barca** Mexico
97A3 **Labé** Guinea
59B2 **Labe** *R* Czech
15D1 **Labelle** Can
17B2 **La Belle** USA
12G2 **Laberge,L** Can
78D1 **Labi** Brunei
13E2 **la Biche,L** Can
61F5 **Labinsk** Russian Fed
94C1 **Laboué** Leb
34C2 **Laboulaye** Arg
7D4 **Labrador** *Region* Can
7D4 **Labrador City** Can
7E4 **Labrador S** Greenland/Can
33E5 **Lábrea** Brazil
78D1 **Labuan** *I* Malay
78B4 **Labuhan** Indon
76A2 **Labutta** Burma
65H3 **Labytnangi** Russian Fed
7C4 **Lac á L'eau Claire** Can
46B2 **La Capelle** France
34C2 **La Carlota** Arg
79B3 **La Carlota** Phil
12J1 **Lac Belot** *L* Can
7C4 **Lac Bienville** *L* Can
83B4 **Laccadive Is** India
47B2 **Lac d'Annecy** *L* France
4G3 **Lac de Gras** *L* Can
47B1 **Lac de Joux** *L* Switz
47B1 **Lac de Neuchâtel** *L* Switz
23A2 **Lac de Patzcuaro** *L* Mexico
23A2 **Lac de Sayula** *L* Mexico
4F3 **Lac des Bois** *L* Can
47A2 **Lac du Bourget** *L* France
25D3 **La Ceiba** Honduras
108A3 **Lacepede B** Aust
48C2 **La Châtre** France
47B1 **La-Chaux-de-Fonds** Switz
94B3 **Lachish** *Hist Site* Israel
107D4 **Lachlan** *R* Aust
32B2 **La Chorrera** Panama
15D1 **Lachute** Can
7D4 **Lac Joseph** *L* Can
15C2 **Lackawanna** USA
5G4 **Lac la Biche** Can
4G3 **Lac la Martre** *L* Can
5H4 **Lac la Ronge** *L* Can
52A1 **Lac Léman** *L* Switz/ France
10C1 **Lac Manouane** *L* Can
15D1 **Lac Megantic** Can
7C4 **Lac Mistassini** *L* Can
13E2 **Lacombe** Can
15D2 **Laconia** USA
50A1 **La Coruña** Spain
10A2 **La Crosse** USA
9C3 **La Cruces** USA
7A4 **Lac Seul** *L* Can
18B2 **La Cygne** USA
84D2 **Ladākh Range** India
85C3 **Lādnūn** India
73B5 **Ladong** China
60D1 **Ladozhskoye Ozero** *L* Ukraine
6B2 **Lady Ann Str** Can
109C4 **Lady Barron** Aust
101G1 **Ladybrand** S Africa
13C3 **Ladysmith** Can
101G1 **Ladysmith** S Africa
71F4 **Lae** PNG
76C3 **Laem Ngop** Thai
56C1 **Laesø** *I* Den
10B2 **Lafayette** Indiana, USA
11A3 **Lafayette** Louisiana, USA
46B2 **La Fère** France
46B2 **La-Ferté-sous-Jouarre** France
97C4 **Lafia** Nig
97C4 **Lafiagi** Nig
48B2 **La Flèche** France
96C1 **La Galite** *I* Tunisia
56C1 **Lagan** *R* Sweden
31D4 **Lagarto** Brazil
96C1 **Laghouat** Alg
35C2 **Lagoa de Araruama** Brazil
29F2 **Lagoa dos Patos** *Lg* Brazil
35C2 **Lagoa Feia** Brazil
32B4 **Lago Agrio** Ecuador
35C1 **Lagoa Juparanã** *L* Brazil
29D2 **Lagoa mar Chiguita** *L* Arg
29F2 **Lagoa Mirim** *L* Brazil/Urug
29B6 **Lago Argentino** *L* Arg
29B5 **Lago Buenos Aries** *L* Arg
29B5 **Lago Cochrane** *L* Arg/Chile
29C5 **Lago Colhué Huapi** *L* Arg
24B2 **Lago de Chapala** *L* Mexico
32A2 **Lago de Chiriqui** *L* Panama
23A2 **Lago de Cuitzeo** *L* Mexico
29B3 **Lago de la Laja** *L* Chile
53A2 **Lago del Coghinas** *L* Sardegna
32C2 **Lago de Maracaibo** *L* Ven
25D3 **Lago de Nicaragua** *L* Nic
32A1 **Lago de Perlas** *L* Nic
52B2 **Lago di Bolsena** *L* Italy
52B2 **Lago di Bracciano** *L* Italy
52A1 **Lago di Como** *L* Italy
47D2 **Lago d'Idro** *L* Italy
52B1 **Lago di Garda** *L* Italy
47C2 **Lago di Lecco** *L* Italy
47C2 **Lago di Lugano** *L* Italy
47D2 **Lago d'Iseo** *L* Italy
47C2 **Lago d'Orta** *L* Italy
29B5 **Lago General Carrera** *L* Chile
52A1 **Lago Maggiore** *L* Italy
29C5 **Lago Musters** *L* Arg
48B3 **Lagon** France
29B4 **Lago Nahuel Haupi** *L* Arg
29B5 **Lago O'Higgins** *L* Chile
53A2 **Lago Omodeo** *L* Sardegna
30C2 **Lago Poopó** *L* Bol
29B4 **Lago Ranco** *L* Chile
32D6 **Lago Rogaguado** *L* Bol
97C4 **Lagos** Nig
50A2 **Lagos** Port
29B5 **Lago San Martin** *L* Arg/Chile
24B2 **Lagos de Moreno** Mexico
30C2 **Lago Titicaca** Bol/ Peru
29B5 **Lago Viedma** *L* Arg
8B2 **La Grande** USA
106B2 **Lagrange** Aust
11B3 **La Grange** Georgia, USA
14A3 **La Grange** Kentucky, USA
19A4 **La Grange** Texas, USA
33E2 **La Gran Sabana** *Mts* Ven
47B2 **La Grave** France
48B3 **Lagronño** Spain
34A3 **Laguna Aluminé** *L* Arg
21B3 **Laguna Beach** USA
34C3 **Laguna Colorada Grande** *L* Arg
79B3 **Laguna de Bay** *Lg* Phil
25D3 **Laguna de Caratasca** *Lg* Honduras
25D4 **Laguna de Chiriqui** *L* Panama
25D3 **Laguna de Managua** *L* Nic
25D3 **Laguna de Nicaragua** *L* Nic
26A4 **Laguna de Perlas** *Lg* Nic
23B1 **Laguna de Pueblo Viejo** *L* Mexico
24C2 **Laguna de Tamiahua** *Lg* Mexico
25C3 **Laguna de Términos** *Lg* Mexico
23A1 **Laguna de Yuriria** *L* Mexico
23B1 **Laguna le Altamira** Mexico

24C2 **Laguna Madre** *Lg* Mexico
34C2 **Laguna Mar Chiquita** *L* Arg
29B4 **Laguna Nahuel Huapi** *L* Arg
34C2 **Laguna Paiva** Arg
29B4 **Laguna Ranco** Chile
9C4 **Laguna Seca** Mexico
23B1 **Laguna Tortugas** *L* Mexico
70C3 **Lahad Datu** Malay
78A3 **Lahat** Indon
38J6 **Lahia** Fin
90B2 **Lāhījān** Iran
46D1 **Lahn** *R* Germany
46D1 **Lahnstein** Germany
84C2 **Lahore** Pak
39K6 **Lahti** Fin
23A2 **La Huerta** Mexico
98B2 **Lai** Chad
73B5 **Laibin** China
76C1 **Lai Chau** Viet
100B4 **Laingsburg** S Africa
44B2 **Lairg** Scot
78A3 **Lais** Indon
79C4 **Lais** Phil
72E2 **Laiyang** China
72D2 **Laizhou Wan** *B* China
34A3 **Laja** *R* Chile
30F4 **Lajes** Brazil
22D4 **La Jolla** USA
9C3 **La Junta** USA
109C2 **Lake Cargelligo** Aust
11A3 **Lake Charles** USA
17B1 **Lake City** Florida, USA
17C1 **Lake City** S Carolina, USA
42C2 **Lake District** Region, Eng
22D4 **Lake Elsinore** USA
106C3 **Lake Eyre Basin** Aust
15C2 **Lakefield** Can
6D3 **Lake Harbour** Can
22C3 **Lake Hughes** USA
16B2 **Lakehurst** USA
19A4 **Lake Jackson** USA
13E2 **Lake la Biche** Can
17B2 **Lakeland** USA
7A5 **Lake of the Woods** Can
20B1 **Lake Oswego** USA
21A2 **Lakeport** USA
19B3 **Lake Providence** USA
111B2 **Lake Pukaki** NZ
109C3 **Lakes Entrance** Aust
22C2 **Lakeshore** USA
108B1 **Lake Stewart** Aust
15C1 **Lake Traverse** Can
8A2 **Lakeview** USA
20B1 **Lakeview Mt** Can
19B3 **Lake Village** USA
17B2 **Lake Wales** USA
22C4 **Lakewood** California, USA
16B2 **Lakewood** New Jersey, USA
14B2 **Lakewood** Ohio, USA
17B2 **Lake Worth** USA
86A1 **Lakhimpur** India
85B4 **Lakhpat** India
84C2 **Lakki** Pak
55B3 **Lakonikós Kólpos** *G* Greece
97B4 **Lakota** Ivory Coast
38K4 **Laksefjord** *Inlet* Nor
38K4 **Lakselv** Nor
34C2 **La Laguna** Arg
32A4 **La Libertad** Ecuador
34A2 **La Ligua** Chile
50A2 **La Linea** Spain
85D4 **Lalitpur** India
5H4 **La Loche** Can
13F1 **la Loche,L** Can
46C1 **La Louvière** Belg
26A4 **La Luz** Nic
7C5 **La Malbaie** Can
23B2 **La Malinche** *Mt* Mexico
50B2 **La Mancha** Region, Spain
9C3 **Lamar** Colorado, USA
18B2 **Lamar** Missouri, USA
19A4 **La Marque** USA
98B3 **Lambaréné** Gabon
32A5 **Lambayeque** Peru
112B10 **Lambert Gl** Ant
16B2 **Lambertville** USA
4F2 **Lamblon,C** Can
47C2 **Lambro** *R* Italy
76C2 **Lam Chi** *R* Thai
50A1 **Lamego** Port
47B2 **La Meije** *Mt* France
32B6 **La Merced** Peru
21B3 **La Mesa** USA
55B3 **Lamía** Greece
42C2 **Lammermuir Hills** Scot
39G7 **Lammhult** Sweden
79B3 **Lamon B** Phil
18B1 **Lamoni** USA
71F3 **Lamotrek** *I* Pacific O
43B3 **Lampeter** Wales
99E3 **Lamu** Kenya
47D1 **Lana** Italy
21C4 **Lanai** *I* Hawaiian Is
21C4 **Lanai City** Hawaiian Is
42C2 **Lanark** Scot
76B3 **Lanbi** *I* Burma
76C1 **Lancang** *R* China
42C3 **Lancashire** County, Eng
21B3 **Lancaster** California, USA
42C2 **Lancaster** Eng
18B1 **Lancaster** Mississippi, USA
15D2 **Lancaster** New Hampshire, USA
14B3 **Lancaster** Ohio, USA
10C3 **Lancaster** Pennsylvania, USA
17B1 **Lancaster** S Carolina, USA
6B2 **Lancaster Sd** Can
78B3 **Landak** *R* Indon
46E2 **Landan** Germany
57C3 **Landeck** Austria
8C2 **Lander** USA
34C2 **Landeta** Arg
57C3 **Landsberg** Germany
4F2 **Lands End** *C* Can
43B4 **Land's End** *Pt* Eng
57C3 **Landshut** Germany
39G7 **Landskrona** Sweden
17A1 **Lanett** USA
56B2 **Langenhagen** Germany
47B1 **Langenthal** Switz
42C2 **Langholm** Scot
38A2 **Langjökull** *Mts* Iceland
77B4 **Langkawi** *I* Malay
13C3 **Langley** Can
108C1 **Langlo** *R* Aust
47B1 **Langnau** Switz
49D2 **Langres** France
70A3 **langsa** Indon
68C2 **Lang Shan** *Mts* China
76D1 **Lang Son** Viet
48C3 **Languedoc** Region, France
29B3 **Lanin** *Mt* Arg
79B4 **Lanoa,L** *L* Phil
16B2 **Lansdale** USA
7B4 **Lansdowne House** Can
16B2 **Lansford** USA
10B2 **Lansing** USA
47B2 **Lanslebourg** France
96A2 **Lanzarote** *I* Canary Is
72A2 **Lanzhou** China
47B2 **Lanzo Torinese** Italy
79B2 **Laoag** Phil
76C1 **Lao Cai** Viet
72D1 **Laoha He** *R* China
45C2 **Laois** County, Irish Rep
46B2 **Laon** France
32B6 **La Oroya** Peru
76C2 **Laos** Republic, S E Asia
49C2 **Lapalisse** France
32B2 **La Palma** Panama
96A2 **La Palma** *I* Canary Is
34B3 **La Pampa** State, Arg
33E2 **La Paragua** Ven
29E2 **La Paz** Arg
34B2 **La Paz** Arg
30C2 **La Paz** Bol
24A2 **La Paz** Mexico
69G2 **La Perouse Str** Japan/Russian Fed
23A1 **La Piedad** Mexico
20B2 **La Pine** USA
19B3 **Laplace** USA
23A2 **la Placita** Mexico
29E2 **La Plata** Arg
13F1 **La Plonge,L** Can
14A2 **La Porte** USA
39K6 **Lappeenranta** Fin
38H5 **Lappland** *Region* Sweden/Fin
34C3 **Laprida** Arg
1B8 **Laptev S** Russian Fed
38J6 **Lapua** Fin
79B3 **Lapu-Lapu** Phil
9B4 **La Purisma** Mexico
95B2 **Laqiya Arba'in** *Well* Sudan
30C3 **La Quiaca** Arg
52B2 **L'Aquila** Italy
91B4 **Lār** Iran
96B1 **Larache** Mor
8C2 **Laramie** USA
8C2 **Laramie Range** *Mts* USA
50B2 **Larca** Spain
9D4 **Laredo** USA
91B4 **Larestan** Region, Iran
Largeau = Faya
47B2 **L'Argentière** France
17B2 **Largo** USA
42B2 **Largs** Scot
90A2 **Lārī** Iran
30C4 **La Rioja** Arg
30C4 **La Rioja** State, Arg
55B3 **Lárisa** Greece
85B3 **Larkana** Pak
92B3 **Larnaca** Cyprus
94A1 **Larnaca B** Cyprus
45D1 **Larne** N Ire
50A1 **La Robla** Spain
46C1 **La Roche-en-Ardenne** Belg
48B2 **La Rochelle** France
47B1 **La Roche-sur-Foron** France
48B2 **La Roche-sur-Yon** France
51B2 **La Roda** Spain
27D3 **La Romana** Dom Rep
5H4 **La Ronge** Can
5H4 **La Ronge,L** Can
39F7 **Larvik** Nor
65J3 **Laryak** Russian Fed
50B2 **La Sagra** *Mt* Spain
15D1 **La Salle** Can
18C1 **La Salle** USA
7C5 **La Sarre** Can
34C1 **Las Avispas** Arg
34A2 **Las Cabras** Chile
5G4 **Lascombe** Can
9C3 **Las Cruces** USA
26C3 **La Selle** *Mt* Haiti
72B2 **Lasengmia** China
30B4 **La Serena** Chile
29E3 **Las Flores** Arg
76B1 **Lashio** Burma
53C3 **La Sila** *Mts* Italy
90B2 **Lāsjerd** Iran
34A3 **Las Lajas** Chile
50A2 **Las Marismas** *Marshland* Spain
96A2 **Las Palmas de Gran Canaria** Canary Is
52A2 **La Spezia** Italy
29C4 **Las Plumas** Arg
34C2 **Las Rosas** Arg
20B2 **Lassen Peak** *Mt* USA
20B2 **Lassen Volcanic Nat Pk** USA
23B2 **las Tinai** Mexico
98B3 **Lastoursville** Gabon
52C2 **Lastovo** *I* Croatia
24B2 **Las Tres Marias** *Is* Mexico
34C2 **Las Varillas** Arg
9C3 **Las Vegas** USA
Latakia = Al Lādhiqīyah
53B2 **Latina** Italy
34B2 **La Toma** Arg
32D1 **La Tortuga** *I* Ven
79B2 **La Trinidad** Phil
109C4 **Latrobe** Aust
94B3 **Latrun** Israel
7C5 **La Tuque** Can
87B1 **Lātūr** India
60B2 **Latvia** Republic, Europe
107D5 **Launceston** Aust
43B4 **Launceston** Eng
29B4 **La Unión** Chile
25D3 **La Union** El Salvador
23A2 **La Union** Mexico
32B5 **La Unión** Peru
107D2 **Laura** Aust
15C3 **Laurel** Delaware, USA
16A3 **Laurel** Maryland, USA
11B3 **Laurel** Mississippi, USA
17B1 **Laurens** USA
17C1 **Laurinburg** USA
52A1 **Lausanne** Switz
78D3 **Laut** *I* Indon
29B5 **Lautaro** *Mt* Chile
46D2 **Lauterecken** Germany
15D1 **Laval** Can
48B2 **Laval** France
22B2 **Laveaga Peak** *Mt* USA
47C2 **Laveno** Italy
31B6 **Lavras** Brazil
4A3 **Lavrentiya** Russian Fed
101H1 **Lavumisa** Swaziland
78D1 **Lawas** Malay
76B1 **Lawksawk** Burma
18A2 **Lawrence** Kansas, USA
15D2 **Lawrence** Massachusetts, USA
111A3 **Lawrence** NZ
14A3 **Lawrenceville** Illinois, USA
9D3 **Lawton** USA
91A5 **Layla** S Arabia
99D2 **Laylo** Sudan
23A2 **Lázaro Cárdenas** Mexico
99E1 **Laz Daua** Somalia
79B4 **Lazi** Phil
8C2 **Lead** USA
13F2 **Leader** Can
18A2 **Leavenworth** USA
58B2 **Leba** Pol
18B2 **Lebanon** Missouri, USA
20B2 **Lebanon** Oregon, USA
15C2 **Lebanon** Pennsylvania, USA
92C3 **Lebanon** Republic, S W Asia
101C3 **Lebombo** *Mts* Mozam/S Africa/ Swaziland
58B2 **Lebork** Pol
47A2 **Le Bourg-d'Oisans** France
47B1 **Le Brassus** Switz
29B3 **Lebu** Chile
47B1 **Le Buet** *Mt* France
46B1 **Le Cateau** France
55A2 **Lecce** Italy
52A1 **Lecco** Italy
47D1 **Lech** *R* Austria
47D1 **Lechtaler Alpen** *Mts* Austria
49C2 **Le Creusot** France
43C3 **Ledbury** Eng
13E2 **Leduc** Can
16C1 **Lee** USA
45B3 **Lee** *R* Irish Rep

41C3 **Leeds** Eng
43C3 **Leek** Eng
56B2 **Leer** Germany
17B2 **Leesburg** Florida, USA
16A3 **Leesburg** Virginia, USA
19B3 **Leesville** USA
109C2 **Leeton** Aust
56B2 **Leeuwarden** Neth
106A4 **Leeuwin,C** Aust
22C2 **Lee Vining** USA
27E3 **Leeward Is** Caribbean S
94A1 **Lefkara** Cyprus
79B3 **Legazpi** Phil
47D2 **Legnago** Italy
59B2 **Legnica** Pol
33F2 **Leguan Inlet** Guyana
32C4 **Leguizamo** Colombia
84D2 **Leh** India
48C2 **Le Havre** France
16B2 **Lehigh** R USA
16B2 **Lehighton** USA
84C2 **Leiah** Pak
59B3 **Leibnitz** Austria
43D3 **Leicester** County, Eng
43D3 **Leicester** Eng
107C2 **Leichhardt** R Aust
56A2 **Leiden** Neth
46B1 **Leie** R Belg
106C4 **Leigh Creek** Aust
43D4 **Leighton Buzzard** Eng
56B2 **Leine** R Germany
45C2 **Leinster** Region, Irish Rep
57C2 **Leipzig** Germany
50A2 **Leiria** Port
39F7 **Leirvik** Nor
45B1 **Leitrim** County, Irish Rep
73C4 **Leiyang** China
73B5 **Leizhou Bandao** Pen China
73C5 **Leizhou Wan** B China
56A2 **Lek** R Neth
96C1 **Le Kef** Tunisia
19B3 **Leland** USA
54A2 **Lelija** Mt Bosnia & Herzegovina, Yugos
47B1 **Le Locle** France
48C2 **Le Mans** France
6D3 **Lemicux Is** Can
8C2 **Lemmon** USA
21B2 **Lemoore** USA
49C2 **Lempdes** France
86C2 **Lemro** R Burma
52C2 **Le Murge** Region, Italy
63C2 **Lena** R Russian Fed
38L6 **Lendery** Russian Fed
73C4 **Lengshujiang** China
65F5 **Leninakan** Armenia
Leningrad = Sankt-Peterburg
112B7 **Leningradskaya** Base Ant
61H3 **Leninogorsk** Tatarskaya Respublika, Russian Fed
68A1 **Leninogorsk** Kazakhstan
65K4 **Leninsk-Kuznetskiy** Russian Fed
69F2 **Leninskoye** Russian Fed
65F6 **Lenkoran'** Azerbaijan
46E1 **Lenne** R Germany
16C1 **Lenox** USA
46B1 **Lens** France
63D1 **Lensk** Russian Fed
53B3 **Lentini** Italy
76B3 **Lenya** R Burma
52B1 **Leoben** Austria
43C3 **Leominster** Eng
16D1 **Leominster** USA
24B2 **Leon** Mexico
25D3 **León** Nic
50A1 **Leon** Region, Spain
50A1 **León** Spain

100A3 **Leonardville** Namibia
106B3 **Leonora** Aust
35C2 **Leopoldina** Brazil
Léopoldville = Kinshasa
60C3 **Lepel** Belorussia
73D4 **Leping** China
49C2 **Le Puy** France
98B2 **Léré** Chad
101G1 **Leribe** Lesotho
47C2 **Lerici** Italy
51C1 **Lérida** Spain
23A1 **Lerma** R Mexico
47D1 **Lermoos** Austria
55C3 **Léros** I Greece
44E1 **Lerwick** Scot
46A2 **Les Andelys** France
26C3 **Les Cayes** Haiti
47B2 **Les Ecrins** Mt France
73A4 **Leshan** China
54B2 **Leskovac** Serbia, Yugos
48B3 **Les Landes** Region, France
101G1 **Leslie** S Africa
61H2 **Lesnoy** Russian Fed
63B2 **Lesosibirsk** Russian Fed
101G1 **Lesotho** Kingdom, S Africa
69F2 **Lesozavodsk** Russian Fed
48B2 **Les Sables-d'Olonne** France
112A **Lesser Antarctica** Region, Ant
27D4 **Lesser Antilles** Is Caribbean S
13E1 **Lesser Slave L** Can
55C3 **Lésvos** I Greece
58B2 **Leszno** Pol
86C2 **Letha Range** Mts Burma
5G5 **Lethbridge** Can
33F3 **Lethem** Guyana
59D3 **Letichev** Ukraine
63D2 **Let Oktyobr'ya** Russian Fed
78B2 **Letong** Indon
46A1 **Le Touquet-Paris-Plage** France
76B2 **Letpadan** Burma
48C1 **Le Tréport** France
47B1 **Leuk** Switz
57A2 **Leuven** Belg
55B3 **Levádhia** Greece
38G6 **Levanger** Nor
47B2 **Levanna** Mt Italy
106B2 **Lévêque,C** Aust
46D1 **Leverkusen** Germany
59B3 **Levice** Czech
47D1 **Levico** Italy
110C2 **Levin** NZ
7C5 **Lévis** Can
15D2 **Levittown** USA
55B3 **Lévka -ri** Mt Greece
55B3 **Levkás** Greece
55B3 **Levkás** I Greece
54C2 **Levski** Bulg
43E4 **Lewes** Eng
40B2 **Lewis** I Scot
16A2 **Lewisburg** USA
111B2 **Lewis P** NZ
8B2 **Lewis Range** Mts USA
8B2 **Lewiston** Idaho, USA
10C2 **Lewiston** Maine, USA
8C2 **Lewistown** Montana, USA
15C2 **Lewistown** Pennsylvania, USA
19B3 **Lewisville** USA
11B3 **Lexington** Kentucky, USA
18B2 **Lexington** Missouri, USA
15C3 **Lexington Park** USA
79C3 **Leyte G** Phil
54A2 **Lezhe** Alb
82D3 **Lhasa** China
86B1 **Lhazê** China
70A3 **Lhokseumawe** Indon

86C1 **Lhozhag** China
68B4 **Lhunze** China
Liancourt Rocks = Tok-do
79C4 **Lianga** Phil
72B3 **Liangdang** China
73C5 **Lianjiang** China
73C5 **Lianping** China
73C5 **Lian Xian** China
72D3 **Lianyungang** China
72E1 **Liaoding Bandao** Pen China
72E1 **Liaodong Wan** B China
72E1 **Liao He** R China
72E1 **Liaoning** Province, China
72E1 **Liaoyang** China
72E1 **Liaoyuan** China
74B2 **Liaoyuang** China
4F3 **Liard** R Can
4F4 **Liard River** Can
46C2 **Liart** France
98B2 **Libenge** Zaïre
9C3 **Liberal** USA
57C2 **Liberec** Czech
97A4 **Liberia** Republic, Africa
18B2 **Liberty** Missouri, USA
15D2 **Liberty** New York, USA
19B3 **Liberty** Texas, USA
48B3 **Libourne** France
23B2 **Libres** Mexico
98A2 **Libreville** Gabon
95A2 **Libya** Republic, Africa
95B2 **Libyan Desert** Libya
95B1 **Libyan Plat** Egypt
53B3 **Licata** Italy
43D3 **Lichfield** Eng
101C2 **Lichinga** Mozam
101G1 **Lichtenburg** S Africa
14B3 **Licking** R USA
22B2 **Lick Observatory** USA
60C3 **Lida** Belorussia
39G7 **Lidköping** Sweden
53B2 **Lido di Ostia** Italy
52A1 **Liechtenstein** Principality, Europe
57B2 **Liège** Belg
58C1 **Lielupe** R Latvia
98C2 **Lienart** Zaïre
57C3 **Lienz** Austria
60B2 **Liepäja** Latvia
46C1 **Lier** Belg
47B1 **Liestal** Switz
15C1 **Lièvre** R Can
57C3 **Liezen** Austria
45C2 **Liffey** R Irish Rep
45C1 **Lifford** Irish Rep
107F3 **Lifu** I Nouvelle Calédonie
109C1 **Lightning Ridge** Aust
46C2 **Ligny-en-Barrois** France
101C2 **Ligonha** R Mozam
47C2 **Liguria** Region, Italy
52A2 **Ligurian** S Italy
21C4 **Lihue** Hawaiian Is
100B2 **Likasi** Zaïre
49C1 **Lille** France
39G6 **Lillehammer** Nor
46B1 **Lillers** France
39G7 **Lillestøm** Nor
13C2 **Lillooet** Can
13C2 **Lillooet** R Can
101C2 **Lilongwe** Malawi
79B4 **Liloy** Phil
54A2 **Lim** R Montenegro/Serbia, Yugos
32B6 **Lima** Peru
50A1 **Lima** Spain
10B2 **Lima** USA
92B3 **Limassol** Cyprus
45C1 **Limavady** N Ire
34B3 **Limay** R Arg
34B3 **Limay Mahuida** Arg
98A2 **Limbe** Cam
101C2 **Limbe** Malawi
57B2 **Limburg** W Germ
31B6 **Limeira** Brazil

45B2 **Limerick** County, Irish Rep
41B3 **Limerick** Irish Rep
56B1 **Limfjorden** L Den
106C2 **Limmen Bight** B Aust
55C3 **Limnos** I Greece
31D3 **Limoeiro** Brazil
48C2 **Limoges** France
25D4 **Limón** Costa Rica
8C3 **Limon** USA
48C2 **Limousin** Region, France
79A3 **Linapacan Str** Phil
29B3 **Linares** Chile
9D4 **Linares** Mexico
50B2 **Linares** Spain
68B4 **Lincang** China
29D2 **Lincoln** Arg
18A1 **Lincoln** California, USA
42D3 **Lincoln** County, Eng
42D3 **Lincoln** Eng
18C1 **Lincoln** Illinois, USA
8D2 **Lincoln** Nebraska, USA
15D2 **Lincoln** New Hampshire, USA
111B2 **Lincoln** NZ
80A **Lincoln** S Greenland
20B2 **Lincoln City** USA
14B2 **Lincoln Park** USA
52A2 **L'Incudina** Mt Corse
57B3 **Lindau** Germany
33F2 **Linden** Guyana
39F7 **Lindesnes** C Nor
99D3 **Lindi** Tanz
98C2 **Lindi** R Zaïre
101G1 **Lindley** S Africa
55C3 **Lindos** Greece
15C2 **Lindsay** Can
105J3 **Line Is** Pacific O
72C2 **Linfen** China
76D2 **Lingao** China
79B2 **Lingayen** Phil
56B2 **Lingen** Germany
73C4 **Lingling** China
73B5 **Lingshan** China
72C2 **Lingshi** China
97A3 **Linguère** Sen
73E4 **Linhai** Rhejiang, China
31D5 **Linhares** Brazil
72B1 **Linhe** China
74B2 **Linjiang** China
39H7 **Linköping** Sweden
72D2 **Linqing** China
35B2 **Lins** Brazil
72A2 **Lintao** China
47C1 **Linthal** Switz
68D2 **Linxi** China
72A2 **Linxia** China
57C3 **Linz** Austria
79B3 **Lipa** Phil
53B3 **Lipari** I Italy
61E3 **Lipetsk** Russian Fed
54B1 **Lipova** Rom
56B2 **Lippe** R Germany
46E1 **Lippstadt** Germany
99D2 **Lira** Uganda
98B3 **Liranga** Congo
98C2 **Lisala** Zaïre
50A2 **Lisboa** Port
Lisbon = Lisboa
45C1 **Lisburn** N Ire
45B2 **Liscannor B** Irish Rep
73D4 **Lishui** China
73C4 **Li Shui** R China
60E4 **Lisichansk** Ukraine
48C2 **Lisieux** France
60E3 **Liski** Russian Fed
46B2 **L'Isle-Adam** France
47B1 **L'Isle-sur-le-Doubs** France
107E3 **Lismore** Aust
45B2 **Listowel** Irish Rep
73B5 **Litang** China
94B2 **Litani** R Leb
33G3 **Litani** R Suriname
18C2 **Litchfield** USA
107E4 **Lithgow** Aust
60B2 **Lithuania** Republic, Europe
16A2 **Lititz** USA

69F2 **Litovko** Russian Fed
19A3 **Little** *R* USA
11C4 **Little Abaco** *I* The Bahamas
110C1 **Little Barrier I** NZ
13E2 **Little Bow** *R* Can
25D3 **Little Cayman** *I* Caribbean S
16B3 **Little Egg Harbor** *B* USA
26C2 **Little Inagua** *I* Caribbean S
77A4 **Little Nicobar** *I* Nicobar Is
11A3 **Little Rock** USA
22D3 **Littlerock** USA
13D2 **Little Smoky** Can
13D2 **Little Smoky** *R* Can
16A3 **Littlestown** USA
15D2 **Littleton** New Hampshire, USA
74B2 **Liuhe** China
73B5 **Liuzhou** China
55B3 **Livanátais** Greece
58D1 **Līvāni** Latvia
12E1 **Livengood** USA
17B1 **Live Oak** USA
21A2 **Livermore** USA
7D5 **Liverpool** Can
42C3 **Liverpool** Eng
4E2 **Liverpool B** Can
42C3 **Liverpool B** Eng
6C2 **Liverpool,C** Can
109D2 **Liverpool Range** *Mts* Aust
8B2 **Livingston** Montana, USA
19B3 **Livingston** Texas, USA
44C4 **Livingston** UK
Livingstone =
Maramba
19A3 **Livingston,L** USA
52C2 **Livno** Bosnia & Herzegovina, Yugos
60E3 **Livny** Russian Fed
14B2 **Livonia** USA
52B2 **Livorno** Italy
99D3 **Liwale** Tanz
52B1 **Ljubljana** Slovenia
38G6 **Ljungan** *R* Sweden
39G7 **Ljungby** Sweden
39H6 **Ljusdal** Sweden
38H6 **Ljusnan** *R* Sweden
43C4 **Llandeilo** Wales
43C4 **Llandovery** Wales
43C3 **Llandrindod Wells** Wales
42C3 **Llandudno** Wales
43B4 **Llanelli** Wales
43C3 **Llangollen** Wales
9C3 **Llano Estacado** *Plat* USA
Z4D2 **Llanos** Region, Colombia/Ven
30D2 **Llanos de Chiquitos** Region, Bol
Lleida = Lérida
50A2 **Llerena** Spain
43B3 **Lleyn** *Pen* Wales
89E7 **Llorin** Nig
5H4 **Lloydminster** Can
30C3 **Llullaillaco** *Mt* Arg/Chile
30C3 **Loa** *R* Chile
49C2 **Loan** France
98B3 **Loange** *R* Zaïre
100B3 **Lobatse** Botswana
98B2 **Lobaye** *R* CAR
34D3 **Loberia** Arg
100A2 **Lobito** Angola
34D3 **Lobos** Arg
47B2 **Locano** Italy
47C1 **Locarno** Switz
44B3 **Loch Awe** *L* Scot
44A3 **Lochboisdale** Scot
44A3 **Loch Bracadale** *Inlet* Scot
44B3 **Loch Broom** *Estuary* Scot
42B2 **Loch Doon** *L* Scot
44B3 **Loch Earn** *L* Scot
44B2 **Loch Eriboll** *Inlet* Scot

44B3 **Loch Ericht** *L* Scot
48C2 **Loches** France
44B3 **Loch Etive** *Inlet* Scot
44B3 **Loch Ewe** *Inlet* Scot
44B3 **Loch Fyne** *Inlet* Scot
44B2 **Loch Hourn** *Inlet* Scot
44B2 **Lochinver** Scot
44B3 **Loch Katrine** *L* Scot
44C3 **Loch Leven** *L* Scot
44D3 **Loch Linnhe** *Inlet* Scot
44B3 **Loch Lochy** *L* Scot
44B3 **Loch Lomond** *L* Scot
44B3 **Loch Long** *Inlet* Scot
44A3 **Lochmaddy** Scot
44B3 **Loch Maree** *L* Scot
44B3 **Loch Morar** *L* Scot
44C3 **Lochnagar** *Mt* Scot
44B3 **Loch Ness** *L* Scot
44B3 **Loch Rannoch** *L* Scot
44A2 **Loch Roag** *Inlet* Scot
44B3 **Loch Sheil** *L* Scot
44B2 **Loch Shin** *L* Scot
44A3 **Loch Snizort** *Inlet* Scot
44B3 **Loch Sunart** *Inlet* Scot
44B3 **Loch Tay** *L* Scot
44B3 **Loch Torridon** *Inlet* Scot
108A2 **Lock** Aust
42C2 **Lockerbie** Scot
15C2 **Lock Haven** USA
15C2 **Lockport** USA
76D3 **Loc Ninh** Viet
53C3 **Locri** Italy
94B3 **Lod** Israel
108B3 **Loddon** *R* Aust
60D1 **Lodeynoye Pole** Russian Fed
84C3 **Lodhran** Pak
52A1 **Lodi** Italy
21A2 **Lodi** USA
98C3 **Lodja** Zaïre
47B1 **Lods** France
99D2 **Lodwar** Kenya
58B2 **Łódź** Pol
38G5 **Lofoten** *Is* Nor
8B2 **Logan** Utah, USA
4D3 **Logan,Mt** Can
14A2 **Logansport** Indiana, USA
19B3 **Logansport** Louisiana, USA
50B1 **Logroño** Spain
86A2 **Lohārdaga** India
39J6 **Lohja** Fin
76B2 **Loikaw** Burma
39J6 **Loimaa** Fin
48C2 **Loir** *R* France
49C2 **Loire** *R* France
32B4 **Loja** Ecuador
50B2 **Loja** Spain
38K5 **Lokan Tekojärvi** *Res* Fin
46B1 **Lokeren** Belg
99D2 **Lokitaung** Kenya
58D1 **Loknya** Russian Fed
98C3 **Lokolo** *R* Zaïre
98C3 **Lokoro** *R* Zaïre
6D3 **Loks Land** *I* Can
56C2 **Lolland** *I* Den
54B2 **Lom** Bulg
98C3 **Lomami** *R* Zaïre
97A4 **Loma Mts** Sierra Leone/Guinea
47C2 **Lombardia** Region, Italy
71D4 **Lomblen** *I* Indon
78D4 **Lombok** *I* Indon
97C4 **Lomé** Togo
98C3 **Lomela** Zaïre
98C3 **Lomela** *R* Zaïre
60C2 **Lomonosov** Russian Fed
47B1 **Lomont** Region, France
21A3 **Lompoc** USA
58C2 **Łomza** Pol
87A1 **Lonāvale** India
29B3 **Loncoche** Chile
7B5 **London** Can

43D4 **London** Eng
45C1 **Londonderry** County, N Ire
45C1 **Londonderry** N Ire
29B7 **Londonderry** *I* Chile
106B2 **Londonderry,C** Aust
30C4 **Londres** Arg
30F3 **Londrina** Brazil
21B2 **Lone Pine** USA
11C4 **Long** *I* The Bahamas
71F4 **Long** *I* PNG
78C2 **Long Akah** Malay
47E1 **Longarone** Italy
34A3 **Longavi** *Mt* Chile
27H2 **Long B** Jamaica
17C1 **Long B** USA
9B3 **Long Beach** California, USA
15D2 **Long Beach** New York, USA
15D2 **Long Branch** USA
73D5 **Longchuan** China
20C2 **Long Creek** USA
109C4 **Longford** Aust
45C2 **Longford** County, Irish Rep
45C2 **Longford** Irish Rep
44D3 **Long Forties** *Region* N Sea
72D1 **Longhua** China
7C4 **Long I** Can
10C2 **Long I** USA
16C2 **Long Island Sd** USA
7B4 **Longlac** Can
73B5 **Longlin** China
8C2 **Longmont** USA
78D2 **Longnawan** Indon
29B3 **Longquimay** Chile
107D3 **Longreach** Aust
72A2 **Longshou Shan** *Upland* China
42C2 **Longtown** Eng
15D1 **Longueuil** Can
34A3 **Longuimay** Chile
46C2 **Longuyon** France
11A3 **Longview** Texas, USA
8A2 **Longview** Washington, USA
46C2 **Longwy** France
72A3 **Longxi** China
77D3 **Long Xuyen** Viet
73D4 **Longyan** China
73B5 **Longzhou** China
47D2 **Lonigo** Italy
49D2 **Lons-le-Saunier** France
11C3 **Lookout,C** USA
99D3 **Loolmalasin** *Mt* Tanz
13D1 **Loon** *R* Can
45B2 **Loop Hd** *C* Irish Rep
76C3 **Lop Buri** Thai
98A3 **Lopez** *C* Gabon
68B2 **Lop Nur** *L* China
50A2 **Lora del Rio** Spain
10B2 **Lorain** USA
84B2 **Loralai** Pak
90B3 **Lordegān** Iran
107E4 **Lord Howe** *I* Aust
105G5 **Lord Howe Rise** Pacific O
6A3 **Lord Mayor B** Can
9C3 **Lordsburg** USA
35B2 **Lorena** Brazil
47E2 **Loreo** Italy
23A1 **Loreto** Mexico
48B2 **Lorient** France
108B3 **Lorne** Aust
57B3 **Lörrach** Germany
49D2 **Lorraine** *Region* France
9C3 **Los Alamos** USA
34A2 **Los Andes** Chile
29B3 **Los Angeles** Chile
9B3 **Los Angeles** USA
21A2 **Los Banos** USA
34B2 **Los Cerrillos** Arg
21A2 **Los Gatos** USA
52B2 **Lošinj** *I* Croatia
29B3 **Los Lagos** Chile
24B2 **Los Mochis** Mexico
22B3 **Los Olivos** USA
34A3 **Los Sauces** Chile
44C3 **Lossiemouth** Scot

27E4 **Los Testigos** *Is* Ven
29B2 **Los Vilos** Chile
48C3 **Lot** *R* France
34A3 **Lota** Chile
42C2 **Lothian** Region, Scot
99D2 **Lotikipi Plain** Sudan/Kenya
98C3 **Loto** Zaïre
47B1 **Lötschberg Tunnel** Switz
38K5 **Lotta** *R* Fin/Russian Fed
48B2 **Loudéac** France
97A3 **Louga** Sen
41B3 **Lough Allen** *L* Irish Rep
45C2 **Lough Boderg** *L* Irish Rep
43D3 **Loughborough** Eng
45C2 **Lough Bowna** *L* Irish Rep
45C1 **Lough Carlingford** *L* N Ire
41B3 **Lough Conn** *L* Irish Rep
41B3 **Lough Corrib** *L* Irish Rep
41B3 **Lough Derg** *L* Irish Rep
45C2 **Lough Derravaragh** *L* Irish Rep
4H2 **Loughead I** Can
45C2 **Lough Ennell** *L* Irish Rep
41B3 **Lough Erne** *L* N Ire
40B2 **Lough Foyle** *Estuary* N Ire/Irish Rep
40B3 **Lough Neagh** *L* N Ire
45C1 **Lough Oughter** *L* Irish Rep
45B2 **Loughrea** Irish Rep
45C2 **Lough Ree** *L* Irish Rep
45C2 **Lough Sheelin** *L* Irish Rep
42B2 **Lough Strangford** *L* Irish Rep
45C1 **Lough Swilly** *Estuary* Irish Rep
14B3 **Louisa** USA
70C3 **Louisa Reef** *I* S E Asia
12E2 **Louise,L** USA
107E2 **Louisiade Arch** Solomon Is
11A3 **Louisiana** State, USA
17B1 **Louisville** Georgia, USA
11B3 **Louisville** Kentucky, USA
38L5 **Loukhi** Russian Fed
48B3 **Lourdes** France
108C2 **Louth** Aust
45C2 **Louth** County, Irish Rep
42D3 **Louth** Eng
Louvain = Leuven
48C2 **Louviers** France
60D2 **Lovat** *R* Russian Fed
54B2 **Lovech** Bulg
21B1 **Lovelock** USA
52B1 **Lóvere** Italy
9C3 **Lovington** USA
38L5 **Lovozero** Russian Fed
6B3 **Low,C** Can
10C2 **Lowell** Massachusetts, USA
20B2 **Lowell** Oregon, USA
16D1 **Lowell** USA
111B2 **Lower Hutt** NZ
43E3 **Lowestoft** Eng
58B2 **Łowicz** Pol
108B2 **Loxton** Aust
5F4 **Loyd George,Mt** Can
54A2 **Loznica** Serbia, Yugos
23A2 **Loz Reyes** Mexico
65H3 **Lozva** *R* Russian Fed
100B2 **Luacano** Angola
98C3 **Luachimo** Angola
98C3 **Lualaba** *R* Zaïre
100B2 **Luampa** Zambia
100B2 **Luân** Angola

73D3 **Lu'an** China
98B3 **Luanda** Angola
100A2 **Luando** *R* Angola
100B2 **Luanginga** *R* Angola
76C1 **Luang Namtha** Laos
76C2 **Luang Prabang** Laos
98B3 **Luangue** *R* Angola
100C2 **Luangwa** *R* Zambia
72D1 **Luan He** *R* China
72D1 **Luanping** China
100B2 **Luanshya** Zambia
100B2 **Luapula** *R* Zaïre
50A1 **Luarca** Spain
98B3 **Lubalo** Angola
58D2 **L'uban** Belorussia
79B3 **Lubang Is** Phil
100A2 **Lubango** Angola
9C3 **Lubbock** USA
56C2 **Lübeck** Germany
98C3 **Lubefu** Zaïre
98C3 **Lubefu** *R* Zaïre
99C3 **Lubero** Zaïre
98C3 **Lubilash** *R* Zaïre
59C2 **Lublin** Pol
60D3 **Lubny** Ukraine
78C2 **Lubok Antu** Malay
98C3 **Lubudi** Zaïre
98C3 **Lubudi** *R* Zaïre
78A3 **Lubuklinggau** Indon
100B2 **Lubumbashi** Zaïre
98C3 **Lubutu** Zaïre
79B3 **Lucban** Phil
52B2 **Lucca** Italy
42B2 **Luce** *B* Scot
19C3 **Lucedale** USA
79B3 **Lucena** Phil
59B3 **Lucenec** Czech
Lucerne = Luzern
73C5 **Luchuan** China
56C2 **Luckenwalde** Germany
101F1 **Luckhoff** S Africa
86A1 **Lucknow** India
100B2 **Lucusse** Angola
46D1 **Lüdenscheid** Germany
100A3 **Lüderitz** Namibia
84D2 **Ludhiana** India
14A2 **Ludington** USA
43C3 **Ludlow** Eng
54C2 **Ludogorie** *Upland* Bulg
17B1 **Ludowici** USA
54B1 **Luduş** Rom
39H6 **Ludvika** Sweden
57B3 **Ludwigsburg** Germany
57B3 **Ludwigshafen** Germany
56C2 **Ludwigslust** Germany
98C3 **Luebo** Zaïre
98C3 **Luema** *R* Zaïre
98C3 **Luembe** *R* Angola
100A2 **Luena** Angola
100B2 **Luene** *R* Angola
72B3 **Lüeyang** China
73D5 **Lufeng** China
11A3 **Lufkin** USA
60C2 **Luga** Russian Fed
60C2 **Luga** *R* Russian Fed
52A1 **Lugano** Switz
60E4 **Lugansk** Ukraine
101C2 **Lugela** Mozam
101C2 **Lugenda** *R* Mozam
50A1 **Lugo** Spain
54B1 **Lugoj** Rom
72A3 **Luhuo** China
98B3 **Lui** *R* Angola
100B2 **Luiana** Angola
100B2 **Luiana** *R* Angola
Luichow Peninsula = Leizhou Bandao
47C2 **Luino** Italy
98B2 **Luionga** *R* Zaïre
72B2 **Luipan Shan** *Upland* China
100B2 **Luishia** Zaïre
68B4 **Luixi** China
98C3 **Luiza** Zaïre
34B2 **Luján** Arg
34D2 **Luján** Arg
73D3 **Lujiang** China
98B3 **Lukenie** *R* Zaïre
64E4 **Luki** Russian Fed
98B3 **Lukolela** Zaïre
58C2 **Łuków** Pol
98C3 **Lukuga** *R* Zaïre
100B2 **Lukulu** Zambia
38J5 **Lule** *R* Sweden
38J5 **Luleå** Sweden
54C2 **Lüleburgaz** Turk
72C2 **Lüliang Shan** *Mts* China
19A4 **Luling** USA
98C2 **Lulonga** *R* Zaïre
Luluabourg = Kananga
100B2 **Lumbala Kaquengue** Angola
11C3 **Lumberton** USA
78D1 **Lumbis** Indon
86C1 **Lumding** India
100B2 **Lumeje** Angola
111A3 **Lumsden** NZ
39G7 **Lund** Sweden
101C2 **Lundazi** Zambia
43B4 **Lundy** *I* Eng
56C2 **Lüneburg** Germany
46D2 **Lunéville** France
100B2 **Lunga** *R* Zambia
86C2 **Lunglei** India
100A2 **Lungue Bungo** *R* Angola
58D2 **Luninec** Belorussia
98B3 **Luobomo** Congo
73B5 **Luocheng** China
73C5 **Luoding** China
72C3 **Luohe** China
72C3 **Luo He** *R* Henan, China
72B2 **Luo He** *R* Shaanxi, China
73C4 **Luoxiao Shan** *Hills* China
72C3 **Luoyang** China
98B3 **Luozi** Zaïre
100B2 **Lupane** Zim
101C2 **Lupilichi** Mozam
Lu Qu = Tao He
30E4 **Luque** Par
45C1 **Lurgan** N Ire
101C2 **Lurio** *R* Mozam
90A3 **Luristan** Region, Iran
100B2 **Lusaka** Zambia
98C3 **Lusambo** Zaïre
55A2 **Lushnjë** Alb
99D3 **Lushoto** Tanz
68B4 **Lushui** China
72E2 **Lüshun** China
43D4 **Luton** Eng
60C3 **Lutsk** Ukraine
99E2 **Luuq** Somalia
99C3 **Luvua** *R* Zaïre
99D3 **Luwegu** *R* Tanz
100C2 **Luwingu** Zambia
71D4 **Luwuk** Indon
46D2 **Luxembourg** Grand Duchy, N W Europe
49D2 **Luxembourg** Lux
73A5 **Luxi** China
95C2 **Luxor** Egypt
61G1 **Luza** Russian Fed
61G1 **Luza** *R* Russian Fed
52A1 **Luzern** Switz
73B5 **Luzhai** China
73B4 **Luzhi** China
73B4 **Luzhou** China
35B1 **Luziânia** Brazil
79B2 **Luzon** *I* Phil
79B1 **Luzon Str** Phil
59C3 **L'vov** Ukraine
44C2 **Lybster** Scot
38H6 **Lycksele** Sweden
100B3 **Lydenburg** S Africa
8B3 **Lyell,Mt** USA
16A2 **Lykens** USA
43C4 **Lyme B** Eng
43C4 **Lyme Regis** Eng
11C3 **Lynchburg** USA
108A2 **Lyndhurst** Aust
15D2 **Lynn** USA
12G3 **Lynn Canal** *Sd* USA
17A1 **Lynn Haven** USA
5H4 **Lynn Lake** Can
5H3 **Lynx L** Can
49C2 **Lyon** France
12G3 **Lyon Canal** *Sd* USA
17B1 **Lyons** Georgia, USA
106A3 **Lyons** *R* Aust
47B2 **Lys** *R* Italy
61J2 **Lys'va** Russian Fed
111B2 **Lyttelton** NZ
13C2 **Lytton** Can
22A1 **Lytton** USA
58D2 **Lyubeshov** Ukraine
60E2 **Lyublino** Russian Fed

M

76C1 **Ma** *R* Viet
94B2 **Ma'agan** Jordan
94B2 **Ma'alot Tarshīha** Israel
92C3 **Ma'an** Jordan
73D3 **Ma'anshan** China
92C2 **Ma'arrat an Nu'mān** Syria
46C1 **Maas** *R* Neth
46C1 **Maaseik** Belg
79B3 **Maasin** Phil
57B2 **Maastricht** Belg
101C3 **Mabalane** Mozam
33F2 **Mabaruma** Guyana
42E3 **Mablethorpe** Eng
101C3 **Mabote** Mozam
58C2 **Mabrita** Belorussia
58D2 **M'adel** Belorussia
35C2 **Macaé** Brazil
9D3 **McAlester** USA
9D4 **McAllen** USA
101C2 **Macaloge** Mozam
33G3 **Macapá** Brazil
35C1 **Macarani** Brazil
32B4 **Macas** Ecuador
31D3 **Macaú** Brazil
73C5 **Macau** Dependency, China
98C2 **M'Bari** *R* CAR
13C2 **McBride** Can
12F2 **McCarthy** USA
13A2 **McCauley I** Can
42C3 **Macclesfield** Eng
6B1 **McClintock B** Can
4H2 **McClintock Chan** Can
16A2 **McClure** USA
22B2 **McClure,L** USA
4G2 **McClure Str** Can
19B3 **McComb** USA
8C2 **McCook** USA
6C2 **Macculloch,C** Can
13C1 **McCusker,Mt** Can
4F4 **McDame** Can
20C2 **McDermitt** USA
13E2 **Macdonald** *R* Can
106C3 **Macdonnell Ranges** *Mts* Aust
50A1 **Macedo de Cavaleiros** Port
55B2 **Macedonia** Republic, Yugos
31D3 **Maceió** Brazil
97B4 **Macenta** Guinea
52B2 **Macerata** Italy
108A2 **Macfarlane,L** Aust
19B3 **McGehee** USA
45B3 **MacGillycuddys Reeks** *Mts* Irish Rep
4C3 **McGrath** USA
35B2 **Machado** Brazil
101C3 **Machaíla** Mozam
99D3 **Machakos** Kenya
32B4 **Machala** Ecuador
101C3 **Machaze** Mozam
87B1 **Mācherla** India
94B2 **Machgharab** Leb
87C1 **Machilīpatnam** India
32C1 **Machiques** Ven
32C6 **Machu-Picchu** *Hist Site* Peru
101C3 **Macia** Mozam
109C1 **MacIntyre** *R* Aust
107D3 **Mackay** Aust
106B3 **Mackay,L** Aust
14C2 **McKeesport** USA
13C1 **Mackenzie** Can
4F3 **Mackenzie** *R* Can
4E3 **Mackenzie B** Can
4G2 **Mackenzie King I** Can
4E3 **Mackenzie Mts** Can
14B1 **Mackinac,Str of** USA
14B1 **Mackinaw City** USA
12D2 **McKinley,Mt** USA
19A3 **McKinney** USA
6C2 **Mackinson Inlet** *B* Can
109D2 **Macksville** Aust
20B2 **Mclaoughlin,Mt** USA
109D1 **Maclean** Aust
100B4 **Maclear** S Africa
5G4 **McLennan** Can
13D2 **McLeod** *R* Can
4G3 **McLeod B** Can
106A3 **McLeod,L** Aust
13C1 **McLeod Lake** Can
4E3 **Macmillan** *R* Can
12H2 **Macmillan P** Can
20B1 **McMinnville** Oregon, USA
112B7 **McMurdo** *Base* Ant
13D2 **McNaughton L** Can
18B1 **Macomb** USA
53A2 **Macomer** Sardegna
101C2 **Macomia** Mozam
49C2 **Mâcon** France
11B3 **Macon** Georgia, USA
18B2 **Macon** Missouri, USA
100B2 **Macondo** Angola
18A2 **McPherson** USA
104F6 **Macquarie** *Is* Aust
109C2 **Macquarie** *R* Aust
109C4 **Macquarie Harbour** *B* Aust
109D2 **Macquarie,L** Aust
17B1 **McRae** USA
112B11 **Mac. Robertson Land** Region, Ant
45B3 **Macroom** Irish Rep
96C1 **M'Sila** Alg
4G3 **McTavish Arm** *B* Can
108A1 **Macumba** *R* Aust
47C2 **Macunaga** Italy
4F3 **McVicar Arm** *B* Can
59B3 **M'yaróvár** Hung
94B3 **Mādabā** Jordan
95A3 **Madadi** *Well* Chad
89J10 **Madagascar** *I* Indian O
95A2 **Madama** Niger
71F4 **Madang** PNG
97C3 **Madaoua** Niger
86C2 **Madaripur** Bang
90B2 **Madau** Turkmenistan
15C1 **Madawaska** *R* Can
96A1 **Madeira** *I* Atlantic O
33E5 **Madeira** *R* Brazil
7D5 **Madeleine, Îsle de la** Can
24B2 **Madera** Mexico
21A2 **Madera** USA
87A1 **Madgaon** India
86B1 **Madhubani** India
86A2 **Madhya Pradesh** State, India
87B2 **Madikeri** India
98B3 **Madimba** Zaïre
98B3 **Madingo Kayes** Congo
98B3 **Madingou** Congo
10B3 **Madison** Indiana, USA
10B2 **Madison** Wisconsin, USA
18C2 **Madisonville** Kentucky, USA
19A3 **Madisonville** Texas, USA
78C4 **Madiun** Indon
99D2 **Mado Gashi** Kenya
47D1 **Madonna Di Campiglio** Italy
87C2 **Madras** India
20B2 **Madras** USA
29A6 **Madre de Dios** *I* Chile
32D6 **Madre de Dios** *R* Bol
50B1 **Madrid** Spain
50B2 **Madridejos** Spain
78C4 **Madura** *I* Indon
87B3 **Madurai** India
75B1 **Maebashi** Japan
76B3 **Mae Khlong** *R* Thai
77B4 **Mae Nam Lunang** *R* Thai

76C2 **Mae Nam Mun** *R* Thai
76B2 **Mae Nam Ping** *R* Thai
101D2 **Maevatanana** Madag
101G1 **Mafeteng** Lesotho
109C3 **Maffra** Aust
99D3 **Mafia** *I* Tanz
101G1 **Mafikeng** S Africa
30G4 **Mafra** Brazil
92C3 **Mafraq** Jordan
32C2 **Magangué** Colombia
34D3 **Magdalena** Arg
24A1 **Magdalena** Mexico
26C4 **Magdalena** *R* Colombia
78D1 **Magdalena,Mt** Malay
56C2 **Magdeburg** Germany
31C6 **Magé** Brazil
78C4 **Magelang** Indon
47C1 **Maggia** *R* Switz
92B4 **Maghâgha** Egypt
45C1 **Magherafelt** N Ire
55A2 **Maglie** Italy
61J3 **Magnitogorsk** Russian Fed
19B3 **Magnolia** USA
101C2 **Magoé** Mozam
15D1 **Magog** Can
23B1 **Magosal** Mexico
13E2 **Magrath** Can
7A3 **Maguse River** Can
76B1 **Magwe** Burma
90A2 **Mahābād** Iran
86B1 **Mahabharat Range** *Mts* Nepal
87A1 **Mahād** India
85D4 **Mahadeo Hills** India
101D2 **Mahajanga** Madag
100B3 **Mahalapye** Botswana
86A2 **Mahānadi** *R* India
101D2 **Mahanoro** Madag
16A2 **Mahanoy City** USA
87A1 **Maharashtra** State, India
86A2 **Māhāsamund** India
76C2 **Maha Sarakham** Thai
101D2 **Mahavavy** *R* Madag
87B1 **Mahbubnagar** India
96D1 **Mahdia** Tunisia
87B2 **Mahe** India
85D4 **Mahekar** India
101D2 **Mahéli** *I* Comoros
86A2 **Mahendragarh** India
99D3 **Mahenge** Tanz
85C4 **Mahesana** India
110C1 **Mahia Pen** NZ
85D3 **Mahoba** India
51C2 **Mahón** Spain
12J1 **Mahony L** Can
96D1 **Mahrès** Tunisia
85C4 **Mahuva** India
32C1 **Maicao** Colombia
47B1 **Maiche** France
43E4 **Maidstone** Eng
98B1 **Maiduguri** Nig
86A2 **Maihar** India
86C2 **Maijdi** Bang
76B3 **Mail Kyun** *I* Burma
84A1 **Maimana** Afghan
14B1 **Main Chan** Can
98B3 **Mai-Ndombe** *L* Zaïre
10D2 **Maine** State, USA
48B2 **Maine** *Region* France
44C2 **Mainland** *I* Scot
85D3 **Mainpuri** India
46A2 **Maintenon** France
101D2 **Maintirano** Madag
57B2 **Mainz** Germany
97A4 **Maio** *I* Cape Verde
29C2 **Maipó** *Mt* Arg/Chile
34D3 **Maipú** Arg
32D1 **Maiquetía** Ven
47B2 **Maira** *R* Italy
86C1 **Mairābāri** India
86C2 **Maiskhal I** Bang
107E4 **Maitland** New South Wales, Aust
108A2 **Maitland** S Australia, Aust
112C12 **Maitri** *Base* Ant
74D3 **Maizuru** Japan
70C4 **Majene** Indon

30B2 **Majes** *R* Peru
99D2 **Maji** Eth
72D2 **Majia He** *R* China
Majunga = **Mahajanga**
70C4 **Makale** Indon
86B1 **Makalu** *Mt* China/ Nepal
98B2 **Makanza** Zaïre
52C2 **Makarska** Croatia
61F2 **Makaryev** Russian Fed
Makassar = Ujung **Pandang**
78D3 **Makassar Str** Indon
61H4 **Makat** Kazakhstan
97A4 **Makeni** Sierra Leone
60E4 **Makeyevka** Ukraine
100B3 **Makgadikgadi** *Salt Pan* Botswana
61G5 **Makhachkala** Russian Fed
99D3 **Makindu** Kenya
88H5 **Makkah** S Arabia
7E4 **Makkovik** Can
59C3 **Makó** Hung
98B2 **Makokou** Gabon
110C1 **Makorako,Mt** NZ
98B2 **Makoua** Congo
85C3 **Makrāna** India
85A3 **Makran Coast Range** *Mts* Pak
96C1 **Makthar** Tunisia
93D2 **Mākū** Iran
98C3 **Makumbi** Zaïre
74C4 **Makurazaki** Japan
97C4 **Makurdi** Nig
79B4 **Malabang** Phil
87A2 **Malabar Coast** India
89E7 **Malabo** Bioko
77C5 **Malacca,Str of** S E Asia
32C2 **Málaga** Colombia
50B2 **Malaga** Spain
101D3 **Malaimbandy** Madag
107F1 **Malaita** *I* Solomon Is
99D2 **Malakal** Sudan
84C2 **Malakand** Pak
78C4 **Malang** Indon
98B3 **Malange** Angola
97C3 **Malanville** Benin
39H7 **Mälaren** *L* Sweden
34B3 **Malargüe** Arg
12F3 **Malaspina Gl** USA
93C2 **Malatya** Turk
101C2 **Malawi** Republic, Africa
Malawi,L = Nyasa,L
79C4 **Malaybalay** Phil
90A3 **Malāyer** Iran
70B3 **Malaysia** Fed, S E Asia
93D2 **Malazgirt** Turk
58B2 **Malbork** Pol
56C2 **Malchin** Germany
18C2 **Malden** USA
83B5 **Maldives Is** Indian O
104B4 **Maldives Ridge** Indian O
29F2 **Maldonado** Urug
47D1 **Male** Italy
85C4 **Malegaon** India
59B3 **Malé Karpaty** *Upland* Czech
101C2 **Malema** Mozam
84B2 **Mālestān** Afghan
38H5 **Malgomaj** *L* Sweden
95B3 **Malha** *Well* Sudan
20C2 **Malheur L** USA
97D3 **Mali** Republic, Africa
78D1 **Malinau** Indon
99E3 **Malindi** Kenya
Malines = Mechelen
40B2 **Malin Head** *Pt* Irish Rep
86A2 **Malkala Range** *Mts* India
85D4 **Malkāpur** India
55C2 **Malkara** Turk
54C2 **Malko Türnovo** Bulg
44B3 **Mallaig** Scot
95C2 **Mallawi** Egypt
47D1 **Málles Venosta** Italy
51C2 **Mallorca** *I* Spain

45B2 **Mallow** Irish Rep
38G6 **Malm** Nor
38J5 **Malmberget** Sweden
46D1 **Malmédy** Germany
43C4 **Malmesbury** Eng
100A4 **Malmesbury** S Africa
39G7 **Malmö** Sweden
61G2 **Malmyzh** Russian Fed
79B3 **Malolos** Phil
15D2 **Malone** USA
101G1 **Maloti Mts** Lesotho
38F6 **Måloy** Nor
28A2 **Malpelo** *I* Colombia
34A2 **Malpo** *R* Chile
85D3 **Mālpura** India
8C2 **Malta** Montana, USA
53B3 **Malta** *Chan* Malta/ Italy
53B3 **Malta** *I* Medit S
100A3 **Maltahöhe** Namibia
42D2 **Malton** Eng
39G6 **Malung** Sweden
87A1 **Mālvan** India
19B3 **Malvern** USA
85D4 **Malwa Plat** India
65F5 **Malyy Kavkaz** *Mts* Azerbaijan/Georgia
61G4 **Malyy Uzen'** *R* Kazakhstan
63D2 **Mama** Russian Fed
61H2 **Mamadysh** Russian Fed
99C2 **Mambasa** Zaïre
71E4 **Mamberamo** *R* Indon
98B2 **Mambéré** *R* CAR
98A2 **Mamfé** Cam
33D6 **Mamoré** *R* Bol
97A3 **Mamou** Guinea
101D2 **Mampikony** Madag
97B4 **Mampong** Ghana
94B3 **Mamshit** *Hist Site* Israel
100B3 **Mamuno** Botswana
97B4 **Man** Ivory Coast
21C4 **Mana** Hawaiian Is
101D3 **Manabo** Madag
33E4 **Manacapuru** Brazil
51C2 **Manacor** Spain
71D3 **Manado** Indon
25D3 **Managua** Nic
101D3 **Manakara** Madag
101D2 **Mananara** Madag
101D3 **Mananjary** Madag
111A3 **Manapouri** NZ
111A3 **Manapouri,L** NZ
86C1 **Manas** Bhutan
82C1 **Manas** China
65K5 **Manas Hu** *L* China
86A1 **Manaslu** *Mt* Nepal
16B2 **Manasquan** USA
33F4 **Manaus** Brazil
92B2 **Manavgat** Turk
93C2 **Manbij** Syria
42B2 **Man,Calf of** *I* Eng
87B1 **Mancheral** India
15D2 **Manchester** Connecticut, USA
42C3 **Manchester** Eng
10C2 **Manchester** New Hampshire, USA
16A2 **Manchester** Pennsylvania, USA
69E2 **Manchuria** *Hist Region*, China
91B4 **Mand** *R* Iran
101C2 **Manda** Tanz
35A2 **Mandaguari** Brazil
39F7 **Mandal** Nor
76B1 **Mandalay** Burma
68C2 **Mandalgovi** Mongolia
8C2 **Mandan** USA
14A2 **Mandelona** USA
99E2 **Mandera** Eth
26B3 **Mandeville** Jamaica
101C2 **Mandimba** Mozam
86A2 **Mandla** India
101D2 **Mandritsara** Madag
85D4 **Mandsaur** India
53C2 **Manduria** Italy
85B4 **Mändvi** India
87B2 **Mandya** India

58D2 **Manevichi** Ukraine
42D3 **Manfield** Eng
53C2 **Manfredonia** Italy
98B1 **Manga** *Desert Region* Niger
110C1 **Mangakino** NZ
54C2 **Mangalia** Rom
98B1 **Mangalmé** Chad
87A2 **Mangalore** India
78B3 **Manggar** Indon
68B3 **Mangnia** China
101C2 **Mangoche** Malawi
101D3 **Mangoky** *R* Madag
71D4 **Mangole** *I* Indon
85B4 **Mängral** India
63E2 **Mangui** China
8D3 **Manhattan** USA
31C6 **Manhuacu** Brazil
101D2 **Mania** *R* Madag
101C2 **Manica** Mozam
7D5 **Manicouagan** *R* Can
91A4 **Manifah** S Arabia
79B3 **Manila** Phil
109D2 **Manilla** Aust
97B3 **Maninian** Ivory Coast
86C2 **Manipur** State, India
86C2 **Manipur** *R* Burma
92A2 **Manisa** Turk
41C3 **Man,Isle of** Irish S
14A2 **Manistee** USA
14A2 **Manistee** *R* USA
14A1 **Manistique** USA
5H4 **Manitoba** Province, Can
5J4 **Manitoba,L** Can
13F2 **Manito L** Can
14A1 **Manitou Is** USA
7B5 **Manitoulin** *I* Can
14A2 **Manitowoc** USA
15C1 **Maniwaki** Can
32B2 **Manizales** Colombia
101D3 **Manja** Madag
106A4 **Manjimup** Aust
87B1 **Mānjra** *R* India
10A2 **Mankato** USA
97B4 **Mankono** Ivory Coast
12D2 **Manley Hot Springs** USA
110B1 **Manly** NZ
85C4 **Manmād** India
78A3 **Manna** Indon
108A2 **Mannahill** Aust
87B3 **Mannar** Sri Lanka
87B3 **Mannär,G of** India
87B2 **Mannärgudi** India
57B3 **Mannheim** Germany
13D1 **Manning** Can
17B1 **Manning** USA
108A2 **Mannum** Aust
97A4 **Mano** Sierra Leone
71E4 **Mankwari** Indon
98C3 **Manono** Zaïre
76B3 **Manoron** Burma
75B1 **Mano-wan** *B* Japan
74B2 **Manp'o** N Korea
84D3 **Mänsa** India
100B2 **Mansa** Zambia
6B3 **Mansel I** Can
19B2 **Mansfield** Arkansas, USA
108C3 **Mansfield** Aust
19B3 **Mansfield** Louisiana, USA
16D1 **Mansfield** Massachusetts, USA
10B2 **Mansfield** Ohio, USA
15C2 **Mansfield** Pennsylvania, USA
71E2 **Mansyu Deep** Pacific O
32A4 **Manta** Ecuador
79A4 **Mantalingajan,Mt** Phil
32B6 **Mantaro** *R* Peru
22B2 **Manteca** USA
48C2 **Mantes** France
52B1 **Mantova** Italy
38J6 **Mantta** Fin
61F2 **Manturovo** Russian Fed
35A2 **Manuel Ribas** Brazil
79B4 **Manukan** Phil
110B1 **Manukau** NZ
71F4 **Manus** *I* Pacific O

Manzanares

50B2 **Manzanares** Spain
25E2 **Manzanillo** Cuba
24B3 **Manzanillo** Mexico
63D3 **Manzhouli** China
94C3 **Manzil** Jordan
101C3 **Manzini** Swaziland
98B1 **Mao** Chad
72A2 **Maomao Shan** *Mt* China
73C5 **Maoming** China
101C3 **Mapai** Mozam
71E3 **Mapia** *Is* Pacific O
79A4 **Mapin** *I* Phil
5H5 **Maple Creek** Can
101H1 **Maputo** Mozam
101H1 **Maputo** *R* Mozam
Ma Qu = Huange He
72A3 **Maqu** China
86B1 **Maquan He** *R* China
98B3 **Maquela do Zombo** Angola
29C4 **Maquinchao** Arg
31B3 **Marabá** Brazil
32C1 **Maracaibo** Ven
32D1 **Maracay** Ven
95A2 **Marādah** Libya
97C3 **Maradi** Niger
90A2 **Marāgheh** Iran
99D2 **Maralal** Kenya
107F1 **Maramasike** *I* Solomon Is
100B2 **Maramba** Zambia
90A2 **Marand** Iran
31B2 **Maranhõa** State, Brazil
109C1 **Maranoa** *R* Aust
32B4 **Marañón** *R* Peru
7B5 **Marathon** Can
17B2 **Marathon** Florida, USA
78D2 **Maratua** *I* Indon
23A2 **Maravatio** Mexico
79B4 **Marawi** Phil
34B2 **Marayes** Arg
50B2 **Marbella** Spain
106A3 **Marble Bar** Aust
100B3 **Marblehall** S Africa
16D1 **Marblehead** USA
57B2 **Marburg** Germany
57B2 **Marche** Belg
50A2 **Marchean** Spain
46C1 **Marche-en-Famenne** Belg
32J7 **Marchena** *I* Ecuador
17B2 **Marco** USA
34C2 **Marcos Juárez** Arg
12E2 **Marcus Baker,Mt** USA
15D2 **Marcy,Mt** USA
84C2 **Mardan** Pak
29E3 **Mar del Plata** Arg
93D2 **Mardin** Turk
99D1 **Mareb** *R* Eth
16B1 **Margaretville** USA
43E4 **Margate** Eng
54B1 **Marghita** Rom
109C4 **Maria I** Aust
104F3 **Mariana** *Is* Pacific O
13E1 **Mariana Lake** Can
104F3 **Marianas Trench** Pacific O
86C1 **Mariāni** India
19B3 **Marianna** Arkansas, USA
17A1 **Marianna** Florida, USA
7G4 **Maria Van Diemen,C** NZ
59B3 **Mariazell** Austria
52C1 **Maribor** Slovenia
99C2 **Maridi** Sudan
112B5 **Marie Byrd Land** Region, Ant
27E3 **Marie Galante** *I* Caribbean S
39H6 **Mariehamn** Fin
46C1 **Mariembourg** Belg
33G2 **Marienburg** Surinam
100A3 **Mariental** Namibia
39G7 **Mariestad** Sweden
17B1 **Marietta** Georgia, USA
14B3 **Marietta** Ohio, USA

19A3 **Marietta** Oklahoma, USA
27Q2 **Marigot** Dominica
60B3 **Marijampole** Lithuania
31B6 **Marilia** Brazil
98B3 **Marimba** Angola
79B3 **Marinduque** *I* Phil
10B2 **Marinette** USA
30F3 **Maringá** Brazil
98C2 **Maringa** *R* Zaire
18B2 **Marion** Arkansas, USA
18C2 **Marion** Illinois, USA
10B2 **Marion** Indiana, USA
10B2 **Marion** Ohio, USA
17C1 **Marion** S Carolina, USA
11B3 **Marion,L** USA
107E2 **Marion Reef** Aust
21B2 **Mariposa** USA
22B2 **Mariposa** *R* USA
22B2 **Mariposa Res** USA
60C5 **Marista** *R* Bulg
60E4 **Mariupol'** Ukraine
61G2 **Mariyskaya Respublika,** Russian Fed
94B2 **Marjayoun** Leb
58D2 **Marjina Gorki** Belorussia
94B3 **Marka** Jordan
99E2 **Marka** Somalia
56C1 **Markaryd** Sweden
43C3 **Market Drayton** Eng
43D3 **Market Harborough** Eng
112A **Markham,Mt** Ant
22C1 **Markleeville** USA
16D1 **Marlboro** Massachusetts, USA
107D3 **Marlborough** Aust
46B2 **Marle** France
19A3 **Marlin** USA
48C3 **Marmande** France
55C2 **Marmara Adi** *I* Turk
92A1 **Marmara,S of** Turk
55C3 **Marmaris** Turk
14B3 **Marmet** USA
52B1 **Marmolada** *Mt* Italy
12D3 **Marmot B** USA
47A1 **Marnay** France
46B2 **Marne** Department, France
46B2 **Marne** *R* France
98B2 **Maro** Chad
101D2 **Maroantsetra** Madag
101C2 **Marondera** Zim
33G3 **Maroni** *R* French Guiana
109D1 **Maroochydore** Aust
98B1 **Maroua** Cam
101D2 **Marovoay** Madag
11B4 **Marquesas Keys** *Is* USA
10B2 **Marquette** USA
46A1 **Marquise** France
109C2 **Marra** *R* Aust
101H1 **Marracuene** Mozam
96B1 **Marrakech** Mor
106C3 **Marree** Aust
19B4 **Marrero** USA
101C2 **Marromeu** Mozam
101C2 **Marrupa** Mozam
95C2 **Marsa Alam** Egypt
99D2 **Marsabit** Kenya
53B3 **Marsala** Italy
49D3 **Marseille** France
12B2 **Marshall** Alaska, USA
14A3 **Marshall** Illinois, USA
14B2 **Marshall** Michigan, USA
18B2 **Marshall** Missouri, USA
11A3 **Marshall** Texas, USA
105G3 **Marshall Is** Pacific O
18B2 **Marshfield** Missouri, USA
26B1 **Marsh Harbour** The Bahamas
19B4 **Marsh I** USA
12H2 **Marsh L** Can
76B2 **Martaban,G of** Burma

78A3 **Martapura** Indon
78C3 **Martapura** Indon
15D2 **Martha's Vineyard** *I* USA
49D2 **Martigny** Switz
59B3 **Martin** Czech
111C2 **Martinborough** NZ
34B3 **Martín de Loyola** Arg
23B1 **Martínez de la Torre** Mexico
27E4 **Martinique** *I* Caribbean S
17A1 **Martin,L** USA
15C3 **Martinsburg** USA
14B2 **Martins Ferry** USA
103G6 **Martin Vaz** *I* Atlantic O
49D3 **Martiques** France
110C2 **Marton** NZ
50B2 **Martos** Spain
78D1 **Marudi** Malay
84B2 **Maruf** Afghan
75A2 **Marugame** Japan
85C3 **Mārwār** India
65H6 **Mary** Turkmenistan
107E3 **Maryborough** Queensland, Aust
108B3 **Maryborough** Victoria, Aust
5F4 **Mary Henry,Mt** Can
10C3 **Maryland** State, USA
42C2 **Maryport** Eng
21A2 **Marysville** California, USA
18A2 **Marysville** Kansas, USA
20B1 **Marysville** Washington, USA
10A2 **Maryville** Iowa, USA
18B1 **Maryville** Missouri, USA
95A2 **Marzuq** Libya
Masada = Mezada
94B2 **Mas'adah** Syria
99D3 **Masai Steppe** Upland Tanz
99D3 **Masaka** Uganda
93E2 **Masally** Azerbaijan
74B3 **Masan** S Korea
101C2 **Masasi** Tanz
25D3 **Masaya** Nic
79B3 **Masbate** Phil
79B3 **Masbate** *I* Phil
96C1 **Mascara** Alg
23A1 **Mascota** Mexico
35D1 **Mascote** Brazil
101G1 **Maseru** Lesotho
66C3 **Mashad** Iran
84B2 **Mashaki** Afghan
90C2 **Mashhad** Iran
98B3 **Masi-Manimba** Zaïre
99D2 **Masindi** Uganda
99C3 **Masisi** Zaïre
90A3 **Masjed Soleyman** Iran
101E2 **Masoala** *C* Madag
10A2 **Mason City** USA
91C5 **Masqat** Oman
52B2 **Massa** Italy
10C2 **Massachusetts** State, USA
15D2 **Massachusetts B** USA
98B1 **Massakori** Chad
101C3 **Massangena** Mozam
Massawa = Mits'iwa
15D2 **Massena** USA
98B1 **Massénya** Chad
14B1 **Massey** Can
49C2 **Massif Central** Mts France
98B2 **Massif de l'Adamaoua** Mts Cam
26C3 **Massif de la Hotte** Mts Haiti
101D3 **Massif de l'Isalo** Upland Madag
98C2 **Massif des Bongo** Upland CAR
49D2 **Massif du Pelvoux** Mts France

101D2 **Massif du Tsaratanana** *Mt* Madag
14B2 **Massillon** USA
97B3 **Massina** Region, Mali
101C3 **Massinga** Mozam
101C3 **Massingir** Mozam
61H4 **Masteksay** Kazakhstan
111C2 **Masterton** NZ
74C4 **Masuda** Japan
98B3 **Masuku** Gabon
100C3 **Masvingo** Zim
92C2 **Maşyāf** Syria
98B3 **Matadi** Zaïre
25D3 **Matagalpa** Nic
7C4 **Matagami** Can
9D4 **Matagorda B** USA
110C1 **Matakana I** NZ
100A2 **Matala** Angola
87C3 **Matale** Sri Lanka
97A3 **Matam** Sen
97C3 **Matameye** Niger
24C2 **Matamoros** Mexico
95B2 **Ma'tan as Sarra** Well Libya
7D5 **Matane** Can
25D2 **Matanzas** Cuba
34A2 **Mataquito** *R* Chile
87C3 **Matara** Sri Lanka
106A1 **Mataram** Indon
30B2 **Matarani** Peru
51C1 **Mataró** Spain
111A3 **Mataura** NZ
24B2 **Matehuala** Mexico
27L1 **Matelot** Trinidad
53C2 **Matera** Italy
59C3 **Mátészalka** Hung
85D3 **Mathura** India
79C4 **Mati** Phil
78D3 **Matisiri** *I* Indon
43D3 **Matlock** Eng
33F6 **Mato Grosso** Brazil
33F6 **Mato Grosso** State, Brazil
30E2 **Mato Grosso do Sul** State, Brazil
101H1 **Matola** Mozam
91C5 **Matrah** Oman
92A3 **Matrûh** Egypt
74C3 **Matsue** Japan
74E2 **Matsumae** Japan
74D3 **Matsumoto** Japan
74D4 **Matsusaka** Japan
74C4 **Matsuyama** Japan
7B5 **Mattagami** *R* Can
15C1 **Mattawa** Can
52A1 **Matterhorn** *Mt* Italy/Switz
26C2 **Matthew Town** The Bahamas
16C2 **Mattituck** USA
18C2 **Mattoon** USA
84B2 **Matun** Afghan
27L1 **Matura B** Trinidad
33E2 **Maturin** Ven
86A1 **Mau** India
101C2 **Maúa** Mozam
49C1 **Maubeuge** France
108B2 **Maude** Aust
103J8 **Maud Seamount** Atlantic O
21C4 **Maui** *I* Hawaiian Is
34A3 **Maule** *R* Chile
14B2 **Maumee** USA
14B2 **Maumee** *R* USA
100B2 **Maun** Botswana
21C4 **Mauna Kea** *Mt* Hawaiian Is
21C4 **Mauna Loa** *Mt* Hawaiian Is
4F3 **Maunoir** *L* Can
4F3 **Maunoir,L** Can
48C2 **Mauriac** France
96A2 **Mauritania** Republic, Africa
100E3 **Mauritius** *I* Indian O
100B2 **Mavinga** Angola
86C2 **Mawlaik** Burma
112C10 **Mawson** Base Ant
78B3 **Maya** *I* Indon
63F2 **Maya** *R* Russian Fed
93D2 **Mayādīn** Syria

11C4 **Mayaguana** *I* The Bahamas
27D3 **Mayagüez** Puerto Rico
97C3 **Mayahi** Niger
98B3 **Mayama** Congo
90C2 **Mayamey** Iran
42B2 **Maybole** Scot
10C3 **May,C** USA
109C4 **Maydena** Aust
46D1 **Mayen** Germany
48B2 **Mayenne** France
13D2 **Mayerthorpe** Can
18C2 **Mayfield** USA
61E5 **Maykop** Russian Fed
65H6 **Maymaneh** Afghan
76B1 **Maymyo** Burma
4E3 **Mayo** Can
45B2 **Mayo** County, Irish Rep
16A3 **Mayo** USA
45B1 **Mayo,Mts of** Irish Rep
79B3 **Mayon** *Mt* Phil
51C2 **Mayor** *Mt* Spain
34C3 **Mayor Buratovich** Arg
110C1 **Mayor I** NZ
30D2 **Mayor P Lagerenza** Par
101D2 **Mayotte** *I* Indian O
27H2 **May Pen** Jamaica
16B3 **May Point,C** USA
47D1 **Mayrhofen** Austria
16B3 **Mays Landing** USA
14B3 **Maysville** USA
98B3 **Mayumba** Gabon
100B2 **Mazabuka** Zambia
84D1 **Mazar** China
94B3 **Mazār** Jordan
53B3 **Mazara del Vallo** Italy
84B1 **Mazar-i-Sharif** Afghan
24B2 **Mazatlán** Mexico
60B2 **Mazeikiai** Lithuania
94B3 **Mazra** Jordan
101C3 **Mbabane** Swaziland
98B2 **Mbaïki** CAR
99D3 **Mbala** Zambia
100B3 **Mbalabala** Zim
99D2 **Mbale** Uganda
98B2 **Mbalmayo** Cam
98B2 **Mbam** *R* Cam
101C2 **Mbamba Bay** Tanz
98B2 **Mbandaka** Zaïre
98B3 **Mbanza Congo** Angola
98B3 **Mbanza-Ngungu** Zaïre
99D3 **Mbarara** Uganda
98B2 **Mbènza** Congo
98B2 **Mbére** *R* Cam
99D3 **Mbeya** Tanz
98B3 **Mbinda** Congo
97A3 **Mbout** Maur
98C3 **Mbuji-Mayi** Zaïre
99D3 **Mbulu** Tanz
96B2 **Mcherrah** Region, Alg
101C2 **Mchinji** Malawi
76D3 **Mdrak** Viet
9B3 **Mead,L** USA
5H4 **Meadow Lake** Can
14B2 **Meadville** USA
7E4 **Mealy Mts** Can
109C1 **Meandarra** Aust
5G4 **Meander River** Can
45C2 **Meath** County, Irish Rep
49C2 **Meaux** France
16C1 **Mechanicville** USA
56A2 **Mechelen** Belg
96B1 **Mecheria** Alg
56C2 **Mecklenburg-Vorpommern** *State* Germany
56C2 **Mecklenburger Bucht** *B* Germany
101C2 **Meconta** Mozam
101C2 **Mecuburi** Mozam
101D2 **Mecufi** Mozam
101C2 **Mecula** Mozam
70A3 **Medan** Indon
34C3 **Medanos** Arg
34D2 **Médanos** Arg
13E2 **Medecine Hat** Can
32B2 **Medellín** Colombia
96D1 **Medenine** Tunisia
8A2 **Medford** USA
54C2 **Medgidia** Rom
34B2 **Media Agua** Arg
54B1 **Mediaş** Rom
20C1 **Medical Lake** USA
5G5 **Medicine Hat** Can
35C1 **Medina** Brazil
80B3 **Medina** S Arabia
50B1 **Medinaceli** Spain
50B1 **Medina del Campo** Spain
50A1 **Medina de Rio Seco** Spain
86B2 **Medinīpur** India
88E4 **Mediterranean S** Europe
13F2 **Medley** Can
61J3 **Mednogorsk** Russian Fed
86D1 **Mêdog** China
98B2 **Medouneu** Gabon
61F3 **Medvedista** *R* Russian Fed
64E3 **Medvezh'yegorsk** Russian Fed
106A3 **Meekatharra** Aust
84D3 **Meerut** India
99D2 **Mēga** Eth
55B3 **Megalópolis** Greece
55B3 **Mégara** Greece
86C1 **Meghālaya** State, India
86C2 **Meghna** *R* Bang
94B2 **Megiddo** *Hist Site* Israel
91B4 **Mehran** *R* Iran
90B3 **Mehriz** Iran
35B1 **Meia Ponte** *R* Brazil
98B2 **Meiganga** Cam
76B1 **Meiktila** Burma
47C1 **Meiringen** Switz
73A4 **Meishan** China
57C2 **Meissen** Germany
73D5 **Mei Xian** China
73D5 **Meizhou** China
30B3 **Mejillones** Chile
98B2 **Mekambo** Gabon
99D1 **Mek'elē** Eth
96B1 **Meknès** Mor
76D3 **Mekong** *R* Camb
97C3 **Mekrou** *R* Benin
77C5 **Melaka** Malay
104F4 **Melanesia** *Region* Pacific O
78C3 **Melawi** *R* Indon
107D4 **Melbourne** Aust
11B4 **Melbourne** USA
9C4 **Melchor Muźguiz** Mexico
61J3 **Meleuz** Russian Fed
98B1 **Melfi** Chad
5H4 **Melfort** Can
96B1 **Melilla** N W Africa
29B4 **Melimoyu** *Mt* Chile
34C2 **Melincué** Arg
34A2 **Melipilla** Chile
60E4 **Melitopol'** Ukraine
6D2 **Meliville Bugt** *B* Greenland
99D2 **Melka Guba** Eth
101H1 **Melmoth** S Africa
34C2 **Melo** Arg
29F2 **Melo** Urug
22B2 **Melones Res** USA
12D1 **Melozitna** *R* USA
47C1 **Mels** Switz
43D3 **Melton Mowbry** Eng
49C2 **Melun** France
5H4 **Melville** Can
27Q2 **Melville,C** Dominica
4F3 **Melville Hills** *Mts* Can
106C2 **Melville I** Aust
4G2 **Melville I** Can
7E4 **Melville,L** Can
6B3 **Melville Pen** Can
45B1 **Melvin,L** Irish Rep
101D2 **Memba** Mozam
106A1 **Memboro** Indon
57C3 **Memmingen** Germany
78B2 **Mempawan** Indon
11B3 **Memphis** Tennessee, USA
19B3 **Mena** USA
43B3 **Menai Str** Wales
97C3 **Ménaka** Mali
14A2 **Menasha** USA
78C3 **Mendawai** *R* Indon
49C3 **Mende** France
99D2 **Mendebo** *Mts* Eth
43C4 **Mendip Hills** *Upland* Eng
20B2 **Mendocino,C** USA
105J2 **Mendocino Seascarp** Pacific O
22B2 **Mendota** California, USA
29C2 **Mendoza** Arg
29C3 **Mendoza** State, Arg
55C3 **Menemen** Turk
46B1 **Menen** Belg
72D3 **Mengcheng** China
78B3 **Menggala** Indon
76B1 **Menghai** China
73A5 **Mengla** China
76B1 **Menglian** China
73A5 **Mengzi** China
107D4 **Menindee** Aust
108B2 **Menindee L** Aust
108A3 **Meningie** Aust
14A1 **Menominee** USA
14A2 **Menomonee Falls** USA
100A2 **Menongue** Angola
51C1 **Menorca** *I* Spain
12F2 **Mentasta Mts** USA
78B3 **Mentok** Indon
14B2 **Mentor** USA
46B2 **Ménu** France
72A2 **Menyuan** China
61H2 **Menzelinsk** Russian Fed
56B2 **Meppen** Germany
78D2 **Merah** Indon
18B2 **Meramec** *R* USA
52B1 **Merano** Italy
71F4 **Merauke** Indon
8A3 **Merced** USA
22B2 **Merced** *R* USA
29B2 **Mercedario** *Mt* Chile
29C2 **Mercedes** Arg
29E2 **Mercedes** Buenos Aires, Arg
30E4 **Mercedes** Corrientes, Arg
29E2 **Mercedes** Urug
110C1 **Mercury B** NZ
110C1 **Mercury Is** NZ
4F2 **Mercy B** Can
6D3 **Mercy,C** Can
99E2 **Meregh** Somalia
76B3 **Mergui** Burma
76B3 **Mergui Arch** Burma
25D2 **Mérida** Mexico
50A2 **Mérida** Spain
32C2 **Mérida** Ven
11B3 **Meridian** USA
109C3 **Merimbula** Aust
108B2 **Meringur** Aust
95C3 **Merowe** Sudan
106A4 **Merredin** Aust
42B2 **Merrick** *Mt* Scot
14A2 **Merrillville** USA
13C2 **Merritt** Can
17B2 **Merritt Island** USA
109D2 **Merriwa** Aust
99E1 **Mersa Fatma** Eth
51B2 **Mers el Kebir** Alg
42C3 **Mersey** *R* Eng
42C3 **Merseyside** Metropolitan County, Eng
92B2 **Mersin** Turk
77C5 **Mersing** Malay
85C3 **Merta** India
43C4 **Merthyr Tydfil** Wales
50A2 **Mertola** Port
99D3 **Meru** *Mt* Tanz
60E5 **Merzifon** Turk
46D2 **Merzig** Germany
9B3 **Mesa** USA
46E1 **Meschede** Germany
93D1 **Mescit Dağ** *Mt* Turk
12C3 **Meshik** USA
99C2 **Meshra Er Req** Sudan
47C1 **Mesocco** Switz
55B3 **Mesolóngion** Greece
19A3 **Mesquite** Texas, USA
101C2 **Messalo** *R* Mozam
53C3 **Messina** Italy
100B3 **Messina** S Africa
55B3 **Messíni** Greece
55B3 **Messiniakós Kólpos** *G* Greece
54B2 **Mesta** *R* Bulg
52B1 **Mestre** Italy
32C3 **Meta** *R* Colombia
60D2 **Meta** *R* Russian Fed
32D2 **Meta** *R* Ven
6C3 **Meta Incognito Pen** Can
19B4 **Metairie** USA
20C1 **Metaline Falls** USA
30D4 **Metán** Arg
101C2 **Metangula** Mozam
53C2 **Metaponto** Italy
44C3 **Methil** Scot
16D1 **Methuen** USA
111B2 **Methven** NZ
12H3 **Metlakatla** USA
18C2 **Metropolis** USA
87B2 **Mettūr** India
49D2 **Metz** France
70A3 **Meulaboh** Indon
46A2 **Meulan** France
46C2 **Meuse** Department, France
49D2 **Meuse** *R* France
19A3 **Mexia** USA
24A1 **Mexicali** Mexico
24B2 **Mexico** Federal Republic, Cent America
24C3 **México** Mexico
23A2 **México** State, Mexico
18B2 **Mexico** USA
24C2 **Mexico,G of** Cent America
94B3 **Mezada** *Hist Site* Israel
23B2 **Mezcala** Mexico
64F3 **Mezen'** Russian Fed
64G2 **Mezhdusharskiy, Ostrov** *I* Russian Fed
85D4 **Mhow** India
23B2 **Miahuatlán** Mexico
11B4 **Miami** Florida, USA
18B2 **Miami** Oklahoma, USA
11B4 **Miami Beach** USA
90A2 **Miandowāb** Iran
101D2 **Miandrivazo** Madag
90A2 **Mīāneh** Iran
84C2 **Mianwali** Pak
73A3 **Mianyang** China
73C3 **Mianyang** China
73A3 **Mianzhu** China
72E2 **Miaodao Qundao** *Arch* China
73B4 **Miao Ling** *Upland* China
61K3 **Miass** Russian Fed
59C3 **Michalovce** Czech
27D3 **Miches** Dom Rep
10B2 **Michigan** State, USA
14A2 **Michigan City** USA
10B2 **Michigan,L** USA
7B5 **Michipicoten I** Can
23A2 **Michoacan** State, Mexico
54C2 **Michurin** Bulg
61F3 **Michurinsk** Russian Fed
104F3 **Micronesia** *Region* Pacific O
78B2 **Midai** *I* Indon
102F4 **Mid Atlantic Ridge** Atlantic O
46B1 **Middelburg** Neth
20B2 **Middle Alkali L** USA
16D2 **Middleboro** USA
100B4 **Middleburg** Cape Province, S Africa

16A2 **Middleburg**
Pennsylvania, USA
101G1 **Middleburg**
Transvaal, S Africa
16B1 **Middleburgh** USA
15D2 **Middlebury** USA
11B3 **Middlesboro** USA
42D2 **Middlesbrough** Eng
16C2 **Middletown**
Connecticut, USA
16B3 **Middletown**
Delaware, USA
15D2 **Middletown** New
York, USA
14B3 **Middletown** Ohio,
USA
16A2 **Middletown**
Pennsylvania, USA
96B1 **Midelt** Mor
43C4 **Mid Glamorgan**
County, Wales
104B4 **Mid Indian Basin**
Indian O
104B4 **Mid Indian Ridge**
Indian O
7C5 **Midland** Can
14B2 **Midland** Michigan,
USA
9C3 **Midland** Texas, USA
101D3 **Midongy Atsimo**
Madag
105G2 **Mid Pacific Mts**
Pacific O
20C2 **Midvale** USA
105H2 **Midway Is** Pacific O
18A2 **Midwest City** USA
93D2 **Midyat** Turk
54B2 **Midžor** Mt Serbia,
Yugos
59B2 **Mielec** Pol
54C1 **Miercurea-Ciuc** Rom
50A1 **Mieres** Spain
16A2 **Mifflintown** USA
75A2 **Mihara** Japan
72D1 **Mijun Shuiku** Res
China
54B2 **Mikhaylovgrad** Bulg
61F3 **Mikhaylovka** Russian
Fed
65J4 **Mikhaylovskiy**
Russian Fed
38K6 **Mikkeli** Fin
55C3 **Mikonos** I Greece
59B3 **Mikulov** Czech
99D3 **Mikumi** Tanz
74D3 **Mikuni-sammyaku**
Mts Japan
75B2 **Mikura-jima** I Japan
32B4 **Milagro** Ecuador
Milan = Milano
51C2 **Milana** Alg
101C2 **Milange** Mozam
52A1 **Milano** Italy
92A2 **Milas** Turk
107D4 **Mildura** Aust
73A5 **Mile** China
93D3 **Mileh Tharthār** L
Iraq
107E3 **Miles** Aust
8C2 **Miles City** USA
16C2 **Milford** Connecticut,
USA
15C3 **Milford** Delaware,
USA
15D2 **Milford**
Massachusetts, USA
18A1 **Milford** Nebraska,
USA
16B2 **Milford**
Pennsylvania, USA
43B4 **Milford Haven** Wales
43B4 **Milford Haven** Sd
Wales
18A2 **Milford L** USA
111A2 **Milford Sd** NZ
13E2 **Milk River** Can
49C3 **Millau** France
16C2 **Millbrook** USA
17B1 **Milledgeville** USA
12F2 **Miller,Mt** USA
61F4 **Millerovo** Russian
Fed
16A2 **Millersburg** USA
108A1 **Millers Creek** Aust

16C1 **Millers Falls** USA
16C2 **Millerton** USA
22C2 **Millerton L** USA
108B3 **Millicent** Aust
109D1 **Millmerran** Aust
45B2 **Milltown Malbay**
Irish Rep
22A2 **Mill Valley** USA
15D3 **Millville** USA
6H2 **Milne Land** I
Greenland
21C4 **Milolii** Hawaiian Is
55B3 **Milos** I Greece
107D3 **Milparinka** Aust
16A2 **Milroy** USA
111A3 **Milton** NZ
16A2 **Milton** Pennsylvania,
USA
10B2 **Milwaukee** USA
51C2 **Mina** R Alg
93E4 **Mina' al Ahmadī**
Kuwait
91C4 **Mināb** Iran
74C4 **Minamata** Japan
78A2 **Minas** Indon
29E2 **Minas** Urug
31B5 **Minas Gerais** State,
Brazil
35C1 **Minas Novas** Brazil
25C3 **Minatitlan** Mexico
76A1 **Minbu** Burma
76A1 **Minbya** Burma
34A2 **Mincha** Chile
44A3 **Minch,Little** Sd Scot
44A2 **Minch,North** Sd
Scot
40B2 **Minch,The** Sd Scot
12D2 **Minchumina,L** USA
47D2 **Mincio** R Italy
79B4 **Mindanao** I Phil
19B3 **Minden** Louisiana,
USA
56B2 **Minden** Germany
108B2 **Mindona L** Aust
79B3 **Mindoro** I Phil
79B3 **Mindoro Str** Phil
45C3 **Mine Hd** C Irish Rep
43C4 **Minehead** Eng
30F2 **Mineiros** Brazil
19A3 **Mineola** USA
23B1 **Mineral de Monte**
Mexico
16A2 **Minersville** USA
108B2 **Mingary** Aust
72A2 **Minhe** China
87A3 **Minicoy** I India
73D4 **Min Jiang** R Fujian,
China
73A4 **Min Jiang** R
Sichuan, China
22C2 **Minkler** USA
108A2 **Minlaton** Aust
72A2 **Minle** China
97C4 **Minna** Nig
10A2 **Minneapolis** USA
5J4 **Minnedosa** Can
10A2 **Minnesota** State,
USA
50A1 **Miño** R Spain
8C2 **Minot** USA
72A2 **Minqin** China
72A3 **Min Shan** Upland
China
60C3 **Minsk** Belorussia
58C2 **Minsk Mazowiecki**
Pol
12E2 **Minto** USA
4G2 **Minto Inlet** B Can
7C4 **Minto,L** Can
63B2 **Minusinsk** Russian
Fed
72A3 **Min Xian** China
7E5 **Miquelon** Can
22D3 **Mirage L** USA
87A1 **Miraj** India
29E3 **Miramar** Arg
84B2 **Miram Shah** Pak
50B1 **Miranda de Ebro**
Spain
47D2 **Mirandola** Italy
84B2 **Mir Bachchen Kūt**
Afghan
78D1 **Miri** Malay
96A3 **Mirik,C** Maur

63A1 **Mirnoye** Russian Fed
63D1 **Mirnyy** Russian Fed
112C9 **Mirnyy** Base Ant
84C2 **Mirpur** Pak
85B3 **Mirpur Khas** Pak
55B3 **Mirtoan S** Greece
74B3 **Miryang** S Korea
86A1 **Mirzāpur** India
23B2 **Misantla** Mexico
84C1 **Misgar** Pak
14A2 **Mishawaka** USA
12B1 **Misheguk Mt** USA
75A2 **Mi-shima** I Japan
107E2 **Misima** I Solomon Is
30F4 **Misiones** State, Arg
59C3 **Miskolc** Hung
94C2 **Mismiyah** Syria
71E4 **Misoöl** I Indon
95A1 **Misrātah** Libya
7B5 **Missinaibi** R Can
20B1 **Mission City** Can
15C2 **Mississauga** Can
11A3 **Mississippi** State,
USA
11A3 **Mississippi** R USA
19C3 **Mississippi Delta**
USA
8B2 **Missoula** USA
96B1 **Missour** Mor
11A3 **Missouri** State, USA
10A2 **Missouri** R USA
10C1 **Mistassini,L** Can
30B2 **Misti** Mt Peru
109C1 **Mitchell** Aust
8D2 **Mitchell** USA
107D2 **Mitchell** R Aust
11B3 **Mitchell,Mt** USA
45B2 **Mitchelstown**
Irish Rep
84C3 **Mithankot** Pak
55C3 **Mitilini** Greece
23B2 **Mitla** Mexico
95C3 **Mits'iwa** Eth
32C3 **Mitu** Colombia
99C3 **Mitumbar** Mts Zaïre
98C3 **Mitwaba** Zaïre
98B2 **Mitzic** Gabon
75B1 **Miura** Japan
72C3 **Mi Xian** China
69F3 **Miyake** I Japan
75B2 **Miyake-jima** I Japan
69E4 **Miyako** I Japan
74C4 **Miyakonojō** Japan
74C4 **Miyazaki** Japan
75B1 **Miyazu** Japan
74C4 **Miyoshi** Japan
72D1 **Miyun** China
99D2 **Mizan Teferi** Eth
95A1 **Mizdah** Libya
45B3 **Mizen Hd** C
Irish Rep
54C1 **Mizil** Rom
86C2 **Mizo Hills** India
86C2 **Mizoram** Union
Territory, India
94B3 **Mizpe Ramon** Israel
112B11 **Mizuho** Base Ant
74E3 **Mizusawa** Japan
39H7 **Mjolby** Sweden
100B2 **Mkushi** Zambia
101H1 **Mkuzi** S Africa
57C2 **Mladá Boleslav**
Czech
58C2 **Mława** Pol
52C2 **Mljet** I Croatia
100B3 **Mmabatho** S Africa
84D2 **Mnadi** India
97A4 **Moa** R Sierra Leone
94B3 **Moab** Region,
Jordan
9C3 **Moab** USA
98B3 **Moanda** Congo
98B3 **Moanda** Gabon
99C3 **Moba** Zaïre
75C1 **Mobara** Japan
98C2 **Mobaye** CAR
98C2 **Mobayi** Zaïre
10A3 **Moberly** USA
11B3 **Mobile** USA
11B3 **Mobile B** USA
8C2 **Mobridge** USA
101D2 **Moçambique** Mozam
76C1 **Moc Chau** Viet
100B3 **Mochudi** Botswana

101D2 **Mocimboa da Praia**
Mozam
32B3 **Mocoa** Colombia
35B2 **Mococa** Brazil
34D2 **Mocoreta** R Arg
23B1 **Moctezuma** R
Mexico
101C2 **Mocuba** Mozam
47B2 **Modane** France
101G1 **Modder** R S Africa
52B2 **Modena** Italy
46D2 **Moder** R France
8A3 **Modesto** USA
22B2 **Modesto Res** USA
53B3 **Modica** Italy
59B3 **Mödling** Austria
107D4 **Moe** Aust
47C1 **Moesa** R Switz
42C2 **Moffat** Scot
84D2 **Moga** India
35B2 **Mogi das Cruzes**
Brazil
60C3 **Mogilev** Belorussia
60C4 **Mogilev Podolskiy**
Ukraine
35B2 **Mogi-Mirim** Brazil
101D2 **Mogincual** Mozam
47E2 **Mogliano** Italy
34B2 **Mogna** Arg
68D1 **Mogocha** Russian
Fed
65K4 **Mogochin** Russian
Fed
50A2 **Moguer** Spain
110C1 **Mohaka** R NZ
86C2 **Mohanganj** Bang
15D2 **Mohawk** R USA
99D3 **Mohoro** Tanz
65J5 **Mointy** Kazakhstan
38G5 **Mo i Rana** Nor
48C3 **Moissac** France
21B2 **Mojave** USA
22D3 **Mojave** R USA
9B3 **Mojave Desert** USA
78C4 **Mojokerto** Indon
86B1 **Mokama** India
110B1 **Mokau** R NZ
22B1 **Mokelumne**
Aqueduct USA
22B1 **Mokelumne Hill**
USA
22B1 **Mokelumne North**
Fork R USA
101G1 **Mokhotlong** Lesotho
96D1 **Moknine** Tunisia
86C1 **Mokokchūng** India
98B1 **Mokolo** Cam
74B4 **Mokp'o** S Korea
61F3 **Moksha** R Russian
Fed
23B1 **Molango** Mexico
55B3 **Moláoi** Greece
60C4 **Moldavia** Republic,
Europe
38F6 **Molde** Nor
54B1 **Moldoveanu** Mt
Rom
100B3 **Molepolole**
Botswana
53C2 **Molfetta** Italy
34A3 **Molina** Chile
30B2 **Mollendo** Peru
60C3 **Molodechno**
Belorussia
112C11 **Molodezhnaya** Base
Ant
21C4 **Molokai** I Hawaiian
Is
61G2 **Moloma** R Russian
Fed
109C2 **Molong** Aust
100B3 **Molopo** R Botswana
98B2 **Molounddu** Cam
8D1 **Molson L** Can
71D4 **Molucca** S Indon
71D4 **Moluccas** Is Indon
101C2 **Moma** Mozam
31C3 **Mombaca** Brazil
99D3 **Mombasa** Kenya
98C2 **Mompono** Zaïre
56C2 **Mon** I Den
44A3 **Monach** Is Scot
49D3 **Monaco**
Principality, Europe

44B3 **Monadhliath** *Mts* Scot
45C1 **Monaghan** County, Irish Rep
45C1 **Monaghan** Irish Rep
27D3 **Mona Pass** Caribbean S
13B2 **Monarch Mt** Can
5G4 **Monashee Mts** Can
41B3 **Monastereven** Irish Rep
47B2 **Moncalieri** Italy
31B2 **Monçao** Brazil
38L5 **Monchegorsk** Russian Fed
56B2 **Mönchen-gladbach** Germany
24B2 **Monclova** Mexico
7D5 **Moncton** Can
9C4 **Monctova** Mexico
50A1 **Mondego** *R* Port
52A2 **Mondovi** Italy
27H1 **Moneague** Jamaica
14C2 **Monessen** USA
18B2 **Monett** USA
52B1 **Monfalcone** Italy
50A1 **Monforte de Lemos** Spain
98C2 **Monga** Zaïre
98C2 **Mongala** *R* Zaïre
99D2 **Mongalla** Sudan
76D1 **Mong Cai** Viet
98B1 **Mongo** Chad
68B2 **Mongolia** Republic, Asia
100B2 **Mongu** Zambia
21B2 **Monitor Range** *Mts* USA
98C3 **Monkoto** Zaïre
43C4 **Monmouth** Eng
18B1 **Monmouth** USA
13C2 **Monmouth,Mt** Can
97C4 **Mono** *R* Togo
21B2 **Mono L** USA
53C2 **Monopoli** Italy
51B1 **Monreal del Campo** Spain
19B3 **Monroe** Louisiana, USA
14B2 **Monroe** Michigan, USA
20B1 **Monroe** Washington, USA
18B2 **Monroe City** USA
97A4 **Monrovia** Lib
20D3 **Monrovia** USA
56A2 **Mons** Belg
47D2 **Monselice** Italy
16C1 **Monson** USA
58B1 **Mönsterås** Sweden
101D2 **Montagne d'Ambre** *Mt* Madag
96C1 **Montagnes des Ouled Naïl** *Mts* Alg
12E3 **Montague I** USA
49C3 **Mont Aigoual** *Mt* France
48B2 **Montaigu** France
53C3 **Montallo** *Mt* Italy
8B2 **Montana** State, USA
50A1 **Montañas de León** *Mts* Spain
49C2 **Montargis** France
48C3 **Montauban** France
15D2 **Montauk** USA
15D2 **Montauk Pt** USA
49D2 **Montbéliard** France
52A1 **Mont Blanc** *Mt* France/Italy
49C2 **Montceau les Mines** France
51C1 **Montceny** *Mt* Spain
49D3 **Mont Cinto** *Mt* Corse
46C2 **Montcornet** France
48B3 **Mont-de-Marsin** France
48C2 **Montdidier** France
30D2 **Monteagudo** Bol
33G4 **Monte Alegre** Brazil
52B2 **Monte Amiata** *Mt* Italy
47D2 **Monte Baldo** *Mt* Italy
15C1 **Montebello** Can
106A3 **Monte Bello Is** Aust
47E2 **Montebelluna** Italy
49D3 **Monte Carlo** Monaco
35B1 **Monte Carmelo** Brazil
34D2 **Monte Caseros** Arg
52B2 **Monte Cimone** *Mt* Italy
52A2 **Monte Cinto** *Mt* Corse
34B2 **Monte Coman** Arg
52B2 **Monte Corno** *Mt* Italy
27C3 **Montecristi** Dom Rep
52B2 **Montecristo** *I* Italy
23A1 **Monte Escobedo** Mexico
53C2 **Monte Gargano** *Mt* Italy
26B3 **Montego Bay** Jamaica
47D2 **Monte Grappa** *Mt* Italy
47C2 **Monte Lesima** *Mt* Italy
49C3 **Montélimar** France
53B2 **Monte Miletto** *Mt* Italy
50A2 **Montemo-o-Novo** Port
24C2 **Montemorelos** Mexico
26B5 **Montená** Colombia
54A2 **Montenegro** Republic, Yugos
35D1 **Monte Pascoal** *Mt* Brazil
34A2 **Monte Patria** Chile
53C3 **Monte Pollino** *Mt* Italy
101C2 **Montepuez** Mozam
8A3 **Monterey** California, USA
15C3 **Monterey** Virginia, USA
8A3 **Monterey B** USA
32B2 **Montería** Colombia
30D2 **Montero** Bol
47B2 **Monte Rosa** *Mt* Italy/Switz
24B2 **Monterrey** Mexico
31C5 **Montes Claros** Brazil
50B2 **Montes de Toledo** *Mts* Spain
29E2 **Montevideo** Urug
52A2 **Monte Viso** *Mt* Italy
27P2 **Mont Gimie** *Mt* St Lucia
11B3 **Montgomery** Alabama, USA
96C2 **Mont Gréboun** Niger
46C2 **Montherme** France
47B1 **Monthey** Switz
19B3 **Monticello** Arkansas, USA
16B2 **Monticello** New York, USA
9C3 **Monticello** Utah, USA
53A2 **Monti del Gennargentu** *Mt* Sardegna
47D2 **Monti Lessini** *Mts* Italy
53B3 **Monti Nebrodi** *Mts* Italy
7C5 **Mont-Laurier** Can
48C2 **Montluçon** France
7C5 **Montmagny** Can
46C2 **Montmédy** France
49C3 **Mont Mézenc** *Mt* France
46B2 **Montmirail** France
50B2 **Montoro** Spain
49D3 **Mont Pelat** *Mt* France
14B2 **Montpelier** Ohio, USA
10C2 **Montpelier** Vermont, USA
49C3 **Montpellier** France
7C5 **Montréal** Can
48C1 **Montreuil** France
52A1 **Montreux** Switz
47B1 **Mont Risoux** *Mt* France
8C3 **Montrose** Colorado, USA
40C2 **Montrose** Scot
48B2 **Mont-St-Michel** France
96B1 **Monts des Ksour** *Mts* Alg
51C3 **Monts des Ouled Neil** *Mts* Alg
51C2 **Monts du Hodna** *Mts* Alg
27E3 **Montserrat** *I* Caribbean S
10C1 **Monts Otish** *Mts* Can
12B1 **Monument Mt** USA
9B3 **Monument V** USA
98C2 **Monveda** Zaïre
76B1 **Monywa** Burma
52A1 **Monza** Italy
100B2 **Monze** Zambia
101H1 **Mooi** *R* S Africa
101G1 **Mooi River** S Africa
108B1 **Moomba** Aust
109D2 **Moonbi Range** *Mts* Aust
108B1 **Moonda L** Aust
109D1 **Moonie** Aust
109C1 **Moonie** *R* Aust
108A2 **Moonta** Aust
106A4 **Moora** Aust
106A3 **Moore,L** Aust
42C2 **Moorfoot Hills** Scot
8D2 **Moorhead** USA
22C3 **Moorpark** USA
7B4 **Moose** *R* Can
5H4 **Moose Jaw** Can
5H4 **Moosomin** Can
7B4 **Moosonee** Can
16D2 **Moosup** USA
101C2 **Mopeia** Mozam
97B3 **Mopti** Mali
30B2 **Moquegua** Peru
39G6 **Mora** Sweden
31D3 **Morada** Brazil
84D3 **Morādābād** India
35B1 **Morada Nova de Minas** *L* Brazil
101D2 **Morafenobe** Madag
101D2 **Moramanga** Madag
27J2 **Morant Bay** Jamaica
27J2 **Morant Pt** Jamaica
87B3 **Moratuwa** Sri Lanka
59B3 **Morava** *R* Austria/Czech
54B2 **Morava** *R* Serbia, Yugos
90C2 **Moraveh Tappeh** Iran
40C2 **Moray Firth** *Estuary* Scot
47C1 **Morbegno** Italy
85C4 **Morbi** India
93D2 **Mor Dağ** *Mt* Turk
5J5 **Morden** Can
61F3 **Mordovskaya Respublika,** Russian Fed
42C2 **Morecambe** Eng
42C2 **Morecambe B** Eng
107D3 **Moree** Aust
14B3 **Morehead** USA
47C1 **Mörel** Switz
24B3 **Morelia** Mexico
23B2 **Morelos** State, Mexico
85D3 **Morena** India
5E4 **Moresby I** Can
109D1 **Moreton I** Aust
46B2 **Moreuil** France
47B1 **Morez** France
19B4 **Morgan City** USA
22B2 **Morgan Hill** USA
14C3 **Morgantown** USA
101G1 **Morgenzon** S Africa
47B1 **Morges** Switz
46D2 **Morhange** France
74E2 **Mori** Japan
27K1 **Moriatio** Tobago
13B2 **Morice L** Can
13E2 **Morinville** Can
74E3 **Morioka** Japan
109D2 **Morisset** Aust
63D1 **Morkoka** *R* Russian Fed
48B2 **Morlaix** France
27Q2 **Morne Diablotin** *Mt* Dominica
106C2 **Mornington** *I* Aust
85B3 **Moro** Pak
96B2 **Morocco** Kingdom, Africa
79B4 **Moro G** Phil
99D3 **Morogoro** Tanz
23A1 **Moroleon** Mexico
101D3 **Morombe** Madag
26B2 **Morón** Cuba
101D3 **Morondava** Madag
50A2 **Moron de la Frontera** Spain
101D2 **Moroni** Comoros
71D3 **Morotai** *I* Indon
99D2 **Moroto** Uganda
61F4 **Morozovsk** Russian Fed
42D2 **Morpeth** Eng
19B2 **Morrilton** USA
35B1 **Morrinhos** Brazil
110C1 **Morrinsville** NZ
16B2 **Morristown** New Jersey, USA
15C2 **Morristown** New York, USA
16B2 **Morrisville** Pennsylvania, USA
21A2 **Morro Bay** USA
23A2 **Morro de Papanoa** Mexico
23A2 **Morro de Petatlán** Mexico
101C2 **Morrumbala** Mozam
101C3 **Morrumbene** Mozam
61F3 **Morshansk** Russian Fed
47C2 **Mortara** Italy
34C2 **Morteros** Arg
33G6 **Mortes** *R* Mato Grosso, Brazil
35C2 **Mortes** *R* Minas Gerais, Brazil
108B3 **Mortlake** Aust
27L1 **Moruga** Trinidad
109D3 **Moruya** Aust
109C1 **Morven** Aust
44B3 **Morvern** *Pen* Scot
109C3 **Morwell** Aust
76B3 **Moscos Is** Burma
Moscow = Moskva
20C1 **Moscow** Idaho, USA
56B2 **Mosel** *R* Germany
46D2 **Moselle** Department, France
46D2 **Moselle** *R* France
20C1 **Moses Lake** USA
111B3 **Mosgiel** NZ
99D3 **Moshi** Tanz
38G5 **Mosjøen** Nor
63G2 **Moskal'vo** Russian Fed
64E4 **Moskva** Russian Fed
35C1 **Mosquito** *R* Brazil
39G7 **Moss** Nor
98B3 **Mossaka** Congo
100B4 **Mossel Bay** S Africa
98B3 **Mossendjo** Congo
108B2 **Mossgiel** Aust
31D3 **Mossoró** Brazil
57C2 **Most** Czech
96C1 **Mostaganem** Alg
54A2 **Mostar** Bosnia & Herzegovina, Yugos
58C2 **Mosty** Belorussia
93D2 **Mosul** Iraq
39H7 **Motala** Sweden
42C2 **Motherwell** Scot
86A1 **Motihāri** India
51B2 **Motilla del Palancar** Spain
50B2 **Motril** Spain
111B2 **Motueka** NZ
111B2 **Motueka** *R* NZ
47B1 **Moudon** Switz
98B3 **Mouila** Gabon
108B2 **Moulamein** Aust
4G2 **Mould Bay** Can
49C2 **Moulins** France
76B2 **Moulmein** Burma

Moulouya

96B1 **Moulouya** R Mor
17B1 **Moultrie** USA
17C1 **Moultrie,L** USA
18C2 **Mound City** Illinois, USA
18A1 **Mound City** Missouri, USA
98B2 **Moundou** Chad
14B3 **Moundsville** USA
12J1 **Mountain** R Can
17A1 **Mountain Brook** USA
18B2 **Mountain Grove** USA
18B2 **Mountain Home** Arkansas, USA
22A2 **Mountain View** USA
12B2 **Mountain Village** USA
16A3 **Mount Airy** Maryland, USA
16A2 **Mount Carmel** USA
108A1 **Mount Dutton** Aust
108A2 **Mount Eba** Aust
108B3 **Mount Gambier** Aust
16B3 **Mount Holly** USA
16A2 **Mount Holly Springs** USA
108A2 **Mount Hope** Aust
106C3 **Mount Isa** Aust
108A2 **Mount Lofty Range** Mts Aust
12D2 **Mount McKinley Nat Pk** USA
106A3 **Mount Magnet** Aust
108B2 **Mount Manara** Aust
107E3 **Mount Morgan** Aust
19B3 **Mount Pleasant** Texas, USA
20B1 **Mount Rainier Nat Pk** USA
43B4 **Mounts B** Eng
20B2 **Mount Shasta** USA
11B3 **Mount Vernon** Illinois, USA
19A3 **Mount Vernon** Kentucky, USA
20B1 **Mount Vernon** Washington, USA
45C1 **Mourne Mts** N Ire
98B1 **Moussoro** Chad
86B2 **Mouths of the Ganga** India/Bang
85B4 **Mouths of the Indus** Pak
77D4 **Mouths of the Mekong** Viet
97C4 **Mouths of the Niger** Nig
47B1 **Moutier** Switz
47B2 **Moûtiers** France
96C2 **Mouydir** Mts Alg
98B3 **Mouyondzi** Congo
46C2 **Mouzon** France
59B3 **M'óvár** Hung
23A1 **Moyahua** Mexico
99D2 **Moyale** Kenya
97A4 **Moyamba** Sierra Leone
96B1 **Moyen Atlas** Mts Mor
100B4 **Moyeni** Lesotho
99D2 **Moyo** Uganda
32B5 **Moyobamba** Peru
84D1 **Moyu** China
101C3 **Mozambique** Republic, Africa
101C3 **Mozambique Chan** Mozam/Madag
61H2 **Mozhga** Russian Fed
60C3 **Mozyr'** Belorussia
99D3 **Mpanda** Tanz
101C2 **Mpika** Zambia
99D3 **Mporokosa** Zambia
100B2 **Mposhi** Zambia
99D3 **Mpulungu** Zambia
99D3 **Mpwapwa** Tanz
60E3 **Mtsensk** Russian Fed
101H1 **Mtubatuba** S Africa
101D2 **Mtwara** Tanz
76C2 **Muang Chainat** Thai
76C2 **Muang Chiang Rai** Thai
76C2 **Muang Kalasin** Thai

76C2 **Muang Khon Kaen** Thai
76B2 **Muang Lampang** Thai
76B2 **Muang Lamphun** Thai
76C2 **Muang Loei** Thai
76C2 **Muang Lom Sak** Thai
76C2 **Muang Nakhon Phanom** Thai
76B2 **Muang Nakhon Sawan** Thai
76C2 **Muang Nan** Thai
76C2 **Muang Phayao** Thai
76C2 **Muang Phetchabun** Thai
86A2 **Muang Phichit** Thai
76C2 **Muang Phitsanulok** Thai
76C2 **Muang Phrae** Thai
76C2 **Muang Roi Et** Thai
76C2 **Muang Sakon Nakhon** Thai
76C3 **Muang Samut Prakan** Thai
76C2 **Muang Uthai Thani** Thai
76C2 **Muang Yasothon** Thai
77C5 **Muar** Malay
78C2 **Muara** Brunei
70B4 **Muara** Indon
78A3 **Muaralakitan** Indon
78A3 **Muaratebo** Indon
78C3 **Muaratewah** Indon
78A3 **Muarenim** Indon
76A2 **Muaungmaya** Burma
99D2 **Mubende** Uganda
100C2 **Muchinga** Mts Zambia
44A3 **Muck** I Scot
109C1 **Muckadilla** Aust
100B2 **Muconda** Angola
35D1 **Mucuri** Brazil
35C1 **Mucuri** R Brazil
100B2 **Mucusso** Angola
69E2 **Mudanjiang** China
109C2 **Mudgee** Aust
76B2 **Mudon** Burma
101C2 **Mueda** Mozam
107F3 **Mueo** Nouvelle Calédonie
100B2 **Mufulira** Zambia
73C4 **Mufu Shan** Hills China
Mugadishu = Muqdisho
93C4 **Mughayra** S Arabia
92A2 **Muğla** Turk
65G5 **Mugodzhary** Mts Kazakhstan
73A3 **Muguaping** China
93D3 **Muhaywir** Iraq
57C3 **Mühldorf** Germany
57C2 **Mühlhausen** Germany
38K6 **Muhos** Fin
77C4 **Mui Bai Bung** C Camb
45C2 **Muine Bheag** Irish Rep
100B2 **Mujimbeji** Zambia
59C3 **Mukachevo** Ukraine
78C2 **Mukah** Malay
69G4 **Muko-jima** I Japan
86A1 **Muktinath** Nepal
84B2 **Mukur** Afghan
18B2 **Mulberry** USA
12C2 **Mulchatna** R USA
34A3 **Mulchén** Chile
56C2 **Mulde** R Germany
71F5 **Mulgrave I** Aust
50B2 **Mulhacén** Mt Spain
46D1 **Mülheim** Germany
49D2 **Mulhouse** France
73A4 **Muli** China
44B3 **Mull** I Scot
87C3 **Mullaitvu** Sri Lanka
109C2 **Mullaley** Aust
106A3 **Mullewa** Aust
16B3 **Mullica** R USA
45C2 **Mullingar** Irish Rep
42B2 **Mull of Kintyre** Pt Scot

45C1 **Mull of Oa** C Scot
109D1 **Mullumbimby** Aust
100B2 **Mulobezi** Zambia
84C2 **Multan** Pak
100B2 **Mumbwa** Zambia
61G4 **Mumra** Russian Fed
71D4 **Muna** I Indon
57C3 **München** Germany
14A2 **Muncie** USA
15C2 **Muncy** USA
56B2 **Münden** Germany
109D1 **Mundubbera** Aust
109C1 **Mungallala** Aust
109C1 **Mungallala** R Aust
99C2 **Mungbere** Zaïre
86A2 **Mungeli** India
86B1 **Munger** India
109C1 **Mungindi** Aust
Munich = München
14A1 **Munising** USA
29B6 **Muñoz Gomero,Pen** Chile
45B2 **Munster** Region, Irish Rep
47C1 **Münster** Switz
56B2 **Münster** Germany
54B1 **Munṭii Apuseni** Mts Rom
54B1 **Muntii Călimanilor** Mts Rom
54B1 **Muntii Carpaţii Meridionali** Mts Rom
54B1 **Muntii Rodnei** Mts Rom
54B1 **Muntii Zarandului** Mts Rom
100B2 **Munyati** R Zim
93C2 **Munzur Silsilesi** Mts Turk
64D3 **Muomio** Fin
76C1 **Muong Khoua** Laos
76D3 **Muong Man** Viet
76D2 **Muong Nong** Laos
76C1 **Muong Ou Neua** Laos
76C1 **Muong Sai** Laos
76C2 **Muong Sen** Viet
76C1 **Muong Sing** Laos
76C1 **Muong Son** Laos
38J5 **Muonio** Fin
38J5 **Muonio** R Sweden/ Fin
99E2 **Muqdisho** Somalia
52B1 **Mur** R Austria
74D3 **Murakami** Japan
29B5 **Murallón** Mt Arg/ Chile
61G2 **Murashi** Russian Fed
93D2 **Murat** R Turk
53A3 **Muravera** Sardegna
75C1 **Murayama** Japan
90B3 **Murcheh Khvort** Iran
111B2 **Murchison** NZ
106A3 **Murchison** R Aust
51B2 **Murcia** Region, Spain
51B2 **Murcia** Spain
54B1 **Mureş** R Rom
46E2 **Murg** R Germany
65H6 **Murgab** R Turkmenistan
84B2 **Murgha Kibzai** Pak
109D1 **Murgon** Aust
86B2 **Muri** India
35C2 **Muriaé** Brazil
98C3 **Muriege** Angola
64E3 **Murmansk** Russian Fed
61F2 **Murom** Russian Fed
74E2 **Muroran** Japan
50A1 **Muros** Spain
74C4 **Muroto** Japan
75A2 **Muroto-zaki** C Japan
20C2 **Murphy** Idaho, USA
22B1 **Murphys** USA
18C2 **Murray** Kentucky, USA
108B2 **Murray** R Aust
13C2 **Murray** R Can
108A3 **Murray Bridge** Aust
71F4 **Murray,L** PNG
17B1 **Murray,L** USA
105J2 **Murray Seacarp** Pacific O

108B2 **Murrumbidgee** R Aust
109C2 **Murrumburrah** Aust
109D2 **Murrurundi** Aust
47B1 **Murten** Switz
108B3 **Murtoa** Aust
110C1 **Murupara** NZ
86A2 **Murwāra** India
109D1 **Murwillimbah** Aust
93D2 **Muş** Turk
54B2 **Musala** Mt Bulg
74B2 **Musan** N Korea
91C4 **Musandam** Pen Oman
Muscat = Masqat
91C5 **Muscat** Region, Oman
106C3 **Musgrave Range** Mts Aust
98B3 **Mushie** Zaïre
14A2 **Muskegon** USA
14A2 **Muskegon** R USA
18A2 **Muskogee** USA
15C2 **Muskoka,L** Can
95C3 **Musmar** Sudan
99D3 **Musoma** Tanz
8C2 **Musselshell** R USA
100A2 **Mussende** Angola
48C2 **Mussidan** France
55C2 **Mustafa-Kemalpasa** Turk
86A1 **Mustang** Nepal
109D2 **Muswelibrook** Aust
95B2 **Mut** Egypt
101C2 **Mutarara** Mozam
101C2 **Mutare** Zim
101C2 **Mutoko** Zim
101D2 **Mutsamudu** Comoros
74E2 **Mutsu** Japan
74E2 **Mutsu-wan** B Japan
45B2 **Mutton** I Irish Rep
72B2 **Mu Us Shamo** Desert China
98B3 **Muxima** Angola
63D2 **Muya** Russian Fed
38L6 **Muyezerskiy** Russian Fed
99D3 **Muyinga** Burundi
98C3 **Muyumba** Zaïre
82A1 **Muyun Kum** Desert Kazakhstan
84C2 **Muzaffarābad** Pak
84C2 **Muzaffargarh** Pak
84D3 **Muzaffarnagar** India
86B1 **Muzaffarpur** India
64H3 **Muzhi** Russian Fed
82C2 **Muztag** Mt China
82B2 **Muztagata** Mt China
100C2 **Mvuma** Zim
99D3 **Mwanza** Tanz
98C3 **Mwanza** Zaïre
98C3 **Mweka** Zaïre
98C3 **Mwene Ditu** Zaïre
100C3 **Mwenezi** Zim
99C3 **Mwenga** Zaïre
99C3 **Mweru** L Zambia
100B2 **Mwinilunga** Zambia
83D4 **Myanaung** Burma
Myanma = Burma
86D2 **Myingyan** Burma
76B1 **Myingyao** Burma
76B3 **Myinmoletkat** Mt Burma
82D3 **Myitkyina** Burma
76B3 **Myitta** Burma
86C2 **Mymensingh** Bang
69F3 **Myojin** I Japan
39F6 **Myrdal** Nor
38B2 **Myrdalsjökur** Mts Iceland
17C1 **Myrtle Beach** USA
20B2 **Myrtle Creek** USA
39G7 **Mysen** Nor
56C2 **Mysiloborz** Pol
64F3 **Mys Kanin Nos** C Russian Fed
59B3 **Myślenice** Pol
69H1 **Mys Lopatka** C Russian Fed
87B2 **Mysore** India
60D5 **Mys Sarych** C Ukraine

16D2 **Mystic** USA
61H5 **Mys Tyub-Karagan** *Pt* Kazakhstan
63G2 **Mys Yelizavety** *C* Russian Fed
64H2 **Mys Zhelaniya** *C* Russian Fed
77D3 **My Tho** Viet
20B2 **Mytle Point** USA
101C2 **Mzimba** Malawi
101C2 **Mzuzú** Malawi

N
21C4 **Naalehu** Hawaiian Is
39JG **Naantali** Fin
45C2 **Naas** Irish Rep
75B2 **Nabari** Japan
61H2 **Naberezhnye Chelny** Russian Fed
12F2 **Nabesna** *R* USA
96D1 **Nabeul** Tunisia
94B2 **Nablus** Israel
101D2 **Nacala** Mozam
20B1 **Naches** USA
101C2 **Nachingwea** Tanz
19B3 **Nacogdoches** USA
76A3 **Nacondam** *I* Indian O
24B1 **Nacozari** Mexico
85C4 **Nadiad** India
50B2 **Nador** Mor
90B3 **Nadüshan** Iran
59C3 **Nadvornaya** Ukraine
56C1 **Naestved** Den
95B2 **Näfürah** Libya
75A2 **Nagahama** Japan
82D3 **Naga Hills** Burma
75B1 **Nagai** Japan
86C1 **Nägäland** State, India
74D3 **Nagano** Japan
74D3 **Nagaoka** Japan
87B2 **Nägappattinam** India
85C4 **Nagar Parkar** Pak
74B4 **Nagasaki** Japan
75B2 **Nagashima** Japan
75A2 **Nagato** Japan
85C3 **Nägaur** India
87B3 **Nägercoil** India
85B3 **Nagha Kalat** Pak
84D3 **Nagina** India
74D3 **Nagoya** Japan
85D4 **Nägpur** India
82D2 **Nagqu** China
59B3 **Nagykanizsa** Hung
59B3 **Nagykörös** Hung
69E4 **Naha** Japan
8A2 **Nahaimo** Can
84D2 **Nähan** India
4F3 **Nahanni Butte** Can
94B2 **Nahariya** Israel
90A3 **Nahävand** Iran
46D2 **Nahe** *R* Germany
72D2 **Nahpu** China
72E1 **Naimen Qi** China
7D4 **Nain** Can
90B3 **Nä'in** Iran
84D3 **Naini Tal** India
44C3 **Nairn** Scot
99D3 **Nairobi** Kenya
90B3 **Najafäbäd** Iran
74C2 **Najin** N Korea
75A2 **Nakama** Japan
74E3 **Nakaminato** Japan
75A2 **Nakamura** Japan
75B1 **Nakano** Japan
75A1 **Nakano-shima** *I* Japan
74C4 **Nakatsu** Japan
75B1 **Nakasaga-gawa** Japan
95C3 **Nak'fa** Eth
93E2 **Nakhichevan** Azerbaijan
92B4 **Nakhl** Egypt
74C2 **Nakhodka** Russian Fed
76C3 **Nakhon Pathom** Thai
76C3 **Nakhon Ratchasima** Thai
77C4 **Nakhon Si Thammarat** Thai
12H3 **Nakina** Can
7B4 **Nakina** Ontario, Can
12C3 **Naknek** USA
12C3 **Naknek L** USA

4C4 **Nakrek** USA
39G8 **Nakskov** Den
99D3 **Nakuru** Kenya
13D2 **Nakusp** Can
61F5 **Nal'chik** Russian Fed
87B1 **Nalgonda** India
87B1 **Nallamala Range** *Mts* India
95A1 **Nälüt** Libya
101H1 **Namaacha** Mozam
65G6 **Namak** *L* Iran
90C3 **Namakzar-e Shadad** *Salt Flat* Iran
65J5 **Namangan** Uzbekistan
101C2 **Namapa** Mozam
100A4 **Namaqualand** Region, S Africa
109D1 **Nambour** Aust
109D2 **Nambucca Heads** Aust
77D4 **Nam Can** Viet
82D2 **Nam Co** *L* China
76D1 **Nam Dinh** Viet
101C2 **Nametil** Mozam
74B4 **Namhae-do** *I* S Korea
100A2 **Namib Desert** Namibia
100A2 **Namibe** Angola
100A3 **Namibia** Dependency, Africa
82D3 **Namjagbarwa Feng** *Mt* China
71D4 **Namlea** Indon
109C2 **Namoi** *R* Aust
13D1 **Nampa** Can
20C2 **Nampa** USA
97B3 **Nampala** Mali
76C2 **Nam Phong** Thai
74B3 **Namp'o** N Korea
101C2 **Nampula** Mozam
38G6 **Namsos** Nor
76B1 **Namton** Burma
86D2 **Namtu** Burma
13B2 **Namu** Can
101C2 **Namuno** Mozam
46C1 **Namur** Belg
100A2 **Namutoni** Namibia
74B3 **Namwön** S Korea
13C3 **Nanaimo** Can
74B2 **Nanam** N Korea
109D1 **Nanango** Aust
74D3 **Nanao** Japan
75B1 **Nanatsu-jima** *I* Japan
73B3 **Nanbu** China
73D4 **Nanchang** China
73B3 **Nanchong** China
49D2 **Nancy** France
87B1 **Nänded** India
109D2 **Nandewar Range** *Mts* Aust
85C4 **Nandurbar** India
87B1 **Nandyäl** India
98B2 **Nanga Eboko** Cam
84C1 **Nanga Parbat** *Mt* Pak
78C3 **Nangapinoh** Indon
78C3 **Nangatayap** Indon
74B2 **Nangnim Sanmaek** *Mts* N Korea
86C1 **Nang Xian** China
67F3 **Nangzhou** China
87B2 **Nanjangüd** India
72D3 **Nanjing** China
Nanking = Nanjing
75A2 **Nankoku** Japan
73C4 **Nan Ling** Region, China
76D1 **Nanliu** *R* China
73B5 **Nanning** China
6F3 **Nanortalik** Greenland
73A5 **Nanpan Jiang** *R* China
86A1 **Nänpära** India
73D4 **Nanping** China
6A1 **Nansen Sd** Can
99D3 **Nansio** Tanz
48B2 **Nantes** France
13E2 **Nanton** Can
72E3 **Nantong** China
10C2 **Nantucket** *I* USA

35C1 **Nanuque** Brazil
72C3 **Nanyang** China
72D2 **Nanyang Hu** *L* China
99D2 **Nanyuki** Kenya
74D3 **Naoetsu** Japan
85B4 **Naokot** Pak
22A1 **Napa** USA
12B2 **Napaiskak** USA
15C2 **Napanee** Can
65K4 **Napas** Russian Fed
6E3 **Napassoq** Greenland
76D2 **Nape** Laos
110C1 **Napier** NZ
Naples = Napoli
17B2 **Naples** Florida, USA
19B3 **Naples** Texas, USA
73B5 **Napo** China
32C4 **Napo** *R* Peru/Ecuador
53B2 **Napoli** Italy
90A2 **Naqadeh** Iran
92C4 **Naqb Ishtar** Jordan
75B2 **Nara** Japan
97B3 **Nara** Mali
107D4 **Naracoorte** Aust
23B1 **Naranjos** Mexico
87C1 **Narasaräopet** India
77C4 **Narathiwat** Thai
86C2 **Narayanganj** Bang
87B1 **Näräyenpet** India
49C3 **Narbonne** France
84D2 **Narendranagar** India
6C2 **Nares Str** Can
58C2 **Narew** *R* Pol
75C1 **Narita** Japan
85C4 **Narmada** *R* India
84D3 **Närnaul** India
60E2 **Naro Fominsk** Russian Fed
99D3 **Narok** Kenya
84C2 **Narowal** Pak
107D4 **Narrabri** Aust
109C1 **Narran** *L* Aust
109C1 **Narran** *R* Aust
109C2 **Narrandera** Aust
106A4 **Narrogin** Aust
109C2 **Narromine** Aust
85D4 **Narsimhapur** India
87C1 **Narsipatnam** India
6F3 **Narssalik** Greenland
6F3 **Narssaq** Greenland
6F3 **Narssarssuaq** Greenland
75C1 **Narugo** Japan
75A2 **Naruto** Japan
60C2 **Narva** Russian Fed
38H5 **Narvik** Nor
84D3 **Narwäna** India
64G3 **Nar'yan Mar** Russian Fed
108B1 **Narylico** Aust
65J5 **Naryn** Kazakhstan
97C4 **Nasarawa** Nig
103D5 **Nasca Ridge** Pacific O
16D1 **Nashua** USA
19B3 **Nashville** Arkansas, USA
11B3 **Nashville** Tennessee, USA
54A1 **Našice** Croatia
85D4 **Näsik** India
99D2 **Nasir** Sudan
13B1 **Nass** *R* Can
26B1 **Nassau** The Bahamas
16C1 **Nassau** USA
95C2 **Nasser,L** Egypt
39G7 **Nässjö** Sweden
7C4 **Nastapoka Is** Can
100B3 **Nata** Botswana
31D3 **Natal** Brazil
70A3 **Natal** Indon
101H1 **Natal** Province, S Africa
90B3 **Natanz** Iran
7D4 **Natashquan** Can
7D4 **Natashquan** *R* Can
19B3 **Natchez** USA
19B3 **Natchitoches** USA
108C3 **Nathalia** Aust
6H2 **Nathorsts Land** *Region* Greenland
13C1 **Nation** *R* Can

21B3 **National City** USA
75C1 **Natori** Japan
99D3 **Natron** *L* Tanz
106A4 **Naturaliste,C** Aust
47D1 **Nauders** Austria
56C2 **Nauen** Germany
16C2 **Naugatuck** USA
57C2 **Naumburg** Germany
94B3 **Naur** Jordan
105G4 **Nauru** *I* Pacific O
63C2 **Naushki** Russian Fed
23B1 **Nautla** Mexico
9C3 **Navajo Res** USA
50A2 **Navalmoral de la Mata** Spain
29C7 **Navarino** *I* Chile
51B1 **Navarra** Province, Spain
34D3 **Navarro** Arg
19A3 **Navasota** USA
19A3 **Navasota** *R* USA
50A1 **Navia** *R* Spain
34A2 **Navidad** Chile
85C4 **Navlakhi** India
60D3 **Navlya** Russian Fed
24B2 **Navojoa** Mexico
55B3 **Návpaktos** Greece
55B3 **Návplion** Greece
85C4 **Navsäri** India
94C2 **Nawá** Syria
86B2 **Nawäda** India
84B2 **Nawah** Afghan
85B3 **Nawrabshah** Pak
73B4 **Naxi** China
55C3 **Náxos** *I* Greece
23A1 **Nayar** Mexico
90C3 **Nay Band** Iran
91B4 **Näy Band** Iran
74E2 **Nayoro** Japan
94B2 **Nazareth** Israel
48B2 **Nazay** France
32C6 **Nazca** Peru
92A2 **Nazilli** Turk
63B2 **Nazimovo** Russian Fed
13C2 **Nazko** *R* Can
99D2 **Nazret** Eth
91C5 **Nazwa** Oman
65J4 **Nazyvayevsk** Russian Fed
98B3 **Ndalatando** Angola
98C2 **Ndélé** CAR
98B3 **Ndendé** Gabon
98B1 **Ndjamena** Chad
98B3 **Ndjolé** Gabon
100B2 **Ndola** Zambia
109C1 **Neabul** Aust
108A1 **Neales** *R* Aust
55B3 **Neápolis** Greece
43C4 **Neath** Wales
109C1 **Nebine** *R* Aust
65G6 **Nebit Dag** Turkmenistan
8C2 **Nebraska** State, USA
18A1 **Nebraska City** USA
13C2 **Nechako** *R* Can
19A3 **Neches** *R* USA
34D3 **Necochea** Arg
86C1 **Nédong** China
9B3 **Needles** USA
14A2 **Neenah** USA
5J4 **Neepawa** Can
46C1 **Neerpelt** Belg
63C2 **Neftelensk** Russian Fed
99D2 **Negelē** Eth
94B3 **Negev** *Desert* Israel
60B4 **Negolu** *Mt* Rom
87B3 **Negombo** Sri Lanka
76A2 **Negrais,C** Burma
32A4 **Negritos** Peru
33E4 **Negro** *R* Amazonas, Brazil
29C4 **Negro** *R* Arg
34D2 **Negro** *R* Urug
79B4 **Negros** *I* Phil
54C2 **Negru Voda** Rom
90D3 **Nehbändan** Iran
73B4 **Neijiang** China
72B1 **Nei Monggol** Autononous Region, China
32B3 **Neiva** Colombia
99D2 **Nejo** Eth

Nek'emtē

99D2 **Nek'emtē** Eth
60D2 **Nelidovo** Russian Fed
87B2 **Nellore** India
69F2 **Nel'ma** Russian Fed
13D3 **Nelson** Can
111B2 **Nelson** NZ
7A4 **Nelson** R Can
108B3 **Nelson,C** Aust
12B2 **Nelson I** USA
97B3 **Néma** Maur
72A1 **Nemagt Uul** Mt Mongolia
54C1 **Nemira** Mt Rom
58C1 **Nemunas** R Lithuania
74F2 **Nemuro** Japan
63E3 **Nen** R China
41B3 **Nenagh** Irish Rep
12E2 **Nenana** USA
12E2 **Nenana** R USA
43D3 **Nene** R Eng
69E2 **Nenjiang** China
18A2 **Neodesha** USA
18B2 **Neosho** USA
63C2 **Nepa** Russian Fed
82C3 **Nepal** Kingdom, Asia
86A1 **Nepalganj** Nepal
45B1 **Nephin** Mt Irish Rep
94B3 **Neqarot** R Israel
34A3 **Nequén** State, Arg
68D1 **Nerchinsk** Russian Fed
52C2 **Neretva** R Bosnia & Herzegovina, Yugos/Croatia
71F2 **Nero Deep** Pacific O
38C1 **Neskaupstaður** Iceland
46B2 **Nesle** France
7E5 **Nesleyville** Can
55B2 **Néstos** R Greece
94B2 **Netanya** Israel
16B2 **Netcong** USA
56B2 **Netherlands** Kingdom, Europe
3M7 **Netherlands Antilles** Is Caribbean S
86C2 **Netrakona** Bang
6C3 **Nettilling** L Can
56C2 **Neubrandenburg** Germany
47B1 **Neuchâtel** Switz
46C2 **Neufchâteau** Belg
48C2 **Neufchâtel** France
46A2 **Neufchâtel-en-Bray** France
56B2 **Neumünster** Germany
52C1 **Neunkirchen** Austria
46D2 **Neunkirchen** Germany
34B3 **Neuquén** Arg
29B4 **Neuquén** State, Arg
34B3 **Neuquén** R Arg
56C2 **Neuruppin** Germany
46D1 **Neuss** Germany
46E2 **Neustadt** Germany
56C2 **Neustadt** Germany
56C2 **Neustrelitz** Germany
46D1 **Neuwied** Germany
8B3 **Nevada** State, USA
18B2 **Nevada** USA
34A3 **Nevada de Chillán** Mts Arg/Chile
23A2 **Nevada de Collima** Mexico
23B2 **Nevada de Toluca** Mt Mexico
94B3 **Nevatim** Israel
60C2 **Nevel'** Russian Fed
49C2 **Nevers** France
109C2 **Nevertire** Aust
27E3 **Nevis** I Caribbean S
58D2 **Nevis** R Belorussia/Lithuania
92B2 **Nevşehir** Turk
61K2 **Nev'yansk** Russian Fed
101C2 **Newala** Tanz
14A3 **New Albany** Indiana, USA
19C3 **New Albany** Mississippi, USA

33F2 **New Amsterdam** Guyana
109C1 **New Angledool** Aust
15C3 **Newark** Delaware, USA
10C2 **Newark** New Jersey, USA
14B2 **Newark** Ohio, USA
43D3 **Newark-upon-Trent** Eng
15D2 **New Bedford** USA
13B2 **New Bella Bella** Can
20B1 **Newberg** USA
11C3 **New Bern** USA
17B1 **Newberry** USA
26B2 **New Bight** The Bahamas
14B3 **New Boston** USA
9D4 **New Braunfels** USA
16C2 **New Britain** USA
7D5 **New Brunswick** Province, Can
16B2 **New Brunswick** USA
16B2 **Newburgh** USA
43D4 **Newbury** Eng
16D1 **Newburyport** USA
16C2 **New Canaan** USA
109D2 **Newcastle** Aust
14A3 **New Castle** Indiana, USA
42B2 **Newcastle** N Ire
14B2 **New Castle** Pennsylvania, USA
101G1 **Newcastle** S Africa
8C2 **Newcastle** Wyoming, USA
42D2 **Newcastle upon Tyne** Eng
106C2 **Newcastle Waters** Aust
45B2 **Newcastle West** Irish Rep
84D3 **New Delhi** India
109D2 **New England Range** Mts Aust
12B3 **Newenham,C** USA
43D4 **New Forest,The** Eng
7D4 **Newfoundland** Province, Can
7E5 **Newfoundland** I Can
102F2 **Newfoundland Basin** Atlantic O
18B2 **New Franklin** USA
42B2 **New Galloway** Scot
107E1 **New Georgia** I Solomon Is
7D5 **New Glasgow** Can
71F4 **New Guinea** SE Asia
12D3 **Newhalen** USA
22C3 **Newhall** USA
10C2 **New Hampshire** State, USA
101H1 **New Hanover** S Africa
43E4 **Newhaven** Eng
15D2 **New Haven** USA
13B1 **New Hazelton** Can
19B3 **New Iberia** USA
10C2 **New Jersey** State, USA
7C5 **New Liskeard** Can
16C2 **New London** USA
106A3 **Newman** Aust
22B2 **Newman** USA
43E3 **Newmarket** Eng
45B2 **Newmarket** Irish Rep
15C3 **New Market** USA
9C3 **New Mexico** State, USA
16C2 **New Milford** Connecticut, USA
17B1 **Newnan** USA
109C4 **New Norfolk** Aust
11A3 **New Orleans** USA
16B2 **New Paltz** USA
14B2 **New Philadelphia** USA
110B1 **New Plymouth** NZ
18B2 **Newport** Arkansas, USA
43D4 **Newport** Eng
14B3 **Newport** Kentucky, USA

20B2 **Newport** Oregon, USA
16A2 **Newport** Pennsylvania, USA
15D2 **Newport** Rhode Island, USA
15D2 **Newport** Vermont, USA
43C4 **Newport** Wales
20C1 **Newport** Washington, USA
22D4 **Newport Beach** USA
11C3 **Newport News** USA
26B1 **New Providence** I Caribbean S
43B4 **Newquay** Eng
6C3 **New Quebec Crater** Can
45C2 **New Ross** Irish Rep
45C1 **Newry** N Ire
New Siberian Is = Novosibirskye Ostrova
17B2 **New Smyrna Beach** USA
107D4 **New South Wales** State, Aust
12C3 **New Stuyahok** USA
18A2 **Newton** Kansas, USA
16D1 **Newton** Massachusetts, USA
19C3 **Newton** Mississippi, USA
16B2 **Newton** New York, USA
43C4 **Newton Abbot** Eng
45C1 **Newton Stewart** N Ire
42B2 **Newton Stewart** Scot
43C3 **Newtown** Wales
42B2 **Newtownards** N Ire
16A2 **Newville** USA
5F5 **New Westminster** Can
10C2 **New York** State, USA
10C2 **New York** USA
110 **New Zealand** Dominion, SW Pacific O
105G6 **New Zealand Plat** Pacific O
61F2 **Neya** Russian Fed
91B4 **Neyrīz** Iran
90C2 **Neyshābūr** Iran
60D3 **Nezhin** Russian Fed
98B3 **Ngabé** Congo
100B3 **Ngami** L Botswana
110C1 **Ngaruawahia** NZ
110C1 **Ngaruroro** R NZ
110C1 **Ngauruhoe,Mt** NZ
98B3 **Ngo** Congo
76D2 **Ngoc Linh** Mt Viet
98B2 **Ngoko** R Cam
68B3 **Ngoring Hu** L China
99D3 **Ngorongoro Crater** Tanz
98B3 **N'Gounié** R Gabon
98B1 **Nguigmi** Niger
71E3 **Ngulu** I Pacific O
97D3 **Nguru** Nig
76D3 **Nha Trang** Viet
108B3 **Nhill** Aust
101H1 **Nhlangano** Swaziland
76D2 **Nhommarath** Laos
106C2 **Nhulunbuy** Aust
97B3 **Niafounké** Mali
14A1 **Niagara** USA
15C2 **Niagara Falls** Can
15C2 **Niagara Falls** USA
70C3 **Niah** Malay
97B4 **Niakaramandougou** Ivory Coast
97C3 **Niamey** Niger
99C2 **Niangara** Zaïre
98C2 **Nia Nia** Zaïre
70A3 **Nias** I Indon
25D3 **Nicaragua** Republic, Cent America
53C3 **Nicastro** Italy
49D3 **Nice** France

26B1 **Nicholl's Town** The Bahamas
83D5 **Nicobar Is** Indian O
92B2 **Nicosia** Cyprus
25D3 **Nicoya,Pen de** Costa Rica
58C2 **Nidzica** Pol
46D2 **Niederbronn** France
56B2 **Niedersachsen** State, Germany
99C3 **Niemba** Zaïre
56B2 **Nienburg** Germany
46D1 **Niers** R Germany
97B4 **Niete,Mt** Lib
33F2 **Nieuw Amsterdam** Surinam
33F2 **Nieuw Nickerie** Surinam
46B1 **Nieuwpoort** Belg
92B2 **Niğde** Turk
97C3 **Niger** Republic, Africa
97C4 **Niger** R Nig
97C4 **Nigeria** Federal Republic, Africa
55B2 **Nigrita** Greece
75C1 **Nihommatsu** Japan
74D3 **Niigata** Japan
74C4 **Niihama** Japan
75B2 **Nii-jima** I Japan
75A2 **Niimi** Japan
74D3 **Niitsu** Japan
94B3 **Nijil** Jordan
56B2 **Nijmegen** Neth
64E3 **Nikel'** Russian Fed
97C3 **Nikki** Benin
74D3 **Nikko** Japan
60D4 **Nikolayev** Ukraine
61G4 **Nikolayevsk** Russian Fed
63G2 **Nikolayevsk-na-Amure** Russian Fed
61G2 **Nikol'sk** Russian Fed
61G3 **Nikol'sk** Russian Fed
60D4 **Nikopol** Ukraine
92C1 **Niksar** Turk
91D4 **Nikshahr** Iran
54A2 **Nikšić** Montenegro, Yugos
71D4 **Nila** I Indon
80B3 **Nile** R N E Africa
14A2 **Niles** USA
87B2 **Nilgiri Hills** India
85C4 **Nimach** India
49C3 **Nîmes** France
109C3 **Nimmitabel** Aust
99D2 **Nimule** Sudan
83B5 **Nine Degree Chan** Indian O
104C4 **Ninety-East Ridge** Indian O
109C3 **Ninety Mile Beach** Aust
73D4 **Ningde** China
73D4 **Ningdu** China
68B3 **Ningjing Shan** Mts China
76D1 **Ningming** China
73A4 **Ningnan** China
72B2 **Ningxia** Province, China
72B2 **Ning Xian** China
73B5 **Ninh Binh** Vietnam
107D1 **Ninigo Is** PNG
12D2 **Ninilchik** USA
8D2 **Niobrara** R USA
98B3 **Nioki** Zaïre
97B3 **Nioro du Sahel** Mali
48B2 **Niort** France
5H4 **Nipawin** Can
7B5 **Nipigon** Can
7B5 **Nipigon,L** Can
7B5 **Nipigon** R Can
14B1 **Nipissing,L** Can
87B1 **Nirmal** India
86B1 **Nirmāli** India
54B2 **Niš** Serbia, Yugos
81C4 **Nisāb** Yemen
69F4 **Nishino-shima** I Japan
75A1 **Nishino-shima** I Japan
75A2 **Nishiwaki** Japan
12G2 **Nisling** R Can

12H2 **Nisutlin** *R* Can
7C4 **Nitchequon** Can
31C6 **Niterói** Brazil
42C2 **Nith** *R* Scot
59B3 **Nitra** Czech
14B3 **Nitro** USA
78C2 **Niut** *Mt* Malay
46C1 **Nivelles** Belg
49C2 **Nivernais** Region, France
38L5 **Nivskiy** Russian Fed
87B1 **Nizāmābād** India
94B3 **Nizana** *Hist Site* Israel
61J2 **Nizhniye Sergi** Russian Fed
65F4 **Nizhniy Novgorod** Russian Fed
61F3 **Nizhniy Lomov** Russian Fed
65G4 **Nizhniy Tagil** Russian Fed
63B1 **Nizhnyaya Tunguska** *R* Russian Fed
93C2 **Nizip** Turk
100B2 **Njoko** *R* Zambia
99D3 **Njombe** Tanz
98B2 **Nkambé** Cam
101C2 **Nkhata Bay** Malawi
98B2 **Nkongsamba** Cam
97C3 **N'Konni** Niger
86C2 **Noakhali** Bang
12B1 **Noatak** USA
12C1 **Noatak** *R* USA
74C4 **Nobeoka** Japan
47D1 **Noce** *R* Italy
23A1 **Nochistlán** Mexico
23B2 **Nochixtlán** Mexico
19A3 **Nocona** USA
24A1 **Nogales** Sonora, Mexico
9B3 **Nogales** USA
23B2 **Nogales** Veracruz, Mexico
47D2 **Nogara** Italy
75A2 **Nogata** Japan
60E2 **Noginsk** Russian Fed
34D2 **Nogoyá** Arg
34D2 **Nogoyá** *R* Arg
84C3 **Nohar** India
75B2 **Nojima-zaki** *C* Japan
98B2 **Nola** CAR
61G2 **Nolinsk** Russian Fed
16D2 **Nomans Land** *I* USA
12A2 **Nome** USA
46D2 **Nomeny** France
72B1 **Nomgon** Mongolia
5H3 **Nonachol L** Can
76C2 **Nong Khai** Thai
101H1 **Nongoma** S Africa
12B1 **Noorvik** USA
13B3 **Nootka Sd** Can
98B3 **Noqui** Angola
7C5 **Noranda** Can
46B1 **Nord** Department, France
64D2 **Nordaustlandet** *I* Barents S
13D2 **Nordegg** Can
38F6 **Nordfjord** *Inlet* Nor
39F8 **Nordfriesische** *Is* Germany
56C2 **Nordhausen** Germany
56B2 **Nordrhein Westfalen** State, Germany
38J4 **Nordkapp** *C* Nor
6E3 **Nordre** Greenland
38H5 **Nord Stronfjället** *Mt* Sweden
1B9 **Nordvik** Russian Fed
45C2 **Nore** *R* Irish Rep
43E3 **Norfolk** County, Eng
8D2 **Norfolk** Nebraska, USA
11C3 **Norfolk** Virginia, USA
107F3 **Norfolk I** Aust
18B2 **Norfolk L** USA
105G5 **Norfolk Ridge** Pacific O
1C10 **Noril'sk** Russian Fed
18C1 **Normal** USA
19A2 **Norman** USA
48B2 **Normandie** Region, France
107D2 **Normanton** Aust
12J1 **Norman Wells** Can
4B3 **Norne** USA
15C2 **Norristown** USA
39H7 **Norrköping** Sweden
39H6 **Norrsundet** Sweden
39H7 **Norrtälje** Sweden
106B4 **Norseman** Aust
63F2 **Norsk** Russian Fed
102J2 **North** *S* N W Europe
42D2 **Northallerton** Eng
106A4 **Northam** Aust
102E3 **North American Basin** Atlantic O
106A3 **Northampton** Aust
43D3 **Northampton** County, Eng
43D3 **Northampton** Eng
15D2 **Northampton** USA
4G3 **North Arm** *B* Can
17B1 **North Augusta** USA
6D4 **North Aulatsvik** *I* Can
13F2 **North Battleford** Can
7C5 **North Bay** Can
20B2 **North Bend** USA
44C3 **North Berwick** Scot
7D5 **North,C** Can
7G4 **North C** NZ
11B3 **North Carolina** State, USA
20B1 **North Cascade Nat Pk** USA
14B1 **North Chan** Can
42B2 **North Chan** Ire/Scot
8C2 **North Dakota** State, USA
43E4 **North Downs** Eng
14C2 **North East** USA
102H2 **North East Atlantic Basin** Atlantic O
4B3 **Northeast C** USA
40B3 **Northern Ireland** UK
27L1 **Northern Range** *Mts* Trinidad
106C2 **Northern Territory** Aust
44C3 **North Esk** *R* Scot
16C1 **Northfield** Massachusetts, USA
12D2 **North Fork** *R* USA
110B1 **North I** NZ
74B3 **North Korea** Republic, S E Asia
North Land = Severnaya Zemlya
19B3 **North Little Rock** USA
1B4 **North Magnetic Pole** Can
17B2 **North Miami** USA
17B2 **North Miami Beach** USA
8C2 **North Platte** USA
8C2 **North Platte** *R* USA
27R3 **North Pt** Barbados
14B1 **North Pt** USA
40B2 **North Rona** *I* Scot
44C2 **North Ronaldsay** *I* Scot
13F2 **North Saskatchewan** *R* Can
40D2 **North Sea** N W Europe
4D3 **North Slope** *Region* USA
109D1 **North Stradbroke** *I* Aust
110B1 **North Taranaki Bight** *B* NZ
9C3 **North Truchas Peak** *Mt* USA
44A3 **North Uist** *I* Scot
42C2 **Northumberland** County, Eng
107E3 **Northumberland Is** Aust
7D5 **Northumberland Str** Can
20B1 **North Vancouver** Can
43E3 **North Walsham** Eng
12F2 **Northway** USA
106A3 **North West C** Aust
84C2 **North West Frontier** Province, Pak
7D4 **North West River** Can
4F3 **North West Territories** Can
42D2 **North York Moors Nat Pk** Eng
12B2 **Norton B** USA
12B2 **Norton Sd** USA
112B1 **Norvegia,C** Ant
16C2 **Norwalk** Connecticut, USA
14B2 **Norwalk** Ohio, USA
39F6 **Norway** Kingdom, Europe
5J4 **Norway House** Can
6A2 **Norwegian B** Can
102H1 **Norwegian Basin** Norewegian S
64A3 **Norwegian S** N W Europe
16C2 **Norwich** Connecticut, USA
43E3 **Norwich** Eng
16D1 **Norwood** Massachusetts, USA
14B3 **Norwood** Ohio, USA
54C2 **Nos Emine** *C* Bulg
74D2 **Noshiro** Japan
54C2 **Nos Kaliakra** *C* Bulg
44E1 **Noss** *I* Scot
91D4 **Nostrābād** Iran
101D2 **Nosy Barren** *I* Madag
101D2 **Nosy Bé** *I* Madag
101E2 **Nosy Boraha** *I* Madag
101D3 **Nosy Varika** Madag
58B2 **Notéc** *R* Pol
5G4 **Notikeuin** Can
53C3 **Noto** Italy
39F7 **Notodden** Nor
75B1 **Noto-hantō** *Pen* Japan
7E5 **Notre Dams B** Can
43D3 **Nottingham** County, Eng
43D3 **Nottingham** Eng
6C3 **Nottingham** *I* Can
6C3 **Nottingham Island** Can
96A2 **Nouadhibou** Maur
97A3 **Nouakchott** Maur
107F3 **Nouméa** Nouvelle Calédonie
97B3 **Nouna** Burkina
107F3 **Nouvelle Calédonie** *I* S W Pacific O
98B3 **Nova Caipemba** Angola
35A2 **Nova Esperança** Brazil
35C2 **Nova Friburgo** Brazil
100A2 **Nova Gaia** Angola
35B2 **Nova Granada** Brazil
35B2 **Nova Horizonte** Brazil
35C1 **Nova Lima** Brazil
Nova Lisboa = Huambo
35A2 **Nova Londrina** Brazil
101C3 **Nova Mambone** Mozam
47C2 **Novara** Italy
7D5 **Nova Scotia** Province, Can
22A1 **Novato** USA
35C1 **Nova Venécia** Brazil
60D4 **Novaya Kakhovka** Ukraine
64G2 **Novaya Zemlya** *I* Barents S
54C2 **Nova Zagora** Bulg
31C2 **Nove Russas** Brazil
54A1 **Nové Zámky** Czech
60D2 **Novgorod** Russian Fed
47C2 **Novi Ligure** Italy
54C2 **Novi Pazar** Bulg
54B2 **Novi Pazar** Serbia, Yugos
54A1 **Novi Sad** Serbia, Yugos
61J3 **Novoalekseyevka** Kazakhstan
61F3 **Novoanninskiy** Russian Fed
61E4 **Novocherkassk** Russian Fed
60C3 **Novograd Volynskiy** Ukraine
58D2 **Novogrudok** Russian Fed
30F4 **Novo Hamburgo** Brazil
65H5 **Novokazalinsk** Kazakhstan
65K4 **Novokuznetsk** Russian Fed
112B12 **Novolazarevskaya** *Base* Ant
52C1 **Novo Mesto** Slovenia
60E3 **Novomoskovsk** Russian Fed
60E5 **Novorossiysk** Russian Fed
65K4 **Novosibirsk** Russian Fed
1B8 **Novosibirskiye Ostrova** *I* Russian Fed
61J3 **Novotroitsk** Russian Fed
61G3 **Novo Uzensk** Russian Fed
59C2 **Novovolynsk** Ukraine
61G2 **Novo Vyatsk** Russian Fed
60D3 **Novozybkov** Russian Fed
58C2 **Novy Dwór Mazowiecki** Pol
61K2 **Novyy Lyalya** Russian Fed
61H5 **Novyy Port** Russian Fed
61H5 **Novyy Uzen** Kazakhstan
58B2 **Nowa Sól** Pol
18A2 **Nowata** USA
86C1 **Nowgong** India
12D2 **Nowitna** *R* USA
109D2 **Nowra** Aust
90B2 **Now Shahr** Iran
84C2 **Nowshera** Pak
59C3 **Nowy Sącz** Pol
12H3 **Noyes I** USA
46B2 **Noyon** France
97B4 **Nsawam** Ghana
99D1 **Nuba** *Mts* Sudan
81B3 **Nubian Desert** Sudan
34A3 **Nuble** *R* Chile
9D4 **Nueces** *R* USA
5J3 **Nueltin L** Can
26A2 **Nueva Gerona** Cuba
34A3 **Nueva Imperial** Chile
9C4 **Nueva Laredo** Mexico
34D2 **Nueva Palmira** Urug
24B2 **Nueva Rosita** Mexico
26B2 **Nuevitas** Cuba
24B1 **Nuevo Casas Grandes** Mexico
24C2 **Nuevo Laredo** Mexico
99E2 **Nugaal** Region, Somalia
6E2 **Nûgâtsiaq** Greenland
6E2 **Nugssuag** *Pen* Greenland
6E2 **Nûgussaq** *I* Greenland
108A2 **Nukey Bluff** *Mt* Aust
93D3 **Nukhayb** Iraq
65G5 **Nukus** Uzbekistan
12C2 **Nulato** USA
106B4 **Nullarbor Plain** Aust
97D4 **Numan** Nig
75B1 **Numata** Japan
98C2 **Numatinna** *R* Sudan
74D3 **Numazu** Japan
71E4 **Numfoor** *I* Indon
108C3 **Numurkah** Aust
12B2 **Nunapitchuk** USA

84D2 **Nunkun** Mt India
53A2 **Nuoro** Sardegna
91B3 **Nurābād** Iran
47C2 **Nure** R Italy
108A2 **Nuriootpa** Aust
84C1 **Nuristan** Upland
Afghan
61H3 **Nurlat** Russian Fed
38K6 **Nurmes** Fin
57C3 **Nürnberg** Germany
108C2 **Nurri,Mt** Aust
93D2 **Nusaybin** Turk
12C3 **Nushagak** R USA
12C3 **Nushagak B** USA
12C3 **Nushagak Pen** USA
84B3 **Nushki** Pak
7D4 **Nutak** Can
12F2 **Nutzotin Mts** USA
86A1 **Nuwakot** Nepal
87C3 **Nuwara-Eliya**
Sri Lanka
6C3 **Nuyukjuak** Can
16C2 **Nyack** USA
99D2 **Nyahururu** Kenya
108B3 **Nyah West** Aust
4C3 **Nyai** USA
68B3 **Nyainqentanglha**
Shan Mts China
99D3 **Nyakabindi** Tanz
98C1 **Nyala** Sudan
86B1 **Nyalam** China
98C2 **Nyamlell** Sudan
64F3 **Nyandoma** Russian
Fed
101C2 **Nyanga** Zim
98B3 **Nyanga** R Gabon
101C2 **Nyasa L** Malawi/
Mozam
76B2 **Nyaunglebin** Burma
61J2 **Nyazepetrovsk**
Russian Fed
39G7 **Nyborg** Den
39H7 **Nybro** Sweden
64J3 **Nyda** Russian Fed
6D1 **Nyeboes Land**
Region Can
99D3 **Nyeri** Kenya
101C2 **Nyimba** Zambia
82D3 **Nyingchi** China
59C3 **Nyíregyháza** Hung
99D2 **Nyiru,Mt** Kenya
38J6 **Nykarleby** Fin
39F7 **Nykøbing** Den
39G8 **Nykøbing** Den
39H7 **Nyköping** Sweden
100B3 **Nylstroom** S Africa
109C2 **Nymagee** Aust
39H7 **Nynäshamn** Sweden
109C2 **Nyngan** Aust
47B1 **Nyon** Switz
98B2 **Nyong** R Cam
49D3 **Nyons** France
59B2 **Nysa** Pol
20C2 **Nyssa** USA
63D1 **Nyurba** Russian Fed
99D3 **Nzega** Tanz
97B4 **Nzérékore** Guinea
98B3 **N'zeto** Angola

O

6F3 **Oaggsimiut**
Greenland
8C2 **Oahe Res** USA
21C4 **Oahu** I Hawaiian Is
108B2 **Oakbank** Aust
22B2 **Oakdale** USA
109D1 **Oakey** Aust
21A2 **Oakland** California,
USA
20B2 **Oakland** Oregon,
USA
14A3 **Oakland City** USA
14A2 **Oak Lawn** USA
22B2 **Oakley** California,
USA
20B2 **Oakridge** USA
14C2 **Oakville** Can
111B3 **Oamaru** NZ
112B7 **Oates Land** Region,
Ant
109C4 **Oatlands** Aust
23B2 **Oaxaca** Mexico
23B2 **Oaxaca** State, Mexico
65J3 **Ob'** R Russian Fed

75B1 **Obama** Japan
111A3 **Oban** NZ
44B3 **Oban** Scot
75C1 **Obanazawa** Japan
47D1 **Oberammergau**
Germany
46D1 **Oberhausen**
Germany
47D1 **Oberstdorf** Germany
71D4 **Obi** I Indon
33F4 **Obidos** Brazil
74E2 **Obihiro** Japan
98C2 **Obo** CAR
99E1 **Obock** Djibouti
58B2 **Oborniki** Pol
60E3 **Oboyan** Russian Fed
20B2 **O'Brien** USA
61H3 **Obshchiy Syrt** Mts
Russian Fed
64J3 **Obskava Guba** B
Russian Fed
97B4 **Obuasi** Ghana
17B2 **Ocala** USA
32C2 **Ocana** Colombia
50B2 **Ocaño** Spain
12G3 **Ocean C** USA
15C3 **Ocean City** Maryland,
USA
16B3 **Ocean City** New
Jersey, USA
5F4 **Ocean Falls** Can
22D4 **Oceanside** USA
19C3 **Ocean Springs** USA
61H2 **Ocher** Russian Fed
44C3 **Ochil Hills** Scot
17B1 **Ochlockonee** R
USA
27H1 **Ocho Rios** Jamaica
17B1 **Ocmulgee** R USA
17B1 **Oconee** R USA
14A2 **Oconto** USA
23A1 **Ocotlán** Jalisco,
Mexico
23B2 **Ocotlán** Oaxaca,
Mexico
97B4 **Oda** Ghana
75A1 **Oda** Japan
38B2 **Ódáðahraun** Region,
Iceland
74E2 **Odate** Japan
74D3 **Odawara** Japan
39F6 **Odda** Nor
50A2 **Odemira** Port
55C3 **Odemiş** Turk
101G1 **Odendaalsrus**
S Africa
39G7 **Odense** Den
56C2 **Oder** R Pol/Germany
9C3 **Odessa** Texas, USA
60D4 **Odessa** Ukraine
20C1 **Odessa** Washington,
USA
97B4 **Odienné** Ivory Coast
59B2 **Odra** R Pol
31C3 **Oeiras** Brazil
53C2 **Ofanto** R Italy
94B3 **Ofaqim** Israel
45C2 **Offaly** County,
Irish Rep
49D1 **Offenbach** Germany
49D2 **Offenburg** Germany
74D3 **Oga** Japan
99E2 **Ogaden** Region, Eth
74D3 **Ogaki** Japan
8C2 **Ogallala** USA
69G4 **Ogasawara Gunto** Is
Japan
97C4 **Ogbomosho** Nig
8B2 **Ogden** Utah, USA
15C2 **Ogdensburg** USA
17B1 **Ogeechee** R USA
12G1 **Ogilvie** Can
4E3 **Ogilvie Mts** Can
17B1 **Oglethorpe,Mt** USA
47D2 **Oglio** R Italy
47B1 **Ognon** R France
97C4 **Ogoja** Nig
98A3 **Ogooué** R Gabon
58C1 **Ogre** Latvia
96B2 **Oguilet Khenachich**
Well Mali
52C1 **Ogulin** Croatia
111A3 **Ohai** NZ
110C1 **Ohakune** NZ

96C2 **Ohanet** Alg
111A2 **Ohau,L** NZ
10B2 **Ohio** State, USA
14A3 **Ohio** R USA
100A2 **Ohopoho** Namibia
57C2 **Ohre** R Czech
55B2 **Ohrid** Macedonia,
Yugos
55B2 **Ohridsko Jezero** L
Macedonia, Yugos/
Alb
110B1 **Ohura** NZ
33G3 **Oiapoque** French
Guiana
68B2 **Oijiaojing** China
14C2 **Oil City** USA
21B2 **Oildale** USA
46B2 **Oise** Department,
France
49C2 **Oise** R France
74C4 **Oita** Japan
22C3 **Ojai** USA
24B2 **Ojinaga** Mexico
23B2 **Ojitlán** Mexico
75B1 **Ojiya** Japan
30C4 **Ojos del Salado** Mt
Arg
23A1 **Ojueloz** Mexico
60E3 **Oka** R Russian Fed
100A3 **Okahandja** Namibia
20C1 **Okanagan Falls** Can
13D2 **Okanagan L** Can
20C1 **Okanogan** USA
20C1 **Okanogan** R USA
20B1 **Okanogan Range**
Mts Can/USA
84C2 **Okara** Pak
100A2 **Okavango** R Angola/
Namibia
100B2 **Okavango Delta**
Marsh Botswana
74D3 **Okaya** Japan
74C4 **Okayama** Japan
75B2 **Okazaki** Japan
17B2 **Okeechobee** USA
17B2 **Okeechobee,L** USA
17B1 **Okefenokee Swamp**
USA
97C4 **Okene** Nig
85B4 **Okha** India
69G1 **Okha** Russian Fed
86B1 **Okhaldunga** Nepal
62J3 **Okhotsk,S of** Russian
Fed
69E4 **Okinawa** I Japan
69E4 **Okinawa gunto** Arch
Japan
74C3 **Oki-shoto** Is Japan
9D3 **Oklahoma** State,
USA
18A2 **Oklahoma City** USA
18A2 **Okmulgee** USA
98B3 **Okondja** Gabon
98B3 **Okoyo** Congo
97C4 **Okpara** R Nig
61J4 **Oktyabr'sk**
Kazakhstan
61H3 **Oktyabr'skiy** Russian
Fed
74D2 **Okushiri-tō** I Japan
38A2 **Ólafsvik** Iceland
39H7 **Oland** I Sweden
108B2 **Olary** Aust
18B2 **Olathe** USA
29D3 **Olavarría** Arg
53A2 **Olbia** Sardegna
12G1 **Old Crow** Can
56B2 **Oldenburg**
Niedersachsen,
Germany
56C2 **Oldenburg**
Schleswig-Holstein,
Germany
15C2 **Old Forge** USA
42C3 **Oldham** Eng
12D3 **Old Harbor** USA
41B3 **Old Head of Kinsale**
C Scot
16C2 **Old Lyme** USA
13E2 **Olds** Can
72B1 **Oldziyt** Mongolia
15C2 **Olean** USA
63E2 **Olekma** R Russian

63D1 **Olekminsk** Russian
Fed
38L5 **Olenegorsk** Russian
Fed
58D2 **Olevsk** Ukraine
69F2 **Ol'ga** Russian Fed
100A3 **Olifants** R Namibia
55B2 **Ólimbos** Mt Greece
35B2 **Olimpia** Brazil
23B2 **Olinala** Mexico
31E3 **Olinda** Brazil
34C2 **Oliva** Arg
29C2 **Olivares** Mt Arg
35C2 **Oliveira** Brazil
13D3 **Oliver** Can
30C3 **Ollague** Chile
30C3 **Ollagüe** Mt Bol
18C2 **Olney** USA
68E1 **Olochi** Russian Fed
39G7 **Olofstrom** Sweden
98B3 **Olombo** Congo
59B3 **Olomouc** Czech
60D1 **Olonets** Russian Fed
79B3 **Olongapa** Phil
48B3 **Oloron Ste Marie**
France
68D1 **Olovyannaya**
Russian Fed
46D1 **Olpe** Germany
58C2 **Olsztyn** Pol
54B2 **Olt** R Rom
47B1 **Olten** Switz
20B1 **Olympia** USA
20B1 **Olympic Nat Pk** USA
Olympus = **Ólimbos**
20B1 **Olympus,Mt** USA
65J4 **Om'** R Russian Fed
75B1 **Omachi** Japan
75B2 **Omae-zaki** C Japan
45C1 **Omagh** N Ire
18A1 **Omaha** USA
20C1 **Omak** USA
91C5 **Oman** Sultanate,
Arabian Pen
91C4 **Oman,G of** UAE
98A3 **Omboué** Gabon
99D1 **Omdurman** Sudan
23B2 **Ometepec** Mexico
99D1 **Om Häjer** Eth
13B1 **Omineca** R Can
13B1 **Omineca Mts** Can
75B1 **Omiya** Japan
12H3 **Ommaney,C** USA
4H2 **Ommanney B** Can
99D2 **Omo** R Eth
65J4 **Omsk** Russian Fed
74B4 **Omura** Japan
74C4 **Omuta** Japan
61H2 **Omutninsk** Russian
Fed
78D3 **Onang** Indon
14B1 **Onaping L** Can
100A2 **Oncócua** Angola
100A2 **Ondangua** Namibia
59C3 **Ondava** R Czech
68D2 **Öndörhaan** Molgolia
83B5 **One and Half Degree**
Chan Indian O
64E3 **Onega** Russian Fed
64E3 **Onega** R Russian
Fed
15C2 **Oneida L** USA
8D2 **O'Neill** USA
69H2 **Onekotan** I Russian
Fed
98C3 **Onema** Zaïre
15D2 **Oneonta** USA
54C1 **Oneşti** Rom
64E3 **Onezhskoye Ozero** L
Russian Fed
100A2 **Ongiva** Angola
74B3 **Ongjin** N Korea
72D1 **Ongniud Qi** China
87C1 **Ongole** India
15C2 **Onieda L** USA
101D3 **Onilahy** R Madag
97C4 **Onitsha** Nig
68C2 **Onjüül** Mongolia
75B1 **Ono** Japan
75B2 **Onohara-jima** I
Japan
74C4 **Onomichi** Japan
106A3 **Onslow** Aust
17C1 **Onslow B** USA

75B1 **Ontake-san** *Mt* Japan
22D3 **Ontario** California, USA
20C2 **Ontario** Oregon, USA
7A4 **Ontario** Province, Can
15C2 **Ontario,L** Can/USA
51B2 **Onteniente** Spain
106C3 **Oodnadatta** Aust
106C4 **Ooldea** Aust
18A2 **Oologah L** USA
46B1 **Oostende** Belg
46B1 **Oosterschelde** *Estuary* Neth
87B2 **Ootacamund** India
13B2 **Ootsa L** Can
69H1 **Opala** Russian Fed
98C3 **Opala** Zaïre
87C3 **Opanake** Sri Lanka
61G2 **Oparino** Russian Fed
59B3 **Opava** Czech
17A1 **Opelika** USA
19B3 **Opelousas** USA
12C2 **Ophir** USA
58D1 **Opochka** Russian Fed
59B2 **Opole** Pol
       Oporto = Porto
110C1 **Opotiki** NZ
17A1 **Opp** USA
38F6 **Oppdal** Nor
110B1 **Opunake** NZ
54B1 **Oradea** Rom
38B2 **Oraefajökull** *Mts* Iceland
85D3 **Orai** India
96B1 **Oran** Alg
30D3 **Orán** Arg
109C2 **Orange** Aust
22D4 **Orange** California, USA
49C3 **Orange** France
19B3 **Orange** Texas, USA
100A3 **Orange** *R* S Africa
17B1 **Orangeburg** USA
101G1 **Orange Free State** Province, S Africa
17B1 **Orange Park** USA
14B2 **Orangeville** Can
56C2 **Oranienburg** Germany
79C3 **Oras** Phil
54B1 **Orăstie** Rom
54B1 **Oravita** Rom
52B2 **Orbetello** Italy
109C3 **Orbost** Aust
46B1 **Orchies** France
47B2 **Orco** *R* Italy
106B2 **Ord** *R* Aust
106B2 **Ord,Mt** Aust
93C1 **Ordu** Turk
39H7 **Örebro** Sweden
8A2 **Oregon** State, USA
14B2 **Oregon** USA
20B1 **Oregon City** USA
39H6 **Öregrund** Sweden
60E2 **Orekhovo Zuyevo** Russian Fed
60E3 **Orel** Russian Fed
61H3 **Orenburg** Russian Fed
34D3 **Orense** Arg
50A1 **Orense** Spain
56C1 **Oresund** *Str* Den/ Sweden
111A3 **Oreti** *R* NZ
55C3 **Orhaneli** *R* Turk
68C2 **Orhon Gol** *R* Mongolia
23B2 **Oriental** Mexico
108B1 **Orientos** Aust
51B2 **Orihuela** Spain
15C2 **Orillia** Can
33E2 **Orinoco** *R* Ven
86A2 **Orissa** State, India
53A3 **Oristano** Sardegna
38K6 **Orivesi** *L* Fin
33F4 **Oriximina** Brazil
23B2 **Orizaba** Mexico
35B1 **Orizona** Brazil
44C2 **Orkney** *I* Scot
35B2 **Orlândia** Brazil
17B2 **Orlando** USA

48C2 **Orléanais** *Region* France
48C2 **Orléans** France
63B2 **Orlik** Russian Fed
82A3 **Ormara** Pak
79B3 **Ormoc** Phil
17B2 **Ormond Beach** USA
46C2 **Ornain** *R* France
47B1 **Ornans** France
48B2 **Orne** *R* France
38H6 **Örnsköldsvik** Sweden
32C3 **Orocué** Colombia
94B3 **Oron** Israel
       Orontes = 'Āsī
79B4 **Oroquieta** Phil
59C3 **Orosháza** Hung
21A2 **Oroville** California, USA
20C1 **Oroville** Washington, USA
47B1 **Orsières** Switz
65G4 **Orsk** Russian Fed
38F6 **Ørsta** Nor
48B3 **Orthez** France
50A1 **Ortigueira** Spain
47D1 **Ortles** *Mts* Italy
27L1 **Ortoire** *R* Trinidad
93E2 **Ürümīyeh** Iran
30C2 **Oruro** Bol
61J2 **Osa** Russian Fed
18B2 **Osage** *R* USA
75B1 **Osaka** Japan
25D4 **Osa,Pen de** Costa Rica
18C2 **Osceola** Arkansas, USA
18B1 **Osceola** Iowa, USA
20C2 **Osgood Mts** USA
15C2 **Oshawa** Can
75B2 **O-shima** *I* Japan
10B2 **Oshkosh** USA
97C4 **Oshogbo** Nig
7B5 **Oshosh** USA
98B3 **Oshwe** Zaïre
54A1 **Osijek** Croatia
65K5 **Osinniki** Russian Fed
58D2 **Osipovichi** Belorussia
18B1 **Oskaloosa** USA
60A2 **Oskarshamn** Sweden
39G7 **Oslo** Nor
92C2 **Osmaniye** Turk
56B2 **Osnabrück** Germany
30F4 **Osório** Brazil
29B4 **Osorno** Chile
50B1 **Osorno** Spain
20C1 **Osoyoos** Can
13C1 **Ospika** *R* Can
107D5 **Ossa,Mt** Aust
16C2 **Ossining** USA
60D2 **Ostashkov** Russian Fed
       Ostend = Oostende
38G6 **Østerdalen** *V* Nor
38G6 **Östersund** Sweden
56B2 **Ostfriesische Inseln** *Is* Germany
39H6 **Östhammär** Sweden
53B2 **Ostia** Italy
47D2 **Ostiglia** Italy
59B3 **Ostrava** Czech
58B2 **Ostróda** Pol
58B2 **Ostroleka** Pol
60C2 **Ostrov** Russian Fed
64J2 **Ostrov Belyy** *I* Russian Fed
64H1 **Ostrov Greem Bell** *I* Barents S
64F3 **Ostrov Kolguyev** *I* Russian Fed
74F2 **Ostrov Kunashir** *I* Russian Fed
64F2 **Ostrov Mechdusharskiy** *I* Barents S
90B2 **Ostrov Ogurchinskiy** *I* Turkmenistan
64G1 **Ostrov Rudol'fa** *I* Barents S
64G2 **Ostrov Vaygach** *I* Russian Fed
1B7 **Ostrov Vrangelya** *I* Russian Fed
58B2 **Ostrów** Pol

59C2 **Ostrowiec** Pol
58C2 **Ostrów Mazowiecka** Pol
50A2 **Osuna** Spain
15C2 **Osweg** USA
15C2 **Oswego** USA
43C3 **Oswestry** Eng
59D2 **Oświęcim** Pol
75B1 **Ota** Japan
111B3 **Otago Pen** NZ
110C2 **Otaki** NZ
74E2 **Otaru** Japan
32B3 **Otavalo** Ecuador
100A2 **Otavi** Namibia
75C1 **Otawara** Japan
20C1 **Othello** USA
55B3 **Othris** *Mt* Greece
16C1 **Otis** Massachusetts, USA
16B2 **Otisville** USA
100A3 **Otjiwarongo** Namibia
72B2 **Otog Qi** China
110C1 **Otorohanga** NZ
55A2 **Otranto** Italy
55A2 **Otranto,Str of** *Chan* Italy/Alb
14A2 **Otsego** USA
75B1 **Otsu** Japan
39F6 **Otta** Nor
39F7 **Otta** *R* Nor
15C1 **Ottawa** Can
18A2 **Ottawa** Kansas, USA
15C1 **Ottawa** *R* Can
7B4 **Ottawa Is** Can
7B4 **Otter Rapids** Can
6B1 **Otto Fjord** Can
101G1 **Ottosdal** S Africa
18B1 **Ottumwa** USA
46D2 **Ottweiler** Germany
97C4 **Oturkpo** Nig
32B5 **Otusco** Peru
108B3 **Otway,C** Aust
58C2 **Otwock** Pol
47D1 **Otz** Austria
47D1 **Otzal** *Mts* Austria
76C1 **Ou** *R* Laos
19B3 **Ouachita** *R* USA
19B3 **Ouachita,L** USA
19B3 **Ouachita Mts** USA
96A2 **Ouadane** Maur
98C2 **Ouadda** CAR
98C1 **Ouaddai** *Desert Region* Chad
97B3 **Ouagadougou** Burkina
97B3 **Ouahigouya** Burkina
98C2 **Ouaka** CAR
97C3 **Oualam** Niger
96C2 **Ouallen** Alg
98C2 **Ouanda Djallé** CAR
96A2 **Ouarane** *Region,* Maur
96C1 **Ouargla** Alg
98C2 **Ouarra** *R* CAR
96B1 **Ouarzazate** Mor
51C2 **Ouassel** *R* Alg
98B2 **Oubangui** *R* Congo
46B1 **Oudenaarde** Belg
100B4 **Oudtshoorn** S Africa
51B2 **Oued Tlélat** Alg
96B1 **Oued Zem** Mor
98B2 **Ouesso** Congo
96B1 **Ouezzane** Mor
98B2 **Ouham** *R* Chad
97C4 **Ouidah** Benin
96B1 **Oujda** Mor
38J6 **Oulainen** Fin
38K5 **Oulu** Fin
38K6 **Oulu** *R* Fin
38K6 **Oulujärvi** *L* Fin
95B3 **Oum Chalouba** Chad
98B1 **Oum Hadjer** Chad
95R3 **Oum Haouach** *Watercourse* Chad
38K5 **Ounas** *R* Fin
95B3 **Ounianga Kébir** Chad
46D1 **Our** *R* Germany
46B2 **Ourcq** *R* France
       Ourense = Orense
31C3 **Ouricurí** Brazil
35B2 **Ourinhos** Brazil
35C2 **Ouro Prêto** Brazil
46C1 **Ourthe** *R* Belg

42D2 **Ouse** *R* Eng
43E3 **Ouse** *R* Eng
40B2 **Outer Hebrides** *Is* Scot
22C4 **Outer Santa Barbara** *Chan* USA
100A3 **Outjo** Namibia
38K6 **Outokumpu** Fin
108B3 **Ouyen** Aust
47C2 **Ovada** Italy
34A2 **Ovalle** Chile
100A2 **Ovamboland** *Region,* Namibia
61H5 **Ova Tyuleni** *Is* Kazakhstan
38J5 **Övertorneå** Sweden
50A1 **Oviedo** Spain
60C3 **Ovruch** Ukraine
63E2 **Ovsyanka** Russian Fed
111A3 **Owaka** NZ
75B2 **Owase** Japan
11B3 **Owensboro** USA
21B2 **Owens L** USA
14B2 **Owen Sound** Can
107D1 **Owen Stanley Range** *Mts* PNG
97C4 **Owerri** Nig
97C4 **Owo** Nig
14B2 **Owosso** USA
20C2 **Owyhee** *R* USA
20C2 **Owyhee Mts** USA
32D6 **Oxapampa** Peru
39H7 **Oxelösund** Sweden
43D4 **Oxford** County, Eng
43D4 **Oxford** Eng
16D1 **Oxford** Massachusetts, USA
19C3 **Oxford** Mississippi, USA
45B1 **Ox Mts** Irish Rep
22C3 **Oxnard** USA
74D3 **Oyama** Japan
13E2 **Oyen** Can
98B2 **Oyem** Gabon
44B3 **Oykel** *R* Scot
39F6 **Øyre** Nor
109C4 **Oyster B** Aust
79B4 **Ozamiz** Phil
17A1 **Ozark** USA
18B2 **Ozark Plat** USA
18B2 **Ozarks,L of the** USA
59C3 **Ozd** Hung
65K5 **Ozero Alakol** *L* Kazakhstan/Russian Fed
65J5 **Ozero Balkhash** *L* Kazakhstan
63C2 **Ozero Baykal** *L* Russian Fed
65J4 **Ozero Chany** *L* Russian Fed
69F1 **Ozero Chukchagirskoye** *L* Russian Fed
69F1 **Ozero Evoron** *L* Russian Fed
60C2 **Ozero Chudskoye** *L* Russian Fed
60D2 **Ozero Il'men** *L* Russian Fed
38L5 **Ozero Imandra** *L* Russian Fed
82B1 **Ozero Issyk Kul'** *L* Kirgizia
69F2 **Ozero Khanka** *L* China/Russian Fed
38L5 **Ozero Kovdozero** *L* Russian Fed
38L5 **Ozero Kuyto** *L* Russian Fed
38L5 **Ozero Pyaozero** *L* Russian Fed
65H4 **Ozero Tengiz** *L* Kazakhstan
38L5 **Ozero Topozero** *L* Russian Fed
65K5 **Ozero Zaysan** *L* Kazakhstan
23B1 **Ozuluama** Mexico

P

100A4 **Paarl** S Africa
44A3 **Pabbay** *I* Scot

58B2	Pabianice Pol
86B2	Pabna Bang
58D2	Pabrade Lithuania
32B5	Pacasmayo Peru
23B1	Pachuca Mexico
105K6	Pacific-Antarctic Ridge Pacific O
22B2	Pacific Grove USA
78C4	Pacitan Indon
35C1	Pacuí R Brazil
70B4	Padang Indon
56B2	Paderborn Germany
5J3	Padlei Can
86C2	Padma R Bang
47D2	Padova Italy
9D4	Padre I USA
43B4	Padstow Eng
108B3	Padthaway Aust
	Padua = Padova
14A3	Paducah Kentucky, USA
11B3	Paducah USA
38L5	Padunskoye More L Russian Fed
74A3	Paengnyŏng-do I S Korea
110C1	Paeroa NZ
100C3	Pafuri Mozam
52B2	Pag I Croatia
79B4	Pagadian Phil
70B4	Pagai Selatan I Indon
70B4	Pagai Utara I Indon
71F2	Pagan I Pacific O
78D3	Pagatan Indon
55C3	Pagondhas Greece
110C2	Pahiatua NZ
21C4	Pahoa Hawaiian Is
17B2	Pahokee USA
39K6	Päijänna L Fin
21C4	Pailola Chan Hawaiian Is
14B2	Painesville USA
9B3	Painted Desert USA
42B2	Paisley Scot
32A5	Paita Peru
38J5	Pajala Sweden
80E3	Pakistan Republic, Asia
76C2	Pak Lay Laos
86D2	Pakokku Burma
13E2	Pakowki L Can
52C1	Pakrac Croatia
54A1	Paks Hung
76C2	Pak Sane Laos
76D2	Pakse Laos
99D2	Pakwach Uganda
98B2	Pala Chad
52C2	Palagruža I Croatia
46B2	Palaiseau France
78C3	Palangkaraya Indon
87B2	Palani India
85C4	Palanpur India
100B3	Palapye Botswana
17B2	Palatka USA
71E3	Palau Is Pacific O
76B3	Palaw Burma
79A4	Palawan I Phil
79A4	Palawan Pass Phil
87B3	Palayankottai India
39J7	Paldiski Estonia
78A3	Palembang Indon
50B1	Palencia Spain
94A1	Paleokhorio Cyprus
53B3	Palermo Italy
94B3	Palestine Region, Israel
19A3	Palestine USA
86C2	Paletwa Burma
87B2	Pālghāt India
85C3	Pāli India
85C4	Pālitāna India
87B3	Palk Str India/ Sri Lanka
61G3	Pallasovka Russian Fed
38J5	Pallastunturi Mt Fin
111B2	Palliser B NZ
111C2	Palliser,C NZ
101D2	Palma Mozam
51C2	Palma de Mallorca Spain
31D3	Palmares Brazil

26A5	Palmar Sur Costa Rica
97B4	Palmas,C Lib
26B2	Palma Soriano Cuba
17B2	Palm Bay USA
17B2	Palm Beach USA
22C3	Palmdale USA
31D3	Palmeira dos Indos Brazil
12E2	Palmer USA
112C3	Palmer Base Ant
112C3	Palmer Arch Ant
112B3	Palmer Land Region Ant
111B3	Palmerston NZ
110C2	Palmerston North NZ
16B2	Palmerton USA
17B2	Palmetto USA
53C3	Palmi Italy
32B3	Palmira Colombia
107D2	Palm Is Aust
21B3	Palm Springs USA
18B2	Palmyra Missouri, USA
16A2	Palmyra Pennsylvania, USA
86B2	Palmyras Pt India
22A2	Palo Alto USA
78B2	Paloh Indon
99D1	Paloich Sudan
21B3	Palomar Mt USA
70D4	Palopo Indon
70C4	Palu Indon
93C2	Palu Turk
84D3	Palwal India
97C3	Pama Burkina
78C4	Pamekasan Indon
78B4	Pameungpeuk Indon
48C3	Pamiers France
82B2	Pamir Mts China
65J6	Pamir R Russian Fed
11C3	Pamlico Sd USA
9C3	Pampa USA
34B2	Pampa de la Salinas Salt pan Arg
34B3	Pampa de la Varita Plain Arg
32C2	Pamplona Colombia
50B1	Pamplona Spain
18C2	Pana USA
54B2	Panagyurishte Bulg
87A1	Panaji India
32B2	Panamá Panama
32A2	Panama Republic, Cent America
26B5	Panama Canal Panama
17A1	Panama City USA
21B2	Panamint Range Mts USA
21B2	Panamint V USA
47D2	Panaro R Italy
79B3	Panay I Phil
54B2	Pancevo Serbia, Yugos
79B3	Pandan Phil
87B1	Pandharpur India
108A1	Pandie Pandie Aust
58C1	Panevežys Lithuania
65K5	Panfilov Kazakhstan
76B1	Pang R Burma
99D3	Pangani Tanz
99D3	Pangani R Tanz
98C3	Pangi Zaïre
78B3	Pangkalpinang Indon
6D3	Pangnirtung Can
76B1	Pangtara Burma
79B4	Pangutaran Group Is Phil
84D3	Panipat India
84B2	Panjao Afghan
74B3	P'anmunjŏm N Korea
86A2	Panna India
35A2	Panorama Brazil
53B3	Pantelleria I Medit S
23B1	Pantepec Mexico
23B1	Panuco Mexico
23B1	Pánuco R Mexico
73A4	Pan Xian China
53C3	Paola Italy
18B2	Paola USA
14A3	Paoli USA
59B3	Pápa Hung

110B1	Papakura NZ
23B2	Papaloapan R Mexico
23B1	Papantla Mexico
44E1	Papa Stour I Scot
110B1	Papatoetoe NZ
44C2	Papa Westray I Scot
107D1	Papua,G of PNG
107D1	Papua New Guinea Republic, S E Asia
34A2	Papudo Chile
76B2	Papun Burma
33G4	Para State, Brazil
31B2	Pará R Brazil
106A3	Paraburdoo Aust
32B6	Paracas,Pen de Peru
35B1	Paracatu Brazil
35B1	Paracatu R Brazil
108A2	Parachilna Aust
84C2	Parachinar Pak
54B2	Paracin Serbia, Yugos
35C1	Pará de Minas Brazil
21A2	Paradise California, USA
18B2	Paragould USA
33E6	Paraguá R Bol
33E2	Paragua R Ven
30E2	Paraguai R Brazil
30E4	Paraguari Par
30E3	Paraguay Republic, S America
30E3	Paraguay R Par
31D3	Paraiba State, Brazil
35B2	Paraiba R Brazil
35C2	Paraiba do Sul R Brazil
97C4	Parakou Benin
108A2	Parakylia Aust
87B3	Paramakkudi India
33F2	Paramaribo Surinam
69H1	Paramushir I Russian Fed
30F3	Paraná State, Brazil
34C2	Paraná Urug
29E2	Paraná R Arg
31B4	Paraná R Brazil
35A2	Paraná R Brazil
30G4	Paranaguá Brazil
35A1	Paranaiba Brazil
35A1	Paranaiba R Brazil
35A2	Paranapanema R Brazil
35A2	Paranavai Brazil
79B4	Parang Phil
35C1	Paraope R Brazil
110B2	Paraparaumu NZ
87B1	Parbhani India
94B2	Pardes Hanna Israel
34D3	Pardo Arg
35D1	Pardo R Bahia, Brazil
35A2	Pardo R Mato Grosso do Sul, Brazil
35B1	Pardo R Minas Gerais, Brazil
35B2	Pardo R Sao Paulo, Brazil
59B2	Pardubice Czech
69F4	Parece Vela Reef Pacific O
10C2	Parent Can
70C4	Parepare Indon
34C3	Parera Arg
70B4	Pariaman Indon
33E1	Paria,Pen de Ven
48C2	Paris France
14B3	Paris Kentucky, USA
19A3	Paris Texas, USA
13B2	Parkersburg USA
109C2	Parkes Aust
16B3	Parkesburg USA
14A2	Park Forest USA
20B1	Parksville Can
87B1	Parli India
47D2	Parma Italy
14B2	Parma USA
31C2	Parnaíba Brazil
31C2	Parnaíba R Brazil
55B3	Párnon Óros Mts Greece
60B2	Pärnu Estonia
86B1	Paro Bhutan
108B1	Paroo R Aust

108B2	Paroo Channel R Aust
55C3	Páros I Greece
47B2	Parpaillon Mts France
34A3	Parral Chile
109D2	Parramatta Aust
9C4	Parras Mexico
6B3	Parry B Can
4G2	Parry Is Can
7C5	Parry Sd Can
14B1	Parry Sound Can
57C3	Parsberg Germany
5F4	Parsnip R Can
18A2	Parsons Kansas, USA
14C3	Parsons West Virginia, USA
48B2	Parthenay France
53B3	Partinico Italy
74C2	Partizansk Russian Fed
33G4	Paru R Brazil
101G1	Parys S Africa
19A4	Pasadena Texas, USA
22C3	Pasadena California, USA
78D3	Pasangkayu Indon
76B2	Pasawing Burma
19C3	Pascagoula USA
54C1	Paşcani Rom
20C1	Pasco USA
46B1	Pas-de-Calais Department, France
39G8	Pasewalk Germany
91C4	Pashū'iyeh Iran
106B4	Pasley,C Aust
29E2	Paso de los Toros Urug
29B4	Paso Limay Arg
21A2	Paso Robles USA
45B3	Passage West Irish Rep
16B2	Passaic USA
57C3	Passau Germany
30E4	Passo de los Libres Arg
47D1	Passo di Stelvio Mt Italy
30F4	Passo Fundo Brazil
35B2	Passos Brazil
47B2	Passy France
32B4	Pastaza R Peru
34C3	Pasteur Arg
5H4	Pas,The Can
32B3	Pasto Colombia
12B2	Pastol B USA
47D2	Pasubio Mt Italy
78C4	Pasuruan Indon
58C1	Pasvalys Lithuania
85C4	Pătan India
86B1	Patan Nepal
108B3	Patchewollock Aust
110B1	Patea NZ
111B2	Patea R NZ
53B3	Paterno Italy
16B2	Paterson USA
111A3	Paterson Inlet B NZ
84D2	Pathankot India
84D2	Patiāla India
32B6	Pativilca Peru
55C3	Pátmos I Greece
86B1	Patna India
93D2	Patnos Turk
63D2	Patomskoye Nagor'ye Upland Russian Fed
31D3	Patos Brazil
35B1	Patos de Minas Brazil
34B2	Patquia Arg
55B3	Pátrai Greece
35B1	Patrocinio Brazil
99E3	Patta I Kenya
78D4	Pattallasang Indon
77C4	Pattani Thai
22B2	Patterson California, USA
19B4	Patterson Louisiana, USA
12H2	Patterson,Mt Can
22C2	Patterson Mt USA
13B1	Pattullo,Mt Can
31D3	Patu Brazil
86C2	Patuakhali Bang

25D3 **Patuca** *R* Honduras
23A2 **Patzcuaro** Mexico
48B3 **Pau** France
4F3 **Paulatuk** Can
31C3 **Paulistana** Brazil
101H1 **Paulpietersburg** S Africa
19A3 **Pauls Valley** USA
76B2 **Paungde** Burma
84D2 **Pauri** India
38H5 **Pauskie** Nor
35C1 **Pavão** Brazil
47C2 **Pavia** Italy
65J4 **Pavlodar** Kazakhstan
61J2 **Pavlovka** Russian Fed
61F2 **Pavlovo** Russian Fed
61F3 **Pavlovsk** Russian Fed
78C3 **Pawan** *R* Indon
18A2 **Pawhuska** USA
16D2 **Pawtucket** USA
47B1 **Payerne** Switz
20C2 **Payette** USA
7C4 **Payne,L** Can
34D2 **Paysandu** Urug
46A2 **Pays-de-Bray** Region, France
54B2 **Pazardzhik** Bulg
13D1 **Peace** *R* Can
17B2 **Peace** *R* USA
13D1 **Peace River** Can
43D3 **Peak District Nat Pk** Eng
108A1 **Peake** *R* Aust
109C2 **Peak Hill** Aust
71E4 **Peak Mandala** *Mt* Indon
42D3 **Peak,The** *Mt* Eng
19B3 **Pearl** *R* USA
21C4 **Pearl City** Hawaiian Is
21C4 **Pearl Harbor** Hawaiian Is
4H2 **Peary Chan** Can
101C2 **Pebane** Mozam
54B2 **Peć** Serbia, Yugos
35C1 **Peçanha** Brazil
19B4 **Pecan Island** USA
38L5 **Pechenga** Russian Fed
64F3 **Pechora** *R* Russian Fed
64G3 **Pechorskoye More** *S* Russian Fed
53C3 **Pecoraro** *Mt* Italy
9C3 **Pecos** USA
9C3 **Pecos** *R* USA
59B3 **Pécs** Hung
108A1 **Pedirka** Aust
35C1 **Pedra Azul** Brazil
35B2 **Pedregulho** Brazil
26B3 **Pedro Cays** *Is* Caribbean S
30C3 **Pedro de Valdivia** Chile
30E3 **Pedro Juan Caballero** Par
34C3 **Pedro Luro** Arg
23B1 **Pedro Mentova** Mexico
87C3 **Pedro,Pt** Sri Lanka
108B2 **Peebinga** Aust
42C2 **Peebles** Scot
17C1 **Pee Dee** *R* USA
16C2 **Peekskill** USA
42B2 **Peel** Eng
12H1 **Peel** *R* Can
4J2 **Peel Sd** Can
108A1 **Peera Peera Poolanna** *L* Aust
13E1 **Peerless L** Can
71E4 **Peg Arfak** *Mt* Indon
111B2 **Pegasus B** NZ
83D4 **Pegu** Burma
78A3 **Pegunungan Barisan** *Mts* Indon
78C2 **Pegunungan Iran** *Mts* Malay/Indon
71E4 **Pegunungan Maoke** *Mts* Indon
78D3 **Pegunungan Meratus** *Mts* Indon
78C2 **Pegunungan Muller** *Mts* Indon
78C3 **Pegunungan Schwanet** *Mts* Indon
78A3 **Pegunungan Tigapuluh** *Mts* Indon
76B2 **Pegu Yoma** *Mts* Burma
34C3 **Pehuajó** Arg
39K7 **Péipsi Järve** *L* Estonia
39K7 **Peipus, Lake** Estonia/ Russian Fed
35A2 **Peixe** *R* Sao Paulo, Brazil
72D3 **Pei Xian** China
78B4 **Pekalongan** Indon
77C5 **Pekan** Malay
78A2 **Pekanbaru** Indon
18C1 **Pekin** USA
Peking = Beijing
77C5 **Pelabohan Kelang** Malay
78D4 **Pelau Pelau Kangean** *Is* Indon
78C4 **Pelau Pelau Karimunjawa** *Arch* Indon
78D4 **Pelau Pelau Postilyon** *Is* Indon
54B1 **Peleaga** *Mt* Rom
63D2 **Peleduy** Russian Fed
14B2 **Pelee I** Can
71D4 **Peleng** *I* Indon
12G3 **Pelican** USA
69F1 **Peliny Osipenko** Russian Fed
34C3 **Pellegrini** Arg
38J5 **Pello** Fin
12H2 **Pelly** *R* Can
6A3 **Pelly Bay** Can
12G2 **Pelly Crossing** Can
12H2 **Pelly Mts** Can
30F5 **Pelotas** Brazil
30F4 **Pelotas** *R* Brazil
47B2 **Pelvoux** Region, France
78B4 **Pemalang** Indon
78A3 **Pematang** Indon
101D2 **Pemba** Mozam
99D3 **Pemba** *I* Tanz
13C2 **Pemberton** Can
13D2 **Pembina** *R* Can
15C1 **Pembroke** Can
17B1 **Pembroke** USA
43B4 **Pembroke** Wales
34A3 **Pemuco** Chile
78D2 **Penambo Range** *Mts* Malay
35A2 **Penápolis** Brazil
50A2 **Peñarroya** Spain
51B1 **Penarroya** *Mt* Spain
50A1 **Peña Trevina** *Mt* Spain
98B2 **Pende** *R* Chad
12J3 **Pendelton,Mt** Can
20C1 **Pendleton** USA
20C1 **Pend Oreille** *R* USA
31D4 **Penedo** Brazil
85D5 **Penganga** *R* India
73D5 **P'eng-hu Lieh-tao** *Is* Taiwan
72E2 **Penglai** China
73B4 **Pengshui** China
71E4 **Pengunungan Maoke** *Mts* Indon
26C4 **Península de la Guajiri** *Pen* Colombia
27E4 **Península de Paria** *Pen* Ven
77C5 **Peninsular Malaysia** Malay
10D2 **Peninsule de Gaspé** *Pen* Can
23A1 **Penjamo** Mexico
87B2 **Penner** *R* India
42C2 **Pennine Chain** *Mts* Eng
16B3 **Penns Grove** USA
10C2 **Pennsylvania** State, USA
6D3 **Penny Highlands** *Mts* Can
108B3 **Penola** Aust
106C4 **Penong** Aust
42C2 **Penrith** Eng
11B3 **Pensacola** USA
112A **Pensacola Mts** Ant
78D1 **Pensiangan** Malay
13D3 **Penticton** Can
44C2 **Pentland Firth** *Chan* Scot
42C2 **Pentland Hills** Scot
61G3 **Penza** Russian Fed
43B4 **Penzance** Eng
10B2 **Peoria** USA
78A3 **Perabumulih** Indon
77C5 **Perak** *R* Malay
78A2 **Perawang** Indon
32B3 **Pereira** Colombia
35A2 **Pereira Barreto** Brazil
61F4 **Perelazovskiy** Russian Fed
12D3 **Perenosa B** USA
34C2 **Pergamino** Arg
7C4 **Peribonca** *R* Can
48C2 **Périqueux** France
25E4 **Perlas Arch de** *Is* Panama
61J2 **Perm'** Russian Fed
Pernambuco = Recife
31D3 **Pernambuco** State, Brazil
108A2 **Pernatty Lg** Aust
54B2 **Pernik** Bulg
46B2 **Péronne** France
23B2 **Perote** Mexico
49C3 **Perpignan** France
22D4 **Perris** USA
17B1 **Perry** Florida, USA
17B1 **Perry** Georgia, USA
18A2 **Perry** Oklahoma, USA
4H3 **Perry River** Can
14B2 **Perrysburg** USA
12C3 **Perryville** Alaska, USA
18C2 **Perryville** Missouri, USA
106A4 **Perth** Aust
15C2 **Perth** Can
44C3 **Perth** Scot
16B2 **Perth Amboy** USA
32C6 **Peru** Republic, S America
18C1 **Peru** USA
103E5 **Peru-Chile Trench** Pacific O
52B2 **Perugia** Italy
52C2 **Perušic** Croatia
93D2 **Pervari** Turk
61F3 **Pervomaysk** Russian Fed
60D4 **Pervomaysk** Ukraine
61J2 **Pervoural'sk** Russian Fed
52B2 **Pesaro** Italy
22A2 **Pescadero** USA
Pescadores = P'eng-hu Lieh-tao
52B2 **Pescara** Italy
47D2 **Peschiera** Italy
84C2 **Peshawar** Pak
54B2 **Peshkopi** Alb
14A1 **Peshtigo** USA
60E2 **Pestovo** Russian Fed
94B2 **Petah Tiqwa** Israel
21A2 **Petaluma** USA
46C2 **Pétange** Lux
23A2 **Petatlán** Mexico
101C2 **Petauke** Zambia
108A2 **Peterborough** Aust
15C2 **Peterborough** Can
43D3 **Peterborough** Eng
44D3 **Peterhead** Scot
6D1 **Petermann Gletscher** *Gl* Greenland
106B3 **Petermann Range** *Mts* Aust
29B3 **Peteroa** *Mt* Arg/Chile
13F1 **Peter Pond L** Can
12H3 **Petersburg** Alaska, USA
85C4 **Petlād** India
23B2 **Petlalcingo** Mexico
25D2 **Peto** Mexico
63D2 **Petomskoye Nagor'ye** *Upland* Russian Fed
34A2 **Petorca** Chile
14B1 **Petoskey** USA
31C3 **Petrolina** Brazil
65H4 **Petropavlovsk** Kazakhstan
35C2 **Petrópolis** Brazil
61G3 **Petrovsk** Russian Fed
68C1 **Petrovsk Zabaykal'skiy** Russian Fed
64E3 **Petrozavodsk** Russian Fed
101G1 **Petrus** S Africa
101G1 **Petrusburg** S Africa
1B7 **Pevek** Russian Fed
46D2 **Pfälzer Wald** Region, Germany
57B3 **Pforzheim** Germany
84D2 **Phagwara** India
85C3 **Phalodi** India
46D2 **Phalsbourg** France
87A1 **Phaltan** India
77B4 **Phangnga** Thai
76C3 **Phanom Dang** *Mts* Camb
76D3 **Phan Rang** Viet
76D3 **Phan Thiet** Viet
17A1 **Phenix City** USA
76B3 **Phet Buri** Thai
76D3 **Phiafay** Laos
19C3 **Philadelphia** Mississippi, USA
16B2 **Philadelphia** Pennsylvania, USA
Philippeville = Skikda
46C1 **Philippeville** Belg
71D2 **Philippine S** Pacific O
71D2 **Philippines** Republic, S E Asia
104E3 **Philippine Trench** Pacific O
15C2 **Philipsburg** Pennsylvania, USA
12E1 **Philip Smith Mts** USA
79B2 **Phillipine S** Phil
6B1 **Phillips B** Can
16B2 **Phillipsburg** New Jersey, USA
6B2 **Philpots Pen** Can
76C3 **Phnom Penh** Camb
9B3 **Phoenix** Arizona, USA
16B2 **Phoenixville** USA
76C1 **Phong Saly** Laos
Phra Nakhon = Bangkok
76C2 **Phu Bia** *Mt* Laos
76D3 **Phu Cuong** Viet
77B4 **Phuket** Thai
86A2 **Phulbāni** India
76C2 **Phu Miang** *Mt* Thai
76D2 **Phu Set** *Mt* Laos
76D1 **Phu Tho** Viet
77D4 **Phu Vinh** Viet
47C2 **Piacenza** Italy
109C2 **Pian** *R* Aust
52B2 **Pianosa** *I* Italy
52C2 **Pianosa** *I* Italy
58C2 **Piaseczno** Pol
54C1 **Piatra-Neamţ** Rom
31C3 **Piaui** State, Brazil
47E2 **Piave** *R* Italy
99D2 **Pibor** *R* Sudan
99D2 **Pibor Post** Sudan
46B1 **Picardie** Region, France
19C3 **Picayune** USA
47B2 **Pic de Rochebrune** *Mt* France
34A2 **Pichilemu** Chile
34C3 **Pichi Mahuida** Arg
42D2 **Pickering** Eng
7A4 **Pickle Lake** Can
96A1 **Pico** *I* Açores
47C1 **Pico Bernina** *Mt* Switz
51C1 **Pico de Anito** *Mt* Spain
24B3 **Pico del Infiernillo** *Mt* Mexico

27C3 **Pico Duarte** *Mt* Dom Rep
31C3 **Picos** Brazil
50B1 **Picos de Europa** *Mt* Spain
109D2 **Picton** Aust
111B2 **Picton** NZ
95A2 **Pic Toussidé** *Mt* Chad
35B2 **Piedade** Brazil
22C2 **Piedra** USA
24B2 **Piedras Negras** Mexico
38K6 **Pieksämäki** Fin
38K6 **Pielinen** *L* Fin
47B2 **Piemonte** Region, Italy
8C2 **Pierre** USA
59B3 **Pieštany** Czech
101H1 **Pietermaritzburg** S Africa
100B3 **Pietersburg** S Africa
101H1 **Piet Retief** S Africa
60B4 **Pietrosu** *Mt* Rom
47E1 **Pieve di Cadore** Italy
13E2 **Pigeon L** Can
18B2 **Piggott** USA
34C3 **Pigüé** Arg
7A4 **Pikangikum L** Can
8C3 **Pikes Peak** USA
100A4 **Piketberg** S Africa
6F3 **Pikintaleq** Greenland
82B2 **Pik Kommunizma** *Mt* Tajikistan
98B2 **Pikounda** Congo
82C1 **Pik Pobedy** *Mt* China/Kirgizia
34D3 **Pila** Arg
58B2 **Pila** Pol
30E4 **Pilar** Par
30D3 **Pilcomayo** *R* Arg/Par
84D3 **Pīlībhīt** India
59B2 **Pilica** *R* Pol
109C4 **Pillar,C** Aust
55B3 **Pílos** Greece
12C3 **Pilot Point** USA
12B2 **Pilot Station** USA
19C3 **Pilottown** USA
33F4 **Pimenta** Brazil
77C4 **Pinang** *I* Malay
26A2 **Pinar del Rio** Cuba
34B2 **Pinas** Arg
46C1 **Pinche** Belg
13E2 **Pincher Creek** Can
31B2 **Pindaré** *R* Brazil
55B3 **Píndhos** *Mts* Greece
19B3 **Pine Bluff** USA
106C2 **Pine Creek** Aust
22C1 **Pinecrest** USA
22C2 **Pinedale** California, USA
22C2 **Pine Flat Res** USA
64F3 **Pinega** *R* Russian Fed
16A2 **Pine Grove** USA
17B2 **Pine Hills** USA
17B2 **Pine I** USA
19B3 **Pineland** USA
17B2 **Pinellas Park** USA
5G3 **Pine Point** Can
47B2 **Pinerolo** Italy
19B3 **Pines,Lo'the** USA
19B3 **Pineville** USA
72C3 **Pingdingshan** China
73B5 **Pingguo** China
72B2 **Pingliang** China
72B2 **Pingluo** China
73D4 **Pingtan Dao** *I* China
73E5 **P'ing tung** Taiwan
72A3 **Pingwu** China
73B5 **Pingxiang** Guangxi, China
73C4 **Pingxiang** Jiangxi, China
31B2 **Pinheiro** Brazil
70A3 **Pini** *I* Indon
55B3 **Piniós** *R* Greece
106A4 **Pinjarra** Aust
13C1 **Pink Mountain** Can
108B3 **Pinnaroo** Aust
Pinos,I de, I = Isla de la Juventud
21A2 **Pinos,Pt** USA
23B2 **Pinotepa Nacional** Mexico
70C4 **Pinrang** Indon
60C3 **Pinsk** Belorussia
32J7 **Pinta** *I* Ecuador
61G1 **Pinyug** Russian Fed
8B3 **Pioche** USA
52B2 **Piombino** Italy
6H3 **Piórsá** Iceland
59B2 **Piotroków Trybunalski** Pol
44E2 **Piper** *Oilfield* N Sea
21B2 **Piper Peak** *Mt* USA
10C2 **Pipmuacan Res** Can
14B2 **Piqua** USA
35B1 **Piracanjuba** Brazil
35B2 **Piracicaba** Brazil
35B2 **Piraçunung**a Brazil
35B2 **Piraí do Sul** Brazil
55B3 **Piraiévs** Greece
35B2 **Pirajuí** Brazil
35A1 **Piranhas** Brazil
35C1 **Pirapora** Brazil
35B1 **Pirenópolis** Brazil
35B1 **Pires do Rio** Brazil
55B3 **Pírgos** Greece
Pirineos = Pyrénees
31C2 **Piripiri** Brazil
46D2 **Pirmasens** Germany
54B2 **Pirot** Serbia, Yugos
84C2 **Pīr Panjāl Range** *Mts* Pak
71D4 **Piru** Indon
22C3 **Piru Creek** *R* USA
49E3 **Pisa** Italy
32B6 **Pisco** Peru
57C3 **Písek** Czech
84B2 **Pishin** Pak
30C4 **Pissis** *Mt* Arg
49E3 **Pistoia** Italy
50B1 **Pisuerga** *R* Spain
20B2 **Pit** *R* USA
32B3 **Pitalito** Colombia
105K5 **Pitcairn** *I* Pacific O
38H5 **Pite** *R* Sweden
38J5 **Piteå** Sweden
54B2 **Piteşti** Rom
63B2 **Pit Gorodok** Russian Fed
38L6 **Pitkyaranta** Russian Fed
44C3 **Pitlochry** Scot
34A3 **Pitrutquén** Chile
13B2 **Pitt I** Can
22B1 **Pittsburg** California, USA
18B2 **Pittsburg** Kansas, USA
14C2 **Pittsburgh** USA
18B2 **Pittsfield** Illinois, USA
16C1 **Pittsfield** Massachusetts, USA
109D1 **Pittsworth** Aust
86A1 **Piuthan** Nepal
47D1 **Pizzo Redorta** *Mt* Italy
38B2 **Pjórsá** Iceland
32A5 **Pjura** Peru
7E5 **Placentia B** Can
22B1 **Placerville** USA
46B1 **Plaine des Flandres** *Plain* Belg/France
96C2 **Plaine du Tidikelt** *Desert* Region
9C3 **Plainview** Texas, USA
22B2 **Planada** USA
30F2 **Planalto de Mato Grosso** *Plat* Brazil
31D3 **Planalto do Borborema** *Plat* Brazil
32A1 **Planalto do Mato Grosso** *Mts* Brazil
19A3 **Plano** USA
17B2 **Plantation** USA
17B2 **Plant City** USA
50A1 **Plasencia** Spain
61K3 **Plast** Russian Fed
69F2 **Plastun** Russian Fed
96C2 **Plateau du Tademait** Alg
46D2 **Plateau Lorrain** *Plat* France
48C2 **Plateaux de Limousin** *Plat* France
51C2 **Plateaux du Sersou** *Plat* Alg
26C5 **Plato** Colombia
65G5 **Plato Ustyurt** *Plat* Kazakhstan
8C2 **Platte** *R* USA
15D2 **Plattsburgh** USA
18A1 **Plattsmouth** USA
57C2 **Plauen** Germany
60E3 **Plavsk** Russian Fed
23A2 **Playa Azul** Mexico
32A4 **Playas** Ecuador
23B2 **Playa Vicente** Mexico
50A1 **Plaza de Moro Almanzor** *Mt* Spain
22B2 **Pleasanton** California, USA
16B3 **Pleasantville** USA
14A3 **Pleasure Ridge Park** USA
76D3 **Pleiku** Viet
110C1 **Plenty,B of** NZ
58B2 **Pleszew** Pol
7C4 **Pletipi,L** Can
54B2 **Pleven** Bulg
54A2 **Pljevlja** Montenegro, Yugos
52C2 **Ploče** Bosnia & Herzegovina, Yugos
58B2 **Płock** Pol
48B2 **Ploërmel** France
54C2 **Ploieşti** Rom
60B3 **Płońsk** Pol
54B2 **Plovdiv** Bulg
20C1 **Plummer** USA
12C2 **Plummer,Mt** USA
100B3 **Plumtree** Zim
22B1 **Plymouth** California, USA
43B4 **Plymouth** Eng
14A2 **Plymouth** Indiana, USA
16D2 **Plymouth** Massachusetts, USA
15C2 **Plymouth** Pennsylvania, USA
43B4 **Plymouth Sd** Eng
43C3 **Plynlimon** *Mt* Wales
57C3 **Plzeň** Czech
58B2 **Pniewy** Pol
38K6 **Pnyäselkä** *L* Fin
97B3 **Pô** Burkina
47E2 **Po** *R* Italy
97C4 **Pobé** Benin
69G2 **Pobedino** Russian Fed
8B2 **Pocatello** USA
15C3 **Pocomoke City** USA
35B2 **Pocos de Caldas** Brazil
47D2 **Po di Volano** *R* Italy
63B1 **Podkamennaya** *R* Russian Fed
60E2 **Podol'sk** Russian Fed
59D3 **Podol'skaya Vozvyshennost'** *Upland* Ukraine
60D1 **Podporozh'ye** Russian Fed
61F1 **Podyuga** Russian Fed
100A3 **Pofadder** S Africa
74B3 **P'ohang** S Korea
112C9 **Poinsett,C** Ant
108C2 **Point** Aust
27E3 **Pointe-à-Pitre** Guadeloupe
48B2 **Pointe de Barfleur** *Pt* France
98B3 **Pointe Noire** Congo
98A2 **Pointe Pongara** *Pt* Gabon
108B3 **Point Fairy** Aust
27L1 **Point Fortin** Trinidad
4B3 **Point Hope** USA
4G3 **Point L** Can
12B1 **Point Lay** USA
16B2 **Point Pleasant** New Jersey, USA
14B3 **Point Pleasant** W Virginia, USA
47B2 **Point St Bernard** *Mt* France
48C2 **Poitiers** France
48B2 **Poitou** Region, France
46A2 **Poix** France
85C3 **Pokaran** India
109C1 **Pokataroo** Aust
63E1 **Pokrovsk** Russian Fed
58B2 **Poland** Republic, Europe
92B2 **Polatli** Turk
78D3 **Polewali** Indon
47A1 **Poligny** France
55B2 **Políyiros** Greece
87B2 **Pollāchi** India
79B3 **Polollo Is** Phil
59D2 **Polonnye** Ukraine
58D1 **Polotsk** Russian Fed
60D4 **Poltava** Russian Fed
52C1 **Pölten** Austria
64F3 **Poluostrov Kanin** *Pen* Russian Fed
61H5 **Poluostrov Mangyshlak** *Pen* Kazakhstan
38L5 **Poluostrov Rybachiy** *Pen* Russian Fed
64H2 **Poluostrov Yamal** *Pen* Russian Fed
38L5 **Polyarnyy** Murmansk, Russian Fed
1B8 **Polyarnyy** Yakutskaya, Russian Fed
105H3 **Polynesia** *Region* Pacific O
32B5 **Pomabamba** Peru
35C2 **Pomba** *R* Brazil
22D3 **Pomona** USA
18A2 **Pomona Res** USA
17B2 **Pompano Beach** USA
16B2 **Pompton Lakes** USA
18A2 **Ponca City** USA
27D3 **Ponce** Puerto Rico
17B2 **Ponce de Leon B** USA
87B2 **Pondicherry** India
6C2 **Pond Inlet** Can
50A1 **Ponferrade** Spain
98C2 **Pongo** *R* Sudan
101H1 **Pongola** *R* S Africa
87B2 **Ponnāni** India
86C2 **Ponnyadoung Range** *Mts* Burma
13E2 **Ponoka** Can
64F3 **Ponoy** Russian Fed
48B2 **Pons** France
35D1 **Ponta da Baleia** *Pt* Brazil
96A1 **Ponta Delgada** Açores
98B3 **Ponta do Padrão** *Pt* Angola
35C2 **Ponta dos Búzios** *Pt* Brazil
30F4 **Ponta Grossa** Brazil
35B2 **Pontal** Brazil
46D2 **Pont-à-Mousson** France
30E3 **Ponta Pora** Brazil
49D2 **Pontarlier** France
19B3 **Pontchartrain,L** USA
52B2 **Pontedera** Italy
52A2 **Ponte Leccia** Corse
50A1 **Pontevedra** Spain
18C1 **Pontiac** Illinois, USA
14B2 **Pontiac** Michigan, USA
78B3 **Pontianak** Indon
48B2 **Pontivy** France
46B2 **Pontoise** France
19C3 **Pontotoc** USA
43C4 **Pontypool** Wales
43C4 **Pontypridd** Wales
43D4 **Poole** Eng
Poona = Pune
108B2 **Pooncarie** Aust
108B2 **Poopelloe,L** *L* Aust
12C2 **Poorman** USA
32B3 **Popayán** Colombia
46B1 **Poperinge** Belg

108B2 **Popilta L** Aust
18B2 **Poplar Bluff** USA
19C3 **Poplarville** USA
107D1 **Popndetta** PNG
23B2 **Popocatepetl** *Mt* Mexico
98B3 **Popokabaka** Zaïre
71F4 **Popondetta** PNG
54C2 **Popovo** Bulg
85B4 **Porbandar** India
13A2 **Porcher I** Can
12F1 **Porcupine** *R* Can/USA
52B1 **Poreč** Croatia
35A2 **Porecatu** Brazil
39J6 **Pori** Fin
111B2 **Porirua** NZ
38H5 **Porjus** Sweden
69G2 **Poronaysk** Russian Fed
47B1 **Porrentruy** Switz
38K4 **Porsangen** *Inlet* Nor
39F7 **Porsgrunn** Nor
45C1 **Portadown** N Ire
8D2 **Portage la Prairie** Can
13C3 **Port Alberni** Can
50A2 **Portalegre** Port
9C3 **Portales** USA
100B4 **Port Alfred** S Africa
13B2 **Port Alice** Can
19B3 **Port Allen** USA
20B1 **Port Angeles** USA
26B3 **Port Antonio** Jamaica
45C2 **Portarlington** Irish Rep
19B4 **Port Arthur** USA
108A2 **Port Augusta** Aust
26C3 **Port-au-Prince** Haiti
14B2 **Port Austin** USA
108B3 **Port Campbell** Aust
86B2 **Port Canning** India
7D5 **Port Cartier** Can
111B3 **Port Chalmers** NZ
17B2 **Port Charlotte** USA
16C2 **Port Chester** USA
15C2 **Port Colborne** Can
15C2 **Port Credit** Can
109C4 **Port Davey** Aust
26C3 **Port-de-Paix** Haiti
77C5 **Port Dickson** Malay
100C4 **Port Edward** S Africa
35C1 **Porteirinha** Brazil
14B2 **Port Elgin** Can
100B4 **Port Elizabeth** S Africa
27N2 **Porter Pt** St Vincent
21B2 **Porterville** USA
107D4 **Port Fairy** Aust
98A3 **Port Gentil** Gabon
19B3 **Port Gibson** USA
12D3 **Port Graham** USA
20B1 **Port Hammond** Can
89E7 **Port Harcourt** Nig
13B2 **Port Hardy** Can
7D5 **Port Hawkesbury** Can
106A3 **Port Hedland** Aust
Port Heiden = Meshik
43B3 **Porthmadog** Wales
7E4 **Port Hope Simpson** Can
22C3 **Port Hueneme** USA
14B2 **Port Huron** USA
50A2 **Portimão** Port
109D2 **Port Jackson** *B* Aust
16C2 **Port Jefferson** USA
16B2 **Port Jervis** USA
109D2 **Port Kembla** Aust
14B2 **Portland** Indiana, USA
10C2 **Portland** Maine, USA
109C2 **Portland** New South Wales, Aust
20B1 **Portland** Oregon, USA
108B3 **Portland** Victoria, Aust
27H2 **Portland Bight** *B* Jamaica
43C4 **Portland Bill** *Pt* Eng
109C4 **Portland,C** Aust
13A1 **Portland Canal** Can/USA
110C1 **Portland I** NZ
27H2 **Portland Pt** Jamaica
45C2 **Port Laoise** Irish Rep
108A2 **Port Lincoln** Aust
97A4 **Port Loko** Sierra Leone
101E3 **Port Louis** Mauritius
108B3 **Port MacDonnell** Aust
13B2 **Port McNeill** Can
109D2 **Port Macquarie** Aust
12B3 **Port Moller** USA
107D1 **Port Moresby** PNG
100A3 **Port Nolloth** S Africa
16B3 **Port Norris** USA
89E7 **Port Novo** Benin
50A1 **Porto** Port
30F5 **Pôrto Alegre** Brazil
33F6 **Pôrto Artur** Brazil
30F3 **Pôrto E Cunha** Brazil
52B2 **Portoferraio** Italy
27E4 **Port of Spain** Trinidad
47D2 **Portomaggiore** Italy
97C4 **Porto Novo** Benin
20B1 **Port Orchard** USA
20B2 **Port Orford** USA
96A1 **Porto Santo** *I* Medeira
31D5 **Pôrto Seguro** Brazil
53A2 **Porto Torres** Sardegna
53A2 **Porto Vecchio** Corse
33E5 **Pôrto Velho** Brazil
111A3 **Port Pegasus** *B* NZ
108B3 **Port Phillip B** Aust
108A2 **Port Pirie** Aust
44A3 **Portree** Scot
20B1 **Port Renfrew** Can
27J2 **Port Royal** Jamaica
17B1 **Port Royal Sd** USA
45C1 **Portrush** N Ire
92B3 **Port Said** Egypt
17A2 **Port St Joe** USA
100B4 **Port St Johns** S Africa
7E4 **Port Saunders** Can
100C4 **Port Shepstone** S Africa
13A2 **Port Simpson** Can
27Q2 **Portsmouth** Dominica
43D4 **Portsmouth** Eng
14B3 **Portsmouth** Ohio, USA
11C3 **Portsmouth** Virginia, USA
109D2 **Port Stephens** *B* Aust
95C3 **Port Sudan** Sudan
19C3 **Port Sulphur** USA
38K5 **Porttipahdan Tekojärvi** *Res* Fin
50A2 **Portugal** Republic, Europe
14A2 **Port Washington** USA
77C5 **Port Weld** Malay
32D6 **Porvenir** Bol
39K6 **Porvoo** Fin
30E4 **Posadas** Arg
50A2 **Posadas** Spain
47D1 **Poschiavo** Switz
6B2 **Posheim Pen** Can
90C3 **Posht-e Badam** Iran
71D4 **Poso** Indon
58D1 **Postavy** Belorussia
14B2 **Post Clinton** USA
100B3 **Postmasburg** S Africa
52B1 **Postojna** Slovenia
74C2 **Pos'yet** Russian Fed
101G1 **Potchetstroom** S Africa
19B2 **Poteau** USA
53C2 **Potenza** Italy
100B3 **Potgietersrus** S Africa
97D3 **Potiskum** Nig
20C1 **Potlatch** USA
15C3 **Potomac** *R* USA
30C2 **Potosi** Bol
30C4 **Potrerillos** Chile
56C2 **Potsdam** Germany
16B2 **Pottstown** USA
16A2 **Pottsville** USA
16C2 **Poughkeepsie** USA
35B2 **Pouso Alegre** Brazil
110C1 **Poverty B** NZ
61F3 **Povorino** Russian Fed
7C4 **Povungnituk** Can
8C2 **Powder** *R* USA
106C2 **Powell Creek** Aust
9B3 **Powell,L** USA
13C3 **Powell River** Can
8C2 **Power** *R* USA
43C3 **Powys** County, Wales
73D4 **Poyang Hu** *L* China
92B2 **Pozantı** Turk
23B1 **Poza Rica** Mexico
58B2 **Poznań** Pol
30E3 **Pozo Colorado** Par
53B2 **Pozzuoli** Italy
97B4 **Pra** *R* Ghana
76C3 **Prachin Buri** Thai
76B3 **Prachuap Khiri Khan** Thai
59B2 **Praděd** *Mt* Czech
49C3 **Pradelles** France
35D1 **Prado** Brazil
Prague = Praha
57C2 **Praha** Czech
97A4 **Praia** Cape Verde
33E5 **Prainha** Brazil
18B2 **Prairie Village** USA
76C3 **Prakhon Chai** Thai
35B1 **Prata** Brazil
35B1 **Prata** *R* Brazil
Prates = Dongsha Qundao
49E3 **Prato** Italy
16B1 **Prattsville** USA
17A1 **Prattville** USA
48B1 **Prawle Pt** Eng
78D4 **Praya** Indon
47D1 **Predazzo** Italy
63B2 **Predivinsk** Russian Fed
58C2 **Pregolyu** *R* Russian Fed
76D3 **Prek Kak** Camb
56C2 **Prenzlau** Germany
76A3 **Preparis** *I* Burma
76A2 **Preparis North Chan** Burma
59B3 **Přerov** Czech
23A2 **Presa del Infiernillo** Mexico
9B3 **Prescott** Arizona, USA
19B3 **Prescott** Arkansas, USA
15C2 **Prescott** Can
30D4 **Presidencia Roque Sáenz Peña** Arg
35A2 **Presidente Epitácio** Brazil
112C2 **Presidente Frei** *Base* Ant
23B2 **Presidente Migúel Aleman** *L* Mexico
35A2 **Presidente Prudente** Brazil
35A2 **Presidente Venceslau** Brazil
59C3 **Prešov** Czech
55B2 **Prespansko Jezero** *L* Macedonia, Yugos
10D2 **Presque Isle** USA
42C3 **Preston** Eng
8B2 **Preston** Idaho, USA
18B2 **Preston** Missouri, USA
42B2 **Prestwick** Scot
31B6 **Prêto** Brazil
35B1 **Prêto** *R* Brazil
101G1 **Pretoria** S Africa
55B3 **Préveza** Greece
76D3 **Prey Veng** Camb
8B3 **Price** USA
13B2 **Price I** Can
60D4 **Prichernomorskaya Nizmennost'** *Lowland* Ukraine
27M2 **Prickly Pt** Grenada
58C1 **Priekule** Lithuania
100B3 **Prieska** S Africa
20C1 **Priest L** USA
20C1 **Priest River** USA
61G4 **Prikaspiyskaya Nizmennost'** *Region* Kazakhstan
55B2 **Prilep** Macedonia, Yugos
60D3 **Priluki** Ukraine
34C2 **Primero** *R* Arg
39K6 **Primorsk** Russian Fed
60E4 **Primorsko-Akhtarsk** Russian Fed
13F2 **Primrose L** Can
5H4 **Prince Albert** Can
4F2 **Prince Albert,C** Can
4G2 **Prince Albert Pen** Can
4G2 **Prince Albert Sd** Can
6C3 **Prince Charles I** Can
112B10 **Prince Charles Mts** Ant
7D5 **Prince Edward I** Can
13C2 **Prince George** Can
4H2 **Prince Gustaf Adolp** *S* Can
5E4 **Prince of Wales** *I* USA
71F5 **Prince of Wales I** Aust
4H2 **Prince of Wales I** Can
4G2 **Prince of Wales Str** Can
4F2 **Prince Patrick I** Can
6A2 **Prince Regent Inlet** *Str* Can
13A2 **Prince Rupert** Can
107D2 **Princess Charlotte B** Aust
13B2 **Princess Royal I** Can
27L1 **Princes Town** Trinidad
13C3 **Princeton** Can
18C2 **Princeton** Kentucky, USA
18B1 **Princeton** Missouri, USA
16B2 **Princeton** New Jersey, USA
4D3 **Prince William** USA
12E2 **Prince William Sd** USA
97C4 **Principe** *I* W Africa
20B2 **Prineville** USA
12E1 **Pringle,Mt** USA
6F3 **Prins Christian Sund** *Sd* Greenland
112B12 **Prinsesse Astrid Kyst** Region, Ant
112B12 **Prinsesse Ragnhild Kyst** Region, Ant
64B2 **Prins Karls Forland** *I* Barents S
25D3 **Prinzapolca** Nic
58D2 **Pripyat'** *R* Belorussia
54B2 **Priština** Serbia, Yugos
56C2 **Pritzwalk** Germany
61F3 **Privolzhskaya Vozvyshennost'** *Upland* Russian Fed
54B2 **Prizren** Serbia, Yugos
78C4 **Probolinggo** Indon
5G5 **Procatello** USA
87B2 **Proddatūr** India
25D2 **Progreso** Mexico
20B2 **Project City** USA
61F5 **Prokhladnyy** Russian Fed
65K4 **Prokop'yevsk** Russian Fed
61F4 **Proletarskaya** Russian Fed
64G2 **Proliv Karskiye Vorota** *Str* Russian Fed
83D4 **Prome** Burma
31D4 **Propriá** Brazil
20B2 **Prospect** Oregon, USA

107D3	**Prosperine** Aust
59B3	**Prostějov** Czech
6E2	**Prøven** Greenland
49D3	**Provence** Region, France
16D2	**Providence** USA
15D2	**Provincetown** USA
49C2	**Provins** France
8B2	**Provo** USA
13E2	**Provost** Can
4D2	**Prudhoe Bay** USA
6D2	**Prudhoe Land** Greenland
58C2	**Pruszkow** Pol
60C4	**Prut** *R* Romania/ Moldavia
60C4	**Prutul** *R* Romania
58C2	**Pruzhany** Belorussia
18A2	**Pryor** USA
59C3	**Przemys'l** Pol
55C3	**Psará** *I* Greece
60C2	**Pskov** Russian Fed
58D2	**Ptich** *R* Belorussia
55B2	**Ptolemaïs** Greece
32C5	**Pucallpa** Peru
73D4	**Pucheng** China
34A3	**Pucón** Chile
38K5	**Pudasjärvi** Fin
87B2	**Pudukkottai** India
23B2	**Puebla** Mexico
23B2	**Puebla** State, Mexico
50A1	**Puebla de Sanabria** Spain
50A1	**Puebla de Trives** Spain
9C2	**Pueblo** USA
34B3	**Puelches** Arg
34B3	**Puelén** Arg
23A2	**Puenta Ixbapa** Mexico
34B2	**Puente del Inca** Arg
32A5	**Puerta Aguja** Peru
30B2	**Puerta Coles** Peru
34B2	**Puerta de los Llanos** Arg
31D3	**Puerta do Calcanhar** *Pt* Brazil
32C1	**Puerta Gallinas** Colombia
23B2	**Puerta Maldonado** *Pt* Mexico
32A2	**Puerta Mariato** Panama
29C5	**Puerta Médanosa** *Pt* Arg
23A2	**Puerta Mongrove** Mexico
25E4	**Puerta San Blas** *Pt* Panama
23A2	**Puerta San Telmo** Mexico
29B5	**Puerto Aisén** Chile
25D4	**Puerto Armuelles** Panama
33F6	**Puerto Artur** Brazil
32B3	**Puerto Asis** Colombia
32D2	**Puerto Ayacucho** Ven
25D3	**Puerto Barrios** Guatemala
32C2	**Puerto Berrio** Colombia
32D1	**Puerto Cabello** Ven
25D3	**Puerto Cabezas** Nic
32D2	**Puerto Carreño** Colombia
25D4	**Puerto Cortes** Costa Rica
25D3	**Puerto Cortés** Honduras
96A2	**Puerto del Rosario** Canary Is
30F3	**Puerto E Cunha** Brazil
32C1	**Puerto Fijo** Ven
31B3	**Puerto Franco** Brazil
32D6	**Puerto Heath** Bol
25D2	**Puerto Juarez** Mexico
33E1	**Puerto la Cruz** Ven
50B2	**Puertollano** Spain
27C4	**Puerto Lopez** Colombia

29D4	**Puerto Madryn** Arg
32D6	**Puerto Maldonado** Peru
23B2	**Puerto Marquéz** Mexico
29B4	**Puerto Montt** Chile
30E3	**Puerto Murtinho** Brazil
29B6	**Puerto Natales** Chile
24A1	**Puerto Peñasco** Mexico
29D4	**Puerto Pirámides** Arg
27C3	**Puerto Plata** Dom Rep
79A4	**Puerto Princesa** Phil
32B3	**Puerto Rico** Colombia
27D3	**Puerto Rico** *I* Caribbean S
27D3	**Puerto Rico Trench** Caribbean S
23A2	**Puerto San Juan de Lima** Mexico
33G4	**Puerto Santanga** Brazil
30E2	**Puerto Suárez** Bol
24B2	**Puerto Vallarta** Mexico
29B4	**Puerto Varas** Chile
30D2	**Puerto Villarroel** Bol
61G3	**Pugachev** Russian Fed
84C3	**Pugal** India
51C1	**Puigcerdá** Spain
111B2	**Pukaki,L** *L* NZ
74B2	**Pukch'ŏng** N Korea
110B1	**Pukekobe** NZ
111B2	**Puketeraki Range** *Mts* NZ
52B2	**Pula** Croatia
15C2	**Pulaski** New York, USA
71E4	**Pulau Kolepom** *I* Indon
70A4	**Pulau Pulau Batu** *Is* Indon
58C2	**Pulawy** Pol
87C2	**Pulicat,L** India
84B1	**Pul-i-Khumri** Afghan
87B3	**Puliyangudi** India
20C1	**Pullman** USA
71E3	**Pulo Anna Merir** *I* Pacific O
79B2	**Pulog,Mt** Phil
38L5	**Pulozero** Russian Fed
58C2	**Pultusk** Pol
30C4	**Puna de Atacama** Arg
86B1	**Punakha** Bhutan
84C2	**Punch** Pak
87A1	**Pune** India
23A2	**Punéper** Mexico
98C3	**Punia** Zaïre
34A2	**Punitaqui** Chile
84C2	**Punjab** Province, Pak
84D2	**Punjab** State, India
30B2	**Puno** Peru
24A2	**Punta Abreojos** *Pt* Mexico
53C3	**Punta Alice** *Pt* Italy
34C3	**Punta Alta** Arg
29B6	**Punta Arenas** Chile
24A2	**Punta Baja** *Pt* Mexico
34A2	**Punta Curaumilla** *Pt* Chile
100A2	**Punta da Marca** *Pt* Angola
101C3	**Punta de Barra Falsa** *Pt* Mozam
29F2	**Punta del Este** Urug
24A2	**Punta Eugenia** *Pt* Mexico
25D3	**Punta Gorda** Belize
17B2	**Punta Gorda** USA
34A3	**Punta Lavapié** *Pt* Chile
34A2	**Punta Lengua de Vaca** *Pt* Chile
53B2	**Punta Licosa** *Pt* Italy
34A1	**Punta Poroto** *Pt* Chile
9B4	**Punta San Antonia** *Pt* Mexico

34A2	**Punta Topocalma** Chile
73C4	**Puqi** China
64J3	**Pur** *R* Russian Fed
19A2	**Purcell** USA
12C1	**Purcell Mt** USA
13D2	**Purcell Mts** Can
34A3	**Purén** Chile
86B2	**Puri** India
87B1	**Pūrna** India
86B1	**Pūrnia** India
76C3	**Pursat** Camb
23A1	**Puruandro** Mexico
33E4	**Purus** *R* Brazil
19C3	**Purvis** USA
78B4	**Purwokerto** Indon
78C4	**Purworejo** Indon
85D5	**Pusad** India
74B3	**Pusan** S Korea
60D2	**Pushkin** Russian Fed
58D1	**Pustoshka** Russian Fed
82D3	**Puta** Burma
34A2	**Putaendo** Chile
110C1	**Putaruru** NZ
73D4	**Putian** China
16D2	**Putnam** USA
87B3	**Puttalam** Sri Lanka
56C2	**Puttgarden** Germany
32B4	**Putumayo** *R* Ecuador
78C2	**Putussibau** Indon
38K6	**Puulavesl** *L* Fin
20B1	**Puyallup** USA
49C2	**Puy de Sancy** *Mt* France
111A3	**Puysegur Pt** NZ
99C3	**Pweto** Zaïre
43B3	**Pwllheli** Wales
76B2	**Pyapon** Burma
61F5	**Pyatigorsk** Russian Fed
74B3	**P'yŏngyang** N Korea
108B3	**Pyramid Hill** Aust
21B1	**Pyramid L** USA
111A2	**Pyramid,Mt** NZ
48B3	**Pyrénées** *Mts* France
58D1	**Pytalovo** Russian Fed
76B2	**Pyu** Burma

Q

94B2	**Qabatiya** Israel
94C3	**Qā'el Hafira** *Mud Flats* Jordan
94C3	**Qa'el Jinz** *Mud Flats* Jordan
68B3	**Qaidam Pendi** *Salt Flat* China
94C2	**Qa Khanna** *Salt Marsh* Jordan
99D1	**Qala'en Nahl** Sudan
84B2	**Qalat** Afghan
94C1	**Qal'at al Hisn** Syria
81C3	**Qal'at Bishah** S Arabia
93E3	**Qal'at Sālih** Iraq
68B3	**Qamdo** China
99E1	**Qandala** Somalia
99E2	**Qardho** Somalia
95B2	**Qara** Egypt
90A3	**Qare Shirin** Iran
91A4	**Qaryat al Ulyā** S Arabia
94C3	**Qasr el Kharana** Jordan
91D4	**Qasr-e-Qand** Iran
95B2	**Qasr Farafra** Egypt
94C2	**Qatana** Syria
91B4	**Qatar** Emirate, Arabian Pen
94C3	**Qatrāna** Jordan
95B2	**Qattâra Depression** Egypt
90C3	**Qāyen** Iran
90A2	**Qazvin** Iran
95C2	**Qena** Egypt
90A2	**Qeydār** Iran
91B4	**Qeys** *I* Iran
94B3	**Qeziot** Israel
73B5	**Qian Jiang** *R* China
72E1	**Qian Shan** *Upland* China
72E3	**Qidong** China
73B4	**Qijiang** China

84B2	**Qila Saifullah** Pak
72A2	**Qilian** China
68B3	**Qilian Shan** China
72B3	**Qin'an** China
72E2	**Qingdao** China
72A2	**Qinghai** Province, China
68B3	**Qinghai Hu** *L* China
72D3	**Qingjiang** Jiangsu, China
73D4	**Qingjiang** Jiangxi, China
72B3	**Qing Jiang** *R* China
72C2	**Qingshuihe** China
72B2	**Qingshui He** *R* China
72B2	**Qingtonxia** China
72B2	**Qingyang** China
74B2	**Qingyuan** Liaoning, China
73D4	**Qingyuan** Zhejiang, China
82C2	**Qing Zang** *Upland* China
72D2	**Qinhuangdao** China
72B3	**Qin Ling** *Mts* China
73B5	**Qinzhou** China
76E2	**Qionghai** China
73A3	**Qionglai Shan** *Upland* China
76D1	**Qiongzhou Haixia** *Str* China
69E2	**Qiqihar** China
94B2	**Qiryat Ata** Israel
94B3	**Qiryat Gat** Israel
94B2	**Qiryat Shemona** Israel
94B2	**Qiryat Yam** Israel
94B2	**Qishon** *R* Israel
63A3	**Qitai** China
73C4	**Qiyang** China
72B1	**Qog Qi** China
90B2	**Qolleh-ye Damavand** *Mt* Iran
90B3	**Qom** Iran
90B3	**Qomisheh** Iran
	Qomolangma Feng = **Everest,Mt**
94C1	**Qornet es Saouda** *Mt* Leb
6E3	**Qôrnoq** Greenland
90A2	**Qorveh** Iran
91C4	**Qotābad** Iran
16C1	**Qquabbin Res** USA
16B2	**Quakertown** USA
77C3	**Quam Phu Quoc** *I* Viet
76D2	**Quang Ngai** Viet
76D2	**Quang Tri** Viet
77D4	**Quan Long** Viet
73D5	**Quanzhou** Fujian, China
73C4	**Quanzhou** Guangxi, China
5H4	**Qu' Appelle** *R* Can
91C5	**Quarayyät** Oman
13B2	**Quatsino Sd** Can
90C2	**Quchan** Iran
109C3	**Queanbeyan** Aust
15D1	**Québec** Can
7C4	**Quebec** Province, Can
35B1	**Quebra-Anzol** *R* Brazil
34D2	**Quebracho** Urug
30F4	**Quedas do Iguaçu** Brazil/Arg
16A3	**Queen Anne** USA
13B2	**Queen Bess,Mt** Can
5E4	**Queen Charlotte** *Is* Can
13B2	**Queen Charlotte Sd** Can
13B2	**Queen Charlotte Str** Can
4H1	**Queen Elizabeth Is** Can
112B9	**Queen Mary Land** Region, Ant
4H3	**Queen Maud G** Can
112A	**Queen Maud Mts** Ant
16C2	**Queens** Borough, New York, USA
108B3	**Queenscliff** Aust

107D3 **Queensland** State, Aust
109C4 **Queenstown** Aust
111A3 **Queenstown** NZ
100B4 **Queenstown** S Africa
16A3 **Queenstown** USA
98B3 **Quela** Angola
101C2 **Quelimane** Mozam
34C3 **Quemuquemú** Arg
13C2 **Quensel L** Can
34D3 **Quequén** Arg
34D3 **Quequén** *R* Arg
23A1 **Querétaro** Mexico
23A1 **Queretaro** *State* Mexico
13C2 **Quesnel** Can
84B2 **Quetta** Pak
25C3 **Quezaltenango** Guatemala
79B3 **Quezon City** Phil
100A2 **Quibala** Angola
98B3 **Quibaxe** Angola
32B2 **Quibdó** Colombia
48B2 **Quiberon** France
98B3 **Quicama Nat Pk** Angola
73A4 **Quijing** China
34A2 **Quilima** Chile
34C2 **Quilino** Arg
32C6 **Quillabamba** Peru
30C2 **Quillacollo** Bol
48C3 **Quillan** France
5H4 **Quill L** Can
5H4 **Quill Lakes** Can
34A2 **Quillota** Chile
Quilon = Kollam
108B1 **Quilpie** Aust
34A2 **Quilpué** Chile
98B3 **Quimbele** Angola
48B2 **Quimper** France
48B2 **Quimperlé** France
21A2 **Quincy** California, USA
10A3 **Quincy** Illinois, USA
16D1 **Quincy** Massachusetts, USA
34B2 **Quines** Arg
12B3 **Quinhagak** USA
76D3 **Qui Nhon** Viet
50B2 **Quintanar de la Orden** Spain
34A2 **Quintero** Chile
34C2 **Quinto** *R* Arg
34A3 **Quirihue** Chile
100A2 **Quirima** Angola
109D2 **Quirindi** Aust
101D2 **Quissanga** Mozam
101C3 **Quissico** Mozam
32B4 **Quito** Ecuador
31D2 **Quixadá** Brazil
108A2 **Quorn** Aust
95C2 **Quseir** Egypt
6E3 **Qutdligssat** Greenland
Quthing = Moyeni
73B3 **Qu Xian** Sichuan, China
73D4 **Qu Xian** Zhejiang, China
76D2 **Quynh Luu** Viet
72C2 **Quzhou** China
86C1 **Qüzü** China

R

38J6 **Raahe** Fin
44A3 **Raasay** *I* Scot
44A3 **Raasay,Sound of** *Chan* Scot
99F1 **Raas Caseyr** *C* Somalia
52B2 **Rab** *I* Croatia
78D4 **Raba** Indon
59B3 **Rába** *R* Hung
96B1 **Rabat** Mor
94B3 **Rabba** Jordan
80B3 **Rabigh** S Arabia
47B2 **Racconigi** Italy
7E5 **Race,C** Can
94B2 **Rachaya** Leb
57C3 **Rachel** *Mt* Germany
76D3 **Rach Gia** Viet
14A2 **Racine** USA
59D3 **Rădăuţi** Rom
85C4 **Radhanpur** India
27L1 **Radix,Pt** Trinidad
58C2 **Radom** Pol
59B2 **Radomsko** Pol
58C1 **Radviliškis** Lithuania
4G3 **Rae** Can
86A1 **Rāe Bareli** India
6B3 **Rae Isthmus** Can
4G3 **Rae L** Can
110C1 **Raetihi** NZ
34C2 **Rafaela** Arg
94B3 **Rafah** Egypt
98C2 **Rafai** CAR
93D3 **Rafhā Al Jumaymah** S Arabia
91C3 **Rafsanjān** Iran
98C2 **Raga** Sudan
27R3 **Ragged Pt** Barbados
53B3 **Ragusa** Italy
99D1 **Rahad** *R* Sudan
84C3 **Rahimyar Khan** Pak
90B3 **Rāhjerd** Iran
34D2 **Raices** Arg
87B1 **Rāichur** India
86A2 **Raigarh** India
108B3 **Rainbow** Aust
17A1 **Rainbow City** USA
20B1 **Rainier** USA
20B1 **Rainier,Mt** USA
10A2 **Rainy L** Can
12D2 **Rainy P** USA
10A2 **Rainy River** Can
86A2 **Raipur** India
87C1 **Rājahmundry** India
78C2 **Rajang** *R* Malay
84C3 **Rajanpur** Pak
87B3 **Rājapālaiyam** India
85C3 **Rājasthan** State, India
84D3 **Rājgarh** India
85D4 **Rājgarh** State, India
85C4 **Rājkot** India
86B2 **Rājmahāl Hills** India
86A2 **Raj Nāndgaon** India
85C4 **Rājpīpla** India
86B2 **Rajshahi** Bang
85D4 **Rajur** India
111B2 **Rakaia** *R* NZ
78B4 **Rakata** *I* Indon
82C3 **Raka Zangbo** *R* China
59C3 **Rakhov** Ukraine
100B3 **Rakops** Botswana
58D2 **Rakov** Belorussia
11C3 **Raleigh** USA
7A5 **Ralny L** Can
94B2 **Rama** Israel
94B3 **Ramallah** Israel
87B3 **Rāmanāthapuram** India
69G3 **Ramapo Deep** Pacific O
94B2 **Ramat Gan** Israel
46A2 **Rambouillet** France
86B2 **Rāmgarh** Bihar, India
85C3 **Rāmgarh** Rajosthan, India
90A3 **Rāmhormoz** Iran
94B3 **Ramla** Israel
91C5 **Ramlat Al Wahibah** Region, Oman
21B3 **Ramona** USA
84D3 **Rāmpur** India
85D4 **Rāmpura** India
90B2 **Rāmsar** Iran
42B2 **Ramsey** Eng
16B2 **Ramsey** USA
43B4 **Ramsey I** Wales
43E4 **Ramsgate** Eng
94C2 **Ramtha** Jordan
71F4 **Ramu** *R* PNG
34A2 **Rancagua** Chile
86B2 **Rānchi** India
86A2 **Rānchi Plat** India
101G1 **Randburg** S Africa
39G7 **Randers** Den
101G1 **Randfontein** S Africa
15D2 **Randolph** Vermont, USA
111B3 **Ranfurly** NZ
86C2 **Rangamati** Bang
111B2 **Rangiora** NZ
110C1 **Rangitaiki** *R* NZ
111B2 **Rangitate** *R* NZ
110C1 **Rangitikei** *R* NZ
76B2 **Rangoon** Burma
86B1 **Rangpur** India
87B2 **Rānībennur** India
8A2 **Ranier,Mt** *Mt* USA
86B2 **Rānīganj** India
109C2 **Rankins Springs** Aust
6A3 **Ranklin Inlet** Can
85B4 **Rann of Kachchh** *Flood Area* India
77B4 **Ranong** Thai
70A3 **Rantauparapat** Indon
18C1 **Rantoul** USA
49D3 **Rapallo** Italy
34A2 **Rapel** *R* Chile
6D3 **Raper,C** Can
8C2 **Rapid City** USA
14A1 **Rapid River** USA
15C3 **Rappahannock** *R* USA
47C1 **Rapperswil** Switz
16B2 **Raritan B** USA
95C2 **Ras Abu Shagara** *C* Sudan
93D2 **Ra's al 'Ayn** Syria
91C5 **Ra's al Hadd** *C* Oman
91C4 **Ras al Kaimah** UAE
91C4 **Ras-al-Kuh** *C* Iran
81D4 **Ra's al Madrakah** *C* Oman
91A4 **Ra's az Zawr** *C* S Arabia
95C2 **Rās Bânas** *C* Egypt
94A3 **Ras Burûn** *C* Egypt
99D1 **Ras Dashan** *Mt* Eth
90A3 **Ra's-e-Barkan** *Pt* Iran
92A3 **Râs el Kenâyis** *Pt* Egypt
81D4 **Ra's Fartak** *C* Yemen
95C2 **Râs Ghârib** Egypt
99D1 **Rashad** Sudan
94B3 **Rashādīya** Jordan
92B3 **Rashîd** Egypt
90A2 **Rasht** Iran
91C5 **Ra's Jibish** *C* Oman
99E1 **Ras Khanzira** *C* Somalia
84B3 **Ras Koh** *Mt* Pak
95C2 **Râs Muhammad** *C* Egypt
96A2 **Ras Nouadhibou** *C* Maur
69H2 **Rasshua** *I* Russian Fed
61F3 **Rasskazovo** Russian Fed
91A4 **Ra's Tanāqib** *C* S Arabia
91B4 **Ra's Tannūrah** S Arabia
57B3 **Rastatt** Germany
Ras Uarc = Cabo Tres Forcas
99F1 **Ras Xaafuun** *C* Somalia
84C3 **Ratangarh** India
76B3 **Rat Buri** Thai
85D3 **Rath** India
56C2 **Rathenow** Germany
45B2 **Rathkeale** Irish Rep
45C1 **Rathlin** *I* N Ire
45B2 **Ráth Luirc** Irish Rep
85D4 **Ratlām** India
87A1 **Ratnāgiri** India
87C3 **Ratnapura** Sri Lanka
58C2 **Ratno** Ukraine
47D1 **Rattenberg** Austria
39H6 **Rättvik** Sweden
12H3 **Ratz,Mt** Can
34D3 **Rauch** Arg
110C1 **Raukumara Range** *Mts* NZ
35C2 **Raul Soares** Brazil
39J6 **Rauma** Fin
86A2 **Raurkela** India
90A3 **Ravānsar** Iran
90C3 **Rāvar** Iran
59C2 **Rava Russkaya** Ukraine
16C1 **Ravena** USA
52B2 **Ravenna** Italy
57B3 **Ravensburg** Germany
107D2 **Ravenshoe** Aust
42E2 **Ravenspurn** *Oilfield* N Sea
84C2 **Ravi** *R* Pak
84C2 **Rawalpindi** Pak
93D2 **Rawāndiz** Iraq
58B2 **Rawicz** Pol
106B4 **Rawlinna** Aust
8C2 **Rawlins** USA
29C4 **Rawson** Arg
78C3 **Raya** *Mt* Indon
87B2 **Rāyadurg** India
94C2 **Rayak** Leb
7E5 **Ray,C** Can
91C4 **Rāyen** Iran
22C2 **Raymond** California, USA
20B1 **Raymond** Washington, USA
109D2 **Raymond Terrace** Aust
12D1 **Ray Mts** USA
23B1 **Rayon** Mexico
90A2 **Razan** Iran
54C2 **Razgrad** Bulg
54C2 **Razim** *L* Rom
43D4 **Reading** Eng
16B2 **Reading** USA
4G3 **Read Island** Can
16C1 **Readsboro** USA
34B2 **Real de Padre** Arg
34C3 **Realicó** Arg
95B2 **Rebiana** *Well* Libya
95B2 **Rebiana Sand Sea** Libya
38L6 **Reboly** Russian Fed
106B4 **Recherche,Arch of the** *Is* Aust
31E3 **Recife** Brazil
107F2 **Récifs D'Entrecasteaux** Nouvelle Calédonie
46D1 **Recklinghausen** Germany
30E4 **Reconquista** Arg
19B3 **Red** *R* USA
77C4 **Redang** *I* Malay
16B2 **Red Bank** New Jersey, USA
21A1 **Red Bluff** USA
42D2 **Redcar** Eng
13E2 **Redcliff** Can
109D1 **Redcliffe** Aust
108B2 **Red Cliffs** Aust
13E2 **Red Deer** Can
13E2 **Red Deer** *R* Can
20B2 **Redding** USA
10A2 **Red L** USA
7A4 **Red Lake** Can
22D3 **Redlands** USA
16A3 **Red Lion** USA
20B2 **Redmond** USA
18A1 **Red Oak** USA
48B2 **Redon** France
22C4 **Redondo Beach** USA
12D2 **Redoubt V** USA
73B5 **Red River Delta** Vietnam
80B3 **Red Sea** Africa/ Arabian Pen
13E2 **Redwater** Can
22A2 **Redwood City** USA
14A2 **Reed City** USA
22C2 **Reedley** USA
20B2 **Reedsport** USA
111B2 **Reefton** NZ
93C2 **Refahiye** Turk
35D1 **Regência** Brazil
57C3 **Regensburg** Germany
96C2 **Reggane** Alg
53C3 **Reggio di Calabria** Italy
47D2 **Reggio Nell'Emilia** Italy
54B1 **Reghin** Rom
5H4 **Regina** Can
100A3 **Rehoboth** Namibia
15C3 **Rehoboth Beach** USA
94B3 **Rehovot** Israel
32D1 **Reicito** Ven
43D4 **Reigate** Eng
46C2 **Reims** France
5H4 **Reindeer** *R* Can

50B1 **Reinosa** Spain
16A3 **Reisterstown** USA
101G1 **Reitz** S Africa
4H3 **Reliance** Can
108A2 **Remarkable,Mt** Aust
78C4 **Rembang** Indon
91C4 **Remeshk** Iran
46D1 **Remscheid** Germany
18C2 **Rend,L** USA
56B2 **Rendsburg** Germany
15C1 **Renfrew** Can
78A3 **Rengat** Indon
34A2 **Rengo** Chile
59D3 **Reni** Ukraine
99D1 **Renk** Sudan
6H2 **Renland** *Pen*
Greenland
108B2 **Renmark** Aust
107F2 **Rennell** *I* Solomon Is
48B2 **Rennes** France
21B2 **Reno** USA
47D2 **Reno** *R* Italy
15C2 **Renovo** USA
16C1 **Rensselaer** USA
20B1 **Renton** USA
70D4 **Reo** Indon
35B2 **Reprèsa de Furnas**
Dam Brazil
30E3 **Reprèsa Ilha Grande**
Dam Brazil
30E3 **Reprèsa Itaipu** *Dam*
Brazil
35A2 **Reprèsa Porto**
Primavera *Dam*
Brazil
35B1 **Reprèsa Três Marias**
Dam Brazil
20C1 **Republic** USA
41B3 **Republic of Ireland**
NW Europe
6B3 **Repulse Bay** Can
15C1 **Réservoir Baskatong**
Res Can
10C1 **Réservoir de la**
Grande 2 *Res* Can
10C1 **Réservoir de la**
Grande 3 *Res* Can
7C4 **Réservoir de la**
Grande 4 *Res* Can
7C5 **Réservoire Cabonga**
Res Can
7C5 **Réservoire Gouin**
Res Can
10D1 **Réservoire**
Manicouagan *Res*
Can
90B2 **Reshteh-ye Alborz**
Mts Iran
72A2 **Reshui** China
30E4 **Resistencia** Arg
54B1 **Resita** Rom
6A2 **Resolute** Can
111A3 **Resolution I** NZ
6D3 **Resolution Island**
Can
101H1 **Ressano Garcia**
Mozam
34B2 **Retamito** Arg
46C2 **Rethel** France
55B3 **Réthimnon** Greece
89K10 **Reunion** *I* Indian O
51C1 **Reus** Spain
47C1 **Reuss** *R* Switz
47D1 **Reutte** Austria
61K3 **Revda** Russian Fed
13D2 **Revelstoke** Can
24A3 **Revillagigedo** *Is*
Mexico
12H3 **Revillagigedo I** USA
46C2 **Revin** France
94B3 **Revivim** Israel
86A2 **Rewa** India
84D3 **Rewari** India
8B2 **Rexburg** USA
38A2 **Reykjavik** Iceland
24C2 **Reynosa** Mexico
48B2 **Rezé** France
58D1 **Rezekne** Latvia
61K2 **Rezh** Russian Fed
47C1 **Rhätikon** *Mts*
Austria/Switz
94B1 **Rhazir** Republic, Leb
56B2 **Rhein** *R* W Europe
56B2 **Rheine** Germany

47B1 **Rheinfielden** Switz
49D2 **Rheinland Pfalz**
Region, Germany
47C1 **Rheinwaldhorn** *Mt*
Switz
Rhine = Rhein
16C2 **Rhinebeck** USA
10B2 **Rhinelander** USA
47C2 **Rho** Italy
15D2 **Rhode Island** State,
USA
16D2 **Rhode Island Sd** USA
Rhodes = Ródhos
49C3 **Rhône** *R* France
43C3 **Rhyl** Wales
31D4 **Riachão do Jacuipe**
Brazil
50A1 **Ria de Arosa** *B*
Spain
50A1 **Ria de Betanzos** *B*
Spain
50A1 **Ria de Corcubion** *B*
Spain
50A1 **Ria de Lage** *B* Spain
50A1 **Ria de Sta Marta** *B*
Spain
50A1 **Ria de Vigo** *B* Spain
84C2 **Riàsi** Pak
50A1 **Ribadeo** Spain
35A2 **Ribas do Rio Pardo**
Brazil
101C2 **Ribauè** Mozam
42C3 **Ribble** *R* Eng
35B2 **Ribeira** Brazil
35B2 **Ribeirão Prêto** Brazil
32D6 **Riberalta** Bol
15C2 **Rice L** Can
10A2 **Rice Lake** USA
101H1 **Richard's Bay**
S Africa
19A3 **Richardson** USA
12G1 **Richardson Mts** Can
8B3 **Richfield** USA
20C1 **Richland** USA
22A2 **Richmond** California,
USA
101H1 **Richmond** Natal,
S Africa
109D2 **Richmond** New
South Wales, Aust
111B2 **Richmond** NZ
107D3 **Richmond**
Queensland, Aust
10C3 **Richmond** Virginia,
USA
111B2 **Richmond Range** *Mts*
NZ
15C2 **Rideau,L** Can
17B1 **Ridgeland** USA
15C2 **Ridgway** USA
27D4 **Riecito** Ven
47D1 **Rienza** *R* Italy
57C2 **Riesa** Germany
29B6 **Riesco** *I* Chile
101F1 **Riet** *R* S Africa
52B2 **Rieti** Italy
50B2 **Rif** *Mts* Mor
58C1 **Riga** Latvia
60B2 **Riga,G of** Estonia/
Latvia
91C4 **Rigān** Iran
20C1 **Riggins** USA
7E4 **Rigolet** Can
39J6 **Riihimaki** Fin
52B1 **Rijeka** Croatia
13E2 **Rimbey** Can
39H7 **Rimbo** Sweden
52B2 **Rimini** Italy
54C1 **Rîmnicu Sărat** Rom
54B1 **Rîmnicu Vilcea** Rom
10D2 **Rimouski** Can
23A1 **Rincón de Romos**
Mexico
39F7 **Ringkøbing** Den
98A2 **Rio Benito** Eq Guinea
32D5 **Rio Branco** Brazil
24B1 **Rio Bravo del Norte**
R Mexico/USA
32C1 **Riochacha** Colombia
35B2 **Rio Claro** Brazil
27L1 **Rio Claro** Trinidad
34C3 **Rio Colorado** Arg
34C2 **Rio Cuarto** Arg
31D4 **Rio de Jacuipe** Brazil

35C2 **Rio de Janeiro** Brazil
35C2 **Rio de Janeiro** State,
Brazil
29E3 **Rio de la Plata** *Est*
Arg/Urug
29C6 **Rio Gallegos** Arg
29C6 **Rio Grande** Arg
30F5 **Rio Grande** Brazil
26A4 **Rio Grande** Nic
25D3 **Rio Grande** *R* Nic
24B2 **Rio Grande** *R*
Mexico/USA
23A1 **Rio Grande de**
Santiago Mexico
31D3 **Rio Grande do Norte**
State, Brazil
30F4 **Rio Grande do Sul**
State, Brazil
103G6 **Rio Grande Rise**
Atlantic O
26C4 **Riohacha** Colombia
49C2 **Riom** France
32B4 **Riombamba** Ecuador
30C2 **Rio Mulatos** Bol
29C3 **Rio Negro** State, Arg
30F4 **Rio Pardo** Brazil
34C2 **Rio Tercero** Arg
33E6 **Rio Theodore**
Roosevelt *R* Brazil
29B6 **Rio Turbio** Arg
35A1 **Rio Verde** Brazil
23A1 **Rio Verde** Mexico
14B3 **Ripley** Ohio, USA
14B3 **Ripley** West Virginia,
USA
42D2 **Ripon** Eng
22B2 **Ripon** USA
94B3 **Rishon le Zion** Israel
16A3 **Rising Sun** USA
39F7 **Risør** Nor
6E2 **Ritenberk** Greenland
22C2 **Ritter,Mt** USA
20C1 **Ritzville** USA
34B2 **Rivadavia** Arg
34A1 **Rivadavia** Chile
34C3 **Rivadavia Gonzalez**
Moreno Arg
47D2 **Riva de Garda** Italy
34C3 **Rivera** Arg
29E2 **Rivera** Urug
22B2 **Riverbank** USA
97B4 **River Cess** Lib
16C2 **Riverhead** USA
108B3 **Riverina** Aust
111A3 **Riversdale** NZ
22D4 **Riverside** USA
13B2 **Rivers Inlet** Can
111A3 **Riverton** NZ
8C2 **Riverton** USA
17B2 **Riviera Beach** USA
7C4 **Rivière aux Feuilles** *R*
Can
7D4 **Rivière de la Baleine**
R Can
7D4 **Rivière du Petit**
Mècatina *R* Can
46C2 **Rivigny-sur-Ornain**
France
93D1 **Rize** Turk
72D2 **Rizhao** China
Rizhskiy Zaliv =
Riga,G of
39F7 **Rjukan** Nor
6B2 **Roanes Pen** Can
49C2 **Roanne** France
17A1 **Roanoke** Alabama,
USA
11C3 **Roanoke** Virginia,
USA
11C3 **Roanoke** *R* USA
45B3 **Roaringwater B**
Irish Rep
38J6 **Robertsforz** Sweden
19B2 **Robert S Kerr Res**
USA
97A4 **Robertsport** Lib
7C5 **Roberval** Can
30H6 **Robinson Crusoe** *I*
Chile
108B2 **Robinvale** Aust
13D2 **Robson,Mt** Can
24A3 **Roca Partida** *I*
Mexico
103G5 **Rocas** *I* Atlantic O

31E2 **Rocas** *I* Brazil
29F2 **Rocha** Urug
42C3 **Rochdale** Eng
48B2 **Rochefort** France
5G3 **Rocher River** Can
108B3 **Rochester** Aust
7C5 **Rochester** Can
43E4 **Rochester** Eng
10A2 **Rochester**
Minnesota, USA
15D2 **Rochester** New
Hampshire, USA
10C2 **Rochester** New York,
USA
10B2 **Rockford** USA
11B3 **Rock Hill** USA
10A2 **Rock Island** USA
108B3 **Rocklands Res** Aust
17B2 **Rockledge** USA
8C2 **Rock Springs**
Wyoming, USA
110B2 **Rocks Pt** NZ
109C3 **Rock,The** Aust
16C2 **Rockville**
Connecticut, USA
14A3 **Rockville** Indiana,
USA
16A3 **Rockville** Maryland,
USA
14B1 **Rocky Island L** Can
13E2 **Rocky Mountain**
House Can
8B1 **Rocky Mts** Can/USA
12B2 **Rocky Pt** USA
56C2 **Rødbyhavn** Den
34B2 **Rodeo** Arg
49C3 **Rodez** France
55C3 **Ródhos** Greece
55C3 **Ródhos** *I* Greece
52C2 **Rodi Garganico** Italy
54B2 **Rodopi Planina** *Mts*
Bulg
106A3 **Roebourne** Aust
46C1 **Roermond** Neth
46B1 **Roeselare** Belg
6B3 **Roes Welcome Sd**
Can
18B2 **Rogers** USA
14B1 **Rogers City** USA
20B2 **Rogue** *R* USA
85B3 **Rohn** Pak
84D3 **Rohtak** India
58C1 **Roja** Latvia
35A2 **Rolândia** Brazil
18B2 **Rolla** USA
109C1 **Roma** Aust
52B2 **Roma** Italy
47C2 **Romagnano** Italy
17C1 **Romain,C** USA
54C1 **Roman** Rom
103H5 **Romanche Gap**
Atlantic O
71D4 **Romang** *I* Indon
60B4 **Romania** Republic,
E Europe
17B2 **Romano,C** USA
49D2 **Romans sur Isère**
France
79B3 **Romblon** Phil
Rome = Roma
17A1 **Rome** Georgia, USA
15C2 **Rome** New York,
USA
49C2 **Romilly-sur-Seine**
France
15C3 **Romney** USA
60D3 **Romny** Ukraine
56B1 **Rømø** *I* Den
47B1 **Romont** Switz
48C2 **Romoratin** France
50A2 **Ronda** Spain
33E6 **Rondônia** Brazil
24F6 **Rondônia** State,
Brazil
30F2 **Rondonópolis** Brazil
73B4 **Rong'an** China
73B4 **Rongchang** China
72E2 **Rongcheng** China
73B4 **Rongjiang** China
73B4 **Rong Jiang** *R* China
76A1 **Rongklang Range**
Mts Burma
39G7 **Rønne** Den
39H7 **Ronneby** Sweden

112B2 Ronne Ice Shelf Ant
46B1 Ronse Belg
46A1 Ronthieu Region, France
9C3 Roof Butte Mt USA
84D3 Roorkee India
46C1 Roosendaal Neth
112B6 Roosevelt I Ant
106C2 Roper R Aust
33E3 Roraima State, Brazil
33E2 Roraime Mt Ven
38G6 Røros Nor
47C1 Rorschach Switz
38G6 Rørvik Nor
27Q2 Rosalie Dominica
22C3 Rosamond L USA
34C2 Rosario Arg
31C2 Rosário Brazil
34D2 Rosario del Tala Arg
48B2 Roscoff France
45B2 Roscommon County, Irish Rep
41B3 Roscommon Irish Rep
45C2 Roscrea Irish Rep
27E3 Roseau Dominica
109C4 Rosebery Aust
20B2 Roseburg USA
19A4 Rosenberg USA
57C3 Rosenheim Germany
13F2 Rosetown Can
54B2 Roşiori de Vede Rom
39G7 Roskilde Den
60D3 Roslavl' Russian Fed
61E2 Roslyatino Russian Fed
111B2 Ross NZ
12H2 Ross R Can
40B3 Rossan Pt Irish Rep
53C3 Rossano Italy
19C3 Ross Barnet Res USA
15C1 Rosseau L L Can
107E2 Rossel I Solomon Is
112A Ross Ice Shelf Ant
20B1 Ross L USA
13D3 Rossland Can
45C2 Rosslare Irish Rep
111C2 Ross,Mt NZ
97A3 Rosso Maur
43C4 Ross-on-Wye Eng
60E4 Rossosh Russian Fed
4E3 Ross River Can
112B6 Ross S Ant
91B4 Rostāq Iran
56C2 Rostock Germany
Rostov = Rostov-na-Donu
61E4 Rostov-na-Donu Russian Fed
17B1 Roswell Georgia, USA
9C3 Roswell New Mexico, USA
71F2 Rota Pacific O
56B2 Rotenburg Niedersachsen, Germany
46E1 Rothaar-Geb Region Germany
112B2 Rothera Base Ant
42D3 Rotherham Eng
42B2 Rothesay Scot
71D5 Roti I Indon
108C2 Roto Aust
111B2 Rotoiti,L NZ
111B2 Rotoroa,L NZ
110C1 Rotorua NZ
110C1 Rotorua,L NZ
56A2 Rotterdam Neth
46B1 Roubaix France
48C2 Rouen France
42E3 Rough Oilfield N Sea
Roulers = Roeselare
101E3 Round I Mauritius
109D2 Round Mt Aust
8C2 Roundup USA
44C2 Rousay I Scot
48C3 Roussillon Region, France
10C2 Rouyn Can
38K5 Rovaniemi Fin
47D2 Rovereto Italy
47D2 Rovigo Italy
52B1 Rovinj Croatia

59D2 Rovno Ukraine
90A2 Row'ān Iran
109C1 Rowena Aust
6C3 Rowley I Can
106A2 Rowley Shoals Aust
79A3 Roxas Palawan, Phil
79B3 Roxas Panay, Phil
111A3 Roxburgh NZ
45C2 Royal Canal Irish Rep
43D3 Royal Leamington Spa Eng
14B2 Royal Oak USA
43E4 Royal Tunbridge Wells Eng
48B2 Royan France
46B2 Roye France
43D3 Royston Eng
59C3 Rožňava Czech
46B2 Rozoy France
61F3 Rtishchevo Russian Fed
99D3 Ruaha Nat Pk Tanz
110C1 Ruahine Range Mts NZ
110C1 Ruapehu,Mt NZ
65D3 Rub al Khālī Desert S Arabia
44A3 Rubha Hunish Scot
35A2 Rubinéia Brazil
65K4 Rubtsovsk Russian Fed
12C2 Ruby USA
91C4 Rudan Iran
90A2 Rūdbār Iran
69F2 Rudnaya Pristan' Russian Fed
54B2 Rudoka Planina Mt Macedonia, Yugos
72E3 Rudong China
14B1 Rudyard USA
46A1 Rue France
48C2 Ruffec France
99D3 Rufiji R Tanz
34C2 Rufino Arg
97A3 Rufisque Sen
100B2 Rufunsa Zambia
43D3 Rugby Eng
39G8 Rügen I Germany
56B2 Ruhr R Germany
73D4 Ruijin China
54B2 Rujen Mt Bulg/Macedonia, Yugos
99D3 Rukwa L Tanz
44A3 Rum I Scot
54A1 Ruma Serbia, Yugos
91A4 Rumāh S Arabia
98C2 Rumbek Sudan
26C2 Rum Cay I Caribbean S
47A2 Rumilly France
106C2 Rum Jungle Aust
101C2 Rumphi Malawi
111B2 Runanga NZ
110C1 Runaway,C NZ
100C3 Rundi R Zim
100A2 Rundu Namibia
99D3 Rungwa Tanz
99D3 Rungwa R Tanz
99D3 Rungwe Mt Tanz
82C2 Ruoqiang China
68C2 Ruo Shui R China
54C1 Rupea Rom
7C4 Rupert R Can
46D1 Rur R Germany
32D6 Rurrenabaque Bol
101C2 Rusape Zim
54C2 Ruse Bulg
18B1 Rushville Illinois, USA
108B3 Rushworth Aust
19A3 Rusk USA
17B2 Ruskin USA
110B1 Russell NZ
18B2 Russellville Arkansas, USA
18C2 Russellville Kentucky, USA
21A2 Russian R USA
62C3 Russian Fed Asia/Europe
93E1 Rustavi Georgia
101G1 Rustenburg S Africa
19B3 Ruston USA
99C3 Rutana Burundi

46E1 Rüthen Germany
23B2 Rutla Mexico
15D2 Rutland USA
84D2 Rutog China
Ruvu = Pangani
101D2 Ruvuma R Tanz/Mozam
99D2 Ruwenzori Range Mts Uganda/Zaire
101C2 Ruya R Zim
59B3 Ružomberok Czech
99C3 Rwanda Republic, Africa
60E3 Ryazan' Russian Fed
61F3 Ryazhsk Russian Fed
60E2 Rybinsk Russian Fed
60E2 Rybinskoye Vodokhranilishche Res Russian Fed
13D1 Rycroft Can
43D4 Ryde Eng
43E4 Rye Eng
20C2 Rye Patch Res USA
60D3 Ryl'sk Russian Fed
61G4 Ryn Peski Desert Kazakhstan
74D3 Ryōtsu Japan
59D3 Ryskany Moldavia
69E4 Ryūkyū Retto Arch Japan
59C2 Rzeszów Pol
60D2 Rzhev Russian Fed

S

91B3 Sa'adatābād Iran
56C2 Saale R Germany
47B1 Saanen Switz
46D2 Saar R Germany
46D2 Saarbrücken Germany
46D2 Saarburg Germany
39J7 Saaremaa I Estonia
46D2 Saarland State, Germany
46D2 Saarlouis Germany
34C3 Saavedra Arg
54A2 Šabac Serbia, Yugos
51C1 Sabadell Spain
75B1 Sabae Japan
78D1 Sabah State, Malay
26C4 Sabanalarga Colombia
70A3 Sabang Indon
87C1 Sabari R India
94B2 Sabastiya Israel
30C2 Sabaya Bol
93C3 Sab'Bi'ār Syria
94C2 Sabhā Jordan
95A2 Sabhā Libya
24B2 Sabinas Mexico
24B2 Sabinas Hidalgo Mexico
19A3 Sabine R USA
19B4 Sabine L USA
91B5 Sabkhat Maṭṭi Salt Marsh UAE
94A3 Sabkhet El Bardawîl Lg Egypt
79B3 Sablayan Phil
7D5 Sable,C Can
17B2 Sable,C USA
7D5 Sable I Can
90C2 Sabzevār Iran
20C1 Sacajawea Peak USA
10A1 Sachigo R Can
57C2 Sachsen State, Germany
56C2 Sachsen-Anhalt State, Germany
4F2 Sachs Harbour Can
47B1 Säckingen Germany
22B1 Sacramento USA
22B1 Sacramento R USA
21A1 Sacramento V USA
9C3 Sacramento Mts USA
81C4 Sa'dah Yemen
54B2 Sadanski Bulg
82D3 Sadiya India
50A2 Sado R Port
74D3 Sado-shima I Japan
85C3 Sädri India
Safad = Zefat

84A2 Safed Koh Mts Afghan
39G7 Saffle Sweden
92C3 Safi Jordan
96B1 Safi Mor
90D3 Safidabeh Iran
94C1 Şafītā Syria
93E3 Safwān Iraq
75A2 Saga Japan
76B1 Sagaing Burma
75B2 Sagami-nada B Japan
85D4 Sāgar India
16C2 Sag Harbor USA
14B2 Saginaw USA
14B2 Saginaw B USA
26B2 Sagua de Tánamo Cuba
26B2 Sagua la Grande Cuba
7C5 Saguenay R Can
51B2 Sagunto Spain
94C3 Sahāb Jordan
50A1 Sahagún Spain
96C2 Sahara Desert N Africa
84D3 Saharanpur India
84C2 Sahiwal Pak
93D3 Şahrā al Hijārah Desert Region Iraq
23A1 Sahuayo Mexico
107D1 Saibai I Aust
96C1 Saïda Alg
94B2 Saïda Leb
91C4 Sa'idabad Iran
51B2 Saidia Mor
86B1 Saidpur India
84C2 Saidu Pak
75A1 Saigō Japan
Saigon = Ho Chi Minh
86C2 Saiha India
68D2 Saihan Tal China
75A2 Saijo Japan
74C4 Saiki Japan
42C2 St Abb's Head Pt Scot
43D4 St Albans Eng
15D2 St Albans Vermont, USA
14B3 St Albans West Virginia, USA
43C4 St Albans Head C Eng
13E2 St Albert Can
46B1 St Amand-les-Eaux France
48C2 St Amand-Mont Rond France
17A2 St Andrew B USA
44C3 St Andrews Scot
17B1 St Andrew Sd USA
27H1 St Ann's Bay Jamaica
7E4 St Anthony Can
108B3 St Arnaud Aust
17B2 St Augustine USA
43B4 St Austell Eng
46D2 St-Avold France
42C2 St Bees Head Pt Eng
47B2 St-Bonnet France
43B4 St Brides B Wales
48B2 St-Brieuc France
15C2 St Catharines Can
27M2 St Catherine,Mt Grenada
17B1 St Catherines I USA
43D4 St Catherines Pt Eng
49C2 St Chamond France
18B2 St Charles Missouri, USA
14D2 St Clair USA
14B2 St Clair,L Can/USA
14B2 St Clair Shores USA
49D2 St Claud France
10A2 St Cloud USA
47B1 Ste Croix Switz
27E3 St Croix I Caribbean S
43B4 St Davids Head Pt Wales
46B2 St Denis France
101E3 St Denis Réunion
46C2 St Dizier France
12F2 St Elias,Mt USA

12G2 **St Elias Mts** Can
48B2 **Saintes** France
49C2 **St Étienne** France
18B2 **St Francis** R USA
100B4 **St Francis,C** S Africa
47C1 **St Gallen** Switz
48C3 **St-Gaudens** France
109C1 **St George** Aust
17B1 **St George** South Carolina, USA
9B3 **St George** Utah, USA
17B2 **St George I** Florida, USA
20B2 **St George,Pt** USA
15D1 **St-Georges** Can
27E4 **St George's** Grenada
45C3 **St George's Chan** Irish Rep/Wales
46A2 **St Germain-en-Laye** France
47B2 **St-Gervais** France
47C1 **St Gotthard** P Switz
43B4 **St Govans Head** Pt Wales
22A1 **St Helena** USA
103H5 **St Helena** I Atlantic O
100A4 **St Helena B** S Africa
17B1 **St Helena Sd** USA
109C4 **St Helens** Aust
42C3 **St Helens** Eng
20B1 **St Helens** USA
20B1 **St Helens,Mt** USA
48B2 **St Helier** Jersey
47B1 **St Hippolyte** France
46C1 **St Hubert** Belg
7C5 **St-Hyacinthe** Can
14B1 **St Ignace** USA
43B4 **St Ives** Eng
18B2 **St James** Missouri, USA
5E4 **St James,C** Can
15D1 **St Jean** Can
48B2 **St Jean-d'Angely** France
47B2 **St-Jean-de-Maurienne** France
10C2 **St Jean,L** Can
15D1 **St-Jérôme** Can
20C1 **St Joe** R USA
7D5 **Saint John** Can
7E5 **St John's** Can
14B2 **St Johns** Michigan, USA
17B2 **St Johns** R USA
15D2 **St Johnsbury** USA
15D1 **St-Joseph** Can
19B3 **St Joseph** Louisiana, USA
14A2 **St Joseph** Michigan, USA
18B2 **St Joseph** Missouri, USA
27L1 **St Joseph** Trinidad
14B2 **St Joseph** R USA
14B1 **St Joseph I** Can
7A4 **St Joseph,L** Can
47B1 **St Julien** France
48C2 **St-Junien** France
46B2 **St-Just-en-Chaussée** France
4B2 **St Kilda** I Scot
27E3 **St Kitts-Nevis** Is Caribbean S
47A1 **St-Laurent** France
7D5 **St Lawrence** R Can
7D5 **Saint Lawrence,G of** Can
4A3 **St Lawrence I** USA
15C2 **St Lawrence Seaway** Can/USA
48B2 **St Lô** France
97A3 **St Louis** Sen
11A3 **St Louis** USA
27E4 **St Lucia** I Caribbean S
101H1 **St Lucia,L** S Africa
44E1 **St Magnus** B Scot
48B2 **St Malo** France
20C1 **St Maries** USA
27E3 **St Martin** I Caribbean S
108A2 **St Mary Peak** Mt Aust

109C4 **St Marys** Aust
15C2 **St Marys** USA
17B1 **St Marys** R USA
46C2 **Ste-Menehould** France
12B2 **St Michael** USA
16A3 **St Michaels** USA
47B2 **St-Michel** France
46C2 **St-Mihiel** France
47C1 **St Moritz** Switz
48B2 **St-Nazaire** France
46C1 **St-Niklaas** Belg
46B1 **St-Omer** France
13E2 **St Paul** Can
10A2 **St Paul** Minnesota, USA
97A4 **St Paul** R Lib
17B2 **St Petersburg** USA
7E5 **St Pierre** Can
15D1 **St Pierre,L** Can
46B1 **St-Pol-Sur-Ternoise** France
59B3 **St Pölten** Austria
46B2 **St Quentin** France
49D3 **St Raphaël** France
101D2 **St Sébastien** C Madag
17B1 **St Simons I** USA
17B1 **St Stephen** USA
14B2 **St Thomas** Can
49D3 **St-Tropez** France
46C1 **St Truiden** Belg
46A1 **St-Valéry-sur-Somme** France
27E4 **St Vincent** I Caribbean S
108A2 **St Vincent,G** Aust
46D1 **St-Vith** Germany
46D2 **St Wendel** Germany
71F2 **Saipan** I Pacific O
84B2 **Saiydabad** Afghan
30C2 **Sajama** Mt Bol
74D4 **Sakai** Japan
75A2 **Sakaidi** Japan
75A1 **Sakaiminato** Japan
93D4 **Sakākah** S Arabia
10C1 **Sakami,L** Can
100B2 **Sakania** Zaire
101D3 **Sakaraha** Madag
60D5 **Sakarya** R Turk
58C1 **Sakasleja** Latvia
74D3 **Sakata** Japan
97C4 **Saketél** Benin
69G1 **Sakhalin** I Russian Fed
69E4 **Sakishima gunto** Is Japan
97A4 **Sal** I Cape Verde
61F4 **Sal** R Russian Fed
39H7 **Sala** Sweden
34D3 **Saladillo** Arg
34C2 **Saladillo** R Arg
34D3 **Salado** R Buenos Aires, Arg
34B3 **Salado** R Mendoza/San Luis, Arg
30D4 **Salado** R Sante Fe, Arg
97B4 **Salaga** Ghana
76C3 **Sala Hintoun** Camb
98B1 **Salal** Chad
81D4 **Salālah** Oman
34A2 **Salamanca** Chile
23A1 **Salamanca** Mexico
50A1 **Salamanca** Spain
15C2 **Salamanca** USA
98B2 **Salamat** R Chad
71F4 **Salamaua** PNG
15C2 **Salamonica** USA
78D1 **Salang** Indon
38H5 **Salangen** Nor
30C3 **Salar de Arizaro** Arg
30C3 **Salar de Atacama** Salt Pan Chile
30C2 **Salar de Coipasa** Salt Pan Bol
30C3 **Salar de Uyuni** Salt Pan Bol
47C2 **Salasomaggiore** Italy
61J3 **Salavat** Russian Fed
70D4 **Salayar** Indon
105L5 **Sala y Gomez** I Pacific O
34C3 **Salazar** Arg

48C2 **Salbris** France
12E2 **Salcha** R USA
100A4 **Saldanha** S Africa
94C2 **Saldhad** Syria
34C3 **Saldungaray** Arg
58C1 **Saldus** Latvia
109C3 **Sale** Aust
18C2 **Salem** Illinois, USA
87B2 **Salem** India
16D1 **Salem** Massachusetts, USA
16B3 **Salem** New Jersey, USA
20B2 **Salem** Oregon, USA
78C4 **Salembu Besar** I Indon
39G6 **Salen** Sweden
53B2 **Salerno** Italy
42C3 **Salford** Eng
54A1 **Salgót** Hung
59B3 **Salgótarjan** Hung
31D3 **Salgueiro** Brazil
55C3 **Salihli** Turk
101C2 **Salima** Malawi
39K6 **Salimaa** L Fin
18A2 **Salina** Kansas, USA
53B3 **Salina** I Italy
23B2 **Salina Cruz** Mexico
30C3 **Salina de Arizato** Arg
34B3 **Salina Grande** Salt pan Arg
34B2 **Salina La Antigua** Salt pan Arg
35C1 **Salinas** Brazil
22B2 **Salinas** USA
22B2 **Salinas** R USA
34B3 **Salinas de Llancaneb** Salt Pan Arg
34B2 **Salinas Grandes** Salt Pan Arg
19B3 **Saline** R Arkansas, USA
27M2 **Salines,Pt** Grenada
31B2 **Salinópolis** Brazil
47A1 **Salins** France
Salisbury = Harare
43D4 **Salisbury** Eng
15C3 **Salisbury** Maryland, USA
6C3 **Salisbury I** Can
43D4 **Salisbury Plain** Eng
38K5 **Salla** Fin
47B2 **Sallanches** France
18B2 **Sallisaw** USA
6C3 **Salluit** Can
86A1 **Sallyana** Nepal
93D2 **Salmas** Iran
38L6 **Salmi** Russian Fed
20C1 **Salmo** Can
8B2 **Salmon** USA
13D2 **Salmon Arm** Can
8B2 **Salmon River Mts** USA
39J6 **Salo** Fin
47D2 **Salò** Italy
49D3 **Salon-de-Provence** France
Salonica = Thessaloníki
54B1 **Salonta** Rom
38K6 **Salpausselka** Region, Fin
34B2 **Salsacate** Arg
61F4 **Sal'sk** Russian Fed
94B2 **Salt** Jordan
30C3 **Salta** Arg
30C3 **Salta** State, Arg
24B2 **Saltillo** Mexico
8B2 **Salt Lake City** USA
34C2 **Salto** Arg
34D2 **Salto** Urug
32C3 **Salto Angostura** Waterfall Colombia
35D1 **Salto da Divisa** Brazil
33E2 **Salto del Angel** Waterfall Ven
30E3 **Salto del Guaira** Waterfall Brazil
32C4 **Salto Grande** Waterfall Colombia
84C2 **Salt Range** Mts Pak
27H2 **Salt River** Jamaica
17B1 **Saluda** USA
47B2 **Saluzzo** Italy

31D4 **Salvador** Brazil
19B4 **Salvador,L** USA
23A1 **Salvatierra** Mexico
91B5 **Salwah** Qatar
76B1 **Salween** R Burma
93E2 **Sal'yany** Azerbaijan
57C3 **Salzburg** Austria
56C2 **Salzgitter** Germany
56C2 **Salzwedel** Germany
68B1 **Samagaltay** Russian Fed
79B4 **Samales Group** Is Phil
27D3 **Samaná** Dom Rep
92C2 **Samandaği** Turk
84B1 **Samangan** Afghan
79C3 **Samar** I Phil
65G4 **Samara** Russian Fed
107E2 **Samarai** PNG
78D3 **Samarinda** Indon
80E2 **Samarkand** Uzbekistan
93D3 **Sāmarrā'** Iraq
79B3 **Samar S** Phil
86A2 **Sambalpur** India
78B2 **Sambas** Indon
101E2 **Sambava** Madag
84D3 **Sambhal** India
78D3 **Samboja** Indon
59C3 **Sambor** Ukraine
46B1 **Sambre** R France
74B3 **Samch'ŏk** S Korea
99D3 **Same** Tanz
47C1 **Samedan** Switz
46A1 **Samer** France
100B2 **Samfya** Zambia
76B1 **Samka** Burma
76C1 **Sam Neua** Laos
55C3 **Sámos** I Greece
55C2 **Samothráki** I Greece
34C2 **Sampacho** Arg
78D3 **Sampaga** Indon
78C3 **Sampit** Indon
78C3 **Sampit** R Indon
19B3 **Sam Rayburn Res** USA
76C3 **Samrong** Camb
56C1 **Samsø** I Den
92C1 **Samsun** Turk
97B3 **San** Mali
76D3 **San** R Camb
59C2 **San** R Pol
81C4 **Şan'ā'** Yemen
98B2 **Sanaga** R Cam
29C2 **San Agustín** Arg
79C4 **San Agustin,C** Phil
90A2 **Sanandaj** Iran
22B1 **San Andreas** USA
25C3 **San Andrés Tuxtla** Mexico
9C3 **San Angelo** USA
53A3 **San Antioco** Sardegna
53A3 **San Antioco** I Medit S
34A2 **San Antonio** Chile
9C3 **San Antonio** New Mexico, USA
79B2 **San Antonio** Phil
9D4 **San Antonio** R Texas, USA
51C2 **San Antonio Abad** Spain
25D2 **San Antonio,C** Cuba
26A2 **San Antonio de los Banos** Cuba
22D3 **San Antonio,Mt** USA
29C4 **San Antonio Oeste** Arg
34D3 **San Augustin** Arg
34B2 **San Augustin de Valle Féril** Arg
85D4 **Sanawad** India
23A1 **San Bartolo** Mexico
24A3 **San Benedicto** I Mexico
22B2 **San Benito** R USA
22B2 **San Benito Mt** USA
22D3 **San Bernardino** USA
34A2 **San Bernardo** Chile
17A2 **San Blas,C** USA
34A3 **San Carlos** Chile
32A1 **San Carlos** Nic
79B2 **San Carlos** Phil

29B4 **San Carlos de Bariloche** Arg
69E4 **San-chung** Taiwan
61G2 **Sanchursk** Russian Fed
34A3 **San Clemente** Chile
22D4 **San Clemente** USA
21B3 **San Clemente** *I* USA
34C2 **San Cristóbal** Arg
25C3 **San Cristóbal** Mexico
32C2 **San Cristóbal** Ven
32J7 **San Cristóbal** *I* Ecuador
107F2 **San Cristobal** *I* Solomon Is
25E2 **Sancti Spíritus** Cuba
78C3 **Sandai** Indon
70C3 **Sandakan** Malay
44C2 **Sanday** *I* Scot
9C3 **Sanderson** USA
13F1 **Sandfly L** Can
21B3 **San Diego** USA
92B2 **Sandikli** Turk
86A1 **Sandīla** India
39F7 **Sandnes** Nor
38G5 **Sandnessjøen** Nor
98C3 **Sandoa** Zaïre
59C2 **Sandomierz** Pol
38D3 **Sandoy** Føroyar
20C1 **Sandpoint** USA
49D2 **Sandrio** Italy
18A2 **Sand Springs** USA
106A3 **Sandstone** Aust
73C4 **Sandu** China
14B2 **Sandusky** USA
39H6 **Sandviken** Sweden
7A4 **Sandy L** Can
34C2 **San Elcano** Arg
9B3 **San Felipe** Baja Cal, Mexico
34A2 **San Felipe** Chile
23A1 **San Felipe** Guanajuato, Mexico
27D4 **San Felipe** Ven
51C1 **San Feliu de Guixols** Spain
28A5 **San Felix** *I* Pacific O
34A2 **San Fernando** Chile
79B2 **San Fernando** Phil
79B2 **San Fernando** Phil
50A2 **San Fernando** Spain
27E4 **San Fernando** Trinidad
22C3 **San Fernando** USA
32D2 **San Fernando** Ven
17B2 **Sanford** Florida, USA
12F2 **Sanford,Mt** USA
34C2 **San Francisco** Arg
27C3 **San Francisco** Dom Rep
22A2 **San Francisco** USA
22A2 **San Francisco B** USA
24B2 **San Francisco del Oro** Mexico
23A1 **San Francisco del Rincon** Mexico
22D3 **San Gabriel Mts** USA
85C5 **Sangamner** India
18C2 **Sangamon** *R* USA
71F2 **Sangan** *I* Pacific O
87B1 **Sangāreddi** India
78D4 **Sangeang** *I* Indon
22C2 **Sanger** USA
72C2 **Sanggan He** *R* China
78C2 **Sanggau** Indon
98B2 **Sangha** *R* Congo
85B3 **Sanghar** Pak
76B2 **Sangkhla Buri** Thai
78D2 **Sangkulirang** Indon
87A1 **Sāngli** India
98B2 **Sangmélima** Cam
9B3 **San Gorgonio Mt** USA
9C3 **Sangre de Cristo** *Mts* USA
34C2 **San Gregorio** Arg
22A2 **San Gregorio** USA
84D2 **Sangrūr** India
30E4 **San Ignacio** Arg
79B3 **San Isidro** Phil
32B2 **San Jacinto** Colombia
21B3 **San Jacinto Peak** *Mt* USA
34A3 **San Javier** Chile
34D2 **San Javier** Sante Fe, Arg
74D3 **Sanjō** *I* Japan
31C6 **San João del Rei** Brazil
22B2 **San Joaquin** *R* USA
22B2 **San Joaquin Valley** USA
32A1 **San José** Costa Rica
25C3 **San José** Guatemala
79B2 **San Jose** Luzon, Phil
79B3 **San Jose** Mindoro, Phil
22B2 **San Jose** USA
9B4 **San José** *I* Mexico
30D2 **San José de Chiquitos** Bol
34D2 **San José de Feliciano** Arg
34B2 **San José de Jachal** Arg
34C2 **San José de la Dormida** Arg
31B6 **San José do Rio Prêto** Brazil
24B2 **San José del Cabo** Mexico
34B2 **San Juan** Arg
27D3 **San Juan** Puerto Rico
34B2 **San Juan** State, Arg
27L1 **San Juan** Trinidad
32D2 **San Juan** Ven
26B2 **San Juan** *Mt* Cuba
8C3 **San Juan** *Mts* USA
34B2 **San Juan** *R* Arg
23B2 **San Juan** *R* Mexico
25D3 **San Juan** *R* Nic/Costa Rica
23B2 **San Juan Bautista** Mexico
30E4 **San Juan Bautista** Par
22B2 **San Juan Bautista** USA
25D3 **San Juan del Norte** Nic
27D4 **San Juan de los Cayos** Ven
23A1 **San Juan de loz Lagoz** Mexico
23A1 **San Juan del Rio** Mexico
25D3 **San Juan del Sur** Nic
20B1 **San Juan Is** USA
23B2 **San Juan Tepozcolula** Mexico
29C5 **San Julián** Arg
34C2 **San Justo** Arg
60D2 **Sankt-Peterburg** Russian Fed
98C3 **Sankuru** *R* Zaïre
22A2 **San Leandro** USA
93C2 **Şanlıurfa** Turk
32B3 **San Lorenzo** Ecuador
34C2 **San Lorenzo** Arg
22B2 **San Lucas** USA
34B2 **San Luis** Arg
34B2 **San Luis** State, Arg
23A1 **San Luis de la Paz** Mexico
21A2 **San Luis Obispo** USA
23A1 **San Luis Potosi** Mexico
22B2 **San Luis Res** USA
53A3 **Sanluri** Sardegna
33D2 **San Maigualida** *Mts* Ven
34D3 **San Manuel** Arg
34A2 **San Marcos** Chile
23B2 **San Marcos** Mexico
52B2 **San Marino** Republic, Europe
34B2 **San Martin** Mendoza, Arg
112C3 **San Martin** *Base* Ant
47D1 **San Martino di Castroza** Italy
23B2 **San Martin Tuxmelucan** Mexico
22A2 **San Mateo** USA
30E2 **San Matias** Bol
72C3 **Sanmenxia** China
25D3 **San Miguel** El Salvador
22B3 **San Miguel** *I* USA
23A1 **San Miguel del Allende** Mexico
34D3 **San Miguel del Monte** Arg
30C4 **San Miguel de Tucumán** Arg
73D4 **Sanming** China
9B3 **San Nicolas** *I* USA
34C2 **San Nicolás de los Arroyos** Arg
101G1 **Sannieshof** S Africa
97B4 **Sanniquellie** Lib
59C3 **Sanok** Pol
26B5 **San Onofore** Colombia
22D4 **San Onofre** USA
79B3 **San Pablo** Phil
22A1 **San Pablo B** USA
34D2 **San Pedro** Buenos Aires, Arg
97B4 **San Pédro** Ivory Coast
30D3 **San Pedro** Jujuy, Arg
30E3 **San Pedro** Par
22C4 **San Pedro Chan** USA
9C4 **San Pedro de los Colonias** Mexico
25D3 **San Pedro Sula** Honduras
53A3 **San Pietro** *I* Medit S
24A1 **San Quintin** Mexico
34B2 **San Rafael** Arg
22A2 **San Rafael** USA
22C3 **San Rafael Mts** USA
49D3 **San Remo** Italy
34D2 **San Salvador** Arg
26C2 **San Salvador** *I* Caribbean S
32J7 **San Salvador** *I* Ecuador
30C3 **San Salvador de Jujuy** Arg
51B1 **San Sebastian** Spain
53C2 **San Severo** Italy
30C2 **Santa Ana** Bol
25C3 **Santa Ana** Guatemala
22D4 **Santa Ana** USA
22D4 **Santa Ana Mts** USA
34A3 **Santa Bárbara** Chile
24B2 **Santa Barbara** Mexico
22C3 **Santa Barbara** USA
22C4 **Santa Barbara** *I* USA
22B3 **Santa Barbara Chan** USA
22C3 **Santa Barbara Res** USA
22C4 **Santa Catalina** *I* USA
22C4 **Santa Catalina,G of** USA
30F4 **Santa Catarina** State, Brazil
26B2 **Santa Clara** Cuba
22B2 **Santa Clara** USA
22C3 **Santa Clara** *R* USA
29C6 **Santa Cruz** Arg
30D2 **Santa Cruz** Bol
34A2 **Santa Cruz** Chile
79B3 **Santa Cruz** Phil
29B5 **Santa Cruz** State, Arg
22A2 **Santa Cruz** USA
22C4 **Santa Cruz** *I* USA
35D1 **Santa Cruz Cabrália** Brazil
22C3 **Santa Cruz Chan** USA
96A2 **Santa Cruz de la Palma** Canary Is
26B2 **Santa Cruz del Sur** Cuba
96A2 **Santa Cruz de Tenerife** Canary Is
100B2 **Santa Cruz do Cuando** Angola
35B2 **Santa Cruz do Rio Pardo** Brazil
22A2 **Santa Cruz Mts** USA
34D2 **Santa Elena** Arg
33E3 **Santa Elena** Ven
34C2 **Santa Fe** Arg
34C2 **Santa Fe** State, Arg
9C3 **Santa Fe** USA
35A1 **Santa Helena de Goiás** Brazil
73B3 **Santai** China
29B6 **Santa Inés** *I* Chile
34B3 **Santa Isabel** La Pampa, Arg
34C2 **Santa Isabel** Sante Fe, Arg
107E1 **Santa Isabel** *I* Solomon Is
21A2 **Santa Lucia** *Ra* USA
21A2 **Santa Lucia Range** *Mts* USA
97A4 **Santa Luzia** *I* Cape Verde
9B4 **Santa Margarita** *I* Mexico
22D4 **Santa Margarita** *R* USA
30F4 **Santa Maria** Brazil
26C4 **Santa Maria** Colombia
21A3 **Santa Maria** USA
96A1 **Santa Maria** *I* Açores
23B1 **Santa Maria** *R* Queretaro, Mexico
23A1 **Santa Maria del Rio** Mexico
32C1 **Santa Marta** Colombia
22C3 **Santa Monica** USA
22C4 **Santa Monica B** USA
29E2 **Santana do Livramento** Brazil
32B3 **Santander** Colombia
50B1 **Santander** Spain
51C2 **Santañy** Spain
22C3 **Santa Paula** USA
31C2 **Santa Quitéria** Brazil
33G4 **Santarem** Brazil
50A2 **Santarém** Port
22A1 **Santa Rosa** California, USA
25D3 **Santa Rosa** Honduras
34C3 **Santa Rosa** La Pampa, Arg
34B2 **Santa Rosa** Mendoza, Arg
34B2 **Santa Rosa** San Luis, Arg
22B3 **Santa Rosa** *I* USA
24A2 **Santa Rosalía** Mexico
20C2 **Santa Rosa Range** *Mts* USA
31D3 **Santa Talhada** Brazil
35C1 **Santa Teresa** Brazil
53A2 **Santa Teresa di Gallura** Sardegna
22B3 **Santa Ynez** *R* USA
22B3 **Santa Ynez Mts** USA
17C1 **Santee** *R* USA
47C2 **Santhia** Italy
34A2 **Santiago** Chile
27C3 **Santiago** Dom Rep
32A2 **Santiago** Panama
79B2 **Santiago** Phil
32B4 **Santiago** *R* Peru
50A1 **Santiago de Compostela** Spain
26B2 **Santiago de Cuba** Cuba
30D4 **Santiago del Estero** Arg
30D4 **Santiago del Estero** State, Arg
22D4 **Santiago Peak** *Mt* USA
31C5 **Santo** State, Brazil
35A2 **Santo Anastatácio** Brazil
30F4 **Santo Angelo** Brazil
97A4 **Santo Antão** *I* Cape Verde
35A2 **Santo Antonio da Platina** Brazil
27D3 **Santo Domingo** Dom Rep
35B2 **Santos** Brazil

35C2 **Santos Dumont** Brazil
30E4 **Santo Tomé** Arg
29B5 **San Valentin** *Mt* Chile
34A2 **San Vicente** Chile
98B3 **Sanza Pomba** Angola
30E4 **São Borja** Brazil
35B2 **São Carlos** Brazil
33G5 **São Félix** Mato Grosso, Brazil
35C2 **São Fidélis** Brazil
35C1 **São Francisco** Brazil
31D3 **São Francisco** *R* Brazil
30G4 **São Francisco do Sul** Brazil
35B1 **São Gotardo** Brazil
99D3 **Sao Hill** Tanz
35C2 **São João da Barra** Brazil
35B2 **São João da Boa Vista** Brazil
35C1 **São João da Ponte** Brazil
35C2 **São João del Rei** Brazil
35B2 **São Joaquim da Barra** Brazil
96A1 **São Jorge** *I* Açores
35B2 **São José do Rio Prêto** Brazil
35B2 **São José dos Campos** Brazil
31C2 **São Luís** Brazil
35B1 **São Marcos** *R* Brazil
35C1 **São Maria do Suaçui** Brazil
35D1 **São Mateus** Brazil
35C1 **São Mateus** *R* Brazil
96A1 **São Miguel** *I* Açores
49C2 **Saône** *R* France
97A4 **São Nicolau** *I* Cape Verde
35B2 **São Paulo** Brazil
35A2 **São Paulo** State, Brazil
31C3 **São Raimundo Nonato** Brazil
35B1 **São Romão** Brazil
35B2 **São Sebastia do Paraiso** Brazil
35A1 **São Simão** Goias, Brazil
35B2 **São Simão** Sao Paulo, Brazil
97A4 **São Tiago** *I* Cape Verde
97C4 **São Tomé** *I* W Africa
97C4 **São Tomé and Principe** Republic, W Africa
96B2 **Saoura** *Watercourse* Alg
35B2 **São Vicente** Brazil
97A4 **São Vincente** *I* Cape Verde
55C2 **Sápai** Greece
78D4 **Sape** Indon
97C4 **Sapele** Nig
74E2 **Sapporo** Japan
53C2 **Sapri** Italy
18A2 **Sapulpa** USA
90A2 **Saqqez** Iran
10C2 **Saquenay** *R* Can
90A2 **Saráb** Iran
54A2 **Sarajevo** Bosnia & Herzegovina, Yugos
90D2 **Sarakhs** Iran
61J3 **Saraktash** Russian Fed
63A2 **Sarala** Russian Fed
15D2 **Saranac L** USA
15D2 **Saranac Lake** USA
55B3 **Sarandë** Alb
79C4 **Sarangani Is** Phil
61G3 **Saransk** Russian Fed
61H2 **Sarapul** Russian Fed
17B2 **Sarasota** USA
54C1 **Sarata** Ukraine
15D2 **Saratoga Springs** USA
78C2 **Saratok** Malay
61G3 **Saratov** Russian Fed

61G3 **Saratovskoye Vodokhranilishche** *Res* Russian Fed
67F4 **Sarawak** State, Malay
92A2 **Saraykoy** Turk
90C3 **Sarbisheh** Iran
47D1 **Sarca** *R* Italy
95A2 **Sardalas** Libya
90A2 **Sar Dasht** Iran
52A2 **Sardegna** *I* Medit S
Sardinia = **Sardegna**
38H5 **Sarektjåkkå** *Mt* Sweden
84C2 **Sargodha** Pak
98B2 **Sarh** Chad
90B2 **Sārī** Iran
94B2 **Sarida** *R* Isreal
93D1 **Sarikamiş** Turk
107D3 **Sarina** Aust
47B1 **Sarine** *R* Switz
84B1 **Sar-i-Pul** Afghan
95B2 **Sarir** Libya
95A2 **Sarir Tibesti** *Desert* Libya
74B3 **Sariwŏn** N Korea
48B2 **Sark** *I* UK
92C2 **Sarkişla** Turk
71E4 **Sarmi** Indon
29C5 **Sarmiento** Arg
39G6 **Särna** Sweden
47C1 **Sarnen** Switz
14B2 **Sarnia** Can
58D2 **Sarny** Ukraine
6E2 **Saroaq** Greenland
84B2 **Sarobi** Afghan
78A3 **Sarolangun** Indon
55B3 **Saronikós Kólpos** *G* Greece
47C2 **Saronno** Italy
55C2 **Saros Körfezi** *B* Turk
39G7 **Sarpsborg** Nor
46D2 **Sarralbe** France
46D2 **Sarrebourg** France
46D2 **Sarreguemines** France
46D2 **Sarre-Union** France
51B1 **Sarrion** Spain
85B3 **Sartanahu** Pak
53A2 **Sartène** Corse
48B2 **Sarthe** *R* France
61H4 **Sarykamys** Kazakhstan
65H5 **Sarysu** *R* Kazakhstan
86A2 **Sasarām** India
74B4 **Sasebo** Japan
5H4 **Saskatchewan** Province, Can
5H4 **Saskatchewan** *R* Can
13F2 **Saskatoon** Can
101G1 **Sasolburg** S Africa
61F3 **Sasovo** Russian Fed
97B4 **Sassandra** Ivory Coast
97B4 **Sassandra** *R* Ivory Coast
53A2 **Sassari** Sardegna
56C2 **Sassnitz** Germany
47D2 **Sassuolo** Italy
34C2 **Sastre** Arg
87A1 **Sātāra** India
4G2 **Satellite B** Can
78D4 **Satengar** *Is* Indon
39H6 **Säter** Sweden
17B1 **Satilla** *R* USA
61J2 **Satka** Russian Fed
84D2 **Satluj** *R* India
86A2 **Satna** India
85C4 **Sātpura Range** *Mts* India
54B1 **Satu Mare** Rom
34D2 **Sauce** Arg
39F7 **Sauda** Nor
80C3 **Saudi Arabia** Kingdom, Arabian Pen
46D2 **Sauer** *R* Germany/Lux
46D1 **Sauerland** Region, Germany
38B1 **Sauðárkrókur** Iceland
14A2 **Saugatuck** USA

16C1 **Saugerties** USA
13B2 **Saugstad,Mt** Can
7B5 **Sault Sainte Marie** Can
14B1 **Sault Ste Marie** Can
14B1 **Sault Ste Marie** USA
71E4 **Saumlaki** Indon
48B2 **Saumur** France
98C3 **Saurimo** Angola
27M2 **Sauteurs** Grenada
54A2 **Sava** *R* Serbia, Yugos
97C4 **Savalou** Benin
17B1 **Savannah** Georgia, USA
17B1 **Savannah** *R* USA
76C2 **Savannakhet** Laos
26B3 **Savanna la Mar** Jamaica
7A4 **Savant Lake** Can
76D2 **Savarane** Laos
97C4 **Savé** Benin
101C3 **Save** *R* Mozam
90B3 **Sāveh** Iran
46D2 **Saverne** France
47B2 **Savigliano** Italy
46B2 **Savigny** France
49D2 **Savoie** *Region* France
49D3 **Savona** Italy
38K6 **Savonlinna** Fin
4A3 **Savoonga** USA
38K5 **Savukoski** Fin
71D4 **Savu S** Indon
76A1 **Saw** Burma
85D3 **Sawai Mādhopur** India
78A2 **Sawang** Indon
76B2 **Sawankhalok** Thai
75C1 **Sawara** Japan
12E1 **Sawtooth Mt** USA
106B2 **Sawu** *I* Indon
97C3 **Say** Niger
84B1 **Sayghan** Afghan
91B5 **Sayhūt** Yemen
61G4 **Saykhin** Kazakhstan
68D2 **Saynshand** Mongolia
61H5 **Say-Utes** Kazakhstan
16C2 **Sayville** USA
13B2 **Sayward** Can
57C3 **Sázava** *R* Czech
51C2 **Sbisseb** *R* Alg
42C2 **Scafell Pike** *Mt* Eng
44E1 **Scalloway** Scot
44C2 **Scapa Flow** *Sd* Scot
15C2 **Scarborough** Can
42D2 **Scarborough** Eng
27E4 **Scarborough** Tobago
44A2 **Scarp** *I* Scot
45B2 **Scarriff** Irish Rep
52A1 **Schaffhausen** Switz
57C3 **Scharding** Austria
46D1 **Scharteberg** *Mt* Germany
7D4 **Schefferville** Can
46B1 **Schelde** *R* Belg
10C2 **Schenectady** USA
47D2 **Schio** Italy
46D1 **Schleiden** Germany
56B2 **Schleswig** Germany
56B2 **Schleswig Holstein** State, Germany
16B1 **Schoharie** USA
71F4 **Schouten** *Is* PNG
7B5 **Schreiber** Can
21B2 **Schurz** USA
16A2 **Schuykill Haven** USA
16B2 **Schuylkill** *R* USA
57B3 **Schwabische Alb** *Upland* Germany
57B3 **Schwarzwald** *Upland* Germany
12C1 **Schwatka Mts** USA
47D1 **Schwaz** Austria
57C2 **Schweinfurt** Germany
101G1 **Schweizer Reneke** S Africa
56C2 **Schwerin** Germany
47C1 **Schwyz** Switz
53B3 **Sciacca** Italy
14B3 **Scioto** *R* USA
109D2 **Scone** Aust

6H2 **Scoresby Sd** Greenland
103F7 **Scotia Ridge** Atlantic O
103F7 **Scotia S** Atlantic O
44B3 **Scotland** Country, UK
112B7 **Scott** *Base* Ant
13B2 **Scott,C** Can
9C2 **Scott City** USA
112C6 **Scott I** Ant
6C2 **Scott Inlet** *B* Can
20B2 **Scott,Mt** USA
106B2 **Scott Reef** Timor S
8C2 **Scottsbluff** USA
17A1 **Scottsboro** USA
109C4 **Scottsdale** Aust
10C2 **Scranton** USA
47D1 **Scuol** Switz
Scutari = **Shkodër**
5J4 **Seal** *R* Can
108B3 **Sea Lake** Aust
18B2 **Searcy** USA
22B2 **Seaside** California, USA
20B1 **Seaside** Oregon, USA
16B3 **Seaside Park** USA
20B1 **Seattle** USA
22A1 **Sebastopol** USA
58D1 **Sebez** Russian Fed
17B2 **Sebring** USA
111A3 **Secretary I** NZ
18B2 **Sedalia** USA
46C2 **Sedan** France
111B2 **Seddonville** NZ
94B3 **Sede Boqer** Israel
94B3 **Sederot** Israel
97A3 **Sédhiou** Sen
94B3 **Sedom** Israel
100A3 **Seeheim** Namibia
111B2 **Sefton,Mt** NZ
77C5 **Segamat** Malay
51B2 **Segorbe** Spain
97B3 **Ségou** Mali
Segovia = **Coco**
50B1 **Segovia** Spain
51C1 **Segre** *R* Spain
97B4 **Séguéla** Ivory Coast
96A2 **Seguia el Hamra** *Watercourse* Mor
34C2 **Segundo** *R* Arg
78D2 **Seguntur** Indon
50B2 **Segura** *R* Spain
85B3 **Sehwan** Pak
46D2 **Seille** *R* France
38J6 **Seinäjoki** Fin
48C2 **Seine** *R* France
46B2 **Seine-et-Marne** Department, France
99D3 **Sekenke** Tanz
99D1 **Sek'ot'a** Eth
20B1 **Selah** USA
71E4 **Selaru** *I* Indon
78D4 **Selat Alas** *Str* Indon
78B3 **Selat Bangka** *Str* Indon
78A3 **Selat Berhala** *B* Indon
71E4 **Selat Dampier** *Str* Indon
78B3 **Selat Gaspar** *Str* Indon
78D4 **Selat Lombok** *Str* Indon
78D4 **Selat Sape** *Str* Indon
78B4 **Selat Sunda** *Str* Indon
71D4 **Selat Wetar** *Chan* Indon
12B1 **Selawik** USA
12C1 **Selawik** *R* USA
12B1 **Selawik L** USA
42D3 **Selby** Eng
55C3 **Selçuk** Turk
12D3 **Seldovia** USA
100B3 **Selebi Pikwe** Botswana
6H3 **Selfoss** Iceland
95B2 **Selima Oasis** Sudan
5J4 **Selkirk** Can
42C2 **Selkirk** Scot
13D2 **Selkirk Mts** Can

22C2 **Selma** California, USA
50B2 **Selouane** Mor
12H2 **Selous,Mt** Can
78B3 **Selta Karimata** *Str* Indon
32C5 **Selvas** Region, Brazil
107D3 **Selwyn** Aust
4E3 **Selwyn Mts** Can
78C4 **Semarang** Indon
61E2 **Semenov** Russian Fed
12C3 **Semidi Is** USA
60E3 **Semiluki** Russian Fed
19A2 **Seminole** Oklahoma, USA
17B1 **Seminole,L** USA
65K4 **Semipalatinsk** Kazakhstan
79B3 **Semirara Is** Phil
90B3 **Semirom** Iran
78C2 **Semitau** Indon
90B2 **Semnān** Iran
46C2 **Semois** *R* Belg
23B2 **Sempoala** Hist Site, Mexico
32D5 **Sena Madureira** Brazil
100B2 **Senanga** Zambia
19C3 **Senatobia** USA
74E3 **Sendai** Honshū, Japan
74C4 **Sendai** Kyūshu, Japan
85D4 **Sendwha** India
15C2 **Seneca Falls** USA
97A3 **Senegal** Republic, Africa
97A3 **Sénégal** *R* Maur Sen
101G1 **Senekal** S Africa
31D4 **Senhor do Bonfim** Brazil
52B2 **Senigallia** Italy
52C2 **Senj** Croatia
69E4 **Senkaku Gunto** *Is* Japan
46B2 **Senlis** France
99D1 **Sennar** Sudan
7C5 **Senneterre** Can
49C2 **Sens** France
54A1 **Senta** Serbia, Yugos
98C3 **Sentery** Zaïre
13C2 **Sentinel Peak** *Mt* Can
85D4 **Seoni** India
Seoul = Soul
110B2 **Separation Pt** NZ
76D2 **Sepone** Laos
7D4 **Sept-Iles** Can
95A2 **Séquédine** Niger
21B2 **Sequoia** Nat Pk, USA
71D4 **Seram** *I* Indon
78B4 **Serang** Indon
78B2 **Serasan** *I* Indon
54A2 **Serbia** Republic, Yugos
61F3 **Serdobsk** Russian Fed
77C5 **Seremban** Malay
99D3 **Serengeti Nat Pk** Tanz
100C2 **Serenje** Zambia
59D3 **Seret** *R* Ukraine
61G2 **Sergach** Russian Fed
65H3 **Sergino** Russian Fed
31D4 **Sergipe** State, Brazil
78C2 **Seria** Brunei
78C2 **Serian** Malay
55B3 **Sérifos** *I* Greece
47C2 **Serio** *R* Italy
95B2 **Serir Calanscio** *Desert* Libya
46C2 **Sermaize-les-Bains** France
71D4 **Sermata** *I* Indon
61H3 **Sernovodsk** Russian Fed
65H4 **Serov** Russian Fed
100B3 **Serowe** Botswana
50A2 **Serpa** Port
60E3 **Serpukhov** Russian Fed
35B2 **Serra da Canastra** *Mts* Brazil
50A1 **Serra da Estrela** *Mts* Port
35B2 **Serra da Mantiqueira** *Mts* Brazil
35A1 **Serra da Mombuca** Brazil
35C1 **Serra do Cabral** *Mt* Brazil
33F5 **Serra do Cachimbo** *Mts* Brazil
35A1 **Serra do Caiapó** *Mts* Brazil
35A2 **Serra do Cantu** *Mts* Brazil
35C2 **Serra do Caparaó** *Mts* Brazil
31C5 **Serra do Chifre** Brazil
35C1 **Serra do Espinhaço** *Mts* Brazil
35B2 **Serra do Mar** *Mts* Brazil
35A2 **Serra do Mirante** *Mts* Brazil
33G3 **Serra do Navio** Brazil
35B2 **Serra do Paranapiacaba** *Mts* Brazil
33F6 **Serra dos Caiabis** *Mts* Brazil
35A2 **Serra dos Dourados** *Mts* Brazil
33E6 **Serra dos Parecis** *Mts* Brazil
35B1 **Serra dos Piloes** *Mts* Brazil
35A1 **Serra Dourada** *Mts* Brazil
33F6 **Serra Formosa** *Mts* Brazil
55B2 **Sérrai** Greece
25D3 **Serrana Bank** *Is* Caribbean S
51B1 **Serrana de Cuenca** *Mts* Spain
35A1 **Serranópolis** Brazil
33E3 **Serra Pacaraima** *Mts* Brazil/Ven
33E3 **Serra Parima** *Mts* Brazil
33G3 **Serra Tumucumaque** Brazil
46B2 **Serre** *R* France
34B2 **Serrezuela** Arg
31D4 **Serrinha** Brazil
6G3 **Serrmilik** Greenland
35C1 **Serro** Brazil
35A2 **Sertanópolis** Brazil
72A3 **Sêrtar** China
78C3 **Seruyan** *R* Indon
100A2 **Sesfontein** Namibia
100B2 **Sesheke** Zambia
47B2 **Sestriere** Italy
74D2 **Setana** Japan
49C3 **Sète** France
35C1 **Sete Lagoas** Brazil
96C1 **Sétif** Alg
75B1 **Seto** Japan
75A2 **Seto Naikai** *S* Japan
96B1 **Settat** Mor
42C2 **Settle** Eng
5G4 **Settler** Can
50A2 **Sêtúbal** Port
93E1 **Sevan,Oz** *L* Armenia
60D5 **Sevastopol'** Ukraine
7B4 **Severn** *R* Can
43C3 **Severn** *R* Eng
1B9 **Severnaya Zemlya** *I* Russian Fed
63C2 **Severo-Baykalskoye Nagorye** *Mts* Russian Fed
60E4 **Severo Donets** Ukraine
64E3 **Severodvinsk** Russian Fed
64H3 **Severo Sos'va** *R* Russian Fed
8B3 **Sevier** *R* USA
8B3 **Sevier L** USA
50A2 **Sevilla** Spain
Seville = Sevilla
54C2 **Sevlievo** Bulg
97A4 **Sewa** *R* Sierra Leone
12E2 **Seward** Alaska, USA
18A1 **Seward** Nebraska, USA
12A1 **Seward Pen** USA
13D1 **Sexsmith** Can
89K8 **Seychelles** *Is* Indian O
38C1 **Seyðisfjörður** Iceland
92C2 **Seyhan** Turk
60E3 **Seym** *R* Russian Fed
108C3 **Seymour** Aust
16C2 **Seymour** Connecticut, USA
14A3 **Seymour** Indiana, USA
46B2 **Sézanne** France
96D1 **Sfax** Tunisia
54C1 **Sfînto Gheorghe** Rom
56A2 **'s-Gravenhage** Neth
72B3 **Shaanxi** Province, China
98C3 **Shabunda** Zaïre
82B2 **Shache** China
112C9 **Shackleton Ice Shelf** Ant
85B3 **Shadadkot** Pak
91B3 **Shādhām** *R* Iran
43C4 **Shaftesbury** Eng
29G8 **Shag Rocks** *Is* South Georgia
90A3 **Shāhabād** Iran
94C2 **Shahbā** Syria
91C3 **Shahdap** Iran
86A2 **Shahdol** India
90A2 **Shāhīn Dezh** Iran
90C3 **Shāh Kūh** Iran
91C3 **Shahr-e Bābak** Iran
Shahresa = Qomisheh
90B3 **Shahr Kord** Iran
87B1 **Shājābād** India
84D3 **Shājahānpur** India
85D4 **Shājāpur** India
61F4 **Shakhty** Russian Fed
61G2 **Shakhun'ya** Russian Fed
97C4 **Shaki** Nig
12B2 **Shaktoolik** USA
61J2 **Shamary** Russian Fed
99D2 **Shambe** Sudan
16A2 **Shamokin** USA
16B1 **Shandaken** USA
72D2 **Shandong** Province, China
73C5 **Shangchuan Dao** *I* China
72C1 **Shangdu** China
73E3 **Shanghai** China
72C3 **Shangnan** China
100B2 **Shangombo** Zambia
73D4 **Shangra** China
73B5 **Shangsi** China
72C3 **Shang Xian** China
41B3 **Shannon** *R* Irish Rep
72D3 **Shanqiu** China
74B2 **Shansonggang** China
63F2 **Shantarskiye Ostrova** *I* Russian Fed
73D5 **Shantou** China
72C2 **Shanxi** Province, China
72D3 **Shan Xian** China
73C5 **Shaoguan** China
73E4 **Shaoxing** China
73C4 **Shaoyang** China
44C2 **Shapinsay** *I* Scot
94C2 **Shaqqā** Syria
72A1 **Sharhulsan** Mongolia
90C2 **Sharifābād** Iran
91C4 **Sharjah** UAE
106A3 **Shark B** Aust
90C2 **Sharlauk** Turkmenistan
94B2 **Sharon,Plain of** Israel
61G2 **Sharya** Russian Fed
99D2 **Shashemanē** Eth
73C3 **Shashi** China
20B2 **Shasta L** USA
20B2 **Shasta,Mt** USA
93E3 **Shaṭṭ al Gharrat** *R* Iraq
94B3 **Shaubak** Jordan
13F3 **Shaunavon** Can
22C2 **Shaver L** USA
16B2 **Shawangunk Mt** USA
15D1 **Shawinigan** Can
19A2 **Shawnee** Oklahoma, USA
73D4 **Sha Xian** China
106B3 **Shay Gap** Aust
94C2 **Shaykh Miskīn** Syria
99E1 **Shaykh 'Uthmān** Yemen
60E3 **Shchekino** Russian Fed
60E3 **Shchigry** Russian Fed
60D3 **Shchors** Ukraine
65J4 **Shchuchinsk** Kazakhstan
99E2 **Shebele** *R* Eth
14A2 **Sheboygan** USA
98B2 **Shebshi** *Mts* Nig
12F1 **Sheenjek** *R* USA
45C1 **Sheep Haven** *Estuary* Irish Rep
43E4 **Sheerness** Eng
94B2 **Shefar'am** Israel
42D3 **Sheffield** Eng
84C2 **Shekhupura** Pak
13B1 **Shelagyote Peak** *Mt* Can
16C1 **Shelburne Falls** USA
14A2 **Shelby** Michigan, USA
8B2 **Shelby** Montana, USA
14A3 **Shelbyville** Indiana, USA
12H2 **Sheldon,Mt** Can
12D3 **Shelikof Str** USA
109D2 **Shellharbour** Aust
111A3 **Shelter Pt** NZ
20B1 **Shelton** USA
93E1 **Shemakha** Azerbaijan
18A1 **Shenandoah** USA
15C3 **Shenandoah** *R* USA
15C3 **Shenandoah Nat Pk** USA
97C4 **Shendam** Nig
95C2 **Shendi** Sudan
72C2 **Shenmu** China
72E1 **Shenyang** China
73C5 **Shenzhen** China
85D3 **Sheopur** India
59D2 **Shepetovka** Ukraine
108C3 **Shepparton** Aust
6B2 **Sherard,C** Can
43C4 **Sherborne** Eng
97A4 **Sherbro I** Sierra Leone
15D1 **Sherbrooke** Can
85C3 **Shergarh** India
19B3 **Sheridan** Arkansas, USA
8C2 **Sheridan** Wyoming, USA
19A3 **Sherman** USA
56B2 **s-Hertogenbosh** Neth
12H3 **Sheslay** Can
40C1 **Shetland** *Is* Scot
61H5 **Shevchenko** Kazakhstan
91B4 **Sheyk Sho'eyb** *I* Iran
69H2 **Shiashkotan** *I* Russian Fed
84B1 **Shibarghan** Afghan
74D3 **Shibata** Japan
95C1 **Shibin el Kom** Egypt
75B1 **Shibukawa** Japan
72C2 **Shijiazhuang** China
84B3 **Shikarpur** Pak
67G3 **Shikoku** *I* Japan
75A2 **Shikoku-sanchi** *Mts* Japan
86B1 **Shiliguri** India
68D1 **Shilka** Russian Fed
68D1 **Shilka** *R* Russian Fed
16B2 **Shillington** USA
86C1 **Shillong** India
61F3 **Shilovo** Russian Fed
75A2 **Shimabara** Japan
75B2 **Shimada** Japan
69E1 **Shimanovsk** Russian Fed

74D3 **Shimizu** Japan
75B2 **Shimoda** Japan
87B2 **Shimoga** India
74C4 **Shimonoseki** Japan
75B1 **Shinano** R Japan
91C5 **Shinäş** Oman
74D4 **Shingü** Japan
75C1 **Shinjö** Japan
74D3 **Shinminato** Japan
94C1 **Shinshär** Syria
99D3 **Shinyanga** Tanz
74E3 **Shiogama** Japan
75B2 **Shiono-misaki** C Japan
73A5 **Shiping** China
16A2 **Shippensburg** USA
72B3 **Shiquan** China
75C1 **Shirakawa** Japan
75B1 **Shirane-san** Mt Japan
75B1 **Shirani-san** Mt Japan
91B4 **Shiraz** Iran
90B3 **Shīr Küh** Iran
75B1 **Shirotori** Japan
90C2 **Shirvān** Iran
12A1 **Shishmaref** USA
12A1 **Shishmaref Inlet** USA
4B3 **Shishmaret** USA
72B2 **Shitanjing** China
14A3 **Shively** USA
85D3 **Shivpuri** India
94B3 **Shivta** Hist Site Israel
101C2 **Shiwa Ngandu** Zambia
72C3 **Shiyan** China
72B2 **Shizuishan** China
75B1 **Shizuoka** Japan
54A2 **Shkodër** Alb
109D2 **Shoalhaven** R Aust
75A2 **Shobara** Japan
87B2 **Shoranür** India
87B1 **Shorāpur** India
21B2 **Shoshone Mts** USA
60D3 **Shostka** Ukraine
19B3 **Shreveport** USA
43C3 **Shrewsbury** Eng
43C3 **Shropshire** County, Eng
72E1 **Shuanglia** China
69F2 **Shuangyashan** China
61J4 **Shubar-Kuduk** Kazakhstan
72D2 **Shu He** R China
73A4 **Shuicheng** China
84C3 **Shujaabad** Pak
85D4 **Shujälpur** India
68B2 **Shule He** China
54C2 **Shumen** Bulg
61G2 **Shumerlya** Russian Fed
73D4 **Shuncheng** China
12C1 **Shungnak** USA
72C2 **Shuo Xian** China
91C4 **Shür Gaz** Iran
100B2 **Shurugwi** Zim
13D2 **Shuswap L** Can
61F2 **Shuya** Russian Fed
12D3 **Shuyak I** USA
82D3 **Shwebo** Burma
76B2 **Shwegyin** Burma
84A2 **Siah Koh** Mts Afghan
84C2 **Sialkot** Pak
Sian = Xi'an
79C4 **Siarao** I Phil
79B4 **Siaton** Phil
58C1 **Šiauliai** Lithuania
65G4 **Sibay** Russian Fed
101H1 **Sibayi L** S Africa
52C2 **Šibenik** Croatia
70A4 **Siberut** I Indon
84B3 **Sibi** Pak
68C1 **Sibirskoye** Russian Fed
98B3 **Sibiti** Congo
99D3 **Sibiti** R Tanz
54B1 **Sibiu** Rom
70A3 **Sibolga** Indon
86C1 **Sibsāgār** India
78C2 **Sibu** Malay
79B4 **Sibuguay B** Phil

98B2 **Sibut** CAR
79B3 **Sibuyan** I Phil
79B3 **Sibuyan S** Phil
73A3 **Sichuan** Province, China
53B3 **Sicilia** I Medit S
53B3 **Sicilian Chan** Italy/ Tunisia
Sicily = Sicilia
32C6 **Sicuani** Peru
85C4 **Siddhapur** India
87B1 **Siddipet** India
86A2 **Sidhi** India
95B1 **Sidi Barrani** Egypt
96B1 **Sidi Bel Abbès** Alg
96B1 **Sidi Kacem** Mor
44C3 **Sidlaw Hills** Scot
112B5 **Sidley,Mt** Ant
20B1 **Sidney** Can
8C2 **Sidney** Nebraska, USA
15C2 **Sidney** New York, USA
14B2 **Sidney** Ohio, USA
17B1 **Sidney Lanier,L** USA
Sidon = Säida
58C2 **Siedlce** Pol
46D1 **Sieg** R Germany
46D1 **Siegburg** Germany
46D1 **Siegen** Germany
76C3 **Siem Reap** Camb
52B2 **Siena** Italy
58B2 **Sierpc** Pol
23B2 **Sierra Andrés Tuxtla** Mexico
34B3 **Sierra Auca Mahuida** Mts Arg
9C3 **Sierra Blanca** USA
51B1 **Sierra de Albarracin** Mts Spain
50B2 **Sierra de Alcaraz** Mts Spain
34B2 **Sierra de Cordoba** Mts Arg
50A1 **Sierra de Gredos** Mts Spain
50A2 **Sierra de Guadalupe** Mts Spain
50B1 **Sierra de Guadarrama** Mts Spain
51B1 **Sierra de Guara** Mts Spain
51B1 **Sierra de Gudar** Mts Spain
23B2 **Sierra de Juárez** Mexico
34C3 **Sierra de la Ventana** Mts Arg
51C1 **Sierra del Codi** Mts Spain
34B2 **Sierra del Morro** Mt Arg
34B3 **Sierra del Nevado** Mts Arg
24B2 **Sierra de los Alamitos** Mts Mexico
50B2 **Sierra de los Filabres** Spain
23A1 **Sierra de los Huicholes** Mexico
23B2 **Sierra de Miahuatlán** Mexico
23A1 **Sierra de Morones** Mts Mexico
50A2 **Sierra de Ronda** Mts Spain
34B2 **Sierra de San Luis** Mts Arg
50B2 **Sierra de Segura** Mts Spain
50B1 **Sierra de Urbion** Mts Spain
34B2 **Sierra de Uspallata** Mts Arg
34B2 **Sierra de Valle Fértil** Mts Arg
23B2 **Sierra de Zongolica** Mexico
34C2 **Sierra Grande** Mts Arg
97A4 **Sierra Leone** Republic, Africa

97A4 **Sierra Leone,C** Sierra Leone
79B2 **Sierra Madre** Mts Phil
23A2 **Sierra Madre del Sur** Mts Mexico
24B2 **Sierra Madre Occidental** Mts Mexico
24C2 **Sierra Madre Oriental** Mts Mexico
34B2 **Sierra Malanzan** Mts Arg
9C4 **Sierra Mojada** Mexico
50A2 **Sierra Morena** Mts Spain
50B2 **Sierra Nevada** Mts Spain
21A2 **Sierra Nevada** Mts USA
32C1 **Sierra Nevada de Santa Marta** Mts Colombia
34B2 **Sierra Pié de Palo** Mts Arg
47B1 **Sierre** Switz
55B3 **Sifnos** I Greece
59C3 **Sighetu Marmației** Rom
54B1 **Sighișoara** Rom
38B1 **Siglufjörður** Iceland
50B1 **Sigüenza** Spain
97B3 **Siguiri** Guinea
85E4 **Sihora** India
93D2 **Siirt** Turk
68B3 **Sikai Hu** L China
85D3 **Sikar** India
84B2 **Sikaram** Mt Afghan
97B3 **Sikasso** Mali
18C2 **Sikeston** USA
55C3 **Sikinos** I Greece
55B3 **Sikionía** Greece
86B1 **Sikkim** State, India
50A1 **Sil** R Spain
47D1 **Silandro** Italy
23A1 **Silao** Mexico
79B3 **Silay** Phil
86C2 **Silchar** India
96C2 **Silet** Alg
86A1 **Silgarhi** Nepal
92B2 **Silifke** Turk
82C2 **Siling Co** L China
54C2 **Silistra** Bulg
39F7 **Silkeborg** Den
47E1 **Sillian** Austria
18B2 **Siloam Springs** USA
19B3 **Silsbee** USA
95A3 **Siltou** Well Chad
58C1 **Šilute** Lithuania
93D2 **Silvan** Turk
35B1 **Silvania** Brazil
85C4 **Silvassa** India
21B2 **Silver City** Nevada, USA
9C3 **Silver City** New Mexico, USA
20B2 **Silver Lake** USA
16A3 **Silver Spring** USA
13B2 **Silverthrone Mt** Can
108B2 **Silverton** Aust
47C1 **Silvretta** Mts Austria/Switz
78C2 **Simanggang** Malay
76C1 **Simao** China
90A3 **Simareh** R Iran
55C3 **Simav** Turk
55C3 **Simav** R Turk
15C2 **Simcoe,L** Can
70A3 **Simeulue** I Indon
60D5 **Simferopol'** Ukraine
55C3 **Simi** I Greece
84D2 **Simla** India
46D1 **Simmern** Germany
13B2 **Simoon Sound** Can
49D2 **Simplon** Mt Switz
47C1 **Simplon** P Switz
4C2 **Simpson,C** USA
106C3 **Simpson Desert** Aust
6B3 **Simpson Pen** Can
39G7 **Simrishamn** Sweden
69H2 **Simushir** I Russian Fed
99E2 **Sina Dhaqa** Somalia

92B4 **Sinai** Pen Egypt
32B2 **Sincelejo** Colombia
17B1 **Sinclair,L** USA
85D3 **Sind** R India
85B3 **Sindh** Region, Pak
55C3 **Sindirği** Turk
86B2 **Sindri** India
50A2 **Sines** Port
99D1 **Singa** Sudan
77C5 **Singapore** Republic, S E Asia
77C5 **Singapore,Str of** S E Asia
78D4 **Singaraja** Indon
99D3 **Singida** Tanz
78B2 **Singkawang** Indon
109D2 **Singleton** Aust
78A3 **Singtep** I Indon
76B1 **Singu** Burma
53A2 **Siniscola** Sardegna
93D2 **Sinjár** Iraq
84B2 **Sinkai Hills** Mts Afghan
95C3 **Sinkat** Sudan
82C1 **Sinkiang** Autonomous Region, China
33G2 **Sinnamary** French Guiana
92C1 **Sinop** Turk
54B1 **Sintana** Rom
78C2 **Sintang** Indon
50A2 **Sintra** Port
32B2 **Sinú** R Colombia
74A2 **Sinüiju** N Korea
59B3 **Siofok** Hung
47B1 **Sion** Switz
8D2 **Sioux City** USA
8D2 **Sioux Falls** USA
10A2 **Sioux Lookout** Can
79B4 **Sipalay** Phil
27L1 **Siparia** Trinidad
69E2 **Siping** China
112B3 **Siple** Base Ant
112B5 **Siple I** Ant
79B3 **Sipocot** Phil
70A4 **Sipora** Indon
79B4 **Siquijor** I Phil
87B2 **Sira** India
53C3 **Siracusa** Italy
86B2 **Sirajganj** Bang
13C2 **Sir Alexander,Mt** Can
91B5 **Sir Banī Yās** I UAE
106C2 **Sir Edward Pellew Group** Is Aust
54C1 **Siret** R Rom
12J2 **Sir James McBrien,Mt** Can
87B2 **Sir Kālahasti** India
13D2 **Sir Laurier,Mt** Can
93D2 **Şirnak** Turk
85C4 **Sirohi** India
87B1 **Sironcha** India
85D4 **Sironj** India
55B3 **Siros** I Greece
91B4 **Sirri** I Iran
84D3 **Sirsa** India
13D2 **Sir Sandford,Mt** Can
87A2 **Sirsi** India
95A1 **Sirte Desert** Libya
95A1 **Sirte,G of** Libya
52C1 **Sisak** Croatia
76C2 **Sisaket** Thai
76C3 **Sisophon** Camb
46B2 **Sissonne** France
90D3 **Sistan** Region, Iran/ Afghan
49D3 **Sisteron** France
63B2 **Sistig Khem** Russian Fed
86A1 **Sītāpur** India
55C3 **Sitia** Greece
4E4 **Sitka** USA
12D3 **Sitkalidak I** USA
12D3 **Sitkinak I** USA
76B2 **Sittang** R Burma
46C1 **Sittard** Neth
86C2 **Sittwe** Burma
78C4 **Situbondo** Indon
92C2 **Sivas** Turk
93C2 **Siverek** Turk
92B2 **Sivrihisar** Turk
95B2 **Siwa** Egypt

84D2 **Siwalik Range** *Mts* India
86A1 **Siwalik Range** *Mts* Nepal
72D3 **Siyang** China
56C1 **Sjaelland** *I* Den
39G7 **Skagen** Den
39F7 **Skagerrak** *Str* Nor/ Den
20B1 **Skagit** *R* USA
20B1 **Skagit Mt** Can
4E4 **Skagway** USA
39G7 **Skara** Sweden
59C2 **Skarzysko-Kamlenna** Pol
5F4 **Skeena** *R* Can
13B1 **Skeena Mts** Can
4D3 **Skeenjek** *R* USA
42E3 **Skegness** Eng
38H5 **Skellefte** *R* Sweden
38J6 **Skellefteå** Sweden
55B3 **Skíathos** *I* Greece
45B3 **Skibbereen** Irish Rep
5E4 **Skidegate** Can
58C2 **Skiemiewice** Pol
39F7 **Skien** Nor
96C1 **Skikda** Alg
74C4 **Skikoku** *I* Japan
42D3 **Skipton** Eng
55B3 **Skíros** *I* Greece
39F7 **Skive** Den
56B1 **Skjern** Den
6F3 **Skjoldungen** Greenland
14A2 **Skokie** USA
55B3 **Skópelos** *I* Greece
54B2 **Skopje** Macedonia, Yugos
39G7 **Skövde** Sweden
63E2 **Skovorodino** Russian Fed
4C3 **Skwentna** USA
58B2 **Skwierzyna** Pol
40B2 **Skye** *I* Scot
39G7 **Slagelse** Den
45C2 **Slaney** *R* Irish Rep
54B2 **Slatina** Rom
78C4 **Slaung** Indon
5G3 **Slave** *R* Can
13E1 **Slave Lake** Can
65J4 **Slavgorod** Russian Fed
59D2 **Slavuta** Ukraine
60E4 **Slavyansk** Ukraine
44B3 **Sleat,Sound of** *Chan* Scot
12C2 **Sleetmute** USA
45C2 **Sleeve Bloom** *Mts* Irish Rep
19C3 **Slidell** USA
16B2 **Slide Mt** USA
45B1 **Sligo** County, Irish Rep
41B3 **Sligo** Irish Rep
41B3 **Sligo** *B* Irish Rep
54C2 **Sliven** Bulg
54C2 **Slobozia** Rom
13D3 **Slocan** Can
58D2 **Slonim** Belorussia
43D4 **Slough** Eng
22B2 **Slough** *R* USA
52B1 **Slovenia** Republic, Europe
59B3 **Slovensko** Region, Czech
56C2 **Slubice** Pol
59D2 **Sluch'** *R* Ukraine
58B2 **Słupsk** Pol
58D2 **Slutsk** Belorussia
58D2 **Slutsk** *R* Belorussia
41A3 **Slyne Head** *Pt* Irish Rep
63C2 **Slyudyanka** Russian Fed
7D4 **Smallwood Res** Can
54B2 **Smederevo** Serbia, Yugos
54B2 **Smederevska Palanka** Serbia, Yugos
60D4 **Smela** Ukraine
15C2 **Smethport** USA
13E1 **Smith** Can
4F3 **Smith Arm** *B* Can
13B2 **Smithers** Can
7C3 **Smith I** Can
13B2 **Smith Sd** Can
15C2 **Smiths Falls** Can
109C4 **Smithton** Aust
13D1 **Smoky** *R* Can
109D2 **Smoky C** Aust
13E2 **Smoky Lake** Can
38F6 **Smøla** *I* Nor
60D3 **Smolensk** Russian Fed
55B2 **Smólikas** *Mt* Greece
54B2 **Smolyan** Bulg
58D2 **Smorgon'** Belorussia
16B3 **Smyrna** Delaware, USA
17B1 **Smyrna** Georgia, USA
42B2 **Snaefell** *Mt* Eng
38B2 **Snafell** *Mt* Iceland
8B2 **Snake** *R* USA
8B2 **Snake River Canyon** USA
56B2 **Sneek** Neth
45B3 **Sneem** Irish Rep
22B2 **Snelling** USA
59B2 **Sněžka** *Mt* Pol/Czech
38F6 **Snøhetta** *Mt* Nor
20B1 **Snohomish** USA
20B1 **Snoqualmie P** USA
76D3 **Snoul** Camb
43B3 **Snowdon** *Mt* Wales
43B3 **Snowdonia Nat Pk** Wales
4G3 **Snowdrift** Can
5H4 **Snow Lake** Can
108A2 **Snowtown** Aust
109C3 **Snowy Mts** Aust
9C3 **Snyder** USA
74B4 **Soan-kundo** *I* S Korea
99D2 **Sobat** *R* Sudan
31C2 **Sobral** Brazil
58C2 **Sochaczew** Pol
61E5 **Sochi** Russian Fed
9C3 **Socorro** USA
24A3 **Socorro** *I* Mexico
34A2 **Socos** Chile
81D4 **Socotra** *I* Yemen
38K5 **Sodankylä** Fin
39H6 **Soderhamn** Sweden
39H7 **Södertälje** Sweden
99C1 **Sodiri** Sudan
99D2 **Sodo** Eth
46E1 **Soest** Germany
101C2 **Sofala** Mozam
Sofia = Sofiya
54B2 **Sofiya** Bulg
69G4 **Sofu Gan** *I* Japan
32C2 **Sogamoso** Colombia
39F6 **Sognefjorden** *Inlet* Nor
82D2 **Sog Xian** China
95C2 **Sohâg** Egypt
84D3 **Sohīpat** India
46B1 **Soignies** Belg
46B2 **Soissons** France
85C3 **Sojat** India
74A3 **Sŏjosŏn-man** *B* N Korea
92A2 **Söke** Turk
97C4 **Sokodé** Togo
61E2 **Sokol** Russian Fed
58C2 **Sokołka** Pol
97B3 **Sokolo** Mali
6H3 **Søkongens Øy** *I* Greenland
99D1 **Sokota** Eth
97C3 **Sokoto** Nig
97C3 **Sokoto** *R* Nig
111A3 **Solander I** NZ
79B2 **Solano** Phil
87B1 **Solapur** India
47D1 **Solbad Hall** Austria
47D1 **Sölden** Austria
12D2 **Soldotna** USA
26C4 **Soledad** Colombia
43D4 **Solent** *Sd* Eng
46B1 **Solesmes** France
58D2 **Soligorsk** Belorussia
61J2 **Solikamsk** Russian Fed
32C4 **Solimões** *R* Peru
46D1 **Solingen** Germany
38H6 **Sollefteå** Sweden
61H3 **Sol'lletsk** Russian Fed
70B4 **Solok** Indon
105G4 **Solomon** *Is* Pacific O
47B1 **Solothurn** Switz
39F8 **Soltau** Germany
22B3 **Solvang** USA
42C2 **Solway Firth** *Estuary* Eng/Scot
100B2 **Solwezi** Zambia
75C1 **Sōma** Japan
55C3 **Soma** Turk
81C5 **Somalia** Republic, E Africa
54A1 **Sombor** Serbia, Yugos
107D2 **Somerset** Aust
43C4 **Somerset** County, Eng
16D2 **Somerset** Massachusetts, USA
15C2 **Somerset** Pennsylvania, USA
100B4 **Somerset East** S Africa
6A2 **Somerset I** Can
16B3 **Somers Point** USA
16B2 **Somerville** USA
19A3 **Somerville Res** USA
54B1 **Somes** *R* Rom
46B2 **Somme** Department, France
46B2 **Somme** *R* France
46C2 **Sommesous** France
86A2 **Son** *R* India
74A3 **Sonch'ŏn** N Korea
39F8 **Sønderborg** Den
6E3 **Søndre Strømfjord** Greenland
47C1 **Sondrio** Italy
76D3 **Song Ba** *R* Viet
76D3 **Song Cau** Viet
101C2 **Songea** Tanz
73E3 **Songjiang** China
77C4 **Songkhla** Thai
74B3 **Songnim** N Korea
77C5 **Sông Pahang** *R* Malay
72A3 **Songpan** China
72C1 **Sonid Youqi** China
76C1 **Son La** Viet
85B3 **Sonmiani** Pak
85B3 **Sonmiani Bay** Pak
22A1 **Sonoma** USA
22B2 **Sonora** California, USA
24A2 **Sonora** *R* Mexico
9B3 **Sonoran Desert** USA
22C1 **Sonora P** USA
25D3 **Sonsonate** El Salvador
71E3 **Sonsorol** *I* Pacific O
10B2 **Soo Canals** Can/USA
13C3 **Sooke** Can
58B2 **Sopot** Pol
59B3 **Sopron** Hung
22B2 **Soquel** USA
53B2 **Sora** Italy
94B3 **Sored** *R* Israel
15D1 **Sorel** Can
109C4 **Sorell** Aust
92C2 **Sorgun** Turk
50B1 **Soria** Spain
38J5 **Sørkjosen** Nor
64C2 **Sørksop** *I* Barents S
61H4 **Sor Mertvyy Kultuk** *Plain* Kazakhstan
35B2 **Sorocaba** Brazil
61H3 **Sorochinsk** Russian Fed
71F3 **Soroi** *I* Pacific O
60C4 **Soroki** Moldavia
71E4 **Sorong** Indon
71E4 **Sorong** Province, Indon
99D2 **Soroti** Uganda
38J4 **Sørøya** *I* Nor
53B2 **Sorrento** Italy
38K5 **Sorsatunturi** *Mt* Fin
38H5 **Sorsele** Sweden
79B3 **Sorsogon** Phil
38L6 **Sortavala** Russian Fed
74B3 **Sŏsan** S Korea
59B2 **Sosnowiec** Pol
65H4 **Sos'va** Russian Fed
98B2 **Souanké** Congo
97B4 **Soubré** Ivory Coast
16B2 **Souderton** USA
27P2 **Soufrière** St Lucia
27N2 **Soufrière** *V* St Vincent
48C3 **Souillac** France
96C1 **Souk Ahras** Alg
74B3 **Soul** S Korea
51C2 **Soummam** *R* Alg
Sour = Tyr
101G1 **Sources,Mt aux** Lesotho
31D3 **Sousa** Brazil
96D1 **Sousse** Tunisia
100B4 **South Africa** Republic, Africa
16B2 **South Amboy** USA
14B2 **Southampton** Can
43D4 **Southampton** Eng
16C2 **Southampton** USA
6B3 **Southampton I** Can
28F6 **South Atlantic O**
7D4 **South Aulatsivik I** Can
106C3 **South Australia** State, Aust
104E5 **South Australian Basin** Indian O
19C3 **Southaven** USA
17B2 **South Bay** USA
14B1 **South Baymouth** Can
14A2 **South Bend** Indiana, USA
20B1 **South Bend** Washington, USA
16D1 **Southbridge** USA
South Cape = Ka Lae
11B3 **South Carolina** State, USA
70C2 **South China S** S E Asia
8C2 **South Dakota** State, USA
16C1 **South Deerfield** USA
43D4 **South Downs** Eng
109C4 **South East C** Aust
111A2 **Southen Alps** *Mts* NZ
5H4 **Southend** Can
43E4 **Southend-on-Sea** Eng
111A2 **Southern Alps** *Mts* NZ
106A4 **Southern Cross** Aust
5J4 **Southern Indian L** Can
27H2 **Southfield** Jamaica
105G5 **South Fiji Basin** Pacific O
12D2 **South Fork** *R* Alaska, USA
22B1 **South Fork** *R* California, USA
28F8 **South Georgia** *I* S Atlantic O
43C4 **South Glamorgan** County, Wales
14A2 **South Haven** USA
5J3 **South Henik L** Can
104F3 **South Honshu Ridge** Pacific O
111A2 **South I** NZ
16C2 **Southington** USA
74B3 **South Korea** Republic, S E Asia
21A2 **South Lake Tahoe** USA
112C8 **South Magnetic Pole** Ant
17B2 **South Miami** USA
16A3 **South Mt** USA
4F3 **South Nahanni** *R* Can
26G1 **South Negril Pt** Jamaica
103F8 **South Orkney** *Is* Atlantic O
8C2 **South Platte** *R* USA
80E **South Pole** Ant
42C3 **Southport** Eng

27R3 **South Pt** Barbados
16B2 **South River** USA
44C2 **South Ronaldsay** *I* Scot
103G7 **South Sandwich Trench** Atlantic O
22A2 **South San Francisco** USA
5H4 **South Saskatchewan** *R* Can
42D2 **South Shields** Eng
110B1 **South Taranaki Bight** *B* NZ
44A3 **South Uist** *I* Scot
South West Africa = Namibia
107D5 **South West C** Aust
105J5 **South West Pacific Basin** Pacific O
103D5 **South West Peru Ridge** Pacific O
43D3 **South Yorkshire** County, Eng
58C1 **Sovetsk** Russian Fed
61G2 **Sovetsk** Russian Fed
101G1 **Soweto** S Africa
98B3 **Soyo Congo** Angola
60D3 **Sozh** *R* Belorussia
46C1 **Spa** Belg
50A1 **Spain** Kingdom
Spalato = Split
43D3 **Spalding** Eng
14B1 **Spanish** *R* Can
26B3 **Spanish Town** Jamaica
21B2 **Sparks** USA
11B3 **Spartanburg** USA
55B3 **Spartí** Greece
69F2 **Spassk Dal'niy** Russian Fed
27R3 **Speightstown** Barbados
12E2 **Spenard** USA
14A3 **Spencer** Indiana, USA
8D2 **Spencer** Iowa, USA
6A3 **Spencer Bay** Can
108A3 **Spencer,C** Aust
108A2 **Spencer G** Aust
6C3 **Spencer I** Can
111B2 **Spenser Mts** NZ
45C1 **Sperrin** *Mts* N Ire
44C3 **Spey** *R* Scot
57B3 **Speyer** Germany
27K1 **Speyside** Tobago
47B1 **Spiez** Switz
12F1 **Spike Mt** USA
20C1 **Spirit Lake** USA
5G4 **Spirit River** Can
Spitsbergen = Svalbard
64C2 **Spitsbergen** *I* Barents S
57C3 **Spittal** Austria
38F6 **Spjelkavik** Nor
52C2 **Split** Croatia
47C1 **Splügen** Switz
20C1 **Spokane** USA
55C3 **Sporádhes** *Is* Greece
20C2 **Spray** USA
56C2 **Spree** *R* Germany
100A3 **Springbok** S Africa
18B2 **Springdale** USA
10B3 **Springfield** Illinois, USA
10C2 **Springfield** Massachusetts, USA
18B2 **Springfield** Missouri, USA
14B3 **Springfield** Ohio, USA
20B2 **Springfield** Oregon, USA
15D2 **Springfield** Vermont, USA
100B4 **Springfontein** S Africa
101G1 **Springs** S Africa
41D3 **Spurn Head** *Pt* Eng
13C3 **Squamish** Can
60E3 **Sredne-Russkaya Vozvyshennost** *Upland* Russian Fed
63B1 **Sredne Sibirskoye Ploskogorve** *Tableland* Russian Fed
61J2 **Sredniy Ural** *Mts* Russian Fed
76D3 **Srepok** *R* Camb
68D1 **Sretensk** Russian Fed
76C3 **Sre Umbell** Camb
83C5 **Sri Lanka** Republic, S Asia
84C2 **Srīnagar** Pak
87A1 **Srīvardhan** India
58B2 **Sroda** Pol
30H6 **Sta Clara** *I* Chile
32J7 **Sta Cruz** *I* Ecuador
56B2 **Stade** Germany
44A3 **Staffa** *I* Scot
43C3 **Stafford** County, Eng
43C3 **Stafford** Eng
16C2 **Stafford Springs** USA
Stalingrad = Volgograd
6A1 **Stallworthy,C** Can
59C2 **Stalowa Wola** Pol
32J7 **Sta Maria** *I* Ecuador
16C2 **Stamford** Connecticut, USA
16B1 **Stamford** New York, USA
100A3 **Stampriet** Namibia
101G1 **Standerton** S Africa
14B2 **Standish** USA
101H1 **Stanger** S Africa
22B2 **Stanislaus** *R* USA
54B2 **Stanke Dimitrov** Bulg
109C4 **Stanley** Aust
29E6 **Stanley** Falkland Is
87B2 **Stanley Res** India
Stanleyville = Kisangani
25D3 **Stann Creek** Belize
63E2 **Stanovoy Khrebet** *Mts* Russian Fed
47C1 **Stans** Switz
109D1 **Stanthorpe** Aust
59C2 **Starachowice** Pol
54B2 **Stara Planiná** *Mts* Bulg
60D2 **Staraya Russa** Russian Fed
54C2 **Stara Zagora** Bulg
58B2 **Stargard** Pol
19C3 **Starkville** USA
57C3 **Starnberg** Germany
58B2 **Starogard Gdanski** Pol
59D3 **Starokonstantinov** Ukraine
43C4 **Start Pt** Eng
60E3 **Staryy Oskol** Russian Fed
15C2 **State College** USA
16B2 **Staten I** USA
17B1 **Statesboro** USA
15C3 **Staunton** USA
39F7 **Stavanger** Nor
46C1 **Stavelot** Belg
61F4 **Stavropol'** Russian Fed
108B3 **Stawell** Aust
58B2 **Stawno** Pol
20B2 **Stayton** USA
12B2 **Stebbins** USA
12F2 **Steele,Mt** Can
16A2 **Steelton** USA
20C2 **Steens Mt** USA
6E2 **Steenstrups Gletscher** *Gl* Greenland
4H2 **Stefansson I** Can
101H1 **Stegi** Swaziland
47D1 **Steinach** Austria
8D2 **Steinback** Can
38G6 **Steinkjer** Nor
13C2 **Stein Mt** Can
23B2 **Stemaco** Mexico
46C2 **Stenay** France
56C2 **Stendal** Germany
110B2 **Stephens,C** NZ
108B2 **Stephens Creek** Aust
14A1 **Stephenson** USA
12H3 **Stephens Pass** USA
7E5 **Stephenville** Can
100B4 **Sterkstroom** S Africa
8C2 **Sterling** Colorado, USA
14B2 **Sterling Heights** USA
61J3 **Sterlitamak** Russian Fed
13E2 **Stettler** Can
14B2 **Steubenville** USA
4D3 **Stevens Village** USA
13B1 **Stewart** Can
21B2 **Stewart** USA
12G2 **Stewart** *R* Can
12G2 **Stewart Crossing** Can
111A3 **Stewart I** NZ
107F1 **Stewart Is** Solomon Is
4E3 **Stewart River** Can
16A3 **Stewartstown** USA
101G1 **Steyn** S Africa
57C3 **Steyr** Austria
12G3 **Stika** USA
12H3 **Stikine** *R* Can
12H3 **Stikine Ranges** *Mts* Can
18A2 **Stillwater** Oklahoma, USA
21B2 **Stillwater Range** *Mts* USA
108A2 **Stirling** Aust
44C3 **Stirling** Scot
16C1 **Stockbridge** USA
59B3 **Stockerau** Austria
39H7 **Stockholm** Sweden
42C3 **Stockport** Eng
22B2 **Stockton** California, USA
42D2 **Stockton** Eng
18B2 **Stockton L** USA
43C3 **Stoke-on-Trent** Eng
38A2 **Stokkseyri** Iceland
38G5 **Stokmarknes** Nor
39K8 **Stolbtsy** Belorussia
58D2 **Stolin** Belorussia
16B3 **Stone Harbor** USA
44C3 **Stonehaven** Scot
19A3 **Stonewall** USA
12D2 **Stony** *R* USA
38H5 **Storavan** *L* Sweden
38G6 **Støren** Nor
109C4 **Storm B** Aust
44A2 **Stornoway** Scot
59D3 **Storozhinets** Ukraine
16C2 **Storrs** USA
38G6 **Storsjön** *L* Sweden
38H5 **Storuman** Sweden
16D1 **Stoughton** USA
43E3 **Stowmarket** Eng
45C1 **Strablane** N Ire
109C4 **Strahan** Aust
56C2 **Stralsund** Germany
38F6 **Stranda** Nor
39H7 **Strängnäs** Sweden
42B2 **Stranraer** Scot
49D2 **Strasbourg** France
15C3 **Strasburg** USA
14B2 **Stratford** Can
16C2 **Stratford** Connecticut, USA
110B1 **Stratford** NZ
43D3 **Stratford-on-Avon** Eng
108A3 **Strathalbyn** Aust
42B2 **Strathclyde** Region, Scot
13E2 **Strathmore** Can
18C1 **Streator** USA
47C2 **Stresa** Italy
53C3 **Stretto de Messina** *Str* Italy/Sicily
38D3 **Streymoy** Føroyar
53C3 **Stroboli** *I* Italy
6E3 **Strømfjord** Greenland
44C2 **Stromness** Scot
18A1 **Stromsburg** USA
38H6 **Stromsund** Sweden
38G6 **Ströms Vattudal** *L* Sweden
44C2 **Stronsay** *I* Scot
43C4 **Stroud** Eng
16B2 **Stroudsburg** USA
54B2 **Struma** *R* Bulg
43B3 **Strumble Head** *Pt* Wales
55B2 **Strumica** Macedonia, Yugos
59C3 **Stryy** Ukraine
59C3 **Stryy** *R* Ukraine
108B1 **Strzelecki Creek** *R* Aust
17B2 **Stuart** Florida, USA
13C2 **Stuart** *R* Can
12B2 **Stuart I** USA
13C2 **Stuart L** Can
47D1 **Stubaier Alpen** *Mts* Austria
76D3 **Stung Sen** Camb
76D3 **Stung Treng** Camb
52A2 **Stura** *R* Italy
112C7 **Sturge I** Ant
14A2 **Sturgeon Bay** USA
14C1 **Sturgeon Falls** Can
18C2 **Sturgis** Kentucky, USA
14A2 **Sturgis** Michigan, USA
106B2 **Sturt Creek** *R* Aust
108B1 **Sturt Desert** Aust
100B4 **Stuttemeim** S Africa
19B3 **Stuttgart** USA
57B3 **Stuttgart** Germany
38A1 **Stykkishólmur** Iceland
59D2 **Styr'** *R* Ukraine
35C1 **Suaçuí Grande** *R* Brazil
81B4 **Suakin** Sudan
73E5 **Su-ao** Taiwan
34C2 **Suardi** Arg
78B2 **Subi** *I* Indon
54A1 **Subotica** Serbia, Yugos
60C4 **Suceava** Rom
45B2 **Suck** *R* Irish Rep
30C2 **Sucre** Bol
35A1 **Sucuriú** *R* Brazil
98C1 **Sudan** Republic, Africa
14B1 **Sudbury** Can
43E3 **Sudbury** Eng
99C2 **Sudd** *Swamp* Sudan
33F2 **Suddie** Guyana
98C2 **Sue** *R* Sudan
4H2 **Suerdrup Is** Can
92B4 **Suez** Egypt
92B3 **Suez Canal** Egypt
92B4 **Suez,G of** Egypt
16B2 **Suffern** USA
43E3 **Suffolk** County, Eng
109D2 **Sugarloaf Pt** Aust
91C5 **Suhār** Oman
68C1 **Sühbaatar** Mongolia
84B3 **Sui** Pak
72C2 **Suide** China
69E2 **Suihua** China
73B3 **Suining** China
46C2 **Suippes** France
41B3 **Suir** *R* Irish Rep
73C3 **Sui Xian** China
72E1 **Suizhong** China
85C3 **Sujāngarth** India
78B4 **Sukabumi** Indon
78C3 **Sukadana** Borneo, Indon
78B4 **Sukadana** Sumatra, Indon
74E3 **Sukagawa** Japan
78C3 **Sukaraya** Indon
60E3 **Sukhinichi** Russian Fed
61F2 **Sukhona** *R* Russian Fed
61F5 **Sukhumi** Georgia
6E3 **Sukkertoppen** Greenland
6E3 **Sukkertoppen** *L* Greenland
38L6 **Sukkozero** Russian Fed
85B3 **Sukkur** Pak
87C1 **Sukma** India
95A2 **Sūknah** Libya
100A3 **Sukses** Namibia
75A2 **Sukumo** Japan

13C1 **Sukunka** *R* Can
60E3 **Sula** *R* Russian Fed
84B3 **Sulaiman Range** *Mts* Pak
70C4 **Sulawesi** *I* Indon
93E3 **Sulaymānīyah** Iraq
54C1 **Sulina** Rom
38H5 **Sulitjelma** Nor
32A4 **Sullana** Peru
18B2 **Sullivan** USA
13B2 **Sullivan Bay** Can
13E2 **Sullivan L** Can
52B2 **Sulmona** Italy
19B3 **Sulphur** Louisiana, USA
19A3 **Sulphur** Oklahoma, USA
19A3 **Sulphur Springs** USA
86A1 **Sultānpur** India
79B4 **Sulu Arch** Phil
70C3 **Sulu S** Philip
30D4 **Sumampa** Arg
70B4 **Sumatera** *I* Indon
70C4 **Sumba** *I* Indon
78D4 **Sumbawa** *I* Indon
78D4 **Sumbawa Besar** Indon
99D3 **Sumbawanga** Tanz
100A2 **Sumbe** Angola
44E2 **Sumburgh Head** *Pt* Scot
78C4 **Sumenep** Indon
69G3 **Sumisu** *I* Japan
13D3 **Summerland** Can
5F4 **Summit Lake** Can
21B2 **Summit Mt** USA
111B2 **Sumner,L** NZ
75A2 **Sumoto** Japan
17B1 **Sumter** USA
60D3 **Sumy** Ukraine
16A2 **Sunbury** USA
34C2 **Sunchales** Arg
74B3 **Sunch'ŏn** N Korea
74B4 **Sunch'ŏn** S Korea
86A2 **Sundargarh** India
86B2 **Sunderbans** *Swamp* India
42D2 **Sunderland** Eng
13E2 **Sundre** Can
15C1 **Sundridge** Can
38H6 **Sundsvall** Sweden
38D3 **Suduroy** Føroyar
78D3 **Sungaianyar** Indon
78A3 **Sungaisalak** Indon
20C1 **Sunnyside** USA
21A2 **Sunnyvale** USA
63D1 **Suntar** Russian Fed
97B4 **Sunyani** Ghana
75A2 **Suō-nada** *R* Japan
38K6 **Suonejoki** Fin
86B1 **Supaul** India
18A1 **Superior** Nebraska, USA
10A2 **Superior** Wisconsin, USA
10B2 **Superior,L** Can/USA
76C3 **Suphan Buri** Thai
93D2 **Süphan Dağ** Turk
71E4 **Supiori** *I* Indon
93E3 **Suq ash Suyukh** Iraq
72D3 **Suqian** China
Suqutra = Socotra
91C5 **Sūr** Oman
61G3 **Sura** *R* Russian Fed
78C4 **Surabaya** Indon
75B2 **Suraga-wan** *B* Japan
78C4 **Surakarta** Indon
109C1 **Surat** Aust
85C4 **Sūrat** India
84C3 **Sūratgarh** India
77B4 **Surat Thani** Thai
85C4 **Surendranagar** India
16B3 **Surf City** USA
64J3 **Surgut** Russian Fed
87B1 **Suriāpet** India
49D2 **Sürich** Switz
79C4 **Surigao** Phil
76C3 **Surin** Thai
33F3 **Surinam** Republic, S America
43D4 **Surrey** County, Eng
47C1 **Sursee** Switz
95A1 **Surt** Libya
38A2 **Surtsey** *I* Iceland

78A3 **Surulangan** Indon
47B2 **Susa** Italy
75A2 **Susa** Japan
75A2 **Susaki** Japan
21A1 **Susanville** USA
47D1 **Süsch** Switz
12E2 **Susitna** *R* USA
16A3 **Susquehanna** *R* USA
16B2 **Sussex** USA
43D4 **Sussex West** Eng
13B1 **Sustut Peak** *Mt* Can
100B4 **Sutherland** S Africa
84C2 **Sutlej** *R* Pak
21A2 **Sutter Creek** USA
14B3 **Sutton** USA
12C3 **Sutwik I** USA
74D3 **Suwa** Japan
58C2 **Suwałki** Pol
17B2 **Suwannee** *R* USA
94B2 **Suweilih** Jordan
74B3 **Suwŏn** S Korea
72D3 **Su Xian** China
75B1 **Suzaka** Japan
73E3 **Suzhou** China
74D3 **Suzu** Japan
75B2 **Suzuka** Japan
75B1 **Suzu-misaki** *C* Japan
64C2 **Svalbard** *Is* Barents S
59C3 **Svalyava** Ukraine
38G5 **Svartisen** *Mt* Nor
76D3 **Svay Rieng** Camb
38G6 **Sveg** Sweden
39G7 **Svendborg** Den
6A1 **Sverdrup Chan** Can
69F2 **Svetlaya** Russian Fed
58C2 **Svetlogorsk** Russian Fed
39K6 **Svetogorsk** Russian Fed
54B2 **Svetozarevo** Serbia, Yugos
54C2 **Svilengrad** Bulg
58D2 **Svir'** Belorussia
59B3 **Svitavy** Czech
69E1 **Svobodnyy** Russian Fed
38G5 **Svolvaer** Nor
107E3 **Swain Reefs** Aust
17B1 **Swainsboro** USA
100A3 **Swakopmund** Namibia
42D2 **Swale** *R* Eng
70C3 **Swallow Reef** *I* S E Asia
87B2 **Swāmihalli** India
25D3 **Swan** *I* Honduras
43D4 **Swanage** Eng
108B3 **Swan Hill** Aust
13D2 **Swan Hills** Can
13D2 **Swan Hills** *Mts* Can
26A3 **Swan I** Caribbean S
5H4 **Swan River** Can
43C4 **Swansea** Wales
43C4 **Swansea B** Wales
101G1 **Swartruggens** S Africa
Swatow = Shantou
101H1 **Swaziland** Kingdom, S Africa
39G7 **Sweden** Kingdom, N Europe
20B2 **Sweet Home** USA
9C3 **Sweetwater** USA
100B4 **Swellendam** S Africa
59B2 **Świdnica** Pol
58B2 **Świdwin** Pol
58B2 **Świebodzin** Pol
58B2 **Świecie** Pol
5H4 **Swift Current** Can
43D4 **Swindon** Eng
45B2 **Swinford** Irish Rep
56C2 **Świnoujście** Pol
49D2 **Switzerland** Federal Republic, Europe
45C2 **Swords** Irish Rep
109D2 **Sydney** Aust
7D5 **Sydney** Can
64G3 **Syktyvkar** Russian Fed
17A1 **Sylacauga** USA
38G6 **Sylarna** *Mt* Sweden
86C2 **Sylhet** Bang

56B1 **Sylt** *I* Germany
14B2 **Sylvania** USA
112C11 **Syowa** *Base* Ant
Syracuse = Siracusa
15C2 **Syracuse** USA
65H5 **Syrdar'ya** *R* Kazakhstan
93C2 **Syria** Republic, S W Asia
61J2 **Sysert'** Russian Fed
61G3 **Syzran'** Russian Fed
56C2 **Szczecin** Pol
58B2 **Szczecinek** Pol
58C2 **Szczytno** Pol
59C3 **Szeged** Hung
59B3 **Székesfehérvar** Hung
59B3 **Szekszard** Hung
59B3 **Szolnok** Hung
59B3 **Szombathely** Hung
58B2 **Szprotawa** Pol

T

90C3 **Tabas** Iran
23A1 **Tabasco** Mexico
32D4 **Tabatinga** Brazil
96B2 **Tabelbala** Alg
76C3 **Tabeng** Camb
13E2 **Taber** Can
79B3 **Tablas** *I* Phil
100A4 **Table Mt** S Africa
12F1 **Table Mt** USA
18B2 **Table Rock Res** USA
78B3 **Taboali** Indon
57C3 **Tábor** Czech
99D3 **Tabora** Tanz
97B4 **Tabou** Ivory Coast
90A2 **Tabriz** Iran
92C4 **Tabūk** S Arabia
23A2 **Tacámbaro** Mexico
82C1 **Tacheng** China
79C3 **Tacloban** Phil
30B2 **Tacna** Peru
8A2 **Tacoma** USA
99E1 **Tadjoura** Djibouti
87B2 **Tādpatri** India
74B3 **Taebaek Sanmaek** *Mts* S Korea
74B3 **Taegu** S Korea
74B4 **Taehŭksan** *I* S Korea
74B3 **Taejŏn** S Korea
51B1 **Tafalla** Spain
96C2 **Tafasaset** *Watercourse* Alg
43C4 **Taff** *R* Wales
94B3 **Tafila** Jordan
60E4 **Taganrog** Ukraine
97A3 **Tagant** Region, Maur
79B4 **Tagbilaran** Phil
96B2 **Taguenout Hagguerete** *Well* Maur
107E2 **Tagula** *I* Solomon Is
79C4 **Tagum** Phil
Tagus = Tejo
96C2 **Tahat** *Mt* Alg
105J4 **Tahiti** *I* Pacific O
18A2 **Tahlequah** USA
21A2 **Tahoe City** USA
21A2 **Tahoe,L** USA
97C3 **Tahoua** Niger
71D3 **Tahuna** Indon
72D2 **Tai'an** China
72B3 **Taibai Shan** *Mt* China
72D1 **Taibus Qi** China
73E5 **T'ai-chung** Taiwan
111B3 **Taieri** *R* NZ
72C2 **Taihang Shan** China
110C1 **Taihape** NZ
72E3 **Tai Hu** *L* China
108A3 **Tailem Bend** Aust
44B3 **Tain** Scot
73E5 **T'ai-nan** Taiwan
35C1 **Taiobeiras** Brazil
73E5 **T'ai pei** Taiwan
77C5 **Taiping** Malay
75C1 **Taira** Japan
78A3 **Tais** Indon
75A1 **Taisha** Japan
29B5 **Taitao,Pen de** Chile
73E5 **T'ai-tung** Taiwan
38K5 **Taivelkoski** Fin

69E4 **Taiwan** Republic, China
Taiwan Haixia = Formosa Str
72C2 **Taiyuan** China
72D3 **Taizhou** China
81C4 **Ta'izz** Yemen
82A2 **Tajikistan** Republic, Asia
50B1 **Tajo** *R* Spain
76B2 **Tak** Thai
74D3 **Takada** Japan
75A2 **Takahashi** Japan
110B2 **Takaka** NZ
74C4 **Takamatsu** Japan
74D3 **Takaoka** Japan
110B1 **Takapuna** NZ
74D3 **Takasaki** Japan
75B1 **Takayama** Japan
74D3 **Takefu** Japan
70A3 **Takengon** Indon
76C3 **Takeo** Camb
75A2 **Takeo** Japan
Take-shima = Tok-do
90A2 **Takestān** Iran
75A2 **Taketa** Japan
4G3 **Takjvak L** Can
99D1 **Takkaze** *R* Eth
13B1 **Takla L** Can
13B1 **Takla Landing** Can
12B2 **Taksleshuk L** USA
12H2 **Taku Arm** *R* Can
23A1 **Tala** Mexico
59B3 **Talabanya** Hung
84C2 **Talagang** Pak
34A2 **Talagante** Chile
87B3 **Talaimannar** Sri Lanka
97C3 **Talak** *Desert* Region, Niger
78A3 **Talangbetutu** Indon
32A4 **Talara** Peru
50B2 **Talavera de la Reina** Spain
34A3 **Talca** Chile
34A3 **Talcahuano** Chile
86B2 **Tālcher** India
82B1 **Taldy Kurgan** Kazakhstan
71D4 **Taliabu** Indon
84B1 **Taligan** Afghan
99D2 **Tali Post** Sudan
78D4 **Taliwang** Indon
12D2 **Talkeetna** USA
12E2 **Talkeetna Mts** USA
17A1 **Talladega** USA
93D2 **Tall 'Afar** Iraq
17B1 **Tallahassee** USA
94C1 **Tall Bisah** Syria
60B2 **Tallinn** Estonia
92C3 **Tall Kalakh** Syria
19B3 **Tallulah** USA
60D4 **Tal'noye** Ukraine
58C2 **Talpaki** Russian Fed
30B4 **Taltal** Chile
109C1 **Talwood** Aust
78D1 **Tamabo Range** *Mts* Malay
97B4 **Tamale** Ghana
96C2 **Tamanrasset** Alg
96C2 **Tamanrasset** *Watercourse* Alg
16B2 **Tamaqua** USA
Tamatave = Toamasina
23A2 **Tamazula** Jalisco, Mexico
23B2 **Tamazulapán** Mexico
23B1 **Tamazunchale** Mexico
97A3 **Tambacounda** Sen
61F3 **Tambov** Russian Fed
50A1 **Tambre** *R* Spain
98C2 **Tambura** Sudan
97A3 **Tamchaket** Maur
50A1 **Tamega** *R* Port
23B1 **Tamiahua** Mexico
87B2 **Tamil Nādu** State, India
76D2 **Tam Ky** Viet
17B2 **Tampa** USA
17B2 **Tampa B** USA
39J6 **Tampere** Fin
23B1 **Tampico** Mexico

Tamsagbulag

68D2 **Tamsagbulag** Mongolia
86C2 **Tamu** Burma
23B1 **Tamuis** Mexico
109D2 **Tamworth** Aust
43D3 **Tamworth** Eng
38K4 **Tana** Nor
99D1 **Tana** L Eth
99E3 **Tana** R Kenya
38K5 **Tana** R Nor/Fin
75B2 **Tanabe** Japan
38K4 **Tanafjord** Inlet Nor
78D3 **Tanahgrogot** Indon
71E4 **Tanahmerah** Indon
12D1 **Tanana** USA
12E2 **Tanana** R USA
Tananarive = Antananarivo
47C2 **Tanaro** R Italy
74B2 **Tanch'ŏn** N Korea
34D3 **Tandil** Arg
78B2 **Tandjong Datu** Pt Indon
71E4 **Tandjung d'Urville** C Indon
78D3 **Tandjung Layar** C Indon
78B3 **Tandjung Lumut** C Indon
78D2 **Tandjung Mangkalihet** C Indon
78C3 **Tandjung Sambar** C Indon
78C2 **Tandjung Sirik** C Malay
71E4 **Tandjung Vals** C Indon
85B3 **Tando Adam** Pak
85B3 **Tando Muhammad Khan** Pak
108B2 **Tandou L** Aust
87B1 **Tāndūr** India
110C1 **Taneatua** NZ
76B2 **Tanen Range** Mts Burma/Thai
96B2 **Tanezrouft** Desert Region Alg
91C4 **Tang** Iran
99D3 **Tanga** Tanz
60E4 **Tanganrog** Russian Fed
99C3 **Tanganyika,L** Tanz/ Zaïre
96B1 **Tanger** Mor
82C2 **Tanggula Shan** Mts China
Tangier = Tanger
78A2 **Tangjungpinang** Indon
82C2 **Tangra Yumco** L China
72D2 **Tangshan** China
79B4 **Tangub** Phil
63C2 **Tanguy** Russian Fed
79B4 **Tanjay** Phil
101D3 **Tanjona Ankaboa** C Madag
101D2 **Tanjona Babaomby** C Madag
101D2 **Tanjona Vilanandro** C Madag
101D3 **Tanjona Vohimena** C Madag
78C4 **Tanjong Bugel** C Indon
78B4 **Tanjong Cangkuang** C Indon
78C3 **Tanjong Puting** C Indon
78C3 **Tanjong Selatan** C Indon
78D3 **Tanjung** Indon
70A3 **Tanjungbalai** Indon
78A3 **Tanjung Jabung** Pt Indon
78B3 **Tanjungpandan** Indon
78B4 **Tanjung Priok** Indon
78D2 **Tanjungredeb** Indon
78D2 **Tanjungselor** Indon
84C2 **Tank** Pak
68B1 **Tannu Ola** Mts Russian Fed
97B4 **Tano** R Ghana

97C3 **Tanout** Niger
23B1 **Tanquián** Mexico
73E4 **Tan-shui** Taiwan
86A1 **Tansing** Nepal
95C1 **Tanta** Egypt
96A2 **Tan-Tan** Mor
4B3 **Tanunak** USA
99D3 **Tanzania** Republic, Africa
72A3 **Tao He** R China
72B2 **Taole** China
96B1 **Taourirt** Mor
60C2 **Tapa** Estonia
25C3 **Tapachula** Mexico
33F4 **Tapajós** R Brazil
34C3 **Tapalquén** Arg
70B4 **Tapan** Indon
111A3 **Tapanui** NZ
32D5 **Tapauá** R Brazil
85D4 **Tapi** R India
86B1 **Taplejung** Nepal
111B2 **Tapuaeniku** Mt NZ
35B2 **Tapuaritinga** Brazil
79B4 **Tapul Group** Is Phil
33E4 **Tapurucuara** Brazil
109D1 **Tara** Aust
65J4 **Tara** Russian Fed
65J4 **Tara** R Russian Fed
54A2 **Tara** R Bosnia & Herzegovina/ Montenegro, Yugos
97D4 **Taraba** R Nig
30D2 **Tarabuco** Bol
Tarabulus = Tripoli
50B1 **Taracón** Spain
110C1 **Taradale** NZ
78D2 **Tarakan** Indon
44A3 **Taransay** I Scot
53C2 **Taranto** Italy
32B5 **Tarapoto** Peru
49C2 **Tarare** France
110C2 **Tararua Range** Mts NZ
96C2 **Tarat** Alg
110C1 **Tarawera** NZ
51B1 **Tarazona** Spain
44C3 **Tarbat Ness** Pen Scot
84C2 **Tarbela Res** Pak
42B2 **Tarbert** Strathclyde, Scot
44A3 **Tarbert** Western Isles, Scot
48C3 **Tarbes** France
106C4 **Tarcoola** Aust
109C2 **Tarcoon** Aust
109D2 **Taree** Aust
96A2 **Tarfaya** Mor
95A1 **Tarhūnah** Libya
91B5 **Tarif** UAE
30D3 **Tarija** Bol
87B2 **Tarikere** India
81C4 **Tarim** Yemen
99D3 **Tarime** Tanz
82C1 **Tarim He** R China
82C2 **Tarim Pendi** Basin China
84B2 **Tarin Kut** Afghan
18A1 **Tarkio** USA
79B2 **Tarlac** Phil
32B6 **Tarma** Peru
49C3 **Tarn** R France
59C2 **Tarnobrzeg** Pol
59C3 **Tarnów** Pol
107D3 **Taroom** Aust
51C1 **Tarragona** Spain
109C4 **Tarraleah** Aust
51C1 **Tarrasa** Spain
16C2 **Tarrytown** USA
92B2 **Tarsus** Turk
44D2 **Tartan** Oilfield N Sea
47D2 **Tartaro** R Italy
60C2 **Tartu** Estonia
92C3 **Tartūs** Syria
35C1 **Tarumirim** Brazil
70A3 **Tarutung** Indon
52B1 **Tarvisio** Italy
80D1 **Tashauz** Turkmenistan
86C1 **Tashigang** Bhutan
82A1 **Tashkent** Uzbekistan
65K4 **Tashtagol** Russian Fed
63A2 **Tashtyp** Russian Fed

78B4 **Tasikmalaya** Indon
94B2 **Tasil** Syria
6E2 **Tasiussaq** Greenland
95A3 **Tasker** Well Niger
110B2 **Tasman B** NZ
107D5 **Tasmania** I Aust
111B2 **Tasman Mts** NZ
109C4 **Tasman Pen** Aust
107E4 **Tasman S** NZ Aust
92C1 **Taşova** Turk
96C2 **Tassili du Hoggar** Desert Region, Alg
96C2 **Tassili N'jjer** Desert Region, Alg
96B2 **Tata** Mor
96D1 **Tataouine** Tunisia
65J4 **Tatarsk** Russian Fed
61G2 **Tatarskaya** Respublika, Russian Fed
69G2 **Tatarskiy Proliv** Str Russian Fed
75B1 **Tateyama** Japan
5G3 **Tathlina L** Can
12E2 **Tatitlek** USA
13C2 **Tatla Lake** Can
59B3 **Tatry** Mts Pol/Czech
75A2 **Tatsuno** Japan
85B4 **Tatta** Pak
35B2 **Tatuí** Brazil
93D2 **Tatvan** Turk
31C3 **Tauá** Brazil
35B2 **Taubaté** Brazil
110C1 **Taumarunui** NZ
101F1 **Taung** S Africa
76B2 **Taungdwingyi** Burma
76B1 **Taung-gyi** Burma
76A2 **Taungup** Burma
84C2 **Taunsa** Pak
43C4 **Taunton** Eng
16D2 **Taunton** USA
46E1 **Taunus** Region, Germany
110C1 **Taupo** NZ
110C1 **Taupo,L** NZ
58C1 **Taurage** Lithuania
110C1 **Tauranga** NZ
110C1 **Tauranga Harbour** B NZ
110B1 **Tauroa Pt** NZ
7A3 **Tavani** Can
7A3 **Tavani** Can
65H4 **Tavda** R Russian Fed
43B4 **Tavistock** Eng
76B3 **Tavoy** Burma
76B3 **Tavoy Pt** Burma
92A2 **Tavsanli** Turk
111B2 **Tawa** NZ
19A3 **Tawakoni,L** USA
14B2 **Tawas City** USA
70C3 **Tawau** Malay
98C1 **Taweisha** Sudan
79B4 **Tawitawi** I Phil
79B4 **Tawitawi Group** Is Phil
23B2 **Taxco** Mexico
23B2 **Taxcoco** Mexico
44C3 **Tay** R Scot
78C3 **Tayan** Indon
12B1 **Taylor** Alaska, USA
13C1 **Taylor** Can
14B2 **Taylor** Michigan, USA
19A3 **Taylor** Texas, USA
18C2 **Taylorville** USA
80B3 **Taymá'** S Arabia
63B1 **Taymura** R Russian Fed
76D3 **Tay Ninh** Viet
63B2 **Tayshet** Russian Fed
68B2 **Tayshir** Mongolia
44C3 **Tayside** Region, Scot
79A3 **Taytay** Phil
90D3 **Tayyebāt** Iran
96B1 **Taza** Mor
95B2 **Tazirbu** Libya
12E2 **Tazlina L** USA
64J3 **Tazovskiy** Russian Fed
65F5 **Tbilisi** Georgia
98B3 **Tchibanga** Gabon
95A2 **Tchigai,Plat du** Niger

97C3 **Tchin Tabaradene** Niger
98B2 **Tcholliré** Cam
58B2 **Tczew** Pol
111A3 **Te Anau** NZ
111A3 **Te Anau,L** NZ
110C1 **Te Aroha** NZ
110C1 **Te Awamutu** NZ
96C1 **Tébessa** Alg
23A2 **Teboman** Mexico
23A2 **Tecailtlän** Mexico
21B3 **Tecate** Mexico
61K2 **Techa** R Russian Fed
23A1 **Tecolotlán** Mexico
23A2 **Tecpan** Mexico
54C1 **Tecuci** Rom
18A1 **Tecumseh** USA
80E2 **Tedzhen** Turkmenistan
65H6 **Tedzhen** R Turkmenistan
42D2 **Tees** R Eng
33E4 **Tefé** Brazil
78B4 **Tegal** Indon
78B4 **Tegineneng** Indon
25D3 **Tegucigalpa** Honduras
21B3 **Tehachapi Mts** USA
21B2 **Tehachapi P** USA
4J3 **Tehek L** Can
90B2 **Tehrän** Iran
23B2 **Tehuacán** Mexico
23B2 **Tehuantepec** Mexico
23B2 **Tehuitzingo** Mexico
43B3 **Teifi** R Wales
50A2 **Tejo** R Port
23A2 **Tejupilco** Mexico
111B2 **Tekapo,L** NZ
82B1 **Tekeli** Kazakhstan
92A1 **Tekirdağ** Turk
55C2 **Tekir Dağlari** Mts Turk
86C2 **Teknaf** Bang
110C1 **Te Kuiti** NZ
25D3 **Tela** Honduras
94B2 **Tel Aviv Yafo** Israel
34B3 **Telén** Arg
21B2 **Telescope Peak** Mt USA
33F5 **Teles Pires** R Brazil
47D1 **Telfs** Austria
63A2 **Teli** Russian Fed
94B3 **Tell el Meise** Mt Jordan
12A1 **Teller** USA
87B2 **Tellicherry** India
77C5 **Telok Anson** Malay
78D2 **Telok Darvel** Malay
71E4 **Tělok Flamingo** B Indon
78C3 **Tělok Kumai** B Indon
78B4 **Tělok Pelabuanratu** B Indon
78D4 **Tělok Saleh** B Indon
78C3 **Tělok Sampit** B Indon
78B3 **Tělok Sukadona** B Indon
23B2 **Teloloapán** Mexico
64G3 **Tel'pos-iz** Mt Russian Fed
58C1 **Telšiai** Lithuania
78C3 **Telukbatang** Indon
71E4 **Teluk Berau** B Indon
78B4 **Telukbetung** Indon
70D4 **Teluk Bone** B Indon
71E4 **Teluk Cendrawasih** B Indon
78D3 **Teluk Mandar** B Indon
71D4 **Teluk Tolo** B Indon
70D3 **Teluk Tomini** B Indon
71D3 **Těluk Weda** B Indon
14B1 **Temagami,L** Can
23B2 **Temascal** Mexico
78A3 **Tembesi** R Indon
78A3 **Tembilahan** Indon
27E5 **Temblador** Ven
77C5 **Temerloh** Malay
65G5 **Temir** Kazakhstan
65J4 **Temirtau** Kazakhstan
15C1 **Temiscaming** Can
109C2 **Temora** Aust

9B3 **Tempe** USA
19A3 **Temple** USA
45C2 **Templemore** Irish Rep
23B1 **Tempoal** Mexico
34A3 **Temuco** Chile
111B2 **Temuka** NZ
32B4 **Tena** Ecuador
87C1 **Tenāli** India
23B2 **Tenancingo** Mexico
76D3 **Tenasserim** Burma
43B4 **Tenby** Wales
99E1 **Tendaho** Eth
83D5 **Ten Degree Chan** Indian O
98B1 **Ténéré** *Desert Region* Niger
96A2 **Tenerife** *l* Canary Is
76B1 **Teng** *R* Burma
78D3 **Tenggarong** Indon
72A2 **Tengger Shamo** *Desert* China
112C2 **Teniente Jubany** *Base* Ant
112C2 **Teniente Rodolfo Marsh Martin** *Base* Ant
87B3 **Tenkāsi** India
100B2 **Tenke** Zaïre
97B3 **Tenkodogo** Burkina
106C2 **Tennant Creek** Aust
11B3 **Tennessee** State, USA
18C2 **Tennessee** *R* USA
34A2 **Teno** Chile
78D1 **Tenom** Malay
25C3 **Tenosique** Mexico
109D1 **Tenterfield** Aust
17B2 **Ten Thousand Is** USA
23A1 **Teocaltiche** Mexico
35C1 **Teófilo Otõni** Brazil
23B2 **Teotihiucan** Hist Site, Mexico
23B2 **Teotitlan** Mexico
23A1 **Tepatitlan** Mexico
24B2 **Tepehuanes** Mexico
23B2 **Tepeji** Mexico
23A1 **Tepic** Mexico
57C2 **Teplice** Czech
110C1 **Te Puke** NZ
23A1 **Tequila** Mexico
23B2 **Tequistepec** Mexico
51C1 **Ter** *R* Spain
97C3 **Téra** Niger
75B1 **Teradomari** Japan
52B2 **Teramo** Italy
96A1 **Terceira** *l* Açores
59D3 **Terebovlya** Ukraine
31C3 **Teresina** Brazil
35C2 **Teresópolis** Brazil
92C1 **Terme** Turk
80E2 **Termez** Uzbekistan
52B2 **Termoli** Italy
71D3 **Ternate** Indon
52B2 **Terni** Italy
59D3 **Ternopol** Ukraine
13B2 **Terrace** Can
53B2 **Terracina** Italy
100B3 **Terrafirma** S Africa
112C8 **Terre Adélie** Region, Ant
19B4 **Terre Bonne B** USA
14A3 **Terre Haute** USA
19A3 **Terrell** USA
56B2 **Terschelling** *l* Neth
51B1 **Teruel** Spain
4C2 **Teshekpuk** USA
4C2 **Teshekpuk L** USA
74E2 **Teshio** *R* Japan
68B2 **Tesiyn Gol** *Mts* Mongolia
12H2 **Teslin** Can
12H3 **Teslin** *R* Can
12H2 **Teslin L** Can
63B3 **Teslyn Gol** *R* Mongolia
96C2 **Tessalit** Mali
97C3 **Tessaoua** Niger
101C2 **Tete** Mozam
23A2 **Tetela** Mexico
96B1 **Tetouan** Mor
61G2 **Tetyushi** Russian Fed
30D3 **Teuco** *R* Arg

23A1 **Teúl de Gonzalez Ortega** Mexico
71D4 **Teun** *l* Indon
52B2 **Tevere** *R* Italy
42C2 **Teviot** *R* Scot
65J4 **Tevriz** Russian Fed
111A3 **Te Waewae B** NZ
78C3 **Tewah** Indon
109D1 **Tewantin** Aust
72A3 **Têwo** China
19B3 **Texarkana** USA
19B3 **Texarkana,L** USA
109D1 **Texas** Aust
9C3 **Texas** State, USA
19B4 **Texas City** USA
56A2 **Texel** *l* Neth
19A3 **Texoma,L** USA
101G1 **Teyateyaneng** Lesotho
23B2 **Teziutlán** Mexico
86C1 **Tezpur** India
76C1 **Tha** Laos
101G1 **Thabana Ntlenyana** *Mt* Lesotho
101G1 **Thaba Putsoa** *Mt* Lesotho
76B3 **Thagyettaw** Burma
76D1 **Thai Binh** Viet
76C2 **Thailand** Kingdom, S E Asia
76C3 **Thailand,G of** Thai
76D1 **Thai Nguyen** Viet
76C2 **Thakhek** Laos
84C2 **Thal** Pak
77C4 **Thale Luang** *L* Thai
109C1 **Thallon** Aust
110C1 **Thames** NZ
43E4 **Thames** *R* Eng
76D2 **Thanh Hoah** Viet
87B2 **Thanjavur** India
85C3 **Thar Desert** India
108B1 **Thargomindah** Aust
55B2 **Thásos** *l* Greece
76B2 **Thaton** Burma
76B2 **Thayetmyo** Burma
5F5 **The Dalles** USA
91B4 **The Gulf** S W Asia
4H3 **Thelon** *R* Can
107E3 **Theodore** Aust
9B3 **Theodore Roosevelt L** USA
55B2 **Thermaïkós Kólpos** *G* Greece
8C2 **Thermopolis** USA
4F2 **Thesiger B** Can
14B1 **Thessalon** Can
55B2 **Thessaloníki** Greece
43E3 **Thetford** Eng
15D1 **Thetford Mines** Can
101G1 **Theunissen** S Africa
19B4 **Thibodaux** USA
5J4 **Thicket Portage** Can
8D2 **Thief River Falls** USA
20B2 **Thielsen,Mt** USA
49C2 **Thiers** France
97A3 **Thiès** Sen
99D3 **Thika** Kenya
86B1 **Thimphu** Bhutan
49D2 **Thionville** France
55C3 **Thira** *l* Greece
42D2 **Thirsk** Eng
87B3 **Thiruvananthapuram** India
39F7 **Thisted** Den
55B3 **Thivai** Greece
48C2 **Thiviers** France
17B1 **Thomaston** Georgia, USA
45C2 **Thomastown** Irish Rep
17B1 **Thomasville** Georgia, USA
6A2 **Thom Bay** Can
5J4 **Thompson** Can
18B1 **Thompson** *R* USA
4G3 **Thompson Landing** Can
13C2 **Thompson R** Can
16C2 **Thompsonville** USA
17B1 **Thomson** USA
107D3 **Thomson** *R* Aust
76C3 **Thon Buri** Thai
76B2 **Thongwa** Burma

47B1 **Thonon-les-Bains** France
42C2 **Thornhill** Scot
48B2 **Thouars** France
15C2 **Thousand Is** Can/ USA
13E2 **Three Hills** Can
7G4 **Three Kings Is** NZ
76B2 **Three Pagodas P** Thai
14A2 **Three Rivers** Michigan, USA
20B2 **Three Sisters** *Mt* USA
6D2 **Thule** Greenland
47B1 **Thun** Switz
10B2 **Thunder Bay** Can
47B1 **Thuner See** *L* Switz
77B4 **Thung Song** Thai
47C1 **Thur** *R* Switz
57C2 **Thüringen** State, Germany
57C2 **Thüringen Wald** *Upland* Germany
45C2 **Thurles** Irish Rep
71F5 **Thursday I** Aust
44C2 **Thurso** Scot
112B4 **Thurston I** Ant
47C1 **Thusis** Switz
108B1 **Thylungra** Aust
73B5 **Tiandong** China
73B5 **Tian'e** China
72D2 **Tianjin** China
73B5 **Tianlin** China
82C1 **Tiàn Shan** *Mts* C Asia
72B3 **Tianshui** China
72A2 **Tianzhu** China
96C1 **Tiaret** Alg
35A2 **Tibagi** *R* Brazil
94B2 **Tiberias** Israel
94B2 **Tiberias,L** Israel
95A2 **Tibesti** *Mountain Region* Chad
82C2 **Tibet** Autonomous Region, China
108B1 **Tibooburra** Aust
86A1 **Tibrikot** Nepal
24A2 **Tiburón** *l* Mexico
97B3 **Tichitt** Maur
96A2 **Tichla** Mor
47C2 **Ticino** *R* Italy/Switz
15D2 **Ticonderoga** USA
25D2 **Ticul** Mexico
97A3 **Tidjikja** Maur
47C1 **Tiefencastel** Switz
74A2 **Tieling** China
46B1 **Tielt** Belg
46C1 **Tienen** Belg
65J5 **Tien Shan** *Mts* China/Kirgizia
72D2 **Tientsin** China
39H6 **Tierp** Sweden
23B2 **Tierra Blanca** Mexico
23B2 **Tierra Colorada** Mexico
29C6 **Tierra del Fuego** Territory, Arg
28C8 **Tierra del Fuego** *l* Arg/Chile
35B2 **Tietê** Brazil
35A2 **Tiete** *R* Brazil
14B2 **Tiffin** USA
17B1 **Tifton** USA
32B4 **Tigre** *R* Peru
33E2 **Tigre** *R* Ven
93E3 **Tigris** *R* Iraq
23B1 **Tihuatlán** Mexico
21B3 **Tijuana** Mexico
85D4 **Tikamgarh** India
60D2 **Tikhin** Russian Fed
61F4 **Tikhoretsk** Russian Fed
93D3 **Tikrit** Iraq
1B8 **Tiksi** Russian Fed
46C1 **Tilburg** Neth
43E4 **Tilbury** Eng
30C3 **Tilcara** Arg
108B1 **Tilcha** Aust
76A1 **Tilin** Burma
97C3 **Tillabéri** Niger
20B1 **Tillamook** USA
97C3 **Tillia** Niger

55C3 **Tilos** *l* Greece
108B2 **Tilpa** Aust
32B3 **Tiluá** Colombia
64G3 **Timanskiy Kryazh** *Mts* Russian Fed
111B2 **Timaru** NZ
60E4 **Timashevsk** Russian Fed
55B3 **Timbákion** Greece
19B4 **Timbalier B** USA
97B3 **Timbédra** Maur
Timbuktu = Tombouctou
97B3 **Timétrine Monts** *Mts* Mali
97C3 **Timia** Niger
96C2 **Timis** *R* Rom
54B1 **Timişoara** Rom
10B2 **Timmins** Can
106B1 **Timor** *l* Indon
106B2 **Timor S** Aust/Indon
34C3 **Timote** Arg
79C4 **Tinaca Pt** Phil
27D5 **Tinaco** Ven
87B2 **Tindivanam** India
96B2 **Tindouf** Alg
96B2 **Tinfouchy** Alg
96C2 **Tin Fouye** Alg
6F3 **Tingmiarmiut** Greenland
32B5 **Tingo Maria** Peru
97B3 **Tingrela** Ivory Coast
86B1 **Tingri** China
71F2 **Tinian** Pacific O
30C4 **Tinogasta** Arg
55C3 **Tinos** *l* Greece
43B4 **Tintagel Head** *Pt* Eng
96C2 **Tin Tarabine** *Watercourse* Alg
108B3 **Tintinara** Aust
96C2 **Tin Zaouaten** Alg
22C2 **Tioga P** USA
77C5 **Tioman** *l* Malay
47D1 **Tione** Italy
45C2 **Tipperary** County, Irish Rep
41B3 **Tipperary** Irish Rep
18B2 **Tipton** Missouri, USA
87B2 **Tiptür** India
23A2 **Tiquicheo** Mexico
55A2 **Tiranë** Alb
47D1 **Tirano** Italy
60C4 **Tiraspol** Moldavia
87B2 **Tirchchiráppalli** India
55C3 **Tire** Turk
93C1 **Tirebolu** Turk
44A3 **Tiree** *l* Scot
54C2 **Tirgoviște** Rom
54B1 **Tirgu Jiu** Rom
54B1 **Tirgu Mureş** Rom
84C1 **Tirich Mir** *Mt* Pak
96A2 **Tiris** Region, Mor
61J3 **Tirlyanskiy** Russian Fed
54B1 **Tirnăveni** Rom
55B3 **Tirnavos** Greece
85D4 **Tirodi** India
47D1 **Tirol** Province, Austria
53A2 **Tirso** *R* Sardegna
87B3 **Tiruchchendür** India
87B3 **Tirunelveli** India
87B2 **Tirupati** India
87B2 **Tiruppattūr** India
87B2 **Tiruppur** India
87B2 **Tiruvannamalai** India
19A3 **Tishomingo** USA
94C2 **Tisiyah** Syria
59C3 **Tisza** *R* Hung
86A2 **Titlagarh** India
54A2 **Titograd** Montenegro, Yugos
54B2 **Titova Mitrovica** Serbia, Yugos
54A2 **Titovo Užice** Serbia, Yugos
52C1 **Titovo Velenje** Slovenia
54B2 **Titov Veles** Macedonia, Yugos
98C2 **Titule** Zaïre
17B2 **Titusville** USA
43C4 **Tiverton** Eng

Tivoli

52B2 **Tivoli** Italy
23B2 **Tixtla** Mexico
99E2 **Tiyeglow** Somalia
23B2 **Tizayuca** Mexico
25D2 **Tizimin** Mexico
96C1 **Tizi Ouzou** Alg
96B2 **Tiznit** Mor
23A1 **Tizpan el Alto** Mexico
23B2 **Tlacolula** Mexico
23B2 **Tlacotalpan** Mexico
23A2 **Tlalchana** Mexico
23B2 **Tlalnepantla** Mexico
23B2 **Tlalpan** Mexico
23A1 **Tlaltenango** Mexico
23B2 **Tlancualpicán** Mexico
23B2 **Tlapa** Mexico
23B2 **Tlapacoyan** Mexico
23A1 **Tlaquepaque** Mexico
23B2 **Tlaxcala** Mexico
23B2 **Tlaxcala** State, Mexico
23B2 **Tlaxiaco** Mexico
96B1 **Tlemcem** Alg
101D2 **Toamasina** Madag
34C3 **Toay** Arg
75B2 **Toba** Japan
84B2 **Toba and Kakar Ranges** Mts Pak
27E4 **Tobago** I Caribbean S
13C2 **Toba Inlet** Sd Can
71D3 **Tobelo** Indon
14B1 **Tobermory** Can
44A3 **Tobermory** Scot
71E3 **Tobi** I Pacific O
21B1 **Tobin,Mt** USA
65H4 **Tobol** R Kazakhstan
70D4 **Toboli** Indon
65H4 **Tobol'sk** Russian Fed
Tobruk = Tubruq
31B2 **Tocantins** R Brazil
17B1 **Toccoa** USA
47C1 **Toce** R Italy
30B3 **Tocopilla** Chile
30C3 **Tocorpuri** Mt Chile
32D1 **Tocuyo** R Ven
85D3 **Toda** India
47C1 **Tödi** Mt Switz
75A1 **Todong** S Korea
9B4 **Todos Santos** Mexico
13E2 **Tofield** Can
13B3 **Tofino** Can
12B3 **Togiak** USA
12B3 **Togiak B** USA
97C4 **Togo** Republic, Africa
72C1 **Togtoh** China
12F2 **Tok** USA
74E2 **Tokachi** R Japan
75B1 **Tokamachi** Japan
95C3 **Tokar** Sudan
69E4 **Tokara Retto** Arch Japan
92C1 **Tokat** Turk
74B3 **Tŏkchŏk-kundo** Arch S Korea
75A1 **Tok-do** I S Korea
82B1 **Tokmak** Kirgizia
110C1 **Tokomaru Bay** NZ
12H3 **Toku** R Can/USA
78C3 **Tokung** Indon
69E4 **Tokuno** I Japan
74C4 **Tokushima** Japan
75A2 **Tokuyama** Japan
74D3 **Tōkyō** Japan
110C1 **Tolaga Bay** NZ
101D3 **Tôlañaro** Madag
30F3 **Toledo** Brazil
50B2 **Toledo** Spain
14B2 **Toledo** USA
19B3 **Toledo Bend Res** USA
101D3 **Toliara** Madag
23B1 **Toliman** Mexico
32B3 **Tolina** Mt Colombia
51B1 **Tolosa** Spain
29B3 **Toltén** Chile
23B2 **Toluca** Mexico
61G3 **Tol'yatti** Russian Fed
74E2 **Tomakomai** Japan
78D1 **Tomani** Malay

58C2 **Tomaszów Mazowiecka** Pol
11B3 **Tombigbee** R USA
98B3 **Tomboco** Angola
35C2 **Tombos** Brazil
97B3 **Tombouctou** Mali
100A2 **Tombua** Angola
34A3 **Tomé** Chile
50B2 **Tomelloso** Spain
50A2 **Tomer** Port
106B3 **Tomkinson Range** Mts Aust
63E2 **Tommot** Russian Fed
55B2 **Tomorrit** Mt Alb
65K4 **Tomsk** Russian Fed
16B3 **Toms River** USA
25C3 **Tonalá** Mexico
20C1 **Tonasket** USA
15C2 **Tonawanda** USA
105H4 **Tonga** Is Pacific O
101H1 **Tongaat** S Africa
73D3 **Tongcheng** China
72B2 **Tongchuan** China
72A2 **Tongde** China
46C1 **Tongeren** Belg
76E2 **Tonggu Jiao** I China
73A5 **Tonghai** China
74B2 **Tonghua** China
74B3 **Tongjosŏn-man** N Korea
76D1 **Tongkin,G of** China/ Viet
72E1 **Tonglia** China
73D3 **Tongling** China
108B2 **Tongo** Aust
34A2 **Tongoy** Chile
73B4 **Tongren** Guizhou, China
72A2 **Tongren** Qinghai, China
86C1 **Tongsa** Bhutan
76B1 **Tongta** Burma
68B3 **Tongtian He** R China
44B2 **Tongue** Scot
72D2 **Tong Xian** China
72B2 **Tongxin** China
73B4 **Tongzi** China
9C4 **Tonich** Mexico
99C2 **Tonj** Sudan
85D3 **Tonk** India
18A2 **Tonkawa** USA
76C3 **Tonle Sap** L Camb
21B2 **Tonopah** USA
12E2 **Tonsina** USA
8B2 **Tooele** USA
109D1 **Toogoolawah** Aust
108B1 **Toompine** Aust
109D1 **Toowoomba** Aust
22C1 **Topaz L** USA
18A2 **Topeka** USA
9C4 **Topolobampo** Mexico
20B1 **Toppenish** USA
99D2 **Tor** Eth
55C3 **Torbali** Turk
90C2 **Torbat-e-Heydarîyeh** Iran
90D2 **Torbat-e Jām** Iran
12D2 **Torbert,Mt** USA
50A1 **Tordesillas** Spain
56C2 **Torgau** Germany
46B1 **Torhout** Belg
69G3 **Tori** I Japan
47B2 **Torino** Italy
99D2 **Torit** Sudan
35A1 **Torixoreu** Brazil
50A1 **Tormes** R Spain
13E2 **Tornado Mt** Can
38J5 **Torne** L Sweden
38H5 **Torneträsk** Sweden
7D4 **Torngat** Mts Can
38J5 **Tornio** Fin
34C3 **Tornquist** Arg
15C2 **Toronto** Can
60D2 **Toropets** Russian Fed
99D2 **Tororo** Uganda
92B2 **Toros Daǧlari** Mts Turk
43C4 **Torquay** Eng
22C4 **Torrance** USA
50A2 **Torrão** Port
51C1 **Torreblanca** Spain
53B2 **Torre del Greco** Italy

50B1 **Torrelavega** Spain
50B2 **Torremolinos** Spain
108A2 **Torrens,L** Aust
24B2 **Torreón** Mexico
47B2 **Torre Pellice** Italy
107D2 **Torres Str** Aust
50A2 **Torres Vedras** Port
16C2 **Torrington** Connecticut, USA
8C2 **Torrington** Wyoming, USA
9C4 **Torrón** Mexico
38D3 **Tórshavn** Føroyar
47C2 **Tortona** Italy
51C1 **Tortosa** Spain
90C2 **Torüd** Iran
58B2 **Toruń** Pol
40B2 **Tory** I Irish Rep
60D2 **Torzhok** Russian Fed
75A2 **Tosa** Japan
74C4 **Tosa-shimizu** Japan
74C4 **Tosa-wan** B Japan
75B2 **To-shima** I Japan
60D2 **Tosno** Russian Fed
75A2 **Tosu** Japan
92B1 **Tosya** Turk
61F1 **Tot'ma** Russian Fed
43C4 **Totnes** Eng
33F2 **Totness** Surinam
23B2 **Totolapan** Mexico
51B2 **Totona** Spain
109C2 **Tottenham** Aust
74C3 **Tottori** Japan
97B4 **Touba** Ivory Coast
97A3 **Touba** Sen
96B1 **Toubkal** Mt Mor
97B3 **Tougan** Burkina
96C1 **Touggourt** Alg
97A3 **Tougué** Guinea
46C2 **Toul** France
49D3 **Toulon** France
48C3 **Toulouse** France
97B4 **Toumodi** Ivory Coast
76B2 **Toungoo** Burma
46B1 **Tourcoing** France
96A2 **Tourine** Maur
46B1 **Tournai** Belg
48C2 **Tours** France
74E2 **Towada** Japan
74E2 **Towada-ko** L Japan
15C2 **Towanda** USA
107D2 **Townsville** Aust
16A3 **Towson** USA
43C4 **Towy** R Wales
74D3 **Toyama** Japan
75B1 **Toyama-wan** B Japan
75B2 **Toyohashi** Japan
75B2 **Toyonaka** Japan
75A1 **Toyooka** Japan
74D3 **Toyota** Japan
96C1 **Tozeur** Tunisia
46D2 **Traben-Trarbach** Germany
93C1 **Trabzon** Turk
22B2 **Tracy** California, USA
34A3 **Traiguén** Chile
13D3 **Trail** Can
41B3 **Tralee** Irish Rep
45B2 **Tralee B** Irish Rep
45C2 **Tramore** Irish Rep
39G7 **Tranås** Sweden
77B4 **Trang** Thai
71E4 **Trangan** I Indon
109C2 **Trangie** Aust
12E2 **Transalaskan Pipeline** USA
100B3 **Transvaal** Province, S Africa
Transylvanian Alps = Muntii Carpaţii Meridionali
53B3 **Trapani** Italy
109C3 **Traralgon** Aust
97A3 **Trarza** Region, Maur
76C3 **Trat** Thai
108B2 **Traveller's** L Aust
56C2 **Travemünde** Germany
14A2 **Traverse City** USA
12C1 **Traverse Peak** Mt USA
111B2 **Travers,Mt** NZ
47C2 **Trebbia** R Italy

59B3 **Třebíč** Czech
54A2 **Trebinje** Bosnia & Herzegovina, Yugos
57C3 **Trebon** Czech
29F2 **Treinta y Tres** Urug
29C4 **Trelew** Arg
39G7 **Trelleborg** Sweden
43B3 **Tremadog B** Wales
15D1 **Tremblant,Mt** Can
13C2 **Trembleur L** Can
16A2 **Tremont** USA
59B3 **Trenčín** Czech
34C3 **Trenque Lauquén** Arg
43D3 **Trent** R Eng
47D1 **Trentino** Region, Italy
47D1 **Trento** Italy
15C2 **Trenton** Can
18B1 **Trenton** Missouri, USA
16B2 **Trenton** New Jersey, USA
7E5 **Trepassey** Can
34C3 **Tres Arroyos** Arg
35B2 **Tres Coraçoes** Brazil
30F3 **Três Lagoas** Brazil
34C3 **Tres Lomas** Arg
22B2 **Tres Pinos** USA
35C2 **Três Rios** Brazil
47C2 **Treviglio** Italy
47E2 **Treviso** Italy
47C2 **Trezzo** Italy
87B2 **Trichūr** India
108C2 **Trida** Aust
46D2 **Trier** Germany
52B1 **Trieste** Italy
45C2 **Trim** Irish Rep
87C3 **Trincomalee** Sri Lanka
33E6 **Trinidad** Bol
29E2 **Trinidad** Urug
9C3 **Trinidad** USA
34C3 **Trinidad** I Arg
27E4 **Trinidad** I Caribbean S
103E6 **Trindade** I Atlantic O
27E4 **Trinidad & Tobago** Republic Caribbean S
19A3 **Trinity** USA
9D3 **Trinity** R USA
7E5 **Trinity B** Can
12D3 **Trinity Is** USA
17A1 **Trion** USA
94B1 **Tripoli** Leb
95A1 **Tripoli** Libya
55B3 **Tripolis** Greece
86C2 **Tripura** State, India
103H6 **Tristan da Cunha** Is Atlantic O
Trivandrum = Thiruvananthapuram
59B3 **Trnava** Czech
107E1 **Trobriand Is** PNG
15D1 **Trois-Riviéres** Can
65H4 **Troitsk** Russian Fed
39G7 **Trollhättan** Sweden
38F6 **Trollheimen** Mt Nor
89K9 **Tromelin** I Indian O
38H5 **Tromsø** Nor
38G6 **Trondheim** Nor
38G6 **Trondheimfjord** Inlet Nor
42B2 **Troon** Scot
102J3 **Tropic of Cancer**
103J6 **Tropic of Capricorn**
96B2 **Troudenni** Mali
7A4 **Trout L** Ontario, Can
17A1 **Troy** Alabama, USA
16C1 **Troy** New York, USA
14B2 **Troy** Ohio, USA
54B2 **Troyan** Bulg
49C2 **Troyes** France
91B5 **Trucial Coast** Region, UAE
21A2 **Truckee** R USA
25D3 **Trujillo** Honduras
32B5 **Trujillo** Peru
50A2 **Trujillo** Spain
32C2 **Trujillo** Ven
109C2 **Trundle** Aust
7D5 **Truro** Can
43B4 **Truro** Eng

71E3 **Trust Territories of the Pacific Is** Pacific O
68B2 **Tsagaan Nuur** L Mongolia
68B1 **Tsagan-Tologoy** Russian Fed
101D2 **Tsaratanana** Madag
100B3 **Tsau** Botswana
99D3 **Tsavo** Kenya
99D3 **Tsavo Nat Pk** Kenya
65J4 **Tselinograd** Kazakhstan
100A3 **Tses** Namibia
68C2 **Tsetserleg** Mongolia
97C4 **Tsévié** Togo
100B3 **Tshabong** Botswana
100B3 **Tshane** Botswana
98B3 **Tshela** Zaïre
98C3 **Tshibala** Zaïre
98C3 **Tshikapa** Zaïre
98C3 **Tshuapa** R Zaïre
101D3 **Tsihombe** Madag
61F4 **Tsimlyanskoye Vodokhranilishche** Res Russian Fed
Tsinan = Jinan
Tsingtao = Qingdao
101D2 **Tsiroanomandidy** Madag
13B2 **Tsitsutl Peak** Mt Can
58D2 **Tsna** R Belorussia
72R1 **Tsogt Ovoo** Mongolia
68C2 **Tsomog** Mongolia
75B2 **Tsu** Japan
75B1 **Tsubata** Japan
74E3 **Tsuchira** Japan
74E2 **Tsugaru-kaikyō** Str Japan
100A2 **Tsumeb** Namibia
100A3 **Tsumis** Namibia
75B1 **Tsunugi** Japan
74D3 **Tsuruga** Japan
74D3 **Tsuruoka** Japan
75B1 **Tsushima** Japan
74B4 **Tsushima** I Japan
74C3 **Tsuyama** Japan
50A1 **Tua** R Port
45B2 **Tuam** Irish Rep
60E5 **Tuapse** Russian Fed
111A3 **Tuatapere** NZ
30G4 **Tubarão** Brazil
94B2 **Tubas** Israel
79A4 **Tubbataha Reefs** Is Phil
57B3 **Tübingen** Germany
95B1 **Tubruq** Libya
16B3 **Tuckerton** USA
9B3 **Tucson** USA
30C4 **Tucumán** State, Arg
34B2 **Tucunuco** Arg
33E2 **Tucupita** Ven
51B1 **Tudela** Spain
93C3 **Tudmur** Syria
101H1 **Tugela** R S Africa
109D2 **Tuggerah** L Aust
12D3 **Tugidak** I USA
79B2 **Tuguegarao** Phil
63F2 **Tugur** Russian Fed
72D2 **Tuhai He** R China
4E3 **Tuktoyaktuk** USA
58C1 **Tukums** Latvia
99D3 **Tukuyu** Tanz
84B1 **Tukzar** Afghan
60E3 **Tula** Russian Fed
23B1 **Tulancingo** Mexico
78A3 **Tulangbawang** R Indon
32B3 **Tulcán** Colombia
60C5 **Tulcea** Rom
100B3 **Tuli** Zim
94B2 **Tulkarm** Israel
48C2 **Tulle** France
19B3 **Tullos** USA
45C2 **Tullow** Irish Rep
18A2 **Tulsa** USA
93C3 **Tulūl ash Shāmīyah** Desert Region Syria/ S Arabia
63C2 **Tulun** Russian Fed
78C4 **Tulungagung** Indon
32B3 **Tumaco** Colombia
109C3 **Tumbarumba** Aust

32A4 **Tumbes** Ecuador
108A2 **Tumby Bay** Aust
74B2 **Tumen** China
87B2 **Tumkūr** India
77C4 **Tumpat** Malay
85D4 **Tumsar** India
97B3 **Tumu** Ghana
109C3 **Tumut** Aust
109C3 **Tumut** R Aust
27L1 **Tunapuna** Trinidad
93C2 **Tunceli** Turk
99D3 **Tunduma** Zambia
101C2 **Tunduru** Tanz
54C2 **Tundzha** R Bulg
87B1 **Tungabhadra** R India
68D4 **Tung-Chiang** Taiwan
38B2 **Tungnafellsjökull** Mts Iceland
12J2 **Tungsten** Can
63B1 **Tunguska** R Russian Fed
87C1 **Tuni** India
96D1 **Tunis** Tunisia
88E4 **Tunisia** Republic, N Africa
32C2 **Tunja** Colombia
12B2 **Tuntutuliak** USA
12B2 **Tununak** USA
34B2 **Tunuyán** Arg
34B2 **Tunuyán** R Arg
73D4 **Tunxi** China
22C2 **Tuolumne Meadows** USA
35A2 **Tupã** Brazil
35B1 **Tupaciguara** Brazil
19C3 **Tupelo** USA
30C3 **Tupiza** Bol
15D2 **Tupper Lake** USA
34B2 **Tupungato** Arg
29C2 **Tupungato** Mt Arg
86C1 **Tura** India
63C1 **Tura** Russian Fed
61K2 **Tura** R Russian Fed
90C2 **Turān** Iran
63B2 **Turan** Russian Fed
93C3 **Turayf** S Arabia
80E3 **Turbat** Pak
32B2 **Turbo** Colombia
54B1 **Turda** Rom
63A3 **Turfan Depression** China
65H4 **Turgay** Kazakhstan
63B3 **Turgen Uul** Mt Mongolia
54C2 **Turgovishte** Bulg
92A2 **Turgutlu** Turk
92C1 **Turhal** Turk
39K7 **Türi** Estonia
51B2 **Turia** R Spain
Turin = Torino
61K2 **Turinsk** Russian Fed
69F2 **Turiy Rog** Russian Fed
99D2 **Turkana,L** Kenya/Eth
80E1 **Turkestan** Region, C Asia
82A1 **Turkestan** Kazakhstan
92C2 **Turkey** Republic, W Asia
80D1 **Turkmenistan** Republic, Asia
90B2 **Turkmenskiy Zaliv** B Turkmenistan
27C2 **Turks Is** Caribbean S
39J6 **Turku** Fin
99D2 **Turkwel** R Kenya
22B2 **Turlock** USA
22B2 **Turlock L** USA
110C2 **Turnagain,C** NZ
25D3 **Turneffe I** Belize
16C1 **Turners Falls** USA
46C1 **Turnhout** Belg
13F1 **Turnor L** Can
54B2 **Turnu Măgurele** Rom
63A3 **Turpan** China
26B2 **Turquino** Mt Cuba
80E1 **Turtkul'** Uzbekistan
18A2 **Turtle Creek Res** USA
13F2 **Turtle L** Can
63A1 **Turukhansk** Russian

68C1 **Turuntayevo** Russian Fed
35A1 **Turvo** R Goias, Brazil
35B2 **Turvo** R São Paulo, Brazil
58C2 **Tur'ya** R Ukraine
19C3 **Tuscaloosa** USA
18C2 **Tuscola** USA
90C3 **Tusharik** Iran
Tutera = Tudela
87B3 **Tuticorin** India
54C2 **Tutrakan** Bulg
57B3 **Tuttlingen** Germany
68C2 **Tuul Gol** R Mongolia
105G4 **Tuvalu** Is Pacific O
63B2 **Tuvinskaya Respublika,** Russian Fed
23A2 **Tuxpan** Jalisco, Mexico
24B2 **Tuxpan** Nayarit, Mexico
23B1 **Tuxpan** Veracruz, Mexico
23B2 **Tuxtepec** Mexico
25C3 **Tuxtla Gutiérrez** Mexico
50A1 **Túy** Spain
76D3 **Tuy Hoa** Viet
92B2 **Tuz Gölü** Salt L Turk
93D3 **Tuz Khurmātū** Iraq
54A2 **Tuzla** Bosnia & Herzogovina, Yugos
60E2 **Tver'** Russian Fed
42C2 **Tweed** R Eng/Scot
109D1 **Tweed Heads** Aust
42C2 **Tweedsmuir Hills** Scot
7E5 **Twillingate** Can
8B2 **Twin Falls** USA
111B2 **Twins,The** Mt NZ
14A2 **Two Rivers** USA
63E2 **Tygda** Russian Fed
19A3 **Tyler** USA
65K3 **Tym** R Russian Fed
69G1 **Tymovskoye** Russian Fed
42D2 **Tyne** R Eng
42D2 **Tyne and Wear** Metropolitan County, Eng
42D2 **Tynemouth** Eng
38G6 **Tynset** Nor
12D3 **Tyonek** USA
94B2 **Tyr** Leb
Tyre = Tyr
45C1 **Tyrone** County, N Ire
108B3 **Tyrrell,L** Aust
53B2 **Tyrrhenian S** Italy
65H4 **Tyumen'** Russian Fed
43B3 **Tywyn** Wales
55B3 **Tzoumérka** Mt Greece

U

99E2 **Uarsciek** Somalia
35C2 **Ubá** Brazil
35C1 **Ubaí** Brazil
98B2 **Ubangi** R CAR
47B2 **Ubaye** R France
75A2 **Ube** Japan
50B2 **Ubeda** Spain
6E2 **Ubekendt Ejland** I Greenland
35B1 **Uberaba** Brazil
35B1 **Uberlândia** Brazil
76C2 **Ubon Ratchathani** Thai
58D2 **Ubort** R Belorussia
98C3 **Ubundi** Zaïre
32C5 **Ucayali** R Peru
84C3 **Uch** Pak
63F2 **Uchar** R Russian Fed
74E2 **Uchiura-wan** B Japan
63B2 **Uda** R Russian Fed
85C4 **Udaipur** India
86B1 **Udaipur Garhi** Nepal
34D3 **Udaquoila** Arg
39G7 **Uddevalla** Sweden
38H5 **Uddjaur** L Sweden
87B1 **Udgir** India
84D2 **Udhampur** India

61H2 **Udmurtskaya Respublika,** Russian Fed
76C2 **Udon Thani** Thai
63F2 **Udskaya Guba** B Russian Fed
87A2 **Udupi** India
75B1 **Ueda** Japan
99C2 **Uele** R Zaïre
56C2 **Uelzen** Germany
98C2 **Uere** R Zaïre
61J3 **Ufa** Russian Fed
61J2 **Ufa** R Russian Fed
100A3 **Ugab** R Namibia
99D3 **Ugaila** R Tanz
12D3 **Ugak B** USA
99D2 **Uganda** Republic, Africa
12C3 **Ugashik B** USA
12C3 **Ugashik L** USA
47B2 **Ugine** France
69G2 **Uglegorsk** Russian Fed
60E2 **Uglich** Russian Fed
60E3 **Ugra** R Russian Fed
44A3 **Uig** Scot
98B3 **Uige** Angola
61H4 **Uil** Kazakhstan
8B2 **Uinta Mts** USA
100B4 **Uitenhage** S Africa
59C3 **Ujfehértó** Hung
75B2 **Uji** Japan
99C3 **Ujiji** Tanz
30C3 **Ujina** Chile
85D4 **Ujjain** India
70C4 **Ujung Pandang** Indon
99D3 **Ukerewe** I Tanz
86C1 **Ukhrul** India
21A2 **Ukiah** California, USA
20C1 **Ukiah** Oregon, USA
58C1 **Ukmerge** Lithuania
60C4 **Ukraine** Republic, Europe
68C2 **Ulaanbaatar** Mongolia
68B2 **Ulaangom** Mongolia
72C1 **Ulaan Uul** Mongolia
82C1 **Ulangar Hu** L China
68C1 **Ulan Ude** Russian Fed
68B3 **Ulan Ul Hu** L China
34B2 **Ulapes** Arg
74B3 **Ulchin** S Korea
54A2 **Ulcinj** Montenegro, Yugos
68D2 **Uldz** Mongolia
68B2 **Uliastay** Mongolia
58D1 **Ulla** Lithuania
109D3 **Ulladulla** Aust
44B3 **Ullapool** Scot
38H5 **Ullsfjorden** Inlet Nor
42C2 **Ullswater** L Eng
74C3 **Ullung-do** I S Korea
57C3 **Ulm** Germany
108A1 **Uloowaranie,L** Aust
74B3 **Ulsan** S Korea
45C1 **Ulster** Region, N Ire
65K5 **Ulungur He** R China
65K5 **Ulungur Hu** L China
44A3 **Ulva** I Scot
42C2 **Ulverston** Eng
109C4 **Ulverstone** Aust
63G2 **Ulya** R Russian Fed
61G3 **Ul'yanovsk** Russian Fed
60D4 **Uman** Ukraine
6E2 **Umanak** Greenland
86A2 **Umaria** India
85B3 **Umarkot** Pak
108A1 **Umaroona,L** Aust
20C1 **Umatilla** USA
38L5 **Umba** Russian Fed
99D3 **Umba** R Tanz
38H6 **Ume** R Sweden
38J6 **Umea** Sweden
101H1 **Umfolozi** R S Africa
4C3 **Umiat** USA
91C4 **Umm al Qaiwain** UAE
91C5 **Umm as Samīm** Salt Marsh Oman
99C1 **Umm Bell** Sudan

98C1 **Umm Keddada** Sudan
99D1 **Umm Ruwaba** Sudan
91B5 **Umm Sa'id** Qatar
20B2 **Umpqua** *R* USA
85D4 **Umred** India
100B4 **Umtata** S Africa
35A2 **Umuarama** Brazil
52C1 **Una** *R* Bosnia & Herzegovina, Yugos/Croatia
35B1 **Unai** Brazil
12B2 **Unalakleet** USA
80C3 **Unayzah** S Arabia
16C2 **Uncasville** USA
101G1 **Underberg** S Africa
60D3 **Unecha** Russian Fed
94B3 **Uneisa** Jordan
7D4 **Ungava B** Can
30F4 **União de Vitória** Brazil
34B3 **Unión** Arg
18B2 **Union** Missouri, USA
17B1 **Union** S Carolina, USA
14C2 **Union City** Pennsylvania, USA
17A1 **Union Springs** USA
15C3 **Uniontown** USA
91B5 **United Arab Emirates** Arabian Pen
36C3 **United Kingdom** Kingdom, W Europe
2H4 **United States of America**
6B1 **United States Range** *Mts* Can
13F2 **Unity** Can
20C2 **Unity** USA
46D1 **Unna** Germany
86A1 **Unnão** India
44E1 **Unst** *I* Scot
13A1 **Unuk** *R* USA
92C1 **Unye** Turk
61F2 **Unzha** *R* Russian Fed
33E2 **Upata** Ven
98C3 **Upemba Nat Pk** Zaïre
6E2 **Upernavik** Greenland
22D3 **Upland** USA
100B3 **Uplington** S Africa
14B2 **Upper Arlington** USA
13D2 **Upper Arrow L** Can
111C2 **Upper Hutt** NZ
20B2 **Upper Klamath L** USA
20B2 **Upper L** USA
45C1 **Upper Lough Erne** *L* N Ire
27L1 **Upper Manzanilla** Trinidad
39H7 **Uppsala** Sweden
72B1 **Urad Qianqi** China
91A4 **Urairah** S Arabia
61H3 **Ural** *R* Kazakhstan
109D2 **Uralla** Aust
61H3 **Ural'sk** Kazakhstan
65G4 **Uralskiy Khrebet** *Mts* Russian Fed
5H4 **Uranium City** Can
75B1 **Urawa** Japan
18C1 **Urbana** Illinois, USA
14B2 **Urbana** Ohio, USA
52B2 **Urbino** Italy
42C2 **Ure** *R* Eng
61G2 **Uren'** Russian Fed
80E1 **Urgench** Uzbekistan
84B2 **Urgun** Afghan
55C3 **Urla** Turk
54B2 **Uroševac** Serbia, Yugos
31B4 **Uruaçu** Brazil
23A2 **Uruapan** Mexico
35B1 **Urucuia** *R* Brazil
30E4 **Uruguaiana** Brazil
29E2 **Uruguay** Republic, S America
29E2 **Uruguay** *R* Urug
82C1 **Ürümqi** China
69H2 **Urup** *I* Russian Fed
84B2 **Uruzgan** Afghan
61F3 **Uryupinsk** Russian Fed
61H2 **Urzhum** Russian Fed

54C2 **Urziceni** Rom
82C1 **Usa** China
75A2 **Usa** Japan
64G3 **Usa** *R* Russian Fed
92A2 **Uşak** Turk
100A3 **Usakos** Namibia
99D3 **Ushashi** Tanz
65J5 **Ush Tobe** Kazakhstan
29C6 **Ushuaia** Arg
63E2 **Ushumun** Russian Fed
43C4 **Usk** *R* Wales
92A1 **Üsküdar** Turk
63C2 **Usolye Sibirskoye** Russian Fed
34B2 **Uspallata** Arg
69F2 **Ussuriysk** Russian Fed
47C1 **Uster** Switz
53B3 **Ustica** *I* Italy
57C2 **Usti nad Labem** Czech
65J4 **Ust'Ishim** Russian Fed
58B2 **Ustka** Pol
65K5 **Ust'-Kamenogorsk** Kazakhstan
63B2 **Ust Karabula** Russian Fed
61J2 **Ust'Katav** Russian Fed
63C2 **Ust'-Kut** Russian Fed
61E4 **Ust Labinsk** Russian Fed
63F1 **Ust'Maya** Russian Fed
1C8 **Ust'Nera** Russian Fed
63E2 **Ust'Nyukzha** Russian Fed
63C2 **Ust'Ordynskiy** Russian Fed
64G3 **Ust'Tsil'ma** Russian Fed
63F2 **Ust'Umal'ta** Russian Fed
75A2 **Usuki** Japan
25C3 **Usumacinta** *R* Guatemala/Mexico
101H1 **Usutu** *R* Swaziland
8B3 **Utah** State, USA
8B2 **Utah L** USA
58D1 **Utena** Russian Fed
85B3 **Uthal** Pak
10C2 **Utica** USA
51B2 **Utiel** Spain
13D1 **Utikuma L** Can
56B2 **Utrecht** Neth
101H1 **Utrecht** S Africa
50A2 **Utrera** Spain
38K5 **Utsjoki** Fin
74D3 **Utsunomiya** Japan
76C2 **Uttaradit** Thai
86A1 **Uttar Pradesh** State, India
65H4 **Uval** Russian Fed
107F3 **Uvéa** *I* Nouvelle Calédonie
99D3 **Uvinza** Tanz
99C3 **Uvira** Zaïre
6E2 **Uvkusigssat** Greenland
39J6 **Uvsikaupunki** Fin
68B1 **Uvs Nuur** *L* China
74C4 **Uwajima** Japan
72B2 **Uxin Qi** China
63B2 **Uyar** Russian Fed
30C3 **Uyuni** Bol
80E1 **Uzbekistan** Republic, Asia
48C2 **Uzerche** France
59C3 **Uzhgorod** Ukraine
60E3 **Uzlovaya** Russian Fed
92A1 **Uzunköprü** Turk

V
101F1 **Vaal** *R* S Africa
101G1 **Vaal Dam** *Res* S Africa
100B3 **Vaalwater** S Africa
38J6 **Vaasa** Fin
59B3 **Vác** Hung
30F4 **Vacaria** Brazil

35C1 **Vacaria** *R* Minas Gerais, Brazil
21A2 **Vacaville** USA
85C4 **Vadodara** India
38K4 **Vadsø** Nor
47C1 **Vaduz** Leichtenstein
38D3 **Vágar** Føroyar
29E3 **Va Gesell** Arg
59B3 **Váh** *R* Czech
87B2 **Vaigai** *R* India
65K3 **Vakh** *R* Russian Fed
60B4 **Vâlcea** Rom
29C4 **Valcheta** Arg
47D2 **Valdagno** Italy
60D2 **Valday** Russian Fed
60D2 **Valdayskaya Vozvyshennost'** *Upland* Russian Fed
32D2 **Val de la Pascua** Ven
50B2 **Valdepeñas** Spain
12E2 **Valdez** USA
29B3 **Valdivia** Chile
46B2 **Val d'Oise** *Department* France
17B1 **Valdosta** USA
20C2 **Vale** USA
13D2 **Valemount** Can
31D4 **Valença** Bahia, Brazil
35C2 **Valença** Rio de Janeiro, Brazil
49C3 **Valence** France
51B2 **Valencia** Region, Spain
51B2 **Valencia** Spain
32D1 **Valencia** Ven
45A3 **Valencia** *I* Irish Rep
50A2 **Valencia de Alcantara** Spain
46B1 **Valenciennes** France
47C2 **Valenza** Italy
32C2 **Valera** Ven
39K7 **Valga** Estonia
54A2 **Valjevo** Serbia, Yugos
39J6 **Valkeakoski** Fin
25D2 **Valladolid** Mexico
50B1 **Valladolid** Spain
47B2 **Valle d'Aosta** Region, Italy
27D5 **Valle de la Pascua** Ven
23A1 **Valle de Santiago** Mexico
47B2 **Valle d'Isére** France
32C1 **Valledupar** Colombia
97C3 **Vallée de l'Azaouak** *V* Niger
97C3 **Vallée Tilemis** *V* Mali
30D2 **Valle Grande** Bol
22A1 **Vallejo** USA
30B4 **Vallenar** Chile
53B3 **Valletta** Malta
8D2 **Valley City** USA
20B2 **Valley Falls** USA
15D1 **Valleyfield** Can
13D1 **Valleyview** Can
47E2 **Valli di Comacchio** *Lg* Italy
51C1 **Valls** Spain
58D1 **Valmiera** Latvia
35A2 **Valparaiso** Brazil
34A2 **Valparaiso** Chile
23A1 **Valparaiso** Mexico
17A1 **Valparaiso** USA
101G1 **Vals** *R* S Africa
85C4 **Valsād** India
60E3 **Valuyki** Russian Fed
50A2 **Valverde del Camino** Spain
38J6 **Vammala** Fin
93D2 **Van** Turk
63C1 **Vanavara** Russian Fed
18B2 **Van Buren** Arkansas, USA
13C3 **Vancouver** Can
20B1 **Vancouver** USA
5F5 **Vancouver I** Can
12G2 **Vancouver,Mt** Can
18C2 **Vandalia** Illinois, USA
14B3 **Vandalia** Ohio, USA
13C2 **Vanderhoof** Can
106C2 **Van Diemen G** *Gulf* Aust

39G7 **Vänern** *L* Sweden
39G7 **Vänersborg** Sweden
101D3 **Vangaindrano** Madag
93D2 **Van Gölü** *Salt L* Turk
76C2 **Vang Vieng** Laos
9C3 **Van Horn** USA
15C1 **Vanier** Can
1C6 **Vankarem** Russian Fed
38H6 **Vännäs** Sweden
48B2 **Vannes** France
47B2 **Vanoise** *Mts* France
100A4 **Vanrhynsdorp** S Africa
6B3 **Vansittart I** Can
105G4 **Vanuatu** *Is* Pacific O
14B2 **Van Wert** USA
47C2 **Varallo** Italy
90B2 **Varāmin** Iran
86A1 **Vārānasi** India
38K4 **Varangerfjord** *Inlet* Nor
38K4 **Varangerhalvøya** *Pen* Nor
52C1 **Varazdin** Croatia
39G7 **Varberg** Sweden
39F7 **Varde** Den
38L4 **Vardø** Nor
58C2 **Varéna** Lithuania
47C2 **Varenna** Italy
47C2 **Varese** Italy
35B2 **Varginha** Brazil
38K6 **Varkaus** Fin
54C2 **Varna** Bulg
39G7 **Värnamo** Sweden
17B1 **Varnville** USA
35C1 **Várzea da Palma** Brazil
47C2 **Varzi** Italy
50B1 **Vascongadas** Region, Spain
60D3 **Vasil'kov** Ukraine
14B2 **Vassar** USA
39H7 **Västerås** Sweden
39H7 **Västervik** Sweden
52B2 **Vasto** Italy
65J4 **Vasyugan** *R* Russian Fed
38B2 **Vatnajökull** *Mts* Iceland
38A1 **Vatneyri** Iceland
54C1 **Vatra Dornei** Rom
39G7 **Vättern** *L* Sweden
9C3 **Vaughn** USA
32C3 **Vaupés** *R* Colombia
13E2 **Vauxhall** Can
87C3 **Vavunija** Sri Lanka
39G7 **Växjö** Sweden
64G2 **Vaygach, Ostrov** *I* Russian Fed
34C2 **Vedia** Arg
38G5 **Vega** *I* Nor
13E2 **Vegreville** Can
50A2 **Vejer de la Frontera** Spain
39F7 **Vejle** Den
57C2 **Velebit** *Mts* Croatia
35C1 **Velhas** *R* Brazil
39K7 **Velikaya** *R* Russian Fed
60D2 **Velikiye Luki** Russian Fed
61G1 **Velikiy Ustyug** Russian Fed
54C2 **Veliko Türnovo** Bulg
97A3 **Vélingara** Sen
87B2 **Vellore** India
61F1 **Vel'sk** Russian Fed
87B3 **Vembanad L** India
34C2 **Venado Tuerto** Arg
35B2 **Venceslau Braz** Brazil
49C2 **Vendôme** France
12E1 **Venetie** USA
47D2 **Veneto** Region, Italy
47E2 **Venezia** Italy
32D2 **Venezuela** Republic, S America
87A1 **Vengurla** India
12C3 **Veniaminof V** USA
Venice = Venezia
87B2 **Venkatagiri** India
56B2 **Venlo** Neth
58C1 **Venta** *R* Latvia

101G1 **Ventersburg** S Africa
58C1 **Ventspils** Latvia
32D3 **Ventuari** R Ven
22C3 **Ventura** USA
60D1 **Vepsovskaya Vozvyshennost'** Upland Russian Fed
30D4 **Vera** Arg
51B2 **Vera** Spain
23B2 **Veracruz** Mexico
23B1 **Veracruz** State, Mexico
85C4 **Verāval** India
47C2 **Verbania** Italy
47C2 **Vercelli** Italy
35A1 **Verde** R Goias, Brazil
23A1 **Verde** R Jalisco, Mexico
35A1 **Verde** R Mato Grosso do Sul, Brazil
23B2 **Verde** R Oaxaca, Mexico
Verde,C = Cap Vert
35C1 **Verde Grande** R Brazil
34C3 **Verde,Pen** Arg
49D3 **Verdon** R France
46C2 **Verdun** France
101G1 **Vereeniging** S Africa
61H2 **Vereshchagino** Russian Fed
97A3 **Verga,C** Guinea
34D3 **Vergara** Arg
50A1 **Verin** Spain
63D2 **Verkh Angara** R Russian Fed
61J3 **Verkhneural'sk** Russian Fed
63E1 **Verkhnevilyuysk** Russian Fed
1C8 **Verkhoyansk** Russian Fed
35A1 **Vermelho** R Brazil
13E2 **Vermilion** Can
10C2 **Vermont** State, USA
22B2 **Vernalis** USA
13D2 **Vernon** Can
46A2 **Vernon** France
9D3 **Vernon** USA
17B2 **Vero Beach** USA
54B2 **Veroia** Greece
47D2 **Verolanuova** Italy
47D2 **Verona** Italy
46B2 **Versailles** France
101H1 **Verulam** S Africa
46C1 **Verviers** Belg
46B2 **Vervins** France
46C2 **Vesle** R France
49D2 **Vesoul** France
38G5 **Vesterålen** Is Nor
38G5 **Vestfjorden** Inlet Nor
38A2 **Vestmannaeyjar** Iceland
53B2 **Vesuvio** Mt Italy
59B3 **Veszprém** Hung
39H7 **Vetlanda** Sweden
61F2 **Vetluga** R Russian Fed
46B1 **Veurne** Belg
47B1 **Vevey** Switz
46A2 **Vexin** Region, France
47A2 **Veynes** France
50A1 **Viana do Castelo** Port
Viangchan = Vientiane
49E3 **Viareggio** Italy
39F7 **Viborg** Den
53C3 **Vibo Valentia** Italy
Vic = Vich
112C2 **Vicecomodoro Marambio** Base Ant
52B1 **Vicenza** Italy
51C1 **Vich** Spain
32D3 **Vichada** R Colombia
61F2 **Vichuga** Russian Fed
49C2 **Vichy** France
19B3 **Vicksburg** USA
35C2 **Vicosa** Brazil
106C4 **Victor Harbour** Aust
34C2 **Victoria** Arg
13C3 **Victoria** Can
34A3 **Victoria** Chile

78D1 **Victoria** Malay
108B3 **Victoria** State, Aust
9D4 **Victoria** USA
106C2 **Victoria** R Aust
26B2 **Victoria de las Tunas** Cuba
100B2 **Victoria Falls** Zambia/Zim
4G2 **Victoria I** Can
108B2 **Victoria,L** Aust
99D3 **Victoria,L** C Africa
112B7 **Victoria Land** Region, Ant
86C2 **Victoria,Mt** Burma
99D2 **Victoria Nile** R Uganda
111B2 **Victoria Range** Mts NZ
106C2 **Victoria River Downs** Aust
4H3 **Victoria Str** Can
15D1 **Victoriaville** Can
100B4 **Victoria West** S Africa
34B3 **Victorica** Arg
21B3 **Victorville** USA
34A2 **Vicuña** Chile
34C2 **Vicuña Mackenna** Arg
17B1 **Vidalia** USA
54C2 **Videle** Rom
54B2 **Vidin** Bulg
85D4 **Vidisha** India
58D1 **Vidzy** Belorussia
29D4 **Viedma** Arg
26A4 **Viejo** Costa Rica
Vielha = Viella
51C1 **Viella** Spain
Vienna = Wien
18C2 **Vienna** Illinois, USA
14B3 **Vienna** W Virginia, USA
49C2 **Vienne** France
48C2 **Vienne** R France
76C2 **Vientiane** Laos
47C1 **Vierwaldstätter See** L Switz
48C2 **Vierzon** France
53C2 **Vieste** Italy
70B2 **Vietnam** Republic, S E Asia
76D1 **Vietri** Viet
27P2 **Vieux Fort** St Lucia
79B2 **Vigan** Phil
47C2 **Vigevano** Italy
48B3 **Vignemale** Mt France
50A1 **Vigo** Spain
87C1 **Vijayawāda** India
55A2 **Vijosë** R Alb
38B2 **Vik** Iceland
54B2 **Vikhren** Mt Bulg
13E2 **Viking** Can
38G6 **Vikna** I Nor
101C2 **Vila da Maganja** Mozam
101C2 **Vila Machado** Mozam
101C3 **Vilanculos** Mozam
Vilanova i la Geltrú = Villanueva-y-Geltrú
50A1 **Vila Real** Port
101C2 **Vila Vasco da Gama** Mozam
35C2 **Vila Velha** Brazil
58D2 **Vileyka** Belorussia
38H6 **Vilhelmina** Sweden
33E6 **Vilhena** Brazil
60C2 **Viljandi** Estonia
101G1 **Viljoenskroon** S Africa
9C3 **Villa Ahumada** Mexico
34B2 **Villa Atuel** Arg
50A1 **Villaba** Spain
23A2 **Villa Carranza** Mexico
52B1 **Villach** Austria
34B2 **Villa Colon** Arg
34C2 **Villa Constitución** Arg
34C1 **Villa de Maria** Arg
23A1 **Villa de Reyes** Mexico

34B2 **Villa Dolores** Arg
47D2 **Villafranca di Verona** Italy
34C2 **Villa General Mitre** Arg
34B2 **Villa General Roca** Arg
34D2 **Villaguay** Arg
25C3 **Villahermosa** Mexico
23A1 **Villa Hidalgo** Mexico
34C2 **Villa Huidobro** Arg
34C3 **Villa Iris** Arg
34C2 **Villa Maria** Arg
30D3 **Villa Montes** Bol
23A1 **Villaneuva** Mexico
50A1 **Villa Nova de Gaia** Port
50A2 **Villanueva de la Serena** Spain
51C1 **Villanueva-y-Geltrú** Spain
34B3 **Villa Regina** Arg
51B2 **Villarreal** Spain
29B3 **Villarrica** Chile
30E4 **Villarrica** Par
50B2 **Villarrobledo** Spain
34D2 **Villa San José** Arg
34C2 **Villa Valeria** Arg
32C3 **Villavicencio** Colombia
49C2 **Villefranche** France
7C5 **Ville-Marie** Can
51B2 **Villena** Spain
46B2 **Villeneuve-St-Georges** France
48C3 **Villeneuve-sur-Lot** France
19B3 **Ville Platte** USA
46B2 **Villers-Cotterêts** France
49C2 **Villeurbanne** France
101G1 **Villiers** S Africa
87B2 **Villupuram** India
58D2 **Vilnius** Lithuania
63D1 **Vilyuy** R Russian Fed
63E1 **Vilyuysk** Russian Fed
34A2 **Viña del Mar** Chile
51C1 **Vinaroz** Spain
14A3 **Vincennes** USA
38H5 **Vindel** R Sweden
85D4 **Vindhya Range** Mts India
16B3 **Vineland** USA
16D2 **Vineyard Haven** USA
76D2 **Vinh** Viet
76D3 **Vinh Cam Ranh** B Viet
77D4 **Vinh Loi** Viet
77D3 **Vinh Long** Viet
18A2 **Vinita** USA
54A1 **Vinkovci** Croatia
60C4 **Vinnitsa** Ukraine
112B3 **Vinson Massif** Upland Ant
100A3 **Vioolsdrift** S Africa
47D1 **Vipiteno** Italy
79B3 **Virac** Phil
87B2 **Virddhāchalam** India
100A2 **Virei** Angola
35C1 **Virgem da Lapa** Brazil
101G1 **Virginia** S Africa
10C3 **Virginia** State, USA
10A2 **Virginia** USA
21B2 **Virginia City** USA
27E3 **Virgin Is** Caribbean S
52C1 **Virovitica** Croatia
46C2 **Virton** Belg
87B3 **Virudunagar** India
52C2 **Vis** I Croatia
21B2 **Visalia** USA
79B3 **Visayan S** Phil
39H7 **Visby** Sweden
4H2 **Viscount Melville Sd** Can
54A2 **Višegrad** Bosnia & Herzegovina, Yugos
50A1 **Viseu** Port
83C4 **Vishākhapatnam** India
47B1 **Visp** Switz
49C1 **Vissingen** Neth

21B3 **Vista** USA
Vistula = Wisla
57C3 **Vitavia** R Czech
87A1 **Vite** India
60D2 **Vitebsk** Belorussia
52B2 **Viterbo** Italy
50A1 **Vitigudino** Spain
63D2 **Vitim** R Russian Fed
50B1 **Vitora** Spain
31C6 **Vitória** Brazil
31C4 **Vitória da Conquista** Brazil
48B2 **Vitré** France
46C2 **Vitry-le-Francois** France
38J5 **Vittangi** Sweden
53B3 **Vittoria** Italy
47E2 **Vittorio Veneto** Italy
69H2 **Vityaz Depth** Pacific O
50A1 **Vivero** Spain
63B1 **Vivi** R Russian Fed
34D3 **Vivorata** Arg
63C2 **Vizhne-Angarsk** Russian Fed
83C4 **Vizianagaram** India
54B1 **Vlădeasa** Mt Rom
61F5 **Vladikavkaz** Russian Fed
65F4 **Vladimir** Russian Fed
59C2 **Vladimir Volynskiy** Ukraine
74C2 **Vladivostok** Russian Fed
56A2 **Vlieland** I Neth
46B1 **Vlissingen** Neth
55A2 **Vlorë** Alb
57C3 **Vöcklabruck** Austria
76D3 **Voeune Sai** Camb
47C2 **Voghera** Italy
101D2 **Vohibinany** Madag
101E2 **Vohimarina** Madag
99D3 **Voi** Kenya
97B4 **Voinjama** Lib
49D2 **Voiron** France
54A1 **Vojvodina** Aut Republic Serbia, Yugos
26A5 **Volcán Baru** Mt Panama
23B2 **Volcán Citlaltepetl** Mt Mexico
30C3 **Volcán Lullaillaco** Mt Chile
34A3 **Volcáno Copahue** Mt Chile
34A3 **Volcáno Domuyo** Mt Arg
Volcano Is = Kazan Retto
29B3 **Volcáno Lanin** Mt Arg
30C3 **Volcán Ollagüe** Mt Chile
34A3 **Volcáno Llaima** Mt Chile
34B2 **Volcáno Maipo** Mt Arg
34A3 **Volcáno Peteroa** Mt Chile
34B3 **Volcáno Tromen** V Arg
23A2 **Volcán Paracutin** Mt Mexico
32B3 **Volcán Puraće** Mt Colombia
34A2 **Volcán Tinguiririca** Mt Arg/Chile
61J2 **Volchansk** Russian Fed
61G4 **Volga** R Russian Fed
61F4 **Volgodonsk** Russian Fed
61F4 **Volgograd** Russian Fed
61G3 **Volgogradskoye Vodokhranilishche** Res Russian Fed
60D2 **Volkhov** Russian Fed
60D2 **Volkhov** R Russian Fed
58C2 **Volkovysk** Belorussia
101G1 **Volksrust** S Africa
61F2 **Vologda** Russian Fed

Volognes

48B2 **Volognes** France
55B3 **Vólos** Greece
61G3 **Vol'sk** Russian Fed
22B2 **Volta** USA
97B3 **Volta Blanche** *R* Burkina
97B4 **Volta,L** Ghana
97B3 **Volta Noire** *R* Burkina
35C2 **Volta Redonda** Brazil
97B3 **Volta Rouge** *R* Burkina
61F4 **Volzhskiy** Russian Fed
12D2 **Von Frank Mt** USA
6J3 **Vopnafjörður** Iceland
47C1 **Voralberg** Province, Austria
47C1 **Vorder Rhein** *R* Switz
56C1 **Vordingborg** Den
64H3 **Vorkuta** Russian Fed
39G6 **Vorma** *R* Nor
60E3 **Voronezh** Russian Fed
38M5 **Voron'ya** *R* Russian Fed
39K7 **Võru** Estonia
49D2 **Vosges** *Mt* France
39F6 **Voss** Nor
63B2 **Vostochnyy Sayan** *Mts* Russian Fed
112B9 **Vostok** *Base* Ant
61H2 **Votkinsk** Russian Fed
46C2 **Vouziers** France
60D4 **Voznesensk** Ukraine
54B2 **Vranje** Serbia, Yugos
54B2 **Vratsa** Bulg
54A1 **Vrbas** Serbia, Yugos
52C2 **Vrbas** *R* Serbia, Yugos
52B1 **Vrbovsko** Bosnia & Herzegovina, Yugos
101G1 **Vrede** S Africa
33F2 **Vreed en Hoop** Guyana
54B1 **Vršac** Serbia, Yugos
52C2 **Vrtoče** Bosnia & Herzegovina, Yugos
100B3 **Vryburg** S Africa
101H1 **Vryheid** S Africa
54A1 **Vukovar** Croatia
13E2 **Vulcan** Can
53B3 **Vulcano** *I* Italy
77D3 **Vung Tau** Viet
38J5 **Vuollerim** Sweden
38L6 **Vyartsilya** Russian Fed
61H2 **Vyatka** *R* Russian Fed
69F2 **Vyazemskiy** Russian Fed
60D2 **Vyaz'ma** Russian Fed
61F2 **Vyazniki** Russian Fed
60C1 **Vyborg** Russian Fed
64G3 **Vym'** *R* Russian Fed
43C3 **Vyrnwy** *R* Wales
60D2 **Vyshiy Volochek** Russian Fed
59B3 **Vyškov** Czech
60E1 **Vytegra** Russian Fed

W

97B3 **Wa** Ghana
13E1 **Wabasca** Can
5G4 **Wabasca** *R* Can
13E1 **Wabasca L** Can
14A2 **Wabash** USA
14A3 **Wabash** *R* USA
5J4 **Wabowden** Can
7D4 **Wabush** Can
17B2 **Waccasassa B** USA
16D1 **Wachusett Res** USA
19A3 **Waco** USA
85B3 **Wad** Pak
95A2 **Waddān** Libya
5F4 **Waddington,Mt** Can
93E4 **Wadi al Bātin** *Watercourse* Iraq
93D3 **Wadi al Ghudāf** *Watercourse* Iraq
94C2 **Wadi al Harīr** *V* Syria

93D3 **Wadi al Mirah** *Watercourse* Iraq/ S Arabia
93D3 **Wadi al Ubayyid** *Watercourse* Iraq
93D3 **Wadi Ar'ar** *Watercourse* S Arabia
91A5 **Wadi as Hsabā'** *Watercourse* S Arabia
92C3 **Wadi as Sirhān** *V* Jordan/S Arabia
94C2 **Wadi az Zaydi** *V* Syria
94C3 **Wadi edh Dhab'i** *V* Jordan
94A3 **Wadi el 'Arish** *V* Egypt
94C3 **Wadi el Ghadaf** *V* Jordan
94B3 **Wadi el Hasa** *V* Jordan
94C3 **Wadi el Janab** *V* Jordan
94B3 **Wadi el Jeib** *V* Israel/ Jordan
95B3 **Wadi el Milk** *Watercourse* Sudan
92A3 **Wadi el Natrun** *Watercourse* Egypt
94B3 **Wadi es Sir** Jordan
94B3 **Wadi Fidan** *V* Jordan
94B3 **Wadi Hareidin** *V* Egypt
93D3 **Wadi Hawrān** *R* Iraq
95B3 **Wadi Howa** *Watercourse* Sudan
98C1 **Wadi Ibra** *Watercourse* Sudan
94C2 **Wadi Luhfi** *Watercourse* Jordan
94B3 **Wadi Mujib** *V* Jordan
94B3 **Wadi Qītaiya** *V* Egypt
80B3 **Wadi Sha'it** *Watercourse* Egypt
99D1 **Wad Medani** Sudan
93E4 **Wafra** Kuwait
6B3 **Wager B** Can
6A3 **Wager Bay** Can
109C3 **Wagga Wagga** Aust
106A4 **Wagin** Aust
95A2 **Wāha** Libya
21C4 **Wahaiwa** Hawaiian Is
18A1 **Wahoo** USA
8D2 **Wahpeton** USA
87A1 **Wai** India
111B2 **Waiau** NZ
111A3 **Waiau** *R* NZ
111B2 **Waiau** *R* NZ
71E3 **Waigeo** *I* Indon
110C1 **Waihi** NZ
110C1 **Waikaremoana,L** NZ
110C1 **Waikato** *R* NZ
108A2 **Waikerie** Aust
111B3 **Waikouaiti** NZ
21C4 **Wailuku** Hawaiian Is
111B2 **Waimakariri** *R* NZ
111B2 **Waimate** NZ
21C4 **Waimea** Hawaiian Is
106B1 **Waingapu** Indon
13E2 **Wainwright** Can
4B2 **Wainwright** USA
111B2 **Waipara** NZ
110C2 **Waipukurau** NZ
111C2 **Wairarapa,L** NZ
111B2 **Wairau** *R* NZ
110C1 **Wairoa** NZ
110C1 **Wairoa** *R* NZ
111B2 **Waitaki** *R* NZ
110B1 **Waitara** NZ
110C1 **Waitomo** NZ
110B1 **Waiuku** NZ
75B1 **Wajima** Japan
99E2 **Wajir** Kenya
75B1 **Wakasa-wan** *B* Japan
111A3 **Wakatipu,L** NZ
74D4 **Wakayama** Japan
42D3 **Wakefield** Eng
27H1 **Wakefield** Jamaica

16D2 **Wakefield** Rhode Island, USA
76B2 **Wakema** Burma
69G2 **Wakkanai** Japan
108B3 **Wakool** *R* Aust
59B2 **Walbrzych** Pol
109D2 **Walcha** Aust
58B2 **Walcz** Pol
46D1 **Waldbröl** Germany
16B2 **Walden** USA
43C3 **Wales** Country, UK
12A1 **Wales** USA
6B3 **Wales I** Can
109C2 **Walgett** Aust
112B4 **Walgreen Coast** Region, Ant
99C3 **Walikale** Zaïre
21B2 **Walker** *L* USA
14B2 **Walkerton** Can
8B2 **Wallace** USA
108A2 **Wallaroo** Aust
109C3 **Walla Walla** Aust
20C1 **Walla Walla** USA
16C2 **Wallingford** USA
105H4 **Wallis and Futuna** *Is* Pacific O
20C1 **Wallowa** USA
20C1 **Wallowa Mts** *Mts* USA
109C1 **Wallumbilla** Aust
18B2 **Walnut Ridge** USA
110C1 **Walouru** NZ
43D3 **Walsall** Eng
9C3 **Walsenburg** USA
9C3 **Walsenburgh** USA
17B1 **Walterboro** USA
17A1 **Walter F George Res** USA
16D1 **Waltham** USA
100A3 **Walvis Bay** S Africa
103J6 **Walvis Ridge** Atlantic O
97C4 **Wamba** Nig
98B3 **Wamba** *R* Zaïre
18A2 **Wamego** USA
84B2 **Wana** Pak
108B1 **Wanaaring** Aust
111A2 **Wanaka** NZ
111A2 **Wanaka,L** NZ
14B1 **Wanapitei L** Can
109C1 **Wandoan** Aust
108B3 **Wanganella** Aust
110C1 **Wanganui** NZ
110C1 **Wanganui** *R* NZ
109C3 **Wangaratta** Aust
99E2 **Wanle Weyne** Somalia
76E2 **Wanning** China
87B1 **Wanparti** India
73B3 **Wanxian** China
73B3 **Wanyuan** China
13D2 **Wapiti** *R* Can
18B2 **Wappapello,L** USA
16C2 **Wappingers Falls** USA
87B1 **Warangal** India
109C4 **Waratah** Aust
108C3 **Waratah B** Aust
108C3 **Warburton** Aust
108A1 **Warburton** *R* Aust
109C1 **Ward** *R* Aust
101G1 **Warden** S Africa
99E2 **Warder** Eth
85D4 **Wardha** India
111A3 **Ward,Mt** NZ
5F4 **Ware** Can
16C1 **Ware** USA
16D2 **Wareham** USA
109D1 **Warialda** Aust
76C2 **Warin Chamrap** Thai
100B3 **Warmbad** S Africa
16B2 **Warminster** USA
21B2 **Warm Springs** USA
56C2 **Warnemünde** Germany
20B2 **Warner Mts** USA
17B1 **Warner Robins** USA
108B3 **Warracknabeal** Aust
108A1 **Warrandirinna,L** Aust
107D3 **Warrego** *R* Aust
19B3 **Warren** Arkansas, USA
109C2 **Warren** Aust

16D2 **Warren** Massachusetts, USA
14B2 **Warren** Ohio, USA
15C2 **Warren** Pennsylvania, USA
45C1 **Warrenpoint** N Ire
18B2 **Warrensburg** USA
101F1 **Warrenton** S Africa
15C3 **Warrenton** USA
97C4 **Warri** Nig
108A1 **Warrina** Aust
42C3 **Warrington** Eng
108B3 **Warrnambool** Aust
 Warsaw = Warszawa
58C2 **Warszawa** Pol
59B2 **Warta** *R* Pol
109D1 **Warwick** Aust
43D3 **Warwick** County, Eng
43D3 **Warwick** Eng
16B2 **Warwick** New York, USA
16D2 **Warwick** Rhode Island, USA
8B3 **Wasatch Range** *Mts* USA
101H1 **Wasbank** S Africa
21B2 **Wasco** USA
4H2 **Washburn L** Can
85D4 **Wāshim** India
10C3 **Washington** District of Columbia, USA
17B1 **Washington** Georgia, USA
14A3 **Washington** Indiana, USA
18B2 **Washington** Missouri, USA
16B2 **Washington** New Jersey, USA
14B2 **Washington** Pennsylvania, USA
8A2 **Washington** State, USA
14B3 **Washington Court House** USA
6D1 **Washington Land** Can
15D2 **Washington,Mt** USA
43E3 **Wash,The** Eng
85A3 **Washuk** Pak
12E2 **Wasilla** USA
7C4 **Waskaganish** Can
26A4 **Waspán** Nic
70D4 **Watampone** Indon
16C2 **Waterbury** USA
45C2 **Waterford** County, Irish Rep
41B3 **Waterford** Irish Rep
45C2 **Waterford Harbour** Irish Rep
46C1 **Waterloo** Belg
10A2 **Waterloo** USA
15C2 **Watertown** New York, USA
101H1 **Waterval-Boven** S Africa
10D2 **Waterville** Maine, USA
16C1 **Watervliet** USA
5G4 **Waterways** Can
43D4 **Watford** Eng
15C2 **Watkins Glen** USA
8C1 **Watrous** Can
99C2 **Watsa** Zaïre
12J2 **Watson Lake** Can
22B2 **Watsonville** USA
71F4 **Wau** PNG
99C2 **Wau** Sudan
7B5 **Waua** Can
109D2 **Wauchope** Aust
17B2 **Wauchula** USA
14A2 **Waukegan** USA
10B2 **Wausau** USA
14A2 **Wauwatosa** USA
106C2 **Wave Hill** Aust
43E3 **Waveney** *R* Eng
14B3 **Waverly** Ohio, USA
46C1 **Wavre** Belg
10B2 **Wawa** Can
95A2 **Wāw Al Kabīr** Libya
95A2 **Wāw an Nāmūs** *Well* Libya
22C2 **Wawona** USA

19A3	Waxahachie USA
17B1	Waycross USA
17B1	Waynesboro Georgia, USA
19C3	Waynesboro Mississippi, USA
16A3	Waynesboro Pennsylvania, USA
15C3	Waynesboro Virginia, USA
18B2	Waynesville Missouri, USA
84B2	Wazi Khwa Afghan
43E4	Weald,The Upland Eng
42C2	Wear R Eng
19A3	Weatherford Texas, USA
20B2	Weaverville USA
14B1	Webbwood Can
16D1	Webster USA
18B2	Webster Groves USA
29D6	Weddell I Falkland Is
112C2	Weddell S Ant
13C2	Wedge Mt Can
20B2	Weed USA
101H1	Weenen S Africa
109C2	Wee Waa Aust
72D1	Weichang China
57C3	Weiden Germany
72D2	Weifang China
72E2	Weihai China
72C3	Wei He R Henan, China
72C2	Wei He R Shaanxi, China
109C1	Weilmoringle Aust
73A4	Weining China
107D2	Weipa Aust
14B2	Weirton USA
20C2	Weiser USA
72D3	Weishan Hu L China
57C2	Weissenfels Germany
17A1	Weiss L USA
99D1	Weldiya Eth
101G1	Welkom S Africa
15C2	Welland Can
43D3	Welland R Eng
106C2	Wellesley Is Aust
12G2	Wellesley L Can
43D3	Wellingborough Eng
109C2	Wellington Aust
18A2	Wellington Kansas, USA
111B2	Wellington NZ
6A2	Wellington Chan Can
13C2	Wells Can
43C4	Wells Eng
110B1	Wellsford NZ
106B3	Wells,L Aust
57C3	Wels Austria
43C3	Welshpool Wales
13D1	Wembley Can
7C4	Wemindji Can
20B1	Wenatchee USA
20C1	Wenatchee R USA
97B4	Wenchi Ghana
72E2	Wenden China
73E4	Wenling China
32J7	Wenman I Ecuador
73A5	Wenshan China
107D4	Wenthaggi Aust
108B2	Wentworth Aust
72A3	Wen Xian China
73E4	Wenzhou China
73C4	Wenzhu China
101G1	Wepener S Africa
12G1	Wernecke Mts Can
57C2	Werra R Germany
109D2	Werris Creek Aust
56B2	Wesel Germany
56B2	Weser R Germany
106C2	Wessel Is Aust
14A2	West Allis USA
104C4	West Australian Basin Indian O
104C5	West Australian Ridge Indian O
19C3	West B USA
86B2	West Bengal State, India
43D3	West Bromwich Eng
16B3	West Chester USA
46D1	Westerburg Germany
56B2	Westerland Germany
16D2	Westerly USA
106A3	Western Australia State, Aust
87A1	Western Ghats Mts India
44A3	Western Isles Scot
96A2	Western Sahara Region, Mor
105H4	Western Samoa Is Pacific O
46B1	Westerschelde Estuary Neth
46D1	Westerwald Region, Germany
49D1	Westfalen Region, Germany
29D6	West Falkland I Falkland Is
16C1	Westfield Massachusetts, USA
15C2	Westfield New York, USA
18C2	West Frankfort USA
109C1	Westgate Aust
43C4	West Glamorgan County, Wales
102E3	West Indies Is Caribbean S
13E2	Westlock Can
14B2	West Lorne Can
45C2	Westmeath County, Irish Rep
18B2	West Memphis USA
43D3	West Midlands County, Eng
43D4	Westminster Eng
16A3	Westminster Maryland, USA
17B1	Westminster S Carolina, USA
100B3	West Nicholson Zim
78D1	Weston Malay
14B3	Weston USA
43C4	Weston-super-Mare Eng
17B2	West Palm Beach USA
18B2	West Plains USA
22B1	West Point California, USA
19C3	West Point Mississippi, USA
16C2	West Point New York, USA
12F2	West Point Mt USA
45B2	Westport Irish Rep
111B2	Westport NZ
40C2	Westray I Scot
13C2	West Road R Can
42E3	West Sole Oilfield N Sea
11B3	West Virginia State, USA
22C1	West Walker R USA
109C2	West Wyalong Aust
42D3	West Yorkshire County, Eng
71D4	Wetar I Indon
13E2	Wetaskiwin Can
99D3	Wete Tanz
46E1	Wetzlar Germany
	Wevok = Cape Lisburne
71F4	Wewak PNG
19A2	Wewoka USA
45C2	Wexford County, Irish Rep
45C2	Wexford Irish Rep
5H5	Weyburn Can
43C4	Weymouth Eng
16D1	Weymouth USA
110C1	Whakatane NZ
110C1	Whakatane R NZ
44E1	Whalsay I Scot
110B1	Whangarei NZ
42D3	Wharfe R Eng
19A4	Wharton USA
111B2	Whataroa NZ
16A3	Wheaton Maryland, USA
8B3	Wheeler Peak Mt Nevada, USA
9C3	Wheeler Peak Mt New Mexico, USA
14B2	Wheeling USA
13C3	Whistler Can
15C2	Whitby USA
42D2	Whitby Eng
18B2	White R Arkansas, USA
12F2	White R Can
14A3	White R Indiana, USA
8C2	White R S Dakota, USA
7E4	White B Can
108B2	White Cliffs Aust
40C2	White Coomb Mt Scot
13D2	Whitecourt Can
14A1	Whitefish Pt USA
7D4	Whitegull L Can
15D2	Whitehall New York, USA
16B2	Whitehall Pennsylvania, USA
42C2	Whitehaven Eng
12G2	Whitehorse Can
110C1	White I NZ
19B4	White L USA
109C4	Whitemark Aust
21B2	White Mountain Peak Mt USA
12E1	White Mts Alaska, USA
15D2	White Mts New Hampshire, USA
99D1	White Nile R Sudan
16C2	White Plains USA
7B5	White River Can
15D2	White River Junction USA
	White S = Beloye More
13B2	Whitesail L Can
20B1	White Salmon USA
17C1	Whiteville USA
97B4	White Volta R Ghana
42B2	Whithorn Scot
17B1	Whitmire USA
21B2	Whitney,Mt USA
12E2	Whittier Alaska, USA
22C4	Whittier California, USA
5H3	Wholdia L Can
108A2	Whyalla Aust
14B2	Wiarton Can
18A2	Wichita USA
9D3	Wichita Falls USA
44C2	Wick Scot
45C2	Wicklow County, Irish Rep
45C2	Wicklow Irish Rep
45C2	Wicklow Mts Irish Rep
109C1	Widgeegoara R Aust
46D1	Wied R Germany
59B2	Wielun Pol
59B3	Wien Austria
59B3	Wiener Neustadt Austria
58C2	Wieprz R Pol
46E1	Wiesbaden Germany
42C3	Wigan Eng
19C3	Wiggins USA
42B2	Wigtown Scot
42B2	Wigtown B Scot
47C1	Wil Switz
20C1	Wilbur USA
108B2	Wilcannia Aust
21B2	Wildcat Peak Mt USA
47B1	Wildhorn Mt Switz
13E2	Wild Horse Can
47D1	Wildspitze Mt Austria
17B2	Wildwood Florida, USA
16B3	Wildwood New Jersey, USA
101G1	Wilge R S Africa
56B2	Wilhelmshaven Germany
15C2	Wilkes-Barre USA
112B8	Wilkes Land Ant
13F2	Wilkie Can
20B2	Willamette R USA
108B2	Willandra R Aust
20B1	Willapa B USA
9C3	Willcox USA
27D4	Willemstad Curaçao
108A1	William Creek Aust
108B3	William,Mt Aust
21A2	Williams California, USA
13C2	Williams Lake Can
15C2	Williamsport USA
16C1	Williamstown Massachusetts, USA
14B3	Williamstown W Virginia, USA
16C2	Willimantic USA
16B2	Willingboro USA
13D2	Willingdon,Mt Can
107E2	Willis Group Is Aust
17B2	Williston Florida, USA
100B4	Williston S Africa
13C1	Williston L Can
8D2	Willmar USA
108A3	Willoughby,C Aust
13C2	Willow R Can
20B2	Willow Ranch USA
21A2	Willows USA
18B2	Willow Springs USA
108A2	Wilmington Aust
16B3	Wilmington Delaware, USA
17C1	Wilmington N Carolina, USA
7A5	Wilnona USA
11C3	Wilson USA
108B1	Wilson R Aust
6B3	Wilson,C Can
22C3	Wilson,Mt California, USA
20B1	Wilson,Mt Oregon, USA
109C3	Wilsons Promontory Pen Aust
43D4	Wiltshire County, Eng
46C2	Wiltz Lux
106B3	Wiluna Aust
14A2	Winamac USA
101G1	Winburg S Africa
16C1	Winchendon USA
15C1	Winchester Can
43D4	Winchester Eng
16C1	Winchester New Hampshire, USA
15C3	Winchester Virginia, USA
42C2	Windermere Eng
100A3	Windhoek Namibia
107D3	Windorah Aust
8C2	Wind River Range Mts USA
109D2	Windsor Aust
16C2	Windsor Connecticut, USA
43D4	Windsor Eng
7D5	Windsor Nova Scotia, Can
14B2	Windsor Ontario, Can
15D1	Windsor Quebec, Can
17B1	Windsor Forest USA
16C2	Windsor Locks USA
27E4	Windward Is Caribbean S
26C3	Windward Pass Caribbean S
13E1	Winefred L Can
18A2	Winfield Kansas, USA
109D2	Wingham Aust
34C3	Winifreda Arg
7B4	Winisk R Can
7B4	Winisk L Can
76B2	Winkana Burma
20B1	Winlock USA
97B4	Winneba Ghana
14A2	Winnebago,L USA
20C2	Winnemucca USA
19B3	Winnfield USA

5J4 **Winnipeg** Can
5J4 **Winnipeg,L** Can
5J4 **Winnipegosis** Can
4J4 **Winnipegosis,L** Can
15D2 **Winnipesaukee,L** USA
10A2 **Winona** Minnesota, USA
19C3 **Winona** Mississippi, USA
15D2 **Winooski** USA
9B3 **Winslow** USA
16C2 **Winsted** USA
11B3 **Winston-Salem** USA
46E1 **Winterberg** Germany
17B2 **Winter Garden** USA
17B2 **Winter Park** USA
22B1 **Winters** USA
47C1 **Winterthur** Switz
107D3 **Winton** Aust
111A3 **Winton** NZ
43E3 **Wisbech** Eng
10B2 **Wisconsin** State, USA
7B5 **Wisconsin Rapids** USA
12D1 **Wiseman** USA
58B2 **Wisla** *R* Pol
56C2 **Wismar** Germany
33F2 **Witagron** Surinam
101G1 **Witbank** S Africa
9D3 **Witchita Falls** USA
43D3 **Witham** *R* Eng
42E3 **Withernsea** Eng
43D4 **Witney** Eng
46D1 **Witten** Germany
56C2 **Wittenberg** Germany
106A3 **Wittenoom** Aust
46D1 **Wittlich** Germany
58B2 **Wladyslawowo** Pol
58B2 **Włoclawek** Pol
58C2 **Włodawa** Pol
109C3 **Wodonga** Aust
47C1 **Wohlen** Switz
71E4 **Wokam** Indon
43D4 **Woking** Eng
71F3 **Woleai** *I* Pacific O
20B2 **Wolf Creek** USA
8C2 **Wolf Point** USA
57C3 **Wolfsberg** Austria
56C2 **Wolfsburg** Germany
5H4 **Wollaston L** Can
5H4 **Wollaston Lake** Can
4G3 **Wollaston Pen** Can
109D2 **Wollongong** Aust
101G1 **Wolmaransstad** S Africa
59B2 **Wolow** Pol
108B3 **Wolseley** Aust
43C3 **Wolverhampton** Eng
16A2 **Womelsdorf** USA
109D1 **Wondai** Aust
74B3 **Wŏnju** S Korea
108B2 **Wonominta** *R* Aust
13C1 **Wonowon** Can
74B3 **Wŏnsan** N Korea
108C3 **Wonthaggi** Aust
108A2 **Woocalla** Aust
16B3 **Woodbine** USA
15C3 **Woodbridge** USA
5G4 **Wood Buffalo Nat Pk** Can
109D1 **Woodburn** Aust
20B1 **Woodburn** USA
16B3 **Woodbury** USA
12F1 **Woodchopper** USA
21A2 **Woodland** California, USA
20B1 **Woodland** Washington, USA
107E1 **Woodlark** *I* PNG
106C4 **Woodmera** Aust
106C3 **Woodroffe,Mt** Aust
14B2 **Woodstock** Ontario, Can
16B3 **Woodstown** USA
110C2 **Woodville** NZ
19B3 **Woodville** USA
108A2 **Woomera** Aust
15D2 **Woonsocket** USA
14B2 **Wooster** USA
43C3 **Worcester** Eng
100A4 **Worcester** S Africa
16D1 **Worcester** USA
47E1 **Wörgl** Austria
42C2 **Workington** Eng
8C2 **Worland** USA
46E2 **Worms** Germany
43B4 **Worms Head** *Pt* Wales
43D4 **Worthing** Eng
8D2 **Worthington** USA
71D4 **Wowoni** *I* Indon
12H3 **Wrangell** USA
12H3 **Wrangell I** USA
12F2 **Wrangell Mts** USA
40B2 **Wrath,C** Scot
43C3 **Wrexham** Wales
17B1 **Wrightsville** USA
22D3 **Wrightwood** USA
4F3 **Wrigley** Can
59B2 **Wrocław** Pol
58B2 **Wrzésnia** Pol
69E2 **Wuchang** China
76E1 **Wuchuan** China
72E2 **Wuda** China
72C2 **Wuding He** *R* China
72A3 **Wudu** China
73C4 **Wugang** China
72B2 **Wuhai** China
73C3 **Wuhan** China
73D3 **Wuhu** China
73D5 **Wuhua** China
84D2 **Wüjang** China
72B1 **Wujia He** *R* China
73B4 **Wu Jiang** *R* China
97C4 **Wukari** Nig
73B4 **Wuling Shan** *Mts* China
97D4 **Wum** Cam
73A4 **Wumeng Shan** *Upland* China
46D1 **Wuppertal** Germany
72B2 **Wuqi** China
72D2 **Wuqing** China
57B3 **Würzburg** Germany
57C2 **Wurzen** Germany
72C2 **Wutai Shan** *Mt* China
71F4 **Wuvulu** *I* Pacific O
72A2 **Wuwei** China
73E3 **Wuxi** China
73E3 **Wuxing** China
72C2 **Wuyang** China
73D4 **Wuyi Shan** *Mts* China
72B1 **Wuyuan** China
76D2 **Wuzhi Shan** *Mts* China
72B2 **Wuzhong** China
73C5 **Wuzhou** China
14B2 **Wyandotte** USA
109C1 **Wyandra** Aust
43C4 **Wye** *R* Eng
43C4 **Wylye** *R* Eng
43E3 **Wymondham** Eng
106B2 **Wyndham** Aust
18B2 **Wynne** USA
4G2 **Wynniatt B** Can
109C4 **Wynyard** Aust
8C2 **Wyoming** State, USA
14A2 **Wyoming** USA
109D2 **Wyong** Aust

X

84D1 **Xaidulla** China
72D1 **Xai Moron He** *R* China
101C3 **Xai Xai** Mozam
23B2 **Xaltinguis** Mexico
100A2 **Xangongo** Angola
46D1 **Xanten** Germany
55B2 **Xánthi** Greece
100B3 **Xau,L** Botswana
14B3 **Xenia** USA
68B4 **Xiaguan** China
72A2 **Xiahe** China
73D5 **Xiamen** China
72B3 **Xi'an** China
73B4 **Xianfeng** China
73C3 **Xiangfan** China
73C4 **Xiang Jiang** *R* China
73C4 **Xiangtan** Province, China
73C4 **Xianning** China
72B3 **Xianyang** China
73C4 **Xiao Shui** *R* China
73D4 **Xiapu** China
73A4 **Xichang** China
23B1 **Xicotepec** Mexico
76C2 **Xieng Khouang** Laos
73B4 **Xifeng** China
86B1 **Xigazê** China
72A1 **Xi He** *R* China
72B2 **Xiji** China
73C5 **Xi Jiang** *R* China
72E1 **Xiliao He** *R* China
73B5 **Xilin** China
23B1 **Xilitla** Mexico
73D4 **Xinfeng** China
72C1 **Xinghe** China
73D5 **Xingning** China
73B4 **Xingren** China
72C2 **Xingtai** China
33G4 **Xingu** *R* Brazil
68B2 **Xingxingxia** China
73A4 **Xingyi** China
72A2 **Xining** China
72E2 **Xinjin** Liaoning, China
73A3 **Xinjin** Sichuan, China
72D2 **Xinwen** China
72C2 **Xin Xian** China
72C2 **Xinxiang** China
73C3 **Xinyang** China
73C5 **Xinyi** Guangdong, China
72D3 **Xinyi** Jiangsu, China
72D1 **Xi Ujimqin Qi** China
74A2 **Xiuyan** China
23B2 **Xochimilco** Mexico
73D3 **Xuancheng** China
73B3 **Xuanhan** China
72D1 **Xuanhua** China
73A4 **Xuanwei** China
72C3 **Xuchang** China
99E2 **Xuddur** Somalia
72A2 **Xunhua** China
73C5 **Xun Jiang** *R* China
69E2 **Xunke** China
73D5 **Xunwu** China
73C4 **Xupu** China
76E1 **Xuwen** China
73B4 **Xuyong** China
72D3 **Xuzhou** China

Y

73A4 **Ya'an** China
108B3 **Yaapeet** Aust
98B2 **Yabassi** Cam
68C1 **Yablonovyy Khrebet** *Mts* Russian Fed
94C2 **Yabrūd** Syria
20B2 **Yachats** USA
30D3 **Yacuiba** Bol
87B1 **Yādgīr** India
95A1 **Yafran** Libya
23A1 **Yahualica** Mexico
98C2 **Yahuma** Zaïre
75B1 **Yaita** Japan
75B2 **Yaizu** Japan
73A4 **Yajiang** China
20B1 **Yakima** USA
20B1 **Yakima** *R* USA
97B3 **Yako** Burkina
98C2 **Yakoma** Zaïre
74E2 **Yakumo** Japan
12G3 **Yakutat** USA
12G3 **Yakutat B** USA
63E1 **Yakutsk** Russian Fed
77C4 **Yala** Thai
23B2 **Yalalag** Mexico
98C2 **Yalinga** CAR
109C3 **Yallourn** Aust
68B3 **Yalong** *R* China
73A4 **Yalong Jiang** *R* China
54C2 **Yalova** Turk
60D5 **Yalta** Ukraine
74B2 **Yalu Jiang** *R* China
74D3 **Yamagata** Japan
74C4 **Yamaguchi** Japan
68D1 **Yamarovka** Russian Fed
109D1 **Yamba** New S Wales, Aust
108B2 **Yamba** S Australia, Aust
99C2 **Yambio** Sudan
54C2 **Yambol** Bulg
71E4 **Yamdena** *I* Indon
Yam Kinneret = Tiberias,L
108B1 **Yamma Yamma,L** Aust
97B4 **Yamoussoukro** Ivory Coast
85D3 **Yamuna** *R* India
86C1 **Yamzho Yumco** *L* China
63F1 **Yana** *R* Russian Fed
108B3 **Yanac** Aust
75A2 **Yanagawa** Japan
87C1 **Yanam** India
72B2 **Yan'an** China
80B3 **Yanbu'al Bahr** S Arabia
108B2 **Yancannia** Aust
72E3 **Yancheng** China
72B2 **Yanchi** China
108B1 **Yandama** *R* Aust
98C2 **Yangambi** Zaïre
72C1 **Yang He** *R* China
73C5 **Yangjiang** China
Yangon = Rangoon
72C2 **Yangquan** China
73C5 **Yangshan** China
73C3 **Yangtze Gorges** China
72E3 **Yangtze,Mouths of the** China
72D3 **Yangzhou** China
73B4 **Yanhe** China
74B2 **Yanji** China
108C3 **Yanko** *R* Aust
8D2 **Yankton** USA
68A2 **Yanqqi** China
72D1 **Yan Shan** *Hills*
108B1 **Yantabulla** Aust
72E2 **Yantai** China
72D2 **Yanzhou** China
98B2 **Yaoundé** Cam
71E4 **Yapen** *I* Indon
71E3 **Yap Is** Pacific O
24B2 **Yaqui** *R* Mexico
61G2 **Yaransk** Russian Fed
32C3 **Yari** *R* Colombia
74D3 **Yariga-dake** *Mt* Japan
82B2 **Yarkant He** *R* China
86C1 **Yarlung Zangbo Jiang** *R* China
7D5 **Yarmouth** Can
94B2 **Yarmūk** *R* Syria/ Jordan
61E2 **Yaroslavl'** Russian Fed
94B2 **Yarqon** *R* Israel
109C3 **Yarram** Aust
109D1 **Yarraman** Aust
109C3 **Yarrawonga** Aust
60D2 **Yartsevo** Russian Fed
63B1 **Yartsevo** Russian Fed
32B2 **Yarumal** Colombia
97C3 **Yashi** Nig
97C4 **Yashikera** Nig
61F4 **Yashkul'** Russian Fed
84C1 **Yasin** Pak
59C3 **Yasinya** Ukraine
109C2 **Yass** Aust
109C2 **Yass** *R* Aust
75A1 **Yasugi** Japan
18A2 **Yates Center** USA
98C2 **Yatolema** Zaïre
74C4 **Yatsushiro** Japan
94B3 **Yatta** Israel
32C4 **Yavari** Peru
85D4 **Yavatmāl** India
74C4 **Yawatahama** Japan
76D2 **Ya Xian** China
90B3 **Yazd** Iran
90B3 **Yazd-e Khvāst** Iran
19B3 **Yazoo** *R* USA
19B3 **Yazoo City** USA
76B2 **Ye** Burma
59D3 **Yedintsy** Moldavia
108A2 **Yeelanna** Aust
60E3 **Yefremov** Russian Fed
61F4 **Yegorlyk** *R* Russian Fed
99D2 **Yei** Sudan

65H4 Yekaterinburg Russian Fed
60E3 Yelets Russian Fed
44E1 Yell / Scot
87C1 Yellandu India
Yellow = Huang He
8B1 Yellowhead P Can
4G3 Yellowknife Can
5G4 Yellowmead P Can
109C2 Yellow Mt Aust
69E3 Yellow Sea China/Korea
8C2 Yellowstone R USA
8B2 Yellowstone L USA
6B1 Yelverton B Can
97C3 Yelwa Nig
81C4 Yemen Republic, Arabian Pen
76C1 Yen Bai Viet
97R4 Yendi Ghana
76B1 Yengan Burma
63B2 Yeniseysk Russian Fed
63B1 Yeniseyskiy Kryazh Ridge Russian Fed
64J2 Yeniseyskiy Zal B Russian Fed
12D2 Yentna R USA
43C4 Yeo R Eng
109C2 Yeoval Aust
43C4 Yeovil Eng
63C1 Yerbogachen Russian Fed
65F5 Yerevan Armenia
21B2 Yerington USA
21B3 Yermo USA
69E1 Yerofey-Pavlovich Russian Fed
94B3 Yeroham Israel
61G3 Yershov Russian Fed
Yerushalayim = Jerusalem
92C1 Yeşil R Turk
94B2 Yesud Hama'ala Israel
109D1 Yetman Aust
96B2 Yetti Maur
93E1 Yevlakh Azerbaijan
60D4 Yevpatoriya Ukraine
72E2 Ye Xian China
60E4 Yeysk Russian Fed
55B2 Yiannitsá Greece
73A4 Yibin China
73C3 Yichang China
69E2 Yichun China
72B2 Yijun China
54C2 Yildiz Dağlari Upland Turk
92C2 Yıldızeli Turk
73A5 Yiliang China
72B2 Yinchuan China
72D3 Ying He R China
72E1 Yingkou China
73D3 Yingshan Hubei, China
72B3 Yingshan Sichuan, China
73D4 Yingtan China
82C1 Yining China
72B1 Yin Shan Upland China
99D2 Yirga Alem Eth
99D2 Yirol Sudan
63D3 Yirshi China
73B5 Yishan China
72D2 Yishui China
55B3 Yithion Greece
38J6 Yivieska Fin
73C4 Yiyang China
38K5 Yli-Kitka L Fin
38J5 Ylilornio Sweden
19A4 Yoakum USA
23B2 Yogope Mexico
78C4 Yogyakarta Indon
13D2 Yoho Nat Pk Can
98B2 Yokadouma Cam
75B2 Yokkaichi Japan
75B1 Yokohama Japan
75B1 Yokosuka Japan
74C3 Yonago Japan
74E3 Yonezawa Japan
73D4 Yong'an China
72A2 Yongchang China
74B3 Yŏngch'on S Korea

73B4 Yongchuan China
72A2 Yongdeng China
73D5 Yongding China
72D2 Yongding He R China
74B3 Yŏngdŏk S Korea
74B3 Yŏnghŭng N Korea
74B3 Yongju S Korea
72B2 Yongning China
16C2 Yonkers USA
49C2 Yonne R France
42D3 York Eng
18A1 York Nebraska, USA
16A3 York Pennsylvania, USA
107D2 York,C Aust
108A2 Yorke Pen Aust
108A3 Yorketown Aust
7A4 York Factory Can
41C3 Yorkshire Moors Moorland Eng
42D2 Yorkshire Wolds Upland Eng
5H4 Yorkton Can
22B2 Yosemite L USA
22C1 Yosemite Nat Pk USA
75A2 Yoshii·R Japan
75A2 Yoshino R Japan
61G2 Yoshkar Ola Russian Fed
74B4 Yŏsu S Korea
41B3 Youghal Irish Rep
45C3 Youghal Harb Irish Rep
73B5 You Jiang R China
109C2 Young Aust
34D2 Young Urug
111A2 Young Range Mts NZ
13E2 Youngstown Can
14B2 Youngstown Ohio, USA
22A1 Yountville USA
73B4 Youyang China
92B2 Yozgat Turk
20B2 Yreka USA
39G7 Ystad Sweden
43C3 Ystwyth R Wales
44C3 Ythan R Scot
73C4 Yuan Jiang R Hunan, China
73A5 Yuan Jiang R Yunnan, China
73A4 Yuanmu China
72C2 Yuanping China
21A2 Yuba City USA
74E2 Yūbari Japan
25D3 Yucatan Pen Mexico
25D2 Yucatan Chan Mexico/Cuba
72C2 Yuci China
63F2 Yudoma R Russian Fed
73D4 Yudu China
73A4 Yuexi China
73C4 Yueyang China
54A2 Yugoslavia Republic, Europe
73B5 Yu Jiang R China
12C2 Yukon R Can/USA
4E3 Yukon Territory Can
76E1 Yulin Guangdong, China
73C5 Yulin Guangxi, China
72B2 Yulin Shaanxi, China
9B3 Yuma USA
68B3 Yumen China
72D2 Yunan China
34A3 Yungay Chile
73C5 Yunlai Dashan Hills China
108A2 Yunta Aust
72C3 Yunxi China
72C3 Yun Xian China
73B3 Yunyang China
32B5 Yurimaguas Peru
73E5 Yu Shan Mt Taiwan
38L6 Yushkozero Russian Fed
82D2 Yushu Tibet, China
73A5 Yuxi China
74F2 Yuzhno-Kuril'sk Russian Fed

69G2 Yuzhno-Sakhalinsk Russian Fed
61J3 Yuzh Ural Mts Russian Fed
46A2 Yvelines Department, France
47B1 Yverdon Switz

Z

56A2 Zaandam Neth
93D2 Zāb al Babir R Iraq
93D2 Zāb as Şaghir R Iraq
68D2 Zabaykal'sk Russian Fed
59B3 Zabreh Czech
59B2 Zabrze Pol
23A2 Zacapu Mexico
24B2 Zacatecas Mexico
23B2 Zacatepec Morelos, Mexico
23B2 Zacatepec Oaxaca, Mexico
23B2 Zacatlan Mexico
23A1 Zacoalco Mexico
23B1 Zacualtipan Mexico
52C2 Zadar Croatia
76B3 Zadetkyi / Burma
50A2 Zafra Spain
95C1 Zagazig Egypt
96B1 Zagora Mor
60E2 Zagorsk Russian Fed
52C1 Zagreb Croatia
91D4 Zāhedān Iran
94B2 Zahle Leb
51C2 Zahrez Chergui Marshland Alg
61H2 Zainsk Russian Fed
98C3 Zaïre Republic, Africa
98B3 Zaïre R Zaire/Congo
54B2 Zajecär Yugos
68C1 Zakamensk Russian Fed
93D2 Zakho Iraq
55B3 Zákinthos / Greece
59B3 Zakopane Pol
59B3 Zalaegerszeg Hung
54B1 Zalău Rom
56C2 Zalew Szczeciński Lg Pol
98C1 Zalingei Sudan
63F2 Zaliv Akademii B Russian Fed
65G5 Zaliv Kara-Bogaz Gol B Turkmenistan
74C2 Zaliv Petra Velikogo B Russian Fed
69G2 Zaliv Turpeniya B Russian Fed
95A2 Zaltan Libya
89H9 Zambesi R Mozam
100B2 Zambezi Zambia
100B2 Zambezi R Zambia
100B2 Zambia Republic, Africa
79B4 Zamboanga Phil
79B4 Zamboanga Pen Phil
58C2 Zambrów Pol
32B4 Zamora Ecuador
23A2 Zamora Mexico
50A1 Zamora Spain
59C2 Zamość Pol
72A3 Zamtang China
98B3 Zanaga Congo
50B2 Záncara R Spain
84D2 Zanda China
14B3 Zanesville USA
84D2 Zangla India
90A2 Zanjān Iran
34B2 Zanjitas Arg
34B2 Zanjon R Arg
99D3 Zanzibar Tanz
99D3 Zanzibar / Tanz
96C2 Zaouatallaz Alg
72D3 Zaozhuang China
93D2 Zap R Turk
39K7 Zapadnaja Dvina R Russian Fed
65H3 Zapadno-Sibirskaya Nizmennost' Lowland Russian Fed
63B2 Zapadnyy Sayan Mts Russian Fed
34A3 Zapala Arg
60E4 Zaporozh'ye Ukraine

93C2 Zara Turk
23A1 Zaragoza Mexico
50B1 Zaragoza Spain
90B2 Zarand Iran
90C3 Zarand Iran
80E2 Zaranj Afghan
33D2 Zarara Ven
58D1 Zarasai Lithuania
34D2 Zárate Arg
90B3 Zard Kuh Mt Iran
12H3 Zarembo I USA
84B2 Zarghun Shahr Afghan
84B2 Zargun Mt Pak
97C3 Zaria Nig
92C3 Zarqa Jordan
94B2 Zarqa R Jordan
32B4 Zaruma Ecuador
58B2 Zary Pol
96D1 Zarzis Tunisia
84D2 Zäskär Mts India
84D2 Zäskär R India
94C2 Zatara R Jordan
Zatoka Gdańska = Gdańsk,G of
69E1 Zavitinsk Russian Fed
59B2 Zawiercie Pol
63C2 Zayarsk Russian Fed
65K5 Zaysan Kazakhstan
82D3 Zayü China
68B4 Zayü Mt China
58B2 Zduńska Wola Pol
46B1 Zeebrugge Belg
94B3 Zeelim Israel
101G1 Zeerust S Africa
94B2 Zefat Israel
97C3 Zegueren Watercourse Mali
99E1 Zeila Somalia
57C2 Zeitz Germany
72A2 Zekog China
61G2 Zelenodol'sk Russian Fed
39K6 Zelenogorsk Russian Fed
47D1 Zell Austria
98C2 Zemio CAR
64F1 Zemlya Aleksandry I Barents S
64F2 Zemlya Frantsa Iosifa Is Barents S
64F1 Zemlya Georga I Barents S
64H1 Zemlya Vil'cheka I Barents S
73B4 Zenning China
47B1 Zermatt Switz
63E2 Zeya Russian Fed
63E2 Zeya Res Russian Fed
50A1 Zêzere R Port
94B1 Zghorta Leb
58B2 Zgierz Pol
72D1 Zhangjiakou China
73D4 Zhangping China
72D2 Zhangwei He R China
72E1 Zhangwu China
72A2 Zhangye China
73D5 Zhangzhou China
73C5 Zhanjiang China
73A4 Zhanyi China
73C5 Zhaoqing China
73A4 Zhaotong China
72D2 Zhaoyang Hu L China
61J4 Zharkamys Russian Fed
63E1 Zhatay Russian Fed
73D4 Zhejiang Province, China
67F3 Zhengou China
72C3 Zhengzhou China
72D3 Zhenjiang China
73A4 Zhenxiong China
73B4 Zhenyuan China
61F3 Zherdevka Russian Fed
73C3 Zhicheng China
68C1 Zhigalovo Russian Fed
73B4 Zhijin China

Zhitkovichi

58D2 **Zhitkovichi** Belorussia
60C3 **Zhitomir** Ukraine
60D3 **Zhlobin** Belorussia
60C4 **Zhmerinka** Ukraine
84B2 **Zhob** Pak
58D2 **Zhodino** Latvia
72B2 **Zhongning** China
112C10 **Zhongshan** *Base* Ant
73C5 **Zhongshan** China
72B2 **Zhongwei** China
68B4 **Zhougdian** China
73E3 **Zhoushan Quandao** *Arch* China
72E2 **Zhuanghe** China
72A3 **Zhugqu** China
73C3 **Zhushan** China
73C4 **Zhuzhou** China
72D2 **Zibo** China
106C3 **Ziel,Mt** Aust
58B2 **Zielona Gora** Pol
76A1 **Zigaing** Burma
73A4 **Zigong** China

97A3 **Ziguinchor** Sen
23A2 **Zihuatanejo** Mexico
94B2 **Zikhron Ya'aqov** Israel
59B3 **Žilina** Czech
95A2 **Zillah** Libya
47D1 **Ziller** *R* Austria
47D1 **Zillertaler Alpen** *Mts* Austria
58D1 **Zilupe** Russian Fed
63C2 **Zima** Russian Fed
23B1 **Zimapan** Mexico
23B2 **Zimatlan** Mexico
100B2 **Zimbabwe** Republic, Africa
94B3 **Zin** *R* Israel
23B2 **Zinacatepec** Mexico
23A2 **Zinapécuaro** Mexico
97C3 **Zinder** Niger
73C4 **Zi Shui** China
23A2 **Zitácuaro** Mexico
57C2 **Zittau** Germany
72D2 **Ziya He** *R* China
72A3 **Ziyang** China

61J2 **Zlatoust** Russian Fed
59B3 **Zlin** Czech
65K4 **Zmeinogorsk** Russian Fed
58B2 **Znin** Pol
59B3 **Znoimo** Czech
100B3 **Zoekmekaar** S Africa
47B1 **Zofinger** Switz
72A3 **Zoigê** China
59D3 **Zolochev** Ukraine
101C2 **Zomba** Malawi
98B2 **Zongo** Zaire
92B1 **Zonguldak** Turk
97B4 **Zorzor** Lib
96A2 **Zouerate** Maur
54B1 **Zrenjanin** Serbia, Yugos
47C1 **Zug** Switz
47D1 **Zugspitze** *Mt* Germany
50A2 **Zújar** *R* Spain
100C2 **Zumbo** Mozam
23B2 **Zumpango** Mexico

97C4 **Zungeru** Nig
73B4 **Zunyi** China
76D1 **Zuo** *R* China
73B5 **Zuo Jiang** *R* China
47C1 **Zürich** Switz
47C1 **Zürichsee** *L* Switz
95A1 **Zuwärah** Libya
95A2 **Zuwaylah** Libya
61H2 **Zuyevka** Russian Fed
100B4 **Zvishavane** Zim
59B3 **Zvolen** Czech
54A2 **Zvornik** Bosnia & Herzegovina, Yugos
97B4 **Zwedru** Lib
46D2 **Zweibrücken** Germany
47B1 **Zweisimmen** Switz
57C2 **Zwickau** Germany
56B2 **Zwolle** Neth
58C2 **Zyrardów** Pol
65K5 **Zyryanovsk** Kazakhstan
59B3 **Żywiec** Pol
94A1 **Zyyi** Cyprus